Yearbook on

International

Communist Affairs

1976

Yearbook on

International

Communist Affairs

1976

EDITOR: Richard F. Staar

Associate Area Editors:

Eastern Europe and the Soviet Union	Milorad M. Drachkovitch
Western Europe	Dennis L. Bark
Asia and the Pacific	Charles P. Ridley
The Americas	William E. Ratliff
Middle East and Africa	George S. Rentz
International Communist Front Organizations	Witold S. Sworakowski

HOOVER INSTITUTION PRESS
STANFORD UNIVERSITY, STANFORD, CALIFORNIA

Hoover Institution Publications 160

International Standard Book Number 0-8179-6601-3
Library of Congress Catalog Card Number 76-286
©1976 by the Board of Trustees of the
    Leland Stanford Junior University

Yearbook on

International

Communist Affairs

1976

CONTENTS

Profiles of Individual Communist Parties

Eastern Europe and the Soviet Union

Western Europe

Asia and the Pacific

The Americas

Middle East and Africa

International Communist Front Organizations (Paul F. Magnelia)

Biographies of Prominent International Communist Figures

INTRODUCTION

The purpose of the 1976 *Yearbook on International Communist Affairs*, the tenth consecutive volume in this series, is to provide basic data about organizational and personnel changes, attitudes toward domestic and foreign policies, as well as activities of communist parties and international front organizations throughout the world. Most of the information comes from primary source materials in the native languages. Innovations are the checklist (pp. xv-xx) with 1975 data unless otherwise indicated, and biographic sketches of nine prominent communist leaders: Khieu Samphan (Cambodia), Chang Ch'un-ch'iao and Teng Hsiao-p'ing (China), Carlos Rafael Rodríguez (Cuba), Georges Marchais (France), Enrico Berlinguer (Italy), Alvaro Cunhal (Portugal), Nguyen Huu Tho (South Vietnam), and Santiago Carrillo (Spain).

Profiles on each party include founding date, legal or proscribed status, membership, electoral strength, leadership, auxiliary organizations, domestic activities, ideological orientation, views on international issues, attitude toward the Sino-Soviet dispute, and principal news media. Although identity as an orthodox Marxist-Leninist party remains the criterion for inclusion, pro-Chinese, Castroite, Trotskyist, and other rival communist movements are treated whenever applicable. Guerrilla groups and elements of the so-called New Left are noted, insofar as they affect policies and activities of major communist organizations.

Excluded from the Yearbook are Marxist liberation movements as well as Marxist ruling parties that specifically disclaim being communist. The Frente de Libertação de Moçambique (FRELIMO), for example, now governs the newly independent Popular Republic of Mozambique. It has announced a Marxist program and is organized on the basis of "democratic centralism" but is not, properly speaking, a communist party. The Movimento Popular de Libertação de Angola (MPLA) claims to be in charge of the newly independent "Popular Republic of Angola"; it derives support from Soviet advisers and Cuban armed forces in its struggle against rival movements. The Partido Africano de Independência de Guiné e Cabo Verde (PAIGC) is the ruling party of Guinea-Bissau. MPLA and PAIGC both share FRELIMO's general orientation; they also have been excluded.

The ruling movement in the Congo People's Republic, the Parti Congolais du Travail, claims to be Marxist-Leninist; its leaders state that they are communists committed to "scientific socialism." But the party is not regarded as an orthodox Marxist-Leninist movement by its peers, and the president of the Congo People's Republic has stated recently that, while Marx's writings remain valid, they must be adapted to local conditions. The Supreme Revolutionary Council of Somalia, while likewise committed to the establishment of "scientific socialism," is in a similar category, as are the National Front in the People's Democratic Republic of Yemen and the Party of the People's Revolution in the People's Republic of Benin (called Dahomey until 30 November 1975).

Leftist organizations of an oppositional type, such as the pro-Chinese Mouvement National pour l'Indépendance de Madagascar (Monima), the Eritrean Liberation Front (ELF), as well as the so-called national liberation movements in Bahrain, the Cabinda enclave, Rhodesia, and South-West Africa are not discussed. Likewise omitted are insignificant groups such as the communist parties of Lesotho, the Malagasy Republic, Malta, and Saudi Arabia even though their Marxist-Leninist orthodoxy may not be in dispute. Some of these organizations sent representatives to the Italian and/or Polish communist party congresses during the year under review, but there is little current information about any of them.

Vadim V. Zagladin, first deputy chief of the International Department, CPSU Central Committee, in an article entitled "Changes in the World and the Communist Movement," *Rabochii klass i sovremennyi mir*, no. 5 (September-October 1975), pp. 3-20, asserts that communist parties have representation outside the Bloc in the national legislatures of 24 countries and that some 40 million voters allegedly support the movement in capitalist states. He gives a total of 89 communist parties, including 14 ruling ones, distributed as follows: Western Europe, 19 (2.4 million); the Americas, 25 (almost 500,000); Asia, 22 (nearly 720,000 without Indonesia); Africa, 9 (nearly 20,000 members). Zagladin's figures may not be reliable. For example, a TASS despatch from Moscow on 12 December 1975 listed 20 communist parties in Western Europe, without mentioning those of Iceland or Ireland. The conference at Havana in June 1975, discussed below, attracted delegates from 24 Latin American movements plus observers from Canada and the United States. What may be accurate and indeed significant is Zagladin's claim of "nearly 60 million" communist party members throughout the world, whereas previous statements from Moscow had referred to "over 50 million." The checklist on the following pages is based on membership figures released by each respective party or estimates by Yearbook contributors.

International Conferences. Almost 20 national party congresses, plus various regional meetings and informational seminars have taken place over the past five years attended by representatives of the 25 million communists in both East and West Europe according to a broadcast over Moscow radio on 16 February 1975. These activities more recently have involved also preparation for an all-European conference of communist parties, as a follow-on to the one held during April 1967 at Karlovy Vary, Czechoslovakia. A consultative meeting of delegates from 28 parties held discussions in Budapest from 19 to 21 December 1974 and agreed that the proposed conference would be convened in East Berlin by mid-1975, that all parties could participate in the drafting commission, and that the final documents would have no binding force. The Socialist Unity Party of East Germany served as host for all preliminary sessions throughout the year under review.

The editorial commission's working group attracted representatives from only 16 European communist parties, and they met from 17 to 19 February 1975 for the first time. Twenty parties sent officials to the second session, which lasted three days, between 8 and 10 April. It also ended with an uninformative communiqué, although reports suggested a negative reaction to the East German draft documents by the seven parties from Britain, Italy, Norway, Romania, Spain, Sweden, and Yugoslavia. The third session included 27 delegations (without San Marino) on 9 and 10 October, and the communiqué mentioned that the draft document would be ready the following month. Twenty-six parties were present at the fourth meeting, held during 17-19 November. The last meeting of the year, involving 22 representatives, discussed the fourth successive East German draft from 16 to 19 December. (*Pravda*, 20 December.)

Helsinki radio on 19 November had described the problem as involving a basic disagreement over whether communists should adopt legal or violent means in pursuit of political power. According to some participants, the final document cannot be binding, autonomy of all parties must be respected, absent parties (i.e., the Chinese) may not be criticized, and internationalism is not and cannot be equated with subservience. The chief Yugoslav delegate to the East Berlin sessions, Aleksandar Grličkov, stated in an interview over Belgrade radio on 30 November that "a uniform political line is simply impossible," because each communist party determines "its own political line on the basis of its own revolutionary conditions." Thus, "a joint strategy and tactics for communist parties . . . is today an anachronism."

By contrast, unity efforts were more successful in other parts of the world. Thus during April

1975 all eight of the Arab communist parties, openly recognized as orthodox by the Soviets, were able to hold a joint meeting. Two months later, all 24 of the Moscow-line communist parties throughout Latin America sent representatives to Havana and even issued a statement condemning the Chinese. Both of these conferences called for a world communist meeting, the context within which the above-mentioned European unity efforts have been developing.

Soviet Union and Eastern Europe. Leonid Brezhnev's political preeminence, occasionally in doubt, appeared strengthened by the resignation from the Politburo in April and then from chairmanship of trade unions in May of Aleksandr Shelepin, reputedly the general secretary's rival. Suppression of intellectual dissidents continued through the year, while the CPSU stressed the need for more effective ideological work and tighter supervision over the economy. The new five-year plan (1976-80) lowered targets for growth, but continued emphasis on heavy industry. The worst harvest in a decade brought in less than 133 million metric tons of grain (plan: 215.7 million), the same as during the year 1913.

Success, as well as setbacks and unresolved dilemmas, characterized USSR foreign policy on both politico-military and party levels. Signing of the Final Act at the Conference on Security and Cooperation in Europe, on 1 August at Helsinki, represented achievement of a long-term Soviet objective. Yet provisions of the Final Act concerning free flow of people, ideas, and information between East and West became the subject of increasingly heated disagreement, an indication of how fragile the spirit if not the meaning of international détente had become. The latter officially still is proclaimed the cornerstone of USSR foreign policy.

In the United States, government policy vis-à-vis the Soviet Union came under attack by political, labor, and former military leaders, as well as by intellectuals. Some of the factors contributing to the loss of enthusiasm for détente included collapse of the proposed U.S.-USSR trade agreement in January; alleged violations on the part of the Soviet government of the SALT I agreement; divergent policies in the Middle East; and covert Soviet activities in both Portugal and Angola. A major editorial in *World Marxist Review* for April by editor Konstantin Zarodov and a lead article in *Pravda* on 6 August discussed current political events in Leninist terms, indicating a hardening of the Soviet ideological stance as well as encouragement of more militant policies by foreign communist parties. The fact that Brezhnev met with Zarodov on 17 September appeared to signify approval of the "Zarodov doctrine" which, in the eyes of some Western observers, foreshadowed a return to bolshevik revolutionary zeal. USSR aid to the Popular Movement for the Liberation of Angola (MPLA) totaled about $100 million and some 200 advisers as well as 7,500 Cuban combat troops flown in Soviet transport aircraft from Havana to Luanda with refueling stops reportedly on the Azores.

Indirect Soviet-U.S. confrontation in Africa and Europe did not prevent the two superpowers from concluding long-term business agreements. After a temporary moratorium on grain sales, the two countries reached an agreement in October under which the USSR will purchase six to eight million tons of grain per year between 1976 and 1980. No visible success, however, could be achieved either in the protracted SALT talks or in separate negotiations on a reduction of military forces in Europe.

In Western Europe, on the other hand, notable progress was made in Soviet relations with Britain. Prime Minister Harold Wilson's visit to Moscow during February resulted in a pledge to expand ties, and an economic agreement provided $2.5 billion in credits to the USSR over the next five years. Contacts with France remained less cordial than during the De Gaulle era, and visits of Premier Jacques Chirac in March and of President Valéry Giscard d'Estaing in October did not produce hoped-for results. Likewise signing of the new Soviet-East German friendship pact in October, with its economic integration aspects, as well as West German-Soviet disagreements over Berlin, did not further détente.

Relations with China continued to be stalemated, but acrimonious polemics continued. An editorial in *Kommunist* for August contended that Maoism represents a "danger to all states, regardless of their social system" and that "smashing Maoism" must be the objective of the "ideology, theory, and practical activity of Marxist-Leninists in the conditions of today." The Hanoi victory in Vietnam was greeted warmly in Moscow. In late October, during an official visit, North Vietnam's party leader Le Duan approved the CPSU formulation on international communist unity. The Soviets agreed in return to provide economic and technical assistance. Contacts with the new regime in Cambodia were less than cordial from the beginning, in contrast to expanding Soviet influence in Laos. No progress was evident during negotiations for a peace treaty with Japan. India continued to be one of Moscow's closest friends. Soviet propaganda media placed even greater emphasis than before on the need for a system of collective security in Asia.

Active diplomacy in the Middle East resulted in many two-way visits, including a trip to Moscow during the spring by Yasir Arafat of the Palestine Liberation Organization. Highlights included Soviet criticism of the Sinai agreement between Israel and Egypt, followed by bitter attacks in October against Egyptian president Anwar al Sadat. The Middle East is one region of the world in which Soviet influence declined. However, the volatility of political life, antagonism among Arabs themselves, and the possibility of a new Arab-Israeli conflict should continue to provide the USSR with renewed chances to improve its position.

It was Africa which in 1975 emerged as the most important target for Soviet foreign policy. Besides the growing involvement in Angola, the USSR had footholds in several other states: Guinea-Bissau, Guinea, Equatorial Guinea, the People's Republic of the Congo (all on the west coast), and Somalia on the east coast. Leaders of these and other African governments traveled to Moscow and concluded agreements for economic and technical cooperation as well as military aid, including advisers. It remains to be seen whether Soviet involvement will result in "recolonization," as charged by some U.S. officials. It does reflect the expansionism of a superpower, which disturbs both the United States and Communist China.

Soviet interest in Latin America appeared especially on two occasions: during the conference of Latin-American parties at Havana in June and by the presence of senior Politburo member M. A. Suslov at the first congress of the Cuban Communist Party in December.

Economic matters dominated relations between the Soviet Union and the states of Eastern Europe. The Council for Mutual Economic Assistance (CMEA) agreed in June on a coordinated plan for multilateral integration during the period 1976-80, corresponding to national five-year plans. CMEA members are facing new terms of trade and higher prices for USSR petroleum. On the other hand, heavy debts to the West have made international banks increasingly reluctant to provide more credits. Politically, leaders of most East European parties echoed the main tenets of Soviet foreign policy, especially those heard during the Helsinki summit. At the same time, they insisted in domestic affairs on stronger party discipline and greater conformity by journalists and artists.

As for individual states, disagreements over Albania's economic policies led to significant changes within its Politburo. Enver Hoxha continued his ideological and cultural revolution, with a campaign against bureaucratism. No significant change occurred in Tirana's foreign policies although some rapprochement with Belgrade took place. Strong emphasis on ideology was noticeable also in Sofia. Contrary to past Soviet unilateral economic aid, Bulgaria will extend credits to the USSR over the next five-year period. Controversy with Yugoslavia over the Macedonian issue persisted. Contacts with Greece improved greatly after the overthrow of the military government in Athens, while relations with Turkey remained cool. Despite purges and other repressive measures, opposition in Czechoslovakia could not be silenced. Letters of protest against harassment and persecution often appeared in the Western press. Despite internal repression, Prague has attempted to improve relations with the West.

CHECKLIST

Eastern Europe and the Soviet Union (9)

Country	Population	Communist party membership	Percent of vote	Status	Sino-Soviet dispute
Albania	2,378,000	100,000 plus	99.9 (1974); Democratic Front	In power	Pro-Chinese
Bulgaria	8,741,000	700,000 plus	99.8 (1971); Fatherland Front	In power	Pro-Soviet
Czechoslovakia	14,804,000	1,100,000 plus	99.8 (1971); National Front	In power	Pro-Soviet
East Germany	17,050,000	1,900,000 plus	98.3 (1971); National Front	In power	Pro-Soviet
Hungary	10,510,000	754,353	99.6 (1975); Patriotic People's Front	In power	Pro-Soviet
Poland	34,022,000	2,453,000	97.0 (1972); National Unity Front	In power	Pro-Soviet
Romania	21,100,000	2,500,000 (1974)	99.9 (1975); Front of Socialist Unity	In power	Pro-Soviet
USSR	254,300,000	15,000,000 plus	99.9 (1974); all 1,517 seats CPSU-approved	In power	Neutral
Yugoslavia	21,352,000	1,192,446	88.0 (1969); Socialist Alliance	In power	Independent
Total	384,257,000	25,699,799 plus			

xv

WESTERN EUROPE (22)

Country	Population	Communist party membership	Percent of vote	Status	Sino-Soviet dispute
Austria	7,600,000	25,000	1.2 (1975); no seats	Legal	Split
Belgium	9,800,000	10,000	3.2 (1974); 4 of 212 seats	Legal	Split
Cyprus	660,000	12,000	30.8 (1970); 9 of 35 Greek Cypriot seats	Legal	Pro-Soviet
Denmark	5,100,000	8,000	4.2 (1975); 7 of 179 seats	Legal	Pro-Soviet
Finland	4,700,000	48,000	19.0 (1975); 40 of 200 seats	Legal	Pro-Soviet
France	53,030,000	500,000	21.3 (1973); 73 of 490 seats	Legal	Pro-Soviet
Germany (FRG)	62,150,000	40,000	0.3 (1972); no seats	Legal	Split
Germany (West Berlin)	2,100,000	8,000	1.9 (1975); no seats	Legal	Pro-Soviet
Great Britain	56,100,000	29,000	0.5 (1974); no seats	Legal	Pro-Soviet
Greece	9,094,000	27,500	3.6 (1974); 8 of 300 seats	Legal	Pro-Soviet
Iceland	218,000	2,500	18.3 (1974); 11 of 60 seats	Legal	Independent
Ireland	3,066,000	300	-- (1973); no seats	Legal	Pro-Soviet
Italy	55,758,000	1,702,600	27.2 (1972); 179 of 630 seats	Legal	Independent
Luxembourg	357,000	500	10.4 (1974); 5 of 59 seats	Legal	Pro-Soviet
Netherlands	13,634,000	10,000	4.5 (1972); 7 of 150 seats	Legal	Independent
Norway	4,014,000	2,500	10.1 (1973); 16 of 155 seats (coalition)	Legal	
Portugal	8,499,000	50,000	12.5 (1975); 30 of 247 seats	Legal	Pro-Soviet
San Marino	19,000	300	23.7 (1974); 15 of 60 seats	Legal	Pro-Soviet
Spain	35,596,000	5,000	-- --	Proscribed	Independent
Sweden	8,192,000	17,000	5.3 (1973); 19 of 350 seats	Legal	Split
Switzerland	6,500,000	6,000	2.5 (1975); 4 of 200 seats	Legal	Pro-Soviet
Turkey	39,219,000	2,000	-- (1973)	Proscribed	Pro-Soviet
Totals	385,406,000	2,506,200			

Middle East and Africa (13)

Country	Population	Communist party membership	Percent of vote	Status	Sino-Soviet dispute
Egypt	37,335,000	500	-- (1971)	Proscribed	Pro-Soviet
Iran	33,200,000	1,000	-- (1975)	Proscribed	Pro-Soviet
Iraq	11,024,000	2,000	No elections since 1958	Allowed	Pro-Soviet
Israel	3,372,000	1,500	1.4 (1973); 4 of 120 seats	Legal	Pro-Soviet
Jordan	2,708,000	400	-- (1967)	Proscribed	Pro-Soviet
Lebanon	2,449,000	3,000	-- (1972); no seats	Legal	Pro-Soviet
The Maghreb					
Algeria	16,794,000	400	-- (1964); no seats	Proscribed	Pro-Soviet
Morocco	17,274,000	500	-- (1970); no seats	Allowed	Pro-Soviet
Tunisia	5,776,000	100	-- (1974)	Proscribed	Pro-Soviet
Réunion	494,000	800	-- (1973); no seats	Legal	Independent
South Africa	24,964,000	300	-- (1974)	Proscribed	Pro-Soviet
Sudan	18,000,000	3,500	-- (1974)	Proscribed	Pro-Soviet
Syria	7,345,000	3,500	-- (1973); 8 of 186 seats	Allowed	Pro-Soviet
Total	180,735,000	17,500			

Asia and the Pacific (21)

Country	Population	Communist party membership	Percent of vote	Status	Sino-Soviet dispute
Australia	13,574,000	2,300	— (1975); no seats	Legal	Split
Bangladesh	73,746,000	2,500	— (1973)	Proscribed	Pro-Soviet
Burma	30,429,000	6,500	— (1974)	Proscribed	Pro-Chinese
Cambodia	7,634,000	10,000	April 1975 coup	In power	Pro-Chinese
China	942,012,000	28,000,000 (1973)	No elections	In power	— —
India	600,297,000	355,000 CPI 106,000 CPI (M)	4.8 (1971); 24 5.2 (1971); 25 of 751 seats	Legal Legal	Pro-Soviet Neutral
Indonesia	131,166,000	800	— (1971)	Proscribed	Split
Japan	110,932,000	330,000	9.4 (1974); 39 of 491 seats	Legal	Independent
Korea (DPRK)	16,507,000	2,000,000	100.0 (1972); all 541 seats	In power	Neutral
Laos	3,336,000	Unknown	December 1975 coup	In power	Neutral
Malaysia	11,860,000	3,000 insurgents	— (1974)	Proscribed	Pro-Chinese
Mongolia	1,444,000	58,000 (1972)	99.9 (1973); all 336 seats	In power	Pro-Soviet
Nepal	12,550,000	5,000	— (1959)	Proscribed	Factions
New Zealand	3,092,000	100 CPNZ 120 SUP	0.1 (1975); no seats 0.2 (1975); no seats	Legal	Split
Pakistan	70,938,000	800 (1973)	— (1970)	Proscribed	Pro-Chinese
Philippines	42,845,000	2,000 insurgents	Elections suspended	Proscribed	Split
Singapore	2,254,000	200	— (1972)	Proscribed	Pro-Chinese
Sri Lanka	13,763,000	2,000 CP/M 1,000 CP/P	8.7 (1970); 19 of 187 seats no seats	Legal	Split
Thailand	42,298,000	8,000 insurgents	— (1975)	Proscribed	Pro-Chinese
Vietnam (DRV)	24,323,000	900,000	99.9 (1975); all 420 seats	In power	Neutral
Vietnam (RV)	20,843,000	180,000	In process of unification with DRV	In power	Neutral
Total	2,175,843,000	31,973,320			

The Americas (26)

Country	Population	Communist party membership	Percent of vote	Status	Sino-Soviet dispute
Argentina	25,030,000	147,000	— (1973); 2 of 243 Chamber seats	Legal	Pro-Soviet
Bolivia	5,272,000	450	No elections	Proscribed	Split
Brazil	107,613,000	7,000	— (1974)	Proscribed	Split
Canada	22,781,000	2,500	— (1974); no seats	Legal	Split
Chile	10,584,000	100,000	No elections	Proscribed	Pro-Soviet
Colombia	22,217,000	12,000	— (1974); 2 of 199 Chamber seats	Legal	Split
Costa Rica	1,968,000	1,500	— (1974); 2 of 57 seats	Legal	Pro-Soviet
Cuba	9,252,000	200,000	No elections	In power	Pro-Soviet
Dominican Republic	4,697,000	1,500	— (1974)	Proscribed	Factions
Ecuador	6,705,000	600	No elections	Legal	Split
El Salvador	4,100,000	175	— (1974)	Legal	Pro-Soviet
Guadeloupe	352,000	3,000	— (1973); 10 of 31 Gen. Council seats	Proscribed	Pro-Soviet
Guatemala	5,853,000	750	— (1974)	Legal	Pro-Soviet
Guyana	811,000	100	26.0 (1973); 14 of 53 seats	Proscribed	Pro-Soviet
Haiti	4,569,000	150	— (1973)	Legal	Pro-Soviet
Honduras	2,749,000	750	No elections	Proscribed	Pro-Soviet
Martinique	347,000	1,000	— (1973); 4 of 36 Gen. Council seats	Proscribed	Pro-Soviet
Mexico	58,075,000	5,000	— (1973); no seats	Legal	Pro-Soviet
Nicaragua	2,153,000	150	— (1972)	Legal	Independent
Panama	1,668,000	500	— (1972)	Proscribed	Pro-Soviet

The Americas (26) *(Cont.)*

Country	Population	Communist party membership	Percent of vote	Status	Sino-Soviet dispute
Paraguay	2,547,000	3,500	— (1973)	Proscribed	Split
Peru	14,819,000	3,200	No elections	Legal	Split
Puerto Rico	900,000	125	— (1972); no seats	Legal	Pro-Soviet
United States	215,000,000	15,000	— (1974); no seats	Legal	Pro-Soviet
Uruguay	3,064,000	30,000	No elections	Proscribed	Pro-Soviet
Venezuela	11,980,000	6,000	— (1973): 11 (MAS, 9; PCV, 2) of 195 Chamber seats; 2 (MAS) of 47 Senate seats	Legal	Pro-Soviet
Total	545,106,000	541,950		Legal	Factions

International Communist Front Organizations

	Headquarters	Claimed Membership
Afro-Asian People's Solidarity Organization	Cairo	No data
Afro-Asian Writers' Permanent Bureau	Cairo	No data
International Association of Democratic Lawyers	Brussels	25,000
International Federation of Resistance Fighters	Vienna	4,000,000
International Organization of Journalists	Prague	150,000
International Union of Students	Prague	No data
Women's International Democratic Federation	East Berlin	200,000,000
World Federation of Democratic Youth	Budapest	100,000,000
World Federation of Scientific Workers	London	300,000
World Federation of Trade Unions	Prague	170,000,000
World Peace Council	Helsinki	(Affiliates in 80 countries)

The German Democratic Republic maintained its intransigent line. A new treaty, concluded for 25 years at Moscow in October, removed the earlier reference to German reunification and reaffirmed the Brezhnev Doctrine. In Hungary, too, the direction was away from liberalism and toward orthodoxy. Budapest's economy experienced difficulties, resulting largely from world-wide inflation, depressed markets in the West, and higher prices for Soviet oil and raw materials. Even the "New Economic Mechanism," which served well for years, deteriorated because its initial promoters lost their influence and the assertiveness of those who advocate centralized planning increased. The Hungarian communist party held its congress in March and reelected János Kádár as first secretary. The party in Poland confirmed Edward Gierek as leader at a congress in December. Both meetings were attended by Leonid Brezhnev. A reform in Poland, enacted by parliament in July, simplified administration and gave a bonus to Gierek by circumscribing the power base of regional party officials. Real and potential economic shortages present complications in Poland. It is noteworthy that the party intends to have its rule officially recognized in a constitutional amendment. This reportedly provoked open opposition by a group of prominent writers at the end of the year.

As in the past, although less conspicuously, Romania again in 1975 confirmed its own brand of national communism. A policy of rotating leading party cadres has resulted in even greater power for Nicolae Ceauşescu. More control was imposed in ideological and literary areas. The country faced serious economic problems, especially in agriculture and a balance of payments deficit. Ceauşescu's own summit diplomacy made foreign policy unusually active. He expressed firm support for the Helsinki conference, called for international communist unity based on equality, and encouraged press articles criticizing supra-national integration within CMEA. A special aspect of Romania's diplomacy involved closer relations with non-aligned states and identification as a developing country eligible for international economic aid. At the same time political and economic relations with the West were expanded, and most-favored nation status was obtained through a trade agreement from the United States. A treaty of friendship and cooperation with Portugal was signed in May, the first between members of the Warsaw Pact and NATO respectively.

Yugoslavia was beset by confrontations between the regime and various opponents, the latter preparing themselves or at least hoping for more decisive action after Tito's demise. With repressive vigor, surpassing other communist-ruled countries with the exception of the Soviet Union, authorities in Belgrade battled a spectrum of adversaries—critics, separatists, terrorists, philosophers, writers, Cominformists, and religious leaders. The Yugoslav economy grappled with stabilization efforts, unattainable due to soaring inflation, a huge foreign trade deficit, and low labor productivity. Relations with the USSR underwent phases of quasi-open hostility over the issue of anti-Titoist activities by so-called Cominformists inside the country. However, in December a trade accord was reached, the largest Yugoslavia had ever signed.

Western Europe. During the past several years, communist parties in Western Europe have emphasized the necessity for détente and focused attention on "unity of action" among the Left on issues of foreign and domestic policy. These two themes continued to receive wide attention throughout 1975. Therefore, the Conference on Security and Cooperation in Europe received almost universal endorsement as a major contribution toward peaceful co-existence. At the same time, most of the communist parties acknowledged that the latter did not imply ideological co-existence. This point assumed increasing significance during the year, not only because 15 of the 22 parties are represented in the parliaments of their respective countries but also because of activities by the two largest non-ruling communist movements of the world, namely, those of Italy and France.

The most striking development occurred in the former, where the Italian Communist Party (PCI) holds almost 30 percent of the seats in parliament. As a result of victories in regional elections during June, it now participates directly in every major city government except for Rome and Palermo. The

PCI, with 1.7 million members, has a more cohesive organization than any other party. It controls the largest labor union, the 3.6 million member General Confederation of Labor. Together with the Italian Socialist Party, the PCI controls the administration of five among the country's twenty regions and participates to a major degree in the administration of five others. These ten regions are the most populous and productive. But most importantly, the PCI succeeded in making the question of its participation in the national government a principal subject of public discussion during the year.

At the party congress in March, Secretary General Enrico Berlinguer stressed PCI support for a policy of "historical compromise" which entails participation in local and national government together with the Socialists and the more conservative Christian Democrats. This policy is not restricted to endorsing unity of action among the Left, along the lines of the electoral coalition between communist and socialist parties in France during 1973 and 1974. The PCI supported 64 of 76 bills proposed by the Italian government in the course of the past year and joined with the Christian Democrats during the fall on the issue of abortion.

Pleading for a "historical compromise," the PCI contended that its basic policies pose no threat to civil liberties, private property, or national independence. In addition, it claimed that communism is not incompatible with the beliefs of the Catholic church (the Vatican rejected this assertion in December), that it is the most democratic of all Italian parties because it enjoys the most widespread popular support, and that it does not endorse violence and privation which communism has brought elsewhere. In this regard the PCI was especially critical, together with the Communist Party of Spain (PCE), of the Portuguese Communist Party's tactics and of its secretary-general, Alvaro Cunhal. At a meeting with Berlinguer in November, PCE secretary-general Carrillo made a special point of rejecting the people's democracy model of Eastern Europe and endorsed instead "the value of personal and collective freedom," "the principle of the secular state [and] its democratic functioning," "religious freedom," and "the freedom of expression, culture, [and] art."

Whether or not the new policy will gain for the PCI predominant influence in the Italian government remains uncertain. Berlinguer made it clear in November that the PCI would devote its major efforts during 1976 toward achieving the "historical compromise." Any Italian government is likely to require communist support to pass legislation, maintain labor peace, and stay in power, as long as the Socialist Party continues in opposition. At the same time if the PCI achieves this "historical compromise," the democratic process is likely to be placed in serious jeopardy.

The Communist Party of France (PCF), headed by George Marchais, stressed unity of the left, especially since it enjoys less electoral support. It depends on its own ability to persuade other elements of the left-wing opposition in France to coordinate actions with the communists. The electoral alliance formed in 1972 between the PCF and the Socialist Party, led by François Mitterand, brought significant gains in the elections to the French National Assembly in 1973 as well as in the following year's presidential election in which Valéry Giscard d'Estaing narrowly defeated Mitterand.

In 1973, however, it appeared that the main beneficiary of this alliance was the Socialist Party, whose popular support, as indicated in public opinion polls, registered at 34 percent (a total higher than that of the Gaullists), while the PCF scored only 18 percent. As a consequence, while it was evident that both parties would continue to require each other's support, polemics dominated relations between the PCF and the Socialist Party during 1975. The PCF criticized Mitterand's cooperation with French government efforts to solve inflation and unemployment as unacceptable compromise. Thus, while some leaders of the PCF did meet with French cabinet officials, including the minister of the interior, General Secretary Marchais refused any cooperation with Giscard d'Estaing.

Another dispute between the PCF and the Socialist Party centered around developments in Portugal. While Marchais accused the Socialists of seeking to take advantage of an alleged anti-communist campaign to strengthen themselves at the expense of the PCF, Mitterand denied this accusation and rejected the PCF contention that the Socialists were preparing to betray the Union of the Left and align themselves with the "Right." This dispute was exacerbated by publication of a book written by PCF Politburo member Etienne Fajon. Marchais is reported during a secret meeting in June 1972 to have explained that concessions made by the PCF in joining the Union of the Left could be turned to its own advantage and that it would be necessary to continue communist party work, while mistrusting the Socialists and criticizing them whenever necessary.

Although Italian and French communist parties adopted different approaches to domestic policy, they did agree to remain independent of the USSR in developing policies within their respective countries. This was made clear in the autumn joint communiqué by Marchais and Berlinguer, who supported "democratic" change in their countries independent of "all foreign interference." The communiqué also stated that all Europeans should be free to travel between countries (a reference to Soviet/East European emigration and travel restrictions, notably the wall dividing Berlin) and concluded that "the right of each people to decide in a sovereign manner its own political and social regime must be guaranteed."

Developments in Portugal during the year did not increase the influence achieved in 1974 by that country's communist party (PCP). Secretary-General Alvaro Cunhal lost his position in the cabinet following national elections for a constituent assembly in April, in which the PCP received only 12.5 percent of the vote. Nevertheless, the communist alliance with radical elements of the armed forces precipitated a violent escalation in the struggle for power, which plunged Portugal into political and economic disarray. Massive protest demonstrations mobilized during August by the Socialist and Popular Democratic parties, which had won a combined 64 percent of the April vote, forced military leaders to assume a moderate stance. Under the new government formed in August the cabinet reflected the electoral mandate and included PCP member Alvaro Veiga Oliveira as minister of public works.

Throughout the fall Portugal remained in turmoil, as the dominant Socialists sought to dismantle the PCP power structure at all levels of government and throughout the mass media as well as in the highest echelons of the armed forces. The Revolutionary Council was restructured to provide the Army and Air Force with more comfortable majorities over the more radical Navy. In addition, occupation by the military of leftist-controlled radio and television stations was ordered so as to halt the provocative campaign against the government. The result was a violent communist and radical-left backlash which included a rebellion by entire military units, street demonstrations, and bombings by leftist as well as rightist paramilitary organizations. President Costa Gomes, who had sought to avert civil war through conciliation among the major political parties, finally declared martial law at the end of November when 1,500 paratroopers seized four air bases and four radio and television stations.

At the end of the year, the struggle between the Socialists and Popular Democrats on one side and the Communists on the other remained unresolved. The confrontation in Portugal is of importance because of the Soviet role in that country. A report early in the year affirmed that the USSR had requested permission from Portuguese officials to grant its fishing fleet the use of port facilities, which would allow electronic listening devices to record NATO military operations. Another report estimated that the Soviet government was sending more than $10 million each month to the PCP, in addition to staffing the USSR embassy in Lisbon well beyond normal diplomatic requirements.

While events in France, Italy, and Portugal warranted major attention during the year, an electoral success was achieved by the Communist Party of Finland (SKP) in September. Its numbers increased in parliament by three to 40 out of 200 seats. The party now has four cabinet positions in the new Finnish government: ministers of labor and of transport and communications plus deputy ministers of the interior and of education. However, the SKP failed in November to gain control over the influential Metal Workers Union.

Left- and right-wing factionalism within other Scandinavian communist parties did not contribute to cohesion. At the end of the year these parties, as well as those in the Federal Republic of Germany, Greece, Cyprus, Belgium, and Austria, endorsed the parliamentary road to participation in their respective governments. Their future, as well as that of the parties in the Netherlands and Great Britain, will be influenced by the success or failure of policies being pursued by the communist parties in Italy, France, and Portugal.

Asia and the Pacific. The second plenary session of the Chinese Communist Party's (CCP) tenth Central Committee was held from 8 to 10 January in Peking, followed only a few days later by the fourth National People's Congress. The latter approved a revised constitution which provides for consolidation of party control over the military: the chairman of the CCP Central Committee, henceforth, will command the armed forces. With Mao Tse-tung in poor health and Chou En-lai's death, effective leadership remains in the hands of Teng Hsiao-p'ing, who may become the next chief of state even though he has made enemies over the years. The largest party in the world, the CCP has a membership of about 28 million. Its tenth Central Committee comprises 193 members and 124 alternates (204 of them had served on the previous one). In addition to Mao and Teng, the Politburo's Standing Committee includes only five other individuals: Wang Hung-wen, Yeh Chien-ying, Chu Teh, Li Teh-sheng, and Chang Ch'un-ch'iao. Two members died during the year, namely, Tung Pi-wu in April and K'ang Sheng in December. The greatest potential challenge to Teng is Chang Chun-ch'iao, whose biography appears in this Yearbook. Chou En-lai died in January 1976.

The period under review once again involved campaigns of criticism on the domestic front. The anti-Lin [Piao] anti-Confucius campaign, which had reached a peak in 1974, continued but at a lower level of intensity, perhaps reflecting the temporary abatement of the leadership crisis. However, two other campaigns were initiated during 1975 which are significant from an economic point of view. The first, launched in early February, promoted study of proletarian dictatorship theory, criticism and restriction of capitalist practices that continue to exist in China, and discouragement of wage incentives. It is this last aspect that may have contributed to labor unrest throughout the country. The other campaign, begun in September, sought to criticize the popular 14th-century novel *Shui Hu Chuan (All Men Are Brothers)*. Its apparent target is those who desire an immediate rise in living standards, as opposed to the long-term goal of gradual improvement.

In foreign affairs, China maintained diplomatic relations with 103 countries, including Cambodia and South Vietnam. A steady stream of foreign government officials from Africa, Europe, and the United States came to Peking during the year. China continued its international trade, although volume with the United States decreased. President Gerald R. Ford's visit to the Mainland in December appeared to indicate Peking's continuing desire to offset Moscow's power. Despite some problems, Japan remained the largest trading partner of China. On the other hand, Sino-Soviet relations are bitter. Two aid agreements between Moscow and Hanoi, as well as a North Vietnamese declaration supporting Soviet views, added to the tension. China's prestige in Southeast Asia has grown, with only Djakarta and Singapore not recognizing Peking de jure. Good relations with communist factions outside the Soviet Bloc were symbolized by greetings received on the 26th anniversary of the PRC from parties or sympathetic groups in Argentina, Australia, Austria, Belgium, France, Germany, Greece, Italy, Japan, the Netherlands, Norway, Peru, Portugal, Sri Lanka, Sweden, and the United States.

On the Korean peninsula, tension continued between North and South, with the former stepping up its propaganda attacks. Two clashes also occurred at sea. North Koreans built a new airfield close to the DMZ and, during the final weeks of war in Vietnam, moved armored divisions close to the 38th parallel. Danger of war being provoked by the North was eliminated because of Chinese opposition to an attack, a view communicated in April to Kim Il-song during his visit to Peking. Nevertheless, the situation remains tense.

In Indochina, communists established their control over South Vietnam and Cambodia during the year under review. The victory by Hanoi may have come as a surprise even to the North Vietnamese themselves, since they appeared pessimistic about the prospects as late as January. Open acknowledgement that the party had directed the insurgency in the South from its earliest days soon followed. Thus, in May 1975, the Lao Dong resumed the older organizational arrangement of northern and southern branches, with the People's Revolutionary Party disappearing. The sudden victory left Hanoi with serious problems. Internally, the leadership is faced with the need to improve living conditions of the North Vietnamese. Party leaders in the South have exercised their authority through provisional people's revolutionary committees. Elections are scheduled for April 1976 to select a national assembly, charged with drawing up a new constitution that will reunify the country.

April 1975 also witnessed victory for the communists in Cambodia, with the result that they now run the state through the National Union of Kampuchea. While there has been little hard information, it appears that the regime has brought about sweeping social changes of a harsh nature, with the ultimate aim of making Cambodia or Kampuchea, as it is now called, self-sufficient economically and independent of other countries.

Compared with the violent transitions in Vietnam and Cambodia, the one engineered by the People's Revolutionary Party of Laos did not appear as traumatic. The Lao Patriotic Front stepped up its activity at the same time that the communist offensive was launched in South Vietnam. As a result, the Pathet Lao assumed territorial and administrative control at all levels below the top. Elections were held throughout the country on 5 November. At a national congress of people's representatives in Vientiane four weeks later, a note of abdication was accepted from the king and the People's Democratic Republic of Laos established.

In neighboring Thailand insurgency activity increased during 1975, concentrated in the northeast. Since the end of the Indochina war, communist guerrillas have stepped up their operations also in the south with the killing of about 125 local government officials in that region. Burma, farther away from these centers of turmoil, has experienced little guerrilla activity. Thakin Ba Thein Tin assumed the chairmanship of the Burmese Communist Party in June, following the deaths of former chairman Thakin Zin and secretary Thakin Chit during a clash with government troops in the Pegu Yoma mountains. Because of the new leader's close Chinese association, his party's policy is now more than ever attuned ideologically with that of Peking.

Malaysia represents another area of growing unrest. Communist guerrilla operations have been relatively successful in the West, with a steadily mounting number of senior police and counter-insurgency officers being assassinated and with continuing ambushes and guerrilla attacks against construction projects and government patrols. By mid-year, Malaysian security officials were becoming apprehensive over broadening terrorist operations in the suburban and even urban areas of the country. As unemployment remains a problem, this can be expected to have a certain radicalizing political effect. On the other hand, tension among factions within the Communist Party of Malaysia continues unabated and thereby weakens the strength of the movement.

As a result of close government supervision, communists in Singapore have been capable of only limited overt activity. In neighboring Indonesia, the communist movement is badly divided and capable of only small-scale guerrilla activity, primarily in the border region of Sarawak adjacent to West Kalimantan (Borneo). While operations by insurgent groups have continued in the Philippines, the communist party is essentially inactive with most members either in detention or under close surveillance.

Also for the Japan Communist Party (JCP), it was a year of setbacks with a poor showing in the April elections and circulation of the official newspaper *Akahata* falling from three to about 2.5 million by September. Candidates for governorships won only in three prefectures, and there was a decline from 103 to 95 in JCP prefectural assembly seats. At present, only nine among 47 incumbent prefectural governors owe their positions to support from the communists. However, as of September the JCP controlled 3,144 seats in prefectural, city, town, and village assemblies, an advance over the 2,809 it had a year ago. Poor relations exist between the JCP and the Japan Socialist Party, and there were no signs of reconciliation with either the Chinese or Soviet communist parties.

The Communist Party of India (CPI) held its tenth congress from late January to early February, with little significant action taking place. CPI candidates suffered a major defeat in the June election in Gujarat. Prime Minister Indira Gandhi's crackdown received communist support, and the party continued to express anti-Maoist sentiments. In neighboring Sri Lanka, there have been internal divisions in the communist party toward participation in a national coalition government. The major Marxist movement in the country remains the Lanka Sama Samaja Party (LSSP or Ceylon Equal Society Party). Both parties were concerned during the year with the increasingly strained United Front relationship and Prime Minister Bandaranaike's subsequent expulsion from the government of the LSSP. In Bangladesh, among the eight different communist groups, only the Communist Party of Bangladesh is pro-Soviet; the others are pro-Chinese. The August 1975 coup produced conflict among communist as well as other Marxist-Leninist movements regarding the prospects for revolution under the new regime.

The Americas. The basic political line among pro-Soviet communist parties remained the same throughout the year, i.e., establishment of broad united fronts. The major event of the year was a conference of communist parties from Latin America and the Caribbean, held during 9-13 June 1975 at Havana and attended by 24 voting delegations, including representatives from Guadeloupe, Martinique, and Puerto Rico. Observers came from Canada and the United States. The first suggestion for such a conference had been made about one year previously by the movements in Central America and Mexico. Continuing divisions among Latin American Marxist-Leninists could be seen from the fact that certain groups were not invited to Havana, namely, the pro-Chinese;* Trotskyist; guerrilla-oriented, such as the ELN in Bolivia, the ERP in Argentina, and the MIR in Chile; independents, like the Movement toward Socialism or the Communist Vanguard in Venezuela.

A conference declaration gave the "orthodox" pro-Soviet view of revolutionary potential throughout Latin America in some 20,000 words. Governments of Ecuador, Mexico, Panama, Peru (under Juan Velasco), and Venezuela, all received praise. (The pro-Soviet parties maintained their support of Peru even after General Francisco Morales replaced Velasco in the August 1975 coup.) The Havana document stressed the need for anti-imperialist action in unity with other leftists and certain middle-class sectors during the "struggle for economic independence and sovereignty." Nationalist tendencies, it was hoped, could be transformed into anti-imperialist and revolutionary positions with sufficiently decisive participation by "people's forces." The Chilean experience of the early 1970s, according to the declaration signed by all voting delegations, showed that "revolutionary movements cannot disregard any method of democratic access to power"; they also must be "fully prepared and ready to defend, with force of arms, democratic achievements." The document, discussed in an appendix to the article on Cuba, called for a world conference of communist parties and condemned the "treasonous" foreign policy of the Chinese Communist Party.

The conference at Havana marked the full alignment of Fidel Castro with the group of pro-Soviet communist parties in Latin America. Cuba's position at this meeting represented only one indication of its excellent relations with the USSR, another being Cuban support for Soviet policies in Angola (see below). The opening to other Latin American states was facilitated by the lifting of OAS

---

* Maoist groups continued to decline from their original insignificance, in large part because the People's Republic of China cultivated warm relations even with the most "reactionary" of governments, including that of Augusto Pinochet in Chile.

sanctions in late July, nationalistic attitudes in many countries, declining U.S. influence in the area, as well as Soviet encouragement which Castro had rejected in the middle and late 1960s. Domestically the year in Cuba was dominated by preparations for the first party congress, ten years after the party's founding in 1965. Convened in mid-December, the congress approved a new constitution for the country that would become effective as of early 1976.

Guerrilla-oriented groups remained generally subdued in most countries, largely because of suppression and alternate roads offered by right-wing (Bolivia, Brazil, Chile, and Uruguay), leftist military (Peru), and constitutional (Venezuela) governments across the continent. Terrorist activity revived to some degree in Colombia for a time but was of greatest importance in Argentina, where the originally Trotskyist People's Revolutionary Army (ERP) and the Peronist Montoneros played a major role in pushing the military once again to the fore in domestic politics. Argentine guerrillas, with extensive extortion funds at their disposal, as well as invaluable experience, continued to assist other Latin American guerrillas, particularly those in Bolivia and Chile.

Efforts to promote armed struggle by means of a so-called guerrilla international were continued by the Junta for Revolutionary Coordination, initiated during 1974 by the Argentine ERP. It includes the Bolivian ELN, the Chilean MIR, and the Uruguayan MLN-Tupamaros, with offices and a press agency (APAL) in Paris. These guerrillas call for a prolonged struggle, continental in scope, and establishment of socialism. They condemn "reformists," i.e., the orthodox communist parties, which are assailed for rejecting armed struggle in favor of agitation or even a "pact with the bourgeoisie." Thus, in verbal terms at least, many guerrillas long labeled Castroite advocated a more militant line than that of the Cuban leader whose statements and policies were once such an inspiration to them.

The Communist Party of the United States (CPUSA) and the Socialist Workers' Party (Trotskyist) remained active in broadly based left-wing movements, particularly those involving support for school busing and black causes, as well as attacks against the present government of Chile. The CPUSA opposes the Equal Rights Amendment (ERA) on the ground that it will eliminate existing protective laws. It supports instead legislation that will extend women's rights. The party is vigorously attacked for this stand by other Marxist-Leninist movements in the United States. The ERA position has apparently created some difficulties within the CPUSA, as have its statements relating to Israel and the Middle East in general.

Party leader Gus Hall has commented that a socialist revolution in the United States is "blowing in the wind." The CPUSA hopes to run candidates in all 50 states during the November 1976 election. It will not work through either major party but calls on "all progressives, independents, and anti-monopoly forces to join in a dialogue now," for the purpose of establishing "a common electoral front against the monarchs of monopoly capitalism." According to Hall, the party seeks the broadest unity possible and does not even insist on an acceptance of socialism as the final goal. The alliance he wants would be able to support a Ramsey Clark and a Bella Abzug as well as individual communists. The CPUSA condemned assassination attempts on President Gerald R. Ford, because objectively they served "only the ruling class," and denounced Puerto Rican terrorist bombings as the work of agents-provocateur.

Middle East and Africa. Communist movements in this part of the world remain small, with memberships for individual countries ranging from several hundred up to a few thousand at most. During the year 1975 legal parties operated in Algeria, Iraq, Israel, Lebanon, Morocco, and Syria, with roles mostly limited to domestic political affairs. For several years now, communists have held cabinet posts in Iraq as well as Syria, and party members have sat in Israel's parliament. Many of these movements aim at enhancing their influence through participation with more influential groups in national fronts, but this strategy has not always been successful. In 1975, for example, the Iraqi communists ran into serious trouble with the ruling Ba'th party.

The principal communist movements in the Middle East continue to be pro-Soviet. Ever since President Richard M. Nixon's visit to Peking in 1972 and the lessening of tension between the People's Republic of China and the United States, elements on the extreme left of the Middle East political spectrum have avoided labeling themselves Maoist. Chinese communist activities and influence in the region remained at a low ebb during the year under review.

The Soviet Union continued to pursue its program of supplying military equipment to Iraq and Syria in massive amounts. As a consequence, in part, the communist parties in those two countries had until recently been among the strongest in the Middle East. In 1975, however, the Iraqi movement lost much ground, and internal dissension may have weakened its Syrian counterpart. As a result of deterioration in relations with Egypt, the USSR withheld military aid from that country. Toward the end of the year, however, signs indicated that the two sides were attempting to resolve their differences, despite Egypt's increasingly warmer ties with the United States. The Communist Party of Egypt resurfaced outside of the country, with a manifesto published at Beirut during August.

The movement in Jordan, which sought to bring Jordanians and Palestinians together under its umbrella, lost the support of some elements which took to calling themselves the Communist Party of the West Bank or the Palestine Communist Party. During the civil conflict in Lebanon in 1975, the communists there came out with statements vigorously criticizing the Christian Phalangists but did not appear as one of the main protagonists in the street fighting.

The parties in the states of the Maghreb (Algeria, Morocco, and Tunisia) had little impact on either internal or external developments of their respective countries. The same was true of the once strong and now fractured and all but impotent movement in Sudan. The Tudeh Party, effectively excluded from its Iranian homeland, attacked the Shah's government persistently from its base in Eastern Europe. Activities inside Iran by less prominent communist organizations seem to have been curbed to a great degree by the secret police, and at the end of December an army tribunal sentenced ten Marxist guerrillas to death for killing three Americans and five Iranians.

MAKI, the smaller of the two communist parties in Israel, lost its identity by merging with a socialist group. The larger RAKAH, membership in which is predominantly Arab, demonstrated its growing strength by winning the Nazareth mayoralty election in December. This victory indicates a trend among Arab citizens of Israel toward greater ethnic nationalism and perhaps even radicalism. RAKAH won widespread recognition from other parties as the only communist movement in Israel during the year under review.

Early in April, representatives from the Iraqi, Jordanian, Lebanese, Sudanese, Syrian, and Tunisian communist parties as well as the Party of Progress and Socialism in Morocco and the Socialist Vanguard Party in Algeria met at an undisclosed place and issued a declaration on the aims and prospects of the Arab national liberation movement. This document condemned U.S. imperialism and Zionism, and strongly supported the Palestine Liberation Organization for its leadership of the resistance movement. The government of Egypt was criticized for undermining the public sector and compromising with imperialism, when it signed the interim agreement with Israel. Saudi Arabia was charged with being linked to imperialism. The abridged text of the declaration did not include the fact that the eight parties had gone on record in support of convening a world conference of communist movements.

In the fall of 1975 the Iraqi Communist Party, the National Front for the Liberation of Bahrain, and the newly surfaced Saudi Arabian Communist Party held a conference at an undisclosed location. They protested against Western imperialism in the Arabian (Persian) Gulf and advocated national investments in the oil industry which, of course, already are being made on a broad scale. The communist party in Saudi Arabia is reported to represent merely a successor to the old National Front for the Liberation of Saudi Arabia, about which little is known.

Fronts. Throughout 1975 the various international communist front organizations addressed themselves to a select number of issues and continued efforts to expand their contacts with what they described as "progressive" sectors of society. In effect, all fronts sought to penetrate and develop working relationships with non-communist groups. This was particularly evident in the policies of the World Peace Council (WPC), the World Federation of Democratic Youth (WFDY), and the International Union of Students (IUS). In this respect, the unity theme of IUS policy could be seen most clearly from its efforts to broaden contacts throughout Western Europe. For the WFTU, expanded contacts meant not only working with non-communist trade unions but also vigorously operating within a variety of other groups, especially the International Labor Organization and the Food and Agriculture Organization.

For the fronts, the Conference on Security and Cooperation in Europe (CSCE) and the question of disarmament were prominent issues which engaged much of the time and effort on their part. Throughout the spring, support activities (rallies, conferences, seminars) were held on behalf of CSCE. After its successful completion, the fronts called for military détente to follow the political détente established at the Helsinki conference. Although "military détente" has never been clearly defined, it certainly refers to the question of disarmament. In this regard, all the fronts participated in a variety of efforts designed to "restrict the arms race." Indeed, the WPC organized a campaign called "The New Stockholm Movement for General and Complete Disarmament," which resembles the old Stockholm Campaign of the 1950s. Linked with this agitation for disarmament was the corollary demand that the West reduce military expenditures. This linkage has been repeated so often by the fronts that it is obvious they consider both aspects equally important.

The fronts continued their activity also in the developing countries. All of them urged an Asian security arrangement; they also spoke out on behalf of the Palestinians and condemned Israel for its "aggressive" policies. Most of the fronts sought to expand their contacts in the so-called Third World, either through conferences and seminars or with training programs which increasingly are being run in the developing states themselves rather than Eastern Europe.

The year 1975 appears to have been a reasonably successful one for the fronts. Most claimed increased memberships (see checklist). Certainly, they have gained more influence in key international groups such as the ILO. They also managed to keep most internal difficulties to a minimum, perhaps because the Chinese chose to remain silent and outside of these international communist front organizations.

*   *   *

The two concepts of communist fragmentation and militancy on a global scale, emphasized in the Introduction to the preceding *Yearbook*, were at least as applicable in 1975 as they were during 1974. Communist fragmentation not only persisted at top levels, as evidenced by the Sino-Soviet conflict, but the inability of the CPSU to convene a conference of European communist parties proved that Moscow needs to exert unprecedented efforts even to assert leadership in its own camp. On the other hand, communist militancy did make gains during 1975—the war in Indochina ended with victories in South Vietnam, Cambodia, and Laos. Communists in Italy achieved impressive electoral successes, and those in Portugal appeared at least temporarily to have been on the verge of seizing power. By dispatching Cuban troops to Angola, Castro made it clear that he views revolution as exportable by choosing a radical path instead of détente with the United States. Above all, the Soviet Union baffled observers by word and action. The Helsinki summit conference with its resounding statement on relaxation of tensions was not implemented by the USSR, as evidenced in the case of Nobel Prize winner Andrei Sakharov and Soviet intervention on the African continent. The latter suggests that confrontation rather than negotiation had become the order of the day. Finally, it would appear that Soviet leaders themselves were not of a single mind whether to pursue genuine détente with the West or to follow the "Zarodov doctrine." The year 1976 will certainly clarify this uncertainty.

*   *   *

Staff members and several of the associate editors were responsible for much of the research and writing of the *Yearbook*. Profiles were prepared by a total of 66 outside contributors, many of whom wrote more than one. Full names and affiliations for most of them appear at the end of the individual essays. Mrs. Ica Juilland assisted in the processing and filing of research material. Much of the final typing was done by Mrs. Louise Doying. Special appreciation is due the curators and their staffs as well as members of the Readers' Services Department at the Hoover Institution. We are indebted particularly to the copy editor, Mr. Jesse M. Phillips, for putting much of the manuscript in its final form.

Sources are cited throughout the text, with news agencies normally identified by generally accepted initials. Abbreviations are also used for the following widely quoted publications:

FBIS	*Foreign Broadcast Information Service*
NYT	*New York Times*
WMR	*World Marxist Review*
IB	and its *Information Bulletin*
YICA	*Yearbook on International Communist Affairs*

January 1976   Richard F. Staar

EASTERN EUROPE AND THE SOVIET UNION

Albania

The Albanian Communist Party was founded on 8 November 1941. At its First Congress, November 1948, the name was changed to the Albanian Party of Labor (Partia e Punës e Shqipërisë; APL). As the only legal political party in Albania, the APL exercises a monopoly of power. Party members hold all key posts in the government and the mass organizations. All 250 seats in the national legislature, the People's Assembly, are held by representatives of the Democratic Front, the party-controlled mass organization to which all Albanian voters belong.

In November 1975 the APL claimed a membership "in excess of 100,000" (*Zëri i popullit*, 8 November). At its Sixth Congress in November 1971, party spokesmen reported that APL membership totaled 86,985. At that time there were approximately 69,000 full members and 18,000 candidates (ibid., 4 November 1971). In 1975, 37.7 percent of APL members were reportedly laborers, 29.2 percent were peasants, and 33.1 percent were white collar workers (ibid., 6 July). Women comprised 26 percent of the party's membership (ibid., 8 November).

The population of Albania in December 1974 was 2,377,600 (Tirana radio, 18 June 1975). According to the most recent census, peasants comprise 49.4 percent of the population; laborers, 36.2 percent; and white-collar workers, 14.4 percent. Approximately 42 percent of the population is under the age of 15 (*Zëri i popullit*, 28 May, 8 June).

Leadership and Organization. Enver Hoxha, who has served as the party's first secretary since its founding, as chairman of the Democratic Front since 1945, and as commander-in-chief of the People's Armed Forces since 1944, is the dominant personality in the ruling elite. Although the 67-year-old Albanian party leader has been reported in the Western European and U.S. press as being in poor health (e.g., *Arbeiter Zeitung*, Vienna, 30 October; *NYT*, 2 November 1975), he nevertheless maintained an active schedule during the year and appeared to be fully in control of the situation in Albania.

In theory, the highest APL authority is the party congress, which, according to the party statute, meets once every five years. In practice, however, the most important APL policy-making organ is its Politburo, currently comprised of 12 full members and 5 candidates. The APL Central Committee, which met only twice during 1975, is generally convened to ratify major Politburo decisions. The exact composition of the Central Committee is at present unknown owing to the purges between 1973-75 that seem to have resulted in the expulsion or demotion of at least a dozen of the 71 full members and 39 candidates elected to this body at the APL Sixth Congress in November 1971.

The full members of the Politburo are Enver Hoxha, Mehmet Shehu, Adil Çarçani, Haki Toska, Hekuran Isaj, Hysni Kapo, Kadri Hazbiu, Manush Myftiu, Pali Miska, Ramiz Alia, Rita Marko, and

Spiro Koleka; while the candidates are Llambi Gegprifti, Pilo Peristeri, Pirro Dodbiba, Qirjako Mihali, and Xhafer Spahiu. In addition to Hoxha, the secretaries of the Central Committee are Hysni Kapo, Ramiz Alia, Haki Toska, and Hekuran Isaj.

For the second consecutive year, there were significant changes in the composition of the APL Politburo. In 1974 Politburo member and Defense Minister Beqir Balluku and Politburo candidate and Armed Forces Chief of Staff Petrit Dume had been expelled from this body and ousted from their state positions (see *YICA, 1975*, pp. 3-4). Following the Seventh APL Central Committee Plenum (26-29 May 1975), deputy prime minister and chairman of the State Planning Commission Abdyl Këllezi and minister of heavy industry and mining Koço Theodosi were both dropped from the Politburo and removed from their government posts.

Këllezi, 56, who had been elected a Politburo candidate in 1966 and to full membership in 1971, had served as a member of the APL Central Committee since 1956. He had headed the State Planning Commission since 1968 and in October 1974 was given the additional designation of deputy prime minister. Since 1959 Këllezi had also been chairman of the Albania-China Friendship Society. In recent years he also seems to have emerged as one of the leading spokesmen for the new Albanian technocracy. Theodosi, 62, was elected to full Politburo membership in 1971 after having been a candidate member of that body since 1956. He had been a Central Committee member since 1952 and had held several responsible state positions in the economic sector since 1944. The downfall of Këllezi and Theodosi apparently stemmed from Hoxha's dissatisfaction with the performance of the Albanian economy during the current five-year plan and from disagreements over the establishment of priorities for the Sixth Five-Year Plan (1976-80) (see *Zëri i popullit*, 13 June; *Rruga e partisë*, June, July).

Two new full members, Hekuran Isaj and Pali Miska, and two candidates, Llambi Gegprifti and Qirjako Mihali, were formally elevated to the Politburo at the Seventh Plenum. Isaj, who was also appointed to the Central Committee Secretariat, had been elected to full Central Committee membership in 1971 and had served as first secretary of the Diber district party organization since 1972. Miska, who was appointed minister of heavy industry and mining in place of Theodosi, had been elected a Central Committee candidate in 1971 and had served as first secretary of the Puke district party organization since 1970. Gegprifti became a Central Committee candidate in 1971 and a deputy defense minister in 1974. Mihali had been a Central Committee candidate since 1966 and in mid 1975 was named first secretary of the Durrës district party organization.

In selecting the new Politburo members and candidates, the APL leadership passed over a number of veteran Central Committee members and party functionaries. It would appear that the ruling elite desired to bring into its ranks relatively young (the new Politburo appointees appear to be in their late thirties to mid forties) vigorous individuals with experience at the grass-roots and district levels who are thoroughly loyal to Enver Hoxha and staunch supporters of his policies.

At the Seventh Plenum, Petro Dode, who had been a member of the Central Committee Secretariat since February 1973, was relieved of this duty and subsequently appointed deputy prime minister and chairman of the State Planning Commission in place of Këllezi. Hekuran Isaj assumed the Central Committee secretaryship vacated by Dode.

Both prior to and, especially, following the Seventh Plenum there were numerous leadership changes at the district level. While the majority of these are attributable to promotions or routine transfers of incumbents, there do appear to have been several dismissals and demotions arising from unsatisfactory performances, particularly in the economic and cultural sectors.

As of December 1975 there had been no public denunciation of Balluku, Dume, Këllezi, Theodosi, or other high-ranking party and state officials who had been deposed during 1974-75. In a speech delivered in early November (*Zëri i popullit*, 9 November), Prime Minister Mehmet Shehu, second-ranking member of the Albanian ruling hierarchy, pointedly ended his catalogue of "party enemies" with Fadil Paçrami and Todi Lubonja, who had been purged from the APL Central Committee at its June 1973 plenum (see *YICA, 1974*, pp. 3-4). It is apparent that the APL leadership, which constantly stresses the theme of a "united people behind a united party" (e.g., *Zëri i popullit*, 8 November), is not eager to acknowledge publicly that divisions have developed within the inner circle of the ruling elite.

Kahreman Ylli, 58, one of the original members of the APL and a member of its Central Committee since 1961, died on 3 September (ibid., 5 September). Ylli had been minister of education in the early 1950s and rector of the State University of Tirana in 1957-70, and was a member of the Presidium of the People's Assembly at the time of his death. In recent years he had become a vigorous advocate of Hoxha's cultural policies.

Auxiliary, Mass and Professional Organizations. Throughout 1975, APL spokesmen repeatedly stressed that the major functions of the mass organizations are to popularize, explain, and implement the party line in their respective areas of concern. They also emphasized that the mass organizations were subordinate to the party and could not under any circumstances operate independently of it (e.g., *Rruga e partisë*, April; *Zëri i popullit*, 11 October). These views reflect the determination of the Albanian leadership to ensure that the party line prevails in every aspect of the nation's life.

In February the United Trade Unions of Albania celebrated its thirtieth anniversary. On this occasion it was noted that laborers comprise 36.2 percent of the country's population, women make up 41 percent of the labor force, the average age of the labor force is 32.5 years of age, and approximately 48 percent of the working class has a complete eight-year or middle school education (*Zëri i popullit*, 11 February). At the March plenum of the Trade Union Central Council, APL theoretician Ramiz Alia severely criticized the organization's leadership for "complacency" and "formalism" in its work (*Rruga e partisë*, April). The Council's July plenum focused on the problem of improving the quality of production and social services in Albania (*Zëri i popullit*, 31 July). Despite the severe criticism of the trade union leadership, Politburo member Rita Marko continued to serve as president of the organization.

At the July Central Committee plenum of the Union of Albanian Labor Youth (UALY), the organization was urged to intensify its efforts to interest younger-generation Albanians in furthering their education in such areas as engineering, agriculture, geology, and other technical fields where there was a pressing need for their services (ibid., 9 July). The UALY November Central Committee plenum was devoted to an examination of the question of how the nation's youth could be encouraged to live and work in the countryside (ibid., 20 November). Rudi Monari, who in 1973 was demoted from UALY first secretary to membership on the Secretariat, had regained the confidence of the APL leadership to the point where he was named to the Secretariat of the Vlorë district party organization (ibid., 29 November).

The Union of Albanian Writers and Artists, which celebrated its 30th anniversary in October, devoted most of its efforts to implementing the ideas and suggestions contained in Enver Hoxha's 20 December 1974 speech, which was not published until January 1975 (ibid., 19 January). In his address Hoxha had characterized the nation's writers and artists as "valuable auxiliaries" of the party in the struggle to build socialism in Albania. To fulfill the responsibilities the party had entrusted to them, the Union sought to strengthen the ideo-political education and outlook of its members, combat all bureaucratic tendencies within its organization, and go to the people for inspiration and to develop new talents (*Nëntori*, February, August). While acknowledging that much progress had been made toward realizing the party directives regarding art and literature issued since 1973, Union Chairman Dritëro Agolli stated that there were still some "shortcomings" in the work and attitudes on the part of some of the nation's artists, writers, and critics (*Zëri i popullit*, 26 October).

Deputy prime minister and Politburo member Spiro Koleka replaced Abdyl Këllezi as chairman of the Albania-China Friendship Society in September (ibid., 12 September). It was revealed in December that APL Central Committee member Ndreçi Plasari had been elected chairman of the Veterans of the Wars of the Albanian People organization in place of the deposed Beqir Balluku (ibid., 9 December).

Party Internal Affairs. There were two APL Central Committee plenums during 1975. The Seventh Plenum met on 26-29 May to discuss and ratify a series of measures, including leadership changes (see above), to "strengthen further" the nation's economy (ibid., 30 May). Both the length of the session as well as the dismissal of Këllezi and Theodosi from their party and state posts underscored the gravity with which Hoxha and his associates viewed the differences regarding economic policy that had arisen within the party. The 8th Central Committee plenum met on 10 October to approve a proposal for drafting a new constitution for the People's Republic of Albania (ibid., 10 October). This action was taken in accordance with the decision of the Sixth APL Congress (1-7 November 1971) directing that the present 1950 constitution be replaced by a new document that would take into account the "revolutionary changes" that have occurred during the 1960s and 1970s (see *YICA, 1972*, p. 6). In November the People's Assembly elected a 51-person commission to draft the constitution. Enver Hoxha was designated chairman of the body. Mehmet Shehu, Hysni Kapo, and Haxhi Lleshi (the Albanian head of state) were named vice-chairmen while Hekuran Isaj was appointed secretary (*Zëri i popullit*, 18 November). APL Central Committee members comprised a majority of the commission.

Domestic Attitudes and Activities. The Ideological and Cultural Revolution continued to dominate the Albanian domestic scene during 1975. Enver Hoxha and other regime spokesmen persisted in emphasizing the position that the root of all problems that arise in a socialist society is ideological (e.g., *Rruga e partisë*, April, June). They maintain that the difficulties Albania has encountered in its efforts to build socialism arise from two sources. The first of these is the ideological, economic, and other pressures applied to Albania from the imperialist-revisionist camp; and the second is the deeply entrenched complex of "bourgeois" and "patriarchal" attitudes from Albania's past (e.g., *Zëri i popullit*, 25 June). The APL leadership apparently believes that the most effective means for assuring the victory of socialism are a comprehensive ideo-political education program and an intensification of the class struggle. Working from these premises, Hoxha and his associates have concluded that the Ideological and Cultural Revolution will be a permanent feature of Albanian life until the "final victory of socialism" has been realized (ibid., 22 February; *Rruga e partisë*, July).

The publication on 3 April of a *Zëri i popullit* editorial titled "When the Class Speaks, Bureaucratism Cannot" marked the beginning of the anti-bureaucratism campaign, one of the major features of the Ideological and Cultural Revolution during 1975. Within days of the appearance of the editorial a nationwide drive was under way to reduce the staffs of government agencies and the number of "non-production" employees in agriculture and industry (*Zëri i popullit*, 3-17 April). Beginning in late April the regime sought to convince both laborers and clerical personnel that it was their duty to volunteer to work in those parts of the country where their skills were required. By early June party spokesmen were beginning to emphasize the concept of rotation of cadres. This appeal was aimed primarily at state and party cadres, who were now being urged to relocate so that their posts might be either abolished or given to other deserving workers. To demonstrate their loyalty to the party, about a dozen deputy ministers and department directors accepted work assignments in local government agencies and in economic enterprises located outside Tirana (ibid., 6 June). By autumn the regime had embarked on a program to "proletarianize" the bureaucracy by recruiting bureaucrats from the ranks of those who were directly engaged in production or who came from a working class background (ibid., 12 September). In the meantime, several thousand administrative positions, mainly in the governmental and economic sectors, had been abolished and the majority of those whose positions had been eliminated were assigned to "productive work." Furthermore, bureaucratic procedures were greatly simplified (ibid., 14 November).

It was reported that between April and November the percentage of cadres in the central bureaucracy who were either workers or came from a working-class background had risen from 18 to 40 (ibid.). While expressing satisfaction over the successes the anti-bureaucratic campaign had enjoyed, the APL leadership declared that it would continue for the foreseeable future (ibid., 12, 17 September).

There appear to have been two primary considerations that inspired the anti-bureaucratism campaign. First, and most important, Hoxha and his associates have no intention of permitting the development of institutionalized opposition or competition to the party in policy making. As one party commentator has observed, "There can be no parallelism or equality between the party and other . . . organs. The party guides and directs in all fields. This is the law of the socialist revolution." (*Rruga e partisë*, April.) Second, the Albanian leadership was genuinely shocked by the increase in the size of the bureaucracy and the growing complexity of its operations. By reducing its size and simplifying its operations, the regime hoped to save money, assign unneeded bureaucrats to productive work, and ease the growing tensions between the masses and an impersonal bureaucracy.

The party has also persevered in its struggle against "bourgeois attitudes and outlooks" which many Albanians, including party members, continue to harbor. It was noted that there are still many Albanians who seek easy jobs and who are overly concerned with promoting their own interests. Unless these and other "unhealthy" attitudes are eradicated, they could, in the opinion of the APL leadership, lead to the "re-bourgeoisification" of Albanian society (ibid., 28 September). It has been further claimed by party spokesmen that the task of combating "alien influences" in Albania has been made especially difficult, since the country has been subjected to "hostile foreign influences and pressures" designed to "corrupt" the party and people in such a manner as to "create favorable conditions for the destruction of the socialist revolution" (ibid., 9 November).

While recognizing the need to keep "revolutionary vigilance" in Albania at a high level, party members were warned against falling into the errors of "leftism" and "sectarianism" in waging the Ideological and Cultural Revolution. It was noted that isolated manifestations of these doctrinal deviations had been detected and that they would be eliminated (ibid.).

In late September Politburo member and party theoretician Ramiz Alia delivered the main address at the "national aktiv" on education held in Tirana. He called for a concerted effort to make the 1969 school reform—which required students to receive instruction in academic studies, production, and physical and military training—a success. Alia also criticized the schools for doing an inadequate job in the ideo-political education of the younger generation. (Ibid., 23 September.)

The party leadership is apparently still unhappy with the administration of the State University of Tirana. During the early stages of the anti-bureaucratism campaign, the university administration and party organization had been accused of moving too slowly in implementing party directives in this area (ibid., 15 May). By early autumn Petrit Radovicka, deputy chairman of the Albanian National Academy of Sciences, had been appointed rector in place of Perikli Prifti, who had assumed that post in July 1973 (ibid., 19 October). Radovicka is the fifth person appointed to the university rectorship since 1970.

The ouster of Dashnor Mamaqi as secretary for propaganda and culture of the Tirana district party organization seemed to reflect the leadership's disappointment at the pace at which intellectuals and bureaucrats in Tirana were embracing the party line on culture and bureaucratism. A Central Committee member since 1961 and a former editor-in-chief of the party newspaper *Zëri i popullit*, Mamaqi had succeeded Fadil Paçrami, the most important victim of the 1973 party purge, in this key party post. Sotir Kamberi, who had served as a member of the Secretariat of the United Trade Unions of Albania since 1952, replaced Mamaqi (*Nëntori*, August). Kamberi is the first non-intellectual to hold this particular post in over a decade, and his appointment apparently signals a tougher party stance against those residents of the Albanian capital city who continue to oppose or remain indifferent to the Ideological and Cultural Revolution.

In response to a series of recommendations by its "workers control group," the members of the Union of Albanian Writers and Artists agreed in April to give up all fees and other forms of compensation which they had received for the publication, performance, or exhibition of their works. The organization further proposed that the salaries of artists, performers, and writers be reduced to bring them more closely in line with workers' wages. These actions, taken at the instigation of the party, reflect Hoxha's determination to make it impossible for intellectuals to become a privileged group within the country.

The Economy. The disappointing performance of the economy during the Fifth Five-Year Plan (1971-75) and the lack of satisfactory progress in the preparation of the preliminary drafts of the Sixth Five-Year Plan (1976-80) became major concerns of the Albanian leadership during 1975. At the January session of the People's Assembly it was reported that during 1974 industrial production was 7.3 percent higher and agricultural output was 11 percent greater than in 1973. The 1975 plan, however, projected only a 4.4 percent rise for industry and an 15.9 percent increase for agriculture (*Probleme ekonomike*, January-March). The adoption of the 1975 economic plan by the People's Assembly indicated that the regime recognized it could not achieve the goals set in the Fifth Five-Year Plan for both industry and agriculture.

In approving the 1975 economic plan the APL leadership had apparently followed the advice of deputy prime minister and chairman of the State Planning Commission Abdyl Këllezi and minister of heavy industry and mining Koço Theodosi, who reportedly had urged that greater emphasis be placed on raising the quality of output rather than on making an heroic effort during 1975 to overcome accumulated production deficits in the industrial sector. By early 1975, however, Hoxha and his associates seem to have developed doubts regarding the wisdom of this course when they learned that, although industrial output was growing at the projected lower rate, there had been no significant improvement in the quality of production (e.g., *Puna*, 16 May). They were apparently further alarmed by the confusion and squabbling that had arisen in the preliminary planning stages for the 1976-80 plan and by the "overly modest" goals which had been proposed for several sectors of the economy (*Rruga e partisë*, June, September).

It was against this background that the Seventh Central Committee Plenum was convened. Këllezi and Theodosi seemed to have been purged not for their errors in judgment, but rather because they and their followers were perceived to have attempted to undermine the influence of the party in economic planning and management by asserting these were areas that required "professional expertise" (ibid., June). A 5 June editorial in *Zëri i popullit* summed up the position of the party leadership when it declared: "Bureaucracy, technocracy, and intellectualism will not be permitted to become dominant in the sphere of economic management. . . . Economic problems . . . are not merely technical matters, but also party matters, ideological matters."

Following the Seventh Plenum, Kiço Ngjela, 55, minister of trade since 1954, was removed from office. Ngjela, who had held a number of posts in the economic sector since 1946, was elected to the APL Central Committee in 1956. Ngjela's downfall apparently stems from the leadership's displeasure at his inability to reduce imports in the consumer sector and to deal effectively with administrative problems which had developed within his Ministry (*Zëri i popullit*, 5, 13 June). Nedin Hoxha, chairman of the People's Executive Committee for the Gjirokaster district since 1971, succeeded Ngjela (ibid., 12 August).

Owing in part to the leadership changes in the economic sector, economic planning for 1976 is behind schedule. The regime has proposed a significant increase in both industrial and agricultural output for 1976. Contrary to reports appearing in the Western press (e.g., *Washington Post*, 28 October; *NYT*, 23 November), there will not be a shift in priorities from heavy to light industry, at least in 1976. The 1976 draft economic plan calls for heavy industry to rise at a much higher rate than light industry. The main responsibilities for light industry are to improve the quality and enlarge the assortment of its output. It is also hoped that Albania will achieve self-sufficiency in bread grains during 1976 (*Zëri i popullit*, 5 December).

Agricultural output continues to lag behind the expectations of the regime. In the hope of improving peasant morale, pensions for collective farmers were raised by 20 to 50 percent in 1975 (Albanian Telegraphic Agency, ATA, 29 December 1974). To stimulate an improvement in agricultural production, the party launched a nationwide campaign to encourage collective farmers to learn from the experiences of the model Kemishtaj Collective Farm of the Lushnje district (ibid., 23-25 September).

On 3 June the People's Republic of Albania (PRA) and the People's Republic of China (PRC) signed four economic aid agreements for the period of the Albanian Sixth Five-Year Plan (ibid., 4 July). As usual, the details of these were not made public.

The Military. The purge of the military leadership which began with the ousters of Beqir Balluku and Petrit Dume in 1974 appeared to have run its course by the close of 1975. Following the Central Committee Sixth Plenum (16-17 December 1974), Sami Mecollari, who had succeeded Dume as armed forces chief of staff, was himself dropped in favor of Veli Llakaj. Llakaj was also named a deputy defense minister. (Ibid., 7 December.) Premier Mehmet Shehu continues to serve as defense minister.

The fall of Balluku and his associates appears to have stemmed from policy differences that had arisen in recent years between the military establishment and the party. The military professionals seemingly wished to strengthen discipline in the armed forces, increase military training at the expense of ideological indoctrination, downplay the concept of "people's war," re-evaluate the Albanian-Chinese relationship, and limit party "interference" in the military sector. Hoxha reacted decisively to eradicate what he viewed as a genuinely serious threat to the primacy of the party in a key area of Albanian life, and to eliminate the possibility of a "putsch" supported by the military (*Rruga e partisë*, July). In his 1975 Army Day speech Chief of Staff Veli Llakaj neatly summarized Hoxha's position on this issue when he declared, "The party commands the rifle and not the rifle the party" (*Zëri i popullit*, 10 July).

International Views and Policies. Albania during 1975 established diplomatic relations with the People's Republic of Mozambique, Laos, and Venezuela, and at the year's end had diplomatic ties with 72 countries. There were no significant shifts in the PRA's foreign policies or international attitudes.

From the Albanian standpoint, the defeats suffered by "U.S. imperialism" in Cambodia and South Vietnam were especially important international developments. The twin victories of the "forces of national liberation and revolution" proved the "correctness" of the Albanian policy of "people's war" (ibid., 17, 30 April).

The Albanians continued to boycott meetings of the Conference on Security and Cooperation in Europe, which they dismissed as nothing more than a device employed by the two "superpowers" both to legitimize their respective spheres of influence in Europe and to force the participating states to recognize the "superpowers' " roles as arbiters on all European questions. They further maintained that the United States and the Soviet Union have sought to come to an understanding in Europe so they can engage in "aggression" in other parts of the world (ibid., 29 July).

Tirana persisted in its view that the policies and activities of the "superpowers" posed the greatest danger to world peace. The Albanians asserted that Moscow and Washington have prevented a settlement of the Cyprus and Middle East crises because neither wishes to see its influence in the Eastern Mediterranean diminish (ibid., 23 July).

In the United Nations the PRA supported the North Korean proposal for the reunification of Korea. Tirana also advocated U.N. membership for both the Democratic Republic of Vietnam and the Republic of South Vietnam (ibid., 30 September). The Albanians also favored extending national territorial waters up to 200 miles (ibid., 24 May).

In October, Misto Treska, chairman of the Albanian Committee for Cultural and Friendly Relations with Foreign Countries, was replaced by Javer Malo, the PRA's ambassador to France (ibid., 13 October). Given the fact that Malo had been an especially vigorous partisan of the Albanian Ideological and Cultural Revolution during its zenith in the mid 1960s, it remains to be seen whether his appointment will be accompanied by any changes in Albania's relations with and attitude toward the outside world.

Albanian-Chinese Relations. Albanian-Chinese relations appeared to be cordial during 1975. It is obvious that, despite some policy differences existing between the two regimes, both seem interested in strengthening their ties. To emphasize the importance he attaches to the PRA's relationship with China, Hoxha and the entire Albanian Politburo attended the reception given by the Chinese embassy on the occasion of the 26th anniversary of the founding of the PRC (ibid., 1 October). Hoxha and the entire leadership also attended the Tirana performance of a Chinese folk ensemble in late October (ibid., 21 October).

Albanian-Chinese cultural, technical, sports, economic, and tourist exchanges continued to grow during the year. The highest-ranking Albanian delegation to visit China was headed by first deputy premier Adil Çarçani. It was this group that concluded the Albanian-Chinese economic agreements for the period of the Sixth Five-Year Plan. While in China, the delegation was received by the hospitalized Chou En-lai (ibid., 17 June) but had no contact with Teng Hsiao-ping. Another important Albanian delegation to China was headed by chief of staff and deputy defense minister Veli Llakaj and deputy defense minister Nazar Berberi (ibid., 8 December).

It appears that the Chinese are continuing to fulfill their economic commitments to the PRA. Aside from their economic ties, the Chinese and Albanians are united by their opposition to Soviet "revisionism" and "social imperialism."

Albanian-Soviet Relations. There was no discernible improvement in Albanian-Soviet relations. Indeed, Albanian-Soviet polemics became extremely bitter during the year. The heightening vehemence with which the Albanians conducted their feud with the USSR seems to have been, at least in part, intended to silence domestic advocates of an Albanian-Soviet détente.

The Soviets ridiculed the notion that the Albanians, as APL spokesmen repeatedly claimed, were building socialism under conditions of an "imperialist-revisionist blockade." They pointed out that Albania maintained diplomatic and economic relations with the East European socialist countries as well as with many Western European and "Third World" countries (Moscow radio, 3 February). It was also reported that the Soviet Union had offered the Albanians "substantial economic aid and other inducements" to normalize relations (*Washington Post*, 8 September). Tirana apparently ignored this overture.

Throughout the year the Albanians were harshly critical of Moscow's domestic and foreign policies. The Soviet Union was characterized as a "militaristic fascist state" which exploited its allies through such organizations as the Council for Mutual Economic Assistance and the Warsaw Pact, and collaborated with the United States to thwart national liberation movements and "popular revolutions" throughout the world (e.g., *Zëri i popullit*, 5 January, 12 March, 21 April, 25 July). The

Albanians further charged that the "restoration of capitalism" in the USSR was responsible for the numerous social and economic problems that plagued the country today (e.g., ibid., 6 August, 20 September, 16 November).

In November the APL made a point of commemorating the 15th anniversary of Hoxha's speech denouncing Khrushchev and Soviet policies delivered at the 1960 Moscow meeting of the 81 world communist parties. According to an APL commentator, the events of the past 15 years attested to the validity of the Albanian party line toward the USSR (ibid., 26 November).

Relations with Eastern Europe. With the exception of her relations with Romania, Albania's ties with the pro-Soviet East European communist states remained limited and cool. It appeared that the new Greek regime wished to maintain a friendly if not cordial relationship with the PRA (*Shqipëria e re*, September).

Inspired by a common fear of Soviet threats to their independence, Albania and Yugoslavia continued to improve their relations. In April, Tito responded favorably to recent overtures by the Albanian leadership (see *YICA, 1975*, pp. 10-11) for closer ties between the two states (*Rilindja*, Prishtina, 5 April). The Yugoslav leader observed that Belgrade and Tirana had "overriding common interests" that necessitated their cooperation. In response to a plea from Tito, the Albanians virtually ended their ideological polemics with Yugoslavia. In a gesture of friendship that was appreciated by the Albanians (*Zëri i popullit*, 6 December), Yugoslavia agreed to transfer to Albania for burial the remains of Albanian partisans who died in Yugoslavia during World War II. The value of Yugoslav-Albanian trade, which has grown steadily since 1971, was expected to total $56 million by the end of 1975 (*Christian Science Monitor*, 2 June).

Relations with Western Europe and the United States. There were no significant developments in the PRA's relations with Western Europe. The Albanians seem to have made a special effort to strengthen their cultural ties with France and the Scandinavian states, both on an official level and through their Friendship Societies in these countries (e.g., *Zëri i popullit*, 2 February, 27 September, 4 October). In late October the West German government formally rejected the Albanian demand for a $2 billion reparation payment as a precondition for the establishment of diplomatic relations between the two countries. Bonn did, however, indicate its willingness to open diplomatic relations without prior conditions. (*Washington Post*, 28 October.)

There were no signs of any mellowing in Albania's attitude toward the United States. Albanian comments on both U.S. domestic and foreign policies were uniformly critical (e.g., ibid., 13 January, 12 September). The Albanians reported without comment President Ford's visit to China (ibid., 3 December).

International Activities and Contacts. During 1975 the APL leadership seemed eager to convince the Albanian people that the anti-Soviet Marxist-Leninist movement was active and growing in influence. Radio Tirana and the Albanian press gave fairly extensive publicity to the activities and pronouncements of Marxist-Leninist parties and groups (e.g., Tirana radio, 15 January, 9 September; *Zëri i popullit*, 30 September). Albania also continued to serve as a mecca for Marxist-Leninist groups, especially from Europe.

Albania hosted delegations from the Marxist-Leninist parties of Norway, Belgium, the Netherlands, Spain, West Germany, Italy, and Australia. Marxist-Leninist youth groups from Norway and West Germany also toured Albania.

The APL used the visit of the secretary of the Spanish Marxist-Leninist party to publicize and endorse "the Spanish people's struggle against the terroristic Franco regime" (Tirana radio, 9 September). In December the Albanian-based Communist Party of Poland, headed by Kazimierz Mijal, was the recipient of a telegram of greeting and support from the APL Central Committee on the occasion of its tenth anniversary (*Zëri i popullit*, 4 December).

The Cambodian foreign minister visited Albania in June to thank the Albanian party, government, and people for their aid during the Cambodian national liberation struggle (ibid., 18 June). Prince Norodom Sihanouk paid a brief state visit to Albania on 9-11 December (ibid., 12 December) and subsequently returned for a lengthier private stay (ibid., 14 December). An Albanian delegation visited Hanoi for the celebration of the 30th anniversary of the establishment of the Democratic Republic of North Vietnam (ibid., 23 August).

In January the first volume of the *Selected Works* of Enver Hoxha in English, French, Spanish, and Russian editions was released for distribution (ibid., 10 January).

Party Publications. The APL daily newspaper (with a claimed circulation of 101,000) is *Zëri i popullit*. The party's monthly theoretical journal is *Rruga e partisë*. Another major publication is *Bashkimi*, the daily organ of the Democratic Front (claimed average circulation of 30,000). The newspapers of the Union of Albanian Labor Youth, *Zëri i rinisë*, and the United Trade Unions of Albania, *Puna*, are published twice weekly. The official news agency is the Albanian Telegraphic Agency.

Western Illinois University   Nicholas C. Pano

Bulgaria

The Bulgarian Communist Party (Bulgarska Komunisticheska Partiya; BCP) was founded under this name in 1919. It draws its origin, however, from the Bulgarian Social Democratic Party of 1891, and its separate existence from the two-way split of that party in 1903, when it assumed the name of "Workers' Social Democratic Party (Narrow Socialists)." The BCP functioned also under other designations, such as the "Workers' Party," from 1927 to 1934, and the "Bulgarian Workers' Party (Communist)," from 1934 to 1948. Its most notorious leader was Georgi Dimitrov, one-time secretary-general of the Third Communist International (Comintern).

The BCP assumed power as a result of the unexpected Soviet declaration of war on Bulgaria and the country's occupation by the Red Army in September 1944, which was accompanied by a coup d'état overthrowing the pro-Western Muraviev government and installing in its stead the Communist-dominated Fatherland Front (Otechestven Front; FF) coalition. The party's quest for complete hegemony caused a split in the coalition and a memorable struggle of the United Opposition, led by the Agrarian Nikola Petkov. By 1948, Petkov was hanged and the Opposition decimated. The BCP has been the only political force ever since, although a subservient wing of the once-powerful Bulgarian Agrarian People's Union (or Party) is allowed to function yet not to compete for power. The BCP remains unswervingly pro-Soviet and domestically most restrictive.

Party membership, last officially reported at the 1971 congress, was nearly 700,000 and consisted of 40.1 percent blue-collar workers, 28.1 percent white-collar workers, and 26.1 percent peasants (*Rabotnichesko Delo*; [RD] 21 April 1971). The BCP holds an absolute majority in the

National Assembly (Parliament), where the FF also selects the non-Communist deputies, who run unopposed. The government is composed almost exclusively of BCP members.

Bulgaria has a population of 8.7 million, which results in a BCP share of about 8 percent.

Leadership and Organization. Todor Zhivkov, in 1975 more than ever the dominant personality, is not only the BCP first secretary (since 1954), but also chairman of the State Council (equivalent to a head of state), and thus combines both the top party and top government positions. There were no changes in the 12-man Politburo, consisting of Zhivkov, Tsola Dragoycheva, Grisha Filipov, Pencho Kubadinski, Aleksandur Lilov, Ivan Mikhaylov, Todor Pavlov, Ivan Popov, Stanko Todorov (also premier), Tano Tsolov, Boris Velchev, and Zhivko Zhivkov, nor in the 6-man candidate group. Unchanged was also the 12-man Central Committee Secretariat, of which the seven secretaries were Zhivkov (first secretary), Grisha Filipov, Penyu Kiratsov, Aleksandur Lilov, Ivan Prumov, Konstantin Tellalov, and Boris Velchev.

The stability of the political leadership is provided by the unchallenged predominance of Zhivkov, who did not hesitate to install his daughter, Lyudmila, as head of the Committee on Art and Culture, the top position in the country's cultural life, in July 1975. Zhivkova soon began a "purge" of her own, by replacing the committee's three deputy chairmen with her own team and showing her influence whenever possible. Another Zhivkov protégé, Politburo member and FF chairman Pencho Kubadinski, was elevated to membership in the State Council in July. Among other changes, the head of the State Planning Commission, Ivan Iliev, was replaced in April by Kiril Zarev, who was appointed also Deputy premier, indicating possible dissatisfaction with the performance of the economy.

Auxiliary and Mass Organizations. BCP members head the usual mass organizations which are subordinate to the party and its goals. The Fatherland Front, the largest so-called "non-partisan mass organization," had about 3.8 million members and included as its collective members the Bulgarian Komsomol (Dimitrovski Komunisticheski Mladezhki Suyuz; Dimitrov Communist Youth Union), with about 1.2 million members, or more than 70 percent of those eligible; the previously-mentioned Agrarian Party (about 120,000); and the trade unions (about 2.5 million).

Party Internal Affairs. Within the general climate of relative tranquility, the BCP held only two plenary sessions in 1975, and their work was apparently conventional. The first plenum, on 27-28 February, was said to have discussed the main features of the country's economic development during the forthcoming Seventh Five-Year Plan (1976-80) and up to 1990, and—more specifically—fate of the agro-industrial complexes, or AIC. (See Radio Free Europe Research, *Situation Report: Bulgaria*, 6 March).

The second plenum, on 22-23 July, was reportedly devoted to the scientific-technical aspects of economic development and to foreign policy (Sofia radio, 23 July). A national conference on 11 July dealt with the role of the primary party organizations (ibid., 14 July; see below).

In July, a brief announcement indicated that the party's Eleventh Congress would be held on 29 March-2 April 1976. It has become customary that the congresses of the BCP take place shortly after those of the Communist Party of the Soviet Union, in order to reflect the Soviet line, and the future congress is no exception.

Domestic Attitudes and Activities. The thrust of party activities in 1975 was on economic planning and party members' attitudes, as exemplified by the main topics of the plenums and national conference. The role of the party in society was much discussed at the July national conference. Boris Velchev, party secretary in charge of cadres (and perhaps the number-three man, after Zhivkov and Premier Todorov, in the Politburo), stressed in his report the great and varied demands on the primary party organizations during the current period of the party's "gradual transformation from a party of the working class into a party of the entire people" (Sofia radio, 14 July), thus characterizing the BCP in Khrushchevian terms. Zhivkov's closing speech (ibid.) identified some major tasks and concerns of the rank-and-file: the need to strengthen members' authority and discipline, which he found partly wanting; the requirement to make the basic party unit a model for the entire labor collective; the need to improve members' attitude and communication, both with fellow Communists and with other groups; and the important task of asserting party leadership in the fulfillment of paramount social and economic goals.

More specifically, Zhivkov stressed that the quality of the membership, its educational and cultural level, left much to be desired and that many elected party officials had been sentenced for legal violations. He called for strengthening the blue-collar component in the party organizations and revealed that rarely in these organizations was a trade union chairman elected party secretary, whereas the opposite move was quite usual, as it was "the easiest way to get rid of undesirable comrades." Zhivkov also called for the greater use of moral incentives, so as to strike a balance between them and material incentives, citing the Soviet Union as an example to emulate. The speech seemed to pin-point the major shortcomings in party work and attitudes, especially the low level of education and consciousness of the cadres, their frequent pursuit of personal gains, and their rudeness toward others.

Ideological matters were treated, as usual, in leading articles of the party daily, which—to select a typical example—extolled communism's "militant and aggressive ideology" and argued that "in the ideological sphere there is not and cannot be any peaceful co-existence," so that people "must be educated in the spirit of intolerance toward hostile ideological influences, bourgeois ideology, and the different brands of revisionism" (*RD*, 7 February).

Specific shortcomings transpired from a national conference on anti-social behaviors of minors, held in March. While praising the "correct party policy" and its successes in this regard, the proceedings, including an address by Politburo member Zhivko Zhivkov, revealed a score of "anti-social acts" by youths and called for "inculcating lasting working habits, a spirit of patriotism and socialist internationalism, and struggle against negative manifestations, such as bourgeois influences," as desirable remedies (Sofia radio, 14 March). Western observers continued to notice a deterioration in ideological reverence and an increase in cynicism and careerism among Bulgarian youth, while official sources complained about admiration for the West and its popular music (*Narodna Kultura*, 15 March).

On the artistic and cultural front, the wholesale dismissal of editorial-board members of the literary magazine *Septemvri*, revealed only through the change of names in the July issue, denoted an ideological tightening, in line with Lyudmila Zhivkova's growing influence. Judging in retrospect, the publication of relatively unconventional works and especially a powerful short story by Georgi Bozhinov in the March 1975 issue, reminiscent of Solzhenitsyn's *Gulag Archipelago*, must have cost the job of editor in chief Kamen Kalchev, himself occasionally critical of literary conformity, and of most of his staff. (See Radio Free Europe Research, *Background Report: Bulgaria*, 21 August 1975). There were indications that the editorial board of the bimonthly *Literaturna Misul* would also be purged since their names were omitted in its fourth-number issue.

In a similar vein, the party literary organ attacked a recent book on the life and work of the country's greatest living poetess, Elisaveta Bagryana, written by Blaga Dimitrova and Yordan Vasilev, as "overtly sympathetic to pre-Communist literary Bulgaria," during which period Bagryana created some of her masterpieces; moreover, the critics identified "a trend toward an uncritical, un-Leninist, non-class interpretation of literary events of the [pre-Communist] past . . . now painted in rosy colors." The party organ even generalized with undisguised discomfort that the very fact of presenting pre-Communist aesthetic values as "non-political" seemed to be appealing today, since "certain young people consider everything that is marked by political ideas as "bombastic," "bookish," and "biased." (*Literaturen Front*, no. 42, 16 October.) The importance attached to this issue was underscored by the reprint of the criticism in the party daily (*RD*, 23 October).

The Economy. Among the most important domestic activities, economics took precedence. The results of the 1974 plan indicated that targets for most key items were not met: national income grew by about 7.5 instead of the planned 10 percent; capital investments were 12.5 percent below the target; and gross industrial output increased 8.5 instead of 11 percent (*RD*, 1 February 1975). It therefore appears that the overall goals of the Sixth Five-Year Plan would be missed, although preliminary results of the first three-quarters of 1975 were better than the corresponding 1974 period (Bulgarska Telegrafna Agentsiya [BTA], 29 October). In an apparent effort to improve matters, planning chief Kiril Zarev mentioned a "new approach" for the next five-year plan by indicating that planning "will begin with the workers' collectives and specialists" and move upward, "contrary to existing practice" (Sofia radio, 1 August). As no follow-up measures were taken, the allusion to decentralized planning must be taken with skepticism.

On the institutional level, the 90-odd state economic trusts were in the process of further concentration, most likely into larger economic combines (*Ikonomicheski Zhivot*, no. 33, 13 August). Also, about a third of the 150 agro-industrial complexes were reported transformed into "unified legal entities," indicating that their constituent state and cooperative farms have lost their autonomy (decree of 14 April published in *Durzhaven Vestnik*, no. 35, 6 May). At the same time, the encouragement to increase livestock numbers and fodder-crop area on the minute personal plots (occupying about 12.8 percent of the country's arable land) confirmed the regime's reliance on their contribution to the deficient farm and livestock sectors.

Major economic problems were the lagging industrial modernization and the shortage of qualified labor and of fuels and other industrial raw materials. Because of the failure to meet investment targets, the planners earmarked an unusually large 55 percent of all investment for industrial modernization and reconstruction during the next five-year plan and placed growing responsibility on the workers' collectives to implement these goals (*RD*, 28 April; *Kooperativno Selo*, 29 April.)

To cope with the aggravated manpower shortage, the regime urged the broader adoption of two and even three shifts in industry (*RD*, 25 February). Concrete measures included new legislation on the employment of idling youths and high-school and university students on a part-time basis, and the mandatory transfer of industrial workers and employees to work on farms or in canning factories by closing down entire departments temporarily (relevant decrees in *Durzhaven Vestnik*, 28 January, 15, 29 April and 16 May). Even the amendment to the Pension Act, now fully applicable to the one million or so cooperative farmers as well, provided incentives for pensioners to continue or seek employment (ibid., no. 53, 11 July). Long-term measures—primarily cash grants for the newly born—tried to cope with the stagnating birth rate (16.3 per 1,000 in 1974 and projected to fluctuate between 14.3 and 16.3 per 1,000; *RD*, 7 January, and *Vecherni Novini*, 7 October). As to the shortage of materials, a new decree outlined a program for the saving and use of wastes (*RD*, 30 July).

Finally, Premier Stanko Todorov in his "accountability report" to the National Assembly not only underscored the above priority problems but called for a reduction in administration and management personnel and their transfer to productive activities (ibid., 26 March).

International Views and Policies. The Bulgarian leadership continued in 1975 its loyal and unswerving support of the Soviet foreign-policy line in various forums.

As member of the CSCE conference, Bulgaria was represented in Helsinki by Todor Zhivkov, who in his 30 July address backed the Soviet positions and specifically praised Brezhnev for his unique contribution to the success of the Conference. The 30th anniversary of the victory over Nazi Germany and the 20th anniversary of the Warsaw Pact offered additional opportunities to reaffirm Bulgaria's commitment to the Soviet-led alliance. At a gala meeting on 16 May, Foreign Minister

Mladenov eulogized the political-military alliance and the principle of "socialist internationalism" and repeated Brezhnev's view that "unity, cohesion, and cooperation" were a must for the success of communism. He specifically endorsed the known Soviet foreign-policy initiatives and vouched Bulgaria's support fot the cause of Vietnam, Cambodia, the Arab peoples, Cyprus, and the national liberation movements in Asia, Africa, and Latin America. Special criticism was allotted to the "enemies of peace in the imperialist camp" and their "worthy assistant—the Maoist leadership of China . . . blinded by nationalism and anti-Sovietism." (*RD*, 17 May.)

Within the country's commitment to the further economic integration and specialization of the CMEA, the major current problem of price revisions was treated cautiously and obliquely. Thus, it was a Soviet author, writing in *Zemedelsko Zname* (23 July), who for the first time referred to price corrections of Soviet oil (sold to Hungary, not Bulgaria), and made the point that the Soviet price would still be well below the world market price (37 rubles as against 110 U.S. dollars per ton). On their part, Bulgarian authors made occasional references to the low pricing of agricultural products on world markets as well as within the CMEA, which products happen to be Bulgaria's major export group. Thus, Professor Zhak Aroyo, noting world market prices from 1963 to 1971, argued for upward adjustments of agricultural prices lest countries which rely heavily on agricultural exports be made to suffer unfair losses and be forced to reorient their production goals to the detriment of their own comparative advantage as well as of that of their trading partners (*Ikonomika na Selskoto Stopanstvo*, no. 1, 1975). It may be mentioned that about four-fifths of Bulgaria's foreign trade is with the "Socialist countries" and that Bulgaria supplies its CMEA allies with 36 percent of all its fresh vegetables, 54 percent of its tomatoes, 57 percent of its fresh grapes, and 70 percent of its canned vegetables and its tobacco (*Studentska Tribuna*, 29 April).

As far as its non-agricultural exports are concerned, Bulgaria seemed to have been experiencing growing difficulties in satisfying its CMEA markets. A decree of 2 March (see Radio Free Europe Research, *Situation Report: Bulgaria*, 6 March) called for improving the quality of Bulgarian products, so as to meet CMEA standards and especially "Soviet requirements."

Relations with the USSR. Todor Zhivkov stressed in his festive address on the occasion of the anniversary of the victory over fascism that "all Bulgarians [have] transformed their profound faith in the Soviet road and experience into a sacred law and an indestructible resolve that Bulgaria will always march together with its double liberator, the great Soviet Union, toward a bright future under any and all conditions" (Sofia radio, 7 May 1975). Foreign Minister Mladenov specified that "the basic goal of Bulgarian foreign policy is the consolidation of the alliance with the USSR . . . which is constantly moving forward and assuming ever-increasing new dimensions" (*RD*, 17 May).

In fact, Bulgaria's "integration" with the Soviet Union "in every way" (Zhivkov in *Nedelya*, Moscow, 13 March) has become a persistent theme. Ideological and cultural cooperation—already overwhelming—proceeded in 1975 as usual, including the signing of a new cultural agreement (ibid., 31 May), and economic integration seemed to have been stepped up noticeably. This refers not so much to conventional trade—the Soviet share exceeded 50 percent of total Bulgarian trade and the Soviet Union supplied about two-thirds of Bulgaria's imports of fuel, minerals, metals, and machinery and equipment, and received most of Bulgaria's agricultural exports and more than a third of its machinery exports (*Studentska Tribuna*, 29 April), as to plan coordination and new areas of cooperation. Thus, while trade was to increase by 10 percent in 1975 over 1974 and by 50 percent in 1976-80 over the current five-year period, including an increased share of machinery and equipment both ways and largely increased Soviet supplies of much needed fuels, power, and raw materials, the protocol on plan coordination for the next five-year plan, solemnly signed in Moscow on 7 October, calls for expanded specialization and cooperation and, specifically, for Bulgarian investments in the development of Soviet resources. (*RD*, 8, 10 October.) Among the projects of the 20-odd cooperation agreements are Bulgaria's participation in extracting Soviet iron ore and other metallurgical raw materials as well as the supply of machinery and equipment for Soviet plants, to be repaid by Soviet exports of iron concentrates and ferroalloys (TASS, 20 December 1974; *RD*, 21 December). Bulgaria has also established its first enterprise with its own labor force on Soviet soil (for joint timber production in the Komi Republic, with repayment to be by deliveries in kind; *Durzhaven Vestnik*, no. 36, 13 May 1975) and is to participate in CMEA projects (e.g., such as the construction of the Orenburg gas pipeline on Soviet territory, against future gas deliveries). A most interesting development is the first open admission that Bulgaria will extend credits to the USSR during the next five-year period, which reverses past experience of unilateral Soviet aid and makes continued Soviet supplies of crucial materials and equipment clearly dependent on a quid pro quo (Radio Free Europe Research, *Situation Report: Bulgaria*, 27 January).

Relations with Yugoslavia. The controversy with Yugoslavia over the Macedonian issue proceeded "as usual" in 1975: Belgrade views the inhabitants of Bulgarian ("Pirin") Macedonia as part of a Macedonian nation and holds that they should be accorded minority rights, while Sofia considers them Bulgarians. This time it was Lyudmila Zhivkova herself who, at a ceremony unveiling a long-term program for the accelerated development of Bulgarian Macedonia, praised the local inhabitants for their "increased feeling of being an inseparable part of the Bulgarian people" (*Narodna Kultura*, no. 6, 8 February). As usual, the Yugoslavs condemned this speech—as well as subsequent Bulgarian references to the important role of the Soviet and Bulgarian armed forces in the liberation of Yugoslavia—as provocative and chauvinistic. However, while the Macedonian controversy acts as a psychological block, it has not prevented the development of friendly relations, especially in the economic field, as the signing of a long-term agreement on economic cooperation indicates (BTA, 22 May 1975; see also Radio Free Europe Research, Robert R. King, *The Macedonian Question and Bulgaria's Relations with Yugoslavia*, 6 June).

International Activities and Contacts. A distinguishing feature of 1975 was the flurry of official visits and the signing of various agreements with non-Communist countries. Besides his participation in the Helsinki conference, Zhivkov scored "firsts" in his official visit to Rome and the Vatican, and to Bonn (no Bulgarian head of state had been received there since World War II). He also saw Turkish premier Demirel and visited several African countries. On his part, Zhivkov received Greek premier Karamanlis as the first post-war Greek head of government to visit Bulgaria and played host to Austrian chancellor Kreisky and Iranian premier Amir Abbas Hoveyda. Also foreign minister Mladenov made several trips, most notably to Bonn and to some Latin American countries.

The major results of these exchanges, besides the enhancement of Zhivkov's stature, involved the signing of economic agreements, which also indicated greater interest in Bulgaria by non-Communist partners. Among the documents were a ten-year cooperation agreement with the Federal Republic of Germany (Bulgaria's major Western trading partner); similar agreements with Italy (the second-largest Western partner) France and Belgium-Luxembourg; and more "spectacular" single contracts with Sweden's Volvo and Britain's Schweppes firms. A package of agreements was signed with Austria, including the granting of long-term Austrian credits of US$120 million. (Radio Free Europe Research, *Situation Report: Bulgaria*, 16 May.) A new series of trials, with stiff sentencing, of Bulgarian foreign trade officials was reported; involved mainly were alleged bribes by Western firms (*RD*, 15 March, 2 April).

There were visits to and from Arab countries, whose cause Bulgaria champions and on whose resources and markets it relies to a certain extent; the signing of the first long-term trade agreement with Portugal; and visits by vacationing Communist leaders Georges Marchais of France and Luigi Longo of Italy.

Relations with Greece and Turkey. Relations with Greece, which had until then been only correct, showed sudden improvement in 1975 after the overthrow of the Greek military government and the dispute with Turkey. As the visit by Premier Karamanlis to Sofia (preceded by that of the Greek foreign minister) and the final communiqué testified, mutual relations became "cordial" and no controversial issues—"neither territorial claims nor minority problems"—existed any longer (Athens Press and Information Secretariat, joint communiqué, 4 July). Greece subscribed to the position of preferring bilateral to multilateral relations in the Balkans, except in technical fields; to the U.N. resolutions on the Middle East; and to the call for a world disarmament conference. Bulgaria confirmed its support for the Soviet pro-Greek position on Cyprus. This new Greek-Bulgarian rapprochement is explained by the Greek desire for assurance of Bulgaria's neutrality in case of a Turkish attack, which allegedly has been given, and by the Bulgarian desire to wean Greece farther away from the United States and NATO, thus helping Soviet designs (*The Times*, London, 3 July). A series of agreements, including mutual preferential treatment of shipments passing through Salonika and Bulgarian Danube ports, respectively, was also signed.

In turn, relations with Turkey seemed to cool off. Even Zhivkov's meeting with Turkish premier Demirel, across the border at Edirne, was a one-day affair aimed primarily at the inauguration of a joint electric-power line and the joint communiqué did not go beyond the trivial (*RD*, 21 July). Disagreement on Cyprus and on intra-Balkan cooperation persisted and there was speculation that high-level meetings (including the subsequent visit of Bulgarian foreign minister Mladenov to Ankara) were used to dispel Turkish suspicions of a Greek-Bulgarian entente.

Relations with the United States. The momentum given by the exchange of visits of then U.S. secretary of commerce Frederick Dent and then deputy premier Ivan Popov in 1974 lost some speed in 1975 as Bulgaria—unlike Romania—refused to take advantage of the U.S. Trade Reform Act which would have granted most-favored-nation status if its freedom-of-emigration provision had been accepted. Despite the fact that it has no Jewish emigration problem, the Bulgarian government backed the Soviet position. Still, trade continued to increase, but remained small in volume and was caused mainly by exchange of Bulgarian tobacco and U.S. agricultural products.

The 1974 consular agreement, covering—among other matters—the unmolested treatment of naturalized U.S. citizens provided they held a Bulgarian visa, entered into force in May and the U.S. deputy secretary of state paid an official two-day visit to Sofia in September. Bulgaria's generally correct tone toward the United States has turned vitriolic as the attack on Senator Henry Jackson demonstrated (*Narodna Mladezh*, 10 January; *Narodna Armiya*, 18 January.)

Publications. The BCP's official party daily is *Rabotnichesko Delo* ("Workers' Cause"). Its two major monthlies are *Partien Zhivot* ("Party Life") and the theoretical journal *Novo Vreme* ("New Times"). Other mass publications are *Politicheska Prosveta* ("Political Education") and *Ikonomicheski Zhivot* ("Economic Life"). The official news agency is Bulgarska Telegrafna Agentsiya, or BTA.

University of Vermont   L. A. D. Dellin

Czechoslovakia

The origins of the Communist Party of Czechoslovakia (Komunistická strana Československa; KSČ) date back to the split which occurred in the Czechoslovak Socialist Democratic Party after the Bolshevik revolution in Russia in November 1917. The KSČ was formally constituted in November 1921 by the dissident left wing of the Socialist Democratic membership who, six months earlier, had decided to join he Communist (Third) International. In contrast to other countries in Central and Eastern Europe at present under communist regimes, the seizure of power by the KSČ was not the result of a gradual process of outside interference and suppression of opposition but was due to a coup d'état, effected in February 1948 and signifying the end of a pluralist system of a fairly long tradition. Three non-communist parties are still nominally represented in the National Front of Working People, the only body authorized to nominate candidates for elections, but the statutes of this formalized coalition guarantee an absolute majority to the KSČ. The incumbents of the two top functions in the government—the president of the republic, Gustav Husák, and the federal premier, Lubomír Štrougal—are both prominent members of the communist party.

Since October 1968, Czechoslovakia has been a federal state including two components: the Czech Socialist Republic and the Slovak Socialist Republic. The constitutional reform which made this transformation possible is the only lasting part of a much broader innovative program introduced, early in 1968, by Alexander Dubček, then party first secretary; the implementation of the rest of the program was prevented by a military intervention of five Warsaw Pact countries, under Soviet leadership, in August of that year. The federal structure of the Czechoslovak state and government has not been duplicated in the organizational structure of the communist party. Although there exists an autonomous party organization for Slovakia, the Communist Party of Slovakia (Komunistická strana Slovenska; KSS), there is no corresponding body for the Czech provinces. Thus, paradoxically, Czechoslovakia is a federal nation ruled by a centralist party.

The KSČ, which in the late forties counted among the strongest communist parties of the world, measured per capita of total population, lost a considerable part of its membership through the resignations and a mass purge following the 1968 invasion. Official information has indicated that approximately 330,000 party card holders, or roughly 20 percent of all organized effectives, were either expelled or simply "struck off the lists" in the post-invasion period. However, according to data given in a newspaper interview by party Presidium member Vasil Bil'ák in September 1975, about 460,000 persons, close to a third of the entire membership, were purged between 1968 and 1975. According to the same source, some 11,000 KSČ members went into exile after the military intervention, a rather curious record in the annals of the ruling communist parties (*Rudé právo*, 13 September; *Daily World*, New York, 6 September).

Party statistics, released earlier in the year, indicated that more than 230,000 individuals had become candidates to membership since the 14th Congress, in 1971, of whom 67,000 were admitted to full membership (*Rudé právo*, 5 March). The present total can thus be estimated at some 1.1 million full members and 160,000 candidates. Czechoslovakia, in 1975, had a population of 14,804,-000. (ČETEKA, 28 August).

Organization and Leadership. The Central Committee and the Presidium are the two highest policy and decision-making organs of the KSČ. The last party congress was held in 1971, actually the fifteenth in succession, but officially marked as fourteenth. The present leadership does not recognize the legitimacy of the extraordinary congress called to Prague in August 1968, after the troops of the Warsaw Pact occupied Czechoslovakia. The next congress has been slated for 12 April 1976. It is expected to demonstrate the "firm unity of the KSČ and the people for further successes in building a mature socialist society" and is to mark the 55th anniversary of the party's founding. The congress will be preceded by a congress of the KSS on 25 March. (*Rudé právo*, 11 October 1975.)

In July 1975 the Central Committee elected Václav Hůla as member and Ján Baryl as candidate to the Presidium. This measure appears, at the moment, to increase the habitual number of Presidium members, which so far has not exceeded 11, but it is generally assumed that Hůla substitutes for the incapacitated former president of the republic, Ludvík Svoboda.

Party Internal Affairs. The protracted illness of the Presidium member Ludvík Svoboda, since 1968 holder of the supreme political function in the state, confronted the party with a difficult problem of succession involving delicate questions of personnel reshuffle. The issue was all the more sensitive, as it laid bare the smoldering conflict over domestic policies between the hard-liners on the one hand, and the more pragmatic group represented by secretary-general Gustav Husák on the other. The former hoped that the replacement of the ailing president of the republic—for which Husák appeared to be the most obvious candidate, as a logical Slovak successor to a Czech incumbent—would vacate to their benefit the critical party post. The election of Husák to the office of the president of the republic (see below), while he at the same time retained his key party position, can therefore be seen as yet another round in the intra-party dispute. It received full Soviet endorsement, direct as well as indirect, but the cumulation of the two titles in the hands of Husák does not lack irony: a situation was thus repeated which used to be the target of the most vehement criticism, precisely by Husák and his friends, when, prior to the Dubček era, Antonín Novotný had held these two functions. It remains to be seen to what extent the reinforcement of the position of Husák will contribute to the stabilization of the party line.

The group in power has to face opposition also from the segments which in 1968 supported the experiment of "socialism with a human face." This opposition has not yet been silenced, despite purges and other repressive measures. Prominent former party personalities protested in various forms against what they called oppression, abuse of power, and manipulation of citizenry. The publication in the Western communist press of the memoirs of the deceased Presidium member and chairman of the Federal Assembly Josef Smrkovský (*Giorni-Vie Nuove*, Rome, 20 February) provoked a very vehement negative reaction in the Czechoslovak party media (*Rudé právo*, 14 March). The letter sent by the former first party secretary Alexander Dubček to the Federal Assembly and published in April (*NYT*, 17 April) made almost headlines in the party press and elicited extensive polemics on the part of the present leaders. Among others, Presidium members Lubomír Štrougal and Vasil Bil'ák, and even the secretary-general himself, refuted Dubček's claims as "counter-revolutionary slander in the service of the bourgeoisie" (*Rudé právo*, 17 April). This campaign was joined also by members of the leadership of the Soviet party (TASS, 7 May).

In late May, prominent Marxist philosopher Karel Kosík sent an open letter to the French writer and existentialist philosopher Jean-Paul Sartre, and made a copy available to Western correspondents accredited in Prague, in which he denounced the persecution of non-conformist Czech and Slovak intellectuals under the present regime (UPI, 26 May). At the close of the year, former minister of foreign affairs Jiří Hájek criticized in a 2,000-word open letter the discrimination against Czechs and Slovaks who do not approve of the 1968 Soviet-led invasion as a violation of the agreements signed by both Czechoslovakia and the Soviet Union at the Helsinki Conference on Security and Cooperation in Europe (CSCE) (*Christian Science Monitor*, 12 November).

Protests by dissident members were the subject of extensive discussion at the Central Committee plenary session held on 24 April. The main topics of this plenum were economic questions, particularly the improvement of the old-age social-security benefits, and questions of domestic and foreign policy (*Rudé právo*, 25 April). The next plenary session, 2-3 July, discussed the convocation of the 15th party congress and the guidelines for the draft of the Sixth Five-Year Plan (ibid., 4 July). Shortly before the third plenum, the party Presidium replaced the editor in chief of the party's central organ, *Rudé právo*, Miroslav Moc, a hard-liner by Oldřich Švestka, a conservative centrist who had been in charge of the paper before 1968. This change was seen as an expression of the party's discontent with the overall performance of mass media, voiced on various occasions (ČETEKA, 1 September; *Tvorba*, 27 August), and possibly as a tactical gain of the Husák leadership. The third Central Committee plenum, 7 October, continued the preparation of the 15th Congress and drafted a letter on this theme which was then sent to all party organizations (*Rudé právo*, 11 October). The report on the further development of agriculture and the food industry was also on the agenda (Radio Prague, 7 October).

Domestic Affairs. A significant event on the state and government level was the election of the new president of the republic on 29 May 1975. An amendment of the current constitution by the Federal Assembly had to be adopted before the election, since there had been no previous provisions for a replacement of the president while the incumbent was alive but unable to discharge his duties (ČETEKA, 28 May). Aware of the fact that the new president, party secretary-general Gustav Husák, represents a rather moderate position, some circles in Czechoslovakia expected an amelioration of the internal political climate, but so far their hopes have not materialized in any notable way. A general amnesty preceded the election; however, it was qualified, and it excluded precisely such cases as would have required most consideration, above all convictions of political dissenters (*Rudé právo*, 9 May).

The Czechoslovak public also followed with great attention the discussions at the CSCE, particularly those concerning free circulation of persons, knowledge, and cultural values. Although Husák in his address to the Helsinki gathering endorsed the principle of free exchange between East and West (Radio Prague, 31 July), the implementation of the so-called third basket of the Helsinki agreements did not make much progress in Czechoslovakia in 1975. Nevertheless, the "Spirit of Helsinki" appeared to hold promise in the eyes of a large segment of the population.

Mass Organizations. The most spectacular public performance by a mass organization in Czechoslovakia in 1975 was the Fourth National Spartakiad, a combined gymnastics and sports contest, organized in Prague jointly by the paramilitary body Svazarm and the Czechoslovak Army, 28-29 June. This festival, like the three preceding Spartakiads, capitalized on the deeply rooted popularity of the Sokol congresses of the past whose century-old tradition they are expected eventually to replace. The Fourth Spartakiad held in the year of the 30th anniversary of Liberation served beyond that to the regime as an opportunity to celebrate the victory of the Red Army in World War II and to promote Czechoslovak-Soviet friendship. Some 150,000 persons from all regions of the country and all walks of life participated (*Mladá fronta*, 30 June). Shortly before the Spartakiad, new official figures were released indicating the size of the membership of Svazarm. According to this information, there are 5,350 Svazarm organizations on the Czechoslovak territory, which include more than 350,000 members. Since membership is not a condition for participating in Svazarm activities, it is estimated that Svazarm reaches, especially as the agency training the population for civil defense, about 1.5 million citizens every year. (*Zemědělské noviny*, 12 June.)

Another mass organization holding an important meeting in 1975 was the Revolutionary Trade Union Movement, whose Central Council gathered in Prague on 20-21 March. Endorsing the resolutions of the party Central Committee plenum of November 1974, the Council, in its address to the working people, stressed the need for greater productivity and efficiency and exhorted the industrial workers to "save raw materials, equipment, and energy, and to reduce material costs wherever possible" (Radio Prague, 25 March).

Culture, Education, and Religion. The efforts of the present party leaders to bring culture and the entire sector of intellectual activities into line with the prevailing ideological course was further pursued all through 1975. In this sphere, not unlike in political life, the voices of dissent were clearly perceptible. The minister of culture of the Czech Socialist Republic, Milan Klusák, admitted early in the year that "the attempts to misuse culture against the people's interest are still frequently made and are likely to continue" (*Rudé právo*, 5 January).

In the spring, a renowned playwright, Václav Havel, sent an open letter to party secretary-general Husák, copies of which he distributed among foreign press correspondents in Prague. In this letter Havel pointed out that there has been no "normalization" of political and social conditions in Czechoslovakia after the Soviet military intervention of 1968; on the contrary, a real deep crisis has affected the whole society. For the drastic suppression of life and the negation of genuine history, said Havel, a terrible price will have to be paid in the future. (Reuter, 12 April.) Regime spokesmen refuted Havel's assertions with great vehemence (*Tvorba*, 30 April).

In the summer, the well-known Czech writer and former party member Ludvík Vaculík submitted an appeal to U.N. secretary general Kurt Waldheim protesting the restrictions of freedom in Czechoslovakia which, according to the text of the appeal, "have assumed Orwellian proportions" (*Die Presse*, Vienna, 14 August).

A protest against undue harassment and persecution came also from a group of Czechoslovak historians who submitted to the International Congress of Historians in San Francisco a list of scholars who had been dismissed, imprisoned, or otherwise discriminated against because of their political views (*NYT*, 22 August). History was not the only science which suffered mistrust and repressive measures by the regime. Another target of sharp party criticism was the social sciences. Various university departments and research centers came under fire because of alleged indulgence in "bourgeois revisionism" (*Rudé právo*, 11 June).

The atheistic propaganda and the anti-religious campaigns continued in 1975, but the regime also persisted in trying to bring at least a part of the clergy to a more positive attitude toward its policies. The Czech and the Slovak congresses of the pro-governmental organization of Catholic priests "Pacem in Terris" and a joint federal congress in Brno served the purpose of "fruitful cooperation between the Socialist state and the clergy" and the manifestation of "unanimous and unconditional support of the peace policies of the Soviet Union" (*Lidová demokracie*, 4 June). Festivals of this kind, however, could not altogether hide serious open problems between the regime and the churches, which seriously deteriorated in the period following the Soviet-led invasion. The visit in Prague of the Vatican secretary for public affairs, Msgr. Agostino Casaroli, was supposed to help the solution of at least some of these problems, such as, for example, filling in the vacant positions of bishops and archbishops. Four of these seats were filled in at that occasion, and hopes were expressed that further progress might be gradually achieved in the relations between the Vatican and Communist Czechoslovakia. (Radio Prague, 24 February.)

Economy. The state economic development plan for 1975 foresaw an increase in the GNP of 5.8 percent—on the whole a 2.7 percent higher growth than the original Five-Year Plan had envisaged. This increase had to be achieved, almost exclusively, by higher productivity of labor. Main stress in the development policies was put on engineering and chemical industry; for the rest, only absolutely necessary capital investment was to be undertaken. These principles were in agreement with the overall development plan of the member countries of the Council for Mutual Economic Assistance (CMEA). The coordination of the national plans with the ultimate goal of achieving an integration of the individual national economies within a larger regional whole has been a serious concern of CMEA since the early sixties (Radio Prague, 29 January). Following the semi-annual report on plan fulfillment, the target figures appeared within reach. Nevertheless, weak spots in several sectors were ascertained in official analyses (*Rudé právo*, 29 July). The main critical areas were affected by shortcomings of structural or global, rather than local, nature: power and general energy shortage, high oil prices, and a less than average harvest. Of particular significance to the Czechoslovak economy was the cost of crude oil which, after a substantial rise in 1974, threatened again to increase. At the end of 1975, it was expected that the prices of Soviet oil would be adjusted to the level set by the OPEC countries, which would mean a jump in price of no less than 100 percent. The price hike is all the more important to Czechoslovakia, as the volume of oil imports from the Soviet Union is to expand considerably under the terms of the recent Czechoslovak-Soviet trade treaty (ČETEKA, 1 September). Czechoslovak media announced in the fall that the forthcoming Sixth Five-Year Plan would be closely coordinated with the Five-Year Plan of the USSR. The drastic revision of the crucial target figures of the national development plan of the Soviet Union, announced in December (TASS, 8 December), could therefore affect also the planning and the performance of Czechoslovak economy.

Armed Forces. No significant military exercises took place in 1975 on Czechoslovak territory, where still some 18,000 Soviet troops are stationed, under the terms of a treaty imposed upon Czechoslovakia in October 1968, after the August invasion. These units serve political rather than strategic purposes, but it is not impossible that their strength might be reduced in the future, if an agreement is reached between the NATO and the Warsaw Pact on military disengagement in Central Europe. The proposals made by the NATO conference in Brussels, at the end of the year, call among others also, for a cut in Soviet army contingents in Czechoslovakia (AFP, 12 December).

Foreign Affairs. An important event in the development of Czechoslovakia's foreign relations in 1975 was its participation in the closing summit meeting of the CSCE in Helsinki, in late July. The Czechoslovak delegation to this summit was led by the president of the republic, Gustav Husák, and the foreign minister, Bohuslav Chňoupek. The official address was read by Husák on 31 July. Husák stressed, above all, the contribution of the Soviet Union to international peace and understanding (*Rudé právo*, 1 August). Observers in Helsinki noted that while Czechoslovakia had accepted all the broad principles agreed upon at the conference, the so-called third basket, containing provisions for free movement of people and ideas in both parts of Europe, was adopted only with certain qualifications. These qualifications were then formulated more explicitly in the Czechoslovak mass media (Radio Prague, 4 August).

Relations between Czechoslovakia and the United States, which had made some progress toward improvement in the previous years, suffered a new setback in 1975. After the U.S. Congress passed an amended trade bill making the attribution to Czechoslovakia of most-favored-nation status and the return of the Czechoslovak gold reserves stolen by the Nazis dependent on full satisfaction of the compensation claims by U.S. owners of assets nationalized in the forties, the climate between the two countries cooled off considerably. Czechoslovak spokesmen and media pointed out that there was an inconsistency in the U.S. position, as Washington in the negotiations with other communist governments in Central and Eastern Europe had already often settled for even less than the 41 percent of the claims which Czechoslovakia was ready to repay (*Rudé právo*, 18 January). The disappointment of some U.S. business circles over the action of the Congress, voiced in a part of the press and officially expressed by David Rockefeller during his visit in Prague, later in the year, was given an extensive coverage (Radio Prague and Czechoslovak Television, 5 June; *Rudé právo*, 6 June).

The Czechoslovak party leadership took initiative to improve relations with other Western powers, particularly France and Great Britain. In January, foreign trade minister Andrej Barčák went to Paris to negotiate the terms of future economic exchanges. In April, minister of foreign affairs Bohuslav Chňoupek discussed in Paris major international political issues, cooperation in technology and culture, and other questions of bilateral interest (Radio Hvězda, 2 April). It is expected that the activities of French diplomatic and cultural agencies in Czechoslovakia will soon expand. At about the same time, the under-secretary of state in the British Foreign Office, Lord Goronwy-Roberts, visited Czechoslovakia for talks on European security questions, East-West relations, and other major world problems (Reuter, Prague, 2 April). Czechoslovak relations with West Germany developed further when a long-term agreement on economic, industrial, and technical cooperation was signed in Bonn (Rudé právo, 22 January). Two months later, the foreign minister of the German Federal Republic, Hans-Dietrich Genscher, arrived in Czechoslovakia for a two-day official visit (Radio Hvězda, 26 March).

The escape of a group of East Germans aboard a helicopter operating from West Germany over Austrian territory, in late August, tended to complicate relations not only with the Federal Republic but also with Austria (ČETEKA, 25 August), whose foreign minister Erich Bielka-Karltreu had in the spring paid an official visit to his Czechoslovak counterpart in Prague (Rudé právo, 28 April). Prior to this, the diplomatic representations of the two countries had been raised to the embassy level (Radio Prague, 8 January). Another prominent Austrian visiting Czechoslovakia in 1975 was the U.N. secretary general Kurt Waldheim, who met with party chief Husák and the federal prime minister, Lubomír Štrougal (Práca, 9 April).

The visit, in the spring, of a delegation of the Supreme Chamber of Control of the Polish People's Republic, headed by the Chairman Mieczysław Moczar, received particular attention in the Czechoslovak press (Rudé právo, 16 April). Concerning the main systems of military and economic alliances in the area, the 20th anniversary of the foundation of the Warsaw Pact organization was duly observed at a national defense conference in Prague (ČETEKA, 28 April). The Czechoslovak Federal Assembly's approval of the modification of the statutes of the CMEA, agreed upon in Sofia in June 1974, was made public at the beginning of the year (Hospodářské noviny, 17 January).

Relations with Arab countries in the Near East, particularly Libya and Syria, were also developed. As for the events in Portugal and, since October 1975, the evolution of the political situation in Spain, Czechoslovak media and party spokesmen faithfully followed the line set by the Soviet Union. They supported, for example, the Portuguese Communist Party but often criticized and rejected the actions of extremist leftist splinter groups, such as the Portuguese Maoist communist organization (Mladá fronta, 28 January).

International Communist Movement. Since the Soviet military intervention in 1968, the situation of the Czechoslovak party in the world communist movement has been one of the most vital and at the same time one of the most sensitive issues for the present regime. On the one hand, the group actually in power has been in need of Soviet support for its political survival; on the other hand, the disagreement among the various communist parties about the legitimacy of the intervention threatens the stability and also the legitimacy of the current course in Czechoslovakia. This disagreement, now more than seven years old, has not yet been overcome. Thus it was essential for the Czechoslovak communists in 1975 that they obtain Soviet backing of the succession by party secretary-general Husák to the office of the president of the republic.

Meetings of top Czechoslovak and Soviet party officials took place several times during the year. In March, Husák went to Moscow for a brief consultation with Leonid Brezhnev, first secretary of the Communist Party of the Soviet Union, and shortly afterwards received a delegation of the CPSU Central Committee in Prague (Rudé právo, 4 March; Radio Prague, 5 March). In May, a high-ranking group of Soviet party functionaries attended the celebrations of the 30th anniversary of the Liberation in Prague (ČETEKA, 7 May). Husák and Brezhnev met also in the Crimea during Husák's vacation, which he chose to take in the Soviet Union (TASS, 10 August).

Of particular significance to the world communist movement was the meeting of communist and workers' parties in Prague in March, which discussed the program of the forthcoming European communist summit. It is known that the Soviet Union has been pressing for such a conference for a long time. Later official commentaries on the preliminary Prague talks expressed satisfaction with the progress of the preparatory work and explicitly denied any differences of opinion among the individual delegations (*Pravda*, Bratislava, 20 June). No mention was made of a protest letter which a former party Presidium member and secretary of the Central Committee, Zdeněk Mlynář, sent to the Prague meeting and in which he accused the Husák leadership of using police and censorship for the purpose of suppressing ideas at variance with the present line. The letter, nevertheless, aroused interest among Western communist parties represented in Prague (RAD Background Report, no. 151, Munich, 3 November). The criticism of the more independent stand of the Romanian communist party, voiced in the Czechoslovak press shortly after the meeting (*Smena*, 13 March), indicated that the impression of unanimity which the Czechoslovak media had tried to convey did not correspond to reality.

Relations on the party level with Yugoslavia appeared to gain in intensity at the beginning of the year, when Presidium member Vasil Bil'ák visited Zagreb and Belgrade and met with members of the Executive Committee of the League of Yugoslav Communists to discuss common concerns in international sphere and the preparations for a conference of European communist and workers' parties (Tanyug, 4 February). The more friendly atmosphere which thus began to develop was again disturbed when the Czechoslovak press lent space to contributions by two Soviet military leaders, Marshals Yakubovski and Grechko. In dealing with the events of World War II, Yakubovski and Grechko extolled the merits of the Red Army in the liberation of the Balkans but passed over in complete silence the role of the Yugoslav partisans and the Yugoslav army led by Tito. This presentation of history (*Rudé právo*, 25 March) was perceived by the Yugoslav observers as "crude anti-Yugoslav propaganda" and blame was given to the Czechoslovak media who had accepted the articles for publication (Radio Zagreb, 3 April). The incident elicited a strong reaction from President Tito himself (Radio Skopje, 2 April).

Czechoslovak communists closely followed the official Soviet line on the People's Republic of China. The policies of Peking were consistently denounced as reactionary and pro-imperialist. Although the Chinese media repeatedly expressed concern over Soviet interference in the internal affairs of Czechoslovakia (see the commentary on the 7th anniversary of the Soviet invasion, *Peking Review*, 29 August), Czechoslovak party spokesmen and press organs did not seem to appreciate Chinese interest; on the contrary, they unconditionally sided with the USSR in all disputes, rejecting, for example, Chinese claims to territories annexed in the past by Czarist Russia in the Far East and forming now part of the Soviet Union (*Pravda*, Bratislava, 30 July).

Publications. The central daily organ of the KSČ is *Rudé právo*. The KSS publishes in Bratislava its own daily, *Pravda*. Theoretical and general policy questions are dealt with by the party weekly *Tribuna*. *Tvorba*, another party weekly of long standing has since 1968 concentrated on questions of international politics and the international communist movement. The counterpart of *Tribuna* in Slovak language is *Predvoj*. Issues concerning party work and questions of party organizations of all levels are addressed by the fortnightly *Život strany*. Among the mass organizations, the Revolutionary Trade Union Movement owns a daily, *Práce*, and its Slovak variant, *Práca*. The Czechoslovak Socialist Youth Union publishes the daily *Mladá fronta* in Prague and *Smena* in Bratislava. ČETEKA or ČTK are the current abbreviations for the official Czechoslovak news agency, *Československá tisková kancelář*.

University of Pittsburgh   Zdenek L. Suda

Germany:
German Democratic Republic

About a month after the end of hostilities of World War II in Europe and the establishment of Allied military occupation zones in Germany, the Soviet Military Administration issued its Order No. 2 of 10 June 1945 which gave permission for the founding of "anti-fascist" political parties in its zone. The Communist Party of Germany (Kommunistische Partei Deutschlands; KPD), an underground organization throughout the Hitler period, was reactivated one day later. The Social Democratic Party of Germany (Sozialdemokratische Partei Deutschlands; SPD) was the next to start its activities, on 16 June. The Christian Democratic Union of Germany (CDU) and the Liberal Party of Germany (LDPD) also received permission to organize. In spite of substantial support given by the Soviet Military Administration to the KPD, the communists were not able to gain the confidence of the population, which had experience both with totalitarianism and with the behavior of the Red Army. Soviet occupation authorities then forced a merger of the KPD and SPD. The new party, the Socialist Unity Party of Germany (Sozialistische Einheitspartei Deutschlands; SED), was founded on 21 April 1946 at a "Unity Party Congress" attended by Communist and Social Democratic delegates who decided "unanimously" to unite. Many Social Democratic leaders and rank-and-file members resisted the merger, with the result that many of them lost their lives or were incarcerated. The objective of the newly created party was to work for the establishment of a "socialist Germany," but the Communist minority succeeded with the aid of the Soviet occupation authorities in assuming control of the party apparatus, and as early as July 1948 the character of the SED had become that of a "party of the new type," on the model of the Communist Party of the Soviet Union (CPSU). On 7 October 1949, a month after the establishment of the Federal Republic of Germany (FRG) in the three Western-occupied zones, a "German People's Congress" unanimously adopted a proposal to create the German Democratic Republic (Deutsche Demokratische Republik; GDR) in the Soviet zone. Wilhelm Pieck, an old-time communist who had spent the Hitler period in the USSR, was unanimously elected president of the GDR. On 10 October the Soviet Military Administration transferred its administrative tasks to the GDR government and on 15 October the USSR extended diplomatic recognition to it. In July 1950 the 3rd Congress of the SED approved the draft of the first GDR five-year plan.

For a few years Moscow believed that its zone of occupation would possibly be the nucleus of a reunited Germany under Soviet supremacy. The first constitution of the GDR, therefore, consciously followed in some respects the constitution of the Weimar Republic, including a federal system and a multi-party arrangement, although the SED was placed in complete control of the non-communist parties. The federal system was eventually abandoned and a centralized system inaugurated. In 1968 the GDR received a new "socialist constitution" which proclaimed it to be the "first socialist state of the German Nation." In September 1974, on the occasion of the 25th anniversary of the GDR, the People's Chamber unanimously adopted a number of significant amendments and supplements to the 1968 constitution, effective on 7 October. Any references to the "German Nation" and to "German reunification" were eliminated.

A program of ruthless socialization of industry, financial institutions, and agriculture, and the elimination of the traditional professional civil service and trade unions, had commenced as early as

1946. Mass intimidation and the employment of terror against entire social groups was justified on ideological grounds. The SED, supported by secret police, succeeded in changing the economic, social, and political structure into a "people's democracy."

Soviet economic exploitation of the GDR meant establishing effective political control and took the form of economic and military integration of the GDR with the USSR and the other communist-ruled countries of Eastern Europe. The integration process has gained momentum through the years. In September 1950 the GDR joined the Council for Mutual Economic Aid (CMEA). In May 1955 it became a full member of the Warsaw Pact. Re-militarization started as early as 3 July 1948 when the Soviet Military Administration gave authorization for armed and garrisoned units of the People's Police (Kasernierte Volkspolizei). These units were renamed the National Armed Forces (Nationale Streitkräfte) in 1952 and became the National People's Army (Nationale Volksarmee; NVA) after the GDR joined the Warsaw Pact.

The SED had in 1975 about 1.9 million members and candidates (*Neues Deutschland*, 6 June). The population of the GDR is 17,050,000 (estimated in 1972).

Government and Party Structure. The GDR is controlled by SED leaders who have shown themselves to be faithful executors of Moscow's directives. The SED Politburo and the Central Committee are the party institutions which hold the decision-making power, including the selection of key personnel within the party and government bureaucracy. The most important position is that of the SED first secretary, held since 1971 by Erich Honecker. Members of the Politburo or of the Central Committee hold the most important ministries and other government positions.

The People's Chamber (Volkskammer) appoints the GDR government, consisting of the State Council (Staatsrat), comprised of 24 members plus one secretary, and the Council of Ministers (Ministerrat). The State Council, like the Soviet Presidium, handles the business of the People's Chamber when that body is not in session. Its chairman, Willi Stoph, is the head of state. As of late 1975, the SED held 16 seats in the State Council (5 by members and one by a candidate member of the Politburo, and 4 by members of the Central Committee). The Council of Ministers consists of the chairman (minister president), Horst Sindermann, two first deputy chairmen, 10 deputy chairmen and 26 members who head various ministries or government commissions. Of the 49 members of the Council of Ministers, 38 belong to the SED (4 members and 3 candidates of the Politburo, 12 members and 5 candidates of the Central Committee).

The latest general election of the 500-member People's Chamber was held in November 1971. The "National Front," the communist-controlled alliance of all political parties and "mass organizations," provided a single list of candidates. In addition to the SED, four parties are represented in the National Front—the CDU, the LDPD, the National Democratic Party of Germany (NDPD), and the Democratic Peasant Party of Germany (DBD), together with the trade unions and other "mass organizations," such as the Free German Youth (Freie Deutsche Jugend; FDJ) and the Democratic Women's League of Germany (Demokratischer Frauenbund Deutschlands; DFD). Before the elections took place, the seats in the People's Chamber were allotted to the different parties of the National Front and the mass organizations: 127 to the SED, 52 each to the four other parties, 68 to the Free German Trade Union Federation (Freier Deutscher Gewerkschaftsbund; FDGB), 40 to the FDJ, 35 to the DFD, and 22 to the German Union of Culture (Deutscher Kulturbund; DKB). More than 98 percent of the eligible voters of an electorate of 11,400,000 participated in the elections as a result of the strong political pressure and fear of severe retaliation for abstention. The National Front list received 99.85 percent of the votes cast. (*Neues Deutschland*, 20 November 1971.) Since its inception the People's Chamber has always voted unanimously on all issues with only one exception: with SED permission, a few deputies were allowed to vote against a bill concerning abortion in March 1972.

The purpose of the other political parties is to appeal to specific segments of the population in order to integrate them into the socialist society, but the importance or need for them as transmission belts seems to be decreasing. In 1975 the CDU had 100,000 members; the LDPD, 70,000; the NDPD, 80,000, and the DBD, 90,000: a total of 340,000 (*Horizont*, East Berlin, no. 20, 1975). In 1954 the CDU had 115,000; the LDPD, 136,000; the NDPD, 172,000; and the DBD, 98,000: a total of 521,000 (Bundesminister für innerdeutsche Beziehungen, Bonn, *Informationen*, 1975, p. 6).

The SED Central Committee in 1974 had 134 full members and 46 candidates. On 5 June 1975, 5 candidate members were elected to full membership to bring the total again to the prescribed number of 135 full members and 41 candidates (ibid., no. 12, p. 9). The 16 members of the Politburo are Hermann Axen, Friedrich Ebert, Gerhard Grüneberg, Kurt Hager, Heinz Hoffmann, Erich Honecker, Werner Krolikowski, Werner Lamberz, Günter Mittag, Erich Mückenberger, Alfred Neumann, Albert Norden, Horst Sindermann, Willi Stoph, Harry Tisch, and Paul Verner; the 9 candidate members are Werner Felfe, Joachim Herrmann, Werner Jarowinsky, Günther Kleiber, Ingeborg Lange, Erich Mielke, Margarete Müller, Konrad Naumann, and Gerhard Schürer. The Politburo is the real power center of the GDR. The 11 members of the Secretariat are assigned control functions within their respective areas of responsibility. Besides Honecker as first secretary, the members are Hermann Axen (international contact), Horst Dohlus (party organs), Gerhard Grüneberg (agriculture), Kurt Hager (culture and science), Werner Jarowinsky (trade and supply), Werner Krolikowski (economy), Werner Lamberz (agitation), Ingeborg Lange (women's affairs), Albert Norden (propaganda directed to the West), and Paul Verner (security). Politburo member Erich Mückenberger is chairman of the Central Party Control Commission (9 full members, 7 candidates). Kurt Seibt is chairman of the Central Audit Commission (23 full members, 5 candidates).

During 1975 three members of the Central Committee died: Karl Maron, Adolf Hennecke, and Otto Winzer, former minister for foreign affairs. Oskar Fischer became the successor to Winzer already before the latter's demise. Politburo member and chairman of the Central Executive of the FDGB Herbert Warnke died and was replaced by Harry Tisch, who was also elected a member of the State Council. (GDR Domestic Service, 5, 19 June.) The numbers of SED leaders who were politically active prior to 1933 is continuously decreasing. The 26 members and candidate members of the Politburo and members of the Secretariat, have an average age of 55.5 years; the oldest is 80 (Friedrich Ebert) and the youngest is 43 (Bundesminister für innerdeutsche Beziehungen, *Informationen*, no. 11, 1975, p. 7).

Mass Organizations. The mass organizations of the National Front assist the SED in its tasks and control functions, provide a mass basis for political indoctrination, and serve as recruiting ground for future party functionaries. The Free German Youth, the most important of these, has some 18,000 units and a membership of close to 2 million young people. Egon Krenz is first secretary. One of the tasks of the FDJ is to supervise the Ernst-Thälmann Youth Pioneer Organization, which enrolls about 1.2 million children. The Free German Trade Union Federation (FDGB) has 8,050,000 members, in 250,848 trade union groups; and represents 96.1 percent of all workers. Almost 4 million members are women. (*Tribüne*, East Berlin, no. 106, 4 June 1975.) During the past five years the annual increase was about 250,000 members (Bundesminister für innerdeutsche Beziehungen, *Informationen*, no. 12, p. 6). In January 1975 about 1.6 million trade unionists began their studies at the schools of socialist work as part of a program to intensify the political-ideological qualification of the workers (*Tribüne*, no. 21, 30 January). The Democratic Women's League of Germany (DFB) has 1.3 million members, in 16,700 groups, and is headed by Ilse Thiele. Additional mass organizations serve specific interests, such as the German-Soviet Friendship Society and the Society for Sport and Technology (GST). The GST is a paramilitary organization providing pre-military training to about a half million young persons before they start their service in the National People's Army.

Party Internal Affairs. The 13th Session of the Central Committee of the SED (12-14 December 1974) and the 14th Session (5 June 1975) referred to the decisions and resolutions of the 8th Congress (1971) as the guidelines for the party in 1975. Party control in industrial enterprises was to be strengthened and the fighting strength of the SED increased as a result of a strict selection process of new party members from the ranks of the best workers. Also the constant education of the membership in Marxism-Leninism was emphasized. (*Neuer Weg*, no. 3, 1975.) For example, the FDJ study year 1974-75 involved 1.4 million FDJ members who studied the Marxist classics in some 60,000 groups. (*Deutschland Archiv*, Cologne, vol. 8, no. 8, p. 894.)

The 14th Session of the Central Committee on 5 June accepted the Politburo proposal to convoke the 9th SED Congress on 18-22 May 1976 in East Berlin, following by two months the 25th Congress of the Communist Party of the Soviet Union (CPSU). According to party statutes, a congress is to be held every five years. The Politburo also proposed the agenda for the 9th Congress. According to Honecker, the congress will evaluate the results of implementing the decisions of the 8th Congress and will also determine the actions the GDR will take in shaping the developed socialist society until the beginning of the 1980s. It is also to adopt a new party program, already in preparation, and new statutes. (*Neues Deutschland*, 6 June.) The commission charged with the revision of the statutes is chaired by Politburo member Paul Verner and has commenced with its work. It is asserted that amendments and additions are required as a result of the profound changes in all fields of social developments and of the position the GDR finds itself in as result of its international recognition and of being an integral part of the socialist community. ("Voice of the GDR," East Berlin, 26 May).

The 15th session of the SED Central Committee (2-3 October) paid tribute to the successful conclusion of the Helsinki conference (CSCE) because it fulfilled a main task of the Soviet peace program. It was also pointed out that as of 1 August, the GDR had established diplomatic relations with 117 states, including all the "main imperialist powers" (*FBIS*, 6 November).

Hardly had the projects dedicated to overfulfillment of production plans in honor of the "30th anniversary of the liberation from fascism" (see below) been terminated, when a new campaign for a worthy preparation for the 9th Congress was initiated. Numerous youth projects and socialist production competitions were programmed to mobilize additional production reserves (*Die Welt*, Hamburg, 7 July). The FDJ, for example, passed a resolution to strive for special achievements in its socialist production competitions and in the learning efforts of its student members. The FDJ considers its culture conference in July and the GDR workers' youth congress in October important climaxes on the way to the party congress. It also intends to prepare for the 100th birthday anniversary of Wilhelm Pieck, to be celebrated in January 1976 (East Berlin domestic service, 27 June).

Domestic Affairs. *Elections.* Elections for the People's Chamber are scheduled for 1976. The political parties and mass organizations of the National Front have already discussed proposed changes of the election law. The SED leadership intends to have the 66 deputies of East Berlin elected directly—a violation of the Four Power Agreement which applies to all of Berlin. At the elections in 1971 the 66 deputies were appointed by the legislature of East Berlin. (*Die Welt*, 29 November 1974.)

Legal Reforms. Crime in the GDR has significantly increased. The Central Statistical Administration was forbidden for the past five years to publish data on the subject, but the GDR prosecutor-general has announced that between 1969 and 1973 an average of 128,000 crimes was registered annually, as compared with 100,000 in 1968. "Property and economic crimes" were responsible for an annual damage of 500 million Marks. Crimes committed by young persons have more than doubled in the past five years. (*Der Spiegel*, Hamburg, 5 May 1975, pp. 42-44.) These figures coincide with those submitted by the Interior deputy minister to the United Nations, stating that the average annual number of crimes between 1970 and 1974 came to 126,961 (*Die Welt*, 6 September).

The extension of jurisdiction of military justice at the end of June 1975 to civilians either employed by the NVA or in enterprises working directly or indirectly for the military may be intended as one method for dealing with the rising crime rate. Military courts also have jurisdiction over criminal offenses of military personnel committed prior to their joining the armed forces. (*Die Welt*, 10 July.) Work-shy individuals are the cause of another serious problem. The number of proceedings against persons because of "endangering the public order as result of asocial behavior" (Paragraph 249 of the Penal Code) is steadily increasing. (Bundesminister für innerdeutsche Beziehungen, *Informationen*, no. 10, 1975, p. 8.)

The most important change in the GDR judicial system was the unanimous adoption of a new Civil Code and a new law concerning civil court procedures by the People's Chamber on 19 June. The new code and court procedures come into force on 1 January 1976 and replace the 1896 Civil Code which is still used in the FRG. Politburo member Ebert stated that there cannot be a common civil code linking the social system of the GDR, which is based on socialist ownership, and the imperialist order of the FRG. (*German Democratic Report*, vol. 24, no. 12, 2 July). The 480 paragraphs are intended to stifle even the most minor opposition against the state authorities, and provide in addition for the commencement of legal proceedings upon arrest and for confinement until trial (*Deutsches Monatsblatt*, Bonn, vol. 23, no. 10, October).

Youth Indoctrination. The increased influence of the FDJ, noted already in 1974, became evident in the decree concerning the setting of examinations at institutions of higher learning, including technological schools, which became effective on 1 September 1975. The top administrative officials of these institutions are obliged to confirm with FDJ officials all basic decisions in regard to the examination procedures. (*Berliner Zeitung*, 20 March.)

Four thousand high school graduates were not able to obtain admission to institutions of higher learning in the 1975/76 academic year. There are 30,000 study openings at universities and 22,000 for Polytechnical training. (*Die Welt*, 5 February.)

Late in May, nearly 280,000 fourteen-year-olds (96 percent of this age group) participated in the so-called youth consecration (Jugendweihe) and pledged allegiance to socialism, in 6,700 local ceremonies. These events paid tribute to the "liberation from fascism through the Soviet Union and the development of the GDR as a stable and internationally respected state." Since 1954, 4 million boys and girls have taken part in youth consecrations. (*Die Welt*, 1 April; *Der Stern*, Hamburg, 5 June.)

GDR Anniversaries. On 8 February the Ministry of State Security celebrated its 25th anniversary. Colonel General Erich Mielke, candidate member of the Politburo and Minister of State Security, stated at a ceremony in East Berlin on 7 February:

> During the years of its existence the Ministry of State Security, while implementing its special tasks and responsibilities, has made an essential contribution to comprehensively strengthening and consolidating our socialist fatherland, to insuring socialist construction and the peaceful life of the citizens, and to safely protecting our state and the entire socialist community. (*Neues Deutschland*, 8/9 February.)

In an article, Mielke wrote:

> A special organ of the dictatorship of the proletariat came into existence with the Ministry of State Security, which is in a position and possesses all the means to protect the workers' and farmers' power and the revolutionary development against all counter-revolutionary activities of external and internal

enemies of the GDR and to provide internal security and all-inclusive order under the leadership of the SED and in cooperation with the other state organs and armed forces in close connection with the workers.

[The] Chekists of the GDR . . . place their knowledge and know-how at the disposition of the further strengthening and reliable security of the socialist social order of the GDR and the consolidation of the entire socialist fraternal community. (*Einheit*, no. 1, 1975.)

SED first secretary Honecker thanked these "fighters on the invisible front who, frequently far away from their socialist fatherland and only relying on themselves, accomplish heroic deeds" (*Die Welt*, 10 February.)

The 30th anniversary of the German People's Police was commemorated on 30 June. The reason for the selection of this date is not clear; the first non-military police forces under Soviet control were authorized on 1 June 1945, and on 9 June communists were placed in the key positions. On 1 October 1946 the police was placed under a German Central Administration of the Interior. On 3 July 1948 the "Garrisoned People's Police" was organized as additional police force under the former General Inspector and present Minister of Defense Hoffmann. These police units were forerunner of the National People's Army, the name they received on 18 January 1956. (*Wehrkunde*, Munich, vol. 24, no. 9, September 1975.)

The SED propaganda apparatus for more than half a year prepared the population of the GDR for the 30th anniversary of liberation from Hitler through the Soviet Union. The various competitions in socialist production and in practically every aspect of public life which were originated in honor of the 25th anniversary of the creation of the GDR in 1974 were continued as contributions to the liberation commemoration on 9 May 1975. For example, the FDJ organized 44,000 meetings and rallies together with members of the Soviet Army, anti-fascist resistance fighters, and activists (*Deutschland Archiv*, 8, no. 6, June: 561), while builders of the GDR section of the natural gas pipeline between the Ural Mountains and the western border of the USSR worked in the spirit of "socialist competition" (*Neues Deutschland*. 7/8 June). On 21 January the SED Central Committee, the Council of State, the Council of Ministers, and the National Front issued a manifesto stating that the victory of the Soviet Union and its allies had profoundly changed the international relationship of forces and calling upon the people of the GDR to fulfill targets for the concluding year of the present five-year plan in order to create proper conditions for the 1976-80 plan (*Foreign Affairs Bulletin*, 15, no. 4, 31 January: 21-25). The celebration itself witnessed an "enthusiastic manifestation of the brotherly friendship between the GDR and the USSR" (ibid., no. 14, 15 May: 101).

State-Church Relations. Pressure by GDR authorities against the churches in 1975 was especially noticeable in the educational sector and in professional training. The Synode of the Protestant Church of Berlin-Brandenburg pointed out in a letter to community church administrators the unavoidable conflicts between state and church because of the confessed educational objective of the GDR to form socialist personalities based entirely on Marxism-Leninism. The Synode forwarded with this letter a copy of the circular letter of the Catholic bishops of November 1974 to the GDR state secretary for church affairs expressing concern about the purely materialistic educational objectives, the rejection of a neutral Weltanschauung, and the emphasis on the correctness of only the socialist morality which includes the indoctrination to hate. (*Die Welt*, 10 April; *Deutschland Archiv*, 8, no. 5, May: 551-55.)

It was asserted that although every second inhabitant of the GDR belongs to a church, practicing Christians comprise only about 10 percent of the population (*Die Welt*, 5 April). The Protestant church estimated that in about 20 years it will have no more than 4,300 lay administrators, a figure which corresponds to the present number of pastors (ibid., 2 October). The Catholic church in the period from 1965 to October 1974 saw 70 priests quit their office. In March 1975 there were about

1,250 working and about 100 retired priests in the GDR. (*Begegnung*, East Berlin, no. 3, 1975.) At present the Catholic church maintains 1,046 parishes, 30 student parishes, 13 retreat houses, 13 seminaries for priests, 11 church-related educational institutions, and 2 publishing houses. In the health and welfare fields, such as homes for the aged, hospitals, and children's homes, the Catholic church operates more than 220 institutions. (Bundesminister für innerdeutsche Beziehungen, *Informationen*, no. 6, 1974, p. 5.)

SED functionaries were attempting to find out who among artists, scientists, technicians, and members of other intellectual groups maintained contact with the churches (*Die Welt*, 11 July). After the visit of Archbishop Agostino Casaroli, the "foreign minister" of the Vatican, to the GDR in mid-June 1975 for the purpose of exchanging views, the first pilgrims from the GDR were permitted to travel to Rome. Archbishop Casaroli celebrated mass for the pilgrims on 28 June. (Bundesminister für innerdeutsche Beziehungen, *Informationen*, no. 13, p. 5.)

Military Affairs. Military matters continued to receive highest priority. The overall strength of the NVA appears to have remained constant (see *YICA, 1975*, pp. 31-32), while the combat groups of the working class (Kampfgruppen der Arbeiterklasse) increased in strength, armament, training, and combat readiness. The numerical strength of the combat groups has reached 500,000. There are two categories of combat groups. Category A is comprised of older workers and employees who have as their assigned tasks the suppression of internal unrest, protection of important installations, and territorial security. Category B units make use of younger men from 25 years up who have completed their compulsory military service in the NVA. Their training is entirely for combat duty in support of the NVA. (*Deutsches Monatsblatt*, vol. 23, no. 6, June.)

Political indoctrination and education to hate the class enemy is continuously emphasized. The minister of defense, Army General Heinz Hoffmann, declared that the most important task for the NVA in 1975 was to acquire the Marxist-Leninist ideology and to assist comrades in their ideological studies (*Wehrkunde*, 24, no. 1, January: 45). It was reported that more than 90 percent of the officers, about 50 percent of the non-commissioned officers, and every ninth soldier were members or candidates of the SED, and that more than 90 percent of the younger soldiers belonged to the FDJ. All commanders of large military units and 85 percent of the commanders of troop units are graduates of military academies; 88 percent of all officers have graduated from institutions of higher learning, including polytechnical schools, and only 22 percent do not have an academic education. About 600 officers have the academic rank of doctor. Thousands know the Russian language. (*Horizont*, no. 20, 1975; *Armeerundschau*, no. 1.)

The militarization process in the GDR surpasses by far that of other communist-ruled countries. About every fourth citizen is directly involved in paramilitary or pre-military mass organizations or in military units (*Die Welt*, 4 February). Members of these organizations are subjected to intensive political indoctrination. It appears that the military policy of the SED pursues domestic and foreign policy objectives. The domestic aims include the intensive militarization of the population of the GDR in order to facilitate control and surveillance. Foreign policy aims are to maintain politically reliable and combat-ready armed forces which, integrated with the armies of the Warsaw Pact, can make a substantial contribution to the implementation of Soviet foreign policy. According to the communist leadership, the military quality and effectiveness of the armed forces depends on the degree of political conviction which in turn is based on the recognition of the correctness of Marxism-Leninism, and the correct evaluation of the imperialist enemy and the deep hatred felt toward him. (See Eric Waldman, *Die Militärpolitik der Sozialistischen Einheitspartei Deutschlands*, Bonn-Bad Godesburg, 1975.)

The GDR held a military parade in East Berlin on 1 May. This violation of the demilitarized status of Berlin was strongly condemned by the Western Allies. (*Die Welt*, 2 May.)

Security Matters. In spite of the perennial negotiations conducted by Bonn and East Berlin allegedly with the intention of improving the relation of the two German states, the GDR continued. in 1975 to build fortifications along the entire western "state border." Reportedly, the cost for one kilometer of such fortifications, consisting of a metal fence with automatic firing devices attached, minefields, watchtowers, and various other obstacles, amounts to 1 million marks. Some 47,000 troops guard the demarcation line; in addition every border company has a platoon of "voluntary border helpers." People's Police patrol the area to the rear. (*Deutsches Monatsblatt*, vol. 23, no. 6, June.) The police have about 125,000 voluntary helpers (*Neues Deutschland*, 30 June).

Nevertheless, escapes from the GDR occurred. During the first four months of this year 1,676 refugees came into the FRG (1,436 during the same period in 1974) (Bundesminister für innerdeutsche Beziehungen, *Informationen*, no. 10, p. 3).

Political Prisoners. In August 1975 the GDR held about 7,000 political prisoners, of whom about 4,500 were under sentence for attempted "flight from the Republic" (Republikflucht) or for having rendered assistance to persons attempting to flee to the West (*Die Welt*, 13 August). In May, after an interruption of five months, the GDR permitted again the "buying" of freedom of prisoners. Most of them were serving time for Republikflucht or for "slander against the state" (among the freed were also a number of criminals). The government of the FRG paid for every freed prisoner a head price of 50,000 Marks (slightly less than $20,000). In 1974 the FRG paid about $1.25 million for the freedom of about 700 prisoners. (For figures from 1969 to 1973 see *YICA, 1975*, p. 34.)

Since 1969 more than 5,000 political prisoners, among them 33 sentenced for life, have been released to the West (*Die Welt*, 28 April 1975). There are some whom the GDR does not let go, such as persons sentenced for espionage and "crimes against the law for the protection of peace" (ibid., 3 May). Conditions under which political prisoners are kept have become more severe since the beginning of the policy of détente. The stated purpose for the imprisonment is to "educate" the prisoner into becoming a socialist personality. (*Deutsches Monatsblatt*, vol. 23, no. 7/8, July/August.)

A state secretary of the Ministry of Justice of the FRG stated that 210 death sentences have been given in the GDR since its founding in 1949 and that most were in all probability carried out (*Die Welt*, 16 October 1975). From September 1945 until the end of 1974 about 12,800 persons were convicted as Nazi or war criminals (ibid., 11 April).

In August 1975 there were 443 citizens of the FRG and West Berlin in GDR prisons: 108 were awaiting trial and 335 were serving sentences in the jails in Berlin-Rummelsburg, Bautzen, Berlin-Lichtenberg, Brandenburg, and in the women's prison at Hoheneck near Stollberg, most in connection with Republikflucht (ibid., 19 August). A number of secret trials of persons accused of belonging to resistance groups have taken place. Most of those were tried by military courts. (Ibid., 27 February.)

The Economy. The GDR in 1974 fulfilled the assigned quotas in most areas of production in spite of experiencing difficulties in transportation and in obtaining raw material. Some industries, such as the chemical industry, did not reach their production objectives. It was reported that in some factories machines were idle more than 50 percent of the time. (Bundesminister für innerdeutsche Beziehungen, *Informationen*, no. 2, 1975, pp. 6-9.)

Trade with CMEA countries and other socialist states showed a favorable though reduced positive balance in 1974 as compared with 1973; $174.5 million as against $438.5 million. Trade with Western industrialized countries showed an increasing negative balance: $888.1 million as against $818.7 million. With developing countries the balance went from a slight positive to a negative balance: −$172.5 million as against +$52.7 million. (*Deutschland Archiv*, 8, no. 8, August 1975: 853. The figures are given in this source in Valuta Marks and have been converted to dollars. The exchange rate in 1974 was $1 = VM 3.53.)

Higher prices for oil, gas, and other raw materials and the growing indebtedness of the GDR placed heavy burdens on the economy. Also a shortage of trained engineers and managers and of labor in general was reported. (Bundesminister für innnerdeutsche Beziehungen, *Informationen*, no. 11, 1975; *NYT*, 8 August.) The GDR relies heavily on women's labor and with 84 percent of all women of working age (between 18 and 60) employed has one of the highest percentages in the world (Peace Movement of the GDR, *Information*, East Berlin, no. 4, 1975). Utilization of students in the production process during the summer months proved to be a failure (*Die Welt*, 20 August).

Even so, implementation of the 1975 economic plan during the first six months reportedly achieved, in comparison with the same period in1974, increases of 5.5 percent in national income, 6.8 percent in industrial production, 6.7 percent in labor productivity, 4.0 percent in investments, and 4.3 percent in personal incomes. (*Democratic German Report*, vol. 24, no. 14, 30 July).

Foreign Affairs. *Relations with the Federal Republic of Germany.* The process of "normalization" between the GDR and the FRG made no appreciable gains in 1975. SED leaders continued their policy of ideological delineation (Abgrenzung), emphasizing the existence of a socialist German nation in the GDR and a capitalist German nation in the FRG. (East Berlin Domestic Service, 7 January; *Foreign Affairs Bulletin*, 15, no. 3, 20 January: 16).

The distinction is made between nation and nationality. GDR and FRG citizens have the same nationality because of their same ethnic background but belong to two different nations which are characterized by insurmountable contrasts (*Neues Deutschland*, 15/16 February). Thus, it is asserted, a common nationality does not lead by necessity to the emergence of nations, because nationality is not the decisive prerequisite for the formation of nations in capitalism and socialism (*Junge Welt*, no. 79, 3 April).

> The question if at a later time when the socialist revolution will also have been victorious in the FRG and a socialist nation has developed, again a uniform socialist German nation can emerge, cannot be answered in the positive nor negative manner. This will depend on historical conditions which nobody can presently predict. (*Deutsche Zeitschrift für Philosophie*, East Berlin, no. 2, 1975.)

GDR foreign minister Oskar Fischer declared at the Plenary Session of the U.N. General Assembly that the "German question" has been irrevocably solved as a result of the development of two independent German states (*Die Welt*, 26 September). The GDR strongly objected to the FRG's attempt to hinder the conclusion of consular agreements between the GDR and Austria and other states on the grounds that only one uniform German citizenship exists for all Germans (*Neues Deutschland*, 21 January, 7 February). Bonn rejected the GDR note of 23 January (ibid., 24 January) which asserted interference by the FRG government in GDR affairs. Holding that the issue of German citizenship has not been settled, the FRG is determined to continue to provide assistance to all Germans who ask for it within the framework of consular relations with third countries. (*Die Welt*, 24 February.)

East Berlin also attacked the activities of the Central Registration Office at Salzgitter, an FRG agency which attempts to record and investigate activities of GDR citizens in regard to the use of violent means in their efforts to prevent people from escaping from the GDR. The published statistics of 1974 refer to 1,342 investigations against GDR citizens, among them 136 cases of attempted manslaughter and bodily injury (ibid., 8 January 1975.) The GDR asserts that these activities constitute "a continuous and flagrant interference in the sovereign affairs of the GDR" (*Foreign Affairs Bulletin*, vol. 15, no. 2, 14 January). On the other hand, East Berlin objects to the fact that organizations in the FRG comprised of refugees and expellees receive support from public funds, and claims that these persons are aided because they are "revanchists." It demands that the political opposition, the Christian Democrats, in the FRG Bundestag be silenced because they allegedly agitate against international law (*Sonntag*, East Berlin, 20 April).

The SED utilizes the German Communist Party (Deutsche Kommunistische Partei; DKP) to establish contacts and influence the population in the FRG. The so-called Western Work (Westarbeit) has been intensified. Special action groups have been formed by the SED Central Committee to support the efforts of the DKP especially in the industrialized area of North Rhine-Westphalia. Summer camps for children of the FRG have been arranged in the GDR and study groups of workers from large factories are invited to visit the GDR. (*Die Welt*, 26 March.) Especially important for influencing the workers in the FRG are the contacts and mutual friendship visits of officials of the FDGB and the German Trade Union League (Deutscher Gewerkschaftsbund; DGB) of the FRG. There were numerous exchange visits throughout 1975. Emphasis is also placed on establishing contacts and good relations with FRG youth organizations and exchange visits of the FDJ with organizations such as the Young Socialists (Jusos) and German Young Democrats (DJD). (*Junge Welt*, no. 88, 14 March.)

Espionage activities of the SED within the FRG have increased, according to the Federal Service for the Protection of the Constitution (*Deutscher Informationsdienst*, Bonn, vol. 26, no. 1415, 15 September). Visitors from the FRG are frequently approached by agents of the GDR Ministry of State Security who propose that they work for the GDR. During the past two years such efforts have quadrupled. (*Die Welt*, 21 May.)

The annual amount Bonn has to pay to the GDR for use of the transit roads to West Berlin was in recent years 234.9 million Marks. This apparently is to become 580 million Marks on 1 January 1976, comprising 290 million Marks for transit fees and 290 million Marks as Bonn's contribution toward repair of the most used road, between Helmstedt and Berlin, but final agreement on the payment for road repair has not yet been reached (ibid., 27/28 September, 16 October).

Attempts to undermine the status of West Berlin continued throughout 1975. A number of incidents were utilized by the SED leaders to restate the fact that West Berlin is not a part of the FRG. When the FRG minister of foreign affairs accompanied U.S. secretary of state Henry Kissinger on a visit to West Berlin on 21 May, it was charged that Bonn had violated the "Quadripartite Agreement on West Berlin" of 1971 and thus was working against détente (*Neues Deutschland*, 22 May). The EEC's decision to establish a European Center for Vocational Training in West Berlin was equally considered a violation (ibid., 22-23 February). The GDR sent a letter to the U.N. secretary-general protesting against the FRG's appointment of the president of the West Berlin-based Federal Cartel Bureau as its representative to the U.N. Intergovernmental Commission on Transnational Corporations. The USSR, the Ukrainian SSR, and Bulgaria also protested. (*Foreign Affairs Bulletin*, 15, no. 11, 14 April: 82.)

As for the Conference on Security and Cooperation in Europe (CSCE), Honecker declared that the part dealing with border changes by peaceful means had no practical importance for the GDR: "We have no border problems with our neighbors, and also not with the capitalist states since socialism and capitalism can never be united" (*Neues Deutschland*, 6 August). However, at the Helsinki conference, he met with the FRG chancellor Helmut Schmidt on 30 July and discussed "matters of security and cooperation in Europe and bi-lateral relations" (*Foreign Affairs Bulletin*, 15, no. 21, 12 August: 161).

Trade between the GDR and FRG increased during 1975, following the same pattern as in 1974, with the FRG emerging as the most important Western trading partner. The GDR has entered into long-term agreements with Friedrich Krupp G.m.b.H., the giant West German steel firm, and with the Hoechst Works, the world-renowned chemical concern (*NYT*, 21 May). During the first six months of 1975 the GDR debt to the FRG increased from 2 to 2.3 billion Marks. The interest free "Swing" credit, presently set at 790 million Marks, is used up. (*Die Welt*, 1 September.) The GDR's effort to obtain markets for its textile products in the FRG took the form of selling at dumping prices; men's suits sold for 7 to 12.50 Marks and shirts for 0.65 to 4 Marks, far below production cost. The FRG Ministry of Economics was forced to take measures to stop this practice. (Ibid., 26 September.)

Relations with the Soviet Bloc. As in previous years, the SED leaders emphasized the indestructible nature of the GDR's alliance with the Soviet Union. The 20th anniversary of the "Treaty on Relations between the GDR and the USSR," signed on 20 September 1955, was celebrated as "an important milestone in the development of the indestructible fraternal alliance" (*Foreign Affairs Bulletin*, 15, no. 27, 1 October 1975: 201).

The integration of the GDR with the socialist community of states was emphasized rhetorically and implemented in practice. The numerous exchange visits of SED officials and leaders of the communist parties and governments of other states of the socialist community offered opportunities for GDR efforts to coordinate the domestic and foreign policies of the socialist fraternity with Moscow's directives and to lay the groundwork for agreements of cooperation in the economic, technological, scientific, health, military, and production areas. The GDR is a member of 31 bi- and multi-lateral organizations of the community of socialist states concerned with research, development, and production (out of a total of 35 organizations of this type in existence) and of 11 such organizations responsible for foreign trade, transportation, and finances (*Einheit*, no. 6, 1975, pp. 673-78; *Foreign Affairs Bulletin*, 15, no. 23, 23 August: 172-73). In addition the GDR has concluded numerous bilateral agreements with communist-controlled governments dealing with specialization and cooperation. In 1974 there were more than 150 of these agreements in force between the GDR and Poland (Bundesminister für innerdeutsche Beziehungen, *Informationen*, no. 6, 1974, p. 14).

SED Politburo member Horst Sindermann wrote in an article in *Pravda* (6 March):

> The coordination of national economic plans for the period 1976 through 1980 and also the long-term coordination of prospects up to 1990, which is now being carried out among the CMEA countries, is of great political and economic significance. Decisive preconditions are being created here for strengthening the unity and cohesion of the socialist community, for increasing the volume and effectiveness of its scientific research and economic potential, and for expanding economic relations with other countries. They exert a considerable influence on the further change of the alignment of forces in the world arena and on the assertion of the principles of peaceful co-existence in international relations.

Sindermann also paid tribute to the coordination of the five-year plans of all CMEA members at the 29th CMEA session in Budapest on 24-26 June 1975, and GDR foreign minister Oskar Fischer asserted earlier:

> The CMEA states have become the most stable and most dynamic economic region of the World. With approximately one tenth of the world population they turn out about 35% of the world industrial production. . . . It was the coordinated policy of peace of the states of the socialist community which has brought about a turn for the better in the situation in Europe. (*Volkstimme*, Vienna, 11 April.)

The document concerning the coordination of the economic plans of the GDR and USSR for 1976-80 was signed in Moscow on 26 July (*Deutschland Archiv*, 8, no. 8, August: 896).

The GDR's trade with the CMEA countries went up by 11 percent in 1974 as compared with 1973 and accounted for about 70 percent of its overall trade (ADN, 25 February 1975). The Soviet Union remained the largest individual trading partner, with Czechoslovakia in the second place, followed by Poland, Hungary, Romania, and Bulgaria (Bundesminister für innerdeutsche Beziehungen, *Informationen*, no. 6, 1974, pp. 13-14). GDR exports during 1974 were valued at 14.1 billion Valuta Marks, including 7.7 billion for exports to the CMEA countries (*Aussenpolitische Korrespondenz*, 19, no. 41, East Berlin, 9 October 1975: 324).

The introduction of passport-and-visa-free tourist traffic with socialist states was held responsible for a substantial increase in contacts across the border (*Neues Deutschland*, 6 August). In 1974, allegedly 17.6 million persons crossed the "friendship borders" of the GDR, Czechoslovakia, and Poland (*Volkstimme*, 11 April).

The 30th anniversary of the "Liberation from Fascism" by the "glorious Soviet Army and its allies" offered the occasion for many celebrations and of a joint conference held in East Berlin on 8 April 1975 attended by delegations from the Soviet Union, Bulgaria, Czechoslovakia, Hungary, Poland, and Romania. Most of the anniversary celebrations of the "Great Fatherland War" took place in the beginning of May 1975, such as the one at the Supreme Command of the Group of Soviet Forces in Germany (GSSD) at Wuensdorf on 6 May (*Neues Deutschland*, 7 May). The main event took place in East Berlin and was addressed by Honecker and by the head of the USSR party-government delegation Fedor D. Kulakov, member of the Politburo and CPSU Central Committee secretary (ibid., 7-8 June). May 9 was declared a state holiday in the GDR (*NYT*, 28 April).

The outstanding event in GDR-USSR relations was the signing of the third Friendship Pact on 7 October, which SED leaders termed a "treaty of historical significance" (*Neues Deutschland*, 9 October). The other two friendship treaties were concluded in 1955 and 1964. Differences in the contents of the 3 treaties have reflected important changes in Soviet foreign policy. In 1955 the sovereignty of the GDR was emphasized, and even "temporary stationing of Soviet troops" required the approval of the GDR government: In 1964 no reference was made to the sovereignty of the GDR; mutual advantages and mutual assistance were stressed, together with the principle of noninterference in domestic affairs. The 1975 treaty replaces any national consideration with the principle of the socialist community by stating that the parties to the pact are determined to work consistently for the strengthening of the unity of the socialist community of states. Following the example set by the amendments of the GDR constitution in 1974, any reference to the "German question" is completely eliminated. (In the 1955 treaty, the main objective was German reunification and even the termination of the pact was set at the time of the restitution of German unity.) Of great significance also is the change of the military support obligation. The new pact no longer limits the rendering of military assistance to the case of an armed attack in Europe (as in the pact of 1964). That means, for example, that the GDR is obliged to come to the aid of the Soviet Union in the event of a military conflict situation with China. (*Die Welt*, 8 October.)

The demands made by Moscow go beyond issues of mutual advantage. For example, the GDR in spite of its own shortage of skilled labor had to send about 6,000 workmen to build 550 kilometers of the 2,800-kilometer-long natural gas pipeline leading from the Ural Mountains to the western border of the USSR (*Rheinischer Merkur*, Cologne, 18 July).

The military integration of the Warsaw Pact countries was hailed by SED Politburo member and GDR defense minister Army General Heinz Hoffman in *Neues Deutschland* (14 May):

> When we speak about the military superiority of the Warsaw Pact in regard to NATO then we refer first of all to the uniformity of our armed forces from its class character and its political task, armament and equipment, tactical and operational concepts, from the level of training, to the unshakable fighting morale and the firm relations of socialist brotherhood of arms [Waffenbrüderschaft].

The plan for the cooperation between the NVA and the Group of Soviet Armed Forces in Germany (GSSD) was signed on 24 January by Hoffmann and Army General Yevgeny Ivanovski, CPSU Central Committee member and GSSD supreme commander (*Volksarmee*, no. 5).

Other International Positions. By 1975 the GDR could claim that it had established relations with the majority of states throughout the world. The breakthrough from its isolation occurred in 1973 after the Basic Treaty was signed with the FRG. Admitted to the United Nations in that year, the GDR joined several U.N. specialized agencies and a number of commissions. Canada, the last of the NATO countries to establish diplomatic relations with the GDR, did so on 1 August 1975 after the conclusion of the Conference on Security and Cooperation in Europe (CSCE) at Helsinki. Consular agreements were concluded with Austria (26 March) and Finland (28 April).

During 1974 the GDR concluded 273 international agreements, of which 163 were with "socialist brother countries, including 22 with the USSR. Another 54 bi-lateral agreements were concluded with Asian, African, and Latin American nation states, while capitalist states accounted for 56 contractual agreements" (*Foreign Affairs Bulletin*, 15, no. 27, 1 October 1975: 206-7.) The GDR also joined the International Labor Organization and acceded "to 38 multilateral conventions to which states with different social-economic systems are parties" (ibid., p. 207). The record for 1975 was equally impressive. Trade agreements were concluded with Japan, Turkey, Switzerland, and several Arab countries, among them Syria, Iraq, and Kuwait. The GDR's emphasis on good relations with the Arab states was witnessed by several exchange visits of leading party and government officials. The Solidarity Committee of the GDR, founded in 1960, and the Peace Council of the GDR are additional organs to implement East Berlin's foreign policy, especially among the countries of the Middle East and the Third World (ibid., no. 23, 23 August: 169). Development aid primarily took the form of sending experts and specialists (more than 1,500 in 1974) to the developing countries and providing vocational training to persons from these countries in the GDR (more than 4,700 in 1974) (Bundesminister für innerdeutsche Beziehungen, *Informationen*, no. 10, 1975, p. 8).

The GDR continued to support every position taken by the Soviet Union in the United Nations during the 29th and 30th Sessions of the General Assembly. U.N. secretary-general Kurt Waldheim during an official visit to the GDR on 7-9 February 1975 stated at a press conference that the GDR was making a very useful contribution to U.N. efforts for peace and for the solution of various problems (*Foreign Affairs Bulletin*, 15, no. 5, 10 February: 29-30). The GDR became a member of the International Atomic Energy Agency (IAEA) and was visited by its director-general, Dr. Sigvard Eklund, on 10-15 March (ibid., no. 10, 2 April, p. 74). The GDR's deputy foreign minister and permanent representative at the United Nations, Peter Florin, advocated the calling of a world disarmament conference because, according to the opinion of his government, of conditions more favorable than ever before (ibid., no. 17, 12 June, p. 129). East Berlin hosted the International Women's Year World Congress, 20-24 October, which was attended by more than 2,000 delegates, representing 131 national and 91 international organizations. Erich Honecker addressed the meeting. Angela Davis and Hortensia de Allende were enthusiastically received. (*Die Welt*, 21 October.)

The Conference on Security and Cooperation in Europe was considered by the SED leadership as an important step toward peaceful co-existence and cooperation between states with different social systems (*Neues Deutschland*, 6 August). The SED emphasized that the results of the conference coincided with the basic interests and foreign policy objectives of the GDR (*Die Welt*, 9 August) and considered the conference a substitute for a peace treaty because the sovereignty and territorial integrity of the participating states, and especially the inviolability of their frontiers, had been acknowledged and reaffirmed (*Neues Deutschland*, 6 August). As for humanitarian issues and the freer exchange of persons and information, Erich Honecker stated that these problems would be attacked from the position of the working class (*Die Welt*, 16 September). At the Vienna talks on mutual reduction of forces and arms in Central Europe, with 19 participating states, the GDR completely endorsed the Soviet position requesting the reduction of troops and arms of 11 directly involved states in the area (*Foreign Affairs Bulletin*, 15, no. 6, 17 February: 42-43). The original concept of "balanced mutual reduction" was eliminated by the participating communist-ruled states.

In spite of a trade and payment agreement between the GDR and the People's Republic of China, signed in Peking on 27 January (Bundesminister für innerdeutsche Beziehungen, *Informationen*, no. 3, p. 2), the SED leadership echoes Moscow's condemnation of the Chinese communists. Maoism was said to be struggling against peace in Europe and intending to provoke a direct clash between the USSR and the United States (*Neues Deutschland*, 8 January). The Chinese leaders were alleged to be preaching "the cult of violence and brutality and [provoking] everything which could aggravate the international situation" (*Sächsische Zeitung*, Dresden, 2 April). In August the SED accused the Chinese leadership of propagating preparations for a war and placed the Peking government on the same level with U.S. Senator Henry Jackson, former British prime minister Edward Heath, Franz Josef Strauss, chairman of the Christian Social Union of Bavaria, and Chile's "fascist dictator" Augusto Pinochet (*Neues Deutschland*, 25 August).

The SED like other Marxist-Leninist parties officially condemns the activities of anarchist terrorists. It is reported, however, that financial support for international terrorist organizations is provided by East Berlin via Cuba and that Finsterwalde in the GDR is a training camp where terrorists are instructed in the use of explosives, machine guns, and sub-machine guns and in the planning and execution of kidnapings and assassinations (*Rheinischer Merkur*, 25 July).

The GDR, like the other countries of the community of the socialist states, provided political and material support to the revolutionary forces in Portugal, especially the Portuguese Communist Party. Exchange visits of party and government officials continued throughout 1975. A five-year trade agreement was signed on 25 January. (*Democratic German Report*, 24, no. 3, 12 February: 18). The GDR-Portugal Friendship Committee, founded on 26 June, served as a channel for the SED effort to provide assistance to the Portuguese communists.

East Berlin also carried on its efforts to improve relations between Yugoslavia and the Soviet Bloc. GDR foreign minister Oskar Fischer visited Belgrade in late April. Discussions on cooperation for the period 1976-80 were held in August, and a doubling of the trade exchange and long-term economic developments of the two states after 1980 were decided upon (East Berlin domestic television, 3 August).

International Party Contacts. The SED continued in 1975 its work on the preparations for a conference of the communist and workers' parties of 28 East and West European countries, originally planned for the early part of 1975. The SED is entrusted with the chairmanship of the working committee which is to draft a final communiqué. This committee met a few times in East Berlin, Warsaw, and Budapest. The draft submitted by the SED met with strong opposition from the Romanian, Italian, Spanish, British, Swedish, and Yugoslav representatives because the proposed unity of action of all would restrict the freedom of action of the individual parties (*Die Zeit*, 12 September). On 9-10 October another preparatory conference attended by representatives from 27 parties took place in East Berlin, where the document drafted by the SED was again not approved. It is believed that the official conference can only be called when all 28 parties agree on a definite text of the final communiqué. (*Die Welt*, 15 October.)

The SED's West Bureau is especially charged with providing material assistance to the DKP in the FRG and to the West Berlin extension, the Socialist Unity Party of West Berlin (SEW) (*Neues Deutschland*, 11-12 January). The FDJ remained in close contact with the communist youth organizations in the FRG and organized exchange visits with the Marxist Students League—Spartakus and the Socialist German Workers' Youth (SDAJ) (*Junge Welt*, 12-13 April).

Publications and Broadcast Media. SED Politburo member and Central Committee secretary Werner Lamberz defined the role of the mass media in the GDR as follows:

> The mass media occupy a conspicuous and ever more important place. For the Socialist Unity Party they have never been media of entertainment or pure and neutral information. For us they are an effective vehicle of objective and partisan information and of our scientific world outlook. The breadth and diversity of the content and forms of expression essential for mass media are not an aim in themselves. They assure effective popularization of our standpoint through political analyses, atheistic essays, and art broadcasts and articles cultivating ethical and aesthetic views. (*WMR*, June 1975, p. 28.)

The daily newspapers in the GDR announced that as consequence of the higher prices for newsprint their Sunday editions would no longer appear as of the beginning of January 1975 (*NYT*, 3 January). Even the official organ of the SED, *Neues Deutschland*, with a claimed daily circulation of 1.1 million copies (issue of 6 August), was affected. The SED also publishes the *Berliner Zeitung* (circulation 500,000) and a number of dailies in other cities of the GDR. The organs of the four other parties, the *Neue Zeit*, (CDU), *Der Morgen*, (LDPD), the *National Zeitung*, (NDPD) and the *Bauern-Echo*, (DBD) which up to January appeared from Tuesday through Sunday also stopped their Sunday editions, but now publish a Monday paper. (Bundesminister für innerdeutsche Beziehungen, *Informationen*, no. 1, p. 6.) The mass organizations of the National Front have their own publications but are required to print only officially approved material. Military publications include the *Armeerundschau*, the *Volksarmee*, and the official publication of the Defense Ministry, *Militärwesen*. *Der Kämpfer* is the organ of the Combat Groups of the Working Class (Kampfgruppen).

The SED's semi-monthly magazine, *Neuer Weg*, is concerned primarily with party issues. Its monthly journal, *Einheit*, deals mainly with theoretical and practical problems of "scientific" Marxism-Leninism.

The FDJ and the Pioneer organization "Ernst Thälmann" produce 15 newspapers and magazines with a total circulation of more than 5 million. The FDJ daily newspaper, *Junge Welt*, has a circulation of 600,000. The FDJ official magazine is *Junge Generation*. The FDJ bi-weekly theoretical organ *Forum* is concerned with intellectual problems faced by young people in the GDR.

A number of publications, some in foreign languages, carry GDR propaganda abroad. *Neue Heimat* and the *FDGB Review* are well-prepared publications for foreign consumption. The *Democratic German Report* and the *Foreign Affairs Bulletin* are forwarded to recipients in the English-speaking world.

Publications from the socialist countries are readily available in the GDR. As of January 1975 there were 3,730 of these publications, of which 1,600 came from the Soviet Union. Almost 550,000 individual issues of newspapers and journals are imported from the socialist countries, including 305,000 from the Soviet Union. (*Neue Zeit*, 27 January 1975.)

TV and broadcasting are strictly controlled by the SED. Radio transmitters are also used to prevent the population of the GDR from receiving broadcasts from the FRG and West Berlin. Contrary to the decision reached at the CSCE in Helsinki, the GDR increased its jamming activities. Several stations were moved into the immediate area surrounding West Berlin, where their strong frequencies interfere with the West Berlin broadcasting stations, whose programs are hardly audible in the GDR. (*Die Welt*, 1 September.) The main propaganda radio station is the "Voice of the GDR."

The GDR has two TV programs. One can be received by 98.5 percent of the population and the other by 83 percent. Almost 64 percent of the viewers can get color TV reception. (*Sächsische Neueste Nachrichten*, Dresden, 26 March.)

University of Calgary, Canada   Eric Waldman

Hungary

Hungarian communists formed a party in November 1918 and became the dominant force in the left-wing coalition that established the Republic of Councils the following March and ruled for four months. Subsequently proscribed, the party functioned sporadically in exile and illegality. With the Soviet occupation at the end of World War II the Hungarian Communist Party emerged as a partner in the coalition government and exercised an influence disproportionate to its limited electoral support. Communists gained effective control of the country by 1947, and the following year absorbed left-wing social democrats into the newly-named Hungarian Workers' Party. On 1 November 1956, during the popular revolt that momentarily restored a multi-party government, the name was changed to Hungarian Socialist Workers' Party (Magyar Szocialista Munkáspárt; HSWP).

The HSWP rules unchallenged as the sole political party, firmly aligned with the Soviet Union. Its exclusive status is confirmed in the revised state constitution of 1972: "The Marxist-Leninist party of the working class is the leading force in society." Coordination of formal political activities, such as elections, is the function of the Patriotic People's Front (PPF). In the 1971-75 Parliament 71 percent of the deputies were party members. Of municipal and local council members 46.9 percent belong to the HSWP. In the police forces 90 percent of officer rank are HSWP members. Party membership on 1 January 1975 stood at 754,353. By current occupation the membership was composed of 45.5 percent physical workers, 6.1 percent "immediate supervisors of production," 40 percent intellectual workers, and 8.4 percent dependents and others. By original occupation, 59.2 percent were workers, 13 percent peasants, 8.9 percent intellectual workers, 16.3 percent white-collar employees, and 2.6 percent others. Of current members 8,212 joined the HSWP prior to the country's liberation in 1945.

The broadest umbrella organization for political mobilization is the PPF. It works through some 4,000 committees with 112,400 members. A related agency is the National Peace Council, with international responsibilities. Trade unions, directed by the National Council of Trade Unions, comprise close to four million organized workers. The Communist Youth League (Kommunista Ifjusági Szövetség; KISZ) has more than 800,000 members, in 25,600 basic organizations. Thirty-one percent of working youths, 56 percent of secondary school students, and 96 percent of post-secondary students belong to the KISZ. In the Workers' Militia 81 percent are HSWP members. Other active mobilizing agents are the National Council of Hungarian Women and the Hungarian-Soviet Friendship Society.

Hungary has a population (estimated 1975) of 10,510,000.

Leadership and Organization. Ultimate political power in the HSWP, and therefore in Hungary, remains in the hands of the first secretary, János Kádár. Current Politburo members are Kádár, György Aczél, Antal Apró, Valéria Benke, Béla Biszku, Jenö Fock, Sándor Gáspár, István Huszár, György Lázár, Pál Losonczi, László Maróthy, Dezsö Nemes, Károly Németh, Miklós Ovári, and István Sarlós. In addition to first secretary Kádár the Central Committee Secretariat includes Biszku, Németh, Ovári, András Gyénes, Imre Györi, and Arpád Pullai. Chairman of the Central Committee is János Brutyó.

The Central Committee elected at the party's 11th Congress in March 1975 has 125 members. County party committees, together with the Budapest Party Committee, number 24. There are also 97 district party committees, 104 city and Budapest district party committees, 1033 plant and office party committees, and 24,450 primary party organizations. The leaders in the latter organizations number 106,692. Of these primary party organizations, 7,066 are active in industry and construction, 4,215 in agriculture, 1,473 in transportation, and 1,216 in commerce.

Auxiliary and Mass Organizations. The Patriotic People's Front is responsible for organizing the political activities of all citizens, party members and non-members alike, who ostensibly support the HSWP's alliance policy. Its major activity in 1975 was to supervise the preparations for the National Assembly elections on 15 June. The secretary-general of the PPF, István Sarlós, is also a member of the Politburo.

The party's concern with the political mobilizaton of young people was illustrated by Kádár's attendance at the KISZ Central Committee meeting of 21 January, when the guidelines for the HSWP's 11th Congress were discussed and approved. The biennial KISZ leadership elections, held 1 February-15 May, were accompanied by an extensive screening of members. In other activities, the KISZ Central Committee called for the first national conference of youth clubs, designed to bring the many licensed and unlicensed clubs under more centralized direction, and organized a political song contest. The KISZ continues to manage voluntary summer labor camps, which during 1975 had more than 25,000 young people working on agricultural, industrial, and construction projects. The implicit political criteria for future educational opportunities serve as an incentive to volunteer. The media meanwhile continue their criticism of the opulent way of life of the children of the "new class." László Maróthy, first secretary of the KISZ, is a Politburo member.

Sándor Gáspár, the secretary-general of the National Council of Trade Unions, is also a member of the Politburo.

Party Internal Affairs. The most notable party event in 1975 was the holding of the 11th Congress. At the Central Committee plenum, also attended by the Central Control Committee, on 26 February, the final version of the Congress documents was approved and the date of the Congress's opening set for 17 March. In the elaborate party-wide preparations, the drafts of the congressional guidelines and of the revised party statutes had been debated by some 200,000 party members at meetings of primary organizations. Of the 4,000 proposals for modifications that reached the Central Committee, more than 100 were incorporated in the final drafts.

Leonid Brezhnev, general secretary of the Communist Party of the Soviet Union (CPSU), arrived in Budapest by train 16 March and met that same evening with Kádár and Béla Biszku, who is generally regarded as Kádár's second-in-command. The HSWP's 11th Congress met 17-22 March (the 10th Congress had been held in November 1970) and was attended by 843 Hungarian delegates, by Brezhnev and the first secretaries of the Bulgarian, Czechoslovakian, East German, and Polish communist parties, and by other foreign communist party delegations.

At the opening session Kádár delivered a general report on developments since the 10th Congress. Appealing for greater ideological unity of all citizens in the construction of socialism, he stressed the role of enterprise democracy and the need for greater worker involvement in decision making (a theme that was taken up by several speakers at the congress). The New Economic Mechanism had proven itself, but the state must provide central direction and supervision, and group and individual interests, useful as incentives, must remain subordinated to the national interest. Hungary must exert the utmost effort to cope with the effects of world-wide inflation by raising productivity and adjusting its price system. Noting that Hungary must rely primarily on the Soviet Union and other members of CMEA (Council for Mutual Economic Aid), Kádár praised the Soviets for their help and understanding in economic relations. In the sphere of social policy, Kádár announced that the pensionable age of agricultural workers would be progressively reduced to that of industrial workers beginning in 1976. He warned that in the social sciences, and generally in education and the arts, more positive action should be taken against non-Marxist views and toward "socialist consciousness."

Turning to internal party matters, Kádár observed that 67 percent of the members had joined since 1956, and stressed the need to unify the different generations of members. He criticized transgressions of democratic centralism and anticipated an exchange of party cards (an occasion to review each member's performance and suitability) to heighten the party's ideological and functional unity. Reflecting on the action of the November 1972 Central Committee plenum in reviewing the implementation of the 10th Congress's resolutions, he recommended that this practice be repeated at mid-points between congresses.

Kádár's comments on foreign and intra-party affairs followed the established pattern of complete accord with the Soviet line. He denounced extremist opponents of détente, praised the anti-fascist forces in Chile, Greece, and Portugal, and endorsed peaceful co-existence with the West. There were "no clouds on the skies of Hungaro-Soviet friendship," and good relations were maintained with the other socialist states, but the "sins of Maoism" and the resultant hostility of Albania and the People's Republic of China were to be deplored. Kádár also voiced support for the projected conferences of European and world-wide communist parties.

Later during the congress Kádár met informally with a group of scientists and other intellectuals, including non-party members, who were attending the congress as delegates or guests, and reassuringly expressed his gratitude for the political understanding and cooperation of party members and non-members alike.

The report of the Central Control Committee, presented by János Brutyó, indicated that between the two congresses 3.9 percent of party members (29,181) had been disciplined and 7,133 expelled. Brutyó singled out cases of abuse of power, of officials behaving like petty monarchs, and cases of laxity and waste of collective property. He lamented the insufficiency of criticism and the incidence of retaliation for justified criticism. Party members must be protected from the deplorable views and habits that seep in from the society at large and which members ought to be fighting to eradicate in the first place. Brutyó's panacea is an improvement in supervision at all party levels.

Other congressional statistics show that since the 10th Congress 148,288 new members were recruited into the party. Of these, 54.2 percent were physical workers, 33.5 percent intellectual workers, and 12.3 percent in other categories. Thirty-two percent of the new recruits were women. In addition to the expulsions noted by Brutyó, 7,478 resigned their membership and another 15,474 memberships were cancelled.

On the second day of the congress, Brezhnev delivered an address full of unstinting praise for Kádár and the HSWP and calling for even closer ideological, cultural, scientific, and economic cooperation. Premier Jenö Fock's speech, on the other hand, had an element of self-criticism that foreshadowed his subsequent demise. He mentioned "portfolio chauvinism" (i.e., the poor coordination of the various ministries' interests) and delays in the implementation of decrees: "In the eight years that I have been premier we have not made any great headway in getting everyone to realize his responsibility for the economy as a whole."

Károly Németh, the secretary in charge of economic affairs, also addressed himself to the shortcomings of economic management. Speaking on the third day of the meeting, he deplored that "the intent of central guidance is not effectively translated into practice at all levels and in every respect." The application of democratic centralism to economic affairs means the strengthening of both central direction and local independence, and the rights of the society as a whole must remain paramount. Németh underscored persistent weaknesses in phasing out unprofitable production, and in modernization, labor management, and labor discipline. He defended, however, the utility of small farms and private plots alongside the large producers' cooperatives. Sándor Gáspár, speaking for the trade unions, stressed the need to improve the living standard of the workers' class but also endorsed selective rewards for performance. He advocated greater and less formalized enterprise democracy, which he called "one of the most important elements of socialist leadership." Several worker-delegates also addressed the congress on the critical importance of worker participation.

Questions of ideology and culture were the principal themes for Valéria Benke, a Politburo member and editor of the party's ideological journal *Társadalmi Szemle*. Quantitative indicators were not enough to measure the building of socialism; it was also essential to collectively evaluate attitudes and behavior. Nationalism, the "most dangerous of bourgeois ideas," persisted in the social sciences. Certain intellectuals had "drifted into the troubled waters of revisionism and ultra-leftist or other turbid streams." Open debate was essential, but there could be no compromise on certain fundamentals: socialist patriotism, proletarian internationalism and Hungarian-Soviet friendship, the leading role of the working class and of the HSWP, and the worker-peasant alliance.

Politburo member Dezsö Nemes was one of the speakers on the fourth day of the congress. Reflecting on détente, he denounced Western obstruction and charged that the "misleading slogan" of free flow of people and ideas aimed at counter-revolutionary subversion. His speech was also notable for a warning, clearly directed against Romania, that "open or concealed anti-Sovietism" within the leadership of a workers' party or socialist state could serve imperialist interests.

On 21 March Kádár delivered an extemporaneous speech in which he thanked the 57 delegates who had spoken in debate for their unanimous endorsement of the congressional reports. Reflecting on earlier allegations that the party's policies might undergo significant change, he said that the congress "gave a clear reply to such queries." Speculation about greater rigidity and a new dictatorship had been dispelled. The dictatorship of the proletariat would remain in force, and 18 years' experience had shown that "it was not such a bad dictatorship after all. One can live under it, create freely, and acquire honor." There were no longer any antagonistic classes, only class allies, and the remaining differences were not over the desirability of socialism but on the rate of development of the socialist revolution. The role of the HSWP was to lead and persuade.

In its final acts, the congress elected the top party leadership and unanimously approved the report of the Central Committee delivered by Kádár, the program declaration of the HSWP, the amendments to the party statutes, the resolution of the 11th Congress, the report of the Central Control Committee, and Kádár's concluding speech. The program declaration was an anodyne statement of general tasks over the next 15 to 20 years serving to transform socialism into communism. The resolution set out the more specific tasks for the next five years. It stated that in the building of socialism "social cooperation, which embraces all progressive and creative forces of the Hungarian population, party members and non-party people alike, the various nationalities and generations, atheists and believers, is being permeated with a socialist content."

In addition to enlarging the Central Committee from 105 to 125, the Congress approved a number of leadership changes. In the Politburo, Kádár, Aczél, Apró, Benke, Biszku, Fock, Gáspár, Nemes, and Németh were reelected. Four new members—Lázár, Maróthy, Sarlós, and Ovári—were elected to fill the vacancies created by the death of Zoltan Komócsin and the dismissal of Nyers, Fehér, and Kállai. Nyers, regarded as a key architect of the New Economic Mechanism (NEM), had been dropped from the Secretariat in March 1974 and is now entirely excluded from the political arena. Fehér, closely identified with agrarian policy through the recent period of modernization, was in ill health and had earlier resigned as deputy premier. Kállai is a former prime minister and head of the Patriotic People's Front.

Among the new Politburo members, István Sarlós is slated to represent the Patriotic People's Front, of which he is secretary-general, at a time when the party's alliance policy requires a reinvigoration of that front organization. Born in 1921, and originally a skilled worker and social democrat, Sarlós became a literature professor and, in 1970, editor in chief of the party daily *Népszabadság* and a member of the Central Committee. László Maróthy, born in 1942, became first secretary of the KISZ and a Central Committee member in 1973. His rapid elevation reflects the party's concern with mobilizing youth. Miklós Ovári, born in 1925, long worked in the Central Committee's agitprop department. He joined the Central Committee as a full member in 1966 and the Secretariat in 1970. Unexpectedly he was promoted ahead of Pullai, a secretary since 1966. György Lázár, born 1924, joined the party in 1945 and had a long career in the National Planning Office. He was minister of labor in 1970-73, joined the Central Committee in 1970, and became deputy prime minister, chairman of the State Planning Committee, chairman of the National Planning Office, and permanent representative to CMEA in 1973. He is expected to share responsibilities for economic affairs with Németh.

The Secretariat gained an additional member in András Gyénes, a former ambassador to East Germany and deputy minister of foreign affairs. Komócsin's old responsibilities for intra-party affairs will presumably be inherited by Gyénes.

Reflecting on the congressional resolution in *Pártélet* (May), Pullai observed that "fundamentally, it merely calls for more consistent pursuit of past political practice." To the extent, however, that the congress indicated a shift in emphasis, the direction was away from liberalism and toward orthodoxy. This was noticeable in the demands for tighter central control of economic management, for stronger leadership by the party and greater worker participation, and for vigilance against deviations in ideology and culture. The personnel changes in the Politburo tend to confirm evidence of such a shift. For the Hungarian public the most significant outcome was the retention at the helm of Kádár, who has been in poor health and repeatedly rumored to be about to resign. He enjoys genuine popularity through his identification with the economic and cultural liberalization of the last decade.

At the Central Committee meeting of 15 May, Gyénes reported on the international situation; the Central Committee apparatus was restructured with the creation of a separate department for industry, agriculture, and transportation; and the replacement of Jenö Fock by György Lázár as premier was approved. The Central Committee's enlarged plenum of 2 July took the unusual step of changing the Politburo's membership between congresses by adding Istvan Huszár and Pál Losonczi. Huszár, a deputy prime minister, had succeeded Lázár as chairman of the National Planning Office in May; together with Fock and Lázár, he will provide economic expertise on the Politburo at a critical time. Losonczi, chairman of the Presidential Council, becomes the first head of state since 1952 to sit on the Politburo. The Central Committee named Sándor Borbély head of the new department for industry, agriculture, and transportation; he was formerly first secretary of the Csepel Iron and Steel Works party committee. The 2 July plenum also issued a communiqué on economic problems.

The enlarged Central Committee plenum of 23 October heard a routine report by Gyénes on international affairs, then turned to the question of the party card exchange, which had been approved in principle by the 11th Congress. In his report Pullai anticipated not "a purge or inspection of the membership" but "sincere conversations and comradely exchanges of views" (*Népszabadság*, 24 October). The plenum recommended a carefully prepared exchange to be completed by the end of 1976. The measure is designed to activize the membership and reinforce the unity and elite character of the party. The amended party statutes ratified by the 11th Congress allow for release of a member on the initiative of the primary organization in addition to the existing provisions for resignation, cancellation for non-payment of dues, and expulsion. This provision should, in the context of the card exchange, facilitate the removal of unenthusiastic party members.

The HSWP's efforts toward political orthodoxy are also evident in general cadre policy. The established criteria are political reliability, professional competence, and leadership qualities, which in recent practice were applied in rough balance. The ongoing shift in emphasis to political reliability is attributable to the perceived impact of closer contacts with the West and of decentralized state and economic administration on political loyalty. A Central Committee analysis of the political qualifications of 32,000 cadres indicated that a large proportion lacked "political education" (*Béke és Szocializmus*, July). In the past the party insisted on intensive political education principally for HSWP leaders, but now this qualification is to be emphasized on a broader front.

The personnel changes and policy initiatives of the HSWP in 1975 were inspired by a number of current problems, chief among which was the acute economic crisis outlined below. The tightening up of party discipline and ideological and cultural guidelines reflected the concern of the HSWP (and, presumably, of the CPSU) leadership over the negative effects of the liberalization of the late 1960s and early 1970s and the potentially disintegrative impact of détente.

Domestic Attitudes and Activities. The rapid deterioration of Hungary's economic health, resulting largely from world inflationary pressures, was the prime focus of official action throughout 1975.

The Central Committee plenum of 5 December 1974 surveyed the relatively positive performance of the economy in 1974 and approved the plan for 1975. According to official statistics, planned rates of increase were surpassed in national income, industrial and agricultural production, and real income, but a substantial deficit had materialized in trade with the West. The 1975 plan made allowances for the effects of the world-wide recession and for the consumer price increases set for 1 January. It projected rather lower rates of growth in economic indicators than for 1974, and aimed at increased socialist imports and dollar exports.

A major shock came with the negotiation of the Hungarian-Soviet trade agreement, which was signed in Moscow on 31 January 1975 but reported by foreign trade minister József Biró only on 21 February (Radio Budapest). The Soviet decision to relate and annually adjust its energy and raw material prices to world market conditions had a serious impact on Hungary, which relies largely on imports for oil and other primary materials. Biró stressed that "the new raw and basic material prices are far more advantageous than those on the world market—e.g., the new price of crude oil is less than 50 percent of the price of oil imported from capitalist countries." In fact, the average price of imported raw materials and sources of energy rose by 52 percent, while the export prices of Hungarian machinery and agricultural produce were increased by 15 and 28 percent respectively. Overall, Hungarian-Soviet trade was projected to increase by 8.3 percent in 1975. The net result of the Comecon price changes has been a deterioration of Hungary's terms of trade with Poland, Czechoslovakia and most seriously, with the Soviet Union. Meanwhile, Hungary's trade balance with the West continued to worsen due to the unfavorable differential in rates of increase in export and import prices and to the European Economic Community's embargo on Hugarian beef. Statistics released in the West by the Hungarian National Bank indicated that in 1974 Hungary had incurred a balance of payments deficit in current terms of $461 million, which was reduced by hard currency loans to $237 million (*Handelsblatt*, 29-30 August).

The HSWP's 11th Congress addressed itself to a number of economic issues. To begin with, the resolution designated the development of enterprise democracy as a major party task—a "fundamental part of socialist democracy" providing for worker participation in management, for increasing the workers' sense of responsibility, and as an incentive for productivity. "The enterprise party organizations are responsible for consistently enforcing enterprise democracy, a task in which their main support is the trade union." The task is to be achieved by inclusion of physical workers in managerial councils and committees, by internal systems of management that better inform workers of the enterprise's operations, and by the discussion of essential matters in workers' assemblies. Enterprise democracy, warned Sándor Gáspár, is not a formality or periodic consultation but daily contact with the workers.

On economic policy, the resolution recommended greater efficiency in economic regulation and state management while retaining the enterprise independence associated with the New Economic Mechanism. "Control over plan implementation and observance of economic discipline must be made more effective on every level." This, said Károly Németh, the party's chief economic spokesman, "is not in conflict with our desire to increase the independence of enterprises and cooperatives in conformity with national economic interests." The resolution noted that rises in energy and raw material prices were far higher than for finished products: "Although our socialist planned economy can ward off their effect to a certain degree, it must nevertheless react to the processes taking place in the world economy." "The permanent changes in world market prices must be reflected—at least to some degree—in domestic producer prices, so that they may contribute to greater efficiency in management. These changes also inevitably affect the prices of certain consumer goods." Kádár warned the congress that these external factors could not be hidden by fictitious prices and state subsidies indefinitely; Fock observed that oil and gas had become so expensive that future power plants had to be based on coal, atomic energy, and water (the latter a reference to the projected Hungarian-Czechoslovak hydroelectric plant on the Danube).

In the transformation of Hungary's industrial profile the resolution gave priority to energy, public transportation, computers, petrochemicals, aluminum, and textiles, while generally recommending modernization, the phasing out of unprofitable production, and closer socialist economic integration. Much stress was laid in the resolution and by speakers on the importance of foreign trade, since exports account for close to 50 percent of national income.

Agrarian policy was left essentially unchanged by the congress, reflecting the successful fulfillment of the previous congressional targets. The party endorses the concentration of resources by the mergers of agricultural cooperatives and also the retention of private plots. One innovation concerns land ownership: sales of state land will be phased out and land used by cooperatives (more than half of which is now legally owned by individual members) is to be gradually transferred to cooperative property.

The resolution projected a 23-25 percent rise in per capita real income during the fifth five-year plan (1976-80), recommending a proportionate rise for workers and peasants, elimination of male-female wage differentials, continued central regulation of prices for essential commodities, and improvements in the supply of housing and child-care services. In their addresses Kádár and Biszku reaffirmed the right of artisans and shopkeepers to private property and acquisition of wealth within limits that must be enforced to fight "non-socialist tendencies." The resolution instructed trade unions to invigorate their activities in political, professional, moral, and cultural education, in the "application of the principles of democracy in their internal operations," and in increasing productivity.

The Central Committee's 2 July communiqué on economic issues focused on slow progress in the transformation of the production structure, low productivity, stockpiling, inadequate investment planning over-plan wage increases and consumption, and unsatisfactory trends in the non-socialist trade balance. It appealed for political support in the implementation of economic goals, particularly on the part of party organizations (*Magyar Nemzet*, 3 July). In a similar vein, an article by Károly Németh (*Társadalmi Szemle*, July) indicated the need for more effective central direction, the replacement of incompetent cadres, a greater concentration of production on exports to the West, and a general austerity program. Premier Lázár's maiden speech to the constituent session of the National Assembly, 4 July, echoed these grim warnings. Symptomatic of official attitudes was the government's reaction to the discovery of unjustifiably high inventories of crude steel in a number of enterprises. The managers responsible for this speculative stockpiling incurred the unprecedented punishment of ministerial sanctions and fines. In August, a new round of price increases affected fuels as well as lumber and other building materials.

Agriculture remains an important economic sector, and the merging of agricultural producers' cooperatives (APCs) continues apace, with the number of APCs down from 4,507 in 1961 to 1,923 in 1974. Some concern was expressed at the December 1974 session of the National Council of APCs at the trend toward more central guidance, but the motive behind the mergers is essentially that of rational utilization of resources. The 18 June session of the NCAPC debated the congressional resolutions and concluded that changes in land ownership should not be effected by "administrative" (i.e., compulsory) measures, since to force the pace of increasing common property would be costly and might alienate some members. The elimination of economic and legal obstacles to closer cooperation between state and cooperative farms was also discussed. Meanwhile, small farms still produce 35 to 39 percent of agricultural output by gross value, and the party endorses the continuing utility of this small-scale production while the costly industrialization of agriculture proceeds. Small farms are important labor-intensive producers of foodstuffs for domestic consumption as well as for export, and they provide jobs for agricultural workers made redundant by closed production system farms. In his address to Parliament on 20 September, agriculture and food minister Pál Romány praised the contribution of private household plots (which provide 30 percent of beef and milk production, 33 percent of the potato crop, 57 percent of paprika, and 33 percent of pigs for slaughter) and deplored the indifference shown by many APCs to this scale of farming. Other difficulties are the chronic shortage of suitable small farm machinery and the taxation of private plot incomes.

At the 29th regular CMEA Council session in Budapest 24-27 June the participants conferred on the coordination of the five-year plans for 1976-80. Hungary's principal concern is to ensure a supply of vital raw materials in the context of the new annually-adjusted pricing system. Development of Soviet resources depends in part on joint investment by CMEA users, a current example being the Orenburg natural gas pipeline under construction. The perennial problems of non-convertibility, bilateral clearing, and disparate domestic planning and price mechanisms remain a hindrance to genuine multilateralism and economic integration.

The gravity of Hungary's economic dilemma was confirmed by an unprecedentedly high unfavorable trade balance in *both* the socialist and the dollar sectors in the first half of 1975. Official statements tended to stress the difficulties in the Western sector. Finance minister Lajos Faluvégi deplored that the proportion of processed goods in exports had not increased: "It is one of the typical features of our production structure that nonprofitable export—which we sell to acquire foreign exchange and not because of the advantages of the international division of labor—is comparatively high" (*Magyar Hirlap*, 18 June). Deputy foreign trade minister Gyula Kovács declared that "the endeavor to increase exports to the capitalist countries must be made virtually the focal point of the efforts of governmental and economic organizations" (Radio Budapest, 10 May). A new decree provides tax and credit incentives for joint Hungarian-foreign enterprises operating outside Hungary. There are now 63 such enterprises operating in Europe, Asia, Africa, and the United States; 41 are engaged in trade, 8 in production, and 14 in the service sector (*Világgazdaság*, 10 May).

Nevertheless, the trade deficit also indicates that CMEA price changes had a major negative effect on Hungary's balance of trade with the Soviet Union, which in the past few years had produced a surplus. Clearly a much greater proportion of Hungarian production will have to be allocated in payment for expensive raw materials, the bulk of which comes from the Soviet Union. This was borne out by the agreement, signed in Moscow on 8 September, on the coordination of Hungarian and Soviet national economic plans for 1976-80. It projects a 40 percent increase (by value) in trade over the preceding five-year period, including a 60 percent increase (by value) in Soviet raw material and power deliveries. More specialization and more cooperative ventures are planned in the production of vehicles and agricultural and electronic machinery. In October a 15-year agreement on growth and specialization in Hungarian agricultural exports and thirteen other cooperation agreements were signed in Moscow. A July announcement indicated that the Soviet Union had alleviated the surplus in Hungarian beef cattle blocked by the EEC embargo and had paid in hard currency. Some general problems in Soviet-Hungarian trade noted in the local press were delays in Hungarian fulfillment of obligations in Soviet investments (which include the Kiembaev asbestos factory, the Kingisepp ammonia phosphate project, the Orenburg natural gas pipeline, and a long-distance electric power transmission line); insufficient market research by Hungarian exporters at a time of aggressive Western sales promotion in the Soviet Union; and the frequently inadequate quality of Hungarian exports. Shortcomings on the Soviet side were not reported.

Hungary has been borrowing heavily to cover its deficits and modernize production. A $40 million loan from Kuwait in December 1974 (the first such transaction between an Arab oil-producing country and the Soviet bloc) was followed in July by a $60 million Hungarian bond issue taken up also by Kuwait, which has invested and will be a supplier of oil in the Adria pipeline. A Western consortium (including the First National City Bank of New York, which is opening a branch in Budapest) has advanced a 100 million Eurodollar loan for export-oriented investments, and in July the Hungarian National Bank floated a 100 million Deutschmark bond issue, the first non-dollar borrowing. Finally, a notable commercial event was the signing in Tokyo on 20 October of a five-year trade and shipping agreement with Japan.

At the fall session of the National Assembly on 25 September Premier Lázár unveiled a series of measures to cope with the crisis. To improve the trade balance, he projected a 5 to 6 percent annual increase in national income over 1976-80 while holding down consumption to a maximum increase of 4.5 percent per annum. The consumer price level will rise, and a slower improvement in the standard of living is forecast for the years ahead. Lázár stated that prices of agricultural equipment and supplies would be raised 1 January 1976, as would the price of meat and other agricultural products. Most significant was the confirmation that a new system of economic regulators, representing a major and complex modification of the NEM, is to be introduced 1 January 1976. The basic purpose of the regulators is to reduce the discrepancies between domestic and world market prices and thereby improve managerial efficiency and competitiveness. Enterprise independence, the profit motive, and the use of economic tools of control are essentially unchanged, although central supervision will be qualitatively and quantitatively increased. The new regulators are designed to reduce retained profits through taxation and to lower direct state subsidies for producer and consumer prices (such subsidies accounted for approximately one-third of the 1974 state budget). Those investments that are left to the enterprises' discretion are to be funded no longer from subsidies but by state and bank loans. Finally, the sectors covered by the centrally regulated wage system are to be expanded and strongly progressive taxes imposed to inhibit inflationary increases.

Whether the fundamental principles of the NEM can survive the economic crisis and the hostility of the more dogmatic centralizers in the HSWP is an open question. As József Bognár, a leading Hungarian economist and architect of the NEM, recognized, "the NEM was a model for a good period, not for an emergency situation. Now we cannot keep up so consistently the whole system as we did before the changes in the world economy. If we want to defend our economy against the world crisis, it has to happen in a more centralized way" (*NYT*, 12 June). For the time being, however, there are no indications that the HSWP leadership is intent on moving back to the old model of a command economy.

At the last session of Parliament (10-11 April) before the election, the National Assembly approved a constitutional amendment extending the parliamentary term from 4 to 5 years in order to make it coincide with the five-year plans and the time of party congresses. On 15 May Premier Fock resigned "for reasons of health." Like Nyers, he had been closely identified with the original conception of the NEM, and his self-criticism at the 11th Congress had raised expectations of his demise, although he retained his seat on the Politburo.

The Patriotic People's Front supervised preparations for the elections in 352 electoral districts, where 34 double candidacies materialized (compared with 48 double and one triple in 1971). In his address to the meeting on 15 April of the PPF National Council, Kádár stressed the party's alliance policy and praised the cooperation of the Roman Catholic church. PPF secretary-general István Sarlós also courted church support at a meeting with church representatives on 15 May. Some 800 nomination meetings were organized by the PPF for the selection of candidates by open vote. The local PPF committees worked with party committees, the KISZ, and other groups to select the most widely acceptable candidates and forestall a contest. In any event the competition is not political but personal since all candidates must support the PPF platform. Of the 345 outgoing deputies, 129 were not renominated, 210 were renominated unopposed, and 6 were renominated in double candidacies.

At the 15 June election, according to official statistics, 97.6 percent of those eligible exercised their franchise, and 99.6 percent voted for the PPF slate. Two candidates received 100 percent of the votes, Biszku and Fock 99.9 percent, Kádár 99.8 percent; the lowest majority in a single-member constituency was 95.9 percent. The new assembly is distinguished by a lower average age, more women, and almost twice the former number of industrial workers. Six out of 7 Central Committee secretaries, 10 out of 15 Politburo members, and 34 out of 125 Central Committee members are among the deputies.

At its constituent session on 4 July the Assembly elected the new government: Premier Lázár, deputy premiers György Aczél, János Borbándi, István Huszár, Gyula Szekér, and Ferenc Havasi (the last named, former first secretary of the Komárom county party committee, replaces Mátyás Timár, who had been appointed president of the National Bank). A notable new appointment was that of the former head of the Central Committee's department of regional economic development, Pál Romány, as minister of agriculture and food. The new council of ministers has 23 members. Three (Lázár, Aczél, Huszár) are members of the Politburo; 19 are also Central Committee members; and only 7 are elected members of parliament. Politburo member Antal Apró was reelected speaker of the National Assembly.

Unusually intensive celebrations marked the 30th anniversary on 4 April of Hungary's liberation from Nazi occupation. They included a military parade, an amnesty, the distribution of State and Kossuth prizes, and heavy media coverage.

In the ideological and cultural sphere, the hard line adopted by Valéria Benke at the 11th Congress has yet to be visibly implemented. The case of the three intellectuals briefly put under arrest in October 1973 on suspicion of "new left" anti-socialist activities appears to have been dropped after quiet negotiations and compromises, and György Konrád's contentious book is to be published. A major literary figure, József Lengyel, died at 79 on 14 July. A founder of the Hungary Communist Party in November 1918, Lengyel lived in exile and, from 1938, in Siberia, until his rehabilitation and return to Hungary in 1955. His semi-autobiographical works exposing the Stalinist terror and his advocacy of cultural tolerance earned him a reputation as Hungary's Solzhenitsyn and brought down official disfavor.

Despite the appreciative gestures made at election time, the HSWP pursues its quiet struggle against religion, notably by mounting party courses on religious criticism. József Cardinal Mindszenty died in Vienna in May, uncompromisingly hostile to communism to the end, as was the HSWP to him.

International Views and Policies. In 1975, as before, the HSWP remained closely aligned to the Soviet Union and dutifully echoed Soviet foreign and intra-party policy in all spheres.

At the 15 May Central Committee plenum, András Gyénes in his report on the international situation hailed the victory of the Vietnamese communists; commended the returning Hungarian contingent from the International Control and Supervision Commission for "having served to insure the implementation of the Paris agreement and having helped to strengthen friendship between the

Hungarian and Vietnamese people"; asserted that political détente must be followed by military détente and supported the socialist position at the Vienna force reduction talks, where Hungary is an observer; hailed the Portuguese revolution and the role of the Portuguese Communist party (the Hungarian press subsequently criticized certain Portuguese factions for forcing the pace of reform and the West German Social Democratic party for giving financial aid to the Portuguese anti-communists); called for a sovereign, united, non-aligned Cyprus; urged the reconvening of the Geneva conference, with participation by the Palestine Liberation Organization, to resolve the Middle East crisis; expressed solidarity with the persecuted communists of Chile and Spain; and pledged active support (to the Soviet line) in the preparatory talks for a conference of European communist parties.

A delegation led by Kádár and including Lázár, foreign minister Frigyes Puja, and deputy foreign minister János Nagy attended the Conference on Security and Cooperation in Europe (CSCE) in Helsinki. Kádár's address at the plenary session was notable for its reference to Hungary's historical role in the Danubian basin and its territorial truncation at Versailles. In expressing general agreement with the "basket three" provisions of the Final Act, Kádár drew attention to Hungary's high tourist trade but noted that "we did not come here to accept each other's ideologies or political systems." His remarks suggested that nothing in the Final Act would require a change in Hungarian policy.

At the Central Committee's 23 October session, Gyénes reported that the conviction was spreading in the West that peaceful co-existence was the only realistic policy; denounced the People's Republic of China for promoting the policy of "extremist imperialist circles"; voiced Hungary's willingness to develop relations with all countries in keeping with the Helsinki principles; and attributed great importance to the U.S.-Soviet SALT negotiations.

A matter of more immediate concern has been Hungary's quest for most-favored-nation status with the United States. Unlike Romania, however, the Kádár regime has followed Moscow's lead and announced that it would not pursue negotiations as long as the U.S. trade law's political stipulations (on free emigration) prevailed.

International Activities and Contacts. The major Hungarian-Soviet encounter in 1975 occurred during Brezhnev's visit to the 11th Congress, which also provided the occasion for a meeting between Brezhnev and the other Warsaw Pact first secretaries (presumably not including Romania's lower-ranking delegation) on 18 March. The latter meeting was described as "a mutual exchange of information on socialist and communist construction," was "frank and cordial," and demonstrated "complete unity of views." Kádár also met with Brezhnev and the other Soviet bloc leaders at Helsinki. Lázár paid his first official visit to Moscow on 21-24 October and conferred with Brezhnev, Kosygin, and other Soviet leaders, principally on the coordination of long-term economic planning.

In January PPF secretary-general Sarlós met in Bratislava with the acting deputy chairman of the Czechoslovak National Front central committee. Foreign minister Puja visited East Germany on 3-5 March and met with foreign minister Oskar Fischer, first secretary Erich Honecker of the East German party, and premier Horst Sindermann; the talks were reportedly cordial and produced full agreement. The Gästerbeiter program with the German Democratic Republic continues. In 1975, 3,200 young Hungarian workers went to the GDR, while some 170 East Germans arrived in Hungary and were assigned to three large enterprises. The real purpose of the program appears to be to relieve the GDR's chronic labor shortage, although the Hungarians derive some benefit in technical training and language acquisition.

Hungary's rapprochement with Yugoslavia has been progressing through cultural agreements, economic cooperation on projects such as the Adria pipeline, and relative harmony on the question of minorities (500,000 Hungarians live in the Voivodina and 100,000 South Slavs in Hungary) who, as foreign minister Puja observed during a visit to Belgrade 7-9 January, "act successfully as bridges between our countries." On 16 April Premier Fock received Nikola Kmezić, president of the executive council of Voivodina, for discussions on economic matters such as local border trade, production cooperation ventures, and joint investments. Tito's deputy, Edvard Kardelj, visited Budapest on 23-26 June for talks with Kádár and Biszku. Yugoslavia is the only socialist country with which Hungary's trade is cleared in convertible currency.

Construction has begun on Hungary's first space telecommunication station, in fulfillment of the 1971 agreement with the Soviet Union and the other socialist states establishing the Intersputnik International Space Telecommunication organization.

Relations with Austria remain cordial. While finance minister Faluvégi conducted economic negotiations in Vienna, Austrian foreign minister Erich Bielka visited Budapest 24-26 February and signed four agreements, on extradition, visas, legal aid, and consular arrangements.

The vice-chairman of the Iraqi Revolution Command Council met with Kádár during his stay in Budapest 7-9 May. The joint communiqué expressed agreement that Zionist forces must be withdrawn from all occupied Arab areas and the national rights of the Palestinian people must be restored in order to secure a just and permanent peace, and noted the good links between the HSWP and the Socialist Arab Ba'th party.

Foreign minister Puja paid a "working visit" to Paris on 5-7 June, and was in Bonn on 11-13 June, returning West German foreign minister Walter Scheel's visit to Budapest in April 1974. In both capitals Hungary's bilateral trade deficits and the EEC's trade barriers were subjects of discussion, but general political relations are officially cordial. Interviewed on West German television, Puja said that Hungary favors "an extensive exchange of people, information, and cultural treasurers, but a so-called free exchange of views and opinions is not a realistic concept at present."

British foreign secretary James Callaghan stopped over in Budapest, 28-29 July, on his way to Helsinki and discussed bilateral relations as well as the CSCE. His insistence on broader East-West contacts at the individual level were not reported by the Hungarian news agency. At Helsinki Kádár held talks with Finnish president Urho Kekkonen and with West German chancellor Helmut Schmidt, who invited the Hungarian leader to visit West Germany in 1976; foreign minister Puja, meanwhile, had an interview with U.S. secretary of state Henry Kissinger.

On a visit to Rome, 12-13 November, Lázár met with Italian premier Aldo Moro and discussed, inter alia, Hungarian-Italian economic relations and the difficulties caused by the EEC beef embargo, which had severely affected Hungary's exports to Italy. Lázár was also received in private audience by Pope Paul.

Publications. The HWSP's principal daily newspaper is *Népszabadság* ("People's Freedom"), with a circulation of 750,000. The theoretical monthly *Társadalmi Szemle* ("Social Review"), edited by Valéria Benke, has a circulation of 40,700. The monthly organizational journal *Pártélet* ("Party Life") has a circulation of 130,000. The official news agency is Magyar Távirati Iroda (Hungarian Telegraphic Agency; MTI).

University of Toronto   Bennett Kovrig

Poland

The communist party in power in Poland is officially the Polish United Workers' Party (Polska Zjednoczona Partia Robotnicza; PZPR), which dates back to the Communist Workers' Party of Poland founded in December 1918, outlawed in early 1919, and renamed the Communist Party of Poland in 1925. The Comintern dissolved the party in 1938 and many members perished in the great Soviet purge, but in January 1942 during World War II it reappeared as the Polish Workers' Party. In 1944-45, following the advance of Soviet forces into Poland, the party quickly achieved dominance in the coalition government that was set up to appeal to the broad masses. After undermining the non-communist parties in the coalition, it merged in 1948 with left-wing remnants of the old Polish Socialist Party to form the PZPR, which since then has controlled all formal political activities through the Front of National Unity (FNU).

Ostensibly the FNU is a coalition of the PZPR with the United Peasant Party (UPP) and the Democratic Party (DP), the one officially representing the peasantry and the other the working intelligentsia and small entrepreneurs. Candidates of various non-party organizations, including Catholic groups, are also allowed to appear on the FNU "preferred lists" at the head of the ballots, which since 1956 have permitted more candidates than seats. To vote against a preferred candidate the voter may cross out the name. Since the PZPR decides who gets on the ballot, the choice allowed has little meaning, but it provides for a vote of protest.

The PZPR has about 2,453,000 members and candidate members. The population of Poland is about 34,000,000.

Organization and Leadership. The basic PZPR unit is the primary party organization, set up in places of work (factories, stores, schools, military units, etc.) and residential locations (villages and small towns in rural areas, streets or housing units in cities). There are about 72,600 civilian and 3,400 military primary party organizations at this local (gmina) level. Above these, until 1975 (see below), were the district units in counties (powiats) and parts of large cities. The province (voivodship) or regional organizations comprise the next level. The highest authority is the PZPR Congress, which meets every four years and elects the Central Committee and the Central Party Audit Commission. The Central Committee elects the Politburo—the supreme policy-making body—and the Secretariat, executive organ for the Central Committee and the Politburo. There are Central Committee departments for various functions, and the Central Party Control Commission oversees party discipline and ideological correctness. There are corresponding simpler structures at lower levels.

Edward Gierek, Politburo and Secretariat member, has headed the PZPR as first secretary since 1970, when he replaced long-time leader Władysław Gomułka. Politburo members Piotr Jaroszewicz and Henryk Jabłoński are respectively premier and chief of state of the Polish government. The Seventh PZPR Congress, 8-12 December 1975, elected a leadership which differs but little from the previous one except for several promotions.

POLITBURO (17)

Members:

1. Edward Babiuch*	7. Wojciech Jaruzelski	13. Jan Szydlak*
2. Edward Gierek*	8. *Stanisław Kania**	14. Józef Tejchma
3. *Zdzisław Grudzień*	9. *Józef Kępa*	*Candidates:*
4. Henryk Jabłoński	10. *Stanisław Kowalczyk*	1. Kazimierz Barcikowski
5. Mieczysław Jagielski	11. Władysław Kruczek	2. *Jerzy Łukaszewicz**
6. Piotr Jaroszewicz	12. Stefan Olszowski	3. *Tadeusz Wrzaszczyk*

SECRETARIAT (10, including 5 above)

Ryszard Frelek	Józef Pinkowski	*Zdzisław Żandarowski*
Wincenty Kraśko	Andrzej Werblan	

Notes: *Secretaries of the Central Committee.   Italics denote promotion.

In addition, one newcomer has been identified as a member of the Secretariat. He is Zdzisław Kurowski, chairman of the Federation of Socialist Unions of Youth.

The only individual who lost his position on the Politburo was Franciszek Szlachcic, at 55 years of age, a potential challenger to Gierek. After leading a guerrilla unit during World War Two, he began work in the secret police and rose to Minister of the Interior. That position is held by Kowalczyk, whereas Kania maintains security responsibilities on the PZPR side and, hence, supervises the Minister. Two other full Politburo members, Grudzień and Kępa, are first Party secretaries in Katowice and Warsaw respectively. PZPR congresses will be held every five years, in order to coincide with the five-year economic plans.

Party Internal Affairs. The Seventh PZPR Congress brought forth very few changes in party leadership and no surprises in its decisions. It confirmed for another five years Edward Gierek as first secretary of the party. His main report to the congress dealt essentially with the most recent and future economic problems, and its title—"For a Dynamic Development of Socialist Construction, For an Improvement in Work Quality and in National Living Standards"—reflected Gierek's hopes for the future, while admitting presently existing shortages of meat, quality clothing, housing, domestic appliances, etc. The congress was attended by Leonid Brezhnev, who addressed it, by the leaders of most other Eastern European communist parties, and by the delegates from much of the rest of the world, even the Israeli and United States communist parties (*NYT*, 14 December).

A few days after the closing of the congress on 18 December, the Sejm set up a special commission with the task to draft a constitutional amendment which would recognize formally the leading role of the Communist party in state affairs and would make the party leader the country's president. Comparable changes have already been enacted in Romania and Bulgaria (ibid., 19 December).

The major development in party organization in 1975 was the administrative reform first publicly disclosed in a press interview by Gierek on 25 April and implemented in a series of steps culminating in a new law passed by the Sejm on 12 July. The reform eliminated one of the three administrative tiers of the party and government structure, the 314 districts, between the regional and local levels. The reform also increased the number of—and rendered considerably smaller—the voivodship areas. There are now 49 voivodships in place of 22 equivalently autonomous areas under the old system, which had been effect for virtually the last 30 years.

The 1975 reform was presented in the official *Trybuna ludu* as building upon the administrative changes of 1973 which had consolidated some 4,300 rural administrative entities into 2,350 larger and more efficient parishes (further reduced to about 1,900 parishes at the beginning of 1974). Officially cited reasons for the 1975 reform emphasized the party's desire for simplified administration, eliminating a source of bottlenecks and inertia between the regional voivodships and the rural parishes. The party press indicated that local popular initiative, embodied in the parish people's councils, would now be capable of greater autonomy and discretion. There would be less red tape, presumably, in the implementation of national and regional as well as local policies. Unofficial comment and speculation emphasized Gierek's and the Politburo's interest in cutting down the leverage and the influence of regional party bosses, whose jurisdiction and resources were diminished.

At the PZPR 17th plenum on 12 May, Gierek, Jaroszewicz, and Politburo and Secretariat member Edward Babiuch emphasized the need to struggle against bureaucracy and for efficiency in socialist administration. Gierek indicated that the old parish cadres, whom he praised for dedication and experience, would be absorbed in the remaining tiers of party and state administration. Jaroszewicz stressed the democratic-participatory aspect, as bringing government closer to the people and making it more sensitive locally. Babiuch emphasized the consistency of the new reform with the principle of party leadership in all phases of the social, political, and economic life of the state. The Central Committee approved the prepared reform and called on the Sejm to pass enabling legislation.

In mid-May the party commemorated the 1945 victory in Europe. Gierek and other party spokesmen emphasized the contribution by the Soviet Union to the Allied defeat of Hitler, and reiterated criticisms of the allegedly ruinously passive policies of the Polish (London) government-in-exile. In a speech to the Sejm, Gierek blamed the Nazi invasion of Poland on the "shortsightedness, class egoism, and anti-Soviet motives" of capitalist states. He made no allusion to the Hitler-Stalin Pact; chief credit for victory was given to the Soviet Union. Gierek acknowledged in one sentence that an "important" contribution was also made by the United States, Britain, and France. He then linked the achievements of the wartime anti-Nazi alliance to the current possibilities of coexistence and détente. Recalling Poland's 6 million dead in World War II, Gierek gave major credit for resistance and victory at home to the Communists, never mentioning the Home Army (Armja Krajowa). He acknowledged, however, that Poles also fought against the Nazis in the West, and paid homage to the heroism and sacrifice of "all anti-Hitlerite groups."

On 30 May, Premier Jaroszewicz installed 36 new governors or voivods; there were no changes in the remaining 13 voivodships. Among voivodship party secretaries the turnover was actually greater: only 11 of the 49 had been at their posts before the reform, and only three had held their positions since the period of Gomulka's leadership before December 1970.

The new party secretaries, according to *Trybuna ludu*, are all relatively young, ranging between 36 and 57 years of age with an average age of 47. Among the 41 whose educational attainments have been publicly mentioned, 37 (90 percent) are university graduates; 25 have been educated in economics and technical subjects; only 8 in the humanities. Despite their youth, the voivodship leaders are long-time activists with 25 years average length of party membership. In class origin, 61 percent are of worker and 19.5 of peasant background. Most importantly perhaps, the appointments represented not the promotion of new elements, but rather a reshuffle of the already ascendant: 16 of the new voivodship secretaries were already members or candidate members of the Central Committee of the PZPR; 24 had previously held positions of equivalent rank in either party or government; none could be said to have risen from obscurity. The most innovative appointments were those of Maria Milczarek, former leader of the Women's League, and Wiktor Kinecki, who had been ambassador to India.

By some estimates, as many as 20 to 30 thousand party functionaries were reassigned in the process of eliminating the middle-level organizations. Many suffered the loss of established positions of influence and a troublesome readjustment. Among veteran party bureaucrats, this has been a source of disaffection toward Gierek's leadership.

A further administrative reform took place through the establishment of "macro-regions," assembling the new 49 voivodships into 8 areas, grouped around Białystok, Gdańsk, Katowice, Kraków, Lublin, Poznań, Warsaw, and Wrocław. The function of the macro-regions is to provide long-range planning and coordination, particularly with respect to managing urban centers, environmental protection, tourism, services, employment, and economic development. Each area is to have its Macro-Regional Development Commission, representing party leaders of the constituent voivodships, and a staff or regional team of planners representing the Council of Ministers' Planning Commission. The macro-region appears to be still another instrument of coordination and control over local party leadership.

Throughout the second half of 1975, party organizations held meetings in preparation for the Seventh Congress in December. In most cases, only the dates and the identities of some of the prominent participants were published.

In late February and early March a series of so-called report-and-election party conferences took place in the voivodships. These were held ostensibly to increase rank-and-file participation and control in party activities. In each voivodship, some 300 delegates attended conferences as representatives of anywhere from 80,000 to 170,000 party members. In each case the incumbent party secretaries were reelected.

A process of party membership card validation, or exchange, was taking place throughout the year. Some old members were not reinstated, and some new recruits were brought in. Up to the eve of the Seventh Congress it was not apparent whether this process would produce a net gain or loss in membership.

Gierek addressed the 16th plenum of the PZPR Central Committee in Warsaw on 8 January. He emphasized as the party's principal goals: improvement in the living standards of the people, particularly workers; modernization of the economy; increased popular support of the party, facilitated by greater responsiveness toward the people's needs by party leaders and workers; and continuing ideological firmness combined with pragmatic flexibility. Gierek praised the USSR's foreign policy and domestic example, and spoke of the need to "enrich" the cultural life and channel the attitudes of the Polish people, particularly the workers, with the help of all the cadres in the arts, letters, and social sciences, all of which would facilitate Marxist-Leninist socialist construction in Poland. He also called for greatly improved party work because of the ideological confrontation with capitalism implicit in the new era of peaceful coexistence and détente.

The 18th plenum, on 4 September, adopted guidelines for the forthcoming Seventh Congress. Party concerns were summarized in the slogan of striving, simultaneously, for a higher quality of work and living conditions. The PZPR took credit for increasing the national income by 62 percent and industrial production by 75 percent between 1970 and 1976. Average monthly wages rose from 2,200 zlotys in 1970 to 3,500 in 1976.

Looking toward 1976-80 the party promised to raise real wages further by a relatively modest average of 16 to 18 percent. It also promised to construct 1.5 million new apartments—built to "higher standards" than heretofore—as compared with some 1,120,000 in the 1970-75 period. The new five-year plan was to increase the national income by 40 to 42 percent. Most critically, overall fulfillment of the plan was said to depend in excess of 90 percent upon increased labor productivity. Among itemized goals, coal production was slated to reach a figure of 200 million tons annually by 1980, electric power 132 billion kwh, and steel 22 million tons. Trade with the USSR, already about a third of all Polish trade, was scheduled to treble by 1980.

The party also promised to broaden the participation of the working people in the government and implied the need for constitutional amendments acknowledging the "historic fact that the Polish

People's Republic is a socialist state and that the PZPR is its leading political force." It promised toleration toward the Church, emphasized that "unbreakable friendship, unshakable alliance, and close all-round cooperation with the Soviet Union" and the Communist Party of the Soviet Union (CPSU) were of "key importance" to Poland, and called the policy of the Maoist leadership in China "one of the most dangerous tendencies in the world situation at present."

The PZPR supported an early convocation of a world conference of the Communist movement, praised the results of the Helsinki Conference on Security and Cooperation in Europe and the policy of détente, and hailed the recent agreement with the Federal Republic of Germany (on exchange of exit visas for ethnic Germans still resident in Poland in return for credits and loans from the FRG) as "opening up possibilities of building lasting foundations of coexistence."

The 19th Congress of the Polish Writers' Union took place in Poznań on 19-22 February. It reelected the aged Jarosław Iwaszkiewicz, a proponent of conformity to party rule, and heard a speech by Politburo member and vice-premier Józef Tejchma warning that literature must not be used as propaganda against the regime.

Increased censorship of the press and dismissals of independent-minded editors, such as those of the weekly *Literatura* and the satirical magazine *Szpilki*, characterized party policy. In April, Central Committee secretary Jan Szydlak declared that it was high time for writers and intellectuals to start taking advice from the party instead of giving it. According to *New York Times* reports in August, more restraint was to be imposed on the pronouncements of deputies to the Sejm, particularly five Catholic independents from the Catholic Znak group.

In spite of these warnings, the proposed amendments which would give constitutional expression to the leading role of the Communist party in the state, were criticized in a manifesto signed by 59 personalities. The manifesto, sent to political leaders in Warsaw, called also for more civil liberties and a more independent role for the trade unions (*NYT*, 17 December).

The Economy. At a conference of party economic chiefs in Warsaw on 15 January 1975, Premier Jaroszewicz called for the stringent conservation of energy and raw materials during the year. Other principal tasks were to increase export capabilities, improve the housing situation, and increase the speed and rate of return on new capital investments in the Polish economy. On 7 February, at the election accountability conference of the PZPR in Warsaw, he credited the fixed price agreements of the CMEA, particularly for fuels, for the stability Poland needed to develop her economy in the current five-year plan. He linked progress in détente to Polish hopes for improved and expanded world trade.

Beginning in March, a new note concerning developing food shortages, particularly meat and vegetables, was sounded by party spokesmen. Bad weather and harvests in 1974, and lack of foreign exchange to finance additional purchases abroad, were cited as reasons for shortages, with likelihood of persistence in the months ahead.

At the 30 June plenary meeting of the party-government commission for modernizing the economy, Jaroszewicz indicated that simplification of organization, greater autonomy for local decision-making units, and more responsiveness to grass-roots opinion were the party's chosen means for improving Polish economic performance. More than that, he claimed, "active and creative attitudes of the working people" were "an important value in socialism ... just as important as economic effects" and "an enrichment of life in the very process of work, which is the distinctive feature of socialist society." (*Trybuna ludu*, 1 July.) On 4 July, Gierek devoted his speech to the party-government economic conference almost wholly to the urgent need for improving and expanding Poland's export capabilities, particularly to the capitalist states.

Official results of economic activity in the first half of 1975, as compared with the first half of 1974, indicated a continuing advance in average real wages. The index for 1975 was 109.6, compared with 100 in 1974. On the other hand, livestock production was only 101.9 in cattle output and 99.3 in pig production. Urban housing construction, in view of the accumulated, massive shortages in this sector, was not very impressive at 105.5. Perhaps the most adverse figures were the officially claimed increases in foreign trade. Exports were said to be at 127.8 percent of the 1974 figure and imports at 124.5 percent. Given the tremendous imbalance between Polish imports and exports, it was clear that the effort to close the gap in the trade deficit was all but ineffectual.

Official statistics, stories in the party press, and speeches by the principal party leaders suggest that the Seventh Congress is likely to be followed by substantial measures of economic austerity. For several years, the party has appeased worker and consumer discontent by relatively low subsidized food prices. In 1975 the demand grew but the supply diminished. Given the poor harvest of 1974, followed by a poor harvest in 1975, rising fuel prices charged by the Soviets as well as by Western suppliers, and the failure to expand Polish hard-currency-earning exports to the West, the regime's ability to finance the subsidies or relieve pressure on the market by more imports was under very severe strain. There were shortages of meats, vegetables and dairy products. The housing shortage was scarcely alleviated.

The regime was paying more in subsidies to Polish farmers for producing food than it was receiving in payment from consumers. Some additional revenues for continuing subsidies were being raised by increases in the prices of alcohol and tobacco. Some meats and dairy products were being diverted from the export market to supply increased domestic demand, though at the cost of still greater import-export imbalance. Gierek appeared to be preparing Polish public opinion for bad news by publicly emphasizing that it was not the absolute level of prices which mattered, but the relationship between prices and wages. Officially, it was claimed that prices had advanced at a rate of about 2 percent through the first three quarters of 1975 while real incomes in wages and pensions were advancing at a rate of more than 10 percent. Paradoxically, however, benefits granted to stimulate productivity and labor discipline, particularly liberalized sick-leave pay, did not produce hoped-for results. Considerable dismay was being expressed over failure to increase labor productivity. Party spokesmen admitted that in many cases wage increases outpaced productivity increases, and that disturbing malingering and labor-absenteeism had infected the Polish economy. Late in the year, the party press was complaining that the rate of absenteeism throughout the economy had reached unprecedentedly high levels, rising from 169 hours annually for each industrial employee in 1970 and 193 hours in 1974 to a rate of 210 hours in 1975. Only an epidemic or a plague, it was argued, could explain such high incidence of missed working days (ibid., 15 September). Against the pressure of increasing popular demands for higher living standards and insufficiently expanding resource capabilities, the party leadership, particularly Gierek, continued to offer a new style of exhortation and persuasion. Traveling around the country, holding meetings and discussions with groups of workers, miners, peasants, professionals, party activists, and ordinary citizens, and utilizing television and press interviews much more extensively than his predecessor, the first secretary of the PZPR attempted to bolster morale and win support for the policies of the party. Growing concern over possible repetition of the violent upheaval of December 1970 was, nevertheless, evident.

Relations with the Catholic Church. While unresolved differences persisted, party-church relations were more nearly free of major conflicts during 1975 than in many previous years. The director of the state Office on Religious Affairs, Kazimierz Kąkol, declared in mid-year that the party would safeguard the existence of the Church so long as citizens desired it to exist. The party realized, he said, that religion in Poland could not be expected to disappear very quickly. Kąkol denied rumors that the regime was trying to negotiate a church-state understanding with the Vatican without consulting the Polish episcopate, and in particular Stefan Cardinal Wyszyński.

Among party concessions to the Church were tax reductions on ecclesiastical property, an increased volume of building permits for the construction of new churches, and a reduction in the cumbersome record-keeping requirements imposed upon the Church's educational activities. Among sources of conflict were blocked appointments of new bishops. The Wrocław see, vacated by the death of Bolesław Cardinal Kominek in 1974, remained vacant in 1975, as the regime rejected nominees for it put forward by the Church hierarchy. Church leaders complained about the regime's restrictive policy in preventing Polish pilgrims from visiting Rome. There was some satisfaction among the episcopate with the regime's consent to the appointment of Bishop Pylak to the vacant Lublin see.

International Party Contacts. In February 1975 the PZPR Politburo issued a statement on Polish foreign policy designed to guide party propaganda in the celebrations of the 30th anniversary of the conclusion of World War II and the 20th anniversary of the Warsaw Pact. Solidarity with the USSR, emphasis on continuing economic integration and development through the CMEA, and the need to further détente as an irreversible process, with progress at the European Conference on Security and Cooperation and reduction of arms in central Europe, were the main themes.

On 7 June *Pravda* published a long article on the role of the PZPR in Poland by Central Committee secretary Edward Babiuch full of praise for the USSR, the CPSU, and Marxism-Leninism. The article emphasized an orthodox view of the party's leading role in Polish state and society and called it "the chief and obligatory precondition of the society's prosperity and fulfillment of the tasks of socialist development." It also emphasized the need for ideological-cultural vigilance and commitment in the party cadres; attention was called to the ongoing program of party card exchange as a means for intensifying the quality of the party's cadres and its work.

A similar note was struck by another PZPR secretary, Jerzy Lukaszewicz, in a *Pravda* article of 21 August:

> Our people's historic achievements are based upon socialist ideology and our party's leading and organizing activity. They confirm conclusively the universality of the general law-governed patterns of socialist building substantiated in great Lenin's works, developed by the CPSU and the other fraternal parties, and consistently implemented in the practice of the Soviet Union and the other fraternal countries. Loyalty to Marxism-Leninism [is] the basis of our victories.

Lukaszewicz dwelled at length on the PZPR's ideological and educational tasks, admitting that "old practices and alien habits" in the Polish society were "tenacious" and required an "implacable struggle against anti-socialist views and theories."

Soviet-Polish party (as well as government) contacts were very frequent and close in 1975. PZPR Politburo members visited Moscow in February, April, May, and June. Particularly significant were the Brezhnev-Gierek talks in Moscow on 23 June and the visit by Soviet premier Kosygin to Poland beginning 11 August. According to Polish party organs, Kosygin received an unusually cordial reception in Warsaw. Although few specific details were immediately disclosed, it appeared that the leaderships of the two parties discussed substantially increased trade between Poland and the USSR, a faster pace of integration of the Polish economy in the CMEA, the diplomatic and propaganda moves related to the Helsinki European summit and to the détente policy more generally, the coordination of Polish and Soviet economic development plans for 1976-80, and issues of common CPSU and PZPR policy for the forthcoming congresses of the two parties. The Polish party spokesmen and press lavished praise on the merits of Brezhnev's contributions to détente, and Polish-Soviet links received the customary accolades of "indissolubility." On 30 June, Henryk Jabłoński, Politburo member and chairman of the Polish State Council, visited in Moscow with USSR Supreme Soviet chairman Podgorny. Satisfaction with the development of Polish-Soviet relations was expressed in a joint communiqué which also noted the urgency of furthering the "irreversible character of détente."

According to an October announcement of the Polish Press Agency, new measures for the integration of the Polish economy within the CMEA and for an increased supply of fuels and raw materials to Poland were taken in 1975. Among agreed-upon projects were gas and oil pipelines to be constructed by Polish workers and technicians in the USSR in exchange for stepped-up deliveries to Poland beginning in 1979.

In January, Gierek visited Cuba and Portugal. He held talks with Fidel Castro in Havana and in Lisbon with President Francisco da Costa Gomes as well as Alvaro Cunhal and other leaders of the Portuguese Communist Party. Expansion of trade and coordination of the policies of peaceful coexistence and détente were the officially publicized subjects of these talks.

In March, Gierek attended the Hungarian Socialist Workers' Party congress. A delegation headed by Babiuch attended the Italian Communist Party's congress in the same month.

Publications. The daily organ of the PZPR is *Trybuna ludu* ("People's Tribune"); its monthly theoretical journal is *Nowe drogi* ("New Roads"). A monthly, *Życie Partii* ("Party Life"), is directed at party activists, and a biweekly, *Chłopska droga* ("The Peasant Road"), is aimed at rural readers. The Central Committee's Department of Propaganda, Press, and Publications puts out the fortnightly *Zagadnienia i materiały* ("Problems and Materials") for the training of party members. A party monthly, *Ideologia i polityka* ("Ideology and Politics"), has been published for several years. Seventeen dailies are printed by voivodship party organizations. Two influential Warsaw weeklies, *Polityka* and *Kultura*, deserve notice though they are not official PZPR publications.

University of California   Alexander Groth
Davis

Romania

The Communist Party of Romania (*Partidul Comunist Român*; CPR) was founded, according to official histories, on 13 May 1921, after the splitting of the Social Democratic Party. The arrival of Soviet troops in 1944, accompanied by a coup d'état, brought the party into participation in the government. In February 1948 the CPR and the Social Democratic Party were merged to become the Romanian Workers Party (*Partidul Muncitoresc Romîn*), but at its 9th Congress, in July 1965, the party reverted to its original name—a move concomitant with the elevation of Romania from the status of a people's republic to that of a socialist republic. Since 1948 the CPR has been the only political party in Romania.

As of 31 December 1974 party membership was officially said to be 2,500,000. The figure includes some 130,000 members who joined the party during that year. Some 50 percent of the membership were classed as workers (up from 43 percent in 1969), 20 percent as peasants (down from 28 percent in 1969), and 22 percent as intellectuals and white-collar personnel. The proportion of women was 25 percent. The party's ethnic composition remained approximately the same as that of the country as a whole—89 percent Romanian, 8 percent Hungarian, and 3 percent German and other nationalities (*Scînteia*, 8 August 1969, 25 July 1975). Total population was estimated at 21,100,000 in early 1975 (*Era Socialistă*, no. 4).

Organization and Leadership. The CPR is organized into basic units or cells in factories, on farms, and in the smaller political subdivisions; in 1974 there were 70,000 such units. The next higher step is represented by the party organizations in communes (rural territorial subdivisions) and municipalities, in which there were 2,706 and 235 organizations, respectively. Finally, there are party organizations for each of the 39 counties and the municipality of Bucharest; these supervise the lower-level party organizations within their territories. (*Scînteia*, 25 July 1975; *WMR*, no. 5, 1973.)

According to the party statutes, the supreme authority of the CPR is vested in the congress, which is held every five years and to which delegates are elected by county party organizations. The 11th Congress, the most recent, was held in November 1974. In fact, however, it is the party's Secretariat, Political Executive Committee, Permanent Bureau, and Central Committee that wield the power.

CPR secretary-general Nicolae Ceauşescu has held this position since March 1965. According to the party statutes the secretary-general is chosen by the party congress, not by the Central Committee as with most communist parties. At the end of 1975 the Secretariat was composed of seven secretaries in addition to the secretary-general: Ştefan Andrei, Iosif Banc, Emil Bobu, Cornel Burtică, Dumitru Popesco, Iosif Uglar, and Ilie Verdet.

The CPR does not have a politburo, but two organizations, the Permanent Bureau and the Political Executive Committee, serve somewhat similar functions. The Permanent Bureau of the party, created by a Central Committee plenum in March 1974 and reduced in size at the 11th Congress, is composed of five individuals whose primary concern is economics—and particularly foreign economic problems. These are Secretary-General Ceauşescu; Central Committee secretary Ştefan Andrei, responsible for the party's international policies; chairman of the Council of Ministers Manea Mănescu; deputy chairman of the Council of Ministers Gheorghe Oprea, who has been active in promoting international economic cooperation; and deputy chairman of the Council of Ministers Ion Paţan, who is also minister of foreign trade and international economic cooperation. It is owing to its small membership and its orientation toward foreign economic problems that the Permanent Bureau does not function as a politburo.

The Political Executive Committee (PEC), on the other hand, is much larger than the average politburo (23 full and 12 alternate members), but it performs somewhat similar functions. As a result of organizational changes during 1974, the PEC became more prominent. It was originally created at the 9th Congress, in 1965, primarily to give Ceauşescu a leading party body in which his own supporters would predominate, since at that time the Permanent Presidium (Politburo) was composed largely of older party leaders not beholden to the new party head. The PEC meets frequently between plenary sessions of the Central Committee, and supervises party affairs. The full members include the secretary-general and all secretariat members except Andrei and Banc, and the members of the Permanent Bureau.

The Central Committee is elected at a party congress to direct party affairs between congresses. It meets in plenary session two to five times a year to consider and approve programs and policies. The committee chosen in November 1974 has 205 full and 156 alternate members.

Auxiliary and Mass Organizations. In 1968, after having opposed the Soviet-led invasion of Czechoslovakia, the party sought to mobilize mass support and created the Front of Socialist Unity (FSU) to replace the largely inactive People's Democratic Front. (The latter was an outgrowth of the National Democratic Front created in October 1944 to link the CRP, the Social Democrats, and other left-leaning political groups in order to achieve a consolidation of power.) The FSU includes trade union, youth, and women's front organizations, as well as associations representing the various national minorities living in Romania. The CPR is the only political party. The FSU provides the permanent organizational framework for mass participation in politics at all levels.

The FSU plays a primary role in coordinating the activities of other front organizations and in the election process. A new electoral law adopted in late 1974 (text in *Scînteia*, 21 December) specifies that the right to nominate candidates for the Grand National Assembly and deputies to the people's councils belongs only to the FSU. During the election process in early 1975 the FSU organized some 36,900 meetings attended by some 6,000,000 people for the purpose of nominating candidates (*România liberă*, 17 February).

The leadership of the FSU includes the leadership of the party. Nicolae Ceauşescu is chairman, 10 full and alternate members of the Political Executive Committee sit on the 31-member FSU Executive Bureau, and all major party and government officials and country party leaders are on the 477-member National Council.

The trade unions represent one of the largest and most significant of the mass organizations that function under the CPR's guidance. In March, Gheorghe Pană was released from his post in the Secretariat and became head of the trade union organization (*Scînteia*, 18 March 1975), a move that reflects the extent of party dominance over this group.

The Union of Communist Youth (UCY), the Union of Communist Student Associations, and the Pioneers represent a second major group of mass organizations. In early November 1975 the three held simultaneous congresses, and party leader Ceauşescu stressed at a joint gathering that the party is the only leader of these youth organizations. Traian Stefanescu was reelected first secretary of the UCY, Ion Sasu was chosen head of the students' associations, and Virgil Rădulian became chairman of the Pioneers. (*Scînteia tineretului*, 3, 4, 5, 6 November.)

The National Council of Women, headed by PEC member Lina Ciobanu, is the party's front organization for women. In a move to upgrade this body during International Women's Year, for the first time its chairman was included, ex officio, on the roster of the Council of Ministers chosen at the Grand National Assembly session after the elections in March (*Scînteia*, 19 March).

Internal Party Affairs. The 11th Congress of the CPR was held on 25-28 November 1974, and party statutes call for the next to be convened five years from that time. During 1975 three plenary sessions of the Central Committee were held. The first, at which certain changes in the party Secretariat were made, took place on 17 March (*România liberă*, 18 March), and on the same day the Central Committee and the National Council of the FSU held a joint plenary session at which the results of recent elections were considered and the reorganization of the Grand National Assembly and the Council of Ministers was decided upon. (*Scînteia*, 18 March.) The second Central Committee plenary session was held jointly with the Supreme Council on Socioeconomic Development on 21-22 July. The main topics were the next five-year plan (1976-80) and the 1976 plan and budget. The Central Committee alone considered the problems of rural party organizations, the strength and composition of party membership, and cadre policy. (*Scînteia*, 22, 23, 24, 25 July.) The third Central Committee plenum was held on 16 December, just prior to the convening of another session of the Grand National Assembly. It approved the 1976 economic plan and state budget (both were subsequently adopted by the assembly), a master plan for forestry development from 1976 to 2010, and the foreign policy conducted by the party and state over the last year. In addition, the Political Executive Commitee held a number of meetings.

A number of important party and related government changes were decided upon at the Central Committee's March plenum (*Scînteia*, 18, 19 March). The most important of these was the transfer of Gheorghe Pană, formerly Central Committee secretary responsible for internal party affairs, to the post of chairman of the central trade union organization. Pană's rise from county party first secretary to the Secretariat in 1969 was meteoric; since then, however, the level and quality of work in party organizations—for which Pană was responsible—has been severely criticized. Although such factors no doubt influenced the transfer, another important reason was probably Ceauşescu's policy of rotating leading cadres. The publicly announced purpose of the rotation policy is to give senior officials experience in different areas, but the real reason appears to be to prevent any individual from holding one position long enough to develop a substantial personal power base. Since Pană had been responsible for the critical area of internal party affairs since 1969, he was ripe for rotation. His transfer to the trade unions suggests certain parallels with the careers of Virgil Trofin and Paul Niculescu who were likewise influential members of the Secretariat and have been rotated into less prominent posts in the last few years.

Pană's release from the Secretariat was accompanied by the designation of two new party secretaries—Emil Bobu, previously minister of the interior, and Josif Banc, party first secretary in Mureş County. Bobu was simultaneously elected vice-chairman of the State Council, and Banc was made chairman of the Central Council of Workers' Control of Economic and Social Activities, which oversees the economic performance of the government. The former head of this organization, Central Committee secretary Ilie Verdeţ, who was elected to the post in March 1974, remains in the Secretariat, but his new field of activity is not known.

Banc's return to the Secretariat is somewhat unusual: he was elected to it in April 1972, but in June 1973 was released to become party first secretary of Mureş County.

Bobu's election to the Secretariat marks a new pinnacle in his career. He served as party first secretary in Suceava County from 1968 until shortly before he became minister of the interior in March 1973. He was elected a member of the Defense Council in May 1974, an alternate member of the Executive Committee in July, and a full member of that body at the party congress in November.

At its March session the Central Committee voted to expel Virgil Actarian, minister of construction of machine tools and electrotechnical machinery, as an alternate member "for serious deficiencies in his activity, for not adhering to principles of socialist ethics and equity, [and] for insincerity toward the party." He was replaced by Constantin Ionescu, a technocrat who has worked in the ministry in the past.

Teodor Coman was designated as minister of the interior, in place of Bobu. Coman, like so many of those who have come to prominence under Ceauşescu, made his career in the county party organizations. Shortly before the 1974 party congress he became first deputy minister of the interior, an indication that this change had been anticipated for several months.

Domestic Attitudes and Activities. The Romanian party sees as its main priority the economic development of the country, and to this end it has been concerned to mobilize the population to achieve its ambitious economic plans. With the approach of the new five-year plan period, the targets to be set have been a major preoccupation of the party. The draft directives on the 1976-80 plan adopted at the 11th Congress indicated that Romania's dynamic economic development is to continue, although the targets for industrial growth were in many cases lower than current rates. National income and industrial production are both to rise by 54 to 61 percent, an annual rate of 9 to 10 percent. Investment is to increase by 65 to 72 percent during the five-year period—a rather steep increase which is one of the more significant features of the new plan. Growth in agricultural output is to increase by a more modest 25 to 34 percent. In his speech to the joint plenary session of the Central Committee and the Supreme Council on Socioeconomic Development in July, however, Ceauşescu called for substantial upward revision of many important plan indicators for the coming five-year period (*Scînteia*, 24 July 1975).

A number of economic problems were encountered by the party during 1975 which may make the achievement of these higher goals difficult. Agriculture registered serious deficiencies. The communiqué on 1974 plan results showed total agricultural production to be some 20 percent below target. Potatoes, sugar beets, vegetables, and fruit were all between 20 and 40 percent below plan goals. Although the land improvement plan was overfulfilled, production of fertilizer lagged. The problems in this sphere prompted a special three-day conference of workers in agriculture, held in Bucharest in early February, at which Ceauşescu enumerated deficiencies and criticized those responsible (ibid., 9 February). The passive attitude of the peasantry was openly discussed. This is potentially one of the most serious problems facing the leadership, because it not only results in a loss of agricultural produce for export and home consumption but also represents a challenge to the party's authority. The Central Committee's discussion of and directives on rural party organizations at the July plenum reflected the concern in this area (ibid., 25 July). A special session of the Political Executive Committee was held to consider measures to ensure "order and discipline in the agricultural sphere," and another special session of all leading party and state officials involved in agriculture was held to hear Ceauşescu discuss the steps that must be taken to increase output (ibid., 2 September).

The most serious problem for both agriculture and the economy in general was the damage by flooding in many parts of Romania in early July. More than 60 persons lost their lives, some 270 industrial installations were damaged, transportation was disrupted, many homes were destroyed, some 800,000 hectares of agricultural land were flooded, and large numbers of livestock and poultry were lost. In many areas the floods were as devastating as those in 1970. In assessing the losses, Ceauşescu said that considerable damage could have been prevented or at least limited if the measures decided upon after the 1970 floods had been carried out. In a number of cases flood-control measures were either not completed or were put into practice only superficially. In the aftermath of the recent floods, the party and government again drew up a comprehensive program for flood control which is to be incorporated into the next five-year plan, although some measures are being taken this year.

In the midst of the floods the government issued a decree increasing the prices of a number of goods and services in order to bring them closer to production costs and world prices. The prices of some 200 items—including fuels, wood products, carpets, leather, cloth, building materials, and drugs—and of some 150 services were increased by from 3 percent to 100 percent. To mitigate the effect of this action, supplementary increases in tariff wages for all categories of personnel were granted at the same time. The presidential decree specifying these measures even claimed that the increase in salaries would more than offset the price increases (ibid., 26 July).

The floods caused difficulty in providing the population with adequate amounts of various food products. As early as August the PEC and the Council of Ministers, in joint session, reviewed the supply of sugar and sugar products and criticized the Ministry of Agriculture and the Food Industry (ibid., 10 August). In October, Western news agencies reported serious shortages of a number of food products and some manifestations of popular dissatisfaction, and Ceauşescu visited the Bucharest markets on several occasions. A series of meetings on the food supply and consumer goods followed. The PEC met specifically to consider this question and decided to make increased food supplies available in the fourth quarter of 1975 and the first half of 1976 (ibid., 15 October); a meeting with county party first secretaries and agricultural and domestic trade officials followed three days later, at which Ceauşescu delivered a long speech detailing shortcomings in food production and distribution (ibid., 19 October; *Era Socialistă*, no. 20). Two weeks later the PEC again considered measures to improve market supplies (*Scînteia*, 5 November). This high-level concern about the food supply obviously reflected a very serious problem, but the full extent of the shortages and the prospects of eliminating them were not discussed in Romanian news media.

A second major area of economic concern was foreign trade. The 1974 plan called for a trade surplus to be generated by increasing exports paid for in convertible currency by 76.3 percent while imports were to rise by 50.8 percent. Instead of a hard-currency surplus, however, the trade balance registered a deficit of 200,000 dollars. To deal with this situation, in mid-February Ceauşescu convened a conference attended by heads of diplomatic missions and officials in Romania responsible for foreign relations and international trade. His speech to this gathering called for significant improvements in the foreign trade sector, and he was critical of a number of specific deficiencies. He also stressed that matters were being made worse by the current changes in the prices of raw materials, economic difficulties in the West, and international financial problems. (Ibid., 15, 20 February.)

The election of deputies to the Grand National Assembly and the people's councils on 9 March marked an important departure from past practice: for the first time since the CPR came to power, more than one candidate was permitted to stand for a single position. The electorate voted for people's councils in 39 counties, the municipality of Bucharest and its eight wards, 46 other municipalities, 169 towns, and 2,706 communes. There were 90,858 candidates for 51,441 people's council constituencies—more than one candidate for 76 percent of the posts.

There were also two candidates for 139 of the 349 seats in the Grand National Assembly (i.e., for 39.8 percent). Although all candidates were designated and approved by the FSU, there were several cases of two Central Committee members running against each other for a single seat. All full and alternate members of the Political Executive Committee were reelected to the national assembly. All were FSU candidates, and none had a rival. The large number of newly elected deputies to the assembly is striking, especially when one remembers that the total was reduced from 465 to 349. Some 225 (64.5 percent) of the deputies elected had not been members of the last parliament. (Reports on the elections were published in *România liberă* and *Scînteia tineretului*, 17 February, and *Scînteia*, 18 March.)

The CPR has also shown concern to strengthen ideology and exercise closer control over this important area. A new chairman of the Writers' Union, Virgil Teodorescu, was designated in April to replace Zaharia Stancu, who had died the previous December. His close links with the party leave little doubt that he will further the trend toward stricter party control over literary output. (*România literară*, 10, 17 April.)

A further step in this process was the establishment, at the end of May, of a Press and Printing Committee, a measure envisioned in the Press Law adopted in 1974 but not carried out until a year later. The new body replaces the former censorship office, the General Press and Printing Directorate, established in 1949. It is responsible to both the party Central Committee and the Council of Ministers, whereas the directorate was responsible only to the government. The new committee also has much broader jurisdiction, including supervision of radio, televison, films, live and recorded performances, and printed matter of all types. Its purpose is to provide unified guidance of all cultural activities in line with the party's ideological directives. (*Buletinul Oficial*, no. 51, 30 May.) A number of interviews with heads of publishing houses, shortly after the new organization was established, confirmed that ideological standards had become the principal yardstick in publishing (*Contemporanul*, 13 June).

International Views and Policies. The CPR views the international situation as undergoing revolutionary economic and social changes which in turn require the establishment of a "new international economic and political system." The new system, of course, should be in keeping with Romania's traditional concerns for sovereignty, national independence and non-interference in a state's internal affairs: "The concept of a new policy implies the imprescriptible right of each nation to defend and create its own history and, equally, to participate as an active, sovereign entity in building a new world." The Romanians have been anxious to codify these principles of international conduct by adopting a set of norms and principles that would be morally binding on all states.

In 1975, consistent with this view, Romania was one of the most persistent supporters and advocates of the statement of principles adopted by the Conference on Security and Cooperation in Europe, at Helsinki in August. The CPR continued to stress the important role of small and medium-sized states in resolving international problems. There was also a noticeable new emphasis on the "positive" role of "the new independent states and developing countries" in international relations—an emphasis related to the CPR's desire to bring Romanian foreign policy closer to that of the nonaligned and developing states. (*Programul Partidului Comunist Român*, Bucharest, 1975; *Era Socialistă*, nos. 2, 9; *Lumea*, 27 February.)

On questions of the party's international views, the CPR continued to insist upon the same rights for Marxist-Leninist parties as it does for other states: "Full equality, respect for each party's right to draw up independently its general political guidelines, strategy, and tactics for its revolutionary struggle." CPR spokesmen in general and Ceauşescu in particular have specified that "it is no longer possible for a center that proposes to coordinate the activity of communist and workers' parties to exist." The CPR considers the international unity of "communist and workers' parties" to be necessary, but this must be "a new type of unity . . . based upon equality and on their common Marxist-Leninist ideology." (*Programul Partidului Comunist Român; Era Socialistă* no. 10.) The Romanians have frequently stressed the importance of maintaining and strengthening relations with all parties—Soviet as well as Chinese, North Korean as well as Czechoslovak. These views have given rise to differences with the Soviet party regarding the holding of a meeting of European communist parties. The CPR, along with the Italian and Yugoslav parties, has opposed the adoption of a binding programmatic document and has insisted upon each party's right to define its own political line, although it has been willing to participate in the activity of the committee preparing for the meeting.

International Activities and Contacts. Foreign relations played a very prominent role in CPR and Romanian government policy in 1975, marked by an unusually large number of trips abroad by Romanian leaders and visits by foreign officials. The predominance of international affairs is attributable to a number of circumstances. First, planning for trade and economic cooperation among the CMEA member countries for the next five-year plan, which begins in January 1976, was in full swing. Second, plans for a meeting of European communist parties were under way. Third, the Romanians have been anxious to participate in and encourage détente between East and West. In 1975 particular emphasis was given to economic matters because the Romanian economy faced serious problems owing to the general economic slowdown in the West and the increased prices of raw materials. This resulted in vigorous efforts to increase trade with the countries of Western Europe, the United States, and Japan. Fourth, political and economic concerns prompted a major effort to expand relations with the developing countries. Fifth, the Romanians continued their attempts to play a role in dealing with international crises in the Middle East and other areas.

The efforts to coordinate foreign economic activity for the next five-year plan period led to a series of reciprocal visits involving the prime ministers, deputy prime ministers, planning chiefs, and various economic ministers of Romania and other CMEA countries. Prime Minister Manea Mănescu held talks in Moscow on economic cooperation with Soviet leaders in August (*Scînteia*, 23 August); Bulgarian party leader Todor Zhivkov visited Bucharest to sign a number of economic agreements drawn up during a visit to Sofia by Mănescu and during numerous exchanges between other ministers. The two countries are to complete a long-projected joint hydrotechnical complex on the Danube River over the next five years, and will construct a joint machine-building plant and engage in various other projects involving economic collaboration. Reflecting the closer degree of cooperation at all levels was the decision announced in February that the two party leaders (who are also heads of state) will meet semiannually.

In addition to visits to Moscow and Sofia, Mănescu also traveled to Belgrade and Warsaw for economic discussions, and among the prominent visitors to Bucharest were Czechoslovak and East German prime ministers Lubomir Strougal and Horst Sindermann. Related exchanges with Asian communist states included a visit by Gheorghe Rădulescu to North Vietnam and China in January and a visit by Le Duan of North Vietnam to Bucharest in November.

Linked to the coordination of five-year plans are indications of revived concern on the part of Romania about CMEA integration projects. On the eve of the meeting of the CMEA Council in Budapest at the end of June, Romanian information media published a series of articles criticizing schemes for supra-national economic integration and calling upon CMEA to implement more fully its pledge to equalize the levels of economic development of its member countries. (*România liberă*, 30 May, 10 June; *Scînteia*, 1, 3 June; *Revista economica*, 6 June.) Mănescu stressed the latter in his speech at the Budapest council meeting, but whether the Romanians were protesting against specific proposals has not become clear (*Scînteia*, 6 July).

The second major concern of Romanian foreign policy was the holding of a meeting of European communist parties. The stand of the Romanian party on the convening of such a conference continues to differ—in some cases sharply—from that of its Warsaw Pact allies. The CPR did not send a Central Committee secretary to the Prague secretaries' conference in March, although it was represented at a lower level. Just prior to the meeting, the CPR secretary responsible for foreign relations, Ştefan Andrei, consulted with Soviet party officials, and during a number of high-level contacts with officials of the Yugoslav League of Communists the European conference was no doubt an important topic. Yugoslav party secretary Stane Dolanc was in Romania for talks in February and October, secretary Aleksandar Grličkov visited Romania in May, and party and state official Edvard Kardelj was there in July. Ceauşescu's talks with Spanish party leader Santiago Carrillo during the latter's visit to Romania also no doubt dealt with this issue, among others. Another important visitor to Bucharest was North Korean party chief and state president Kim Il-song, who made Romania his first stop on a tour that subsequently included Yugoslavia, Bulgaria, Algeria, and Mauritania. Not only are the policies of Romania and North Korea alike, but Kim and Ceauşescu have similar styles of leadership; the close personal relationship they appear to have established is therefore not surprising.

The third concern of Romanian foreign policy during 1975 was to expand political and economic relations with the West. The final phase of the Conference on Security and Cooperation in Europe, in August, was regarded by the CPR as having two major benefits. First, it gave certain principles of international relations (sovereignty, fully equal rights, non-interference in internal affairs, etc.) greater moral strength by codifying them in an international document signed by the heads of state and government at the conference. A second matter of interest to Romania was the conference's measures to encourage economic, scientific, and technological cooperation among European states. The Romanian delegation in Helsinki was led by Ceauşescu, who presented Romania's position to the gathering, reiterating the concern of his government to see the principles of equality, independence, and sovereignty put into practice. He also departed from his prepared text to launch into a spirited defense of communism in Romania. He voiced Romania's concern that the follow-up to the Helsinki conference be effective, and described the provisions for a review session in Belgrade in 1977 as inadequate.

In a display of activity in support of détente, the Romanians entertained a number of Western government officials—U.S. president Ford and secretary of state Kissinger; British prime minister Harold Wilson; French premier Jacques Chirac; Austrian chancellor Bruno Kreisky; and Turkish premier Suleyman Demirel. Ceauşescu also made trips to a number of Western countries, including working visits to Washington and London and an official tour of Japan. Among the more significant visits exchanged during the year were those of Portuguese president Francisco da Costa Gomes to Bucharest in May and the return visit paid by Ceauşescu to Lisbon in October. During the May visit a treaty of friendship and cooperation between the two countries was signed—the first between a member of the Warsaw Pact and a member of the North Atlantic Alliance.

The Helsinki conference, coupled with a new government in Greece, gave new impetus to Romania's interest in regional cooperation in the Balkans. Although the Greek government has taken the initiative in encouraging multilateral collaboration, the Romanians, who have traditionally been in the forefront of such efforts, have also thrown their weight behind proposals to that end.

For Romania the most significant and long-sought gain was the signing of a U.S.-Romanian trade agreement which granted most-favored-nation treatment to Romanian exports to the United States. The agreement encountered opposition in Congress, however, because of criticism of Romania's emigration policies towards its Jewish citizens. En route home from a Latin American visit Ceauşescu made a special stop in Washington to meet with members of Congress and American Jewish leaders, and there were indications that Romania eased its emigration policy somewhat in order to win congressional approval of the trade agreement.

The fourth major foreign policy concern was to expand relations with the developing countries. Although there are also political motives behind this action, the main emphasis has been on economic aspects. Romania wants to be identified as a developing country in order to be eligible for the preferential benefits granted by the developed states. Since the fall of 1974 the CPR has been advocating the creation of a new international economic order (in which significant efforts would be made to aid the poorer countries) and the establishment of an equitable system of sharing the world's resources; a declaration on this topic was circulated by the Romanian delegation to the U.N. General Assembly's special session on economic cooperation and development in August and September.

As part of its effort to improve relations with the developing countries and to identify itself with them, Romania requested observer status at the Lima conference of foreign ministers of nonaligned countries (and also at the Colombo conference to be held next year), but was accorded the lower status of invited guest owing to its membership in the Warsaw Pact. The Romanians are nevertheless continuing their attempts to be identified with the nonaligned states.

Expansion of economic relations with the developing countries is seen as an important way of coming to grips with Romanian economic problems. The CPR's 11th Congress set as a goal the raising of trade with third-world countries from the 1974 level of 14 percent of total trade to some 30 percent by 1980. Through his summit diplomacy Ceauşescu has played a major role in the effort to expand third-world markets. In April, for example, he made an extended tour which included visits to the Philippines, Pakistan, Tunisia, and Jordan, and in June he visited Brazil, Venezuela, Mexico, and Senegal. Although various declarations of principle and a number of cultural cooperation agreements were signed, the focal point in each case was economic cooperation. The Romanians have been anxious to trade their industrial products and know-how in fields where they have achieved some recognition (oil extraction and refining, for example) for raw materials.

A fifth consistent theme in Romania's foreign relations is its interest in playing an active role in international crises—an effort to enhance its diplomatic prestige. The Middle East crisis provided Bucharest with frequent opportunities to attempt such a role. It was high on the list of topics discussed during Ceauşescu's official visits to Jordan and Tunisia in April, and a few days after returning home he paid previously unannounced one-day visits to Syria and Egypt for talks with their two presidents. Israeli foreign minister Allon also paid a visit to Bucharest to discuss the Middle East situation, and Romanian foreign minister Macovescu went to Cairo not long thereafter. But despite Romania's vigorous efforts to play a significant role in mitigating the crisis and to win a seat at the Geneva talks, there have been few indications of success thus far. The Romanian and Syrian prime ministers exchanged visits (the former was in Damascus in January and the latter in Bucharest in November), but Romania continues to maintain ties with Israel, and this has caused some problems with the Arab states.

Romania's willingness and desire to enhance its international prestige through active diplomacy were also pointed up by Macovescu's visits to Greece and Turkey in March—a continuation of Romanian efforts to play a constructive role in the Cyprus dispute.

Romania's election to a two-year term as a non-permanent member of the U.N. Security Council in September coincided with a vigorous campaign to play a prominent role in this world body. At the special U.N. session on development questions in August and September the Romanian delegation presented a long document calling for the creation of a new international economic order. At home, in the fall two long proposals, one on disarmament and the other on strengthening the United Nations, were presented for discussion at the Grand Assembly session.

The primary concern of Romania in foreign policy, of course, remains its relations with the Soviet Union, with regard to which it continues to perform a delicate balancing act. Coverage of President Ford's visit, for example, was carefully offset by articles commemorating the 30th anniversary of the reestablishment of Romanian-Soviet diplomatic relations, and Prime Minister Mănescu went to Moscow a few weeks later. Nevertheless, Romania's other policies have resulted in differences of view between the two countries. The question of CMEA integration is obviously one important area on which they do not agree, and their positions differ with regard to the European communist parties conference. Romania's successful effort to obtain most-favored-nation treatment for its exports under terms of a trade agreement with the United States, after the Soviet Union had repudiated its own agreement with that country over the question of Jewish emigration, can hardly have pleased Moscow, nor can Romania's efforts to identify itself with the developing countries or its application for observer status at the nonaligned conference next year. A symptom, though not a cause, of these differences was the exchange over a Romanian novel dealing with the World War II period. A Soviet critic accused the author of treating Romanian marshal Ion Antonescu in too favorable a light, but a Romanian literary critic defended the novel against this attack. Other works on Antonescu and the history of this period suggest a nationalistic Romanian view, which the Soviets probably found irritating. (See *Literaturnaia Gazeta*, Moscow, 14 May; *România literară*, 29 May.)

Publications. *Scînteia* is the official daily of the CPR Central Committee. *Era Socialistă* is the party's popularized theoretical-political fortnightly, and *Munca de partid* the fortnightly that deals with questions of organization and methods of party activity. Other important publications include *Munca*, the weekly of the trade union confederation; *România liberă*, the FSU daily; *România literară*, the weekly of the Writers' Union; and *Scînteia tineretului*, the daily of the Union of Communist Youth. Agerpres is the Romanian news agency.

Radio Free Europe   Robert R. King
Munich

Union of Soviet Socialist Republics

The Communist Party of the Soviet Union (Kommunisticheskaia Partiia Sovetskogo Soiuza; CPSU) traces its origins to the founding of the Russian Social Democratic Labor Party in 1898. The party split into Bolshevik ("majority") and Menshevik ("minority") factions at the Second Congress, held at Brussels and London in 1903. The Bolshevik faction, led by Vladimir I. Lenin, was actually a minority after 1904 and, unable to regain the policy-making dominance attained at the Second Congress, broke away from the Mensheviks in 1912 at the Prague congress to form a separate party. In March 1918, after the seizure of power, this party was renamed the "All-Russian Communist Party (Bolsheviks)." When "Union of Soviet Socialist Republics" was adopted as the name of the country in 1925, the party's designation was changed to "All-Union Communist Party (Bolsheviks)." The party's present name was adopted in 1952 at the 19th Congress. The CPSU is the only legal political party in the U.S.S.R.

Party membership reached the 15,000,000 mark early in 1975, when the exchange of party cards, approved by the 24th Congress in 1971 and initiated in 1973, was officially declared to be completed (*FBIS*, 7 February). This figure represents an increase of only 30,000 (or 0.2 percent) over the one reported the previous March, and continues the trend toward stabilization of party size. The present party membership now constitutes approximately 10 percent of the adult population, and less than 6 percent of the total USSR population of 254.3 million.

According to party sources, almost three-fourths of the membership consists of people employed in the "field of material production" and approximately 56 percent are workers and collective farmers (*Pravda*, 9 June 1974). More than 5.5 million members work in rural regions, of whom 2.6 million are directly employed in agricultural production (*Partiinaia zhizn'*, no. 4). Evaluating the results of the exchange of party cards, TASS reported that the CPSU was "consistently implementing the policy of ensuring that the leading place" in its social composition should belong to the working class. It added, however, that "more care has to be shown for selecting for party membership young people from the working class, the kolkhozes, the student body, above all Komsomol members, and also women." (*FBIS*, 7 February.)

The most recent quadrennial elections for the Supreme Soviet, the country's nominal legislature, were held in June 1974. The supreme Soviet has 1,517 members and is divided into two equal chambers—the Soviet of the Union, in which each deputy represents about 300,000 persons, and the Soviet of the Nationalities, in which deputies represent the republics, regions, and national areas of the USSR. All candidates of the single slate supported by the CPSU were elected. Elections to the soviets existing below the all-union level, from the republic to the village, were held on 15 June 1974. With 99.98 percent of the registered voters participating, official candidates received the majority of votes cast in all but 68 of the 2.2 million election districts (*Pravda*, 21 June).

The Supreme Soviet meets twice each year for two or three days to ratify decrees issued or drafted between sessions by its Presidium and the Council of Ministers and to formalize official appointments. In its July 1975 session the Ninth Supreme Soviet adopted measures aimed at ensuring the "careful and efficient use" of underground mineral resources, including provisions for mining safety and the reclamation of mined land and "specific procedures whereby underground resources will be handed over for exploitation" (Moscow radio, in *FBIS*, 9 July). The December session heard the report on 1975 economic performance and approved the 1976 plan (see below).

Organization and Leadership. The structure of the CPSU parallels the administrative organization of the Soviet state. There are 380,000 primary party organizations. Above this lowest level, there are 2,810 rural *raion* committees, 448 urban *raion* committees, 760 city committees, 10 *okrug* committees, 142 *oblast'* committees, six *krai* committees, and 14 union-republic committees. There is no separate subsidiary organization for the Russian republic (RSFSR), largest constituent unit of the Union. At the top, the All-Union Congress is, according to the party rules, the supreme policy-making body. The 24th Congress, in 1971, set the maximal interval between congresses at five years. Between congresses, the highest representative organ is the Central Committee, to which 255 full members and 141 candidate members were elected at the 1971 congress. At this level, power is concentrated in the Politburo, the Secretariat, and the various departments of the Central Committee.

The present composition of the Politburo is shown in the accompanying list.

POLITBURO

Members:

Brezhnev, Leonid I.	General secretary, CPSU Central Committee
Podgorny, Nikolai V.	Chairman, Presidium of the USSR Supreme Soviet
Kosygin, Aleksei N.	Chairman, USSR Council of Ministers
Suslov, Mikhail A.	Secretary, CPSU Central Committee
Kirilenko, Andrei P.	Secretary, CPSU Central Committee
Pel'she, Arvid I.	Chairman, Party Control Committee
Mazurov, Kiril T.	First deputy chairman, USSR Council of Ministers
Poliansky, Dimitri S.	Minister of agriculture, USSR Council of Ministers
Grishin, Viktor V.	First secretary, Moscow City Party Committee
Kunaev, Dinmukhamed A.	First secretary, Kazakh Central Committee
Shcherbitsky, Vladimir V.	First secretary, Ukrainian Central Committee
Kulakov, Fedor D.	Secretary, CPSU Central Committee
Andropov, Yuri V.	Chairman, Committee of State Security (KGB)
Grechko, Andrei A.	Minister of Defense, USSR Council of Ministers
Gromyko, Andrei A.	Minister of foreign affairs, USSR Council of Ministers

Candidate members:

Ustinov, Dimitri F.	Secretary, CPSU Central Committee
Demichev, Piotr N.	Minister of culture, USSR Council of Ministers
Rashidov, Sharaf R.	First secretary, Uzbek Central Committee
Masherov, Piotr M.	First Secretary, Belorussian Central Committee
Solomentsev, Mikhail S.	Chairman, RSFSR Council of Ministers
Ponomarev, Boris N.	Secretary, CPSU Central Committee
Romanov, Grigori V.	First secretary, Leningrad *oblast'* Party Committee

The present Central Committee Secretariat is composed of nine men: Brezhnev, Suslov, Kirilenko, Kulakov, Ustinov, Ponomarev, Vladimir I. Dolgikh, Ivan V. Kapitonov, and Konstantin F. Katushev.

Republic first secretaries were as follows: Karen S. Demichyan (Armenia), Geidar A. Aliev (Azerbaidzhan), Piotr M. Masherov (Belorussia), Ivan G. Kebin (Estonia), Eduard A. Shevardnadze

(Georgia), Dinmukhamed A. Kunaev (Kazakhstan), Turdakun U. Usabaliev (Kirghizia), August E. Voss (Latvia), Piatras P. Griskiavicus (Lithuania), Ivan I. Bodiul (Moldavia), Dzhabar R. Rasulov (Tadzhikistan), Mukhamednazar G. Gapurov (Turkmenia), Vladimir V. Shcherbitsky (Ukraine), Sharaf R. Rashidov (Uzbekistan).

Auxiliary and Mass Organizations. The most important of the many "voluntary" organizations allied with the CPSU is the Communist Youth League (Kommunisticheskii Soiuz Molodezhi; Komsomol). Its membership of some 34 million young people is led by 47-year-old Yevgeny M. Tyazhelnikov, first secretary of the Komsomol central committee. The committee held plenary sessions twice during 1975 (January, October). The Komsomol's major task during the year was a membership-wide purge ("exchange of documents") aimed at increasing the "labor and social-political activeness of its members and improving the work of its organizations" in fulfilling the tasks set for it by CPSU general secretary Brezhnev at the 17th Komsomol Congress in April 1974 (*Izvestiia*, 26 February).

An even larger mass organization—more than 100 million strong—is the All-Union Central Council of Trade Unions (AUCCTU). Its chairman, Aleksandr N. Shelepin, was active on the international labor front early in the year. He led the Soviet delegation to the European Trade Union Conference in Geneva at the end of February—the first such gathering since European labor split into communist and non-communist federations in 1949. In April, Shelepin led an AUCCTU delegation to Britain for talks with the Trade Unions Congress, but the visit turned into a disaster when angry demonstrations forced the Soviet emissaries to cut short their stay (*Trud*, 2 April). Two weeks later, Shelepin was removed from the CPSU Politburo. At an AUCCTU plenum on 22 May he stepped down as the organization's chairman; the position remained vacant the rest of the year.

Other mass organizations under the direction of the CPSU include the Soviet Voluntary Society for the Promotion of the Army, Aviation and Navy (DOSAAF), whose 70 million members seek to "instill patriotism and pride" in the armed forces; the Union of Soviet Societies for Friendship and Cultural Relations with Foreign Countries; and the Soviet Committee of Women.

Party Internal Affairs. Two CPSU Central Committee plenums were held during 1975. On 15 April, after hearing a report from Brezhnev, the Central Committee set the date for the convening of the 25th Congress on 24 February 1976. The plenum also heard a report from foreign minister and Politburo member Gromyko on the international situation and Soviet foreign policy. Finally, the plenum acted to remove Shelepin from the Politburo "at his own request." (*Pravda*, 16 April.)

In August, TASS reported a Central Committee resolution "on socialist emulation in honor of the 25th CPSU Congress." Approving the "initiative" of collectives who had assumed "increased socialist pledges and worked shock labor shifts for a worthy welcome" to the congress, the resolution invited all the country's organizations to give the "socialist competition in honor of the Congress a nationwide scope." (*FBIS*, 22 August.)

The 1 December Central Committee plenum heard an undoubtedly sobering (and unpublished) major report from Brezhnev on the performance and prospects of the Soviet economy. The Central Committee approved the draft of the 1976-80 Tenth Five-Year Plan and the annual plan and budget for 1976. In addition, it formally set the agenda for the 25th CPSU Congress, assigning Brezhnev to deliver the opening Central Committee report and Kosygin to deliver the report on the Tenth Plan. (*Pravda*, 2 December.)

The removal of Shelepin from the Politburo brought the first change in that body's membership in two years. This action ended a rivalry between Shelepin and Brezhnev which had apparently existed for more than a decade, and it was viewed as a sign of the general secretary's continued strength in the Soviet leadership. It put to rest, at least temporarily, rumors of a high-level challenge to Brezhnev's leadership which had been spurred by major setbacks to his policy toward the United States and Egypt and his absence from official view for a period of seven weeks at the beginning of the year. (*NYT*, 17 April.) The April plenum formally endorsed Brezhnev's détente policies, and his high personal standing was reaffirmed by the presentation to him the following month of the Marshal's Star, an insigne usually awarded only to army generals still on active duty (*Pravda*, 9 May).

Although rumors of a political illness of the Soviet leader were thus quieted, signs of a genuine medical illness continued to be present. Brezhnev was absent from official receptions for an additional five weeks in the spring. Moreover, he excused himself from functions held during the Helsinki summit in July and the visit of the French president in October. Though he displayed occasional vigor, Brezhnev's speech was said to be markedly slurred, causing Western correspondents to speculate that he had a recurrent problem with his jaw (*NYT*, 10 December).

Speculation about the state of Brezhnev's health and about a possible retirement at the 25th Congress focused attention on the relative standing and qualifications of the other Politburo members. One indication came in the pre-election period, when *Pravda* reported that Brezhnev had received 26 nominations to the RSFSR's Supreme Soviet; Podgorny and Kosygin, 13 each; Kirilenko and Suslov, four, and Mazurov and Kulakov, two apiece. When combined with reports in the regional press, the final rankings showed Podgorny slightly ahead of Kosygin, Kirilenko in front of Suslov, and Mazurov somewhat ahead of Kulakov. (*Christian Science Monitor*, 16 June.)

A number of republic-level leadership changes occurred in the spring. The "second secretaries" in three republics were removed in connection with their transfer to other posts (*FBIS*, 30 April, 9 May, 9 June). One other republic received a new second secretary in slightly different circumstances: in Georgia, A. N. Churkin was removed for "Gross errors and shortcomings" and replaced (*Zaria Vostoka*, Tbilisi, 15 April).

An unusually large number of republic and regional-level officials were singled out for criticism during the year; this phenomenon was "no accident" but stemmed from a sharpened concern at the central level of the party with the norms and performance of party leadership. The December 1974 plenum of the Central Committee had appealed to the party to "persistently implement the Leninist style of work in all links of the economic and state apparatus, to resolutely oppose bureaucracy, local patriotism and lack of responsibility, to develop criticism and self-criticism, to boldly uncover shortcomings and to eliminate everything that hampers successful work." An article in *Pravda* (21 January) by P. Rodionov, first deputy director of the Institute of Marxism-Leninism, which quoted this appeal, proceeded even further, suggesting some unrest over party leadership performance at the very highest level. Declaring that the "principle of collectiveness." was firmly established in all echelons of the party, Rodionov stressed the need for an "influx of new, fresh faces from the very midst of the people," and commented that "Taking into consideration the opinion of the party masses in solving questions of domestic and foreign policy has a beneficial influence on the growth of the creative activity of the Communists." Party leadership, he added, must be "political and not administrative." The party organ must lead "without allowing itself to act in the stead of and exercise petty tutelage over soviet, economic, and other organizations. It is regrettable, however, that such phenomena can still be observed."

A month later *Pravda* (28 February) published a Central Committee resolution "on the state of criticism and self-criticism in the Tambov oblast party organization." Nothing that the oblast's industry and agriculture had fallen behind planned growth, the resolution noted that the party obkom was not setting an example of self-critical analysis; it lacked due exactingness toward non-fulfillment of plans, it took a liberal attitude toward violation of discipline, and its reports focused on the positive, depersonalizing any criticism. Citing cases of suppression of criticism, the resolution stressed that criticism and self-criticism were acquiring an "increasing great importance as a means of raising the standards of organization and ideological educational work."

In the summer, an editorial in *Kommunist* (no. 8) declared that the Central Committee's resolution was "of essential significance for the whole party." The editorial quoted Brezhnev on the need for less noisy phraseology and campaign-mindedness, and a little more responsibility and ability to delve calmly and in a business-like manner. There was a tendency to view with indifference and complacency cases of individual leaders "embarking on the path of deception of the state, misrepresentation, and delusion in an attempt to give at any price the impression that all is well."

The Central Committee's importuning called forth a flood of criticism in the republics. In the Ukraine, first secretary V. V. Shcherbitsky described to a Central Committee plenum an "unsatisfactory" state of criticism and self-criticism in the republic, resulting in a situation in which individual leaders "tolerate or engage in book-doctoring, eye-washing, grabbing, and abuse of official status for self-interest" (*Radianska Ukraina*, 23 May). In Kirgizia, the same central committee plenum which appointed Yu. N. Pugachev (a former superviser of purges in the Transcaucasus) as second secretary, heard first secretary T. U. Usabaliev indict slackness, formalism and embezzlement in the republic. In September, the republic newspaper blasted official connivance "at instances of mismanagement, extravagance, deceit, and even actual theft of socialist property." Some of the kolkhozes and enterprises in the republic, it noted, were run by "rogues and rascals." (*Sovetskaia Kirgizia*, 30 April, 6 September.)

In Georgia, widespread purging of corrupt officials had already been in progress since 1972, reportedly involving 25,000 arrests (*Sunday Times*, London, 2 November). In February, first secretary Eduard Shevardnadze complained that there were still persons "among us" who started morbid rumors, spread fables, fabricated slander, and sowed mistrust or doubt as to the correctness of measures being implemented. He assured his audience that "we have established a good, business-like atmosphere" and he appealed to the central party leadership to "accept our firmest assurances that we can cope with any difficulties and fulfill any tasks." (*Zaria Vostoka*, Tbilisi, 1 March.) The removal of Churkin in April showed precisely how high in party ranks such loose standards had spread, and the presence of two Central Committee officials at the Georgian plenum indicated a certain lack of confidence in the republic party's ability to cleanse its own house (ibid., 15 April).

In the other republics of the Transcaucasus, the party leaders were also attempting to overcome a "lack of exactingness" toward corruption. In Armenia the new first secretary, K. S. Demichyan, lashed out at certain "widespread negative phenomena," including "embezzlement of socialist property, abuse of official position, bribe taking, influence peddling, speculation, avarice, hooliganism, and other negative manifestations." In short, he complained, there were "serious shortcomings and crude violations of plan discipline" throughout the economy. (*Kommunist*, Yerevan, 5 February.) In Azerbaidzhan, first secretary G. A. Aliev told the republic central committee that, although there had been positive changes since 1969, there were still substantial shortcomings and unsolved problems in the economy, in organizational and ideological work, and in the selecting, placing, and education of cadres. He then proceeded to detail the activities of a veritable rogue's gallery of Azerbaidzhani officialdom, noting cases of nepotism, corruption, and favoritism. (*Bakinskii rabochii*, 31 July.)

Much of the Central Committee's concern for improved criticism stemmed from a perceived need to increase the effectiveness of the party in supervising the implementation of economic policies and plans. In contrast to Rodionov's warnings against "petty tutelage"—issued in January, a time when Brezhnev was apparently inactive—the press emphasized the need for more active supervision by the party as the year wore on, and the pressures for fulfillment of the Ninth Five-Year Plan increased. Recalling that the 24th Party Congress had extended to many primary party organizations the right to check up on administrative activities, *Pravda* (18 August) called for the pre-congress period of reporting on elections to be used to discuss how effectively these organizations were using their new opportunities to step up party influence. According to V. Kharazov, not every party organization in the ministries had correctly understood its new task: "Some of them still fail to exert an appreciable influence on their collectives and have resigned themselves to an unexacting atmosphere and low responsibility for the allotted work" (*Sotsialisticheskaia industriia*, 24 August). The party, a *Pravda* editorial (29 July) concluded, "must take constant pains to step up party influence in management collectives."

Domestic Attitudes and Activities. In addition to the substantial amount of attention it paid to its own internal governance, the CPSU focused during 1975 on the problems of the Soviet economy and on certain topics relating to the maintenance of order (including cases of individual dissent and of nationalist or religious agitation) which seemed to point up the need for more effective "ideological upbringing."

In January the Central Statistical Administration reported mixed results in the effort to fulfill the 1974 plan. Overall industrial production had risen 8 percent—higher than the revised plan target of 6.8 percent but somewhat below the original goal. Heavy industry had grown by 8.3 percent, well above the revised target, but light industry had fallen short of its planned growth, achieving a rate of 7.2 percent as against a target of 7.5 percent. Completed construction of new housing had fallen by 0.5 percent, while overall agricultural production was 3.7 percent below the previous year's performance and 10 million tons below the 1974 goal. (*Izvestiia*, 25 January.)

Evaluating this record, the Central Committee appealed at the beginning of the year for a higher rate of productivity. "We have tremendous economic power; splendid socialist workers, collective farmers, and experts; great scientific-technical potential; and a wealth of natural resources. However, we cannot shut our eyes to existing shortcomings." A further increase in labor productivity would be of "decisive importance"; 86 percent of the year's planned increase in production would depend on this factor. Moreover, economizing on the use of raw materials, electricity, and capital goods, to the point of achieving a one percent reduction of waste in production output, could add four billion rubles to the national income. (*FBIS*, 6 January.) The party and government declared an economy-wide socialist competition for fulfillment of the 1975 plan ahead of schedule and successful completion of the Ninth Five-Year Plan. (Ibid., 13, 14 January.)

Despite the shortfalls in consumer goods production, housing, and agriculture, the CPSU could and did point with pride toward signs of a rising standard of living for the Soviet people. In his Lenin anniversary speech, Mikhail Suslov declared that annual expenditures by the state on measures to raise the people's living standard in the Ninth Five-Year Plan period were more than double the expenditure level of the previous five years. Two-thirds of Soviet families owned a television set, as against half in 1970; half had refrigerators, as against a third in 1970. Suslov seemed to see particular merit in further concentration on production as a measure toward improving the economy's performance; he noted approvingly the establishment of 1,500 industrial production associations and 5,800 inter-farm organizations. (Moscow radio, *FBIS*, 23 April.)

Fedor Kulakov also pointed to "specialization and concentration" as the "main line of development" in agriculture. Speaking to an all-union scientific-theoretical conference on problems of agricultural policy—held on the anniversary of the March 1965 Central Committee plenum—Kulakov had nothing but praise for the policies adopted a decade ago. He pointed to the "enormous personal contribution" of Brezhnev as contributing to such positive results as a sharp rise in income of kolkhoz workers. Yet at the same time he showed particular concern over the continuing low profitability of investment in agriculture. (*Pravda*, 25 March.)

The initial target for Soviet grain production in 1975 was 215.7 million metric tons, but it was soon clear—from both the poor weather and the absence of harvest statistics in the press—that the results would fall far short of that figure. The weather received much of the blame, but the "shortcomings" and "miscalculations" of certain agriculture specialists who "did not withstand the tests of their efficiency" were also singled out for criticism (*Izvestiia*, 4 November). Beginning early in the summer, the Soviet Union purchased some 20 million tons of grain from the West in the effort to cushion the blow of the bad harvest.

When the final accounting was in, the results were so bad that they were not even announced to the December session of the Supreme Soviet. However, figures released by *Izvestiia* put the average grain output over the five-year period at 180 million metric tons per year. This would bring the total for the period to 900 million metric tons. After subtracting known output for 1971-74 of 767.6 million, Western experts came to the figure of 132.4 million metric tons as the result of the 1975 Soviet harvest—the worst in a decade (*NYT*, 4 and 27 December).

Gosplan chairman Baibakov's December report on plan performance revealed precisely how vulnerable the Soviet economy was to failings in agriculture. Whereas the 1975 growth rate of industry was said to be 7.5 percent, the rise in national income was only 4 percent (as against the revised goal of 6.5 percent). Moreover, the planned industrial growth rate for 1976 was announced as 4.3 percent; Baibakov himself attributed this low figure to the shortage of agricultural raw materials and the continuing failure to commission new industrial plants on time. (Ibid., 3 December.)

According to *Pravda* (6 December), it was necessary to "concentrate maximum attention, efforts, and material resources" on increasing grain production. "If we work well, use all reserves to increase yields, and, where conditions permit, expand the sown area, such a task can be fulfilled successfully." In the next plan period, agricultural production would be "intensified," and its material and technical base would be systematically strengthened. "The Tenth Five-Year Plan will allocate large capital investments to agriculture, and increase the supplies of equipment, machinery and mineral fertilizers."

Brezhnev himself put the best possible light on the results of the Ninth Plan, telling the December Central Committee plenum: "If we bear in mind the scale of the absolute growth of public production, the Ninth Five-Year Plan is the best . . . in the history of our country. Our motherland has become even richer and stronger. The Soviet people have begun to live better, and this is the highest possible appraisal of the party's activity." (Ibid.) These encouraging words notwithstanding, the outline of the Tenth Five-Year Plan made public on 14 December moderated hopes for economic growth and announced that expenditures on agriculture would be increased nearly a third over the next five years. At the same time the new plan scrapped for the rest of the decade previous efforts to redirect the economy in favor of the consumer; instead, the traditional reliance on heavy industry was reasserted (*NYT*, 15 December).

In a number of spheres, the CPSU manifested a continuing concern with the task of enforcement of law and maintenance of order in Soviet society. That the general problem of controlling crime was beyond the capability of the Soviet militia was evident from a *Pravda* editorial in March which revealed that some of the authority of the municipal police was to be transferred to the civilian auxiliary (*druzhiniki*) (*NYT*, 3 March). In an interview in October, the head of the country's regular police force, Interior minister Nikolai Shchelokov, asserted that the incidence of crime had been greatly reduced during the years of Soviet power. He conceded, however, that the "eradication of crime is a long and complex process." (Tass, 28 October.)

In a detailed study, criminologist N. F. Kuznetsova argued that special attention was required in cases of crimes committed by minors, serious crimes of violence, mercenary offenses against socialist and personal property, criminal recidivism, crimes committed in the home, hooliganism, and crimes of negligence, especially those involving motor vehicles. According to statistics in her report, 9 to 10 percent of all crimes in the Soviet Union were committed by minors, 50 percent were committed by persons under the influence of alcohol, and 50 percent were motivated by personal material self-interest. Kuznetsova described the general causes of crime in Soviet socialist society as "negative socio-psychological phenomena and processes in the form of anti-social and anti-legal traditions, mores and customs left over from past class antagonisms." Among the particular social and economic conditions which fostered crime were commodity shortages, housing problems, unskilled labor, and the inadequate provision of material goods to "upbringing institutions." She also cited ineffective activity on the part of the criminal justice system, pointing out that culprits were punished for only one in five crimes occurring in the country. Kuznetsova recommended, as steps in the combating of crime, measures to improve the material well-being of the Soviet people, the establishment of mandatory legal education in the schools, and the strengthening of Soviet agencies of criminal justice. (*Sovetskoe gosudarstvo i pravo*, no. 3.)

It was the threat to Soviet order posed by political dissenters to which KGB chairman Yuri Andropov addressed himself in his election speech in June. Socialist democracy, he declared, was not only rights and freedoms; it also presupposed "duty and strict discipline." The opponents of détente, emphasizing ideological sabotage, were seeking through deception and falsification to distort Soviet policies and to call forth "anti-social manifestations within the country." Such "anti-social" elements, disguising themselves as advocates of the democratization of socialism were, in Andropov's view, in reality seeking to undermine Soviet power from within and liquidate the gains of socialism. (*Pravda*, 10 June.)

The special prominence of Andrei D. Sakharov among Soviet dissenters was underscored in October, when the Soviet physicist was awarded the Nobel Peace Prize. The award was greeted with derision by the Soviet press, which unleashed a full-scale propaganda campaign against Sakharov. Seventy-two members of the Soviet Academy of Sciences denounced the Nobel award to Sakharov as a blasphemy against the ideals of humanism, peace, and international friendship (*NYT*, 26 October). The newspaper *Trud* depicted the prize as a reward for traitorous activities; Sakharov was a Judas and his views were "political pornography" (ibid., 29 October). On 12 November it was announced that Soviet authorities had denied Sakharov's request for a visa to travel to Oslo to accept his prize; they cited as grounds for their refusal his possession of state secrets from his work as a nuclear scientist. Instead of Sakharov, his wife Yelena, who was already in the West for medical treatment, went to Oslo and on 12 December accepted the award. She also read the acceptance speech which Sakharov had managed to send out from the Soviet Union (excerpts from the speech were published in *New York Times*, 13 December).

Sakharov's current political opinions were published in the form of a long essay, "My Country and the World," which he released in July on the eve of the Helsinki summit meeting of the Conference on Security and Cooperation in Europe (CSCE). Criticizing "leftist-liberal fetishness," he attacked Western intellectuals for seeking to explain away the faults of Soviet society and he called upon the United States to be more resolute and consistent in dealing with the Soviet Union. Sakharov wrote that since 1917 the Soviet Union had undergone a moral decline and an uprooting of traditions vital to social stability, resulting in a deprivation in both welfare and freedom. As a program for dealing with these ills, he advocated a multi-party system, a general amnesty for political prisoners, a partial break-up of collective farms, limited restoration of private trading in industry, an end to censorship, and a guaranteed right of secession to Soviet minority nationalities. (*NYT*, 14 November.)

Another well-known Soviet dissident, Roy Medvedev, was identified in March as the editor of a new underground journal, entitled *Twentieth Century*. Shortly after its appearance, Medvedev reportedly was called to the office of the Moscow prosecutor and warned to cease production of the new journal. (Ibid., 22 March). Medvedev's latest political views were also circulated in the West in essay form during 1975. In a contribution to a book entitled *Détente and Socialist Democracy*, he speculated on the manner in which political change was likely to come to the Soviet Union. Downplaying the influence of Western public opinion, he argued that substantial change could come only through internal forces. And since the Soviet Union had as yet developed no effective public opinion, the impetus for change must be provided by a segment of the Soviet elite. The country's only hope, Medvedev concluded, was in a cooperative alliance of moderates in the party leadership (centered around Brezhnev and Kosygin) with rising young technocrats who sought to modernize the Soviet economy. In Medvedev's view, a Western boycott on cooperation with the Soviet Union, as advocated by Senator Henry Jackson, would only work against the formation of such a coalition and play into the hands of right-wing forces in the leadership. (*Manchester Guardian*, 14 May.)

While Sakharov and Medvedev continued to escape arrest for the publication of their views in the West, a host of their lesser-known colleagues were dealt with more harshly by the Soviet authorities. Amnesty International reported in the fall that a total of 10,000 persons were being held as political and religious prisoners in the USSR. Soviet officials refused an invitation to comment on the accuracy of this statistic. (*NYT*, 18 November.)

One of the more prominent dissenters to be convicted in 1975 was Sakharov's close associate, biologist Sergei Kovalyov. His arrest in December 1974 had been protested in a petition from 50 leading dissidents the following month. But, with Sakharov standing outside the courtroom in Vilnius, Kovalyov was sentenced on 12 December to seven years in exile for "systematically for many years fabricating and propagating material of a subversive nature in the Lithuanian republic and other regions." Specifically, Kovalyov was charged with circulating an underground journal, *Chronicle of the Catholic Church in Lithuania*, and with distributing books written by Solzhenitsyn.

The Kovalyov case was described in issue no. 35 of the *Chronicle of Current Events*, which appeared in Moscow in May. The best known of regular Soviet *Samizdat* publications, *The Chronicle* also related the story of Boris Vinokurov, cadres chief of the State Radio and Television Committee, who reportedly disrupted a February meeting of the party *aktiv* with a plea for the formation of an alternative political party. According to the *Chronicle*, Vinokurov was incarcerated in a mental hospital. (BBC, 1 May.)

Other dissenters arrested during the year included Vladimir Osopov, a Russian nationalist who was sentenced to eight years of hard labor for circulating the underground journal *Veche*. Georgy Vins, a leading Baptist minister, who was sentenced to five years in a labor camp and five years in exile; Andrei Tverdokhlebov, secretary of the Moscow chapter of Amnesty International, whose arrest in April called forth a petition from 60 leading dissenters; and Anatoly Marchenko, who was arrested in February for allegedly violating his parole, and was sentenced the following month to four years in exile. (*NYT*, 1, 19 April, 28 September.)

Two Soviet Jews, Mark Nashpits and Boris Tsitlyonok, who had demonstrated in Moscow in February on behalf of the right to emigrate, were tried and sentenced the following month to five years' exile (ibid., 1 April).

According to official Ministry of Internal Affairs statistics, the interest in emigration among Soviet Jews was declining sharply. Applications for emigration visas had dropped a third since the October 1973 Middle East war, from a rate of 2,200 to 2,300 per month in the first nine months of 1973 to an average rate of 850 per month in the subsequent period. In 1974, a total of 16,000 Jews had emigrated, 50 percent less than in 1973. In the first six months of 1975, the Ministry of Internal Affairs asserted, only 1,400 applications for emigration had been received. Over the entire postwar period, according to this report, 115,000 Soviet Jews—5 percent of the total Jewish population—had been allowed to emigrate to Israel. (Radio Moscow, in *FBIS*, 9 October.)

The survival of religious and nationalist sentiment among other Soviet minority nationalities received attention from CPSU officials during the year. In Lithuania, republic first secretary Griskiavicus wrote in *Izvestiia* (23 August), "the questions of the struggle against nationalist survivals must be, today and in the future, at the focus of our attention." A Latvian journal published an article on the "enormous Western propaganda apparatus" using bourgeois nationalism as an ideological weapon and seeking to drive a wedge between peoples of the Soviet Union. Toward this end, reactionary émigré circles were joining in an anti-Soviet bloc with the Maoists and with international

Zionism. (*Sovetskaia Litva*, 1 June.) In Kirgizia, in Central Asia, the party's central committee heard that there were shortcomings in the atheistic education of working people, and that the basic principles of the party's nationality policy were not being adequately disseminated (*Sovetskiaia Kirgiziya*, 29 January). Similarly, from Armenia came the complaint that atheistic propaganda, especially among young people, was a long way from meeting the demands made of it (*Kommunist*, Yerevan, 3 June). Moreover, an "active, aggressive struggle" was needed against "such manifestations of the antipodes of socialist internationalism as national narrow-mindedness, national exclusivity, and conceit" (ibid., 5 February).

Also from the Ukraine came attacks on the stepped-up activity of bourgeois nationalists, and again the hands of "Maoism" and "anti-Sovietism" were said to be joined in support of this activity (Kiev radio, *FBIS*, 20 February). According to one Western report, the purge against Ukrainian nationalists (especially intellectuals), which had been under way since 1972, was by mid-year approaching a climax (*Christian Science Monitor*, 10 July).

Most imprisoned political, religious, and nationalist dissenters were excluded from the two partial amnesties declared by Soviet authorities in May. The first, in connection with the 30th anniversary of the victory over Germany, decreed the release or shortening of sentence of certain categories of male and female prisoners who had served honorably during World War II (*Izvestiia*, 7 May). The second, announced in observance of International Women's Year, extended to women under age 18 serving terms of less than five years, women with children under 18, pregnant women, women over 55, and female invalids (*NYT*, 18 May).

In the light of the persistence of "alien" political, religious and nationalist sentiments among segments of the Soviet population, continuing emphasis was placed by CPSU leaders on the need for more intensive ideological education and struggle. In his Lenin anniversary speech, Mikhail Suslov saw a reason to be pleased with Soviet progress, asserting: "a firm bridgehead has been established for the next goal, Communism." Nevertheless, it was necessary to strengthen ideological work "in all its forms and directions," waging an "irreconcilable struggle against anti-Communism and anti-Sovietism, against bourgeois ideology and revisionism and also against harmful survivals of the past and views and morals alien to our society." In this enterprise, Suslov declared, success largely depended "on the quantity and primarily on the level of training of ideological cadres." (Moscow radio, *FBIS*, 23 April.)

Picking up on this theme, two other Politburo members stressed the importance of proper training of young people. Viktor Grishin, first secretary of the Moscow city committee, noting that almost half of the city's party members had been admitted in the past ten years, called for special care to be taken with the ideological training of the younger party members (*Pravda*, 23 September). In the Ukraine, V. V. Shcherbitsky declared: "One still comes across manifestations of a negligent attitude toward work, drunkenness, hooliganism, and petty bourgeois and philistine moods" among young people. In the task of further improving the ideological education of youth, he said, a "great role" belongs to the growing movement of youth mentors. In his own republic there were 170,000 youth mentors, half of whom were party members, who had assumed responsibility for teaching young people to work productively and efficiently and instilling in them class consciousness and a Communist attitude toward work. (*FBIS*, 7 April.)

International Views and Policies. Foreign policy in 1975 again pursued the themes set forth in 1971 by Brezhnev at the 24th CPSU Congress as the Soviet "peace program." In the wake of the December Central Committee plenum, *Pravda* (6 December) declared that "thanks to the consistent, vigorous activity of the CPSU Central Committee and its Politburo headed by Comrade Leonid Brezhnev . . . great successes have been achieved in implementing the peace program, in intensifying and developing détente, and in strengthening peace and people's security. The authority and influence of our homeland in the world have grown stronger." And yet, despite the confident and positive tone taken in this editorial, the year brought some setbacks and periods of doubt for the Soviet leaders in the international arena.

In fact, 1975 opened with the cancellation of Brezhnev's visit to the Middle East, the abrogation of the Soviet-U.S. trade pact, and Brezhnev's own temporary disappearance from public view. However, reaffirming its commitment to the course of détente, and buoyed by failures of U.S. policy in Portugal, the Middle East, and Indochina, the Soviet leadership appeared by springtime to have worked out an agenda of foreign policy triumphs leading to the 25th Party Congress. The plans seemed to call for a summit-level conclusion to the CSCE, to be followed by a conference of European Communist parties working out a common program and concluded with a triumphful visit by Brezhnev to the United States for the signing of a new SALT accord. Shortly after it was formulated, however, the new agenda was apparently stalled. Only the Helsinki summit was held, but the pleasure in even this meeting was spoiled by an unpleasant aftermath in the fall. By year's end, the United States seemed to have strengthened its position in the Middle East, Soviet allies in Portugal were in disarray, and a new atmosphere of uncertainty and even bitterness seemed to have settled over the Kremlin.

All of the themes in the current Soviet interpretation of the international situation were present in the resolution adopted by the Central Committee at its April plenum. Declaring that the basis for the outstanding successes of its policy was to be found in the achievements of the Soviet Union and its allies in strengthening their economic and defense capabilities, ensuring their stable unity, and adhering to principle, the Central Committee concluded that the imperialist policy of the cold war is suffering defeat." It affirmed that the necessary conditions for a just and peaceful settlement of international conflicts existed, that political détente must now be bolstered by military détente, and that regular summit meetings could play an important part in achieving this end. At the same time, the resolution noted, the forces of war, reaction, and aggression had not abandoned their attempts to torpedo the positive processes of détente, and it was necessary to keep a vigilant eye on the "intrigues of the foes of peace." Finally, the resolution reaffirmed the Soviet Union's "immutable solidarity with the champions of social and national liberation." (*FBIS*, 17 April.)

Even the more conservative forces in the Soviet leadership were publicly voicing the conviction that détente could not be merely a temporary phenomenon on the international scene. Suslov, in his Lenin anniversary address, described the prevailing line in the development of the present situation as "the strengthening and deepening of the reduction of tensions and the translation into life of the principles of peaceful co-existence." However, he stated, the dangerous actions of the opponents of détente made the "unmasking of imperialist subversion and aggression" a part of the "struggle for strengthening peace." But, he concluded, even though "détente is the objective of acute political and ideological confrontation," the "fundamental change in the correlation of forces in the international arena to the benefit of peace and socialism is the basis of détente. This is a continuing factor, a factor truly of not merely passing importance." (*FBIS*, 23 April.)

Brezhnev, a month earlier, had expressed the point somewhat differently: although détente might be rooted in objective factors, one could not be complacent about its enduring health, especially as the opponents of détente became more active. The consolidation of détente and peace, he said, "is a permanent, ceaseless process which demands constant progress. To stop on this road would jeopardize everything we have attained up to now." (*Pravda,*, 19 March.)

Georgi Arbatov, the leading Soviet "Americanologist," reiterated the need for continuing progress in détente later in the year. He seemed to address "those sober-minded politicians" in the West who had been willing to take the first steps on the path of détente, but who had now fallen silent in the face of pressure from its opponents. Just as it was impossible to be "a little pregnant," he said, it was impossible to have a little détente and a little cold war, or a little limitation of arms and continued arms race. If the United States had experienced difficulties in Indochina or in the "southern flank" of the Mediterranean, this was not attributable to détente but to the remnants of the cold war. In the struggle for détente, the Soviet Union did not and could not assume a commitment to guarantee the social status quo. But on the other hand, Arbatov concluded, there was no alternative to peaceful co-existence or to the continuation of a course aimed at détente. (*Izvestiia*, 4 September.)

One "important question, becoming more acute and urgent every day," on which Brezhnev believed progress was necessary was the conclusion of an agreement "banning the creation of new types of weapons of destruction"—weapons more terrible than nuclear weapons (*Pravda*, 14 June). The precise nature of such weapons remained unspecified when Gromyko, in his address to the U.N. General Assembly in September, formally called for such an agreement to be negotiated (*Washington Post*, 24 September).

But the main agreement for which the Soviets had long struggled in the process of consolidating détente was achieved in 1975—though in a manner which only called for further disagreement. This was the summit-level gathering convened in Helsinki in July for the signing of the Final Act of the Conference on Security and Cooperation in Europe. The campaign for the CSCE had been the centerpiece of Soviet diplomacy in Europe for almost a decade, and its concluding event should have been a moment of triumph for Brezhnev. The tone of the general secretary's remarks at the summit was positive and confident: "The main result of the conference is that it is making international détente increasingly substantive. . . . The main conclusion, which is reflected in the Final Act, is that no one should attempt on the basis of a foreign-policy consideration to dictate to other peoples how they should run their internal affairs. . . . The results of the long negotiations are such that there are no victors and no vanquished, no winners and no losers; this is a victory of reason." (*Pravda*, 1 August.)

In the wake of the summit, *Pravda* and *Izvestiia* published the entire text of the Final Act, and the Soviet party and government leaders, endorsing the results of the conference, declared that the Soviet Union would "act precisely" to live up to the agreements (*Pravda*, 7 August).

But a week later Brezhnev told a delegation of U.S. congressmen that the Soviet Union would insist on further bilateral discussions before implementing the "humanitarian" provisions of the Final Act. In Brezhnev's view, some provisions of the final act were binding; others would be specifically fulfilled only when agreements were reached on the part of the participating states. (*NYT*, 16 August.)

It was precisely the "Basket Three" issues concerning the East-West free flow of people, ideas, and information which many Westerners valued most highly in the Final Act, and a campaign was soon under way aimed at pressuring the Soviet Union to relax its restrictions on "free flow." The Soviets, however, were adamant in resisting "co-existence" of ideas; when French president Giscard d'Estaing proposed during his visit to Moscow during October that détente be extended to ideology, Brezhnev replied that "international détente in no way puts an end to the struggle of ideas" (ibid, 26 November).

The Soviets soon launched a counterattack. They charged Western governments with hypocrisy on the "civil rights" issue, citing, for example, the domestic spying activities of the CIA and FBI in the United States and noting that more Western literature is published in the Soviet Union than vice versa. Arbatov, claiming that the USSR had "far surpassed the West and particularly the United States" in honoring the humanitarian provisions of the Final Act, denied that Moscow was obliged by the agreement to open its doors to "anti-Soviet subversive propaganda" and "pornography." Challenging the United States to solve its own social problems rather than pressure the Soviet Union, he quoted the maxim: "physician, heal thyself." (*Izvestiia*, 4 September.)

Brezhnev reacted to the Western pressure even more harshly. He charged that the "bourgeois world," together with "traitors to the cause of socialism," was "slinging mud" and employing ideological infiltration and economic levers to weaken the unity of the socialist community. Western leaders who had not even lived up to the requirement of widely disseminating the Final Act to their publics, were taking portions of it out of context, in a campaign of misinformation and slander, in order to poison the international atmosphere. Calling on the West to join in seeking cooperative agreements in the fields of environmental protection, transport, energy, and military relaxation, he pledged: "We Communists will further do everything depending on us for our planet never to be engulfed in a nuclear conflagration, for the peoples to live, develop, and solve their tasks in conditions of lasting peace, independence, and freedom." (*NYT*, 10 December.)

Brezhnev's reference to "economic levers" revealed the lingering bitterness with which the Soviets regarded the collapse of the trade agreement with the United States in January. The Congressional amendments sponsored by Senators Jackson and Stevenson had been rejected by the Soviets as "insulting conditions," "impermissible interference," and "political blackmail." The press jeered at the "absurd concoctions" which maintained that the Soviet Union required U.S. trade in order to develop its economy, and suggested that orders from Soviet traders could be redirected from the United States to Western Europe (*Izvestiia*, 19 January).

Yet Moscow hastened to add that the collapse of the trade agreement need not put a halt to the further development of Soviet-U.S. détente. Boris Ponomarev, speaking to a conference of military ideological cadres, voiced the assurance that the Soviet leadership still regarded the Vladivostok summit as valid and still relied on the intention of President Ford and Secretary Kissinger to continue improving relations despite "complications" in trade (*Christian Science Monitor*, 30 January). And in the spring, when the collapse of U.S. policy in Indochina again raised doubts about the durability and value of détente, the Soviet press, foregoing the opportunity to rub salt in American wounds, emphasized the gain for world peace as much as the gain for socialism. Brezhnev himself declared that from the victory of the Indochina "patriots" the "cause of international détente gains—including, we hope, relations with the United States" (*Pravda*, 9 May).

Even Marshal Grechko spoke during the year of the need to make détente "irreversible" and praised the "advance toward relaxation of tensions and constructive and mutually profitable coopera- tion." But he also continued to put emphasis on the heightened activity of "aggressive and reactionary" forces, the "war preparations of imperialist countries," and the persisting danger of new military provocations that could aggravate the international situation to a dangerous point," all of which demanded "constant strengthening of the defense capacity" of the socialist community and "readiness to repulse any reactionary imperialist encroachment." (*Pravda*, 8 November; *WMR*, no. 3.)

The effect of détente and the "crisis of capitalism" upon the revolutionary strategy of the non-ruling Communist parties in capitalist countries was a subject of intense discussion in 1975, as it had been in the previous year (see *YICA, 1975*, pp. 90-91). The issue was a complex one and there were numerous signs that it was provoking controversy not only within the CPSU but also between the Soviet party and some of its West European counterparts.

That the effects of the "crisis of capitalism" were not simple was explicitly acknowledged by Ponomarev in his January speech to ideological workers in the armed forces. In contrast to his statement of the previous summer, which had stressed the opportunities opened up to revolutionary forces by the "crisis," Ponomarev now stressed the danger that "fascist" forces might be strengthened by capitalism's crisis. And although the democratic forces had succeeded in winning victory over the previous generation of fascists, "in the nuclear century, the strengthening of fascism and even more, the seizure of state power by fascists, would be more dangerous for humanity." (*Christian Science Monitor*, 30 January.)

The ambivalence in Kremlin thinking on this issue was reflected in an analysis appearing in *Kommunist* in the spring. While denouncing persons who underestimated the crisis of capitalism and ignored the favorable conditions it created for upsurge of the workers' movement, the article also warned against those adventurists who overestimated revolutionary prospects and called for a purely proletarian revolution. It stressed that the crisis was a protracted one, which would be experienced in waves, and it advised Communist parties of the need during the first stages of the revolution to find allies in the armed forces and among the bourgeois strata. (*Washington Post*, 29 May.)

But later an article in *Pravda* (6 August) by Konstantin Zarodov, editor of the journal *Problemy mira i sotsializm*, seemed to be far less cautious about revolutionary prospects. Recalling Lenin's writings on the intertwining of the democratic and socialist stages of the revolution, Zarodov stressed the need not to stop at the first stage of revolution. He indirectly criticized those European communist parties ("present-day conciliators") which seemed to be prepared to "dissolve themselves" in alliances with social-democratic parties, and he emphasized that the only true way to socialism was through exercise of the "hegemony of the proletariat." The true revolutionary would not be beguiled by elections and the search for an "arithmetical majority," but would seek a majority in its "political" sense—that is, in the course of direct revolutionary action by the masses.

The significance of this article was heightened on 17 September when the author was summoned to an audience with Brezhnev, who reportedly bestowed his high approval upon the journal Zarodov edited (*Pravda*, 18 September). European Communists seemed concerned with the possible consequences for their own parties; later in the autumn the French communist newspaper *L'Humanité* went so far as to offer a direct rebuttal to Zarodov's views.

In addition to its effect in retarding the process of assembling the European Communist parties for the enunciation of a common strategy, this controversy had direct implications for the Communist strategy in Portugal. Apart from the control of political power in Portugal itself, two other matters were involved. First, Secretary Kissinger had made it clear that the United States regarded Soviet non-intervention in Portugal as a requirement for the further advance of détente. And second, the fortunes of Communist parties in France, Italy, and other West European countries—both in increasing their popular standing and in forging alliances with non-communist parties—seemed to be tied to the degree of restraint exercised by the Portuguese Communists.

The Soviet Union's awareness of the circumstances was evident in the assertion in April that it "has not interfered and does not intend to interfere in the internal and international affairs of Portugal and even less to influence any of her political parties" (*Pravda*, 20 April). Moreover, in May a Soviet analysis of the spring elections in Portugal recognized the heavy obstacles confronting Portuguese Communists and declared that "only a broad coalition of social and political forces is capable of building a new, democratic Portugal" (*Mezhdunarodnaia zhizn', no. 6*).

As the course of the struggle in Portugal turned against the Communists in late summer, Soviet commentaries grew more insistent in their assertions that the forces of international reaction, including NATO, the leadership of the European Economic Community, and international social democracy were flagrantly interfering in Portugal's affairs. (Parallel with this, according to *Pravda*, 19 August, imperialist forces and their Chinese allies were seeking to fan a civil war in Angola: the situation, reminiscent of that in the days before the "fascist coup" in Chile, was one to which no friend of democracy could remain indifferent, but the Soviet people, while displaying mass solidarity with their Portuguese comrades, would continue to uphold the principle of non-interference and to insist that the problems in Portugal should be solved by the Portuguese people themselves.)

The removal of General Vasco Gonçalves as Portuguese prime minister in September was viewed by the Soviets as a sign of the gathering pace of counter-revolution in Portugal. In Moscow's view the period of the "carnation revolution" was at an end and a new period of acute class struggle had begun. It was precisely such a situation to which Ponomarev's and Zarodov's theoretical contributions had been addressed. In the final analysis, as evidenced by an article which appeared in September, the practical advice rendered to the Portuguese comrades by the Soviet press came down on the side of caution. The Portuguese Communist Party believed, the article asserted, that the present conditions demanded talks and compromises from all anti-fascist forces. "Only revolutionaries who do not believe in themselves are incapable of understanding that talks and compromises are necessary in the sharp bends of the revolutionary path." Naturally, this referred only to compromises "which would not affect the basic achievements of the Portuguese revolution." Nevertheless, it was at present the task of progressive forces in Portugal to secure a "breathing space to repulse the onslaught of reaction and to consolidate the positions won." (*Za rubezhom*, no. 38.)

Just as Portugal was the major test in 1975 of the Soviet strategy of "social liberation," so the former Portuguese colony of Angola was the primary arena for Soviet encouragement of "natural liberation." Of the three factions struggling for control in the new African state, declared independent on 11 November, the Popular Movement for the Liberation of Angola (MPLA) had received Soviet arms and support for more than a decade. A massive infusion of Soviet arms, estimated by one source at 150,000 tons, together with the introduction of Cuban troops into units of the MPLA gave that faction a clear advantage over its rivals by the end of the year (*NYT*, 14 December).

The Soviet press depicted the struggle in Angola as a clash between the "truly patriotic forces" and the "enemies of the Angolan people"—U.S. imperialists and Maoists and their instrument, Holden Roberto's National Front for the Liberation of Angola (*Pravda*, 18 July, 9 September). Clearly, Angola's strategic location and reservoir of natural resources was turning the civil war into a major struggle for influence by the three external powers, and thus into a possible obstacle to "détente." In December, Secretary of State Kissinger warned that the United States would try to prevent "one party, by means of outside equipment, from achieving dominance," and added that Angola "cannot but affect" Soviet-U.S. relations if Moscow continued its massive military support. (*NYT*, 13 December.)

The other party to this triangular struggle—the People's Republic of China—was the object of sharp polemical attack from Moscow throughout the year. According to a *Pravda* editorial published in February, the Maoist leadership had emerged, in the wake of the National People's Congress, even more brazenly on the side of aggressive imperialist circles. The Chinese, it said, were again trying to prove that a new world war was inevitable, and were claiming that such a conflagration would be useful for the cause of socialist revolution. Guided by annexationist designs, they were systematically organizing border provocations against "neighboring socialist states" and subversive activities against other states in South and Southeast Asia. Striving to impose themselves as leaders of the "third world," the Maoists were seeking to use the developing countries as a tool in achieving their great-power chauvinist designs, but were willing to abandon leftist allies and strike deals with right-wing forces when it suited their purposes. For its part, the USSR had advanced numerous constructive proposals aimed at normalizing relations with China, but Peking, "by repeating what are known to be unacceptable preconditions," had spurned all such overtures. (*Pravda*, 22 February.) Moreover, the Maoists had amended the 1954 constitution, replacing a statement calling for friendship with the USSR with one embodying anti-Soviet attacks, and had stripped the political system of all its democratic features, holding that "power rests on bayonets, and not on the people" (ibid., 21 January, 5 February).

Climaxing the long Soviet media campaign against every aspect of contemporary Chinese politics was an editorial in *Kommunist* in August (no. 12), widely disseminated by TASS. Concluding that Maoism constituted a "danger to all states, regardless of their social system," and that it was "unrealistic" to count on a basic change in Chinese policy and unconscionable to adopt a neutral or conciliatory stance, the editorial declared: "The ideology, theory and practical activity of Marxist-Leninists in the conditions of today is aimed at smashing Maoism in its theory and its politics as an anti-Marxist and anti-Leninist movement hostile to the entire contemporary revolutionary movement."

As a concrete instrument for combating the Chinese challenge in the region in which it most immediately manifested itself, the Soviets put even greater emphasis in 1975 on the need for a "system of collective security in Asia." That the Asian security campaign would shift into higher gear following the conclusion of the European security conference was quite predictable. An article in August, summing up the current themes in the campaign, cited the ten principles from the CSCE Final Act as universally applicable to all other countries and continents. It was ridiculous to assert, the article said, that such a security system could be used to establish Soviet hegemony; rather, Peking's refusal to participate was based precisely in its own desire to achieve hegemony in Asia. (*Izvestiia*, 28 August.)

International Activities and Party Contacts. The development of Soviet-U.S. détente lost considerable momentum during the year. Although Ford and Brezhnev met briefly during the Helsinki summit, and Kissinger and Gromyko conferred on four occasions during the year, the planned visit by Brezhnev to the United States for the purpose of signing a new agreement on strategic arms limitations was postponed repeatedly. The year began with the collapse of the Soviet-U.S. trade agreement, followed by some of the shrillest press treatment of the United States to come from Moscow in years. This uncertain atmosphere further deteriorated as the two sides began to encounter difficulties in applying the guidelines laid down at the Vladivostok summit to a final SALT agreement, and as the Soviets began to express resentment at being excluded from Kissinger's Middle East negotiations. It was in this context that Kissinger and Gromyko met in Geneva on 16-17 February for what Kissinger described às talks in a "constructive atmosphere with candid interludes" (*Washington Post*, 17 February). And while the shrill tone of Soviet press treatment of the United States subsided following this meeting, both sides continued to express doubt about the other's seriousness in pursuing détente. Thus, Gromyko, inserting a statement not in the text of a speech he delivered in May, rebuked Kissinger for defending a large military budget increase while at the same time allegedly advocating relaxation of tension (*NYT*, 15 May).

Later in May the two foreign ministers gathered for another meeting in Vienna. Much of the discussion concerned the Middle East, with the Soviets reportedly leaving the impression that they were prepared to explore a "cooperative approach" to the conflict. Some progress was said to have been made on the SALT issues, and another meeting was set for July. In the interim, the Soviet press again complained that a U.S. cabinet member was doing violence to the policy of relaxation of tension by advocating a stepped-up military posture, but this time it was Secretary of Defense Schlesinger who was singled out as the villain. (*Pravda*, 1 June, 12 July.) After Kissinger and Gromyko met again in Geneva in the second week of July for further discussions about SALT and the Middle East, Kissinger reported that some progress had been made in narrowing their differences, and there was renewed talk about a possible fall summit meeting (*Washington Post*, 11 July). Similarly, the brief meeting between President Ford and General Secretary Brezhnev in Helsinki was said to have achieved "encouraging progress" on the SALT issues.

But in the wake of this latter meeting the Soviets began to feel that undue pressure was being placed on them to modify their policies and positions to accord with the West's interpretation of the CSCE Final Act. Ford himself warned, in a speech on 19 August, that Soviet actions in Portugal would be viewed as a test of their willingness to abide by the Helsinki accord, and he pointedly added a warning that the nuclear arms race might well speed up if no SALT agreement had been reached by the end of the year (*NYT*, 20 August). At about the same time, the President, under intense domestic political pressure and amid reports of a serious Soviet crop failure, placed a moratorium on sales of grain to the USSR.

As if this seeming pressure were not enough, the Soviet leaders soon had reason to fear that the United States might succeed in bringing about the collapse of their positions in the Middle East and Portugal. But while the tone of the Soviet press commentary on the United States again grew strident, there was some progress on two fronts. On 21 September the Soviet Union agreed, as an implementation of the Helsinki accord, to grant multiple-entry visas to U.S. correspondents in Moscow. And a month later it was reported that the U.S. moratorium on grain sales had been lifted and that the two countries had reached a five-year agreement, to become effective in October 1976, under which the Soviets would buy 6 to 8 million tons of U.S. grain per year. The U.S. effort to reach an agreement on purchase of Soviet oil at a price below the world level was, however, unsuccessful. (*NYT*, 21 October.)

There was failure also in the renewed U.S. effort to produce a compromise on SALT. A proposal submitted by Kissinger to Gromyko in September was rejected by the Soviets. Plans for a 1975 Soviet-U.S. summit in Washington prior to the 25th CPSU Congress were apparently dead, and even a planned Kissinger trip to Moscow in mid-December for further SALT discussions was postponed until January. By the end of the year, the "spirit of détente" appeared to be very fragile indeed.

Like its relationship with the United States, Moscow's position in the Middle East at the beginning of 1975 stood at a low point. Both the Soviet Union and Egypt attempted to treat the cancellation of Brezhnev's visit as a temporary postponement, but it was soon evident that President Sadat was harboring some deep grievances against his Soviet ally.

Just prior to the start of Kissinger's peace mission, Gromyko arrived for visits in Syria and Egypt. In Damascus he found an "atmosphere of complete mutual understanding" and an agreement that any Middle Eastern settlement must embrace all parties and resolve all questions. The Geneva conference, the communiqué stated, must be resumed immediately—certainly no later than February or early March. (*Pravda*, 4 February.)

The reception in Cairo was somewhat chillier; *Pravda* (6 February) noted that Gromyko and Sadat had an "exchange of opinions in a friendly and business-like atmosphere." Three minor agreements were signed and trade talks between the two countries (apparently to discuss debt rescheduling) were set for later in the month. The communiqué noted that a Middle East settlement must be "all-embracing," with the Soviets participating at all stages, and that the "most suitable" forum for talks was the Geneva conference, which should be immediately resumed. Evidently this represented sufficient progress for the Soviets to decide to resume arms shipments to Egypt and to halt their press attacks on the Sadat government (*Washington Post*, 9 February).

The failure of Kissinger's mission to mediate an interim agreement for Israeli withdrawal from the Sinai did not displease the Soviets, who saw reaffirmation of "the hopelessness of attempts at so-called partial solutions" (*Pravda*, 27 March). As the United States withdrew for a policy review, the Soviets sought to fill the negotiating vacuum with their own version of "shuttle diplomacy," aimed at working out a unified Arab position on the basis of which the Geneva conference could be reconvened.

In the space of two weeks in April, four separate Arab delegations traveled to Moscow for high-level talks. First to arrive was Iraqi leader Saddam Hussain, who was welcomed by Kosygin on 14 April with a warning to the Arabs that they must be more unified or risk being put at a disadvantage at the Geneva conference (*NYT*, 15 April). Then came Egyptian foreign minister Fahmy for talks with Gromyko and Brezhnev on 19-22 April. He was told by Gromyko that it was not incompatible to say that the Geneva conference should be both speedily convened and seriously prepared. As for bilateral Soviet-Egyptian relations, Gromyko told Fahmy that improvement in that sphere depended upon Egypt. (*Pravda*, 28 April.) On 23 April, Syrian foreign minister Khaddam was Gromyko's guest for dinner. Gromyko proposed a three-point agenda for the proposed Geneva conference: first would come the accord on liberation of occupied Arab lands; second, an agreement safeguarding the legitimate rights of the Palestine people; and third, an accord ensuring and guaranteeing the rights of all states in their region, including Israel, to independent existence and development. Gromyko declared: "Israel may get, if it so wishes, the strictest guarantees with participation, under an appropriate agreement, of the Soviet Union." (Ibid., 24 April.)

The last visitor (28 April-5 May) was Yasir Arafat of the Palestine Liberation Organization (PLO), who had an "exchange of views" with Gromyko and Ponomarev, at the conclusion of which the Soviets failed to issue their usual call for an immediate return to the Geneva conference table. It was clear from *Pravda*'s repetition on 5 May of its plea for Arab unity that little progress had been made by Soviet diplomats. In fact, shortly thereafter Gromyko revised his earlier offer to the Israelis, stating that Israel could receive "sufficient guarantees" provided it withdrew from all occupied territories and recognized the right of the Palestinians to create their own state (*NYT*, 15 May).

The next Arab state to hear the Soviet plea for unity was Libya, which received a visit from Kosygin on 12-15 May. Knowing how to please his host, Kosygin presented Colonel Qaddafi with an ancient copy of the Koran. The Soviet premier also arranged to sell the Libyans a large quantity of arms ($800 million worth, according to the Libyans) and a nuclear research reactor. (*Washington Post*, 13 June.) This largesse did not exactly call forth a spirit of unity from Qaddafi's rival, Sadat. The Egyptian press wrote that the Soviet Union was planning to build a base in Libya—a story which *Pravda* denounced as a "crude fabrication" (27 May).

In the summer Egypt was reportedly applying pressure on the Soviets by hampering the movement of Soviet naval and air forces from Egyptian bases, in order to revise the financial basis of their relationship. This strategy at least succeeded in calling forth an invitation to the Egyptian finance minister to visit Moscow. (*NYT*, 27 July.) But the Soviets also knew how to apply pressure. In August it was reported that the Egyptian Communist Party—which had been dissolved in 1965 at Soviet behest—had reemerged, operating to pressure Sadat not to place his bets on the Americans (ibid., 6 September).

Soviet diplomacy was also seeking to increase its flexibility by opening contacts with the Israelis. In April, during the intensive Soviet drive to reconvene the Geneva conference, two Soviet representatives reportedly visited Israel to discuss the conference with Prime Minister Rabin (ibid., 12 April). In June a delegation of Israeli communists visited Moscow for talks, and in September a five-member Israeli delegation came to the Soviet Union for further discussions (*Pravda*, 15 June; *Washington Post*, 26 September). Other Soviet Middle Eastern activities during the summer included a June visit by Ponomarev to Damascus, where he met with both Syrian and PLO officials, and the signing of economic agreements between the Soviet Union and Iraq, and between Iraq and the Council for Mutual Economic Assistance (*Pravda*, 5, 10 July).

As the end-of-summer diplomacy of Henry Kissinger, aimed at a Sinai agreement, came nearer to bearing fruit, *Pravda* (30 August) denounced the projected agreement as a "partial agreement of limited signifance that not only does not replace a general political settlement in the Middle East but also does not bring one any nearer." The possible stationing of U.S. personnel in the Sinai was viewed as a "new complicating element." The actual signing of the accord was greeted by only a two-sentence reaction from TASS, but a later commentary characterized it as a blow to Arab unity. The Syrians, who also opposed the partial Sinai accords, sent two high-level delegations to Moscow in the following weeks. President Hafiz al-Asad visited on 9-10 October to emphasize that "no one will be allowed to shake or harm" Soviet-Syrian friendship, and Foreign Minister Khaddam came later in the month for talks with Gromyko and Grechko (*Pravda*, 11, 16 October).

Soviet bitterness over Sadat's turn to the Americans was expressed in an authoritative and critical article in *Pravda* (25 October) on the eve of his visit to the United States. "Observer" reviewed in the article the history of Soviet support—especially military support—for Egypt, and criticized the Egyptians' "brazen distortion" of the history of this relationship. The Soviet Union, the article declared, was trying to develop cooperation in accordance with existing agreements, but, "as is well known, this is a two-way affair. Cooperation cannot be developed if one of the sides is trying to undermine it."

The Soviets then reportedly conducted a thorough policy reassessment, but what emerged was simply a renewal of the call for a Geneva conference, and a renewed assertion that the "road of partial measures" could not promote an overall solution. One new and complicating element in the Soviet formulation was the insistence that from the very beginning all parties directly concerned in the conflict should take part in the conference on an equal footing—a move away from the previous suggestion that the PLO might have only observer status in Geneva. (*Baltimore Sun*, 17 November.)

Another conference which the Soviets had difficulty in convening on their own terms was the projected meeting of European Communist parties, originally designed to be held in mid-1975, at the conclusion of the CSCE (see *YICA, 1975*, pp. 91-92). The process of working out a draft of a common programmatic statement was proving extremely difficult. A draft proposed by the German Democratic Republic and supported by the Soviet and Danish parties was rejected in the summer by the five remaining members of the drafting committee: the parties of Yugoslavia, Romania, France, Italy, and Spain. Reportedly, the issues in dispute concerned the Soviet role as ideological center of the communist movement, whether China would be criticized in the statement, and the question of future Communist policy in Western Europe. A two-day session of preparation for the conference was held on 9-10 October in East Berlin, and it concluded in an agreement to resume work on a new draft declaration. But no date was set for the conference itself, and the statement issued by the East Berlin meeting spoke of a "constructive democratic exchange of opinion," indicating disagreement at the session. Reportedly, the only proposed binding clause acceptable to all the parties represented at the meeting was an expression of approval of the principles of peaceful co-existence as laid down at Helsinki. (*NYT*, 12 October.) The drafting process was resumed on 17 November, but this meeting also broke up without setting a final date for the proposed conference.

The distance between the CPSU and the French and Italian parties appeared to grow markedly during the year. The Italian Communists were engaged in the process of attempting to forge a long-term alliance with the Christian Democratic Party, thus arranging for themselves a place in the government. Events in Portugal, including especially the exclusion of Portuguese Christian Democrats from the electoral process, were seriously complicating the strategy of the Italian party. A dramatic moment in the negotiations came in March, during that party's 14th Congress, which was attended both by a group of Italian Christian Democrats and by a high-ranking CPSU delegation led by Andrei Kirilenko. The Christian Democrats walked out in protest of the events in Portugal. But the Soviets were not pleased at the congress by Italian party chief Berlinguer's opening speech, which praised Yugoslav foreign policy, urged a Sino-Soviet détente, and criticized the strategy of the Portuguese Communist Party. (Ibid., 14 April.) At the end of June, Gromyko, on a visit to Italy, met with the Italian Communist leaders. The Soviet characterization of the conversation as an "exchange of opinion" indicated that disagreements between the two parties continued (*FBIS*, 30 June). Later the Italian Communist newspaper *L'Unità* (13 November) went so far as to join in the criticism of the Soviet Union for its refusal to grant a visa to Andrei Sakharov. The event was viewed by the Italians as evidence of the existence of a problem of dissent which should be "faced and solved through the confrontation of ideas and positions."

The French Communist newspaper *L'Humanité* had also during the fall had been critical of the CPSU, angrily rejecting the thesis of Zarodov concerning proper revolutionary strategy. The joining of forces between the free-wheeling Italians and the traditionally pro-Soviet French Communists, as represented by the joint statement issued by the two parties in November, signaled a serious problem for the CPSU in its relations with West European communists. (*NYT*, 18 November.)

The League of Communists of Yugoslavia (LCY) was another party which was disagreeing with the CPSU on the basis of a common strategy for European Communists. The two parties were in intensive contact in the spring, as Yugoslav prime minister Bijedić visited Moscow in April for talks with Kosygin and Brezhnev, Soviet deputy prime minister Mazurov led a Soviet delegation to Belgrade in May for the victory-day celebrations and a talk with Tito, and LCY Executive Committee secretary

Aleksandar Grličkov conferred in Moscow the same month with Ponomarev. The greatest controversy between these two parties occurred in the fall and concerned the activities of the illegal pro-Soviet party, the "Communist Party of Yugoslavia." The leader of the party was captured by Yugoslav police in November, and the group was denounced by Tito for seeking to "take power" in Yugoslavia. A speech by another LCY leader a week later specifically linked Moscow with the activities of the illegal faction (*Washington Post*, 12 November.) This allegation was followed by a meeting in Moscow between LCY secretary-general Stane Dolanc and CPSU secretaries Kirilenko and Katushev. In "frank and useful" talks, Dolanc reportedly demanded of the Soviets that they stop meddling in Yugoslav affairs (*NYT*, 25 November).

In contacts with the rest of their East European neighbors, the Soviet leaders were concerned largely with economic matters. Some of this activity was centered in the CMEA, whose Council met in June to work a coordinated plan of multilateral integrative measures for the period 1976-80. Earlier in the year, the CMEA had had its first—and largely unsuccessful—official contact with the European Economic Community (ibid., 8 February).

The Soviets were reportedly seeking to work out new terms of trade with their East European partners. Apparently calling for a doubled price for Soviet petroleum and a program of East European investment in the USSR, the Soviet plan was discussed in Brezhnev's meeting with other East European leaders (except Romania's Ceauçescu) at the Hungarian party congress in March (*Manchester Guardian*, 3 May). Hungary's prime minister Lazar was in Moscow in the fall for further talks on plan coordination. Similar talks were held between Poland and the Soviet Union in August during Kosygin's visit to Warsaw. And another multilateral gathering of the top East European leaders with Brezhnev occurred in December at the Polish party congress.

Gustav Husák of Czechoslovakia was in Moscow for talks on three occasions during the year: in March for a "brief, friendly visit" with Brezhnev, in August for a meeting with Brezhnev in the Crimea, and in November for an official visit.

East German party leader Erich Honecker met with Brezhnev in Moscow twice on matters relating to European security and the status of Berlin. The second occasion was in the second week of October, when he headed a high-powered East German delegation for the signing of a revised Soviet-GDR treaty. Taking into account the Helsinki agreement, the new version removed earlier references to German reunification and substituted mention of "the inviolability of state frontiers in Europe." It also changed the treaty's formulation on West Berlin, from the 1964 version's description of West Berlin as "an independent political unit" to a declaration that West Berlin "is not a constituent part of the Federal Republic of Germany and shall not be administered by it in the future." (*NYT*, 8 October.)

The question of Berlin was also raised in the Soviet talks with the leaders of West Germany. The Soviet press had raised complaints about activities by the Bonn government regarding West Berlin on several occasions during the year. These formed the background for discussions between Soviet leaders and FRG president Walter Scheel in November. Disagreement over the inclusion of West Berlin in agreements on exchanges in the cultural, scientific, and legal fields further delayed the conclusion of pacts on the subjects and symbolized the slowed pace of Soviet-West German détente. (Ibid., 14 November.)

Notable progress was made in Soviet relations with Britain during the year. These relations had been in a state of disrepair for some years—a fact which Brezhnev noted during Prime Minister Harold Wilson's visit to Moscow in February. The meeting resulted in a mutual pledge for a "systematic expansion of relations" in the signing of several political and economic agreements, including one making available credits to the Soviet Union valued at about $2.4 billion over a five-year period. On the whole. Wilson's visit raised Anglo-Soviet relations to the approximate level of Moscow's ties with other major west European states. (*Washington Post*, 18 February.)

Soviet relations with France continued to limp along at a level far below that of the De Gaulle era. Suslov told a visiting delegation of the French Socialist Party that the USSR deplored the French government's "unconstructive positions" on disarmament and on relations with NATO, and declared that "anti-Soviet campaigns mounted in France by the media cannot leave us indifferent" (*FBIS*, 5 June). Later in the summer, TASS attacked the French Minister of the Interior for his remarks warning French Socialists against cooperation with the French Communists (*Washington Post*, 3 August). Official visits to Moscow by Premier Chirac in March and President Giscard d'Estaing in October produced little in the way of concrete results.

Other West European government leaders visiting Moscow during the year included President Leone and Foreign Minister Rumor of Italy (in November), King Baudoin and the Belgian premier (in June), the Grand Duke and Duchess of Luxembourg and Prime Minister Thorn (also in June), President Kekkonen of Finland (in March), and the foreign minister of Iceland (the first visit by an Icelandic official of his rank, in April).

Soviet relations with two northern European neighbors were marked by controversy. Norwegian and Soviet officials gathered in Oslo in November for discussions on the long-standing dispute over the Barents Sea boundaries and the status of Spitsbergen. An area potentially rich in oil deposits and a strategic ice-free route from European waters to Soviet ports, this territory had been the object of controversy in September when the Soviet fleet conducted maneuvers and fired missiles in the disputed waters. (*NYT*, 2 October.)

Twice during the spring the Soviet press renewed its attacks on the non-communist press of Finland for spreading "anti-communist fabrications and slanderous attacks" concerning Soviet involvement in the affairs of the Finnish Communist Party. These allegations were countered by a Communist-front group in Finland which gathered 580,000 signatures on petitions pledging peace and good relations with the USSR. This expression of good will was personally presented to Podgnorny by the Finnish foreign minister. (Ibid., 11 May.) Toward the end of the year, the Finnish Communists reentered the government, participating in a five-party national emergency coalition (ibid., 1 December).

Soviet policies toward Portugal were manifested in several contacts between the two governments during 1975. In January, Pedro Soares, then Portuguese foreign minister, visited Moscow for talks with Gromyko on European security, Portuguese decolonization policies, and the Middle East (*Pravda*, 4 January). Two months later, Portuguese labor minister José de Costa Martins, was received in Moscow by Kosygin (ibid., 27 March). In the interim, a rumor surfaced in the Western press that the Soviets had asked Lisbon for port facilities for use by the Soviet fishing fleet. *Pravda* attacked such "provocational rumors" and published a denial attributed to Portuguese officials (4 February).

The setbacks suffered during the year by Communist forces and their allies in Portugal did not prevent Moscow from welcoming President Francisco da Costa Gomes for a state visit in October. He met with Brezhnev and signed agreements with Podgorny establishing scientific and economic cooperation and calling for regular consultations on international issues. The joint communiqué reiterated Soviet support for the sovereign right of the Portuguese people to decide their own destiny without outside interference. (*Christian Science Monitor*, 6 October.)

A major event in Asia in 1975 was the Communist victory in Vietnam, and North Vietnamese party leader Le Duan was warmly received in Moscow for an "official friendship visit" in late October. He and his comrades met with Brezhnev, Kosygin, Podgorny, Gromyko, Grechko, and Katushev "in a comradely atmosphere and spirit of complete mutual understanding." The joint declaration called the visit a "splendid expression of irremovable friendship and solidarity" which "ushered in an important stage of continuing consolidation and development of fraternal relations." The North Vietnamese delegation approved the Soviet (and anti-Chinese) formulation of international communist unity "based on Marxism-Leninism and proletarian internationalism," expressed gratitude for Moscow's "effective and invaluable assistance" in the war and in postwar rehabilitation, and supported the Soviet efforts toward peace and social progress" that were "making the course of détente irreversible." The Soviets in turn signed agreements calling for economic aid and technical assistance in the development of Vietnamese industry and agriculture. (*Pravda*, 31 October.)

Soviet relations with the new Communist regime in Cambodia were less than cordial from the very beginning; Soviet envoys were among the foreigners expelled by the new government following the spring victory. One high-level conversation did occur, however; on 2 September, Mikhail Solomentsev met with Cambodia's Prince Sihanouk in Hanoi.

Soviet influence in Laos was greater. In May a delegation of the Laotian National Political Consultative Council met in Moscow with Podgorny in a "friendly atmosphere." Later in the year it was reported that a protocol had been signed by the two governments on coordination of their national plans. (Ibid., 6 May, 4 October.) The Western press reported that a contingent of 300 to 500 Soviet diplomats, pilots and engineers were working franticly to expand Soviet influence in the newest Communist state (*NYT*, 9 October).

The Soviet press expressed hope during the year that relations with Thailand might improve as that state "slowly but steadily" reexamined its foreign policy of "blindly following the United States." But it warned that reactionary forces still held important positions in the country, and voiced apprehension over the prospects that Peking might interfere in Thailand's political development. (*Pravda*, 23 June.)

Even stronger concern over Peking's influence was evident in Soviet commentaries on Japan. Japanese foreign minister Miyazawa visited Moscow in January, but no progress was evident during the year on the conclusion of a peace treaty between the two states. A major point of controversy was the projected treaty between Japan and China, the draft of which included a pledge to resist efforts of any third nation seeking to establish hegemony in Asia. The Soviets clearly understood that the Peking-authored clause referred to them, and they sought—through the press and in a statement delivered by Gromyko to the Japanese ambassador in June—to dissuade the Japanese from concluding a treaty so detrimental to the development of Soviet-Japanese relations. (*Izvestiia*, 25 April, 1 July.)

India continued to be one of Moscow's closest friends in Asia. Marshal Grechko paid a visit to New Delhi in February for talks on defense and foreign policy cooperation. The pro-Moscow Communist Party of India held to a line of basic support of the Indian government and strong encouragement for the further strengthening of Soviet-Indian relations, and a strong CPSU delegation, headed by Sh. R. Rashidov, signaled its support for this line in its activities at the CPI's 10th Party Congress (*Pravda vostoka*, 30 January). The Soviet press issued statements throughout the spring supporting Indira Gandhi against the attacks of "right reaction and imperialism," and assumed an approving stance in its commentary on the 26 June proclamation of emergency rule in India. (*Pravda*, 27 June, 4 July.)

Pravda also approved the "progressive program" of the government of Sheik Mujib in Bangladesh, and it applauded the imposition of emergency rule there in January, arguing that such measures were necessary in the face of "Peking-inspired extremist sabotage" (2 January). Not unexpectedly, the Soviets voiced serious apprehension at the assassination of Mujib and change of government in Bangladesh in August. "Observer" warned in *Pravda* (22 August) that forces inimical to the national-liberation movement, including imperialism, Maoism, and internal reaction, were seeking to strengthen their influence in Bangladesh.

Soviet relations with Afghanistan continued to be close and undisturbed by political instability. A government delegation visited Kabul in February for the signing of an agreement on economic and technical cooperation, and Soviet president Podgnorny made his sole trip outside the bloc in December to pay a state visit to Afghanistan.

A number of African leaders paid visits to the Soviet Union in a year in which that continent was beginning to loom larger in Moscow's strategy. In February, a party and government delegation from Guinea-Bissau came to Moscow to sign a number of agreements on economic and cultural cooperation and to discuss "questions of further deepening of cooperation" between the CPSU and the African Party for the Independence of Gunea-Bissau and the Cape Verde Islands. The final communiqué condemned the "anti-Soviet and anti-communist policies" of forces which sought to isolate the African states from their true friends—the states of the socialist commonwealth. (*Pravda*, 26 February.)

Gambia's president K. K. Jawara paid an official visit to Moscow on 17-25 March, and Congo's president Marien Ngoubai came immediately thereafter. The latter was given the honor of a meeting with Brezhnev, and he joined with the Soviets in urging vigilance against efforts to split the ranks of the African states. Like Guinea-Bissau, Congo also concluded a number of agreements calling for greater economic and technical cooperation with the USSR (*Pravda*, 30 March). Earlier in the year, the CPSU sent a delegation to attend the second congress of the Congolese Labor Party in Brazzaville (*FBIS*, 3 January).

One other African visitor to Moscow was Muhammad Ali Samatur, vice-president of the Supreme Revolutionary Council of Somalia, who met in May with Podgnorny and V. G. Kulikov, chief of staff of the Soviet armed forces. Somalia is a heavy user of Soviet arms aid, and the Soviets had been led in April to deny publicly that Soviet bases were being constructed there (*Izvestiia*, 12 April). The Somalis went even further in July, opening the Berbera facilities for inspection by a team of U.S. journalists and congressmen—in an attempt to reaffirm their desire not to become overly dependent on Moscow (*Washington Post*, 13 July).

A conference of Latin American communist parties was the object of Soviet press attention in July. Meeting in Havana, the conference gave a "highly positive assessment" of the Soviet peace program, and "strongly refuted the slanderous fabrications" of assorted imperialists and Maoists aimed against the USSR. In addition to issuing a "categorical statement on the devisive and anti-Soviet policies of Maoism," the assembled parties came out in support of a new international communist conference. (*Pravda*, 19 July.)

The Soviets had bilateral contacts with a number of Latin American parties: the leaders of the Argentine and Uruguayan parties met with Brezhnev after the October anniversary celebrations, and a Soviet delegation traveled to Colombia to meet with leaders of the party in that country. The most significant visit, however, was undertaken by M. A. Suslov, who traveled to Cuba in December to attend the first congress of the Cuban Communist Party.

Publications. The main CPSU organs are the daily newspaper *Pravda*, the theoretical and ideological journal *Kommunist* (appearing 18 times a year), and the twice-monthly *Partiinaia zhizn'*, journal on internal party affairs and organizational party matters. *Kommunist vooruzhennikh sil* is the party theoretical journal for the armed forces, and *Agitator* is the journal for party propagandists, both appearing twice a month. The Komsomol has a newspaper, *Komsomolskaia pravda* (issued six times a week); a monthly theoretical journal, *Molodoi kommunist*; and a monthly literary journal, *Molodaia gvardia*. Each USSR republic prints similar party newspapers and journals in local languages, and usually also in Russian.

Vanderbilt University   Robert H. Donaldson

Yugoslavia

Yugoslav communists date the beginning of their party back to April 1919 when a "unification congress" in Belgrade established a "Socialist Workers' Party of Yugoslavia (Communists)," including both communist and non-communist elements. In June 1920 this organization disbanded, and a "Communist Party of Yugoslavia" was formed. In November 1952, at the Sixth Congress, the name was changed to the League of Communists of Yugoslavia (Savez komunista Jugoslavije; LCY).

In June 1975, the LCY reported a total of 1,192,446 members, of whom 344,280 were blue-collar workers and 62,956 peasants (*Borba*, 10 June). The population of Yugoslavia is 21,352,000 (ibid., 27 December).

Leadership and Organization. The 10th Congress of the LCY (27-30 May 1974) elected the 166-member Central Committee and the Central Committee Presidium of 39 members (38 plus Tito, who was proclaimed president of the LCY for life). The Presidium elected the 12-member Executive Committee: six members from the Presidium and six from the Central Committee in general.

At the plenary session in Belgrade on 25-26 February 1975, the Presidium was enlarged to 48 members (47 plus Tito): another six members of the Executive Committee (those who were not given the title of secretary at the 10th congress, and had therefore not been included in the Presidium) became members of the Presidium, along with three new members (from Montenegro, Croatia, and Slovenia). In March, Veljko Vlahović, one of Yugoslavia's top leaders, died; his place in both the Central Committee and the Presidium remains vacant. The current Executive Committee consists of the following, with year of birth and nationality:

Jule Bilić (1922), Croat
Stane Dolanc (1925), Slovene
Aleksandar Grličkov (1923), Macedonian
Ivan Kukoč (1918), Croat
Todo Kurtović (1919), Serb
Nikola Ljubičić (1916), Serb
Munir Mesihović (1928), Moslem
Dušan Popović (1921), Serb
Mirko Popović (1923), Serb
Ali Shukri (1919), Albanian
Vojo Srzentić (1934), Montenegrin
Dragoljub Stavrev (1932), Macedonian
Dobrivoje Vidić (1918), Serb

The presidents of the LCY's six republican central committees and two provincial committees (Vojvodina and Kosovo) and the secretary of the army party organization (nine altogether) are ex officio members of the Presidium:

> Dr. Tihomir Vlaškalić (1923), Serbia
> Mme Milka Planinc (1924), Croatia
> Angel Čemerski (1923), Macedonia
> Franc Popit (1921), Slovenia
> Branko Mikulić (1928), Bosnia-Hercegovina
> Veselin Djuranović (1925), Montenegro
> Dušan Alimpić (1921), Vojvodina
> Mahmut Bakalli (1936), Kosovo
> General Džemail Šarac (1921), for the Army

Besides that of Vlahović, who died, the place of Jože Smole on the Central Committee and its Presidium must also be filled, since Smole became Yugoslavia's ambassador in Moscow in October 1975.

At the 25-26 February plenary session Jure Bilić, Executive Committee secretary in charge of party affairs, reported that the LCY at that time had "more than 1,100,000 members" (*Borba*, 26 February) and gave the following breakdown of party membership:

Blue-collar workers	313,000
Humanistic intelligentsia	147,000
Technical intelligentsia	60,000
White-collar workers	129,000
Army	83,000
Students and pupils	60,000
Housewives and pensioners	116,000
Peasants	60,000
Others	30,000

This makes a total of 998,000, because Bilić gave round rather than detailed figures.

Auxiliary and Mass Organizations. As the only political party in the Socialist Federative Republic of Yugoslavia (SFRY), the LCY exercises power through its leading role in the Socialist Alliance of the Working People of Yugoslavia (Socijalistički savez radnog naroda Jugoslavije; SAWPY), a front organization which includes all mass auxiliary political organizations, as well as individuals representing various social groups. The present name (formerly it was the People's Front) was adopted in 1953 in response to Tito's suggestion. The SAWPY's main publication is the daily *Borba*. The SAWPY has "about 8,000,000 members" (*Politika*, 20 November 1975).

The supreme body of the SAWPY is the Federal Conference (FC) which numbers 203 members delegated by the republican and provincial socialist alliances and by political and professional organizations (*Borba*, 18 April). The executive branch of the FC is the 51-member Presidium. The Chairman of the SAWPY is the Serb Dušan Petrović, a member of the LCY Presidium. His deputies are Marin Cetenić, a Croat, and Dimče Belovski, a Macedonian. The Secretary of the FC is the Slovene Marjan Rožič. Among the 51 members of the FC Presidium, 11 are members of the LCY Central Committee (of whom 7 are party Presidium members, including 3 in the Executive Committee).

The Confederation of Trade Unions of Yugoslavia (Savez sindikata Jugoslavije; CTUY) is, according to the constitution, "the broadest organization of the working class." In 1974, the CTUY had a total membership of 4,108,000. Its publication is the daily *Rad* (Labor).

According to the official Yugoslav formulation "the trade unions operate in an organized way for the promotion of the Marxist ideological-political education of workers, provide varied forms of on-the-job training in socioeconomic education and, in particular, in education for self-management" (*Yugoslav Survey*, May 1975, p. 17). One of the TU's main functions is "to ensure protection of workers' self-management rights and create conditions conducive to greater industrial safety" (ibid., p. 11).

Since 1957, workers' strikes in Yugoslavia (or "work stoppages" as they are officially called) have been tacitly recognized as a legitimate and necessary form of exerting pressure on the Yugoslav party and state organizations. Legally, strikes are not permitted, although there is no law forbidding them.

The CTUY cooperates with other labor groups, regardless of whether they are affiliated with one of the international labor organizations or not. Its cooperation has been especially fruitful with the WFTU (World Federation of Trade Unions), with the WCL (World Confederation of Labor), and with the ILO (International Labor Organization). As far as cooperation with the ICFTU (International Confederation of Free Trade Unions) is concerned, the official Yugoslav stand is described as follows: "Bilateral cooperation with unions affiliated with the ICFTU has created favorable conditions of cooperation with this international union organization, especially since the American Federation of Labor and the Congress of Industrial Organizations (AFL-CIO) have withdrawn from it" (ibid., p. 21).

The League of Socialist Youth of Yugoslavia (Savez socijalističke omladine Jugoslavije; LSYY) has "more than 3,500,000 members," which is 60 percent of the total number of young people in Yugoslavia between the ages of 14 and 27 (*Borba*, 14 May). The Ninth LSYY Congress was held in Belgrade on 21-23 November 1974. Azem Vlasi (b. 1948), a student of Albanian origin, was elected president of the LSYY, and Matko Topalović (b. 1944) was elected secretary. The Presidium of the LSYY is composed of 30 members, plus 8 presidents of republican and provincial youth organizations. The Secretariat is composed of 10 members elected from among the Presidium members. The main LSYY publication is the weekly *Mladost* (Youth) whose 30th anniversary was celebrated in January 1975.

Party Internal Affairs. The plenary session of the LCY Central Committee on 25 February 1975 dealt with ideological-political organization. In the major report, Jure Bilić, of the Executive Committee, stressed that "the LCY must not assume the role of a guardian, or impose itself on account of the strength of its authority." In this connection he mentioned the necessity of gaining respect for "democratic centralism," which "is not contrary to self-management." All tendencies to confine the individual republics and provinces within their own boundaries must be fought, Bilić said. He attacked not only the various exile organizations in Western countries, but also those "internal enemies who want to force on us a psychosis of uncertainty regarding the future." He also dealt with the problem of the "New Left" in Yugoslavia—a label given to the intellectuals associated with the banned philosophical bimonthly *Praxis*, who he said were not philosophers but rather "political manipulators" attempting to assume power. They had combined "bourgeois liberalism, anarchism, and dogmatism" and sought help abroad, Bilić added, further maintaining that only a dozen or so Yugoslav intellectuals (of approximately 200,000 in the party) have been involved in the anti-party struggle (*Borba*, 26 February).

In another report, distributed to the Central Committee members in advance, the Presidium reviewed the period since the 10th congress and also dealt with the problem of the LCY's participation in the conference of the European communist parties. The report emphasized that at the communist consultative meetings in Warsaw (October 1974) and Budapest (December 1974), the Yugoslav delegates insisted that a future conference of European communist parties (originally scheduled to take place in East Berlin in June 1975) "should be of a political, rather than ideological, character," and that no party whatsoever should be attacked, because such a conference must be an occasion "for a free and equal exchange of opinions." The report also stated that the LCY had not yet made a "final decision" about attending such a conference, but that an announcement would "come at the proper time" (ibid., 24 February).

The Presidium held nine sessions in 1975. On 30 January it discussed the work of the Presidium since the 10th LCY congress in May 1974, the ideological-political and organizational strengthening of the LCY, and suggested the election of new Presidium members. On 18 March it discussed the country's internal policy and defense. The 5 April session dealt with Aleksandar Grličkov's report concerning cooperation among the European communist parties. Economic problems were discussed on 22 April, in particular "economic crimes." On 8 May the ideological-political aspects of the country's economic developments in 1975 were reviewed. The 24 May session discussed the problems of banking and crediting. That of 9 July probed into LCY members' activities. On 15 October the Presidium examined preparations for the European communist conference and "inimical activities" in the country. The session of 11 December discussed implementation of the decisions made at the previous session concerning party cadre policy and approved the LCY delegation's stand at the 17-19 November meeting in East Berlin (see below). In addition, an extraordinary session, on 8 March commemorated the death of Veljko Vlahović.

The LCY took active part in the preparations for a conference of 28 European communist parties, for which there were seven preparatory meetings, all in East Berlin. The LCY delegation, headed by Aleksandar Grličkov, attended all but the meeting on 12-14 May. At none of the meetings was full agreement reached, especially not on the question of just when the conference should take place. Supported by the Italian, Romanian, Spanish, Swedish, and British communist parties, the LCY delegates refused to attend any conference which did not accept in advance the following basic conditions: complete autonomy for every party to determine its own policy; the conference to be open to the public and debate to be entirely free; all decisions to be unanimous—that is, the final resolution to be accepted by all participants; and no "directives" to be issued to the international communist movement by any "single center." (*Komunist*, Belgrade, 20 January; *Borba*, 12 March, 30 June; *Politika*, 20 August; *Borba*, 31 October; *Komunist*, 1 December; and Radio Zagreb, 10, 15 December.) At the 17-19 November session, in addition to the text of the final resolution supported by the LCY and some other parties, the conference was confronted by an East German text which the Yugoslavs described as "a great step backward" in that it tried to reconvert a "political document" into an "ideological platform" (*Sueddeutsche Zeitung*, Munich, 11 December). Despite existing differences concerning the text of the final resolution of the planned conference, the Yugoslavs believed that by January 1976—"unless something unforeseen happens"—agreement would be reached and the date for the conference set (Radio Zagreb, 20 November).

Domestic Affairs. *Committee for Defense of Constitutional Order.* The State Presidency of the SFRY, headed by Tito, decreed on 20 February 1975 the formation of a Committee on the Defense of Constitutional Order. It is composed of the eight most powerful LCY personalities, and is headed by Vladimir Bakarić, the most prominent Croatian communist. The other members of the committee are Lazar Koliševski, Macedonian; Vidoje Žarković, Montenegrin; Stane Dolanc, Slovene, secretary of the LCY Central Committee's Executive Committee; Džemal Bijedić, Moslem, premier of Yugoslavia; General Franjo Herljević, Croat, federal secretary for Internal Affairs; General Nikola Ljubičić, Serb, federal secretary for National Defense; and Miloš Minić, Serb, Yugoslavia's foreign minister. In a message to the army party conference, made the same day as the formation of the new Committee was announced, Tito warned that "the enemy at home and abroad aims at weakening the unity of the Yugoslav nations and nationalities" and "would especially like to weaken our defense capabilities" (Tanjug, 20 February). The establishment of the Committee was considered as a means to counteract internal enemies' activities, and also to help in maintaining order in the case of a possible Tito's succession crisis.

Internal Dissidents, Arrests, and Trials. The year was characterized by a series of oppositional activities of different kinds, repressed in one way or another by the authorities and sternly condemned by LCY leaders. In his annual summary of action against spies, saboteurs, political dissidents, and other critics of the government, Franjo Herljević, secretary for Internal Affairs, reported that about 200 political criminals from 13 different underground groups had been arrested in Yugoslavia during 1975 (*NYT*, 25 December). They belonged mainly to two groups: "bureaucratic statist Cominformists" implicated in different pro-Soviet activities (for details, see section on Yugoslav-Soviet relations, below) and "reactionary rightists and neo-fascists" linked with the West or pursuing their anti-Yugoslav activities in Western countries. On 17 February a court in Zadar sentenced 15 Croatians to prison terms ranging from 18 months to 13 years for subversive activities. They were indicted and condemned for being in contact with Croatian exiles of the Ustashi movement (which ruled Croatia during World War II), and for attempting as members of a so-called Croatian Liberation Revolutionary Organization to disrupt present Yugoslavia and establish an independent Croatian state (ibid., 18 February). A few days earlier, four Yugoslavs of Albanian origin were sentenced to terms of three to nine years for plotting against the state and the LCY (ibid., 16 January). Because of security considerations, 750 foreigners were barred or expelled from Yugoslavia in 1975 (ibid., 25 December).

In a different field of political dissidence, the state parliament of Serbia dismissed eight professors from the philosophy department of the University of Belgrade on 28 January, because of their persistent criticism of the LCY. Their activity was said to be "opposite to the aims and practice of the Yugoslav socialist society and the fundamental principles of the constitution, the self-managing development, and policy of the LCY" (Tanjug, 28 January). The dismissed professors were Mihajlo Marković, Ljubomir Tadić, Miladin Životić, Zagorka Pešić-Golubović, Svetozar Stojanović, Dragoljub Mićunović, Triva Indjić, and Nebojša Popov. Later in the year, the suspended professors appealed against their dismissal to the Yugoslav constitutional court, arguing that the special law passed by the Republic of Serbia in December 1974, which made possible their dismissal, was anti-constitutional and contrary to the principles of self-management socialism (*Neue Zürcher Zeitung*, 12 August). On 21 February, the internationally well-known magazine *Praxis* was forced to close. Published by the Croatian Philosophical Society of Zagreb, affiliated with the university, *Praxis* was the voice of Yugoslav Marxists strongly critical of the LCY. For years, in the magazine's articles, they argued that Yugoslav workers had no real decision-making role in or through the LCY, whose policies were assailed as verging at times on Stalinism.

Mihajlo Mihajlov, the Russian-born writer who had been released from prison in March 1970, after serving a three-and-one-half-year sentence for criticizing the Titoist regime, was arrested 7 October 1974, and on 28 February 1975 was sentenced again to seven years' imprisonment for offenses against Article 118 of the Criminal Code ("spreading hostile propaganda"). He was specifically charged with writing critically about the Yugoslav government in articles published by foreign periodicals, including the *New York Times.* After losing an appeal, Mihajlov was transferred to the main federal prison at Sremska Mitrovica where, on 6 December he was reported to have begun, with two other political prisoners, a hunger strike (*NYT*, 22 December).

The Eighth Congress of the Writers' Union of Yugoslavia. The holding of this congress (postponed several times), at Belgrade on 2-4 October, indicated on the one hand the regime's intention to strengthen its influence over the Yugoslav writers, and on the other hand the opposition of the most prominent writers to toeing the party line. Although 1,556 authors, including editors, were present at the congress, the most prominent Yugoslav writers of all nationalities did not attend the congress or simply boycotted it. The fact that the main speaker at the congress was not a literary man, but Stane Dolanc, secretary of the LCY Executive Committee, underlined the regime's determination to fight nonconformism in the literary life. Consequently, Dolanc warned the congress that the LCY "will always be against those in the cultural sphere who try to use the slogan of freedom of creativity as a political weapon against our revolution. . . . [Freedom] cannot be used as a bunker form which to fire at the freedom of others in the name of reaction and counter-revolution." He added: "The progressive forces of society, with the League of Communists at their head, cannot allow development to be spontaneous. These forces must work to establish a favorable socio-political climate in which the criteria with regard to creativity will be based upon a stream of humanistic creativity directed toward realization of a socialist self-managed society." (*Borba*, 3 October.) The new statutes of the Writers' Union, adopted at the congress, reflected Dolanc's views: the union was organically linked with the SAWPY, the LCY's "transmission belt" in implementing its domestic and foreign policies. Moreover, the "party aktivs," small groups of dedicated party members, will be permanently engaged in controlling the implementation of the LCY policies in all the federated writers' unions, on both republican and province levels.

Still in the field of political controversies implicating prominent literary figures, *Borba* (8 June) published an open letter from the president of the Slovenian Academy of Sciences, Josip Vidmar, to the German Nobel Prize author Heinrich Böll, who had written in defense of the 70-year-old Slovenian poet and philosopher Edvard Kocbek. The latter, a left-wing Catholic, who had fought with the Yugoslav partisans during the war, and after the war had assumed the highest governmental functions, had provoked a storm of official criticism for lamenting in an interview in the Trieste Slovenian-language periodical *Zaliv* about the fate of more than 12,000 Slovenian anti-communist fighters executed after the war by the partisans.

Ivo Andrić, the Yugoslav writer who won the Nobel Prize for literature in 1961 for his novel-chronicle, *The Bridge on the Drina*, and other works, died on 13 March in a Belgrade hospital at the age of 82. His works were translated into 24 languages.

State-Church Relations. Organized religion, and especially the Roman Catholic church, was under increased attack by the Yugoslav authorities throughout 1975. A member of the executive committee of the Croatian party openly attacked the Catholic church in Croatia for anti-socialist activity, charging it with "using a whole arsenal of various methods, from open attacks to covert criticism. Such are the attempts of the clergy, using its publications with a circulation of over 1 million copies monthly, and ideological schools in which about 4,000 students are being trained and ideologically indoctrinated" (*Borba*, Zagreb, 26 January). On its side, the largest Yugoslav Catholic paper, *Glas Koncila*, published in Zagreb, in a 16 March editorial openly accused the state officials of a number of illegal and anti-constitutional acts directed against the church and the faithful. Speaking in the name of religious freedom, the editorial pleaded with the authorities to cease their discriminatory practices and engage in a sincere dialogue with the Christians. At a 26 November meeting of the Coordination Committee for Nationwide Defense and Public Self-Protection, its president, General Djoko Jovanić of the Yugoslav army, exclaimed: "We shall fight against the class enemy, and also against economic crime and against activity of the church, bearing in mind that the political opponent is constantly active" (*NYT*, 22 December). Harsh new laws governing activities of all churches are in preparation and expected to be soon enacted.

Economy. Unfavorable international and domestic factors contributed to general instability in the Yugoslav economy in 1975. Industrial production between January and May was 8.6 percent higher than for that period in 1974 but down from the average 11 percent increase for 1974 as a whole (*Quarterly Economic Review: Yugoslavia*, London, no. 3, 1975, p. 8). Wheat harvest of 4,415,000 tons was below the average for the last ten years and 33 percent below the 1974 record harvest (Tanjug in English, 15 September). The possibility exists that before the next harvest Yugoslavia will be forced to import wheat in order to supplement the country's needs.

The foreign trade deficit continued to be heavy. During the first ten months Yugoslavia exported goods worth 3,289,000,000 dollars, 6 percent more than in the corresponding 1974 period. The value of imports, though recording an increase of only 2 percent compared with last year, was still nearly double that of exports. From January to the end of October 1975, goods totaling 6,350,000,000 dollars were imported (ibid., 14 November). This slight improvement was the result of a 21 June governmental decision (in force until the end of the year) to introduce tighter import restrictions on a 117-item list including certain basic food items, beverages, records, cosmetics, detergents, household appliances, and automobile tires (*Quarterly Economic Review*, no. 3, p. 14; *Politika*, 21 June). Better prospects for Yugoslavia's foreign trade, and consequently for the economy at large, are in view because of expanding trade relations with both the United States and the Soviet Union (for details see below, in "Foreign Affairs" section dealing with the Yugoslav-Soviet and Yugoslav-U.S. relations). Likewise, Yugoslav enterprises have greatly expanded business relations with developing countries in recent years.

Soaring inflation of about 30 percent, low labor productivity (with an alarming high rate of absenteeism from work), the unresolved problem of illiquidity of enterprises, and loss of anticipated hard currency from invisible earnings because of the contracted volume of remittances from emigrant workers and an unsatisfactory tourist season were other economic woes with which the new 1976-80 plan will have to cope.

In June Yugoslavia celebrated the 25th anniversary of its self-management system, that most distinctive mark of the Titoist regime. The tightening of LCY controls during the last few years and the imperative of a genuine democratic decentralization required by self-management continued to represent the fundamental contradiction of Tito's Yugoslavia, without a solution in sight.

Foreign Affairs. *The Soviet Union.* In 1975, Yugoslav-Soviet relations were pursued under the impact of two conflicts: the first over the convocation of the conference of European communist parties (see above), and the second in connection with "Cominformist activities" in Yugoslavia. On the other hand, there was a favorable trend in economic relations, although not all of Moscow's promises were fulfilled. In his concluding speech at the LCY Central Committee plenum on 25 February, Tito denied that Yugoslavia was in danger "from other socialist countries, particularly the Soviet Union" (*Borba*, 27 February). Bilić, in his report did not refer to "Cominformist dangers," but did mention the influence of "fascist groups" from abroad (ibid., 26 February).

Tito's and Bilić's friendly words about the Soviet Union obviously were inspired by the approaching visit of a Soviet economic delegation, which conferred in Belgrade on 1-8 March about trade, industrial and scientific-technical cooperation (*Politika*, 9 March). Preparations were made for a session of the Soviet-Yugoslav Committee for Economic Cooperations, which took place in Moscow between 24 and 31 March. The Yugoslav delegation, led by Vice Premier Berislav Šefer, discussed economic cooperation for the next five years (1976-1980) with Soviet Vice-Premier Vladimir Novikov. This year's trade beween Yugoslavia and the Soviet Union was expected to amount to "about 2,000 million dollars" (ibid., 1 April). But, despite progress of this sort, there remained structural problems in the development of economic relations between the two countries, especially the problem of 990,000,000 dollar Soviet credit (agreed upon on 2 November 1972) which could not be solved, despite several mutual visits between economic and political leaders during the course of the year.

Yugoslavia's Premier Džemal Bijedić made his first official visit in this capacity to the Soviet Union between 9 and 15 April. During the visit, both sides took pains to avoid publicly any differences arising. Concerning the quarrel over the role of Yugoslav Partisans in World War II, and the "minimizing" of this role by Soviet Marshals Yakubovsky (in the Prague daily *Rudé Právo* of 25 March) and Grechko (in the Czechoslovak army newspaper *Obrana Lidu* of 3 April), Bijedić and Kosygin reached a "compromise" according to which the Yugoslavs recognized that the Soviet Union "bore the main burden of the war and played a decisive role in the victory over fascism," while "the Yugoslav peoples, led by the Communist Party of Yugoslavia, waged, from the very first days of the war, a heroic struggle for their national and social liberation and did everything in their power to help bring about general victory" (*Borba*, 16 April). Aleksandar Grličkov's visit to Moscow on 14-17 May was devoted to an examination of differences concerning the conference of European communist parties (ibid., 18 May).

In June, Yugoslavia marked the 10th anniversary of the Belgrade Declaration (signed on 2 June 1955 by Nikolai Bulganin and Tito), considered the basis for the idea of "various roads to socialism" recognized by Moscow seven years after Tito's expulsion from the Cominform in June 1948. From the very beginning of 1975, there were arrests of "Cominformist elements" throughout the country. The intensification of the anti-Cominformist campaign began when it was reported that former Yugoslav army colonel Vlado Dapčević, 62, a pro-Moscow exile holding a Belgian passport and living in Brussels, was kidnaped on 9 August in Bucharest by the agents of Yugoslavia's secret police (with the connivance of the Romanian authorites) and spirited across the border into Yugoslavia (*Sunday Times*, London, 26 October). The full-fledged anti-Cominformist campaign, launched by the announcement of the arrest of a dozen "Cominformist elements," was stepped up after the Presidium session on 15 October. As noted above, that session discussed two topics: the East Berlin preparatory meeting for a conference of communist parties and "inimical activities" in the country. The very coupling of these two "hot" topics indicated that relations between Moscow and Belgrade were not too good. On 17 October, Stane Dolanc spoke in Novi Sad, saying that Stalinists and Cominformists were "traitors to our country, to our working class, and to our party" (*Borba*, 18 October). A few days later, Vladimir Bakarić accused the pro-Soviet groups of being "the instrument of alien influence, whose political line amounts to compelling Yugoslavia to join the Warsaw Pact" (*Tanjug*, in English, 21 October). Tito, on 30 October (*Politika*, 31 October), and again Bakarić, on 20 November (*Vjesnik*, 22 November), repeated anti-Cominformist accusations, clearly implying Moscow's influence.

After a long silence, the Moscow *Pravda* (27 November) published an article dissociating itself from "conspiratorial sectarian groups" in Yugoslavia (that is, from the Cominformists,) "who represent no one but themselves." But the Soviet party daily attempted to put the whole blame on "reactionary circles" in the West, who were allegedly trying to discredit the Soviet Union by inventing anti-Yugoslav activities and implicating the USSR in them. The subsequent visit to Moscow of Yugoslav foreign minister Miloš Minić 8-11 December was said to have brought about "full unanimity" of views (*Borba*, 12 December), although, in a radio commentary during Minić's visit in Moscow, the Yugoslavs emphasized that "the CPSU has not changed its stand on relations and cooperation in the communist movement and among socialist countries" (Radio Zagreb, 10 December). Minić's talks with Gromyko and Kosygin supplied no evidence that their efforts to take the strain out of Soviet-Yugoslav relations were successful. Dolanc's short stopovers in Moscow on 20 October (on his way to Mongolia) and 9 November (on his way back home) were no more successful. On the other hand, the economic talks in Belgrade (9-12 December) between Soviet vice-premier Ivan Arkhipov and Berislav Šefer seemed more successful (*Borba*, 13 December). On 8 December the

Soviet foreign trade minister Nikolai Patolichev and his Yugoslav counterpart, Emil Ludviger, signed in Moscow a five-year economic accord under which bilateral trade is to increase by 150 percent over the next five years, amounting to 14,000 million dollars (the 1971-75 trade exchange between the two countries totaled only 5,000 million dollars). Ludviger stated that the new agreement was "the largest Yugoslavia had ever signed (ibid., 9 December).

Yugoslavia appointed Jože Smole its new ambassador to Moscow in October (ibid., 11 October).

People's Republic of China. The improvement in Chinese-Yugoslav relations which took place in 1974 was strengthened in 1975. Yugoslavia's opposition to Moscow's domination within the international communist movement found favorable backing in China. A Chinese military delegation, headed by General Hsiang Chung-hua, deputy chief of staff, paid an official visit to Yugoslavia on 30 May-7 June. General Hsiang hailed Yugoslavia's struggle for "state sovereignty and national independence" (NCNA, 31 May). The culminating point in Yugoslav-Chinese relations was an official visit to Peking by Džemal Bijedić (6-12 October), the first Yugoslav premier to visit China. Bijedić was received by Mao Tse-Tung, who extended his greetings to President Tito (*Borba*, 13 October). During a toast by Chinese vice-premier Teng Hsiao-ping, the Soviet ambassador to Peking and his Warsaw Pact collegues (with the exception of Romania) walked out of the banquet hall during Teng's speech (*Vjesnik*, 12 October). Teng was invited to visit Yugoslavia, an invitation which he accepted "with pleasure." The date of the visit will be fixed later. According to the joint communiqué, the two sides declared they were "ready to develop and strengthen many sided cooperation . . . based on equality, independence, and mutual trust" (*Borba*, 13 October). Both the Chinese and the Yugoslavs did their utmost to stress how their mutual relations had improved, even though the Yugoslavs avoided saying anything that would involve their country in the Sino-Soviet conflict. A press commentary emphasized that "the improvement of Yugoslav-Chinese relations does not harm the Soviet Union (which has recently proposed normalization of interstate relations to Peking) or the United States (whose President is preparing to visit Peking, as did his predecessor, Nixon)" (*Vjesnik*, 12 October).

As for economic relations between the two countries, Bijedić's visit to Peking should boost trade, which increased, from 1969 to 1974, from 1,600,000 dollars to 144,000,000 dollars (*Komunist*, 13 October).

Albania. Yugoslav-Albanian relations are characterized by the fear shared by both countries of the Soviet Union and by the existence of a huge Albanian national minority in Yugoslavia (more than 1,300,000 according to the March 1971 census). During Tito's visit to Kosovo, in April 1975, both he and Bakalli emphasized "good neighborly relations" between the two countries. Tito said that, because Albania and Yugoslavia wanted to preserve their independence, "we can construct our cooperation on that basis," and that Albanian leaders would see that "occasional attacks" on Yugoslavia "harm mutual relations." Tito added, however, that the Yugoslavs "should not be too sensitive" over such attacks. (*Borba*, 5 April.) Later, however, an Albanian-language paper (*Rilindja*, Priština, 9 November) charged the "Cominformists" with the aim "of bringing about the secession of Kosovo and other regions of Yugoslavia in which Albanians live." The publication of Enver Hoxha's Collected Works in Tirana also provoked a Yugoslav reaction, because of some "crude attacks" against Yugoslavia.

Albanian-Yugoslav economic relations developed favorably. Yugoslavia is Albania's second most important partner, after China, in the foreign trade field (*Nedeljne novosti*, Belgrade, 8 June). While the value of trade in both directions amounted to a mere 5,000,000 dollars in 1970, by 1974 the 40,000,000 dollar mark had been reached (*Review of International Affairs*, 20 June). For 1975, a 53,000,000 dollar trade (in both directions) was envisaged. By the end of March, Albania had imported Yugoslav goods valued at 26,000,000 dollars, while exporting to Yugoslavia goods valued at 12,000,000 dollars (Tanjug in English, 9 April).

Bulgaria. During the whole of 1975, Yugoslav information media were full of various types of attack against Bulgaria. Four familiar points constantly recurred in the controversy: (1) the inhabitants of both Yugoslav Macedonia and Pirin Macedonia (in Bulgaria) are not Bulgarians, but Macedonians; (2) they have their own language, which differs from both Serbian and Bulgarian; (3) the Bulgarian troops that were the "fascist occupiers" of Macedonia between 1941 and 1945 did not play a decisive role in the liberation of Yugoslavia; and (4) "Greater Bulgarian chauvinism" had been an obstacle, not only to the improvement of Yugoslav-Bulgarian relations, but also to the consolidation of the situation in the Balkans as a whole. The official visit to Belgrade of Bulgarian foreign minister Petar Mladenov (11-13 November) was seen in Yugoslavia as a "sign of new developments in the relations between the two countries" (Radio Belgrade, 13 November), even though the fact that Tito did not receive Mladenov indicated that the existing difficulties had not been fully solved. In a joint communiqué, it was said that the "disputed questions" would be solved "during a meeting between Josip Broz Tito and Todor Zhivkov on a date to be agreed upon later by the two sides" (*Borba*, 14 November). One day after Mladenov left for home, the Skoplje daily *Nova Makedonija* (14 November) sharply attacked the preparations for the census that was to be taken in Bulgaria (1-8 December) as designed to "eradicate" the Macedonian national minority in Bulgaria. In addition, the paper accused the Bulgarian leaders of "glorifying the Bulgarian fascist army, i.e., Bulgarian fascism."

The culminating point in this bilateral squabbling was reached during and after the census in Bulgaria, although no final results were announced. The Yugoslavs claimed that while the 1956 census in Bulgaria reported 178,862 people in Pirin Macedonia who declared themselves to be Macedonians, the 1965 census found only 8,750 (ibid.). How many Macedonians there were after the December 1975 census was not published. However, the Yugoslavs anticipated that only a few would have been courageous enough to declare themselves Macedonians. In an interview given to the Belgrade tabloid *Večernje novosti* (15 December), first secretary of the Blagoevgrad District party committee Petar Dyulgerov, a candidate-member of the Bulgarian party's Central Committee, said that only people with "anti-socialist and anti-Bulgarian" feelings declared themselves Macedonians in the last census. Dyulgerov said there were no Macedonians in Bulgaria at all, and that the Bulgarian party had corrected "past mistakes," when people were forced to declare themselves Macedonians.

Despite all the political difficulties, trade relations between the two countries developed normally. The trade protocol for 1976, signed in Sofia on 7 November, provides for a 260,000,000 dollar exchange of goods "in both directions," about 20 percent higher than in 1975 (*Borba*, 8 November). On 15 December, a five-year trade agreement (1976-80) was signed in Sofia providing for an exchange of goods to the value of 1,280 million dollars, three times higher than the present, 1971-75, five-year agreement (*Borba*, 16 December).

Romania. Romania is the only Warsaw Pact country with which Yugoslavia maintains good and really friendly relations. Meetings between top party and state leaders of the two countries took place over the whole course of the year. On 31 January and 1 February Nicolae Ceauşescu conferred with Stane Dolanc in the Romanian town of Timesoara (ibid., 3 February). On 6-8 February, Romanian defense minister Ion Ionita paid an official visit to Yugoslavia (ibid., 9 February). How close Yugoslav-Romanian cooperation was can best be demonstrated by a report in April that the two countries had designed and manufactured a prototype fighter aircraft to be used by both their air forces (Agerpres and Tanjug, 15 April). On 28-30 April, Romania's foreign minister, Gheorghe Macovescu, paid an official visit to Belgrade, during which he formally requested Yugoslavia's support for Romania's request to be granted observer status at the nonaligned conference scheduled for Colombo, Sri Lanka, in 1976 (ibid., 3 May). On 22 May, Ceauşescu received Aleksandar Grličkov to discuss the conference of European communist parties (ibid., 23 May). On 2 July, Ceauşescu met with Edvard Kardelj, Yugoslavia's number two man, who came to Bucharest on 30 June after having visited Budapest and Prague. Romanian media reported that Romanian-Yugoslav relations, the international situation, and the world communist movement were discussed at the meeting (Radio Bucharest, 2 July). At the same time, it was reported that three young Romanians who tried to escape to the West through Yugoslavia took poison when they were caught and two of them died (*Le Monde*, 4 July). Romanian premier Manea Manescu paid an official visit to Yugoslavia on 26-29 September. Manescu and Bijedić signed a protocol providing for mutual goods exchanges worth 1,000 million dollars in 1980 (Radio Bucharest, 28 September). Between 6 and 9 October, Cornel Burtică, secretary of the Romanian party, suddenly arrived in Belgrade and had talks with Stane Dolanc and Todo Kurtović (*Komunist*, 13 October). Only hours after his talks with Burtică, Dolanc unexpectedly flew to Bucharest on 9 October to confer with Ceaușescu (*Borba*, 11 October). It was later reported (AFP, 10 October) that Ceaușescu would visit Belgrade on 14-17 October. Western news agencies (AFP, Reuter) reported on 13 October that Ceaușescu's visit was "indefinitely postponed," without giving any explanation. On 14 October, Reuter reported that the Yugoslav Foreign Ministry confirmed the postponement of Ceaușescu's visit, which led to various conjectures about alleged differences between the two countries. Finally, on 10-15 December, a delegation of the Romanian Grand National Assembly, headed by its president, Nicolae Giosan, visited Belgrade and was received by Tito (ibid., 16 December).

Trade between Yugoslavia and Romania in 1975 totaled about 350,000,000 dollars (ibid., 3 November).

Poland. Tito's 10-13 March visit to Poland took him not to Warsaw but to Rzeszow, capital of Poland's southeastern voivodship (*Vjesnik*, 14 March). The communiqué did not include any reference to the planned conference of communist parties. Western correspondents pointed out certain nuances in the toast by Tito and Edward Gierek that indicated diverse appraisals of certain problems, especially different approaches to the question of the role of the Soviet Union. Gierek, for example, praised the role of the Soviet Union, and of Leonid Brezhnev, in the pursuit of peace, while Tito, in his reply, ignored both the Soviet Union and Brezhnev (*Frankfurter Allgemeine Zeitung*, 13 March).

Poland's premier Piotr Jaroszewicz paid an official visit to Yugoslavia on 23-25 April, where he engaged chiefly in economic talks, and was also received by Tito (*Borba*, 26 April). On 4-6 June, Edward Babiuch, a member of the Polish Politburo and central committee secretary, came to Belgrade for discussions with Aleksandar Grličkov about the convocation of the conference of communist parties (Tanjug, 5 June). Between 7 and 13 July, a delegation of the Polish parliament paid an official visit to Yugoslavia. The delegation of the LCY to the congress of the Polish party held in Warsaw on 7-12 December was headed by Vojo Srzentić, a member of the LCY Executive Committee (*Borba*, 13 December).

During the first eight months of the year, Polish-Yugoslav trade came to 246,000,000 dollars (Yugoslav exports, 112,000,000; imports, 134,000,000) out of a total of 350,000,000 dollars projected for 1975 (ibid., 20 September). On 24 October, a trade protocol was signed in Belgrade noting that the 1976 volume of Yugoslav-Polish trade was planned to reach the 490,000,000 dollar mark (Tanjug, 25 October). A long-term trade agreement between the two countries for the 1976-80 period, signed in Belgrade on 20 November, stipulated that the value of the total volume of commodity trade during the next five years reach 3,300 million dollars, which is about 2.5 times larger than the value of trade in the last five-year agreement (ibid., 20 November).

Czechoslovakia. On 3-5 February, Vasil Bil'ák, Presidium member and Central Committee secretary of the Czechoslovak party had talks in Belgrade with Stane Dolanc and Aleksandar Grličkov about bilateral relations and the situation within the international communist movement (*Borba*, 6 February). An article by Czechoslovak General Vaclav Horaček in a Yugoslav weekly (*Narodna armija*, Belgrade, 1 May) attracted great interest, because Horaček quoted Tito as having said the following in October 1973, during a visit to Yugoslavia by Czechoslovak party and state delegation:

"Formally, we are not in the Warsaw Pact, but, if the cause of socialism and communism should be at stake, we know well where our place is. We want you never to doubt where we stand. Our goals are common with yours, with the Soviet Union's." On 18 July, the editor in chief of *Narodna armija* denied that Yugoslavia was returning to the Warsaw Pact, and put the blame for such rumors on "certain reactionary political circles both in Europe and outside it."

In May, an agreement was concluded between Belgrade and Prague providing for the unrestricted employment of Yugoslav labor in Czechoslovakia. This is the first agreement of its kind that Yugoslavia has reached with an East European country. At that time, there were about 7,000 Yugoslav workers in Czechoslovakia (*Politika*, 19 May). According to the agreement, about 2,000 Yugoslav workers could annually get jobs there (ibid., 22 May).

Between 26 and 30 June, Edvard Kardelj visited Bratislava and Prague where he conferred with Vasil Bil'ák and was received by Gustav Husák (Radio Prague, 30 June). Tito and Husák met in Helsinki on 11 August (*Borba*, 12 August). On 8-10 December, Czechoslovak premier Lubomír Štrougal paid an official visit to Yugoslavia, where he was received by Tito, and conferred with Bijedić (ibid., 11 December). Yugoslavia's defense minister, General Nikola Ljubičić, headed an army delegation which visited Czechoslovakia between 13 and 17 October (Tanjug, 17 October).

Trade between the two countries in 1975 was expected to be 700,000,000 dollars (*Politika*, 21 June). On 10 December, a five-year (1976-80) trade agreement was signed in Belgrade providing for a 4,300 million dollar trade turnover, twice as much as in the previous five-year period. A trade protocol for 1976 was also signed, projecting a trade valued at 742,000,000 dollars (*Borba*, 11 December).

Hungary. Hungarian foreign minister Frigyes Puja made an official visit to Belgrade on 7-9 January, 1975. Puja's visit came at a time when "no major problems" existed between Yugoslavia and Hungary (Tanjug, 6 January). The Yugoslavs emphasized their excellent treatment of the Hungarian national minority in Yugoslavia (it numbers about 500,000 and there are about 100,000 Yugoslavs in Hungary), making comparisons with the bad treatment meted out to Yugoslav nationals in Austria and Bulgaria (*Vjesnik*, 5-6 January). According to the Yugoslav press, there were some disagreements "over some international problems," but these differences were not of a nature "to harm the real cooperation existing between the two countries also on the international plane" (*Komunist*, 13 January). Strangely enough, Puja was not received by Tito, as was his predecessor in May 1967.

Jure Bilić represented the LCY at the congress of the Hungarian Socialist Workers' Party in Budapest (17-22 March). Bilić especially defended the policy of nonalignment (*Borba*, 20 March). Edvard Kardelj visited Hungary on 23-26 June, where he talked with János Kádár (ibid., 27 June). In August, it was reported that Yugoslavia had succeeded in obtaining the necessary financing for the construction of its first oil pipeline (the Adria Pipeline) which will run through Yugoslavia to Hungary and Czechoslovakia; the two countries will contribute 25,000,000 dollars each to the project, in addition to funds to be provided by Kuwait, Libya, the World Bank, and Yugoslavia itself (a total of about 400,000,000 dollars). Construction is scheduled to begin in the spring of 1976 (*Vjesnik u srijedu*, 6 August; *Vjesnik*, 7 August). An agreement was signed in Budapest on 16 September providing for a 30,000,000 dollar credit from Hungary (Radio Budapest, 16 September).

The volume of Yugoslav-Hungarian trade (in both directions) was projected to be 270,000,000 dollars (*Economic Review*, Belgrade, August 1975). During the first eight months, however, only 128,000,000 dollars were realized, which was below the level envisaged. Industrial cooperation was particularly unsatisfactory (Tanjug, 15 October). Following a visit by the Hungarian trade minister in April, the two countries decided to double their trade, to more than 840,000,000 dollars in the next five years (Reuter, 25 April).

East Germany. Three top East German communist state and party functionaries visited Yugoslavia in 1975: Foreign Minister Oskar Fischer (21-23 April), Premier Horst Sindermann (11-15 June) and Politburo member Hermann Axen of the East German party (18-20 June). During the first two visits, mainly bilateral relations between the two countries were discussed, while Axen's visit was in connection with interparty relations and with the preparations for the convocation of the conference of European communist parties. The fact, however, that Fischer also met with Aleksandar Grličkov, in charge of relations with other communist parties (*Politika*, 23 April), indicated that LCY participation in the conference was also discussed. The volume of trade for 1975 was projected to be about 500,000,000 dollars (*Borba*, 10 June), while the five-year (1971-75) trade was expected to amount to 1,300 million dollars (*Politika*, 10 June). The signing of a trade protocol for the next five-year period (1976-80) in East Berlin on 3 August provided for trade amounting to 3,000 million dollars (*Borba*, 4 August). The signing of a new friendship treaty between the Soviet Union and East Germany in Moscow on 7 October provoked criticism in the Yugoslav press. It was claimed that the new treaty, signed nine years before the old one's 20-year term expired, contained the same formulation used by the Warsaw Pact countries in 1968 to explain the invasion of Czechoslovakia (*Politika*, 10 October).

Cuba. On 17-19 March, 1975, the third ministerial meeting of the Co-ordinating Bureau of the Nonaligned Countries took place in Havana, at which Miloš Minić, Yugoslavia's foreign minister, was present (*Review of International Affairs*, 20 April). At the First Congress of the Cuban Communist Party in Havana (16-23 December), Todo Kurtović, a member of the Executive Committee, represented the LCY (*Borba*, 18 December). An economic delegation from Cuba paid a two-week visit to Yugoslavia (6-19 November), discussing economic relations between the two countries (ibid., 20 November). No results of the visit were reported in the Yugoslav information media. In May 1975, it was reported that the value of Yugoslav-Cuban trade in 1974 was 25,000,000 dollars, but that there was "a large Yugoslav deficit" of more than 20,000,000 dollars (*Economic Review*, May 1975).

West and Central Europe; the Balkans. Except for his participation in the Conference on European Security and Cooperation at Helsinki (29 July-1 August), President Tito did not pay a visit to any Western country in 1975. Yugoslavia's foreign minister, however, visited several countries and received many visitors from abroad. Except for President Ford's visit, the Yugoslav-Italian accord on the frontiers between the two countries was considered in Yugoslavia the most important event of the year involving a Western country. The so-called Trieste Agreement came after 30 years of quarreling between Belgrade and Rome about Zone A and Zone B. Boundaries were fixed in 1954, in a Memorandum of Understanding, which assigned the port of Trieste and some land around it (Zone A) to Italy, and the rest of the disputed territory (Zone B) to Yugoslavia. Neither government was then ready to surrender any legal claims, so the agreement was officially a "provisional" one, leaving open the chance of a revival of the dispute (*NYT*, 9 October). On 10 November, Yugoslavia's foreign minister and his Italian counterpart signed the agreement in Ancona, Italy, formally recognizing, with only minor changes, the borders drawn up in 1954 (*Politika*, 11 November).

Another significant event was a two-day official visit (4-5 June) by Greek premier Constantine Karamanlis. Received by Tito, Karamanlis discussed problems involved in Balkan cooperation (*Borba*, 5 June). In August, Yugoslav information media reported a message from Karamanlis concerning the initiative taken by him "to convoke a conference of Balkan countries for the purpose of furthering mutual cooperation in the economy, communications, energy and pollution" (*Politika*, 22 August). Tito gave a favorable answer on 22 September (*Borba*, 23 September). However, because of the Greek-Turkish conflict over Cyprus and the Yugoslav-Bulgarian dispute over Macedonia, the convocation of a Balkan conference (originally planned by the Greeks to take place on 25 October) was postponed to next year. Albania refused to be present, while Turkey accepted in principle (*Politika*, 11 October).

Other noteworthy visits to Yugoslavia were those of President Urho Kekkonen of Finland (21-25 March); Swedish Prime Minister Olof Palme (16-18 March); Foreign Minister Jean Sauvagnargues of

France (21-25 May); Willy Brandt, chairman of the West German Social-Democratic Party (24-25 June); President Francisco da Costa Gomes of Portugal (23-25 October); and Annemarie Renger, president of the West German Bundestag (17-22 November).

In addition to his above-mentioned visits, Yugoslavia's Foreign Minister Miloš Minić also went to the following countries: Portugal (12-14 October); West Germany (3-5 November); Norway (5-7 November); and the Netherlands (3-5 December).

European Economic Community. Relations between Yugoslavia and the EEC were disturbed at the beginning of 1975 because of the embargo on Yugoslav meat exports to the EEC (*Borba* 5 February). On 12-15 June, the president of the EEC Commission, François Ortoli, paid an official visit to Belgrade to discuss the implementation of the Yugoslav-EEC nonpreferential trade agreement, which went into force on 1 September, 1973 (ibid., 17 June). Yugoslav trade with the EEC normally represents 40 percent of Yugoslavia's foreign trade, but it was running a mounting balance-of-payments deficit with the EEC this past year. Difficulties appeared following the EEC's 1974 decision to ban all beef imports, in order to cut down surpluses within the community. Ortoli's visit led to new talks in July concerning the EEC's help to correct Yugoslavia's worsening balance-of-payments deficit (ibid., 24 July). Since it proved impossible to achieve an improvement, new talks began in Brussels in October (Tanjug, 21 October), and continued in Belgrade in November (ibid., 24 November). It was said that the final decision would be made only in January 1976 (ibid., 10 December).

Most of Yugoslavia's 1,100,000 workers employed in the West were to be found in the EEC countries, especially in West Germany, where 707,800 Yugoslavs (with family members) lived (*Nedeljne informativne novine*, Belgrade, 26 October).

The United States. Yugoslav-U.S. relations in 1975 were highlighted by two visits: Yugoslavia's Premier Bijedić visited Washington from 19-21 March, and U.S. President Gerald Ford paid a short call in Belgrade on 3-4 August. Both visits were given great publicity in Yugoslavia. Bijedić's visit to Washington was keyed to economic and commercial considerations. There were no major problems in U.S.-Yugoslav bilateral relations, although the two governments did not see eye-to-eye on every issue. In January, two U.S. opera singers were detained, and then expelled the following month, in connection with a suspected importing of "oppositional literature" while visiting Yugoslavia (Tanjug, 13 February). While in Washington, Bijedić was received by President Ford and conferred with the President of the World Bank about two loans amounting to 140,000,000 dollars (*Politika*, 21 March). A 600,000,000 dollar joint venture by the U.S. Dow Chemical Company and a Yugoslav oil firm in Zagreb, for the construction of a major petrochemical complex in the Yugoslav port of Rijeka, was also agreed upon (*Ekonomska politika*, Belgrade, 24 March). The contract was initialed in January.

There was great interest in the United States in doing business with Yugoslavia. In May, six commissions, composed of 85 American businessmen representing 45 companies, and 150 managers representing 90 Yugoslav enterprises, met in New York to discuss intensification of Yugoslav-U.S. economic cooperation (*Vjesnik*, 14 May). The trade between the two countries was expected to reach the 700 million dollar mark (*Journal of Commerce*, 5 November). By June 1974, the United States had concluded only eight joint-venture contracts, amounting in value to 7,500,000 dollars (*Borba*, 8 June). Between June 1974 and 1975, nine additional contracts were concluded, and 18 others were under consideration. This made the United States the third in the list of states with which Yugoslavia had undertaken such ventures. With approximately 600,000,000 dollars invested in Yugoslavia thus far, the United States now occupied first place in point of value.

The problem of U.S. sales of arms to Yugoslavia was also discussed during President Ford's stay in Belgrade, according to the Western information media (*Christian Science Monitor*, 6 August; *Baltimore Sun*, 16 August). During the visit of a group of U.S. Congressmen to Belgrade, Tito denied

Western reports that he had submitted a list of weapons he wanted to buy from the United States. What Yugoslavia wanted, Tito said, was to buy only military spare parts, some electronic equipment, and ammunition (UPI, 26 August). In September, Foreign Minister Minić met with U.S. Secretary of State Henry Kissinger in Washington (*Borba*, 27 September), and in November the U.S. Secretary of Agriculture paid an official visit to Belgrade (ibid., 21 November). Several days later, a U.S. citizen of Yugoslav origin was sentenced to seven years imprisonment, in a secret trial, for alleged espionage (*NYT*, 27 November).

Yugoslavia's new ambassador to the United States is Dimče Belovski, a Macedonian, whose appointment was announced in October (*Borba*, 25 October).

Nonalignment. There were two important nonaligned meetings in 1975: the meeting of the Co-ordinating Bureau of Nonaligned Countries in Havana (17-19 March), and the Fifth Ministerial Conference on Nonaligned Countries in Lima (25-30 August). The meeting in Cuba passed the 53-point Havana Declaration, and a short Resolution on Palestine (*Review of International Affairs*, 20 April), while the Lima conference adopted 13 resolutions dealing with various international problems (ibid., 5 October). In Lima, it was decided that the Fifth Nonaligned Summit should take place in Colombo (Sri Lanka) on 16-19 August 1976.

During 1975, President Tito and his chief aides made several statements reaffirming Yugoslavia's nonaligned stand. Of particular importance was Edvard Kardelj's September speech in Zagreb about Yugoslavia's nonaligned policy (ibid., 12 September).

Other Countries. Among visits to Yugoslavia in 1975 by officials of Asian, African, and Latin American countries were those of the presidents of Gabon, Tanzania, Egypt, North Korea, Indonesia, Mongolia, Senegal, People's Republic of Congo, and India; the King of Nepal; the prime ministers of Singapore, Australia and New Zealand; Prince Sihanouk of Cambodia; and the U.N. secretary-general, Kurt Waldheim.

Various high Yugoslav officials visited India, Mexico, Venezuela, Egypt, Syria, North Vietnam, Sri Lanka, Singapore, and Canada.

Publications. The chief publications of the LCY are *Komunist* (weekly) and *Socijalizam* (monthly). The most important daily newspapers are *Borba* (with Belgrade and Zagreb editions), *Politika* (Belgrade), *Vjesnik* (Zagreb), *Nova Makedonija* (Skoplje), *Oslobodjenje* (Sarajevo), and *Delo* (Ljubljana). The most important weeklies are *Vjesnik u srijedu* (Zagreb), and *Nedeljne informativne novine* (Belgrade). Tanjug is the official news agency.

Radio Free Europe   Slobodan Stanković
Munich

WESTERN EUROPE

Austria

The Communist Party of Austria (Kommunistische Partei Österreichs; KPÖ), founded on 3 November 1918, has enjoyed legal status during the entire democratic period of the Austrian Republic (1918-33 and since 1945). The party's political insignificance—it never has had more than three percent of Austria's parliamentary representation, and none since 1959—has been aggravated by two circumstances. First, Austria's position next to some of the People's Democracies caused the party to suffer from the Soviet interventions in Hungary (1956) and Czechoslovakia (1968). Second, the party does not unite all of Austria's communists. Trotskyists continue to compete in a few elections, and Maoists are active in student affairs.

In a country with a population of 7,575,000, and with a voting population of five million (with participation in excess of 90 percent), the KPÖ currently obtains no more than 55,000 votes. Membership estimates differ, but the number appears to be between 20,000 and 25,000.

The most important event for the KPÖ in 1975 was the parliamentary election of 5 October, where its showing was, if anything, poorer than usual. Its fate was noted by the respected *Salzburger Nachrichten* 6 October): "As regards the Communists, the decision of the Austrian voter was unmistakable. This party lacks significance."

The change in the Communist vote was small: 1.2 percent of the total, as against 1.4 percent in the previous election of 1971. The Socialists (Sozialistische Partei Österreichs; SPÖ) won 50.6 percent, the People's Party (ÖVP) 42.8 percent, and the Freedom Party (FPÖ) 5.4 percent, which came to a difference from 1971 of less than one percent for the SPÖ and ÖVP, and no change for the FPÖ. (*Arbeiter Zeitung*, Vienna, 6 October, preliminary results without absentee ballots.) In the final count the distribution of seats was unchanged: 93 for the SPÖ, 80 for the ÖVP, 10 for the FPÖ, and none for the Communists (*Wiener Zeitung*, 8 October).

There were provincial elections in Carinthia (2 March) and Tyrol (8 June). In Carinthia the election initially appeared hopeful for the KPÖ's effort to regain the one seat (of 36) they had lost in 1970. The Socialists, traditionally the party representing the Slovene minority, had made their peace with nationalist German circles, which caused the chairman of the Slovenes' central organization to leave the SPÖ and, early in the campaign, urge Slovenes to vote either for the KPÖ or for the KEL, a mostly Slovene unity list (*Volksstimme*, 11 February). The ethnic issue apparently cost the Socialists close to two percent of the vote, though they kept the majority of votes and seats, while the Communists and the KEL ended up with 2 percent each and neither gained a single seat. In Tyrol, the KPÖ increased its vote share to 0.6 percent (from 0.2).

Local elections took place in Lower Austria (6 April) and Styria (27 April), where Communists were among the serious competitors in some communities, and in Vorarlberg (13 April), where they were not. While the KPÖ vote in Lower Austria declined from 1.2 percent to 1.1, the party maintained its representation in a number of municipalities, especially in Brunn near Vienna, where it held its four council seats (with 14 percent) (ibid., 8 April). The total vote of the party in Styrian communities was slightly higher than in Lower Austria, an average of 1.4 percent (*Die Presse*, Vienna, 28 April). In Vorarlberg the KPÖ did not invade a single local council, but its province-wide votes increased from 168 to 475 (ibid., 14 April).

Toward the end of the year a number of corporations (including some nationalized ones) held elections of shop stewards. In 1972, Communists had been a strong minority, especially in nationalized steel works. In 1975 they generally lost the greater part of their seats on works councils (*Arbeiter-Zeitung*, 27 September; *Wiener Zeitung*, 16 October). In the major VÖEST-Alpine firm the KPÖ vote dropped to 9 percent, from 18 in 1971 (*Wiener Zeitung*, 17 October).

Austria's students voted on 14 and 15 May, in the first elections since the enactment of the Kreisky government's University Organization Act. The new law, attacked by the majority of the academic profession as dangerous to academic liberty, was attacked by the KPÖ as providing for only show student participation (*Weg und Ziel*, May 1975, pp. 202-4). There was no change in Communist representation: as in 1974, four seats (of 53) were divided among three Communist groups (*Arbeiter-Zeitung*, 17 May). Possibly more interesting than the student elections was a survey about students' voting preference in parliamentary elections, conducted by the Ministry of Science in 1973 and released in 1975. Two percent of the student sample answered that they would vote Communist. A further breakdown showed that this Communist voting preference was 2 percent among students from white-collar families, 5 percent among students from professional families; while elsewhere the ratio of Socialist to Communist voters among students was above ten to one, it was less than four to one in the case of students with professional family backgrounds. (Ibid., 24 July.)

Leadership and Organization. The organizational life of the KPÖ in 1975 was under the influence of the federal general election of 5 October. In December 1974 the call went out for an all-Austrian party conference on 25 January to set the tone for the election year. In a press conference, Franz Muhri, the party's chairman, pronounced the KPÖ's chief goal for 1975: "The gaining of a parliamentary seat in Vienna, and thus the [re]entry of the KPÖ into Parliament" (*Volksstimme*, 14 December 1974). When the conference convened, it found itself faced with a banner which read: "In the interest of all who work, Communists into Parliament" (ibid., 26 January 1975).

At the conference, the KPÖ's leading candidates for each provincial list were announced. There was the usual duplication. Franz Muhri led the lists in Vienna and Styria; Erwin Scharf, the veteran secretary of the Central Committee, in Lower Austria, Salzburg, and Tyrol; Anton Hofer, the Communist trade union chief, in Upper Austria and Vorarlberg; Hans Kalt, the editor of the *Volksstimme*, in Carinthia and Burgenland.

During 1975, party finances became a matter of public policy. According to the Party Finance Act, all parties receiving more than one percent of the vote are, upon application, entitled to a public subsidy. At various times during the discussion of the matter among the parties represented in Parliament, Muhri asserted that the KPÖ would spurn money that was also available to the neo-Nazi NDP—a red herring, as the NDP never polled one percent of the vote. Muhri finally announced formally the refusal of public funds on 13 August, stating also that the KPÖ had already collected 750,000 schillings (about U.S. $40,000) toward a proposed election budget of 1.5 to 2 million schillings (*Die Presse*, 14 August).

Another organizational issue in 1975 gave the Communist wing of the Trade Union Federation the opportunity to assert its autonomy. The SPÖ and its majority wing of the Trade Union Congress called a conference for 26 June to which Christian (Catholic) and Communist trade unionists were invited as individuals, not as organizations. The ÖVP wing of the movement declined immediately, attacking the proposed conference as Socialist election propaganda (ibid., 20 June). The KPÖ's negative answer came on 25 June. It also suspected Socialist election propaganda and further complained about lack of opportunity for a full discussion (*Arbeiter-Zeitung*, 26 June).

Domestic Attitudes and Activities. The KPÖ's four-point "alternative program,"passed by its party conference of 25 January 1975, addressed three major domestic issues: recession, inflation, and stabilization. As means against recession, the party proposed increased purchasing power for the masses, much of which would come about through tax reform. Measures proposed against inflation were to be an immediate freeze on prices, transportation and energy rates, and rents, and a reduction of sales profits. Stabilization was to be brought about through a massive public works program, to be financed by the elimination of tax favors and the rigorous collection of a tax debt claimed to amount to 8 billion schillings (close to U.S. $500 million). Programmatic speeches at the conference were made on behalf of workers, renters, women, and youth. Representing the latter, Willi Rau made the most militant speech, calling for extra-parliamentary agitation in factories, schools, and housing units.

In a theoretical article for the *World Marxist Review* (February, pp. 5-15), Muhri applied a Marxist-Leninist analysis to what he called the new state-monopoly capitalism. Pointing to an increase of controls of workers' rights, of the sheer number of wage and salary earners, and of alienated small producers, he found that the problem of the time, was to make clear to workers their true class interest, in the face of "the ideology and policy of social partnership which the reformist Social Democrat leaders are inculcating" (p. 14).

The Communist platform for the 1975 election was decided on by the meeting of the KPÖ's Central Committee on 22 May (*Volksstimme*, 28 May). The main domestic plank was headed "Right to Work for All." It dealt with the points raised at the January conference: recession, inflation, stabilization. Other planks dealt with housing, health, and the "Democratization of all Public Domains." More democracy was demanded for all levels of government, for unions, for the economy, for broadcasting, and for schools. A special plea for women's rights was added.

There was one more domestic initiative the party took. Just before the election, Nazi-hunter Simon Wiesenthal announced that Friedrich Peter, leader of the Freedom Party since 1963 and an admitted former Nazi, had been an active SS officer. The question soon became a major political football, involving also Chancellor Kreisky, as Peter would presumably have become vice-chancellor had there been no Socialist majority after 5 October. In a press release during the controversy, the KPÖ demanded "that Peter leave Austria's political scene" (*Wiener Zeitung*, 3 November).

International Views and Positions. The four-point program of the KPÖ's January 1975 conference contained one international item: foreign trade. Austria's allegedly one-sided Common Market orientation was opposed, and long-range trade arrangements with Socialist countries were urged.

In the March issue of *World Marxist Review* Erwin Scharf said about Austrian neutrality (pp. 20-21):

> To be sure, neutrality has proved unstable more than once since it was proclaimed, and has been a constant target of direct attacks and various manipulations by NATO and EEC. But Austrian neutrality has had powerful political and economic support from the socialist community, first of all from the Soviet Union. The existence of the socialist world system has been a decisive factor which Austria's Communists have constantly used in upholding their country's independence and neutrality and campaigning against attempts to draw Austria into the EEC. The progress of the European Conference on Security and Cooperation has shown their position to be correct.

The 1975 election platform had mostly domestic content. A notable exception was the following rationale for a proposed reorientation of Austria's foreign trade: "Growing exports into socialist countries that are free of crisis have greatly helped in still keeping the capitalist crisis less noticeable in Austria" (*Volksstimme*, 28 May).

In June, the KPÖ Politburo issued a statement voicing strong support for the Armed Forces Movement in Portugal, and castigating the Kreisky government for its support of the Portuguese Socialists (ibid., 22 June).

International and Party Contacts. A KPÖ delegation led by Franz Muhri visited the Central Committee of the Communist Party of Czechoslovakia on 23-26 March. The Austrians traveled to Prague and Bratislava, and though they met with the first secretary of the Slovak party, there was no indication that they conferred with top leaders in Prague. Among the communiqués was an appreciation of the role of the Red Army in Hitler's defeat 30 years earlier. (CTK, 27 March.)

On 11 April a delegation of the Central Committee of the Communist Party of the Soviet Union arrived in Vienna to participate in celebrating the 30th anniversary of the liberation of Austria (*Volksstimme*, 11 April). In mid-May, KPÖ delegations visited Budapest and Sofia. In July, there were visits to Bucharest and again to Sofia.

Publications. The KPÖ publishes the daily *Volksstimme* (People's Voice) in Vienna, and the monthly *Weg und Ziel* (Path and Goal). A circulation of about 70,000 is claimed for the daily paper.

The University of Alberta   F. C. Engelmann

Belgium

The Communist Party of Belgium (Parti Communiste de Belgique; PBC) was founded in 1921. Although the party is of only peripheral importance in Belgian politics, it is the largest of several contending Marxist-Leninist organizations. Other extreme-left parties include the Maoist Marxist-Leninist Communist Party of Belgium (Parti Communiste Marxiste-Léniniste de Belgique; PCMLB), the Flanders-based All Power to the Workers (Alle Macht ann de Arbeiders; AMADA), which is also Maoist in orientation, and the Trotskyist Revolutionary Workers' League (Lique Révolutionnaire des Travailleurs/Revolutionaire Arbeiders Liga; LRT/RAL). The PCB does not publicize net membership figures, but, rather, issues data on new members that join during a given year (without offering statistics as to those who left the party or did not renew their membership cards). In 1975, the PCB announced that, as of 20 October, 914 new members had joined the party (634 from Wallonia and 216 from Flanders). It was indicated, at that time, that nine of the party's federations (all in Wallonia and Brussels) had attained higher total memberships than at the same period in 1974. (*Le Drapeau Rouge*, 27 October). The PCB is believed to have between 10,000 and 12,500 members; the combined total membership of the other groups is probably around 2,000. The population of Belgium is some 10 million (estimated 1975).

In terms of electoral support, the PCB received 169,668 votes (3.2 percent) in the 10 March 1974 elections to the Chamber of Representatives. Although this represented a small increase from the previous (1971) parliamentary elections, when the party received 162,463 votes (3.1 percent), the PCB obtained one seat less in the 212-member Chamber, bringing its representation down to four. In simultaneously held elections to the Senate, the party retained its single representative. The Senate has 181 members: 106 directly elected, 50 appointed by provincial councils, and 25 co-opted by secret ballot. Finally, in the elections to the nine provincial councils' 720 seats (706 in 1971), the PCB obtained 9 seats (8 in 1971). The only other extreme-left party that participated in the 1974 elections was the Flemish Maoist AMADA. Contesting only four districts (Anvers, Gand, Hasselt, and Alost), it obtained a total of 19,784 votes. Most of these came from Anvers, where AMADA obtained 14,923 votes (2.8 percent). None of AMADA's candidates was elected.

Leadership and Organization. The PCB held its Twenty-first Congress on 14 to 16 December 1973. The Congress elected a 63-member Central Committee (see *Le Drapeau Rouge*, 21 December 1973), which, in turn, elected the party's Politburo, Secretariat, president and vice-presidents. The Politburo consisted of: Jean Blume, Urbain Coussement, Jan Debrouwere, Albert De Coninck, Augustin Duchateau, Robert Dussart, George Glineur, Claude Renard, Jef Turf, Frans Van den Branden, and Louis Van Geyt. The four-member Secretariat comprised Coussement, Debrouwere, De Coninck, and Renard. The party was headed by Louis Van Geyt, as president, with Jean Terfve and Jef Turf acting as vice-presidents for Wallonia and Flanders, respectively. The PCB has regional councils for Wallonia, Flanders and Brussels. At its conference, in April 1975, the Walloon regional council elected a new leadership. Claude Renard replaced Jean Terfve as president. Terfve, however, remained vice-president of the PCB. (For further details, see *Le Drapeau Rouge*, 22 April.) Other changes in 1975 included the deaths of Central Committee members Alex Liénard (in January) and Isabelle Blume (in March).

The PCB directs a youth organization, the Communist Youth of Belgium (Jeunesse Communiste de Belgique; JCB), which, in 1975, was led by Marc Somville (president) and Prosper Grunewald (secretary-general), a student group called the National Union of Communist Students (Union Nationale des Etudiants Communistes; UNEC), and a children's organization, the Union of Pioneers (Union des Pionniers). The party does not have its own labor union, but exerts peripheral influence in the country's largest trade union, the General Workers' Federation of Belgium (Fédération Générale du Travail de Belgique; FGTB).

Domestic Attitudes and Activities. With only a small base of support in the country, the PCB has repeatedly stressed the need for alliances with other "progressive" political formations. The most important of the latter has been the Belgian Socialist Party (Parti Socialiste Belge; PSB). The PCB's courtship of the Socialist Party had suffered a setback in 1973, when the Socialists formed a coalition government with the Christian Social Party (Parti Social-Chrétien/Christelijke Volkspartij; PSC/CVP) and the Liberal Party (Parti de la Liberté et du Progrès/Partij voor Vrijheid en Vooruitgang; PLP/PVV), under the premiership of PSB leader Edmond Leburton. The PSB went back into toe opposition in 1974, and a new government was formed under Christian Social leader Léo Tindemans. During 1975, the PCB paid close attention to PSB views and activities, quickly pointing out any perceived signs of moderation in the Socialists' role of opposition party and/or trends toward reintegration into government.

The PCB's own stance was one of total opposition against any measures that would help the government surmount the country's economic difficulties. It repeatedly stressed that it would not accept calls for self-sacrifice and austerity, which, it claimed, were directed solely at the workers. Instead, throughout the year, the PCB publicized and participated in agitation and labor disputes. In the early months of the year, in particular, the communiqués of the party's Politburo almost invariably included expressions of "support with all workers struggling against the policy of austerity" (see, e.g., *Le Drapeau Rouge*, 9 and 25/26 January, and 6 March). At a press conference, following a meeting of the party's Central Committee at the end of March, Louis Van Geyt emphasized that "moderation would only aggravate the country's economic crisis" (ibid., 26 March). Within this context, the Socialist Party was often a target of crticism for its alleged lack of militancy. As noted in an editorial in *Le Drapeau Rouge* (4 July), the PSB leadership's response to government policy was guardedly limited. A month later, the party newspaper claimed that the PSB co-president, André Cools, was ready to carry through the government's policy of austerity, and asked whether this was a sign that the Socialists were ready to join the Tindemans government (ibid., 6 August). The party reacted strongly (ibid., 22 September) to suggestions made by Edmond Leburton that the PSB should reintegrate into the government. Although it expressed relief (ibid., 13 October) when the Socialist Party's Congress affirmed that the PSB would remain in the opposition, the PCB remained wary of the Socialist leadership's intentions.

Aside from industrial agitation, the PCB devoted considerable attention during the first half of the year to publicizing its campaign against the spending of an alleged 30 billion francs for the replacement of Belgium's combat aircraft (within the framework of NATO's decision to up-date its F-104 G's for newer planes). As early as mid-January, Louis Van Geyt had stated in a speech to the Chamber of Representatives that the party's domestic activity was "indissolubly linked" with its struggle against "Atlanticism" and for détente (ibid., 15 January). The campaign against the replacement of the F-104 G's was seen in the same context (see, e.g., ibid., 10 April and 7/8 June).

The PCB's stance regarding Belgium's regional and ethnic problems was reiterated in an interview given by Louis Van Geyt in mid-July. He stressed that the PCB called for the creation of regional assemblies elected by direct universal suffrage, with executive bodies responsible to them. The regions would have to have adequate financial support to carry out policies of regional interest. (Ibid., 14 July).

International Views and Positions. While it has generally supported the views of the Soviet Union and the Communist Party of the Soviet Union (CPSU), the PCB has at times (as in the case of the Soviet-led invasion of Czechoslovakia) offered relatively strong criticism. The party has also tended to take a guardedly conciliatory attitude vis-à-vis the Chinese. During 1975, the PCB continued to publicize the "achievements" of the Soviet Union, but made few pronouncements on its relationship with the CPSU, except to insist that the latter was governed by the documents adopted at the 1969 World Conference of Communist Parties (see, e.g., *Le Drapeau Rouge*, 11 August). The joint communiqué issued at the end of Louis Van Geyt's visit to Moscow, in May, referred to the "community of the two parties views on all the essential questions discussed" (ibid., 23 May). The communiqué issued at the end of a visit in October made by a PCB delegation to the strongly pro-Soviet Communist Party of Czechoslovakia (CPCZ) noted "with gratification" that "the relations of comradely cooperation and international unity between the CPCZ and the PCB are successfully developing," and added that the talks had demonstrated "the full identity of opinions held by the two parties" on the questons discussed (*Pravda*, Bratislava, 1 November). This communiqué also stressed "the significance of the resolute ideological fight against all manifestations of anti-communism and anti-sovietism," and condemned "the harmful splitting policy of China's Maoist leadership." (Ibid.)

The PCB's criticism of Chinese policies was stronger than in previous years, particularly in response to Peking's calls for West European military preparedness against the Soviet Union. On the occasion of Tindemans' visit to China, in April, the PCB welcomed the development of relations between the two countries, but attacked Chinese alignment with "those forces that are most opposed to the strengthening of détente" (*Le Drapeau Rouge*, 21 April). Peking's comparison of Soviet policies with those of Hitlerian Germany (made on the occasion of the thirtieth anniversary of the end of the Second World War) were strongly denounced by the PCB, which asked whether the Peking leadership had acquired these ideas as a result of China's "excellent relations" with the Pinochet government in Chile (ibid., 10/11 May). The Visit of a Chilean economic delegation to Peking, in September, engendered further strong PCB attacks against the Chinese leadership (ibid., 12 September).

In its comments on developments in Portugal, the PCB consistently defended the views and activities of the Portuguese Communist Party. In contrast to the attitude taken by the French Communist Party, however, the PCB's criticism of the Portuguese Socialists was relatively guarded. At least on one occasion, the PCB intimated that the Portuguese Communists might have made some errors, notably in the affair of the closure of the Socialist-oriented newspaper *Republica* (ibid., 6 August). The main thrust of the party's comments on Portugal, however, was that developments in that country were being misrepresented and/or blown out of proportion by right-wing commentators in order to further anti-communism and to sabotage détente. The PCB was also careful to insist that, while the Portuguese Communists' objectives were the same as the Belgians', the situations in the two countries were quite different (see, e.g., ibid., 31 May).

In the debates concerning the holding of a pan-European Communist Party conference, the PCB's stance seemed to be closest to that held by the French Communist Party (see *France*), at least in its insistence that détente should not hamper in any way the activities of the Western Communist parties. As stated by Claude Renard, in an editorial in *Le Drapeau Rouge* (24 October): "Peaceful coexistence and international cooperation, yes. It is both necessary and possible. Ideological détente, no. That's nothing but a hoax."

International Party Contacts. In addition to its participation in the major preparatory meetings for a pan-European Communist party conference, and all the year's West European Communist party conferences, the PCB engaged in a number of bilateral party contacts. In January, it hosted the visit of a delegation from the Communist Party of Czechoslovakia, led by Jozef Lenart (for joint communiqué, see *Le Drapeau Rouge*, 27 January). During the month of March, the party leadership met with a Chilean delegation, led by Julieta Campusano, Politburo member of the Communist Party of Chile, and sent delegations to the Eleventh Congress of the Hungarian Socialist Workers' Party and the Fourteenth Congress of the Italian Communist Party, led respectively by Frans Van den Branden and Louis Van Geyt. At the end of the month, the party's youth movement organized a "young communists' anti-imperialist day," which brought a number of communist youth delegations to Brussels, including representatives from Portugal, Spain, South Vietnam, Chile, the USSR, and the World Federation of Democratic Youth (for details, see ibid., 1 April).

In April, the PCB hosted a delegation of the Popular Movement for the Liberation of Angola (MPLA), led by its president, Agostinho Neto, and helped organize the Second Assembly of Representatives of Public Opinion for European Security and Cooperation (held in Brussels and Liege on 26-29 April). In May, PCB leaders met in Brussels with Santiago Carrillo, secretary-general of the Communist Party of Spain, and Louis Van Geyt led a delegation to the Soviet Union. Van Geyt met the following month in Paris with Georges Marchais, secretary-general of the French Communist Party. In July, Central Committee member Jacques Nagels spent a fortnight in Portugal (for a report on his activities there, see ibid., 14, 15, and 16 July). During the month of August, PCB leaders traveled primarily in East Europe and the Soviet Union: Claude Renard was in Bulgaria, Jean Blume in Romania, Albert De Coninck in East Germany, Louis Van Geyt in Poland, and Frans Van den Branden in the USSR. In early September, Albert De Coninck returned from a visit to Portugal. In October, Robert Dussart led a delegation to Bulgaria, while Jef Turf led one to Czechoslovakia. Louis Van Geyt met, once again, with Georges Marchais, in Paris, on 13 October. At the end of November, Augustin Duchateau led a delegation to Hungary.

Publications. The PCB publishes a daily newspaper, *Le Drapeau Rouge*, and a weekly, in Flemish, *De Rode Vaan.* The party's theoretical journal is the monthly *Cahiers Marxistes.* The JCB publishes a bi-monthly, *L'Offensive.*

Stanford University   Milorad Popov

Cyprus

The original Communist Party of Cyprus (Kommounistikon Komma Kiprou), secretly founded by Greek-trained Cypriots, held its First Congress in August 1926 while the island was a British Crown Colony. Outlawed in 1933, it emerged in April 1941 as the Progressive Party of the Working People of Cyprus (Anorthotikon Komma Ergazomenou Laou Tis Kiprou; AKEL). Outlawed again in 1955, when all political organizations were proscribed by the British, it has been legal since the proclamation of the Cypriot Republic in 1960. The oldest and best-organized political party in Cyprus, it commands a following far in excess of its estimated 12,000 to 14,000 members. Virtually all AKEL support comes from among the Greek Cypriot majority, about 80 percent of the island's estimated 650,000 total population. In proportion of party members to national adult populace AKEL ranks second only to its Italian counterpart among non-ruling communist parties.

Despite its overall strength and legal status, AKEL has never held a cabinet post. For tactical reasons, it played down its strength in the latest parliamentary elections, in 1970. The party contested only nine of the 35 seats reserved for the Greek Cypriot majority. In winning all nine, AKEL increased its representation by five seats and received a surprising 39.7 percent of the actual vote, or 30.2 percent on the basis of the total Greek Cypriot registered electorate. Some 29 percent of the eligible Greek community voters did not turn out, which meant that apathy on the part of the nationalists was a significant factor in the communist success. The leading nationalist parties also suffered from fragmented voting because President Makarios did not express a preference among the parties.

AKEL's reluctance to show its true potential acknowledged two realities: first, the fact that the 1959 Zurich and London agreements—which gave Cyprus independence—provide a rationale for the three guarantor powers (Greece, Turkey, and England) to intervene against an internal subversion of the government; and second, the probability that a legal push for power by AKEL would unite the splintered nationalist parties against the leftists. While AKEL continues to have friction with the four Greek Cypriot non-communist parties, it has consistently in recent years given open support to the domestic and foreign policies of Archbishop Makarios. AKEL supported Makarios for a third consecutive term as president in 1973 and has played down its differences with the Church of Cyprus. The autocephalous church has traditionally been most influential in secular politics, and AKEL has learned that it cannot appeal to the Greek Cypriots by attacking their Orthodox faith.

The current socio-economic situation of Cyprus is a fragile calm because of the Turkish control of nearly 40 percent of the northern part of the island, yet political life among the Greek Cypriots in the southern zone continues. Though AKEL is the only professed Marxist-Leninist party, there has been growing competition and often convergence on issues with the active Socialist Party (EDEK), headed by Makarios's former personal physician, 55-year-old Dr. Vassos Lyssarides. In a 1975 radio interview with a Yugoslav journalist—in which AKEL was also featured—Lyssarides summarized his party in this manner:

> Our party is a socialist party and is based on scientific socialism. It was formed approximately 6 years ago and it has very good relations with all national liberation movements in the world, particularly in this Middle East area. . . . The party membership is composed of the workers class, peasants and scientific workers, who in Cyprus are a part of the workers class. They are not employers and their status is not very different from the status of workers. They belong under a wider definition of the workers class.
> Our primary concern is the national liberation of Cyprus, the struggle against imperialism and the struggle aimed at not allowing Cyprus to deviate from the policy of non-alignment. Our foreign policy has always been based on non-alignment and on non-interference in the internal affairs of other countries. Within the local framework we are fighting for a socialist transformation within the Cyprus reality. However, after the tragedy inflicted by the Turkish occupation, it is clear that the socio-economic policy of the party must be completely reoriented in accordance with the newly arisen situation. (Belgrade Domestic Service, 10 January 1975.)

EDEK holds two seats in the Greek Cypriot parliament, and reportedly sponsors a private band of armed militants (*trambucos*) which has been in the forefront of much of the gunfighting that has characterized Cypriot life in recent years. There are standing allegations in Cyprus that Lyssarides was once a member of AKEL, but he has always denied these charges.

Leadership and Organization. The leading figures in AKEL are the general secretary, Ezekias Papaionnou, in office since 1949, and his deputy, Andreas Fantis. Both were reelected in April 1974 at the party's Thirteenth Congress. The leadership structure follows the usual pattern of communist party organization. (For names of Politburo and Secretariat members see *YICA, 1975*, p. 142.) The party leadership is notable for its stability and the comparatively advanced age of each individual, most of whom are 60 and older.

The total membership for all elements within the AKEL apparatus, including various fronts and allowing for overlapping memberships, is estimated at some 60,000. AKEL controls the island's largest trade union organization, the Pan-Cypriot Workers' Confederation (Pankiprios Ergatiki Omospondia; PEO), which has some 35,000 members—about 45 percent of the overall membership in labor unions—and is an affiliate of the communist-front World Federation of Trade Unions. Many businessmen prefer to deal with PEO because it is well run, historically trustworthy, and usually not excessive in bargaining demands. Andreas Ziartides, a labor leader since 1943, was reelected as the PEO general secretary in April 1975, with Pavlos Dinglis as his deputy (*Ta Nea*, Nicosia, 19 April). Influential in AKEL's decision-making structure, Ziartides has been mentioned from time to time as a possibility for the post of minister of labor and social insurance in the Makarios cabinet.

The AKEL-sponsored United Democratic Youth Organization (Eniaia Dimokratiki Organosis Neolaias; EDON), is headed by a 28-year-old London-trained lawyer, Mikhail Papapetrou, elected in 1975 (*Kharavyi*, 31 January). EDON claims to have 10,000 members and is believed also to operate a branch in England. Through sport and social programs, it influences some 30,000 young persons. The EDON organization of secondary-school students—known as PEOM—has an estimated 2,000 members. EDON holds a seat on the Executive Committee of the communist-front World Federation of Democratic Youth. About this relationship, Papapetrou has said:

> The plentiful international connections of the organization should be utilized for the further enlightenment of young people throughout the world and for the encouragement of the moral and material support which has been shown for the just struggle of the youth and people of Cyprus (ibid., 29 January 1975).

Other AKEL-dominated organizations include the Pan-Cypriot Confederation of Women's Organizations (POGO); the pan-Cypriot Peace Council (PEE), a member of the communist-front World Peace Council; the Cypriot-Soviet Association; and the Cyprus-East German Friendship Society. The communists continually work on strengthening their front groups, "with special emphasis on the party's activities among the intellectuals, professionals, the youth and women (ibid., 21 May), but have been less effective in organizing the first two groups. AKEL and its adjuncts exchange fraternal delegations with the communist parties of Eastern Europe and the USSR. In 1970 the Soviet Union opened a cultural pavilion in Nicosia, which is regularly used in various communist front-group activities.

The AKEL-sponsored the Union of Greek Cypriots in England has an estimated 1,250 members, with support many times that figure. Of the estimated 40,000 Turkish Cypriots who reside in England, a few are open members of the Communist Party of Great Britain and a few others are undoubtedly crypto-communists of the Cyprus-Turkish Progressive Association. Some leftist tension in mainland Turkey is thought to be abetted in part by Turkish Cypriot communists living in London. In July 1975 a highly unusual meeting was held in Paris between AKEL and EDEK officials and representatives of underground "progressive forces of Turkey." The joint resolution was totally opposite to anything that has been advocated by Turkish Cypriots. For example, the call for a ban on exports of products from and imports to the "Turkish zone of occupation" must have been particularly offensive to both mainland and island Turks. (*I Vradini*, Athens, 9 July.)

While professed communists are unknown within the Turkish Cypriot community on the island, some of its young people, especially those enrolled in mainland Turkish universities, are Marxist-influenced. The same may be said, to differing degrees, about the two political parties in opposition to the present Turkish Cypriot leader, Rauf Denktash. AKEL has made continual overtures for membership to the Turks in Cyprus (as has EDEK also) and has tried to infiltrate the one Turkish Cyprit labor union. During the height of the Turking "intransigence" on the negotiations between the two communities, and after the February 1975 declaration of a "Turkish state within a Federal Republic of Cyprus," Papaioannou made this conciliatory gesture:

> We extend our hand to our Turkish Cypriot compatriots. We lived together harmoniously for hundreds of years, and we shall live together in the future. We are all victims of the same implacable enemy – imperialism and Turkish expansionism. (*O Anexartitos*, Nicosia, 14 April.)

Such overtures to this tempting minority have had little success. Papaioannou's gesture drew such criticism that, in order to appease the nationalist forces, the AKEL Central Committee later made a violent attack on the same Turkish Cypriots for their treatment of Greeks living in the north zone:

> During the last few days Turkish occupation forces and the Turkish Cypriot leadership, which is under their power, have applied themselves in an organized and systematic way to the forcible and mass uprooting of hundreds of Greek Cypriots enslaved in Karpas. The Central Committee strongly and unreservedly denounces this new crime of the occupation forces and the Turkish Cypriot leadership. Our party expresses its wholehearted support for and solidarity with our enslaved compatriots, who are suffering so much and whose anxiety, uncertainty and anguish have been increased by these criminal activities, which make their lives a nightmare. (*Kharavyi*, 2 July.)

The Greek Cypriot communists have been embarrassed in their relations with Cypriot Turks because of the Soviet Union's desire to keep good relations with mainland Turkey. The Russians seldom consult their Cypriot comrades prior to a major foreign policy declaration. Meeting in September with the Turkish president, the Soviet ambassador delivered an oral message from the Kremlin that noted "the pleasure felt over the development of relations between the two countries" and expressed "the hope that relations between Turkey and the Soviet Union would be further broadened and deepened" (Ankara Domestic Service, 9 September). AKEL seldom, if ever, comments on such initiatives directly.

Party Internal Affairs. The Central Committee and Central Control Committee (or Auditing Commission) of AKEL convene in plenary session every two or three months to deal with both international and domestic political developments. While there are supposed to be plenums at regularly scheduled intervals, the two committees can easily meet in "extraordinary" sessions. This was the case on 14 June 1975, when they met to review the period since the "second ordinary plenum" of 21-22 February (*Kharavyi*, 19 June). This meeting resulted in a lengthy set of resolutions, indicating a great deal of preparatory work in advance. In essence, the resolutions amounted to a six-month report which covered everything from the communist victories in Indochina to the need to "crush bureaucracy" in order to reactivate the Cyprus economy.

One important matter which is probably discussed at the plenums is the "problem of financial resources." Due to the disruptive events of 1974, "AKEL did not manage to hold its traditional annual collection last year" (ibid., 31 August) and went into debt. It set a 1975 collection goal of 25,000 Cypriot pounds in an appeal "to all party members, all its friends and supporters–despite the financial difficulties which we know they are facing" (ibid.).

Party congresses are held every four years, the latest on 25-28 April 1974. At this Thirteenth Congress, "900 delegates and representatives from 400 Party organizations took part, as well as delegations from 16 Communist and Workers' parties of other countries including a delegation from the Soviet Communist Party" (*IB*, May 1974). Since the congress was convened prior to the coup d'état and Turkish intervention in July, the resolutions did not hold any surprises.

Domestic Attitudes and Activities. AKEL has consistently exploited anti-colonialist sentiment in its protest against the restrictions placed on Cyprus by the 1959 Zurich and London agreements and against the continuing presence of two British bases on the island. Because as a mass party it seeks to attract the Turks, AKEL had shown little favor for the purely Greek objective of enosis–the union of Cyprus with Greece.

After the Cypriot coup in July 1974, which temporarily deposed President Makarios and brought on the Turkish invasion, the issues of enosis was kept alive by the efforts of an extreme political group called ESEA, (Coordination Committee for the Enosis Struggle) in conjunction with remnants of terrorist guerrilla forces (EOKA). Papaionnou has continually referred to rifts in the "internal front" caused by the reappearance of illegal bands allegedly "guided by the same CIA and NATO circles that organized the July coup." He claims there are 14,000 illegal weapons among these die-hards, and has called upon the state to take "immediate and effective measures," since the amnesty and pardon granted in 1974 by President Makarios "do not mean that coupist elements should be left alone to repeat their horrible criminal adventures." (*Kharavyi*, 25 February 1975.) AKEL called for a "purging of the state machinery and security forces of those elements that played a leading role during the coup" (ibid., 19 June), but apparently without much effect:

> Some changes have been made in the national guard and the police, and AKEL appreciates what has been done. But this is not enough. Both in the national guard and police there are still many coupists in key positions who must be replaced ... [others] should be arrested and, as has been the case in Greece, tried for their crime ... but instead they publish newspapers and dare to blame others for the evil that they have caused Cyprus through the fascist coup d'état that was guided by foreigners. (Ibid., 31 August.)

By year's end, the communists appeared even more frustrated with the Greek Cypriot domestic conditions:

1. Since the coup leaders and murderers are roaming the streets freely and, moreover, still holding their previous posts, what kind of a democratic order has been established in the island?
2. Since we have not yet divorced our responsibility, as a State, from the Henous crimes committed by fascism against Turkish Cypriot women and children, and thousands of democratic elements within the Greek community, what sort of democracy do we have?
3. Since lawlessness is formally accepted and the State lives in harmony with armed terrorists, what kind of justice do we have? (Ibid., 22 November.)

Other main domestic issues included the refugee problem, revitalization of the economy, the declaring of a separate Turkish-Cypriot state, demilitarization of the island, and the need to "internationalize," outside NATO, the security of Cyprus. AKEL's tactic was to urge "the unity of the domestic front." This insistence became increasingly stronger so that by the end of the year the communists were almost demanding the formation of a coalition government with the nationalists.

The approach early in 1975 was low-keyed:

Naturally, under the present conditions the party is fighting to liberate Cyprus from the foreign intervention and to make the country really free and independent. The main, short-term goal of our party is to force, *in cooperation with all other patriotic forces*, the withdrawal of all foreign troops from the Cyprus territory, to return refugees to their homes and to solve the Cyprus problem in a peaceful manner, through talks between the Greek and Turkish communities. (Belgrade Domestic Service, 10 January; emphasis added.)

In February, the pressing need was for "the formation of a government of national unity and a joint Athens-Nicosia line" (*Kharavyi*, 25 February). Instead of that, Makarios created a six-member national council to advise him, which AKEL saw as "a very significant step toward unity at the top," according to AKEL, but one which "in no way replaces the government of national unity, which was not formed." Even though one AKEL official was included in the council, it still was seen as more "devisive than unifying." Papaioannou ruefully felt that "all parties agreeing with the joint course and tactics for the solution of the Cyprus problem should be represented on the national council." (Ibid.)

At an extraordinary plenum of the Central Committee in June, AKEL again declared that "the unity of the internal front can be considerably strengthened through the formation of a political government that will represent all the political forces," and that "to meet the general popular feeling" the president "must proceed without delay" (ibid., 19 June). The same theme of "an all party (*politiki*) government' was echoed two months later, because it would "inspire confidence both at home and abroad and would contribute in the many-sided strengthening of our liberation struggle" (ibid., 31 August). A similar plea was made for a "fully representative delegation" to be sent to the fall meeting of the U.N. General Assembly since "it could develop useful activities among the delegates of the other member states with positive results (ibid., 13 September). In fact, Papaioannou, as well as the socialist leader Lyssarides, were both members of the Greek Cypriot delegation which attended the General Assembly debate on Cyprus (ibid., 22 November). The resolution which resulted was most favorable to the Greek Cypriots.

The issue of "political government" became so heated at one point that AKEL openly criticized President Makarios personally, probably for the first time in recent years. When Makarios was asked in mid-year about his intentions to carry out the AKEL proposal, he answered: "I have it in mind but it is a far cry between thinking about something and carrying it out. There is a difference in concept among the parties and this difference must at least be removed before I give the question any serious consideration." An editorial in *Kharavyi* (28 June) quote this and declared that the answer "does not satisfy the mass popular sentiment":

First of all it is incomprehensible that there should be a difference in concepts among parties as to whether there is a need for a "political government" under the tragic conditions through which this place is passing. . . . Public opinion expects precisely the opposite from His Beatitude: that he give serious consideration to the question so that he can contribute to the removal of the differing concepts, if they exist; that he approach the question of implementation with determination and not keep on "thinking" about it, which may mean nothing.

This uncharacteristically harsh rejoinder was apparently seen as a serious mistake, and on the occasion of the first anniversary of the July coup Papaioannou in laudatory phrases spoke of how the Soviet tanks and artillery given Makarios in 1964 were the only defense the duly elected president and his government had against the coupists (Nicosia Domestic Service, 15 July). Two days later the AKEL Central Committee called upon its followers to attend the mass rally to hear Makarios speak and to protest the Turkish invasion (ibid., 17 July). Typically, the communists turned out en masse to add to an overflow throng. Further, an editorial in *Kharavyi* on 7 July challenged published reports that the Makarios government was rent with dissension, claiming "there is no crisis of leadership in Cyprus."

Back in good graces by August, Archbishop Makarios received a three-member AKEL delegation which issued a statement that its views on the forthcoming fourth phase of the intercommunal talks were "in full agreement with those of the National Council and the Council of Ministers" (Nicosia Domestic Service, 22 August). AKEL deputy general secretary Fantis at an "exceptionally successful" communal gathering of AKEL sympathizers in Limassol "hit" at those who were dissenting from the Makarios government's policy concerning the intercommunal talks (*Kharavyi*, 26 August). The Central Committee later in the month sounded more like its former self, promising to "hold high, as has always been the case, the banner of patriotic unity," "contribute to the peoples rallying around President Makarios," and "fully meet the serious and urgent obligations it shoulders within the framework of the Cypriot people's liberation struggle" (ibid., 31 August).

Despite its efforts to back Makarios and his government as far as possible, AKEL was inexorably pushed to one last criticism. When the foreign minister said that "the Cyprus government does not rule out—indeed it would accept with satisfaction—a new initiative by the U.S. State Department," an editorial in *Kharavyi* (9 October) responded that the statement was "unfortunate" because "no initiative by machinator Kissinger could aim at a just settlement of the Cyprus issue." AKEL has blamed the CIA and "NATO circles" for planning the coup last year and gone so far as to say that another was being hatched for both Greece and Cyprus. The arrest of a number of Greek officers in Athens early in the year "confirmed the authenticity of the AKEL charges" that the new fascist coup was "instigated by the Americans" (ibid., 27 February).

The United States was involved in another domestic issue by its use of a British base in Cyprus for U-2 flights to observe Arab-Israeli troop movements in conjunction with agreed Middle East peacekeeping activities. Makarios reportedly declared that he had authorized this operation and that it had been kept secret "in order to assure that no misunderstanding would occur between the Greek Cypriot administration and the Arab countries" (SWB, 4 March). Papaioannou had asked previously in the parliament whether British bases were being used "in violation of their Treaty of Establishment" (*Kharavyi*, 28 February). He went no further in his questioning, nor did he choose to criticize Makarios on allowing their use, but the Soviet ambassador made a personal call to Makarios to express his government's concern (Athens Domestic Service, 2 March, and when the Soviet Union takes the lead in a Cypriot domestic issue, AKEL traditionally steps aside.

Controversy arose later because of a report that the Cyprus government had consented to the reopening of one of the U.S. communications facilities in an annex to the American Embassy in the Greek part of Nicosia. Claiming that this decision "contradicts the declared non-aligned policy of Cyprus," AKEL's deputy leader Fantis thus described the communications facility:

As organs in the service of CIA and the Pentagon, these radio stations are used for the collection and transmission of espionage information against countries friendly to the Cyprus Republic, for hostile cold war purposes and, generally, for activities that poison the relations among the various countries in our area (*Rizospastis*, Athens, 30 July).

An editorial in *Kharavyi* (7 October) extended to the small Marine detachment which customarily serves as Embassy guards:

The government has not realized that by "legalizing" the presence here of American marines, spy radio stations, American bases within the "sovereign" British bases and so forth, it makes internationally questionable the consistency of its anti-imperialist stand. It must undertake a serious struggle for the complete demilitarization of the island.

In contrast, relations with the Soviet Union were in February in glowing terms:

The Soviet Union ... showed during the entire Cyprus crisis, and even very recently that it decisively supports the legitimate Cyprus Government.... The Soviet Union opposes a bizonal federation and has strongly condemned the Turkish coup of proclaiming the federated Turkish Cypriot state. The Soviet union, with the other socialist countries, has been proven to be the best and most selfless supporter of the just struggle of the Cyprus people. (*Kharavyi*, 25 February.)

At that time Makarios was already on record expressing a "deep appreciation and gratitude for the Soviet Union's stand on the Cyprus issue" (Nicosia Domestic Service, 18 February).

The most obvious diplomatic initiative by the Soviet Union was a carryover from the previous year. In August 1974 it proposed an 18-nation "broadly representative conference" to consider the Cyprus problem. The idea was to give the Soviet Union a bigger hand in the island's internal affairs and future, and to move the negotiations out of "NATO circles." Disregarding the Soviet bid, the U.N. Security Council on 12 March 1975 adopted a resolution (no. 367) which called for resumption of the inter-communal talks between Greek and Turkish Cypriots. Disappointed, the Soviet delegate to the United Nations made this comment: "We regret that the fair proposal of the USSR has met with such stubborn opposition from the NATO countries and China" (*Izvestiia*, 14 March). Following this diplomatic rebuff, the Soviet Union toned down its demands for an "international conference" but did not stop its efforts to "internationalize" the Cyprus dilemma.

AKEL spokesmen took every opportunity to promote Soviet involvement. The theme played over and over was that the "main effort of the imperialist elements" was to "find a solution to the Cyprus issue within the narrow framework of NATO and behind the back of the Cyprus people" (*Kharavyi*, 19 June). Later the AKEL line became more diffuse: "When we talk about internationalization of the Cyprus issue we mean the utilization of all, without exception, the international factors to the benefit of Cyprus" (ibid., 28 September). Even though the Soviet Union simultaneously was mentioned as the "true friend and unselfish supporter" of Cyprus, it would seem that the original idea of a Soviet-sponsored international conference had been greatly watered down.

As to the ravaged, but resilient economy of divided Cyprus, Papaioannou stressed the "need for quick implementation of the emergency economic reactivation program" that AKEL had submitted to the government the year before (ibid., 3 October). On the exodus of Cypriot workers to other countries, he harkened back to a familiar Marxian rubric:

The people want deeds. They want bread and work. We should not be forcing them to emigrate in order to live. We must take from those who have, who have a lot, and give to those who have not or have very little. (Ibid.)

Some of the 100,000 Greek refugees from the north of the island, had been living in tent cities for more than a year. The AKEL leader said that they should be allowed to go into productive farming, and raised an old controversy with the Orthodox church about land distribution:

> . . it is inconceivable for our peasants to lack land to cultivate and for the churches and monasteries to have large tracts of land at their disposal. The land will have to be given to the peasants to cultivate it so that they may produce what we need and what our national economy in general requires. (Ibid.)

Soviet Union political support for the Markarios government—particularly in the U.N. debates on the problem—extended ito the economic area before the year ended. For the first time the USSR and Cyprus entered into a technical and economic cooperation agreement, which over a 10-year-period would assist the establishment of industrial units on the island (Nicosia Domestic Service, 3 October). AKEL was overjoyed at this development, which furthered a growing assumption in Cyprus that the Soviet Union was the "only true friend of the people":

> While also strengthening the economic endurance front of our struggle, the 10-year economic and technical cooperation agreement simultaneously strengthens the international standing and foundations of the lawful Cypriot State at a time when Cyprus' implacable enemies are systematically undermining its existence, having so far failed to abolish it through the fascist coup and the Turkish-NATO invasion. Within the economic agreement also coexist the dynamic elements of moral and political help for the militant propping up of the Cyprus state and our people. (Ibid., 4 October.)

Trade between Russia and the Eastern Bloc countries also picked up, especially in the export of Cypriot vine products. Still Makarios is cautious in his dealing with the Soviet Union because he knows they are not interested in closing the gap which has opened between greece and Turkey. Nonetheless, the United States and NATO fell into the lowest ebb of popularity with the Greek Cypriots.

International Views and Positions. AKEL's general secretary made a statement at the end of 1974 reaffirming his view that "The solution of the Cyprus question is closely related to the Middle East problem and also to the continuing process of international détente." He thought that "the Mediterranean can and should be made a peace zone, and Cyprus a bridge of peace, friendship, mutual understanding and cooperation among the peoples of the Mediterranean and the three continents." (*WMR*, December.) In the March 1975 issue of *World Marxist Review*, he discussed international involvement in the events of 1974 on Cyprus and drew the following conclusions about certain foreign powers:

> — Turkey's ruling circles, far from being interested in the restoration of constitutional order, which they hypocritically said was their aim to justify somehow the invasion of Cyprus, are out to liquidate Cyprus as an independent, sovereign and territorially integral state;
> — aggressive NATO circles and the Pentagon follow an anti-Cyprus policy and support Turkey's claims;
> — Britain, one of the "guarantors," did not meet its commitments; moreover, its pro-junta and pro-Turkish policy abetted the first coup and then the Turkish invasion;
> — the Soviet Union again showed itself to be the most loyal, trustworthy and disinterested friend of the Cypriot people and their legitimate government.

AKEL has consistently been in favor of non-armed struggle for communist goals. According to Papaioannou, AKEL has not made any of its own armed units ready for action in strife-torn Cyprus. His reasoning may explain why the communists opted not to fight against Britain in the 1950s:

It is obvious that violence and extremism have nothing in common with patriotic militancy or devotion to the cause of Cyprus. In our country today, a revolutionary patriot is not he who resorts to individual terror or illegally carries arms, but he who fights unrelentingly for the people's unity and proves his patriotism by joining the ranks of the armed forces of the republic. Revolutions are made neither through revolutionary rhetoric nor by shooting from ambush. We communists consider that arms are an extreme means of solving any problem. (*WMR*, March 1975.)

After the two Turkish ambassadors were slain in Vienna and Paris, *Kharavyi* editorialized on 26 October that "such murderous activities do not constitute the correct manner for promoting any political struggle." In the final analysis, the editorial continued, "these terrorist methods—which actually express the element of despair, lack of faith and confidence in the people and their just cause—benefit the enemies of the people's cause and serve imperialist aims."

The decision by the U.S. Congress to place an embargo on arms shipments to Turkey was another international issue on which AKEL expressed itself on numerous occasions. Favoring the initial cutoff in February, AKEL had some kind words to say about certain members of Congress who were leading the fight against the restoration of arms to Turkey. Senator Thomas Eagleton was specifically praised:

The American senator very correctly stressed that the United States of America should not pay ransom to Turkish blackmail by accepting or even tolerating its aggressive policy. These statements and actions by Mr. Eagleton and a number of his honest colleagues constitute moral help and support for our struggle and are fully appreciated by our people. (*Kharavyi*, 22 August.)

AKEL called President Ford "a very cheap state leader" because of his "pressure for the resumption of military aid to Turkey" and "indifference to the Cyprus drama" (ibid., 9 August). When the embargo was partially lifted in October, AKEL was muted in its criticism:

It is not right, naturally, for us to turn out backs on the factor of democratic public opinion in the United States. Whatever positive [support]can be offered by Congress and the American people so that Cypriot rights may prevail is welcome and valuable. We must continue efforts in this direction as well by continuous enlightenment. In Congress, too, we have consistent supporters. (Ibid., 5 October.)

On 8 December, when President Ford submitted his required report to the Congress on "efforts to resolve the Cyprus problem," an editorial in the 11 December issue of *Kharavyi* asserted that the report was not "objective" but aimed to prevent the reimposition of the arms embargo against their "powerful ally" Turkey. The editorial continued:

President Ford has spoken of narrowing down of differences on most key issues . . . but these are rebutted by the UN Secretary General's report to the Security Council (9 December 1975) . . . It is not known how the majority of American Congressmen will react to Ford's report. They know that their President does not give an accurate picture of the situation. It cannot escape their attention that in the most vital points the report is misleading for reasons which it is easy to understand. It is up to them to define their attitude. Our people will judge them accordingly. (Ibid., 11 December.)

Preoccupied with its criticism of the United States and "NATO circles," the Cyprus communists said comparatively little about their long-standing hatred of the Peoples Republic of China, whose ambassador to Cyprus professed early in the year his government's interest in President Makarios and "support for the independence, sovereignty and territorial integrity of the Republic" (Nicosia Domestic Service, 28 January). The Chinese communists held that "the primary condition for a solution to the Cyprus problem was for the United States and the Soviet Union to stop their meditation and intervention in the issue" (Ankara Domestic Service, 28 February).

International Activities and Contacts. AKEL's policy on international solidarity and relations with other communist parties has been dictated by Moscow. Accordingly, numerous AKEL delegations visit Eastern Bloc countries for ceremonial purposes and individual members for vacations and health treatments. In turn, Cyprus is a favorite stop-over for communists from these countries, and many delegations are personally received by President Makarios. In 1975, representatives of the newly legalized Communist Party of Greece also made a visit.

The communist-front World Peace Council (WPC) took an active part in the Cyprus problem during the year. Its president, Romesh Chandra, was received in March by Makarios. He pledged full support of his organization for the Greek Cypriot government and declared that actions would be taken toward the "immediate implementation of the U.N. resolutions on Cyprus" (Nicosia Domestic Service, 15 March). A step in this direction was the convening of a WPC conference in London in May, attended by delegates from Cyprus, members of the British Parliament, representatives of 16 international organizations, peace movement delegates from 24 countries, and a number of "progressive turks" (ibid., 14 May). Papaiaonnou summarized the impact of the conference:

> We would certainly utulize to the utmost degree the resolutions of the international conference on the implementation of the U.N. resolutions on Cyprus. Beyond what has been mentioned by my colleage Mr. Lyssarides there are many other ways through which we could utilize in different countries these resolutions and insure the solidarity. (Ibid.)

The above fraternal allusion to Lyssarides is not surprising. The Socialist Party leader has long been active in leftist international organizations, notably the Afro-Asian Peoples' Solidarity Organization (AAPSO), of which he he is vice-president. The AAPSO international conference at Cairo, in May, declared its support for "the lawful government of President Markarios" and chose to hold its Executive Committee session in Cyprus on 15-16 May (ibid., 14 April). At that meeting Lyssarides scored "world imperialism headed by the United States" and managed to have a number of resolutions passed which were favorable to the Makarios government (ibid., 16 May. An AAPSO meeting in the Soviet Union on 17-20 September was also attended by Lyssarides (*Na Nea*, 14 September). While AKEL could support practically everything AAPSO stands for, it does not attend their meeting nor does it give much coverage to such activities in its press.

Although at least two members of the Makarios cabinet visited the USSR during the year, the widely publicized state visit of the president himself did not materialize. It had been expected in May, after the USSR again made known its strong support for his government. The reason for this trip was reportedly to seek more "diplomatic and military aid from Soviet leaders," as was urged in a campaign by the island's press. It was not known whether Moscow told Makarios that the trip would be inopportune, or whether he heeded Greek officials who "opposed a Moscow visit." (Agence France Presse, 23 June.)

Publications. AKEL enjoys influential press channels. Its central organ is the large circulation daily newspaper *Kharavyi* ("Dawn") edited by the 57-year-old Costas Partassides, but there are also sympathetic writers and editors on most of the island's periodicals. AKEL's occasional theoretical journal is *Theoritikos Dimokratis* ("Theoretical Democrat"); and a weekly magazine is *Neoi Kairoi* ("New Times"). The PEO publishes a weekly newspaper, *Ergatiko Vima* ("Workers' Stride"). EDON publishes a newspaper, *Dimokratia* ("Democracy") and a monthly, *Neolaia* ("Youth"). The communist publications in Cyprus appeared with their usual regularity during the year. In London a weekly called *To Vima* ("The Stride") has been published by the Greek Cypriot communists for the past 36 years.

The Middle East Educational Trust, Inc.   T. W. Adams
Washington, D.C.

Denmark

The Communist Party of Denmark (Danmarks Kommunistiske Parti; DKP) sprang from the left-wing portion of the Social Democratic Party (SDP) during the agitated aftermath of World War I. It was organized on 9 November 1919 and has been legal ever since, with the exception of the period of German occupation during World War II.

The DKP draws most of its followers from among industrial workers and farm laborers, together with leftist intellectuals in Copenhagen and other urban centers. Membership has edged up to an estimated 8,000. The population of Denmark is about 5,200,000.

The DKP has continued to capitalize on the rising discontent of Danish workers and taxpayers—first expressed in a high maverick vote in the national election of 4 December 1973. The last parliamentary election, on 9 January 1975, with ten parties vying for representation and none winning a majority, reflected an ongoing trend of political turmoil in this normally tranquil country. The communists gained 0.6 percent in the popular vote for a total of 4.2 percent. This tally represented the highest percentage achieved by the DKP since the September 1953 election, when it won 4.3 percent of the votes cast. The party's representation in the Folketing (Parliament) rose in 1975 from six to seven.

Some observers considered the communist victory to be part of an overall shift to the left. The Left Socialists (Venstresocialisten; VS), who had fallen below the 2 percent threshold for parliamentary representation at the last election, cleared the barrier this time and got the minimum 4 seats. The SDP increased its representation from 46 to 53 seats and gained 4.4 percent in popular votes for a total of 30 percent.

Recent communist advances contrast sharply with what had been a fairly consistent downhill slide. Party power had peaked in 1945, owing in large part to the DKP's effective role in the Danish resistance. The expulsion of the late Aksel Larsen (party chairman, 1932-58) for "Titoist revisionism" in 1958, the formation of the Socialist People's Party (Socialistik Folkeparti) in 1959, the emergence of the Left Socialists in 1967, and the DKP's continuing loyalty to Moscow had all whittled away at the communist constituency. The DKP has subsequently been able to capitalize on the pervasive malaise of Social Democracy throughout Scandinavia and the special economic challenges of burgeoning inflation, unemployment, and deficits on current account occasioned, in part, by the energy crisis.

Leadership and Organization. Supreme party authority is the DKP's triennial congress, next scheduled for 1976. It discusses the report of the Central Committee, adopts the Party Program and Rules, and elects the leading party bodies, consisting of the Central Committee (41 members and 11 alternates), a five-member Control Commission, and two party auditors. The Central Committee elects the Executive Committee (14 members) and Secretariat (5).

Knud Jespersen is DKP chairman, a post to which he was first elected in 1958 and to which he was re-elected at the most recent congress, in January 1973. Poul Emanuel is party secretary. The party's youth affiliate is the Communist Youth of Denmark (Danmarks Kommunistiske Ungdom; DKU).

A major development for Danish communists in 1975 was the formation of the Communist Party of the Faroe Islands (FKP) in Torshavn, 14-15 June. Egon Thomsen was elected party chairman. Although Thomsen stressed the independence of the DKP and FKP from each other, he also emphasized the need for close cooperation between the two parties.

Domestic Attitudes and Activities. Danish politics revolved around economic questions in 1975. Such problems brought down the Hartling government in January and continued to demand primary attention from the new Social Democratic minority government of Anker Jorgensen. And, not surprisingly, it was to such issues that the Danish communists repeatedly returned.

DKP spokesman IB Nørlund faulted Hartling for a crisis plan that allegedly put the main burden on the workers, but claimed that the January elections "created better conditions for the defense of the interests of the working class" (*Land og Folk*, 14 January). A DKP Executive Committee statement declared: "The communists are ready to support the new government in any step that will ease the burdens of the capitalist crisis on the broad masses of the people." Included in the six-point program of action were cheap loans for the modernization of old housing; repeal of the value-added tax on food, medicine, and construction; and a freeze on increases on land and real estate values. (Ibid., 13 February.)

DKP chairman Jespersen made clear that, "if Anker Jorgensen wants a viable government . . . he must learn to look to the Left and to seek the support of those forces in the population whose activities primarily brought about the fall of Hartling" (ibid., 15-16 February). When the government proceeded to promote a law for the settlement of labor contract negotiations, Jespersen stressed his opposition and urged instead that Social Democrats "undertake compulsory measures where they are needed against big capital, the speculators, militarism, and profits" (ibid., 8-19 March). The communists charged further that the law abrogated "the right to have a voice in wages and working conditions" (ibid., 13 March). These sentiments reflected the more general program of the DKP set forth at a plenum of the Central Committee in Copenhagen, 1-2 March. The statement adopted there indicated that the communists intended to pursue new economic policies providing for "elimination of unemployment; nationalization of insurance companies, medical institutions, and power stations; introduction of effective control over the administration's activities at enterprises; and reduction of military allocations." The statement underlined the need to rally all Danish workers in the struggle against big capital, "which is trying to shift the consequences of the economic crisis in the country onto the shoulders of the working people." (TASS, 3 March.)

Defense questions, long a target for communist concern, took on new domestic urgency because of Denmark's serious economic recession. Villy Fuglsang, a DKP spokesman, objected to the purchase of expensive aircraft when the nation faced problems of unemployment and deficits in its balance of payments. He asserted that "patriotism is not measured in aircraft purchases." (Ibid., 12 March.)

The "energy crisis" commanded attention in Denmark, as elsewhere in Western Europe. In a booklet entitled "Energy and the Future," Ib Nørlund charged that the "oil crisis" was not a genuine crisis since "the monopolies manipulate oil in the interest of profits" (ibid., 31 May-1 June).

As the year progressed, the communists found that they "could not participate in the confident talk of the Social Democrats." Economically, the times did not seem to be improving. The DKP saw instead "the misanthropic and cynical profile of the capitalistic system" and the spreading economic malaise in the 24 OECD countries. They asserted further that membership in the European Community (EC) had opened Demmark to the domination of big capital. (Ibid., 20 June.) By July, the communists believed that the Jorgensen government was little improvement over its predecessor: "We got a new government but not a new attitude toward the problems and not at all a new political line" (ibid., 10 July, 2-3 August).

Despite the DKP's stress on policies to benefit Danish workers, the party failed to gain ground in the nation's important labor union movement. The president of the Danish Trade Union Federation (LO), successfully defended himself and the LO leadership at the federation's quadrennial congress, 12-16 May. The divisive EC referendum campaign of 1972 and continuing rivalry between the SDP majority and DKP minority within the LO had colored the previous four years and threatened to complicate the congress. Instead, the LO president succeeded in withstanding DKP attacks on the federation's policy with regard to EC membership, multi-national corporations, alleged passivity about unemployment, and LO concurrence in the SDP government's intervention to solve the nation's spring stalemate on wage negotiations.

The DKP and Socialist People's Party opposition failed to achieve their major objective of placing one communist on the LO executive board in order to provide a "platform" for communist opinion. The combined opposition could only muster less than 125 votes out of 994 voting delegates for their three candidates. The net effect of the communists' active campaign for power within the labor movement was no improvement over their position in 1971.

International Views and Positions. Commitment to the genuine national independence of Denmark was the alleged cornerstone of DKP foreign policy in 1975. The theme recurred in communist references to the EC, NATO, "U.S. imperialism," and energy exploitation.

Ib Nørlund faulted the government for surrendering Danish sovereignty to the EC and, because of NATO membership, saddling the nation with substantial increases in military expenditures, while cutting the budget elsewhere (*Land og Folk*,, 4-5 January). In August, the DKP called a mass demonstration for Denmark's pullout from NATO under the slogan, "Against Militarism and War, for Peace and Security." The communist newspaper criticized a former Danish foreign minister for proposing that the EC be gradually expanded into the United States of Europe (ibid., 10 July). Chairman Jespersen argued that multi-national corporations, "most of them of U.S. parentage," used the Rome Treaty to strengthen their hold on EC member states. He focused, in particular, on "a series of concession deals between the Danish ruling circles and U.S. capital" whereby "multi-national monopolies" gained exclusive rights to "exploit the natural wealth" of Greenland. Further, he contended that "the crisis of the capitalist world" gave U.S. imperialism another opportunity to grip Western Europe in the "vise of dependence." (*WMR*, June.)

Détente was a point for continuing DKP emphasis. The party, according to its chairman, expected détente to lead to a "system of cooperation based on the equality and sovereignty of states" and so serve as a counterbalance to "the policy of the monopolies, the EEC, and to NATO, which are of a distinctly aggressive character." The communists seized as their "main task" making the problems of European security and cooperation the "cause of broad sections of the public and all the peace forces of our country." (Ibid., December 1974.)

Parliamentary debate on foreign policy drew out communist sentiments on several other predictable international issues. Nørlund expressed satisfaction with the collapse of "fascist regimes" in Greece and Portugal" and stressed that Denmark had an obligation to "show solidarity with the anti-fascist forces." He criticized Denmark's attitude in the United Nations toward the Mideast—in particular, the refusal to "recognize the rights of the Palestinian people." And he urged sending an ambassador to Cuba. (*Land og Folk*, 19 March.)

Many of the above themes were echoed by the party's youth affiliate at its congress in May. The DKU policy statement featured Danish secession from NATO and the EC, claiming that Denmark ought to maintain an independent foreign policy. It welcomed the major achievements made by the world socialist system in building peace and declared that the Soviet Union and other socialist countries constituted a strong bulwark for world peace (TASS, 19 May).

International Party Contacts. Emphasis on exchanges of visits with their European counterparts and loyalty to the Communist Party of the Soviet Union continued to characterize Danish communist activity in 1975. The joint communiqué issued at the conclusion of a visit to Denmark by a delegation of the French Communist Party, 4-7 March, stressed that "there exist new possibilities for developing joint action by the communist parties and all working class and democratic forces with the aim of countering the Europe of monopolies by a Europe of the working people" (*L'Humanité*, Paris, 11 March). Soviet news services publicized French and Danish communist support for the holding of a conference of communist and workers parties of Europe (Moscow domestic service, 12 March).

DKP official IB Nørlund attended the Seventh World Conference of the Comintern, held 8-10 April in Prague. A delegation of the DKP Central Committee, headed by Poul Emanuel, visited Bulgaria, 26 May-2 June, to exchange views with a delegation of the Central Committee of the Bulgarian Communist Party. Both groups attributed the easing of international tension primarily to "the peaceful policy of the Soviet Union" and both stated that a well-prepared world conference of communist and workers' parties would make a major contribution to the solidarity of the international communist movement.

In late June, DKP chairman Jespersen led a Danish communist delegation to the German Democratic Republic and a meeting with East German party chief Erich Honecker. The parties affirmed their solidarity with the fight of the Portuguese Communist Party and with the historic victory of the Vietnamese and Cambodian peoples. DKP Central Committee members visited their counterparts in Czechoslovakia in early July and those in Bulgaria in late August. The Danes received a warm welcome from the French party's Politburo in September.

Publications. *Land og Folk* ("Nation and People"), a daily newspaper, is the DKP central organ. It enjoys a daily circulation of about 8,000 and on weekends about 11,500. *Tiden-Verden Rund* ("Time round the World") is the party's theoretical journal. The DKU publication is *Fremad* ("Forward").

Finland

Social Democratic dissidents—"reds" escaping from Finland's bloody civil war—established the Communist Party of Finland (Suomen Kommunistinen Puolue; SKP) in Moscow on 29 August 1918. Until 1930, the SKP operated through a variety of front organizations. The party reverted to illegal activities in the 1930s because of its own internal division and the government's ban on its operations. It became legal in 1944, as stipulated by the Finnish-Soviet armistice that year.

Most SKP members are drawn from either the industrialized urban areas of southern Finland or the small farming communities of the northern and eastern districts, where a radical tradition thrives. SKP members number an estimated 48,000. Finland's population is about 4,700,000.

The party's major political achievement for 1975 was gaining in the parliamentary elections and winning a place in the new Finnish government. Prime Minister Kalevi Sorsa's four-party coalition of

Social Democratic, Swedish People's, Center, and Liberal parties–in power since September 1972–resigned in June under pressure of a 17 percent annual inflation rate, a fourfold increase in the Finnish trade deficit, and bitter wrangling between the Social Democrats and the agrarian Center Party.

General elections were set for 21-22 September. That vote produced only minor shifts in the overall political balance of the nation. With twelve parties vying for representation in the 200-seat unicameral Parliament (Eduskunta), only one seat shifted from the non-socialist to the socialist side. The Social Democrats remained the nation's largest party despite a drop from 56 to 54 seats. The communists, running under their traditional label of the Finnish People's Democratic League (Suomen Kansan Demokraattinen Liitto; SKDL), picked up three seats for a total of 40 and ranking as Finland's second-largest party.

A caretaker government of civil servants held power pending the formation of a new government. That decision was deferred, pending the outcome of the critical election for the Metalworkers' Union (Finland's largest trade union) in November. Following the Social Democrats' victory over the Communists in that bitter and scandal-ridden contest, President Urho Kekkonen interceded on 27 November with a sudden demand for the formation of a "national emergency" government to meet Finland's critical economic problems.

Finland's 58th government in as many years was sworn in on 30 November, just in time for the country's celebration of independence on 6 December. Headed by Martti Miettunen, the government is composed of representatives of the Social Democratic, Center, Swedish People's, Liberal, and Communist parties and has the support of 140-152 members of the Parliament (the difference being the twelve Stalinist faction communists who cannot be counted on to support the Miettunen government). The communists holding portfolios include Olavi Hänninen (second minister of the interior), Kalevi Kivisto (second minister of education), Kauko Hjerppe (minister of transport and communications), and Paavo Aitio (minister of labor).

Kekkonen put strong pressure on all five parties, including the communists. He warned that any party shirking responsibility for Finland's "national emergency" must take the blame for any disaster befalling the country as a result of the politicians' inability to perform. The president went out of his way to make it possible for the communists to reverse their prior decision to stay out of the government by saying that he agreed with their contention that "assuring employment" was the nation's top priority and assuring them that a strong government could take on the Bank of Finland (notable for its tight credit policy).

Participation in the Miettunen government poses special problems for the communists. First, it underscores the internal schism within the SKP. Party votes on government involvement split strictly along factional lines. This division put into serious doubt the staying power of the communists in the Miettunen government–as in the case of the Karjalainen government in 1970–given the constant pressure which the Stalinists can exert on the liberal majority of the SKP. In addition, the communists hold several tough ministries which could force them to make difficult and potentially embarrassing politico-economic choices. Kekkonen clearly had sought their participation in order to avoid their irresponsible opposition outside the government and to curry points with Moscow. Given those factors and the fact that the communists have made their continued participation in the government contingent on resolution of some previously irreconcilable program points, the prospects for lengthy SKP involvement in the Miettunen government or, indeed, for long life for that coalition itself, seemed bleak at the year's end.

Leadership and Organization. Aarne Saarinen, "liberal" communist and former union leader, was reelected SKP chairman at the party's Seventeenth Congress, in Helsinki on 16-18 May 1975. He had been first elected to that position in 1966. The congress also reelected the Stalinist Taisto Sinasalo and liberal Olavi Hänninen as vice-chairmen and liberal Arvo Aalto as general secretary. The relative strength of the two factions of the SKP, established at an extraordinary congress in 1970, remained the same—with the ratio of liberals to Stalinists at 20-15 in the Central Committee, 9-6 in the Politburo, and 503 in the Secretariat.

Eight new members and five new deputy members were elected at the congress to serve on the Central Committee for the next three years. During the interim between congresses, the Central Committee is the highest decision-making organ of the party.

Party Internal Affairs. Deep division continued to mar SKP action during 1975. The conflict between the "liberal" majority and the Stalinist minority harked back to the ideological turmoil following the 1956 "de-Stalinization" congress of the Communist Party of the Soviet Union (CPSU). Different reactions to the Warsaw Pact invasion of Czechoslovakia in 1968, fluctuating party fortunes within Finland, and seemingly ambivalent signs from Moscow only widened the gap between the two ideological camps.

The convening of the SKP's Seventeenth Congress appeared to bring intra-party friction even closer to the fore. Chairman Saarinen noted in February that dissatisfaction with the internal state of the party was widespread, that the leadership had split into two parts, and that the break seemed more serious than during the previous congress. Exchanges between the Stalinist newspaper, *Tiedonantaja*, and the liberal *Kansan Uutiset* exemplified the schism. The former faulted the activity of certain trade union officials—a continuation of the "Hautala affair" of 1974 (*Tiedonantaja*, 12, 13 February). The latter criticized the Stalinists for "division of roles" and continuing "parallel activities" in contravention of democratic centralism (*Kansan Uutiset*, 11, 16 February). Saarinen deplored party disunity which led to split positions in union elections and on such issues as income policy and a national investment fund.

The intra-party attacks and counter ripostes became so sharp that both factions went to Moscow, 26-28 February, to thrash out their differences with CPSU officials. The USSR continued to be concerned about SKP disunity, as was evident in a *Pravda* article in March criticizing right-wing forces in Finland which were said to be trying to slander communists and imperil friendly Finnish-Soviet relations. Saarinen termed those talks beneficial with regard to the SKP's internal situation. Stalinists echoed the belief that the talks "improved the conditions for creating an atmosphere for strengthening unity prior to the Seventeenth Congress of the SKP" (*Tiedonantaja*, 6 March).

Such hopes, if they were every seriously held, proved illusory. Although speakers of both SKP factions stressed unity at the party congress in May, genuine rapport existed more on paper than in fact. Saarinen admitted after the meeting that the atmosphere had become tense and that it was not clear that proposals to end separate organizational structures could be realized.

The congress did issue an important statement on the subject, entitled "On Strengthening Party Unity" (*Kansan Uutiset*, 20 May). However, subsequent debate over settling which newspaper could speak for the party, dissension in the communist youth movement, and criticism of SKDL chairman Alenius belied any new consensus or inner party peace.

Domestic Attitudes and Activities. Some themes seem to remain constant with the SKP. Among those are continuing concern with the perennial economic difficulties of Finland and cooperation with the Social Democrats. The pattern persisted in 1975.

On the economic front, the SKP focused on the worsening situation of unemployment (*Kansan Uutiset*, 15 April). It faulted the Social Democrats for having no economic policy alternative to pulling "the wagon of bourgeois policy"—that is, limiting consumer demand, directing foreign trade toward the European Community (EC), allowing record-breaking price increases, and upping taxation on small and medium incomes (*Tiedonantaja*, 8 May). The SKP's statement on the domestic political situation, approved in mid-June, criticized the fallen Sorsa government for having worked contrary to the needs of the people. It went on to affirm the view, set forth at the Party congress, that the "most urgent tasks of today" were the increase of real income for workers, an end to unemployment, increasing social security, and protection of health. It proposed "broadening of state-controlled industry, the nationalization of commercial banks and large industrial and insurance monopolies, and the realization of democratic control." (*Kansan Uutiset*, 17 June.) As part of their election campaign, the communists stressed that "the SKP alone was able to present a clear alternative to the current bourgeois politics" (ibid., 28 June, 11 August). They also emphasized increased trade and cooperation with the Soviet Union as a means to alleviate Finland's economic problems (*Tiedonantaja*, 1 August). Saarinen set reduction of interest rates as one of the conditions for SKP participation in a new government (*Kansan Uutiset*, 31 August). A plenary session of the SKP Central Committee, 3-4 October, asserted that the results of the September elections indicated the voters' trust in the SKP program for a "radical alteration of domestic policy in the interests of the working people" (*Tiedonantaja*, 7 October).

Olavi Hänninen, SKP vice-chairman, emphasized that bringing together the working class and promoting collaboration between its parties had traditionally been—and remained—a key matter for Finnish communists (*WMR*, February). Ele Alenius contended that "the great question in Finnish politics is the building of left-wing cooperation in the same way the left-wing in France has attempted to do" (*Helsingin Sanomat*, 10 May). The SKP congress approved a "Program of Cooperation between Democratic Forces" which was, according to Saarinen, the expression of "the main strategic aim" of that gathering (*Kansas Uutiset*, 20 May). However, at the Social Democrats' congress in June, Kalevi Sorsa ruled out cooperation with the communists. Subsequent pressure from Kekkonen, as noted above, helped overcome some obstacles to the two parties' political cooperation.

A key index to leftist rivalry—SKP proclamations and coalition politics notwithstanding—was competition for control of the crucial Metalworkers' Union. The Social Democratic incumbents captured 259 of the 506 delegate seats for the union's quadrennial congress late in the year. The communists won 240 seats in the challenge for union control in November—seen as a bellwether contest following the September election and prior to the formation of a new government.

In other domestic matters, the communists advocated a strengthened role for parliament, condemned the activities of the conservative National Coalition Party, and endorsed Kekkonen for reelection in 1978.

International Views and Positions. Promotion of the Conference on Security and Cooperation in Europe (CSCE), opposition to the EC and NATO, support for the Portuguese Communist Party, and allegiance to the Soviet Union (versus the People's Republic of China) were the dominant points in the SKP's foreign policy for 1975.

According to the Finish communists, the CSCE represented a means for the strengthening of peace in general and for increased respect for the rights of small nations like Finland in particular (*Kansan Uutiset*, 30 July). The SKDL and SKP thus welcomed the final Helsinki summit in late July as a "revolutionary event, a visible milestone on the road to a lasting peace . . . on our continent" (*Tiedonantaja*, 30 July) and condemned the anti-détentist backlash in the Western press to that summit (*Kansan Uutiset*, 2 August).

Based on their concern for Finland's growing economic crisis, the communists emphasized the economic disadvantages caused by Finland's affiliation with the EC. They proposed instead that the nation sever connections in Brussels and "take the course of increasing and deepening economic cooperation between Finland and the Soviet Union" (*Tiedonantaja*, 3 September). They resented that bourgeois link much as they objected to the alleged recourse of rightist circles to the "rattle of arms" in the September election. It was considered inappropriate in the post-CSCE atmosphere for NATO to have invited Finnish journalists to Norway where they were briefed on Soviet military activity on the northern flank. This invitation was condemned as a calculated interference in Finnish affairs and an effort to damage Finnish-Soviet relations and provoke increased armaments in Finland. (Ibid., 9 September.)

The SKP statement—"For Peace, Security, and Progress—at the Seventeenth Congress gave the most comprehensive presentation of these points and of communist concern with the general status of imperialism and shifting power relationships. In that regard, the party welcomed the political and military defeat of "U.S. imperialism" in Indochina and the new prospects for workers in Greece and Portugal. The SKP put particular emphasis on solidarity with the Portuguese Communist Party and condemned "reactionary slander" against that party and the Social Democrats' support for the Portuguese Socialists.

The SKP remained resolutely in the pro-Soviet camp—whether in advocacy of specific economic programs or general loyalty in the international communist movement. According to the Finnish communists, the policies of the Chinese Communist Party and the leadership of China's foreign policy were "in definite conflict with the interests of the struggle against imperialism . . . and the principles of Marxism-Leninism and proletarian internationalism." They condemned the "irrational super-state theory of Maoist ideology" and the Chinese opposition to the CSCE and approval for the "reactionary aspirations" of NATO and the EC. (*Kansan Uutiset*, 21 May.)

International Party Contacts. Moscow remained the ideological and operational mecca for the Finnish communists. The aforementioned meeting between the SKP and the CPSU on 26-28 February was the apt reflection of this key linkage. A. P. Kirilenko, CPSU Politburo member and Central Committee secretary, and B. N. Ponomarev, alternate member of the Central Committee, were among the Soviets receiving a large Finnish delegation headed by Saarinen. They stressed the need to make détente irreversible, to achieve complete liberation of all Arab territories occupied by Israel, to persevere in efforts to improve Soviet-Finnish relations, and to try to hold an all-European conference of communist and workers' parties. Both *Tiedonantaja* and *Kansan Uutiset* stressed the value of the Moscow trip for preparations for the May congress.

The communist press gave extensive coverage to the first meeting in history between the heads of the Finnish and French communist parties, 11-13 June. Saarinen and Georges Marchais affirmed peace and socialism to be their respective parties' inseparable goals. They noted, further, that "the prevailing trend in the present international situation is the weakening of imperialism." (*Kansan Uutiset*, 14 June.)

In other exchanges, SKDL chairman Alenius led a delegation to Romania, 12-18 June, and met with President Ceauşescu; SKP vice-chairman Sinisalo visited party counterparts in Leningrad in July; the East German party's Central Committee sent condolences in July on the death of SKP Politburo member Erkki Tuominen; and members of the Polish party's Central Committee received SKP Politburo member Erkki Kivimäki in August.

Publications. The SKP's central organ is *Kansan Uutiset* ("People's News"), published daily in Helsinki and notable for its more "liberal" orientation. *Kommunisti* is the party's monthly theoretical journal. *Tiedonantaja* and *Hämeen Yhteistyö* serve as the voices of the SKP's Stalinist faction. The weekly *Folktidningen* ("People's News") is the communist newspaper for Finland's small Swedish-speaking minority. Finnish Maoists circulate such publications as *Punalippu* ("Red Flag"), *Kiina Sanoin ja Kuvin* ("China in Words and Pictures"), and *Punakaarti* ("Red Guard").

France

The French Communist Party (Parti Communiste Français; PCF) was founded in December 1920. Although it remained, in terms of membership figures, the largest left-wing party in France, the PCF, in 1975, clearly lost its electoral preeminence to an increasingly influential Socialist Party (Parti Socialiste). Other small Marxist-Leninist organizations continued to challenge the PCF from the left, but their political significance was relatively marginal.

At the beginning of the year, in a report to the party's Central Committee meeting of 20-21 January, Jean Colpin (candidate-member of the Politburo) claimed that the PCF had 450,000 members (*L'Humanité*, 21 January). This figure was accepted, with no commentary, by the independent weekly *L'Express* (20-26 January). In a press conference on 10 February, the party's secretary-general, Georges Marchais, referred to the PCF's 400,000 members (*L'Humanité*, 11 February). During a radio interview in August, Marchais increased the membership figure to 500,000 (ibid., 29 August), a claim that was reiterated at the PCF's Central Committee meeting of 5-6 November (*Le Monde*, 13 November).

The most recent elections to the National Assembly, held on 4 and 11 March 1973, had given the PCF 5,026,417 votes (21.29 percent) on the first ballot. The Socialist Party entered the first round together with the small Movement of Left Radicals (Mouvement des Radicaux de Gauche) under the ticket of the Union of the Socialist and Democratic Left (Union de la Gauche Socialiste et Démocratique; UGSD) The UGSD ticket obtained just under five million votes (19.6 percent), of which some 350,000 (1.43 percent) were received by Left Radicals. An electoral alliance between the UGSD and the PCF called for a withdrawal in the second round in favor of the allied candidate in any given single-member constituency who had the greatest chance of winning. The PCF obtained 73 seats, the Socialists 89, and the Left Radicals 12, out of a total of 490. (See *YICA, 1974*, pp. 133-34.) In 1975, the PCF had 74 seats (including one held by a representative of the Guadeloupe Communist Party); the Socialists and Left Radicals had a total of 107 seats. In the 283-seat Senate, the PCF had a total of 20 members; the Socialists were represented by 52 Senators, there was no Left Radical representation.

In the presidential elections of 5 and 19 May 1974, the PCF did not present its own candidate in the first ballot. Instead it joined the Socialists and Left Radicals in the so-called Union of the Left (Union de la Gauche), which presented Socialist Party First Secretary François Mitterrand as its candidate. Mitterrand received 12,971,604 votes, a total that came close to that obtained by Valery Giscard d'Estaing (13,396,203). (See *YICA, 1975*, pp. 162-63.)

Leadership and Organization. The national leadership of the PCF was elected at the party's Twentieth Congress, held on 13-17 December 1972. The Central Committee numbered 90 full and 28 candidate members. Representing the party's Politburo were: Gustave Ansart, Guy Besse, Jacques Duclos, Etienne Fajon, Benoît Frachon, Georges Frischmann, Henri Krasucki, Paul Laurent, Roland Leroy, Georges Marchais, René Piquet, Gaston Plissonnier, Claude Poperen, Georges Séguy, André Vieuguet, and Madeleine Vincent. Mireille Bertrand, Jean Colpin, and Guy Hermier were candidate members of the Politburo. The Secretariat consisted of: Etienne Fajon, Roland Leroy, Georges Marchais, René Piquet, Gaston Plissonier, and André Vieuguet. Georges Marchais remained secretary-general of the party. In October 1973, Paul Laurent was appointed to the Secretariat. The PCF's Extraordinary Twenty-first Congress, held on 24-27 October 1974, did not include elections to the party's leading bodies. It was followed, however, by a Central Committee meeting which appointed Jacques Chambaz to the Politburo. On 25 April 1975, the veteran Jacques Duclos—PCF presidential candidate in 1969 and head of the party's Senate group—died. He was replaced on the Politburo, on 28 May, by Jean Kanapa, the head of the Central Committee's foreign affairs section. Duclos' role in the Senate was taken over by Marie-Thérèse Goutmann, Senator from Seine-Saint-Denis, the first woman to ever head a French parliamentary group. (The PCF's vice-president in the Senate, Louis Talamoni, also died at the end of April. His post was taken by Roger Gaudon, Senator from Val-de-Marne.) another veteran PCF leader, Politburo member Benoît Frachon, died on 4 August. A long-time trade union activist, Frachon had been president of the Communist-controlled Confédération Générale du Travail (CGT). He had resigned his post at the CGT's Thirty-ninth Congress, in June (see below), and had been elected honorary president. The PCF has scheduled to hold its Twenty-second Congress at Saint-Ouen on 4-8 February 1976.

At the beginning of the year, the PCF claimed to have 21,340 cells in its 97 federations (*L'Humanité*, 21 January). The most notable development during the year was the emphasis placed by the party to increase the number of its industrial cells, from 6,500 to a target level of 8,000. By mid-year, the PCF's organizational secretary, André Vieuguet, was to claim that the net total of industrial cells had increased to 7,339 (ibid., 10 July).

The PCF's primary auxiliary organization is the General Confederation of Labor (Confédération Générale du Travail; CGT), the largest trade union in France. The CGT held its Thirty-ninth Congress on 22-27 June, at which time it claimed 2,400,000 members from 16,000 trade unions (*Flashes*, organ of World Federation of Trade Unions, no. 26, 9 July). Although only some 10 percent of the CGT membership adheres to the PCF, the union's leadership is controlled by the party. The secretary-general of the CGT is PCF Politburo member Georges Séguy.

The other major PCF auxiliary organization is the Movement of Communist Youth (Mouvement de la Jeunesse Communiste; MJC). At its most recent Congress, held on 1-4 May, the MJC claimed a membership of 70,000. The organization's secretary-general is Jean-Michel Catala, member of the PCF Central Committee.

Among students the PCF controls a splinter group of the National Union of Students of France (Union Nationale des Etudiants de France; UNEF). Originally referred to as UNEF-Renouveau, this group is now designated by the PCF simply as UNEF. A contending UNEF is led by Trotskyists. The principal PCF-controlled high-school organization during the year continued to be the National Union of High School Action Committees (Union Nationale des Comités d'Action Lycéenne; UNCAL), a body formed in 1968.

Party Internal Affairs. During the previous year, Georges Marchais, a leading advocate of electoral alliance with the Socialist Party, had seen the latter party increase its influence at the expense of the PCF. This development had, in turn, brought about a reaction within the PCF's leadership and an apparent erosion of Marchais' authority (see *YICA, 1975*, pp. 160-61). Marchais accepted the swing toward polemical confrontation with the Socialists, which dominated the latter part of the year. However, the issue of Marchais' leadership was brought sharply back into question on 14 January when the secretary-general suffered a heart attack. Non-communist political observers focused their attentions on the PCF's leading critics of the Socialist Party (Etienne Fajon, Paul Laurent, Roland Leroy, Gaston Plissonnier, and André Vieuguet) in their speculations as to who might succeed Marchais. In response, the party's Politburo issued a declaration on 15 January which stated that

Marchais' duties would be assumed by the Politburo "collectively" until the secretary-general's recovery. At a press luncheon on 22 January, Etienne Fajon commented: "The speculations on the imaginary differences between the leaders of our party . . . are perfectly ridiculous" (*Le Monde*, 24 January). In an article published in *L'Humanité* (23 January), Roland Leroy claimed: "The truth of the matter is that there are no imaginary internal party problems." By early February, Marchais had recovered, and, at a press conference on 10 February, he insisted: "Even if I have to disappoint those who support factions and view their existence as the acme of democracy, I assert that we have no factions" (*L'Humanité*, 11 February). Marchais actively participated in party affairs during the rest of the year, and his personal involvement in polemics with the Socialist Party (see below) appears to have satisfied his Politburo critics. The issue of Communist-Socialist relations did, however, continue to have repercussions on party unity at lower levels, and there were several reports during the year of demotions and censures of activists for complacency in their attitudes toward the Socialists.

During the year, the PCF leadership took a notably hard line against the Giscard d'Estaing government (see below). This, also, provoked some friction within the party. Thus, in March, the Paris federation of the PCF, led by Central Committee member Henri Fiszbin, requested an audience with Giscard d'Estaing. This move was denounced by both Marchais and the party's Politburo, and the Paris federation retracted its request and issued a self-criticism. (For details, see *Le Monde*, 8 March.)

Domestic Attitudes and Activities. With only some 20 percent of electoral support, the PCF's bid for power rests on the party's ability to persuade other elements of the left-wing opposition to coordinate their actions with communist policy. A major step in this direction had been taken in 1972 when the PCF, the Socialist Party and a splinter group from the Radical-Socialist Party, ultimately designated as the Movement of Left Radicals, adopted a Common Program and an electoral alliance for the March 1973 elections to the National Assembly. This alliance brought significant gains to the left opposition in the Assembly elections and in the following year's presidential contest. But the main beneficiary was the Socialist Party, whose popular support and influence was soon out-distancing the Communist Party's. In fact, by early 1975, public opinion polls were giving the Socialists 34 percent of the vote (a total even higher than the Gaullists). At the same time, the Communists had dropped to 18 percent. Although both parties still needed each other's support, the trend was such that there could come a time when the Socialists would no longer need the PCF and/or would be tempted into aligning themselves with centrist parties.

While the alliance had never been entirely smooth, the results of by-elections held in the autumn of 1974 (see *YICA, 1975*, pp. 164-65) precipitated a hardening in the PCF's attitude to the Socialist Party. Polemical disputes dominated the rest of the year, and were to continue with varying degrees of intensity through 1975.

A theme of accusations developed by the PCF against its Socialist partners was that the latter were not responding with militant action to the alleged economic crisis that the government had brought about, most notably in the field of unemployment. On 7 January, in a radio interview, Marchais attacked Mitterrand directly for the first time: "I implicate the first secretary of the Socialist Party, for he is responsible for his party in the same way as I am responsible for mine. When I see François Mitterrand act as if there were no problems, as if the real facts which all of you have been able to verify did not exist, I say: He is covering them up. That's all." (*L'Humanité*, 8 January; *Le Monde*, 9 January.)

A meeting of the PCF's Central Committee, held on 20-21 January, reiterated the theme of Socialist inactivity. "In politics, as in life," Politbury member Jean Colpin emphasized, "facts and deeds are more important than statements of intent." The PCF, he stated, had proposed to the Socialists to "jointly wage on a national scale a struggle against the policy of austerity pursued by the grande bourgeoisie and its government," but the proposals had not been accepted. (*L'Humanité*, 21 January). In the meeting's closing speech, Gaston Plissonnier emphasized: "All the speeches have stressed the necessity for pursuing with perseverance our action to preserve the union and bring it up to the level of the political demands and of the objectives to be achieved. This implies presenting to the workers and to the country the problems relating to the behaviour of the Socialist Party." "The discussion has shown," he added, "that the problems raised by the Socialist Party's behaviour are linked with the question of the differences in nature between our two parties—that is, class struggle or reformism." (Ibid., 22 January.) The differences between the two parties was stressed by Roland Leroy in a radio interview on 21 January. These, he stated, "do not depend on present circumstances and did not start a few weeks ago. It is a question of profound differences of nature. It so happened that François Mitterrand was the Union of the Left candidate for the presidential election. But that has never made him the leader of the left opposition. We believe that the left is made up of an alliance based on the equal rights of its constituent parties." Leroy then went on to warn: "The signing of the Common Program for Government drew the Socialist Party away from its policy of class collaboration, but there remains the risk of seeing it return as a result of the solicitations from the right." (Ibid., and *Le Monde*, 23 January.)

The Socialist Party held a national Congress from 31 January to 2 February. In a move calculated to influence the more militant delgates (most notably the 25 percent or so aligned with the Center for Studies and Research in Socialist Education—CERES), the PCF Politburo issued a statement, which emphasized: "The Politburo believes that the joint action on a national scale proposed to the Socialist Party as long ago as last September is more necessary than even. Four months having elapsed since this proposal was advanced, and considering that the Socialist Party Congress will take place very soon, it believes that the persistent refusal to take such action greatly harms the struggle against Giscard d'Estaing's government." (*L'Humanité*, 31 January.) In the same issue of the party's newspaper, an article on Mitterrand asked whether there was a calculation in the Socialist leader's failure to attack Giscard d'Estaing in a recent press conference: "Was this deliberate? One may wonder. Especially when one knows that the Socialist Party does not rule out the 'possibility' of assuming power in answer to a call by the president now in office." (Ibid.)

The challenge from the left that the PCF had hoped for was kept within bounds. Mitterrand retained his control of the party, and, although none of its leaders was reelected to the Socialist Party's Secretariat, the CERES did not break rank. The PCF's response came in a strongly-worded article by Politburo member Paul Laurent, published in *L'Humanité* (4 February):

> . . . François Mitterrand and the main spokesmen of the majoirty group continued to give negative answers to the questions which were discussed. The Socialist Party's first secretary, in the name of "tolerance" and the "fear of monolithism," condoned the actions of those of his party's leaders who have justified austerity or fought against the basic ideas of the joint program. Much less tolerance was shown toward the minority group, which expressed anxiety about the Socialist Party's present orientations. . . . The Socialist Congress, which hardly heard the voices of direct representatives of the working class, made no decisions on actions for the defense of the workers' interests or for the victory of the Joint Program. It remained very ambiguous on the problem of municipal alliances. It did not rectify François Mitterrand's ambitions to weaken the PCF. All observers concluded, as we did, that there has been a shift to the right, ill-concealed by the accentuation of a left-wing vocabulary.

In a press conference, on 10 February, Georges Marchais stated: "In contrast to our behaviour, it is now clearly apparent that the Socialist Party leaders are using the strategy of union and the reference to the Joint Program for essentially partisan ends. It is doing this to reinforce itself and weaken others, taking support if necessary from the campaigns developed against us by the adversary. . . . Lulled by the deceptive music of the opinion polls, certain people in the Socialist Party see themselves coming to power without us, to pursue, obviously, a policy which would have nothing to do with the Joint Program." Marchais also leveled a personal attack against Mitterrand, describing him as "increasingly sure of himself and domineering." (Ibid., 11 February.)

Although several Socialist leaders, most notably Pierre Mauroy, responded with indignation at the PCF's "aggression" against the Socialist Party (see commentaries in *Le Monde*, 12 February), Mitterrand's press conference of 13 February was relatively moderate in tone. Although his stance differed little from earlier positions (including pronouncements made at the Socialist Party Congress), the editor of *L'Humanité*, René Andrieu, asked whether there hadn't been indications of "a certain evolution" (*L'Humanité*, 14 February). It was apparent that both parties had come to realize that their relationship had come to the brink of a break, which neither could afford. For the PCF, however, the strong personal attacks against Mitterrand had brought some benefits. A public opinion poll, carried out by SOFRES (from 8 to 11 February), showed that within a period of one month Mitterrand's popularity—in terms of questions relating to political figures that respondents wished to have increased influence—had dropped from 55 percent to 47 percent (nationally) and from 83 percent to 65 percent (among the Communist electorate).

The Liaison Committee of the Union of the Left met on 27 February, the first such meeting since 28 June 1974. While the contending parties agreed on some joint protest actions against government policy, the meeting did not signal the end of Communist-Socialist polemic. It was at this time that President Giscard d'Estaing decided to visit Marseille, where he was hosted by the city's mayor, Gaston Deferre, a prominent Socialist Party spokesman. The coincidence of the two events was emphasized by PCF spokesmen. In a speech in Romainville, Jean Kanapa noted the "positive side" of the Liaison Committee's decision to organize joint meetings in 100 cities to publicize opposition to the government's economic policy, but added:

> This positive decision is belated. This delay is due to the Socialist Party. For several months it rejected joint political action, asserting that we should first cease to draw the workers' attention to certain worrying aspects of the Socialist Party's behaviour. But how could we Communists, who have a highly developed sense of our responsibilities to the workers, fail to alert them when the defense of the union and the success of the joint program are at stake? We do this and will do it every time that it is necessary. And the welcome given by the Socialist leader Gaston Deferre to Giscard d'Estaing confirms that we are right to do it.

According to Kanapa, Giscard d'Estaing's visit to Marseille was part of a government plan to "recreate political conditions conducive to collaboration between the Right and the Socialist Party," which included, as one of its first steps, the "development of 'cooperation' " with "certain municipalities governed by prominent Socialists whose penchant for collaboration with the Right is well known." "It is obvious," Kanapa concluded, "that the coincidence between the Giscard-Deferre meeting and the Liaison Committee meeting was intended, in particular, to undermine the decisions for joint action made at the latter meeting." (Ibid., 1 March.)

The issue of relations with President Giscard d'Estaing had a further significance to the PCF. While elections to the National Assembly are scheduled for 1978, presidential elections are not due till 1981. Thus, the situation could arise whereby there would be a left majority in the Assembly even though there was no change in the presidency. There would then be a temptation for the Socialists to cooperate with Giscard d'Estaing and accept to form a government under him, which would not include Communist representation. The PCF's strong denunciations against any contacts with the Presidency (including those of its own militants—see above, *Party Internal Affairs*), its refusal to cooperate in any government-sponsored measures to alleviate the country's economic problems, its increased militancy in labor and other social conflicts, and its insistence that the Socialists join in these stands were calculated to counteract against any such eventuality.

That the PCF was concerned about Giscard d'Estaing's role was clearly brought out in early March. While a number of Communist delegations held meetings with various Cabinet officials, including the Prime Minister and the Minister of the Interior, the PCF expressed strong opposition to any similar meetings with the President. The latter's invitation for a meeting was denounced by Georges Marchais, who stated that the move by the President was a "maneuver" to "compromise" the PCF in the government's "extreme reactionary policy." "We have already said that we will not lead ourselves to any deception," he concluded, "we will not sanction the demagogy of the President of the republic. No, definitely, we will not go to the Elysée." (Ibid., 7 March.) (Marchais had initially indicated—in the summer of 1974—that he would be willing to meet with Giscard d'Estaing; he reversed his stance in the autumn of that year. The attitude of the PCF made it difficult for Mitterrand to engage in dialog with the Presidency, even though he had indicated that if he were President he would approve of such meetings.)

The PCF held a meeting of its Central Committee on 14-15 April. In his speech, Marchais drew a balance sheet concerning his party's activities since the Twenty-first Congress of October 1974. Dismissing speculations that the party had "changed its strategy," he emphasized that militancy had been a constant characteristic of the PCF. Moreover, from an international point of view, the PCF, Marchais stated, was "more determined than ever to seize every new opportunity opened up for the class struggle by the weakening of imperialism in order to advance the united struggle of the workers and our people for democracy and socialism." "To put it another way," he explained, "we will overlook nothing in order to put an end to the Giscard regime." (Ibid., 17 April.) Questioned by reporters as to whether the PCF would participate in other conflicts, such as the strikes that had confronted the Renault factories in the early part of the year, Marchais replied: "Not only will we support the demands of all of the workers, as at Renault, but we will do our best to create other conflicts" (*Le Monde*, 18 April).

With the PCF's attention focused primarily on anti-government agitation, a temporary lull ensued, in early May, with relation to Communist-Socialist polemic. But, Mitterand's proposal for regular contacts between the two parties, made on 4 May, received an evasive response from the PCF, whose Politburo responded that this would have to be discussed at the party's Central Committee meeting of 27-28 May. By the end of the month, however, relations had once again deteriorated. The developments in Portugal were placing a severe strain on Communist-Socialist relations in France (see below—*International Views and Positions*), and a by-election in the Tarn reaffirmed the growing strength of the Socialists. The latter, who had not previously contested the district, received 24 percent of the vote; the PCF candidate's vote dropped from 14.22 percent to 12.90.

In his speech to the Central Committee meeting, Marchais accepted the idea of a summit meeting between the leaders of the Union of the Left, but the thrust of his remarks was critical of the Socialist Party. He focused, in particular, on the fact that the Socialists had on several occasions made favorable reference to their historical genesis in the Section Française de l'Internationale Ouvrière (S.F.I.O.) and to its most notable leader, the late Léon Blum. Retracing Socialist-Communist differences back to 1920, date when the PCF was formed as a result of a split from the S.F.I.O., Marchais stressed the working-class nature of the Communist party and claimed:

> In contrast, the Socialist Party is characterized by a lack of theoretical coherence, by the predominance within its ranks of non-working-class elements and forces that for a long time, and even in certain cases today, are associated with the Right, by hesitation when confronted by class struggle against big capital, and even the tendency toward compromise with the latter.

Noting that the Socialist Party was attempting to extend its activities in the industrial arena, particularly in those sectors where the PCF was strong, Marchais warned that while the Socialist Party retained its present characteristics such a move would only serve "to divert the workers from consistent class positions." "We have stated," he went on, "and we repeat it now, the victory of the left cannot be built on the basis of a weakening of the Communist Party and of the influence of its ideas upon the working-class." (*L'Humanité*, 29 May, and *Le Monde*, 30 May). At the same Central Committee meeting, Politburo member Guy Hermier also attacked the Socialist Party for its alleged attempts to extend its influence among youth organizations, at the PCF's expense (*Le Monde*, 31 May).

On 19 June, for the first time in over a year, the three leaders of the Union of the Left (Marchais, Mitterrand and Robert Fabre) met in summit conference, within the framework of the Liaison Committee. (The last such meeting had taken place on 29 May 1974.) In response to developments in Portugal, the meeting was dominated by polemics over the issue of liberties, with Marchais accusing the Socialists of wishing to take advantage of an alleged campaign of anti-communism to strengthen themselves at the expense of the PCF. "Such a stance," Marchais emphasized, was "intolerable." Mitterrand, in turn, focused on PCF accusations that the Socialists were ready to betray the Union of the Left and align themselves with the Right, and labeled these as "intolerable." (*Le Monde*, 21 June). The polemics continued.

At the end of July, in an interview given to the PCF's weekly *France Nouvelle* (28 July), Paul Laurent noted that the debate between Socialists and Communists was not over and that "problems remained." During that month, Politburo member Etienne Fajon had published a book, entitled "Union is Combat," which included hitherto secret extracts of a speech made by Marchais at a Central Committee meeting in June 1972, shortly after the signing of the Joint Program with the Socialists. The speech had explained the concessions made by the Communists, but had noted that these could still be turned to future advantage. It had insisted on the importance of continuing party work, while mistrusting the PCF's new allies and criticizing them whenever necessary. Laurent explained that the publication of the 1972 speech was undertaken in response to charges that the PCF had changed strategy only in the autumn of 1974. "By publishing what we then said," Laurent stated, "we wanted to show that our policy has been consistent."

On 16 September, the president of the Left Radicals, Robert Fabre, announced that he would seek an audience with Giscard d'Estaing. An editorial by René Andrieu in *L'Humanité* (17 September) labeled Fabre a "turn-coat," but intimated also that the move by the Left Radical leader complemented the stances taken by Mitterrand. In his speech to a Central Committee meeting of 17-18 September, Marchais referred to the Fabre visit as a "serious matter, a very serious one" (*L'Humanité*, 19 September). The PCF secretary-general also dwelt at length over relations with the Socialists since the summit meeting of June, claiming that the PCF had been "the object of harassment, pursued with methods hardly in keeping with the rules governing relations between political partners" (ibid.). According to Marchais, the "most frequent pretext" taken by the Socialists was to question the PCF's commitment to individual freedoms, often over the issue of developments in Portugal. The PCF had developed two hypotheses: either the Socialist Party's criticisms were a "convenient screen" behind which "undertakings could be developed to obstruct the Union of the Left, or even break it up," or by its campaign of attacking the PCF over the issue of freedoms, the Socialist Party was attempting to strengthen itself at the Communists' expense. In either case, Marchais stated, the "victory of the Left" can "under no circumstances be built. . . . On the contrary, if it continues, it could cause the Union to be called into question." "That is why," Marchais concluded, "we are asking the Socialist Party to stop its criticism of us concerning our attachment to freedoms. The Communists will not longer tolerate it without reacting in the most vigorous way." (Ibid.). A few days later, at a public meeting in Paris, Marchais returned to the subject of the party's commitment to freedom. Claiming that the PCF had defended freedom consistently, even when it concerned developments in the Soviet Union, Marchais added: "Therefore, let accusations aimed at weakening us cease. We cannot be bettered in the economic and social sphere where we are unbeatable. Therefore, attempts are being made to implant the idea that freedoms are our weak point. This is not true—also in this sphere we are unbeatable." (Ibid., 26 September).

Following by-elections, held in Vienne on 12 and 19 October, Marchais attempted to put further pressure on the Socialists by claiming that, in the second round, not all Communist voters had given their support to the Socialist candidate, Edith Cresson. Their attitude could be explained, he stated, by their perception of the Socialists' "lack of loyalty." (*Le Monde*, 23 October.) The PCF secretary-general's thrust was, however, somewhat deflected by Mrs. Cresson's rejoinder that her own investigation had revealed that there had been no withdrawal of Communist support (ibid., 24 October).

Communist-Socialist relations at the municipal level were a source of friction throughout the year, with the PCF repeatedly accusing the Socialists of preferring cooperation with the forces of the right and criticizing them for not refusing to vote on local budgets. The Socialists' response, as expressed by Mitterrand, was that there would be no municipal alliances "under threat" (ibid., 29 October), and that the PCF's attitude regarding communal budgets was "demagogic and hasty" (ibid., 25 November).

The Liaison Committee met once again in plenary session on 20 November, but the relations between the PCF and its partners remained tense during the rest of the year. Indeed, the Liaison Committee meeting itself had engendered further fruction as a result of a Socialist suggestion for joint industrial action. Responding to this call, Politburo member Jean Colpin had stated: "Let us say this clearly: one should not count on us to help the ambitions of the Socialist Party, which wants, in the industrial arena also, to strengthen itself at our expense, using unity as a Trojan horse, which would be carried by our cells and our militants" (ibid., 2 December).

International Views and Positions. While occasionally expressing guarded disagreement with Soviet views and policies, and, at the end of the year, claiming a rapprochment with the Italian Communist Party, the PCF reaffirmed during the year its traditional alignment with the Soviet Union.

The disagreements with the Soviet Union were of a relatively minor nature, and were generally in response to a Soviet action. On occasion the disagreement was the result of no more than lack of communication between Moscow and its foreign-stationed officials. Thus, President Giscard d'Estaing's decision to abolish the commemoration on 8 May of the victory over Nazi Germany brought strong attacks from the PCF. However, the Soviet Ambassador in Paris was to state that the decision was one made "by the people of France and, therefore, an internal affair" (*Le Monde*, 13 May). The PCF responded by emphasizing that "far from being a decision of the people of France, it was one taken by Giscard d'Estaing alone, with no consultation" (*L'Humanité*, 13 May). The organ of the CPSU, *Pravda* (13 May), while not using the same arguments as the PCF, also criticized the President's decision. A similar incident, again involving Giscard d'Estaing, but, this time, directed at the Polish newspaper *Trybuna Ludu*, occurred a month later. Prior to the President's visit to Warsaw, *Trybuna Ludu* (11 June) had written that "the goal of French policy" was "peace and détente in the whole world." This enterpretation of the French government's foreign policy did not correspond to the PCF's, and *L'Humanité* (13 June) was quick to correct the "journalists from Warsaw." More substantive disagreement took place in August as a result of the publication in *Pravda* (6 August) of an article on Leninist tactics by Konstantin Zarodov (editor-in-chief of the *World Marxist Review*). The article argued that democracy and electoral arithmetic had nothing to do with one another, and urged Western Communists not to be deceived by calls for moderation. It claimed that to create a socialist revolution a communist party could well have to resort to violence. The PCF's initial response following queries as to the party's own stance, was one that has been reiterated for several years. Commenting on the article, Georges Marchais stated: "In all spheres of politics, the French Communist Party determines its stands in Paris and not in Moscow" (*Le Monde*, 10-11 August). It was not till a month later that *L'Humanité* (4 September), in an article by Politburo member Jacques Chambaz, developed more substantive arguments in opposition to Zarodov's theses, taking pains to insist that the PCF was committed to Western style democracy.

On the occasion of Giscard d'Estaing's visit to the USSR (14-18 October), Soviet officialdom was obliged to engage in some censorship of PCF pronouncements. A declaration of the PCF Politburo (adopted on 10 October and published in *L'Humanité* on 13 October), devoted to the President's trip, was condensed by *Pravda* (15 October) in such a way as to eliminate all potentially controversial phrases. Thus, whereas the PCF had stated that "it would under no conditions abandon or abate its struggle to substitute as soon as possible a democratic unity government for the present 'grande bourgeoisie' power structure that would put into practice the new policies defined by the Joint Program of the Left," *Pravda* reported only that the PCF "will never abandon or abate its struggle for the realization of the objective defined in the Joint Program." *Pravda* made no reference to the PCF Politburo's views concerning the position of "the workers and the French people who are suffering from the crisis that has hit our country, from the policy of austerity, authoritarianism, and national recklessness being carried out by the conservative right now in power." The Soviet party organ, also, eliminated the PCF statement which noted that the USSR had never publicly protested the "gross provocation" against the PCF by Prime Minister Chirac, in March 1975 during a visit to Moscow. (Chirac had reportedly asked Brezhnev to instruct the PCF to cease agitational activity within the French armed forces.) *Pravda* made reference only to Chirac's "attempt to use his stay to put pressure on the PCF." The PCF Politburo declaration ended with the statement that the party's policy could not be changed by "any interference, pressure or foreign reprisals whatsoever." This part was eliminated in its entirety by *Pravda*. According to *Le Monde* (16 October), the publicity engendered by the *Pravda* censorship brought the following comment from an unidentified Soviet leader: "It is probably time for the PCF to understand that Soviet foreign policy is defined in Moscow, and only in Moscow." (In contrast to its treatment of the PCF declaration, the same issue of *Pravda* carried verbatim a speech by Giscard d'Estaing, in which the French President had called for a "détente with respect to ideological competition.") Later in the month, however, an article in *Pravda* (26 October) on Franco-Soviet relations emphasized the PCF's "immense contribution" to its development. It also pointedly noted that the Soviet Union's commitment to "peaceful coexistence" in no way precluded its "strong and unflinching adherence to Marxist-Leninist tenets of proletarian solidarity with workers' and liberation movements," and insisted that "international détente in no way eliminates ideological struggle, which is an objective phenomenon."

The PCF has on occasion criticized Soviet treatment of political dissidents, albeit highly guardedly. In 1975, within the context of the party's repeatedly publicized campaign over its "Declaration on Liberties" (published in mid-May), the PCF expressed somewhat stronger criticism. On 23 October, a number of left-wing organizations (but not the PCF) had held a meeting to protest the imprisonment of Soviet mathematician Leonid Plyushch. In response to criticism of its failure to attend the gathering, an editorial in *L'Humanité* (25 October) claimed that the party had not been invited, but added: ". . . the Leonid Plyushch case is of interest to us and we have for a long time sought to obtain information on this matter. If it is true—and unfortunately up to now the proof to the contrary has not been produced—that the mathematician is interned in a mental asylum solely because he has taken a stand against certain aspects of Soviet policy or against the regime itself, we cannot but confirm most categorically our total disapproval and demand that he be released as quickly as possible." The PCF took a similar stance in mid-December, following the television presentation (on 11 December) of a documentary on Soviet labor camps. A declaration of the PCF Politburo, issued on 12 December, stated:

> The film shows an intolerable view of the conditions in the camp. Moreover, the commentator declared that some of the inmates are political prisoners. This affirmation elicits all the more attention in that

there are, in fact, trials in the Soviet Union against citizens pursued because of their political stands. Under these circumstances, the Politburo of the French Communist Party declares that, if the reality corresponds to the scenes shown, and if it is not publicly disproven by the Soviet authorities, it will express its deep surprise and most formal reprobation. Such unjustified facts cannot but bring prejudice to socialism and to the renown that the Soviet Union has with merit acquired among the workers and peoples of the world . . . (*L'Humanité*, 13 December.)

Aside from the above differences, the PCF's stance on other aspects of Soviet policy and its alignment within the international communist movement showed no notable variation from its traditional orientation. The publication in mid-November of a joint statement by the PCF and the Italian Communist Party (ibid., 18 November) gave rise to speculation that the French party was aligning itself with the views of its more independent Italian counterpart. In part this was brought about by the emphasis placed by Georges Marchais on the statement's significance. Noting that discussions with the Italians had lasted from 29 September to 15 November, Marchais claimed that they had been concluded with a "joint statement which had no precedent as far as the relations between our two parties are concerned . . . a truly historical document" (ibid., 20 November). A reading of the statement, however, showed that on a number of sensitive issues, such as inter-party relations within the communist movement, there was either no reference or no more than a reiteration of previously expressed stands. While claiming that the statement had "expressed the agreement of the Italian and French communists on all the main problems with which they are faced," Marchais was careful to add: "Obviously, all this does not mean that the PCI and the PCF will standardize their activities and tactics in all spheres . . ." (Ibid.)

In the turtuous preparatory negotiations for a European Communist Party conference, which took place in East Berlin in February, April, May, July, October and November, the PCF's stance differed notably from that of the PCI. Following a deadlock at the April meeting, a special "balanced" sub-committee was formed to iron out differences. The PCF was lined up with the Soviet, East German and Danish representatives, while, on the other negotiating side were the parties from Yugoslavia, Romania, Italy and Spain. According to a report in *L'Humanité* (14 May), the differences had nothing to do with any confrontation between "centralists" and "autonomists." The PCF, the party newspaper claimed, was "no less attached to its independence than the League of Communists of Yugoslavia and the PCI." The real issue, it went on, was: "Does action necessary to consolidate détente and progress toward collective security call for a determined struggle against imperialism? Or, on the contrary, should imperialism be dealt with gently for diplomatic reasons and in view of domestic circumstances" "It is generally known," *L'Humanité* noted, "that the PCF supports the first of these two theses." Elaborating on the theme, *L'Humanité* stated:

> Can the Communists agree with the idea that the workers should accept sacrifices in a crisis situation affecting the capitalist system? Or should they, on the contrary, intensify their class struggle to extricate their country from the crisis? The PCF opposes the first of these two views. Furthermore, it is very attached to the view that peaceful coexistence can in no way mean that the social and political "status quo" should be maintained. . . . It is absolutely out of the question that they support documents likely to spread confusion in this sphere.

That there were other issues involved in the preparatory meetings was evidenced by comments made by Politburo member Jean Kanapa to Agence France-Presse (11 October) in an interview at the conclusion of the October meeting. With apparent dissatisfaction over the decisions reached, Kanapa stated that the eventual conference would take official positions only on "problems of peace, security, and cooperation" in Europe following the Helsinki conference. The PCF, as a "revolutionary party," he said, regretted this limitation of the subjects to be discussed. He went on, then, to list a number of topics that would not be covered: the class struggle in capitalist countries; questions of alliances between communist parties and other "democratic forces"; problems raised by "the building of socialism" in the East European regimes—there could be no question of the conference giving approval to the policies of this or that party, and, finally, Kanapa noted that the Chinese issue and developments in Portugal were not discussed at the meeting, and would not be mentioned in the final document. He also indicated that none of the parties had wanted to put the subject of a world conference of communist parties on the agenda. As for the PCF, this issue was "not topical at all."

With its own hard-line approach to domestic "class struggle," the PCF expressed strong solidarity during the year with the militant stance taken by the Portuguese Communist Party. The PCF's attitude engendered bitter polemics with the French Socialists, but also friction with the Italian and Spanish Communist parties, both of which criticized Portuguese communist tactics. A major issue involved the Communist organized closure of the Socialist-oriented newspaper, *Republica* (see *Portugal*). On his return from leading a CGT delegation to meet with the counterpart, communist-controlled Portuguese Intersyndical, Georges Séguy held a press conference to reveal his interpretation of the *Republica* affair. He described a situation in which the newspaper had lost almost half of its readership, and this had aroused the fears of its printers and journalists. "There followed," he claimed, "a very classical collective work conflict." In a speech to the Central Committee meeting of 27-28 May, Georges Marchais stated: "The *Republica* affair is a lot of hot air. Georges Séguy has clearly demonstrated that." In response, a Socialist leader, Robert Pontillon, labeled Séguy "a liar," and the Socialist weekly, *L'Unité*, published a special supplement on Portugal, including an editorial by Claude Estier and articles by Mitterrand, Portuguese Socialist Party leader Mario Soares and the editor-in-chief of *Republica*, Socialist deputy Joao Gomes, who gave an account of the closure that contradicted Séguy's version. In his contribution, Mitterrand made a point of noting that "the communist parties of Italy and Spain, to speak only of Western countries, have already taken a stand in condemnation of the operation" against *Republica*. The PCF, however, did not change its stance, and charges and counter-charges dominated the summer months. The polemics did not decrease till the late autumn, by which time the Portuguese communist bid for power had been temporarily thwarted.

During the year, the PCF remained highly critical of the Chinese leadership. At the time of the visit to Paris of Chinese Deputy Premier Teng Hsiao-ping, Marchais commented on the Chinese Communist Party leaders' "abandonment of the fundamental positions of Marxism-Leninism and proletarian internationalism," and their defense of "the Europe of trusts by means of anti-Sovietism" (*L'Humanité*, 15 May). An earlier, unattributed, article in *L'Humanité* (12 May) claimed: "The professional anti-Sovietism of the Chinese leaders is likely to satisfy the French Government, which is pursuing an anti-communist campaign reminiscent of the Cold War years."

PCF commentary on the French Government's foreign policy was invariably polemical, with emphasis placed on its alleged pro-American nature, manifested by France's "de facto reintegration into NATO" (see, e.g., Roland Leroy's speech in the National Assembly, *L'Humanité*, 28 June). In its continuing appeal to French nationalist sentiment (and potential Gaullist electoral support), the PCF remained opposed to the search for greater European political unity. In response to an invitation to meet with Belgian Prime Minister Léo Tindemans, for discussions regarding European union, Marchais responded: "[Tindemans'] mission consists of seeking ways and means of achieving the integration of the European Community countries into a supranational group. A plan of this type, if carried through, would seriously undermine France's freedom of action and sovereignty. . . . We consider it unacceptable that, on the pretext of cooperation, our country should ultimately be stripped of its essential prerogatives in economic, social and monetary policy, foreign policy or defense policy, all of which govern the free determination of our people. . . . In reality, 'European union' could only mean a Europe of national surrender, a Europe of sacrifices for the workers. . . . There could be no question of our party's participating in this enterprise of national surrender and, in so doing, sanctioning a policy so ardently desired by Giscard's government. " (Ibid., 12 August.)

International Party Contacts. In addition to attending all the preparatory meetings for a European Communist party conference (see above), PCF leaders held a number of bilateral meetings during the year. In mid-January, the PCF hosted a delegation from the Communist Party, U.S.A., led by Chairman Henry Winston. At the end of the month, a meeting was held between the PCF and representatives from the Communist parties of France's overseas departments of Guadeloupe, Martinique and Réunion, and Jean-Michel Catala led a MJC delegation to East Berlin. Also in January, Roland Leroy led a delegation to Algeria. In early February, Paul Laurent led a delegation to Poland. For the first time since the 1930s, a PCF delegation visited Spain. It was hosted by the Communist Party of Spain's Madrid provincial committee (see *L'Humanité* 1 March for joint communiqué issued on 28 February). Gustave Ansart led a PCF delegation to Denmark from 4 to 7 March. At the same time, the PCF sent a delegation, led by René Piquet, to Portugal. The PCF was represented at the Fourteenth Congress of the Italian Communist Party by a delegation, led by Paul Laurent. René Piquet headed the PCF representation at the Eleventh Congress of the Hungarian Socialist Workers' Party.

In early April, Etienne Fajon led a PCF delegation to Guadeloupe and Martinique. During the second half of the month, the PCF hosted a visit from a delegation of the South African Communist Party. Jacques Duclos' funeral was attended by a number of foreign party representatives, including Boris Ponomarev, candidate-member of the Politburo and Secretary of the CPSU, and Dolores Ibarruri, chairman of the Communist Party of Spain. At the beginning of May, Henri Fiszbin headed a delegation to East Berlin. At the end of the month, the PCF hosted a delegation from the Mongolian People's Revolutionary Party, and representatives from the African People's League for the Independence of Djibouti. George Séguy headed a CGT delegation to Portugal.

In June, Paul Laurent led a high-level delegation to Lebanon and Syria. Meetings were held with the leaderships of the Lebanese and Syrian Communist parties and with Yasir 'Arafat of the Palestine Liberation Organization. Roland Leroy headed a delegation to Greece. Two PCF delegations, led by Guy Hermier and Mirielle Bertrand respectively, visited the Soviet Union at the end of the month. Georges Marchais went to Bulgaria. During the month, the PCF hosted a delegation of the Communist Party of Finland, led by its chairman, Aarne Saarinen, and met with representatives of the Congolese Labor Party. On 24 June, a high-level meeting took place in Paris between Georges Marchais and Louis Van Geyt, president of the Communist Party of Belgium. A women's meeting, organized by the PCF on 7 June, was attended by several foreign representatives, including Angela Davis, of the CPUSA, Valentina Tereschkova, of the CPSU, and Julieta Campusano, member of the Politburo of the Communist Party of Chile.

In early July, the PCF hosted a visit from a delegation of the Norwegian Communist Party, led by its vice-chairman, Rolf Nettum. A delegation of the PCF, led by Marcel Zaidner, was in the Soviet Union from 7 to 17 July. Jacques Chambaz also visited the Soviet Union, in mid-July. At the end of the month, Roland Leroy spent time in Budapest. Georges Marchais returned from his stay in Bulgaria on 2 August. Benoît Frachon's funeral at the beginning of August was attended by party representatives from numerous countries, including Belgium, Bulgaria, Cambodia, Chile, Czechoslovakia, Germany (both East and West), Greece, Guadeloupe, Haïti, Hungary, Italy, Morocco, Martinique, Nicaragua, Paraguay, Poland, Portugal, Romania, Senegal, Spain, Turkey, USSR, and North and South Vietnam (for details, see *L'Humanité*, 7 August). At the beginning of the month, André Vieuguet visited the Soviet Union, while at the end of August a high-level PCF delegation, led by Gustave Ansart, left for Hanoi to attend the 2 September thirtieth anniversary of the founding of the Democratic Republic of Vietnam.

The PCF's annual *L'Humanité* festival, in mid-September, was attended by a number of foreign party representatives, including Werner Felfe, from East Germany, Grigori Romanov, from the Soviet Union, and Oldrich Svestka, from Czechoslovakia. A delegation of the MJC, led by its secretary-general, Jean-Michel Catala, visit the Soviet Union from 24 to 27 September. Also, at the end of the month, Georges Marchais conferred with Enrico Berlinguer, secretary-general of the Italian Communist Party, in Paris. On 30 September, Robert Ballanger, president of the PCF group in the National Assembly, left with a PCF delegation for a visit to sub-Saharan Africa (including Guinea, Guinea-Bissau, Senegal, Niger, and the Congo).

In mid-October, a delegation of the PCF, led by Paul Laurent, was hosted by the Japanese Communist Party. During the same period of time, Georges Marchais met in Paris, once again, with Louis Van Geyt of the Communist Party of Belgium. Later in the month, Marchais led a delegation to East Berlin. The PCF's secretary-general met with Enrico Berlinguer, in mid-November, in Rome, and with Santiago Carrillo, secretary-general of the Communist Party of Spain, on 28 November, in Paris. A high-level Italian Communist Party delegation, led by Gian Carlo Pajetta and Giorgio Amendola, met with PCF representatives, in Paris on 24 November. At the beginning of December, it was announced that Georges Marchais would lead a PCF delegation to the upcoming Cuban Communist Party Congress. Madeleine Vincent attended the Seventh Congress of the Polish United Workers' Party.

Publications. The main publications of the PCF in 1975 were: the daily newspaper *L'Humanité*; the weekly *France Nouvelle*; the monthly theoretical journal *Cahiers du Communisme*; a popular weekend magazine, *L'Humanité Dimanche*; a peasant weekly, *La Terre*; an intellectual monthly, *La Nouvelle Critique*; a literary monthly, *Europe*; a bimonthly economic journal, *Economie et Politique*; a philosophically oriented bimonthly, *La Pensée*; and a historical bimonthly, *Cahiers d'Histoire de l'Institut Maurice Thorez*. In addition the party has a number of provincial newspapers. For intra-party work the Central Committee published *La Vie du Parti*. In May, at the Congress of the MJC, it was decided to transform the MJC's monthly, *Avant-Garde*, into a fortnightly. A similar decision was made with regard to *Le Nouveau Clarté*, organ of the Union of Communist Students.

Stanford University   Milorad Popov

Germany: Federal Republic of Germany

The history of the Communist Party of Germany (Kommunistische Partei Deutschlands; KPD) goes back to the period of World War I when a revolutionary group within the Social Democratic Party of Germany (Sozialdemokratische Partei Deutschlands; SPD) formed the Spartacist League under the leadership of Rosa Luxemburg and Karl Liebknecht. Following the November Revolution of 1918, the Spartacist League founded the KPD on 31 December of that year. The German communists believed that the SPD betrayed the revolution and therefore their attitude toward the republic during the Weimar period was uncompromisingly hostile. The KPD steadily increased its influence primarily as a result of the severe economic depression in Germany. In November 1932, at the last elections prior to the appointment of Adolf Hitler as Reich chancellor, the party received almost 6 million votes out of a total of about 35 million valid votes. From 1933 until 1945 the KPD was outlawed. It continued activities underground, with little result except in the party's support of Soviet espionage.

In 1945 after the end of World War II in Europe, the KPD was reconstituted in the four allied occupation zones of Germany and in the area of Greater Berlin. The first organizational efforts occurred in the Soviet zone. Soviet occupation authorities proposed the merger of the SPD with the much smaller KPD when the latter failed to receive the expected support from the population. However, only in the Soviet zone could this merger be enforced. The new party thus formed was called Socialist Unity Party of Germany (Sozialistische Einheitspartei Deutschlands; SED). In the three Western zones of occupation, which in 1949 emerged as the Federal Republic of Germany (FRG), the KPD was outlawed as an unconstitutional party on 17 August 1956 after the Federal Constitutional Court found the party's objectives and methods in violation of Article 21/2 of the Basic Law of the FRG.

In the first elections in the FRG, in 1949, the KPD obtained 5.7 percent of the vote and was able to send 15 deputies to the Bundestag. In the next elections, in 1953, the communists won only 2.2 percent and thus lost their representation in the federal legislature. The KPD operated as an underground organization after it was outlawed. Its chairman, Max Reimann, continued to direct the activities of the party from East Berlin. In 1965, the German Peace Union (Deutsche Friedensunion; DFU) was formed by communists, former socialists, and pacifists. The DFU participated in the federal elections of the same year and polled only 1.3 percent of the vote. The DFU is still in existence and operates as an ineffective communist front organization in spite of its merger with the International of War Resisters (Internationale der Kriegsdienstgegner; IDK) and the Association of War Service Resisters (Verband der Kriegsdienstverweigerer; VK).

Since 1967 the German communists have conducted a campaign to legalize the outlawed communist party, in spite of the fact that the German Communist Party (Deustsche Kommunistische Partei; DKP) was founded on 22 September 1968. At the time of the founding of the DKP, the undergroupnd KPD had about 7,000 members. Almost all of the underground members joined the new DKP, following the example set by the leadership, who became the leaders of the new party. There is little doubt that the DKP is a successor organization to the outlawed KPD, an assertion which can be proven by the composition of the leadership group of the DKP during the initial organization phase (see *YICA, 1975*, p. 174).

The DKP considers itself a part of the communist world movement and maintains close relations with fraternal parties throughout the world. The 1974 report of the Federal Service for the Protection of the Constitution (Bundesverfassungsschutz; BVS) gave an overview of the leftist extremist organizations in the FRG, including West Berlin. The number of these organizations had decreased to 302 (from 317 in 1973), while the number of members rose to 102,000 (from 87,000). Orthodox communist (Moscow-loyal) organizations numbered 113 (110 in 1973) and the groups of the new left 189 (207 in 1973), the latter accounting for approximately 16 percent of all members of leftist extremist organizations. (*Handelsblatt*, Düsseldorf, 28 May 1975.) The population of the FRG is just over 60 million (not including West Berlin).

Leadership and Organization. The illegal KPD is still in existence, with now about 6,000 members, although its significance to Moscow has probably declined because of the operations of the DKP, although it is generally recognized by Moscow that underground organizations provide fertile recruiting ground for Soviet espionage. The obvious reason for the continuation of the KPD is to provide the organization for underground activities in case the DKP should be outlawed as an unconstitutional party.

As for the DKP, federal Interior minister Werner Maihofer declared in 1975 that the program of the party "clearly violates essential goals of the free democratic basic order" (*Handelsblatt*, Düsseldorf, 28 May). Also the parliamentary secretary of state in the Interior ministry, Gerhard Rudolf Baum (a member of the Free Democratic Party; FDP), stated in writing; "the federal government declared repeatedly in public—lastly in the publication of the 1974 report of the BVS—that the DKP pursues, according to its [BVS] opinion, unconstitutional objectives" (*Deutscher Informationsdienst*, Bonn, 26, no. 1410, 27 June 1975: 7). Yet it is most unlikely that the FRG's present socialist-liberal government will outlaw the DKP, especially since former chancellor Willy Brandt while in office characterized the DKP as a constitutional party to Soviet party chief Brezhnev at their Crimea meeting.

There are no reports by the DKP about its membership in 1975. The number of members is believed to have increased slightly from the 39,344 reported at the Third Party Congress in November 1973 to somewhat above 40,000. The relatively small number of members does not reflect the influence the party has among trade unions and institutions of higher learning. In 1974 there were 1,423 left extremists in the public service. Of the 911 *Land* employees of this total, 415 were teachers and 269 scientific or "other" personnel at the universities. The 1974 BVS report stated that left extremists (most of them Moscow-loyal) held 37 percent of all chairs at the universities and colleges, an alleged decline from 44 percent in 1973.

The DKP headquarters is in Düsseldorf. The organizational structure is that of a typical communist party. At the lowest level are the industrial and residential primary organizations. Next above are the approximately 200 district (Kreis) organizations and the regional (Bezirk) headquarters. No important changes of personnel occurred during 1975. The party chairman is Herbert Mies and the deputy is Hermann Gautier. (For names of other high officials see *YICA, 1974*, p. 149.) The Party Directorate (Parteivorstand), the equivalent of a central committee, has 91 members; the Presidium, 16; and the secretariat, 7. The Central Auditing Commission has 7 members, and the Central Arbitration Commission, 9.

Cooperation between the DKP and the ruling SED of the German Democratic Republic (GDR) continued throughout 1975, with the SED providing substantial financial aid, direct supervision of DKP activities, and schooling of communists from the FRG at East German installations.

The Socialist German Workers' Youth (Sozialistische Deutsche Arbeiterjugend; SDAJ), founded on 4 May 1968, (i.e., before the founding date of the DKP), is the youth organization of the DKP in spite of its claiming to be "independent." The SDAJ in all its publications and actions supports the DKP, especially in election campaigns. The SDAJ also maintains close relations with the SED youth organization in the DGR and the Soviet Komsomol (Union in Deutschland, *Dokumentation*, no. 34/35, Bonn, 1975). The SDAJ chairman is Wolfgang Gehrke; the deputy is Dieter Gautier. The headquarters is in Essen. Membership at the time of its Fourth Congress, in May 1974, was given as 27,442. If the report covering the second half of 1974 by the Interior minister of North Rhine-Westphalia, Willi Weyer, is an indication of the growth rate of the SDAJ, then the present number of members may be considerably higher. Weyer reported that the SDAJ groups had increased from 104 to 142, the number of newspapers for apprentices and young workers from 81 in 38 cities to 108 in 47 cities, SDAJ—published factory newspapers from 30 to 40, vocational school papers from 11 to 13, and newspapers for high school students from 7 to 8 (*Deutscher Informationsdienst*, 26, no. 1400, 25 January 1975: 10). Another report placed the number of SDAJ groups and local organizations in the same *Land* at 185 (ibid., no. 1401, 9 February, p. 4). It also was reported that in Lower Saxony the SDAJ had increased its influence among high school students and was able to take over the youth magazine *Kern*, the organ of the "Youth Press of Lower Saxony" (ibid., 25 January, p. 11). On 1 March 1975 the SDAJ organized in Bremen a socialist high school student congress which served to broaden its propaganda basis (ibid., no. 1402, 27 February: 3).

The struggle to become accepted in city and district Youth Committees, and especially in the

German Federal Youth Committee (Deutscher Bundesjugendring) has been a primary objective of the SDAJ for at least two reasons. First, member organizations of these committees receive substantial monetary contributions from public funds, which in the case of the SDAJ can be used for communist propaganda. Second, membership provides a basis for contact with other youth organizations and the opportunity to form unity of action programs. It also can be used to expel or deny membership to "right wing" groups, as in the case of the denial of admission to the Association of Christian-Democratic Students (RCDS) in Bielefeld because of its alleged unconstitutional policy. By mid-1975, the SDAJ had been admitted to some 60 city and district Yough Committees and to the *Land* Youth Committees of Bremen and Saar. This could only be achieved with the assistance of representatives of other youth organizations, like the Nature Friend Youth and the Young Socialists of the SPD. (*Deutschland-Union-Dienst*, Bonn, 29, no. 139, 25 July: 2-4.)

The Marxist Student Union-Spartakus (Marxistischer Studentenbund-Spartakus; MSB-Spartakus), founded in Bonn in 1971, has developed since into the strongest student organization, with representation in all university cities of more than 4,700 members, organized in 145 groups. Its national chairman is Steffen Lehndorff, who was reelected at the Fourth Federal Congress (8-9 October). The MSB-Spartakus in coalition with the Socialist Student League (Sozialistischer Hochschulbund; SHB), the former SPD student organization, controls the student governments in many institutions of higher learning. For example, in North Rhine-Westphalia this was the case in 7 of the 13 institutions (*Deutscher Informationsdienst*, vol. 26, no. 1400, 25 January 1975). These two organizations together control also the National Union of Students. The DKP maintains DKP University Groups (DKP-Hochschulgruppen) at institutions of higher learning, with a total of about 3,500 members (*Wehrkunde*, Munich, 24, no. 7, July: 353).

The Young Pioneers (Junge Pioniere; JP), the "socialist childrens' organization" founded by the DKP on 1 June 1974, has increased its membership to about 5,000 (ibid.). Its chairman is Achim Krooss. During the first five months of its activities, 141 pioneer groups were founded—in North Rhine-Westphalia alone, 22 groups (*Deutscher Informationsdienst*, 25, no. 1395/96, 10 November 1974: 8.; *Frankfurter Allgemeine*, 16 January 1975). Thousands of children from the FRG were sent to summer camps in the GDR and other East European countries. The JP maintains close relations with more than 20 like organizations abroad (*Deutscher Informationsdienst*, 26, no. 14/15, 15 September: 3) and has applied for membership in the world children's organization, CIMEA (*Deutsche Lehrerzeitung*, East Berlin, no. 49, 1974).

The Working Committee of Democratic Soldiers (Arbeitskreis Demokratischer Soldaten; ADS) has about 300 members and carries on the DKP's "anti-militaristic struggle" within the Federal Armed Services (Bundeswehr). (*Wehrkunde*, 24, no. 7, July 1975: 353, 355).

The DKP also controls several affiliated groups, such as the DFU, VK, and Nature Friend Youth, and exerts considerable influence over the German Young Democrats (Deutsche Jung-Demokraten; DJD), the Union of Independent Socialists (Vereinigung Unabhängiger Sozialisten; VUS) and a number of left extremist "professional" organizations among lawyers and artists, such as the Democratic Culture League of the FRG (Demokratischer Kulturbund der BRD) and the League of Democratic Scientists (Bund Demokratischer Wissenschaftler) (*Deutscher Informationsdienst*, 26, no. 1409, 14 June: 6).

The "Working Committees of Democratic Soldiers" are estimated to number between 90 and 100, in groups of 3 to 24 members (*Die Welt*, 24 April).

Party Internal Affairs. At its session on 14-15 June 1975 the Party Directorate decided to schedule the DKP's Fourth Congress for 19-21 March 1976 in Bonn. This session adopted a resolution addressed to all members, party organizations, and executive committees to "strengthen and extend contact with the working masses and the youth." The report of the Presidium and Secretariat contained as usual the arguments for establishing "unity of action" of Communists and Social Democrats and the unity of all progressive forces of the left. The "essential struggle for democratic rights and freedom and against the undemocratic prohibition to carry on one's profession (Berufsverbot)" was considered an important basis for common action. The main topics set for the party congress were the strengthening of party work among the masses combined with intensification of the unity of action policy, opportunities for socialism in the FRG, increased participation of the DKP in creating unity and fraternal ties in the international communist and workers' movement, and support of the anti-imperialist struggle directed by Moscow. The congress will also elect the party chairman, deputy chairman, and officials of the Party Directorate, Auditing Commission, and Arbitration Commission. (*Unsere Zeit*, 19 June; *Deutscher Informationsdienst*, 26, no. 1410, 27 June: 9-10.) Delegates for the congress will be elected according to the Party Statute at regional (Bezirk) delegates' conferences. One delegate will be elected for the first 80 members and one delegate for each additional 80 members or less. One guest-delegate will be elected for the first 300 members and one for each additional 300 members or less. (*DKP Pressedienst*, no. 58, 14 June.)

The session of the Party Directorate on 8 August discussed the tasks the DKP is facing in the struggle for the implementation of the results of the CSCE in the FRG and for military détente and disarmament (*Deutscher Informationsdienst*, 26, no. 1413, 16 August: 2).

The DKP receives most of its financial support from the SED, estimated at 30 million marks annually. This, however, constitutes only a part of the approximately 100 million Marks supplied in support of all communist organizations in the FRG, such as the SDAJ, MSB-Spartakus, and the Young Pioneers, and of the communist newspaper *Unsere Zeit*. Part of this money is used to pay for trips of delegations and for the schooling of officials. Most of the funds come from the GDR and other Eastern Bloc countries via firms in Austria and Switzerland. (*Die Welt*, 29 January, 20 February, 29 August.) This support for the DKP is organized by the "West Department" of the SED Central Committee and the "West Sectors" of the regional SED headquarters, to which specific support areas in the FRG are assigned. The number of invitations into the GDR have increased and also the travels of SED functionaries, 1,650 being recognized who came with political missions to the FRG during 1974. The DKP's own resources provide only a fraction of the total budget. For 1973, the DKP reported the sum of 9.3 million Marks as its total budget, of which 6.4 million allegedly derived from donations. (*Die Welt*, 29 May 1975.) Additional income sources are the over 30 collective bookshops in the FRG. The financial contributions of the party members are between 30 and 50 Marks monthly. (*Wehrkunde*, 24, no. 7, July: 354.)

On 18 January the DKP organized in Solingen a central Lenin-Liebknecht-Luxemburg celebration which started the "week of the DKP" during which all DKP organizations were supposed to present to the public in the FRG the party's short-range objectives such as a price freeze and job security (*Unsere Zeit*, 10 January). More than 1,000 information stands were set up, in various cities and communities. DKP propaganda material was distributed in 50,000 homes visited by party members. 40,000 signatures were collected for a DKP draft law on the implementation of a price freeze and democratic price controls. Local initiatives against rent profiteering, against the increase of fares and tariffs, and for job security were carried out, with demonstrations organized by the party in more than 50 cities in support of these demands. (Ibid., 30 January.)

On 1 May the DKP demonstrated or held meeting in at least 19 cities in the FRG (*Deutscher Informationsdienst*, 26, no. 1407, 28 April: 1). On 28-29 June the DKP sponsored a theoretical conference on the topic, "The Seventh World Congress of the Communist International [1935] and the Policy of the DKP." Chairman Mies concentrated in his presentation on the lessons to be learned and applied to the struggle for unity of action by Communists and Social Democrats and for a "broad alliance of all progressive forces" (i.e., for a popular front). He called attention to the many successful examples of practical unity of action in factories, in extra-parliamentary activities, and in muncicipal councils. (*Rheinischer Merkur*, Cologne, 11 July.)

On 20-21 September the DKP held its "UZ-Press Festival" (*Unsere Zeit*, the official newspaper of the DKP) in Düsseldorf, which like the one in 1974 was considered a most successful event. The party asserted that 400,000 visitors attended the two-day-long "UZ-People's Festival 1975"; the police estimate was 160,000. Among the visitors were the GDR permanent representative in the FRG, Michael Kohl, and the Soviet ambassador to the FRG. (*Die Welt*, 22, 23 September.)

The SDAJ organized a "Siemens Tribunal" at Bottrop in March and several "actions" against a number of other giant enterprises, such as Krupp, Hoesch, Thyssen, and Mannesmann (*Deutscher Informationsdienst*, 26, no. 1401, Bonn, 10 February, p. 4). The MSB-Spartakus held its Fourth Federal Congress on 8-9 October 1975 in Cologne. (*Deutscher Informationsdienst*, 26, no. 1416, Bonn, 6 October, p. 3.)

The DKP is also greatly concerned with the ideological schooling of its members. In Munich a Marxist evening school (MASCH) was founded with an extension division in Augsburg, the latter designed for "organized self-instructions." The DKP is particularly interested to provide dialectical education to factory and trade union officials. (*Die Welt*, 26 July 1975.)

Domestic Attitudes and Activities. The year 1975 provided the DKP with several opportunities to participate in *Land* and municipal elections. The party utilized the election campaigns to present its short-range objectives to the voting public as well as its proposals for unity of action by "all progressive forces." The DKP organized "voters' initiatives" and "citizen's initiatives" of party sympathizers in support of its candidates in the various *Land* elections (*Unsere Zeit*, 11 April). In North Rhine-Westphalia, for example, delegates from voters' initiatives, comprised of soldiers, students, scientists, and artists, addressed a DKP election congress at Essen. As usual, a high percentage of the party's candidates were trade unionists, (35 of the 55 DKP candidates in North Rhine-Westphalia). Of the 512 delegates at the elections congress in Essen, 227 were members or officials of trade unions or shop stewards. (*Deutscher Informationsdienst*, 26, no. 1401, 10 February: 8.) All the *Land* elections (except in Schleswig-Holstein, where the party held on to the 0.4 percent of the vote) showed marked declines in DKP support (see table).

The DKP achieved some success in few communal elections. In the Baden-Württemberg communal elections the DKP participated in 16 cities and communities with 470 candidates, of whom 55 were non-party people. The party obtained in Tübingen 7.2% of the votes and 2 city councilmen and in Heidenheim reached almost 4% and has 1 deputy. However, in Mannheim the DKP lost and has presently only one city councilman. In Stuttgart, the former DKP representative lost by 0.2%. (*DKP Pressedienst*, no. 38, Düsseldorf, 28 April.) The best election results were in Bottrop where the DKP candidates received 9,170 votes (1971: 2,570) and increased its number of councilmen from 2 to 4. (*Unsere Zeit*, 9 May 1975.) However, it is of interest to note that on the same day the DKP received in the same voting district only 2.3% in the *Land* elections in North Rhine-Westphalia. (*Der Spiegel*, Hamburg, 12 May 1975.) *Unsere Zeit* (5 April 1975) gave its reasons why people should vote for DKP candidates:

> Communist deputies are supported directly by the actions and demands, the initiatives of the people outside of parliament. They bring into parliament what moves the man on the street, what he demands of the deputies. This cooperation between extra-parliamentary and parliamentary activity is the first prerequisite to seeing that city councils and municipal administrations do not pursue policies behind closed doors which go over the heads of the people and come down from above.

The DKP has been able to penetrate many of the German Trade Unions (DGB). According to Mies, about 85 percent of the party members belong to trade unions (*Frankfurter Allgemeine*, 22 January). The trade unions provide the party with one of the two main opportunities to gain

Land Elections in 1975

Land	Date		Votes cast	Per-cent	Last previous Land elections	Votes cast	Per-cent	Federal elections 1972, percent
Berlin	2 March	DKP	25,583	1.9	1971	33.845	2.3	
		KPD[a]	10,277	0.7		— —	— —	
		KBW[b]	802	0.1		— —	— —	
Rhineland-Palatinate	2 March	DKP	11,096	0.5	1971	17.849	0.9	0.3
		KPD	2,015	0.1		— —	— —	— —
Schleswig-Holstein	13 April	DKP	5,919	0.4	1971	5,278	0.4	0.2
		KPD	696	— —		— —	— —	— —
North Rhine-Westphalia	4 May	DKP	54,779	0.5	1970	76,964	0.9	0.3
		KPD/ ML[c]	1,735	— —		— —	— —	— —
		KPD	7,558	0.1		— —	— —	— —
Saarland	4 May	DKP	6,859	1.0	1970	17,344	2.7	0.7
Bremen	30 Sept	DKP	9,230	2.1	1971	12,561	2.8	0.7

[a] KPD: Kommunistische Partei Deutschland (not identical with the underground and Moscow-loyal KPD)
[b] KBW: Kommunistischer Bund Westdeutschlands
[c] KPD/ML: Kommunistische Partei Deutschland/Marxist-Leninist

influence among the masses, the other being its "unity of action" activities. The DKP therefore supports all trade union objectives and wherever possible incoporates them in its own program. *Unsere Zeit*(16 January) declared:

> In contrast to all other political parties, the DKP supports a form of co-determination for white- and blue-collar workers and for unions, which reduces and circumscribes the profit-oriented decision-making powers of big business on all levels. In contrast to all other parties, the DKP supports co-determination based on active negotiations by workers, employees and the unions.

In some trade unions, such as the Education and Science Union, DKP influence has caused concern among union leaders, while in others, such as the Metal Workers' Union and the Paper and Printers' Union, the communists are considered valuable members (*Unsere Zeit*, 30 January). The DGB and various unions adopted resolutions excluding "extremist" communists belonging to splinter groups such as the new "KPD," KBW, and KPD/ML (see below) and to the Revolutionary Labor Union Opposition (RGO) (*Frankfurter Allgemeine*, 22 January).

The "unity of action" tactic continued to be emphasized by the DKP and has proven effective in a number of cases. The Berufsverbot remained an important issue and even was utilized to obtain sympathies outside the FRG for the "progressive democrats" persecuted by the "right-wing" forces in Bonn. *Pravda* (24 April) attacked the "undemocratic practice of depriving people of work because of their progressive political convictions."

In May, a working committee for "Defense of the Constitutional Rights" organized a public meeting that was held in Frankfurt on 5 June under the topic "Defend the Constitutional Rights." The signatures on the appeal for this event, indicating the broad spectrum of this unity of action, included Pastor Martin Niemöller, several trade union officials, SPD and FDP members of the *Land* legislature of Hesse, the deputy chairman of the Young Democrats, and various officials of communist front organizations. This meeting was also intended to prepare for the "International Hearing" on 7 June in Bonn, which received considerable support from Communists and left-wing Social Democrats of other West European countries. The "Hearing" was attended by about 500 persons, many of them from abroad. It addressed an appeal to the "democratic public" to protest the Berufsverbot and asked the trade unions to demonstrate "political and practical solidarity" with those who were affected by this "unconstitutional practice" and to use the influence of the workers to bring it to an end. (*Deutscher Informationsdienst*, 26, no. 1409, 14 June: 7-9.) DKP chairman Mies also used the Berufsverbot to draw the "attention of the West European public to the violation of basic political rights and freedom in the· FRG" by sending statements to governments, parliamentary groups of various political parties, and socialist and Social Democratic parties of West Europe (TASS, 31 July). The Association of Persons Persecuted by the Nazis (VVN), a communist front organization, reported that appeals were circulated in various West European countries and that a committee "For Freedom of Opinion and against the Berufsverbot in the FRG" was founded early in July in Paris, comprising about 30 professors, lawyers, trade unionists, and shop stewards (*Deutscher Informationsdienst*, 26, no. 1413, 16 August: 5). Following the conclusion of the CSCE, the DKP declared that compliance with the principles of Helsinki demanded the termination of the Berufsverbot (ibid., no. 1415, 15 September). Professor Wolfgang Abendroth, former political science professor at the University of Marburg, wrote that the solidarity action of the European Left was justified since the FRG had by joining the United Nations accepted also the Human Rights Declaration which demands the free access to public offices for everybody (ibid., no. 1416/17, 6 October: 6).

The DKP also used day-to-day issues on the local level and in factories for "unity of action" activities, such as a "Red Point" action in Hanover against an increase in fares for public transportation, in which *Unsere Zeit* (4 April) claimed that 30,000 persons took part. International issues utilized for unity of action included the mobilization of "democratic forces" against the "fascist military regime in Chile" and in support of the new Portuguese revolutionary government. On 26 June a "Committee for Peace, Disarmament, and Cooperation," comprised mainly of communist and pro-communist organizations, held an information meeting at the University of Bonn, calling for "Solidarity with the New Portugal! No interference in the internal affairs of the Portuguese people! " (*Deutscher Informationsdienst*, 26, no. 1410, 27 June: 2). The pro-communist *Deutsche Volkszeitung* initiated an appeal under the heading "Portugal must not become a Chile in Europe." Allegedly 300 scientists, writers, journalists, shop stewards, trade union officials, political personalities, and churchmen signed this appeal calling for solidarity with the Portuguese people and for an end of the anti-communist hate campaign (ibid., no. 1415, 15 September: 3).

The formerly highly active DKP-controlled "Initiative International Vietnam-Solidarity" (IIVS) held a "victory celebration" on 15 June in Frankfurt attended by members of the DKP Party Directorate and representatives of North and South Vietnam (ibid., no. 1411, 14 July: 3).

On the occasion of International Women's Day, 8 March, the DKP organized more than 300 meetings and actions throughout the FRG, calling for job security, equal rights, and social security for women, and for reform of the abortion laws (*Unsere Zeit*, 14 March).

On 11 June, 36,000 students massed in a so-called star march (Sternenmarsch) on Dortmund in support of various demands, including those dealing with Berufsverbot, disarmament, and protection of civil liberties. The League of Democratic Scientists, youth groups of the trade unions, the SDAJ, Nature Friend Youth, and many shop stewards and workers expressed their solidarity with the students and the MSB-Spartakus, one of the organizers of this event. (Ibid., 30 June.)

The DKP also organized a "workers' train" for a two-week propaganda trip through the Soviet Union (8-20 June). Soviet trade unions used the occasion of the 30th Anniversary of the Liberation from Fascism to invite 300 workers from the FRG on this trip (*Deutscher Informationsdienst*, 26, no. 1409, 14 June: 5).

The 30th Anniversary of the Liberation from Fascism (8 May) was also utilized for a unity of action campaign. A committee was founded at the end of January and charged with the preparations for this event, which included the dissemination of an appeal signed by some 3,000 persons. On 10 May about 40,000 "anti-fascists," communists, Social Democrats, trade unionists, Young Democrats, and soldiers demonstrated in Frankfurt. (Ibid., no. 1407, 28 April: 8-9; *Unsere Zeit*, 12 May.) The DKP held its own celebration on 7 May in Nuremberg, which was attended by about 1,500 persons, including the Soviet Ambassador to the FRG and the GDR's permanent representative in the FRG. The latter was greeted as the "ambassador" of the first socialist state on German soil. (*Unsere Zeit*, 9 May; *Die Welt*, 9 May.)

The "anti-militarist" campaign, directed against the Bundeswehr and military expenditures was carried on throughout 1975. DKP deputy chairman Hermann Gautier wrote in *Trud* (Moscow, 25 April) that the FRG currently has the highest per capita military expenditure, and that its military budget shows the highest increase. "Therefore the democratic movement in the FRG is demanding with growing persistence that political détente be followed by military détente." The Bundeswehr has remained a special target for infiltration and propaganda. (*Wehrkunde*, 24, no. 7, July: 355-57.)

East-West German Relations. The DKP is most critical of the policies of the FRG and accuses the government of obstructing international détente by failing to normalize relations with the GDR. The FRG's insistence of a unitary German citizenship represents a variation of the old claim to sole representation of Germany by Bonn. Chancellor Helmut Schmidt is accused of sharing the views of the "reactionary" Christian Democratic opposition, which allegedly is not interested in improving relations with East Berlin ("Voice of the GDR," East Berlin, 31 January 1975).

The Basic Treaty between Bonn and East Berlin, ratified by the Bundestag in 1973, contributed significantly to the process of détente in Europe, according to the DKP, which claims that improved relations between the two German states have in turn benefited the people of the FRG. Trade with the GDR is said to be in the interest of employment. The DKP appeals to all "peace loving and progressive people" in the FRG to work together to see that good-neighborly relations with the GDR are developed through strict observation of the Basic Treaty, through taking up the "constructive proposals" of the GDR, and by rejecting anti-communism. (*Unsere Zeit*, 1 February.)

The DKP, taking up the argument used by the SED, accuses FRG foreign minister Hans-Dietrich Genscher of interfering in the GDR's relations with third countries by insisting that they recognize the exclusive right of Bonn to represent all Germans, including GDR citizens. According to the SED, Chancellor Schmidt justifies this position on grounds of certain provisions of the Basic Law of the FRG and thereby places the laws of FRG above international law. "The relations between the FRG and the GDR are regulated in the Basic Treaty under which apply both the international law principle of sovereign equality (section 2) and the provision 'that neither of the two states can represent the other internationally' (section 4) as well as the stipulation that both sides respect 'the independence and sovereignty of each of the two states in its domestic and foreign affairs' (Article 6)" (*Neues Deutschland*, East Berlin, 19 February). The communists, therefore, call on the "progressive forces" of the FRG to require the federal government to revert to a policy of realism (ibid.)

International Views and Party Contacts. The international views of the DKP are identical with those of East Berlin and Moscow. Also the DKP propagates détente and peaceful co-existence between capitalism and socialism, but at the same time emphasizes that "internationally the democratic and socialist forces are on the advance," as exemplified by the "severe defeat" of the counter-revolution in Portugal and in Asia, and that "the national liberation movement is spreading" (*Unsere Zeit*, 27 March 1975).

DKP chairman Mies stressed the necessity of the consistent observance of the treaties Bonn had concluded with Moscow, Warsaw, East Berlin, and Prague because these treaties recognized the political and territorial realities in Europe. Their implementation was seen as contributing to the cause of peace and advancing the normalization of the situation in Europe. (TASS, 5 June), and also as provoding a solid basis for long-term economic and technological cooperation and trade with the Soviet Union and the other East European countries, thereby creating thousands of jobs in the FRG (*Unsere Zeit*, 25 April). Mies declared that the DKP "in fraternal alliance with the CPSU, would do everything possible to make the achieved successes in peace and détente policy irreversible" (ibid., 27 January).

The Soviet-sponsored campaign to hold the concluding summit meeting of the Conference on Security and Cooperation in Europe (CSCE) as soon as possible received complete support from the DKP. Mies stated that his party strongly favored the earliest successful completeion of the CSCE because this would have positive effect on the strengthening peace in Europe (TASS, 19 March). Deputy chairman Gautier claimed that the peoples of Europe desire an all-European security and cooperation system and the consistent implementation of the principles of peaceful co-existence between states with different social systems (*Trud*, 25 April). The KPD Directorate on 8 August paid tribute to the initiative of the Soviet Union in bringing about the CSCE and appealed to the working people of the FRG to implement the principles and tenets of this conference. The appeal contained the standard communist demands, for termination of all attempts to misinterpret the unambiguous international treaties, acceptance of the inviolability of the borders, and ending the Berufsverbot. (*DKP Pressedienst*, no. 82, 8 August; "Voice of the GDR," 9 August.)

The Portuguese Communist Party received strong support from the DKP in a solidarity statement approved by Party Directorate at its session on 14-15 June. The statement also protested against the "attempt at interference in Portugal's internal affairs by the CDU/CSU, the Federal Government, and rightist forces of the FDP and SPD leaderships" (*Unsere Zeit*, 19 June). A DKP delegation visited Portugal at the invitation of the Portuguese Communist Party on 10-13 September and declared its "solidarity with the revolutionary-democratic process in Portugal" (*Deutscher Informationsdienst*, 26, no. 1416/17, 6 October: 5).

On 8-16 March a delegation of the Party Directorate, headed by Chairman Mies, visited Cuba at the invitation of the Cuban Communist Party (*Unsere Zeit*, 21 March). Mies also led a delegation on a friendship visit in May to Romania at the invitation of the Central Committee of the Romanian Communist Party. (AGERPRES, 15 May). Mies visited Poland in August and met with leading communists. (PAP, 11 August.) The closest contact was maintained with the SED Central Committee, which, according to West Berlin intelligence sources, severely criticized the DKP for its poor showing in the elections. The SED expressed its intention, in order to achieve greater influence in the FRG, to increase its direct contacts with various social groups. (*Die Welt*, 3 May.)

Visits also were exchanged with communist parties in capitalist countries. In January, Mies received leading representatives of the Communist Party of Indonesia (*Unsere Zeit*, 24 January). A common protest of the French Communist Party and the DKP against the stationing of French tactical nuclear "Pluton" missiles on FRG territory was issued in Paris by the two party leaders, Georges Marchais and Mies (*Die Welt*, 24 June).

The attendance of two members of the DKP Party Directorate and the editor in chief of *Unsere Zeit* at the congress of the Communist Party, USA, in Chicago in June, was prevented by the "anti-democratic and discriminatory act" of U.S. authorities who refused to issue entry visas (TASS, 25 June).

A conference of the communist parties of the capitalist countries of Europe took place on 28 February-1 March 1975 in Düsseldorf at the DKP headquarters. The topic of the meeting was "the crisis of the automobile industry in the capitalist countries of Europe, the struggle of the working class, and the position of the communist parties." Representatives of parties in Belgium, Denmark, France, Great Britain, Italy, Austria, Sweden, Spain, Turkey, and the FRG participated and decided to organize in several countries an action week on 13-19 April against the "crisis policy of the monopolies in the automobile industries." (*DKP Pressedienst*, no. 23, 1 March.)

On the invitation of the DKP Party Directorate, a delegation of the "Committee of Soviet Women" visited the FRG on 5-12 March (*Deutscher Informationsdienst*, 26, no. 1404, 25 March: 4).

The DKP position concerning the Chinese communists completely supports that of Moscow. Günther Weis, chairman of the Central Party Control Commission of the DKP, writing in *World Marxist Review* (no. 4, April, pp. 113-19), accused the Chinese of making anti-Sovietism an official political doctrine in the new constitution of the People's Republic of China. He also stated:

> . . . the Constitution repeats the wholly false Maoist theory about the sources of the present war danger. It stems, they claim, from the "imperialist and social-imperialist policies of aggression and war" and from the "hegemonism of the superpowers." Such statements at the National People's Congress which adopted the Constitution, *L'Humanité* (January 1, 1975) says, can only create "confusion, by depicting the USSR as a 'superpower' along with the USA . . ." (P. 114.)

> The picture is clear enough: the Maoists are giving open support and encouragement to the revanchist plans of "reuniting" Germany. They are among the most inveterate opponents of the socialist Germany state, in flagrant violation of the 1955 Treaty of Friendship and Cooperation with the GDR which expressly speaks of the sovereignty of the two contracting parties. (P. 117.)

The SDAJ together with the MSB-Spartakus participated in an "International Friendship Camp," 19 July 3 August, near Bernau in the GDR (*Deutscher Informationsdienst*, 26, no. 1409, 14 June: 6). A SDAJ delegation traveled in October to Cuba to assist in the preparation of the 11th World Festival of Youth and Students to be held there in 1978. The delegation also visited Mexico and Venezuela and participated in meetings and seminars concerned with the solidarity movement for Chile, (ibid., 26, no. 1416/17, 6 October: 3-4.) A delegation of the leadership of the MSB-Spartakus led by its chairman Steffen Lehndorff visited in February 1975 the GDR at the invitation of Central Council of the FDJ (*Junge Welt*, 7 February). The summer camp activities of the Young Pioneers included the sending of 4,500 children to vacation in East European countries. Young Pioneers delegations visited a number of Pioneer camps in Poland, the GDR, Crimea (USSR), Bulgaria, Hungary, and Czechoslovakia. (*Deutscher Informationsdienst*, 26, no. 1415, 15 September: 2.)

Publications. The DKP official organ is the daily *Unsere Zeit*, printed in Düsseldorf, with a claimed circulation of about 60,000 (estimated at 17,000 by *Die Welt*, 8 August 1975). The former weekly edition has been discontinued. *Unsere Zeit* has a number of local supplements. The DKP publishes also *DKP-Pressedienst* and a "theoretical-scientific" periodical, *Marxistische Blätter* (at Frankfurt), with a circulation of about 8,500. The latter periodical produces and distributes the series of *Marxistische Taschenbücher* and *Marxistische Lehrbriefe*, both used in the "educational work" of the party. Other DKP publications include the theoretical quarterly *Marxismus Digest, Praxis*—examples of the democratic struggle. The illustrated *Sozialismus Konkret-DKP Report* is published by the Public Relations Section of the Party Directorate. The SDAJ weekly organ *Elan* (Dortmund) has a circulation of some 20,000. The Young Pioneers' papers are *Mach mit* and *Willibald*. The MSB-Spartakus publishes the monthly *Rote Blätter*, the bimonthly *facit*, and for the institutes for higher learning in Bavaria, *unireport*, in addition to its 170 newspapers at most universities in the FRG with a total circulation of about 200,000 per semester. The newspaper of the DKP University Groups is *DKP-Kommunist*.

The DKP utilizes numerous district, local, and factory papers for its propaganda. Also factory papers for foreign workers, printed in their mother tongues, have made their appearance. In July 1975, the 400th SDAJ newspaper, *Lokomotive Lanstrop*, a local paper, came out. The SDAJ publications include, in addition to local papers, those intended for young factory workers, apprentices, vocational students, and high school students. The SDAJ is also responsible for the communist soldiers' papers *Links-um* and *Rührt Euch*, and the Munich soldiers' paper *Neue Lage*.

In addition to the publications of the DKP and its fronts there are a number of leftist periodicals, such as the *Sozialistische Korrespondenz* (Hamburg), *Express* (Offenbach), and *Links-Sozialistische Zeitung* (Offenbach). A chain of over 30 bookstores throughout the FRG is connected with the DKP; these stores offer communist literature, mostly from he GDR, at very reasonable prices.

The previously mentioned BVS report for 1974 noted that there were 1,271 orthodox-communist and pro-communist publications in the FRG, with a weekly output of 1,073,000 copies. The average weekly edition of these publications in 1974 increased almost 100 percent, as compared with 1973. (*Deutscher Informationsdienst*, 26, no. 1411, 14 July: 8.)

Other Leftist Groups-Rival Communists. In addition to the Moscow-loyal communist organizations, numerous extremist leftist groups propagate their special brand of revolutionary activities, including terrorism. Some of the groups consider themselves to be political parties and participate as such in various *Land* and municipal elections, though they tend to be in a state of continuous flux. They emerge, combine with other groups, break up into splinter groups, and frequently disappear as quickly as they were organized. Even the BVS has difficulties in keeping track of them. The BVS report for 1974 stated that the decisive groups of the new left are Maoist-oriented and represent dogmatic Marxism-Leninism, and that total membership was about 19,200 (18,500 in 1973).

The most important Maoist "party" is the new "KPD," which is not to be taken as a successor organization of the outlawed Moscow-oriented KPD which still exists as an insignificant underground party. (For background, see *YICA, 1975*, pp. 183-84.) Recognized as a "party" by the German courts, the new KPD participated in a number of elections during 1975 (see table). Its central Committee and the editorial office of its organ, *Rote Fahne*, moved in February 1975 from Dortmund to Cologne. In North Rhine-Westphalia the KPD has more than 1,000 full members. Its student organization has 1,200 members and its youth group 800. The KPD maintains 7 local headquarters. (*Bayernkurier*, Munich, 22 February.) The Communist Youth League (Kommunistischer Jugendverband Deutschlands; KJVD) is the youth organization of the KPD. In May, it held its first conference of delegates in Hanover, attended by about 150 delegates representing cells and committees in factories, hospitals, and communities. It considered itself as the "fighting organization of the working youth and the reserve of the party." (*Deutscher Informationsdienst*, 26, no. 1410, 27 June: 3.) The KPD-affiliated student organization, the Communist Student League (Kommunistischer Studentenverband; KSV) is highly active in many universities. The Communist High School Student League (Kommunistischer Oberschüler-Verband; KOV) has its own central organ, the *Schulkampf*. KPD-controlled "mass organizations" include the Rote Hilfe, the product of the merger of several Rote Hilfe groups which took place at a conference in Frankfurt on 25-26 May 1974 (ibid., 26, no.

1405, 10 April 1975: 11). Another is the League against Imperialism (Liga gegen den Imperialismus), which celebrated its fourth anniversary on 14 July 1975. It has headquarters in Cologne, with units in several *Länder*, and an official organ, *Internationale Solidariaät* (ibid., no. 1412, 25 July: 4). The Association of Socialist Artists (Vereinigung Sozialistischer Kulturschaffender; VSK) was founded at Whitsuntide 1975 at a conference in Birkesdorf near Düren, attended by about 250 persons. The VSK has local groups in at least 12 cities. Its organ is *Kulturzeitschrift-Kämpfende Kunst.* (Ibid., no. 1410, 27 June: 5.)

The KPD started on a "Marxist workers' education" program on 13 June in 13 cities in North Rhine-Westphalia in order to prepare the workers for intensified confrontation with "Soviet social imperialism" (ibid., no. 1411, 14 July: 5-6).

The KPD held its own May Day demonstrations, calling for its version of "unity of action" based on "the common fight against the two imperialist superpowers, against the main warmongers Brezhnev and Ford" (ibid., no. 1407, 28 April: 5). The most publicized action was the demonstration in May against the USSR by 18 KPD members in East Berlin in front of the Soviet War Memorial. They were promptly arrested but eventually were released and sent back. (*NYT*, 2 June.) To mark the 36th anniversary of the beginning of World War II about 5,000 KPD followers concentrated in Frankfurt and demonstrated against the Soviet Union and the United States (*Die Welt*, 1 September).

The Communist Party of Germany/Marxist-Leninist (Kommunistische Partei Deutschland/ML; KPD/ML) was founded on 31 December 1968 and is the oldest Maoist "party" in the FRG. Ernst Aust is chairman. It publishes an official organ, *Roter Morgen*, and a "theoretical" periodical, *Der Weg der Partei*. The KPD/ML refuses to disclose the party's strength. The BVS report for 1974 estimated the membership at about 700 concentrated in a few cities in North Rhine-Westphalia, where in the *Land* elections (4 May 1975) its candidates received 1,735 votes. The party has followers in a number of large industrial enterprises. The best results were obtained in the factory elections at the Howaldt Werke in Kiel, where the "Red List" of the KPD/ML obtained almost 25 percent of the votes (*Deutscher Informationsdienst*, 26, no. 1407, 28 April: 2).

The KPD/ML's youth organization, the Rote Garde, publishes 11 periodicals for young workers, 17 for secondary schools and universities, and 4 for soldiers in various garrisons. (For a list see *Deutscher Informationsdienst*, 26, No. 1407, 28 April: 13-17.) A pamphlet entitled "What Does the KPD/ML Want? " has been widely distributed; it openly advocates violent revolution. Young workers and students are encouraged to join the Bundeswehr in order to learn how to handle weapons and to destroy the armed forces from within. (*Die Welt*, 29 July.)

The KPD/ML front organization, Rote Hilfe Deutschlands, was founded on 26 January 1975 in Dortmund by 50 delegates from Rote Hilfe groups in 25 communities. Great emphasis is placed on the production and dissemination of KPD/ML publications, which in 1975 included 87 factory newspapers (17 new since May), 5 papers for hospitals, and 14 for different communities. The KPD/ML owns at least six bookstores, in various cities.

On May Day and 1 September, the day dedicated to the struggle against imperialist wars, the KPD/ML called for common action by all Maoist groups. It was reported that after the return of KPD and KPD/ML delegations from a visit to China, discussions were held with the aim of combining the two parties (*Deutscher Informationsdienst*, 26, no. 1411, 14 July: 5). This objective has not yet been reached.

A third Maoist organization is the Communist League of West Germany (Kommunistischer Bund Westdeutschlands; KBW), which publishes the *Kommunistische Volkszeitung*. The KBW held its Second Conference of Delegates on 28-29 March in Ludwigshafen. The 98 delegates represented 1,700 members, organized in 46 local groups. Representatives from 76 communist groups from all parts of the FRG attended as guests. A 15-member central committee was elected, which in turn appointed a 5-member "permanent committee." (Ibid., no. 1405, 10 April: 4.) The KBW was able to have one of its members elected in 1975 to the city council in Heidelberg. On 21 September it organized a demonstration in Bonn against the law prohibiting abortion; about 20,000 persons participated. The KBW had organized committees and initiatives in 166 localities for this event. (Ibid., no. 1416/17, 6 October: 7.) The KBW also is attempting to infiltrate the Bundeswehr. In Hanover, it succeeded in organizing a "Soldiers' and Reservists' Committee" (ibid., no. 1409, 14 June: 3).

The Communist Workers League of Germany (Kommunistischer Arbeiterbund Deutschlands; KAB) also is Maoist. Its central organ is *Rote Fahne*. The KAB youth organization, the Revolutionary Youth League of Germany (Revolutionärer Jugendverband Deutschlands), began publishing in February a youth magazine, *Stachel* (ibid., no. 1403, 10 March: 2).

The left-nationalistic Independent Workers' Party (Unabhängige Arbeiterpartei; UAP) held its Seventh Congress on 26 January in Essen. Its chairman is Erhard Kliese. The UAP has about 2,000 members. (Ibid., no. 1401, 10 February: 2.)

The Trotskyists are represented by several small groups, among them the Group of International Marxists (Gruppe Internationale Marxisten; GIM), the German section of the Fourth International. The GIM held a national conference in Frankfurt on 7-9 March and 6 April, with 170 delegates representing more than 50 local branches and supporter groups. A new central committee was elected. (*Intercontinental Press*, New York, 23 June.) Another Trotskyist organization is the Spartacus League (Spartacusbund), with headquarters in Essen.

Several foreign left-radical groups are active in the FRG among students and guest workers. Since May 1975, for example, the Turkish Maoists have been reported to have increased their activities. (*Deutscher Informationsdienst*, 26, no. 1415, 15 September: 5.)

Terrorist activities in the FRG have continued in 1975 in spite of the fact that a number of the leaders of the "Red Army Faction" (the Baader-Meinhof Gang) and the "Second June Movement" were apprehended and are in jail with trials pending or in process. The kidnaping in February of Peter Lorenz, the leader of the Christian Democrats, in West Berlin and the assault and murders committed at the German Embassy at Stockholm were the most dramatic events of this kind in 1975. However, there were many other terrorist acts, including bank robberies and bombings. There is evidence that the German terrorist groups, especially the Second June Movement and the Revolutionary Cell in the Heidelberg-Manheim area, have contacts with terrorists organizations abroad (*Die Welt*, 4 September).

The DKP dissociates itself as a matter of principle from the "adventurist activities of anarchist and pseudo-revolutionary groupings because they are hostile to the workers' movement" (TASS, 5 March).

* * * *

WEST BERLIN. The three Western Sectors of Berlin are not a part of the FRG. The U.S., British, and French troops stationed in West Berlin are not part of the NATO contingents of these countries. Berlin has up to the present day a "special status," based on the Allied agreements of 1944 and 1945 and restated in the Quadripartite Agreement concerning Berlin of 3 September 1971. All of these arrangements were supposed to apply to the area of Greater Berlin, which includes the Soviet Sector. However, the German Democratic Republic (GDR) has for all practical purposes incorporated East Berlin, with Moscow's approval, declared "Berlin" as its capital, and repeatedly ignored provisions of the Allied agreements such as the demilitarization of the entire city. Both the Soviet Union and the GDR have pursued the policy of attempting to isolate West Berlin from the FRG as part of their efforts to absorb West Berlin eventually into East Germany. One important phase of this policy is the insistence that the three Western Sectors constitute an "independent political entity." (See Eric Waldman, *Die Sozialistische Einheitspartei Westberlins und die sowjetische Berlinpolitik*, Boppard am Rhein, 1972.)

The FRG maintains close ties with West Berlin which have been approved and encouraged by the

United States, France, and Great Britain, and also have been reaffirmed by the Quadripartite Agreement of 1971.

The special status of Berlin, though only applied to the Western Sectors, made it possible for the Socialist Unity Party of Germany (SED) to establish a branch in West Berlin. Thus the present Socialist Unity Party of West Berlin (Sozialistische Einheitspartei Westberlins; SEW) is the creation of the SED of the GDR and was not founded by communists in West Berlin. Originally it was the SED organization in the three Western Sectors of Berlin. Therefore, up to the time of the alleged separation from the "mother party," it has the same history as the SED.

In the spring of 1959, five months after Khrushchev had demanded the transformation of West Berlin into a "free city," a separate leadership for the SED in the Western Sectors of the city was appointed in order to give the impression of an independent political party. In November 1962, a "Conference of Delegates" was organized by the West Berlin headquarters. This conference gave the party the name Socialist Unity Party of Germany-West Berlin (SED-W) and adopted a new set of rules (Parteistatuten). The separation of East and West Berlin as the result of the Wall (13 August 1961) made this organizational division, at least for the outside world, a necessity. In February 1969 at a special congress of the SED-W the name was changed once more, to its present SEW form. The elimination of "Germany" from the name is part of the implementation of the short-range Soviet policy of stressing the concept of the "independent political entity of West Berlin" and the assignment of the term "Germany" only to the ruling communist party in the GDR, making clear thereby that the other German communist parties (DKP and SEW) are merely carrying out the tasks assigned to them by the SED.

Leadership and Organization. The SEW is a small party with a membership of about 8,000. (West Berlin's population is about 2.1 million.) The organizational pattern is that of a typical communist party. The 47-member Party Directorate (Parteivorstand) is the equivalent of a central committee. The Party Directorate, the 12-man Bureau (Politburo equivalent) and the 7-member Secretariat form the leadership group. The party organization follows the administrative subdivisions of West Berlin and has 12 district (Kreis) organizations, each of them having a District Directorate (Kreisvorstand) and Secretariat. The primary party organization is comprised of factory and residential groups (Betriebs- and Wohngruppen), and party groups in institutions of higher learning. The present 12 leaders, including party chairman Gerhard Danelius and deputy chairman Erich Ziegler, were all reelected to the Bureau at the Fourth Party Congress in 1974 (15-17 November). (The only former party leader dropped was Gerd Ellert. For other names see *YICA, 1974*, p. 158.)

In the effort to increase its influence among the population of West Berlin and to infiltrate the trade unions, the SEW utilizes a number of mass and front organizations. The Free German Youth-West Berlin (Freie Deutsche Jugend-Westberlin; FDJ-W) has about 1,000 members and is responsible for the communist children's organization in West Berlin, the Pioneer Groups. Other SEW subsidiaries are the German-Soviet Friendship Society-West Berlin (including "Club DSF" and the "Mayakovski Gallery"), the Democratic Women's League of Berlin, the Alliance of Victims of the Nazi Regime, and a few others. (See Waldman, *op.cit.*, pp. 101-9.)

The impact of the SEW among students in West Berlin either through its own SEW groups or by means of the Action Union of Democrats and Socialists (ADS) is considerable.

Party Internal Affairs. Most of the SEW's activities following the Fourth Party Congress in November 1974 were concentrated on the forthcoming elections in West Berlin on 2 March 1975. The Party Directorate session on 8 January was primarily concerned with current issues of the election campaign. This session also appointed the members of the SEW Court of Arbitration. (*Die Wahrheit*, 8 January.) The next Session, in March, passed the party's resolution for May Day. It was pointed out that after the election it was even more than ever necessary to establish unity of action, to defend democratic rights and liberties, and preserve labor union unity. The communists were called upon to prepare for 1 May together with Social Democrats, non-party colleagues, and trade unionists. (Ibid., 21 March.)

SEW chairman Danelius spoke on 5 April at a conference of the party *aktiv* on the election results and some of the conclusions to be drawn for the future struggle. He expressed his conviction that the "fierce anti-communist campaign of all other political parties, including the Maoist 'CPG' [KPD,] and the mass media, and the 'Lorenz Affair' [the kidnaping of the leader of the Christian Democrats in West Berlin by members of the terrorist Second of June Movement]" were responsible for the poor election results. The main effort was not to be directed toward establishing and developing firm and good relations with the broad masses of the working people on the basis of the "12 Basic SEW Demands" of September 1973 and the election program. (*IB*, no. 9, 15 May, pp. 26-28.)

Domestic Attitudes and Activities. The main emphasis of the activities of the SEW during the early part of 1975 were in connection with the elections in West Berlin which took place on 2 March. The party's program, marked by the standard communist objectives, such as nationalization of large economic enterprises and the eventual socialist transformation of society, also contained short-range goals on the order of wage demands, price and rent controls, job security and control and co-determination by the workers, factory councils, and trade unions. It was supposed to provide the basis for an appeal to the "masses" to elect communist delegates to the legislature. It also declared that the SEW would continue to fight for these objectives both within "parliament" and outside: "The SEW has resolutely decided to utilize the Chamber of Deputies as a tribune in the great struggle of classes." (*Die Wahrheit*, 19 November 1974.) SEW voters' initiatives were organized, especially in the party's stronghold at the universities. The president of the Free University, Rolf Kreibich, a member of the SPD, has worked together on many issues and occasions with the SEW, which in turn at its election congress declared that the party was very firmly anchored in all the fields (24 subject areas) of the university (*Frankfurter Allgemeine*, 15 January). In spite of the prohibition of election propaganda within the buildings of institutions of higher learning, the SEW and the Maoist communist groups disregarded entirely this official directive (*Die Welt*, 18 January). The election appeal of the SEW, published by the "Emergency Committee for a Free University," carried 135 signatures, among them 94 faculty members and assistants (ibid., 30 January). The emphasis was on workers and youth in the SEW's selection of its 80 candidates for the Chamber of Deputies. The social composition was 62 blue- and white-collar workers (77.5 percent), 11 intelligentsia (13.7), 7 students (8.8). The age distribution was as follows: up to 30 years of age, 38 percent (47.5); 30 to 35 years, 10 (12.5); 35 to 40 years, 4 (5.0); 40 to 50 years, 19 (23.7); 50 to 60 years, 5 (6.3); and over 60 years, 4 (5.0). (*Die Wahrheit*, 14/15 December 1974.)

The outcome of the elections was most disappointing for the communists. The SEW lost 8,262 votes, as compared with the 1971 elections, receiving a total of 25,583 votes, or 1.9 percent (2.3 percent in 1971). The SEW lost votes to the Maoist KPD and KBW (see below). Its best results were in districts with a large student population. For example, in Zehlendorf the SEW obtained 3.5 percent of the vote and in Schöneberg 5.2. (*Die Welt*, 12 May.)

The election defeat did not slow down the SEW activities at the universities. The emphasis continued to be on creating a unity of action of the "left-wing cartel." At a meeting at the Free University, about 2,000 persons were addressed by a representative of the SEW Party Directorate, and several professors in an attempt to reach the "liberal" and "progressive" elements. (*Rheinischer Merkur*, 20 June.)

The other main activity of the SEW was directed toward increasing its contact with the masses, with communist infiltration into trade unions considered as one of the best methods. The SEW was most successful in the Education and Science Union (Gewerkschaft Erziehung und Wissenschaft; GEW). The Federal Executive Broad of the GEW had adopted the DGB's demarcation resolution excluding "left extremists" from membership in the unions on the grounds that they regarded union work merely as the means to an end. The DGB policy did not exclude followers of the Moscow-loyal DKP and SEW. However, because of the success of the SEW in West Berlin in obtaining control of the union through a "people's front" tactic, GEW Chairman Frister declared at the Federal Congress of the GEW that also SEW members are excluded. (*Handelsblatt*, Düsseldorf, 15 January; *Die Welt*, 11 September.) On 28 September 1974 the *Berliner Stimme*, an SPD weekly, reported that some 1,500 members had left the GEW in Berlin since January of that year.

International Views and Party Contacts. There is not one single issue concerning the position of West Berlin as spelled out in the agreements of the Western Allies and the Soviet Union, or with regard to the city's relations with the FRG or DGR, on which the views of the SEW diverge from those expressed in East Berlin. Chairman Danelius stressed early in 1975 that West Berlin must become a city open to the world and maintain good relations with both German states (*Die Wahrheit*, 23 January). He added later: "The most important thing for West Berlin is the consolidation of peace [and] the further successful establishment of the policy of détente.... But everything begins with strict observation, full application, and realization of the treaties concluded, in letter and spirit." (Ibid., 28 January.) Danelius accused the West Berlin Senate of avoiding direct talks with the GDR on its proposals of 9 December 1974 on a number of issues of serious interest (*IB*, no. 9, 1975, p. 30). His emphasis on direct talks between the authorities of West Berlin and the GDR was entirely in agreement with the aforementioned Soviet concept of West Berlin as an "independent political entity." The communist interpretation of the "special status" of Berlin pertains only to the three Western Sectors, according to *Neues Deutschland* (30 May 1975), the official organ of the SED:

> It is absolutely clear that Berlin is the capital of the German Democratic Republic. Our capital is an inseparable, integral component part of, and has exactly the same legal status as every other part of the territory of the German Democratic Republic. France, Great Britain, and the United States have no original noncontractual rights with regard to Berlin, nor have they ever had them. Berlin has never been extracted territorially from the former Soviet Occupation Zone of Germany. The four powers affirmed all this when they concluded the Quadripartite Agreement on West Berlin.
>
> Completely different, but just as clear, is the situation of Berlin-West. West Berlin is still an occupied area. Its status and its relations have been settled in the Quadripartite Agreement.
>
> Consequently West Berlin, which is located on the territory of the German Democratic Republic, is a special structure which, as before, is not a component part of the Federal Republic of Germany and will not be governed by it in the future either.

The views expressed by Danelius about some of the international conferences held in 1975 also restated opinions frequently heard from Moscow and East Berlin. He pointed out that conferences such as the World Population Conference of the United Nations, the Raw Materials Conference, disarmament talks, the Law of the Sea Conference, and, most important, the CSCE, were defined by the class struggle:

> ... since ideology extends through all areas of life, every conference in which states with different social orders participate becomes at the same time a complicated class struggle of contrary combatants at the conference table. And the fact that a solution can only go as far as the power relationship has developed is an old lesson which the communists have learned, especially in Europe. (*Die Wahrheit*, 4 February.)

The SEW maintained contacts with several communist parties. Its closest relations were with the

SED. Danelius met with SED first secretary Erich Honecker on several occasions in East Berlin. A meeting of the two party leaders on 10 January was "characterized by the spirit of fraternal affection" (ibid., 11/12 January). Both sides underscored the significance of the results achieved so far in the struggle for international détente, especially for European security. Danelius was received on 4 June in East Berlin by the Soviet ambassador to the GDR. A delegation of the FDJ-W, headed by its chairman, visited the Soviet Union at the invitation of the Central Committee of the Komsomol and the USSR Youth Organization Committee (*Komsomolskaya Pravda*, Moscow, 19 June).

Publications. *Die Wahrheit*, published six times weekly in about 15,000 copies, is the official and most important publication of the SEW. The party has its own printing plant. The twice-weekly *Berliner Extradienst* 4,500 to 5,000 copies, is not officially a mouthpiece of the SEW but endorses most of the party's positions and also advocates unity of action; its editor in chief is a member of the SPD. The SEW publishes at irregular intervals a number of factory and residential newspapers. A quarterly publication, *Konsequent*, addresses itself to theoretical issues and practical problems of party activities. The "Europäische Buch" is a party bookshop which sells Marxist literature, mostly printed in the GDR, at very reasonable prices.

The various subsidiary organizations of the SEW have their own publications, such as *Signal*, the FDJ-W monthly, and the *DSF-Journal* of the German-Soviet Friendship Society. (For other publications of the "mass organizations" see *YICA, 1975*, p. 191.)

Other Leftist Groups–Rival Communists. The "left extremists" are represented in West Berlin by numerous groups and organizations, each of them claiming to possess the only correct interpretation of Marxism-Leninism. Especially the Free University has been the matrix for the development of the various Maoist, Trotskyist, anarchist, dissident-left wing socialist, and left communist groups. They form the so-called APO, or Extra-Parliamentary Opposition.

Two Maoist parties, the "new" Communist Party of Germany (Kommunistische Partei Deutschlands; KPD) and the Communist League of West Germany (Kommunistischer Bund Westdeutschlands; KBW) participated in the 2 March 1975 elections. The KPD obtained 10,277 votes (0.7 percent) and the KBW 802 (0.1). The Maoist Communist Student Union (Kommunistischer Studenten-Verband) appeared to have an increasing following in West Berlin's institutions of higher learning in 1975.

The SEW is strongly opposed to these "left extremists" and has called upon its members to combat the "chaoten" because of their "policy of provocation" (*Die Welt*, 13 May).

University of Calgary   Eric Waldman

Great Britain

The Communist Party of Great Britain (CPGB) was founded in 1920. Its traditional preeminence as the oldest communist movement in Great Britain has been steadily attacked since 1973 by other Marxist-Leninist groups and the "ultra left" (see below).

The CPGB is a recognized political party and its candidates contend for national and local offices. There have, however, been no members in the House of Commons since 1950. In national elections in February and October 1974 the party contested 73 seats, all unsuccessfully. Overall results are shown in the accompanying table.

In 1975 the CPGB at its Thirty-Fourth Congress (15-18 November) reported a loss of membership from 29,943 (1973) to 28,519—about 3 percent. About 46 percent of the membership was in arrears with party dues. (*Morning Star*, 19 November). The population of Great Britain is 6,102,000.

Leadership and Organization. The National Congress is the supreme authority and policy-making organ of the CPGB. It meets biennially when called by the Executive Committee, but a special congress can be convened under extraordinary circumstances. The National Congress elects the 42-member Executive Committee, which is the highest authority between congresses. At its first meeting after a congress has been convened the Executive Committee elects the party officers and the Political Committee. The Executive Committee meets every two months; the Political Committee usually meets weekly or when the need arises. Below the leadership level, the CPGB is organized into district committees, then area and borough committees, and finally into party branches. Wales and Scotland do not have separate parties, but have area branches of the main party. During 1975, party officers and departmental heads were Gordon McLennan (general secretary), Irene Swann (chairman), Reuben Falber (assistant general secretary), Bert Ramelson (industrial), Jack Woddis (international), Dave Cook (organization), George Matthews (press and publicity), Jean Styles (women), Betty Matthews (education), Dennis Elwand (treasurer), and Malcolm Cowle (election agent). The 16-member Political Committee included McLennan, Falber, Ramelson, Woddis, and G. Matthews.

The Young Communist League (YCL) has been affiliated to the CPGB since the latter's founding. The YCL has a 40-member Executive Committee, whose principal members include Tom Bell (national secretary) and Phil Green (chairman). YCL membership rose from 2,355 in 1974 to 2,800 in 1975.

The CPGB derives its greatest strength from the trade union movement, in which it exercises significant influence. But in 1975 the party was not so prominently involved in industrial agitation as before; the level of polemics was high but direct responsibility in shop-floor stoppages diminished. The main reason was government pressure on the labor movement and a general awareness of the critical national economic condition.

Formerly the CPGB has been most influential in the Amalgamated Union of Engineering Workers (AUEW), Britain's second-largest union, with 1.4 million members. The AUEW had about 175 communists in official positions but elections for the union executive in November produced a massive swing to the right, in effect a 5-2 majority for the moderates. Especially significant was the defeat of James Reid of the CPGB Political Committee by 12,000 votes. The Transport and General Workers Union (TGWU) is the largest, with a membership of about 2 million. Of the 36 members of its executive committee, 15 follow the CPGB line. The party continued to promote its Liaison Committee for the Defense of Trade Unions (LCDTU), an "umbrella" organization for unofficial rank-and-file bodies set up throughout the country and in key industries, which was founded in 1966.

Party Internal Affairs. Unlike the preceding congress in 1973 (see *YICA, 1974*), the Thirty-fourth Congress was not controversial. The dissent of hard-liners was not so prominent, being mainly confined to exchanges of correspondence in the press before the congress. Among visiting delegations were representatives from the Communist Party of Spain, the Palestine Liberation Organization (PLO), and the Communist Party of Chile. For the party the most important event was the formal retirement of John Gollan as general secretary and his replacement by Gordon McLennan. There was little dissent on most of the resolutions on domestic affairs such as education, agriculture, steel and transport. But the resolution on Northern Ireland was opposed by the delegate from Norwich who criticized the party's call for Irish reunification as "republican dogma" which the left can only advocate through "bourgeois metaphysical disputes" that contradict Leninist theories (*Economist*, 22 November 1975). In traditional manner, the Norwich appeal was defeated and the final resolution advocated a united Ireland and a carefully worded compromise proposal on the withdrawal of British troops.

The most keenly debated resolution dealt with the party's poor performance in the elections. In October 1974, 29 communist candidates polled 17.008 votes (an average of less than 600 each). "There were many weaknesses in [the] campaign, including inadequate preparation and organisation," according to the resolution, which went on to note that "Contesting elections and preparing for them more effectively is an important part of the activity of the party" (Congress document). The party's election defeat and its dismal showing in the 1975 EEC referendum focused attention on the decrease in membership. Blame was placed on the governing Labour Party in calling elections and a referendum at a time that was unhelpful to the CPGB, which during the campaigns "did not find the way to maintain sustained attention to membership advance" (ibid.).

Declining membership and electoral failure were matched by lack of money, both for the party and for its organ, *Morning Star*. The party has an annual income of about £130,000 made up of subscriptions and donations, but in May it launched a major fund-raising campaign to bring in a further £30,000. The condition of the *Morning Star* has become an annual problem: "Of key importance for further political development is our fight to extend the circulation of the *Morning Star*, especially as the circulation has declined since our last Congress" (ibid.). As an incentive, a monthly target of £6,000 was set in November 1974, a target which was easily reached. In two years, the price of the newspaper was increased three times.

The Titoist line of the CPGB was maintained during the 1975 congress. Its position was made easier because the Stalinists (see *YICA, 1974*) of the previous congress were generally reticent. This encouraged the congress to call on the Soviet Union to allow dissidents to express and publish their views freely. An executive resolution said that political dissent and the "combating of anti-Marxist ideas should be handled by political debate and not by administrative measures" (*Daily Telegraph*, 17 November).

The YCL closely followed the policies of the adult party. Its membership remained sluggish and the low recruitment rate was emphasized at the YCL's Thirtieth Congress (12-13 April): "We have done insufficient in the fight to implement our last Congress resolution, and there must be a new effort to fulfill the aims set out in that resolution. This demands that ... we conduct activity amongst youth as a political party of all working people" (Congress document).

Domestic Attitudes and Activities. The CPGB campaigned on a wide range of issues during 1975: trade union rights and industrial democracy, social freedoms, race relations, Northern Ireland, government devolution, the armed forces, police and prison reforms. But two main issues predominated, the national economic crisis and British entry into the Common Market. Industrial closures, rising unemployment, falling exports and rising imports put the British Government on the defensive. The gravity of the crisis and the governnment's intention to create a socialist system provoked numerous confrontations in both private and public sectors. Within the government there was a distinct rift between left and right—the former supporting a central market system, the latter preferring a mixed economy in which market forces were encouraged. The CPGB attacked the government for its ambivalence: "The full united strength of the working class movement must now be brought into action for an alternative policy and to force a change of direction in the government" (*Morning Star*, 13 January). Among its proposals the party called for higher wages, an end to closures and dismissals, an extension of public ownership, and cuts in defense expenditure.

Government efforts to control the rate of inflation were broadly welcomed by the Trades Union Congress (TUC), even though the government warned that there might be an unavoidable reduction in living standards. But the CPGB claimed that the government's economic strategy would assist the return of a Conservative government: "It will not solve the crisis. It places the government on a course of confrontation with the unions and the Labour movement." (*Comment*, 12 July.) The CPGB's program received a setback when key unions like the TGWU, the National Union of Mineworkers (NUM) and the AUEW finally rallied to the government. Events in the AUEW were especially unfavorable to the CPBG after two elections within the union produced a marked shift to the right. The CPGB's explanation for the shift was unrealistic: "Massive interference in elections in the engineering union, by the press, television and bosses has resulted in the unseating of Mr. Bob Wright from the union's executive council" (*Morning Star*, 19 November). What the party chose to overlook was that the AUEW elections had been conducted by a democratic postal ballot. James Reid described his defeat as "a setback for the working class" (ibid.).

On 5 June, Great Britain voted overwhelmingly in a referendum in favor of joining the Common Market. The CPGB's policy toward European integration has led to an ideological contradiction. Though firm in its allegiance to the international communist movement, the CPGB has been opposed to the EEC since the early 1960s, which puts it at odds with West European communists. The contradiction is that the CPGB sees itself as the custodian of British nationalism (see *YICA, 1974*). In January, the battle lines were drawn. The CPGB stated: "The real issue is not the so-called terms. It is whether to remain in this monopolist, rich man's club or come out to save Britain's future." (*Morning Star*, 25 January). Undeterred by the failure of its campaign (67.2 percent voted to stay in the EEC), the CPGB planned future strategy which was to "resist through mass struggle, all attempts to use Common Market membership laws and regulations'" (*WMR*, August).

Policy statements on other domestic issues, like Northern Ireland, racism, and women's equality altered little from previous years. What emphasis was made was directed at the right-wing movement, the National Front (NF), which is neo-Nazi and committed to the repatriation of immigrants. During the year there were minor skirmishes between communists and NF militants, but none were allowed to escalate. In February there was a brief diversion in CPGB affairs when a listening device was found in the party headquarters: "Whoever was responsible, we consider it an outrageous invasion of our democratic right" (*Morning Star*, 6 February). An investigation was inconclusive.

The revival of Scottish and Welsh nationalism contrived to unsettle the CPGB, especially as the nationalist vote cut into traditional communist areas. Nationalist gains were one reason for the CPGB's poor electoral effort: "In Scotland and Wales, the nationalist advance was an additional factor. It created the fear of losing some marginal constituencies." (Congress document.)

International Views and Party Contacts. In 1975 the CPGB campaigned on South-East Asia, European security, southern Europe, and Africa. Communist success in Cambodia, Laos, and South Vietnam was enthusiastically acclaimed: "The victory . . . marks a further fundamental and irreversible shift in the world balance of power to the forces of peace, democracy, national liberation and socialism" (Congress document).

Although détente between the United States and the USSR cooled a little during the year, the CPGB closely followed the Soviet line and called for an end to NATO: "A key role [in European security] has been played by the Socialist countries, especially the Soviet Union, which has worked tirelessly to initiate peace policies and activities commanding wide popular support." The only problem it seemed was China: "China's attitude in European questions . . . can only bring satisfaction to the imperialists. This is the harsh logic of the anti-Soviet policy pursued by China's present leaders." (Ibid.)

Political developments in southern Europe—Portugal, Greece, and Spain—were interpreted by the CPGB as a shifting of the balance toward progress. In August the party organ devoted four lengthy articles by Jack Woddis and Dave Cook to the Portuguese revolution. The ideological confusion of the Portuguese armed forces movement presented Woddis with problems of classification: "The AFM . . . represents a complex problem. It is by no sense a united, homogeneous organisation. They are surrounded by political crisis and rapid change." In many cases the rapid pace of revolution was criticized: there was "Ultra-leftism in the armed forces too, in many forms—sometimes in elementary forms of anarchism, indiscipline, impatience and lack of experience" (*Morning Star*, 20-23 August). A meeting of the London district of the CPGB on 2 September passed a resolution urging members of the labor movement to make contact with Portuguese progressives and to "counter the grossly biased reporting by the British media" (ibid., 3 September).

European communist parties devoted a great deal of attention to organizing a pan-European conference. But the proposed aim ran into problems, not the least of which was that such a conference would be an unequal one of the non-ruling parties of western Europe and those of Warsaw Pact countries. Repeated delays in holding such a conference provoked press speculation that there were rifts in the ranks of European communists. This was denied by the CPGB in a statement by Reuben Falber (ibid., 29 October), but he conceded that polycentrism was a fact: "Each party decides its own strategy."

Foreign visits made by CPGB members included those of Woddis to the Soviet Union in May, where he had talks with Boris Ponomarev, and of Falber to Yugoslavia in April as a guest of the League of Communists. Woddis and Cook visited Portugal (28 July-3 August) and wrote up their impressions in August editions of the party organ. In August, two Political Committee members were guests of the Romanian Communist Party, holidaying at the invitation of its Central Committee. In October, Falber attended a meeting in Berlin to discuss preparations for a conference of European communists. CPGB guests included Santiago Carrillo of the Communist Party of Spain and party workers from Romania and East Germany.

Publications. The London daily *Morning Star* is the CPGB's principal organ. Other major publications are *Comment* (a fortnightly magazine), *Marxism Today* (a monthly theoretical journal), and *Labour Monthly*, which provides a commentary on political events. The YCL publishes *Challenge* (monthly) and *Cogito*, a monthly theoretical journal.

*   *   *

Workers Revolutionary Party. Among the Marxist-Leninist parties and groups that challenge the CPGB's leadership in the communist movement, the largest and most influential (particularly in the trade union movement) is the Workers Revolutionary Party (WRP). It was formed on 4 November 1973 and is the reconstituted Socialist Labour League, which was founded in 1959. The WRP is an affiliate of the Trotskyite International Committee of the Fourth International.

The WRP claims about 2,000 members. Its youth movement, the Young Socialists (YS), claims to have 20,000 members and is the largest Marxist-Leninist organization to have existed in Britain.

The WRP is led by Gerry Healy (general secretary). The party issues a daily newspaper, *Workers Press*, and a quarterly, *Fourth International*. The YS is led by Maureen Bambrick (national secretary). Its organ is a weekly, *Keep Left*.

The WRP controls the All Trade Union Alliance (ATUA), a group similar to the CPGB-controlled LCDTU. The WRP's domestic activity in 1975 was largely devoted to industrial agitation. On 19 January, the miners' section of the ATUA called for a revolutionary program for industrial reform, in particular for the complete communization of the coal industry. This call was renewed at the fifth annual conference of the ATUA (*Workers Press* 11 March).

The impact of the WRP was weakened by bitter internal disputes on doctrine and personalities. Moreover, the year was punctuated by bitter debates with rival groups. Following a controversial legal battle between Vanessa Redgrave and Alan Thornett—both members of the WRP—the latter broke away and formed his own splinter group in December 1974 (see below). Thornett's defection and his views were scathingly attacked by the WRP; he was accused of "arrogance, trickery, inventing fables" and having organized a slander campaign against the WRP.

Ideological skirmishes with the CPGB were fitfully conducted. The CPGB is considered as Stalinist and was regularly attacked for obstructing WRP activities in industry. The CPGB was asked to reject its "right-wing" leadership.

In October the WRP's most publicized efforts were the attempts of Vanessa Redgrave and her brother to seize control of Equity, a 23,000-strong actors' union. The voting was inconclusive.

The YS supported WRP policies in the trade unions and continued its activities among youth groups. The YS 15th Annual Conference in Scarborough (12-13 April) passed resolutions on the crisis of capitalism, student welfare, and means of raising more money for the production of *Keep Left*.

*   *   *

None of the several other several Marxist-Leninist groups in Britain has been able to muster numerically significant support. The four main ones are the Workers Socialist League (WSL), the International Socialists (IS), and the International Marxist Group (IMG), and the Communist Party of Great Britain (Marxist-Leninist) (CPBML).

The WSL emerged in December 1974 as a splinter of the WRP. It is led by Alan Thornett and has a membership of about 200. It is Trotskyist and has a weekly organ, *Socialist Press*.

The IS has about 3,500 members. Its principal leaders were Tony Cliff, Paul Foot and Jim Higgins. It is mainly active in industrial affairs. Its activities at the grass-roots level are coordinated by the Rank and File Movement (RFM), founded in 1974, which though small claims to have the support of teachers, local government offices, and blue-collar unions. The IS organ is the weekly *Socialist Worker*.

The IMG claims to be the British section of the United Secretariat of the Fourth International. The national secretary is Pat Jordan. The IMG issues a monthly organ, *International*, and a fortnightly, *Red Weekly*. In 1975 the group was interested in Ireland, Portugal, and the economic crisis.

The CPBML is pro-Chinese. Reg Birch, its leader, is a member of the Executive Committee of the AUEW. In September, he was elected to the General Council of the TUC. The CPBML has a membership of about 400. Its impact is insignificant and is conditioned by amicable Sino-British relations. The party's main organ is a fortnightly, *The Worker*.

London   D. L. Price

Appendix A

Great Britain National Election of 10 October 1974

Party	Votes cast	Percent of total votes	Number of seats won	Percent of total seats
Communist				
Comunist Party of Great Britain	17,008	0.5	— —	— —
Non-communist left:				
Labour	11,272,762	39.6	315	50.7
Center:				
Liberal	5,228,017	18.4	11	1.7
Conservative:				
Conservative	10,255,822	36.0	217	43.6
Other parties	1,683,952	5.5	22	4.0
Totals	28,457,561	100.0	619	100.0

Greece

The Communist Party of Greece (Kommounistikon Komma Ellados; KKE) evolved from the Socialist Workers' Party of Greece, a basically social-democratic party affiliated with the Second International, which was formed in November 1918. KKE went through a series of internal convulsions during the 1920s, remaining throughout this period a small and rather ineffectual organization. The party's fortunes improved after the appointment of N. Zakhariades to its leadership by the Comintern in 1931, but its progress was seriously disrupted by the Metaxas dictatorial regime, established on 4 August 1936. During the country's occupation by the Axis (1941-44), the communist party succeeded in organizing a very successful resistance movement (National Liberation Front; EAM) and a guerrilla force (Greek Popular Liberation Army; ELAS). In December 1944, shortly after the country's liberation, an attempt by KKE/ELAS to seize power by force was crushed by the British, but the party remained a legitimate organization until 1947, when it was outlawed because of the guerrilla campaign it had launched the year before. The campaign was eventually crushed by the Greek army in August 1949. During the 1950s and 1960s the communist left was represented by a front organization known as United Democratic Left (EDA). The Papadopoulos dictatorial regime, imposed after a successful coup on 21 April 1967, banned EDA together with all other parties. Following the student demonstrations of November 1973 and their violent suppression by the government, Papadopoulos was replaced by a group of hardliners led by a former colleague, Brigadier General Dimitrios Ioannides, chief of the military police. The Ioannides government collapsed on 23 July 1974 as a result of its disastrous policies on Cyprus, which opened the way to the Turkish invasion and occupation of a large part of the island republic. With the fall of the dictatorship and the return of Constantine Karamanlis to the premiership (held by him in 1955-63), the communist party regained legitimate status after a hiatus of almost 28 years.

The party's legitimacy was marred by the continuing split which had occurred during the years of the dictatorship. One section, dominated till December 1972 by Kostas Koliyannis and since then by Harilaos Florakis, claimed to be the genuine KKE. Because its leadership and most of its followers had lived in Eastern Europe and the Soviet Union since the collapse of the 1946-49 guerrilla campaign, the faction became known as the KKE (Exterior). The other group, led by Babis Drakopoulos and veteran communist Dimitrios Partsalides, was primarily based within Greece and thus became known as the KKE (Interior). The first continues to have the support of the Soviet Union. The second has tried to follow a somewhat independent and moderate course.

Any review of the communist Left in Greece which limits itself to the two communist parties will be unrealistic and superficial. The "anti-imperialist, anti-fascist, anti-capitalist, anti-American" Left which in years past could be identified with the KKE and its front organizations is currently represented by several political organizations which are not necessarily related—in fact are often antagonistic—to the communist party.

The United Democratic Left (EDA), under the leadership of Illias Iliou, reemerged immediately after the fall of the dictatorship in July 1974 and participated in the first parliamentary election together with the two communist parties in an electoral coalition labeled the United Left (EA). Since the beginning of 1975, EDA has been making a serious effort to play the role of an "independent and autonomous party of the Left" while cooperating with the leadership of the KKE (Interior). Its relations meanwhile with the KKE (Exterior) have been steadily worsening. On 4 February EDA held a "broad conference" in which Iliou expounded on the role of an independent party and attacked the "dogmatism" of KKE (Exterior) while at the same time praising KKE (Interior) for its "earnest efforts on behalf of an up-to-date policy on Greece's political affairs." KKE (Exterior) responded by accusing "Iliou and those who cooperate with him" of trying to "reap the fruits of EDA's long and rich record." The party's statement went on to say: "The present EDA bears no relation to the old EDA. . . . It was the KKE that played a leading role in establishing EDA, and KKE's members and followers were the heart of EDA's activities." Exchanges of this type between EDA and its organ *Avgi* (which also serves KKE (Interior), on the one side, and KKE (Exterior) and its organ *Rizospastis* on the other, continued through the year. At this point there is no accurate estimate as to the EDA's political following but considering the role the KKE members played in EDA prior to 1967 and the existence now of two communist parties in Greece one may safely assume that EDA's political strength is currently quite limited. Loosely, there may be 25,000 to 30,000 persons, in Greece and abroad, who could be labeled as communist party members or followers, but this estimate would also include the numerous small Left groups (see below) and is to be regarded with caution. The population of Greece is just over 9 million.

Another political organization with a pronounced "anti-imperialist, anti-fascist, anti-capitalist, anti-American" ideological orientation is that of the Panhellenic Socialist Movement (PASOK) established in September 1974 by Andreas Papandreou. In an article published on 26 September 1975 in *Athinaiki* (an Athens daily friendly to Papandreou) the leader of PASOK declared that his party is Marxist but not Leninist and proceeded to criticize the Soviet Union as following a "course of retrogression toward capitalism—a capitalism of a new type, of course, which some identify as state capitalism." In his article Papandreou indicated that he favors a form of "commune-type" socialism somewhat along the Chinese model. He is strongly anti-American and anti-NATO, and his ideology reflects some of the orientations which became associated with the "New Left" in the late 1960s. In a statement last July Papandreou accused KKE (Interior) of being "a lackey of the Right" and claimed that "its conciliatory posture toward the Establishment . . . is undermining the people's movement." Papandreou aims his message primarily at the intellectuals and young adults. While one should not consider PASOK a "communist" organization, one can say that PASOK, EDA, and the two communist parties comprise the four major political parties of the "anti-imperialist" Left.

Beyond these four parties—which sent 20 representatives to the Chamber of Deputies (Vouli) in the November 1974 parliamentary election (see *YICA, 1975*, p. 202)—several other organizations of the "extreme Left" made their appearance during 1975. All told, there are at least 23 such organizations currently operating in Greece. Most of them are marginal in terms of mass following. To the extent that reliable information exists about their membership, it appears that most of these organizations draw their following primarily from young adults, with university students and young technicians accounting for most of their limited constituencies. Some have been successful in fomenting demonstrations against the wishes of the major parties of the Left. The most significant among them are:

1. Organization of Marxist-Leninists of Greece (OMLE). This organization was initially formed in June 1964 by certain elements from the "Lambrakis Youth Organization" and KKE cadres who were dissatisfied with EDA's "lukewarm" policies. During the dictatorship OMLE went underground and in June 1967 established the Liberation Front of Greeks Abroad (AMEE) which published the newspaper *Laiki Enotita* and was very active among Greek workers and university students in France and West Germany. Since the fall of the dictatorship this organization (OMLE) has been operating primarily through "syndicalist" outfits: the university student Pan-student Progressive Syndicalist Parataxis [Camp] (PPSP), the worker-oriented Progressive Workers Syndicalist Parataxis (PESP), and the younger (secondary school) students Progressive Students Syndicalist Parataxis (PMSP). These organizations publish respectively *Laikos Dromos, Spoudastikos Kosmos,* and *Mathitiki Genia*, the last being distributed free of charge among secondary school students "for the growth of an anti-fascist, anti-imperialist younger student movement."

2. Revolutionary Communist Movement of Greece (EKKE). This organization was founded by Greek university students in West Berlin in 1970 and for almost four years its main activity was the publication of the Periodical *Kommounistis*, whose issues were published in book form in 1975 under the title "Basic Political Texts, 1970-1974." At present EKKE is considered to be the best-organized and largest "extremely radical" leftist group. It has a Maoist orientation and aspires to be the nucleus for a truly "Maoist-Leninist communist workers party in Greece." EKKE is also operating through organizations known as the Anti-imperialist, Anti-fascist Student Parataxis of Greece (AASPE) and the Anti-imperialist, Anti-fascist Student Parataxis of Working Technicians (AASPET). EKKE now publishes the weekly *Laikoi Agones.* In student elections at the universities of Athens and Salonica its candidates received 630 and 225 votes out of a total number of votes cast of 16,053 and 7,227 respectively.

3. Greek Revolutionary Liberation Front (EEAM). This is a group of "Marxist-Leninists opposed to the opportunism of KKE and to the Khrushchevite revisionism which led to the ideological-political degeneration of KKE since 1956." EEAM was formed in the spring of 1973 by cadres who left OMLE as a result of personal and ideological feuds. The EEAM cadres are Stalinists and Maoists and consider the present Soviet leadership out of step with true Marxism-Leninism. EEAM operates among the university students through its Union of Struggle of Leftist Students (EPAS). Its effect among students remains so far limited, the only exception being the Athens medical school, where the organization succeeded in electing one of its candidates to the student government. Its publica-

tion, *Neoni Agones*, closed down recently for lack of funds.

4. Greek Communist Party/Marxist Leninist (KKE/ML). The officers of this organization were initially associated with OMLE. In 1969 they disagreed with the OMLE leadership on its inability to launch "decisive action" against the dictatorship. Those who left OMLE at that time established a splinter organization which they labeled the Organization of Greek Marxist-Leninists (OEML). On 3 November 1974 the name was changed to KKE/ML. It does not have separate student or worker organizations, but forms "militant groups" within the legitimate student or syndicalist organizations and promotes its political views through individual spokesmen. At the present time KKE/ML is planning to hold its first congress and to take part in the next parliamentary election when it is held. KKE/ML publishes a monthly periodical, *Kokkini Simaia*, and controls the "Poreia" publishing house at 77 Solonis Street in Athens. Stalinist in orientation, it defends the positions of N. Zakhariades, KKE's leader between 1931 and 1956.

5. Several small groups with Trotskyite leanings have also made their appearance, especially during and after the dictatorship. The Revolutionary Communist League (EKS) is associated with the monthly periodical *Neoi Stokhoi*. The Socialist Revolutionary Organization (OSE) is currently operating through its Militant Students Parataxis (APS), whose candidates received 267 votes in the latest elections for the student government at the University of Athens; its newspaper, *Agonistiki Poreia*, has stopped publication for lack of funds. The Greek Internationalist Union (EDE), strongly opposed to both communist parties and to the Maoist organizations, is associated with the weekly newspaper *Socialistiki Allagi*. During 1975 the paper caused a sensation with its running argument that a war with Turkey would only serve the interest of the Greek bourgeoisie "because the Greek workers and farmers have nothing to fight about with the Turkish masses." The Organization of Communist Internationalists of Greece (OKDE) is currently the recognized branch of the Fourth International in Greece. It publishes a weekly, *Ergatiki Pali*, and a monthly, *Marxistiko Deltio*. The ODKE operates also through the Socialist Syndicalist Movement (SSK), active in the construction and industrial workers trade unions, and the Socialist Student Struggle (SSP), which elected two of its candidates to the student government, in the architectural school and in the dental school, at the University of Athens. The Socialist Revolutionary Union (SEE) was established abroad in November 1973. It preaches the theory of permanent revolution and publishes the periodical *Kommounismos*. The group "Gia to Socialismo" (For Socialism) publishes a bimonthly periodical of the same name, and is associated with a picturesque Trotskyite, K. Raptis, who has close ties with Andreas Papandreou. This group is relatively moderate and politically near to PASOK.

6. There are also some smaller Maoist groups vying for public support, so far with but limited appeal. One of them is "Kritiki Syspeirosis" (Critical Rally). Another is the Movement of Greek Marxist-Leninists (KEML), which was established in 1974 and has made its existence visible primarily through placards during demonstrations organized by the major groups. The movement of the Revolutionary Left (KEA) is a small organization which so far has not played any noteworthy role.

7. One should also mention the existence of some groups of anarchists who have participated in demonstrations with totally blank placards or anarchist slogans. Ideologically they are influenced by Bakunin and anarcho-Trotskyism and in true anarchist fashion they do not have a structured organization. The best-known group is identified by the acronym "KRAK" which means Kato Rossia, Ameriki, Kina (Down with Russia, America, China).

Party Internal Affairs. Following the Second Plenum of the KKE (Exterior) Central Committee in late December 1974, several party-affiliated organizations held regional and local meetings. The leadership of the Athens-Piraeus Communst Youth of Greece (KNE) met on 1 February 1975, followed by its Salonica organization on 5 February. The party's organization of Ipeiros held a plenum on 5 February. The party-supported United Anti-dictatorial Syndicalist Movement (ESAK) held a broad assembly in Athens on 4 February.

On 23 February the Central Committee of KKE (Interior) announced its intention to hold a party congress sometime in November 1975, "with the participation of the broadest possible representation of the renewal forces to create a united Marxist-Leninist party." Statements issued by KKE (Interior) with regard to the projected congress revealed a significant reorientation of its views on organization. KKE (Interior) favors a "mass party" as opposed to the Leninist model: "Our party is no longer a party following the narrow sectarian line that isolated it from the broad masses." In a lengthy resolution issued on 15 April by the "expanded plenum of the Central Committee," KKE (Interior) made an interesting reference to democratic centralism, "which can also be adjusted to the new conditions that today dictate stressing the aspect of democracy which has been neglected, and went on, "This does not mean in any way, however, neglecting the aspect of discipline."

The anti-dictatorial demonstrations held on 21 April to denounce the anniversary of the defunct Papadopoulos regime brought to the foreground the EKKE and its student affiliate AASPE. When violence broke out, the demonstrations were forcibly dispersed by the police and were denounced by both communist parties and by PASOK. The Politburo of the KKE (Exterior) attributed the violence to "a plan of great provocation prepared in advance ... by the dark enemies of the Greek people [and] the dark circles of the American domination and its various domestic lackeys—reactionaries, junta followers, neofascists and others." The statement went on to say these "dark forces" were "helped by the provocative activites of EKKE." On its part, EKKE proudly claimed responsibility for the demonstration.

On 1 April municipal elections were held throughout Greece. The Karamanlis government decided against giving them a partisan character and refused to endorse any candidates. By contrast, the opposition parties—Center Union/New Forces, PASOK, KKE (Exterior), KKE (Interior), and EDA—used the municipal elections as an opportunity to attack the Karamanlis government for allegedly being slow in removing junta elements from the armed forces and the civil service, and for its inability to solve the mounting economic problems and particularly the inflationary spiral. The opposition parties also used anti-Americanism and the emotions generated by the continuing Turkish occupation of Cypriot soil as an additional rallying point. As a result, the opposition candidates won a majority of seats in the municipal councils of Athens, Piraeus, Patrai, Salonica, Volos, Kavala, Larisa, Khalkis, Irakleion, Khania, and many smaller towns. Considering that the Karamanlis party of "New Democracy" had won close to 60 percent of the popular vote in the parliamentary elections of November 1974, the reversal was a significant achievement for the opposition, including the communist parties. Yet the Left proved unable to capitalize on its apparent success, primarily because of the continuing rivalries in its ranks. An agreement among the leaders of PASOK, KKE (Exterior), KKE (Interior), and EDA to avoid the use of partisan slogans during the May Day demonstrations was violated by the KKE (Exterior) affiliates ESAK and KNE, leading to bitter recriminations. In July, PASOK and KKE (Interior) traded charges. Speaking in Larisa on 7 July, Papandreou accused KKE (Interior) of being "the lackey of the Right," adding that "its conciliatory posture toward the establishment ... is undermining the people's movement." The following day, KKE (Interior) accused Papandreou of seeking to disintegrate the anti-imperialist and anti-dictatorial forces of the Left.

Two major domestic issues preoccupied the political parties during 1975: the new constitutional draft and the trial of 21 April protagonists. Both within the Chamber of Deputies and in party declarations and commentaries, the two communist parties, EDA, and PASOK (and to a considerable extent the major opposition party, Center Union/New forces) pressed for changes relating to civil rights, the authority of the President of the Republic, and the functions of the executive, favoring a weaker executive in general and fewer restraints on the activities of political organizations. The position of KKE (Exterior) was summed up in a Central Committee statement published in *Rizospastis* on 9 May. The party denounced the draft constitution as an "anti-democratic text" and declared: "The Greek people, headed by the working class, will not be impressed by the number or the identity of those who will approve it. The people will continue their efforts to have it revised and to enact a truly people's democratic constitution." Comparable opposition was voiced by PASOK, KKE (Interior), and EDA.

The leading personalities of the Papadopoulos government were tried for sedition in the summer, and three of them were sentenced to death. The Karamanlis government immediately issued a statement declaring its intention to commute the sentences to life imprisonment. With varying degrees of intensity, all opposition parties denounced the hasty announcement and pressed for "a more rapid de-juntaization of the armed forces and the civil service."

An important issue for the communist Left during the year was the prospective return to Greece of those who fled to Eastern Europe following the collapse of the guerrilla campaign of 1946-49. On the basis of a census taken in 1965 by refugee associations, the total number has been estimated at approximately 50,000. The total includes children born abroad, as well as 28,000 children abducted during the campaign. Of these the largest numbers are in the Soviet Union (14,000), Czechoslovakia (12,000) and Poland (8,000), with the rest in Romania (6,000), Bulgaria (6,000), Hungary (4,000) and East Germany (1,700). Both communist parties have called for the repatriation of all refugees but the government is prepared only to review each case individually. In reality, many of these expatriates who have lived abroad for almost thirty years and whose children have been born there will be reluctant to return to Greece unless their relatives can help them find employment. In a gesture of good will, Interior minister C. Stefanopoulos announced on 11 August that steps will be taken to restore Greek citizenship to the refugees.

International Views and Positions. Between 27 January and 10 February 1975 a delegation representing the Central Committee of KKE (Exterior) visited Moscow and other East European capitals in an effort to renew the party's authority in view of the continuing challenge by KKE (Interior). The delegation, headed by the party's secretary-general Harilaos Florakis and including Politburo members G. Farakos and K. Tsolakis, met with Soviet party secretaries Boris Ponomarev and Ivan Kapitonov. On 30 January, Florakis was awarded the Order of Friendship by N. V. Podgorny during a ceremony at the Kremlin. The delegation then visited East Berlin, where Florakis had talks with Erich Henecker, and Sofia, where he met with Todor Zhivkov. In May, Politburo member Kostas Loules visited Cuba. In June, another delegation held talks with representatives of the French Communist Party.

On its side, KKE (Interior) was active in participating in meetings abroad and in forging ties with other elements of the Left. Late in November 1974, representatives of its youth organization "Rigas Feraios" participated with PASOK youth representatives as observers at the Ninth Congress of the Youth Federation of Yugoslavia. However, among the communist parties of Eastern Europe only that of Romania appears to be friendly to KKE (Interior). On 20 September, Romanian party chief Ceauşescu met with Babis Drakopoulos and D. Partsalidis, who were visiting Romania at the invitation of his party's Central Committee.

The major international issue for all parties was the continuing presence of Turkish troops in Cyprus. Both communist parties and PASOK spoke out against the "continuing imperialist aggression," which was attributed primarily to U.S. machinations. KKE (Interior) in a statement on 17 April summed up the views of the Left when it called for a new foreign policy that "would unite all true patriots and democrats so that the country will break the chains of dependency." All three parties strongly opposed any "bi-zonal solution" for Cyprus and rejected any mediation by the United States, whose motives they consider suspect. In November, reports of a renewed initiative by the West and allegedly by U.S. secretary of state Kissinger to break the deadlock in the Cypriot inter-communal talks drew severe denunciations from both communist parties and PASOK. Also attracting the opposition of the three was the presence of U.S. or NATO installations on Greek soil. Although the Karamanlis government has taken steps to review the status of U.S. bases and has withdrawn Greece from the NATO military structure, both KKE (Exterior) and PASOK continued to press for a complete end to U.S. facilities on Greek soil and a total withdrawal from NATO. EDA and KKE (Interior) took a less pronounced stand, avoiding the articulation of precise demands and confining their statements to broad denunciations of "imperialism" and "foreign domination."

Publications. Since the fall of the dictatorship, the number of extreme Left publications has increased manifold. Several of these weekly or monthly publications are mentioned above in connection with the organizations publishing them. Views with considerable leaning to the Left often appear in such non-communist publications as *Ta Nea; Athinaiki*, which is friendly to Papandreou; and *Epikaira*. However, the major publications of the communist left are the daily *Avgi*, affiliated with KKE (interior) and EDA, and *Rizospastis*, the daily organ of KKE (Exterior), and *Kommounistiki Epitheorisi*, its monthly. PASOK is associated with *Exormisi*.

Howard University   D. George Kousoulas

Iceland

Iceland, with its egalitarian culture and fervent nationalism, is fertile ground for nationalism—and clearly ideological turf on which various incarnations of communism have capitalized over the years. The communist-dominated People's Alliance (Altýdubandalagid; PA) is a socialist labor party that draws support from a disparate assemblage of trade union members, radical teachers and students, die-hard nationalists, and disenchanted Social Democrats. It has an estimated 2,500 members, out of a total Icelandic population of about 218,000. Its main strength rests in the urban areas (particularly Reykjavik) and the small fishing and processing towns along the eastern and northern coasts.

The PA is only the most recent version of the communist party in Iceland. It first developed from a secessionist left-wing splinter from the Social Democratic Party (SDP) in 1930. It has enjoyed legal status ever since. In 1938—now considered its birth year—the communist party withdrew from the Third International, reconstituted itself to include more radical Social Democrats, and took the name of United People's Party-Socialist Party (UPP-SP). For some time, the communist and social democratic elements sustained a semblance of joint control. By 1949, however, pro-Soviet communists assumed full control of the UPP-SP. Seven years later the communists again joined with leftist Social Democrats—primarily from the Iceland Federation of Labor (IFL)—to form an electoral front known as the People's Alliance. That front became an openly avowed "Marxist political party" in November 1968 and so replaced the UPP-SP. It split from the two other main factions in the Icelandic communist movement—Hannibal Valdimarsson's Organization of Liberals and Leftists (OLL) and the pro-Soviet, politically insignificant Organization of Icelandic Socialists (OIS).

Despite its small membership and incessant internal division, the PA has parlayed an effective organization, concentration in the Icelandic labor movement, and a sharp eye for appealing political issues into relative success. It has been one of the few Western European communist parties to participate in a democratically elected government. Since World War II, it has polled between 12 and 20 percent of Iceland's popular vote. In the 1971 parliamentary election, the PA received 17.1 percent of the vote and won 10 of the 60 seats in the Althing (parliament). The PA thus joined the OLL and the Progressive Party in a left-center coalition under Prime Minister Olafur Johannesson. Two PA veterans, Ludvik Josefsson and Magnus Kjartansson, participated in the seven-man cabinet as the ministers of commerce and fisheries and of health, social security, and industries, respectively.

Parliamentary elections on 30 June 1974 brought mixed blessings for the PA. On the one hand, the party gained one seat in the Althing and rose to 18.3 percent of the popular vote. On the other hand, the PA lost direct participation in the cabinet. The mid-summer elections had resulted in a 30-30 stalemate between the opposition parties (the conservative Independence Party and the SDP) and the former coalition parties. After two months of intense political bargaining, Geir Hallgrimsson formed a new coalition of his own Independence Party (which had jumped to 42.7 percent of the popular vote) and the Progressive Party on 27 August. Together, they commanded 42 seats in the Althing. The loss of direct participation, combined with an important substantive setback on defense matters (see below), tended to overshadow the PA's modest electoral gain.

Leadership and Organization. Ragnar Arnalds, former leader of the anti-NATO National Opposition Party, continued in 1975 as PA chairman and Adda Bara Sigfusdottir as vice-chairman. The Management Council is the party's highest authority between meetings of the 32-member Central Committee.

Party Internal Affairs. Like all Nordic communist organizations, the PA has suffered from a surfeit of factionalism. Its parliamentary strength has fluctuated more because of intra-party disagreement than from lost popular support. The most dramatic example was the power struggle between the communists and "Hannibalists" for control of the PA in 1968. The latter managed to hold five seats in the Althing during 1971-73, which might have gone to the PA otherwise.

Friction has also been sparked by interplay between the PA's two most influential members, Joseffson and Kjartansson. The former has often tried to score immediate political points—especially on the question of extending Iceland's jurisdiction over fishing territory—at the expense of the governmental stability and international good-will espoused by the latter. The two have also diverged in the past on tactics regarding the European Community (EC) and the Iceland Defense Force (IDF).

Factionalism has taken an even clearer tool on that colorful remnant of the communist movement, the OLL. In 1974 it shrank to a miniature of its former might. It was, in part, the victim of internal bickering and an ill-fated effort to merge with the Social Democratic Party. In the June 1974 election it dropped from 8.9 to 4.7 percent of the popular vote and from five to two seats in the Althing. It was no longer the party of the remarkable Hannibal Valdimarsson. It attracted instead those anti-IDF voters who were disgruntled with all older parties and yet would not vote for the PA because they were anti-communist and pro-NATO.

Domestic Attitudes and Activities. If economic problems prevailed in Western Europe, they were particularly acute in Iceland. Inflation soared upward from 40 percent in 1974 to over 50 percent in 1975. Falling output, a deteriorating current-account balance, and allegedly insufficient anti-inflationary measures fed the malaise. Despite these severe problems, the PA seemed unable to counter with an effective economic program and thus drive a wedge into Geir Hallgrimsson's coalition government. Instead, the fishing issue resurfaced as the major point for domestic and international concern. Iceland derives about 75 percent of its export earnings from the sales of fish and fish by-products. The fishing and fish processing industries are the country's largest employers. During the past decade, Iceland's economic prosperity has been increasingly threatened by the expanded operations of foreign fishermen, tougher competition for foreign markets, and declining fish re-sources.

Iceland has for some years tried to control foreign access to its fishing grounds. A four-mile fishing limit, declared in 1952, was extended to 12 miles in 1958, and to 50 miles in 1972. Despite the growing restrictions, foreigners still catch more than half of the fish netted around Iceland. In addition, each extension has provoked a "Cod War" between the Icelandic coast guard and foreign fishermen that had ultimately to be settled at the governmental level. The 1973 pact with the United Kingdom was written for only two years because Iceland believed that the U.N.-sponsored conference on the Law of the Sea might set international limits greater than 50 miles. Early in 1975, Iceland announced that it was unilaterally extending its fishing limits to 200 miles on 15 October, just 29 days before the expiration of the pact with the United Kingdom.

The ability of the current Icelandic coalition to negotiate was restricted throughout most of 1975 by history and domestic political considerations—not least of all, pressure from the communists. Past fishing agreements more frequently than not were negotiated in the wake of bitter disputes over fishing rights, and no previous government had begun negotiations in a spirit of compromise. To adopt an easy line would leave the Hallgrimsson government vulnerable to charges that it was not protecting Iceland's vital interests. The opposition, indeed, argued that the coalition failed in just that regard.

Deep political divisions, the link between fishing and the national economic well-being, and a chauvinism bred of relative physical isolation militated against an easy compromise. By early September, numerous public and private organizations had petitioned the government to allow no foreign fishing within the old 50-mile limit, where most fish are caught, and sharp limitations in the 50 to 200 mile area. The PA, as principal opposition party holding 11 of the 60 parliamentary seats, eagerly championed this line.

International Views and Positions. The PA remained strongly opposed to Icelandic membership in NATO and to retention of the IDF in any form. The communists' long-term objective has been and is an unarmed and neutral Iceland.

The PA brought that sentiment to bear with its hardline in Icelandic negotiations with the United States over the Keflavik NATO base in 1974. The fact that both the pro-IDF Independence Party and the anti-IDF People's Alliance gained in the 1974 election underscored the commingling of economic and defense issues in voter minds. Many backed the Independence Party—or "business party"— because it seemed more likely to cope effectively with the growing economic crisis and because the parties of the left seemed to be placing Iceland's only form of defense in jeopardy. The modest gain achieved by the PA, on the other hand, may have indicated some growing support for that party's clear position on the defense issue and the belief of many workers that the PA would best protect their interests in a period of economic reform. The PA thus won and lost from a polarization of opinion which undercut the middle parties most conspicuously.

All was not lost with regard to the defense issue for the PA, however. The ink was barely dry on the 1974 agreement before Prime Minister Hallgrimsson and Progressive Party chairman Johannesson warned the United States that—unless the Federal Republic of Germany withdrew its veto of EC tariff concessions on Icelandic fish products and both the British and the West Germans agreed to stop fishing within Iceland's 50-mile zone—there was pressure from their parties and the communist opposition to retaliate against the Keflavik base and reconsider Icelandic membership in NATO. The prime minister felt under increasing pressure during the year to develop closer economic ties with the

USSR to offset losses prompted by the United Kingdom and West Germany. Some younger members within his Independence Party felt that the PA should replace the Progressive Party as a coalition partner—a change possible only if the Independence Party were willing to make some concessions to the PA on defense matters.

International Party Contacts., The Icelandic communists have traditionally stayed at arms length from the international communist movement. In fact, no other Western European communist party has maintained such an isolationist position.

The PA has not participated officially in international communist conferences at either the global or the regional level. On the few occasions when Icelandic "observers" have shown up at such meetings, the PA leadership has later felt compelled to offer elaborate justifications to the rank and file. Furthermore, the PA has consistently stressed the "national road" and dismissed the idea of one center of international communism. Any increase in PA activities abroad is more an index to efforts—as in 1974—to gain foreign support for Iceland's fishing rights than a fundamental change from that pattern.

The PA does not maintain formal ties with the Communist Party of the Soviet Union and has made clear its condemnation of the Warsaw Pact invasion of Czechoslovakia in 1968. It has made a point of siding with communist parties, most notably those of the Romanians and Yugoslavs, which are known for their own independent or nationalistic views.

Publications. *Thjodviljiin* ("Will of the Nation"), a daily newspaper in Reykjavik, is the PA's central organ. The party also publishes a bi-weekly theoretical journal, *NY Utsyn.* Outside the capital, there are at least two pro-communist weeklies, *Verkamadhurinn* in Akureyri and *Mjolnir* in Siglufjordhur. The publication of the fledgling Maoist organization is *Stettabarattan* ("Class Struggle").

Ireland

A profile on the activities of the Communist Party of Ireland does not appear in this edition of the *Yearbook on International Communist Affairs.*

In the last decade the Communist Party of Ireland has steadily lost influence and strength. The major reason is the changing social and political conditions in the Republic of Ireland. Other factors include the revival of interest in traditional republicanism which has been manifest by the paramilitary organization, Official Sinn Fein, and the interest taken in it by the Soviet Union. Urban violence in the North since 1968, has aggravated these trends. Should the activities of the Communist Party of Ireland so warrant, the profile on the CPI will be resumed in the next edition of the *Yearbook on International Communist Affairs.*

Italy

The Italian Communist Party (Partito Comunista Italiano; PCI) was founded in January 1921.

The PCI enjoys legal status. In the 1972 general election it gained 8,121,117 votes, or 28.3 percent of the total. This gave it control of 179 seats out of 630 in the Chamber of Deputies. Although it does not formally participate in the government, the party wields vast influence on Italy's social and political life, with 1.7 million members, who come proportionately from every walk of life (farmers excepted), out of a national population of 55.7 million.

In 1975 the PCI was literally the center of political life in Italy, with more adherents than all other political organizations combined. In the 1975 municipal and regional elections its candidates—together with those of the small Italian Socialist Party of Proletarian Unity (PSIUP), incorporated into the party after the 1972 electons—received 11,263,173 votes, or 33.7 percent of the total cast. Together with the Italian Socialist Party (PSI), with which it has shared control of some of its most important mass organizations since the 1930s, the PCI controls the administration of five of the country's twenty regions, and participates more or less directly in the administration of five more. These ten are the nation's most populous and productive ones. In addition, the PCI participates directly in the administration of every major Italian city except Rome. Most importantly, it has made the question of its participation in the government of Italian society—not merely in the cabinet—the principal subject of public discussion in Italy.

The PCI was formed in 1921 out of that faction of the PSI which voted to accepted the 21 conditions for membership in the Comintern. Palmiro Togliatti, one of its founders, took over its leadership in 1926 and held it until his death in 1964. From 1926 until 1943 the party's illegality in Italy made its leadership more than normally dependent upon the Comintern. Togliatti worked in that organization's Moscow offices for 12 years. (In February 1975, Davide Lajolo, then a member of the PCI Central Committee, published some remarks allegedly made by Togliatti, in which the leader acknowledged that participation in Stalin's purges had been part of his job). But if the PCI was dependent on Moscow, the PSI, also banned, was dependent on the PCI. During those years the pattern of joint Communist-Socialist control of social and labor "mass organizations" became established—a pattern which endures today.

Between 1934 and 1948, the PSI and PCI, joined by the "unity of action" pact, behaved as one party. They fought the 1948 election as a bloc on the slogan: "Washington or Moscow." Since suffering massive defeat in that election, the two parties have run under separate labels. There was, however, no "break." On the eve of the 1953 elections, Nenni, then as now leader of the PSI, returned from the USSR with the Stalin Peace prize, and placed the PSI firmly within the framework of Stalin's policy of "peaceful co-existence." The PCI lent its indispensable support within the mass organizations for the PSI's drive throughout the 1950s and early 60s to convince the Christian Democrats (DC), Italy's relative majority party, that the nation would not be free of violent strikes until the PSI was allowed a share in the government. When the DC agreed to the "opening to the left," the PSI refused to abandon its special relationship with the PCI in local governments and mass organizations. Also, in every presidential election in the Italian Parliament since, the PSI has collaborated with the PCI against its government partners. Today the PSI is committed to helping the PCI convince the DC that Italy cannot expect domestic peace and government stability until "all democratic and popular forces"—that is, the Communists, Socialists, and those Christian Democrats disposed to dealing with them—agree on how to govern the nation. PSI secretary Francesco De Martino has refused to consider supporting any new government as long as the DC refuses the "new relationship" and the Communists remain in opposition (*Corriere Della Sera*, 16 July 1975). The achievement of this new relationship, which PCI general secretary Enrico Berlinguer first proposed in 1974 under the title "historic compromise," is the PCI's great objective. If achieved, it would not necessarily, at least at first, mean Communist participation in the cabinet. The PCI is more interested in exercising influence than in the question of who holds what ministerial portfolio.

The party has successfully portrayed itself as a far more coherent, disciplined, and efficient group than its main rival. Also, since it knows that many who vote Communist do so to avenge themselves on "the system," it has catered to the Italians' general feeling of revulsion against their government by letting it be known that, so far as it has the power, it will "get back" at those responsible for Italy's troubles (*L'Unità*, 18 June 1975). But the PCI is aware that being known as anti-system is also what stands between it and the exercise of power. Given its other assets, and the ineptitude of its enemies, the PCI would have been in possession of government power long ago were it known as "safe." So, its public utterances throughout 1975 were aimed at one goal above all others: to convince those who might stand in the way of the "historic compromise" that the PCI is no threat to civil liberties, prosperity, religion, or national independence. The PCI claims that its goals for government are anything but incompatible with the spirit of a Catholic church whose head eulogizes the "spirit of Helsinki" (ANSA, 28 July). Likewise it calls itself the firmest supporter of the U.S. policy of détente, without which, it knows, the "historic compromise" would be out of the question. Following this logic, the party has sought support in the United States for the view that any American pronouncement of disfavor for the "historic compromise" would be an interference in Italy's internal affairs, motivated solely by anti-communism, and therefore incompatible with the spirit of détente. To big businessmen it has offered labor peace and guaranteed sales; to small businessmen it has promised subsidies and support against the pressures of large competitors. To the nation as a whole, it presents itself as the only available "great force which presses for new solutions" (*L'Unità*, 12 April).

The PCI works within a political system which it has been able to manipulate. Its traditional allies are still close. Its DC adversaries, split into at least six factions, have been rendered dependent on the support of the Communists' PSI allies. Should some DC factions attempt to govern against the wishes of the PCI/PSI, they would be faced (as in 1960, 1969, and 1972) with the often-threatened violent "popular riposte to provocation." The sources from which the PCI's traditional enemies once drew their encouragement and support, the Catholic church and the United States, appear no longer willing to act to bar the party's way. Nevertheless, mindful of the Chilean experience, the PCI has chosen to gather political power in ways calculated to arouse no more opposition at any given time than it can easily dispose of at that time.

Leadership and Organization. The PCI's 1.7 million members are organized into 11,000 sections, established in places of work and residence. Above the sections are plant committees and town or area committees. These in turn are subordinated to 93 provincial federations, which are under 20 regional committees. There are also special federations for Italians abroad. All are under the national party organization. The federations are based on central committees (in practice selected by the next higher level) and secretariats. At congresses and plenums all resolutions and elections are effected unanimously. The strongest federations are in Emilia, long under joint PCI-PSI administration, where one in nine inhabitants is a party member; the weakest are in Veneto, where the ratio is one to 53, and in the South, one to 54. Growth in party membership averaged 8.95 percent in 1974, and was highest in large cities.

At the national level are the 177-member Central Committee, 53-member Central Control Commission, 6-member Central Auditing Committee, 33-member Directorate, and, above all, the 9-member Secretariat. Enrico Berlinguer is general secretary; Luigi Longo holds the post of party president. At CPI the offices in Rome are 17 "working sections" meant to resemble shadow government departments.

The party's three most senior men, Giancarlo Pajetta, Pietro Ingrao, and Giorgio Amendoia head "institutes" for international policy, state reform, and economic policy. These men, definitely not in disgrace and very active, are obviously not confined to their "institute" tasks. Pajetta is also a member of the Secretariat. Moreover, the party has "commissions" for foreign policy-relations with Communist parties, democratic institutions and Parliament, economic and social affairs, press, propaganda and ideological activities, and organization and party life. The jurisdiction of these commissions clearly overlaps that of other party bodies. Their heads are party personages of the first order. In sum, the PCI's published organization scheme suggests: (1) tight control of subordinate by superior echelons, (b) a very substantial part of the party's active talent is channeled to activities not specified by the scheme, and (c) the PCI follows the traditional pattern of assigning overlapping tasks to competing top party bureaucracies.

Early in 1975 the PCI published a financial balance sheet for 1974 (L'Unità, 26 January). The budget totaled 23,812,000,000 lire, or about 40 million dollars—as published the largest budget of any Italian party. About 44 percent of the income was from public financing. The party also reported taking in about 5 billion lire from membership dues, 4.5 billion from festivals and press subscriptions, 1.5 billion from the salaries of Communist members of Parliament, and 55 million from the salaries of their staff. (Actually, all party members who hold official positions; mayors and local councilmen, as well as deputies and senators, turn in their entire state-issued check to the party treasury, from which they then receive a party salary for a lesser amount. This not only benefits the treasury and gives the party leadership great control over subordinates, but underscores the fact that Communist officials are working for the PCI first of all, for the state only secondarily. Thus while various individuals of other parties earn the title "corrupt" for demanding various levels of kickbacks from the people they place in official positions, the PCI gains money, cohesion, and a reputation for both self-sacrifice and candor by fixing and collecting such contributions publicly.)

But the budget mentions nothing about the contributions from the salaries of Communist officials on any but the parliamentary level. This suggests that the published budget covers only a portion of PCI operations. The budget also specifies that no contributions were received from labor unions or companies. This means that the party has chosen to deny, at least for budget purposes, the existence of its ties with the labor movement, and of any connection with businesses, even with Fiat through the PCI federation in Turin. Moreover the PCI's extensive local operations do not exist on the revenue side and barely appear on the expenditure side. Also, the name of the National League of Cooperatives, a party-controlled commercial organization, does not appear in the budget. Indeed, the only "mass organization" which appears is the 119,000-member Communist youth federation—and that for only 240,000,000 lire ($400,000) on the expenditure side. In sum, the published budget indicates neither now much nor what the party is doing.

The undisputed leader of the PCI is Enrico Berlinguer, born on the island of Sardinia in 1922 of a wealthy PSI family and associated with the party since his teens. His urbane ways are well-fitted to the image he has been fostering of the PCI as a serious, thoroughly professional, and not intolerant organization. His marriage to a practicing Catholic has been widely publicized. Below him are three somewhat older and very able men who were once considered rivals to his leadership: Amendola, Ingrao, and Pajetta. The first two were long thought to represent incipient "soft" and "hard" factions within the PCI. They were known to be rivals. The third today provides a high-level link with the Soviet Union. He shares this role with Tullio Vecchietti, who has risen rapidly in the PCI since leading his PSIUP to merge with the party in 1972. Also worthy of mention are Giorgio Napolitano and Armando Cossuta, now in charge of the Party's two most important areas of operation: labor, and regional and local government, respectively.

Auxiliary Organizations. At the 14th Congress, in the spring of 1975, Berlinguer said: "A broad and sturdy democratic fabric has indeed been created in Italy through an effort extending over decades. This is one of the great achievements of the socialist movement and also of the other popular movements, such as those which are Catholic-inspired." (*L'Unità*, 19 March.) The network of mass organizations is one of the most important of the PCI's fields of action. Only a few of these uncounted organizations can be mentioned here.

Foremost is the Italian General Confederation of Labor (CGIL), with 3,827,000 members not only the largest labor group in Italy but also the one around which all the others have coalesced in a unity of action pact. The general council of the smaller Catholic CISL has voted to accept the offer of the CGIL to merge in a single trade union movement. Within the CISL, a minority led by Vito Scalia was resisting further amalgamation with the communist movement, citing the fate of the Portuguese Catholic trade unions after unification of the labor movement in that country (*Economist*, 29 March). In September the official Italian news agency reported that Scalia has been suspended for six months by the CISL council for his opposition to the CGIL (ANSA, 18 September). Thus the fabric of which Berlinguer spoke is becoming stronger.

Traditionally, the president of the CGIL was a member of the PCI Politburo and the vice-president a member of the PSI Politburo. But in 1975 the leaders of the CGIL did not appear on the leadership rosters of the parties. The reason, according to the *World Marxist Review*, was "to emphasize the autonomy of this and other mass organizations" (*IB*, no. 6-7, 1975). Virtually the same words were used in *L'Unità*, 27 March. The party has every reason to emphasize the autonomy of the CGIL: it facilitates the CGIL's assumption of leadership over other labor groups and makes it easier for the PCI to disassociate itself from the Unions' violence when it miscarries. Nevertheless, control of the CGIL, easily the party's single greatest asset, is as important to it as ever. The greatest threat to PCI control, and indeed the only one about which Berlinguer has expressed concern, is the influence of ultra-left organizers whose appeals to workers are often more exciting. Heading off that threat is the job of the labor section of the PCI, which was placed under Secretariat member Napolitano after Fernando di Giulio, member of the lower-ranking Directorate, was unable to exercise sufficient control over the metalworkers union.

The other great PCI mass organization is the National League of Cooperatives. It has 2,412,000 members and an annual volume of business equivalent to about US$4 billion. In addition to retail sales, the League is very active in East-West trade. Berlinguer has referred to it as the leading part of a larger cooperative movement with 6 million members, which also includes Catholic and lay groups. The president is Vincenzo Galetti, a member of the PCI Central Committee and former secretary of its Bologna federation. He is not on the high leadership bodies, again in order "to emphasize the autonomy of this and other mass organizations" (*IB*, no. 6-7).

Until 1974 the Union of Italian women, part of the (Communist-front Women's International Democratic Federation, did not enjoy special priority among the PCI organizations. It is Berlinguer's judgment, however, that cultural trends have made it possible to greatly diminish the overwhelming support which Italian women had heretofore been giving to Catholic social organizations and the DC. The PCI has, therefore, tried to place itself conspicuously, though soberly, on the side of women's liberation. The Union of Italian Women became an important part of the PCI plans during the campaign against the repeal of the divorce law in 1974. In 1975 the PCI issued a communiqué declaring the year one of "struggle, unity, and real achievement for Italian women" (*L'Unità*, 11 January). The PCI publishing house now puts out a magazine called *Donne e Politica* (Women and Politics).

Among other mass organizations are the Italian Communist Youth Federation, the Association of Democratic Lawyers, and the Association of Democratic Journalists, all affiliated with their respective international Communist associations.

The PCI is undertaking the building of wholly new, usually small, territorially based mass organizations for the purpose of organizing sectors of the population normally beyond its reach. It has been particularly successful in publicly owned apartment complexes, where it has organized blocs of tenants and forced the authorities to rescind rent increases or make improvements. But the most important auxiliary organizations covering territories are, of course, the local and regional governments in which the PCI participates. The coordination of these was once confided to the National League of Democratic Municipalities. Given both advances in local elections and the strategy of the "historic compromise," the task of building ruling coalitions at the local level, of asserting influence where direct participation is unfeasible, as well as of coordinating the political and financial advantages to be drawn from local influence, has grown important enough to warrant entrusting it to a special party "working section" for Regional and Local Government. Its leader, already noted, is Cossuta (*L'Unità*, 12 April), former member of the Secretariat, now member of the Directorate. As president of Italturist, an organization specializing in travel between Italy and the USSR, he has long been considered particularly close to the Soviet leadership.

Party Internal Affairs. The PCI's 14th Congress adopted a resolution favoring the simplification of the structure of the party's leading bodies (*L'Unità*, 27 March 1975). The main differences between the present and past published schemes are as follows: (1) The Politburo has been entirely eliminated. (2) The Secretariat, now the only small-membership top organ, has been increased in membership from 7 to 9. (3) No leader of "mass democratic organizations" appears in the ranks of the top PCI leadership at a time when the work of these organizations is more important to the party's strategy than ever.

The fact that Cossuta's name was removed from the list of members of the Secretariat caused *New York Times* reporter Paul Hoffman to speculate that "all is not well between the Italian party and Moscow (14 April). The French biweekly *Est et Ouest* (no. 552, May) saw Cossuta's removal from the Secretariat as related both to his having been placed at the head of a vast front-like operation, and to personal differences with Berlinguer.

Davide Lajolo, who published a "Secret History of the Italian Communist Party" in March, in which he said that Palmiro Togliatti as secretary of the Comintern had taken part in Stalin's purges (noted above), was not reappointed to the Central Committee. Nevertheless, the Lajolo incident did tend to strengthen the present "third-generation" leaders who were not prominent during Stalin's lifetime.

Domestic Attitudes and Activities. In 1975 the PCI sought to induce other Italian political forces to accept the "historic compromise." In this enterprise it received powerful aid from the results of the 1975 local and regional elections, which increased the party's prestige and allowed it to gather uncounted hundreds of additional official posts under its control. The year also saw development of the party's six-year-old crusade against the rightist Italian Social Movement (MSI), pursuit of its public relations effort for respectability (to which events in Portugal posed some difficulties), continued appeals to most of the nation's interest groups, and the initiation of party activity aimed at the reorganization of the armed forces.

On 15 June elections were held in 15 of Italy's 20 regions, 92 of the 93 provinces, and 7,727 of the 8,065 communes. Given that even local elections in Italy are contests between national parties and are fought largely over national issues, the results show how each party has risen or fallen in popular favor and prefigure future general electoral returns. The PCI increased its overall share of the vote by nearly 6 percent over the previous local electons, while the PSI increased its share by nearly 2 percent. The Christian Democrats saw their own poll decline by more than 2 percent. (For the PCI's definite analysis of the vote, see the special edition of *L'Unità*, 22 June.) As Giacomo Sani has pointed out (paper delivered at the American Political Science Association's 1975 annual meeting), the aggregate size of the change in the relative strength of the parties between the elections of 1970 and 1975 was not significantly greater than the average change in the strength of Italian parties between other postwar elections. The changes that did occur, however, were of one kind only: the PCI and its allies won, while the DC, the Right, and the moderates lost what, by Italian standards, is significant strength. More importantly, the changes made it arithmetically possible in many places for the PSI and PCI to form majority coalitions, leaving the DC and the moderates, with whom the PSI is joined at the national level, in opposition. In some cases, notably that of Milan, the nation's most important city, where the PCI-PSI fell a few seats short of the majority in the council, the two parties were able to lure enough leftist DC council members with offers of jobs in the administration to constitute a ruling coalition. In Asti it was councilors from the Italian Social Democratic Party (PSDI) who were persuaded to cooperate. Even where PCI-PSI coalitions did not have the opportunity to constitute a majority, the PCI was in a position to demand that nothing be done of which it did not approve. Moreover, since the Communist gains were heaviest in the most important urban centers and in the most important regions, the PCI has shown that the political wind is blowing its way — something very important in Italy. For example, in Naples where after the elections the PCI-PSI together controlled only 33 out of 80 seats, the Left was able to exercise enough influence among the parties of the majority to keep them from coalescing to elect a city administration, whereupon the PCI-PSI set up a minority administration and made a Communist the mayor (ANSA, 29 September). This feat was accomplished on the basis of anti-fascism. That is, the PCI-PSI were able to persuade the Christian Democrats, Social Democrats, and Republicans that if they accepted MSI votes to stave off a Left administration, there would be trouble.

Were the results of the 1975 elections to be directly translated into general election results, coalition politics at the national level would be affected first by the arithmetic elimination of the possibility of majority coalitions either of the Center (Christian Democrats, Liberals, Social Democrats, Republicans) or of the Center-Right (Christian Democrats, Liberals, Social Movement), but, more important, by the new political position in which the DC, PSI, and PCI would find themselves. Although the PCI-PSI would still be about 35 seats (or about 5 percent of the vote) short of a majority, they would be dealing with a DC reduced to only two options: the Center-Left coalition based on alliance with the PSI, or some arrangement with the Communists. Since the PSI has already made it clear it will not be a party to any exclusion of the Communists, the DC would not only have to deal with the PCI, but would be compelled to do so on the latter's own terms. The compulsion would be all the greater because two of the DC's six major factions (Basisti and Forze Nuove), which have a long record of cooperation with the PCI in labor and local affairs, and which would probably command at least the number of seats required for a PCI-PSI majority, would certainly be eager to act as vanguard for those members of the DC who would now, not wholly unreasonably, regard Berlinguer's offer of a "historic compromise" as magnanimous.

Analysis of the election results shows that the Christian Democrats and their moderate allies lost to the Left in three ways: they suffered more than the Left (PCI-PSI) from the attrition of older voters (their supporters belong disproportionately to older age groups); the Left gained an estimated half million new voters more than the Center-Right parties (18-to-21-year-olds, who were voting for the first time); and about a half million voters who had previously supported the Center-Right voted the Left, resulting in the net shift of one million votes. (Sani, in the paper noted above.) These shifts occurred both because the Left's organization and propaganda worked as designed, and because in 1975 the DC had neither the will, the organization, nor the audience which had won for it in the past.

In 1975, for the first time since World War II, the Conference of Italian Bishops failed to issue its customary pre-election appeal for the "unity of Catholics." This was only the most obvious of the Church's many acts of omission in behalf of the moderate forces in Italian politics in recent years. (Warnings against the "priorities and character" of Marxist-Leninist parties such as appeared in the 14 August Vatican City *Osservatore* are rare.) The top hierarchy is split over the role the Church ought to play in society, as well as over the question of whether the Church can best protect the faith in Italy and around the world by supporting the self-proclaimed defenders of Western civilization or by attempting to establish a modus vivendi with the revolutionaries. The lower clergy was thus left without political leadership this year. Furthermore, the local organizations of Catholic students, housewives, and so on were suffering from demoralization and a decade of neglect in recruitment. The Catholic labor unions (CISL) had recently joined a unity of action agreement with the Communist-Socialist CGIL. This "Cooperation for common human goals" has resulted in the Catholic group's joining in support of PCI goals, but has made the CISL unavailable for Christian Democratic political purposes. Finally, polls have shown that today's Italian Catholic no longer looks to the Church for guidance in politics as he once did. In short, the Church's social attitudes in the last decade have cooled the ardors of its strongest supporters, made recruitment into its organizations difficult, and lowered the level of authoritativeness of the clergy in social matters, but have not compensated for these losses by spreading the Church's influence to strata of the population which its competitors control.

The PCI, for its part, did its best throughout the campaign to court Catholic voters by means of appeals, while holding on to its own by means of organization. The party repeatedly claimed that Communism and Catholicism are not incompatible, that only a now-discredited brand of Catholicism ever held them to be, that the Communists are the most democratic of Italian parties because they have the most widespread and intense popular support, that the Party's commitment to democracy and civility is demonstrated by its opposition to the rightist MSI—which the Party claims is responsible for the violence and disorder plaguing Italy—and that Italian Communists are so different from foreign Communists that Italians need not fear that their advent to power would bring the violence and privation which Communism has brought elsewhere. Examination of the PCI's treatment by the major mass media prior to the election reveals only sporadic and lukewarm opposition to these contentions on the part of Italian elites. Months prior to the election, the Italian Radio and Television System, which has a monopoly on broadcasting, had reacted to the forced resignation of it Christian Democratic president Ettore Barnabei by giving more favorable treatment to the Left. The organization's instincts proved correct, for on 24 May 1975 Beniamino Finocchiaro of the PSI was named to replace Barnabei. In Italy as elsewhere, public opinion usually follows the opinion leaders. A glance at public opinion polls shows that, for example, the percentage of those who thought Communism and Catholicism compatible rose from 28 to 55 between 1963 and 1972, and that the percentage of those who thought Communism so dangerous to freedom as to preclude any agreement with it dropped from 44.8 to 26.2 between 1970 and 1974 (Sani, see above). Not surprisingly, those younger voters who have been exposed to less unfavorable attitudes toward Communism on the part of non-Communist elites proved more susceptible to the party's arguments. Less surprisingly, the more the government parties deal with the PCI on a day-to-day basis, the less credible do their anti-Communist appeals at election time appear.

At its 14th Congress, labeled in advance the "congress of the 'historic compromise,'" in Rome on 18-22 March 1975, the PCI expounded the several themes of its continuing campaign for the "compromise." The following is an account of the most important of those themes:

(1) The political, economic, and social institutions of the West are in the painful process of disintegration, while those of the Socialist world are giving proof of their vitality. According to Berlinguer, "It is now ... almost universally recognized that a higher moral climate exists in these countries whereas the capitalist societies are being increasingly hit by a decline of ideals and ethical values and by increasingly broad processes of corruption and disintegration" (*L'Unità*, 19 March). Italians ought not to delude themselves; the disintegration they see around them cannot be healed by Western means. Only the advent of socialism will bring moral health. Nor will the cure kill those elements of the Western way of life to which Italians are attached. Alfredo Reichelin, editor of the Party weekly, argued that Communists in general, and Italian ones in particular, would preserve everything worth preserving better than those under whose care everything seems to rot. To support this view he quoted the French political scientist Maurice Duverger: "The West no longer believes in its basic values. And I am wondering whether Communism is not, in a certain manner, taking up those basic Western values, all those things that someone like myself, who attended schools of Christian character, now rediscover more readily in the Communists" (*Rinascita*, 2 July). The PCI presents itself as the party of order and seriousness to a country sick of chaos and decay.

The PCI claims that the desire for order and certainty is so strong that even those sectors of society which one would least expect—that is, private industry—"now ask the public power for an indication of new national goals and an atmosphere of certainty for all social forces." (Ibid.) Democracy, claims the PCI, does not preclude strength in government. Democracy is a means of organizing the adherence of the people. Consent is that against which every political action is necessarily measured. (*L'Unità*, 24 August.) But it is wrong to say that the "direct" forms of democracy, which the party practices, are incompatible with representative forms: Under communist guidance "universal suffrage also assumes a new significance—a confirmation of consent." The rule of the working class, which is the truest democracy," is never achieved once and for all; it is a historical victory and must be continually reaffirmed and checked against a vast and complex system of social alliances." Berlinguer has described a "strong democracy" as one which would "know how to gain everyone's respect for the decisions made." (Ibid., 1 December 1974.)

(2) The PCI contends, in fact, that in large part thanks to its efforts, Italy has never been as democratic as it is today. That is, never before have so many people become active in the cause of the working class—the great majority of the population. According to Berlinguer, the development of democracy in Italy has entered a new phase "which introduces some elements of socialism itself into the structures of society, into income distribution, into life habits, into the exercise of power" (Ibid., 19 March 1975.) This is occurring not because the government is committed to it, but rather because of what the masses themselves, following the leadership of the working class, have done. Most symptomatic of the democratic conquests of recent years, according to Berlinguer, was the forced abandonment of the Centrist Andreotti cabinet which, after the 1972 elections, was an attempt by the ruling classes (that is, the DC) to go back on the "Opening to the Left" and do without the PSI.

The departure from the Center Left had been made possible, among other causes, by the rise in the popularity of the rightist MSI, which resulted from the wave of violence of 1969-71, for which the Left had been blamed. The Andreotti coalition had been prefigured in the Parliament in December 1971, when the DC (minus some of its leftists) joined with the moderate Social Democrats and Liberals, with the votes of the MSI making up for the loss of the DC left, formed a majority coalition and elected a president of the republic. (Ibid.) Since then the PCI has put major stress on the anti-fascist theme, treating the elimination of the MSI as a very important end and also as a means by which diverse groups might be mobilized.

The PCI has built a network of "anti-fascist committees" which are meant, according to Berlinguer's report to the 14th Congress, to accomplish three tasks. First, they must "spur all public authorities on so that they will do their duty completely and totally" to bring the enemies of public order to justice. This requires that a relationship of mutual confidence and collaboration be established between the police and the committees. To help bring this about, the PCI has ceased its attacks on the police—and their salaries—in Parliament, and has publicly supported improved working conditions for them. Second, the committees are meant for the "aggressive and tempestuous mobilization of the masses whenever the necessity arises," as it did in Milan on 18-19 April 1975 after a "left-wing youth" was shot by a "presumed fascist thug" (ANSA, 18 April). There followed a one-hour general strike by all labor unions and two days of violent demonstrations in the course of which the offices of the MSI and the PSDI and a café known to be frequented by rightists were ransacked. Third, the committees have gathered the required signatures and formally proposed to the Parliament a "people's bill" to outlaw the MSI and all organizations connected with it. In his pre-Congress document, Berlinguer warned that any attempts at "subversion," even ones "which try to hide behind a veil of legal mystification," would meet with "powerful and irrepressible" 'people's answers' (*L'Unità*, 11 December 1974).

The PCI's relationship with domestic violence is ambiguous. On the one hand the anti-fascist committees—so important to the party—can only function as intended if there is some. In addition, the maintenance of the massive street apparatus indispensable for exerting the kind of political pressure which served the party so well in 1960, 1969, and 1972 appears far less unreasonable if there is a "fascist threat" in the air. On the other hand, the violence, even the 'anti-fascist' kind practiced by the unions and the committees, is at least a potential embarrassment for the Communists. Moreover, when groups with names such as "Red Brigades" and "Armed Proletarian Nuclei" (ANSA, 21 March 1975) claim credit for terrorist acts, the party must reiterate they have not "anything in common with the Italian workers' movement." This is precisely the sort of disclaimer that the MSI issues when suspected terrorists are alleged to belong to its camp. The precise responsibility for the acts of terrorism may never be clear. As Paul Hoffman has reported (*NYT*, 15, 22 March), the highly politicized Italian judiciary, split along partisan lines, appears incapable of resolving the maze of countercharges of provocation. The assessment of blame, it appears, will continue to be accomplished politically.

(3) Italy's economic troubles are no doubt to some extent responsible for the disaffection which has so benefited the PCI. Its economic statements are meant to accomplish the following: to blame the troubles on the capitalist system in general and on corrupt Italian politicians in particular; to argue that the solution to the troubles will require what the party has to offer; and to assure the party's supporters that they won't have to tighten their belts, while assuring capitalists at home and abroad that they need not fear for their money if the PCI comes to power.

The PCI's own economic plans were made clearest in an interview granted by Luciano Barca (*Die Welt*, Hamburg, 19 July). The PCI recognizes, Barca said, that the market is the best measure of economic profitability, and that Italy is a part of the Western market economy. However, since the market is not working well for Italy now, the state must make the fundamental choices. "For that, however, we in the PCI are looking for as broad a consensus as possible among all forces active in economy and society." The party, says Barca, is not interested in nationalizing industries, not even the giant Fiat. Rather, it is interested in socializing demand. Firms should be free to produce what they wish, but the state would provide guaranteed sales at guaranteed prices for socially desirable products, and guaranteed investment capital for financing them. This would produce both the achievement of national priorities, and the certainty for which everyone hungers, for everyone knows the PCI is a good manager.

(4) At the 14th Congress, Berlinguer declared: "Let no one think that there is room among us for any insinuations or exhortations to the effect that we break with the principles and practices of proletarian internationalism, that we withdraw from that line of solidarity and common struggle with all of the worker, socialist, and revolutionary forces anywhere in the world, the line which we have

chosen and which we intend to pursue through our free choice and amid the fullness of our autonomy" (*L'Unità*, 19 March). Several weeks later, after the fall of Saigon (*Rinascita* 9 May 1975), Berlinguer exhulted in an article entitled "The World is Freer": "Only the enemies of the people and of national independence are less free in Saigon today." In dozens of interviews, PCI officials have had to confront the question, how can anyone be sure, given that every Communist regime has deprived its people of civil liberties, that the PCI, once in power, would not do the same? Uniformly, instead of arguing directly that brother parties in power only restrict the liberties of the fascist enemies of the people, PCI spokesmen argue that the transition to socialism necessarily takes place in different ways in different places and that given the character of the Italian people as well as the policy of the PCI, violence and despotism will not characterize the way Italy must travel to socialism. In an interview published in *Der Spiegel*, Hamburg 4 August, Amendola reduced this refrain to the formula: "Well, other countries, other conditions. We are in Italy.") If anything upset the workings of the 14th Congress, it was the brusque revival of this question by the Portuguese Communist Party, a group with long fraternal ties to the PCI which, in the course of its own struggle, found it expedient to bar Portugal's own Christian Democrats from participation in the country's elections. Berlinguer found himself making his offer of a "historic compromise" with Italy's Christian Democrats in a chillier atmosphere than he had expected. The DC's secretary, Amintore Fanfani, withdrew his party's observer from the PCI congress in protest. In a closing address to the congress (*L'Unità*, 24 March), Berlinguer stated the PCI is "not in agreement with decisions in which just and necessary acts, intended to strike at the direct responsibilities of persons whose participation in reactionary putschist attempts has been recognized, appear to us to have been mixed up with other actions which strike at the parties to which these persons belong." He went on to say that these actions were perfectly understandable in the Portuguese political context, and that the Portuguese Communists had done more than any other group for liberty and democracy in Portugal, but added: "The historic and political conditions that have evolved in Italy are completely different, as is our own political strategy." These points were amplified when Napolitano (*Rinascita*, 4 April) pointed out to the DC that its withdrawal from the PCI congress because of events in Portugal would not change the political facts in Italy which compel it to be attentive to the PCI's offer of a "historic compromise."

(5) Berlinguer first used the term "historic compromise" in one of a series of articles (ibid., 12 October 1973) in which he analyzed the failure of the Allende government in Chile. Allende had been constitutionally but narrowly elected to a position of power, and powerful political and social forces remained in opposition. When Allende attempted the transformation of society, he aroused more opposition than his narrowly based supporters were able to deal with. Simply put, one cannot wisely undertake the dictatorship of the proletariat simply because one has received a relative—or even an absolute—majority at the polls. One must be careful that one's victory not relegate one of the country's great political forces to opposition, that is to a position in which it will have both the opportunity and the inclination to gather to itself all elements disaffected by the process of social transformation, and use them to make reactionary trouble. So, said Berlinguer, the problem in Italy is not to build up an eventually successful PCI-PSI front which would garner 51 percent of the vote and push the CD into opposition, but "instead to get the forces of the Center to shift to coherently democratic positions" and therefore achieve "the great new historic compromise between the forces which really represent the great majority of the Italian people." In the preparatory document for the 14th Congress (*L'Unità*, 11 December 1974), Berlinguer again cited the "tragic Chilean experience" as authority for a policy meant to "avoid a vertical break up of the people and the country into two clearly opposed and hostile fronts." He therefore denounced as "illusory" the proposition that "the winning of 51 percent of the votes by the left forces" could be "conclusive." On the eve of the 1975 elections, Berlinguer again addressed the key point of the "historic compromise," that is, the co-option of as much of the potential opposition's organization as possible. "The central idea of the

compromise is simple: to give Italy a political leadership with a strong and authoritative basis which will make it possible to govern and democratically overcome resistance to the necessary task of reform. In order to do this, 51 percent of the votes is not enough, not even if this 51 percent is made up of leftwing votes." (*Corriere Della Sera* 1 June). But would there not be something anomalous about a PCI-PSI-DC coaliton that would include more than four-fifths of the electorate? Where would the opposition be? Berlinguer was certain that plenty of opposition would surely manifest itself once reforms began (*L'Unità*, 19 March). Given the "historic compromise," the individuals who would go into opposition from the "compromised" DC organizations would leave their organizations behind them.

The PCI does not see the "historic compromise" as primarily a deal with the DC organization on the parliamentary level. In fact, the PCI terms any talk of parliamentary line-ups as symptomatic of a lack of understanding of the real problems of power. Berlinguer has repeatedly stated that the PCI is "not in a hurry" to enter the national government. Rather, it seeks substantive influence via "constructive relationships" with the holders of power—be they industrialists, clergy, bureaucrats, local or national politicians. These, it hopes, will allow the party to wield substantive power while raising a minimum of alarm and opposition, and leave it free to attack its informal partners when they show recalcitrance.

To an extent, the "historic compromise" has been functioning for some time. Fiat's director, Giovanni Agnelli, is only the best known of many top Italian businessmen who have decided to cooperate with the PCI in labor, local government matters, and financing. Of course, unity of action, which continued to prevail in 1975 among the various components of the labor movement, was seen as very much a part of the "compromise." Even at the national parliamentary level, explained Alessandro Natta, leader of the PCI's deputies, though what is going on only foreshadows the "compromise," the indispensaiblity of the Communist's good will has been recognized: "The majority of laws passed . . . carry the PCI's mark" (*Corriere Della Sera*, 30 September). The party's effect on legislation, continued Natta, is out of proportion to the number of its deputies. The PCI is consulted because, as a Socialist deputy opined in the same article, "The theory of delimitation to the left of the majority has been defeated mainly thanks to the PSI, and the opposition is finding more space for a positive contribution." Whoever is responsible, and whatever the "historic compromise" might mean, the PCI proudly reports that a public opinion poll taken in December 1974 showed 38 percent of the Italian public in its favor, 34.9 opposed and 27.1 undecided.

(6) What the PCI precisely means by the "historic compromise" is to be seen in its explanations of its intentions toward the two political forces most directly concerned: the PSI and the DC. American journalists (e.g., *Washington Post*, 12 February) have generally seen the PCI's proposal of the "historic compromise" as an attempt by Berlinguer to forego the laborious process by which a joint PCI-PSI majority would have to be built, and to leap over the heads of his PSI allies to strike a bargain directly with the DC, which bargain would give the PCI a share of the governmental spoils. Berlinguer, however, in the preparatory document for the 14th Congress (*L'Unità*, 11 December 1974) stated: "The development of unity between the PCI and the PSI contstitutes an essential condition for pushing ahead all the processes of renewal, including those necessary and possible within the Catholic world and in the DC itself." In other words, the alliance with the PSI is not an alternative to, but a prerequisite of, the "historic compromise." In this discussion, specifically reaffirmed in his speech at the congress, Berlinguer stated that the "compromise" was a joint PCI-PSI enterprise and that the PSI was an "integral part of the workers' movement," though with its own specific physiognomy and autonomy."

On 1 February the PCI and PSI held a high-level public colloquium on the "historic compromise," led by Ingrao for the PCI and Alessandro Manca for the PSI. Manca said in part:

From 1969 on, there developed an awareness of the fact that a process of true renewal cannot be planned without establishing a relationship that will gradually assume the forms permitted by political conditions, but that, in any case, dialectically involves Communists and Christian Democrats in a complex and profound integration. This conviction does not contradict the other—equally important and decisive—which is based on the essential nature of a special relationship between the two parties of the working movement. An underestimation of the essential nature and of the special nature of this relationship involves dangerous distortions and errors. . . .

[The] Communist proposal of the "historic compromise" was inspired by a line which the PSI urged and is urging the PCI to adopt.

At the end of the colloquium, after reaffirming the indispensability of PCI-PSI unity, Ingrao said: "We have firmly rejected the interpretation of our proposal as a power agreement between Christian Democrats and Communists. . . . We have asked not only for change of men and directions, but for the liquidation of the system of Christian Democratic power." (*Avanti*, 2 February.)

(7) The PCI's statements and actions regarding the Christian Democrats are therefore most important. The most immediate objective of the "historic compromise" is clearly the resolution of Catholicism, in all its social and political manifestations, from the greatest obstacle to Communist power into several different elements, only some of which would remain hostile, while others would be either neutral or objectively associated with Communism. In his pre-Congress document, Berlinguer said:

Profound contradictions exist in the DC Party. It is a party tied to the interests of big economic concentrations, of vested interests, and of parasitic groups. But it is also a party which, by virtue of its origins, of some of its traditions, and of the presence in it and in its electorate of broad masses of the middle classes, peasants, women, and workers must also take account of popular demands and aspirations.

Our initiatives must play on these contradictions so that the weight of the popular, anti-fascist, democratic and unitary components within and around the DC may grow, and that of the more conservative, narrow-minded, and factious groups may diminish. (*L'Unità*, 11 December 1974.)

How is the process to be pursued? Ingrao spoke of "striving for genuine divisions, real cleavages, within the DC," and said that these should accomplish more than "driving out a few corrupting influences in the DC" or merely detaching fringe elements" (*Rinascita*, 21 February 1975). These profound divisions, this winnowing process, would take place as the Catholic forces reoriented themselves "in a coherently democratic and antifascist sense" (Berlinguer, *L'Unità*, 19 March 1975) and joined the Marxist ones in "the indispensable struggle of the subordinate classes for their emancipation" and in the transformation of Italian society. The implication is simple: as the DC is induced to adopt new ways, new men associated with those ways will gain prominence over partisans of old ways. The very controversy over whether to cooperate with the PCI is transforming the DC.

In the aftermath of the June elections, Berlinguer called on the DC to oust its leader of the past quarter-century, Amintore Fanfani. Not surprisingly, within the DC Fanfani's most vigorous opponents were men confident of PCI support for their own position in the DC. Fanfani was ousted from the DC chairmanship by a vote of 103-69 on 22 July. The electoral defeat at the hands of the PCI which made possible the ouster of Fanfani strengthened the position, within the DC of men who have long urged and practiced cooperation with the Communists.

In a speech on 16 September, Italian premier Aldo Moro said that if the Communist Party used its influence on the labor unions to keep them from pressing for the sort of wage settlements that would worsen Italy's near 20 percent rate of inflation, the government would find "some way" of associating the PCI with its work. (ANSA, *NYT*, and *Corriere Della Sera*, 17 September.)

International Views and Positions. If the PCI sees the prospects for its success as very largely dependent on the progress of détente between the United States and the Soviet Union (*Rinascita*, 25 July, 1975), it sees détente itself as founded on firm and irreversible facts: the enemies of peace and socialism have lost so much ground that they no longer control absolutely even the citadel of imperialism, the United states (see Berlinguer's preparatory document for the 14th Congress and his speech to the congress (*L'Unità*, 11 December 1974, 19 March 1975; also Pajetta over Soviet radio, 20 August, *FBIS*, 26 August). During 1975, according to Berlinguer, three major events advanced the cause of world détente: "the final defeat of the imperialist aggression in Indochina"; "the reopening of the Suez Canal, which has opened up positive prospects for a solution to the involved Middle East situation"; and "the new steps forward in the Soviet-American dialogue ... as a result of the now imminent concluding Conference of European states." Therefore "even the Western countries are realizing that it is only within the process of détente that there can be any future for individual peoples and countries." (*L'Unità*, 13 July.) The strengthening of the PCI at the expense of imperialism's Italian partners was therefore seen as not only compatible with but essential to the progress of détente in Europe.

The weakening of imperialism, especially in Europe, was seen as giving Europeans a chance to reestablish an important role for themselves in the world: "It is Lenin's idea that socialism will be achieved only when it is established in the more developed nations" (ibid., 11 December 1974). In order to take advantage of this opportunity, said Berlinguer, Europeans—and Italians in particular—must reject the view that the United States is "head of the European countries—a theory which means servility and the abandonment of national autonomy" (ibid., 10 June 1975). Those who hold it "seek to revive a relationship between the United States and individual European countries ... which no longer exists because it has been repudiated or abandoned by all or almost all the European countries as well as—as Fanfani seems not to have heard—by the United States itself" (ibid., 29 May). Most important, the kind of relationship they envisage is one in which the socialist and imperialist blocs confront one another internationally, while within nations politics is reduced to the clash between clearly delineated reactionary and progressive forces. In such a dangerous cold-war situation, progress is very difficult. The PCI, on the other hand, wants to bury the cold war and build Europe's friendship with both the United States and the Soviet Union. The PCI, however, makes it clear that its choice of friendship with both the United States and the Soviet Union is not an "agnostic choice" or a denial of its nature. Rather, it is a political choice for a given set of circumstances. (Ibid., 3 August). Berlinguer was, he said, very eager to explain his policy of friendship to the American people, for whom Italians have always had special affection.

The PCI's appeals for understanding in the United States did not go unheeded. Columns praising one or another aspect of the PCI have appeared in the *New York Times* (5 October), *Los Angeles Times* (9 July) and *San Francisco Examiner* (20 July). Daniel Yergin (Harvard International Affairs Council on Foreign Relations) published a very favorable article on the PCI in the *New Republic* (November) which ended with the words "we need them." The Council on Foreign Relations scheduled a dinner in New York in October in honor of Sergio Segre, head of the PCI working group on foreign affairs. Segre was, however, denied a visa, precisely because such reception of a PCI dignitary would be read in Italy as the kind of acceptance of the PCI by American which the PCI has been seeking. Segre did receive a visa for a visit to the United States in November, but only as a member of a mixed Italian parliamentary delegation.

If Americans are worried that the growth of the PCI would mean the withdrawal of Italy from NATO, the PCI seeks to reassure them. " ... so long as the Atlantic Alliance ... struck and maintained an aggressive and provocatory attitude, we openly fought to get Italy out of that context and onto a line of neutrality and peace. But ever since, partly with our help, we have seen the dawning in he world ... of a new era [the PCI has no longer sought] unilateral withdrawal from the Atlantic

Alliance, but rather . . . energetic and consistent action so that the quest may develop favorably and so that, as a consequence, the conditions can be brought about which will make it possible to supersede and do away with the opposing military blocs" (*L'Unità*, 17 June). This, says Berlinguer, does not deny the party's judgment of NATO: "It was designed to perpetuate the rupture of anti-fascist unity on the world scale and in single nations. . . . [It] was to impose on the entire world through force and blackmail . . . the so-called American way of life. . . . It was initiated by the United States . . . when it was not possible to hypothesize and fear any threat from the Soviet Union, which had always provided proof of a firm and coherent policy of peace." But NATO failed. The process of détente now makes it possible for each nation to work autonomously "within the blocs themselves" to end blocs. (Ibid., 11 December 1974.) Fanfani characterized the PCI position on NATO as follows: "Ever since the Italian Communists have been saying that they can tolerate the Atlantic Alliance, the suspicion has been growing that they may be tolerating it because they consider it useless" (*Stampa Sera*, 5 May 1975). It is clear, in any case, that in 1975 the PCI considers NATO less troublesome to it and to the socialist world than the turmoil which would be caused by its insistence that Italy leave the alliance.

Intimately connected with the party's stand on international security matters was its 1975 campaign for the reform of the Italian armed forces. In a nine-point plan presented to Parliament on 16 February the PCI asked, in the name of détente, for the cessation of development and deployment of offensive weapons and the redeployment of Italy's armed forces away from the northeast corner of the country. In the name of democracy and anti-fascism, it asked for the abrogation of "authoritarian" practices in the military, a reorganization of the intelligence services in which all parliamentary forces (including the PCI) would participate, the exercise of closer parliamentary control over the "democratic" character of the general staff, and the removal from the general staff of exclusive authority over promotion of officers. The Party had previously asked for greater freedom of political activity in the ranks, for shorter periods of obligatory service, and for a law dispensing soldiers from the necessity of following orders which might endanger their physical integrity (*L'Unità*, 2, 4 November 1973; 17 March 1974).

The PCI regularly comments on world events. When Saigon fell to the North Vietnamese on April 30th, Berlinguer wrote: "We have lived and are living through unforgettable times. Why? Because of the immense and legitimate satisfaction we Communists, we revolutionaries feel every time our ideals and our policy assert themselves and, to a greater or lesser extent prevail: and this time they have asserted themselves and prevailed to the greatest extent imaginable. April 30 marks a decisive moment in world history: it is a victory of freedom over oppression, of peace over war, of life over death, or unity and of right over oppression and violence." (Ibid., 4 May 1975.) In its letter of congratulations to the National Front for the Liberation of South Vietnam, the PCI Central Committee, besides praising "with brotherly friendship" the NLF's dedication to liberty and peace, remarked on its "extraordinary political intelligence which, at any moment during the struggle, was always careful to create the broadest popular consensus around it in Vietnam and throughout the world" (ibid., 1 May).

When the United Nations voted to define Zionism as a form of racism, the PCI stated that it does not agree "with the fact that the United Nations should have wanted to take a vote" asserting what it did. The party also said it considers the existence of the state of Israel an indisputable fact, "But of that state's internal organization, of its non-secular character, of the discriminations which it retains, we have never ceased to express our condemnation and our criticism" (ibid., 21 October). Of course, without its "non-secular character" and "discriminations," Israel would be Arafat's "secular state in which Jews and Moslems could live in democratic equality." That is, it would not be the state of Israel at all. The PCI's position on the Arab-Israeli conflict is one of thorough-going support for the Arab cause. This was expressed very succinctly in *L'Unità* (24 December 1974) after a high-level PCI committee visited Lebanon, Syria, Iraq, and the Palestine Liberation Organization headquarters. The PCI statement also singled out Iran to share the blame cast upon Israel and the United States for tension in the Mid-East.

When India's prime minister jailed her political opponents and imposed press censorship, citing a CIA plot as her reason for acting so, the PCI, following the lead of TASS and the World Peace Council, declared that the Indian state of emergency had foiled plans by "reactionary forces" to "unleash a mutiny" (*NYT*, 27 June).

As mentioned above, the international issue to which the PCI paid most attention during 1975 was the acceptability of the tactics employed by the Portuguese Communist Party (PCP) in its drive for power. The PCP's success in excluding Portugal's Christian Democrats from the April elections came at the beginning of the PCI's 14th Congress, billed as the Congress of the "historic compromise," and caused much embarrassment. In his concluding speech Berlinguer declared that the PCI disagreed with the PCP's decision to ban the Christian Democratic Party from the elections. Rather, in the PCI's view, the PCP should have struck at those individual Christian Democrats it considered dangerous, and left the shell of the party for the use of those it deemed not dangerous. (*L'Unità*, 24 March.) This statement contains the strongest negative reference to the PCP to be found in all the PCI's statements on Portugal. The PCI's innumerable references to "previously stated disagreements" with the PCP (e.g., *L'Espresso*, 30 March) refer primarily to it.

Since the congress the PCI has spoken out on Portugal as follows. After the takeover of the Socialist newspaper *Republica*, the PCI expressed "worry," and said: "Intolerant methods, or, at any rate, methods which lead to clashes between the workers' political and social organizations cannot find us in agreement" (ibid., 20 May). However, the statement was full of praise for the PCP. On 12 July the PSI organ *Avanti* published a letter of encouragement to Mario Soares's Portuguese Socialists, coupled with an attack on Communism "from Moscow to Prague to Lisbon" and with praise for the PCI for its adherence "to the spirit and the letter of democratic principles."

On 8 August 1975, the PCI issued a statement jointly with the Soviet party on a wide range of international issues. On portugal, the statement called for the unity of action of all progressives and expressed solidarity with the Portuguese Communists. In an editorial (*L'Unità*, 12 August) the PCI said that even though the Soviet and Italian parties had taken a common position, the PCI was wholly independent and restated the necessity that in Italy "the affirmation of socialism pass through and not against the schemes of representative democracy."

The Party strongly disapproved of Soares's withdrawal from the government in Portugal in protest over Communist tactics. On 29 July *L'Unità* stated in an article on Portugal that fundamental political freedoms should be defended "as a specific banner" of the workers movement. On 20 August it denounced as "calumny" and as "politically unacceptable opinions" U.S. suggestions that the Soviet Union was interfering in Portugal. It also disagreed with *Pravda*'s evaluation of the Portuguese Socialist Party (PSP) as hopeless, saying that although the PSP's present policy was indeed "provocative" and its leadership was responsible for the reverses the Communists were suffering, the blame for non-cooperation of the Socialists and Communists in Portugal ought to be placed on both sides. Thus the PCI accepted in principle, as did all foreign parties invited, Soares's bid for a conference of the Socialists and Communists of Italy, France, Spain, and Portugal. The meeting did not take place in 1975. But the PCI and PSI did send a joint note to the Portuguese Communists and Socialists urging on them the kind of cooperation their Italian counterparts were practicing. In an interview published in the French Socialist journal *L'Unité* (24 October) they again urged cooperation between the PCP and the PSP.

The PCI had several occasions to speak on the subject of Czechoslovakia. On 20 February, in the course of a television public affairs show, Berlinguer had just finished saying that Communism in Italy would not be illiberal, as it is elsewhere, because Italy is a developed country with a history of liberalism, when he was asked about Czechoslovakia. He answered that its characteristics would have allowed a liberal Communism, "But this appertains to a fact which we have criticized and to a reality which, while maintaining our critical opinion, is explained, if not by specific reasons in that country, by reasons stemming from the international situation. In other words, from that division into blocs which must be made obsolete in order also that the countries of both blocs are allowed increasing freedom and autonomy in terms of their own internal affairs." (*L'Unità*, 21 February.) PSI secretary Francesco De Martino said of the PCI's attitude: "The Italian Communists show they favor democratic forms of socialism in Italy. But then they favor authoritarian forms in Eastern Europe and in all Communist countries." (*NYT*, 23 October.)

International Party Contacts. Only a few of the PCI's many contacts with the Communist Party of the Soviet Union (CPSU) and with Moscow-line movements throughout the world (45 of which sent delegations to the 14th Congress) can be mentioned here. The PCI has no relations with anti-Moscow Communists anywhere. Relations between the PCI and CPSU are frequent and very cordial. Multi-member working delegations of PCI leaders and leaders of PCI mass organizations are often in Moscow, and, on 23 July 1975, the leadership of the PCI even held a regular session in the Soviet capital. The primary business of the session, Tass reported, was the conference of European Communist Parties originally proposed by the Italian and Polish parties and originally scheduled for late 1975 (postponed until 1976). The place of honor at the PCI 14th Congress was reserved for A. P. Kirilenko, candidate member of the CPSU Politburo, who brought greetings for the party, the Order of Lenin for its president, Luigi Longo, and praise for "Enrico Berlinguer ... our big friend." (*IB*, no. 6-7). In his speech to the Congress, Kirilenko assured the delegates: "We see in you people who hold the same views and champion the same cause that we do." The CPSU Central Committee's message stated that the PCI's vigilance and unification of all progressive forces was "the right way" to proceed. (*Pravda*, 18 March; *FBIS*, 20 March.)

On 6 August, on the occasion of the 70th anniversary of Lenin's publication of "Two Tactics of Social Democracy" and also the day of the arrival in Moscow of a high-level PCI working group, *Pravda* published an article by Konstantin Zaradov, an expert on foreign Communist parties, which pointed out that when Communist parties enter into wide political alliances, they expose themselves to the dangers of compromising the principle of hegemony of the working class, and of forgetting that a majority is not an arithmetical but a political concept. This was seen by *Le Monde* the next day as a criticism of the PCI. On 9 August *L'Unità*, said that only "certain newspapers ... thought they could see a polemical intent" in Zaradov's words on alliances and majorities, which were written "inter alia" in the context of the Lenin anniversary. The PCI pointed out that principles must be put into practice in very different situations, and that experience has taught it the Italian situation requires the interweaving of democracy, socialism and liberty.

On 17 October *Rinascita*, in a reference to the Zaradov article, made a distinction between the situation in Russia in Lenin's time and that in present-day Italy. In the latter, political hegemony must be understood in terms of a "very wide and articulated" alliance of forces, including even industrialists, and hegemony must be seen "in the sense of capacity for direction, conquest of consent, and construction of alliances." This sort of hegemony provided "the real guarantee that socialism can develop protected from reactionary counterattacks," whereas a narrow understanding of hegemony would expose socialism in the West to what befell the Allende regime in 1973. In the West (in implied contrast with East Europe and Asia), it was impossible to simply transfer "democratic centralism" from the Party to the State "as has happened in other countries and under other historical conditions with results that are rather indisputable." This article elicited headlines in Western newspapers like that in the 30 October *Christian Science Monitor*: "Italy's Communist Party refuses Moscow's Rule."

Singled out for the honor of addressing the PCI's 14th Congress, besides the CPSU, were the

Communist parties of Chile, Czechoslovakia, France, Greece, Hungary, Japan, North Korea, Portugal, and South Vietnam. Between 23 and 30 June, a PCI working group visited Bulgaria. The Italian and Bulgarian parties traded their highest decorations. When Spanish Communist leader Santiago Carillo visited Italy in July, he was featured in the Party press, and honored by a mass demonstraton at which he appeared alongside Berlinguer.

Publications. The PCI's daily newspaper, *L'Unità*, published in both Milan and Rome, has a circulation of 400,000 and is one of Italy's largest newspapers. The editor in chief and the co-editor responsible for the Milan edition are members of the Central Committee. The PCI also has local organs. These, together with the Party ideological school system and the Editori Riuniti publishing house, are under the supervision of Renato Zangheri, Central Committee member and mayor of Bologna. Products of the publishing house are: the weekly *Rinascita* and the bimonthly *Critica Marxista*; *Politica ed Economia*, a journal of political economy; *Riforma della Scuola*, which deals with educational matters; *Studi Storici* a historical journal; *Donne e Politica*, a women's political magazine; and *La Nuova Rivista Internazionale*, a journal of international affairs.

*   *   *

Competing Communist Groups. The PCI is to be distinguished from the following minor groups:

Party of Proletarian Unity for Communism (Partito Di Unità Proletaria; PDUP) founded July 1974 from a merger of the *Manifesto* group expelled from the PCI in 1969, and that portion of the Italian Socialist Party of Proletarian Unity which did not integrate itself into the PCI in 1972.

Continuing Struggle (Lotta Continua; LC), founded in 1968.

Workers' Vanguard (Avanguardia Operaia; organized on a national scale since 1971.

Communist Party of Italy, Marxist-Leninist (Partito Comunista d'Italia Marxista-Leninista or PCI (ML), founded in 1966.

Italian Communist Party (Marxist Leninist), or PC(M–L)I, founded informally out of four associated mini-groups in 1968, formally in 1972.

Workers' Autonomy (Autonomia Operaia; AO), active since 1969.

Red Brigades (Brigate Rosse), active since 1971.

Armed Proletarian Nuclei (Nuclei Armati Proletari; NAP), first appeared in 1975.

Revolutionary Communist Groups (Gruppi Comunisti Rivoluzionari; GCR).

The Party of Proletarian Unit has a membership estimated at about 15,000. It publishes the daily *Il Manifesto*, which expresses strong opposition to both the PCI and the Soviet Union, but shows no commitment to China. The PDUP is most comparable with the French Unified Socialist Party (PSU). In November and December 1974. The PDUP and the PSU exchanged visits. In the 1975 local and regional elections, the PDUP presented joint lists with Workers' Autonomy (AO) and gained a little over one percent of the vote. Some PDUP militants retain the influence in the labor movement they gained while members of the PCI or PSI. They are active in all three labor confederations, often outbidding the PCI for the allegiance of the most embittered workers.

Continuing Struggle (also the name of the group's daily newspaper) held its third national convention in Naples on 19-21 July 1975. It is a Trotskyite group, but the Revolutionary Communist Groups (GCR), who are the official Italian section of the Fourth International, accuse LC of excessive reliance on working-class self-guidance (*Intercontinental Press*, New York, 28 July). LC's main strength lies among unskilled workers, although one of its branches, the Military Movement, has recruited enough soldiers to cause worry among Italian military authorities. The Movement's slogan is "Today soldiers, tomorrow partisans."

Workers' Vanguard has an estimated membership of 25,000. It publishes daily and weekly newspapers and a quartery journal, *Politica Comunista*. The group is based in the labor movement in Milan, but has attempted to branch out into universities. Its members include dissident Communists, dissident Maoists, and dissident Trotskyites.

The Communist Party of Italy, Marxist-Leninist, led by Fosco Dinucci since 1966, is the largest Maoist group in Italy. It regularly exchanges visits and messages with China (May 1975), Albania, (September-October) and Maoist groups around the world (e.g., the joint declaration with the Communist Party of Brazil (Marxist-Leninist). It publishes a weekly, *Nuova Unità* and a periodical *La Voce Della Cella*, but has not held a congress since 1973. The PCI (ML) is reported to have taken an interest in terrorism.

The Italian Communist Party (Marxist Leninist) is led by Aldo Brandirali and publishes a journal, *Servire il Popolo*. In the 1972 general election, it gained about 85,000 votes. Although it is avowedly Maoist, the group has no·known connection with China.

Workers' Autonomy is the result of the amalgamation of a left-wing split from Lotta Continua and the remnants of the defunct Workers' Power (PO). It has no national coordination, and works closely with the GCR.

The GCR publishes a fortnightly, *Bandiera Rossa*. News about it appears in the Fourth International's *Intercontinental Press*. Its field of action is the labor movement, but it is quite isolated.

The Red Brigades and Armed Proletarian Nuclei are terrorist organizations, specializing in kidnapings, bombings, and prison uprisings.

Hoover Institution   Angelo Codevilla

Luxembourg

A profile on the activities of the Communist Party of Luxembourg (Parti Communiste de Luxembourg; PCL) during 1975 has not been prepared for this edition of the *Yearbook on International Communist Affairs*. The leadership and organization of the PCL remained essentially unchanged, and domestic attitudes and activities, as well as international views and positions, remained generally the same as in 1974 (see *YICA, 1974*, pp. 217-219).

During the latest national elections, held on 26 May 1974, the ruling conservative Christian Socialist Party (Parti Chrétien Social; PCS) suffered an unexpected loss of 3 seats. The result was the creation of a center-left coalition which ended 55 years of unbroken rule by the PCS alone or in coalition.

In the new assembly, expanded to 59 seats (1968: 56 seats), the Christian Socialists remain the largest single party, with 18 seats (1968: 21 seats). But the Socialist Party, with 17 seats (1968: 18 seats), commands a straight majority of 31 together with the 14 seats held by the "Liberal" Party (Parti Démocratique; PD). The PCL captured approximately 10.4 percent of the vote (1968: 15.5) and 5 seats in parliament (1968: 6 seats).

The profile on the activities of the PCL during 1975 and 1976 will appear in the 1977 edition of the *Yearbook on International Communist Affairs*.

Hoover Institution   Dennis L. Bark

Netherlands

The Communist Party of the Netherlands (Communistische Partij van Nederland; CPN) was founded as the Communist Party of Holand in 1918. The official founding date, however, is that of affiliation to the Comi ern, 10 April 1919. The present name was chosen at the party congress in December 1935. The party has always been legal (with the exception of the war years).

CPN policy is based on the "new orientation" proclaimed at its 1964 congress, which gives primary importance to the realization of domestic political goals: relations with the international communist movement are subordinated to the realization of a united front of which communists and socialists form the pivot. In 1975, however, a tendency of more involvement of the CPN in the international communist movement was noticeable. The autonomous attitude of the CPN to the Sino-Soviet dispute has led to the formation of both pro-Soviet and pro-Chinese groups outside the party. Their influence on CPN politics is small.

The number of CPN votes received in elections has been increasing since the low point of 2.4 percent in 1959, when the party was split. In the November 1972 general elections the CPN received 4.5 percent of the votes, which means 7 seats out of 150 in the Lower House of the parliament. In the provincial governing bodies the CPN has 19 seats out of 670, in the municipal governing bodies 130 seats out of 12,000. In 16 out of more than 800 municipalities the CPN has aldermen.

The CPN does not publish figures, but the number of members is estimated at 10,000 and the number of subscribers to its daily paper, *De Waarheid*, at 16,000. CPN followers are irregularly spread over the country, with centers of activity in Amsterdam, the highly industrialized "Zaanstreek," and the province of Groningen. The population of the Netherlands ia bout 13,634,000.

Leadership and Organization. The CPN's 25th Congress, in June 1975, elected a new Central Committee which does not differ much from the previous one. The principal policy-making body is the 12-member Executive Committee of the Central Committee, including H. J. Hoekstra (chairman), M. Bakker (chairman of the CPN fraction in parliament), G. Hoogenberg (charged with work in industry), and J. IJisberg (administrative secretary). The Secretariat, consisting of 5 or 6 members of the Executive Committee, is the organizational and administrative center of the party. The Central Committee, consisting of 37 members and 3 deputy members, only meets a few times per year. Former leader P. de Groot still has a strong influence on CPN politics.

The significance of the CPN front organizations has decreased considerably since the breaking of their ties with the international front organizations because of the party's autonomous policy. The most active is the General Netherlands Youth Organization (Algemeen Nederlands Jeugd Verbond; ANJV). The activities of the Netherlands Women's Movement (Nederlandse Vrouwen Beweging; NVB), like those of the ANJV, supported CPN demands. The organization of former resistants, "Verenigd Verzet 1940-1945," is politically of no importance.

Party Internal Affairs. The CPN held its 25th congress on 6-8 June 1975. Because of the intention to make the aims and activities of the party more public, the party members—for the first time since the 19th party congress, in 1959—were given the opportunity to conduct a public discussion in advance of the congress. For this purpose the daily *De Waarheid* started a special column.

The functioning of the party is still one of the main concerns of its leaders. In a speech for the Central Committee in January, chairman Hoekstra said that the measures which had been taken in 1974 to intensify central control on the regional and local bodies had led to some improvement, but that it had become clear that a much stronger control was necessary (*De Waarheid*, 15 January 1975). In the preparatory report on the work of the Central Committee for the party congress it was also stated that in spite of a different approach to the work to be done, the regional conferences had shown differing results, ranging from strong growth to arrest of growth and here and there even decline (*Politiek en Cultuur*, no. 4).

Tn the Central Committee's theses for the congress—published in *De Waarheid* of 4 April—self-criticism was expressed on an attitude of waiting and on the leaving of initiatives for action to the "reformists" in the trade-union movement. The theses also noted that attention to the training of party members was "necessary for the struggle inside the party against bourgeois influence, infiltration and interference from outside, embassies of other countries included." Moreover, drastic measures were said to be necessary to strengthen the party in Rotterdam, an "important proletarian center."

Domestic Attitudes and Activities. The CPN has been inclined, in accordance with its policy of a united front of communists and socialists, to wage a constructive opposition agains the present Den Uyl coalition government, hoping to be able to exert some influence on government policy. This attitude change in 1975, and policy was more directed at the change of this government for a "real progressive government." The latter, Hoekstra said in his speech for the party congress "is not possible in this country if the CPN does not take part in the policy-making process of such a government" (*De Waarheid*, 7 June).

The extra-parliamentary mass action of the CPN is mainly directed against the replacement of military aircraft, Dutch participation in the building of a nuclear power station at Kalkar (a small place in the Federal Republic of Germany), unemployment, and cuts in many fields. In these activities the independent role of the CPN is increasingly stressed, at the cost of the idea of a united front with the socialists. Nevertheless the CPN states that it wants cooperation with other parties, without being used by them and while keeping its own character.

The CPN used the economic recession by launching an appeal in which it proposed a "broad national cooperation to fight against the scourge of this time, the crisis," particularly through: protection and increase of buying-power and standard of living, improvement of employment (also through extension of trade with the socialist countries, and protection of social and cultural attainments (ibid., 3 October 1975).

These demands will shape the policy of the CPN in the near future. It believes that these measures can be financed by cutting the defense budget, stopping the contribution to the EEC, finishing neo-colonial development aid, and raising the revenues from the production of natural gas.

The CPN's activity in the trade union field was limited to propaganda and agitation efforts in industry to influence trade unions and to avoid the closing down of factories.

International Views and Positions. In the party policy ("new orientation") proclaimed at the CPN's Twenty-first Congress, in 1964, it was affirmed that international policy is determined more by the domestic political situation than by the internationalist communist movement line. A turn in this policy was begun in the course of 1975, caused by the wish of the party leaders to normalize relations with the Communist Party of the Soviet Union (CPSU). Still, however, the CPN gives priority to domestic affairs. "Views and statements on world events only have a real significance, if in [our] own country efforts are made to force a policy which ends the cold war and the arms race and which, also in the field of trade and culture, practices peaceful co-existence" (*De Waarheid*, 4 April).

The process of normalized international relations was begun in a remarkable series of articles by former CPN chairman Paul de Groot, who still has a strong influence (ibid., 16, 17, 18 January). He wrote about the possibilities of adjustment of CPN views on international communist affiars to the views of the CPSU and allied parties, particularly in regard to peaceful co-existence and proletarian internationalism. Contrary to his previous view of the two superpowers dividing the power in the world among themselves, he now stated that the CPN had always fought "side by side with the Soviet Union and the other socialist countries" because the interests of the Dutch people stood with those of the socialist countries. The détente policy was no longer qualified as revisionism, but positively judged. Other attacks on Soviet revisionism were left out.

On the request of the Executive Committee of the CPN, informal talks were held with a delegation of the Central Committee of the CPSU in Amsterdam at the end of May. The subject was "problems of contents and forms of relations between the CPSU and the CPN in the past and in the future as well as possibilities of developing these relations positively" (ibid., 2 June). The party congress made it clear that the CPN does not want to follow the CPSU line in every respect straight away. Chairman Hoekstra expressed himself positively on the détente policy of the socialist countries and urged stronger action of all communists all over the world, particularly unified action for specific purposes. On the other hand he stressed the independence of the CPN and its responsibility to the working class and indicated that the contribution of the CPN to the international struggle will be limited to the struggle in its own country for "national independence," which includes dissociation from NATO and EEC. He repeated the old view that ideological struggle against revisionism and dogmatism will be necessary to reunite the international communist movement, without excommunication of any party (*Politiek en Cultuur*, no. 4).

As a symptom of the wish for normalization of international relations may also be regarded the intensified interest of the CPN in developments in Portugal. The CPN backed the Portuguese Communist Party without any reservation. Such an identification with an other communist party was something unheard of in the past. Hoekstra explained this in a public meeting by saying that the Communist Party of Portugal acts as an autonomous party which is only responsible to the workers of Portugal (*De Waarheid*, 8 September).

While following the main lines of CPSU policy, the CPN sought to show the continuation of its autonomous policy by stressing its own views on certain minor questions. For instance, at a meeting in Belgrade on 9-11 April on Europe and the developing countries, the CPN representative reproached the revisionists in regard to Indonesia, saying that they practiced a sort of "conspiracy of silence" (ibid., 12 April). In another instance, with regard to the measures taken by the Gandhi government in India in June, the CPN turned against those measures and took sides with those communist groups in India which are not recognized by the Soviet Union.

In the Middle East, the CPN advocated a peace agreement in which the rights of all countries concerned would be respected and the interests of the socialist countries would be taken into account (ibid., 3 September).

International Party Contacts. Improvement during 1975 in the relations between the CPN and the CPSU did not lead to an increased participation worth mentioning of the CPN in the international communist movement. A follow-up of the CPN-CPSU talks in Amsterdam in May was a trip through the Soviet Union made by two journalists from *De Waarheid* at the invitation of the Central Committee of the CPSU. Otherwise the CPN press only mentioned Hoekstra's visit to the Portuguese party in June, and de Groot's visit in November. As was the practice in previous years, the CPN did not invite other communist parties to attend its congress.

The CPN was not involved in the preparations for a conference of European communist and workers' parties. Taking into account the changed relations, however, it is not likely that the CPN will withdraw from participation in the conference.

Publications. The CPN daily, *De Waarheid* ("The Truth"), is the main source of information for party members. The paper is in constant financial trouble, which the party tries to overcome by collections from time to time. The bimonthly *Politiek en Cultuur*, devoted to the theory and practice of Marxism-Leninism under the leadership of the CPN Central Committee, is used for training purposes. The ANJV (youth) and NVB (women) have their own monthly papers. The CPN institute for political and social research, Instituut voor Politiek en Sociaal Onderzoek (IPSO), issues a quarterly, *Info*, which draws attention to articles which have been published by other parties on problems of present-day communism. The CPN has its own publishing house and bookshop, "Pegasus." In the importation of Russian publications, the pro-Soviet bookshop "Sterboek" competes with "Pegasus." The CPN has two commercial printing plants, one for *De Waarheid* and one for other printed matter.

*   *   *

Dissident Groups. The pro-Soviet communists in the Netherlands do not have organizational unity. Most are members of the "Nederland-USSR" friendship society, which is not engaged in domestic politics; it promotes cultural relations between the Netherlands and the Soviet Union, hoping to foster appreciation for the socialist system. Its monthly paper is *NU* (Standing for "Netherlands-USSR"). An important part is played by the travel agency "Vernu BV," which organizes an increasing number of tourist visits to the Soviet union. The chairman of the friendship society, who is also director of the travel agency, is W. Hulst. He has been awarded the Soviet "Order of the Friendship of the Peoples" for "his promotion of better relations between the peoples of the Netherlands and the Soviet Union" over many years. Highlights in the life of this society are the annual "Month of the Soviet Union" and the signing of the yearly cultural plan. Similar activities, but on a smaller scale and directed at the Balkan states and the German Democratic Republic (GDR) are fostered by a society for cultural exchange, "Vereniging voor Culturele Uitwisseling" (VCU), which seeks to coordinate its activities with those of the Netherlands-GDR friendship society.

Young members of Nederland—USSR founded in 1973 a new organization, Jongeren Kontakt voor Internationale Solidariteit en Uitwisseling (Youth Contact for International Solidarity and Exchange; JKU). It issues a paper, *Solidair*. In cooperation with Vernu BV, travels to Eastern Europe are organized, with the principal aim to learn more about the system of socialist society. The JKU maintains contacts with similar organizations in other West European countries and with the coordinating Soviet youth organization. JKU is a member of the World Federation of Democratic Youth.

As a rival of the CPN-oriented organization of former resistants, "Verenigd Verzet 1940-1945," pro-Soviet communists have founded an organization of anti-fascist resistants, Anti-Fascistische Oud-Verzetsstrijders Nederland" (AFVN).(It has a paper, *Antifascist*). The AFVN is a member of the International Federation of Resistance Fighters.

Soviet views are also presented by the "Nederlands Comité voor Europese Veiligheid en Samenwerking" (Dutch Committee for European Security and Cooperation) and by a monthly paper, *Communistische Notities* (Communist Notes), edited by a former CPN Executive Committee member, F. Baruch. As the unofficial mouthpiece of the CPSU, this paper played a role in the rapprochement between the CPN and the CPSU.

Although originally splinter groups of the CPN, the pro-Chinese groups find their followers among students and young workers who have no past or present connection with the CPN. There are six competing pro-Chinese groups. The two main groups are the Netherlands Communist Unity Movement-Marxist-Leninist (Kommunistische Eenheidsbeweging Nederland-marxistisch-leninistisch: KEN-ml) and the Socialist Party (SP). Both are small. The SP issues a monthly, *De Tribune*, and the KEN-ml a fortnightly, *De Rode Tribune*. The SP took part in the municipal electons in May 1974, for the first time, and received a total of 15,000 votes in 12 municipalities.

Oost-West Instituut   C. C. van den Heuvel
The Hague

Norway

The Norwegian Communist Party (Norges Kommunistiske Parti; NKP) is small and is facing the prospect of greater fragmentation and isolation. Its alliance with other leftist parties—formed in 1973 and responsible for NKP representation in the parliament (Storting)—may be on the rocks. That could mean new political frustrations for the NKP rank and file, most of whom are drawn from industrial workers in Oslo and low-income groups in the northern province of Finnmark and the eastern region of Hedmark. Members may number 2,500; other estimates range from 2,000 to 5,000. The population of Norway is about 4 million.

The NKP was organized on 4 November 1923 when a few radical politicians and trade unionists split from the Norwegian Labor Party (Det Norske Arbeiderparti; DNA). The NKP, in contrast to the parent DNA, conformed to Comintern principles. It started with an inherited 14 seats in the parliament and about 16,000 members, but (except for some electoral success in 1945, due to communist participation in wartime resistance against the Germans and in the liberation of northern Norway by the Soviets) has subsequently lost some of its political ground.

The communists have clearly suffered from being sandwiched between the nation's traditionally strongest political organization—the DNA—on the one side, and the Socialist People's Party (Sosialistisk Folkepartei; SF) and a motley collection of tiny extremist groups on the other. The NKP broke out of this vise in 1973 through participation in the Socialist Electoral Alliance (Sosialistisk Valgforbund; SV). Whereas, in the previous parliamentary election of 1969 the NKP got only one percent of the vote and no seats, in 1973 it got one of the 16 places won by the SV. That alliance—of the NKP, SF, and dissidents who had bolted the DNA in 1972 over the issue of Norwegian membership in the European Community (EC)—garnered 11.2 percent of the votes cast.

The SV holds the balance of power between the minority Labor government and the combined rightist and centrist opposition in the 155-member Storting. Both the DNA and the SV, however, may be in growing political trouble. Returns from the September municipal elections indicated that conservative parties might well gain control of Parliament in 1977 (the next general election, since each parliament must sit its four-year term) and that the SV, with a precipitous drop to 5.5 percent of the vote, would be hard pressed to catch up.

Leadership and Organization. Fragmentation is a large part of the Norwegian Left's problem. Besides the NKP, the following organizations exist: the Norwegian Communist Youth League, which split from the NKP in the late 1960's; Communist Youth, the NKP's youth organization after the split; the Socialist Youth League/Marxist-Leninist; the Socialist Youth League; the Norwegian Communist Workers (Marxist-Leninist) Party (Arbeidernes Kommunistpartei-Marxist-Leninist, AKP-ml); and several discussion groups, consisting primarily of intellectuals.

Much of the pressure of this fragmentation came to bear on the NKP at its Fifteenth Congress, on 1-2 November 1975. Delegates capped a year of anguished debate in the pages of *Friheten* and elsewhere with the decision not to merge with three other leftist parties into the Socialist Left Party.

The NKP congress named party vice-chairman Martin Gunnar Knutsen to replace Reidar Larsen as chairman. Larsen was a strong advocate of the planned merger and issued an open declaration at the congress opposing the party decision. He and 29 others announced plans to continue to work actively for a merger with the Socialist Left Party. The merger had been a divisive issue among the communists since the "unity congress" of the Socialist Left Party in April. At that time, the four component parties of the alliance—the communists, Socialist People's Party, Democratic Socialists, and independent Socialists—set a timetable for the eventual union, but put off important ideological differences. The communists were the main holdouts. Although they have said that they will continue to cooperate as an independent party, their decision all but dooms the Socialist Left Party. Without the communists, the leftist alliance does not have enough strength to threaten the Labor Party.

Internal divisions within the NKP were further aggravated when the National Council of the SV met in early November and agreed that its unification process should be accelerated and that a decision on the expulsion of the NKP should be taken by the SV congress in February 1976. Meanwhile, the SV council challenged supporters of the NKP congress majority decision (which repudiated the SV timetable for dissolution of the NKP and other SV component parties) to "take the organizational consequences" and quit the SV.

In a press conference announcing the SV council decision, SV leaders made it clear that they expected the February 1976 congress to give the communists a relatively short period to leave the NKP or be thrown out of the SV. Rune Fredh, SV secretary and until recently an NKP Central Committee member, has predicted that most NKP officers and members—except in Oslo, Bergen, and Norway's three northernmost provinces—will leave the NKP for the SV. He believed that this development would be particularly true of communist trade union officers and that so little would be left of the NKP that it would have difficulty functioning. Those like himself who had left the NKP would, however, work for revolutionary policy within the SV. Berit Ås, elected to head the SV in 1975, has the challenging task of bridging these ideological and tactical differences over the next year. Berge Furre has replaced Finn Gustavsen as parliamentary leader for that shaky alliance.

Domestic Attitudes and Activities. Debate over the nature and timing of full "organizational unification" of the Norwegian Left dominated NKP considerations in 1975, as it did in 1974. Pleas from SV leaders that the NKP put left-wing unity above party interests were to no avail. The "period for reflection" on that cooperative course ended in a clear repudiation of NKP chairman Larsen's coalition line.

For the Norwegian communists—like their counterparts elsewhere in the Nordic area—trade unions continue to be a major area of concern. The unions are well organized and represent tremendous economic and political power. Unfortunately for the NKP, it has been impossible to break the linkage between the DNA and the Norwegian Federation of Trade Unions (Landsorganisasjonen Norge; LO). The communists thus have no national officer in the LO and control no national labor union. At the local level, the NKP is most significant in the construction workers' union and, to some extent, in the metal, wood, transport, and electro-chemical fields. The party directs a "Baltic Sea Committee' which sends delegations to the "Workers' conferences of Baltic Nations, Norway, and Iceland," held annually in Rostock, East Germany.

Concern over how to use Norway's new oil and gas deposits continued to attract NKP attention in 1975. The communists stressed keeping firm Norwegian control of these new resources and a judicious utilization of the reserves. They opposed development by the large international oil companies and expressed satisfaction in parliament with the report that the state planned to take over the refining facility and distribution apparatus of the Norwegian-British oil company (BP) (*Friheten*, 9-14 June).

Even the discovery of oil did not spare Norway some of the economic problems plaguing the rest of Western Europe. An NKP official stated in an interview with *France Nouvelle*, (Paris, 7 July) that the Labor government was making the working people pay for the crisis of capitalism and was thus losing the support of the labor movement. He noted, in addition, that Norway was still faring better than many inside the European Community and that those who had opposed EC entry in the 1972 referendum felt vindicated.

Berit Ås, SV leader, and Finn Sjue, editor of *Klassekampen*, elaborated on the general theme of socio-economic disenchantment. As claimed that Norway has "a dictatorship of the bourgeoisie with control of the mass media and a strong power of influence over our interests and consumer habits." Sjue claimed that his ideal was not the USSR but Albania—"a small country like Norway, equally stingy but a rich country [where] any worker can go up to the ministry and check that the job is being done properly." (*Aftenposten*, Oslo, 10 October.)

International Views and Positions. There were no surprises in the international stance of the NKP during 1975. It gave, for example, full and total support to the proposal to reconsider the Finnish plan declaring Scandinavia a nuclear-free zone. Such a zone, the communist argued, would contribute constructively to the successful outcome of the Conference on Security and Cooperation in Europe (CSCE) and help break the "vicious circle of armaments" (*Friheten*, 10-15 March). The national conference of the NKP also demanded that the Norwegian government break off diplomatic relations with "the detested Saigon government" and support "the demand of the Cambodian people for the peaceful reuniting of their country" (ibid.). The NKP expressed solidarity with the Chilean people "resolutely fighting the Fascist coup regime in their country" and hoped that the Mideast crisis could be solved peacefully and in a way that met "the justified demands of the Palestinian people."

Portugal ranked high on the roster of international issues for communists throughout Europe. The NKP stressed that it fully supported "the call of the Portuguese Communist Party to establish an all-out democratic anti-fascist front" (TASS, 12 September). The communists struck back sharply and consistently at the Norwegian press and media for their "inflammatory and lying propaganda against the revolutionary process" in Portugal (*Friheten,* 9-14 June).

The communists challenged the proposition that "Norway exhaust its oil resources for the sake of the United States." They accused those who had tried to lure Norway into the EC of seeking insidious access to North Sea oil via Norwegian affiliation with the International Energy Agency (*Friheten*, 2-4 January).

The NKP found occasion to reaffirm its traditional opposition to Norwegian membership in NATO. Chairman Larsen claimed that it was vitally important to break out of NATO so that Norway could chart its own independent course. The communists urged opposition to the decision of Norway, Belgium, Denmark, and the Netherlands to buy the American F-16 and so further subordinate Norwegian national interests to the NATO Supreme Command. (*Friheten*, quoted by TASS, 5 April.)

International Party Contacts. In 1975, the NKP sustained its usual brisk pace of fraternal visits.

Herman Axen, Politburo member of the East Germany SED Central Committee received NKP Chairman Larsen in January for an exchange of views on European security and the international communist movement. Visits were exchanged in February, September, and October between the Norwegian Communist Workers (Marxist-Leninist) Party and the Albanian Communist Party. A delegation of the same group, led by its chairman Sigurd Allern and secretary Sverre Knutsen visited the Chinese People's Republic on 9 January-5 February. Arne Pettersen represented the NKP at a symposium organized by the *World Marxist Review* in Prague. The Norwegian communists relayed to their Soviet counterparts, during a visit to Moscow, 30 June-5 July, reports of their efforts to "insure comprehensive cooperation among all leftist-oriented, progressive anti-monopolistic forces in Norway." In Berlin in July, on behalf of the SED and the NKP, members of the respective East German and Norwegian politburos welcomed the decisions of the CSCE and stressed that the conference of European communist and workers' parties was of "great importance for the continued struggle for peace, security, cooperation and social progress" (GDR Domestic Servcie, East Berlin, 16 July). Georg Ovesen, member of the NKP Politburo, met with members of the Politburo Executive Committee of the Romanian Communist Party on 20 August.

Publications. The NKP press consists of *Friheten* ("Freedom"), the party's central organ, and several "in house" publications of party district organizations. First published during the wartime resistance, *Friheten* reached a peak circulation of 100,000 in 1945. Financial hard times and dwindling demand caused its transition from daily to weekly publication in 1967. The KU publishes a bulletin, *Fremad* ("Forward"). The primary voice of the AKP (m-l) is *Klassekampen* ("Class Struggle"). The new newspaper of the SV is *Ny Tid* ("New Times"), intended to absorb much of the staff and readership of the SF publication, *Orientering.*

Portugal

The oldest, largest, and most powerful communist organization in Portugal is the Portuguese Communist Party (Partido Comunista Português; PCP). It has operated since 1921, though for 47 years it stayed underground. National elections in 1975 for a constituent assembly clearly established it as a minority party, with only 12.5 percent of the vote, but that was scarcely a measure of its true strength and influence. Following the April 1974 overthrow of the Caetano government, it rapidly extended its control over student and labor organizations, news media, and local administration, and it strengthened its influence within the armed forces. By the end of 1975, however, its sway over the Armed Forces Movement (Movimento dos Forzas Armadas; MFA) and the news media was much diminished.

Another left-wing group, the Portuguese Democratic Movement (Movimento Democrático Português; MDP), was generally regarded as a "satellite" of the PCP. Formed as a coalition of opposition parties during the last years of the Caetano government, it was transformed into a political party in 1974. In the April 1975 elections, the MDP won 4 percent of the vote.

After the elections, there were widespread reports that the PCP and MDP had lost many members to more militant and ultra-left groups of Maoists and Trotskyites (*NYT*, 27 September). These radicals were the most actively involved in leftist acts of violence following the April 1974 revolution. They rejected the PCP's more moderate program of developing Marxism "gradually" and were as fiercely opposed to the "revisionist" Communists as to the parties to their right. They called PCP members "social fascists"; the latter, in turn, charged that the ultra-leftists were really middle-class reactionaries "masquerading with extreme-left ideas" (ibid., 7 July).

There were reported to be some 12 different groupings of far leftists, only six of which participated in the April elections for a constituent assembly. They received a combined 4 percent of the returns. Two offshoots of the Socialist Party, the Popular Socialist Front (Frente Socialista· Popular; FPS) and the Socialist Left Movement (Movimento da Esquerda Socialista; MES) received the highest vote count among these groups—about 1 percent each. They were described by some as fronts through which the PCP could manipulate acts of violence. A combined 1.6 percent of the votes went to three Maoist parties: the Popular Democratic Union (União Democrática Popular; UDP), the only ultra-left party to win a seat in the constituent assembly; the Electoral Communist Front-Marxist-Leninist (Frente Eleitoral de Comunistas-Marxista-Leninista; FEC-ML); and the Popular Unity Party (Partido de Unidade Popular; PUP).

Two Maoist parties were banned from the elections: the Movement for the Reorganization of the Proletariat (Movimento Reorganizativo do Partido do Proletariado; MRPP), which was also declared illegal as a party, and the Workers and Peasants Alliance (Aliança Operária e Camponesa; AOC). Three other Maoist groups scorned participation in the elections: the Revolutionary Party of the Proletariat-Revolutionary Brigades (Partido Revolucionário do Proletariado-Brigadas Revolucionárias; PRP-BR); the Organization for the Reconstruction of the Marxist-Leninist Party (Organização para a Reconstrução do Partido Marxista-Leninista; ORPML); and the Communist Party of Portugal-Marxist-Leninist (Partido Comunista do Portugal-Marxista-Leninista; PCP-ML).

The Trotskyite Internationalist Communist League (Liga Comunista Internacionalista; LCI) also took part in the elections, but received the lowest vote count of the 12 participating parties—0.2 percent. One additional group, which did not offer candidates, was the League of Revolutionary Union and Action (Liga para a Unidade e Ação Revolucionária; LUAR).

Most of these parties were formed following the April 1974 revolution. The most militant and heavily armed were two Maoist groups organized in earlier years—the PRP-BR (formerly the Frente Popular de Liberação Nacional; FPLN) and the MRPP. The latter was thought to be financed by the Chinese; it adhered closely to Maoist ideas. Less overtly Maoist was the PRP-BR; "Portugal is not China," was the explanation of its well publicized leader, Isabel do Carmo. The latter was said to be a close friend of the armed forces security chief, the radical Brigadier General Otelo Saraiva de Carvalho (ibid., 14 October).

Acts of violence by these and other leftist groups were principally deployed through several paramilitary organizations. These were illegal but were tolerated benevolently by General Carvalho and other radical officers. The biggest private army, said to be backed by the PCP, was called "Soldiers United Will Overcome" (Soldados Unidos Vencerão; SUV).

Leadership and Organization. Even after it was legalized in 1974, the PCP continued operating through many small cells in business and educational organizations, on rural estates, and in the armed forces. Party congresses meet periodically to establish policy guidelines and to elect the Central Committee. The latter supervises activities between congresses and selects the Secretariat and other executive organs. (For a list of members of the Central Committee and of the Secretariat see *YICA, 1975*, p. 229).

The secretary-general is Alvaro Cunhal, who became one of Portugal's most influential political leaders immediately following the April 1974 revolution. He had been admired for his many years of tenacious resistance, much of the time in jail, to the Salazar and Caetano dictatorships. He held a portfolio in all but the last of the cabinets that have been formed by the revolutionary government.

Communist Influence in the Armed Forces. The exact extent of communist influence on the military remained in dispute during 1975, but it was generally believed that only a small nucleus of officers embraced the ideologies of the PCP and other more militant groups. The bulk of the Armed Forces Movement appeared inclined vaguely toward a "socialistic path," open to "any kind of experiment by the people" that might lead to a "Portuguese kind of socialism" (*NYT*, 25 March, 5, 15 April). Most leading members of the MFA were said to have no illusion about the motives of Communist leaders but appreciated their "consistent support" and, while ideologically closer to the Socialists, resented the latter's criticism and wish "to take over from us" (ibid., 27 May). Others, even though suspicious of the PCP itself, allegedly felt that a truly radical thrust as recommended by the party was required to wrest conservative Portugal from its semi-feudal stagnancy (*Christian Science Monitor* [*CSM*], 21 January.)

Among the MFA officers, the chief advocate of PCP positions appeared to be General Vasco Gonçalves, premier until removed from power in August. An exiled former member of the MFA Coordinating Committee characterized the premier as a secret member of the PCP, determined to orchestrate a Communist take-over of the country. Gonçalves himself was publicly quoted as saying that the political analysis of the PCP had always been right (*CSM*, 13 March; *NYT*, 23 April).

Many officers, especially in the Navy, were said to be partial to Maoists and other groups of the extreme left. Prominent in this contingent were Admiral Antónia Rosa Coutinho, known as the "Red Admiral," and the aforementioned General Carvalho, head of the internal security forces and also military governor of Lisbon (*NYT*, 23 April).

The only "moderate" military officer who continued to hold a major position of power throughout the year's turmoil was the President, Francisco da Costa Gomes, who conceived his proper role as that of conciliator. Many regarded him as being too indecisive and pliant to the will of the leftists (*Veja*, São Paulo, Brazil, 11 December 1974; *NYT*, 23 April 1975).

Domestic Attitudes and Activities. The PCP in alliance with radical elements of the armed forces precipitated during 1975 a violent escalation of the struggle for power. This plunged Portugal into almost total political and economic disarray. Even though exasperated with the "sterile" bickering of the political parties and their inability to reach a consensus on policy, the Armed Forces Movement itself vacillated between moderate and extremist options. It permitted elections in April that confirmed the overwhelming non-communist preferences of the electorate. On the other hand, a minority of key military leaders appeared to be maneuvering the government during the first half of the year toward a markedly leftist military dictatorship. Massive protest demonstrations mobilized in August by the Socialist and Popular Democratic parties, which won a combined 64 percent of the April vote versus just over 16 percent for the PCP and MDP, wrenched the military back into a moderate stance under a new government. That regime in turn was paralyzed for almost three months by the resistance of leftist military and civilian dissidents and by the threat of civil war.

Prior to the elections, polls made it clear that the PCP could not expect to command a significant following (*NYT*, 20 January). This reinforced the party's decision to continue girding up its power base through close ties with the MFA. The strategy was to wangle through as many pro-communist decisions as possible before elections and to try to persuade the AFM either to cancel or delay elections or at least to stay in power with a veto over whatever democratic decisions might be taken (*CSM*, 12 February).

The first successful ploy was passage of a law in January merging the country's more than 180 trade unions into a single confederation. Since control of most unions had already been secured by the Communists, it was charged that the new grouping would also be dominated by them. To Socialist Party claims that a majority of workers were opposed to this maneuver, the PCP's Alvaro Cunhal countered that 40,000 supporters who paraded in Lisbon could hardly be called an Anti-Communist "silent majority." He suggested that real freedom was not possible with a pluralistic division of unions since many were controlled, and thereby "enslaved," by political parties or even by the owner class itself (*NYT*, 18 January; *Avante*, 23, 30 January).

Socialists were frustrated in their efforts to demonstrate popular opposition to the law. When the party summoned a protest rally, the PCP and two far-left movements announced mass meetings of their own for the same day, thereby providing the MFA with an excuse to ban the four simultaneous demonstrations as threats to public order (*NYT*, 31 January). Socialists and centrists in the cabinet did succeed in attaching amendments to the law providing for review of the measure after a year and specifying that membership in the confederation would not be compulsory. Meanwhile, Communists continued maneuvering into control of new unions. After their candidates lost elections in an important chemical workers union in Lisbon, they used their influence to have the election voided by the Ministry of Labor and the victorious candidates arrested. The latter were members of the Maoist AOC. (Ibid., 27 January, 23 March.)

Radicalization of the MFA. A second decisive advantage was gained by the PCP when it capitalized to the hilt on an abortive, awkwardly executed coup attempt in March by a military group of conservatives and moderates. An air assault by two training planes on the headquarters of a left-leaning artillery regiment outside Lisbon quickly collapsed and was branded by the Communists as part of a "reactionary, right-wing plot." Accused of leading the conspiracy was former president General António Spînola, whose arrest was ordered and who fled into exile (*NYT*, 12 March).

There was much speculation that the uprising was slyly provoked by the Communists and military leftists. They purportedly let the impression be conveyed to Spînola that his name headed a list of 500 officers and 1,000 civilians to be eliminated in an operation coded the Great Easter Massacre. It was presumably anticipated that he would launch a pre-emptive strike to prevent this and thereby fall into a trap. The effect was to provide the leftists with an issue that permitted them to galvanize MFA opinions against Spînola—for whom support had been growing in the military—and behind a more aggressive leftist program in order to "defend the revolution" (*NYT*, 13, 16, 26 March; *The Economist*, 15 March; *Paris Match*, 5 April). More than 1,500 persons were arrested on charges of complicity in the uprising and a purge of the armed forces was undertaken (*NYT* 10 April). A more leftist cabinet was installed, bringing in for the first time members of the Communist-front MDP and giving the PCP and MDP the same representation—two members each—as the Socialists and Popular Democrats (*CSM*, 27 March).

The most important upshot of the new swing of the pendulum was that it hardened MFA opinion in favor of an extended military stewardship of the country's political life. In January, the group had announced its intention of continuing to exercise an important political role only until presidential and legislative elections (*O Século*, Lisbon, 14 January; *NYT*, 19 February). Following the coup attempt in March, a Supreme Revolutionary Council was set up as an executive body to "direct the revolution," and in April political parties were required, as a condition for participation in the elections, to sign a contract conferring on the Council veto power over all political and government decisions for the next three to five years. Presidential candidates were required to be military men and the Council was to be responsible only to a new general assembly of the armed forces. The outlines of a new constitution were in effect dictated in advance to the future constituent assembly (*NYT*, 13 March, 5 April).

The PCP clearly welcomed the institutionalization of the military role in politics, declaring that a permanent alliance between the "people" and the MFA was the "axis of the revolutionary process." Other parties were dismayed. However, only six far-left groups refused to endorse the pact—on grounds that the military was not being revolutionary enough and was merely perpetuating "bourgeois power." The moderate parties reluctantly signed the agreement in the hope that success in the elections would at least give them more leverage and strengthen the moderates in the MFA (*The Economist*, 22 March; *NYT*, 12 April).

The leftists made further use of their new muscle by rushing through a series of nationalizations more extensive and precipitous than the MFA had previously been willing to sanction. Affected were all domestic banks and insurance companies and many key and middle-sized industries (*NYT*, 17 April, 15 May). The rationale for these moves had already been amply provided by the PCP as it campaigned against the "monopolists." It insisted that there could be no political democracy without economic democracy. As unemployment mounted and as bankruptcies became commonplace and investments declined, businessmen became easy marks for charges of economic "sabotage" and financial irregularities (*Neue Zürcher Zeitung*, Zurich, 21/22 December 1974; *NYT*, 19 December 1974, 8 February 1975; *O Século*, 13 January). Many firms were paralyzed by strikes and by the rash actions of workers' committees—encouraged by the PCP—that took over management functions in many firms without assuming financial resonsibility. This provided the government with the opportunity to intervene directly in the firms (*Chicago Tribune*, 17 April; *CSM*, 23 May). An anti-business bias was further reinforced when more than a dozen prominent industrialists and bankers were arrested on suspicion of having financed the 11 March plot against the government (*NYT*, 13 March).

Election Campaign. During the election campaign, the Communists directed their attention primarily to the areas where they expected to draw their main electoral strength—the industrial centers of Lisbon and Setúbal and rural Alentejo Province. Drought had diminished production and boosted unemployment in that southern farm land, but "reactionary" estate owners were blamed by the PCP for this "economic and social sabotage" and for conspiring to bring back "fascism." Confiscation of their lands and goods was therefore urged, by direct action of landless peasants as well as by legislation ("Rádio Clube Português," 6 January, 3 February; *NYT*, 10 February). The new Revolutionary Council obliged with a program of land reform limiting owners of irrigated farm property to 125 acres and providing for a government take-over of large unirrigated estates (*NYT*, 17 April).

A major PCP attempt to narrow the presumed breach between the party's popular support and that of its opposition—especially in the conservative North—was made through an intensive campaign to discredit other parties and to disrupt their campaign activities. The usual tactic was to identify all criticism of the party and of the MFA, particularly criticism coming from Socialists and Popular Democrats, as "fascist" and "anti-revolutionary" (*NYT*, 17, 21 March, 10 April; *To the Point International*, Antwerp, 5 April). The Socialist Party was even regarded as "dispensable" because it did not represent the people (*The Economist*, 22 March). An effort was made to implicate the left-of-center Popular Democrats and the conservative Christian Democrats in the March coup attempt, but the government only banned the latter group from elections on this charge (*NYT*, 19 March).

Socialists further complained of the infiltration of Communist "submarines" who sought to weaken the party by encouraging rifts among its more radical elements. The Popular Socialist Front (FSP) and the Movement of the Socialist Left (MES) were two such splinter groups that became Communist "fellow-travelers." Similar subterfuge was said to take place within the Popular Democratic Party. Thus politicians in Lisbon came to speak of Communist Party No. 1, No. 2, No. 3, and so on (ibid., 31 March).

The biggest impediment to campaign freedoms was the wave of leftist terrorism that involved disruption of rallies, sacking of party offices, and threats to lives. Police protection was either tardy, inadequate, or simply not provided. Most rioters were said to be Marxists to the left of the PCP, but, although the latter publicly deplored the violence, it was charged that its members also participated in and even manipulated many of the incidents (*NYT*, 27 January, 9 March, 3 April; *The Economist*, 15 March). The Social Democratic Center, the only conservative party permitted to field candidates, was so intimidated by the violence that it stopped holding political meetings and even considered withdrawing altogether from the elections (*NYT*, 23 March).

The PCP executed its campaign through a powerful political apparatus said to be lavishly financed from abroad. The number of party workers hired, branch offices opened, and posters affixed to walls far exceeded what other parties were able to muster. In spite of all this activity and superior organizational prowess, reinforced by the party's influence in the MFA as well as by its extensive control over organized labor and over most communications media, its electoral showing turned out, as expected, to be unimpressive: 12.5 percent for the PCP and 4 percent for the MDP. The Communists had been unable to induce the military to cancel elections or to postpone them long enough to permit the "revolutionary process" to "enlighten" the population and liberate it from the control of "reactionaries." Voters were "intimidated, coerced, corrupted and duped" and prejudiced against the Communists, it was repeatedly charged before and after the elections. Therefore, the results "could not be considered valid." Cunhal warned the victorious Socialist Party—which won 38 percent of the votes—that if it did not cooperate with the "progressive and revolutionary" forces and stop its "flirtation with bourgeois democracy," it would inevitably be dragged into opposition to the MFA (*NYT*, 20 January, 28 April; *Avante*, 26 April; TASS, 27 April).

A number of military men also began early in the year to downgrade the elections and the "power-hungry" political parties. Security chief Carvalho said that the party with the most votes did not necessarily represent the best interests of the people (*NYT*, 10 February). The minister of information, Commander Jorge Correia Jesuino, and Admiral Coutinho tried unsuccessfully to win MFA support for bypassing the regular parties in favor of a single armed forces party (*NYT*, 11, 15 April; *The Economist*, 3 May). Apparently in order to win an indirect public endorsement of the armed forces, Coutinho and some authorities advised voters to submit blank ballots if they did not feel "sufficiently informed" to choose between the different parties. Since polls had marked about half the electorate as "undecided," his expectation was that a high percentage would comply with his suggestion; actually, only 8 percent did (*NYT*, 15 April; Lisbon domestic radio, 17 April; "Rádio Clube Português," 28 April).

Radical officers seemed shocked at this seeming rejection by the electorate of their self-assumed role of public defender, but they were undeterred. Admiral Coutinho let it be known that the armed forces would hold on to political power for so long as it took to build a socialist society—for 20 or 30 years or more (*Washington Star*, 27 June). "Cultural enlightenment" teams of officers and enlisted men continued—as before the elections—to be sent around the country, especially to the "unreconstructed" North. Their charge was to indoctrinate the people in support of the MFA and the "Socialist Revolution" (*NYT*, 9 June).

Socialist-Communist Power Struggle. The obtrusive pro-Communist behavior of Premier Gonçalves and other radical officers, even following the elections, set the stage for a major confrontation with the Socialists and their anti-Communist allies. The episode that precipitated the engagement was the seizure of a Socialist newspaper, *República*, by the paper's Communist printers. They instructed the publisher that his ideology was mistaken: he had published what they alleged was a "falsified" secret PCP document urging the military to purge more Communists out of the radio and television systems (*NYT*, 20, 31 May; *U.S. News & World Report*, 2 June). Information minister Jesuino called the matter a labor dispute and ordered the paper closed down until the matter could be settled by the courts. Socialist leader Mário Soares, indignant at what he regarded as discrimination in favor of the Communist Party, said he would boycott cabinet meetings until the paper was returned to its owner (*NYT*, 23 May, 1 June). Then the Communist-dominated communications union demanded a sweeping revision of the country's "class-conscious" press law so as to give broader worker control over editorial policies. The government promised that the law would be changed to accommodate their demands (*NYT*, 17, 20 June).

Leftist employees—militants of the Popular Democratic Union—also seized a Catholic Church radio station, Rádio Renascença, in June in a dispute over personnel layoffs and over news policy. The military sought to settle the problem in July by nationalizing all the nation's radio stations (*CSM*, 9 June; *NYT*, 4, 7 July).

The Revolutionary Council expressed its impatience with the Socialists and pressed for a prompt settlement and for a reconciliation of the parties. When this was not forthcoming, the MFA acceded in July to a proposal of the radical officers for a system of "direct democracy" that would purportedly merely parallel the party system but would in effect short-circuit it. A series of neighborhood and worker committees was to be set up with direct links to the armed forces. The aim was to defend the revolution against reactionary forces and to win the "battle of production" by extending worker control and participation in business decisions. Such popular assemblies were denounced by the Socialists as the framework for a dictatorship; they were welcomed by the PCP as "highly favorable to the revolutionary process" (*NYT*, 28 May, 10, 12 July).

In desperation the Socialists and Popular Democrats formally withdrew in July from the cabinet, which was then dissolved. A military commission was immediately assigned to publish *República* (*NYT*, 12 July). Weeks of mass protests and violent attacks on PCP and MDP members and offices followed, with Soares demanding the removal of Gonçalves as premier. The leftist-dominated Revolutionary Council, in which opposition to Gonçalves was growing but remained divided, lashed back by setting up a junta of three generals—Costa Gomes, Gonçalves, and Carvalho—to give a "strong political direction" to the government. Though Carvalho promised "very hard repression" to put down the "counter-revolutionaries," the government remained paralyzed. The turmoil threatened to escalate into civil war (*NYT*, 26 July; *The Economist*, 9 August).

Finally, on 29 August, Gonçalves was replaced by Vice-Admiral José Batista Pinheiro Azevedo, who, as Navy chief of staff, had remained aloof from the power struggle. Antagonism to Gonçalves even within the armed forces had crystallized to such an extent that there was fierce resistance to his simultaneous nomination by Costa Gomes to be armed forces chief of staff. Consequently, his name was withdrawn and he was even stripped of his seat in the Revolutionary Council (*NYT*, 6 September).

The Azevedo cabinet was constructed to reflect the mandate of the April elections. It included, in addition to five moderate military men, four Socialists, three independents (two of whom were close to the Socialists), two Popular Democrats, and one Communist. The latter, Alvaro Veiga Oliveira, was assigned the unimportant Public Works ministry. The dominant Socialists set as their primary objective the dismantling of the PCP's power structure at all levels of government and the mass media and in the highest levels of the armed forces. The Revolutionary Council was promptly restructured to give the Army and Air Force more comfortable majorities over the more radical Navy. Also the armed occupation of leftist-controlled radio and television stations was ordered so as to halt a "provocative campaign of seditious attitudes" against the government. (*NYT*, 13, 22 September, 10 October.)

A violent Communist and radical-left backlash was immediate. Many soldiers, strongly swayed by the PCP, simply refused to obey orders to interfere with broadcasting operations; throughout the military services, in fact, large numbers of enlisted men openly defied their superiors. Entire military units even rebelled, contending that the aims of the revolution were being betrayed. Anti-government street demonstrations by civilians and mutinous enlisted men became almost daily affairs. PCP militants reportedly joined in the agitation, but the party itself stayed in the background (*NYT*, 26

September, 1, 5, 23 October).

The threat of civil war was rekindled as Socialists and Popular Democrats fought back with their own demonstrations (ibid., 10 October). A number of leftist and rightist paramilitary organizations, which had supplied themselves amply with arms from the military arsenals—with the connivance of sympathetic soldiers—contributed to the chaos with bombings and other violence (*Washington Post*, 22 September; *Visión*, New York, 30 October; *U.S. News & World Report*, 20 November). A government order to civilians to surrender all weapons or face fines and imprisonment brought in only 11 guns. Arms violations went unpunished (*NYT*, 19 October, 2 November).

The massive breakdown of authority led to repeated demands for a shake-up in the government and armed forces. Soares declared that it was "intolerable" for the Communists to remain in the government and "sabotage" it by backing military leftists' attempts to bring it down (*NYT*, 12 October; *CSM*, 14 October). On 20 November, amid rumors of an impending leftist plot to overthrow the government, the Socialists and Popular democrats announced that they would remain in the cabinet but would refuse to govern until steps were taken to assure their safety. They made it clear that they wanted the removal of radicals such as General Carvalho, who was giving his undisguised support to the military rebellion. The Revolutionary Council, though resentful of the cabinet strike, did agree to replace Carvalho the following day with a moderate officer (*CSM*, 22, 21 November; *NYT*, 22 November).

President Costa Gomes, who had been trying to avert civil war by being conciliatory, was finally pushed into taking decisive action when about 1,500 paratroopers seized four airbases and four radio and television stations on 25 November. He declared martial law and dispatched loyal troops in tanks to put down the rebellion. The revolt collapsed the next day with only four casualties and after most units surrendered without a fight (*CSM*, 28 November).

International Views and Positions. There was a flurry of alarm in Western countries early in the year when the USSR was reported to have sounded out Portuguese officials on the possibility of letting the Soviet Atlantic fishing fleet use Portuguese port facilities. The concern was based on the belief that their fleet's spying equipment would be used to watch over NATO operations. Portuguese officials denied that such a request had been made (*NYT*, 1, 2 February 1975).

Western governments also showed much nervousness over the open and covert support provided the PCP by the USSR. According to an alleged CIA estimate, the USSR was channeling over $10 million a month to the Portuguese Communist Party (*NYT*, 10 June). This would considerably exceed the more than $800,000 supplied, according to a Czech defector, to the Portuguese Communists and to the African colonies in an "average year" (*San Francisco Examiner*, 10 August). Additional evidence that the USSR was extending much more backing than mere declarations of "massive solidarity" with the Portuguese Communists was the heavy staffing of its Lisbon Embassy beyond its normal diplomatic needs. Six known KGB agents were said to be assigned there (*Aktuelt*, Copenhagen, 21 April; *NYT*, 10 June; *CSM*, 20 August). Concrete offers of economic aid to the Portuguese government itself, which might have fortified the Communists' position, appear to have been modest. After Premier Gonçalves had been removed in August, the Soviet press accepted the Communist retreat in Portugal without protest (*CSM*, 6 October).

Even while disclaiming that there was Soviet aid to the PCP, the latter party and the USSR repeatedly denounced CIA and other Western "interference" in Portugal during the year (ibid., 6 October). General Carvalho implicated U.S. Ambassador Frank Carlucci in the 11 March coup attempt and told reporters that Carlucci had better leave the country or else he could not guarantee his safety (*NYT*, 12 March). It was widely assumed in Portugal that the Embassy was in the hands of the CIA (ibid., 20 January). U.S. President Ford, in contrast, said it was "very tragic" that the limitations imposed on the CIA because of the congressional investigations kept the United States from participating with other Western European governments in supporting the anti-Communist struggle in Portugal (ibid., 4 August). A month later, there were newspaper reports that the CIA was sending millions of dollars to the Portuguese Socialist Party through West European Socialist parties and trade unions. The latter groups reportedly extended considerable support of their own, with money and supplies, to Soares's party. (Ibid., 6, 26 September.)

U.S. secretary of state Henry Kissinger was said early in the year to be very pessimistic about democratic prospects in Portugal; he reportedly predicted privately in April that by the following year Portugal would be a Communist nation or a neutralist nation under heavy Communist influence (ibid., 17 April). At the end of 1974, the United States had cautiously announced a modest economic aid program for Portugal, but it was not until after Gonçalves was pushed out that enthusiasm was shown for extending assistance. An immediate offer of $85 million in emergency aid was made. Kissinger said he was encouraged by the anti-Communist gains in Portugal. The European Common Market, which had also deferred a decision on financial aid to the left-leaning Gonçalves government, offered the Azevedo regime $80 million in guaranteed loans. (Ibid., 10 September, 12 October; *CSM*, 20 October.)

The United States also protested Soviet intervention in Angola, the last of the Portuguese colonies to be granted independence during 1975 (ibid., 2, 3, 4 December). The Russians reportedly supplied large quantities of sophisticated weaponry and "military advisers" to one of the three rival liberation movements engaged in civil war for control of the area (ibid, 19 November). The Soviet-backed group, the Popular Movement for the Liberation of Angola (MPLA), was also joined in the fighting by an estimated 5,000-6,000 Cuban troops and some "volunteers" from East Europe. To counterbalance this, military support from China, the United States, France, and neighboring Zaire and South Africa reportedly went to the other two groups, which joined forces to resist the MPLA after the latter repudiated an agreement to govern an independent Angola through a coalition. Some observers thought the divisions among the groups was tribally oriented rather than basically ideological and that even if the MPLA prevailed it would soon be pursuing a non-aligned policy independent of the Soviet Union (*Manchester Guardian*, 5 November; *CSM*, 7, 12, 17, 24, 26 November, 2, 4 December). Many white refugees from Angola complained of MPLA atrocities against them and blamed their plight on Admiral Coutinho, who was said to have openly supported the MPLA as the only legitimate representative of the Angolan people (*CSM*, 11 November).

Rivalry among three independence groups was also reported in East Timor, with a left-wing group claiming by December to control most of the colony. When the Revolutionary Front for the Independence of East Timor (FRETILIN) unilaterally declared its independence on 28 November, Portugal sought a negotiated settlement through the United Nations. Uneasy about the prospect of a neighboring Maoist regime, Indonesia then invaded and annexed the colony, much to the consternation of a Portuguese government that was powerless to intervene. (*CSM*, 7 March, 24 April, 22 August, 1, 8 December; Far Eastern Economic Review, Hong Kong, 1 August.)

Macao was the only Portuguese colony that appeared likely to continue its dependent—though largely autonomous—status. Reportedly, when Portugal offered to turn it over to Communist China, the latter refused, apparently because the foreign-owned status of the enclave facilitates the channeling to the West of opium, textiles, and other goods that are high foreign-exchange earners. Peking did warn in April, when pro-Soviet attitudes were ascendant in the Lisbon government, that it would not tolerate any activity in Macao inimical to China (*CSM*, 1, 6, 11 April: *Manchester Guardian*, 26 July).

PCP Media. The PCP's principal publication was its newspaper *Avante*, which was transformed from a weekly to a daily during 1975. Its broadcast medium was the station "Rádio Clube Português." The party also had a pronounced influence on other media through its control over "workers' committees" The television and radio networks were state-run and even all private radios were nationalized in July. After 15 March, when banks were nationalized, most newspapers also fell under state ownership since the majority had been in the hands of the banks. One news supervisor resigned because his department had been shaken up to put Communists in charge. Only Communists and their allies had regular access to broadcast time and to space in the newspapers. These groups denounced as "reactionary" efforts to make television an independent organ, declaring that it had to be "at the service of the people" and of the provisional government (*NYT*, 15, 30, 31 March, 10 April).

Actually, the popularity of newspapers was said to decline markedly after they fell under Communist domination. For example, the circulation of *República* reportedly fell from 80,000 to 8,000 after it was taken over by its Communist printers; the Socialist publisher then started a new paper, *A Luta*, which was soon selling 80,000 copies (*CSM*, 28 October).

Elbert Covell College   H. Leslie Robinson
University of the Pacific

San Marino

The world's smallest republic, with 19,000 inhabitants, San Marino is entirely surrounded by Italy, which provides it with connections to the world. Politics in San Marino are an extension of politics in Italy. Although treated by the world's Communist parties as an independent entity, the Communist Party of San Marino (Partito Comunista di San Marino; PCS) is a branch of the Italian Communist Party (PCI). Members are estimated to number about 300. The PCS sent three delegates to the PCI's 14th Congress in March 1975. (They sat with the foreign delegates).

As a result of the 1974 elections, the PCS controls 15 seats in the San Marino's 60-member General Council—an increase of one (*WMR*, November 1974). Its domestic line, like that of the PCI, is based on a proposed coalition of all left-wing forces regardless of party.

At a meeting of European Communist parties in April 1975, PCS chairman Ermenegildo Gasperoni, stressed the importance of left-wing unity. Under Gasperoni, the PCS has remained an orthodox disciple of Moscow, proud of "its modest contribution" to "the general consolidation of the socialist community, the intensification of the people's struggle against Imperialism" (ibid., December 1974).

Hoover Institution   Angelo Codevilla

Spain

The Communist Party of Spain (Partido Comunista de España; PCE) is the best organized and most widely established political group in Spain. It has been active since 1920 and clandestine since 1939. It is reported to be the third largest communist party in Western Europe, with one of the highest operating budgets, and claims to have a larger membership than any illegal party in history. Its number of hard-core militants has been estimated at 5,000 within Spain—out of a total population of some 35.6 million—and 20,000 abroad. The party emphasizes its working-class base but says it has many sympathizers as well as members among professional people, merchants, tradesmen, intellectuals, and students. The main strength is in the big cities and the highly industrial areas. Since taking a line independent of the USSR after the Soviet invasion of Czechoslovakia in 1968, the PCE has had to rely on outside contributions primarily from anti-Franco exiles and from a few Communist parties that share its independent stance.

Because of the PCE's dissident attitude, the Soviet Union until recently openly supported a rival party that had been expelled from the PCE in 1970. This splinter group, led by Enrique Líster, eventually came to be called the Spanish Communist Workers' Party (Partido Comunista de Obreros Españoles; PCOE). It succeeded in attracting no more than a few hundred members in Spain and was ineffectual. In an October 1974 reconciliation with the PCE, the Soviets agreed to withdraw support from the Líster party (see *YICA, 1975*, p. 243).

Though there are semi-autonomous PCE branches that exploit the sentiments of various regional separatists, such as the Catalan United Socialist Party and the Basque (Euzkadi) Communist Party, the principal separatist movements are the rival factions of ETA (Euzkadi ta Askatasuna, "Basque Homeland and Liberty"). ETA has been active since 1959 as a guerrilla group seeing "national liberation" for the Basque region. Hard-core activists are believed to number only a few hundred in a Basque population of 2 million. In 1970 the movement separated into a terrorist wing called ETA-V and a military-political wing called ETA-VI. The latter was an outgrowth of ETA's Sixth Assembly which opposed the Fifth Assembly's resolutions calling for violence. A Marxist ideology is said to inspire about a third of the ETA militants, with the ETA-VI having merged in 1974 with a Trotskyite organization to become the Revolutionary Communist League-ETA-VI (Liga Comunista Revolucionaria-ETA-VI). The League was itself a rival of the Trotskyite Communist League of Spain (Liga Comunista de España; LCE).

The principal terrorist groups in Spain are the ETA-V and a Maoist party called the Patriotic and Revolutionary Anti-Fascist Front (Frente Revolucionario Antifascista y Patriótico; FRAP).

Leadership and Organization. The PCE operates through party cells in each of Spain's 50 administrative provinces. National direction comes from a 7-member Secretariat, 24-member Executive Committee, and 118-member Central Committee. The PCE chairman is 79-year-old Dolores Ibarruri, and the secretary-general is 60-year-old Santiago Carrillo, who directs party activities from exile in Paris.

Carrillo led his party in forming an alliance in 1974 with various leftist-to-rightist opponents of the government in a "Democratic Junta of Spain." The Junta claimed 2,000 branches in 1975, including 123 in Madrid alone. Some PCE youth groups opposed to making "collaborationist" pacts with "unrepresentative conservative sectors" were said to be pushing for the replacement of Carrillo by a younger secretary-general. (Madrid domestic radio, 3 May, 7 June).

Party workers also occupied positions of leadership in the illegal trade unions called Workers' Committees (Comisiones Obreras, or "CC OO"), which they used to promote strikes and other labor agitation. When the government decided in May to authorize strikes, "CC OO" leaders took advantage of fresh elections to move into key positions also within the government-sponsored National Confederation of Trade Unions.

Domestic Attitudes and Activities. Though Spain was crippled by fresh onslaughts of terrorism and strikes during 1975, Premier Carlos Arias Navarro continued to affirm his commitment to a gradual liberalization of political life. He said the 1974 law allowing limited political association was broad enough to give a voice to left-leaning Spaniards but that it did exclude communists and separatists (*NYT*, 20, 27 February). Juan Carlos, who ascended the throne on 28 November following the death of dictator Francisco Franco, was said to agree with moderates in the regime that communist activities may have scuttled Spain's hopes for a pluralist democracy by strengthening the hand of alarmed hard-liners (ibid., 27 October; *Christian Science Monitor* [*CSM*], 31 January, 25 June, 27 October). The king's intention reportedly was to try to outflank the extremists on the right and the left by allowing gradual formation of a center-right Christian Democratic Party and a non-Marxist center-left Socialist Party. In this way, these moderate parties would become better equipped to compete for popular support against the superior underground apparatus of the Communists. (*NYT*, 28 October, 3 November; *CSM*, 5 December).

Actually, no headway was made during the year in encouraging any but a few far-right political organizations to seek official sanction. Since the ideology of the Franco movement could not be opposed and since recognition had to be supported by a petition of 25,000 signatures, opposition groups regarded as suicidal any notion of thereby handing the government "on a platter" so many names of potential future guests of Spanish prisons (*Visión*, New York, 30 December 1974). It remained to be seen whether liberal voices and policies in the post-Franco government would persuade party leaders to put aside their hesitation.

Polls published at mid-year indicated that in free elections, 60 to 70 percent of the votes would go to Christian Democrats and two Socialist parties and only 10 percent to the Communists (*Manchester Guardian*, 19 July). Some moderate party leaders took the view that even the Communists should be legalized immediately on the ground that they would soon lose strength if exposed "to the light of day," but would continue to be disruptive if kept clandestine. Others countered that the PCE's potentialities would be "multiplied by two" if it were legalized: it would be able to function both above ground and underground. (*Wall Street Journal*, 21 November.)

The PCE made a concerted effort to dispel widespread fears, aroused by Communist conduct in Portugal, concerning the reliability of its declared democratic intentions. Denouncing the devious tactics of Portuguese Communists, PCE secretary-general Carrillo declared that his party shared with Italian Communists a belief in democracy and socialism, not as a tactical expedient but as a strategic concept. He asserted that Communist despotism in Spain was "unimaginable." (*Manchester Guardian*, 27 June; *U.S. News & World Report*, 4 August.) The party, he said, wanted to see the major means of production become the property of society as a whole, but in the context of a pluralistic party system in which Marxism-Leninism would not be the official state philosophy. Even though acknowledging that there is as yet no historical model for this arrangement—Marxist socialism with freedom— he insisted that it was not utopian. (*Der Stern*, Hamburg, 13 March; *Corriere della Sera*, Milan, 7 May; *NYT*, 29 October.) Carrillo even declared that it was "indispensable" for small business to remain in private hands (*NYT*, 23 July).

The PCE was unsuccessful in efforts to attract the major opposition parties to the "Democratic Junta," which it organized in 1974 along with some socialists, liberal monarchists and scattered individuals, and regional opposition groups (see *YICA, 1975*, p. 241). The Christian Democrats, the Spanish Socialist Workers Party—the main socialist force in Spain—and the Social Democrats appeared to be dubious about the sincerity of the Communists. In June the latter groups formed their own center-left alliance called "Democratic Convergence." (*NYT*, 13 June, 22 September, 28 October.) In September the two groups reached agreement to establish a joint platform as a common alternative to Franco, but they remained divided on the key issue of the succession. The Convergence favored giving the king a chance, while the Junta demanded an immediate provisional government independent of him. (ANSA, Buenos Aires, 12 October; *NYT*, 28 October.)

As a means of "forcing the building of democracy" without violence, the Democratic Junta staged during the year a few so-called "democratic action movements." These involved appeals to employees, professional people, and students for one-day abstentions from all activities in the private and public sectors. Housewives were urged to refuse to make purchases or to send their children to school. Public response was not sensational. Some 30 associations of housewives were dissolved by the police for three months because of their participation in the first action movement in February. In June, the PCE claimed that about a million working people responded to a similar call. (*Der Stern*, 13 March; *L'Humanité*, Paris, 12 April; *NYT*, 29 October.)

A number of publications and journalists were closed or fined during the year for reporting on activities of the Democratic Junta and other leftist groups. One journalist was ordered to stand trial for attending and reporting on a secret meeting of the Junta and for having made an apology for the group in an article published abroad. Three professional people were arrested in January on suspicion of having organized a clandestine press conference in Madrid to promote the Junta. (*Washington Post*, 23 January; *CSM*, 11 March.)

The PCE was able to continue exploiting labor restlessness in the face of economic recession and a near 20 percent rate of inflation. The illegal Communist-dominated Workers' Commissions ("CC OO") led an aroused labor force in over 2,200 strikes in the first eight months alone. This was more than in all of 1974, when a record had been set for the previous decade. (TRUD, Msocow, 22 August; *Peking Review*, 29 August.) The fining, arrest, and discharge or temporary suspension of hundreds of workers provoked even more agitation. In an effort to defuse the growing ferment, the government early in the year drastically reduced the harsh sentences imposed the previous December on ten "CC OO" leaders for illegal assembly (see *YICA, 1975*, p. 240). The authorities reaffirmed, however, that the "CC OO" were inspired by the illegal PCE (*NYT* 16 February; *CSM*, 19 February).

Early in the year, pressures began to build even within the government-controlled labor syndicates for a reform of the system. One representative, describing himself as a "man of the system" and a staunch anti-Communist, said he favored recognition of the right to strike along with more independence from government (*NYT*, 2 February). Finally, in May the government relented by legalizing strikes "as a last resort in support of economic demands." Politically motivated strikes were still proscribed (Ibid., 10 May.) Under the new conditions, Communist "CC OO" workers found it useful to participate the following month in the election of labor representation in the syndicates. The results were interpreted by a government official as a defeat for the PCE and a victory for the moderate left; actually, more than 80 percent of the "CC OO"-supported—i.e., Communist-backed—candidates reportedly won election to syndicate posts. (*AEI News Digest*, Washington, 3 July.)

There was speculation about the possibility of a leftist military putsch in Spain, following the example of Portugal. There seemed to be general agreement with Carrillo, among political observers, that such a development was "out of the question," even though the Spanish army was indeed becoming politicized to a degree that alarmed ultra-rightists. Most officers were judged to be moderates who would welcome evolution toward democracy but who would intervene to prevent seizure of power by leftist or rightist extremists. Officers were said to be largely middle class with a stake in defending Spain's rising standard of living. Moreover, they had not been demoralized, as had their Portuguese counterparts, by a long and unsuccessful colonial war, nor had their ranks swollen by conscript officers who might have been more susceptible to leftist ideology. (*Der Stern*, 13 March; *CSM*, 1 May; *NYT*, 5 July, 22 September.)

On the other hand, one officer, Major Julio Busquets, maintained that the social class of the army has been moving downward. In a sociological analysis of the professional soldier, he wrote that the military academies were mostly attracting young men from the lower middle class, with the sons of traditional officers choosing not to follow military careers. Busquets suggested that the breach between new officers' low income level and their upper-class cultural pretensions might lead to Nasserism or the development of a leftist army on the Peruvian model. (*Manchester Guardian*, 29 March.)

Junior officers were said to be engaged increasingly in secret political discussions within a so-called "Democratic Military Union" (Unión Democrafica Militar; UDM). Its membership was variously estimated at 600 to 900; there were allegedly thousands of sympathizers as well. It was claimed that some 2,000 officers were among 160,000 Spaniards who signed a petition early in the year seeking amnesty for political prisoners. (*CSM*, 21 February; *NYT*, 28 October.) As the year progressed, UDM members were said to have contact with every political organization in Spain, including the PCE and the Democratic Junta—which claimed some officers in its membership; however, most UDM officers were reputedly anti-Franco moderates who did not believe the army should initiate political change. Carrillo concurred with this when he said that if in Portugal the army had made the change with the support of the people, in Spain the people would do it with the backing of the army or a fraction of it. (*Visión*, New York, 15 February; *NYT*, 3 August, 28 October.)

Such political activism was condemned by old-guard top commanders of the armed forces. In February, Major Busquets and a captain were held in "preventive detention" for unspecified reasons and in the following months some 12 officers were arrested on charges of sedition. In one of his last official acts before he was felled by a heart attack, General Franco replaced four of the country's eight regional commanders and named a hard-liner to head the paramilitary Civil Guard. (*CSM*, 21 February; *U.S. News & World Report*, 3 November.)

The PCE was encouraged not only by the "growing movement for democracy" within the army but also by the anti-Franco attitude of the Catholic church, which for so long had, along with the army, supported the dictatorship. Carrillo claimed "very close to friendly relations" between the Communists and "wide circles of the Church." He said he believed it possible to be a practicing Catholic and Communist at the same time. The biggest obstacles to democratization, he asserted, were, apart from the "ultras," Premier Arias and Juan Carlos. Though acknowledging that Arias was more flexible than his predecessor had been, he pointed out that precisely because of that he was actually more dangerous. This was because his "supposed liberalization" won him a "broader base" so that he could avoid making a genuine "opening" (*apertura*). (*Der Stern*, 13 March.)

Carrillo considered Juan Carlos an obstacle because he was sworn to perpetuate Francoism. If monarchy had to be accepted, Carillo said, the prince's liberal father, Don Juan, would be a more suitable king. (*NYT*, 23 July.) After Franco died, the PCE at first dropped its outright opposition to Juan Carlos as successor. It merely called for a provisional government of all opposition forces and a "realistic program capable of achieving the broadest national unity." (*CSM*, 21 November.)

By the end of the second week of December, Carrillo announced that since this prescription had not been followed, the government would encounter hostility and resistance and could not last more than a few months. Communists and extremist groups had not been mollified by a partial amnesty immediately extended to political prisoners by Juan Carlos on becoming king. About 4,000 prisoners, including 1,000 jailed for political crimes, were released, the prison terms of others were reduced, and all death sentences previously imposed were commuted to 30 years' imprisonment. Right away, many of the released prisoners were again jailed as they defiantly denounced the amnesty as being "insufficient" and a "fraud." Left-wing opposition groups called for general strikes to fight "Franco-ism without Franco." Police denounced the "intensive campaign of agitation conducted by clandestine organizations of a Communist nature." (*CSM*, 9 December.)

Communists also professed to be unimpressed with the cabinet changes announced on 12 December. Actually, even though Juan Carlos did include some conservatives in his cabinet and was forced by the Council of the Realm to retain Arias as premier, he was able to replace the important interior, foreign affairs, and justice ministers with advocates of democratic change. The cabinet was described by observers as a reflection of the king's desire for cautious but far-reaching change in the regime he inherited.

International Views and Positions—Party Contacts. The trial and execution of Basque and FRAP terrorists in September 1975 (see below) sparked a wave of international protest, especially in Western Europe. There were demonstrations, some of them violent, in most major cities of Europe as well as in Ankara, Mexico City, and Bogotá. Ambassadors from 15 European countries were recalled from Madrid and Mexican president Luis Echeverría called for the expulsion of Spain from the United Nations. Spain's diplomatic staff was evacuated from Lisbon just before rioters sacked the Embassy there. The Vatican, even though denouncing terrorist acts, reportedly termed the killings "muderous repression." The foreign ministers of the West European Common Market even suspended negotiations aimed at liberalizing trade with Spain. (*NYT*, 2, 3, 7 October; *Intercontinental Press*, New York, 2 October.)

The Spanish government's reaction was to rally thousands of supporters in Madrid and Seville to protest the "hypocritical" European outcry and to acclaim Franco as "savior of Spain." It was charged that Spain was under attack from Marxism and Communism; General Franco spoke of a "leftist Masonic conspiracy." (*NYT*, 2, 5 October.)

Since the executions came at a time when the United States was negotiating for continued use of four military bases in Spain, Washington maintained official silence about the Franco represssion. Secretary of State Henry Kissinger was reported to have said privately that whatever the United States might think about the government's conduct, it had to give high priority to maintaining access to Spanish bases. (*NYT*, 5 October.) When President Ford, during an earlier European tour, stopped off in Spain to discuss the bases, the Democratic Junta protested this infusion of life to a "dictatorial regime unable to survive of itself." It said this would unnecessarily jeopardize future relations between the United States and a democratic Spain. Especially criticized was the timing of the visit, which was said to "presuppose approval" of Franco's oppressive acts. (*CSM*, 30 May; "Radio Independent Spain," 3 May, 3 June.)

Carrillo claimed the prestige of the United States had been compromised in the eyes of the Spanish public, but said he was not proposing that U.S. forces withdraw from the bases. On the other hand, he did think they should leave Spain "one day, just as the Soviets should leave Czechoslovakia." (*Time*, 28 July.) The PCE Central Committee announced that it was "high time" for Spain to draw up a policy of neutrality, "which is the best guarantee of its defense and security." ("Radio Independent Spain," 3 May).

Within the U.S. government, there was said to be disagreement over the future of the bases in the post-Franco era. Some Pentagon analysts were reportedly alarmed about a possible strengthening of left-wing pressures in the Spanish military for removal of the U.S. presence and for a neutralist foreign policy. State Department sources, on the other hand, apparently felt the army would remain essentially apolitical. (*CSM*, 31 October.)

The PCE's rapprochement with the Communist Party of the Soviet Union (CPSU) in October

1974 (see *YICA, 1975*, p. 243) did not restrain the Spanish Communists from continuing their criticism of the CPSU or the parties loyal to it in other countries. In fact, Carrillo boasted about the "great concessions" the CPSU had made, which were "successes" in his struggle for the independence of his party. He still insisted on the need to "institutionalize internal criticism," denying at the same time that this should be interpreted as "anti-Sovietism." (*Radio Free Europe Research*, 13 March.)

The main thrust of Carrillo's attacks during 1975 was directed at the alleged lack of evolution in the political system of socialist countries—that is, the Soviet Union and its satellite states—and, especially, the uncompromising Stalinist behavior of old-line Communists in their struggle for power in Portugal. Calling for pluralist democracy in socialist countries, he insisted that Spaniards would not accept a "people's democracy" on the East European model. He declared that if capitalism could afford democratic freedoms, socialism ("which we hold to be the better system") should certainly be able to do so. (Ibid., 13 March, 14 May; *Rinascita*, Rome, 2 May; *Frankfurter Allgemeine*, 19 November.)

The PCE continued to stress its friendly relations with the Romanian Communist Party, the League of Communists of Yugoslavia, and the Italian Communist Party (PCI), to whom Carrillo paid "friendship" visits during the year. During one stay in Italy, he and PCI secretary-general Enrico Berlinguer expressed their disapproval of the Portuguese model of Communist conduct and cited the PCI's flexible approach as more appropriate for Spain and other Western nations (*Rinascita*, 2 May; *L'Unità*, Rome, 12 July). Carrillo pointedly snubbed Portuguese Communist Party (PCP) leaders when he attended a Portuguese Socialist Party convention in Lisbon at the end of 1974. He criticized PCP secretary-general Alvaro Cunhal as a "narrow-minded man who doesn't see reality" and praised Socialist Mário Soares as softer, less combative, and wiser. (*Expresso*, Lisbon, 14 December 1974; "Radio Independent Spain," 9 January 1975; *Vorwaerts*, Bonn, 17 April; *NYT*, 23 July.)

Carrillo also cited as an example to be avoided the Chilean experience that led to the overthrow of the Socialist regime of Salvador Allende. In a new book, *Demain l'Espagne* (Tomorrow Spain), he offered three lessons to be learned; the working class must remain allied to the middle sectors of society; power must be relinquished if civil war is threatened and majority support is lacking; and if there is a will to hold on to power, the necessary precautions must be taken to fight (*Manchester Guardian*, 29 March).

PCE Media. Published by the PCE abroad, with clandestine distribution within Spain, are a quarterly theoretic journal, *Nuestra Bandera*, and the official organ, *Mundo Obrero*. In March 1975, the latter was transformed from a semi-monthly to a weekly. It also announced plans to become a daily as soon as the political situation in Spain made this possible, and it appealed for contributions from Spanish emigrants to a "fighting fund" to finance acquisition of the necessary equipment. (*Morning Star*, London, 22 January, 3 March.)

Short-wave broadcasts with party messages reach Spain over "Radio Independent Spain" from facilities in Bucharest. Prior to 1973, the radio had functioned in Prague, but that unit was closed after the PCE insisted on independence from Soviet party positions. (*CSM*, 15 May.)

* * *

Activities of Basque and Rival Communist Organizations. During 1975 two terrorist groups kept Spain in turmoil, especially in northern Basque areas. These militants included the Basque guerrillas called ETA-V and the Maoist movement called FRAP. Both extremist organizations set as their prime targets the Franco security forces, described by Basques as the "army of occupation." They killed more than 20 policemen and carried out bombings, bank robberies, kidnapings, and other sabotage. (*CSM*, 25 April, 9 October.)

The police and military presence in two Basque provinces was intensified, and hundreds of terrorist suspects or sympathizers were arrested. In April a three-month "State of Exception"—in effect, martial law—was declared for the two provinces in an effort to curb the wave of violence. (*NYT*, 26 April; *CSM*, 24 June.) On 28 August a new law mandated the death sentence for any convicted killer of a policeman and also called for fines or imprisonment of those expressing sympathy for accused or convicted terrorists or criticizing any government action against them. Organizations of Communists, anarchists, and separatists were singled out as subject to prosecution for taking part in violent political activities. (*NYT*, 28 August.) Incidentally, in an apparent effort to discredit the regular PCE, government officials and some newspapers regularly confused it with Marxist terrorist groups (ibid., 22 September).

In the three weeks following decree of the anti-terrorist law, 11 accused ETA and FRAP terrorists received death sentences. The PCE Executive Committee condemned the "flagrant violation of the most basic human rights," saying that confessions of the accused had been elicited from them by brutal torture. Amnesty International also charged that Basque prisoners were tortured "on a massive scale." ("Radio Independent Spain," 28 August; *NYT*, 1 October.) During the trial of five FRAP terrorists, the defense lawyers were expelled for raising legal objections. They were replaced by five court-appointed army officers untrained in law who were given five hours to prepare the defense. A guilty verdict followed a three-hour trial. (*Wall Street Journal*, 2 October.) Massive demonstrations of protest over the sentences erupted in the Basque region and clemency was urged from Catholic church pulpits as well as by the Pope himself. Franco responded by sparing the lives of all but five, who were executed in September. (*NYT*, 27 September, 12 October.)

The governor of one Basque province pled in June for the cooperation of residents to root out the terrorism, but most Basques, even though reportedly not sympathetic with the violence, refused to be informers. The governor saw in the ETA activities an attempt to introduce communism "disguised in its multiple facets." (ANSA, 26 June.)

Police and right-wing groups reportedly were in despair not only because of the protection given guerrillas by Basques within Spain but especially by the protection afforded by the French border. Commandos were said to use the French Basque provinces as a refuge and stronghold from which to launch their attacks into Spain. Outraged rightist extremists began to launch their own terrorist campaigns in both Spanish and French Basque country, bombing property and killing anyone suspected of being an ETA sympathizer or protector. Two organizations were reportedly active—the "Guerrillas of Christ the King," who were believed to consist essentially of Spanish policemen or at least to have their tacit support, and ATE (Anti-ETA Terrorists), a group professing to be "sick and tired of seeing so many crimes go unpunished." (*NYT*, 25 May, 13 June; *L'Espresso*, Rome, 6 July; IPS, Buenos Aires, 23 July; ANSA, 9 August.) In September, after a security agent was killed in Barcelona, hundreds of right-wing demonstrators—including policemen in uniform—paraded to demand tougher action against leftist urban guerrillas. (*NYT*, 17 September).

Less sensational were the activities of the dissident Basque and Trotskyite separatist group, the non-violent Revolutionary Communist League—ETA-VI. Arrests of several members were reported in April and October on charges of engaging in subversive propaganda. (Madrid domestic radio, 11 April, ANSA, 14 October.)

Elbert Covell College   H. Leslie Robinson
University of the Pacific

Sweden

The Swedish Communist Party (Sveriges Kommunistiska Parti; SKP) grew from a left-wing dissident faction of the Social Democrats. It has been legal since its establishment in 1921. Most of its support comes from organized workers in the urban industrial areas of Stockholm, Gävleborg, and Göteborg, and from Sweden's northernmost province of Norrbotten.

The party name was changed in 1967 to Left Party—Communists (Vänsterpartiet Kommunisterna; VPK) in an effort to broaden appeal to young Swedes of the New Left. The change was in vain. Young leftists have either gravitated toward Maoist splinter groups or found satisfaction in Sweden's politically savvy Social Democratic Party (Sodialdemokratiska Arbetarparti; SDP). In early 1973, the Communist League, Marxist-Leninist (Kommunistiska Förbundet Marxist-Leninisterna; KFML) compounded the insult of waning VPK allure by appropriating the SKP name for its own party.

Despite Maoist and SDP incursions into its natural consituency, the VPK has managed to achieve some significant political leverage. Though the party claims an estimated membership of only 17,000 out of the total Swedish population of about 8 million, it has often parlayed its parliamentary representation into a pivotal role. During 1970-73, Prime Minister Olof Palme, with only 163 seats to the non-socialist opposition's 170 in the 350-seat Riksdag (parliament), sometimes had to use the VPK's 17 votes for crucial legislation or the survival of his government.

The VPK edged up to 19 seats in the latest parliamentary elections, 16 September 1973. Since the SDP dropped back to 156 places, there was a 175-175 split in the unicameral Riksdag between the socialist left and the three so-called bourgeois parties. Even so, the VPK's hopes for advantage from this situation have not materialized. First, though the party did improve its representation in the Stockholm area, it lost some of its traditional support in the northern "forest" districts. Second, in practice during 1975, Palme was able to gain increased non-socialist support for key votes and thus increase his own political latitude vis-à-vis the VPK—thus enhancing his chances of staying in power until the next scheduled parliamentary election in September 1976. Opinion polls taken in late 1975 suggest that the VPK—particularly its new chairman—has been slipping in popularity and may have trouble getting the four percent of the popular vote required for representation for that election.

Leadership and Organization. Lars Werner was elected new VPK chairman at the party's Twenty-fourth Congress, held on 12-16 March 1975 in Stockholm. He replaced the charismatic Carl-Henrik Hermansson, who had led the communists since 1964.

The choice of Werner reflected the continued split within the VPK. Despite pleas from Hermansson, there was strong opposition to his chosen candidate, Werner. Almost a third of the 239 assembled delegates backed other contenders. Werner, age 39, is a former mason who won his party spurs in the construction workers' union.

Theoretically, all important questions of policy and organization are decided at the triennial party congress. That meeting elects the 35-member Central Committee, known since 1964 as the Party Board. The Board supervises party activities and selects the Executive Committee (Politburo), which controls daily operations. Eivor Marklund is VPK vice-chairman, and the members of the Executive Committee are Lars Werner, C. H. Hermannsson, Eivor Marklund, Urban Karlsson, Tore Forsberg, Bror Engstrom, and Jörn Svensson. Elections to the party leadership reflected a definite move toward younger members, an attempt to weed out Stalinist dissidents, and an effort to increase the number of women represented.

There are 28 party districts, which correspond to the nation's 28 electoral regions. Below these are the workers' communes, which are the main local units responsible for the coordination of fund raising, propaganda, and training.

Despite reliance on support from "the workers," the VPK enjoys control neither over a national trade union nor in Sweden's powerful Federation of Trade Unions (LO). The VPK controls about 80 of the nation's 9,000 union locals, primarily in the construction, forestry, and mining industries.

Kommunistisk Ungdom (KU) is the youth wing of the party.

Party Internal Affairs. Ideological and tactical scuffles between the VPK and SKP and within the VPK itself continued in 1975. The controversy inside the VPK—between the party leadership and its Stalinist competitors in northern Sweden—took a turn for the worse in late October. The party's Executive Committee dismissed a northern district chairman, and the chairman and three others were banned from the Executive Committee. VPK party secretary Tore Forsberg said that the offenders had "pursued activities in violation of the party program and decisions by the party congress" (Stockholm Domestic Service, 23 October).

The long-time dispute had flared up previously at the March meeting of the party congress. The Stalinists had demanded that the VPK follow more orthodox lines and attacked the Hermansson leadership for its past criticism of the Soviet invasion of Czechoslovakia and the expulsion of Solzhenitsyn from the USSR. The Stalinists—clustered around former party chairman Hilding Hagberg—met defeat at the March meeting but continued their attacks in their daily newspaper, *Norrskensflamman*. Hagberg and company had never trusted the "revolutionary credentials" of Hermansson—in part because of his bourgeois background and marriage to one of Sweden's wealthy heiresses, and in part because of his common-front tactics for the VPK. Despite Hermansson's success in convincing many Swedes that the VPK was politically housebroken and able to behave itself responsibly in a democratic system, the Stalinists remained suspicious and continued to attack VPK maneuvering for political co-existence with the Social Democrats.

Norrskensflamman opened the year with blasts against Hermansson's policies. Writers there contended that attitudes toward the USSR constituted "the watershed between socialism and capitalism," that there should be no contacts with the Chinese leadership until after it changed its perspectives, and that VPK views on energy did not accord with the interests of northern Sweden (15, 24, 31 January). Hermansson opened the VPK congress in March with a strong attack against opposition groups, claiming that the party was not a "discussion club" and that conscious discipline was needed to overcome factionalism (Swedish Domestic Service, 12 March). The question of financial support for *Norrskensflamman*, as well as other points of intra-party divergence, surfaced at the congress (*Norrskensflamman*, 12-17 March; *Ny Dag*, 19-20 March).

As if this kind of schism were not enough, there were other outbreaks of factionalism on Sweden's Far Left. The KFML(r)—Kommunistiska Förbundet Marxist-Leninisterna—Revolutionärerna—split again over the question of student leftism and many of its Stockholm members joined the SKP. Its youth branch formed a separate study group because of alleged differences over international policies.

Domestic Activities and Attitudes. Old issues—better benefits for workers—and new—formulation of a national energy policy—provided a mix for the VPK domestic focus in 1975.

Hermansson's criticism of the Palme government's budget set the tone for much of the year. He charged that the Social Democrats had "completely abandoned the demand for enhanced equality" and expressed regret that the Social Democrats had digressed from coalition with the communists to collaboration with the non-socialist parties. He asserted, further, that "today's problems are connected with the long-term changes in Swedish capitalism and the increased differences there," and that such developments were "undermining understanding between labor and capital upon which the Social Democrats build their activity." (*Dagens Nyheter*, Stockholm, 20 January.)

VPK spokesman Tore Forsberg embellished on such themes in his evaluation of May Day celebrations. He admitted that the "Communist Party and its influence on the job sites and in the unions are not yet strong enough" to break the Social Democratic and reformist grip on the trade union movement. It was "high time to take the ideological offensive" and work for a "socialist renewal of the Swedish labor movement in combination with the task of creating a united front of communists, Social Democrats, and unaffiliated voters" against monopoly capital. (*Ny Dag*, 30 May-3 June.)

The communists' new chief underscored many of these same themes at a big VPK meeting in Södertalje in August and so set the stage for the party's 1976 domestic election platform. Werner stressed that "the working-class struggle is directed against the capitalist system and toward planned economy and socialism" and that the following specific political goals should be achieved in 1975-76: a shorter working day, more day-care space, a price halt to all vital necessities, greater employee power in business, and nationalization of private commercial banks, insurance, energy, the drug industry, and arms production (*Norrskensflamman*, 30 August).

Debate over energy policy consumed much attention. VPK leaders Werner and Svensson opposed the government view that more energy meant more jobs and urged Palme to put the question of nuclear power to a popular referendum (*Dagens Hyheter*, 28 May). A public opinion poll had reportedly indicated that most VPK members opposed the immediate expansion of nuclear power (*Ny Dag*, 26-27 February). There was not, however, unamimity within communist ranks. The Stalinist factions to the north criticized the VPK position on the grounds that "Norrbotten inhabitants believe more in increased future consumption of energy than their comrades in Stockholm and Göteborg do." The northern "country folks" saw no way to achieve increased industrialization and upgraded agriculture with reduced energy consumption. (*Norrskensflamman*, 26 February.)

Finally, both VPK and SKP joined forces to protest alleged government encroachment on individual rights. The catalyst for concern was the complaint of telephone taps by the Swedish Security Policy (SAPO) on party members. VPK representatives in the Riksadag charged that surveillance was "part of the growing level of political reaction." (*Ny Dag*, 2-10 July; *Gnistan*, 25 July; *Dagens Nyheter*, 27 June.)

International Views and Positions. Distinctions continued to blur between domestic and international concerns of the VPK and the positions on foreign policy adopted by the communists and Social Democrats. Developments in Iberia, the military junta in Chile, the outcome of the Conference on Security and Cooperation in Europe (CSCE), and, to a lesser extent, the international oil problem were the dominant issues for 1975.

The broadest outline of VPK international interest—and the one which will probably govern the party's approach to the 1976 parliamentary campaign—emerged in a presentation by Chairman Werner. He rejoiced that the banner of the National Liberation Front waved over Ho Chi Minh's city (Saigon) as a symbol of the victory over U.S. imperialism and the restored freedom of the Vietnamese people. He affirmed solidarity with the Chilean people," who are now being terrorized by a muderous fascist government—installed by U.S. imperialism," and asserted that the Swedish Tennis League should oppose the Davis Cup match with Chile. He urged that "all forces for peace" follow up on the CSCE's "normalization and recognition of the present boundaries in Europe" with "arms limitations as a step toward disarmament by both NATO and the Warsaw Pact countries." (*Norrskensflamman*, 29 August.)

Solidarity with Portuguese revolutionaries was a key point in that presentation and others by VPK leaders. Werner protested against fascists and reactionary forces for their "witch hunt against Portuguese communists" and warned that "Portugal must not become another Chile" (ibid.). He claimed that the Swedish press and media were using Oriana Fallaci's interview of Portuguese communist leader Alvaro Cunhal to attack the VPK unfairly for its attitude toward democracy. He asserted that Cunhal's views had been distorted and that "we condemn the terror against the Portuguese communists just as we condemn other violations of democratic liberties and rights."

Swedish policy toward Spain came in for comparable fire. Werner demanded that "Sweden should put all relations with Spain on ice while Franco's murderous regime exists" and "adapt an international boycott of Spain" (*Dagens Nyheter*, 3 October).

Sensitivity to onslaughts against Sweden's traditional neutrality prompted the VPK to question the nation's ties to the International Energy Agency. Such affiliation to the "oil club" suggested undue outside influence on domestic policy and, together with Sweden's ties to the European Community, indicated that the Riksdag was "proceeding with a reinterpretation of the concept of neutrality" (*Ny Dag*, 21-25 February).

On less publicized matters of international policy, the VPK protested the use of Swedish workers' money for anti-communist activity in Finland (a reference to the transfer of Swedish funds before the Finnish metalworkers' meeting in the autumn of 1975) and urged support for the oppressed peoples of southern Africa and efforts to bring about a peaceful Mideast settlement "with regard for the legitimate rights of the Arab people of Palestine" (TASS, 15 March). On 21 August, left-wing groups arranged a demonstration against the USSR on the seventh anniversary of the Soviet occupation of Czechoslovakia. And finally, the KU published an "International Resolution" which urged carrying on discussions according to the principles of mutual respect for different views and so taking no position for or against the communist parties of the USSR or China.

International Party Contacts. Like most of the Nordic communist parties, the VPK sustained an active pace of fraternal talks and visits in 1975.

Many foreign delegations attended the Twenty-fourth Congress of the VPK in March. Among the most notable attendees were representatives from the Central Committees of the East German and Soviet parties.

Interviews in Stockholm with visiting Spanish Communist Party Politburo member Manuel Azcarate helped dramatize VPK concern with political conditions in Spain. Azcarate stressed recourse to a national strike as the instrument to overthrow the Franco government (*Ny Dag*, 4-8 April).

Lars Werner headed a VPK delegation in late May to Poland, where party chief Edward Gierek received the Swedish group for talks focused on the need to maintain an anti-imperialist front in the Third World and to continue preparations for a conference of communist and workers' parties in Europe.

There were ups and downs in VPK dealings with its Asian counterparts. The Swedes hailed the victory of the Vietnamese people over U.S. imperialism (ibid., 16-20 May) but were surprised to have their visa requests denied by the Chinese Communist Party (*Norrskensflamman*, 5 June). The refusal to let the VPK representative join a study delegation from the Swedish parliament prompted renewed acrimony within the VPK (ibid., 15 May). On the occasion of the 26th anniversary of the founding of the People's Republic if China, the Chinese pointedly sent National Day greetings to Roland Pettersson of the SKP and not to the VPK.

The CSCE and the planned conference of European communist and workers' parties figures most prominently in talks between VPK chairman Werner and first secretary János Kádár, of the Hungarian ruling party, in Budapest in July. Karl Hallgren led a VPK delegation to Bucharest in early August.

Publications. The VPK's central organ. *Ny Dag* ("New Day"), is published twice weekly in Stockholm. It appears under the name *Arbetar-Tidningen* ("Worker News") in western Sweden. The party's only daily is *Norrskensflamman* ("Blaze of Northern Lights"), published in Luleå. Its theoretical quarterly is *Socialistisk Debatt*. The weekly voice of the SKP is *Gnistan* ("Spark").

Switzerland

The Swiss Labor Party—Partei der Arbeit (PdA), Parti du Travail (PdT), Partito del Lavoro (PdL), here referred to as PdA—is the oldest and main Moscow-oriented communist party in Switzerland. It was founded as the Swiss Communist Party on 5-6 March 1921, banned by emergency decree (wartime legislation) on 27 November 1940, and re-formed under its present name on 14 October 1944.

Three other communist organization of later origin have some prominence. The Swiss Popular Party (Parti populaire suisse; PPS) was founded as dissident, pro-Chinese party in 1963 under the name of Communist Party, Switzerland. Its present name was taken in 1967. The Marxist Revolutionary League—Ligue marxiste révolutionnaire (LMR), Marxistische Revolutionäre Liga (MRL), here referred to as LMR—was founded in 1969 by some 100 young intellectuals in Geneva and Lausanne who had been excluded from the PdA. It advocates violent overthrow of the system and is a member of the Trotskyite Fourth International. The Progressive Organizations, Switzerland (Progressive Organisationen, Schweiz; POCH—CH being the car number-plate letters for Switzerland) was founded in 1972 by a congress of local and cantonal progressive groups; the oldest group, POB (Progressive Organisation, Basel), dates back to a congress of extraparliamentary leftist opponents in 1968. It comprises young people, some below voting age, dissatisfied with the over-age, rigid PdA leadership. While disagreeing with the PdA on tactics and many points of domestic policy, it follows the pro-Soviet line of the PdA in the foreign field.

The PdA lost one of its five seats (out of 200) in the National Council in the 1975 parliamentary elections of 25-26 October 1975. It claims to have five seats still, because of voting support of one maverick (see below). The party has no seat in the senate (out of 44). It is not, and has never been, represented in the seven-member Executive Cabinet (Federal Council), which continues its traditional composition of two Liberal-Democrats, two Catholics, two Socialists, and one Popular Party (former Artisans' and Farmers' Party) member. It has two National Councillors (unchanged) in the canton of Vaud (capital: Lausanne) and two (formerly three) in Geneva, where it combined forces with the

Socialists, who went from two seats to three, confirming the generally unfavorable experience communists have had recently with "Popular Front" tactics in Western Europe. The PdA has 53 representatives in the legislatures of 6 cantons and one in the executive of the canton of Geneva. According to its own estimates, it polled around 2.5 percent of the national vote, or about 0.2 percent less than in 1971.

The PdA is losing strength in its traditional centers—Geneva, Lausanne, Basel, and Zurich—to radical New Left groups, as its leaders admit readily. Also, according to its own analysis, it has failed to gain back elements lost during recent years of prosperity to the emerging anti-foreign (racist) groups of the extreme right. But it is gaining members as it spreads to formerly conservative cantons, and has a total of 5,000 to 7,000.

Among the other parties noted, the PPS is only intermittently active and no membership estimates are available. The LMR ran candidates in 11 cantons, with the avowed aim of disrupting and ridiculing the electoral process, and failed everywhere, but took votes away from the PdA. Observers call the LMR the most disciplined and militant group of the Left. It has a hard core of about 800 members, all trained agitators with a flair for showmanship. The POCH had candidates in 9 cantons and elected one in the Italian-speaking canton of Ticino. This case illustrates the futility of trying too hard to codify New Left groups. The new National Councillor represents the Autonomous Socialist Party (Partito Socialista Autonomo; PSA) that exists in the Ticino only, after a local revolt of young Socialists against a sclerotic party machine there. The PSA resembles Germany's Jusos (Young Socialists) more than anything else, although it has no links to JUSO groups in the rest of Switzerland. It joins forces with some POCH groups occasionally, and during the elections it received POCH support. The newly elected PSA candidate, however, pledged himself to vote with the PdA fraction of four in national matters (hence the PdA claims of still having five National Councillors). POCH strength is difficult to gauge; there are no regular members in the strict sense, and many of its followers appear as cadres of other, more or less permanent groups. The hard-core followers of POCH, nationwide, are estimated at 2,000 to 4,000. The population of Switzerland is about 6,524,000.

Numerous other New Left groups are promoting marginal protests and disruptions. One sampling would be: the Women's New Left, Autonomous Women's Group—Bern, Women's Liberation Movement of Switzerland, Movement of Fighting Women (the latter immediately famous for bitter infighting that led to dissident Fighting Women's groups in four cities), Progressive Women, Women for Self-Aid, Homosexual Women's Group—Zurich. These and others show a handful of leaders and have marginal followers that change from event to event. There are "anti-congress" groups that disrupt gatherings they dislike. Young Socialists (Junge Sozialisten; JUSO) are addressing protests to the Socialist Party, which regularly declares that the protests are unacceptable and the JUSO is out of order as it is "not a recognized section of the Socialist Party." In the midst of this constant and growing hum of disruptive activities the parties of the Left—Socialists as well as the PdA—have trouble controlling the extreme left fringe. Leftist groups also multiply initiatives at the communal, cantonal, and federal level to strain the system and keep a steady stream of "legal" protest against "arbitrary government" rolling.

The PdA is definitely on the defensive; the main reproach of dissidents is that in spite of self-criticism at its 10th Party Congress last year (see *YICA, 1975*, p. 250) and the inclusion of 20 new young members in its 50-man Central Committee, key positions have remained in the hands of old-timers. The result has been a dispersion of radical Young Left elements into all possible movements, including the left wing of the Socialist Party. Politically, the main result has been a radicalization of that party whose left wing has become more influential.

The Socialists (2nd International) were by far the most aggressive party of the Left in Switzerland in 1975, with elements of their radical wing teaming up openly with communist efforts in social, military, and foreign affairs. With their two seats in the seven-member Executive and their position as strongest party of the governing coalition, they are the conduit for throwing the noise on the Left into political gear within the system. Their trend is that of most European Socialists: strengthening their membership by recruiting the disciplined "apparatchnik" soldier of the communists who is disgusted by the stand-patting of national communist leaders and the disruptive, "socially counter-productive" activities of the New Left. To keep their strengthened left wing satisfied, the Socialists are adopting a shriller tone and a wider range of anti-capitalist, anti-defense and generally anti-private-enterprise themes—while saying privately to coalition partners on the right that their way is the lesser of two evils.

PdA Leadership and Organization. The PdA's leadership was determined at the party's Tenth Congress, in Basel, 1-3 June 1974. Of the 50 members of the Central Committee, 32 are French-speaking, 15 German-speaking, and 3 Italian-speaking. Diffuse membership in formerly rather conservative cantons has been growing, essentially in the German-speaking part of the country, and there are 4.5 million German-speaking Swiss against barely 1 million French-speaking. There is a Political Bureau of 14 members, and a Secretariat of 5, led by Jean Vincent (Geneva), chairman, and comprising André Muret (Lausanne), Jakob Lechleitner (Zurich), Hansjörg Hofer (Basel), and Armand Magnin (Geneva).

The PdA is a "party of cadres" and its membership of 5,000 to 7,000 does not reflect actual voting strength. Although there has been a trend to accept more regular members, the pulling power of the party has diminished. This is due to an overcareful party program formulated in 1974, when the party tried to keep the middle of the road, to act as "elder statesman" among the leftist proliferation and to play an avuncular role within the parliamentary system. In the midst of the agitation of the New Left, of the new militancy of the Socialists, and the gnawing recession of 1975, this just has not been good enough, as election results showed.

The PdA's problem shows in the composition of its auxiliary organization. The Swiss-Soviet Society (Gesellschaft Schweiz-Sowjetunion; GSS), Swiss Association for Culture and the People (Schweizerische Vereinigung Kultur und Volk; SVKuV), Union for Culture, Education, and Science (Gewerkschaft Kultur, Erziehung und Wissenschaft; GKEW), and several other similar groups organize meetings and lectures on topics like "Problems of Realism among Soviet Avant-Garde Artists," "Socialist Humanism," or "Political Posters" and launch drives for medical aid to Vietnam—aimed mostly at leftist intellectuals. The Swiss Communist Youth Union (Kommunistischer Jugendverband der Schweiz; KJVS) launched with headlines in the party paper (*Vorwärts*, 28 November 1974), has been rather tame so far. Its delegates have appeared on international forums and national panels for the participation of students in determining their curriculum, and in campaigns for "education, no bombs" and to "free armaments outlays in capitalist countries for education," but have said that "the pressure of working and studying youths in Switzerland has not yet reached the intensity it has in other countries" (ibid., 13 February 1975). The GKEW has made a name for itself as a militant force of New Left teachers, but with this and few other exceptions the real impact on the masses and in the media has been achieved by New Left groups that were, on the whole, either roundly criticized by the PdA or supported rather late and lamely.

Planned PdA activities were dominated by the parliamentary elections, which the party leaders approached with seeming bravado but, as PdA sources revealed, with the fatalistic conclusion that they were going to lose strength. The outcome—only one loss, more or less recouped by an arrangement with the maverick Ticino PSA man—was a pleasant surprise, but the PdA still does not seem to know exactly where it is heading. In this respect, the PdA still clings to its strict pro-Soviet line; POCH has been following suit so far. The LMR and other groups, who keep taunting the PdA, tend to favor the Chinese or at least to play both ends against the middle.

Domestic Affairs. The domestic scene in Switzerland was dominated in 1975 by one long-range aspect—the recession—and by four events: The second Jura Plebiscite on 16 March; the occupation of a nuclear power plant site near Basel, in April, that lasted until summer; the arrest of a gang that had systematically burglarized army ammunition dumps, in March; and the national elections (see below) in October.

Switzerland's special position during prosperity, with close to a million foreigners working in the country, took most of the sting out of unemployment, which was "exported" by the voluntary departure of tens of thousands of foreign workers—also weakening the position of the ultra-right anti-foreign groups that had launched two initiatives against foreign workers in 1970 and 1974 (see *YICA, 1975*, p. 252). In autumn 1975, official statistics reported just above 10,000 unemployed; but government economists officially pointed out that with the diminishing foreign work force, reduced working hours in many industries, and the dismissal of wives, teen-agers, and other "second earners" that never registered as unemployed, the country, by late autumn, had lost the equivalent of close to 200,000 jobs. This would put Switzerland squarely into the same league with other Western European countries, but the feeble impact of what remained as "unexported" unemployment on the Swiss market thwarted plans—especially of the LMR—to exploit the economic and social situation for violent action.

The second Jura Plebiscite was to determine the boundary between French-speaking districts that had decided, last year, to secede from the mainly German-speaking canton of Bern, and other, equally French-speaking districts that had decided to stay. There was some violence and much bitterness, but although tactics on both sides were inspired by leftist confrontation techniques—and the LMR especially tried to inject ideological elements into the struggle—the Left as such had strictly no say in the matter. It was a question of Catholics against Protestants, the Catholics having been added to the canton without their consent after the French Revolution, while the Protestants had been willing Bernese subjects long before. Language came second, and social ideology was practically forgotten.

The occupation of the nuclear power plant site at Kaiseraugst near Basel followed similar maneuvers against other planned sites in neighboring countries. It developed into a lengthy confrontation because Federal authorities awoke too late to the need for real grass-roots information. The Non-Violent Action Kaiseraugst (Gewaltfreie Aktion Kaiseraugst; GAK) consisted mainly of concerned moderates, although the impetus and the planning came from New Left groups. As Federal authorities finally agreed to a dialogue, early in summer, the front cracked between GAK and the more militant Non-Violent Action Against the Nuclear Power Plant Kaiseraugst (Gewaltfreie Aktion gegen das Atomkraftwerk Kaiseraugst; GAGAK). As of now, Federal authorities are still engaged in an intermittent mediation, henpecked between GAK and GAGAK. For all its poultry-yard acronyms and noises, Kaiseraugst proved that basic confidence still exists between a majority of citizens and authorities, as soon as the latter climb down from their mountain of laws and regulations, leaving extremists an insignificant minority.

A group of anarchists, two of them Swiss, three of foreign origin, was arrested in March. They had stolen ammunition, grenades, weapons, and explosives from Swiss army dumps. Some of the materiel was recovered, but essentially, false identity documents, systematic plans for further burglaries, and proof of international connections with groups of the Baader-Meinhof type abroad were found. Two factors were duly noted: first, that the Swiss militia system with its decentralized mobilization facilities will have to be much more thoroughly guarded, and second, that extremely dangerous groups of that type still operate in Switzerland with very little support in their environment and tend to be isolated branches of international movements.

The National Elections. Parliamentary elections, for the National Council (200 representatives) and The Council of States (44 senators), were held on 25-26 October. Turnout was light, 52.4

percent, confirming an abstentionist trend that dates back two decades, which the women's vote, introduced in the meantime, has not altered.

The Socialists made the only "substantial" gain (Swiss style) of 9 seats in the National Council, while the Senate remained practically unchanged. However, the center of the four-party coalition of Liberal-Democrats, Catholics, Socialists, and Popular Party has shifted to the left much more than figures and labels indicate. The Catholics have a trade union wing that is increasingly militant in response to general militancy on the Left, and some smaller parties gravitating around the coalition have adopted platforms calling for state intervention, increased social benefits, and a general "anti-rich" policy.

The coalition now holds 169 instead of 162 seats: 55 Socialists (+9), 46 Catholics (+2), 47 Liberal-Democrats (−2), 21 Popular Party members (−2). The brunt of the loss was carried by small parties on the extreme right and left. As noted before, the PdA lost officially 1, dropping to 4 (but says it recouped thanks to the autonomous socialist). The two anti-foreign rightist parties dropped from 11 to 6.

While the PdA was rather silent, the Socialists were vocal, demanding a change of the basic Cabinet structure that would have introduced a two-bloc confrontation instead of the traditional "consensus-and-coalition" formula. This would have changed the whole mechanism of parliamentary committee work where, for decades, the procedure has been one of whittling down differences by compromise to obtain a consensus; the Socialists' proposal would have introduced an open fight between a majority and a minority that would have had to re-form with every new major subject. The Socialists dropped the idea after realizing that the change in numbers was insufficient for their demands; but issues will be fought over harder during the next four years.

There were a record 170 electoral lists and 1,960 candidates for the 200 National Council seats. Only two parties, the Liberal-Democrats and the Socialists, contested in all cantons. Three others had electoral lists in 10 to 20 cantons—one of them the LMR with candidates in 11 cantons, none of whom came close to being elected. Combinations of lists were frequent, but with few exceptions, PdA (with candidates in 9 cantons, POCH (9 cantons), and LMR refused to merge their tickets.

The leftist trend, often named the "European trend toward socialism" in the United States, has a basis in the fear of each party that its lower- and lower-middle-class voters might defect to the Socialists if it should fail to advocate state aid and compulsory social benefits. Thus there is also the shriller militancy of originally religious groups (Catholics, Evangelical People's Party) that created their own unions to combat socialism and are now carried away by their need to keep their workers' organizations from looking second best in comparison with the Socialists. Together, Socialists and the PdA hold only 26.64 percent of the 244 National Council and Senate seats, the PdA alone only 0.2 percent. LMR and POCH, whose agitation has become a constant humming around the margins of Swiss political life aren't even represented. The trend to the left, although very real, can no longer be defined on the basis of party labels and numbers.

Publications. The PdA publishes journals in three languages: *Vorwärts*, Basel, weekly (circulation 12,000). in German; *Voix Ouvrière*, Geneva, daily (8,000), in French; and *Il Lavoratore*, Lugano, weekly (less than 1,000), in Italian.

New Left groups, some of whom run into financial difficulties regularly and reemerge under other names, publish about thirty periodicals or occasional pamphlets. The *POCH-Zeitung*, weekly, is mostly about protest actions and planned demonstrations, prints some appeals to overthrow the system, and is pro-Soviet in world affairs (circulation about 4,000). *Bresche* ("The Breach") fortnightly, Trotskyist, is the organ of the LMR. A fight has started around the *Zürcher Student*, formerly a nonpolitical magazine (9 issues per year) distributed to all Zurich students and financed by part of the tuition fees; it was taken over by a radicalized students' council who found its certified circulation of 37,000 useful. Moderate students are now fighting to get it back on a non-political basis. *Konzept*, a Marxist supplement to the *Zürcher Student*, with a mysterious financing history, is now running out of funds. *Focus*, an illustrated monthly on glossy paper, is edited by a "collective [whose members] are part of the New Left and cooperate with all groups of this movement" (masthead of *Focus*). Lately *Focus* has been published in common with another magazine, *Agitation*. The number of smaller publications and pamphlets published by the LMR and directed essentially at schools and army draftees has multiplied. (All circulation figures, PdA included, are estimates, except for the *Zürcher Student*.)

Martigny   Richard Anderegg

Turkey

The year 1975 was marked by several important political developments which markedly affected the various elements of the left in Turkey. The Communist Party of Turkey (TKP) remained outlawed, as has been the case for fifty years. Moreover, Articles 141 and 142 of the Penal Code, outlawing the propagation or advocacy of Communist ideology, remained on the books as well, although they were not as systematically invoked as had been the case during the years of military dominance (1971-73).

The most important political development of the year was the increasing polarization of Turkish politics in general, especially among young persons and university students. This polarization was exacerbated by the formation of a right-wing coalition government late in March consisting of: the right-centrist Justice Party (JP) (approximately 150 seats, whose leader, Süleyman Demirel, became prime minister; the conservative Republican Reliance Party (RRP) led by Turhan Feyzioğlu (approximately 10 seats); the religiously oriented National Salvation Party (NSP) of Necmettin Erbakan (approximately 50 seats); and the radical, proto-fascist National Movement Party (NMP) of former colonel Alparslan Türkeş (3 seats). This coalition, adopting the name "National Front" (NF), came into being primarily to solidify the opposition to the Republican People's Party (RPP), and in particular to forestall early general elections, advocated by the RPP as a means of resolving the political stalemate which resulted from the inconclusive results of the 1973 Parliamentary elections.

A second major development was the arms embargo imposed by the U.S. Congress from 5 February until early October. The embargo constituted a boon of sorts for the political left, for it lent considerable credence to the general anti-U.S. stance so consistently assumed by leftists of varying shades. But the embargo also produced an uncharacteristic unanimity among all political leaders, from Türkeş on the right to the clandestine TKP (and beyond) on the left.

The stage for the political drama of 1975 was set by several events late in 1974. On 29 November, for the first time in the history of the Turkish Republic, the Parliament cast a resounding vote of no confidence in the moderate non-partisan government of Professor Sadi Irmak, which had been formed in the wake of the collapse of the RPP-NSP coalition led by Bülent Ecevit. This unprecedented Parliamentary action provided a powerful impetus for the formation of the conservative National Front coalition which succeeded in coming to power some four months later.

On 14-15 December the RPP held a national convention which constituted a major test of Ecevit's leadership. The party, clearly identified as moderately left-of-center, had under its new leader come a long way: it had emerged from the 1973 elections with a plurality of votes as well as seats in the lower house of Parliament, the National Assembly; it had controlled the government as the dominant partner in an unwieldy and unlikely coalition for the better part of a year; this government had enacted a political amnesty releasing the bulk of the leftists who had been jailed on a variety of charges by the quasi-military regime of 1971-73; it had defied the United States by permitting the resumption of cultivation of the opium poppy; and it had presided over the military operation on the island of Cyprus, temporarily propelling Ecevit to a position of popularity unrivaled since the death of Kemal Atatürk. The party convention resulted in a victory for Ecevit's moderate leadership. His supporters achieved an overwhelming majority in the newly elected national-policy-making party Council. As 1975 opened, therefore, the question was whether the more extreme leftist factions would continue to see the RPP as worthy of their support, or would once again attempt to strike out on their own. This question assumed immediate importance because of the general expectation that the RPP's desire for early general elections would soon be realized in the wake of Parliament's refusal to accept the Irmak government.

The formation of the NF and its success in establishing a government and winning a vote of confidence in the Parliament (though by the barest majority: 222 affirmative votes, 218 negative, 2 abstentions, and 4 members not voting) frustrated the RPP's hopes of winning a sufficient number of additional seats in an early election to allow it to come to power in a more stable political setting.

Both before and after the establishment of the NF government, major incidents of violence punctuated the political atmosphere, which seemed to have assumed the character of a perpetual election campaign, particularly on the part of Ecevit and the RPP. Major incidents occurred in mid-February when the leftist Turkish Teachers' Unity and Solidarity Organization (TÖBDER) carried out nationwide demonstrations against fascism, inflation, and unemployment. On 21 June, Ecevit himself became the target of violent attacks on a crowd which had gathered in the county seat of Gerede to hear him speak. Two days later, in Diyarbakır, violence erupted prior to a speech by Alparslan Türkeş, now a deputy prime minister in the NF. There were also frequent disturbances among students at universities and other institutions of higher education. These usually took the form of violent, sometimes armed, clashes between leftist and rightist groups, and sometimes resulted in serious injuries and deaths. A number of these institutions, including units of the universities of Istanbul and Ankara, were forced to suspend operations for varying periods. In some instances, confrontations between students and university administrations also occurred; there was, for example, a major boycott of classes and examinations by students at the once-prestigious Middle East Technical University, in Ankara, resulting in the dismissal of a number of faculty members suspected of supporting the students.

The political struggle reached a climax of sorts in the partial Senate elections of 12 October in 24 of the 67 provinces. The campaign was marked by vitriolic exchanges between the leaders of the two major parties, Demirel and Ecevit, and by the fact that the parties of the NF coalition failed to present a united front. In the election, the two large parties scored important gains at the expense of the smaller parties. The RPP garnered 43.4 percent of the vote (33.3 in 1973). The JP was a close second with 40.8 percent (29.8 in 1973). The NSP could only muster 8.8 percent (11.9 in 1973), and the Democratic Party and the NMP about 3 percent each (the Democrats had 11.8 in 1973, the NMP about 3.0). Of the 54 Senate seats at stake, the JP took 27, the RPP 25, and the NSP 2. Of six lower house seats also at stake, the JP took 5 and the RPP 1. The election did not, however, affect the distribution of party strength in the National Assembly, which has the power to make and unmake cabinets. Thus the NF coalition remained precariously in the saddle, at least for the time being.

What was the reaction of Marxist groups to these developments? Before attempting to answer this question, let us briefly review the Marxist groups which existed or which came into being during 1975. The largest of these is the Turkish Socialist Workers' Party (TSWP), formed in June 1974 (see *YICA, 1975*, p. 261). By mid-1975 this party reportedly had a membership of 2,500 and functioning organizations in some 21 provinces with important concentrations of labor. The party did not participate in the October Senate elections because it failed to meet the legal requirements of having local (sub-provincial) organizations in at least 15 provinces and convening a national congress at least six months prior to the election. The party reportedly organized "Work, Bread and Freedom" rallies in six major provincial centers, although it was barred from doing so by martial law authorities in Ankara and Istanbul (martial law had initially been proclaimed in connection with the Cyprus operation in the summer of 1974; it was extended on a monthly basis until August 1975 in four provinces—Ankara, Istanbul, Adana, and Içel). In addition, several provincial officials of the TSWP in Ankara were arrested and charged with distributing communist propaganda and forming underground organizations early in May.

Two former leaders of the outlawed Turkish Labor Party (TLP) established new organizations during 1975. On 30 April, Behice Boran announced the formation of a new Turkish Labor Party. Included among its leaders were several former Members of Parliament (including Mrs. Boran) and members of the central executive committee of the old party. While some observers noted that this party might attract dissident radicals from the RPP as well as from other socialist parties, it was also rumored that the official announcement of the formation of the party had to be postponed due to difficulties in lining up adequate support (*Yankı*, 14 April). At the party's first meeting of provincial heads on 22 November, with Soviet bloc representatives present, Mrs. Boran denounced Turkey's western ties (NATO, CENTO, the Common Market, etc.) as benefiting only the bourgeoisie, and charged that U.S. pressures were driving true patriots to rebel (*Cumhuriyet*, 23 November).

The second former TLP leader to form a new party was Mehmet Ali Aybar, one of the most durable of Turkey's socialists. He announced the formation of the Socialist Party on 30 May, after also reportedly experiencing difficulty lining up support. Although he is rhetorically as militant as any, Aybar has established a reputation as a comparative moderate. He reportedly earned Moscow's enmity by supportiug the Czech leader Alexander Dubček in 1968. Above all, Aybar believes in a pragmatic approach to socialism, grounded in a realistic appraisal of the Turkish social and economic context; and he believes in Parliamentary elections as the means for the working class and its allies to come to power. (See Jacob M. Landau, *Radical Politics in Modern Turkey*, pp. 147-54 and passim. This major work in English on Turkish radicalism of both right and left was published in 1974 by E. J. Brill, Leiden, Holland.)

Finally, there were two very minor parties organized and led by men who were alleged to have once been members of the Communist Party. These were Mihri Belli's Turkish Workers' Party and the Motherland (Vatan) Party formed by associates of Hikmet Kıvılcımlı. Both of these men had been prime targets of the political repression of 1971-73. Their efforts at a political comeback in 1975 were not visibly impressive. Nevertheless, Belli was again arrested 20 November for refusing to comply with a judicial order.

The continued fragmentation of the Marxist left in Turkey is graphically illustrated by the fact that one review of the scene as of mid-April listed no fewer than 19 periodicals and newspapers, with a twentieth in the planning stage. Many leftists, however, were understandably gun-shy after the experiences of 1971-73. As one of them remarked, "There is no point to forming a party without a wide base. As long as Article 141 and 142 remain in the Turkish Penal Code, there will be no way to conduct a revolutionary struggle. The jails will be filled again if anyone dares." A wiser strategy appeared to be to support the RPP in the hope that it would win sufficient votes to come to power in its own right, repeal "fascist" laws, and thus pave the way for the formation of a genuine socialist party which could then realistically expect to gain mass support (*Yankı*, 14 April). On the other hand, Mehmet Ali Aybar noted in an interview that the RPP had already benefited substantially from the support of the left, and that it was considerably disturbed by the renewed activity of the socialists and Marxists (*Yanki*, 17 March).

Support for the RPP in preference to the above-mentioned socialist splinter groups and parties was also evident among such interest associations as the labor confederations. In fact, the national congress of the relatively militant DISK, the leftist trade union, openly called for cooperation with the RPP (though one report noted that this resolution passed by a razor thin majority). Moreover, the moderate Türk Iş began to speak in more militant tones, possibly in an effort to counteract what press reports depicted as inroads into its support within organized labor by DISK.

The pro-RPP strategy gained credence with the formation of the National Front government in the spring of 1975. The coalition turned the Justice Ministry over to the NSP. The responsibility for prosecuting alleged violations of the law was thus placed in the hands of a group whose abhorrence for leftism is second only to that of Türkeş and his NMP. Open advocacy of recourse to violence was therefore clearly most unwise. For that matter, the coalition protocol identified communism as the chief danger confronting contemporary Turkey, and JP leader and prime minister Demirel repeated this point on numerous occasions.

Nonetheless, there were frequent outbursts of violence, as has been noted above, and each produced a spate of finger-pointing. NF leaders, particularly of the JP and NMP, blamed the leftists and particularly Ecevit and the RPP, who, they claimed, encouraged and sheltered communists and other extremists. Ecevit and the RPP, on the other hand, accused the government of complicity in the incidents. In this connection, they emphasized the prominent role of Türkeş in the coalition. It was charged that the youthful armed "komando" units which he had organized and trained, and which were characterized as political thugs reminiscent of the Nazi SS, had become virtual auxiliaries of the law enforcement authorities. On the other hand, Ecevit was moved on at least one occasion to warn extremists of both right and left to desist from further provocative or violent acts. There were also reports of anarchist plans for bank robberies, kidnapings, and infiltration of the armed forces outside of the larger metropolitan centers (*Tercuman*, 27 November).

Paradoxically, the one development which might have been expected to gain support for leftist groups failed to do so. Thus the U.S. arms embargo seemed to justify fully the consistently and often stridently anti-U.S. stance of the leftists, by emphasizing the heavy dependence of Turkey on its great-power ally. The left failed to benefit from this development, however, for all parties from Türkeş's NMP on the right to the most extreme leftists responded in strongly nationalistic terms. Only such nuances as how far Turkey should go in divesting itself of the U.S. connection and asserting control over its own affairs distinguished the parties from one another. Predictably, the opposition criticized the NF government for not defending Turkish interests with sufficient vigor. Thus, although the anti-Americanism of the left became more pervasive than ever, leftist groups failed to capitalize on this development in terms of visibly increased political support.

In short, as 1975 drew to a close, the future of the Turkish left was as clouded as ever. On the one hand, deep-seated social changes were reflected in the proliferation and relatively free (though harassed) expression of socialist ideas, both Marxist and non-Marxist. On the other hand, the continuing political polarization and the outbursts of violence associated with it raised serious questions not only regarding the left, but regarding the very health of Turkish democracy.

University of Illinois
  at Chicago Circle

Frank Tachau

ASIA AND THE PACIFIC

Australia

The state of the Australian left in 1975 remains problematical. Fragmentation and diversification have, if anything, magnified, while at the same time there seems, in some of the groups, to be emerging a degree of theoretical health, which has not been noticeable before. Indicative of their fragmentation is the considerable number of leftist groups now in existence. These include the Communist Party of Australia (CPA), the oldest and largest of the left parties, and its two offspring, the CPA (Marxist-Leninist), born from the 1963 split, and the Socialist Party of Australia (SPA), which emerged from the 1971 split of the CPA. There are in addition the various "Trotskyist" (or non-mainstream) groups: the fraternal organizations of the Socialist Youth Alliance and the Socialist Workers League (SYA-SWL), the Communist League (CL) and its splinter, Melbourne Revolutionary Marxists (MRM), the Socialist Labour League (SLL), the Spartacist League (SL) and the Socialist Workers Action Group (SWAG—or International Socialists as it is now known).

A bad omen for the left is the revival of the far right, and in particular the growth of a new type of "respectable right" group. The "fall" of Portugal, Laos, Cambodia, South Vietnam and Timor, coupled with the "economic crisis," has prompted the re-emergence of left- and union-baiting organizations. The year 1975 has witnessed the revival of extraparliamentary attacks from the right, in the form of "People Against Communism" (PAC), and the growth of laissez-faire anti-governmentalism in the form of the "Workers Party" (WP). Disguised as a saviour of democracy, and anticipating a Red Australia within three years, PAC seeks the banning of the CPA. The WP are not as single-minded as PAC. They seek an individualism of the "every man for himself" variety. This results in a massive castigation of all and sundry "bludgers" and leftists (the terms are used interchangeably).

The Communist Party so far is bearing the brunt of these potential right-wing attacks single-handedly. For some reason the officially constituted party always receives the most blame for alleged left misdeeds. Perhaps there is justification for this, for the CPA is much healthier, in terms of theory if not organization, than its critics on the left will allow. Melbourne Revolutionary Marxists (MRM), for example, consider the CPA to be not only "transparently reformist" but also "mummified." ("A Call for the Revolutionary Regroupment of the Australian Left," MRM pamphlet, September 1975). Central to the MRM critique is the idea that a bankrupt CPA spends its time busily leaping upon passing bourgeois bandwagons in order to promote its ailing cause (that is, either Stalinism or reformism). To this end MRM argues that the CPA wasn't really upset about Czechoslovakia, which provided, on the contrary, a chance to display anti-CPSU crocodile's tears.

Though the CPA still conceives of itself as being a vital left force, it no longer has claims to vanguard exclusivity. Its theoretical basis in this sense is the concept of the left coalition. This concept hovers around two principles: firstly, the recognition of the necessity for a total revolution; secondly, the recognition that qualitative (not quantitative) reforms can achieve much in the meantime (or even suffice to supplant the first thread, given that revolution is not forthcoming). Jack Blake, a veteran communist, ably sums up CPA policy in 1975 thus: "The path to a massive transformation of consciousness appears to be in systematic struggle for a number of qualitative reforms which challenge and strike at the value system, and consequently the hegemony of the bourgeoisie." (*Arena*, No. 40, 1975, p. 26).

What many critics of the CPA, including those on the left, fail to consider is that the CPA is, in tendencies and historical layers, far more amorphous than rash generality will allow. It has radical and revolutionary people in its ranks; it has some members who can remember the I.W.W. and others who could only be referred to as the generation of '68. It has some members who should, perhaps, have joined SPA; it has others who are as critical of the Soviet Union as the International Socialists themselves. The CPA, more so than any other left group, is an amalgam of fractions.

Organizationally, the CPA's health is not as glowing as it is theoretically. The party was dealt a bad blow in 1975 by the demise of the New South Wales Builders' Labourers Federation (NSW BLF). Through the implementation of environmental blackbans, which came to be known as "Green Bans," the CPA leadership of the NSW BLF was able to spearhead the development of Gramscian tactics. The Builders' Labourers were able to utilize their industrial power to give themselves a say in the use of their labor-power. By 1974 the NSW BLF had tied up construction operations worth $3000 million in forty-one sites, because it considered these operations to be other than in the interests of the working class and society in general. Further, the NSW BLF was able to use its industrial power to support the struggle for Women's Studies in Philosophy at Sydney University and to support a homosexual expelled from Macquarie University.

All the while, however, the collapse of the Green Bans was thought to be inevitable because of the oncoming economic downturn, which foreshadowed a return to standard economist tactics on the union's behalf. So it was that Norm Gallagher, Federal Secretary of the BLF (and then vice-chairman of the CPA (ML)) set about intervening in the affairs of the NSW branch. He launched a takeover bid by attempting to set up a bogus branch and flush out the legitimate branch. (See *YICA 1975*, pp. 277-8). In late February of this year Gallagher's takeover bid was still thought to be failing (*Tribune*, 25 February): the bogus Federal branch had only recruited 450 ticketholders while the NSW branch maintained 8000. Gallagher was, however, able to succeed: the Master Builders' Association (MBA) locked out NSW branch members by employing only the holders of Federal tickets. In return, Gallagher broke selected Green Bans. Thus there arose the bitter cry of class collaboration.

On 1 April the NSW BLF Green Ban on Centennial Park was broken. Militants with NSW tickets were excluded from work sites. On 22 April the bogus Federal branch proceeded to lift the Victoria Street ban and expelled the twenty-six elected personnel of the NSW BLF for life. The remaining militants decided to join the new branch in order to attempt to excerise a policy of entrism—apparently a futile exercise. The *Tribune*'s editorial of 22 April conceded that because of the power of the class enemy—the MBA forces combined with the Federal BLF—its Gramscian vanguard had been defeated. The bogus branch installed by the Federal BLF had won.

The Socialist Party (SPA) and the Australian Socialist Group (ASG), though slow to act in unity with the NSW BLF, were quick to offer explanations for its defeat. (The ASG, led by Alf Watt, left the CPA at the same time as did those who were to become SPA. ASG remains a group because of its conviction that there should be one only communist party. This prevents it from joining SPA, so it awaits the "reform" of the CPA). Their principle suggestion was obvious: that the NSW BLF had not given adequate pursuit to the development of a wide union base for its policies. There was a related sentiment in the CPA's Victorian Section: that the union had brought about its own downfall by its inclination to work on a policy of "all rights, no duties." Generally it seems that no one really anticipated the defeat of the NSW BLF, but all were quick to point out its mistakes after the event.

The Gramscian inclination of the CPA has not been too badly bruised by this episode. It has been accepted as a defeat for the NSW BLF in particular rather than for counterhegemonical tactics per se. (It remains a virtual *a priori* that the CPA is never defeatist.) The NSW BLF has now apparently turned a full circle, reverting to its early 1960's condition, characterized by class collaboration and a corresponding stifling of the rank and file. Certainly the existing leadership was in some senses responsible for its own undoing. Its administrative methods were allegedly sloppy, it overestimated its own progressive role (and thus detracted from the character of potential allies). Its sole supporter was the Federated Engine Drivers' and Firemen's Association (FEDFA). But as far as the consequences of the defeat for the CPA go, the loss of the NSW BLF seems to be little more than a classic case of "one step forward, two steps back."

Thus, the CPA continued to pursue its international relations. In April a delegation consisting of Dave Davies, Joyce Stevens and Richard Walsham visited Romania. Davies went on to visit Yugoslavia, and attended the Fourteenth Congress of the Italian Communist Party. His reports on this Congress in *Tribune* led to a debate on the relevance or irrelevance of the "historic compromise" to the Australian situation in the letters columns from May to July. Brian Aarons visited Laos in April also, and in September he, Mavis Robertson and Pat Healy met representatives of the French communist Party at the l'Humanité festival. In November Robertson and Aarons met with the Spanish Communist Party in exile.

Otherwise, with the exception of the Constitutional Crisis and the ensuing emergency election campaign, 1975 has been relatively quiet for the CPA. In September Denis Freney (CPA) and Dave Holmes (SWL) debated the nature of the MFA and the PCP in Portugal. Though this kind of "dialogue" may be looked upon warmly in principle by the groups involved, it was in this instance not overproductive. On the weekend of 1-2 November the CPA celebrated its 55th birthday with a solid program of lectures, discussions and films, and a display of relics from the early years. Over three hundred attended.

The Communist Party of Australia (Marxist-Leninist) (CPA-ML) puts itself out of the competition for counterhegemony in several ways, the most monolithic of which is its theoretical crudity. Clearly a party which does not believe in the necessity of breaking bourgeois hegemony, indeed, which seems to ignore its existence, could hardly itself play a key counterhegemonical role. The Maoists still believe that the existence of the bourgeois state is perpetuated by naked class power alone. They seem to possess a faith, perhaps reminiscent of Bakunin, in the "socialist instinct" of the masses, who can be won over to the revolutionary cause not by a program of socialist education but by sloganizing and police-baiting. Further, the CPA (ML) was responsible—at least in the early seventies—for the revival of the "social fascism" theory of the "third period," which specified that the ALP was a worse enemy than those who actually professed themselves tory. This theory of socialism fascism tends to be coupled with an abstentionist program regarding parliamentary politics. Another theoretical crudity—the tendency to regard "American Imperialism" as Public Enemy Number One—allows possibilities for collaboration with the national bourgeoisie against the foreign running-dogs. This is a consequence of succumbing to a two-state (Menshevik) theory of revolution, and becoming fully absorbed in the first stage.

In the international arena, the lot of the CPA (ML) has not improved in 1975. Apparently quotes from the Maoist weekly *Vanguard* appeared in years past with "unremitting regularity" in Peking news handouts. It would appear that, with few exceptions, this is no longer the case. It has been suggested that this decline, when considered with other incidents such as the visits fo China of Herral Waten of the SPA, and Ian Turner, a member of the Socialist Left of the ALP who was in the CPA in the fifties, mark the fall from grace of Ted Hill. Perhaps this is to overemphasize the point, and to ignore Peking's continued inclination, since entering the world through détente, to be friendly to people of a far wider political variety than the local outpost of red flagwavers alone.

If Hill has not fallen from grace with Peking, though, it is not so clear that ex-vice chairman and

National secretary of the BLF Norm Gallagher has not fallen from grace within the CPA (ML). Charges against Gallagher of "collusion" with the Dillingham Corporation, as well as with the MBA, apparently outweighed the service he performed for the party in winning over the NSW branch of the BLF. The internal affairs of the CPA (ML) rarely see the light of day, but it is known that Clarrie O'Shea is now the lone vice-chairman, Gallagher having been returned to the rank and file for his misdeeds. He also lost his position as building industry representative on the executive of the Australian Council of Trade Unions (ACTU), to the SPA's Pat Clancy. Apparently Gallagher's support for wage indexation endeared him to neither Maoists nor unionists.

Organizationally, the CPA (ML) remains a mystery. Its unofficial youth offshoot, the Worker-Student Alliance, was disbanded; it is unclear as to whether the Young Communist League, formed to help the CPA (ML) "direct" the WSA, still exists or not. If student Maoism is in decline, as it would appear to be, it is not dying quietly. Particularly at Latrobe University, Maoist violence has not been on the decrease. (See for example *Australasian Spartacist*, April 1975). The most stunning example of the Maoist version of "right to tendency" was that in July, in which a Spartacist was pushed through a plateglass window at Latrobe (*Australasian Spartacist*, August). Maoists were responsible for assaulting SWL members in March, and were also involved in Zionist-Palestinian street fighting on May Day (*Australasian Spartacist*, June).

Since its growth from the CPA split of 1971, the Socialist Party has seen the CPA as playing the role of "old-style Trotskyites," left-wing deviationists. The SPA thus claims to be the legitimate heir of the CPA "in its good (read orthodox) years." Organizationally SPA is strong, for the present at least. It maintains much of the influence of the old CPA in the maritime sectors in Sydney, Newcastle and Melbourne. It has been suggested, however, that the party is chronically lacking in recruitment of youth, despite the existence of its youth group, the Young Socialist League, and its children's group, the Eureka Children's Movement. This would seem to put a question mark over the SPA's long term future; the CPA, by comparison, has increased incoming youth membership and is actually growing.

At the SPA's Second Congress (13-16 June), the party reinforced its partiality for the popular front. A central feature was the development of the cause of the opposition to monopoly capitalism. (The SPA also took part in the Adelaide "People Versus Monopoly" Conference in November). The SPA sees itself as playing the leading role in this potential "popular alliance" and in the Australian revolution also. The SPA will play the historic role of vanguard: Bill Brown, its major theoretician, suggests that, like the Russian Bolsheviks, the SPA is "such a party."

Overall, then, the SPA does not emerge as a major competitor for counterhegemony. Unlike the CPA (ML) it does recognize that it is necessary to break bourgeois hegemony in order to introduce a period of radical social change, but it seems reluctant to take action on this basis. In some senses it, too, seems to be mesmerized by a two-stage theory of revolution. This being the case, the SPA seems happy to follow a policy of trade union activism internally, and meanwhile play the role of Soviet Union publicity center.

Trotskyism seems to have considerable historical roots in Australia perhaps as far back as the late twenties. While it has in no sense of the word been successful, it has redeveloped through a typically convoluted sequence of events. In Brisbane there existed a Trotskyite Labour Action Group. It split in 1971 into Healyites—who were to become the Socialist Labour League (SLL)—and Mandelites, who came to be the Socialist Workers League (SWL). The Mandelites in the SWL eventually came to be a minority, while followers of the American Socialist Workers Party (SWP) who were in the majority, came to inherit the name and organizational machine of the SWL. The exiting followers of Mandel formed the Communist League (CL).

In Melbourne, the Tocsin group of the Victorian Labour College produced the Melbourne SLL and also the Socialist Workers Action Group (SWAG), now called the International Socialists (IS) (after the British group to which they have long loosely adhered).

Meanwhile, in Sydney in the late sixties two groups, Australian Revolutionary Marxists (Pabloites) and Bob Gould's Resistance group (based on Vietnam as an issue and the Third World bookshop as an organization) vied for the hegemony of the Sydney left. The former spawned the Revolutionary Socialist Alliance (RSA) and died (as the RSA later did itself); the latter group grew into the Socialist Youth Alliance (SYA) at the hands of Jim Percy rather than Bob Gould. From the outset the SYA was modelled on the American SWP's youth front, the Young Socialist Alliance.

Consequently the SYA came to affiliate with the SWL, establishing groups around Australia, with the SYA as youth group and the SWL as "parent" group. The SLL likewise set up groups around the country, as did the CL. Thus while most eyes were on the CPA/SPA split—in the foreground, as it were—Trotskyism was blossoming in the background. Further developments have not been of substance until this year, when MRM split from the CL in Melbourne. Apparently MRM was a majority in the CL before the split. At any rate it was the MRM which inherited the CL's post office box, while the CL, or what was left of it, has in effect lost its entire Melbourne branch. Rumors that the CL will reaffiliate with SYA-SWL are still circulating, although this would seem unlikely given their differences. All that has happened in the area of amalgamation is that the Tasmanian Socialist League has fused with the SYA at the latter's Sixth Conference in October. Apart from some rank and file members in the Tramways and BLF, the SYA-SWL is based on the most transient element of the "new mass vanguard," radical youth and students in particular.

In some senses the theoretical condition of the SYA-SWL is as shaky as its organizational basis. There is a consistent tendency in this group to assume that, with "economic crisis," there is necessarily provoked a process of ongoing mass radicalization. This is the central thrust of the Draft Political Resolution read to the Sixth National Conference of the SYA in Melbourne, 4-5 October; it is also the binding basis of the Draft Program of the SWL. It comes as no surprise, therefore, that the slogan of the SYA's Sixth Conference was "to make a revolution . . . it takes revolutionaries!" This concern with "building the revolutionary party" leaves a void as far as the masses are concerned. In a way this puts the SYA-SWL out of the competition for counterhegemony, for successful counterhegemony is dependent not only on the party formulation of socialist hegemony, but on the mass confirmation of it in practice.

The Communist League (CL) is the "Australian Sympathizing Organization of the FI (Fourth International)." The faction within the FI with which it associates itself is the International Majority Tendency (Pierre Frank, Ernest Mandel). Organizationally, the CL is centered in Sydney, where the loss of its "base" in the NSW BLF, coupled with the loss of the Melbourne branch, means that the CL is not in the best of shape. The CL shares with SYA-SWL the same emphasis on building the revolutionary party, but unlike the latter it is not attracted (or distracted) by single issues. It is this factor, however, that could be held to account for the CL's apparent lack of success and numbers. As the SYA-SWL has proven, the issues orientation is certainly good for recruitment. In contrast to SYA-SWL, the CL exudes a little less of that characteristic Trotskyite optimism displayed so frequently by the former organization.

At the national Conference of the CL in July, the Melbourne branch split from the remainder of the CL over the very basic question of transposition. The contention of those who were to become Melbourne Marxists (MRM) was that the CL's attempt to grapple with the Australian situation was irrelevant, as it was based on a carbon copy of the analysis and proposed tactics of its foreign guiding light, the IMT of the Fourth International. The split came about when the membership of one Melbourne member, who did not hold an orthodox position on the nature of the Soviet Union, was questioned. The Tendency, which was to grow into MRM, saw this as a collective attack on the Tendency and so resigned in sympathy.

MRM came to make a name of sorts for itself in September, when it published its pamphlet "A Call for the Revolutionary Regroupment of the Australian Left." MRM's call for regroupment is based on the impeccable analysis that "the foremost objective factor obstructing the growth of the revolutionary left in Australia is the present acute degree of fragmentation isolating the members of the various groups from one another" as well as from its potential allies in the working class and elsewhere. The MRM pamphlet proceeds to argue that Australian left groups tend to be derivative sects based on carbon copies of overseas groups, and that each group tends to present itself as vanguard.

It seems that MRM's call for regroupment has in fact motivated interest; MRM itself considers the response remarkable. One cannot help but feel, though, that the outcome of the call will not be the fulfillment of MRM's desires. Its analysis of left groups in the call could only succeed in winning over the few dissidents within these groups. MRM's expectation that interested people and parties come to it, rather than MRM seeking them out, is unlikely to leave MRM in a form any more infuential than any other of the string of smaller left groups.

MRM thus stakes its claim to authentic Leninism. However, it will probably not pursue a course of dialogue with the "Intervention" group, or the Adelaide group, of the CPA. Nor does MRM seem likely to pursue relations with the International Socialist (IS), the one group of all those of the left which bears some similarities to itself. MRM's call for regroupment ends with a plea for a communal left newspaper, a discussion bulletin and debates. This cynical critic doubts whether "regroupment" will come to much more than that.

In the Constitutional Crisis, MRM has been guarded in its advocacy of support for the ALP government. The title of one of its leaflets expressed this position quite aptly: "Defend the Labor Government—but not its policies." The leaflet went on, not only to document the case against Fraser, but also the "black record" of the ALP in office. Another MRM leaflet concluded that workers should "vote Labor, but place no trust in it. Rely on your *own* strength."

The Socialist Labour League (SLL) is the Australian section of the so-called International Committee of the Fourth International (Healyite). As such it vehemently opposes the renegades attached to the FI United Secretariat (that is, SYA-SWL and CL). The SLL seems to be based mainly in Sydney, organizationally and numerically speaking. The SLL's national secretary is Jim Mulgrew.

There is not a streak of pragmatism in the SLL. That its purism leads to a degree of ineffectuality is hardly surprising. In the Constitutional Crisis the SLL saw the alternative as fascist dictatorship or proletarian revolution. (The headline of "Weekly Workers News" 23 October read: "Build the Revolutionary Party! Prepare for Power"). The road to power was perceived as consisting of a general strike, snap nationalization and the expulsion of the right wing of the ALP. Presumably the SLL was to spearhead this revolution-to-be; it views all other groups as either Stalinist or reformist. As the SLL has neither a transitional program nor even a minimum program of its own, the only way in which it manages to keep itself in peoples' minds is through its reputation for sectarianism and violence. (Spartacists, for example, were victims of SLL attacks during Healy's visit to Australia in June.)

The SLL's youth group, the Young Socialists (YS) publish the monthly "Young Socialist" and were involved in organizing a Right to Work march in Sydney (25 October) and running dances to aid the "politicization of youth" around mainly economic demands. Much of its youth organization must, consequently, be more committed to Saturday nights out than to a revolutionary program.

The Spartacist League (SL) first developed in New Zealand under the leadership of Owen Gager, on the basis of the American Spartacist League's 1966 "Declaration of Principles." Its transplantation to Australia was accompanied by Gager's exit. The SL now seems at least partially to associate with the Revolutionary International Tendency in the United Secretariat of the FI. (This Tendency was expelled from the SWP in 1974.) The SL sees its role as being the agent for crystallization of Leninist regroupment. It claims to adhere strictly to the Transitional Program, castigating other "Trotskyist" groups for their failure to do so. For the SL, the central feature of the Transitional Program is Trotsky's specification that the task of the FI consists in overcoming the contradiction between the maturity of objectively revolutionary conditions and immaturity of the proletariat and the revolutionary party.

The SL sees the SYA-SWL as being the local variant of Pabloism. The growth of the SYA before the SWL indicates to the Spartacists the poverty of the "new mass vanguard" line, which it interprets as an attempted replacement of class struggle with student alienation as the central contradiction of capitalist society. That is, it interprets the "new mass vanguard" as a blatant manifestation of naked revisionism. In its eyes, the CPA is decadent in its reformism: the CPA is, in fact, seeking the mantle of the ALP so it can engage in a PCI trick. Thus, the SL strives for revolutionary purity, standing opposed to ultraleftism and reformism, Pabloist revisionism and Stalinist substitutionism.

Student Spartacists—along with members of other left groups—were involved in the Printing and Kindred Industries Union (PKIU) strike in August. (This strike was at least partially over the closed shop.) Unlike other left groups, the SL consistently joined in picketing. In this dispute the SL showed the difference between themselves and the legalistically inclined SYA-SWL. For the Spartacists, class violence can only be replied to with class violence. This principle was applied against police. It hardly succeeded in putting fear into the hearts of the ruling class, though.

August marked another incident, of numerical insignificance, but of symbolic importance to the SL. The Bolshevik Tendency of the CPA—two members—was expelled and joined the Spartacists. Steve Haran, who had previously been expelled from the Left Tendency of the CPA's Sydney group (thus setting an incredible precedent: that of faction discipline), was further expelled from the CPA. Doug Fullerton resigned in sympathy and the duo joined the SL. The SL's conclusion, unavoidable in the circumstances, was that there was (is) no left opposition in the CPA (as the Left Tendency had effectively identified with CPA leadership) (*Australian Spartacist*, September).

Though typically tagged Trotskyites, the Socialist Workers Action Group (WAG) sees orthodox Trotskyism as bankrupt. SWAG grew from an earlier group called the Marxist Workers Group, and is concentrated in Melbourne, where it has links with the Revolutionary Communists at Monash and La Trobe Universities. SWAG's stance is basically akin to that of the British International Socialists, their disagreement with the orthodox being over the alleged class nature of the post-capitalist states. On this issue there is no concrete SWAG line other than an agreement that the Soviet Union is not authentically socialist. Consequently SWAG, unlike SYA-SWL, feels no obligation to defend the post-capitalist world against the western imperialists.

In domestic policy, SWAG concentrates on the building of rank and file groups in unions. To date its efforts have been concentrated in white collar unions; now SWAG is seeking to move into the industrial sector proper. This strategy is a consequence of SWAG's analysis that middle-class radicalism is in decline and thus that the development of genuine working class roots is necessary. Despite its Leninism, SWAG does not appear to claim the historical role of exclusive vanguard of the Australian revolution. Still, it makes a point of denying this role to the CPA and all other reformists. In this sense the members of SWAG remain ardent revolutionists.

On 14 November, in an anti-Fraser protest meeting in Melbourne, SWAG was responsible for leading a march on the Stock Exchange. This occurred after the protest had apparently been closed by its official ALP and CPA patrons. (*Battler*, 29 November). SWAG took the success of this further march as a rejection of CPA reformist and an encouragement of SWAG initiative.

The Left Groups in the December Election. Like most sections of Australian society, the left groups were caught off-balance by the unexpected precipitation of this year's election which was held on 13 December. Thus, although the SWL was able to launch a wide campaign for the Senate, the CPA only ran candidates for five years in the House of Representatives. Similarly, the SPA only put together a Senate team for South Australia.

Due to awkward timing of this election, only incomplete, but nevertheless indicative, results are available at the time of this writing. The figures indicate votes counted as of 17 December.

CPA. Ian Fehring, standing for the seat of Melbourne, scored 570 votes of the 46,937 counted (the total of electors enrolled being 58,090). Laurie Aarons stood for Sydney, receiving 2052 votes of 42,544 counted (the total enrolled being 55,567). David Ross, in the seat of Newcastle, gained 781 votes of 51,120 counted (total enrollment 58,664). Rob Durbridge, standing for Bonython, received 3577 of 79,833 votes counted (total enrollment 87,805). Finally, Vic Slater in the seat of Perth scored 678 of 57,945 votes counted (total enrolled 68,274).

SWL. With 85 percent of the vote counted, Victorian candidates Peter Conrick and Diane Ewin scored 809 and 359 votes, respectively. This constituted 0.1 percent of the total vote. In New South Wales, benefiting from the number one position on the ballot paper, Helen Jarvis gained 22,308 votes—an abnormally high score even allowing for the donkey vote—and Gordon Adler 1835. With 79 percent of the vote counted, they thus scored one percent of the total vote. South Australians Brett Trenery and Peter Abrahamson, with 89 percent of the vote counted, scored 333 and 47 votes respectively (a negligible percentage of the total votes cast). In Queensland, with 76 percent of the vote counted, Renfrey Clarke had collected 102 votes. Rod Quinn, in the Australian Capital Territory won 177 with 89 percent of the vote counted, and John Tully, in Tasmania, scored 196 votes with 87 percent of the vote counted.

SPA. The SPA's Adelaide team, Bob Pointer, Muriel Goss and Alan Miller, gained 572, 41 and 100 votes respectively. This constituted 0.1 percent of the total vote (and 0.01 of a quota).

Thus, as the Australian left stands in 1975, it is characterized by fragmentation and confusion, with nine mutually antagonistic groups in existence. Comprised of some 4000 "revolutionaries" they find more to disagree about amongst themselves than they do with their class enemies. SYA-SWL and CL share some possibilities, as MRM and SWAG (IS) would appear to, though there is no doubt that neither of the latter would care to acknowledge this. Each group tends to consider itself the receptacle of Australian Marxist Truth and thus waits for the world to beat a path to its door. Regroupment—whether of the left coalition variety preferred by the CPA or the pure Leninist form of MRM—if achieved, would still leave the enormous problem of *mass* consciousness. For all the serious left groups readily acknowledge the need for substantial popular support, there are amongst their ranks few would-be putschists.

In all its varieties, the Australian left appears, thus to be not unhealthy, but at the same time, not potent. Communism has for more than fifty years been and without doubt will remain an important thread in Australian society. But it is equally certain that it will not, in our time, become the dominant thread.

Publications. The CPA continues to publish its weekly newspaper *Tribune. Australian Left Review* continues to serve its purpose as a general forum, while *Praxis* fulfills the role of intra-party discussion. The Young Comunist Movement, which apparently principally serves the purpose of recruitment, publishes its own journal *Red Pen.*

Monash University   Peter Beilharz

Bangladesh

In a faction-ridden polity such as the one in Bangladesh, political parties undergo recurrent and almost routine schisms. The communist parties are particularly vulnerable to factional splits, in part because of their insistence on correct ideology and in part, in Bangladesh, because of the socio-cultural milieu of factionalism. In Bangladesh, as the year 1975 began, there were eight communist parties, one pro-Soviet and the rest of various pro-Chinese orientations. Early in the year, the ruling Awami League (AL) government of Sheikh Mujibur Rahman, formally non-communist, discarded parliamentary democracy and adopted a presidential, one-party system. But within six months, on 15 August, AL leader Rahman was killed together with his extended family by a small group of junior officers in the army. All political parties and the single national party, Bangladesh Krishak Sramik Awami League (BAKSAL), founded after the constitutional changes in January, were banned. Although a return to parliamentary democracy was promised and elections were scheduled for February 1977, the new governing coalition was toppled by a counter-coup on 3 November by senior officers of the army. A new government with a politically neutral civilian as president was sworn in on 7 November, but was mainly a military regime with the chiefs of the army, navy, and air force as deputy martial law administrators. The advisers to the new government appear to be generally right-wing, pro-West, and pro-Pakistan Islamists. The pledge of a return to parliamentary democracy and of elections in February 1977 was affirmed.

The pro-Soviet CPB is estimated to have, or have had, about 2,500 members. The other communist parties have fewer members and their actual strength is only conjecturable. The population of Bangladesh is 73,746,000.

In order of their founding, the eight parties are as follows:

1. Communist Party of Bangladesh (CPB). After the emergence of Bangladesh in December 1972, the formerly banned East Pakistan organization of the Pakistan Communist Party was allowed to function openly as the Communist Party of Pakistan. The origins of this party—the pro-Soviet CPB—go back, however, to British Indian days, when it was part of the Communist Party of India (CPI). After the birth of Pakistan in 1947, there were some 12,000 members of the CPI who remained in Eastern Bengal and became the East Pakistan communist orgnization. Banned in 1954, the organization went underground and its membership was reduced. It is to factional splits and sub-splits from this party, the present CPB, that most of the various other Marxist-Leninist parties of what is now Bangladesh owe their origin.

2. East Pakistan Communist Party—Marxist Leninist (EPCP-ML). As the Sino-Soviet dispute intensified, members of the original communist party who leaned toward China split off and formed the EPCP-ML in 1966.

3. East Bengal Communist Party-Marxist Leninist (Purba Banglar Communist Party-Marxist Leninist; PBCP-ML). This party originated in 1968 when those members of the EPCP-ML who believed capitalism, rather than feudalism, to be the principal contradiction in Bangladesh society were expelled—they then formed the PBCP-ML.

4. Purba Banglar Sammayabadi Dal (PBSD). This party originated in 1972 out of a factional split in the EPCP-ML during the 1971 Bangladesh liberation movement. Those members of the EPCP-ML who favored an armed struggle against both the Pakistan army and the Awami League remained with the party, while those who favored an armed struggle against the Pakistan army and political struggle against the AL formed the PBSD.

5. Communist Party of Bangladesh—Leninist (Bangladesher Communist Party Leninbadi; BCP-L). This party originated in 1971 during the liberation movement when five pro-Chinese groups joined in a Somonny (consultative) Committee in a bid to unify the leftist forces of the country behind the movement. The BCP-L consists of four of the five groups who originally formed the committee.

6. Communist Party of Bengal (Banglar Communist Party; BCP). This party consists of the fifth group of the Somonny Committee, which did not join the BCP-L. Factional differences arose because this group viewed China as more of a potential leader of Bangladesh's struggles than did the BCP-L.

7. Purba Bangla Sorbohara Party (PBSP). This party was founded in 1971 during the liberation movement and is composed mostly of new members.

8. Bangladesh Communist League (BCL). The BCL originated in 1972 and was composed mostly of dissidents from the AL's student front, the Chatra League, who believed in establishing scientific socialism in the country.

Of the eight parties, four operated solely as underground parites: the EPCP-ML, PBCP-ML, PBSD, and PBSP. The other four—CPB, BCL, BCP, and BCP-L—have had both open fronts and underground cells. In the 1973 national election, the first to be held in Bangladesh, they took part through their mass front parties: the National Awami Party-Muzaffar, or NAP(M), affiliated with the CPB; Jatiya Samajtantrik Dal (JSD), affiliated with the BCL; and National Awami Party-Bhashani, or NAP(B), affiliated with various leftist forces including the BCP and BCP-L.

The JSD won two seats in the parliament, and the NAP(B) one seat. The NAP(M), which failed to win a seat, polled 8 percent of the votes, as against the JSD's 6 percent and NAP(B)'s 5 percent. The ruling Awami League won 292 seats out of the 300 general seats in the parliament and polled 73 percent of the votes. The CPB and NAP(M) proved to be the second-largest vote-getting organization, and additionally were only nominally in the opposition: they supported the major domestic and foreign policy objectives of the ruling party, earning the nickname of the "B team" of the AL. Indeed, they tried very hard to persuade the AL to incorporate them as partners in a coalition government. The AL refused to share power with them, but at the end of 1973 formed an alliance—the Gono Oikkya Jote (People's United Front)—with them, and this put the two parties in a supportive role.

The CPB and NAP(M) recruited support mainly from the same mobilized urban groups—lawyers, students, and workers—as did the AL. The other parties were more clearly in opposition to the AL. Those which had mass party fronts had national organizational structures and support bases, though they also recruited support among the urban mobilized groups. The BCL and JSD had strong support particularly among students, former freedom fighters, enlisted men in the armed forces, and workers. It is, however difficult to analyze the social composition of the support bases of the various parties. All their leaderships belonged to the university-educated urban middle class, but the support bases were distinguishable more by geographical location than by social grouping.

The underground parties operated at the village level, where presumably they had some peasant support. None of them had nationwide support of any particular social groups. The EPCP was active in the western and northern regions. The BCP operated in the Feni, Chittagong, Tangail, and Sylhet districts. The PBCP had support in northern districts. The PBCP-ML had launched an armed insurrection very early after the independence of Bangladesh, and many of its supporters were in prison. In the three years after independence the PBSP rapidly picked up support and was reportedly responsible for most of the attacks on police stations and other law-and-order agencies. It had a distinctly large urban student support. Since the BCP-L was composed of four factions, its support base was scattered to the four areas where those factions operated. It is, naturally, difficult to discern the impact of any of the eight parties on the nation's millions of poor people, most of whom are either small farmers or landless peasants.

After the emergence of Bangladesh the right political parties, which also happened to be pro-Pakistan, were banned. All the constitutional parties were moderate to far left. The ruling party, the AL, believed in socialism, though in early 1975 it gave up parliamentary democracy and opted for a one-party state. The CPB supported the ruling party's preference for socialism and parliamentary democracy, and though it later was the strongest supporter of the AL when the regime shifted to the one-party system. Both the AL and the CPB wanted friendly relations with India and the Soviet Union.

The other communist or Marxist-Leninist parties looked upon India and the Soviet Union as enemies, and the PBSP, PBSD, EPCP-ML, and PBCP-ML did not believe in parliamentary politics. Despite their common belief in armed revolution and their agreement on common enemies at home (the AL) and abroad (India and the Soviet Union), all efforts to form a united front of leftist parties failed, in part because of personality differences among the factional leaders and in part because of differences in tactics.

Leadership and Organization. The CPB was headed by its 24-member Central Committee, with Moni Singh as chairman and Mohammad Farhad as general secretary. The leadership was old—generally over sixty—and in the hands of the old CPI members who joined the party before 1947. Since the party leadership was dominated by CPI members, few Muslims joined. The chairman and three of the eight secretaries of the party were Hindus.

Data about the leadership and organizational structure of other Marxist-Leninist parties are sketchy. All were headed by Central Committees and all had party cells in the various districts of their operation. Some, which were engaged in armed insurrection (PBSP, PBSD, and PBCP-ML), had formed national liberation fronts to fight the AL government. Each party had one or two well-known leaders.

Auxiliary and Mass Organizations. The communist and Marxist-Leninist parties which believed in competitive parliamentary politics had their student, labor, peasant, women's, and mass party fronts.

The CPB's student front, Bangladesh Chatra Union (BCU), and the AL's student front, Bangladesh Chatra League, dominated the Dacca University Central Students' Union (DUCSU), long considered to be one of the major centers of political power in the country. The CPB's labor front was led by one of the secretaries of its Central Committee. A women's social organization, Mahila Parishad, was the party's women's front. Most of the Parishad leaders were former members of the BCU. The peasant front, Bangladesh Krishak Samity, was headed by CPB president Moni Singh. As mentioned earlier, the NAP(M) was its mass political front. The NAP(M) president was Muzaffar Ahmad, a Muslim professor in his mid-fifties; the general secretary was Pankaj Bhattacharya, a Hindu in his early thirties.

The BCL's student front, Bangladesh Chatra League, was composed of a dissident faction of the AL's student front of the same name. This front challenged the Mujibbad ideology of the AL front and vowed to establish scientific socialism. When the elections to the DUCSU could not be completed in 1973 due to the stealing of ballot boxes, it was widely believed that the boxes were stolen by the rival AL front and the BCU to prevent the BCL's front from winning. The labor front of the BCL was composed of the dissident faction of the AL's labor front. It did not have any affiliated women's organization, its women's front being the women's wings of its mass and student party fronts. The mass party front of the BCL was the JSD, formed in 1972 and led by Major Jalil, a Muslim former freedom fighter in his late thirties. The majority of JSD's Central Executive Committee members were former student leaders in their early thirties. The BCL had also a peasant front and had the support of the dissident faction of the AL's affiliated freedom fighters association.

The BCP(L) also had student, labor, and peasant fronts. Operating as an open party, it also used the NAP(B) as a mass party front. The BCP also had student and labor fronts and operated in part as an open party and in part used the NAP(B) as a mass party front. It had, however, only limited support.

The other parties–PBSP, PBSD, PBCP-ML, and EPCP-ML–did not believe in parliamentary politics. They operated solely as underground parties with secret party cells and with no publicized student, labor, or peasant fronts.

Party Internal Affairs. When the AL rejected parliamentary democracy and initiated its "second revolution" (the one-party presidential system) in early 1975, the major support for the move came from the CPB, which for a long time had advocated the cause of a "national" government composed of the patriotic elements, meaning the AL, CPB, and NAP(M). It saw the single-party system as providing them with an opportunity for partnership in a ruling party coalition. Indeed, CPB and NAP(M) leaders were incorporated in the various fronts of BAKSAL. Between January and August the CPB nearly merged with the ruling party whereas the BCL, PBSP, PBSD, PBCP-ML and EPCP-ML were violently opposed and did not join the BAKSAL, and BCP and BCP-L were divided in their attitude toward the single party.

The August and November coups (see above) led to the loss of the CPB's partnership in governmental powers. The PBSD, PBCP-ML, and NAP(B) welcomed the August coup and supported the new regime, mostly because of its attempt to establish friendly relations with China. The stands of the PBSP and BCL on the political changes were not clear. The BCL claimed that it instigated the army mutiny of 7 November, but it failed to take over governmental power and subsequently appeared to be in opposition to the new government.

PBSP lost its founder-leader, Siraj Sikdar, in early 1975 when he was imprisoned and killed by Bangladesh police. What impact his death would have on the party's rapidly growing support base was unclear. Since Sikdar was the party's main theoretician and himself a romantic figure, his loss would certainly reduce the party's support, particularly among urban youths. The PBCP-ML lost many of its prominent leaders through their imprisonment. The BCL and PBSD leadership escaped imprisonment, but the leadership of the BCL's mass front, the JSD, had been in police custody since early 1974. After 3 November 1975, some of the JSD leaders were set free and then rearrested within a few days.

In sum, 1975 saw the CPB lose its share in governmental powers, and it also lost popular support because of its pro-Soviet, pro-India leanings. The PBSP, which picked up rapid support during 1971 to 1974, received a setback when its leader was killed. The fortunes of PBSD remained unchanged. With the AL in disarray following the coups of August and November, the BCL appeared to be in a very strong position, and in any forthcoming election its JSD front is likely to emerge as a strong party. Additionally the 7 November mutiny showed that the BCL had picked up the support of factions in the army and the paramilitary Rakkhi Bahini.

Domestic Attitudes and Activities. The communist and Marxist-Leninist parties differed with regard to their attitude towards the Bangladesh movement and the ruling AL. The CPB looked upon the AL as a progressive party of the middle class and urged cooperation with it. The AL was progressive, according to the CPB, because of its policy of nationalization of industries and public sector planning and its policy of land reform (putting a ceiling on landholding over 33 acres). The CPB regarded the constitution framed by the AL as a forward step in the direction of democratic national development, and it supported the four principles of state ideology: nationalism, socialism, democracy, and secularism. Additionally the CPB regarded the foreign policy of AL as progressive, especially its policy of friendly relations with India and the Soviet Union. The CPB accused the other Marxist-Leninist parties as reactionaries which had both ultra-leftists and communalists within their fold. It branded the BCL and other Maoist parties as enemies of national independence and deplored their armed attacks on law-and-order agencies of government. While the CPB urged the AL to give up its policy of "going it alone" and criticized the presence of some corrupt, reactionary, and imperialist forces within the AL fold, it still regarded the AL's overall policy as progressive and called on all patriotic parties, meaning the CPB and NAP(M), to strengthen the hands of the AL as against the other Marxist-Leninist parties. In January 1975 the CPB and NAP-M published numerous pamphlets about the Tanzanian model of a one-party system and argued that its adoption would help Bangladesh consolidate its independence.

The other Marxist-Leninist parties however considered the AL regime as a dependent or puppet of India. PBSP believed that Bangladesh had not yet completed its nationalist revolution since it was stopped too short by the intervention of India which put the puppet AL government in power and maintained Indian military presence through arming and training the paramilitary Rakkhi Bahini. The PBSP formed a national liberation front composed of peasants, laborers, students, and "oppressed" minorities (the tribal groups and the Biharis). It believed that since Bangladesh was surrounded on three sides by India no outside help would be available for the revolution and the liberation front would have to raise its own resources, thus justifying attacks on the thanas and banks to loot arms and money. It also assassinated AL supporters and social miscreants (i.e., smugglers).

Like the PBSP, the PBSD looked upon the Bangladesh movement as an unfinished revolution. During the 1971 liberation movement it opposed and fought both the Pakistan army and the Bangladesh "Mukti Bahini" (freedom fighters). It also regarded the AL government as a puppet in the hands of Indian and Soviet social imperialists. But it differed from PBSP in that while the latter saw the principle contradiction as between India and East Bengal, the former saw it as between the socialist and anti-socialist forces. The PBSD attacked the PBSP as a counter-revolutionary terrorist force supported by the U.S. Central Intelligence Agency to oust the influence of Delhi and Moscow from Bangladesh.

The PBCP-ML regarded the 1971 liberation movement in Bangladesh as a fight between two "bourgeoisie dogs" and it opposed both the Pakistan army and the Mukti Bahini. Differing from the PBSD and other Marxist-Leninist parties, it favored collaboration with the revolutionaries in India, especially the Naxalites.

The EPCP-ML did not recognize the independence of Bangladesh at all, and hence retained "East Pakistan" in its name. It regarded the 1971 liberation movement as an "expansionist move by India" and considered Bangladesh to be an Indian colony. Its movement aimed at resurrecting old East Pakistan.

The BCL differed from the other parties in that it looked upon the 1971 liberation movement as completing the nationalist revolution in Bangladesh, and urged the continuation of the third and final phase of the revolution for the establishment of the dictatorship of the proletariat. For favoring an immediate class struggle to establish scientific socialism, the BCL was branded as Trotskyite by the PBSP and PBSD.

The overthrow of Sheikh Mujibur Rahman by the August coup led to another conflict among the parties regarding the stage of revolution in the post-Mujib phase. The CPB, which supported Sheikh Mujib's policy of friendship with India and the Soviet Union, looked upon his successors as communalists (i.e., Islamists) and imperialists (i.e., pro U.S./China forces). The rest of the parties welcomed the August coup. After the November coups, particularly the mutiny in the army, the Marxist-Leninist parties were divided in their attitude. While the BCL, which claimed to have instigated the 7 November army mutiny, called for an immediate class struggle to establish scientific socialism, the PBSD and BCP-L urged a moratorium on immediate class struggle and called for united support behind the military regime to deter Indian intervention in Bangladesh.

International Views, Policies, Activities, and Contacts. As mentioned earlier, the CPB was aligned with the Soviet Union and the major reason behind CPB support of the AL was the argument that the latter pursued a policy of friendship toward India and the Soviet Union. The other Marxist-Leninist parties, especially the EPCP-ML, PBCP-ML, and PBSD, were virulently anti-India and anti-Soviet, and supported friendship with China. The PBSP and BCL, though anti-Indian and anti-Soviet, were more concerned with domestic issues than with international ones. Their objective was to establish a revolutionary government in Bangladesh first, and then to hope for friendship and support from China and other countries. Both had originated not out of any factional split over international issues but as parties promising different strategy and tactics on domestic issues. Of all the Marxist-Leninist parties, only the BCL believed the country to be ripe for launching an immediate class struggle to establish a dictatorship of the proletariat. The BCL's arguments were that, since the August and November coups, the three pillars of the bourgeoise and semi-feudal state—the bureaucracy, the army, and the police—had been so shaken and shattered that it would be easy to destroy the corroded remnants of the bourgeois government and establish a proletarian administration based on the "unity of the revolutionary soldiers, peasants, workers, and students." The BCL was the only party which formed its wing in the army—known as the people's revolutionary army (PRA). The PRA was behind the 7 November army mutiny and called for the establishment of a "revolutionary army" where the "armed forces of the country will build themselves as the protector of the interests of the country's poorer class." In the post-Mujib phase in Bangladesh, the principal contradiction according to BCL was between the moribund Bengali bourgeoisie and semi-feudal elements on one side and the proletariat and poor peasantry on the other. The PBSD, BCP-L, and BCP on the other hand saw the principal contradiction as between the independence and sovereignty of Bangladesh and the threat of Indian expansionism backed by the social imperialism of the Soviet Union. They argued in favor of postponing the class struggle for the time being to support national independence.

The various parties took a very predictable line on international issues—that is, on national liberation movements and other international conflicts. The CPB supported the Soviet-backed movements. The other parties supported the Chinese-backed. With the exception of the CPB, the parties did not spend much time on internatinal issues. The CPB organized demonstrations and conferences on Vietnam, Chile, and the Middle East. It was, also, the only party which could send delegations to conferences abroad. The other had only clandestine contact with their counterparts abroad. Since the ruling AL leaned toward the Indo-Soviet line in international conflicts, the government itself came out strongly in favor of North Vietnam, the Viet Cong, and Cambodia in Indochina and of the Arabs in the Middle East. The overthrow of the AL regime and the establishment of a military government in Bangladesh, however, implied certain policy changes at the government level. The present government may not follow the Indo-Soviet line in all international conflicts; it may veer toward the U.S.-China-Pakistan line.

Party Publications. Only those communist and Marxist-Leninist parties which operated as open parties had party newspapers and publications with open circulations. The underground parties published newspapers and pamphlets, but their circulation was restricted. The CPB and NAP(M) had a daily newspaper published in Bengali, *Sangbad* (News). From February to August 1975 *Sangbad* temporarily ceased publication when the government limited the number of newspapers to four national dailies, two in English and two in Bengali. After August, *Sangbad* had resumed publication. The editor of *Sangbad*, Ahmedul Kabir, was for a long time associated with the NAP(M). The NAP-M had a weekly—*Nutan Bangla* (New Bengal)—which was the official mouthpiece of the party. It was published in Bengali. The CPB and NAP(M) were prolific in publishing pamphlets which explained the party's policies on various issues. Additionally the CPB published the proceedings of the party's Second Congress, held in Dacca in 1973.

The BCL had a Bengali-language daily newspaper, *Gonokantha* (Voice of the people), edited by a radical poet, Al Mahmud. The AL regime tried to close down *Gonokantha* a number of times in 1973. After January 1975 *Gonokantha* ceased publication when the government limited the number of newspapers. Like the other parties, the BCL published numerous pamphlets, some of which had restricted underground circulation. Pamphlets published by the JSD had open circulation.

The BCP-L and NAP(B) had an English-language weekly, *Holiday*, which ceased publication from February to August and resumed afterward. The NAP(B) published a number of Bengali-language weeklies, which the AL government banned. The PBSP published a Bengali weekly, *Lal Jhanda* (Red Flag) and a news bulletin, *Sangbad Bulletin*. The PBSD's official weekly was *Gonoshakti* (People's Strength), published in Bengali and edited by Mohammad Toaha, leader of the party. The PBCP-ML's mouthpiece was *Purba Bangla* (East Bengal). The EPCP-ML's official news paper was *Jono Juddha* (People's War), edited by the party leader, Abdul Haq. All these newspapers published by the underground parties had restricted underground circulation, as did the parties' pamphlets on various ideological and tactical issues.

Dacca University   Rounaq Jahan

Burma

The Burma Communist Party (BCP) was established on 15 August 1939 with probably 13 members and Thakin Soe as secretary-general. After participating in the struggle for the liberation of Burma under the leadership of the "Anti-Fascist People's Freedom League" (AFPFL), the communists more and more disagreed with the socialists in the AFPFL. In March 1946, Thakin Soe and some followers split from the BCP, where Thakin Than Tun had taken over the leadership, and founded the Communist Party of Burma, also known as the "Red Flag." The Red Flag soon went underground and its armed insurrection against the British resulted in its being declared an unlawful association in January 1947. The BCP or "White Flag" communists under Thakin Than Tun collaborated for some time with the AFPFL, though without much success, even after Burma attained independence on 4 January 1948. They went underground at the end of March 1948 and were declared illegal in October 1953.

Except for the years 1948 to 1950 when the government of Prime Minister U Nu nearly collapsed, communist activities were confined to certain areas (especially the Irrawaddy delta, the Pegu Yoma highlands, and the Shan State) and therefore were a local, but constant, harassment to the Union government. Large-scale counter-insurgency operations of the Burmese army, undertaken in cooperation with local "People's Militia," together with internal party struggles and purges of "revisionists," critically weakened the BCP after 1967-68. After the death of Thakin Than Tun in

September 1968, leadership was taken over at most levels by men subservient to Peking. With Communist Chinese aid given openly after June 1967 and continued secretly after the resumption of full diplomatic relations between Burma and China in 1971, the BCP stepped up its guerrilla activities in the Shan State, first north of Lashio and about 1971 in the Kunlong area east of the Salween River which it has controlled since the end of 1973.

The Red Flags, whose main base was in the Arakan region and for some time also in the Irrawaddy delta, did not reach any major importance. The capture of their leader Thakin Soe and the loss of other leaders at the end of 1970 critically weakened the group. Thus, the Red Flag and its splinter group, the Arakan Communist Party, have lost even the small local importance they were able to claim during the mid-1960s. As there was hardly any information on them during 1975, they are not noted further in the following survey (for their leadership and organization see *YICA, 1975*, p. 296).

Reliable figures on the membership of the BCP are not available. In the past few years it was estimated as having a strength of at least 6,000 men under arms (*YICA, 1974*, p. 405, and 1975, p. 296). In view of the loss of at least 1,000 men during 1975, the estimate, "according to conservative observers," of "below 10,000 men" (*NYT*, 7 August 1975) seems a little too high, but might be correct as the losses were probably more than replaced by new recruits from the tribes residing on both sides of the China border. Burma's population is just over 30 million.

Leadership and Organization. Thakin Zin and Thakin Chit, who had become chairman and secretary of the BCP after Thakin Than Tun's death in 1968, were killed in a clash with government troops in the Pegu Yoma on 15 March 1975. In addition, Tun Sein, alias Barkeh, was captured in November 1974, and Toke was killed on 26 February 1975. According to government sources both had been members of the BCP Central Committee (*Forward*, Rangoon, 1 May 1975, p. 20). At an expanded meeting of the Central Committee of the BCP in May, elections were held to the Central Committee and the Politburo. According to a statement of the clandestine "Voice of the People of Burma" (*VPB*) of 1 June (*FBIS*, 2, 9 June), the Central Committee now consists of Thakin Ba Thein Tin as chairman (up to then first vice-chairman and head of the group's permanent delegation in Peking), Thakin Pe Tint as vice-chairman, and members Kyaw Mya, Kyin Maung, Khin Maung Kyi, Soe Kyi, Saw Han, Zaw Myaing, Taik Aung, Ne Win, Pe Thaung, Fran Gan Di, Myo Myint, Ye Tuni, Thet Tun and another person from the northwest command, Than Shwe, and one person from the delta. In addition 14 candidate members were elected, in three cases (Arakan, delta region, second member from Tavoy) without identification as to names as yet. The new Politburo comprises Thakin Ba Thein Tin, Thakin Pe Tint, Khin Maung Kyi, Myo Myint, Kyaw Mya, Kyin Maung, and Ne Win.

The organizational structure extends from the Politburo and the Central Committee through divisional and district committees down to township and, in some areas, even village committees. Divisional committees exist, as the elections to the Central Committee reveal, for all parts of Burma, though sometimes only in name, and other committees only in regions where the BCP is active. At the Central Committee meeting a "border area people's administrative body was set up to comprehensively strengthen the bases in the border area and to develop the revolution" (*VPB*, 12 June; *FBIS*, 16 June). The BCP's "People's Army" is structured along traditional communist lines with party political cadres superior to military commanders at all levels.

Party Internal Affairs. The main event in 1975 was the change of leadership in the BCP due to the deaths of chairman Thakin Zin and secretary Thakin Chit. In the Central Committee statement on their deaths both were celebrated for having "shed their last drop of blood, dying martyrs' deaths in fighting valiantly with proletarian heroism against the enemy." The statement admits that the party now faces difficulties. These are regarded, however, as "temporary difficulties which revolutionaries constantly encounter in the course of their advance." (*Peking Review*, 30 May, pp. 15, 16; also *FBIS*, 20 May.)

The new elections to the top committees, due for some time and now forced upon the party, took place in the Central Committee meeting in May (ending 16 May?) in an unidentified place, situated perhaps even outside Burma. With Thakin Ba Thein Tin and Thakin Pe Tint two long-time Peking residents of the BCP came to power. Ba Thein Tin has been a member of the Central Committee probably since the BCP's Second Congress on 20 July 1945. He became one of the eleven generals of the "People's Army" when it was founded in 1950, and early in the 1950s was elected vice-chairman. He went in May 1953 to China where he was soon named head of the party's permanent delegation in Peking and was given special permission to marry. It is not known how long Pe Tint has lived in China (also since 1953?); he has been at least since 1965 a member of the Central Committee. Besides these two, it appears that only Myo Myint, Kyaw Mya, and Than Shwe are veteran, Central Committee members. If last year's list (*YICA, 1975*, p. 296) was right, a major reshuffle has taken place and a second generation of BCP leaders, surely all trained in China, got into the Central Committee.

The programmatic first speech of the new chairman, broadcast by the VPB on 16 May (*FBIS*, 22 May), reflects, much more than the speeches of Thakin Zin, his long ideological training in the PRC. Thus, the BCP's policy is now also ideologically more than ever an offspring of the Chinese policy and follows the principles of "our revolutionary teachers" (ibid.). This concerns the attitude toward revisionism and subjectivism as well as Mao Tse-tung's guerrilla warfare tactics.

The main problem of the Burmese communists in 1975 was apparently the breakdown of their organizational structure which was also indicated by the vacancies in the Central Committee. As can be seen from Ba Thein Tin's "instructions to party organizations in various regions," the influence of former red guards was to be cut down:

> Veteran and mature comrades of party organizations in various regions, you must take responsibility and give leadership in respective regions. As leaders you should train resourceful youths and women with political conviction and include them in leadership. The rich experience of mature comrades should be combined with the good points of the active youths and they should help each other and share their experience. (Ibid.)

At the same time Ba Thein Tin appealed for an end to the internal ideological struggle which obviously still followed, at least partly, the "Demote, Dismiss, Destroy" line of 1967:

> A group of comrades or a comrade who has political and ideological differences must not be punished physically. . . . A comrad who commits a mistake must be allowed to see and correct his mistake. We must consider him as a sick person and save him by giving medical treatment. (Ibid.)

In aiming to shape discussions along the line of "Consolidating ideology with practice, criticism and self-criticism following the mass line," Ba Thein Tin applied a more intellectual and less aggressive policy than his predecessors Thakin Than Tun and Thakin Zin. Regarding the overall situation as quite favorable for the Burmese communists, he sought to form his party into a consolidated bloc which could be presented as an alternative to the present government of U Ne Win, chairman of the Council of State and president of the Union.

Domestic Activities and Armed Struggles. As in previous years, the Burmese communists continued their armed struggle against the "Ne Win-San Yu military government" (referring to U Ne Win and army chief General San Yu). However, it was more difficult than before to discern the scenario evolving during 1975. No doubt, the most important battle was fought in March in the jungles of Kyauktaga township on the eastern slopes of the Pegu Yoma. From earlier days until party chairman Thakin Than Tun was killed there in September 1968, the headquarters of the BCP had been in this mountain range. In and after 1972 Thakin Zin, with 800 followers, again set up the headquarters in the Pegu Yoma. In spite of several attempts, government troops did not succeed in breaking them up until the all-out "Aung Soe Moe" ("Famous Victory") offensive in March 1975. Thakin Zin and Thakin Chit were found dead, 172 of their followers were also killed, and 149 captured (*Far Eastern Economic Review* [*FEER*], 23 May, p. 35). The government's claim to have wiped out the communist forces in the area could be generally correct, but the communists will surely try to win back a foothold in the vast and dense jungles of the Pegu Yoma, which are strategically well situated for their guerrilla warfare and hard for the government forces to control.

The communists, on their part, claimed to "have our people's army and liberated bases in the northwest, delta, Arakan, Tenasserim, Kengtung, Myitkyina, Momeik, northeast military region, and the central Shan State District" (*VPB*, 17 May; *FBIS*, 22 May), a statement which sounds very bold for areas like the delta, Arakan, and Tenasserim. In early 1975, a main operation area of the BCP was the opium-growing Kengtung region where they launched, as in December 1973, a major attack in January, but were repulsed. According to government reports, the BCP lost 450 men, whereas the government forces "suffered 96 killed, 132 wounded and 66 missing" (*FEER*, 23 May, p. 35). This victory was, however, most probably also due to the fact that the balance of power between the insurgent forces operating in this area (rightist Shan rebels, Kuomintang remnants, and others) was in danger, so that those forces also opposed an advance by the communists.

The BCP therefore switched to other places. After securing domination of the eastern bank of the Salween in January and February, they tried by the end of June, for the first time in this long secret war, to establish a base in Tangyan township, Northern Shan State, on the western bank. In 17 close-range bayonet battles between 22 and 26 June, with Air Force planes also participating, 120 communist and 32 government troops are reported to have lost their lives (*Burma Broadcasting Service*, 28 June; *FBIS*, 30 June). Another center of communist activities was, also in January and February, the region north of Lashio, between Lashio and Kutkai and around Muse. Both sides suffered heavy casualties. In all other regions, activities were apparently restricted to minor guerrilla attacks.

It is interesting to note that neither side reported major operations after June. This could be a result of Ba Thein Tin's new line of consolidating the party and giving a new image to it. In his eyes it would be "wrong to abandon the armed struggle in favor of other forms of struggle" (*VPB*, 17 May). But also in military actions he wanted to apply more than before Mao Tse-tung's flexible guerrilla tactics to avoid further heavy losses among his troops. It appears as if propaganda activities, executed in a well-planned manner, were to be given similar weight in the party's future struggle. Toward the ruling government, the communists contented themselves with pointing at its general problems without going into details: "Although they were shouting about socialist construction, they are facing hardship in all areas. They are facing great difficulties on the political, economic, social, education, health and military fronts." (*VPD*, 17 May 1975.) Besides that, the communists were profiting by the demonstrations of students and urban population in June 1974, December 1974 (arising from the government's refusal to concede a state funeral to former U.N. secretary-general U Thant), and June 1975. The BCP did not play a major role, if any, in launching the 1974 demonstrations, during which many persons were killed and, in December, nearly 3,000 were detained (most of them released in early 1975). Nevertheless, leaflets indicated that some of the students were inspired by communist ideas. The BCP supported their case in a long statement on 10 June which the government, for the first time, regarded as important enough to answer the same day by a statement of the minister of information. The communists predicted that the demonstrations would be abortive, but strenuously urged "all oppressed people of various classes and strata throughout the country to support the demands and movements of the university students enthusiastically, join in the struggle and render mutual assistance" (*VPB*, 10 June; *FBIS*, 11 June).

In several statements of the communist leaders a new note can be discovered: the attempt to address specific groups and instigate them to engage in active resistance. A favorite target was the army, especially the lower ranks:

> The Ne Win-San Yu military clique, which cannot improve the people's life, can never improve the lives of the lower stratum in its armed forces. Now the people will surely expect the privates and corporals not to allow the Ne Win-San Yu military authorities to trick them but rather point their guns at the Ne Win-San Yu clique [and] not toward the people. (Ibid.)

Other groups addressed in their propaganda were the peasants and workers. In these cases the communists put their finger on the general decline of the Burmese economy and called for "sustained, multiformed struggles in your respective areas to win victory" (*VPB*, 1 May; *FBIS*, 2 May).

The BCP also continued "its efforts to consolidate and develop the National and Democratic Front of Unity founded in 1959, and build a broad united front with armed forces of all nationalities opposing the Ne Win-San Yu military regime" (*Peking Review*, 16 May, p. 16). However, no significant progress was made in the party's relations with the minorities. The offer of aid to the "Kachin Independence Army" (*FBIS*, 21, 22 August) apparently went unanswered by that group, which generally considered the BCP to be as anti-minority-minded as the Rangoon government.

International Views and Contacts. The BCP remains firmly aligned with the People's Republic of China in spite of officially good diplomatic relations between the governments in Rangoon and Peking. The new BCP leaders obviously have their headquarters in China and their broadcasting station is also situated there. After omitting the Burmese communists from its pages since 1971, the *Peking Review* in its issue of 30 May 1975, printed the statement of the BCP Central Committee on the deaths of Thakin Zin and Thakin Chit. The continuing Chinese support for the BCP evidently caused the visits to the PRC by Burma's foreign minister U Hla Phone in August and president U Ne Win between 11 and 15 November. On his arrival in Peking, U Ne Win alluded to "differences" between Peking and Rangoon which they "should resolve . . . with patience, mutual understanding and accommodation" (*The Working People's Daily*, Rangoon, 13 November 1975). The following AFP report on the visit was reprinted by Burmese newspapers:

> It cannot be ruled out that the Burmese government obtained from Chinese leaders a greater discretion in their support of these rebels. But China has always made a distinction between government-to-government relations and party-to-party relations.

> It wants to have good relations with the regime in power in Rangoon but it is doubtful, diplomatic circles believe, that the Chinese Communist Party will abandon its material aid to the Burmese Communist Party (*The Working People's Daily*, 17 November).

The Soviet Union, without partners among the numerous insurgency groups in Burma, but very interested in winning Burma as a close partner and perhaps even a foothold, condemned Peking for the support given to the BCP:

> While paying lip service to friendship with Burma, Peking, after the failure of its attempts to make it the bulwark of its influence in South Asia, has been keeping the country in a constant state of tension more than 10 years now. Peking is regularly sending to Burma armed units of peoples of the same origin as the nationalities populating the border areas of Burma. Their task is to undermine the economy, discredit the social measures taken by the authorities and create chaos and lack of confidence in the country. (*Pravda*, 14 April; *FBIS*, 17 April.)

On 3 May the BCP sent a message to the Vietnam Workers' Party and the National Front for the Liberation of South Vietnam congratulating them on their "great victory of historical and international significance" (*FBIS*, 12 June). The victories of the communists in Cambodia and South Vietnam were taken as an example and as a challenge for the Burmese communists: "The world situation is excellent for revolution and the Southeast Asian situation is also excellent. . . . The local situation is also excellent for the development of revolution." (*VPB*, 17 May.)

The relations with the Malaysian underground communists seem to have become closer, with exchanges of greetings on anniversaries. On 3 July the (clandestine) "Voice of the Malayan Revolution" broadcast also (in Mandarin) the appeals of the Rangoon Students' General Strike Committee of 6 and 8 June (*FBIS*, 7 July), and on 28 August the station aired a quite out-of-date BCP attack against "renegade" Thakin Soe (ibid., 4 September).

The BCP also greeted the Indonesian Communist Party and the Thai Communist Party on their anniversaries, thus giving the appearance of close contacts between the underground communist forces in the still non-communist countries of Southeast Asia.

Publications. The only first-hand information on the BCP comes from the broadcasts of its clandestine radio station, the "Voice of the People of Burma," inaugurated on 28 March 1971 and supposedly situated in southwest Yunnan Province in China (*The Economist*, 23 November 1974, p. 49). No regular publications are known. Occasional leaflets are distributed illegally and therefore not available.

Köln-Weiss   Klaus Fleischmann
Federal Republic of Germany

Cambodia

The Khmer Communist Party (KCP) is the name usually given by Western writers to the communist political organization in Cambodia, which directed a five-year struggle against Lon Nol's Khmer Republic government and on 17 April 1975 seized control of the capital, Phnom Penh, and the rest of the country. (The Khmer-language version of the country's name, Kampuchea, is now used officially, in place of Cambodia.)

Even after achieving victory, the KCP remains a highly secretive organization, governing the country through the Royal Government of National Union of Kampuchea (French acronym, GRUNK). The publicly announced GRUNK cabinet membership is believed to overlap partially with the secret KCP Central Committee, which actually rules Cambodia.

The KCP traces its lineage to Ho Chi Min's pre-World War II Indochina Communist Party, which was reconstituted as the Lao Dong (Workers) Party in 1951. During most of the subsequent period until 1962, Prince Norodom Sihanouk, who ruled Cambodia, allowed the Khmer communists some leeway to take part in the political process. In this period, the legal and semi-open communist movement in Cambodia was known by the Khmer name Pracheachon, loosely translated as "People's Revolutionary Party." The communist and fellow-traveler *maquis* was dubbed *Khmer rouge* by Sihanouk.

Since 1962 the communist movement in Cambodia has operated through various front organizations, which have rarely if ever acknowledged being communist. Undoubtedly the movement has meanwhile gone through a complex series of divisions and reorganizations. Most observers of Cambodian politics seem to assume that during the 1970-75 war the KCP gained a position of dominance over all left-wing elements in the country. If so, it certainly did not occupy such a position before the war or during its early stages, when scattered bands of dissidents gradually coalesced into an army under strong Vietnamese communist tutelage.

In 1972, most Vietnamese communist forces left Cambodia for the final stages of the Vietnam war. Thereafter, traditional Khmer-Vietnamese hostility rapidly asserted itself between the Khmer guerrilla forces and the Vietnamese communists. However, a sense of common struggle against "U.S. imperialism" evidently provided a strong bond between leading elements of the two groups, who held meetings (publicized by their propaganda organs) from time to time to sort out differences, probably relating more to territory than to ideology. Unity of all Khmer leftists under communist control may have been inadvertently fostered by the uncompromising approach of Lon Nol's U.S.-supported right-wing government. This contrasted with the more flexible divide-and-rule tactics which Sihanouk used in the 1950s and 1960s to keep potential domestic opponents off balance.

The main indigenous elements comprising the leftist camp in Cambodia during the 1970-75 war were probably: (1) the *Khmers rouges* dissidents, who at various times in the 1960s opted out of a society tightly controlled by Sihanouk; (2) a few thousand Khmers who went to North Vietnam in the 1950s, received military and political training, and reentered Cambodia after Sihanouk's overthrow; and (3) peasants recruited by these more highly motivated and indoctrinated groups during the 1970-75 war.

Sihanouk's overthrow in March 1970 and his formation of an avowedly pro-communist exile regime (GRUNK) based in Peking, in May 1970, coincided with the beginning of a rapid increase of communist influence in Cambodia. During the winter of 1973-74 most GRUNK ministerial portfolios were transferred from exiled politicians (pro-Sihanouk and generally non-communist) to members of the anti-Lon Nol guerrilla forces in Cambodia. The latter by this time were generally pro-communist and had little or no grounds for personal loyalty to Sihanouk, who has, however, remained the figurehead chief of state of GRUNK.

Membership in the KCP is believed to have reached about 10,000 during its wartime expansion. The population of Cambodia is estimated at 7.6 million.

Leadership and Organization. The KCP and (since 17 April 1975) all of Cambodia are run by the Central Committee of the party. Although its membership is secret, press speculation has focused on a few individuals, most of them long active in left-wing political activities in Cambodia. Saloth Sar has been variously described as "chairman," "secretary-general," and "secretary" of the KCP. He probably played an important organizing role in the buildup of party membership during the war. He was born in 1928, took a radio technicians' course in France, married one of the elite Khieu sisters (the other married Ieng Sary), and entered the *maquis* in 1963. Despite his credentials, he is probably an unimpressive personality. The fact that he holds no GRUNK cabinet post may mean either that he is preoccupied with KCP affairs or that he is less able than some of his colleages—or both.

The three deputy premiers of GRUNK—Khieu Samphan, Ieng Sary, and Son Sen—are almost certainly members of the KCP Central Committee and probably the dominant political personalities in Phnom Penh. All are in their early forties, French-educated, and have been pro-communist or communist all their adult lives. They have also shared the rigors of life in the *maquis* for a number of years, and they probably feel that their personal survival, as well as that of their party and country, depends on their close collaboration. However, there are interesting differences in the backgrounds and probable political orientation of these three leaders.

Khieu Samphan was always one of the most outstanding members of his age group, since working his way through school and helping to support his widowed mother in Kompong Cham. Physically slight, morally ascetic, and brilliant, he earned scholarships that led to a doctorate in economics at the Sorbonne. In 1962 he was one of the outstanding young leftist deputies in the National Assembly to whom Sihanouk entrusted the government (to stifle their criticism and harness their energies). By 1966 their radical experiments with state control had brought the economy to a virtual standstill, and Sihanouk allowed older rightist elite members to regain control. He probably also approved police intimidation of the most prominent leftist intellectuals. Khieu Samphan and others (including Hou Yuon and Hu Nim, who are in the GRUNK cabinet and possibly the KCP Central Committee) were believed at the time to have been secretly executed. But they fled to the *maquis*, and played a well-publicized role as leaders of it during the war.

Khieu Samphan was publicly described as GRUNK defense minister and commander-in-chief of the "Cambodian Peoples National Liberation Forces" (CPNLF), a term for the anti-Lon Nol guerrilla army that journalists usually shortened to "Khmers rouges." In addition, he was named deputy premier of GRUNK. (Penn Nouth, Sihanouk's aging and very ill political adviser, retained the title of premier although he, like Sinahouk, spent the war years in Peking.)

In late spring 1974, Khieu Samphan made an extended tour of friendly nations, beginning with a lavish reception by Mao in Peking that seemed to put him on terms at least of equality with Sihanouk. This produced speculation that he was being groomed by the Chinese to replace or supplement Sihanouk as the focus for Chinese influence in Cambodia and Chinese orchestration of Third World support for the KCP struggle. His absence from Cambodia at a time when leftist military operations increased in tempo also made it obvious that he was not involved in day-to-day military command.

Khieu Samphan was favorably regarded, even by prominent officials of the Lon Nol regime, as a Khmer nationalist, a man of rare integrity, and an opponent of the Vietnamese. This also made him seem to some observers an ideal instrument of Chinese indirect influence in Cambodia. While there is no evidence that China has sought direct political control in Cambodia, denying such control to Hanoi is a probable Chinese objective. The fact that Sihanouk makes no bones about being non-communist—and his generally free-wheeling contacts with the Western press even during his exile in Peking—may well make many Chinese officials uncomfortable or even hostile toward him. Khieu Samphan, being younger and less well established on the world scene—and a genuine communist—may seem a more suitable instrument for Chinese influence.

Since 17 April 1975, Khieu Samphan has played a prominent but not preeminent role in the very limited public activity of the new government. He retained the title of vice-premier (now designated for "general affairs") in the August revision of the GRUNK cabinet. But Son Sen became vice-premier for "defense affairs," confirming the belief of some former officers of Lon Nol's army that he was the main military figure in the leftist camp. Son Sen subsequently began to figure more prominently in official announcements of government activities by Radio Phnom Penh.

Ieng Sary, named vice-premier for foreign affairs in August, has traveled to Peking and to the non-aligned nations conference in Lima (also in August) and in the following month attended the U.N. General Assembly. In November, he led a group to Bangkok and negotiated the reestablishment of bilateral economic and diplomatic relations.

Khieu Samphan also visited Peking in August, and went on to Pyongyang, where he evidently persuaded Sihanouk to make his first return visit to Phnom Penh since his overthrow in 1970. It is not known whether Khieu Samphan and Sihanouk now accept Mao's public admonition (in May

1974) that they must work together as comrades. It is unlikely that their deep and long-standing political and substantive differences can be bridged except by Sihanouk's willingness to play a very subordinate role. However, events since 17 April 1975 support the evidence of more than twenty years that both men are first and foremost Khmer nationalists.

The other two vice-premiers of GRUNK are comparatively unknown quantities. Son Sen was born in South Vietnam in 1930, Ieng Sary in southeastern Cambodia in the same year. Both are of "Khmer Krom" families (Khmers long domiciled in South Vietnam), which might make them more pro-Vietnamese than the average Cambodian. They both received some education in France (Ieng Sary after an undistinguished academic career in Phnom Penh). Ieng Sary probably owes his political affiliation and much of his prominence to his marriage to Khieu Thirith, daughter of a wealthy, leftist Phnom Penh family. She is now GRUNK minister of popular education and youth. Her sister married Saloth Sar, as noted above, and probably shaped his career as well.

Ieng Sary and Son Sen took to the *maquis* together in 1963 to escape arrest by Sihanouk's police. Ieng Sary subsequently visited Hanoi and formed close ties with Vietnamese communists. He went to Peking early in the 1970-75 war to "represent" the Khmer guerrillas and probably to watch Sihanouk on behalf of the pro-Vietnam faction (or simply on behalf of Hanoi). The prince was publicly outraged by Sary's efforts to monitor his contacts with the press; he said Sary was too much of a "Stalinist" for his taste, and evidently engineered his return to Cambodia in 1973. Sary subsequently accompanied Khieu Samphan on his extended tour abroad in 1974; some observers thought he was again serving as "watchdog" for the pro-Hanoi faction of the KCP.

If Ieng Sary is, or has been, a leading proponent of cooperation with the Vietnamese communists, this has not prevented him from making a number of official visits to Peking since 1970; nor did it prevent him from negotiating the terms of Cambodia's economic and diplomatic rapprochement with Bangkok in 1975. This action was fostered by Peking, which had just normalized its own relations with Thailand in an obvious effort to limit or counter Hanoi's influence in Southeast Asia. Peking loaned Cambodia the airplane in which Ieng Sary traveled to Thailand, and he was met at Bangkok's airport by the newly arrived Chinese ambassador to Thailand, who feted the Cambodians during their stay. The Thai-Cambodian rapprochement came at a time when Thai leaders publicly acknowledged that their efforts to normalize relations with Hanoi were at least suspended; Thai forces were engaged in small-scale clashes with Hanoi-supported Pathet Lao forces along the Mekong River border.

Further evidence that Ieng Sary is not Hanoi's puppet lies in the fact that many observers credit him with formulating the program for radical restructuring of Cambodian society that was implemented in occupied areas during the war and in the rest of Cambodia immediately after the 17 April communist victory. This program contrasts sharply with the approach taken by the Vietnamese communists in consolidating their victory in South Vietnam. There is no public evidence that Ieng Sary was, in fact, the architect of the more brutal Khmer communist approach—and he is known to have spent a large part of the war in Peking. Nevertheless, he explained and defended the Khmer communist program at the non-aligned conference in Lima in August. This at least indicates that he supports this very un-Vietnamese method of internal administration. However, it should be noted that Sihanouk's press attaché has described Ieng Sary as a "stooge of Hanoi" in an interview published in *Far Eastern Economic Review* (Hong Kong, 17 October; *FBIS*, 20 October). Sihanouk's extreme personal dislike of Sary might be a factor in this judgment.

Several other members of the GRUNK are almost certainly not members of the KCP Central Committee. Hence their influence over policy is based on other factors or is non-existent. First and foremost in this group is Prince Sihanouk himself. The prince was allowed by the KCP to visit Cambodian soil only once during the war, and he cautiously and reluctantly assumed the role of figurehead chief of state and roving ambassador after the war's end. Sihanouk's strongly negative reaction to the new KCP regime during his three-week visit to Phnom Penh (9-28 September) was described by his press attaché in the above-mentioned interview, which is interesting also because it alleges that Peking took a very dim view of the KCP's brutal efforts to reconstruct Cambodia.

Sihanouk's long-standing differences with the leftists were reportedly exacerbated by their failure to notify him formally in Peking of their 17 April victory and by their almost unpardonable failure to take note of the death of his mother, Queen Kossamak, eleven days later. In early May, Sihanouk went to North Korea. He may have been urged by Chinese leaders either to return to Cambodia or to go where he would have less access to foreign journalists. Apparently urged by Khieu Samphan, who visited him in Pyongyang in late August, he visited Phnom Penh in September. The day after his arrival, he presided over a GRUNK cabinet meeting, but reportedly was not allowed to speak. He and his small retinue were virtually confined to the royal palace during their stay; they went accompanied even in Phnom Penh and were allowed to go only ten miles outside the city. They reportedly found virtually no evidence of popular support for Sihanouk in their carefully limited contacts with the people.

In marked contrast with prewar days, Sihanouk delivered a brief and obviously prepared speech at a reception during his visit; the recorded speech was broadcast by Radio Phnom Penh a few days later. At the U.N. General Assembly, which he visited next, Sihanouk again delivered a written speech (this time of about 45 minutes' duration).

After next stopping in France for a meeting with President Giscard-d'Estaing, Sihanouk attended the National Day ceremonies in Peking, went to Pyongyang for the 30th anniversary of the Korean Workers' Party, and returned to Peking for his 53rd birthday on 31 October. He then embarked on a good-will visit to some twenty countries that had supported the Khmer leftist struggle. Meanwhile, most members of his wartime retinue in Peking had opted for residence in France or Great Britain.

Sarin Chhak was the first, and possibly the only, member of Sihanouk's wartime retinue in Peking who returned to Phnom Penh and assumed an important function there—as GRUNK foreign minister. A non-communist career diplomat of marked ability and scholarly bent, Sarin Chhak would undoubtedly be limited in his influence by the desire of Ieng Sary and possibly other communists to control foreign policy. Penn Nouth, who continued to hold the title of GRUNK premier, returned to Phnom Penh with Sihanouk in September. But he seemed excluded from power by his age (75), ill-health, and the fact he was non-communist and long identified with Sihanouk.

The list of prominent GRUNK personalities who might or might not be members of the KCP Central Committee is relatively long. Hou Yuon (Interior and Security and Communal Reform) and Hu Nim (Information and Propaganda) have backgrounds very similar to that of Khieu Samphan, with whom they fled to the *maquis* in early 1967. Prince Norodom Phurissara (Justice), Sihanouk's cousin, was regarded during the war as the main Sihanoukist in the GRUNK cabinet. Toch Phoen (Public Works, Telecommunications and Reconstruction) was named a member of the Liberation Committee for Phnom Penh during the war, as was Phurissara. This may suggest that both are non-communist.

Chou Chet (Religious and Social Affairs) was a member of the Central Committee of the Pracheachon, precursor of the KCP, and hence is almost certainly a communist. Thiounn Thioeun (Public Health) was a prominent surgeon before the war and is a member of a socially prominent though leftist family. Madame Ieng Thirith (Popular Education and Youth) has been involved in communist organizations since the early 1950s; married to Ieng Sary, she is now quite possibly a KCP Central Committee member. Chau Seng, one of the leading leftists in Sihanouk's entourage before the war, spent the war years mainly on his estate in France, although he sometimes held a GRUNK portfolio. It is conceivable that he might forego his luxurious life in France and return to Cambodia to try to find a place in the KCP hierarchy.

Other GRUNK cabinet members, who may possibly also be members of the KCP Central

Committee, are: Koy Thuon (Economy and Finance), Men San (Armaments and Military Equipment), Sok Thuok (vice-minister, Interior and Security), Kong Sophal (vice-minister, Defense), Tiv Ol (vice-minister, Information and Propaganda), and Ros Chetor and Van Piny (vice-ministers, Foreign Affairs).

Auxiliary and Mass Organizations. During the 1970-75 war, refugee reports indicated that the usual range of mass organizations (e.g., for peasants, women, students, and Buddhist monks) was created by the KCP to aid in the reconstruction of Cambodian society; this was the central non-military goal of the KCP during the war and is its main concern after military victory. There are not enough data to determine how important a role mass organizations have actually played in the process of reconstruction, though they have undoubtedly had some importance in transmitting the policies of the KCP Central Committee to the masses of ordinary people. Many refugees from KCP-controlled areas have reported that virtually their only contact with the new regime was with gun-wielding teen-age guerrillas and anonymous cadres, who lectured them on political subjects or on practical matters such as agriculture.

Party Internal Affairs. Because of the highly secretive nature of the KCP, virtually nothing has been published on its internal deliberations. For a discussion of the political views of particular leaders, based on circumstantial evidence, see earlier sections of this profile.

Domestic Attitudes and Activities. Following their military victory in April 1975, the communists extended their wartime program of reconstruction of Cambodian society to all portions of the country and population. The hallmarks of this program seem to be a ruthless indifference to popular sentiment, an urgent desire to implement sweeping social changes as rapidly as possible, and an ultimate aim of making Cambodia economically self-sufficient at a low level of consumption and hence independent of all other countries. In each of these respects, the Khmer communist approach has been the exact opposite of the one followed by Vietnamese communists in South Vietnam. In their relatively few statements to the outside world, the new Khmer regime has implicitly or explicitly affirmed this approach. At his press conference at the Lima meeting of non-aligned nations in August 1975, Ieng Sary defended his government's decision to force all urban dwellers to move to the country and clear new land. He said that it was necessary to move the people to available food supplies because there was not enough transport or fuel to move the food supplies to the towns.

Just how much food the GRUNK had succeeded in stockpiling in rural areas remains uncertain, as is their effectiveness in organizing the distribution of necessary commodities and basic health and educational services. A picture of extremely harsh and primitive living conditions and brutal punishments for disobedience toward cadres emerges from press reports of interviews with some of the more than 10,000 Khmer refugees in Thailand. Even assuming that these reports may give a somewhat exaggerated impression, it appears certain that Cambodia is being transformed into a highly regimented and puritanical society, run by a faceless elite for ends that it does not even deign to describe. In many ways, this reverses the prewar situation in which Sihanouk's benevolent autocracy barely touched the lives of the roral masses but somehow conveyed to them a feeling that they belonged to a protective, over-arching family. By so doing, Sihanouk was able to enlist the support of the rural masses against the less compliant urban elite.

International Views and Policies. Communist Cambodia leans toward China for much the same non-ideological reasons as did Sihanouk's prewar Cambodia. (Ideologically, Cambodia under KCP rule may be even harder for Peking to swallow than prewar neutralist Cambodia, which pursued Sihanouk's ersatz view of socialism. But China is just as anxious now as before the war to deny influence over Cambodia to Hanoi and Moscow.)

Cambodia's main foreign policy aim appears to be to avoid Vietnamese dominance or encroachment by maintaining good relations with China and correct relations with Bangkok, and by holding open the possibility of relations with other opponents of Vietnamese expansion. The possibility of Vietnamese encroachment, in the eyes of KCP leaders, is not merely a theoretical one. Vietnamese communist forces occupied extensive areas of Cambodia, particularly during the years 1970-72. During the war there were frequent reports of armed clashes, in eastern Cambodia and in the Gulf of Thailand, between Khmer and Vietnamese communist forces, and reports of such clashes have continued since.

The KCP regime received a Chinese mission shortly after seizing control of Phnom Penh. By the end of 1975 only China and North Vietnam, perhaps also North Korea, had embassies in Phnom Penh. GRUNK established diplomatic relations with more than 60 other countries during the war, but it has not as yet exchanged embassies with any of them.

Of some 60-odd countries that did not recognize or support GRUNK diplomatically during the war, many offered to recognize the new Khmer regime after 17 April; GRUNK acknowledged most of these offers, in some cases after long delay. Thailand was the only country—of the group that withheld recognition during the war—that Cambodia actually recognized during 1975. Liaison offices were established at the Thai-Cambodia border to facilitate trade (fuel and salt from Thailand, fish and timber from Cambodia, according to official announcements). But it was not expected that Thailand and Cambodia would exchange embassies in the near future. Nor, at the year's end, did France or Japan seem likely to reach agreement with Cambodia on an early reestablishment of relations.

There was even less sign that relations would soon be reestablished with the United States or with the USSR. The latter maintained its Embassy in Phnom Penh until 17 April, an affront that may have been compounded in the eyes of many KCP members by Moscow's support for Hanoi during and after the Indochina war. As for the United States, Sihanouk was met at the airport in New York, when he attended the U.N. General Assembly, by a U.S. deputy assistant secretary of state, a protocol gesture that seemed to please him. Although his General Assembly speech inevitably contained many references to "U.S. imperialism," it was delivered in a mild and relatively inoffensive tone. U.S. secretary of state Henry Kissinger spoke in general terms about the prospects for normalizing relations with Cambodia and Vietnam in his 24 November speech to the Economic Club of Detroit.

International Activities and Contacts. Ieng Sary's participation in the Lima conference of non-aligned nations in August and the U.N. General Assembly in September, and Sihanouk's participation in the U.N. General Assembly in October, have been noted above.

Publications. Radio broadcasts have formed by far the most important medium for official statements by the KCP organization—or rather by the Royal Government of National Union of Kampuchea, which carries out KCP policies. Prior to 17 April, GRUNK's statements were broadcast by the Hanoi government over transmitters on North Vietnamese territory. Since then, Radio Phnom Penh has been GRUNK's prime medium for making known its policies to the Khmer people (although it is believed that a lack of batteries for transistor radios has limited this form of communication). The two stations comprising Radio Phnom Penh are not powerful enough to reach far beyond Cambodia's borders. The broadcasts are intercepted by *FBIS*, which publishes selected items. Most broadcasts are in Khmer. The GRUNK Ministry of Information apparently does not issue a printed information bulletin as previous Cambodian regimes have done.

Legislative Assistant   Peter A. Poole
Washington, D.C.

China

The First Congress of the Chinese Communist Party (Chung-kuo kung-ch'an tang; CCP) was held in Shanghai in July 1921. Mao Tse-tung, the present party chairman, who turned 82 years of age in December 1975, was one of the twelve delegates known to have attended. The party celebrates its anniversary each 1 July.

The People's Republic of China (PRC) was established 1 October 1949. State organs and all other organizations of society are in all important respects provided leadership by the CCP, which is the sole legal party. The Tenth Party Constitution, adopted in 1973, makes this clear: "State organs, the People's Liberation Army (PLA) and the militia, labour unions, poor and lower-middle peasant associations, women's federations, the Communist Youth League, the Red Guards, the Little Red Guards and other revolutionary mass organizations must all accept the centralized leadership of the Party" (Chap. II, Art. 7; see *Peking Review*, 24 January, 1975, pp. 12-17).

The CCP is the largest communist party in the world. It had 28 million members as of August 1973, an increase of 11 million members since the previously reported figure of 17 million in 1961. The population of China was officially reported at the World Population Conference in Bucharest in August 1974 to be "nearly 800 million." This phrase was repeated by Premier Chou En-lai on 13 January 1975 (*Peking Review*, 24 January). The U.S. Central Intelligence Agency estimated the population to be 920 million in mid-1974 (*NYT*, 16 July). The Taipei *China News* reported that the PRC would conduct a new census in October 1975 (AFP, 22 August).

Organization and Leadership. According to the party constitution, the "highest leading body" of the CCP is the national party congress, which is to be convened every five years, although under often-invoked "special circumstances" the congress may be convened early or postponed. The party congress elects the Central Committee, which leads when the congress is not in session and which elects the Politburo, the Standing Committee of the Politburo, and the chairman and the vice-chairmen of the Central Committee. Membership in these high offices is said to embody the combination of the old, the middle-aged, and the young. This is meant to reflect a determination to have the three generations of leaders work together in a way that shows that while experience is still respected and utilized, there is in China "no lack of successors."

The Tenth Central Committee, elected at the party's most recent national congress, in August 1973, consists of 195 members and 124 alternate members (319 total). The previous Ninth Central Committee, elected in 1969, had 170 members and 109 alternates (279 total). Only 115 members of the Tenth Central Committee were newly seated; 204 members were continued from the previous committee. About 100 seats are said to be assigned to representatives of the masses, that is, outstanding workers, peasants, soldiers, and leaders of the recently reconstructed mass organizations. Some members of the Tenth Central Committee are rehabilitees who served on the Eighth Central Committee (elected in 1956) but not on the Ninth. Nine provincial leaders who were purged during the Great Proletarian Cultural Revolution (GPCR) are on the Tenth Central Committee. The committee has a greater representation of central government officials than did the Ninth, but their numbers are below levels known before the GPRC. Officials involved in foreign affairs are prominently present, including foreign minister Chiao Kuan-hua and former foreign minister Chi Peng-fei; the ambassador to the United Nations Huang Hua; the head of the PRC Liaison Office in Washington, D.C., Huang Chen; the head of the China-Japan Friendship Association, Liao Cheng-chih; and rehabilitated former vice foreign minister Wang Chia-hsiang.

Five vice-chairmen (Chou En-lai, Wang Hung-wen, Kang Sheng, Yeh Chien-ying, and Li Teh-sheng) were elected to the Tenth Central Committee in August 1973, although previously only one person had this office. Another vice-chairman, Teng Hsiao-ping, was elected in January 1975 at the Second Plenary Session of the Tenth Central Committee. It appears that Li Teh-sheng may have been removed as a vice-chairman as early as his transfer to Shenyang in early 1974. Given the age and frailty of Chou, Yeh, and Kang, among the vice-chairmen of the CCP only Wang and Teng appear to be in good health and fully active.

Effective policy-making power within the party rests with the Central Committee and, at higher levels, particularly the Politburo and its Standing Committee, both of which are elected by the Central Committee.

The members of the Politburo's Standing Committee are: Mao Tse-tung, Wang Hung-wen, Yeh Chien-ying, Chu Teh, Li Teh-sheng (who may have been removed from the Standing Committee), Chang Chun-chiao, Chou En-lai, Kang Sheng (deceased 16 December 1975), Tung Pi-wu (deceased 2 April 1975), and Teng Hsiao-ping (elected in January 1975). (Listed, with the exception of Teng Hsiao-ping, in the order of the number of strokes in their surnames, as are those following.)

The other members of the Politburo are Wei Kuo-ching, Li Po-cheng, Chiang Ching, Hsu Shih-yu, Hua Kuo-feng, Chi Teng-kuei, Wu Teh, Wang Tung-hsing, Chen Yung-kuei, Chen Hsi-lien, Li Hsien-nien, and Yao Wen-yuan. The alternate members are Wu Kuei-hsien, Su Chen-hua, Ni Chih-fu, and Saifudin. Sixteen of the above members of the Tenth Politburo had been on the previous Politburo; the three former alternates among them were promoted to full membership. Thus, the Politburo added to its ranks in August 1973 five new full members and four alternates. All of these had been on the Ninth Central Committee except for Su Chen-hua, a rehabilitee of the Eighth Central Committee. Three Politburo members are labor heroes: Chen Yung-kuei, head of the model Tachai Commune; Ni Chih-fu, a Peking worker-inventor; and Wu Kuei-hsien, a woman textile worker from Sian. Four of the new members are provincial party first secretaries.

Below the Central Committee there is a network of party committees at the provincial, special district, county and municipal levels. A similar network of party committees exists within the PLA, from the level of the military region down to that of the regiment. According to the party constitution, primary organizations of the party, or party branches, are located in factories, mines and other enterprises, people's communes, offices, schools, shops, neighborhoods, PLA companies and elsewhere as required.

Except within the PLA, the national structure of party organization was shattered in the course of the GPCR. Reconstruction began in late 1969 and by mid-August 1971 the last of the privincial-level party committees was reestablished. Reconstruction at the lower and intermediate levels was probably completed during 1973. The "revolutionary committees," which were created at all levels during the GPCR in order to provide leadership in the temporary absence of regular party and government organizations, have been confirmed as "permanent organs" of local government at various levels (and officially replacing the people's councils) by the new constitution of the PRC, released in January 1975. However, the revolutionary committees are now clearly subordinate to reconstituted party committees.

The long overdue Fourth National People's Congress (NPC) met in Peking on 13-17 January 1975. While the Third NPC had been held with great fanfare and lasted for three weeks in the winter of 1964-65, the Fourth NPC was unheralded (not even in the New Year's Day message two weeks earlier) and its session was short and secret. The meeting was preceded by the Second Plenary Session of the Tenth Central Committee on 8-10 January, which dealt with the final preparatory work of the impending NPC, and which submitted to it the draft revised text of the PRC constitution, a report on the revision of the constitution, a report on the work of the government, as well as lists of nominees for membership on the Standing Committee of the NPC and the State Council. This Plenary Session also elected Teng Hsiao-ping as a vice-chairman of the Central Committee and a member of the Politburo's Standing Committee.

Chairman Mao Tse-tung did not attend either the Second Plenary Session or the Fourth NPC. He received two visitors from abroad during the time of the meetings—Prime Minister Dominic Mintoff of Malta on 9 January and West German political leader Franz-Joseph Strauss on 16 January. This may have been the first time Mao ever missed a plenum of the Central Committee or an NPC. It is not clear that Mao's absence necessarily indicated disapproval of the decisions taken at the meetings. Only Politburo member Chi Teng-kuei, who was named a vice-premier at the meeting, two provincial first party secretaries, Wang Chia-tao of Heilungkiang and Hsieh Chen-hua of Shansi, and Mao's bodyguard Wang Tung-hsing were also absent. Otherwise the NPC was well attended by principal party luminaries. All provincial first party secretaries, except for the two above, attended. Ranking members of the provincial party committees of the four provinces without first party secretaries were in attendance. All eleven regional military commanders were present. In all, there were 2,864 delegates at the NPC.

The Fourth NPC finally terminated the anomalous constitutional situation which had prevailed ever since the GPCR. The 1954 PRC constitution had long been a dead document although it had never been officially rescinded or supplanted, something only a new NPC could do. The constitutional stipulation that annual sessions of the NPC be held was ignored for ten years. Also ignored had been the stipulation that a new NPC be elected every four years. In the meanwhile, a number of actions took place that were clearly extra-constitutional. Only the NPC had been empowered to elect and remove the chairman of the PRC and approve the members of the State Council as recommended by the premier. Nevertheless, since the GPCR there have been many personnel changes in government that did not receive the NPC's approval, although it could be that the Standing Committee of the Third NPC performed the necessary functions despite the fact that its legal term expired six years ago. It is known, however, that Liu Shao-chi was removed from all posts within and without the party by the Twelfth Plenum of the party's Eighth Central Committee in October 1968. Thus, the Fourth NPC in January cleared the air in a number of respects and conferred a new aura of legitimacy in Chinese government.

The NPC reaffirmed Chu Teh as chairman of the NPC Standing Committee, a post he has held since the Second NPC in 1959. Under Chu Teh are 22 vice-chairmen, all of whom are on the Tenth Central Committee. Three of these (former vice-premier Tan Chen-lin, Ulanfu of Inner Mongolia, and Li Ching-chuan, the former head of the Southwest Party Bureau), had not had a known position until now.

The Fourth NPC Standing Committee

Chairman:	Chu Teh	
Vice-chairmen:	Tung Pi-wu (deceased 2 April)	Tan Chen-lin
	Soong Ching Ling	Li Ching-chuan
	Kang Sheng	Chang Ting-cheng
	Liu Po-cheng	Tsai Chang
	Wu Teh	Ulanfu

Wei Kuo-ching	Ngapo Ngawang-Jigme
Saifudin	Chou Chien-jen
Kuo Mo-jo	Hsu Teh-heng
Hsu Hsiang-chien	Hu Chueh-wen
Nieh Jung-chen	Li Su-wen
Chen Yun	Yao Lien-wei

The NPC confirmed the new State Council, which reflects many changes since before the GPCR. Chou En-lai was reelected premier. Twelve vice-premiers were named, four less than the number approved by the Third NPC in 1965. Of the 16 pre-GPCR vice-premiers, only two have been retained—Teng Hsiao-ping and Li Hsien-nien. All but four of the vice-premiers are members or alternates of the Politburo. The only military man is Chen Hsi-lien, the Peking regional military commander, who is also a member of the Politburo.

The State Council

Premier: Chou En-lai

Vice-premiers:

Teng Hsiao-ping	Chen Yung-kuei
Chang Chun-chiao	Wu Kuei-hsien
Li Hsien-nien	Wang Chen
Chen Hsi-lien	Yu Chiu-li
Chi Teng-kuei	Ku Mu
Hua Kuo-feng	Sun Chien

Ministers	Ministries and Commissions
Chiao Kuan-hua	Foreign Affairs
Yeh Chien-ying	National Defense
Yu Chiu-li	State Planning Commission
Ku Mu	State Capital Construction Commission
Hua Kuo-feng	Public Security
Li Chiang	Foreign Trade
Fang Yi	Economic Relations with Foreign Countries
Sha Feng	Agriculture and Forestry
Chen Shao-kun	Metallurgical Industry
Li Shui-ching	First Ministry of Machine Building
Liu Hsi-yao	Second Ministry of Machine Building
Li Chi-tai	Third Ministry of Machine Building
Wang Cheng	Fourth Ministry of Machine Building
Li Cheng-fang	Fifth Ministry of Machine Building
Pien Chiang	Sixth Ministry of Machine Building
Wang Yang	Seventh Ministry of Machine Building
Hsu Chin-chiang	Coal Industry
Kang Shih-en	Petroleum and Chemical Industries
Chien Cheng-ying	Water Conservancy and Power
Chien Chih-kuang	Light Industry
Wan Li	Railways

Yeh Fei	Communications
Chung Fu-hsiang	Posts and Telecommunications
Chang Ching-fu	Finance
Fan Tzu-yu	Commerce
Yu Hui-yung	Culture
Chou Jung-hsin	Education
Liu Hsiang-ping	Public Health
Chuang Tse-tung	Physical Culture and Sports Commission

The 26 ministries and 3 commissions of the new State Council reflect the simplification and streamlining of administration that has taken place in the several years since the GPCR. Some of the streamlining came about as the result of combining ministries. Thus the Ministry of Petroleum and Chemical Industries (known for a while after the GPCR as the Ministry of Fuel and Chemical Industries) represents a merging of the three earlier ministries of Chemicals, Coal, and Petroleum. Among the pre-GPCR ministries not to be revived are those of Labor, Internal Affairs, and Allocation of Materials. The erstwhile Overseas Chinese Affairs Commission has not been resuscitated. Reemerging at the Fourth NPC were the Machine Building Ministries two through seven and the Ministries of Culture and of Education. No information was given on other groups or special agencies of the State Council if they still exist.

Of the 29 ministers, 16 are new at their posts, and of these only half have previously served in some capacity on the State Council. The new ministers are: Yeh Chien-ying, Hua Kuo-feng, Liu Hsi-yao,* Li Chi-tai, Pien Chiang,* Wang Yang, Hsu Chin-chiang,* Kang shih-en,* Chien Cheng-ying,* Wan Li, Yeh Fei, Chang Ching-fu,* Yu Hui-yung,* Chou Jung-hsin,* and Chuang Tse-tung (*Current Scene*, March-April; (the asterisk indicates previous formally acknowledged service with the State Council).

The year 1975 saw further consolidation of party control over the military. The new constitution passed by the Fourth NPC (Chap. I, Art. 15), states that "The Chinese People's Liberation Army and the people's militia are the workers' and peasants' own armed forces led by the Communist Party of China; they are the armed forces of the people of all nationalities." The new constitution also gives command of the armed forces to the chairman of the CCP Central Committee, in contrast to the previous constitution, which invested command in the chairman of the PRC, a post which itself was now eliminated. Mao Tse-tung, therefore, became the supreme commander of China's armed forces in 1975, a development which probably has more symbolic significance than substantive; it makes explicit the principle of party domination over the military.

Other significant changes in leadership took place. It was announced on 29 January that Teng Hsiao-ping had been made chief of staff of the PLA (in addition to his first vice-premiership in the State Council and his vice-chairmanship in the party (*NYT*, 30 January). The position of chief of staff of the PLA had been vacant since the former occupant, Huang Yung-sheng, dropped from sight in 1971. Given Teng Hsiao-ping's many responsibilities, it is likely that Yang Cheng-wu, the first of ten deputies, plays a key role. It was revealed inadvertently in a New China News Agency (NCNA) report in August that Wang Hung-wen is a deputy chairman of the party's important Military Affairs Commission (*NYT*, 2 August). The NCNA report was immediately withdrawn. It is of interest to note, additionally, that the Military Affairs Commission was mentioned at different times in 1975, and is active again after several years of apparent inactivity. Chang Chun-chiao, who ranks just behind Teng Hsiao-ping among the State Council's vice-premiers and who is also a member of the Politburo's Standing Committee, was also announced on 29 January to be the head of the General Political Department of the PLA. These new appointments, coupled with the remarkably few military appointments in the higher reaches of the party and the government, demonstrate a firming-up of the party's control over the military. Among the noted rehabilitees during the year was former chief of the general staff Lo Jui-ching, who had reportedly tried to commit suicide during the GPCR. He was present at the Army Day reception in Peking.

Perhaps reflecting the diminishing influence of the military in the party and government, China's defense spending continued to decline. An analyst for the CIA reported that "production and procurement of military hardware in 1972-74 [was] about 25 percent lower than during the peak period of 1970-71" and this drop apparently was "continuing in the first quarter of 1975" (*NYT*, 16 July). According to the same report, which was issued by the Joint Economic Committee of Congress, the Chinese "may be regarded as possessing the third military force in the world; even in the present reduced phase they devote one-tenth of their gross national product to military purposes. Yet they spend only one-fifth as much for equipment per man as the U.S. and the Soviet Union and only one-half as much as NATO." (*Christian Science Monitor*, 16 July.) The Chinese navy, however, has been developing apace, with coastal defense having been built-up threefold since the early 1960s. According to the International Institute for Strategic Studies in London, the Chinese navy is larger than the French and British navies combined. (*NYT*, 10 August.)

Among the deaths of notable figures was that of Li Fu-chun, a member of the Central Committee and former vice-premier of the State Council, on 9 January. Chairman Mao presented wreaths at the funeral on 16 January in Peking (interestingly placing Mao back in Peking before the conclusion of the Fourth NPC). Tung Pi-wu, aged 90, a founding member of the CCP, a member of the Politburo's Standing Committee and vice-chairman of the NPC's Standing Committee, died on 2 April. A prominent rehabilitee is Wang Ping-nan, a former deputy foreign minister during the GPCR, whose appointment as president of the People's Association for Friendship with Foreign Countries was announced in August (AP, Tokyo, 24 August).

The new PRC constitution that the Fourth NPC adopted in January 1975 is much shorter than the 1954 constitution that it replaced, containing only 30 articles, as against 106. It reflects many of the great changes that have taken place in the intervening 20 years. To begin with, it redefines the PRC as a "socialist state of the dictatorship of the proletariat" rather than as a "people's democratic state."

The new constitution eliminates the posts of PRC chairman and vice-chairman. As noted above, the function of commander in chief of the armed forces (which now specifically includes the people's militia) is vested in the chairman of the CCP (Art. 15).

The new Constitution defines more explicitly the relationship between the CCP and state organization. Article 16 states: "The NPC is the highest organ of state power under the leadership of the Communist Party of China." This contrasts with Article 21 of the 1954 constitution, which merely defined the NPC as "the highest organ of state authority in the PRC." Furthermore, the new constitution explicitly states that the exercise of its powers are "on the proposal of the Central Committee of the Communist Party of China" (Art. 17). Chang Chun-chiao in his report on the revised draft constitution explained: "All this will certainly help strengthen the party's centralized leadership over the structure of the state."

The new constitution endorses the "four big's," that is, "speaking out freely, airing views fully, holding great debates and writing big-character posters." It also sets conditions for such forms of expression: "The state shall ensure to the masses the right to use these forms to create a political situation in which there are both centralism and democracy, both discipline and freedom, both unity of will and personal ease of mind and liveliness, and so help consolidate the leadership of the Communist Party of China over the state and consolidate the dictatorship of the proletariat." (Art. 13.)

Article 27 guarantees the right of the people "to lodge complaints of transgression of law or neglect of duty on the part of any person working in an organ of state." It also warns that "No one shall attempt to hinder or obstruct the making of such complaints or retaliate." This warning is an innovation, not having been included in the earlier document.

The Preamble to the new constitution succinctly summarizes the current domestic and international line, extolling the CCP, the GPCR, Marxism-Leninism-Mao Tse-tung Thought, continued revolution, the three great revolutionary movements of class struggle, production, and scientific experimentation, and the building of socialism independently by means of self-reliance, hard work, diligence, and thrift. Internationally, the constitution declares that the PRC will "never be a superpower" and upholds proletarian internationalism, unity with socialist countries and all oppressed peoples, and the five principles of peaceful co-existence.

Chapter I of the constitution discusses basic social, cultural, and economic policies. It clarifies, and narrows, policy with regard to intellectual expression. For example, the 1954 constitution (Art. 95) at least theoretically safeguarded "the freedom of citizens to engage in scientific research, literary and artistic creation and other cultural pursuits." It went on: "The state encourages and assists creative work in science, education, literature, art and other cultural pursuits." The new constitution simply states: "The proletariat must exercise all-round dictatorship over the bourgeoisie in the superstructure, including all spheres of culture. Culture and education, literature and art, physical education, health work and scientific research work must all serve proletarian politics, serve the workers, peasants and soldiers, and be combined with productive labor." (Art. 12.)

With regard to national minorities, the 1954 constitution stipulated that "all nationalities have freedom to use and foster the growth of their spoken language and to preserve or reform their own customs or ways." The new constitution abridges this to read: "All the nationalities have the freedom to use their own spoken and written languages." Both "big-nationality chauvinism" and "local-nationality chauvinism" are denounced. (Art. 4.)

The country's movement towards socialism and collectivization are reflected in the new constitution, but the articles dealing with the economy are moderate, compared with the policies of the Great Leap Forward or the GPCR periods. Article 10 confirms the principles of "taking agriculture as the foundation and industry as the leading factor" as the basic policy for development. Article 9 says that the state applies the socialist principle: "He who does not work, neither shall he eat" and "from each according to his ability, to each according to his work." Article 5 declares that "there are mainly two kinds of ownership of the means of production at the present stage: Socialist ownership by the whole people and socialist collective ownership by working people." However, Article 9 "protects the citizens' right of ownership to their income from work, their savings, their houses, and other means of livelihood." No longer guaranteed is the right to individual ownership of means of production, or the right to inherit private property. Chang Chun-chiao, in his accompanying address, warned that in some enterprises "the form is that of socialist ownership, but the reality is that their leadership is not in the hands of Marxists and the masses of workers."

The rural communes are described as an organization which "integrates government administration and economic management," and confirms the continuation "at the present stage" of three-level ownership: commune, production brigade, and production team. The latter is the basic level and the basic accounting unit. Also condoned are "small plots," "limited household sideline production," and the keeping of a "small number of livestock" for personal needs, provided that the "development and absolute predominance of the collective economy are ensured." (Art. 7.) Chang Chun-chiao explained that these provisions "integrate the principle of adherence to socialism with the necessary flexibility and are sharply demarcated from such fallacies as those advocated by Liu Shao-chi and Lin Piao on the fixing of farm output quotas for individual households with each on its own and the abolition of farm plots for personal needs."

To freedom of speech, correspondence, the press, assembly, association, procession, and demonstration, Article 28 adds the freedom to strike, which Chang Chun-chiao stated was "in accordance with Chairman Mao's proposal." This article includes the freedom to believe in religion or not, and the freedom to propagate atheism.

Chapter II of the new constitution discusses the structure of the state, but has been reduced from 64 to 10 articles. The basic institutions of the NPC, State Council, and local and judicial organs are retained, but the description of their powers and functions is highly abbreviated. Then enumerated powers of the NPC are cut from 19 to 5, and the exercise of these is contingent upon recommendation by the party's Central Committee. The NPC's enumerated powers are "to amend the Constitution; make laws; appoint and remove the Premier and members of the State Council on the proposal of the Central Committee of the CCP; approve the national economic plan, the state budget and the final state accounts; and exercise such other functions and powers as the NPC deems necessary." The term of the NPC was increased from four years to five. It is to be convened annually.

The enumerated specific functions of the State Council were reduced from 17 to the following: to formulate administrative measures and issue decrees and orders; exercise leadership over ministries and commissions and local state organs; draft and implement the national economic plan and the state budget; and direct state administrative affairs. It is also to exercise such other functions and powers as are vested in it by the NPC or its Standing Committee. No longer listed specifically are functions relating to foreign and domestic trade, culture, educational and public health work, national minorities affairs, foreign affairs, guidance of the defense forces and protection of the interests of the state, maintenance of public order and the safeguarding of the rights of citizens. However, since there are ministries of the State Council which deal with such functions, there can be no particular significance to their omission from the constitution.

The Supreme People's Procuratorate is not mentioned in the 1975 constitution. Under the 1954 constitution, that organ exercised procuratorial functions over the State Council and local organs of state to ensure compliance with the law. The local procuratorial organs previously exercised "independent power, without the interference of local organs of state," and were responsible to the higher-level procuratorate. The new constitution indicates that the "functions and powers of procuratorial organs are exercised by the organs of public security at various levels." This obviously strengthens the Ministry of Public Security.

Mass organizations are a significant component of socio-political life in China, but they have not figured prominently in the news in either 1974 or 1975. Mass organizations had been very important from 1949 to GPCR, but were dismantled during that great upheaval. They were reconstructed largely in 1973, and again play their important roles. The Communist Youth League is involved in the educational system. The Women's Federation was active in the Criticize Lin, Criticize Confucius campaign. The trade unions are the most important of the mass organizations. This is seen in the large trade union representation in the Tenth Central Committee, in which they have one-ninth of the regular and one-sixth of the alternate membership. Twenty-two of the chairmen and vice-chairmen of the 28 known trade union committees are members of the Central Committee, and 19 are alternate members. Their top representative in the CCP is Wang Hung-wen, who is regarded as the number-three man of the party. This representation contrasts with that of the Women's Federation, which has only three top officers among its local committees who are members of the Central Committee, and only eight are alternate members. Of top officers from Communist Youth League local committees, seven are members of the Central Committee, and only one is an alternate member.

It appears that there is a concerted effort to bring women into junior leadership positions and this is seen in CCP recruitment and cadre promotion, and in trade union and Communist Youth League leadership changes. As the aging leadership is replaced, these junior-level women cadres will probably play an increasingly larger role (see Joan Maloney, "Women Cadres and Junior-Level Leadership in China," *Current Scene*, March-April 1975).

Domestic Party Affairs. The year 1975 was another marked by important campaigns. Continuing from 1974 was the Criticize Lin, Criticize Confucius campaign, which had reached high points of intensity in the late winter and summer of 1974, but which by early 1975 was apparently flagging. It would continue, however, through 1975. Suggestions of an impending Great Leap Forward-like spurt in economic activity that were heard in December 1974 were not followed up in 1975. The Fourth NPC provided a respite from movements in January. Premier Chou En-lai delivered to the NPC a "Report on the Work of the Government" (*Peking Review*, 24 January, pp. 21-25). Chou hailed the GPCR as the most important event in the past ten years of China's political life. He praised the three-in-one revolutionary committees, the proletarian revolution in literature and art exemplified by the model revolutionary theatrical works, which were "developing in depth," and the revolution in education and in health work, which was "thriving." Chou noted that cadres, workers, peasants, soldiers, students, and commercial workers were "persevering on the May 7th road." He said that more than a million barefoot doctors were "becoming more competent," and that nearly 10 million school graduates had gone to mountainous and other rural areas. The Marxist theoretical contingents were expanding, with the participation of workers, peasants, and soldiers. "The emergence of all these new things," Chou exclaimed, "has strengthened the all-round dictatorship of the proletariat over the bourgeoisie in the realm of the superstructure, and this further helps consolidate and develop the socialist economic base."

Chou spoke of the PRC's economic successes, and of the plans for the future. He said that the Third Five-Year Plan was overfulfilled and the Fourth Five-Year Plan would be successfully fulfilled in 1975. China had "won good harvests for thirteen years running." The total value of agricultural output was estimated to be 51 percent higher in 1974 than in 1964, "fully" demonstrating "the superiority of the people's commune." Chou held that while China's population had increased 60 percent since 1949, grain output increased 140 percent and cotton 470 percent. Gross industrial output for 1974 was estimated to be 190 percent more than 1964; steel increased 120 percent, coal 91 percent, petroleum 650 percent, electric power 200 percent, chemical fertilizer 330 percent, tractors 520 percent, cotton yarn 85 percent and chemical fibers 330 percent. He pointed out that through relying on "our own efforts" 1,000 big and medium-sized projects were completed, hydrogen bomb tests were successfully carried out, and man-made earth satellites were launched. He said that "in contrast to the economic turmoil and inflation of the capitalist world," the PRC maintained a balance between national revenue and expenditure and contracted no external or internal debts. He said that prices had remained stable, while the people's livelihood had steadily improved and socialist construction had flourished.

Chou recalled that on Mao's instructions it was suggested in the report on the work of the government to the Third NPC in 1964 that the PRC might envisage the development of the national economy in two stages, beginning from the Third Five-Year Plan: "The first stage is to build an independent and relatively comprehensive industrial and economic system in 15 years, that is before 1980; the second stage is to accomplish the comprehensive modernization of agriculture, industry, national defense and science and technology before the end of the century, so that our national economy will be advancing in the front ranks of the world." Chou said that the Fourth Five-Year Plan in 1975 should be fulfilled or over-fulfilled in order to reinforce the foundations for completing the first stage of this plan. The next ten years, then, "are crucial for accomplishing what has been envisaged for the two stages." Accordingly, Chou reported that the State Council will draw up a long-range ten-year plan, five-year plans, and annual plans, with this objective in mind. "In order to keep on expanding our socialist economy," Chou asserted, "we must persist in the general line of 'going all out, aiming high and achieving greater, faster, better and more economical results in building socialism' and continue to apply the policy of 'taking agriculture as the foundation and industry as the leading factor' and the series of policies of walking on two legs. We should work out the national economic plan in this order of priorities: agriculture, light industry, heavy industry. We should give full play to the initiative of both central and local authorities under the state's unified planning. We should implement the 'Charter of the Anshan Iron and Steel Company' still better and deepen the mass movements— 'In industry, learn from Taching' and 'In agriculture, learn from Tachai.' "

Chou discussed the international situation (see next section) and completed his report with a series of elaborated-upon quotations from Chairman Mao:

"Dig tunnels deep, store grain everywhere, and never seek hegemony." "Be prepared against war, be prepared against natural disasters, and do everything for the people."

"Practise Marxism, and not revisionism; unite, and don't split; be open and aboveboard, and don't intrigue and conspire."

"Of the seven sectors—industry, agriculture, commerce, culture and education, the Army, the government and the Party—it is the Party that exercises overall leadership."

Democratic centralism is to be practiced in order to achieve "unity in thinking, policy, plan, command and action."

The mass line is to be implemented persistently: "From the masses, to the masses."

"We should maintain the same vigor, the same revolutionary enthusiasm and the same daring death-defying spirit we displayed in the years of revolutionary war, and carry on our revolutionary work to the end."

Proletarian internationalism is to be upheld and China is to "get rid of great-power chauvinism resolutely, thoroughly, wholly and completely."

"Under the guidance of Chairman Mao's revolutionary line," Chou declared, "let us 'unite to win still greater victories! ' "

Chou's report had pointed up the importance of the Criticize Lin, Criticize Confucius campaign: "Our primary task is to continue to broaden, deepen and persevere" in it. However, while this campaign would continue through the year, a vigorous new campaign began in early February which was probably intended to provide firmer theoretical underpinnings for the Criticize Lin, Criticize Confucius campaign. An editorial in *People's Daily* (9 February), entitled to "Study Well the Theory of the Dictatorship of the Proletariat," revealed that Mao had recently given an instruction on the matter, pointing out: "Why did Lenin speak of exercising dictatorship over the bourgeoisie? This question must be thoroughly understood. 'Lack of clarity on this question will lead to revisionism. This should be made known to the whole nation.' " (*Peking Review*, 14 Febuary.) In addition to the study of the theory of the proletarian dictatorship, the new movement has criticized and sought to restrict "bourgeois right," meaning capitalist practices which continue to exist in China. Later in February, attention was focused on Mao's observation that China, even though it is a socialist country "practices an eight-grade wage system, distribution to each according to his work and exchange by means of money, which are scarcely different from those in the old society." Noting "it would be quite easy for people like Lin Piao to push the capitalist system if they [should] come to power," Mao warned against the revival of a bourgeois style of life in China. He quoted Lenin: "Small production engenders capitalism and the bourgeoisie continuously, daily, hourly, spontaneously, and on a mass scale" Mao declared: "Both within the ranks of the proletariat and among the personnel of state organs there are people who follow the bourgeois style of life." ("Marx, Engels and Lenin on the Dictatorship of the Proletariat," ibid., 28 February.)

Mao's sentiments were echoed in well-publicized articles by two prominent leaders who have generally been regarded among his closest supporters. Politburo member Yao Wen-yuan, in an article,

"On the Social Basis of the Lin Piao Anti-Party Clique," in the third number of *Red Flag* strongly attacked bourgeois tendencies and their practitioners. In the next number, higher-ranking Chang Chun-chiao wrote an essay, "On Exercising All-Round Dictatorship over the Bourgeoisie," which struck a particularly telling blow at the Soviet leadership, saying that while the post-Stalin leaders have had a good class background, their subsequent betrayal of their own class "accomplished what Hitler tried but failed to accomplish." Chang was making the point—not only to the Russians, but also to his domestic audience—that the importance of technocratic competence should not be overestimated. Both Yao and Chang spoke of the need for gradual change in the system of collective ownership, and of the need to eradicate corruption and back-sliding among cadres and young persons. These were the principal pronouncements of the campaign, which, however, continued with numerous articles throughout the year.

One aspect of the campaign—the discouragement of wage incentives—may have contributed to labor unrest that became widespread in some areas and threatened production. How the unrest began is unclear, but it was not resolved without some difficulty. Apparently a visit by Wang Hung-wen was insufficient to settle factional differences in Hangchow. Subsequently, some 10,000 troops were distributed among 18 Hangchow factories in July and August (*NYT*, 12 August). Teng Hsiao-ping reportedly visited Hangchow, and there was a shake-up in the administrations of both Hangchow and Chekiang province (Leo Goodstadt, *Far Eastern Economic Review* [*FEER*], Hong Kong, 29 August). Strikes and disturbances were reported in Heilungkiang and special measures were implemented to protect railroads in some areas in the early part of the year.

Early September saw the beginning of yet another campaign, apparently to reinforce the other continuing movements. This campaign featured criticism of the popular old 14th century novel, the *Shui Hu Chuan* or *Water Margin* (translated into English as *All Men Are Brothers* by Pearl Buck). Mao's instructions of 4 September indicated that *Water Margin* portrays capitulation, and serves as teaching material by negative example. Mao explained that the heroes of the novel were against corruption, but not the emperor. Sung Chiang, the principal hero, pushes "capitulationism, practises revisionism . . . and accepts the offer of amnesty and enlistment." A *People's Daily* editorial (4 September) stated: "This is another struggle of great importance on our country's political and ideological front and is a component part in the implementation of Chairman Mao's important directives on studying theory and combating and preventing revisionism; it will give a powerful impetus to deepening the study of the theory of the dictatorship of the proletariat." (*Peking Review*, 12 September).

The *Water Margin* campaign scanned a number of targets, but it too seemed to be concentrating on those who desire an immediate improvement in living standards. Such improvement would have to be at the expense of the national plan to finance new investments, which it is hoped will double national income between 1976 and 1980. Thus the campaign was addressed basically to the various interest-based factions which reflect such short-term aspirations. Related to this, it has been said that another major purpose of the campaign was to strengthen the national will against possible Soviet sabre-rattling (Leo Goodstadt, *FEER*, 19 September). Leo Goodstadt reported that Peking has sought to mollify disgruntled workers by means of a three-pronged strategy: (1) tougher management and a refusal to allow violations of factory rules and regulations; (2) encouragement of more direct worker participation in management (in 1975 "workers' management groups" were again highly visible in factories); and (3) improved welfare and facilities as a substitute for higher wages. (Ibid.)

International Views and Positions. "Chairman Mao's revolutionary line in diplomacy" continued to be implemented successfully in 1975. This outwardly oriented policy began in May 1969 and is in contrast to the diplomacy of the GPCR period, in the course of which ambassadors were withdrawn from all posts except Cairo. Diplomatic relations were established with eight more countries in 1975, and with the fall of both Phnom Penh and Saigon, the new formally installed regimes there are henceforth listed among the nations with whom the PRC has diplomatic relations. There are now diplomatic ties with 103 countries. The PRC also extended recognition to newly independent Papua New Guinea on 16 September, and an agreement was reached on 10 May for the establishment of official relations with the European Economic Community (Common Market). The accompanying three tables provide a comprehensive overview of China's diplomatic relationships:

I.   Countries which established diplomatic relations with China before 1970, exclusive of those which later suspended relations (44):

Afghanistan	Iraq	Southern Yemen (P.D.R.)
Albania	Kenya	Sri Lanka
Alberia	Korea (North)	Sudan
Bulgaria	Laos	Sweden
Burma	Mali	Switzerland
Congo	Mauritania	Syria
Cuba	Mongolia	Tanzania
Czechoslovakia	Morocco	Uganda
Egypt	Nepal	USSR
Finland	Netherlands	United Kingdom
France	Norway	Vietnam (North)
Germany (East)	Pakistan	Yemen Arab Republic
Guinea	Poland	Yugoslavia
Hungary	Romania	Zambia
India	Somalia	

II. Countries which have established diplomatic relations with China since 1970, listed chronologically with date of establishment of diplomatic relations (or, in the cases of Cambodia and South Vietnam the date of capture of Phnom Penh and Saigon respectively) (59):

Canada	13 October 1970	Malagasy Republic	6 November 1972
Equatorial Guinea	15 October 1970	Luxembourg	16 November 1972
Italy	6 November 1970	Zaire	19 November 1972
Ethiopia	3 December 1970	Jamaica	21 November 1972
Chile	15 December 1970	Chad	28 November 1972
Nigeria	10 February 1971	Australia	21 December 1972
Kuwait	22 March 1971	New Zealand	22 December 1972
Cameroon	26 March 1971	Dahomey (resumed)	29 December 1972
Austria	26 May 1971		(first est. 12 Nov. 1964)
Sierra Leone	29 July 1971	Spain	9 March 1973
Turkey	4 August 1971	Upper Volta	15 September 1973
Iran	16 August 1971	Guinea-Bissau	15 March 1974
Belgium	25 October 1971	Gabon Republic	20 April 1924
Peru	2 November 1971	Malaysia	31 May 1974
Lebanon	9 November 1971	Trinidad and Tobago	20 June 1974
Rwanda	12 November 1971	Venezuela	28 June 1974
Senegal	7 December 1971	Niger	20 July 1974
Iceland	8 December 1971	Brazil	15 August 1974
Cyprus	12 January 1972	Gambia	17 December 1974
Mexico	14 February 1972	Botswana	6 January 1975
Argentina	19 February 1972	Cambodia	17 April 1975
Malta	25 February 1972		(capture of Phnom Penh)
Ghana (resumed)	29 February 1972,	South Vietnam	30 April 1975
	(first est. 5 July 1960)		(capture of Saigon)
Mauritius	15 April 1972	Philippines	9 June 1975
Netherlands (resumed)	16 May 1972,	Thailand	1 July 1975
	(first est. 19 Nov. 1954)		

Greece	5 June 1972	Sao Tome and	
Guyana	27 June 1972	Principe	12 July 1975
Togo	19 September 1972	Bangladesh	4 October 1975
Japan	29 September 1972	Fiji	5 November 1975
Germany (West)	11 October 1972	Comoros	13 November 1975
Maldives	14 October 1972	Western Samoa	15 November 1975

III.   Countries which have diplomatic relations with Taiwan (28):

Barbados	Liberia
Bolivia	Libya
Central African Republic	Malawi
Columbia	Nicaragua
Costa Rica	Panama
Dominican Republic	Paraguay
El Salvador	Portugal
Guatemala	Saudi Arabia
Haiti	South Africa
Honduras	Swaziland
Ivory Coast	Tonga
Jordan	United States
Korea (South)	Uruguay
Lesotho	Vatican

Again in 1975, despite the phenomenon of intensive ideological campaigns and indications of scattered strikes and discord earlier in the year, a steady succession of important dignitaries and many others continued to visit the PRC. U.S. visitors included President Gerald Ford in early December, Secretary of State Henry Kissinger on his eighth visit in October and his ninth in December, a 15-member Congressional delegation led by Representatives Carl Albert and John Rhodes in late January and February, a Congressional delegation led by Senators Charles Percy and Jacob Javits in early August, and yet another, led by Representative John B. Anderson, in mid-August. Other prominent foreign government visitors included the presidents of North Korea, the Philippines, Gambia, Gabon, Yugoslavia, West Germany, Burma and Sao Tome and Principe; the vice-president of Iraq; the prime ministers of Malta, Trinidad and Tobago, Republic of the Congo, Guyana, Tunisia, Belgium, and Cambodia; the deputy prime ministers of Romania, North Vietnam, and Cambodia; the foreign ministers of the Netherlands, Zambia, Singapore, Morocco, Lesotho, Australia, Thailand, Guinea-Bissau, Burma, and Rwanda; the vice foreign minister of El Salvador; and such other luminaries as Franz-Josef Strauss, chairman of the West German Christian Social Union (in January and again in September); the presidents of the Liberation Front of Mozambique and of the African National Congress of South Africa; the general commander of the National Union for Total Independence of Angola; the vice-president of the Commission of the European Economic Community; Prince Norodom Sihanouk of Cambodia; former prime minister Edward Heath of Great Britain; and the wife of the président of the Republic of Mali. Mao's continuing support for this kind of diplomacy was suggested by his having met with no less than 19 of these visitors and delegations during the year (19 in 1974).

China's international trading pattern continued to reflect its expanding and intensifying global relationships. (Because of the delay in receiving statistics we shift our focus primarily to the previous year.) In 1974 the PRC's foreign trade continued to experience growth, but was bedeviled by the effects of world-wide inflation and recession. The PRC's total trade rose from US$9,870 million in 1973 to US$13,705 million in 1974. However, it is estimated that real growth probably accounted for only one-third to one-half of the increase in dollar value, the remainder being attributable to price inflation and adjustments in exchange rates. The terms of trade deteriorated greatly and unex-

Table I
PRC Foreign Trade
(US$ Million)

	Total Trade	Exports	Imports	Balance
1950	1,210	620	590	+ 30
1955	3,035	1,375	1,660	− 285
1960	3,990	1,960	2,030	− 70
1965	3,880	2,035	1,845	+ 190
1970	4,290	2,050	2,240	− 190
1971	4,720	2,415	2,305	+ 110
1972	5,920	3,085	2,835	+ 250
1973	9,870	4,895	4,975	− 80
1974	13,705	6,305	7,400	−1,095

Non-Communist

	Total Trade	Exports	Imports	Balance
1950	860	410	450	− 40
1955	785	425	360	+ 65
1960	1,370	625	745	− 120
1965	2,715	1,385	1,330	+ 55
1970	3,430	1,570	1,860	− 290
1971	3,635	1,830	1,805	+ 25
1972	4,645	2,345	2,300	+ 45
1973	8,170	3,900	4,270	− 370
1974	11,405	4,935	6,470	−1,535

Communist

	Total Trade	Exports	Imports	Balance
1950	350	210	140	+ 70
1955	2,250	950	1,300	− 350
1960	2,620	1,335	1,285	+ 50
1965	1,165	650	515	+ 135
1970	860	480	380	+ 100
1971	1,085	585	500	+ 85
1972	1,275	740	535	+ 205
1973	1,700	995	705	+ 290
1974·	2,300	1,370	930	+ 440

pectedly, with imports of US$7.4 billion outdistancing exports of US$6.3 billion. This caused the balance of trace deficit to mushroom from US$80 million in 1973 to US$1,095 million in current dollar terms. Japan remained the PRC's first-ranking trade partner in 1974, and the United States remained in second place. In 1974 the direction of PRC trade continued to favor the developed non-communist countries over Hong Kong, the less developed countries, and the socialist world. Petroleum exports to non-communist countries amounted to 8 percent of China's exports by value, represented an increase from one percent in 1973, but these earnings offset weak foreign demand for

Table II
Major Trading Partners

Country	Total Trade (US$ million)		Rank		
	1974	1973	1974	1973	1972
Japan	3,330	2,021	1	1	1
United States	1,070	876	2	2	11
Hong Kong	895	796	3	3	2
West Germany	650	487	4	4	4
Canada	575	409	5	6	3
Malaysia/Singapore	550	460	6	5	6
Australia	465	247	7	10	12
France	345	231	8	11	10
United Kingdom	330	340	9	7	8
Romania	300	265	10	9	7
USSR	280	272	11	8	5
Italy	220	196	12	12	9

traditional exports rather than provided an increase in export revenues. There was an increase in machinery and equipment in PRC imports in 1974.

The accompanying three tables provide a useful overview of the PRC's trading picture since 1950, a listing of major trading partners in 1972-74, and an analysis of trade by area and country for 1973 and 1974 (source: *Current Scene*, vol. XII, no. 12, December 1974, for 1950-73 data, and vol. XIII, no. 9, September 1975).

Although the PRC has been adversely affected by world-wide inflation, it has been successful, as noted in Chou En-lai's address at the Fourth NPC in January, in avoiding that problem within the country. In order to ensure that domestic market prices are not influenced by price fluctuations internationally, the PRC has persisted in differentiating prices in domestic and foreign trade. It has "cut the links between prices on the domestic and foreign markets by fixing different prices for each" (*Peking Review*, 10 October, p. 9). The domestic economy continues to improve, again as described in Chou En-lai's report, and this continues to assure the PRC an ever stronger position vis-à-vis the global economic situation.

During the first half of 1975 it was reported that PRC industrial output continued to pick up momentum, rising by an estimated 9 to 11 percent over the same period in1974. The development of the petroleum industry, which is generally regarded as a major asset in China's future trading plans, continued to figure prominently. Crude oil output was up 24 percent in the first half of 1975 over the same period in 1974, and this figure is close to the long-run growth rate. It was estimated that if the established trend continued, the production figure for all of 1975 should surpass 80 million tons. (*Current Scene*, October, pp. 8-9). Selig Harrison, of the Carnegie Endowment for International Peace, concluded on the basis of a year-long study, that China might rival Saudi Arabia as an oil producer by 1988 or soon thereafter. As China develops its oil potential, Japan's dependence on oil imports presumably will shift from the Middle East to China. (*NYT*, 4 September.)

The PRC's increasing role in international relations, shored up as it is by an improving domestic economy, appears to be, in practice, a stabilizing element in the world. As noted above, military influence in on the decline in China and defense spending has continued to decline. On the other

Table III
China: Trade by Area and Country
(US$ Million)
(Chinese Exports FOB; Imports CIF)

	Total	Exports	Imports	Balance	Total	Exports	Imports	Balance
Total	9,870	4,895	4,975	− 80	13,705	6,305	7,400	−1,095
Non-Communist countries	8,170	3,900	4,270	− 370	11,405	4,935	6,470	−1,535
Developed Countries	5,260	1,805	3,455	−1,650	7,665	2,375	5,290	−2,915
Japan	2,020	925	1,095	− 170	3,330	1,245	2,085	− 840
Western Europe	1,690	665	1,025	− 360	2,170	820	1,350	− 530
United States	875	65	810	− 745	1,070	115	955	− 840
Canada	410	55	355	− 300	575	60	515	− 455
Australia and New Zealand	265	95	170	− 75	520	135	385	− 250
Less-developed countries	2,075	1,270	805	+ 465	2,810	1,650	1,160	+ 490
Southeast Asia	825	660	165	+ 495	855	660	195	+ 465
Near East and South Asia	450	260	190	+ 70	760	440	320	+ 120
Africa	470	285	185	+ 100	610	420	190	+ 230
Latin America	300	45	255	− 210	530	90	440	− 350
Southern Europe[a]	30	20	10	+ 10	55	40	15	+ 25
Hong Kong and Macau	835	825	10	+ 815	930	910	20	+ 890
Communist countries	1,700	995	705	+ 290	2,300	1,370	930	+ 440
Far East	480	355	125	+ 230	735	580	155	+ 425
USSR	270	135	135	− −	280	140	140	− −
Eastern Europe[b]	605	305	300	+ 5	660	345	315	+ 30
Other Communist countries[c]	345	200	145	+ 55	625	305	320	+ 15

Note: Data are rounded to the nearest US$5 million. The statistics are adjusted to show China's imports CIF and exports FOB. Data for 1974 are preliminary.

[a] Spain, Portugal, Malta, and Greece.   [b] Excluding Albania and Yugoslavia.   [c] Albania, Yugoslavia, and Cuba.

hand, there are uncertain implications in the ideological campaigns that dominate China, and there remains the oft-repeated sentiment expressed by Chou En-lai at the Tenth Party Congress in August 1973 that "Relaxation is a temporary and superficial phenomenon, and great disorder will continue." Chou's report at the Fourth NPC in January continued this theme:

> The present international situation is still characterized by great disorder under heaven, a disorder which is growing greater and greater. The capitalist world is facing the most serious economic crisis since the war, and all the basic contradictions in the world are sharpening. On the one hand, the trend of revolution by the people of the world is actively developing; countries want independence, nations want liberation, and the people want revolution—this has become an irresistible historical current. On the other hand, the contention for world hegemony between the two superpowers, the United States and the Soviet Union is becoming more and more intense. Their contention has extended to every corner of the world, the focus of their contention being Europe. Soviet social-imperialism "makes a feint to the east while attacking in the west." The two superpowers, the United States and the Soviet Union, are the biggest international oppressors and exploiters today, and they are the source of a new world war. Their fierce contention is bound to lead to world war some day. The people of all countries must get prepared. Detente and peace are being talked about everywhere in the world; it is precisely this that shows there is no detente, let alone lasting peace, in this world. At present, the factors for both revolution and war are increasing. Whether war gives rise to revolution or revolution prevents war, in either case the international situation will develop in a direction favourable to the people and the future of the world will be bright.
>
> We should continue to implement Chairman Mao's revolutionary line in foreign affairs, always keep the people in mind, place our hopes on them and do our external work better. We should uphold proletarian internationalism and strengthen our unity with the socialist countries and all the oppressed people and oppressed nations of the world, with each supporting the other. We should ally ourselves with all the forces in the world that can be allied with to combat colonialism, imperialism and above all superpower hegemonism. We are ready to establish or develop relations with all countries on the basis of the Five Principles of Peaceful Coexistence.
>
> The third world is the main force in combating colonialism, imperialism and hegemonism. China is a developing socialist country belonging to the third world. We should enhance our unity with the countries and people of Asia, Africa and Latin America and resolutely support them in their struggle to win or safeguard national independence, defend their state sovereignty, protect their national resources and develop their national economy. We firmly support the just struggles of the people of Korea, Viet Nam, Cambodia, Laos, Palestine and Africa. We support the countries and people of the second world in their struggle against superpower control, threats and bullying. We support the efforts of West European countries to get united in this struggle. We are ready to work together with the Japanese Government and people to promote friendly and good-neighbourly relations between the two countries on the basis of the Sino-Japanese Joint Statement. (*Peking Review*, 24 January, p. 24.)

Relations with the Soviet Union. Sino-Soviet relations remained tense and bitter in 1975. Except for a Soviet greeting on 1 October calling for normalization of relations, there was no real follow-up to the apparent conciliatory gestures of late 1974. Although there continued to be certain minimal kinds of normal relationships, the overall relationship would have to be characterized as hostile. Chou En-lai's report to the Fourth NPC in January summarized the basic differences:

> The Soviet leading clique have betrayed Marxism-Leninism, and our debate with them on matters of principle will go on for a long time. However we have always held that this debate should not obstruct the maintenance of normal state relations between China and the Soviet Union. The Soviet leadership have taken a series of steps to worsen the relations between the two countries, conducted subversive activities against our country and even provoked armed conflicts on the border. In violation of the understanding reached between the Premiers of China and the Soviet Union as early as 1969, they refuse to sign the agreement on the maintenance of the status quo on the border, the prevention of armed conflicts and the disengagement of the armed forces of the two sides in the disputed areas on the border, an agreement which includes the non-use of force against each other and mutual non-aggression. Hence the negotiations on the Sino-Soviet boundary question have so far yielded no results. They even deny the existence of the disputed areas on the Sino-Soviet border, and they even refuse to do anything about such matters as the

disengagement of the armed forces of the two sides in the disputed areas on the border and the prevention of armed conflcits; instead they talk profusely about empty treaties on the non-use of force against each other and mutual non-aggression. So what can their real intention be if not to deceive the Soviet people and world public opinion? We wish to advise the Soviet leadership to sit down and negotiate honestly, do something to solve a bit of the problem and stop playing such deceitful tricks. (Ibid., pp. 24-25.)

It is clear that the Chinese are not taking the possibility of an attack from the Soviet Union lightly, hence all the underground bomb shelters which have been excavated over the past several years and the new diplomacy which has won support for the PRC throughout the world. Concern was expressed especially in July over the staging of large-scale maneuvers by Soviet troops in Mongolia close to the Chinese border, in conjunction with unprecedentedly large exercises by the Soviet Pacific Fleet in the East China Sea. (*FEER*, 18 July). For its part, according to *Aviation Week and Space Technology*, China deployed two intercontinental ballistic missiles in western China, capable of reaching Moscow and other key Soviet targets with three megaton nuclear warheads (UPI, Washington, D.C., 14 October). The PRC launched its third earth satellite on 26 July (*Current Scene*, July-August).

The Chinese lost few opportunities during the year to castigate the Soviet leadership in the harshest terms. Although both superpowers, the United States and the Soviet Union, were regularly taken to task for various policies, the criticism of the Soviet Union was the sharper. For example, both countries were criticized for continuing to "pay lip-service to disarmament to deceive people while stepping up the nuclear arms race," but the Soviet Union was said to show "a great zeal for this" (*Peking Review*, 18 July, p. 14). "As in their contention in other parts of the world," it was said, the stance of the Soviet Union in Latin America was "an offensive one, with the United States making every effort to keep it out of the Western Hemisphere while looking for a chance to strike back" (ibid., p. 12). With regard to the joint U.S.-Soviet space program (the "handshake in space" linking-up of the Apollo and Soyuz missions), the Chinese charged that Moscow "tries to cover up its intensified contention for hegemony on earth with superficial 'detente in space' " (ibid., 1 August, p. 9). Also: "To contend with U.S. imperialism in its bid for hegemony and to explore the cosmic space for the purpose of arms expansion and war preparations and carrying out espionage activities, Soviet revisionism has invested vast sums of money and huge amounts of manpower and materials in this field. This has resulted in a still more lopsided development of the already bleak Soviet national economy beset with difficulties, imposed heavier burdens on the people which caused discontent among them." (Ibid., 25 July, p. 7.) On the European situation: "Facts show that over the past few years since preparations started for the 'security conference,' the intensity of Soviet-U.S. rivalry in Europe has increased and their war preparations [have become] more frenzied. In this desperate struggle the Soviet Union generally is on the offensive while its rival, the United States, more often than not, finds itself at the receiving end." (Ibid., 8 August, p. 9.) On Cyprus: "The past year has witnessed the most odious manoeuvres by the two superpowers around the Cyprus question. The performance by the men who run the Kremlin is particularly disgusting." (Ibid., 25 July, p. 9). On the Third World: "Like the other superpower, Soviet social-imperialism is a super-exploiter of the third world. . . . The Soviet revisionists, who style themselves as the 'natural ally' of the developing countries, are actually loan sharks, the most merciless exploiters." (Ibid., 15 August, p. 25.) On Southeast Asia: "Now that the United States has readjusted its strategy in Asia following its defeat in and withdrawal from Indochina, the Soviet Union is making a fresh attempt to step into the shoes of the United States and establish hegemony in Southeast Asia" (ibid., p. 20).

Where direct comparisons with the United States were lacking, Chinese criticism of Soviet policies was even harsher. Some examples: "The Brezhnev clique is following Hitler's beaten track. Compare their words and deeds with Hitler's and you can see that the Soviet revisionists not only indulge in a Hitler-like pipe dream to rule the world, but behave in an astonishingly similar manner to achieve this wild ambition. [However,] earth-shaking changes have taken place in the world since that time. Following in Hitler's footsteps, the Brezhnev clique, another paper tiger, will come to an end worse than Hitler's." (Ibid., 18 July, pp. 4-6). "By jacking up the prices of raw materials and fuel sold to other CMEA [Council for Mutual Economic Assistance] member states, the Soviet revisionists are clearly making profits at the expense of others, and yet they use such claptrap as 'it is in the interest of all' to deceive people" (ibid., 25 July, p. 11). "Aggression, intervention, bullying, attempts at control and subversion—such are the counter-revolutionary activities the Soviet social-imperialists carry out day in and day out against third world countries. In speeches, statements and official documents, however, they are sweet reasonableness itself, saying only the nicest things but never speaking the truth. This is just what Soviet revisionism's 'aid' to the third world countries amounts to—honey on its lips and murder in its heart." (Ibid., 1 August, p. 14.) "To realize their aim of controlling Angola, the Soviet social-imperialists have resorted to the most despicable tactics—sowing dissension and creating splits among the liberation organizations" (ibid., p. 8).

For their part, the Russians lost few opportunities to assail the Chinese leadership. *Pravda* denounced the PRC's new constitution as a serious infringement of the rights and freedoms of Chinese citizens and proof that in China democracy is "grossly flouted." It also criticized the institutionalization of current Soviet-Chinese hostility in the new document. (AP, Moscow, 5 February.) On the campaign begun in February to study the theory of the dictatorship of the proletariat, Soviet editorialists charged that its call to "restrict bourgeois rights" would "victimize the entire Chinese people," and averred that the campaign was aimed at "consolidating the Maoist military bureaucratic dictatorship" (AFP, Moscow, 12 June). The charge was made that Mao Tse-tung "was a real Marxist" (AP, Moscow, 4 June). Soviet diplomats stalked out of a banquet for visiting Yugoslav president Džemal Bijedić in Peking following Teng Hsiao-ping's remark that the Soviet Union was "the most dangerous source of war." The Russians were joined in the walkout by Czech, Hungarian, Polish, Bulgarian, East German, and Mongolian envoys; the representatives of North Korea, Romania, Albania, Cuba, and North and South Vietnam kept their seats. (AP, Tokyo, 7 October.) A month later, the Chinese ambassador to the Soviet Union walked out on the military parade marking the 58th anniversary of the October Revolution when defense minister Andrei Grechko attacked the Chinese leadership (AP, Moscow, 7 November).

Despite all of these indications of mutual hostility, the chief Soviet delegate to the Sino-Soviet border talks was in Peking between 13 February and 5 May, during which time talks were presumably continued. On 24 July the PRC and the Soviet Union signed in Moscow a goods exchange and payments agreement for 1975 (*Current Scene*, July-August).

Relations with the United States. During 1975 the Sino-American relationship continued on the less-than-normal diplomatic basis which characterizes it, with some strains here and there. On the whole the relationship remained intact and seemed to strengthen somewhat near the end of the year with President Gerald Ford's visit to Peking. Throughout the year the United States received its share of rhetorical criticism as one of the two superpowers, though, as we have seen, this criticism was somewhat lighter than that directed toward the Soviet Union. The concern expressed over the Taiwan issue in late 1974 as being a major barrier to a continuation of improving relations was not seriously pursued in 1975. On the U.S. side, however, Senate majority leader Mike Mansfield called for removal of the 5,000 U.S. troops on Taiwan (AP, Washington, 3 February). The report issued in November by Senator Charles Percy's delegation to China indicated that full diplomatic ties would not be possible until the United States severed relations with Taiwan and removes its troops (using the figure 3,000) from the island (UPI, Washington, 3 November). The State Department indefinitely postponed in March the visit to the United States of a troupe of Chinese musical artists because of a Chinese refusal to remove from their intended repertoire a song expressing the PRC's determination to liberate Taiwan (Washington Post Service, 28 March). Later in the year, the Chinese objected to the inclusion of the mayor of San Juan, Puerto Rico, in a delegation of U.S. mayors who were scheduled to visit China. The objection reflected Chinese support of the Puerto Rican independence movement. The flap led to the cancellation of the visit by the U.S. Conference of Mayors on the grounds that Peking had introduced a "political element" into the intended visit. This decision was in turn sharply criticized by the Chinese, who accused the United States of "one-sidedly making public the cancellation of the visit and directing groundless charges" (UPI, Hong Kong, 17 September). On the eve of Secretary of State Henry Kissinger's October trip, the allowing of supporters of the exiled Dalai Lama to operate in the United States was blasted as "undisguised interference in China's internal affairs" and was regarded as a "flagrant violation" of the Shanghai communiqué of 1972 (UPI, Hong Kong, 14 October). But most of all Peking criticized the U.S.-Soviet détente, which would be the chief topic of discussion during the Sino-American high-level meetings of October and December.

Despite the Chinese criticisms, and the minor mishaps of the year, it remained clear that both sides were desirous of protecting the relationship. Hence, incidents that might have provided occasion for far greater disharmony were dealt with quietly. A Chinese diplomat stationed in Canada who was allegedly involved in espionage in the United States was asked to leave Canada; apparently the indirect handling of the matter was arranged by the U.S. Federal Bureau of Investigation (*Christian Science Monitor*, 12 May). Fear that Chinese elation over the fall of U.S.-supported governments in Phnom Penh and Saigon would endanger the visit of President Ford to Peking proved to be unfounded (e.g., UPI, Paris, 5 May). If anything, the Chinese seemed anxious that the United States not entirely abandon its presence in Asia in the wake of the Indochina debacle, and this impression was specifically received by U.S. Congressman Paul Findley in a talk with Teng Hsiao-ping in August (AFP, 26 August). The death of Chiang Kai-shek and the ceremonial funeral visit to Taiwan by Vice-President Nelson Rockefeller was not made an issue of by Peking. For its part, the United States reportedly blocked two U.S. companies from drilling for oil in waters claimed by China, so as not to provoke the Chinese (Washington Post Service, quoting Selig Harrison's above-noted report, 5 September). Other indications of normalizing relations were the opening by the Bank of America, the world's largest commercial bank, of a direct banking channel with the Bank of China (AP, 8 October) and the approval by the U.S. Federal Communications Commission of radio contact between U.S. amateur radio operators and those in the PRC (*Honolulu Star-Bulletin*, 8 October).

The most important Chinese visit to the United States was that of a high-ranking trade mission which toured the country and met with President Ford and Congressional leaders in September. The 10-man mission was led by Li Chaun, deputy chairman of the China Council for the Promotion of Foreign Trade; it was hosted by the National Council of United States-China Trade (*NYT*, 13 September). Considering the fact that the United States, which has become China's second trading partner but which also saw cancellation of large Chinese grain orders during the year, such a visit has special significance.

Secretary of State Kissinger, during his visit to Peking on 19-22 October, held talks with ranking Chinese leaders including Mao Tse-tung and Teng Hsiao-ping. The discussions, preparatory to President Ford's visit, were friendly. However, the Chinese made clear their displeasure at the U.S.-Soviet détente. Subsequently there appeared to be some difficulty in making last-minute arrangements for the presidential visit, but these were cleared up.

President Ford, accompanied by his wife and daughter, the secretary of state, and other officials and newsmen, arrived in Peking on 1 December. He met with Chairman Mao on 2 December for an hour and 50 minutes, which was roughly twice as long as former President Nixon's meeting with Mao. Their talk was described by the Chinese as "earnest and significant . . . wide-ranging" and as having taken place "in a friendly atmosphere." (UPI, Peking, 2 December). Ford called the talk "significant" (ibid., 3 December). Perhaps in coordination with the Presidential mission in Peking, where the chief topic was détente, U.S. ambassador to the United Nations Daniel Moynihan asserted that Moscow intends to "colonize Africa," although he later admitted that his remarks were "somewhat hyperbolic" (Washington Post Service, 3 December). After four days of discussions between the top U.S. and Chinese leaders, primarily between President Ford and Vice-Premier Teng and between Secretary of State Kissinger and Foreign Minister Chiao Kuan-hua, the visit concluded without a formal joint communiqué. Kissinger and Chiao had decided against a communiqué in a late-night meeting prior to the third round of talks. White House sources reportedly said that the principle obstacle to a communiqué was Chinese opposition to U.S. insistence on seeking peaceful accommodations with the Soviet Union (Washington Post Service, Peking, 4 December).

The Chinese provided Ford with detailed information, presumably elicited from Hanoi, on seven dead U.S. servicemen previously listed as missing in action in Indochina. This was the only observable "concrete" result of the visit. At the farewell banquet in the Great Hall of the People, Teng Hsiao-ping diplomatically ignored the unresolved impasse over détente, and stressed confidence that Sino-American relations were "full of vitality" and bound to improve. Ford reaffirmed the U.S. commitment to "complete the normalization of relations with the PRC." Kissinger later disclosed at a briefing for reporters that the United States had indicated interest during the talks in a tentative Chinese formula for getting around the complex, sensitive Taiwan issue. He said that the Chinese had made it clear that they wanted "something similar to the Japanese model," in which Japan broke relations with Taiwan and extended recognition to the PRC in September 1972, but maintained trade and other relations with Taiwan. Kissinger said: "I think we have also made clear that it will take time for this process to mature and for certain circumstances to exist." He did not elaborate further, but did suggest that the Chinese were sensitive to domestic political pressures on Ford because of the 1976 elections. In a toast at the banquet, Ford reaffirmed U.S. opposition to "the efforts of others to impose hegemony in any part of the world," without, however, specifically mentioning the Soviet Union. Kissinger later said that he was not prepared to announce in Peking that he was ready to go to Moscow later in December to pursue negotiations on a new strategic arms limitation treaty, but that the question would be decided in the next week or so (UPI, AP, Peking, 5 December). The President departed Peking on 5 December, and returned home via Indonesia, the Philippines, and Honolulu.

Relations with Japan. This was the third year of normal Sino-Japanese relations, but overshadowing all else throughout 1975 was the so-called hegeomony issue, by which Japan is caught up in the Sino-Soviet dispute.

In the Sino-Japanese joint communiqué of September 1972 the two countries declared that neither of them should seek hegemony in the Asian-Pacific region and that "each is opposed to efforts by any other country or group of countries to establish such hegemony." The point at issue now is this last phrase. The Chinese insist that it be included into the yet-to-be-concluded Japan-China peace and friendship treaty. The Russians, on the other hand, have repeatedly warned the Japanese that the inclusion of the "anti-hegemony" clause might affect Soviet-Japanese relations. In any case, the Japanese are not anxious to offend the Soviets, especially since the Chinese have made it clear that the clause is aimed at the Soviet Union specifically.

Otherwise, Sino-Japanese relations continued to show progress. In August, the two governments signed a fisheries accord, the fourth and last agreement, following ones on trade, air, and navigation, under the terms of the 1972 joint communiqué. Trade continued to expand, with Japan securely the biggest bilateral trader with China. Oil has become the most important import item, and accounts for more than 40 percent of Japan's total purchases. The PRC chose to ignore both the resumption of Tokyo-Taipei air service, and the visit to Japan of U.S. secretary of defense James Schlesinger. The Chinese have championed very vocally the Japanese claim to the four northern islands held by the Soviet Union (*FEER*, 3 October, pp. 26-27).

Relations with Elsewhere. Among the significant developments of 1975 was the PRC's continued cultivation of the "Second World," which it credits with a struggle to free itself "from the control, threats, bullying and exploitation by one or the other superpower." It was commended for a "positive attitude" in favoring a "dialogue with the Third World countries." Such was the thrust of comments made on 2 September by Li Chiang, minister of foreign trade and chief delegate to the Seventh Special Session of the U.N. General Assembly. (*Current Scene*, November, p. 18.) This attention to Europe was seen also in the state visit of Teng Hsiao-ping to Paris for six days in May, and to the attention given to such visitors to China as Franz-Josef Strauss and Edward Heath, and in the establishment of relations with the EEC. In Portugal, the Peking-oriented communist faction supported the more popular Socialists over the Moscow-oriented communists (*Christian Science Monitor*, 18 July).

In Southeast Asia the PRC's prestige continued to gain. Only Indonesia and Singapore stand out in the region in not recognizing Peking. Singapore appears to be considering recognition. Indonesia claims that the relations were never formally broken, but merely suspended, making it unnecessary to extend formal recognition again (dispatch from Bangkok, *NYT*, 2 July). In little more than a year, the PRC had established relations with Malaysia, the Philippines, and Thailand, members of the Association of Southeast Asian Nations, which was once regarded as a potential bulwark against communism. The PRC has pleased governments in the region by calling upon overseas Chinese to integrate with the people in the countries in which they live, "to become naturalized in their countries of domicile, to live in amity with the natives and to obey the laws of the land" (AFP, Hong Kong, *Washington Post*, 13 July).

Kim Il-sung, president of North Korea, visited Peking in April-May, and clearly the Chinese dissuaded him from seriously taking actions calculated to capitalize upon the communist success in Indochina or test U.S. resolve in Korea at this point (*Peking Review*, 2 May).

At the United Nations, PRC representatives have partly dropped their self-imposed isolation and are beginning to participate and mingle more freely with other delegates in lounges and at parties. This is, however, a change in style and reflects no policy change. The Chinese permanent delegation of 30 is roughly a third that of the Soviet Union. (*International Herald Tribune*, Paris, 7 November.) The PRC consistently supported Third World positions and attacked the superpowers throughout the year. Chen Mu-hua led the PRC delegation at the U.N. Industrial Development Organization conference, 12-27 March, in Lima, Peru. The Chinese model of developing an agricultural base, followed by light and heavy industries was preferred, with stress on self-reliance and the acceptance of foreign aid only if no ulterior motives on the part of the donor were involved (*Peking Review*, 21 March). The Third Session of the Third United Nations Sea Law Conference ended after eight weeks in Geneva on 9 May, failing to reach agreement on any important substantive matter. The head of the Chinese delegation said that the reason for this was that "the two superpowers still maintain their positions of maritime hegemonism, and assiduously cling to the outdated legal regime of the sea and refuse to abandon their control and monopoly over the seas and oceans" (ibid., 23 May, p. 27). Li Su-wen led the Chinese delegation to the International Women's Year World Conference, 19 June to 2 July, in Mexico City. Li argued that the superpowers were "doing their utmost to lead the women's movement astray." Li Chiang represented the PRC at the Seventh Special Session of the U.N. General Assembly in September. Foreign Minister Chiao-Kuan-hua addressed the 30th Session of the General Assembly on 26 September, providing a comprehensive review of the PRC's policies (ibid., 3 October, pp. 10-17). Yang Li-kung, head of the Chinese delegation and vice minister of agriculture and forestry, spoke to the 18th session of the U.N. Food and Agriculture Organization, meeting in Rome on 8 November.

Publications. The official and most authoritative publication of the CCP is the newspaper

Jen-min jih-pao ("People's Daily"), published in Peking. The theoretical journal of the Central Committee, *Hung chi* ("Red Flag") is published approximately once a month. The daily paper of the PLA is *Chieh-fang-chun pao* ("Liberation Army Daily"). The weekly *Peking Review* is published in English and several other languages. It carries translations of important articles, editorials, and documents from the three aforementioned publications. The official news agency of the party and government is the New China News Agency (Hsinhua; NCNA).

University of Hawaii, Manoa   Stephen Uhalley, Jr.

India

Indian communists give December 1925 as the founding date of the Communist Party of India (CPI). Since the formal split of 1964, two main parties have existed independently. One is commonly referred to as the "right" or pro-Soviet party, and the other as the "left" or "independent" party. They call themselves, respectively, the Communist Party of India—the CPI, and the Communist Party of India (Marxist)—the CPI(M). In 1969 a new, Maoist communist party, the Communist Party of India (Marxist-Leninist)—the CPI (M-L)—was created, largely by defectors from the CPI(M). This group derives its inspiration from the peasant revolt it instigated in 1967 in Naxalbari, West Bengal. Its members, along with other numerous but smaller Maoist organizations, continue to be referred to popularly as Naxalites.

On a nationwide basis the two large parties, the CPI and the more militant CPI(M), have competed against each other on more or less equal bases of strength. Active membership in each is probably between 80,000 and 100,000, although the CPI claims a membership of over 350,000. While the strength of the CPI(M) is concentrated heavily in Kerala and West Bengal, that of the CPI is more widely distributed—in Bihar, Andhra Pradesh, Kerala, West Bengal, Uttar Pradesh, and Tamil-nadu.

The March 1971 parliamentary elections gave the CPI and CPI(M) almost equal shares (about 4 percent for each) of the seats in the Lok Sabha. The CPI has 24 MPs in the Lok Sabha, compared with the CPI(M)'s 25. In the fifth general elections for the state and union territory legislative assembly seats, held in March 1972, the CPI won a total of 112 seats while the CPI(M) won only 34 (as against CPI's 110 seats and CPI(M)'s 160 at the end of 1971). Subsequent state elections have increased to 162 the CPI's total strength in state and territorial legislative assemblies.

The CPI(M-L) and other Naxalite groups oppose parliamentary methods and have not participated in any elections. Membership in these groups has declined sharply in recent years (from an estimated 10,000 in 1972) due to the government's armed campaign and detention policy against them. Eight separate "Naxalite" Communist organizations were formally proscribed by the government, under the "emergency" legislation, in July.

The CPI and the CPI(M) operate legally, although members of both parties have been arrested or detained from time to time. In fact, the CPI leads the government coalition (with Congress party participation) in the state of Kerala, although the defection of one of its partners left it in a precarious position for most of the year.

Other national parties in India are: the Indian National Congress or the Congress(R), the moderate socialist party led by Indira Gandhi; Congress(O), the breakaway conservative ("Syndicate") faction of the Indian National Congress; Bharatiya Lok Dol (BLD, a new rightist party formed in August 1974 by a merger of Swatantra and 6 regional parties); Bharatiya Jan Sangh (often referred to as the Jan Sangh), a militant Hindu-Nationalist and conservative party; the Socialist Party (SP; formed out of the merger of the Praja Socialist Party and the Samyukta Socialist Party in August 1971), seeking to develop the image of a moderate socialist party; and the Dravida Munnetra Kazhagam or the DMK, an ardently sub-nationalist party of Tamilnadu which has now split into two factions, the breakaway faction calling itself Anna-DMK. Most of the non-communist opposition parties have been tactically united since mid-1974 in support of the national anti-government agitation movement led by Jayaprakash Narayan, a disciple of Mahatma Gandhi. The CPI(M) has given only limited support to this movement, whereas the CPI has been prominent in defending Mrs. Gandhi's government against Narayan's attacks.

The CPI. Leadership and Organization. The central leadership of the CPI, elected at its Tenth Congress in 1975, includes the party chairman, Sripad Amrit Dange; the general secretary, C. Rajeswara Rao; the Central Secretariat (chairman, general secretary, and 7 secretaries); the Central Executive Committee (31 members); the Auditing Commission (11 members); and the National Council (125 full members and 13 candidate members). There are also party secretariats and state councils in each state in India. Bhupesh Gupta is the party's spokesman in the Parliament. The following are members of the Central Executive Committee (members of the Central Secretariat are indicated by asterisks):

*S. A. Dange	S. G. Sardesai
*C. Rajeswara Rao	Avtar Singh Malhotra
*N. K. Krishnan	Bhogendra Jha
*Bhupesh Gupta	Phani Bora
*Indrajit Gupta	Kalshankar Shukla
*Yogindra Sharma	H. K. Vyas
*Rajashekhara Reddy	C. K. Chandrappan
*Indradeep Sinha	Romesh Chandra
*S. Kumaran	Jagannath Sarkar
Z. A. Ahmad	Bhikhalal
M. Farooqi	Homi Daji
Mohit Sen	Parvarti Krishnan
Gopal Banerjee	Raj Bahadur Gour
Bswanath Mukherjee	Tammareddy Satyanarayana
M. Kalyanasundaram	M. N. Govindan Nair
P. K. Vasudevan Nair	

Auxiliary and Mass Organizations. Chief among the CPI's major fronts is the All-India Trade Union Congress (AITUC), in which the CPI and the CPI(M) exercised joint leadership until the two parties' differences led to a formal split of the AITUC in 1970. The CPI retained control of the original AITUC, leaving the CPI(M) to form a new organization. CPI chairman S. A. Dange is the secretary-general of the AITUC as well; its president is S. S. Mirajkar. Its membership is claimed to be 1,984,778 (*New Age*, New Delhi, 4 February 1973).

Another important front, the All-India Kisan Sabha (Peasants' Association; AIKS) split on 1969 into two separate organizations—one controlled by the CPI and the other (the larger one) controlled by the CPI(M), both continuing the AIKS name. Other major mass organizations dominated by the CPI include the All-India Youth Federation (AIYF), the All-India Student Federation (AISF), the National Federation of Women, and for agricultural laborers, the All-India Khet Mazdoor Union.

Party Internal Affairs. As the CPI entered its 50th anniversary year, the party convened its Tenth Congress at Vijayawada, in the state of Andhra Pradesh, from 27 January to 2 February. Perceiving an urgent threat of a double "counter-revolutionary pincer" of "right reaction," led by Jayaprakash Narayan, and "U.S. imperialism," the Congress focused its discussions on the desired form and extent of CPI cooperation with the ruling Congress Party, and particularly on the possibility and desirability of further "Kerala-type coalitions" in the states and at the center. On the international front, the Congress discussed the "favorable change in the international situation" brought about by Soviet policies and stressed the need for strengthening Indo-Soviet ties and combatting the threat of U.S. imperialism in the Indian Ocean.

Yogindra Sharma's organizational report to the Congress presented a picture of a party which, contrary to press reports of serious divisions over the degree of support to be rendered to the ruling party, had never in its history been so unified. Sharma claimed that the party's membership had increased by 125,000 since the Ninth Congress, to a new level of 355,000. The CPI's 16,000 branches were reportedly led by 3,000 full-time and 40,000 part-time party cadres. The training of cadres was carried on at party schools existing at both the center and in several of the states. Sharma reported to the Congress on plans to organize a volunteer corps—the Jana Seva Dal—in every state and district of India. Trained both in physical combat and in Marxism-Leninism, it would exist both to defend the party and to engage in struggles on its behalf during the "coming storm." On the negative side, Sharma admitted that the party's growth was not commensurate with either the need or the possibilities. Acknowledging Jayaprakash Narayan's strength among the urban petty bourgeoisie and the CPI's continued weakness among India's peasantry, he stressed the need to build up the party's working-class membership. Sharma also admonished the Congress of the necessity for waging a "stern battle against wrong habits and styles" of party work. (*The Hindu*, Madras, 1 February.)

The first post-Congress meeting of the CPI's National Council occurred in April. This body approved a 17-point minimum program, including sections on agrarian reform, food distribution, price control, and further nationalization, on the basis of which the CPI would conduct itself in the coming national elections. Pointing to the continuing threat posed by Narayan's movement, the National Council called on the government to pay more attention to the economic front in order to soothe mass discontent, and it denounced the policy of the CPI(M), which served only to sow utter confusion among masses. (*Hindustan Times*, New Delhi, 6 April.)

The party's Central Executive Committee convened a 2-day meeting four days after Mrs. Gandhi proclaimed a nation-wide Emergency. Proclaiming her action to be "necessary and justified," the CEC urged Mrs. Gandhi to put forward a program of progressive economic reforms. In light of the changed circumstances, the party called off its plans for a nation-wide agitation among the peasantry aimed at the forcible seizure of surplus land. (*Far Eastern Economic Review*, 18 July.) In September, taking note of the national concern over political corruption, the party directed all members of its national and state councils to declare their property holdings and incomes.

Domestic Attitudes and Activities. The party's long-range goal is the establishment of a "national democracy" composed of a coalition of "left and democratic forces" led by the communist party and based on a worker-peasant alliance. This coalition would be composed of the "patriotic" elements of the national bourgeoisie, the intelligentsia, the peasants (including the "rich peasants"), and the workers, with the working class gradually rising to a position of leadership under the guidance of the communist party, ultimately forming a "genuinely socialist" society. At its Tenth Congress, the CPI set forth a detailed analysis of the domestic situation, and outlined its strategy. Party Chairman S. A. Dange asserted in his opening speech that the two arms of the counter-revolutionary pincers—imperialism and right reaction (especially as represented by Jayaprakash Narayan)—could not be combatted by the Congress Party alone. It was the task of the CPI to work for the "broadest mobilization of left and democratic forces of the country and particularly those of the Congress" in order to fight counter-revolution and to "prepare the ground for a radical advance toward the left." (*Hindustan Times*, 28 January.) As the CPI saw it, the urgency of the situation had forced the centrists in the Congress Party, including Mrs. Gandhi herself, to come out against right reaction. This was still a vacillating element, and it was still necessary for the CPI to fight against all anti-democratic policies of the present government as well as against all attempts to replace it with a right wing coalition. But on the whole, it was now possible to work toward the formation of a progressive coalition which would include such centrist forces from the ruling Congress. Dange noted at the Congress that the CPI was using the slogan for "Kerala-type" coalitions loosely; the party was not advocating the establishment of such coalitions everywhere. (*The Hindu*, 30 January.) Only in those states where "the democratic sections" within the Congress achieve a dominant position, could the slogan of united front governments of the CPI, Congress, and other left and democratic forces, be advanced. (*World Marxist Review*, number 5.) The party stood ready to cooperate in the formation of such a government, "freed from all rightist elements" and constituted on the basis of a minimum agreed program, at the central level; Dange felt that the opportunity for this should come before too long. (*The Hindu*, 30 January.) Discussions at the Congress made clear, however, that the formation of such progressive coalition governments would result from more than mere electoral struggle, but would entail efforts of mass struggle as well. The CPI, Dange said, was not contemplating armed struggle, but if any party tried to force the communists' hands, the CPI stood ready to fight against it. (*The Hindu*, 30 January.)

Discussing the prospects for unity between his party and the parallel CPI(M), Rajeswara Rao asserted that such unity was desired both by the CPI and by India's masses. (*The Hindu*, 3 February.) The CPI insisted, however, that such unity could not be built on the basis of "blind anti-Congressism." Such was apparently the perceived motivation for the CPI(M)'s flirtation with Narayan's movement; as Rao put it, although the CPI(M) keeps up a "fig leaf of demarcation," it was for all practical purposes acting with Narayan's counter-revolutionary movement. (*World Marxist Review*, number 5.)

The Tenth Congress documents portrayed the coming period as one of increasingly sharpened struggle over India's road of development. In the party's opinion, the government had laid the foundation for progressive development through the public sector, but was allowing India's monopoly houses to continue to rob the people. The party's own view of a proper economic course was contained in the 17-point program promulgated by the National Council in April, on which it was proposed that the party fight the coming election campaign.

An indication of the mood of India's voters was provided in June in the state elections in Gujarat. Earlier in the year, the state Congress organization had rejected the suggestion put forward by D. K. Barooah—the national Congress president and himself a former member of the communist party—that the Congress Party form an electoral coalition in the state with the CPI. The June election, widely regarded as a test of anti-government sentiment, resulted in a shattering defeat for the Congress, and a coalition supported by Narayan formed a government in the state. Although the CPI contested only five and the CPI(M) only three of the state's 181 legislative seats, neither party won a single contest.

In the wake of the Gujarat repudiation and the almost simultaneous court ruling voiding her 1971 election to parliament, Mrs. Gandhi thoroughly transformed the internal situation on 26 June with a proclamation of nation-wide emergency. In the widespread arrests of political opposition leaders which followed, the CPI emerged virtually unscathed. Alone among the opposition parties, the CPI supported the government crackdown, finding it justified by the activities of "reactionary forces" and their "imperialist" supporters. Following the lead of *Pravda*'s own analysis, the party's CEC described the emergency in July as a preemptive strike against a rightist attempt to seize power. Mrs. Gandhi's 20-point program, announced later in the month, was hailed by the CPI as laying the basis for progressive unity. Although it incorporated some of the party's own demands, the CPI urged the government to go even farther in the direction of nationalizing additional sectors of Indian industries. (*Far Eastern Economic Review*, 18 July.) The July CEC statement called on other leftist parties to give up their blind opposition to the government, while cautioning Mrs. Gandhi that the emergency should not be used to restrict the rights of the working people. (*FBIS*, 7 July.) The CPI stood by the ruling party during the subsequent parliamentary session, supporting it especially in its efforts to assert parliamentary supremacy over the courts. (*Washington Post*, 10 August.)

International Views and Policies. The reports delivered to the Tenth Congress hailed the "radical" and "favorable" changes in the international situation which had occurred in the last five years, thanks to the "peace program" of the Soviet Union. Bhupesh Gupta's report on the international situation described a turn away from cold war toward détente, and argued that the cause of world peace has a big stake in the steady improvement of relations between the United States and the Soviet Union. And yet the "American imperialists" were harshly criticized by the party for "once again trying the path of brinksmanship and blackmail" and even applying the threat of military intervention. According to Dange, American activities in the Indian Ocean were aimed at shattering the freedom and democracy of Asian and African states. (*Hindustan Times*, 28 January.) Calling for the liquidation of the American "base" on Diego Garcia, the CPI urged the government of India to call a conference of littoral states to work out joint measures to foil the "imperialist conspiracy." (*Hindustan Times*, 31 January.) Declaring its intention to continue to defend the "anti-imperialist stands" of the Indian government, the CPI resolved to work toward strengthening India's relations with "the socialist and democratic countries" and toward extricating her from the world capitalist system.

The CPI continued throughout the year to make harsh attacks on the policies of the Chinese "Maoist leadership" and to link China's activities with the schemes of the "imperialists" and forces of internal "reaction." Rajeswara Rao chose to stress this theme in the context of a statement hailing the victory of "patriotic forces" in Vietnam. Warning his compatriots not to be lulled into complacency by the "debacle of U.S. imperialism" in Indo-China, Rao asserted that the Chinese Maoists would continue to work hand in glove with U.S. imperialism to "destabilize" South Asia—with India as their main target. He called upon the government to rally other countries in the region in common defense against this threat, and particularly urged that "no stone be left unturned" in the effort to normalize relations with Pakistan. (*Information Bulletin*, number 11.)

The need for heightened vigilance was restated by the CPI's National Council in an August resolution describing the coup in Bangladesh as a "definite link in the chain of U.S. imperialism's global strategy of destabilizing the internal situation" in the nonaligned world. (*The Patriot*, Dehli, 27 August.)

International Activities and Contacts. Twenty-eight delegations from foreign communist parties attended the CPI Tenth Congress at the beginning of the year. Among them was a delegation from the Communist Party of the Soviet Union led by alternate Politburo member Sh. R. Rashidov, who congratulated the party for its "highly important" stands and urged it to new efforts in strengthening Indo-Soviet friendship. Greetings from 23 other foreign communist parties were received by the

Tenth Congress. Included among them was the first such message sent by the North Korean party since the CPI split of 1964.

In the resolutions of the Tenth Congress, the CPI reiterated its stand in favor of the convocation of an international meeting of the communist parties.

Twice during the year CPI leaders travelled to Moscow to meet with Boris Ponomarev and R. A. Ulyanovsky of the International Department of the CPSU's Central Committee. The first occasion was during the political crisis of early June, when N. K. Krishnan met with the Soviet officials in an atmosphere of "complete mutual understanding." (*FBIS*, 10 June.) On 14 October the Soviet comrades received CPI Chairman S. A. Dange. According to *Pravda* Dange described his party's activities in further uniting democratic forces in the struggle against reaction and for implementation of the progressive socio-economic reforms proclaimed by Indira Gandhi. This meeting was said to have occurred in an "atmosphere of mutual understanding."

At about the same time, Yogindra Sharma was leading a CPI delegation to Czechoslovakia. The two parties noted their "unanimity of views on all questions of common interest," and joined in condemning the harmful, splitting, anti-Soviet policies of the Chinese Maoist leadership. (*FBIS*, 28 October.)

*   *   *

The CPI(M). Leadership and Organization. The CPI(M) is led by P. Sundarayya as general secretary and Jyoti Basu as chairman, and by its Politburo (which includes, in addition to the above, B. T. Ranadive, M. Basavapunniah, E. M. S. Namboodiripad, A. K. Gopalan, Promode Das Gupta, Harkishan Singh Surjeet, and P. Ramamurthy), the party Central Committee (31 members), and state secretariats and committees.

Auxiliary and Mass Organizations. The CPI(M) acquired its own trade union federation in May 1970 when a CPI(M)-dominated "All-India Trade Union Conference" created a new organization, the Center of Indian Trade Unions (CITU) and elected B. T. Ranadive and P. Ramamurthy (who were leaders in the undivided AITUC) as its president and general secretary, respectively. In 1971, a new General Council of CITU, consisting of 191 members, was elected at the second conference of the organization, held at Cochin on 18 to 22 April. The conference confirmed Ranadive and Ramamurthy in their offices and elected seven vice-president (Jyoti Basu, Mohammad Ismail, Sudhin Kumar, S. M. Chowhury, S. Y. Kolhatkar, E. Balanandan, and K. Ramani), four secretaries, a treasurer, and a Working Committee of 32—which was elected by the new General Council. The CITU (with more than 2,000 affiliated unions) has a membership of about a million.

The CPI(M) has been somewhat stronger than the CPI in organizing the peasantry. The party's AIKS probably has about a million members with close to two-thirds of the membership in West Bengal. The leadership includes the Politburo member A. K. Gopalan as president and Central Committee member Harekrishna Konar as general secretary. The CPI(M) also controls an agricultural laborers' union which probably has a membership of about 300,000. The CPI(M)'s former student organization (All-India Student Federation; AISF) was reorganized in December 1970 as the Students' Federation of India.

Domestic Attitudes and Activities. The CPI(M) emerged from the split of the CPI in 1964. Initially it was more militant than its parent organization in supporting armed revolts by workers and peasants, and was oriented toward, but not a partisan of, China. In the first year of its existence it had no agreed-upon ideology. In 1966 the Chinese Communist Party (CCP) attempted unsuccessfully to have at least a strong minority of CPI(M) leadership adopt the Maoist line and break away from the parliamentary tradition of the CPI.

With the adoption in 1967 of the "Madurai line," the CPI(M) assumed an internationally "independent" policy—abandoning its pro-Chinese sentiments and the ramifications of these domestically. It has adopted a stance in recent years which has been "anti-revisionist," "anti-dogmatist," and against "left-wing opportunism."

The CPI(M) has constantly criticized the CPI for the latter's willingness to form coalitions with various "reactionary parties." However, the CPI(M)'s practice in making alliances has not been inflexible. Consequently, it has had to face counter-criticism from the CPI on this issue.

The CPI(M)'s long-range goal is the establishment of a "people's democracy" in India. In the political resolution adopted at the Ninth Congress, the CPI(M) took the position that "the traditional Marxist concept of self-determination by nationalities was not applicable in the Indian context and that in the interests of the working class the unity of the country should be preserved." According to this resolution, the party would oppose secessionist and separatist trends. However, it had deemed that the real threat to unity arose from the increasing centralization of powers by the present Congress government. Thus the party would also support "real autonomy," for all nationalities—aimed at strengthening the unity of the people and based on the party's perception of the voluntary character of the Indian Union: "real equality and autonomy" for various nationalities that have found expression in the form of linguistic states, combined with the party's opposition to centralization and its repudiation of separatism. In terms of party tactics, the political resolution had proposed the continuation of the "parliamentary path," revival of united fronts, and, for the present, not an armed struggle. Sundarayya, summing up the achievements of the Ninth Congress, stated that the party had overcome threats from "right deviationism and left adventurism from within" and succeeded in projecting to other "left and democratic parties" in the country an "alternative line to the ruling classes." (See *YICA, 1973*, p. 463.)

By 1975, following a series of electoral reverses, the party's leadership was declaring that unless substantial reforms could be achieved, including the institution of a system of proportional representation, there was no point in participating further in elections. (*Hindustan Times*, 14 January.)

The CPI(M) agreed to participate in Jayaprakash Narayan's conference on electoral reform, and they supported the veteran Gandhian in certain other facets of his nation-wide agitation. But they refused to make an unconditional commitment to his movement, finding his stand on economic issues inadequate and taking particular exception to the right wing cast of his coalition of supporters. Pledging to campaign independently for implementation of Narayan's "democratic demands," the CPI(M) asserted that unity of left and democratic forces in India was incompatible with unity with the right. (*Hindustan Times*, 4 March.) According to Jyoti Basu, Narayan would not succeed, given the nature of his present supporters, in achieving an "overall revolution." (*FBIS*, 13 March.)

Despite their distaste for Narayan's coalition, the leaders of the CIP(M) found the thrust of his anti-government agitation to their liking. Jyoti Basu declared in March that the "biggest enemy of our country today is Mrs. Gandhi and her party," and he sternly condemned the CPI for its support of the Congress. (*FBIS*, 13 March.)

Not surprisingly, the party used the occasion of the June court decision to call for Mrs. Gandhi's resignation. And yet its top leaders wery not included among the political opponents jailed by the Indian government following the imposition of emergency rule. (*Manchester Guardian*, 19 July.) In Kerala, the CPI(M) leadership virtually courted arrest when it defied the emergency and attempted to lead a general strike; although its cadres were taken into police custody, they were later released. (*Far Eastern Economic Review*, 22 August.)

International Views and Attitudes. The CPI(M) maintains a policy of independence and refuses to be aligned with either the Chinese Communist Party or the CPSU, neither of which has accorded international recognition to it. Since 1967 the party has condemned with equal intensity Chinese "left-sectarianism" and Soviet "revisionism." The party in 1974 centered its efforts on establishing relations with "like-minded" communist parties in Cuba, North Korea, Romania, and North Vietnam. Unlike the CPI, the CPI(M) has not endorsed the Soviet campaign for a new international meeting of communist and workers' parties, and would not be likely to attend one.

The CPI(M) supports close Indo-Soviet relations, but also urges Sino-Indian rapprochement. It has criticized the CPI for "willy-nilly advocating that Soviet aid is a panacea for India's economic crisis" while failing to fight against the "exploiting ruling classes for misusing [such aid] for their narrow partisan interest." (*People's Democracy*, Calcutta, 16 December 1973.)

The CPI(M) has been far less circumspect than the CPI on the subject of harm to third-world interests arising from closer U.S.-Soviet relations. Like the CPI, the CPI(M) has been vigorous in condemning U.S. plans for expanding the naval facilities on Diego Garcia, though it has also engaged in broader criticism of all superpower naval activity in the Indian Ocean.

The continuing even-handedness of the CPI(M) in its attitude toward the USSR and China was evidenced in April, when party leader E. M. S. Namboodiripad characterized the victory of the communists in Vietnam as an historic event which could be compared to both the Russian revolution and the Chinese revolution. (*Hindustan Times*, 1 May.)

*   *   *

The CPI(M-L) or Naxalites. The Communist Party of India (Marxist-Leninist) was formed in 1969. Oriented toward and approved by the Chinese Communist Party, it advocated the organization of peasants for armed struggle to seize power, condemning the CPI as "revisionist" and the CPI(M) as "neo-revisionist." The Naxalite violence in rural and urban areas led to the government's armed campaign and strong detention policy against them. Disapproving of the party's failure to build a mass base before launching an armed struggle, the Chinese have ceased to mention the CPI(M-L) in their publications. Following the death of their leader Charu Mazumdar in July 1972, the imprisonment or detention of most of their leaders, and persistent factionalism within their ranks, the Naxalites have generally been demoralized. The CPI and CPI(M) have campaigned for better treatment in prisons, grant of political status, and release of the Naxalite prisoners.

During the year, Naxalite activity (particularly in the states of Bihar, Orissa, Andhra Pradesh and West Bengal) was again on the increase. Following a clash in Bihar in June, in which 15 of the rebels were killed, the government announced the discovery of documents containing a Naxalite plan to seize power in India by 1980. (*Hindustan Times*, 11 June.)

In July the government, acting under the Emergency rules, formally proscribed the following Naxalite groups: CPI(M-L), both pro- and anti-Lin Piao factions; United CP(M-L), the "S. N. Sing-Chandra Pully Reddy group"; Andhra Pradesh Revolutionary Communist Committee, the "T. Nagi Reddy groups"; (CPI(M-L), "Suniti Ghosh-Sharmar faction"); Eastern India Zonal Consolidation Committee of CP (Communist, Leninist); the Maoist Communist Center; the Unity Center of Communist Revolutionaries of India (Marxist-Leninist); and the Center of Indian Communists. (*Hindustan Times*, 15 July.) The last-named group is apparently the newest, having been formed in December 1974 in Kerala at a convention of disgruntled members of the CPI(M) who favored a Maoist armed revolution. (*FBIS*, 17 December 1974.)

Publications. The communist parties and groups in India publish dailies, weeklies, and monthlies, issued in English and various vernacular languages. The central organization of the CPI publishes the English weekly *New Age* in New Delhi (1971 circulation 7,500). It also publishes the weekly *Party Life*, in English. In 1973, it started publishing a daily, *Janyug* ("People's Era"), in Hindi; and a journal, *Problems of Peace and Socialism*, in English, in New Delhi. Moreover, it has dailies in five states; two in Kerala, and one each in Andhra Pradesh, West Bengal, Punjab, and Manipur.

The CPI(M)'s central organ is the weekly *People's Democracy*, published in Calcutta, in English (1971 circulation 10,000). The party also publishes dailies in Kerala, West Bengal, and Andhra

Pradesh and weeklies in Tamilnadu, Karnataka, West Bengal, Punjab and Jammu and Kashmir. The CPI(M-L)'s publications (see *YICA, 1973*, p. 468) have virtually ceased to appear.

Vanderbilt University   Robert H. Donaldson

Indonesia

The Communist movement in Indonesia is badly divided and widely scattered. It is thus faced with serious internal organizational problems, and is largely limited to occasional small-scale guerrilla activity primarily in the Sarawak border region adjacent to the Indonesian province of West Kalimantan (Borneo). In the aftermath of the abortive coup attempt on 30 September 1965 at Djakarta and other places in Java, in which Communist leaders and front groups as well as dissident military units were seriously implicated, party members and sympathizers were hounded down, and in 1966 the Communist Party of Indonesia (Partai Komunis Indonesia: PKI) was for the second time in its history formally banned and the teaching of Marxist-Leninist doctrine, except in an academic context, was proscribed.

The pro-Soviet wing of the PKI has adherents primarily in Moscow, and in Prague and other East European capitals, with a handful also in India and Sri Lanka. It has at the moment a minimal following in Indonesia. The pro-Peking wing of the PKI calls itself the "Delegation of the Central Committee of the Indonesian Communist Party," while the pro-Moscow wing sometimes has referred to itself as the "PKI-Marxist-Leninist." Most followers of the "Delegation" are in Tirana and Peking, and all of the Indonesian guerrillas operating along the Sarawak-Indonesian border, usually in conjunction with the equally ethnic Chinese "North Kalimantan People's Guerrilla Force" (NKPGF), are members of the "Delegation" or sympathizers with its views. In Indonesia, since 1966 the crushing of the "remnants" of Gestapu (from Gerakan Tigah Puluh September, or Thirty September Movement, i.e., the previously noted coup attempt of that date in 1965) and a posture of "unrelenting vigilance" against the alleged latent threat of continuing domestic Communist subversion (sometimes linked in official statements to supposed support from People's China) have been official principles of the present government of President Suharto, repeatedly affirmed in policy statements. The threat of subversion has also been linked since 1974 to what officials call the "New Left" among students. This continues to be the case even though criticism in the Soviet and Chinese media, quite sharp in the later sixties, has been greatly mitigated in the past few years.

History. Founded on 23 May 1920, during the Dutch colonial period, the PKI has the distinction of being the oldest Communist movement in Asia. Its origins were not so much Indonesian as Dutch, since Dutch Marxists, among them the prominent Comintern agent Hendrik Sneevliet ("Maring"), had taken the lead in 1914 when they formed the "Indies Social Democratic Association." With the PKI's founding, however, Indonesians assumed leadership of the movement. Soon afterward the PKI threw itself into intense trade-union organizing and strike agitation.

In part because of a poorly defined policy relationship with the Comintern, and despite the opposition of some of its prominent leaders, the PKI launched a coup attempt in 1926-27 in West Java and West Sumatra. Quickly quelled, this resulted in the arrest and confinement in a West New Guinea concentration camp of scores of suspected participants and sympathizers, and plummeted the party into a steep decline as a number of the remaining cadres left the country. Some like the veteran PKI leader Tan Malaka, became prominent Comintern representatives in Asia. According to PKI history, the development of the party has proceeded through such periods of "white terror" (anti-Communist) repression, consequent on a number of years of party activity of varying intensity, usually culminating in a coup attempt.

Underground Party agitation in the budding Indonesian labor movement continued during the 1930s, especially in and around the East Java port of Surabaya, and it was not until the Indonesian independence proclamation (17 August 1945) that the PKI became a legal party once again. The party's record during World War II had been ineffectual, not least because of prominent Indonesian nationalist collaboration with the Japanese occupation forces. Although there were a few scattered instances of anti-Japanese resistance, at no time did organized anti-Japanese guerrilla Communism develop to an extent comparable to that in Malaya and the Philippines. After 1945 relations between the PKI and other political parties in the fledgling Indonesian Republic, struggling against returning Dutch colonial authority, gradually polarized, even as some PKI members attained high office in some Indonesian cabinets during the Indonesian revolution (1945-59). The promulgation by Moscow of its new hard-line "two camp doctrine," ending wartime collaboration with Western allies, and the Communist Youth Conference in Calcutta in February 1948, may have given impetus to PKI reorganization and the imposition of a new line of tighter organizational discipline and tactical militancy.

On 18 September 1948 a handful of second-echelon party and front-group leaders with support from local Army personnel launched a coup attempt in the East Java city of Madiun which was quickly nipped in the bud by regular Indonesian forces. The action almost certainly did not have the approval of principal party leaders, but PKI prestige suffered greatly, although the party was not proscribed when Indonesia formally won independence at the so-called Round Table Conference in The Hague at the end of December 1949.

From the nadir of its Madiun debacle the PKI was to rise within a few years to the point of winning the fourth-largest number of seats and about 16 percent of the popular vote in the republic's first general elections, in 1955. This was accomplished largely thanks to the leadership of younger party leaders, notably the Sumatran Dipa Nusantara Aidit, who eventually became party chairman. Under Aidit the PKI followed a militantly nationalistic policy stressing its "Indonesian" character in forging ahead with a policy of promoting a "national democratic" and anti-colonial revolution not just for Indonesia but also for the rest of the Third World, and particularly leaning leavily on President Sukarno and his nationalist ideology with its many verbal symbols. In Sukarno's intricate Power struggle with the Army, the PKI eventually became a powerful ally of the President. Aidit and other prominent party leaders even rose to minor cabinet posts, but subsequently Communist and other critics of Aidit were to allege that the PKI had been co-opted by the Sukarno establishment and had succumbed to "opportunism" through its espousal of parliamentary tactics. By early 1965 the party had seemingly reached the pinnacle of its power, having nearly three million members and candidate members, and additional tens of thousands in a network of interlocking trade-union, women's, youth, cultural affairs, and other front organizations. Coordination of the vast party structure proved far from effective, however, and the domestic power struggle with anti-Communist Muslim and military elements did little to create a secure environment for future growth. In the Sino-Soviet dispute the PKI under Aidit followed an officially independent policy, but in reality drifted, like the Indonesian government, ever closer into Peking's orbit.

On the night of 30 September 1965 a number of major PKI leaders, among them chairman Aidit, as well as elements of the party's youth and women's front organizations who had received paramilitary training at an airbase near Djakarta with the agreement of Communist-sympathizing Air Force officers, attempted a coup d'état. In this action, generally referred to as the Gestapu affair, they were supported by reportedly left-wing "progressive" Army officers and a small number of Army and Air Force units. Confined largely to the capital of Djakarta and parts of West and Central Java, it was virtually quelled within 72 hours. The circumstances surrounding the preparation and the question of primary responsibility for the coup remain controversial, but its failure and the isolated Communist resistance in its wake unleashed an extensive massacre of tens of thousands of PKI members, sympathizers, and, it is to be feared, innocents by various anti-Communist groups, particularly Army-supported Muslim youth organizations. The question of President Sukarno's and the Chinese government's foreknowledge of or assistance to the Gestapu plotters also remains controversial, but on 12 March 1966, as Sukarno was steadily sliding from power, the PKI was formally banned, and on 5 July the Provisional People's Constituent Assembly (the country's highest policy-making body) proscribed the dissemination of Marxism-Leninism, confining it to study in an academic context only.

Covert Communist activity continued, and by the middle of 1966 two wings within the shattered PKI underground, one pro-Peking, the other pro-Moscow, had emerged, each denouncing the other and elaborating on the causes of the party's debacle. Principal PKI leaders like Aidit were killed in Gestapu's aftermath, and scores of other prominent party leaders and cadres who escaped the immediate pogrom were arrested and tried in the following months and years. Tens of thousands were arrested on grounds of actual or suspected Gestapu involvement, PKI membership, or mere sympathy and were often held for years without trial.

Pro-Peking party *kompros* ("project committees") attempted to rally scattered elements during 1967, and a short-lived Communist "Indonesian People's Republic" was proclaimed near Blitar, East Java, under former PKI editor B. Hutapea in 1968, but military and police action cut short this revival. Since then PKI activity has engaged the few hundred expatriate party members, the "people's war" insurgents along the Sarawak border, and a number, generally considered small, of underground activists in Java. With the advent of General Suharto to power, government warnings of the Communist threat to Indonesia have continued, accentuated in various policy pronouncements by the rise of Communist power in Indochina and more recently by the instability in neighboring Eastern (Portuguese) Timor.

Organization and Tactics. Inside Indonesia the two wings of the PKI are limited to deep-cover proselytizing, periodic "execution" of allegedly rapacious landlords, and continuous attempts at infiltrating likely front organizations, including trade unions, peasants' cooperative associations, students' groups, and—according to official sources—even Muslim organizations. Only the Maoist wing of the party is involved in the small-scale, irregular guerrilla struggle along the Sarawak border.

In September 1966 the Politburo of the pro-Maoist PKI issued an *otokritik* (self-criticism) setting forth policies that have remained in effect ever since. Ascribing the disaster that overtook the party in the Gestapu incident to a too accommodating attitude taken by PKI chairman Aidit toward the Sukarno regime, the Maoist self-criticism raises "three banners" for the party to follow. The first is the building of a Marxist-Leninist party, free from "subjectivism, opportunism, and modern revisionism." The second is the promotion of the "armed people's struggle which, in essence, is the armed struggle of the peasants," in an anti-feudal agrarian revolution which is, however, under the direction of the "working class." Thirdly there is the needed development of a "revolutionary united front" based on the alliance between workers and peasants and also led by the "working class." (*Build the PKI along the Marxist-Leninist Line to Lead the People's Democratic Revolution in Indonesia*, published by the Delegation of the Central Committee of the PKI, Tirana, 1971, p. 199.) A new Maoist-wing PKI party program, published in November 1967, stresses that the "Indonesian people must arm themselves, build a people's armed force, and wage a people's war. Only through people's war will the Indonesian people achieve their liberation." (Ibid., p. 264.)

On 23 May 1975, the Peking-based "Delegation" issued a statement on the occasion of the PKI's fifty-fifth anniversary, lauding the "very great victories" won by the "fraternal peoples of Indochina, Vietnam, Cambodia and Laos," and noting again that the historical mission of the PKI could be realized only by true mastery of "Marxism Leninism Mao Tse Tung Thought" and particularly by "persistently and perseveringly" working with the masses in the countryside (Peking Review, 30 May, p. 17). The anniversary statement further emphasizes that the working class "must establish" a revolutionary united front by bringing together "all classes and revolutionary levels that can be united," particularly the proletariat, the peasantry, the petty bourgeoisie, and, to a degree, the national bourgeoisie, which, generally, has a "greedy nature" and is "not consistent" in the struggle against feudalism and imperialism (FBIS, 30 May).

On 17 August the Maoist "Delegation" issued, over the signature of Jusuf Adjitorop, a statement on the national independence anniversary of Indonesia, celebrated that day. It charged that "Suharto's clique of traitors" was using the name of the Indonesian Republic as a cover to insure that "imperialists, colonialists, compradors and feudalistic landlords" could "rob the Indonesian people" with impunity. Also the "Indonesian revisionist clique" was charged with taking a stand "identical to that of the bourgeoisie" who were trying to sabotage the PKI and the Indonesian revolution." (Ibid., 18 September.) The statement was broadcast over the transmitter of the Malaysian Communists' "Voice of the Malayan Revolution," which increasingly has served as the international channel of communication for the Peking-based "Delegation" as Peking's own international media have spent less time on "Delegation" pronouncements.

The Moscow wing, which in the past, but not in recent years, has called itself the "Marxist-Leninist Group of the PKI," also has published several authoritative statements of policy. The February 1969 document entitled "Urgent Tasks of the Communist Movement in Indonesia," allegedly issued in Djakarta, is perhaps most important. This document calls attention to the need for "new tactics" based on the premise that while it is necessary to prepare for possible armed struggle, "it would be premature" to launch such action now before the "completion" of careful preparatory party activity and before the emergence of a "clear cut revolutionary crisis" in the country that would lead to a "revolutionary situation." (IB, Prague, no. 7, 1969, p. 27.) Berating the Maoist wing's otokritik, the pro-Moscow group notes that "In armed struggle victory does not fall from the sky" and that "nobody can foretell exactly what form the armed struggle will take." It stresses these immediate tactical concerns: rehabilitation of the party and restoration of its "ideological prestige," creation of a "staunch Marxist-Leninist nucleus of leaders," careful organizational preparation among the masses, publication of periodicals that will form a rallying point for the "healthy forces" of the PKI and thus also "clearly"reveal the "anti-Leninist groups," and, finally, rejection of armed struggle at this stage, even though "secret weapons caches" for future armed action are being made ready. (Ibid., pp. 33-37.)

On 23 May 1975 Pravda, in an article commemorating the PKI's anniversary, stressed that the party program prescribes "the possibility of creating a broad anti-imperialist progressive national front." Without criticizing the Suharto government directly, the Pravda article cited the program document to the effect that the class struggle in Indonesia is now intensifying because of the inroads of foreign monopoly capital, the restriction on civil liberties, the suppression of movements favoring a more democratic social life, and the raising of the standard of living. (FBIS, 29 May.) The article affirmed that the Maoist concept of the countryside as the leading center of mass movements has been shown to be false by recent mass actions in Indonesia looking toward the democratization of political and social life and against the domination of foreign monopoly capital, which have all been centered in the cities. It added that there is need to work toward overcoming anti-Communist prejudices which the "reaction" has been fostering, and that Indonesia's "progressive" elements advocate the establishment of a broad "national unity front" and then the creation of a "national democratic state" that can speak for the concerns of the "broadest strata" of the people. (Ibid.)

The pro-Moscow PKI faction thus appears to seek to pursue a "national democratic" strategy, predicated on stressing the party's peaceful but progressive character. By identifying itself with the non- or even anti-Communist critics of the regime—who have repeatedly protested or demonstrated against the influx of foreign, particularly Japanese capital (*YICA, 1975* p. 341), against the alleged corruption of high-living leading officials while the mass of Indonesians have benefited but little from Suharto's "New Order," and against the tight controls over the press and over all freedom of political opinion—the PKI may be able to "rehabilitate" itself and so become relegitimized. In a way this policy is like that pursued by the PKI under Aidit in the early 1950s when the PKI also sought to recover from a debacle (i.e., the coup attempt at Madiun). The difference is that today neither the Moscow-oriented faction nor the Peking group possesses a significant organizational base (the PKI was not outlawed after the 1948 attempt) and neither "people's war" tactics nor a "national democratic" united front building and relegitimization strategy is likely to have any effect on the Suharto government. Rather, the low level of covert Communist activity and the foreign-based anti-Suharto propaganda being disseminated by the two PKI branches suffice to lend a certain credibility to the government's persisting warnings about the threat of subversion. For example, at the close of May 1975, in an address to government officials and leaders of political parties in South Sumatra, Attorney-General Ali Said reminded Indonesians "to be more vigilant against underground activities of the defunct Communist party," adding that the fall of Vietnam and Cambodia to Communists would "in some ways affect Indonesia" (*Indonesian Times*, Djakarta, 31 May). On the other hand, there is an on-going if controlled undercurrent of criticism of and opposition to the regime resulting from alleged corruption, the dominance of foreign capital, the lack of press and political freedoms, and the plight of the Indonesian masses suffering from double-digit inflation—all of which remain ready for political exploitation.

Especially the publications of the Maoist wing of the PKI stress the economic crisis. In an interview over Radio Tirana on 28 November 1974, Setiati Surasto of the "Delegation" group declared:

> The Suharto fascist regime has thrown the door wide open for foreign capital investment and has sold out the country's riches to imperialist monopoly capital. That being the case, Indonesia has again become a cheap source of raw materials and labour and an outlet for the increasingly high priced industrial products of the imperialist countries. The working people are suffering more heavily. The total number of unemployed and semi-employed people has reached 28 million. Living costs and prices of basic necessities continue soaring. Peasants are being subjected to exploitation and oppression by the landlords, bureaucrat capitalists and imperialists. Democratic rights are being trampled under the heels." (*Indonesian Tribune*, 8, no. 4, 1974: 4.)

An undetermined number of former PKI members and suspected sympathizers continue to be held by the government in various detention camps. Some estimates of their number have gone as high as 760,000 (*FBIS*, 27 June 1975). Officially the government declines to use the term "tapol" (from *tabanan politik*, "political resisters"), claiming that those being detained have committed various statutory crimes not of a political nature. But by its own admission at least 10,000 prisoners are being held on the island of Buru in the Moluccas. Against these prisoners there is, according to the government, not enough evidence to permit a trial, but they are in process of being "rehabilitated." At least an additional 24,000 in this category are estimated as being held elsewhere, also without prospect of trial. Another group of about 2,000 prisoners (described as "hard-core" Communists or Gestapu participants by officials), on whom sufficient evidence is available, have been or are eventually to be brought to trial. (About 850 of these had been tried by March 1975, with about 250 receiving death sentences.) Additionally, there are perhaps as many as 10,000 other detainees, belonging to neither of the above two classifications, and whose release in the near future is officially described as likely (see also *YICA, 1975*, p. 337). At the end of June, Admiral Sudomo, chief of staff of the national security agency, offered a new set of data. Some 34,000 prisoners were still being held for "rehabilitation" (10,000 on Buru), he said, but some 1,300 of this group had been released in 1975 under surveillance and after having given assurances that they had abandoned the Marxist-Leninist ideology. As for the "hundreds of thousands of Communist sympathizers" arrested after the 1965 coup attempt, 540,000 had been released since 1966, Sudomo said, and 128,000 had been allowed to keep their government jobs till they retired. (*FBIS*, 2 June.)

Also at the end of June, presidential decree 88/1975 provided a new classification of those prisoners, whether military or civil officials, who allegedly were indirectly involved in the 1948 or 1965 coup attempts. According to the decree, a so-called C group will be composed of those "suspected of" or "indirectly involved in" the coup attempts, presumably those with the greatest degree of culpability. They will be dismissed dishonorably from government service. A second group, called C-1, is to consist of those who were involved in the 1948 attempt or in the "aftermath" of the 1965 one, or who "are regarded" as sympathizing or having sympathized with the Communists, or who did not oppose the Communist movement though they were able to do so. A C-2 category, is to consist of former members of the PKI and its mass and front organizations. Finally, a C-3 group will comprise "those persons whose involvement could not be established" but who are believed to be sympathetic to the PKI or Communism or the 1965 coup attempt through behavior or utterances. (*Antara Daily News Bulletin*, 30 June; *FBIS*, 30 June; *Indonesian Times*, 28 June.) Especially the last classification, which again raises questions as to why persons whose culpability cannot be established nevertheless are under detention and for how long they will be, is likely to afford new ammunition to critics. Among others, the "British Campaign for the Release of Indonesian Political Prisoners" and its founder, Mrs. Carmel Budiardjo, wife of a tapol, have been attempting to provide information abroad on the tapol question (*Christian Science Monitor*, 21 May), particularly on the allegedly severe living conditions of the prisoners held on Buru ("Ten Buru Tapols Found Dead," *Tapol*, publication of the "British Campaign . . . ," London, August, p. 2). The Indonesian government has sought to counter this campaign by pointing to improved conditions on Buru and also by alleging past Communist sympathies on the part of Mrs. Budiardjo and her husband. At the close of August, a foundation in Djakarta chaired by the Indonesian foreign minister, Adam Malik, established an "Institute for the Rehabilitation and Education of Detainees or Former Detainees Charged with Subversion." The new Institute is to have a humanitarian as well as a social role in seeking the adjustment of tapols. (*Indonesian Current Affairs Translation Service Bulletin*, August, p. 622.)

Domestic Developments. Trials of alleged Communist leaders and/or participants in the 1965 coup attempt and disclosures by Indonesian officials of presumably new threats of subversion to the nation continued during 1974-75 as in previous years. On 26 December 1974 a former infantry major, Sukarlan, described as a PKI "leader," was sentenced to 20 years in jail for having attempted to overthrow the government on the island of Bali during the course of the Gestapu affair (*FBIS*, 7 January 1975), and at the close of January 1975 military tribunals in West Sumatra and Riau provinces began the trials of six former military described by the prosecution as "Gestapu-PKI and subversion cases" (ibid., 31 January). On 28 January a military court in Bogor, West Java, sentenced two military to 10 and 12 years imprisonment for Gestapu "involvement" (ibid., 30 January). In mid-June a Central Java district court sentenced three women, one of whom had been the third secretary of the PKI women's front, to prison terms ranging from 15 to 20 years. All of the defendants had pleaded guilty to violating statutes on "subversive activities" and had been charged with Gestapu participation. (*Indonesian Times*, 17 June.) On 1 July the Indonesian Antara news agency announced that a district court at Balikpapan, East Kalimantan, had sentenced a "prominent member" of the PKI to 17 years in prison for "subversion against the state," a statutory offense formulated in the heyday of the Sukarno era and continued by the Suharto government.

Non-Communist, but presumably "New Left" activists, especially among university students who around the turn of 1973/74 had demonstrated their opposition to some of the regime's policies (*YICA, 1975*, p. 341), have been sentenced on such grounds as well. For example, one Sjachrir, described as a "former student leader of the University of Indonesia," was sentenced to six and a half years, having been found guilty of "committing subversion." According to the presiding judge, the defendant had invited political leaders from outside the university to a panel discussion in the university student center to speak on the recent course of Indonesian politics. During this discussion, according to the judge, Sjachrir had said that the existing political system in Indonesia should be eliminated and a new "political order" created (Antara dispatch, Djakarta, 17 June 1975). At about the same time police sources in Djakarta disclosed that "certain individuals and circles" were taking "undue advantage" of the "integrity" of President Suharto, his wife, and various high officials. The actions described, according to police, were designed to create a negative image of the state leadership and the resulting creation of an "atmosphere of unrest" in the government and armed forces. Behind these charges, however, appeared to lie at least in part a simple swindling scheme, whereby the perpetrators, using forged signatures of officials and purloined official stationery, were soliciting monetary contributions. (*Indonesian Times*, 21 June.) But in the present context of political controls in Indonesia even simple fraud may assume the dimensions of "subversion."

Toward the end of 1974 East Java authorities disclosed activities of a new "underground organization of Gestapu-PKI remnants" in the province, including a business called itself USPROD (Usaha Produksi, or "Production Enterprise"), engaged in transportation and trade, run by funds and attempting to make East Java into a "supply depot and a struggle base" for the underground organization (*FBIS*, 6 January 1975). In February military information sources in Bandung, West Java, reported distribution of illegal pamphlets designed to create "tension" by inciting members of the religious communities against each other. In view of the contents, according to official sources, "it was obvious" that the leaflets had been distributed by PKI-Gestapu "remnants." (Ibid., 7 March.) In May, also in Bandung, police uncovered an "illegal immigration network" engaged in smuggling Chinese from Hong Kong and People's China. False travel documents had been seized, and arrested suspects reportedly admitted to smuggling back into Indonesia 30 Chinese who had returned to China in 1960. Concern about the "political aspects" of the case was openly expressed by military spokesmen who raised the issue of possible infiltration of Chinese Communist agents. (*Indonesian Current Affairs Translation Service Bulletin*, May, pp. 381-82; *FBIS,*, 28 May.)

At the close of July, Major General Yasir of the Central Java Security Command declared that underground Communists were busy attempting to undermine the government and people, and that especially in facing the forthcoming 1977 general elections Indonesians should be "continuously vigilant and alert" against the Communists (*FBIS*, 30 July). The previous month, Major General Amir Murtopo, chairman of the government's party Golkar (from Golongan Karya or "Functional Group"), which wholly dominates the membership of Indonesia's parliament, called for the cultivation of a "sense of hereditary hostility" against Communism, adding that Communism could not be fought with weapons, but rather by the cultivation of mental attitudes based on the official national ideology of Indonesia, the so-called Pantjasila or "Five Pillars" of the state: belief in God, democracy, nationalism, social justice, and humanitarianism (or internationalism) (ibid., 3 July). Murtopo also called for "continued vigilance" against the PKI underground.

In meeting the alleged Communist threat at home Indonesian leaders also stress the importance of what they call "national resilience" (*ketahanan nasional*), a total mobilization of the spiritual and material resources of Indonesia but solely for defensive purposes. Thus, commenting on the fall of Saigon to Communist control, Indonesian defense minister and armed forces commander General Maraden Panggabean declared that this fall had had a "moral impact" on the Communist underground in Indonesia, which needed to be confronted by a strengthened "national resilience" (ibid., 5 May). Official exhortations to religious groups in Indonesia not to fall into the "trap of subversive elements" which are attempting to set one group against another have similarly been frequent (ibid., 18 April). The periodic flare-up of insurgent activity in Thailand and Malaysia generally also finds ready Indonesian press comment, with papers reflecting the government's Golkar party position usually linking such flare-ups to a boost in the morale of the PKI underground (ibid., 12 April).

Apart from such generalizations, however, specific concern is particularly focused on the only area of more or less if small-scale continued Communist guerrilla resistance in Indonesia: along the Sarawak frontier in West Kalimantan (Borneo). In mid-April the military commander of West Kalimantan, Brigadier Seno Hartono, attempted to reassure Indonesians that his command was prepared for any eventualities, including possible stepped-up activities by insurgents in the event the latter felt encouraged by developments in Vietnam. Hartono said, however, that Vietnam developments had had no bearing on the "stable security situation" in his command area (ibid., 17 April). Somewhat earlier Hartono expressed concern that the area might be infiltrated by North Kalimantan Communists who had been released by the Malaysian government as part of its recent amnesty program for Communist guerrillas in Sarawak (see *Malaysia,*) (ibid., 12 March).

In June the Djakarta daily *Suara Karya* published a series of on-the-spot reports on the security situation in West Kalimantan. The paper noted that in the past few years more than 10,000 Indonesian troops and about the same number of Malaysian forces had taken part in security operations there. Owing to the rugged terrain, total elimination of the insurgent threat was held to be difficult and some 150 armed guerrillas remained active. According to the paper, it was "obvious that uneasy security still prevails in the border area." (*FBIS*, 1 July.) Problems in the border area are aggravated by the evacuation of Chinese civilians from the scene of guerrilla operations, which has created a "vacuum of middlemen" and traders and thus adversely affected the general population as well (ibid.). On 19 July the Indonesian army chief of staff, General Makmun Murod, was reported by Djakarta radio to have stressed that the government would continue it operations against "remnants" of the Sarawak border insurgent force. He noted that Malaysia's policy of granting amnesty to insurgents "should not influence and cause us to slacken our determination" to obliterate the guerrillas. Murod also claimed success in recent counter-insurgency operations, including the "destruction" of the PKI underground network in West Kalimantan. (Ibid., 21 July.)

In the face of foreign criticism of Indonesia's policies toward its political prisoners and of its preoccupation with the threat of domestic subversion generally, efforts were being made toward the close of the year to improve the image of the Djakarta government abroad. On 22 November, ranking Indonesian diplomats, including ambassadors, posted in the United States, Britain, France, Japan, Belgium, and Australia, met in Djakarta to hear a detailed explanation of the security policies of the Suharto government from Admiral Sudomo, chief of staff of the "Security and Order Restoration Command" (KOPKAMTIB). Sudomo reportedly explained the government's policies on returning the tapol (political prisoners) to society as well as the "tasks of Indonesian envoys in facing the activities of G-30-S/PKI remnants (i.e., Communists and participants in the 1965 coup) abroad" and the need to remain "vigilant" (*FBIS*, 26 November). The Suharto regime officially remains concerned, however, that there may be a slackening in domestic vigilance against Communist elements. On 12 December, the military commander of the Twelfth (Tanjungpura) Military District declared that while "militarily" the Communist insurgents in West Borneo "had no meaning," it was necessary to remain on guard against what he termed "pseudo-stability," that is, presumably a condition of seeming normalcy as the enemy was "constantly looking for an opportunity to act" (*Antara Daily News Bulletin*, 15 December, p. ii).

International Aspects. The Communist ascendance in Indochina during the course of 1975 resulted in a number of official Indonesian reactions in which caution was mixed with hope of improved relationships with the Communist world. Interviewed by the French paper *Le Monde*, in May, Foreign Minister Malik emphasized that the collapse of U.S. power in Indochina had come as no surprise to the ASEAN countries, adding that U.S.-Indonesian relations would perhaps be limited in future to "the economic sector" and that, with regard to People's China (with which Indonesian diplomatic relations have been suspended since 1967) "everything has been readied" for a resumption of ties" (*FBIS*, 16 May). By the end of June, Malik was saying that the Vietnamese Communists would be too preoccupied with domestic problems to be interested in exporting revolution. Malik expressed hope that the United States, while it would eventually give up its Thai and Philippine military bases, would retain its role "as a Pacific power and a superpower." (*NYT*, 29 June.)

About the same time, Admiral Sudomo, chief of staff of the national security agency, said that Indonesia was prepared to cooperate with all Communist countries and more specifically with its Indochinese "neighbors" after they had had a chance to consolidate and "clarify" their position toward Southeast Asia. Indonesian appreciation of the U.S. role was changing, Sudomo added, and although there was no question of Indonesia's changing its traditional policy of non-alignment, he preferred a "more positive regional cooperation" against future Communist subversion in the region instead of "the current 'panicky rush' " of ASEAN countries to Peking. (*FBIS*, 2 July.) A week later, President Suharto, commenting on his discussions with government leaders in Iran, Yugoslavia, Canada, and the United States during his recent twelve-day tour to those countries, said that he had "particularly" clarified in these discussions "the situation after the conclusion of the Vietnam war." Suharto said that he had explained that the end of the war in Vietnam had not come as a shock to Indonesia, first because of Indonesia's "vast experience" in facing Communists at home, and, second, because Indonesia was aware that U.S. and other countries' aid to South Vietnam had not reached its goal. There had been a belief in various circles that it would be sufficient to face the Communists with arms, but actually, according to Suharto, Communist strength itself did not lie in force of arms but in "ideological fanaticism." Hence, Communist strength could only be met effectively by "national ideological fanaticism," and this fact, he claimed, had been "grossly neglected" by countries confronting Communism. (Ibid., 10 July.)

With the capture of Saigon and Phnom Penh by Communist forces the Suharto government moved toward formal diplomatic recognition of the new Communist regimes of South Vietnam and Cambodia. In early April a government spokesman in Djakarta had already announced that Indonesia was making "indirect contacts" with the Khmer Rouge rebels in Cambodia, ostensibly in order to "reduce casualties," and on 28 April formal recognition of the Royal Government of National Union was announced (ibid., 9, 28 April). Technically diplomatic relations with Hanoi had never been ruptured since their establishment more than a decade ago.

Relations with People's China remained suspended. A message broadcast by Radio Peking on 23 May, commemorating the fifty-fifth anniversary of the PKI, elicited a sharp reaction from the Indonesian foreign minister. Malik said that "whatever group attempts to intervene in Indonesia will be wiped out by the entire people." He recalled that a former Chinese foreign minister, Chi P'eng-fei, had promised two years before that China would not interfere in Indonesian internal affairs. (Ibid., 27 May.) The Peking broadcast had relayed the greetings of the Central Committee of the Chinese Communist Party to the "Delegation" of the PKI Central Committee. This message, among other things, had said:

> At present the Indonesian Revolution has suffered temporary setbacks and the Communist Party of Indonesia is in a difficult position. But no matter how frantic the counter-revolutionary forces may be, the Indonesian Communists have neither been cowed nor subjugated. . . . Our two Parties and two peoples have always sympathized with and supported each other in the protracted friendship and militant unity on the basis of proletarian internationalism. (*Peking Review*, 30 May, p. 3.)

The deputy speaker of the Indonesian parliament, Isnaei, said that this message was one of Peking's methods to divert attention from current problems on the Chinese mainland (*FBIS*, 29 May). On 16 August, in his annual address of state to the Indonesian parliament on the eve of the republic's Independence Day celebratons, President Suharto noted that "Other countries that keep on protecting former leaders of the PKI revolt, or that openly support the reemergency of the PKI in this country," were considered by Indonesia as "interfering in our domestic affairs" and as being unfriendly. Therefore, according to Suharto, "it is still difficult to de-freeze diplomatic relations with the People's Republic of China." (*Merdeka*, Djakarta, 18 August; *Indonesian Current Affairs Translation Service Bulletin*, August, p. 566.) While other ASEAN powers like Thailand and the Philippines moved toward mutual diplomatic recognition with China during 1975, Indonesia, like Singapore, has not been persuaded thus far that Radio Peking's pronouncements and other support of local Communists can be reconciled with ordinary state-to-state relations.

Indonesia's relations with the Soviet Union continued to improve slowly after the period of tension and mutual recrimination in the late 1960s (unlike the Chinese case, Soviet-Indonesian diplomatic relations were never suspended in the aftermath of the Gestapu incident, although bad strains developed during the height of the domestic anti-Communist campaign). Trade between the two countries has increased significantly. In 1973 Soviet exports to Indonesia amounted to about $3.5 million and in 1974 had risen to $13 million. Soviet imports from Indonesia rose from $5.5 million in 1973 to almost $29 million in 1974, with Indonesian rubber, coffee, pepper, and other commodities being traded for Soviet textile manufacturing machinery, pharmaceuticals, and chemical fertilizer (*Antara Daily News Bulletin*, 20 June 1975, p. 5).

In line with the Suharto government's efforts to improve its relations with the Soviet Union and to diversify the sources of support for its long-range plans for national economic development, the government on 18 November approved a Soviet offer of assistance in the construction of two electric power plants, a 400 megawatt station at Sakuling, West Java, and a 600 megawatt facility at Mrica, Central Java. The Soviet Union is expected to bear most of the financial burden of the project, estimated at about US $100 million, as well as to send technical advisers. This is the first aid package extended by Moscow to Indonesia since General Suharto assumed power in 1966. (*FBIS*, 19 November; Dan Coggin, "Indonesia, A Soviet Fund Package," *Far Eastern Economic Review*, 12 December, p. 48).

The Soviet position toward the Suharto government remains ambivalent, however. On the one hand, authoritative Soviet commentators like Y. Lugovskiy, writing in *Izvestiia* on 17 August on the occasion of Indonesia's Independence Day anniversary, noted the widening belief of Indonesian "business and official circles" in the need to diversify economic relations, and in the danger of foregoing "the opportunity of cooperation with the socialist countries" in a manner that "has helped India and other Asian nations" to develop production in the public sector. The USSR, according to Lugovskiy, is ready to develop "comprehensive ties" with the Indonesian Republic on the basis of "non-interference in domestic affairs, equality and mutual benefit" (*FBIS*, 22 August). On the other hand, Indonesia's continuing search for a new post-Vietnam regional security system has begun to arouse Soviet criticism. Writing in *Pravda* on 31 August, a Soviet commentator, Yuriy Aninskiy, warned of the danger in alleged attempts by Indonesian military to turn ASEAN (the Association of Southeast Asian Nations, founded in 1967 and including the Philippines, Thailand, Malaysia, Singapore, and Indonesia) "into a military bloc with a distinct anti-Communist orientation." Such efforts, according to Aninskiy, fly in the face of historical experience in the region, which suggests that the existence of anti-Communist military blocs "has been a constant source of the threat of conflicts between the Asian countries and of interference in their internal affairs." (Ibid., 8 September.) Soviet strategy toward the ASEAN powers, and particularly countries like Indonesia with avowed domestic anti-Communist policy priorities, remains that of encouraging a broadening of and a greater independence in the entire field of international relations, breaking down residual Cold War rigidities, and encouraging domestic liberalization of politics, particularly in making a place for the Left, with an eventual relegitimization of a Moscow-oriented Communist party and a movement toward establishment of a more "progressive" regime.

This Soviet strategy, the implications of which are well appreciated in top Indonesian government circles, also continues to meet with suspicion and opposition from various influential elements in Indonesian society, such as the orthodox Muslim leadership, which are sensitive to allegedly anti-religious slurs in Communist materials. Thus, in June 1975, Kjai H. Masjkur, chairman of the Islamic Solidarity Committee in Djakarta, demanded that the government bar the import into Indonesia of a book entitled "Roses," by Ludvic Venera, originally published in Czechoslovakia but translated into English and circulating through the West. According to Masjkur, the book contained distortions concerning the life of the Prophet Muhammad and his family. Masjkur called on Indonesians to be alert "against Communist attempts to make Islam the target of their propaganda campaign." A protest against the book has been lodged by the World Islamic League in Mecca, and in Pakistan the book has been banned. (*Antara Daily News Bulletin*, 27 June.)

Meanwhile, Indonesian trade with East European countries other than the USSR has also begun to increase. In March a bilateral trade agreement was signed in Prague under which Czechoslovakia is expected to increase rubber imports to 15,000 tons per year, and imports of other Indonesian commodities, such as tin, also are expected to accelerate (*Indonesia Perspective*, Djakarta, June, p. 19). The volume of Indonesian-Polish trade in 1974 was almost $43 million; in 1973 it was only a fourth of that figure (Antara dispatch, Djakarta, 25 July). Polish exports to Indonesia include chemical products, machinery and factory equipment, and Indonesian exports to Poland have been primarily rubber and tin. In mid-May 1975 as a result of a visit by a Bulgarian trade mission to Djakarta, a comprehensive trade agreement was signed, providing for direct exports of Indonesian rubber up to 10,000 tons per annum (previously Indonesian rubber was shipped via Singapore). The agreement is likely to bring about a better balance in Bulgarian-Indonesian trade relations (Indonesia's exports to Bulgaria in 1974 were valued at only $200,000 and its imports from Bulgaria at around $30 million) and also broaden the range of exports to include tin, spices, and tobacco. (*Kompas*, Djakarta, 12 May; *Indonesian Current Affairs Translation Service Bulletin*, May, p. 363.)

Developments in Eastern Timor, a Portuguese possession in a rapid state of decolonization and originally promised independence in 1978, have become a source of acute concern to the Suharto government (*Far Eastern Economic Review*, Hong Kong, 1 August 1975, pp. 22-23). The split in political sentiments in Eastern Timor (Western Timor is Indonesian Territory), led, according to Djakarta radio, to streams of political refugees from Eastern Timor into Indonesian territory as the Leftist "Timorese Liberation Front" (known as Fretilin) assumed political ascendancy and bloody clashes erupted with followers of the Apodeti Party, which reportedly seeks union of East Timor with Indonesia and other groups. Indonesian officials have accused Fretilin leaders of being communists and have said that most East Timorese desire union with Indonesia (*NYT*, 13 September). As early as February 1975 the correspondent of the Indonesian news agency Antara claimed that a "hate Indonesia" campaign was intensifying among East Timor's 600,000 inhabitants as key government positions were being taken over by Communists and as the Fretilin launched a campaign of intimidation and fear among the inhabitants (*FBIS*, 28 February). Mediating efforts by Portuguese officials in Macao and by an emissary from Lisbon appear to have had little effect, and by early

September the Indonesian government was accusing a special envoy of the Portuguese government, Dr. Antonio Almeida Santos, sent to Djakarta and Timor to mediate the Timor dispute, of violating an agreement not to come to a separate understanding with the Fretilin alone at the possible expense of other parties (Antara dispatch, Djakarta, 9 September). On 17 September Indonesia sent a naval flotilla to East Timor and threatened retaliation if the Fretilin continued its armed action against its opponents (*NYT*, 18 September). By this time, Fretilin dominance of most of East Timor's de facto government had become an established fact and the prospect of a Leftist, if not Communist-dominated government located directly on Indonesia's doorstep greatly disturbed Djakarta decision makers committed to maintaining a domestic anti-Communist policy momentum.

Initially, Indonesia seemed concerned with exerting a pattern of indirect political pressures on Eastern Timor, including a blockade, even as the opposition to Fretilin, was gravely weakening (*Far Eastern Review*, 19 September, p. 9). However, at the same time, the prospect of direct Indonesian intervention also began to loom larger and President Suharto declared on 17 September that "attention" was being paid to a petition to Djakarta signed by East Timorese to have East Timor join the Indonesian Republic, and that "in principle" Indonesia did not reject the wish of the inhabitants of East Timor for such a merger (*Antara Daily News Bulletin*, 19 September). Meanwhile one Timorese organization opposed to Fretilin, the Democratic Union of Timor (UDT), changed its name in mid-September to "Anti-Communist Movement" and, reportedly, also sought a merger with Indonesia.

On 7 December, Indonesian forces, subsequently described as "volunteers" responding to an invitation by pro-Indonesian parties wishing a merger of East Timor with Indonesia, stormed ashore at Dili, the capital of Eastern Timor, driving the leftist Fretilin units into the hills. Both the Fourth Committee of the United Nations General Assembly and the Security Council condemned the invasion, but by the end of the year and in spite of particularly vigorous criticism from Peking, the process of merger of East Timor into Indonesian territory was apparently irreversible. Djakarta had acted out of obvious concern that an independent, leftist East Timorese government might provide a haven for PKI and other dissidents (Justus M. van der Kroef, "The Problem of Portuguese Timor," *Asian Affairs*, November-December).

During the year discussions continued between Malaysian and Indonesian military representatives on joint action against Communist insurgents in the Sarawak border area and Communist infiltration generally. In mid-April, Malaysian and Indonesian military representatives after a three-day meeting in Sumatra endorsed a new joint operations program for 1975-76, looking toward combating "enemy subversion, inflation and other illegal activities threatening both countries" (*FBIS*, 25 April). Measures to ensure the security of territorial waters were also discussed. Early in July at the conclusion of another conference of the military, held on the island of Bali, agreement was reached on stepping up operations against the Sarawak insurgents. The conference was the third of its kind held since 1973 and dealt with a number of joint operations, among them border crossings by military helicopters. (Ibid., 10 July.)

During the year Malaysian Communists expressed solidarity with their Indonesian counterparts. On 24 May the Central Committee of the Communist Party of Malaya sent a congratulatory message to the Central Committee of the PKI on the occasion of the latter's anniversary, stating: "Our parties and peoples have always supported and encouraged each other in our common struggle against old and new colonialism," and added that the PKI was "waging an extraordinarily difficult struggle to overthrow the fascist regime of the U.S. imperialists and their running dogs, the Suharto clique," but still would "attain the genuine liberation of the people" (ibid., 10 June). The PKI also received greetings from the North Kalimantan (i.e., North Borneo) Communist Party, whose message stated that "the road taken by China is the only road for the colonial and semicolonial people to seek liberation," and that in taking this road the Indonesian Communists had dealt "a heavy blow at the

Suharto fascist regime" and at "U.S. imperialism and Soviet revisionism," and thus had greatly "inspired" the "Indonesian revolutionary people" (ibid., 25 July). On 30 May, North Vietnamese media reported a congratulatory message to the National Liberation Front of South Vietnam sent by Jusuf Adjitorop, the Peking-based head of the "Delegation of the Central Committee of the PKI." Adjitorop declared that the "great victory" of the Vietnamese people marked a total and "shameful" setback for the U.S. policy of "aggresson and intervention" in Vietnam, thus providing "great encouragement to the struggle of the world people against imperialism and its henchmen and for national salvation" (ibid., 4 June).

Publications. Inside Indonesia the two underground wings of the PKI do not now have publications that appear with any regularity or frequency; only mimeographed or poorly printed pamphlets and leaflets are used. An example is *Front Rakjat* ("People's Front"), an irregular mimeo publication of the Maoist PKI in Kalimantan (Borneo). The Indonesian Communists do not have a clandestine radio transmitter of their own, but in the past two years an increasing number of messages of the PKI Central Committee have been broadcast over the "Voice of the Malayan Revolution," the transmitter of the major, Peking-oriented faction in the Communist movement in West Malaysia. Only very occasionally do Chinese media now carry statements by the "Delegation" group, in contrast to frequent publication in previous years.

The "Delegation" continues to publish its main journal, *Indonesian Tribune*, about five or six times a year. This is edited and produced in Tirana, as is the faction's youth-front publication *API (Api Pemuda Indonesia)* ("Fire of Indonesian Youth"), which now appears only once or twice a year. *Suara Rakjat Indonesia* ("Voice of the Indonesian People"), the publication of the "Indonesian Organization for Afro-Asian Solidarity," headquartered in Peking, did not appear in 1975; since 1972 it has been published more and more irregularly.

The Moscow-wing of the PKI has over the years relied heavily on the Prague-based *World Marxist Review* and *Information Bulletin* for publication of its principal policy statements. While such media continue to publish policy statements made by the Moscow-oriented PKI faction representatives at various Soviet conferences, in general the Soviet media have reduced the space allocated for such purposes in the past two years. *Tekad Rakjat* ("People's Will"), edited in Moscow, has increasingly become this group's main publication. It has a very limited circulation outside the Soviet-bloc countries.

University of Bridgeport   Justus M. van der Kroef

Japan

The Japan Communist Party (Nihon Kyosanto; JCP) was founded in 1922. It operated illegally until October 1945 when the Allied Occupation restored freedom of organization to all political parties. In 1949, the party elected 35 members to the House of Representatives, but condemnation by the Cominform the following year and a succession of "red purges" ordered by General MacArthur resulted in the loss of all communist seats in the elections of 1952 and a reduction in the party's popular vote from 9.7 percent in 1949 to 2.5 percent in 1952. In 1955, the party was reorganized, and under a policy of "power through parliamentary means" began a steady ascent in membership and seats in the Diet.

Membership in the JCP remained in 1975 the same as that estimated in 1974, about 330,000. The party holds 20 seats (out of 252) in the (upper) House of Councillors and 38 (out of 491) in the House of Representatives, and is third in each house, after the Liberal Democratic Party (LDP) and the Japan Socialist Party (JSP).

Because of the alienation between the JCP and the communist parties of the Soviet Union and China, two splinter parties have been formed: the Voice of Japan (Nihon no Koe), which is pro-Soviet and has an estimated 400 members, and the Japan Communist Party (Left), which is pro-Peking, with about 1,000 members; the latter party has recently split into two rival factions. Several other small Marxist-Leninist groups exist, but are insignificant in size and influence.

The population of Japan in 1975 was estimated at 111,110,000.

Except for the JSP, the JCP is the only left-wing force in Japan to be represented in the parliament and to exert measurable influence on public opinion. Because of its independent stance, including denunciations of policies and actions taken by the communist parties and governments of both the People's Republic of China and the Soviet Union, and a "soft" policy line which underplays orthodox Marxism-Leninism, the JCP has been able to develop an appeal which has until recently won increasing popular support. Nevertheless, party spokesmen are concerned over the "communist allergy" which still prevails among Japanese: a public opinion poll recently revealed 41 percent of respondents designated the JCP as a party they could "never like" (*Sankei*, 19 November). JCP leaders, seeking power in a capitalist industrial society, find more affinity with their sister parties in Italy and France than with those of Asian countries. They continually emphasize in public statements and propaganda their policy of "power through parliamentary means," their support of the freedoms of press, speech, and religion, and their objective of a "democratic coalition government." The party organs gave prominent coverage to the joint declaration issued in mid-November 1975 by the heads of the communist parties of Italy and France expressing commitment to independence, democracy, and human rights—principles which parallel those of the JCP (*Akahata*, 19 November).

Organization and Leadership. The affairs of the JCP are directed by the Central Committee, whose 168 members (120 regular and 48 alternate) were elected by the Twelfth Congress in 1973. The 14-member Standing Committee of the 38-member Presidium (elected by the Central Committee) controls the party. Nosaka Sanzo, 83 years of age and a member of the House of Councillors, is chairman of the Central Committee and thus senior official of the party. Miyamoto Kenji, effective leader of the JCP, is chairman of the Presidium; he is assisted by three deputies: Oka Masayoshi, Senaga Kamejiro, and Hakamada Satomi. These four and the ten following comprise the Standing Committee: Fuwa Tetsuzo, Kurahara Korehito, Matsuhara Harushige, Nishizawa Tomio, Ichikawa Shoichi, Iwabayashi Toranosuke, Ueda Koichiro, Kaitani Harumatsu, Kaneko Mitsuhiro, and Murakami Hiroshi. A second organ which has recently assumed increased authority is the 15-member Secretariat, headed by Fuwa Tetsuzo, the third-ranking party official after Nosaka and Miyamoto. Other important party organs are the Control Committee (6 members), and Central Party Organ Publications Committee (21 members). There are also some 22 special committees; the most important of these runs the newspaper *Akahata*, which maintains full-time correspondents in Moscow, Berlin, Prague, Bucharest, and Hanoi. Other committees are charged with responsibility for such varied matters as: party policy, international affairs, party theory, mass movements, sports, culture, propaganda, party construction, education, magazine publishing, elections, and policy toward military bases, nuclear weapons and the U.S.-Japanese security treaty. In addition, the party maintains a "Research Institute for Social and Scientific Problems." The 58 Diet members are organized in each of the parliamentary houses.

Auxiliary and Mass Organizations. The JCP controls or has the support of some 40 principal national organizations which include peace movements, cultural societies, professional groups, and international friendship associations, and relate to youth, labor, students, women, businessmen, doctors and nurses, lawyers, consumers, writers, journalists, scientists, athletes, and many other professions and interests. The youth movement receives most attention and is considered to be the most important of the JCP-affiliated organizations.

The Youth Movement. The Democratic Youth League (Minseido), which dates from 1923, has an estimated membership of 200,000 and branches in all 47 prefectures. The JCP sees Minseido as a recruiting ground for full-fledged party members and has, therefore, placed great emphasis on the expansion of Minseido membership and on training and education. Furthermore, Minseido is looked upon as a useful auxiliary force to be mobilized in election campaigns for JCP candidates.

In an important meeting of Minseido's Central Committee in September 1975, resolutions were passed calling for the realization of the "four demands" of youth: healthy and sane livelihood, peace and security for the motherland; democracy, freedom, and human rights; and clean culture and morals. Other, more practical goals were an increase in Minseido membership as a stimulus to a bigger party membership and more seats for the JCP in the expected forthcoming general elections. The committee discussed the principal obstacles to the party's much touted renovationist front: the strength of reactionary elements and the activities of radical, Trotskyite, and terrorist groups. Leaders pointed out that general membership had declined since the 1974 congress and appealed for redoubled efforts to obtain new recruits and new subscriptions to Minseido's newspaper.

A recent development in party activities, in which the members of Minseido have been mobilized, is the use of legal action to secure redress against acts of violence or discrimination. Many young Minseido and JCP members are lawyers or law students and their talents are being utilized to press suits in three general classes of action: criminal acts, libel in anti-JCP writings, and discriminatory actions against Minseido and JCP members by industrialists and factory owners. Suits against several of Japan's best-known industrial firms have charged unfair treatment respecting wages and promotions of employees with communist party affiliations.

Labor. The JCP has never been able to achieve dominance in the Japanese labor movement. The General Council of Trade Unions (Sohyo) represents the largest percentage of organized labor (4,470,000 members) and has traditionally operated under the influence of the Japan Socialist Party which it has consistently backed. The JCP has made constant and strenuous efforts to break the JSP hold on Sohyo, without success. Communist union representatives propose each year at Sohyo's annual congress a motion to establish the principle of "freedom of political party choice" (members of the federation are expected to vote for JSP-backed candidates) and thus far have been consistently voted down. At the 50th Sohyo congress meeting in Tokyo on 21-24 July 1975, the pro-JCP motion gained six more votes than in 1974, but still failed of passage by a large majority. The principal attention of the congress was directed to the "failure" of the annual "spring struggle," which achieved only an average 13.1 percent wage hike, in contrast to the 32.9 percent won in 1974.

The Japan Teachers' Union (Nikkyoso), with 619,000 members, has long been characterized by significant communist influence, earning from its antagonists the sobriquet "red union." In fact, a third of its local chapters are controlled by communists. The 47th congress of the national union was held on 1-4 July in Akaishi, Hyogo prefecture, after several other cities had refused hospitality. The meetings, attended by 1,700 delegates, saw a fierce confrontation between the mainstream (pro-JSP) and anti-mainstream (pro-JCP). The latter mustered nearly 35 percent of the votes in favor of the "freedom of party choice" resolution. *Akahata* gave daily and extensive coverage to the congress, severely attacking the chairman of Nikkyoso for remarks such as: "The criticism and comments recently aimed at labor unions by the JCP have exceeded the bounds of responsible leadership to be expected from a renovationist party" (4 July). At the conclusion of the congresss, *Akahata* labeled "totally bankrupt" the line taken by Nikkyoso's executive committee, and called for abandonment of its "misguided policy based on the support of one specific party" (5 July).

Early in the postwar period the JCP and Nikkyoso emphasized the class consciousness of teachers as workers. Later, the idea gained currency that teachers were " specialists." In 1974, the JCP, noting the spiritual and cultural characteristics of the teaching profession and the great and direct influence brought to bear by it on the formation of the nation's children, evolved the phrase "sacred profession" to describe teachers who had previously been labeled workers and specialists. In 1975, Miyamoto broadened his categories to announce that government workers should be regarded as "public servants," since their wages were paid from taxes rather than by private employers and they shared with the general public the responsibilities for a "people's administration." Both of these slogans, "teaching as a sacred profession" and government workers as "public servants," were designed to curry public favor, to enhance the benign image of the JCP, and to gain votes in elections. Most members of Nikkyoso opposed the new labeling, and the issue became another element in the ongoing dispute between the JCP and the JSP. Some impression of the unpopularity of the JCP position can be gained from a poll taken among Nikkyoso members in Miyagi Prefecture which resulted in 83.6 percent of the respondents favoring classification of teachers as "both workers and specialists," and only 1.8 percent approving the JCP-proposed "teaching as a sacred profession."

If anything, JCP influence in Nikkyoso appeared to be declining in 1975. JCP representatives attending a Nikkyoso special convention in March 1975 numbered 139 (out of 476) in contrast to attendance at meetings in 1974 and 1973 of 166 and 159. The number of JCP supporters in local Nikkyoso unions has also been reported as diminishing while the JSP has gained in strength.

The JCP energetically supported Japan's longest and largest-scale strike involving employees of government-owned enterprises and corporations, which began 26 November and ended at midnight 3 December, two days earlier than the ten days planned. The issue was the right of government employees to strike; this right had been prohibited by General MacArthur during the occupation in an ordinance issued in July 1948. The JCP claimed that the loss of this right, by fiat of a foreign occupier, violated fundamental human rights guaranteed by the Japanese constitution, particularly article 28 which guarantees to workers the right "to organize and to bargain and act collectively." The government refused to accede to the unions' demands and the strike failed to gain its objective. The JCP expressed determination to carry on the struggle to secure this right inside and outside the Diet; thus a continuing battle with the government on the issue can be expected in 1976.

Peace Movement. The principal manifestation of the Japanese peace movement continues to be the annual meetings to commemorate the nuclear bombing of Hiroshima and Nagasaki. The Japan Council Against Atomic and Hydrogen Bombs (Gensuikyo) was organized in 1955. It split in 1963 over the issue of the partial nuclear test ban treaty. Since that time, three organizations have existed, the JCP-supported Gensuikyo, the JSP- and Sohyo-oriented Gensuikin, and a third, Kakkin, allied to the Democratic Socialist Party (DSP).

Early in 1975 spokesmen for these organizations issued statements pointing out the folly of rivalry within the anti-nuclear bomb movement and calling for reunification. A committee representing seven concerned organizations was established, and discussions, which culminated in July, were directed to resolving the outstanding differences. These efforts failed, as they had in previous years, and the JCP and JSP supporters blamed each other for the breakdown of the talks. As a result, the principal organizations, Gensuikyo and Gensuikin, held separate mass meetings in Tokyo, Hiroshima, and Nagasaki during the anniversary week of the 1945 attacks. Attendance was reported as 10,000 at each meeting, but Gensuikyo boasted of more foreign delegates to emphasize the international character of the movement: 76 from 24 countries, including the United States (23), Cuba, North and South Vietnam, "Democratic Chile," and Micronesia (Gensuikin drew 26 foreign delegates from 15 countries). Well-known representatives attending Gensuikyo meetings were Nobel Peace Prize winner Philip Noel-Baker from the United Kingdom, and John McBride, former Irish foreign minister. No delegates attended either convention from the Soviet Union or the People's Republic of China (PRC).

Observers noted that many of those attending the meetings were doing so for the first time: a generational change had become manifest in the ban-the-bomb movement. Some journalists found in this a "new stirring in the Japanese peace movement after thirty years" (*Asahi*, Tokyo, 10 August). There were still no signs of restored unity among the participants; this would probably have to await reconciliation between the JSP and JCP on other issues. Meanwhile, public attitudes toward nuclear weapons appeared to have changed little. An opinion poll taken during the summer resulted in a 77 percent majority favoring strict adherence to the three "non-nuclear principles" (i.e., not to make, possess, or permit the entry into Japan of nuclear weapons). Although 59 percent agreed that "we must never forget the bombing of Hiroshima and Nagasaki," indifference to the anti-bomb movement seemed to be increasing, only 41 percent of respondents expressed "interest in" Gensuikyo and Gensuikin; 50 percent were negative.

International Friendship Association. The three most important international friendship associations affiliated with the JCP are the Japan-Korea Association (Ni-cho Kyokai), the Japan-Soviet Association (Nisso Kyokai), and the Japan-China Friendship Association (Ni-chu Kyokai).

The Japan-Korea Association, with 14,000 members, is allied to the General Federation of Korean Residents in Japan (Chosen Soren), which in turn is regarded as an arm of the Workers Party of North Korea. A rival organization is Mindan, the organization of Koreans in Japan loyal to the Republic of Korea. Chosen Soren, with 290,000 members, is the successor to a postwar organization dominated by the JCP. The present chairman of Chosen Soren stated in May 1975 that his organization was "not partial to any specific political force in Japan" (*Mainichi*, Tokyo, 24 May). However, since the JCP supports the policies of the Democratic People's Republic of Korea, there is general ideological affinity between Chosen Soren and the JCP.

Two rival societies exist for the promotion of friendly relations with the Soviet Union. The Japan-Soviet Association, with 10,000 members, is dominated by the JCP. The Japan-Soviet Friendship Association, with 4,000 members, is supported by the JSP and other anti-JCP elements. In a July visit to Moscow by a delegation from the Japan-Soviet Association, the Russian counterpart (Soviet-Japan Association) agreed to provisional arrangements for cultural exchanges but refused to consider "regularization" of relations between the two groups. It has been Soviet policy to deal cautiously with both of the Japanese friendship societies. The Soviet Embassy in Tokyo regularly sends representatives to the annual meetings of both.

As a result of the JCP's quarrel with the Chinese Communist Party in 1966, two friendship societies to promote Chinese-Japanese relations were established. One is the pro-JCP Japan-China Friendship Association, the other, the anti-JCP Japan-China Friendship Association (Orthodox). The pro-JCP group, with a reported 35,000 members, set a goal for 1975 of 50,000 members. It attacked its rival for blind subservience to the PRC and calculated indifference to the U.S.-Japan security treaty issue, to Prime Minister Miki's "two-faced policy toward China," to U.S. "world domination," and to the "five principles of peaceful co-existence." It called for opposition to the proposed Japan-China treaty of peace and friendship with its anti-hegemony clause. (*Chugai Tokuho*, Tokyo, 20 August.)

Party Affairs. Realization that the growth of the JCP had slowed down was brought home to the party leadership during 1975 by setbacks in the April local elections and by the slump in party membership and in the circulation of *Akahata*. The Japanese press described the JCP variously as having "reached a ceiling," "suffered a retreat," and "met defeat" (*Asahi*, 4 November). Party leaders began soul-searching and found various explanations, among them a lackadaisical attitude toward the election campaign, arrogance among party workers which alienated voters, and, more important, continuing hostility toward communism by the Japanese public.

The JCP regards the circulation of its official organ *Akahata* as the barometer of the party's progress. In December 1974, the combined circulation of the daily and Sunday editions had surpassed three million, but by September 1975, the number of copies sold was estimated by a non-communist source to reach only 2.5 million (550,000 daily, 1.95 million Sunday). Because of extraordinary efforts to enlist new subscribers, these figures may have increased somewhat by the end of the year. Miyamoto explained the problems of *Akahata* in a magazine interview, stating that efforts to convince readers that "one newspaper is enough" had not succeeded since an increasingly politically sophisticated clientele demanded newspapers which pretended to be "neutral" and to give both sides of every question. This attitude, he said, was the greatest obstacle to the expansion of *Akahata*'s circulation. Still, Miyamoto pointed out, other parties, such as those in Italy and France, were astounded at *Akahata*'s three-million readership. (*Shukan Asahi*, Tokyo, 30 May.)

For the future, the party's activities are to be based on mass struggle and party building. The general elections, expected during the first half of 1976 are the next goal in sight. Some independent analysts have predicted that the JCP will win no more than three new seats in the House of Representatives beyond the 39 which the party now holds (*Nikkei-kyo Joho*, Tokyo, 10 September). Others forecast a possible new total of as many as 50 seats.

In June, the party published the details of its receipts and disbursements. Income for the fiscal year 1974 was reported to have been 10 billion yen (U.S.-$32.3 million). More than 93 percent of the party revenues came from its publishing enterprises, including *Akahata* and numerous books, periodicals, and pamphlets. Only 5 percent was said to come from party membership dues (*Akahata*, 26 June.)

The fifth meeting of the Central Committee of the JCP (numbered from the party Congress of November 1973) was held on 17-19 January. Attention was directed principally toward the forthcoming local elections to be held in April, although other highlighted problems included obstacles to a renovationist united front, the *Dowa* (assimilation) problem involving *burakumin* (outcast-communities—see below), and the international situation. The policies set forth in a platform for the election campaign were designed to appeal to local interests: abolish "money" politics and elections; reduce inflation; resolve local financial crises; promote welfare; develop land democratically; stimulate local industry and economy, abolish violence; effect just local government; fulfill educational demands; develop art, culture, and sports; free Japan of nuclear weapons and military bases; promote democratic local politics through expanding the autonomy of local entities and the reform of local financial systems. The committee's resolutions emphasized the necessity of wiping out the obstructions to a united front, which consisted of the DSP's proposed anti-JCP union of opposition parties, the negative attitudes of the Komeito, the JSP's unrealistic proposal for an alliance of all opposition parties, and the insistence of the labor unions on the principle of support for a "specified party" (JSP). The committee went on record to condemn the anti-JCP "League for the Liberation of Special Communities"—the burakumin—as posing a problem affecting national and local politics, people's security and rights, and threatening local governments and the labor unions. A special report was approved noting the danger of war in the Middle East and condemning the United States for policies in Vietnam. A protest to President Ford was sent in the name of the Central Committee, calling on the United States to stop aggression in the Middle East and Vietnam, vacate military bases on Japanese soil, revive the Vietnam agreements and stop aid to the Thieu regime, halt the temporary stationing of nuclear weapons on Japanese soil, and withdraw all nuclear weapons and nuclear forces from Japan.

It became public only in July that the fifth plenum of the Central Committee had secretly approved a ten-year agreement between the JCP and the Soka Gakkai, the Buddhist organization that founded the Komeito. The agreement had been signed 28 December 1974 by Ueda Koichiro, member of the Standing Committee of the Presidium of the JCP, and Nozaki Isao, executive director of the Soka Gakkai. (*Tokyo Shimbun*, 28 July.)

The sixth meeting of the Central Committee, 6-9 July, brought opportunities for a review of the results of the April elections and for reassessment of the party's present and future, at a "testing time" for the JCP, in the words of its leaders. In his opening statement, Miyamoto warned: "We are not at the point where our party's prospects have reached an immovable ceiling. However, it is evident that if we become complacent and spiritless, far from reaching a ceiling, we will instead go downwards, even to defeat." (*Akahata*, 7 July.) Anxiety and frustration were reflected in the statements and reports presented at the conference. A party which had grown spectacularly from its Seventh Congress in 1958 to its Twelfth in 1973 had suddenly met stagnation; the dramatically and widely publicized program for a democratic coalition government had lost all prospects of realization, the widespread "communist allergy" had not been dissipated, and election results in both 1974 and 1975 had been discouraging. Pointing out the rise of "bureaucratism" among party officials and the loss of revolutionary spirit among the rank and file, the leadership sought to restore the JCP to a "vanguard" position and nurture a new revolutionary consciousness among the members. Skepticism about the future of a united front was voiced repeatedly, with sharp hostility directed to the JSP for collaborating with the LDP instead of entering a joint struggle, and to the Komeito for not reversing its anti-communist stand.

The most significant act of the Central Committee at its sixth plenum was the dismissal of a member of the Presidium, Fujiwara Ryuzo, concurrently chairman of the Miyagi party prefectural committee. Fujiwara was relieved of his positions in the Presidium, the Central Committee, and the prefectural committee, but was allowed to remain an ordinary member of the party. Miyamoto in his greetings to the opening committee session pointedly remarked that participation in the leadership of a vanguard party did not guarantee a permanent reserved seat. The public charges against Fujiwara were violation of party regulations and "taking a bureaucratic attitude." The facts were that Fujiwara, in order to gain credit with party headquarters, had reported to the center inflated circulation figures for *Akahata*. When the discrepancy was discovered by a member of the circulation department, Fujiwara proceeded to have him expelled as a "spy." Apparently, Fujiwara's practice was a common one among chiefs of local party branches and the severity of the punishment meted out to him was intended as a lesson and a warning to others—in Miyamoto's words, "one punishment for a hundred crimes." (Akiyama Junichi, "The Essence and Direction of the Sixth Meeting of the JCP," *Koan Joho*, Tokyo, August).

In further efforts to rejuvenate and tighten control over party affairs, several organizational changes were effected. A series of bureaus was set up to replace sub-committees; these included Education, Organization, Election Policy, Local Government and Citizens, Mass Movements, and Propaganda. Whereas the sub-committees had reported to the Standing Committee for the Presidium, bureau chiefs were now made directly responsible to the Secretariat. Thus, the Secretariat, headed by Fuwa Tetsuzo, which had already progressed toward the position of true management organ of the party, was invested with greater power than before. Henceforward, the controlling authority in the party seemed to be divided equally between the Standing Committee of the Presidium and the Secretariat. (Ibid.)

At the seventh meeting of the Central Committee on 20-23 December, Fuwa Tetsuzo denounced the Soka Gakkai for its failure to observe the ten year agreement signed with the JCP in December 1974, but the communists pledged to defend the substance and spirit of the agreement while criticizing the activities of the Soka Gakkai. The party condemned both the Soka Gakkai and the Komeito for their anti-communist policies of "unity of politics and religion."

Domestic Attitudes and Activities. As usual, JCP representatives in the Diet vigorously opposed the Miki government on every issue, trying to bring about its downfall and to block important legislation to which the Prime Minister was committed. Three bills, which had been presented as a result of the scandals surrounding the previous Tanaka administration, drew particular Communist fire. These were the laws regulating public elections, political contributions, and monopolies. The first two were finally passed on 4 July as a result of agreement among the LDP, JSP, and DSP. The JCP objected to the first bill because it would limit campaign practices, including the number of handbills to be distributed; this, in Communist eyes, would unconstitutionally restrict freedom of speech, popular sovereignty, and parliamentary democracy. The principal criticism of the political contributions bill was that it would regulate trade unions, as well as other organizations and, by requiring detailed reports, would interfere in the internal affairs of political parties.

The JCP found yet another opportunity to proclaim unflinching loyalty to the Japanese constitution in the Inaba incident, which caused suspension of Diet business for 12 days in May. The Justice minister, Inaba Osamu, attended a meeting on 3 May, "Constitution Day," sponsored by the Conference for an Autonomous Constitution. Inaba had long been an advocate of constitutional reform, but his attendance at such a meeting in the capacity of Justice minister aroused immediate attack by the JCP and other opposition parties, on the grounds that article 99, which requires public officials to "respect and defend" the constitution, had been violated. Inaba insisted that his personal advocacy of revision, for which procedures were stipulated, in no way contradicted his legal obligation to defend the present constitution so long as it remained in effect. Although Inaba apologized on 8 May for his "indiscretion," the opposition parties brought all Diet action to a halt until the 22nd, when a consensus for resumption of business was reached. The JCP, which had taken the leadership in the incident, refused, however, to subscribe to the final agreement.

Relations with Other Parties. The JCP's relations with both the JSP and the Komeito deteriorated during 1975. In late May, chairman Miyamoto confessed: "There is now no basic strength on which to form a true united struggle." He noted ruefully that the LDP had been joined by the JSP in 10 mayoralty elections and by the Komeito in 15 or 20. He concluded: "There will be no progress for renovationist politics if we avoid the question of overcoming the anti-communist splitting policy which is the first element in the breakup of the joint front." (Interview, *Shukan Asahi*, 30 May.)

JSP-JCP hostility developed to such an intense degree that the JSP's Central Committee formally decided on 12 June to break off all joint action with the JCP in the Diet. At the July meeting of the JCP Central Committee, Miyamoto castigated the JSP in unusually strong language: "The Socialist Party has openly embarked on a course toward degeneration which is extremely dangerous." He went on to accuse the Socialists of betraying the principles of renovationism and of blatantly cooperating with the LDP and the DSP. (*Akahata*, 7 July.)

In addition to the instances in which the JSP joined the LDP in certain election constituencies and Diet debates, other events exacerbated JCP-JSP relations. One was the revelation by the JCP that the Socialists had accepted a donation of 30 million yen (U.S.$100,000) from the Japan Automobile Manufacturers' Association. Another was the publication by the JSP of a "secret" document purporting to be instructions sent to all local branches of the JCP Central Headquarters confirming to all party members that "the enemy of the JCP for the present is the Socialist Party." (See *Akahata*, 9 June, for text.) Secretariat director Fuwa promptly denied the authenticity of the document and demanded a formal apology; on 10 June, the party filed a formal court action against the JSP for criminal libel. At the same time, the latter's secretary-general admitted that the payment from the Automobile Association was a fact, but explained that after "self-reflection" the party had discontinued the practice of receiving business contributions. Because of its form and unlikely language, the "secret" document unearthed by the JSP was generally regarded as false. Fuwa, in a vitriolic press conference on 12 June, denounced the JSP as "unprincipled" and "immoral," and as embarked on a path of collaboration with the LDP, thus tying itself to a "Japanese style of fascism" which must inevitably face bankruptcy (ibid., 13 June).

The issue which has created the most serious and continuing cleavage is the so-called Dowa problem which relates to outcast communities existing in Japan for several hundred years. These mainly underprivileged and socially segregated citizens, referred to as *eta* in ancient times and as *burakumin* at present, number between two and three million and, for the most part, inhabit the area adjoining Kobe, Osaka, and Kyoto. Their organizations, formed in the prewar period under leftist influence, were re-established during the Occupation. In 1965, the Communists among them split from the national organization, the Buraku Liberation League (Buraku Kaiho Domei), and in 1970 founded a separate organization, the "Liaison Council for a Return to Correct Conditions within the League." Since that time, the two organizations, under JSP and JCP influence respectively, have confronted each other politically. Essentially, the contention has been over the government funds, both national and local, which are appropriated for the welfare of the buraku people. The Liberation League has insisted that the funds be administered through its branches and the JCP has fought this monopoly, an issue which became crucial in the April elections for the governors of both Tokyo and Osaka. In Tokyo, the JCP refused to support Governor Minobe Ryokichi until he reversed the policy of funneling burakumin aid through the League (see below) and in Osaka the JSP withdrew support from the renovationist candidate when he refused to deal exclusively with the League.

In addition to its effect on elections, the Dowa problem has been the cause of numerous incidents, including violence, which have embittered relations between the JSP and JCP. The presence of buraku students in schools, the occurrence of discriminatory practices, including verbal insults (terms such as "eta" and "four legs"), and attempts to form rival clubs to study buraku problems, have brought the controversy into school rooms and teachers' unions. In one incident in a high school north of Kobe, in which 53 out of 1,200 students were burakumin, League supporters physically fought pro-communist teachers, resulting in the hospitalization of 13 out of the 52 teachers for periods of six weeks and more. The police failed to intervene and the incident was given little publicity outside of the communist press. (Thomas P. Rohlen, "Violence at Yoka High School: The Implications for Japanese Coalition Politics of the Confrontation between the Communist Party and the Buraku Liberation League," unpublished manuscript.)

The membership in the League includes only a small percentage of the burakumin (less than 100,000 according to police estimates) and the opposing pro-JCP Liaison Council is even smaller (28,000); there are two other organizations, a small LDP-supported group, the Japan Assimilation Society, and a larger non-party association, the Muto-ha. The JCP has successfully exploited the issue, posing as the true champion of human rights, non-discrimination, and desegregation, and the staunch defender of the burakumin against the violence and confrontation tactics of the JSP-supported League. In terms of coalition politics, the problem appears to be deep-seated and immensely difficult to resolve.

In spite of the fundamental differences which separate the JSP from the JCP, their leaders make periodic efforts to reestablish some form of cooperation, particularly within the Diet. On 2 September the JSP secretary general met with the JCP Secretariat chief, Fuwa Tetsuzo, and the two agreed on a nine-point agenda of cooperation, principally on specific bills before the Diet, efforts to overthrow the Miki cabinet, and foreign policy issues (Japan-U.S. security cooperation, the Korean question, and support for the Palestine Liberation Organization) (*Asahi*, 3 September). Such cooperation on specific issues or on specific candidates for election can be expected but any form of united front between the two parties seems farther away than ever.

The biggest political bombshell of 1975 was the simultaneous announcement on 28 July in *Akahata* and *Seikyo Shimbun*—the organ of the Buddhist Soka Gakkai (Value Creation Society)—that a ten-year agreement had been signed six months earlier, 28 December 1974, by representatives of the Soka Gakkai and the JCP. The accord stipulated that the JCP would unconditionally uphold freedom of religion, that the Soka Gakkai would not regard communism with hostility, and that both organizations, while refraining from interference in each other's affairs, would work for social justice, improved welfare, eternal peace in the world, and the abolition of fascism and its attempts to curb democracy and fundamental human rights. The parties to the agreement revealed that discussions had begun as early as October 1974 and that Ikeda Daisuke, president of the Soka Gakkai, and Miyamoto Kenji, chairman of the JCP's Presidium, had themselves held extended conversations at least twice, on 29 December 1974 and 12 July 1975. The publication of this unprecedented "treaty" between a Buddhist society and a communist party stirred Japan's political world as few events have done, and was particularly embarrassing for the Komeito, political offspring of the Soka Gakkai, whose members had apparently been unaware of the agreement before its publication.

Differences of interpretation of the document immediately became apparent and the net effect was a worsening of relations between the Komeito and the JCP, which had never been good. Ikeda's motives in the dialogue were described as Buddhist humanism rather than politics, a search for a higher level of mutual understanding with those holding differing philosophies. Miyamoto, in a lengthy magazine article, sought earnestly to justify and to rationalize the unusual phenomenon of a communist pact with religion. Marx and Lenin, he pointed out, must be read in the context of history. When they lived, Germany and Russia were authoritarian anti-modern nations and religion, in the name of "God's discipline" had become within them a reactionary social force. "It was clear that Marx did not intend simply to disparage religion itself. His was only a criticism of the role which religion was then in reality playing." (Miyamoto Kenji, "Standing at the Crossroads of History: The JCP and Soka Gakkai," *Bungei Shunju*, October.) Another JCP apologist for the agreement, Kurahara Korehito, member of the Standing Committee of the Presidium, interpreted Marx's famous dictum "Religion is the opium of the people" to mean that religion is only a "comfort" to people in trouble, not a poison (*Akahata*, 31 August). Miyamoto himself found it natural that in certain circumstances people will turn to spiritual solace (op.cit.).

The most controversial point to emerge from the joint accord was the issue of "joint struggles" between the JCP and the Komeito. Miyamoto interpreted the agreement to mean "mutual cooperation, mutual effort, and, on occasion, joint struggle" (ibid.). Soka Gakkai officials, including Ikeda Daisuke, were prompt to deny vehemently any implication of joint political struggle. The leaders of Komeito were clearly shocked and embarrassed by what their parent organization had done. Immediately after publication of the pact, the Central Committee of the Komeito announced: (1) "suspicions over JCP respect for freedom of religion have not been removed; (2) the majority of

Japanese do not approve the realization of communism; (3) there can be no joint Komeito-JCP struggles; (4) Komeito agrees that no joint Soka Gakkai-JCP struggles can be envisaged; and (5) Komeito's belief that the JCP may inject ideological self-righteousness and dictatorship into the fight against fascism has not changed" (*Asahi Evening News*, 6 August). At the national convention of the Komeito, 14-16 October, the delegates closely questioned the leadership on the meaning of the accord and were only satisfied when the party's "suspicion toward the JCP" was emphatically confirmed. Again in November, Komeito's newspaper characterized the JCP's professed attachment to religious freedom as "make-believe," a stand which "merely reflects the JCP's intention of fully exploiting religion in its political strategy" (*Komei*, December, quoted in *Hokubei Mainichi*, San Francisco, 25 November).

The Miyamoto-Ikeda dialogues and the 10-year accord intensified hostility between the Komeito and JCP and, in addition, created serious rifts between the Komeito and the Soka Gakkai. The JCP accused its Buddhist "partners" of bad faith and the Komeito and Soka Gakkai went to extraordinary lengths to convince their members that the Gakkai had not sold out to communism. Observers generally agreed that the Budhists had lost while the Communists had won. The JCP came out of the dispute with the benign image of a party valiantly defending the freedom of religious thought and activity while seeking concord and cooperation in the political arena. Still, some commentators detected dissenting voices within the JCP, critical of Miyamoto for his self-aggrandizement and for his unorthodox interpretations of the teachings of Marx and Lenin.

Elections. The elections for prefectural governors, mayors, and members of local assemblies on 13 and 27 April produced disappointing results to the JCP, whose candidates for governor won in only three prefectures and whose seats in prefectural assemblies were decreased by eight (95 as against 103 in the previous elections). "No seat" prefectures were increased from three to seven. Results in the prefectural assemblies proved particularly discouraging since prefectural committee chairmen had predicted the capture of as many as 150 seats. The party's only outstanding victory was the reelection in Osaka Prefecture of the incumbent governor with the sole support of the JCP. The latter was opposed by two candidates, one nominated by the LDP and a second put up by three opposition parties (JSP, Komeito, DSP). Two other prefectures, Tokyo and Kanagawa, elected governors supported by the renovationist parties, thus bringing to nine (out of 47) the number of prefectural executives who owe support to the JCP.

The Communists did better in the local assembly elections, but principally because they ran more candidates than ever before. Taking into account certain elections subsequent to those in April, the JCP as of September controlled 3,144 seats in prefectural, city, town, and village assemblies, an advance over the 2,809 which they occupied in 1974. In numbers of votes, JCP-supported candidates for prefectural assemblies received 4.3 million as against 3 million in the previous local elections, representing a gain of 2.1 percent.

The elections were characterized by the large number of candidates who ran as independents, abjuring especially the Liberal Democratic label, by the significant number of candidates jointly supported by the LDP and DSP, and by the marked inability of the JCP and JSP to cooperate. JCP officials attributed the party's lack of greater success to complacency and unskillful tactics. Fuwa Tetsuzo commented that "a scientific socialist political party carried out an unscientific election campaign" (*Yomiuri*, Tokyo, 19 April). In Tokyo, only a last-minute agreement between the JSP and JCP prevented the kind of split that occurred in Osaka. Minobe Ryokichi, incumbent governor of Tokyo, announced early in the year that he would not become a candidate and only after a semblance of unity was established between the Communists and Socialists (over the Dowa problem) did he reconsider his position. His margin of victory was reduced, however, from 1.7 million votes in 1971 to only 350,000 in 1975. Total votes cast numbered 5.2 million.

International Views and Policies. In an interview, Miyamoto Kenji stated that "after the Chinese revolution, the communist victory in Vietnam was the greatest historical event in the postwar period" (*Shukan Asahi*, 30 May 1975). The JCP concluded that the outcome in Indochina had proved the correctness of the Party's line. Reports to the sixth meeting of the Central Committee in July stressed that the bankruptcy of both the Soviet Union's "unprincipled policy of cooperation with the United States," and of China's policy of equating the Soviet Union with the United States, had been demonstrated (*Koan Joho*, August).

The communist parties with which the JCP leadership continued to find the most compatibility were those of Vietnam and North Korea in Asia, France, Italy, Romania, and Yugoslavia, in Europe, and Cuba in the Americas. Both Hanoi and Pyongyang were appearing to maintain equal distance with Moscow and Peking, which was precisely the line of the JCP. As for relations with the parties of France and Italy, Miyamoto made the JCP's policy quite clear. "We are not at the stage of a socialist revolution in Japan. Independence, democracy, peace, neutrality: we are building this kind of Japan. For this purpose, we must have a united front. The French and Italian examples show that we must emphasize the democratic stage." (*Shukan Asahi*, 30 May.)

Following the cessation of hostilities in Indochina, Asian attention focused on Korea. In early August the JCP viewed with alarm the confirmation in the Miki-Ford joint communiqué that Korean security was identified with Japan's security, and protested the formation of a U.S.-Japan-South Korea military alliance as a threat to the peace of Northeast Asia. Supporting Kim Il-song fully, party spokesmen called for the immediate withdrawal of U.S. forces from the Republic of Korea and denounced the resumed talks on economic cooperation between Tokyo and Seoul. The visit to Japan in late August of U.S. secretary of defense James Schlesinger provided an additional occasion for the JCP to signal the dangers of a strengthened U.S.-Japan-ROK military structure, including a challenge to the South Korean people's right to self-determination (*Akahata*, 30 August). In an earlier interview, Ueda Koichiro, member of the Standing Committee of the Presidium, quoted Kim Il-song's insistence that an advance to the south was out of the question, and declared that the removal of U.S. forces was essential to the peaceful, autonomous unification of the Korean peninsula (*Asahi*, 25 June).

On nuclear policy, the JCP continued to oppose Japan's ratification of the nuclear non-proliferation treaty. The treaty review conference at Geneva, in May, provided occasion for the party to restate its objections, namely, that the treaty, far from contributing to nuclear disarmament, only strengthens the nuclear monopoly structure of those nations possessing weapons, permits the United States and other powers to bring nuclear weapons into other nations, and keeps the non-nuclear nations under the so-called "nuclear umbrellas" of the weapon-possessing powers (*Akahata*, 6 June).

Relations with the Chinese Communist Party. In a New Year's television interview, Chairman Miyamoto stated categorically: "There is no indication of reconciliation between our party and the Chinese and Soviet parties" (Tokyo JOAK-TV, 2 January 1975). The facts behind this statement had not changed by the year's end. The columns of *Akahata* were filled with anti-Chinese propaganda and the same complaints, dating from the 1966 break between Miyamoto and Mao Tse-tung in Peking, were repeated periodically. Especially galling to the JCP was the Chinese tolerance, and even encouragement, of the Japan-U.S. security relationship.

The issue which drew most attention, however, was the so-called hegemony problem (*haken mondai*) which was the stumbling block to signature of a peace treaty between the governments of Japan and the People's Republic of China. The Chinese insisted that a clause confirming opposition to the hegemony of third powers be included in the body of the treaty. Because the Russians protested, claiming that the clause was directed against them, the Japanese government hesitated to agree. The JCP, accusing both the Soviet Union and the PRC of hegemony, found the proposed clause in conflict with Japan's autonomous diplomacy. The JCP defined hegemony as "Big Powerism" and cited as examples the Soviet Union's occupation of Japan's northern territories and its invasion of Czechoslovakia in 1968, and China's efforts to destroy the JCP and to interfere in the revolutionary and democratic movements in Japan. Condemning all hegemony, the JCP rejected Chinese efforts to win Japan's collusion in attacking the Soviet Union by means of an anti-hegemony clause in the Sino-Japanese peace treaty. (*Akahata*, 27 May.)

Hegemony became another issue in the conflict between the JCP and the JSP when a Socialist delegation to Peking signed a joint communiqué with the Chinese opposing hegemony by "the two superpowers." *Akahata* (13 May) excoriated the JSP for its submissive capitulation to "another great power's chaivinism" by endorsing the anti-hegemony clause.

Relations with the Communist Party of the Soviet Union. Relations between the Soviet and Japanese parties continued cool, with no change in the positions of either. The one event relating to Japanese-Soviet relations which shook the political world and the mass media was the appearance in the October issue of the U.S. magazine *Foreign Affairs* of an article entitled "Japan's Emerging Foreign Policy," by Hirasawa Kazushige, a news commentator and informal adviser to Prime Minister Miki, which recommended that Japan agree to place the two northern islands in the Kurile chain, Kunashiri and Etorofu, now in the possession of the Soviet Union, "on ice" until the 21st century. Such a "solution" would presumably remove the principal obstacle to a Japanese peace treaty. The Foreign Office and prominent LDP members reacted immediately and forcefully, denying that Hirasawa in any way spoke for the government and insisting that the Russians must agree to the return of the islands as a condition for any treaty. The JCP, through Fuwa Tetsuzo at a press conference, at first welcomed the Hirasawa proposal as a "step in a realistic direction." Fuwa added, however, that the JCP would not wish to wait until the 21st century for a settlement and that it would demand reversion of all the Kurile Islands, not just those in the southern part of the chain. (*Asahi*, 19 September.) A few days later *Akahata* (25 September) revised the party's stand, pronounced the Hirasawa proposal a "sell-out" of Japanese territory and accused "anti-communist" critics of distorting Fuwa's word. The paper repeated the JCP position on the northern territories: an immediate peace treaty with return of the Habomais and Shikotan followed by return of all the Kurile Islands (including the northern group which even the Japanese government does not claim) when the U.S.-Japan security treaty is abrogated and U.S. forces and bases are withdrawn from Japan.

The United States. Through Diet interpellations, statements of party leaders, and the columns of *Akahata*, the JCP kept up throughout 1975 a barrage of attacks against the United States and "U.S. imperialism," deemed Japan's prime enemies in the international arena. Typical was Fuwa Tetsuzo's extended interpellation before the House of Representatives Budget Committee on 31 January. He pursued the prime minister and the foreign minister on the application of the security treaty to Taiwan, the uses of U.S. bases in Japan, and the presence of nuclear weapons on Japanese soil. Fuwa questioned the consistency between the U.S. commitment to defend Taiwan, using Japanese bases, and Japan's recognition of "one China"; cited documents to prove that the United States was conducting training for nuclear warfare in Okinawa as well as on Taiwan; and warned that Japan was being made the base for a nuclear war. Both the prime minister and foreign minister denied that nuclear weapons had been, or would be, brought into Japan, and defended the security treaty as the basis for collective self-defense. (*Akahata*, 2 February.)

Until the end of hostilities in Indochina, the JCP attacked the United States for prolonging the war and for disregarding the Paris accords. After the U.S. withdrawal, party organs proclaimed that U.S. "aggressive" policy had not changed and still threatened the independence of small nations: the Korean peninsula was likely to be next. This line was fortified by reference to the security of Korea in the Ford-Miki communiqué issued in Washington on 6 August and Secretary Schlesinger's subsequent visit to Tokyo, noted earlier. The recurring communist propaganda theme became "the U.S.-Japan-ROK military structure."

From the time of its first announcement, the Emperor's visit to the United States was opposed by the JCP. An editorial in *Akahata*, (1 March) was captioned "The Political Use of the Emperor Is Intolerable." The theme of JCP objections was that the visit was a violation of the constitutional restriction which made the Emperor a "symbol" but not a chief of state. Visits to foreign countries were not included in the ceremonial acts to be performed by the Emperor as specified in article 7 of the constitution. The LDP, according to *Akahata*, already preparing a revision of the constitution, was seeking to revert to the prewar concept of the Emperor as chief of state, thus violating the principle of people's sovereignty guaranteed by the postwar constitution. After the Emperor's return to Japan, his press conference statement to the effect that the the atomic bombing of Hiroshima was "regrettable" but that "it could not have been helped," incited the JCP to denounce Hirohito for "failing to feel his responsibility for the war." The secretary-general of the LDP, replying to JCP criticism, declared that "the large majority of the people oppose the words and actions of the JCP and *Akahata*" (*Yomiuri*, 2 November).

In February an *Akahata* reporter was for the first time admitted to the United States and his reports of his cross-country tour were published in twenty-eight installments, 5 March to 11 April. While, not unexpectedly, he emphasized poverty, unemployment, economic depression, and crime, many of his impressions cannot fail to have aroused interest among *Akahata* readers. Perhaps reflecting the JCP's position as staunch defender of the Japanese constitution, the reporter found noteworthy the respect of Americans for their constitution. He ended his series from New York: "The pledge of allegiance to the Stars and Stripes is linked with the formation of the American people's feelings toward the constitution. And, without this feeling toward the constitution, this mammoth country America would inevitably fall apart." (*Akahata*, 2 April.) The U.S. government, making a distinction between a journalist and an official delegation, refused visas to members of the JCP wishing to attend the 21st Congress of the Communist Party, U.S.A., held at Chicago in June. The press later reported, however, that the U.S. assistant secretary of state for East Asian and Pacific affairs had stated to a congressional subcommittee that if the JCP wished in the future to send a delegation to the United States, the matter would be given "serious consideration" (*Sankei*, Tokyo, 19 November). A State Department spokesman subsequently clarified that U.S. policy toward the JCP had not changed (*Mainichi*, 20 November).

International Activities and Contacts. The exchanges of visits between the JCP and other communist parties reveal the nature of the JCP's relationships in the international communist movement. The principal foreign parties which either received or sent missions in 1975 were those of Romania, Yugoslavia, Cuba, Laos, Vietnam, Lebanon (Palestine Liberation Organization; PLO), Italy, and France.

The first visits during the year were made to Yugoslavia and Vietnam, in January and in February. The delegation to Yugoslavia was led by Nishizawa Tomie, member of the Standing Committee of the Presidium.

Two delegations visited Romania, one in March and another in August, both led by Nishizawa. President Nicolae Ceauşescu spent six days in Tokyo (4-9 April), during the course of which time he held discussions with Miyamoto Kenji. On 3-12 September a four-man delegation from the Romanian Communist Party visited Japan at the invitation of the JCP.

On 10-19 May a JCP delegation led also by Nishizawa visited Cuba, where a call was made on Fidel Castro and a joint communiqué issued which expressed the solidarity of the JCP with the Cuban Communist Party and with the Cuban people.

In June the JCP named a delegation to the 21st Congress of the Communist Party, U.S.A., to be headed by Senaga Kamejiro, vice-chairman of the Presidium. As already noted, visas were refused by the U.S. government.

In July and August a delegation led by Kaneko Mitsuhiro, deputy chief of the Secretariat, visited Laos, Vietnam, and Lebanon. In Laos the JCP group met with officials of the Laotian Patriotic Front and signed a communiqué welcoming the victory of the Pathet Lao over the "new colonialist domination" of the United States and the attainment of the "people's national democratic revolution throughout the whole country." The delegation stopped briefly in Saigon and Hanoi but no meetings or joint declarations were publicized. The visit to Lebanon (1-12 August) was for the purpose of holding conversations with Chairman Yasser Arafat and officials of the PLO. In addition to a joint declaration of solidarity, the JCP members strongly supported the establishment in Tokyo of an office of the PLO as the "sole, legitimate representative of the Palestinian people" (*Mainichi*, 14 August). Upon his return to Japan, Kaneko made his appeal for recognition of the PLO in a press conference and personally to the foreign minister.

From 28 August to 12 September, Nosaka Sanzo, chairman of the Central Committee, led a delegation to Hanoi to attend the celebration of the 30th anniversary of the establishment of the Democratic Republic of Vietnam. The visit attracted press attention in Japan when Nosaka shook hands with the chairman of the delegation from the People's Republic of China.

A three-member Italian Communist Party group spent 20-28 September in Japan, returning an earlier visit to Italy (18-23 March) by a JCP delegation led by Senaga Kamejiro.

Significant meetings were held during an eight-day visit (12-19 October) by a delegation from the French Communist Party led by Paul Laurent, a member of the Politburo. A joint communiqué noted the similarity of circumstances in whcih both parties operated (unemployment, inflation, pollution, worsening of people's livelihood: the greatest crisis for the capitalist system since World War II) and emphasized the "communist allergy" present in both Japan and France. The parties agreed that to overcome this allergy arising out of the ideas of "violence and dictatorship" associated with Marxism-Leninism they must base their appeals on guarantees of human rights and of a democratic political system, including the tolerance of opposing political parties under a communist-led coalition. The "historical compromise" of the Italian Communist Party was cited as an example to follow. The emphasis on autonomy and independence was described by a non-communist Japanese commentator as a shift in nuance for the French party, which has traditionally been closely allied to the Soviet party ("The Joint Communiqué of the Communist Parties of France and Japan," *Koan Joho*, October).

On 10-11 October the communist parties of France, Vietnam, and Romania sent representatives of their party journals to attend the annual "Akahata Festival" sponsored in Tokyo by the JCP.

JCP Publications. As already stated, more than 93 percent of the JCP's annual income derives from its publications. In addition to numerous books, pamphlets, and tracts, periodicals include the following:

Party organs: *Akahata*, daily, circulation 550,000; Sunday, 1,950,000; Vanguard (*Zenei*), monthly magazine, 110,000; Documents of World Politics (*Sekai Seiji Shiryo*), semi-monthly, 30,000; Problems of Peace and Socialism (*Heiwa to Shakaishugi no Sho Mondai*), monthly, 10,000; Parliament and Self-Governing Organizations (*Gikai to Jichitai*), monthly, 15,000; Students' News (*Gakusei Shimbun*), 26,000; Studies Monthly (*Gekkan Gakushu*), guidance for new party members, 110,000; Cultural Critique (*Bunka Hyoron*), Monthly, 20,000; Akahata Picture News (*Akahata Shashin Nyusu*), every 10 days, 7,000.

Semi-party organs: Economics Monthly (*Gekkan Keizai*), 30,000; New Women's News (*Shin Fujin Shimbun*), weekly, 160,000; Democratic Youth news (*Minshu Seinen Shimbun*), 300,000; Youth Movement (*Seinen Undo*), monthly, 20,000; Friend of Learning (*Gakushu no Tomo*), monthly, 120,000; The Farming Village Worker (*Noson Rodosha*), semi-monthly, 10,000; The Workers and Farmers Movement (*Rodo Nomin Undo*), monthly, 20,000; Democratic Literature (*Minshu Bungaku*), monthly, 20,000.

Splinter Parties. Numerous small leftist political parties oppose the JCP. Ten of these splinter groups—including such minor organizations as the Voice of Japan, Japan Labor Party, Japan Communist Revolutionary Party, Japan Workers Party, and Fourth International—endorsed among them 68 candidates in the nation-wide elections for local assemblies in April 1975. Of these, 39 were elected, one to a prefectural assembly, 29 to municipal assemblies, 4 to Tokyo district assemblies, 4 to town assemblies, and one to a village assembly. (*Chugai Tokuho*, 20 June.)

The most important splinter parties are the pro-Soviet Voice of Japan (Nihon no Koe) and the pro-Chinese "JCP (Left)." The Voice of Japan was formed around Shiga Yoshio, once a member of the JCP Central Committee and of the House of Representatives, who was expelled from the JCP in 1964 at the time when the partial nuclear test ban treaty was passed by the Diet. Shiga's group numbers approximately 400 and continues to support Soviet policy. Shiga, who has backed the anti-JCP Buraku Liberation League, has recently and apparently successfully cultivated relations with the JSP. The policy line of the Voice of Japan is indicated by one of Shiga's statements in the New Year's editorial of the party organ: "If a treaty which recognizes the status quo of international boundaries is signed between Japan and the Soviet Union, this will bring about collective security in Asia and will emasculate the American-Japanese and U.S.-ROK security treaties" (*Chugai Tokuho*, 20 February).

The JCP (Left) has within the past year split into two factions over the present direction of Chinese policy. The division within the party, which had been growing for some time, came to a climax at the 25th meeting of its Central Committee on 20 March. The Central, or mainstream, faction (also called the Yamaguchi Prefecture group) disagrees with the diplomatic line being taken by Peking, which encourages Japanese-U.S. relations and bases diplomatic policy on confrontation with the USSR. The opposing group, or Kanto-ha (Eastern Japan faction), supports the Japan-China Friendship Association (Orthodox) in its acceptance of Chinese policy, and describes the Central faction as leftist opportunists, exclusionists, and sect-ists. The party's publication, *People's Star*, accused the Kanto-ha of factionalism, ignoring party regulations, and attempting to split the party. The Central group on 20 March expelled four members from the committee and carried out a complete reorganization of the party's administration. The Chinese have apparently been embarrassed by the split and have so far refrained from intervention. Both groups reportedly sent delegations to Peking and were unable to get clear-cut and satisfactory direction from the Chinese Communist Party (*Chugai Tokuho*, 20 September). Membership in the two factions is estimated at 600 in the mainstream and 400 in the opposing Kanto group.

Hoover Institution   John K. Emmerson
Stanford University

Korea: Democratic People's Republic of Korea

The Korean Communist Party (Choson Kongsan-dang; KCP) was formed at Seoul in 1925 during the time of the Japanese rule; in 1928, due chiefly to suppression, it ceased to function. Shortly after World War II, a revived KCP appeared briefly in Seoul. Control of the communist movement in Korea soon shifted to the northern part of the country, then occupied by Soviet forces, where the "North Korean Central Bureau of the KCP" was formed in October 1945 under Soviet auspices. The three major factions of the movement—comprising Korean communists who during the Japanese period had gone to China, or to the Soviet Union, or had remained in Korea—subsequently merged, and on 23 June 1949 the Korean Workers' Party (Choson Nodon-dang; KWP) was established. The KWP is today the ruling party of the Democratic People's Republic of Korea (DPRK).

Kim Il-song, Korean-born but Soviet-trained, who had been an anti-Japanese communist guerrilla leader in southern Manchuria in the 1930s, consolidated his power by eliminating rival factions, and today his Manchurian partisan group (the Kapsan faction) holds unassailable supremacy in the North Korean leadership.

The number of the KWP members was estimated in 1972 at 2,000,000 by the party newspaper, *Nodong Shinmun* (editorial, 29 August). A recent outside estimate is 1.6 million. The estimated population of the DPRK (North Korea) is 16.5 million.

Leadership and Organization. North Korea has a typical communist administrative structure. The center of the decisionmaking is in the KWP, and the government merely executes party policy. All important leaders hold concurrent positions in the party and government.

The present top leaders of the DPRK, most of whom were elected at the KWP's Fifth Congress on 13 November 1970, include the following:

KWP Political Committee	Other Positions Held Concurrently
Regular (Voting) Members	
Kim Il-song	KWP secretary-general; DPRK president; supreme commander of armed forces; chairman of KWP Military Committee; marshal
Choe Yong-gon	KWP Central Committee (CC) secretary; DPRK vice-president; member of Central People's Committee; deputy marshal
Kim Il	KWP CC secretary; premier of State Administration Council; member of Central People's Committee
Choe Hyon	Colonel general; minister of People's Armed Forces; vice-chairman of National Defense Commission of Central People's Committee
O Chin-u	KWP CC secretary; Armed Forces chief of staff; colonel general; vice-chairman of National Defense Commission of Central People's Committee

Pak Song-chol	Deputy premier of State Administration Council; member of Central People's Committee
Kin Tong-kyu	KWP CC secretary; DPRK vice-president, member of Central People's Committee
Kim Yong-chu	Kim Il-song's younger brother; KWP CC secretary; deputy premier of State Administration Council; member of Central People's Committee; co-chairman of South-North Coordinating Committee
Kim Chung-nin	KWP CC secretary; Director of KWP Liaison Bureau (General Bureau of South Korea); member of Central People's Committee
Han Ik-su	KWP CC secretary; colonel general; member of Standing Committee of Supreme People's Assembly
Yon Hyung-muk	KWP CC secretary; member of Central People's Committee
So Chol	Colonel general; chairman of KWP Inspection (Control) Committee; member of Standing Committee of Supreme People's Assembly
Yang Hyong-sop	KWP CC secretary; member of Central People's Committee
Yi Yong-mu	Colonel general; chief of Political Bureau of (North) Korean People's Army
Yi Kun-mo	Deputy premier of State Administration Council (machinery and heavy industry expert); member of Central People's Committee

Candidate (Non-Voting) Members

Hyon Mu-kwang	KWP CC secretary; member of Central People's Committee; chairman of Transportation and Communications Committee of State Administration Council
Chon Mun-sop	Colonel general; director of Escort Bureau
O Paek-yong	Colonel general; vice-chairman of National Defense Commission of Central People's Committee; Kim Il-Song's former bodyguard
Kim Yong-nam	KWP CC secretary; director of International Department of KWP CC; member of Standing Committee of Supreme People's Assembly
Choe Chae-u	Deputy premier of State Administration Council; member of Central People's Committee
Chong Chung-ki	Deputy premier of State Administration Council; member of Standing Committee of Supreme People's Assembly
O Tae-pong	KWP CC secretary; member of Central People's Committee; O Paek-yong's cousin
Im Chun-chu	Secretary and member of Central People's Committee
Yu Chang-sik	Director of External Affairs Department of KWP CC; deputy foreign minister
Yi Chong-ok	Member of Central People's Committee; chairman of Heavy Industry Committee of State Administration Council
Hong Won-Kil	Member of Central People's Committee; chairman of Machine Building Industry Committee of State Administration Council

Kang Song-san   Chief secretary of KWP Pyongyang Municipal Committee;
                                 member of Standing Committee of Supreme People's Assembly

The 27-member KWP Political Committee (created during the Fourth Party Congress, 1961) and the 13-member Secretariat constitute the core of important decision-makers in the DPRK and act as a controlling nucleus for the Central Committee (117 regular and 55 alternate members).

The present central government structure consists of three pillars of power: the 25-member Central People's Committee (which is basically a policy-making and supervisory body under KWP guidance); the 29-member State Administration Council (an organ to execute policies already made by the Central People's Committee); and the 19-member Standing Committee of the Supreme People's Assembly (a symbolic and honorific body which functions as a legislative branch).

The KWP controls the following mass organizations: the 2-million-member General Federation of Trade Unions of Korea (GFTUK); the 2.7-million-member League of Socialist Working Youth of Korea (LSWY); the Union of Agricultural Working People; the Korean Democratic Women's Union; and the General Federation of Korean Residents in Japan (Chongnyon, or Chosen Soren).

At least two subordinate political movements under the tight KWP control exist in North Korea: the Korean Democratic Party (Choson Minju-dang) and Young Friends' Party of the Chondogyo Sect (the sect being the Society of the Heavenly Way—Chondogyo Chong-u-dang). No membership figures are available on these movements. Their function is to enhance acceptance of the United Democratic Fatherland Front (Choguk Tongil Minjujuui Chonson), created by 71 political and social organizations in June 1949, which is assigned the task of uniting "all the revolutionary forces of North and South Korea" under the leadership of the KWP, in order to implement the "peaceful unification and complete independence of the country." The KWP also controls the "Committee for Peaceful Unification of the Fatherland," established in May 1961 and consisting of representatives from the KWP, the subordinate "democratic" parties, and the mass organizations.

In recent months, the membership of the KWP Political Committee has been enlarged from 15 (11 full and 4 candidate members) to 27 (15 full and 12 candidate members) since the Fifth Party Congress of November 1970. Newly elected as full members were Yi Kun-mo and Yon Hyung-muk, and as candidates: O Paek-yong, Kim Yong-nam, Choe Chae-u, Chong Chun-ki, O Tae-pong, Kang Song-san, Im Chun-chu, Yi Chong-ok and Hong Won-kil. The new candidates were promoted from positions as Central Committee members. (A former candidate member, Chong Chun-taek, died recently, and another, Kim Man-gum, was eliminated from party leadership and the government.) The reasons for this enlargement and realignment of the powerful Political Committee prior to the forthcoming Sixth Party Congress have not been given or become known.

According to the party constitution, the National Party Congress is scheduled to convene every four years to elect central KWP organs and to discuss and make decisions on major problems facing the party and the nation. In the past, however, congresses have generally been convened in line with the fulfillment of past economic plans and the beginning of new ones. The Third, Fourth, and Fifth Party Congresses set up the Five-Year Plan in 1956, the Seven-Year Plan in 1961, and the Six-Year Plan in 1970. Accordingly, the Sixth Party Congress is likely to be held sometime in 1976, when it is expected to evaluate the outcome of the current economic plan and schedule the next one. The congress is also likely to be highlighted—as was the previous one—by a new overall reshuffle or some realignment in the North Korean power structure.

The DPRK rests squarely under the broad thumb of the Beloved Leader, Ever-Victorious Commander of the Korean People, President Kim Il-song, whose personality cult is far more extensive than any known in our times and continues unabated. Coincidentally, the cult has produced nepotism and intrigues. In the past few years, Kim Il-song's younger brother, Kim Yong-chu, and eldest son, Kim Chong-il, have each reportedly played political roles in the fashion of ancient dynasties.

For a while it was speculated that Kim Yong-chu would be the successor to his brother. Quite recently, however, Kim Il-song's son, rather than his brother, has begun to receive attention as the likely heir apparent. For example, according to officials of the pro-Pyongyang General Association of Korean Residents in Japan (Chongnyon) who recently visited North Korea, Kim Il-song's son was holding an important position in the North Korean party hierarchy—possibly as a candidate member of the KWP Political Committee, a secretary of the party Central Committee, and a member of the party's propaganda division (Tokyo Kyodo News Service in English, 2 August 1975). They said that they had seen pictures of Kim Chong-il side by side with those of his father in all the homes they visited in North Korea. They also said that their association had been told in Pyongyang that a "party central figure" often mentioned in party directives stood for Comrade Kim Chong-il. DPRK Foreign Ministry officials told the Chongnyon officials that Kim Chong-il's official appointment would be announced possibly at the forthcoming Sixth Party Congress.

All the speculations about Kim Chong-il, intriguing as they may be, must remain conjecture. Besides, Kim Il-song is only in his early 60s and is not expected to step down for some time. Additional time is needed to make a reliable assessment, and more detailed and credible information may emerge in the quite near future when the party congress is convened.

Nepotism has also pushed other members of Kim Il-song's family into powerful positions. The president's second wife, Kim Song-ae, is chairman of the Central Committee of the Korean Democratic Women's Union, a regular member of the KWP Central Committee and a member of the Standing Committee of the Supreme People's Assembly. Kang Yang-uk, former Methodist preacher, who is now DPRK Vice-President and a regular member of the KWP Central Committee, is a maternal relative (Kim's grandfather-in-law). A female cousin, Kim Jung-suk, is deputy chairman of the General Federation of Trade Unions of Korea. Her husband is Ho Tam, a regular member of the KWP Central Committee and DPRK foreign minister. Her sister is Kim Sin-suk, deputy director of the ideological Institute of National Social Science Research. This woman's husband, Yang Hyong-sup, is a regular member of the all-powerful KWP Political Committee and party Central Committee secretary for ideology. The husband of Kim Il-song's niece is Kim Byung-ha, head of the powerful National Security and Political Affairs Bureau—North Korea's intelligence and secret police organization. One of the President's nephews, Hwang Chang-yop, is chairman of the Standing Committee of the Supreme People's Assembly, while a cousin, Kang Hui-won, is chairman of the Pyongyang Municipal People's Committee, a sort of mayor of the DPRK capital. The degree of interconnection by marriage within the party hierarchy can be considered quite high, if the appointments mentioned above are any indication.

Domestic Attitudes and Activities. The 10th plenum of the 5th KWP Central Committee was held from 11 to 17 February 1975 in Pyongyang. Kim Il-song, who presided over the week-long session, advised a continued firm building of the revolutionary base politically, economically, and militarily by strengthening the party power base—the people's army—and promoting socialist construction.

The 5th session of the 5th Supreme People's Assembly was held form 8 to 10 April at Mansudae Assembly Hall in Pyongyang. Finance Minister Kim Kyong-yon reported on the settlement of accounts for the fulfillment of the DPRK state budget for 1974 and also on the 1975 state budget at the 8 April opening session. State revenue for 1974 amounted to 10,015,250,000 won instead of the planned 9,801,000,000 won. (The exchange rate of the won is estimated to be 2.05 to US$1.) This was 2 percent more than the planned target and 17 percent more than the 1973 figures. State expenditures for 1974 were 9,672,190,000 won, or 99 percent of the planned figure and 16 percent over the previous year. That is to say, state income exceeded expenditures by 343,060,000 won.

Both revenues and expenditures in the DPRK state budget for 1975 were scaled at 11,517,200,-000 won. In 1975, in other words, the state budgetary revenues would increase 15 percent as against 1974, and the state budgetary expenditures 19 percent as against the past year. The KWP and DPRK government envisaged the allotment of 16.4 percent of the total state budget expenditure for defense spending. (The actual defense budget would be higher because the Pyongyang regime makes it a rule to hide defense expenditures in other sectors.) Total armed forces in 1975 were believed to number around 467,000 actives and 1,600,000 civilian militia.

Kim Sok-gi, chairman of the education committee of the Supreme People's Assembly said at the 9 April session that universal compulsory 11-year education would be introduced on a full scale throughout the DPRK from 1 September 1975. He noted that the Supreme People's Assembly in April 1973 adopted a law to enforce universal compulsory 10-year senior middle school education and 1-year pre-school education during the Six-Year-Plan. The DPRK, he said, had made full preparations for fulfilling this law far ahead of schedule. In 1972-74 some 60,000 teachers had been trained, and there were in 1975 more than 200,000 teachers amounting to one teacher for every 25 students. He also stated that large-scale construction of schools was being carried and and that in 1975 the DPRK had 60,000 nurseries and kindergartens, 4,700 primary schools, 4,100 senior middle schools, 600 higher specialized schools, and 150-odd universities and colleges. (On 4 October the North Korean Central News Agency in Pyongyang said that 5,600,000 children, almost a third of the population were enrolled.)

During 1975 the regime had consistently urged the North Koreans to fulfill the major targets of the Six-Year Plan before 10 October—the 30th anniversary of the founding of the North Korean Central Bureau of the Korean Communist Party, the KWP's predecessor. On 22 September the Central Statistical Board reported that the plan had been fulfilled by 5,126 factories and enterprises as of the end of August. Annual gross industrial output was 2.2 times greater than 1970. The average annual rate of growth of industrial production reached 18.4 percent—considerably higher than the projected 14 percent, and industrial production in 1975 showed a 25 percent increase above 1974.

With the production of more than 7 million tons of grain in 1974, according to the same report, the grain target of the plan was reached two years ahead of schedule. A rare bumper crop bigger than 1974's harvest was expected in 1975.

South Korea. During 1975, more than three years after a limited dialogue between North and South Korea started, relations between them continued to deteriorate. Talks on rapprochement between the two Koreas have been suspended for more than two years. Meanwhile the DPRK in the north resumed violent propaganda attacks on the Republic of Korea in the South, and the tension and animosity reached a new peak. Moreover, incidents threatened the peace in the Korean peninsula. North Korean infiltrations tunnels under the Demilitarized Zone (DMZ), discovered by the South Korean army both in November 1974 and in March 1975, were in themselves symbols of the more tense atmosphere. North and South Korea clashed twice at sea in February, the second clash drawing U.S. Air Force planes into a chase over the Yellow Sea. According to the *New York Times* (23 May), during the last two weeks of the Vietnam War the North Korean High command moved elements of armored divisions into position near the DMZ to reinforce troops already there. Furthermore, the DPRK built a new airfield located near the DMZ which brought its aircraft within a few minutes' flight time of Seoul. (The DPRK deploys about 600 combat aircraft, the most modern being 130 MIG-21 interceptors.)

Since the collapse of the rapprochement talks, the North Korean line has been that the road to unification lies through a revolution in the South. On 14 February, for example, a *Nodong Shinmun* editorial called upon the South Korean people to overthrow President Park Chung-hee's government in Seoul. If such a revolution takes place, said Kim Il-song in Peking on 18 April, North Korea, "as one and the same nation, will not just look at it with folded arms but will strongly support the South Korean people" (*Peking Review*, 25 April, p. 17).

During the spring the DPRK launched propaganda campaigns on the theme that the danger of war between North and South Korea was steadily increasing and that a situation had been created by the U.S. and South Korean governments in which "a war might break out at any moment." On 9 August *Nodong Shinmun* carried an article headlined "Threat of Southward Invasion Is a Terrible Lie Invented by Park Chung-hee Puppet Clique."

It is possible that the recent communist victories in Indochina emboldened Kim Il-song's ambitions toward the South. To many observers, after the end of the Indochina conflict, the principal danger spot in Asia seemed to be the Korean peninsula. Indeed, the military situation in Korea in 1975 was potentially as dangerous as ever. More than a million men were under arms in the divided peninsula, each side possessing the most sophisticated modern weapons short of the nuclear variety. South of the DMZ, which became the de facto boundary after the 1953 truce which ended the Korean War, were the last U.S. combat troops committed on the Asian mainland, equipped with a frightening array of tactical nuclear weapons. While none of the great powers was encouraging either Pyongyang or Seoul to attempt to reunify the peninsula by force, Korea represented at least as great a threat to world peace as did the Middle East.

International Views and Positions. During 1975 Pyongyang supplemented its efforts on the reunification issue by becoming extremely active on the foreign policy front, partly to undermine the international position of its rival regime in South Korea and partly to develop world support for North Korean policies. Parliamentary, trade, and other good-will missions were dispatched abroad and invited to North Korea, and friendly diplomatic gestures were made to every corner of the earth, especially the "Third World" countries whose bloc has increasingly dominated actions at the United Nations. In particular, the DPRK's foreign policy sought (a) to prevent recognition of "the two Koreas" concept by the world community, (b) to isolate South Korea from both the Third World and the communist bloc, (c) to gain full membership for the DPRK in the non-aligned movement, and (d) to drum up diplomatic support for the forthcoming U.N. vote on the withdrawal of U.N. (actually U.S.) forces from South Korea. President Kim Il-song undertook an international offensive designed to achieve these objectives. His opening visit in April—significantly—was to Peking and came immediately after the U.S. debacle in Indochina. He traveled to Romania, Algeria, and Mauritania in May, and to Bulgaria and Yugoslavia in early June.

A high point in North Korea's world-wide diplomatic campaign was its entry in August to the non-aligned Third World at the conference of foreign ministers of 80 non-aligned states in Lima, Peru. (South Korea's membership application was rejected.) During the year, the DPRK established diplomatic relations with Portugal, Thailand, the Republic of Cape Verde Islands, and Singapore.

On 24 July the North Korean Central News Agency reported that the DPRK had become a member of the International Telecommunication Union by majority vote.

On 6 November Pyongyang broke diplomatic relations with Australia because of "unpardonable unfriendly acts committed by the Australian Government and the Australian Embassy against our country and our people." The real reason was apparently that Australia failed to support North Korea diplomatically at the 30th session of the U.N. General Assembly.

On 19 April the DPRK regime sent a message of greetings to the Cambodian communist leaders upon the occupation of Phnom Penh. Shortly afterward, Prince Norodom Sihanouk and Khieu Samphan, the real leader of the Khmer Rouge, made a good-will visit to North Korea.

Upon the collapse of the Thieu government in Saigon in April, Pyongyang congratulated the Vietnamese communist leaders and the Vietnamese people "on their great historic victory in the heroic struggle against United States aggression and for national salvation." Shortly after the end of the Vietnam war, North Korea and North Vietnam signed two agreements on economic, scientific, and technological cooperation for 1975-76 in Pyongyang.

Severe weakness in the North Korean economy was reported by numerous sources during the year (and this would be an important factor in Pyongyang's decision not to employ a military offensive against the South). Western and other creditors were miffed by the DPRK's inability to honor contracts and finance its growing trade deficits and there was much talk of "bad faith." Acccording to a report in the *New York Times* (8 August), estimates of the DPRK's debts in 1975 to trading partners in Western Europe, Japan, and the communist bloc ran from $700 million to as high as $1.7 billion. Perhaps $200 million of this was already overdue in delinquent payments to non-communist countries.

The DPRK's payments troubles began chiefly because of its ambitious decision in late 1970, before the start of the Six-Year Plan, to import industrial plants and other heavy machinery from the West in vast quantity, in an effort to push ahead of South Korea's rapidly growing economy.

It was believed in diplomatic circles that Kim Il-song went to China and Eastern Europe in the spring of 1975 to solve these payments problems, rather than to gain backing for a military offensive against the South. According to some unverifiable reports obtained in Hong Kong (*NYT*, 8 August), the DPRK leader won a reduction of $150 million in North Korea's debts to the Chinese.

Relations with China and the Soviet Union. Currently, the DPRK's chuch'e" (self-identity, or national identity) policy in communist-bloc affairs is exemplified by its opposition to both Soviet "revisionism" and Chinese "dogmatism." But relations with the Soviet Union and China continued in 1975 to be equally warm and cordial.

Kim Il-song and his DPRK delegation arrived in Peking on 18 April. If the North Korean leader came to obtain Chinese support for his militant revolutionary strategy toward South Korea, apparently timed to take advantage of the disillusionment in the United States over the Indochina debacle, the message he received may have disappointed him. Chinese deputy premier Teng Hsiao-ping, in his speech welcoming the DPRK delegation, expressed resolute support for North Korean efforts to unite Korea but re-emphasized Pyongyang's "reasonable proposals for the peaceful reunification of the fatherland," thereby making clear that the Chinese leaders did not want to see a revival of the Korean War. (See *Peking Review*, 25 April, pp. 11-14.) The general atmosphere of détente among the great powers seemed to lead China (and the Soviet Union) to discourage military adventurism by Kim Il-song in 1975.

Some outstanding points in the 26 April joint communiqué issued by North Korea and China were renewed emphasis on the "independent and peaceful reunification" of the divided Korean peninsula, Peking's affirmation of the status of North Korea as the "sole legitimate sovereign state of the Korean nation," absence of criticism of "Japanese militarism," emphasis upon the growing strength of the numerous "Third World countries," and China's repeated calls for the dissolution of the U.N. military command and withdrawal of the 40,000 U.S. troops from South Korea (ibid., 2 May, pp. 8-11).

It is conceivable that with his government facing a severe balance-of-payments problem, Kim Il-song may have discussed financial aid with the Chinese leaders. The joint communiqué threw no light on this beyond confirming that DPRK economic experts had taken part in the talks.

The Soviet Union's reaction to the DPRK leader's China trip was cool. The DPRK ambassador to the Soviet Union, Kwon Hui-kyong, visited Soviet foreign minister Andrei Gomyko on 10 April, according to Moscow Radio, apparently to inform Moscow of Kim's trip. But the Soviet news agency delayed its brief report on the visit until the last day of Kim's stay in China.

Kim Il-song apparently planned to visit the Soviet Union as well, but it was reported that such a visit was discouraged at that time by the Soviets. Moscow reportedly gave Leonid Brezhnev's "illness" as the reason. It was believed that the Soviets were reluctant to risk possible adverse U.S. reaction to the DPRK leader's visit to Moscow.

During the course of 1975 Moscow was castigating its Chinese adversaries harder than ever. The major anti-Chinese blast was a 10,000-word unsigned editorial in the August issue of *Kommunist*, the doctrinal journal published by the Central Committee of the Communist Party of the Soviet Union. It was a call on communists to adopt a policy of "smashing Maoism." Communists who remained neutral in the Sino-Soviet conflict, the editorial said, would serve the anti-Marxist interests of China—presumably a warning meant for North Vietnam and North Korea, as well as the communist parties of Romania and Yugoslavia, that had sought to strike a balance between the two communist giants. This message seemed to have fallen on deaf ears among the DPRK leaders.

Relations with Japan. While highly critical of the growing Japanese "imperialistic" stakes in South Korea, the DPRK in 1975 was openly bidding for Japanese diplomatic recognition and closer economic ties. Suspicions and hostility toward Japan were still profound in North Korea. Pyongyang viewed Tokyo as being excessively partial to Seoul, pursuing a policy of "two Koreas" and hostility toward the DPRK. On 10 March a *Nodong Shinmun* commentary assailed Japanese prime minister Miki's assertion that "Japan's recognition of North Korea must presuppose some sort of understanding with South Korea." The commentary added: "Japan must give up the reinvasion of South Korea and the hostile policy toward North Korea and 'two Koreas' plot."

During 1975 the Pyongyang-Tokyo relations seemed to have deteriorated somewhat, due to the DPRK's denunciations of the alleged collusion of Japan and the United States to preserve their "colonial interests" in South Korea. On 19 April a *Nodong Shinmun* commentary blasted the Japanese Foreign Ministry for its 17 April announcement that U.S. bases in Japan could be used "for defense of South Korea" and that Japan would "cooperate" with the United States in accordance with the provisions of the Japan-U.S. security treaty. About two weeks later (4 May) *Nodong Shinmun* bitterly denounced the Japanese government for agreeing to comply with Washington's request for the introduction of nuclear weapons into Japan in case an emergency situation was created in South Korea.

Relations with the United States. It was apparent in 1975 that in the short run the Indochina debacle probably strengthened the commitment of the United States to South Korea, where it still had 40,000 troops, 80 fighter planes, and an artillery brigade with new surface-to-surface missiles, plus an undisclosed number of nuclear warheads under U.S. control.

Shortly after the end of the Vietnam conflict, the United States renewed its pledge to support South Korea, emphasizing the strategic importance of the Korean peninsula in the post-Vietnam era. Needless to say, the primary objective of doing this was to deter the DPRK from initiating military adventurism in the South. President Ford said: "We have a treaty with South Korea and I think it is important that we let them, as well as others, know that at least this administration intends to live up to our signed obligation" (*NYT*, 21 May). Later his remarks were elaborated upon by Secretary of State Kissinger: "There can be no ambiguity about our treaty commitment that was ratified by Congress"(*Wall Street Journal*, 25 June), and "We believe that the defense of Korea is important for the security of the whole Northeast Pacific" (*Washington Post*, 29 June). Reinforcing these statements, Secretary of Defense Schlesinger stated that if South Korea were invaded by the North, it would be "necessary to go for the heart of the opponent's power [and] destroy his military forces," rather than simply be "involved endlessly in ancillary military operations" (*U.S. News & World Report*, 26 May). Schlesinger also said: "The United States cannot foreclose any option to use nuclear weapons or introduce more ground troops in the event of a North Korean invasion of the South" (*Korea Week*, 30 June).

In early May the DPRK charged that the United States was planning another war in Korea in which it would use nuclear weapons. On 27 June a *Nodong Shinmun* commentary bitterly denounced "the nuclear blackmail of Ford the villain, the warlike boss of U.S. imperialism, against the Korean people at a press conference held on 25 June at the notorious White House." The article asserted that North Korea would meet any weapon with proper retaliation and punishment.

During 1975 the DPRK was vigorous and a good bit more shrill in demanding (a) the end of all U.N. involvement in Korea, (b) the withdrawal of the 40,000 U.S. troops in South Korea, with their nuclear arms, and (c) the replacement of the current armistice, signed at the end of the Korean War in 1953, with a bilateral "peace" agreement with the United States, without the participation of Seoul. President Kim Il-song reportedly asked President Ford, through Prime Minister Miki of Japan, for direct talks to settle outstanding issues on the troubled Korean peninsula.

The United States, by agreement with South Korea, formally offered on 27 June to dissolve the U.N. Command in Korea on 1 January 1976, provided that China and North Korea agreed to alternative arrangements for maintaining the 1953 armistice. (Termination of the command would not affect the 40,000 U.S. troops in South Korea, which are covered by a separate 1954 military agreement with the Seoul government.) In September, Washington informed the U.N. Security Council that the U.N. flag was no longer flying over military installations in South Korea, except for units directly connected with enforcement of the armistice agreement, involving fewer than 300 non-Korean military personnel. Following up the U.S. proposal of 27 June, Secretary Kissinger, in an address to the U.N. General Assembly on 22 September, called for a new conference of the United States, China, and North and South Korea to discuss ways of keeping the Korean armistice of 1953, including the possible convention of a larger body to negotiate a Korean peace (*NYT*, 23 September). Pyongyang's response to both U.S. proposals was negative.

One major topic at the time of Kissinger's October visit to China was Korea. The Chinese repeated their position that Washington should withdraw its troops from South Korea and engage in direct talks with North Korea. Kissinger was said to have answered that the United States would remove its troops only after the permanent arrangements for security in Korea had been worked out and that these could be negotiated only along with South Korea.

Meanwhile, *For the Independent Peaceful Reunification of Korea*, a selection from the works of Kim Il-song, was published in the United States by International Publishers, in New York. Many statements made by Kim on various subjects were also advertised in leading U.S. newspapers.

United Nations. The Korean question was brought up again in the 1975 fall session of the U.N. General Assembly. The Seoul government sought again the simultaneous admission into the world organization of South and North Korea, and the DPRK government stuck to its previous proposal that the two sides join the United Nations as a single unified body under the name of Confederal Republic of Koryo after the abolition of the U.N. military command in Korea and the withdrawal of all U.S. troops. (In mid-June the DPRK again rejected the South's call for renewed talks via the South-North Coordinating Committee, asserting among other things that Seoul's request for dual U.N. membership must be withdrawn.) On 6 August the U.N. Secrutiy Council refused to consider South Korea's application for membership in the world organization.

The General Assembly's Political Committee, which took up the Koren question in October, had two draft resolutions before it. One, introduced by Japan, had the backing of the United States, a group of its European allies, Thailand, the Philippines, and other countries. The text expressed hope that "all parties directly concerned will enter into negotiations on new arrangements to replace the armistice agreement" of 1953 and reduce tensions. The draft also called for talks on dissolving the U.N. Command in Korea by 1 January 1976. The other draft resolution, sponsored by China, the Soviet Union, and a group of non-aligned Afro-Asian nations, called for ending the U.N. involvement in Korea and for withdrawal of U.S. troops without anything to replace the truce agreement.

The two seemingly contradictory resolutions on Korea were approved by the General Assembly's Political Committee later. The 30th session of the U.N. General Assembly did the same thing. The pro-Seoul revolution was approved 59 to 51 with 29 abstentions; and the pro-Pyongyang resolution 54 to 43 with 42 abstentions. Victory was promptly claimed by North Korea on the one hand and South Korea on the other.

Publications. The KWP publishes a daily organ, *Nodong Shinmun*, and a journal, *Kulloja.* The DPRK government publishes *Minju Choson*, the organ of the Supreme People's Assembly and the cabinet. The *Pyongyang Times, People's Korea,* and *Korea Today* are weekly English-language publications. The official news agency is the Korean Central News Agency.

Washington College   Tai Sung An

Laos

The communist party of Laos, which has been described by its secretary-general as "the leader in all the victories in the Lao revolution," was revealed during 1975 to have changed its name from the People's Party of Laos (Phak Pasason Lao; PPL) to the People's Revolutuionary Party of Laos (Phak Pasason Pativat Lao; PPPL). The change in nomenclature occurred on the eve of the party's formal seizure of power in Laos, the circumstances of which are described below.

The PPL has operated through the medium of the Lao Patriotic Front (Neo Lao Hak Xat; NLHX—sometimes NLHS), which was founded on 6 January 1956 when conditions were propitious for a switch from a primarily military to a primarily political strategy.

In a long documentary article published in 1975 tracing the history of party activities in Laos, the NLHX Central Committee refers to the expansion of the influence of Marxist-Leninist doctrine in Laos, then a French protectorate, beginning in 1930. "In 1934 the Lao Restoration Party was installed under the patronage of the Indochinese Communist Party . . . Pursuing the spirit of the Indochinese Communist Party, on 22 March 1955 the Lao people established the Marxist-Leninist Lao People's Party, which today is the Revolutionary Lao People's Party, to lead the Lao revolution" (Radio Pathet Lao, 26 September 1975; *FBIS*, 2 October 1975). Thus, the common root of communism in Laos with the Vietnamese communist movement has been historically established.

The membership of the PPL has recently been estimated at 15,000 (*NYT*, 5 October 1975). The total population of Laos is approximately three million.

Leadership and Organization. So far as is known, the Central Committee of the PPL comprises the following 11 members: Kaysone Phomvihan, secretary-general; Nouhak Phoumsavan, deputy secretary-general; Prince Souphanouvong, first committee member (and chairman of the NLHX Central Committee); Phoumi Vonvichit, foreign affairs; Sisomphone, PPL organization and membership; Samseun, PPL internal security; Sanan; General Khamtay Siphandone, commander in chief of the Lao People's Liberation Army (LPLA, better known as the Pathet Lao); General Sisavat, chief of staff, LPLA; General Saman, chief of staff, political affairs, LPLA; Khamsouk, first secretary, South Laos (Joseph J. Zasloff, *The Pathet Lao*, Lexington, Mass.: Heath, 1973, p. 33).

Auxiliary and Mass Organizations. The NLHX, as the principal mass-mobilizing instrument of the PPL, serves as the coordinator for more specialized front groups. As Phoumi Vongvichit described it in an interview with a German newspaper, "the NLHX is a political organization which units several anti-imperialist organizations of the people" (*Unsere Zeit* (Essen), 27 June 1970; JPRS 51,104, 6 August 1970).

Party Internal Affairs. No major leadership or organizational changes were reported in party organs during 1975.

Domestic Attitudes and Activities. The seizure of power in Laos by the PPL proceeded in several distinct phases, the outline of which may be traced by a reconstruction of the events of the period, throughout which the NLHX and its armed forces, the Pathet Lao, played the catalytic role. Nevertheless, such a reconstruction, with the help of the communists' own retrospective statements, can provide only broad clues to decision-making within the PPL.

In the first phase the NLHX was not in a dominant position. The ceasefire agreement of 1973, the so-called Vientiane Agreement, had left the Pathet Lao in control of a zone established by years of warfare. This zone was large in terms of territory, but sparse in population. The establishment of the Provisional Government of National Union (PGNU) on 4 April 1974, however, gave the NLHX one-half the Cabinet posts, and the NLHX proceeded to exploit this participation to expand its influence in the rightist-controlled zone through political propaganda both overt and covert, "neutralization" of Vientiane and Luang Prabang (the two capitals), and other means. The NLHX, meanwhile, denied the PGNU any exercise of authority within the Pathet Lao zone.

The rightist faction still possessed great assets, however, including the continued receipt of American aid and the goodwill of the Prime Minister and veteran Lao leader, Prince Souvanna Phouma. It seemed at first as if the balance of forces of the war years (1963-1973) might be preserved. For this to have occurred, however, the rightists would have had to implement a reform program.

The combination of NLHX propaganda and continued rightist corruption exploded in October 1974 in the mutiny of the rightist garrison at Ban Houei Sai, which had allegedly not received its pay for several months. The trouble was papered over, but NLHX agents in the town were active among soldiers and students, and in December a second and more serious uprising took place, in which a list of demands was set forth, including the dissolution of the rightist-dominated National Assembly in Vientiane.

The dissolution of the National Assembly became a central NLHX demand. The PGNU expressed its willingness to sanction this on 6 December, but when King Savang Vatthana referred the matter to his Privy Council, NLHX propaganda organs attacked the council as a tool of the rightists. The King, under Laos' Constitution, had the authority to dismiss the National Assembly. However, a new Assembly would have been required to meet within 90 days, and the NLHX was clearly unwilling to agree to fresh elections until it had managed to secure control over the election machinery.

A "compromise"on the issue was finally worked out whereby the members of the new National Assembly would be appointed by each side and by the King, thereby obviating the need for holding elections in the near future, and King Savang signed the decree dissolving the National Assembly in April. The action had the effect of depriving the rightist side of its last claim to parliamentary legitimacy and placed the rightists on the same footing with the NLHX as contenders for power. This signal success marked the end of the first phase of the PPL's drive to seize power.

The opening of the second phase coincided with the Communist offensive in South Vietnam. Pathet Lao troops launched offensive actions in both north and south Laos, claiming prior provocation and the right of self-defense. Simultaneously, NLHX proselytizers fomented mutinies in units of the armed forces of the rightist side. The principal objective of this phase became to "eliminate the reactionaries" (see, e.g., Radio Pathet Lao, 16 May; *FBIS*, 22 May). Three rightist ministers fled to Thailand, as did a number of military commanders of various ranks. The disarray of the rightist side was further increased by the temporary assumption of the duties of the absent defense minister, at the critical moment, by his NLHX vice-minister. Simultaneously, Pathet Lao units moved into all major population centers in the rightist zone, claiming to be acting in response to the appeals of various "steering committees" set up by pro-NLHX activists. Rightist functionaries were intimidated.

Territorially and administratively, the NLHX had now achieved a dominant position in Laos, having succeeded in maintaining exclusive control over its own zone and having virtually neutralized rightist control over the nominally rightist zone. All this while, the NLHX continued to affirm that it upheld the Vientiane Agreement, a claim that was made more plausible by the PGNU's willingness to delegate negotiating authority in order to settle disputes involving demonstrators in the provincial towns, who frequently occupied administrative offices until such time as rightist functionaries agreed to step down. In launching the third phase of its action, however, the PPL aimed at consolidating the gains already won by the complete replacement of existing administrative organs by NLHX cadres at all levels except at the national level, where the PGNU remained in office, thus finally dispensing with the veneer of the Vientiane Agreement and its stipulation that each side would continue to exercise authority in its separate zone until the holding of general elections, the formation of a permanent government, and the integration of the two zones.

In an important statement issued on 27 June following a meeting of the NLHX Central Committee, sanction was given to the new campaign, which was already under way in districts and towns in the rightist zone.

> The NLHX believes that the simultaneous uprisings by the people of all strata, students, schoolchildren, workers, farmers, soldiers, policemen and civil servants to overthrow the decadent administration, as well as the military machinery which served as the tools of the U.S. imperialists' neocolonialism in our country, and to seize administrative power, are just and correct. ("On the New Situation in Laos," Radio Pathet Lao, 27 June; *FBIS*, 30 June.)

The seizure of power was termed "the most urgent task of the Lao people" in a Pathet Lao News Agency commentary broadcast on 18 July (*FBIS*, 21 July). The campaign culminated with the formation on 23 August of a revolutionary committee in Vientiane city.

The opening of the fourth and climactic phase of the PPL's seizure of power could be deduced from the importance the NLHX attached to the celebration of the 30th anniversary of the 12 October 1945 proclamation of Laos' independence from France. Always celebrated as independence day by the NLHX, 12 October was to be marked in Vientiane by a mammoth rally and speeches by NLHX leaders.

The decision to launch this phase must have been decided upon in September at the latest, for on 1 October typesetters at the National Printing Office in Vientiane had reportedly already received instructions to work evenings to produce the text of a major speech by Kaysone Phomvihan (*New York Times* [*NYT*], 5 October). While the anniversary ceremonies at Viengsay were attended by an important DRV party-government delegation headed by Truong Chinh, Kaysone himself was not listed among the greeting party of NLHX Central Committee Standing Committee members, leading one to suppose he had traveled from Hanoi with the delegation (Radio Pathet Lao, 11 October; *FBIS*, 14 October).

In his speech at Viengsay, Kaysone declared that "the revolution will speed up" (Radio Pathet Lao, 12 October; *FBIS*, 15 October). He also emphasized the role played by the PPL, which he said was not called the Lao People's Revolutionary Party, "which was the leader in all the victories in the Lao revolution" (ibid.). On 8 October, the newspaper *Siang Pasason*, central organ of the Lao People's Revolutionary Party, declared that the Lao revolution was entering "a new stage" (Pathet Lao News Agency, 8 October; *FBIS*, 9 October).

Timed to coincide with the anniversary preparations, Radio Pathet Lao on September 26 broadcast the text of a lengthy article signed by the Cultural Propaganda and Training Committee of the NLHX Central Committee titled "30 Years of the Lao Revolution." The Article contained a rare elucidation of the strategy dictated by the party in the achievement of the revolutionary takeover.

> Four-fifths of Lao territory—the old liberated areas—have been turned into areas with a popular democratic system in accordance with our policy of achieving a socialist system. Following the people's uprisings to seize power, the remaining one-fifth of Lao territory has now begun advancing toward achieving a popular democratic system.
>
> The progressive changes are the result of two things. First, the clear-sighted initiative and independent leadership of the Lao People's Revolutionary Party. In each stage of the revolution, the party has correctly evaluated the balance of forces between our people and the enemy, understood who is the real enemy, and led our people to carry out revolutionary struggle in line with the realities in Laos, in Indochina, in Southeast Asia and the world. On this basis, the party has set forth suitable policies and pointed out how to correctly implement them; suitably marked out the stages of the revolution; rationally coordinated the national revolutionary task with democracy and the interests of the Lao revolution and those of the three Indochinese countries with world peace; suitably employed an offensive strategy and tactics; taken advantage of the internal contradictions in the ranks of the enemy; and made all efforts to overthrow the real enemy. This is why our people defeated the enemy step by step, won victories part by part, and were able to march forward to complete victory. . .
>
> We understood when to stop and when to start the struggle in each period, and we knew well when it was necessary to struggle and when to negotiate—and we would negotiate only when we had the necessary conditions to do so. We understood when to take advantage of the situation and to create the opportunities to achieve as big victories as possible. We firmly upheld the banner of the nation and the banner of democracy. While the banner of the nation has always been raised high, it has always been related to the banner of democracy. At the same time, we profoundly understood the fact that in our country, the original forces to carry out the national, democratic revolution are the peasants. This is why we went to the rural areas to build the strength of the worker-peasant alliance and to mobilize the peasants of various nationalities to rise up and carry out the people's war. . .
>
> The popular uprisings have been successful because the policy of the party Central Committee is correct, the leadership of the party Central Committee is clear-sighted, the leading committee of the local party committee of each level has directed the uprisings in a timely manner, taken advantage of the situation, firmly grasped the line of thinking on revolutionary offensive, upheld the attitude of using revolutionary violence, powerfully coordinated the three strategic blows, and made use of the lawful support of the various organizations and applied it to the realities in each locality. . .
>
> The second factor responsible for the progressive changes is the profoundly patriotic spirit, the dauntless determination, and the fine combat tradition against foreign aggression of our Lao people . . . (Radio Pathet Lao, 26 September; *FBIS*, 2 October.)

On 3-5 October the National Political Consultative Council (NPCC), which had been established by the Vientiane Agreement as a coequal body with the PGNU, held a hastily-summoned session in Luang Prabang and was addressed by its chairman, Prince Souphanouvong, who said:

> I believe that the current objective and subjective conditions and circumstances in our country are favorable for us now to hold general elections in order to form a National Assembly and the permanent coalition government as stipulated in Article 6 of the 1973 Vientiane Agreement. (Vientiane Radio, 3 October; *FBIS*, 6 October.)

The NPCC went on to approve unanimously two bills specifying the modalities for holding nation-wide elections to be carried out "level by level from the grassroots to the central level and from the local to the national level" (ibid.). Afterward, a PGNU spokesman announced that general elections would be held on April 4, 1976.

The NLHX, however, lost no time in getting the election process started, and for its own ends, as was to become evident. Beginning on 5 November, elections were organized throughout the country (i.e. in both zones) on the lowest level and proceeded in a number of rounds to higher levels. Hints of the direction in which events were moving were provided by the title of a Radio Pathet Lao editorial on 11 November, "Laos Will Majestically March Forward Along the Path of Independence, Popular Democracy, Prosperity and Strength" (*FBIS*, 12 November), and by a reference in *Siang Pasason* on 13 November to "this democratic election—the first one in our history" (*FBIS*, 14 November).

On 25-26 November in Viengsay a "special joint conference" of the PGNU and NPCC was held, news of which was disseminated by NLHX organs following an interval of three days. By this time, movements of members of both these bodies were being effected entirely by Soviet-provided aircraft of the LPLA Aviation Department. The conference was chaired by Prince Souphanouvong (Pathet Lao News Agency, 28 November; *FBIS*, 1 December), but Prince Souvanna Phouma, who in the meantime flew from Vientiane to Luang Prabang in the company of Phoumi Vongvichit (who then flew on to Viengsay), was not in attendance. The conference ended after unanimously adopting "an important resolution" (Pathet Lao News Agency, 29 November; *FBIS*, 1 December).

The pace of events quickened, with the NLHX firmly in control at every step. Vientiane Radio reported a demonstration in Vientiane of 100,000 people on 28 November demanding the dissolution of the PGNU and the NPCC "because they do not conform to the current situation" and calling on the NLHX Central Committee to hold a national congress of people's representatives (Vientiane Radio, 29 November; *FBIS*, 1 December). Again events were orchestrated in such a manner as to make it appear that the NLHX was responding to the popular will. An editorial in *Siang Pasason* on 28 November titled "The People's Legitimate Demand" declared "The national democratic revolution has so far been mainly completed throughout Laos" (Pathet Lao News Agency, 29 November; *FBIS*, 1 December). A demonstration in Vientiane on 1 December demanding the abdication of the King was reported by non-Communist sources.

In response to "the people's demand," the NLHX Central Committee convened a national congress of people's representatives in Vientiane on 1-2 December. Vientiane Radio reported on 3 December that the congress adopted a note of abdication from King Savang and a note on the dissolution of the PGNU and NPCC, and unanimously decided on a resolution to abolish the monarchy and establish a people's democratic republic, to appoint the President of the People's Democratic Republic of Laos, and to appoint the Government of the People's Democratic Republic of Laos (*FBIS*, 3 December).

The following day the radio gave further details of the proceedings. On 1 December, Souphanouvong had made a 12-and-one-half-minute opening speech. Souvanna Phouma had made an 8 minute speech announcing his resignation as Prime Minister and the dissolution of the PGNU. Crown Prince Vongsavang made a 9 minute speech in which he read a note of abdication of King Savang effective at 0144 GMT 1 December. Souphanouvong then made a 6 minute speech announcing the dissolution of the NPCC. Kaysone Phomvihan then made a political report lasting 70 minutes (*FBIS*, 4 December). On 2 December, Kaysone again addressed the congress to propose Souphanouvong as President of the Democratic People's Republic of Laos. This was unanimously approved. Souphanouvong accepted and pledged to "closely cooperate with the Supreme People's Council and the Government of the People's Democratic Republic of Laos under the leadership of the People's Revolutionary Party of Laos." The congress then proceeded with the election of a 44-member Supreme People's Council, with Souphanouvong as chairman and other NLHX Central Committee Standing Committee members as officers. Kaysone then presented in a 52 minute speech a program of action and a list of the members of the government, which he headed as Prime Minister (ibid.).

The Cabinet comprised in all 39 members. The main ministerial posts, all distributed to NLHX Central Committee members, were as follows:

Kaysone Phomvihan	Prime Minister
Nouhak Phoumsavan	Deputy Prime Minister and Minister of Finance
Phoumi Vongvichit	Deputy Prime Minister and Minister of Education, Sports and Religion
Phoun Sipraseuth	Deputy Prime Minister and Minister of Foreign Affairs
Khamtay Siphandone	Deputy Prime Minister and Minister of National Defense
Somseun Khamphithoun	Minister of Interior
(May be same name as Samseun of PPL Central Committee)	
Sisana Sisane	Minister of Information, Propaganda, Culture and Tourism
Sanan Soutthichak	Minister of Communications, Public Works and Transport
Souk Vongsak	Minister of Public Health
Kou Souvannamethi	Minister of Justice
Maisouk Saisompheng	Minister of Industry and Commerce
Khampheng Boupha	Mnister of Posts and Telecommunications

(Radio Vientiane, 4 December; *FBIS*, 4 December)

Following the precedent established by the Vietnamese communists in 1945 in the case of the Emperor Bao Dai, the NLHX appointed King Savang an "adviser" to the Supreme People's Council. This marked the end of the fourth phase; the Vientiane Agreement and the coalition government that went with it were scrapped, having outlived their usefulness.

Prince Souvanna Phouma must have viewed the events of 1975 with strongly mixed feelings. The viceregal family of which he and his two brothers were members had historically been the rival of the royal family. Nevertheless, he had in the end remained more loyal to his kind than either Phetsarath or Souphanouvong, both of whom were partial to republican ideas. In the long and trying period of Laos' recent history in which he had held the Prime Ministership, Souvanna Phouma had made it his first task to try to reintegrate the NLHX into the mainstream of Lao politics. Three coalitions had eventuated. In the last, while the PPL behind the NLHX talked in terms of the "national democratic revolution," Souvanna Phouma talked in terms of "national reconciliation." The two things could be perceived as identical for some time, and his brother surely tried to convince him to look at things in this way. As the shape of the "reintegration" became manifest during 1975, Souvanna Phouma's friends on the right deserted him. Powerless in the end to forestall the inevitable, Souvanna Phouma acquiesced. The NLHX victory left Souphanouvong as President. But Souvanna Phouma must have asked himself how long his brother could maintain his influence with Kaysone and the Hanoi-liners now in complete control of the government and the revolution. Perhaps he foresaw the day when Souphanouvong, too, would be compelled to "abdicate"for the good of the revolution, and follow his two elder brothers into enforced retirement.

International Views and Policies. The PPL continued in 1975 to maintain its closest working relationship with the Vietnam Workers Party and to follow the views of this party in international relations, according the DRV a predominant position in expressions of solidarity and gratitude for assistance rendered over both the USSR and the PRC. The documentary article "30 Years of the Lao Revolution," previously referred to, was careful to avoid giving offense by mentioning the history of

Vietnamese intervention in Laos during the 19th century, which went so far as actual annexation of certain regions, and merely referred to the depredations of Siam. Up to October 1975, there were an estimated 30,000-40,000 North Vietnamese troops still in Laos (*NYT*, 5 October).

International Activities and Contacts. Exchanges of visits by delegations with the DRV continued to be frequent. The PPL or its front organizations also exchanged visits with the USSR, the PRC, Eastern European and other countries, however. A CPSU delegation headed by Alexei Shibayev visited Viengsay in January 1975 at the invitation of the NLHX Central Committee (Radio Pathet Lao, 9 January; *FBIS*, 10 January).

Party Publications. An important development was the beginning of publication in Vientiane of the newspaper *Siang Pasason*, which was described as the "central organ" of the People's Revolutionary Party of Laos. *Siang Pasason* was reported to be distributed throughout Laos.

Silver Spring, Maryland   Arthur J. Dommen

Malaysia

Following the basic geographic division of Malaysia—between West Malaysia, consisting of the Malay Peninsula, and East Malaysia, comprising the states of Sarawak and Sabah in the northern and western sections of the island of Borneo (also called Kalimantan)—Malaysian Communism consists of the splintered underground Communist Party of Malaya (CPM) and its guerrilla forces, operating on the peninsula and also in Singapore, and a number of local revolutionary and guerrilla groups limited to East Malaysia, collectively designated by various terms, among which Sarawak Communist Organization (SCO), North Kalimantan Communist Party (NKCP), and North Kalimantan People's Guerrilla Force (NKPGF) occur particularly frequently both in government usage and in popular parlance, at least at present (terminology has tended to change over the years).

Except for the period of the "confrontation" campaign carried out by the Indonesian government against Malaysia (1963-65), there has been and is now no organization or tactical coordination or any other significant interaction between the two geographic wings of the Malaysian Communist movement, even though the program and ideology of both is laced with Maoism and despite the fact that both wings should be considered as essentially Peking-oriented. The main reason is that Communists and their sympathizers in both parts of Malaysia regard the formation of Malaysia in 1963 to have been the culmination of a U.S. and British "imperialist" scheme and to have occurred illegally and undemocratically. The factions of the CPM continue to favor a "merger" of Malaya (the peninsula states) with Singapore (which, originally part of Malaysia in 1963, seceded and became an independent republic in 1965), but believe that the Malaysian states of Sarawak and Sabah on Borneo should determine their own future and preferably acquire independence.

West Malaysia has a population of about 9,200,000 and East Malaysia about 1,800,000.

History. During the 1920s, predominantly Chinese trade unions, school associations, and other interest groups in Singapore, Penang, and other Malay Peninsula towns provided the first seedbed of Malaysian Communism. In 1928 a "Communist Party of the South Seas" was formed under Comintern direction to coordinate Malayan, Philippine, Thai, and even some expatriate Indonesian Communist activity, but complaints over a lack of leadership led to various local splits and to the formal establishment of the CPM on 26 April 1930 in Singapore. Indonesian Communists, escaping from the consequences of a failed Communist coup attempt in Indonesia in 1926-27, appear to have been active in the early CPM, maintaining Comintern contacts in the Soviet Union, Britain, the Netherlands, and much of the Far East.

The effects of the world depression during the 1930s on the tin miners, rubber estate workers, and Chinese trade unions in Malaya proved a relative boon to the CPM, whose new party constitution in 1934 reflected new organizational strength, but effective British colonial government surveillance, and the CPM's failure to link up with the budding and generally moderately conservative Malay nationalist movement tended to limit the party's effectiveness. This failure, then and to almost the same degree today, can be said to have stemmed in large part from the predominantly Chinese ethnic character of the CPM and from the complex pattern of racial differentiation and occasional hostility in virtually all phases of public life between Malays and Chinese, who, together with inhabitants of ethnic Indian and Pakistani origin, form the principal population groups on the Malay Peninsula.

Perhaps only during World War II, when the CPM's initiatives in organizing an anti-Japanese guerrilla movement in Malaya provided it with popularity and prestige, did a significant degree of solidarity develop between the Chinese, Malay, and other population groups. After the war, as Britain proceeded with plans for the eventual independence of Malaya, the CPM, seeking to dominate the decolonialization process, launched in 1948 a protracted guerrilla struggle against British rule from its jungle strongholds in the interior of the peninsula. Thus there began an "Emergency" period which was not officially proclaimed to have ended until 1960, although by the mid-1950s the CPM's "people's war" had lost all chance of success, and the net effect was that the Communists alienated themselves from Malay nationalism, and the formal independence of Malaya on 31 August 1957, cut the ground from under whatever further nationalist appeal the Communists might once have been able to develop. (See Edgar O'Ballance, *Malaya: The Communist Insurgent War, 1948-1960*, London, Faber, 1966.) Malays, Indians, and others refused to join the CPM guerrilla struggle, deepening their communal and political differences with the Chinese.

As British and Malayan government counter-insurgency tactics became more sophisticated and effective, the CPM's "people's army," numbering about 100, was driven to the jungle frontier area between Malaya and Thailand. (See Richard Clutterbuck, *Riot and Revolution in Singapore and Malaya, 1945-1963*, London, Faber, 1973.) Calling their forces the Malayan National Liberation Army (MNLA) or less frequently the Malayan Revolutionary Liberation Army (MLRA), the guerrillas here reorganized themselves for a continuing hit-and-run campaign, slowly developing new "regiments," encampments, and channels of recruitment on both sides of the border among both local Chinese estate workers and secession-minded Muslim Malays and Thais dissatisfied with their respective governments. (See Justus M. van der Kroef, *Communism in Malaysia and Singapore: A Contemporary Survey,* The Hague, Nijhoff, 1967.)

Although long-time CPM secretary-general Chin Peng continued to be the overall leader of the Guerrillas, their relative ineffectiveness over the years in winning significant new popular support, and the containment imposed on their operations by extensive government intelligence, bred suspicion and leadership quarrels which, by the early 1970s had hardened into permanent fissures. In August 1974 there came from various sources confirmation of a three-way division in West Malaysian Communism. Two organizations reportedly had broken off from the parent CPM. One refers to itself as the Communist Party of Malaya (Revolutionary Faction), or CPM-RF, and since February 1970 (when, according to the government, it was formed) appears to have drawn followers primarily from among the MNLA's "Eighth Regiment." The other splinter group calls itself the Communist Party of Malaya (Marxist-Leninist), or CPM-ML. Both splinter groups claim to have their own fighting forces, both called the "Malayan People's Liberation Army" (MPLA). The CPM-ML's founding was announced by its leaders on 1 August 1974. Adherents of the CPM-ML are said to have come primarily from the "2nd district" unit of the MNLA's "Twelfth Regiment," although some "Eighth Regiment" regulars also joined. The immediate (as opposed to deeper, long-term) cause of the CPM's splintering was the increasing suspicion of some CPM leaders during the later 1960s regarding the loyalty of some leading cadres and recent recruits. Orders in January 1970 to kill those suspected were ignored, and the dissension was fortified by long-festering criticism among younger cadres of Chin Peng's strategy and alleged ineffectiveness over the need to implement a more militant and aggressive policy, and possibly also over ideological differences regarding potential collaboration with the budding Malay and Chinese radical "New Left" in university towns. CPM appeals continue to be made in terms of Chinese pride and identity, and charges that the Malaysian government of Premier Abdul Razak is hampering or destroying Chinese schools in Malaysia remain the CPM's stock in trade (see, e.g., *FBIS*, 1 October 1974, and "Voice of the Malayan Revolution" broadcast report entitled "Another Crime of the Razak Clique in Wiping Out Chinese Schools," 26 September 1974).

In Eastern Malaysia, Communism arose primarily among the Chinese of Sarawak, particularly in the towns of Sibu and Miri. Given a major impetus by the Chinese schools of those towns before World War II, the Communist movement crystallized initially in various "progressive" youth clubs and during the later 1930s into the "Sarawak Advanced Youths Association" (SAYA). The last-named group, along with such organizations as the underground "Sarawak Liberation League" and the "Sarawak Anti-Fascist League," were active in the anti-Japanese resistance during the early 1940s. By 1951 a number of Communist groups and "self-criticism" clubs among Chinese school youths, Peking-oriented shop assistants, and Chinese planters had accepted general direction from an umbrella organization, the "Sarawak Overseas Chinese Democratic Youth League," which reportedly maintained contact with the Communist party in China. Urban youths, particularly in the Chinese schools, and front organizations of planters like the "Sarawak Farmers' Association" (SFA), formed the backbone of a developing Communist underground complex in the early 1940s, generally designated by the government as the Sarawak Communist Organization. Vigorously opposed to Sarawak's entry into the Malaysia Federation in 1963, the SCO was subsequently also able to exercise some influence in the predominantly Chinese Sarawak United People's Party (SUPP), although by the early 1970s the SUPP had virtually purged itself of its radical Leftists and joined the government coalition of parties. Well before 1963 the SCO had begun mobilizing for a "people's war" in the Sarawak jungles, a struggle which intensified after Sarawak became part of the Malaysian Federation.

During the Indonesian "confrontation" of Malaysia (1963-65) the SCO received assistance from both the Indonesian Communist Party (PKI), and from leftist Indonesian military commanders across the border in Indonesian Kalimantan. However, the failure of the coup attempt in Indonesia on 30 September 1965 and the collapse of the PKI, which had been heavily involved in it, led to a sharp change in Indonesian policy and to intensified campaigns against SCO guerrillas by the governments at both Malaysia and Indonesia. Beginning in October 1973 with the launching of the Malaysian government's "Sri Aman" (Lasting Peace) campaign, which promised rehabilitation to SCO guerrillas who laid down their arms, more than 560 insurgents, comprising nearly 70 percent of the SCO's total "People's Army," came out of the Sarawak jungle. But even before the termination of the Sri Aman campaign in June 1974 there had been re-defections back to the NKPGF. Some 100 continue small-scale occasional hit-and-run guerrilla struggle today (government reports tend to exaggerate the extent of this activity). There has also been evidence of recent assistance to the NKPGF by underground PKI elements across the Indonesian border.

In Sabah, underground Communist activity is virtually negligible, being largely confined to deep-cover proselytizing among Chinese school youths and shop personnel in the towns. There has been some apprehension over the illegal influx of Chinese aliens with Communist sympathies from Indonesia and mainland China.

Organization and Tactics. In West Malaysia, despite internal CPM fissures and the extensive government surveillance and counter-insurgency programs in the guerrilla affected Thai-Malaysian border areas, the CPM and its MNLA fighting arm are estimated today to have together from 2,000 to 3,000 hard-core members, with additional supporters among Chinese and radical "New Left" Malays and Indians at various levels of sympathy, numbering perhaps about 4,000 and scattered throughout the peninsula. Official estimates vary and are much smaller. According to (very considerably underestimated) data released by the Malaysian government in mid-1975, Communist forces on the Malaysian side of the border totaled only 877, among them 732 Chinese, 107 Malays, 2 ethnic Indians, 11 Malayan aborigines, 23 Chinese "Masquerading as Malays," and 2 Japanese (presumably World War II stragglers); on the Thai side there were said to be 1,177, all "Thais" (*Far Eastern Economic Review*, Hong Kong, 4 July, p. 10). There is little reliable information on the extent of cooperation of the CPM and its splinter groups with the Thai Communist organization across the border. The CPM has, on a number of occasions, proselytized effectively among border Thais, particularly Chinese, and there has probably been considerable, if informal, participation by them in and alongside CPM ranks. Because of this, and because of the equally unverified extent to which the CPM may have begun to develop a fluid urban following, the very exactitude of official figures on Communist insurgent strength suggests a seemingly high intelligence quality that is belied, however, by the relative success of continuing Communist guerrilla operations; the steadily mounting number of senior Malaysian police and counter-insurgency intelligence officers assassinated by the CPM, the ever ongoing ambushes and guerrilla attacks on construction projects and government patrols which it seems impossible to forestall, and so on.

Some Malaysian police sources view the CPM-ML and CPM-RF as little more than relatively small "nuisance" factions of from 100 to 150 followers, respectively, whose leadership personnel have remained unpublished, although both factions claim to have a central committee and a chairman and other executive officers.

The parent CPM, the CPM-ML, and the CPM-RF are divided into political organizations (the formal party structure) and military units, though individual adherents participate in both aspects. The CPM's political wing is called the Malayan National Liberation League (MNLL). Its military organization has since the middle 1960s generally been designated the Malayan National Liberation Army, although occasionally the name Malayan Revolutionary Liberation Army is still used. The CPM-ML and the CPM-RF, both employ the name Malayan People's Liberation Army for their armed forces. To add to the confusion, the *political* organization of the CPM-RF and the *military* wing of the CPM-ML call themselves the Malayan People's Liberation League (MPLL), while approximately the same latter name, *Persekutuan Pembebasan Rakyat Malaya* or Malayan People's Liberation Front (or League) is used by the CPM-ML for its *political* organization. (See Malaysian home affairs minister Ghazali Shafie's statement on the CPM split in *New Straits Times*, Kuala Lumpur, 2 November 1974, and Chandran Jeshurun, "The Security Situation in Peninsular Malaysia," in *Southeast Asian Affairs, 1975*, Institute of Southeast Asian Studies, Singapore, 1975, p. 99.)

The CPM-RF and CPM-ML defections have not altered the MNLA's battle order of three "regiments" which together number about 1,300 men and women. One regiment, the "Eighth," is stationed near the Thai-Malaysian border in the upper region of Kedah State. Another, the "Twelfth Regiment" which includes the MNLA command as well as the CPM central party secretariat, operates in and around Grik, in the northern parts of Perak State and around Kroh in Kedah; the third, the

"Tenth Regiment," is located in Kelantan State around Tanah Merah and Pasir Mas. The "Tenth" is predominantly composed of Malays. Additionally, there have been reports of separate MNLA "Assault Units": an "Eighth Assault Unit" in southern Kedah around the towns of Kulim and Serdang, and a small "Fifth Assault Unit" in the Sungei Siput region of Perak (this unit appears to be an entity distinct from an occasionally reported but unconfirmed MNLA "Fifth Regiment" also operating in Perak) (Jeshurun, op. cit., p. 100). The specific operational areas of the two rival MPLA organizations and of the CPM-ML and CPM-RF have not been reported thus far, although during the first half of 1975, when guerrilla activity was stepping up (see "Domestic Developments," below), Malaysian officials occasionally attributed insurgent attacks to CPM-ML or CPM-RF followers (*Asia Research Bulletin*, Political Supplement, 30 April, p. 77; *The Nation*, Bangkok, 21 June). Other informed Malaysian sources see the CPM splinter groups at present as little more than paper organizations of two small leadership factions.

It is unlikely that the splintering of the CPM reflects basic or irreconcilable ideological or even tactical differences; though such differences may be there, the rifts seem more the result of intra-personnel suspicions and enmities. The appearance of the CPM-ML in 1974, for example, could erroneously be interpreted—in line with the emergence of secessionist, self-styled "Marxist-Leninist" organizations elsewhere in the Communist world—as the activity of Peking-oriented dissidents concerned with establishing their own separate party in the face of a "revisionist" line in their parent party. The parent CPM, however, is and has been consistently and avowedly Maoist in orientation, and in the course of 1974 in particular strongly acknowledged the role of "Mao Tse-tung Thought" in its doctrine, stressed the tactical primacy of armed struggle, and branded the "Soviet revisionist renegade clique" in Moscow as being in league with "imperialist" designs in Malaysia (*YICA, 1975*, p. 378). CPM dissidents in the early 1970s have been variously described as opposed to the official CPM line of "encircling the cities from the countryside" (M. G. G. Pillai, "The Problems of Chin Peng," ibid., 8 November 1974, p. 15). Then, too, one senior Malaysian police official has claimed that the CPM-ML was propagating an orthodox Marxist and Leninist ideology, in contrast to the "Mao Tse-tung concept" followed by the parent CPM (*Sarawak Tribune*, Kuching, 2 November 1974). One perceptive Malaysian press comment on the CPM split has noted, however, that the ML breakaway faction has apparently had to concentrate so much of its efforts on urging its Communist friends to try and recognize the alleged "differences" between itself and the parent CPM's "revisionist political cheats" as to suggest that the differences in fact are not being recognized by the Communist rank and file (editorial, "MCP vs MCP," *New Straits Times*, Kuala Lumpur, 25 October 1974; *FBIS*, 31 October).

Probing beneath the general expressions of calumny which the CPM factions routinely hurl at each other reveals the real reason for the CPM split to have had its roots during the 1967-68 period when the CPM Central Committee, aware of younger rank-and-file criticism of the frequently absent (from Malaya) CPM secretary-general, Chin Peng, and of his cautious tactic of concentrating on building an infrastructure of popular support in the Thai-Malayan border region, began committing itself to a new and aggressively militant guerrilla strategy. On 1 June 1968 the CPM Central Committee issued a statement (reaffirmed on 25 April 1970) which, as a recent CPM analysis of the ML dissidents puts it, "summed up" the party's experience "in our revolution" and "clearly pointed out the need to use the countryside to besiege the cities," adding that "since then the Malayan National Liberation Army has won victory after victory" ("Voice of the Malayan Revolution," 11 February 1975, in *FBIS*, 14 February). However, even before the formal issuance of the 1968 statement there were dissidents' plans, according to the Malaysian government, to depose the Central Committee, and opposition continued afterward, particularly in the MNLA's "Eighth Regiment." Matters reached a point late in 1969 where the Central Committee ordered an investigation and (as noted above) in January 1970 ordered the killing of its opponents in the party, including suspected recent recruits, numbering several score. "Eighth Regiment" commanders and cadres refused to implement the order and by February 1970, according to the Malaysian government, the "Eighth Regiment" dissidents had established their own rival Central Committee and party organization, the CPM-RF.

Tensions between the two factions deepened when the CPM-RF armed units (now called the MPLA) ran into ambushes set by government forces and believed that their positions had been betrayed by the CPM parent. The CPM Central Committee attempted to continue its purge in the early 1970s, sending an investigator to the "second unit" of the MNLA's "Twelfth Regiment," where there were reportedly sympathizers with the CPM-RF. Here, too, executions were ordered, and "Twelfth Regiment" commanders also disobeyed, slipping into the jungle with those who had been marked for liquidation. Even so there was no complete break between the "second unit" dissidents and the CPM until March 1974, when the dissidents established a new "revolutionary committee." Statements issued by this committee denounced the parent CPM's contention that those whom it had marked for execution were government spies and that party organizations had been infiltrated by the "enemy." On 1 August the "revolutionary committee" took the final step, proclaiming a new party, the CPM-ML, with its own armed wing, the MPLA. On 22 October, CPM-ML leaflets were discovered and CPM-ML flags and banners surreptitiously put up in various public places in Kuala Lumpur and in major towns in the states of Selangor, Negri Sembilan, Malaka, and Johore—apparently a CPM-ML attempt to call attention to the split and to the new direction that West Malaysian Communism would be taking. But there have been no repetitions of this incident, and CPM-ML and CPM-RF statements, which remain very few and are primarily concerned with denouncing the parent CPM and its "traitorous" and "revisionist" leaders, reveal nothing of any distinctive ideological or tactical course which they intend to pursue. (*New Straits Times*, 2 November 1974; *Far Eastern Economic Review*, 15 November, pp. 20-21; Jeshurun, op. cit., pp. 99-100.)

CPM statements, issued primarily over its clandestine radio transmitter, "Voice of the Malayan Revolution," which is believed to be located in Yunnan Province in southern China, attempt to give the impression that the parent party has been little affected by the secessionist developments. Although (according to a statement by the Thai armed forces staff chief, General Tan Sri Kriangsak Chomanan, in January 1975) CPM secretary-general Chin Peng has been gone from the CPM guerrilla operational area along the Thai-Malaysian border since 1961, and is no longer in command of the insurgents (*Sarawak Tribune* Kuching, 9 January 1975), CPM pronouncements continue to make it clear that Chin (who is believed to reside in Peking for protracted periods) remains the principal party leader. In a 1975 New Year's Day editorial, the "Voice of the Malayan Revolution," reviewing the past year, declared that the "fighters" of the MNLA, "closely united around the party Central Committee headed by Comrade Chin Peng," had carried out the party's correct line on developing revolutionary armed struggle in our country," and a CPM forty-fifth anniversary statement of 26 April exhorted party followers thus: "Let us hoist even higher the great red banner of Marxism-Leninism-Mao Tse-tung Thought, follow the leadership of the Malayan Communist Party Central Committee headed by Comrade Chin Peng, and valiantly forge ahead along the path of encircling the cities from the countryside and of seizing political power by armed force" (*FBIS*, 3 January, 1 May).

In various comments on the fissures within its ranks, the CPM has alleged that in 1968, when in compliance with new Central Committee directives the MNLA intensified its struggle, an "anti-party clique," teamed up with "individualist careerists," began plotting to "launch an armed rebellion within the national liberation army," and that the plot failed and "ended in total defeat." According to the CPM, it was the "Selangor Liberation League," which was a major source of the dissension within the CPM (ibid., 31 January 1975). Subsequently, CPM commentaries over the "Voice of the Malayan Revolution" began referring to the CPM-ML as "enemy agents" who were following the orders of "the Razak clique" (i.e., the Malaysian government of Premier Tun Abdul Razak) and surviving "by fabricating rumors and telling lies," and who had vainly attempted to disrupt "our party's line of using the countryside to besiege the cities and wresting political power with armed force" (ibid., 11 February). While some CPM pronouncements emphasize that the CPM-ML ("hidden agents ... dressed in Marxist-Leninist trappings") has not been able to stop the "revolutionary currents" that are "flowing onward with irresistible force" in Malaysia, others emphasize the necessity of strengthening party discipline, referring to the CPM's new constitution of 30 April 1972 as stipulating that the MNLA, the party's Youth League, and other organizations "must accept party leadership," and that "no disorganized or factional activities of cliques" or any "disruption of party unity" can be permitted (ibid., 5 February).

The CPM's anniversary statement on 26 April 1975 reaffirmed its basic ideological principles. The CPM is said to "consistently" with the Chinese Communist Party and to be applying the "universal truth" of "Marxism-Leninism-Mao Tse-tung Thought" to the "concrete practice" of the "Malayan revolution." This application involves, tactically, the establishment of a "united national and democratic front," with the worker-peasant alliance as base but comprising "all classes," which will support the principle of encircling the cities from the countryside and seizing political power by armed force, and which, headed by the proletariat and led by the Communist Party, will direct the revolution toward the overthrow of imperialism and "the landlord and bureaucrat-capitalist classes" and the establishment of "the People's Republic of Malaya." This republic will have a "people's democratic dictatorship." To that end, CPM cadres and members must adhere to "democratic centralism" and to three fundamental organizational principles: "practice Marxism and not revisionism," "unite and don't split," and "be open and aboveboard and don't intrigue and conspire" (ibid., 1 May). In the seizure of power the same statement notes:

> Armed struggle is the main form of strugle, the armed unit is the main form of organization and the united front is the main front for carrying out armed struggle. To consolidate and expand the united front, it is essential to launch various forms of struggle with armed struggle as the mainstay [and] and put the stress of work on the rural areas; fully mobilize the masses, primarily the agricultural workers, peasants and other laboring masses in the rural areas; and extensively launch mass movements to support the national liberation army and to join the national liberation army. (Ibid.)

Despite claims of mass support, the CPM's attempts to weld the existing and not inconsiderable popular discontent into a united front has met with indifferent success thus far. The plight of Malayan rubber smallholders, squeezed between dropping world prices for their latex, rapacious rubber dealers, and galloping inflation (about 18 percent at the close of 1974), led for the first time in a generation to smallholders' and peasants' protest marches. The largest of these occurred on 21 November 1974 in the Baling district when some 12,000 peasant demonstrators had to be subdued by tear gas thrown by police. Malaysian university students rallied in support of the peasants, and student pamphlets attacked the "imperialists' plunder" of the country's natural resources and the exploitation of "our workers and peasants." The extent of CPM involvement in this unrest is not clear, but it would appear that Communists did not provide the driving force or the leadership, which instead appeared to emanate from the Islamic Youth Front of Malaysia (Angkatan Belia Islam Malaysia), an organization of Malay youths finding in their Islamic faith a justification for action on behalf of social justice and equality, and from the People's Party (Party Ra'ayat), a small group of Malay and Chinese urban socialist intellectuals, frequently though incorrectly perceived as a CPM front (Denzil Peiris, "The Emerging Rural Revolution," (*Far Eastern Economic Review*, 10 January 1975, pp. 29-31).

The CPM, through "Voice of Malayan Revolution" broadcasts in early December 1974, reported on the peasants' "struggle against hunger" and on the "sympathy and support of the people of all strata" for it, including students "filled with great indignation" against the "Razak cliques' crimes" and "reactionary" policies (*FBIS*, 7 December). But, while smallholders' and peasants' discontent over high food prices and other inflationary pressures continued to simmer during the first half of 1975, and the Kuala Lumpur government's stiffly threatening attitude toward student demonstrators quieted but by no means removed the anti-government sentiment on the campuses, the CPM has not been able to capitalize significantly on the lingering unrest, despite periodic government warnings of alleged Communist infiltration of student groups. On 19 December 1974, in the aftermath of the student unrest, the government published a "white paper" purporting to show that since the middle of 1971 the CPM has seized control of the Chinese Language Society of the University of Malaya and used its publications, theatrical performances, and even picnics and greeting cards as channels for the spread of Communist propaganda (ibid., 23 December). These charges have struck some observers as somewhat contrived, although CPM infiltration attempts undoubtedly occur and the need to mobilize student support is explicitly recognized in CPM literature (see Justis M. van der Kroef, "Current Communist Tactics in Indonesia, Malaysia, and the Philippines," *Lugano Review* (Lugano, Switzerland), 1975, no. 2, pp. 25-35).

The reason why the government's claim of CPM influence must be discounted (though by no means wholly set aside) is that, as in Singapore, the amorphous "New Left" radicalism in student and intellectual circles, for visceral and cerebral reasons, is as opposed to what is perceived to be the allegedly inhumane doctrinaire rigidities of Communist practice as to the supposedly equally dehumanizing exploitative dimensions of Western capitalism. Then, too, the CPM's internal difficulties, and the criticism by former or present party insiders of its aging leader, Chin Peng, are widely known, not least because of government publicity, and have tended to make the organization as little attractive as the Barisan Sosialis and its chairman, Lee Siew Choh, are to Singapore "New Left" students.

The CPM's attempt to reach out to Muslim supporters and to the peasantry has largely been confined to two paper front groups, the Malayan Islamic Fraternal Party (MIFP) and the Malayan Peasant Front (MPF). Toward the close of 1974, the MIFP's Central Committee, through a "Voice of the Malayan Revolution" broadcast, announced a new program for Muslims to "liberate" Malaya and Singapore. Program provisions ranged from launching "people's war" and the overthrow of the "fascist rule of the Razak-Lee Kuan Yew clique" to efforts to increase workers' wages, issuance of landownership certificates to peasants, nationalization of "all properties of the foreign monopoly capitalists and traitors," and support for the "just struggles waged by the Moslems in Southern Thailand and the Philippines" and for the "just struggles of the Arab people and the people of the whole world." (*Asia Research Bulletin*, 30 November, p. 28.) On the occasion of the Hadji (Pilgrimage) festival on 24 December 1974, an MIFP Central Committee extended greetings to all Muslims, wishing them "greater victories" in their struggle to improve their lives and in achieving "liberation." Castigating the "reactionary Razak regime" for alleged persecution and oppression, and for the arrest and torture of "Islamic students" in Kuala Lumpur, the message went on to say that the "people" were demanding lower prices, an end to corruption, the raising of prices of rubber and other agricultural products, and a reduction in the land tax. The message ended with a call on all "Islamic believers in our country" to support the CPM and the MNLA. (*FBIS*, 30 December.)

Meanwhile the other CPM satellite, the Malayan Peasant Front, also using the "Voice of the Malayan Revolution," reviewed the "oppression and exploitation carried out by the imperialists, bureaucratic capitalists and feudalists" in Malaya, and the resulting "heavy tax burden and unreasonable commodity prices" from which the Malayan peasantry is allegedly suffering. Possible benefits from recent increases in rice production, according to the MPF, have been vitiated by "market speculation by the bureaucratic capitalist class," so that, in effect, peasants now have less food available for themselves and "some peasants even have died from starvation." Peasants should therefore unite with "the working class, students and other people who support their just struggle" against the "Razak clique." (Ibid., 14 January 1975.)

Organizational data and names of the leaders of the MIFP and MPF have never been published; the groups seem primarily to be propaganda megaphones of the CPM. Neither have the CPM-RF nor the CPM-ML published party constitutions up to this time. The CPM is nominally governed by its Constitution of 30 April 1972, which commits the party to the principles of "Marxism-Leninism-Mao Tse-tung Thought" and to the accomplishment of a "new democratic revolution" as a prelude to the eventual establishment of "socialism and communism" in Malaya. Party branches are to be established in "every mill, mine, estate, village, school, platoon and within the armed working units of the National Liberation Army," with a party National Congress having "supreme leadership" and daily executive authority placed in the hands of a Central Committee, a Politburo, a secretary-general, and a deputy secretary-general ("New Constitution of the Communist Party of Malaya," *Journal of Contemporary Asia*, 3 no. 2, 1973: 233-37).

During 1974-75, while Chin Peng officially continued to be acknowledged as head of the Central Committee and as party secretary-general, the membership of the CPM Politburo and of other party executive organs has become unclear. The present position and role of party veterans like Control Commission (party discipline) chairman Li On, Agitprop section chairman Chen Tien, deputy secretary-general (sometimes referred to as CPM vice-chairman) and commander of the predominantly Malay "Tenth Regiment" of the MNLA, Abdul Rashid bin Maidin, Chin Peng's personal deputy Musa Ahmad (occasionally described in public media as party chairman, although neither this office nor the office of vice-chairman is provided for in the 1972 CPM constitution), and others, is uncertain, though they appear to have remained loyal to the parent CPM organization. A small staff of CPM cadres assists in operations of the "Voice of the Malayan Revolution."

In East Malaysia, a relative abundance of organizational names obscures the fact that the Communist movement there essentially consists of two operational wings, one political, the other military (though personnel and leaderships overlap). The North Kalimantan Communist Party and the youth and peasant front-group remnants (the previously named SAYA and SFA), numbering about 150 primarily ethnic Chinese in their later twenties and thirties (who also form the core of the movement's military forces) constitute the political wing. The military units of East Malaysian Communism were during most of the 1960s confined to the North Kalimantan People's Army (Pasokan Rakyat Kalimantan Utara or Paraku) and the Sarawak People's Guerrilla Force (Pergerakan Gerilja Rakyat Sarawak; PGRS), which together were usually referred to as the North Kalimantan People's Armed Forces (NKPAF). In 1973, Malaysian and Indonesian authorities claimed that both Paraku and the PGRS had been decimated, but this was contradicted by reports of continuing counter-insurgency operations. Since then, the term North Kalimantan People's Guerrilla Force has been most commonly used to designate the East Malaysian Communist movement's military wing, consisting of approximately 200 armed insurgents engaged in small-scale, hit-and-run attacks on government forces and posts in the interior of Sarawak.

There was a heavy loss of supporters (approximately 560, or nearly 70 percent of the NKPGF) as a result of the aforementioned 1973-74 Sri Aman amnesty and rehabilitation campaign. Additionally, Sabah-Sarawak military commander Major General Datuk Mahmood bin Sulaiman, at the beginning of 1975, declared that in 1973 there were 96 guerrillas killed and 69 captured, while 73 surrendered, and in 1974 there were 10 killed and 17 captured, while 11 surrendered (*Sarawak Tribune*, 11 January). However, several score NKPGF members who came out of the jungle under the Sri Aman plan subsequently returned to the guerrillas, and by early May the Sarawak police commissioner was quoted as saying that there were now 130 guerrillas operating in the Rajang Security Command (Rascom) area of Sarawak, and a further 45 in Sarawak's First Division (*FBIS*, 6 May). Some observers would add an additional two or three dozen insurgents engaged in training, communications, and agitation-propaganda work in other areas of Sarawak. The entire East Malaysian Communist movement frequently is still designated generically as the Sarawak Communist Organization.

Although the 1973 surrender of the NKPAF's "political commissar" (and de facto the NKCP's principal leader) Bong (or Wong) Kie Chok and the hundreds of party amnesty takers under the Sri Aman program dealt a heavy blow to the SCO complex, and although SCO defectors have claimed extensive internal conflict and a power struggle among the organization's leaders (*Sarawak Tribune*, 31 December 1974), a new NKCP chairman, Wen Min-chuan, and new Central Committee were announced in 1974, and the basic structure of NKCP and NKPGF has continued, at least on paper. The NKPGF, before Sri Aman, was divided into six companies and a separate headquarters section, all with political commissars and their deputies, and with defined operational areas. On 9 March 1975 Sarawak's chief minister and director of anti-insurgent operations, Abdul Rahman Ya'kub, disclosed a list of 48 guerrillas who at first had come out of the jungle under the Sri Aman program but within a few months had rejoined the NKPGF. Among them were "deputy political commissars" of NKPGF companies, section leaders and members of the "Logistics." "Publications," "Quartermaster." and "Medical" sections of NKPGF headquarters, and rank-and-file troops; many had had a Chinese primary and in some cases secondary education, and eleven were Indonesian Chinese. Typical employment experience of the 48 ranged from construction laborer and pepper planter, to newspaper typesetter and shop assistant. (*Sarawak Tribune*, 10 March.) In a comment over the "Voice of the Malayan Revolution" on 21 January it was admitted that the NKPAF had "decreased quantitatively," but it was said to have "become better qualitatively" and to be repulsing enemy attacks, and also that, since the "anti-communist, anti-popular activities of the reactionaries were hated by the people," resistance in North Kalimantan would grow (*FBIS*, 23 January).

The SCO evidently is in a state of reconstruction at present. There has been speculation that the surrender of hundreds of NKPGF members during Sri Aman was part of a deliberate Communist tactic, designed to win some breathing space for the organization, badly battered as it was by recent government counter-insurgency activity, and possibly with the hope of slowing such activity in the future. Certainly little ammunition was surrendered, and the weapons turned in were of poor, homemade quality, suggesting that the better arms which the NKPGF is known to possess are being kept back in the jungle for future use. (*Far Eastern Economic Review*, 4 April, pp. 24-25.) The slow but steady growth of the NKPGF after the Sri Aman surrenders and the return to the jungle of scores of guerrillas who refused to be rehabilitated suggest continuing sources of popular appeal and reasons for insurgency in Sarawak. Seeming contradictions in government statements on the guerrilla problem support this. Claims that the insurgents now lack popular support and in their desperate search for food are compelled to ransack even grocery stores (*Sarawak Tribune*, 24 November 1974, 11 January 1975) are belied by the government's continuing appeals to the Sarawak population not to help the insurgents with food and money (*Sarawak Gazette*, Kuching, 30 November 1974, p. 248), and by the announcement of the discovery of no less than 20 guerrilla food and arms dumps in the Binatang district of Sibu, including "large quantities of rice" and other food, electrical wiring, printing materials, and even weed killer (*FBIS*, 5 February 1975). On 3 May 1975 Sarawak's chief minister Ya'kub announced that on 16 April "62 Communist terrorist supporters" in the First Division area had been arrested because they had, despite warning, "persisted in their anti-national activities by providing donations and food supplies to the terrorists" (*Sunday Tribune*, Kuching, 4 May).

No extensive party program and military guidelines have been published. But long-term NKCP tactics are known to include foundation of an independent "North Kalimantan Unitary State" (centered on Sarawak, but which might include Brunei and Sabah if there were popular support in those areas for a merger with Sarawak) whose "new democratic" government would establish socialism and end all racial inequality and "imperialist" and "bureaucrat landlord" domination. NKPGF tactics, like those of the MNLA, look to the building of a broad-based "people's" army, capable of "encircling the cities from the countryside" and gaining victory by "armed force." It is uncertain what future allies the SCO may be able to muster in the parliamentary and legitimate political party arena of Sarawak and Malaysia. The SUPP's identification in the past three years with the government's National Front alliance of parties has limited the parliamentary activity of the more radical, younger Chinese Left. (The extent to which the SUPP was actually a partner in the SCO organizational complex in the past remains controversial.) The principal Sarawak opposition party at present, the Sarawak National Party (SNAP), has shown no desire for and given little indication of making explicit appeals to SUPP's former left-wing constituency.

Domestic Developments. Despite government claims of success in counter-insurgency operations in both West and East Malaysia, Communist guerrilla activity has not slowed down. In June 1975, Malaysia's home affairs minister, Ghazali Shafie, declared that since 1973 security forces had killed "160 Communist guerrillas, captured 108 others, and recovered 121 weapons" in West and East Malaysia together. Fifty guerrillas had been killed in West Malaysia, according to this statement, and 110 in Sarawak. Shafie also said that in 1973 "the Communists launched a seven-year plan to make a comeback in the country from their jungle hideouts in Sarawak and along the Thai-Malaysian border," and that when the plan failed because of "government operations" the insurgents had launched yet another "seven-year plan to create country-wide disorder," sending out small "killer squads" to assassinate government officials. Ten government intelligence officers had been killed since 1973, according to Shafie. (*Bangkok Post*, 24 June.) The insurgents, according to other government statements, further suffered reverses because of the killing of a prominent terrorist leader, Tan Tak Weng, who was shot in Betong, early in December 1974, and because of the refusal of local villagers (e.g., at Kampong Weng, near Baling) to accept proffered candy, cigarettes, medicine, and propaganda talk by a visiting band of rebels (instead villagers informed security forces, who attacked the insurgent band, killing one of their number) (*Sarawak Tribune*, 14, 24 December 1974).

In February 1975, Malaysian police uncovered booby-trapped Communist flags and banners, along with quantities of propaganda materials, in Selangor, Negri Sembilan, and several places in the Kuala Lumpur federal district area, and a group of 50 uniformed guerrillas attacked a train near the Rimba Mas military camp outside Padang Besar, derailing five wagons and robbing train personnel (ibid., 4, 18 February). About the same time the government instituted a "screening" procedure for workers at the Temenggor (Temenggong) hydroelectric-power dam construction site in upper Perak State, and at the East-East Highway project in the northern part of Western Malaysia, both frequent targets of insurgent attacks in the past. The "screening" was reportedly designed to prevent "subversive elements" from infiltrating the work force and committing sabotage. (Bernama dispatch, Grik, 1 February.)

On the night of 31 March insurgents fired about a dozen rockets into the Kuala Lumpur military airbase and set off bomb explosions at army camps at Simpang Renggam, in Johore State, and at Port Dickson in Penang. There were no injuries. Malaysian intelligence sources were said to believe that the bombings were staged in celebration of the Communist victory at Danang, South Vietnam. In April, guerrillas staged new attacks in the Thai-Malaysian border region which left 12 Malaysian soldiers dead and wounded 29. In the Mong Gajah area on 8 April, ten miles from the border, insurgents ambushed a military convoy, using land mines and concentrated firepower, and on the same day a military vehicle near the Temenggor (Temenggong) dam project was attacked and four military personnel were wounded. Another ambush, on 11 April, on the Nakan-Gubin road near Kota Ayer, left five military dead and set off intensified government counter-action, including artillery shelling of suspected rebel strongholds in the jungle border area. (*Asia Research Bulletin*, Political Supplement, 30 April, p. 77.) Malaysian cabinet ministers appeared to be contradicting themselves on the reasons for the new upsurge in guerrilla activity, Home Minister Ghazali Shafie alleging that the recent attacks were the work of the CPM-ML, whose leaders were trying to prove that they were more active than the CPM parent organization, and that the attacks had "no real connection" with the developments in

Indochina (ibid., and *FBIS*, 16 April), while Premier Tun Abdul Razak was quoted as saying that they indeed could have been inspired by events in Indochina (*NYT*, 13 April).

Top Malaysian officials, in the wake of the guerrilla attacks, announced "new security arrangements," including increased coordination of security operations under a senior executive councillor in each of the four northern states of Keday, Penang, Perlis, and Perak. Minister Shafie, speaking in Johore Bharu on 22 April, declared that "the government knows the movements of communist terrorists and their activities in both urban and rural areas," and that if the insurgents "felt elated by the Communist thrusts in Cambodia and Vietnam" and believed they would also succeed in Malaysia they were dreaming, since the "people of Malaysia" would not tolerate them. (*FBIS*, 11, 17, 18, 24 April.)

Nevertheless, insurgents continued operations, although which CPM faction was involved was not apparent. Police Special Branch (intelligence) and other officers continued to be singled out for assassination. On 21 June, for example, a Special Branch officer was shot dead in broad daylight in Ipoh, the capital of Perak State, the third killing of police officers in two months (*The Nation*, Bangkok, 21 June). Ambushes also continued, with eleven Malaysian and four Thai border patrol policemen being killed on 18 June in a surprise attack during a Thai-Malaysian border survey. On the occasion of this last attack Malaysian Home Minister Shafie said that "more than 2,000" guerrillas were now operating on both sides of the border, including "over 1,000 Thais of Chinese and Malay" origin, and that, unlike in the past, Thailand "was now giving priority to suppression of the guerrillas on its southern border" (ibid.).

Whether Shafie's estimate of the size of guerrilla forces was accurate or not, Malaysian security officials seemed by mid-1975 to be becoming particularly apprehensive over a broadening of terrorist operations into the suburban and urban areas of the country and over the implicit or overt support which youthful radicals in the towns might be beginning to give to such tactics. Early in July, leaflets were discovered in the city if Ipoh, signed by a group calling itself the "People's Army for the Liberation of Malaysia." The connection between this group and any of the three CPM factions has been controversial, but some informed Malaysian sources speculated to the author that the new "People's Army" consists primarily of unaffiliated urban radicals. The leaflets stated that "urban guerrilla warfare is inevitable" in Malaysia, and warned: "Be prepared for our urban civil strife, which is the result of the Government's actions over the years." The leaflets further alleged that the government had practiced racial and class discrimination, and urged Malaysians to be prepared to stand up for their just rights. (*Straits Times*, Singapore, 4 July.)

In response to the insurgents' attempt to broaden their popular base, Premier Razak on 21 June announced that the government intended not only to expand police and armed forces, but also to create neighborhood defense forces, reflecting, he said, "a new strategy to involve them (i.e., the people) in the defense of the security and peace of their own neighborhoods, be they in the urban or the rural areas." The exact structure and leadership of the new neighborhood defense units remains to be developed, but it is believed that retired or currently inactive police officers and military men resident in particular areas will form the units' core. This same technique has been applied to the establishment and development of settlements along the East-West Highway, which will connect Penang and Kota Baru in the rebel-infested northern frontier zone. The insurgents have vowed that the highway will never be completed, since it will serve as an important logistical artery in the government's counter-insurgency program, connecting a lengthening string of new villages and settlements, inhabited by former government officials, particularly retired police and military whose loyalty to the government seems assured. (*Far Eastern Economic Review*, 4 July.)

On 26 August a number of bomb explosions severely damaged Malaysia's National Monument, in the heart of Kuala Lumpur. The explosions were attributed to Communists, possibly rival CPM factions, "competing to demonstrate their revolutionary fervor" (ibid., 5 September, p. 28). On 2

September, two young Chinese, believed to be Communists, hurled hand grenades into a formation of Malaysian police during their morning drill, killing two and wounding 39. These developments have underscored the popular Malaysian belief that the Communist threat to wage "urban guerrilla war" was not an idle one. In early September the government announced that it would enforce federal provisions of the Internal Security Act (heretofore, according to the government, only enforced on a "selective basis"), imposing the death penalty for illegal ownership or possession of firearms, bullets, or explosives. The government, according to the same announcement, had decided to "take more stringent measures" to overcome acts of terrorism. (*FBIS*, 9 September.)

In Eastern Malaysia, government reaction to the upsurge of insurgent activity in the western part of the country had its echo. Government radio dispatches announced on 14 May that the Sarawak government had launched a "full offensive to wipe out Communist terrorists" and "achieve total peace in the state" (ibid., 14 May). Sarawak government appeals seemed particularly directed toward the Chinese Community. In a Chinese New Year's message on 13 February Sarawak governor Tun Patinggi Tuanku Haji Bujan said that Malaysian Chinese should recognize the fact that there was no future in Malaysia for those with divided loyalties, and especially urged them to assist those of their "national compatriots" who might be economically backward (*Sarawak Tribune*, 15 February). The government also continued to appeal to school principals and teachers in Sarawak asking them to make sure that their schools would not be infiltrated by Communists, in view of the fact that the SCO, historically, had attempted to win recruits in the schools (*Sarawak Gazette*, 31 October, p. 222). This particular appeal, while not naming Chinese schools as such, nevertheless seemed especially directed at them, since government accounts have consistently stressed that Chinese educational institutions in Sarawak have been fertile ground for Communist proselytizing and propaganda. Mindful of SCO standard tactics of using Chinese cultural and ethnic pride, the government also sought to quiet what it termed a "great deal of agitation" recently concerning possible threats to Chinese-language education in the schools as a result of the new national educational policy aimed at making the Malay language the main medium of instruction. Other languages could be taught in schools, a government statement said in January 1975, but it went on to note that "all Malaysians" would be expected to strive to "bring about the development of one country, one people and one language consciousness" (*Sarawak Tribune*, 8 January). Perhaps in further accord with its policy emphasis on urging Chinese Sarawakians to identify with Malaysia, government statements have emphasized that several Chinese, all former members of the SCO, who had requested that they be sent to People's China, had been denied entry there and had returned to Malaysia (ibid., 7 February). Prominent attention is continuously given in the Sarawak media to the favorable adjustment to society being made by former guerrillas who have come out of the jungle in order to be rehabilitated (or be "self-renewed," as officials put it) and on the $3.5 million spent by the government in 1974 alone to help the former insurgents in finding a place for themselves in society (ibid., 11 December 1974, 6, 7 February and 4 May 1975).

At the same time it is apparent that political tensions are destabilizing Sarawak. Top officials keep complaining that the population is not informing authorities of the nearby presence of guerrillas or of their jungle supply caches (ibid., 28 February 1975). The re-arrest by Special Branch police on 11 March of a prominent Sarawak opposition politician, Datuk James Wong of the SNAP, the moment he stepped out of a Kuching court where he had been ordered released because of a previous arrest ruled unlawful by the court, was viewed by some as a government effort to intimidate all, even lawful and parliamentary, opposition by means of the Internal Security Act. The act, a modified version of a statute dating from the colonial era, permits detention and incarceration without trial of persons for broadly stated reasons of national security. Its application in Malaysia as in Singapore (where a similar measure is in operation) has been a political issue exploited by the Left and opposition parties.

During the year the political polarization of Malaysia has deepened, and although the government claimed that in its 1975 budget of about 7 billion ringgit 27 percent is spent on social services (as compared with 20 percent on defense), critics allege that government economic planning priorities and steadily rising living costs particularly adversely affect lower social strata. There are indications that, as in East Malaysia, so in West Malaysia, the problem of finding suitable employment for the ever growing number of secondary school and university graduates has had a radicalizing political effect despite a rising income level for other population segments. Literacy rates among young Malaysians between the age of 15 and 20 is now 92 percent for women and 95 percent for men (*Sarawak Tribune*, 7 December 1975), and while there is some indication of rising affluence among a part of the population, the problem of the educated unemployed in the country today is illustrated by the fact that "over 1,800 young people recently applied for 100 white collar jobs in a Perak factory—symptomatic of a massive influx of educated rural youths into urban areas in search of non-existent jobs" (editorial, *Far Eastern Economic Review*, 10 January 1975, p. 9).

Beginning in September 1974 and lasting through part of the following January, there was much unrest among students at the University of Malaya and the National University. Three thousand students demonstrated in front of the premier's office on 20 and 21 September, demanding release of two officers of the University of Malaya Students Union (UMSU) who had been arrested a few days previously for attempting to prevent police from demolishing illegally built squatters' huts in Johore. A UMSU seizure of the Administration Building on the University of Malaya campus in Kuala Lumpur on 21 September was undone within hours by a rival pro-government group of students, and the subsequent clashes between student groups appeared to have some ethnic basis since predominantly Chinese students opposing the government confronted Malay students belonging to the "right-wing" Malay Language Society. Despite government warnings, students in subsequent weeks continued street demonstrations against inflation, the plight of the rural poor, and the low rubber prices. After Malay rubber smallholders had demonstrated in Baling on 21 November and the following days some 2,000 students demonstrated on 3 December at the Selangor Club Padang, where fighting erupted between police and students. Ultimately 1,095 were arrested for unlawful assembly and demonstrating against the police. (*Asia Research Bulletin*, Political Supplement, 31 December, p. 37, and *Sarawak Tribune*, 5 December.) As student agitation continued, the "Voice of the Malayan Revolution" repeatedly in lengthy broadcasts reported on the demonstrations, extolling the "dauntless fighting spirit of the younger generation in our country," and noting that students had acted to demonstrate solidarity with "the struggle by the broad masses of peasants against starvation and hunger" (*FBIS*, 12, 21 December).

A Malaysian government "white paper," released on 19 December, asserted that the University of Malaya Chinese Language Society had become the vehicle of the CPM (faction not specified), using concerts and literary and drama presentations as a means of fostering Communist ideology and of portraying the government as oppressive. The society had maintained close contact with the UMSU and the university's Socialist Club in order to provoke student unrest, according to the white paper. (*Sarawak Tribune*, 20 December.) Unrest continued intermittently during the early months of 1975, and in April the Malaysian parliament passed an amendment to the University and University Colleges Act of 1971 which provided for expulsion from school, fining, or jailing of any student engaged in any way in partisan political or trade union activity, and also established close administrative and government controls over any student organization permitted to exist (*Far Eastern Economic Review*, 20 June, p. 30). The extent to which any faction of the CMP had, in fact, established its influence, let alone control, over segments of the university of Malaya student leadership remains controversial.

During the closing weeks of the year the government's new security regulations aimed at combating the Communist terrorists elicited a good deal of discussion and strong opposition was voiced by a few members of the opposition in parliament. Under the *Rukun Tetangga* (neighborhood association) concept of the regulations, individual households and villages are responsible for the movements of family members, neighbors, strangers and visitors in their area and compulsory village and neighborhood vigilante organizations engage in patrolling their localities (*Asia Research Bulletin*, 30 November, p. 144). In early October, premier Tun Abdul Razak stressed that the new security measures contain "adequate safeguards" for the protection of the innocent, that Malaysia adheres to democracy and the rule of law, and that the new measures had become necessary because of "the cruel and inhuman acts carried out by Communists and anti-national elements" (*FBIS*, 7 October). The fact that witnesses in security cases may give testimony in secret and need not reveal their identities and that spouses and even children may give testimony against family members under the new regulations has caused concern even among those aware of the evidentiary problems in security cases and of the intimidation of witnesses. How effective the new measures will be is a matter of speculation. In previous years, the Razak government had expected a stabilizing influence in the terrorist infested border areas in West Malaysia to result from the so-called "new villages," settlements of villagers drawn from communities earlier suspected of having been infiltrated by guerrillas and now reorganized under close government surveillance. Early in November, premier Razak warned residents of the new villages that they might be subjected to still further regroupment in new areas under security control if they persisted in supporting the Communists. He announced that inhabitants of two new villages in the Jerantut district would soon be moved because of the security threat. Razak also warned that land given the new villagers would be taken away if they did not cooperate with the government against the terrorists (*New Straits Times*, Kuala Lumpur, 10 November; *FBIS*, 12 November).

International Aspects. The Communist victories in Indochina during the first half of 1975 provoked contradictory reactions in Malaysian official circles as to any connection with the stepped-up Communist activity along the Thai-Malaysian border (see above). In July, Premier Razak declared that the emergence of Communist governments in Cambodia and South Vietnam would not pose a threat to Malaysia or other Southeast Asian countries (*Philippines Evening Express*, Manila, 8 July). On 12 April he had stated that the government was reviewing Malaysia's whole defense posture because of the developments in Indochina, but on 2 May Malaysia extended formal diplomatic recognition to the new Communist regime in Saigon. At the same time the premier said that a "close watch" was being kept on the possibility of arms being smuggled to the Communists in Malaysia in the wake of the surrender of the old Saigon government. (*FBIS*, 18 April, 2 May.)

Similar ambivalences were becoming apparent in official Malaysian attitudes toward People's China, with which reciprocal diplomatic recognition had been arranged on 31 May 1974. On 29 April 1975 the Central Committee of the Chinese Communist Party sent greetings and "warm fraternal congratulations" to the Central Committee of the Communist Party of Malaya," marking the CPM's forty-fifth anniversary. The Chinese party's message, while not mentioning the Razak government by name, extolled the CPM's "liberation struggle" against "imperialism, feudalism and bureaucrat-capitalism" and its adherence to "the road of armed struggle." (*Peking Review*, 2 May, p. 6.) Several weeks passed before the Malaysian government formally protested these "fraternal congratulations" to the Peking government, with Premier Razak saying that if the practice of greeting Communist guerrillas continued "our relations with China will not be as cordial" (*Hong Kong Standard*, 24 June).

The incident may have been particularly embarrassing to the Razak government, anxious to placate restive anti-Communists in the United Malays National Organization (the largest party in the ruling coalition of parties), because almost simultaneously with the publication of the Chinese party's anniversary greetings to the CPM, Razak said that he had been reassured by the Chinese ambassador to Malaysia that China was not "exporting subversion" to Malaysia (*FBIS*, 5 May). This reassurance had been solicited by Razak when he sought "clarification" from the ambassador on a New China

News Agency dispatch of a few days earlier which reported that the Chinese Communist Party had hailed recent terrorist activity in Kuala Lumpur (ibid.).

Later the "Voice of the Malayan Revolution" greeted the twenty-fifth anniversary of the People's Republic of China in a broadcast that also extolled the "profound revolutionary friendship and militant unity" between the Malayan and Chinese peoples. It added that under CPM leadership the Malayan people were "triumphantly" persisting in "protracted revolutionary armed struggle." (Ibid., 4 October.) The "Voice" had previously carried extended commentaries on the Malaysian government's diplomatic recognition of People's China, declaring that such recognition marked the "bankruptcy" of the "Razak clique's" earlier policy of hostility toward the Peking government, but stressing also that the CPM's armed struggle would continue, and that China had consistently supported this struggle (ibid., 28 May). Although the Sino-Malaysian reciprocal diplomatic recognition may have initially embarrassed the CPM (V. Suryanarayan, "Malayan Communism at the Crossroads," *China Report*, Delhi, 10, no. 4, 1974: 69), continuing Chinese vocal support for the CPM and stepped-up Communist insurgent activity in 1975 suggest that the various CPM factions have been able to adjust themselves to the diplomatic exchange.

On 18 April, Malaysia recognized the new Royal Government of National Union in Cambodia, expressing desire for cooperation "particularly in the cultural and economic fields," but on the basis of a policy of strict neutrality (ibid., 18 April). The "Voice of the Malayan Revolution" in a broadcast on 22 April sent its "warmest greetings" to the new Cambodian government, declaring not only that the "U.S. imperialist aggressive policy" had met with "an extremely disastrous failure," but adding also that the USSR had only at the last moment "adorned itself as a supporter of the Cambodian people's revolutionary struggle," thus revealing its predicament as a "renegade and gambler" (ibid., 25 April).

On 22 December 1974 a statement issued by the Malaysian Ministry of Agriculture and Rural Development said that an agreement had been reached with the USSR whereby the latter would cooperate in the near future in Malaysia's economic development, particularly in rice and fish production projects. The statement expressed hope that the USSR would provide technical aid in developing the Malaysian fishing industry. (Ibid., 23 December.)

During 1975, as in the past, the Thai-Malaysian and Indonesian-Malaysian border committees met, addressing themselves to cooperative efforts in containing the insurgents on both frontiers. Early in January the Thai-Malaysian committee expressed confidence that the terrorists eventually would be eliminated, while noting that, even though there was a split in the Communist organization, the insurgents were continuing their futile struggle (ibid., 8 January). The value of the meetings came under attack in the Thai press, one leading daily declaring them to be a waste of time and money, and accusing the Malaysian home minister of hypocrisy in saying (see above) that Thailand was giving priority to its southern border rebel problem only for the first time (*Bangkok Post*, 23 June). There was no indication that such criticism suggests an impending end to the meetings, although the stepped-up activity of the insurgents on both sides of the border led to concern in many circles over the existing degree of joint military operations.

On 19 April, Malaysian and Indonesian military commanders signed a new agreement in Medan, Sumatra, Indonesia, designed to provide for joint operations against "enemy subversion" infiltration and other "illegal activities" (*FBIS*, 25 April). The agreement apparently not only envisages cooperation in combating the traffic of underground Communist activists across the Straits of Malacca, but also smuggling, black marketing, and price manipulation that could affect food prices in both countries. According to an announcement by the Indonesian Antara news agency, the Medan discussions also were concerned with the security of the territorial waters of both countries, specifically as regards illegal entry and piracy. During 1975 there were frequent consultations between Indonesian and Malaysian military commanders regarding the Sarawak insurgency, and cooperation between the two countries, particularly in sharing intelligence concerning the insurgents' movements, appeared to be better than that prevailing between the Thai and Malaysian governments.

Malaysian-Japanese relations have also been affected by Communist terrorism. The Japanese are major financial backers of the Temenggor (Temenggong) dam project, which the CPM has vowed will never be completed. The CPM reportedly has communicated with the Japanese Embassy in Kuala Lumpur and with Japanese contractors building the dam in order to stop construction. The Japanese have ignored such pressure, and on 2 July Japan extended a new $66 million loan, at 3.25 percent annual interest, to complete the dam (*Straits Times*, 3 July). Japanese Red Army terrorists seized scores of hostages in a Kuala Lumpur office building on 4 August, and after the Japanese government agreed to release a number of Red Army prisoners in Japan, the terrorists flew with them to Libya.

Publications. The "Voice of the Malayan Revolution," the clandestine radio transmitter, said to be located in Yunnan Province in the Chinese People's Republic, has become the principal means of communication for the CPM, at least with the world beyond Malaysia. All three CPM factions occasionally issue leaflets, but the profusion of names of organizations allegedly issuing them makes it frequently difficult to identify their source among the factions. Most "Voice" broadcasts have been in Mandarin Chinese, which the front-group leaflets use also, along with Malay.

Neither the CPM nor the SCO has dailies or regularly appearing periodicals. The principal organ of CPM sympathizers in London, the *Malayan Monitor & General News*, has since 1974 appeared infrequently. SCO publications like the *Masses News* and *Liberation News* appear occasionally, sometimes with different titles. Reports on alleged CPM victories and operations, which used to be carried frequently in the People's Chinese media, have appeared much less often in the past three years.

University of Bridgeport   Justus M. van der Kroef

Mongolia

A fusion of two revolutionary groups in 1921 produced the Mongolian People's Party, which held its First Congress in March of that year at Kyakhta, on Soviet territory. It became known as the Mongolian People's Revolutionary Party (MPRP) in 1924.

Fiftieth-anniversary celebrations in November 1974 commemorated the shift to "socialism" in 1924, but Russian dominance had already been established in 1921. In 1924 the designation "Mongolian People's Republic" (MPR) was adopted, and the present name of the capital city, Ulan Bator (formerly Urga). A non-capitalist and anti-bourgeois line was announced by the party's Third Congress and the first Great Khural (structural equivalent of the USSR Supreme Soviet) at this same time.

In 1972 the MPRP claimed 58,048 members, or about 5 percent of the population of the MPR. The population was estimated at 1,444,000 in 1975, with the city of Ulan Bator accounting for about 300,000 of the total.

Organization and Leadership. The MPRP is organized approximately along the same lines as the Communist Party of the Soviet Union. No changes were noted during 1975 in either the Politburo or the Secretariat. See *YICA, 1975*, p. 389, for memberships of these two bodies.

Domestic Attitudes and Activities. Several developments combined to precipitate important change during 1975. What had remained of traditional culture and substantive Mongolian autonomy suffered considerable erosion. Soviet concern about China is probably the principal underlying reason for the acceleration and intensification of a trend already clearly evident for a long time.

Maidar, one of the Politburo members in Mongolia, in September spoke of "developing the process of political and economic consolidation of Mongolia with the Soviet Union," and provided many examples of close and direct connection. Few of the examples were entirely new in 1975, but most of them have become more important because they are more systematic and far-reaching than before, and because their total cumulative and aggregate impact is becoming so great as to constitute a qualitative and substantive change.

Maidar's examples included: direct economic relations over the past 50 years; joint Mongolian-Soviet enterprises in the MPR such as Erdenet, which will provide copper and molybdenum to the USSR; direct connection between 13 governmental ministries and commissions of the MPR with 20 ministries and commissions of the Soviet Union (e.g., a representative of the USSR Ministry of Agriculture is stationed in Mongolia to work directly with the Mongolian counterpart, and the two agencies communicate directly without any "higher" sanction by government or ruling party in the MPR); a joint commission, "Mongol'sovtsvetmet," to control mining of non-ferrous metals; direct connection between 40 Mongolian research institutes or laboratories and 80 Soviet counterparts; joint investigation of the resources in eastern Mongolia; joint preparation and coordination of the next Five Year Plan, 1976-80; and direct connection between Soviet oblasts and Mongolian aimaks, bypassing normal central government channels. Maidar himself, a Politburo member since 1963, serves concurrently as first deputy prime minister, chairman of the State Committee for Science and Technology, and co-chairman of the Mongolian-Soviet Intergovernmental Commission for Economic, Scientific, and Technical Cooperation. Soviet influence, thus, is penetrating the MPR at more levels than ever before, so that a complex infrastructure undergirds the more orthodox government-to-government and party-to-party relations.

Hints of political or physical weakness raise speculation that Tsedenbal's dominant leadership position is threatened. The appointment of Batmunkh as premier in June 1974 logically suggested a change in the political calculus; some of the photographs in Mongolian newspapers when Brezhnev visited Ulan Bator in November 1974 show Batmunkh in the center between Tsedenbal and Brezhnev; the large portraits appearing on May Day 1975 included the likenesses of both Tsedenbal and Batmunkh. On the other hand Tsedenbal met with Brezhnev in April and again in August, while Batmunkh met only with Kunaev at Alma Ata during the latter month. However, when an important Yugoslav communist delegation visited the MPR from 21 to 27 October, Tsedenbal remained absent, not greeting the arrival at the airport nor participating in any of the events; he was described as "recovering from illness." The fact that he had met with Tito in Yugoslavia during July adds to the riddle within the enigma.

The visit with Tito and vacation in Yugoslavia continued an already evident publicity campaign for Tsedenbal's wife, Anastasia Ivanovna Filatova-Tsedenbal (of Russian extraction). She also received notice in the official press for work as chairperson of the Children's Fund in Mongolia.

Further suggestion of factional struggle derives from changes in the leadership of the Culture Ministry, the Writers' Union, and the Revsomol Youth Movement, all three closely involved with ideology and propaganda. Ts. Namsrai became minister of culture on 10 June, finally ending some 16 months of Luvsanvandan being listed as "acting minister." L. Tudev took over as first secretary of the

Revsomols on 20 June, replacing the veteran of two decades in that post, Purevjav. Tudev had served as chairman of the Writers' Union from 22 July 1974 to 3 October 1975; no replacement was announced immediately. In July, two new organizations held their first congresses: Workers in the Arts, and Young Creative Workers. The reason for their establishment is not clear.

International Views and Activities. Military emphasis increased during 1975. It involved publicity and focus more than any substantive increase in force levels. Soviet troops remain in Mongolia, and the indigenous army continues as before. But numerous visits by USSR generals (usually combat veterans from fighting in Mongolia during 1939 and 1945) and celebrations of various anniversaries, with parades and ceremonies, particularly highlighted Soviet-Mongolian military collaboration in the defeat of the Japanese at Nomonkhan (1939) and claims of a decisive Soviet-Mongolian defeat of the Japanese (1945) in Manchuria and North China.

Accompanying this was a clear escalation in attention to and praise of Choibalsan, Mongolia's "Little Stalin," who died in 1942. Much of Choibalsan's rehabilitation appeared to be specifically military in nature, with Soviet army journals providing much of the impetus. Another, though smaller, indicator of increased public attention to military matters came from repeated reference to activities of the military attaché at the Soviet Embassy in Ulan Bator, Major General G. S. Voronin.

This attention to military affairs often became linked directly and blatantly, at other times indirectly and subtly, to the Sino-Soviet dispute. It was claimed that the Soviet-Mongolian forces in 1945 had "played a basic role in the development of the Chinese revolution" and "averted the complete occupation of China by the American imperialists." It also was claimed that the Chinese were receiving nuclear assistance from the anti-Communist West and even suggested that U.S.-trained Chinese nuclear scientists were not defectors but agents. Yet that kind of anti-U.S. comment in connection with Chinese affairs in no way limited praise of U.S.-Soviet détente or the joint Apollo-Soyuz space mission.

Mongolia claimed that China was developing an anti-Indian nuclear capability in Tibet and vigorously attacked China's supposed expansionist aims in Southeast Asia. It recalled often and in detail China's "cartographic aggression" by distributing maps showing Mongolia and many other areas as belonging to China. It also presented economic analyses supporting the argument that China devoted extraordinary sums to military weapons, particularly nuclear, and exploited the masses of its people mercilessly to support such expenditures. Along with this went fulsome praise for the USSR's proposed collective security plan in Asia.

Most of the strident anti-China campaign in 1975 involved recalling incidents and policies during the Cultural Revolution and actions by Red Guards; few new actions were reported. But the Mongolians did accuse China of violating MPR borders and, in particular, of driving diseased livestock into Mongolia in what sounded like a "germ warfare" story.

There were also serious and detailed analyses of assimilation of Mongols in China; of elimination of Mongols from all leading political positions, thoroughgoing sinification through language, and extensive Chinese settlement in Inner Mongolia; and of administrative border manipulation of the Inner Mongolian Autonomous Region (IMAR). Considerable genuine as well as spurious ancient and modern history was cited throughout the year to discredit the legitimacy of Chinese claims to predominance or sovereignty over Mongols anywhere.

The joint Soviet-Mongolian preparatory development of the huge Erdenet copper and molybdenum mining operation continues, with essential completion of a 100-mile rail connection to the main Trans-Mongolian line, a 112-mile asphalt highway linked with the main north-south highway, and a 40-mile water pipeline from the newly dammed Selenga River to the mine site. The new town of Erdenet, about 250 miles northwest of Ulan Bator, already had a population of 13,000 in November 1975 and is expected to reach at least 60,000 by 1979 when actual mining operations are scheduled to begin.

The copper and molybdenum product of Erdenet is scheduled to go to the USSR and it is hoped that this will correct the persistent trade imbalance between the two countries. More than three-fourths of total Mongolian foreign trade continues to be with the Soviet Union, which receives far less in imports than it exports. However, with considerable pride Mongolia announced in October that a record grain harvest of 875,000 tons would permit, for the first time, fulfillment of all domestic needs and also provide 40,000 tons for export.

The Buddhist church in Mongolia continues to play a propaganda role in pushing for peace and specifically the USSR's collective security plan for Asia. On the Soviet pattern, a communist chairman of the State Council for Religious Affairs, Baljinyam, is in effect the government's watchdog over Buddhist leader Gombojav, the so-called Khambo Lama. This colorfully robed symbolic and ceremonial figure presides over the "Asia Buddhist Conference for Peace," which met in Moscow during October to plan for its fourth conference, to be held at Tokyo in 1976.

The cover enveloping the bland Buddhism of official propaganda was badly torn by the appearance of an illegal *Samizdat* publication in the USSR with details about the arrest, torture, and untimely death on 26 October 1974 of the Buryat Buddhist scholar Bidya Dandaron.

Other relevant but scattered developments included the following:

Local Khurals (patterned after "soviets" in the USSR) held elections in June 1975 that endorsed official candidates, some 61 percent of whom were members or candidate members of the MPRP and another 14 percent of Revsomols (equivalent to Komsomols).

On 20 December 1974 Ch. Suren, former economic adviser at the MPR Embassy in Moscow, replaced B. Dugersuren as one of the government's deputy premiers. Dugersuren had held the post since July 1963.

A major campaign in 1975 stressed the rule and role of law as well as "socialist legality."

Diplomatic recognition by Mexico and several other states brought the countries maintaining diplomatic relations with the MPR to a total of 74. (The United States is not among them.)

A trade union delegation visited Japan in February.

Some 2,300 foreigners visited Mongolia during the first ten months of 1975, and growing tourism led the State University to establish a special training section for interpreters and guides.

Young Pioneer organizations from all Soviet bloc countries met at Ulan Bator in June.

The new USSR super-jet airplane, the TU 154-A, began regular Moscow-to-Ulan Bator service in January.

Noted Soviet diplomat and historian Ivan Maiskii, significant in Mongolian affairs because of a classic book he wrote in 1921 and also because of his active part in the controversy about Genghis Khan in 1962, died on 5 September at 91 years of age.

A declining birth rate and slightly growing death rate led to net drop in births over deaths per thousand, from 33 in 1969 to 28.5 in 1972.

Publications and Communications. Principal MPRP publications include *Unen* ("Truth"), circulation 110,000; *Namyn Amdral* ("Party Life"); the Russian-language *Novosti Mongolii* ("News of Mongolia"), circulation 10,000; and a chinese-language weekly, *Meng-ku Hsiao-hsi Pao* ("News of Mongolia"), circulation 1,000. The Central Committee began publication of *Ediyn Dzasag* ("Economics") on 1 January 1975. The Ministry of Agriculture issues *Shine Hodoo* ("New Countryside"). The MPR assigns a representative to the editorial board of the international communist organ *Problems of Peace and Socialism.*

Mongolian radio now broadcasts in Mongolian, Russian, English, Chinese, and Kazakh. Television broadcasting was begun in 1970.

University of North Carolina   Robert A. Rupen
Chapel Hill

Nepal

The Communist Party of Nepal (CPN) was formed in 1949, and its membership is estimated at about 5,000. All political parties have been banned since 1960 when the late King Mahendra dissolved the Nepali Congress party (NC) government headed by B. P. Koirala.

A "partyless" panchayat (assembly) system of government was later established. The CPN's major competitor among active political groups is the democratic socialist NC. Nepal's population is approximately 12,600,000.

Leadership and Organization. The CPN has been openly split since 1960 when the King's actions exacerbated internal ideological and personal disagreements. The moderate faction, led by General Secretary Keshar Jung Raimajhi, retained party control. Through its pro-monarchy stance and support of "progressive" government measures such as land reform, the Raimajhi CPN and its sympathizers have gained positions in government and officially-sponsored political organizations.

Revolutionaries Pushpa Lal Shrestha, Tulsi Lal Amatya and their supporters who were militantly opposed to the monarchy, however, fled to India where they formed a parallel CPN organization at the May 1962 "Third Party Congress." Further factionalization has developed in the revolutionary CPN. Pushpa Lal remains in India, but the less militant Man Mohan Adhikari, a CPN founder who was imprisoned for several years, now leads an extremist faction in Nepal.

Both CPN organizations operate within Nepal, concentrating their activities in the Kathmandu Valley and in the Tarai, the southern plans adjoining India, but in general their influence appears limited. Communist sympathizers seem strongest among students, educators and urban elements.

Among student groups, the pro-revolutionary CPN All Nepal National Independent Students' Union (ANNISU) competes with the National Student Union, sponsored by the moderate CPN. Their major non-Communist rival is the NC student organization, the Nepal Students' Union.

Domestic Attitudes and Activities. Although the moderate CPN has supported the monarchy, its policies and views as outlined at Raimajhi's own "Third Party Congress' in 1968 were critical of the present political system. The Congress criticized the ban on parties, demanded the release of all political prisoners, and proclaimed the need for restoring democratic rights. Working with the system, the moderate faction's ultimate aim was establishment of a national democracy. Immediate targets in this task were "workers, peasants, students, youth, traders, and professionals." (*New Age*, New Delhi, 12 January 1969.)

The extremist CPN has called for reinstatement of political parties, restoration of parliamentary democracy, and distribution of surplus land among the peasants. Pushpa Lal and Adhikari differ over strategy: while Pushpa Lal has advocated overthrow of the King, Adhikari has been working for domestic political reforms.

Terrorist activity in Napel, allegedly involving CPN extremists as well as Nepali Congress dissidents, has declined since 1974. Those arrested during that year for subversive activities included a number of revolutionary CPN members, including Adhikari's nephew, and members of its student affiliate, the ANNISU. (*YICA, 1975*, p. 392.)

Communist elements participated in the widespread political debate on reforms of the panchayat system which followed King Birendra's announcement in December 1974 of a Constitutional Reform Commission. The seven-member Commission included D. P. Adhikari, associated with the extremist CPN. Both the moderate and extremist factions proposed liberalization measures.

Raimajhi called for direct elections to the National Panchayat (legislature) through adult franchise, fundamental rights of speech and association, and a government more responsible to the people. (*Dainik Nepal*, Kathmandu, 30 May 1975.) Shambhu Ram Shrestha, a pro-Chinese extremist faction figure, proposed formation of organizations with "political party objectives," full religious freedom and fundamental rights, and a cabinet responsible to the legislature as well as the King. He did support, however, the existing indirect election system. (*Charcha*, Kathmandu, 11 June.)

Student activity increased during the spring when a three-month long strike for academic and political demands began and led to sporadic violence and arrests. All student organizations took party, including the ANNISU and the Raimajhi-affiliated National Student Union, although at times there were disagreements and clashes among these factions.

In addition to the student arrests, in August the government cracked down on opposition political activity. Several National Panchayat members linked to the student disturbances were arrested and a number of university employees, including Pushpa Lal Shrestha's wife, were dismissed or retired. Seven newspapers were banned in order to control the activity of "irresponsible elements." (*Gorkhapatra*, Kathmandu, 27 August.) Among those banned were the Raimajhi and Soviet oriented *Samiksha*, the pro-Chinese *Matribhumi*, and three pro-Indian papers. (*Christian Science Monitor*, 10 September.)

International Views and Policies. The moderate CPN is recognized and given financial assistance by the Soviet Union. The Raimajhi party Congress in 1968 praised the USSR as a "bulwark of peace, Socialism and national liberation," while criticizing China's views. (*New Age*, New Delhi, 12 January 1969.) The moderate faction would prefer closer Nepal-Soviet relations, and the pro-Raimajhi *Samiksha* has criticized the state of these relations several times. The paper has opined that the Soviets face "cool behavior" and also claimed the "severance of economic ties." (30 May; 11 July.)

Commenting on the issue of "Collective Security for Asia" in the *World Marxist Review*, the Secretary General of Nepal's Afro-Asian Solidarity Committee, K. P. Shrestha, said that the "humanism of Asian collective security proposals has been warmly received in Nepal." (No. 6, 1975.) During the year delegations from the World Peace Council and the Soviet Committee for World Peace visited Kathmandu.

Competing factions of the revolutionary CPN have appealed to China for closer working relationships, but Chinese involvement appears limited to some financial support.

Party Publications. The now banned weekly *Samiksha* has reflected the views of the moderate CPN. The Pushpa Lal Shrestha revolutionary faction reportedly publishes *Nepal Patra*.

Alexandria, Va.   Barbara Reid

New Zealand

New Zealand has two Communist parties—the pro-Chinese Communist Party of New Zealand (CPNZ), founded in 1921, and the pro-Soviet New Zealand Socialist Unity Party (SUP), founded in 1966 after groups of Moscow-supporters had defected or had been expelled from the CPNZ. The major Trotskyist group in the country is the Socialist Action League (SAL) founded in 1969 by mostly young people, few of whom had previously been associated with any Communist organization. Attempts have been made in the last few years to establish other Marxist groups in New Zealand, but they have almost invariably failed to gain a firm foothold. The most recent effort in this direction is the founding of a youth group in Auckland by an Australian Trotskyist organization, the Socialist Labour League.

All Marxist-Leninist groups are able to function legally in New Zealand. The CPNZ is in fact one of the few Communist Parties in the world which has never been banned throughtout its history, although its journal *People's Voice* was suppressed between 1940 and 1943. This unusual toleration of Communism is probably related to the fact that the CPNZ has never been able to exert any significant influence. It has failed consistently in its efforts to place members in the national Parliament or in any City Council, and its membership has declined from a peak of 2,000 in 1944/45 to an estimated 100 today.

Membership of the SUP is probably somewhat above that of the CPNZ. The party is particularly strong in the trade unions where its members hold some important positions, but it too has failed to make any impact in national or municipal elections. Both CPNZ and SUP have their headquarters in Auckland, New Zealand's largest city, where the bulk of their mainly working-class supporters are concentrated. The SAL, with an estimated membership of 40-50, is predominantly university-based with its major strength and head office in Wellington, the capital city.

In a total population of 3,100,000 the combined strength of the Marxist-Leninist organizations is slight, certainly so in comparison with the huge Labour Party. There has been little evidence of Communist growth over recent years, and where election figures can be compared, they actually show a decline in the already infinitesimal Communist vote.

Leadership and Organization. The CPNZ for years now has not publicized the names of its leading officials, with the exception of V. G. Wilcox, who has been the party's general secretary since 1951. Other key figures in the leadership are understood to be R. C. Wolf, R. Taylor and A. G. Rait. The highest authority under the party's constitution is the national conference which is required to meet at intervals not exceeding three years, but no such conference has been held since 1966. The conference elects the next highest body, the National Committee, which in turn elects the National President, the General Secretary and the Political Committee. The day-to-day work is the responsibility of a still smaller body, the National Secretariat, which is elected by the Political Committee. Through deaths, defections and expulsions the national leading bodies are badly depleted and there is some doubt whether the party actually has a national President.

The SUP is similarly organized, with a triennial conference which last met in 1973, and which elects a National President, National Secretary and the remainder of the National Committee. This committee in turn elects from its members a still smaller National Executive. The current president of the SUP is G. H. ("Bill") Andersen, who is also secretary of the powerful Northern Drivers Union and a National Council member of the N.Z. Federation of Labour, the sole national trade union body. Vice-president is Mrs. E. Ayo and the national secretary since the party's inception is G. E. Jackson, who had earlier been president of the CPNZ. (For the names of the remaining members of the National Committee, see *YICA, 1975*, p. 394.)

Under the SAL constitution a national conference has to meet at least every two years. The 3rd national conference of the league was held in January at Palmerston North attended by 55 delegates and observers, 63 percent of whom were under the age of 25. The conference elected a new National Committee whose most prominent members are K. Locke, G. Fyson and Ms. K. Goodger.

Auxiliary Organizations. The three major Marxist-Leninist groups have each tried to establish youth organizations under their influence. First in the field was the CPNZ which helped form a Youth Action Committee on Vietnam in Auckland in 1965. A year later the committee changed its name to the Auckland Progressive Youth Movement. After much activity in the late sixties, particularly in the Vietnam protest movement, the group suffered a decline and today its membership and influence are very restricted. One of its major activities is the publication of an irregular newssheet *Rebel*, the hundredth issue of which appeared in February 1975.

The Democratic Youth Front sponsored by the SUP is still a very shadowy body confined to Auckland. The only truly national organization among the three is the Young Socialists sponsored by the SAL. Clubs of Young Socialists had been formed earlier in the main university centers and were affiliated with the local student associations. In April 1975 they took a step forward by holding their first national conference in Wellington attended by more than 120 people, at which they adopted a basic code of organizational principles and a constitution, discussed future policy, and elected a National Council of nine full and three alternate members. M. Tucker was elected national coordinator and T. Lane national secretary. 1975 also saw the publication of a new national magazine, *Young Socialist*, three issues of which appeared during the year.

There are no women's auxiliaries in New Zealand but the SUP exerts some influence in the Union of New Zealand Women, an Auckland group whose secretary, Mrs. E. Katz attended the World Congress for International Women's Year in Berlin in October.

Party Internal Affairs. The CPNZ has been rent by dissensions in recent years: the expulsion of the Manson-Bailey group in 1970, the defection of R. Hegman in 1973, and the expulsions of W. McAra in 1973 and of F. N. Wright in 1974. Most of these rebels against Wilcox's leadership have kept their supporters together in a loosely organized fashion, but Wright has gone so far as to promote a minuscule new party, the Communist Party of Aotearoa (the ancient Maori name of New Zealand). These groups continue to publish circulars and other publications setting out their differences with current CPNZ policy and, reading between the lines of official party publications, it seems that this propaganda onslaught is having some effect within the CPNZ.

In a move to reestablish its authority the CPNZ held what it called a plenum of its National Committee in September. This was an enlarged meeting of the committee attended also by invited members representing different areas of party work. The lead-in statement by the National Secretariat stressed that a major problem facing the CPNZ was "the development of party leadership" and the breaking down of "departmentalism" which had produced an uncoordinated party, had obstructed united effective action, and had led to "formalism and routinism and operation as a narrow sect isolated from the working class." (*New Zealand Communist Review*, Auckland, Oct.)

The statement also claimed that whereas social democracy had once been the main obstruction in the broad revolutionary movement, today its place had been taken by modern revisionism: "With social democracy losing its influence, it is the revisionists who step in to fill the vacuum, and serve the class enemy with their delusion, disruptions and sell-outs. This is the role played clearly by the Socialist Unity Party, more cunningly by the Manson-Bailey group and the self-inflated McAra sitting in his ivory tower and using his brand of Marxism-Leninism as a dogma to serve his own interests." (Ibid.)

To the McAra group on the other hand it is the CPNZ leaders who are revisionists guilty of imposing a Lin Piao-Khrushchevite line on their remaining followers. One of their circulars gives details of the resignations of five middle-ranking activists in 1975, which went unreported in the party press. The CPNZ however claims that "for every resignation over the last three years there have been three new members." (*New Zealand Communist Review*, July). The SUP too, for the first time in recent years, has hinted at internal dissension by announcing the expulsion of a group of five Wellington members, among them J. Brinklow, a member of the party's National Committee. (*New Zealand Tribune*, Auckland, 1 Sept.)

Domestic Attitudes and Activities. The main political event of the year was the general election in November. The CPNZ, which had not taken part in elections since 1969, again refused to put up candidates and advised its supporters not to vote at all. "Parliament has now reached the stage," declared its election statement, "when there is no longer any point in a workers' party or other exploited sections standing candidates in order to expose its fraudulent role of concealing a very real dictatorship. . . . That is why the Communist Party urges the development of struggle outside Parliament—so the people can realise that the real power lies with them." Nevertheless the CPNZ took a more active part in the election campaign than in previous years. The National Committee plenum in September had urged the party to make its presence known and to show its independent face, breaking "with an outlook which sees things so bleakly that nothing can be done in the immediate future and so sit back to await more favorable times." (*New Zealand Communist Review*, Oct.) Following these directives the party held what it called "non-election meetings," issued leaflets and statements, put on "guerrilla theatre" productions, and made increased efforts to sell its publications in the streets.

The SUP and the SAL both contested the elections as did a third Marxist party, the Socialist Party of New Zealand (SPNZ), which is linked with the Socialist Party of Great Britain. The SUP put up 15 candidates which gave it the right, for the first time in New Zealand, to free television time during the campaign. Eleven of these candidates stood in the Auckland province. The party did not seriously expect to win any seats—the highest Communist vote ever gained in New Zealand was in 1931 when a CPNZ candidate obtained 6.15 percent—and it deliberately contested safe Labour seats to avoid any accusation of vote-splitting which might help the conservative opposition. Where no party candidates were standing the SUP urged its supporters to vote for the Labour Party, not because it was likely to introduce any fundamental social changes but because it was preferable to the National Party.

The SAL took a similar stand with its slogan of "Return a Labour Government and vote Socialist Action in 1975." Its criticism of the Labour Party was somewhat stronger than the SUP's. It accused the Labour leaders of having deserted the cause of socialism but it accepted that the Labour Party was still "the party of the unions, retaining the support of the overwhelming majority of workers and underprivileged people." (*Socialist Action*, 25 April). "To raise the banner of socialism" the league put forward four candidates, two in Auckland and two in Wellington.

The Paper, a journal close to the Manson-Bailey group, also advised its readers to vote for the Labour Party which it described however as "a thoroughly capitalist party" which largely represented manufacturing interests. (*The Paper*, Nov.). The SPNZ, which put forward seven candidates, all in the Auckland province, asked its supporters to vote socialist in these seven electorates but to invalidate their votes elsewhere by writing "Socialism" across the ballot paper.

The election resulted in an overwhelming defeat for the ruling Labour Party. The tiny number of votes given to the Marxist parties is shown in the table which follows:

	SUP	SAL	CPNZ
Total number of candidates	15	4	7
Average vote per candidate	28	38	16
Combined vote of candidates	413	152	111
Combined vote as percentage of total vote in seats contested	0.16	0.24	0.08

The SAL did not contest the previous general election in 1972, but both the SUP and the SPNZ suffered a further decline in popularity. In 1972 the average vote per SUP candidate was 89 compared with 28 in 1975. In fact, with only five candidates in 1972 the SUP gained a higher combined vote in 1972 than it did with 15 candidates in 1975.

International Activities and Contacts. No CPNZ visits to Peking were reported during the year. The party did however send greetings to China, Albania, Cambodia and Vietnam, to the Communist Parties of Indonesia and Malaya, and to Chongrynn, the General Association of Korean Residents in Japan. G. E. Jackson, the national secretary of the SUP, visited Eastern Europe in February, including the G.D.R., Bulgaria (where he attended the 10th congress of the BCP) and the Soviet Union. A National Committee meeting of the SUP held after his return "endorsed the need for a world meeting of Communist and Workers' Parties" which was rendered urgent by "the present crisis of the capitalist world." (*New Zealand Tribune*, 14 April). In June, Jackson was present in Sydney at the second congress of the Socialist Party of Australia but later in the year he and P. Cross were refused entry visas to attend the 21st convention of the CPUSA.

The SAL national conference in January was attended by representatives from three Australian Trotskyist organizations, the Socialist Workers League, Communist League, and Socialist Youth Alliance. American and Australian delegates attended the founding conference of the Young Socialists in April.

Party Publications. The CPNZ's main organ is the *People's Voice,* which is published weekly in Auckland. A theoretical journal *New Zealand Communist Review* appears monthly. The SUP journal *New Zealand Tribune* is now published fortnightly, also in Auckland, together with a theoretical journal *Socialist Politics*, which appeared three times during the year. The SAL journal *Socialist Action* is published fortnightly in Wellington where its main rival is the independent radical journal *The Paper.* Some of the sponsors of *The Paper* had hoped that it would become the nucleus of a new Marxist-Leninist party. However, not only did it fail in this respect but declining sales also led to a reassessment of the journal's role at a supporters' conference in February. *The Paper* still appears monthly, with occasional gaps, but its size has been drastically cut. Its main objective now is to express the needs and struggles of two groups, factory workers and Polynesian people. (*The Paper*, March.)

No circulation figures have been published for these journals. The CPNZ claimed in September that the *People's Voice* had increased its sales by 3 percent (*New Zealand Communist Review*, Oct.) but probably in no case does regular circulation within New Zealand exceed 2,500 copies.

University of Auckland   H. Roth

Pakistan

The Communist Party of Pakistan (CPP) is essentially a vestigial entity, more a state of mind than a functioning programmatic political organization. This state of mind is characterized by an anti-establishment, anti-imperialist, anti-western bias which finds its roots in the pro-Sovietism of the Third World intellectuals of the 1930s and 1940s, and, to a lesser extent, in the economies of scarcity and exploitation so characteristic of the developing world. The younger generation of Pakistani communists have also been influenced by the "Afro-Asianism" nurtured at Bandung and supported thereafter by both the Soviet and the Chinese communists.

Founded in 1947, following the partition of British India into the two independent dominions of India and Pakistan, the CPP (like its opposite number in Bangladesh) traces its origins to the original Communist Party of India. Proscribed as a subversive organization by the Government of Pakistan (GOP) in 1954, the CPP's current legal position is unclear as a result of subsequent constitutional developments. The East Pakistani branch of the party was always more active and better organized than its West Wing counterpart and the secession of Bangladesh in 1971 has reduced the remainder of the CPP to a shadowy existence. A recent estimate placed the party's membership in 1973 at approximately 800 (or fewer). The CPP would thus appear to be a negligible factor in the lives of Pakistan's some 70 million inhabitants.

Curiously, the Communist Party of India's publication, *New Age* (2 February 1975) included greetings to that party's congress from the CPP. The same newspaper also noted the presence of an undesignated Pakistani delegation to the meeting, although no Communist Party of Pakistan as such is formally recognized by the USSR.

As we have noted before, the ruling Pakistan People's Party (PPP) of Prime Minister Zulfikar Ali Bhutto has tended to co-opt many of the leftist radical intellectuals who considered themselves communists during the military dictatorship of Muhammad Ayub Khan. The PPP's radical rhetoric and "Islamic Socialist" ideology permitted considerable latitude in its membership, especially during the early years of the Bhutto regime.

In addition to the PPP, the National Awami Party (NAP), led by Khan Abdul Wali Khan, has been a congenial home for Pakistani communists. Indeed, some have called it a proxy for the CPP since the latter was banned. Domestically, the NAP has pressed the demands of various ethnic minorities within Pakistan for greater regional autonomy. Although the NAP has traditionally been pro-Soviet internationally, that aspect of its platform was eclipsed by its drive for greater political power and economic benefits for such depressed groups as the Pathans of the North-West Frontier Province (NWFP), the Baluch of Baluchistan, and the Sindhis of Sind. Most recently, the NAP had dominated the small opposition in Pakistan's National Assembly. However, the overwhelming PPP majority deprived opposition forces of anything but token influence and nuisance value.

The Government of Pakistan moved against the NAP in February 1975, following the assassination by bombing of a senior PPP minister in the NWFP government. Blaming the NAP for the terrorist incident, the GOP banned the party, arrested Wali Khan and over 300 other party leaders, and confiscated the party's funds and property. Referring to the party's alleged foreign connection with

Afghanistan (and indirectly with India and the Soviet Union), Bhutto told his National Assembly that "all politics of violence with its tentacles abroad should be ended" (*Washington Post*, February 12, 1975, p. A11). Shortly thereafter, the Pakistan Government also took over direct rule of the NWFP for three months.

Although the banning of the NAP was challenged by party lawyers in Pakistan's Supreme Court, the judgment was upheld unanimously in an October 30 ruling by the six-man bench. The justices held that the NAP had been guilty of attempting to establish an independent "Pakhtunistan" [Pathan and Baluch state] in place of the North-West Frontier and Baluchistan provinces by means of large-scale insurgency, terrorism, and sabotage. Officers of the banned party were barred from seeking provincial or federal elective office for five years.

Late in November, against a background of divisive splintering within Bhutto's own People's Party, Sherbaz Khan Mazari, leader of the independents in the National Assembly and himself chief of one of the more peaceful Baluch tribes, announced the formation of a new National Democratic Party. As the year drew to a close, a number of erstwhile NAP members who were not behind bars, including Mrs. Naseem Wali Khan (wife of the NAP leader), were joining the new party in an effort to regroup against the latest Bhutto assault.

Other leftists who might be active in a communist party if such a body existed, consist of dissident groups in the North-West Frontier Province and Baluchistan. One, the Kisan Mazdoor (Peasants and Workers) Party (KMP), is active in certain districts of the NWFP. Although the KMP was allied with the PPP after the 1970 general election, that relationship ended with the fall of the NAP-led coalition government in the NWFP in February 1973. Unlike the NAP, the KMP is not involved in the regionalist dispute. It emphasizes the radical redistribution of land among poor tenant farmers through forceful seizure of property from landlords. Its members are even more extreme than the NAP radicals who have occasionally planted bombs and sabotaged such symbols of government authority as railways and radio stations.

The most radical group in Baluchistan is a collection of former members of the Baluchistan Students Organization which calls itself the Popular Front of Armed Resistance (PFAR) against National Oppression and Exploitation in Baluchistan. This is a small pro-Soviet student group emphasizing regional autonomy headquartered in the remote hills of the province; it also may have some links with the traditionalist Baluch tribal insurgents. The establishment of the PFAR reflects considerable discontent among recent Baluch college graduates because of the depressed economic conditions and shortage of jobs in the province, as well as dissatisfaction with the continuing action of the Pakistan Government against the Baluch nationalists. Some observers claim that the NAP was promoting the development of the PFAR and was even inducing young Pathans to join the front in order to dramatize Pathan-Baluch unity.

The Pakistan Government has charged that the Baluch tribal insurgents, including the PFAR, have received arms of Soviet and East European origin via neighboring Afghanistan. That country has traditionally been a source of weapons for the Baluch, a number of whom live on the fruits of banditry, but there is no conclusive evidence that the Afghan Government is involved in the arms traffic.

To the extent that they have taken sides in the Sino-Soviet dispute, a number of Pakistani leftists have supported the People's Republic of China. This preference for the PRC would appear to relate equally as much, if not more, to that country's support for Pakistan internationally, as to a conscious preference of the Chinese version of the socialist way. There is, at the same time, continuing Soviet pressure on Pakistan to improve its "correct" relations with Moscow at a faster pace than has been the case until now. Bhutto did praise the Soviet Union publicly on the occasion of the signing of the Helsinki agreement.

Moscow has also tried to influence Pakistan to upgrade the level of its participation in such

Soviet-dominated front organizatons as the Afro-Asian Peoples' Solidarity Organization and the World Peace Council. The most prominent Pakistani permitted to attend such meetings in recent years had been noted poet and journalist Faiz Ahmad Faiz, a Lenin Peace Prize winner. Faiz, one of the older generation of Pakistani communists which traces its origins to the pre-independence Progressive Writers group of Indian communists, was appointed a senior adviser to Bhutto on art and cultural matters shortly after the latter's accession to power. He was, however, subsequently downgraded to a less elevated position. In a related move, Bhutto's wife led a Pakistani delegation invited to the USSR by the Soviet Women's Committee for a ten-day visit in late summer.

With the declaration of the emergency in neighboring India and a confusing succession of coups and counter-coups in Bangladesh, Pakistan would appear to have become the most nearly democratic nation in South Asia by year's end. Bhutto's adroit mixture of parliamentary procedure and autocratic rule, plus active courting of such actual and potential foreign benefactors as the United States, Iran, and the Arab oil states of the Middle East, has achieved for Pakistan a degree of political and economic stability found in few other states of the region. Aid flows reached a record high (over $1 billion) in the past year; about half came from the oil-producing countries, and the balance from the United States, the international lending institutions, and other western countries. As a consequence, Pakistan's relatively poor economic performance was reduced to manageable proportions.

Pakistan's major foreign policy problem area remained its relations with Afghanistan over the issue of Pashtunistan (against a background of fears that India and the Soviet Union are behind Afghan efforts to undermine Pakistan's continued territorial integrity). The domestic repercussions of this problem have been discussed above in connection with the banning of the NAP. Shortly after the announcement of the Supreme Court verdict upholding the ban, Bhutto publicly warned Afghanistan that he would not tolerate the interference of any outside power in Pakistan's internal affairs. Air service between the two countries remains suspended, although the border remains open and trade continues.

The U.S. decision to lift its 10-year embargo on the sale of lethal weapons to Pakistan (and India) following a visit to Washington by Bhutto in February 1975 underlined the cordial relationship which has developed between the two countries in recent years. All sales are to be on a case-by-case basis and the United States has declared that it neither intends to fuel an arms race in the region nor sell sophisticated offensive weapons. In addition to this development, Pakistani forces for the first time in over a decade participated in a CENTO military exercise in late 1974.

Although Pakistan cannot avoid facing the reality that it is part of a South Asia dominated by India, it is making the most of its ties with China, the United States, and the Muslim world. At the same time, there has been some slow progress toward normalization of relations with India and steps have been taken toward the establishment of diplomatic ties with Bangladesh.

Library of Congress   Joel M. Woldman
Washington, D.C.

Philippines

Communism in the Philippines is confined to two illegal and underground organizations, one pro-Peking, with an active guerrilla force, the other oriented toward Moscow, which has all but abandoned its erstwhile small "people's army." Both assert that they are national Philippine organizations with predominant national interests. The persisting Muslim insurrection in the South has, according to Philippine authorities, meshed itself in part with the operations of Peking-oriented guerrillas, but cooperation between the two groups, if any, must be considered quite limited and confined to occasional tactics. Some leaders of the Moscow-oriented faction have surrendered to authorities and appear ready to collaborate with the Marcos government, possibly in the hope of driving for a new legitimization of the Left in a country that is now completing its fourth year under martial law.

History. During the 1920s Chinese and Indonesian Communists as well as Philippine trade unionists disseminated Marxist-Leninist doctrines and tactics, but the islands were a relatively low Comintern priority, and furthermore considered to be an operational terrain also of the distant Communist Party, USA (CPUSA). The Philippine Communist Party (Partido Komunista ng Pilipinas; PKP) was therefore not officially established until 7 November 1930, although it had already completed its organization several weeks previously, on 26 August. Almost wholly dependent from the start on the support of the more radical trade unions like the Marxist labor federation, Katipunan ng mga Ankpawis sa Pilipinas ("Association of the Sons of Sweat of the Philippines") or KAP, and on a handful of lower-middle-class clerical workers and intellectuals, the party under its first general secretary Crisanto Evangelista, a major KAP figure, soon threw itself into a series of ill-considered strike ventures and anti-government demonstrations. On 14 September 1931 both the PKP and KAP were officially banned, which was considered also a policy blow for the CPUSA, which had sought to provide some organizational direction to the Philippine Communists. Evangelista and other PKP leaders were sentenced to eight years for sedition.

Largely on Comintern instructions, those Philippine Communists not in jail during the early 1930s devoted efforts to building front groups, in the hope of developing a larger united complex of organizations that could cooperate with the legitimate political parties in quick realization of national independence. Organizations like the "League for the Defense of Democracy" filled such a limited front-group function. Following the decision of the 1935 Seventh Comintern Congress to mobilize a world-wide united front struggle against fascism, however, Sol Auerbach (traveling under the name of James S. Allen), a CPUSA functionary, mediated between the jailed Evangelista and the Philippine Commonwealth president, Manuel Quezon, eventually securing Evangelista's release on 31 December 1963 and subsequently also effecting a merger of the PKP (now relegalized by Quezon to a degree) with the aboveground, but minuscule, Socialist Party of the Philippines. The merger was announced during the PKP's third national congress, held in Manila on 29-31 October 1938. (Alfredo B. Saulo, *Communism in the Philippines*, Manila, Ateneo Publications, 1969, pp. 33-34.) The merger was one of convenience for the PKP, and reflected also a general consensus among most Philippine political and public leaders of the need for as much national unity as possible if independence was to be achieved.

When Japan invaded the Philippines during World War II the PKP played a major role in organizing the resistance, taking the lead in the formation of an "Anti-Japanese National United Front," whose military committee on 29 March 1942 initiated the formation of an "Anti-Japanese People's Army" (Hukbo ng Bayan Laban sa Hapon, or Hukbalahap—"Huks" in everyday parlance). A separate "squadron" of Chinese Communists operated alongside the Huks but remained organizationally independent. As in the case of the Communist resistance in Malaya, and in a somewhat different context also in Indochina, PKP leaders apparently expected that the wartime united front and the military successes of the Huks would catapult the party into a commanding political position after the restoration of peace and the proclamation of Philippine independence. This expectation was not realized. On 6 March 1948, having refused to surrender their arms, the Huks were outlawed. Later that year on 29 August, a prominent Huk leader, Luis Taruc, who earlier had been expected by the government to lead a new Huk accommodation with government policies, attacked Philippines president Elpidio Quirino for failure to keep his commitments on the release of imprisoned Huks, on promised social and agrarian reforms, and on the Huks arms disposal problem. This attack, according to government sources, marked the resumption of organized armed Huk hostilities. (*The Communist Movement in the Philippines*, Southeast Asia Treaty Organisation Short Paper, no. 46, Bangkok, March 1970, p. 23.)

The revived Huk organization called itself the "People's Liberation Army" (Hukbo ng Mapagpalaya ng Bayan; HMB), and was formally established on 7 November 1948 under the nominal leadership of Luis Taruc (who later emphasized in conversation with the author that he personally had never been a Communist). The PKP, using the HMB "people's war," organized itself for a combined political and military assault on the Philippine government, which it claimed would fall by 1 May 1952. The government did not collapse, however, and after 18 October 1952, when the PKP's secretary general, José Lava, and most of its Politburo fell into government hands, the political effectiveness of the party was again shattered. Combined PKP-HMB membership, which after initial Huk military gains had reached about 25,000 by the end of 1950, soon began to decline, particularly as an extensive, U.S.-assisted aid and counter-insurgency program, and the reform policies initiated by Philippine defense secretary and later president Ramon Magsaysay, gradually began to take effect in the early 1950s.

On 17 June 1957, with the passage of Philippine Republic Act 1700 both the HMB and the PKP were formally outlawed. (Outlawing legislation, proposed earlier, had been postponed so as not to impede implementation of amnesty policies and in order to win over the more moderate Philippine Left.) By then, effective PKP organization and HMB resistance had ceased, though neither the underground party structure in the cities, nor the HMB (degenerating into mere brigandage and extortion rackets, even as some of its leaders professed social reformist goals) wholly vanished. Indeed, the scattered operations of what were again commonly called "Huks"—criminality combined with occasional rough, Robin Hood-style justice for rent-gouging Philippine landlords—through the later 1950s and early 1960s became a not insignificant domestic political factor, in that both the Philippine armed forces establishment and elites within the political parties employed the existence of the Huks as justification of their own ends (e.g., in demanding higher defense budgets). Within the PKP itself, and also in part as an expression of Leftist and nationalistic currents that also began stirring Philippine student, intellectual, labor, and even some business circles during the early 1960s, demands for new organizational and tactical directions arose. As a result, a new pattern of essentially urban-based front organizations began to develop, all strongly nationalistic, with generally "progressive," socialistic, and anti-U.S. leanings, which were infiltrated, though by no means necessarily dominated, by the PKP. Among these were the Kabatang Makabayan (National Youth) or KM, the

Lapiang Manggagawa (Labor Party) or LM, and, in the rural towns and countryside, the Malayang Samahang Magsasaka (Free Peasants Union) or Masaka. Non-Communist support for such groups from industrial workers, youths, the rural proletariat, and impoverished tenants was considerable.

On 12 May 1964 the PKP's last major underground leader, Jesús Lava (who had succeeded his brother as secretary general), was arrested, but this did not impede the newly developing front-group complex. It did, however, give increased prominence in radical underground circles to young Philippine intellectuals—many of them attracted to Maoist doctrines and militant "people's war" tactics—whose allegiance the divided and discredited HMB organization steeped in racketeering, and the PKP, which kept nominal relations with it, seemed unable to develop. During 1966-67 a decisive breach took place in the underground PKP leadership, and on 26 December 1968 (Mao Tse-tung's 75th birthday) to 7 January 1969 a "Congress of Re-establishment of the Communist Party of the Philippines" was held near the town of Capas, in southern Tarlac Province, Luzon. The congress resulted in the establishment of a new Communist party, described in its constitution as the "Communist Party of the Philippines—Marxist-Leninist" (CPP-ML) or "Communist Party of the Philippines—Mao Tse-tung Thought." (On these developments see Eduardo Lachica, *Huk! Philippine Agrarian Society in Revolt*, Manila, Solidaridad Publishing House, 1971, and Justus M. van der Kroef, "The Philippine Maoists," *Orbis*, Winter 1973, pp. 892-926.)

On 29 March 1969, probably again at a meeting near Capas, CPP-ML cadres and sympathizers, some with old Huk or HMB experience, formed a "New People's Army" (NPA), and almost immediately began planning not only for "people's war" in the countryside, but also, according to unverified Philippine government sources, for a campaign of urban terrorism, with the aim of bringing down the government. Meanwhile, the PKP core, though retaining its "national" orientation, came generally to be considered pro-Moscow in orientation, and henceforth both the Soviet and Chinese media were to publicize the statements and exploits of their respective rival wings of Philippine Communism. Though it denounced the militant "cowboy ideology" of the CPP-ML, the PKP did sever its vestigial relatons with some of the remaining Huk leaders, and, according to Philippine armed forces intelligence, created in 1969 a new fighting organization of its own, the Army ng Bayan (National Army), which had little formal structure, and, unlike the NPA, was not destined to win headlines with guerrilla raids.

During 1970-72, NPA attacks and student unrest inside the capital aggravated domestic political tensions over the position of President Ferdinand Marcos and partisan disagreements over a new Philippine constitution then being drafted by a special convention. On 22 September 1972, Marcos, blaming a state of rebellion in the country attributable to the operations of the CPP-ML and the NPA, proclaimed martial law, suspending all normal political processes. According to Marcos the Maoist insurgents were in control of "33 municipalities" and had established "communal farms and production bases." Though repeatedly upheld in the courts and approved by various popular referendums since then, the new authoritarian structure of government imposed by Marcos continued to create serious if muted dissension in Philippine society, while among the Philippine resident community in the United States various anti-Marcos groups, including those sympathetic to the strivings fo the CPP-ML and NPA, made headway. In the Philippines itself, however, the threat allegedly posed by the NPA soon came to be overshadowed by the insurrection of Muslims, some seeking an independent state, in the Mindanao Island and Sulu Archipelago area in the south of the country.

There has been considerable speculation that Marcos unduly accentuated the NPA danger in order to impose a new structure of government. Although hundreds of political and media figures and others who had been arrested in the immediate aftermath of the martial-law declaration were subsequently released, and although a measure of press freedom returned by the end of 1974, the new regime continued to have difficulties with Philippine clergy, intellectuals, and expatriate opponents seeking to influence U.S. public opinion, although seeming political stability had a favorable effect on foreign business interests. Allegations by the Philippine government of NPA inroads in the southern Muslim rising appear to be only minimally substantiated, although, particularly since June 1975, NPA activity, independent of the Muslim rebels, appears to be increasing in the Mindanao area.

Organization and Tactics. The present internal structure of the PKP and its major policies were established by the Fifth Congress of the party, meeting in a condition of "illegality" somewhere "on Luzon," on 10-11 February 1973. The Central Committee also issued a "new policy orientation" toward the state of martial law and the Marcos government, on 22 November 1974. According to the program adopted at the congress, the party is committed to create a "national democratic government" in the Philippines, established by a "national united front" in which political power will be shared by "parties representing the working class, the peasantry, the patriotic members of the national bourgeoisie, and the left and progressive elements among the youth, intellectuals, in the churches and in the armed forces" (*IB*, Prague, vol. 11, 1973, no. 17-18 (249-50), p. 16). An alteration in state power in the Philippines must be achieved (the "national democratic revolution"), but the PKP, along with the national united front, "will wage every form of open and legal struggle, including electoral struggle," and rejects specifically "putschism, coup d'état, foco guerrillaism or anarcho-terrorist revolutionism that stands apart from the sentiment of the masses." However, the PKP "upholds the right" of the people to use force against those who have committed violence against the people. The PKP program asserts also that the "main driving forces" of the national democratic revolution are "the working class, the peasantry, the working intellectuals, and the progressive ranks of the studentry." There are also "patriotic young members of the Filipino clergy" and young officers and other military who are developing a "patriotic and anti-imperialistic consciousness," whose tactical collaboration is seen as having a potential the advantages of which should be considered.

The "immediate demands" of the party include restoration of political liberties, termination of the martial law emergency, release of political prisoners, and discussion of the proposed draft constitution (which subsequently won referendum approval). Other programmatic demands include removal of all U.S. military bases and installations, abrogation of all "unequal treaties" with the United States, repeal of the Anti-Subversion Law, protection of academic freedom in the universities and of the freedom of labor, peasants, women, youths, and other groups to organize, and the nationalization of banks, insurance companies, the copper and nickel mining industry, foreign trade, and oil enterprises. As for the Roman Catholic church, the 1973 program says that the church "should serve the religious needs" of the people, not the material or financial interests of "foreign religious orders or corporations." The state must also prevent political subversion "through religious conduits." (Ibid., pp. 18-25).

The Political Resolution of the 1973 congress, in a section on the international situation states that "working class struggles are exerting tremendous pressures for radical democratic changes" in the principal capitalist countries and that the new states have entered a new phase in their liberation movement: "the struggle for what Lenin called "economic liberation" (ibid., no. 13 (245), pp. 18, 21.). At the same time, however, according to the resolution, a new form of "imperialist controlled industrialization" is beginning to develop in Southeast Asia, a process in which the economies of a number of Asian countries, like the Philippines, Indonesia, Malaysia, Singapore, South Korea, and Thailand, are being integrated under the "aegis of multinational corporations." This process in the Philippines is exemplified by the fact that more and more agricultural lands are being controlled by modern corporate farms and more lands are being placed under "labor administration," so that they in fact become elements of a modern agro-business establishment controlled by the "imperialist" multinational corporations.

The current new phase in U.S.-Philippine relations, according to the resolution, is merely designed to "remove the more brazen" aspects of political and economic U.S. imperialism, so as to facilitate the imposition of the new, less direct pattern of U.S. dominance through the multinational and other foreign business structures. While granting that the reforms being instituted by the new "military-technocratic regime" under Marcos will produce "some amount of economic progress," the resolution states that false hopes about their welfare are being raised among the peasantry and other groups that cannot possibly be fulfilled. At the same time the "CIA forces" in the Philippines—"the subversive agents of multinational corporations"—are using the "Maoist 'communist' vehicle" to drum up an "anti-Communist hysteria." In this crisis, the task of the PKP is to establish close links with the Philippine masses, combat terrorism that may isolate the party, and prevent the PKP from being dragged into "left adventurist" policies by "infantile revolutionary phrase-mongering." (Ibid., pp. 33-36.)

The "new policy orientation" in November 1974 welcomed what appeared to be new political and economic developments in the country, and seemed to suggest that the party was beginning to move toward a qualified, limited endorsement of Marcos's policies. At about the same time, according to the government, some "10,000 Communist rebels" led by PKP secretary-general Felicisimo Macapagal and PKP military commander Alejandro Briones surrendered to the Philippine authorities, pledging cooperation with the government (FBIS, 18 November). Doubt has been expressed that those who surrendered were all, in fact, PKP members, although the circumstance that Briones and Macapagal did give themselves up unquestionably was a significant portent of the PKP's new policy approach to the martial law regime. Earlier, Philippine military sources were quoted as saying that the PKP might soon win government recognition in view of the recent surrender of other top leaders (ibid., 17 October). According to the 22 November 1974 PKP statement, the party "supports the restructuring of the trade unions, based on the one federation-one industry principle," while objecting to the abolition or suspension of the right to strike. Remarkably, the PKP said that it "accepts the basic principle of the present land reform program" of the Marcos government, though it also pledged itself to struggle on behalf of the peasants for lowering the prices at which family-size farms are being sold. The PKP, further, praised the government's employment program, and at the same time noted the growth of the proletariat in the country as affording a necessary context for an intensified class struggle in the future. The fundamental PKP concern remained, however, the political liberalization of the country and the halting of multinational inroads of power. As to the former, according to the statement, the party wishes to test its own program "in an open free election," and therefore "does not aim to overthrow by force of arms" the present regime but instead wishes to make that government serve the "interests of the broadest ranks" of the Philippine working people through "mass struggles, electoral means and the exercise of democratic rights." Hence the party claims that it should be free to conduct its political activities and should be accorded status as a legal political party. (IB, 1975, no. 3, pp. 23-26). According to a PKP Central Committee member, a pattern of international and domestic political and economic changes is having its effect on the Philippine ruling circles, and important sections of society, from landowning oligarchs to the local bourgeoisie, are moving toward a confrontation with an increasingly hard-pressed Marcos dictatorship. Clearly, the PKP sees new tactical advantages in what it perceives as a developing "national democratic, anti-imperialist and anti-feudal front." (Francisco Balagtas, "Trends of Change in the Philippines," WMR, July, p. 44-46.)

Organizationally, the PKP today is in a state of limbo. Some older party leaders, like Jesús Lava and his brother José, have been released from detention; others have surrendered and pledged cooperation with the government; all are under close surveillance, however, and despite the current party line of seeking relegitimization through a pledge of adhering to non-violent conduct and constitutional political participation, there remains formidable opposition, particularly in top Philippine military sources, to granting legal status to the PKP or even to giving party activists a measure of freedom to propagate their ideas. PKP front groups once active in the late 1960s and early 1970s, like the National Workers Federation (Pambansang Kilusan ng Paggawa) or student groups like the Democratic Union of Filipino Youth (Malayang Pagkakaisa ng Kabataang Pilipino, or MKPK, an offshoot of the KM), leftist nationalist and pacifist groups like the Movement for the Advancement of Nationalism (MAN), and the Bertrand Russell Peace Foundation, or industrial workers' self-help organizations like the Brotherhood for Our Development (Ang Kapatrian sa Ikauunlad Natin, or AKSIUN), have to all intents and purposes become paper organizations or have ceased to exist. The peasant organization Masaka, where both factions of the PKP today have supporters, is closely supervised by police and military authorities. It is claimed that the PKP still has a functioning Central Committee, a Politburo, and a provincial organization on the island of Luzon. But since the surrender of Macapagal (see also *YICA, 1975*, pp. 402-3) these party organs appear to be in disarray or suspended operation.

The CPP-ML program sets forth ten general guidelines for the party to follow: (1) destruction of U.S. "imperialism," (2) creation of a "people's democratic state" and a united front coalition government, (3) a continuing struggle for national unity and democratic rights, (4) observance of "democratic centralism" in the party organization, (5) maintenance of a "people's army" whose principal purpose is to fight for and secure the "people's democratic state," (6) satisfaction of the demand for land by the poor peasants and agricultural laborers, (7) creation of a national industry with state, cooperative, and private sectors of production, (8) fostering of a "people's democratic cultural revolution" to rid the nation of "imperialist" and "feudal" cultural traits, (9) integration of national minorities and encouragement of a new type of revolutionary leadership among the minorities, and (10) pursuance of a foreign policy, inspired by "proletarian internationalism," that regards People's China as a bastion of the world proletarian revolution and as a reliable friend of all oppressed peoples, including the Filipino people (*The Maoist Communist Party of the Philippines*, SEATO Short Paper, no. 52, Bangkok, September 1971, pp. 14-15). As laid down by CPP-ML chairman Sison (under the pseudonym "Amado Guerrero"), the Philippine Communists must fight not only for a national revolution that "seeks to assert national sovereignty against U.S. imperialism and its local running dogs," but also for a "democratic revolution" that attempts to meet the peasants' need for land against the encroachments of "domestic feudalism" (Amado Guerrero, *Philippine Society and Revolution*, Manila, Pulang Tala Publications,1971, p. 230).

Like the PKP, the CPP-ML has been committed to development of a broad-based-mass support group. The National Democratic Frònt (NDF), organized in 1973, serves as the vehicle of this mass action. The NDF's "Preparatory Commission" in April 1973 issued a manifesto which basically repeats the ten guidelines above, adding a clause demanding "public trial" of the U.S.-Marcos "fascist gang" for their alleged crimes to be followed by punishment and the confiscation of "all their ill-gotten wealth" (*People's War in the Philippines*, published by the Union of Democratic Filipinos, August 1974, p. 49). In its present state of dispersed continuous guerrilla attacks on government installations and forces, the CPP-ML's fighting arm, the New People's Army—which according to the CPP-ML constitution "shall be the main weapon of the Party in the people's democratic revolution and in the subsequent socialist stage"—has found it increasingly difficult to maintain liaison with the party organization and the NDF. The NDF seems to have little effective influence in the Philippines at present, but serves as a recruiting channel among the more radical elements in the anti-Marcos Philippine community in the United States and Canada.

Like the PKP, by constitutional prescription the CPP-ML maintains a central committee and politburo, and recognizes the party's national congress as the ultimate originator and legitimizer of party policies. The size of both party organizations, according to Philippine intelligence sources, cannot be precisely calculated, owing to continuing defections and losses in lives among the insurgent bands. The NPA force which in the middle of 1974 was still officially estimated at about 1,400 is now put at about half. Defense Secretary Juan Ponce Enrile stated in July 1975 that Communist activity was "very limited," and that there had been no "unusual" movement among pro-Peking elements in the country (*NYT*, 3 July). Early in December 1974, 1,032 "members and supporters" of the NPA under 15 of their commanders formally surrendered before Enrile at Calbigas, western Samar, according to the Defense Department. They took an oath of allegiance to the government and were temporarily released, pending a decision on their applications of amnesty (*FBIS*, 4 December). In February 1975, the Philippine Constabulary command in Panay Island reported that the NPA had abandoned its expansionist drive in the whole of the Visayas "due to continuous government pressure" (ibid., 28 February). NPA guerrilla activity nevertheless has persisted, even according to the government's news reports, and its tactical pattern throughout 1975 in no way suggested abandonment of traditional small-scale but continuous attacks. Only a few weeks after Enrile's downgrading of NPA activity, "Maoist guerrillas" led by "Commander Gerry" attacked villagers on an estate in Porac town, Pampanga Province. This was the first reported Maoist activity in recent months in Pampanga. (Ibid., 8 August.) In the course of previous months the chain of NPA incidents suggested persistent organizational strength. In November 1974, 80 NPA elements overran a Constabulary detachment in Aurora subprovince, killing three and capturing six, and in January 1975 three separate clashes occurred in Davao Del Norte, Pampanga, and Samar provinces, in which six Maoists were killed and three captured (ibid., 20 November 1974, 27 January 1975). Undoubtedly, the NPA has suffered significant leadership losses, as in February 1975 when "Commander Rico" (Teofilo Valenzuela) was shot and killed. He had a $5,700 (40,000 peso) price on his head for having killed three U.S. Navy officers the previous April (ibid., 11 February). Something of the losses suffered by the NPA, as well as the size of its forces, may perhaps be gleaned from the announcement on 12 September by a Philippine military spokesman that for the one-year period ending 5 September 1975 a total of 162 NPA guerrillas had been killed in the Bicol Peninsula area alone. As a result NPA leadership in this area was said to be "fast dwindling" (ibid., 16 September).

While the NPA membership may be said to equal and overlap that of the CPP-ML the same does not apply to the National Army and the PKP. The role of the latter "army" has been very small, and reports of the mass surrender of "Communist rebel" followers of PKP secretary-general Macapagal are misleading as to the army's likely strength. Little certainty as to the PKP's size can be derived from such government announcements as the one, at the close of December 1974, that some 9,000 "PKP followers" had surrendered in recent months and taken advantage of the amnesty offer (ibid., 2 January 1975). Total PKP hard-core membership is probably between 1,200 and 1,500, and the army's core about 100. The population of the country is 42,845,000.

Domestic Developments. President Marcos on 5 May 1975 warned against the danger of massive infiltration from abroad "in support of any indigenous force seeking to overthrow the government," in a "new type of aggression" favored by "most predatory countries." Preparation for this type of aggression would be useless unless the people were "properly motivated." (*FBIS*, 7 May.) His warning sounded a persisting theme of Philippine officials on the danger of plots and subversion. On 1 September 1974 it was reported that Philippine authorities had uncovered an alleged Communist plot calling for the creation of a "national democratic front" uniting all anti-martial-law elements led by the Communist Party (wing not specified). The plotters included 38 "suspected Communist Party officers" and men recently arrested because of arms smuggling. (Ibid., 3 September.) A few days later security authorities disclosed that they had uncovered a well-established network for supplying insurgents with Chinese-made weapons. The 78 persons arrested were accused of smuggling arms and maintaining contact between "Maoist agents" in the Philippines and "their patrons in China." (Ibid., 6 September.)

In November Defense Secretary Enrile offered amnesty to the NPA and the CPP-ML; in the context of a similar recent offer to the PKP, adding that "only four members" of the CPP-ML's Politburo remained to be accounted for, including Sison, Jess Luneta, and two journalists, Antonio Zumel and Satur Ocampo. Also not yet accounted for were two top NPA commanders, "Commander Dante" (Bernabe Buscayno) and a former army lieutenant, Victor Corpuz. Although Corpuz, according to Enrile, was a "mere insignificant training officer," other reports have identified him as the main NPA commander, and have stressed Buscayno's reported differences with Sison's leadership). Enrile's attempt to downgrade the NPA found limited credence, in the light of continued Communist insurgent activity.

In December there was confirmation that some lower-ranking members of the Roman Catholic clergy, as the government has contended, had identified themselves formally or informally with the NPA. Virtually since the inception of the martial law regime, some leaders of the Roman Catholic church, including highly placed members of the church hierarchy, have criticized—sometimes quite severely—the regime's policies (Cirilo A. Rigos, "The Posture of the Church in the Philippines under Martial Law," in *Southeast Asian Affairs 1975*, Singapore, FEP International Ltd., 1975, pp. 127-32). On 23 December 1974, Enrile announced that Fathers E. La Tore and Manuel Lahoz had been arrested for "consorting" with leftist subversives. La Tore, according to the testimony of a CPP-ML official, had been active in that party's National Democratic Front, heading a committee for the participation of Christians in the NDF. (*FBIS*, 24 December 1974, 9 January 1975.)

In subsequent weeks, as the two priests went on a hunger strike in prison, to protest alleged tortures perpetrated on their co-detainees at Camp Olivas in Pampanga, a protest movement developed. The "Association of Major Religious Superiors in the Philippines" initiated a letter-writing campaign, and protest telegrams were sent to Marcos from opposition groups in Hong Kong, the United States, and Canada (*Ang Katipunan*, Oakland, Calif., April 1975, p. 4). Repeatedly, prominent Roman Catholic clergy had protested allegedly brutal treatment of martial-law prisoners in the past. During February 1975, members of other religious groups, among them the Iglesia ni Cristo, reportedly joined in the protest movement against martial law "repression." On 21 February some 5,000 persons, "utilizing the form of a religious rite," marched in Manila during the Lenten season, singing "revolutionary songs" and chanting "anti-dictatorship slogans." (Ibid.) By this time, Defense Secretary Enrile had ordered five military officers, including a lieutenant colonel, to stand trial on charges of torturing martial-law prisoners held in Camp Olivas (*FBIS*, 7 February). Earlier reports on torture of the prisoners, including subjecting them to addictive drugs "in order to break their minds," had brought little official reaction (*Amnesty International Newsletter*, September 1974, p. 2). Partisan accounts, however, popularized the issue (see, e.g., Concepcion Guila, "Detention Camp: Manila," *Bulletin of Concerned Asian Scholars*, November-December 1974, pp. 39-42). On 11 December 1974 Marcos ordered release of 622 of the 5,234 persons arrested since the martial-law declaration, in line with a new policy of "national reconciliation" which drew praise from the Archbishop of Manila (*NYT*, 12 December). In the context of the arrests of Fathers La Tore and Lahoz, the government announced subsequently that it had destroyed a CPP-ML "communications network" during the previous month in raids on underground party establishments in Manila and Baguio, arresting 30 "Communist figures." At the same time it announced the killing of NPA leader and CPP-ML Central Committee member "Commander Goody" (Segundo Miranda). (*FBIS*, 2, 6 January 1975.)

Despite opposition particularly in clerical, intellectual, and labor circles, the Marcos government continued to find substantial popular backing, especially in the more distant provinces, and saw its legitimacy repeatedly upheld in the courts. On 17 September 1974, for example, the Philippine Supreme Court, in a lengthy majority decision, said that Marcos had been justified in declaring martial law and that, in fact, a national emergency within the meaning of the Philippine Constitution existed at the time he did so (Rolando V. del Carmen, "Philippines 1974: A Holding Pattern-Power

Consolidation or Prelude to a Decline" *Asian Survey*, February 1975, pp. 136-47). On 28 February 1975 a nationwide referendum registered nearly 90 percent approval of the president's position and voted yes on the questions whether (a) he should continue to rule by degree and proclamation, and (b) voters approved of his previous rule by decree and proclamation. On a third question, voters overwhelmingly approved the appointment instead of election of local officials.

Still, significant, if scattered, pockets of resistance to Marcos remain, and Muslim rebels in Mindanao opened fire on Cotabato city in an attempt to drive away voters going to the polls (*FBIS*, 28 February). The Philippine press, experiencing a greater degree of freedom in recent months, has, with an obvious measure of popular approval, criticized the short-lived spirit of reform among government officials. In the words of one columnist:

> The most expensive places in town are patronized by government officials; the costliest couturiers cater to government officials' wives; the biggest diamonds are bought by government officials' mistresses; the most dazzling summer resorts are owned by government officials. (Kerima Polotan in *The Evening Post*, Manila, 8 July.)

The government's land reform program, though broadly conceded to be the most effective of a number of such programs undertaken in the past, has not escaped serious question from unbiased quarters. On the one hand, government sources have claimed that by mid-1975 283,163 certificates of land transfer had been issued to 199,906 farmers, covering a total of more than 350,000 hectares in 64 provinces (*Philippine Daily Express*, Manila, 9 July). On the other hand, some small landowners and renters, who could hardly be considered as legitimate targets of the land-tenure restriction laws, have protested the unrealistic limits on the size of holdings now set, and in the course of 1975, reportedly, an appeal to the government for a limit of 24 rather than the currently prescribed 7 hectares was "snowballing" among "thousands of small landowners in Central Luzon" (*Bulletin Today*, Manila, 10 July). Criticism from various quarters (e.g., Dennis Shoesmith, "Land Reform in the Philippines: Emancipating or Emaciating the Tenant Farmers" *Australian Outlook*, December 1974, pp. 274-89; "Philippine Land Reform—Trick or Treat" *Journal of Contemporary Asia*, vol. 4, 1974, no. 3, pp. 390-97) is likely to surround the entire land-reform program, however, opening possibly continuing tactical opportunties to both wings of the Communist party.

The government strenuously sought an accommodation with the Muslim secessionist movement in the Southern Philippines. Already in June 1974, as a total of 30,000 Philippine Constabulary and an additional 30,000 army troops were confronting the insurgents, a full amnesty had been offered to all Muslim rebels who would lay down their arms and surrender (Lim Yoon Lin, "Marcos' 'New Society,'" in *Southeast Asian Affairs 1975*, p. 119). In January 1975, through the auspices of a number of Muslim countries, Marcos began a new negotiating effort to end the rebellion (*NYT*, 11 January). Amid reports of continuing attacks by the secessionist Moro National Liberation Front (MNLF), of surrender and acceptance of amnesty by rebels, and of government counter-attacks and the retaking of towns held by the rebels, peace efforts continued, even though early in February the president publicly reported that his peace effort had failed. According to Marcos, MNLF leader Nur Misuari, formerly a university teacher and KM activist (Misuari's KM affiliation is one reason why the government has occasionally announced that a link exists between the NPA and the Muslim rebellion), wanted establishment of a separate "Moro" state, carved out of Mindanao, Basilan, and other southern islands. (*FBIS*, 3 February.) Reportedly, threatening to "wage a real war" if negotiations were unsuccessful, Marcos in mid-February requested Indonesian mediation, even though earlier negotiations in January with the rebels at Jeddah, Saudi Arabia, had failed. At the same time the government began beefing up its armed forces, a move perhaps designed to heal the reported rifts between Marcos and his military commanders who saw little point in the relatively low level of government counterattack strategy. (*The Economist*, London, 1 March.)

Government successes in a stepped up-army offensive were undercut again by new peace talks that started in Zamboanga on 17 April with some 190 Muslim rebel leaders attending. There were new surrenders of scores of Muslim insurgents (*FBIS*, 16, 28 May 1975) but by the end of June one informed source reported that the rebels were continuing effective attacks and in control of "much of the countryside" in the southern islands, while the well-organized MNLF, operating with a central committee, politburo, and intelligence service, and financially supplied by foreign Muslim governments (particularly Libya), continued to be in a position to purchase large quantities of modern arms, including American M-16 rifles and 105 mm. howitzers (*Far Eastern Economic Review*, Hong Kong, 27 June). On 14 August the government announced that MNLF rebels had accepted a ceasefire and that a spokesman for the front, Abdul Hamid Lukman, had called the Presidential Palace in Manila to announce acceptance (*NYT*, 15 August). Shortly thereafter, however, a segment of the MNLF forces led by Misuari declared that it would continue to fight, and on 19 August, in a dispatch from Tripoli, Misuari (described as "chairman of the Central Committee" of the MNLF) denied that a ceasefire had been worked out (*FBIS*, 26 August). By early September, despite the government's announcement that a large measure of autonomy, including application of Muslim law where appropriate, would be provided to the Muslim communities, MNLF resistance was clearly continuing.

Unlike the previous year, there was no evidence of extensive NPA tactical collaboration with the MNLF which had included joint attacks on government facilities and towns. Early in September 1975, however, the state-owned Philippines News Agency reported that four Maoist guerrillas had been killed and an undetermined number wounded in a clash with police and "home defense" guards in Zamboanga del Sur Province. According to a military source, these NPA insurgents had been attempting to recruit followers in the area (*FBIS*, 5 September).

While NPA involvement in the Muslim rebellion of the southern Philippine islands must be considered minimal, this is not to say that on its own the NPA has not sought to obtain a stronger foothold in the region. Since June 1975, particularly in southern Mindanao, NPA units, first having developed an infrastructure of support in some villages, have become active, resorting to the assassination of local government officials and military. Also in northern and northeastern Mindanao, especially around the town of Gingoog in Misamis Oriental Province, NPA influence is penetrating. It has been speculated that the NPA has begun to establish base areas for its operations here. (Bernard Wideman, "Stepping Up Terror in Mindanao," *Far Eastern Economic Review*, 10 October, p. 16). Because of the tendency of Philippine government sources to magnify the NPA threat, caution must be particularly exercised in assessing NPA influence in the South.

Both the CPP-ML and the PKP, in their respective programs, have promised a large measure of autonomy to the southern Muslim community, but both Communist parties also oppose at this time any formal secession of the South or the formation of an independent Moro republic.

Relations with Communist Countries. On 21 September 1974, the second anniversary of the nationwide martial law declaration, President Marcos said that in line with a "development-motivated policy," and taking into account "changes in the international order," the Philippines (after establishing diplomatic relations with Yugoslavia and Romania in 1973) had opened diplomatic relations with East Germany, Bulgaria, Hungary, Poland, Czechoslovakia, Romania, and the People's Republic of Mongolia, and would be "expanding trade, cultural and diplomatic relations with more socialist countries in the coming months" ("Report to the Nation," *Philippine Geographical Journal*, special issue, January-March 1975, pp. 33-34). In an announcement of five new Philippine foreign policy "guidelines," Marcos ranked "more vigorous" pursuit of diplomatic relations with "socialist states, in particular with the People's Republic of China and with the Soviet Union" as second (naming regional cooperation with the Association of Southeast Asian Nations [ASEAN] as first), while finding a "new basis" for relations with the United States was mentioned last (*Far Eastern Economic Review*, 13 June).

Certainly, the warming trend in relations with People's China was accompanied by much official Philippine publicity. On 20 September 1974 Mrs. Imelda Marcos, the President's wife, and his son, Ferdinand Marcos, Jr., arrived in Peking, where they were subsequently received by party chief Mao Tse-tung. Mrs. Marcos, upon the invitation of Mme Chiang Ch'ing, Mao's wife, extended her stay, a sign widely interpreted as heralding a state of particular cordiality. On 7 June 1975 Marcos, accompanied by his wife, also visited Peking, to establish formal diplomatic ties between the two countries. Reportedly Mao assured Marcos that People's China would seek neither to overthrow nor to exploit the Philippines, saying, "We are one family now" (*NYT*, 8 June). Marcos reportedly declared: "All subtle forms of foreign intervention must disappear in the new era dawning in Asia." On 9 June a seven-point joint communiqué was issued, signed by Marcos and Chinese premier Chou En-lai. Simultaneously with the issuance of the communiqué the Philippine government announced termination of "all existing official relations between the Philippines and Taiwan." The Chou-Marcos communiqué, among others, noted that differences in political, economic, and social systems between the two countries should not be a stumbling block to peaceful coexistence and the development of friendly relations on the basis of "mutual respect for sovereignty and territorial integrity, mutual non-aggression, non-interference in each other's internal affairs, equality, and mutual benefit." With what appeared to be a slap in the direction of the USSR, the communiqué also condemned "any attempt by any country" or by any group of nations to "establish hegemony or to create spheres of influence" anywhere on the globe. (*Peking Review*, 13 June, pp. 7-8.)

Paradoxes during and after Marcos' trip to Peking were duly noted in the press. For example, given the frequently tense and acrimonious historic relationship between the Chinese minority in the Philippines and the Philippine government, "there was deep irony" for Filipino Chinese in Marcos's words at a Peking banquet about the bridges that had always existed between the Philippine and Chinese peoples (*Far Eastern Economic Review*, 20 June, p. 15). And upon his return from the Chinese capital, Marcos promptly announced that new relations with the Chinese government would not be permitted to "prejudice any relations existing on mutual trust with other nations." "We opened our windows to the Socialist world," Marcos said, "but we do not close those windows to our friends and allies." (*NYT*, 12 June.) Trade relations between China and the Philippines are expected to improve rapidly as a result of Marcos's Peking visit. Already in September 1974 China had announced readiness to ship to the Philippines some 62,500 tons of crude oil a month, and to keep doing so throughout 1975, thus meeting an estimated 8 percent of the country's oil needs for the year. In April 1975 the Marcos government approved exports of three major products (copper concentrates, crude coconut oil, and sawn logs and plywood) to China in a total value of $4.45 million (*FBIS*, 11 April).

Philippine officials have let it be known that China now looks favorably on Southeast Asian regionalism. On 8 August, Philippine foreign secretary Carlos Romulo said that People's China had given full support to the ASEAN proposal of making Southeast Asia into a zone of "peace, freedom, and neutrality" (ibid., 11 August). Skepticism remains, however, that despite the Marcos visit to Peking, Sino-Philippine relations will improve rapidly. Relations between the two countries have been marred by suspicion and hostility for many decades (Hsiao Shi-ching, *Chinese-Philippine Diplomatic Relations 1946-1975*, Quezon City, Bookman Printing House, 1975). Moreover, the position of the Chinese in Philippine society has often been difficult and is likely to continue to cause friction between Manila and Peking. There are about 120,000 officially registered Chinese in the Philippines, but unofficial estimates go as high as 600,000. Most of these Chinese are said to be sympathetic to the Republic of China on Taiwan. The recognition of the Peking government has created a major rift in the ranks of the Sino-Philippine community, splitting the powerful Chinese Trade Federation in the Philippines (a major business interest bloc composed of Philippine Chinese) into hostile factions (*South China Morning Post*, Hong Kong, 24 June). Few Chinese have availed themselves of recent government regulations facilitating the Filipinization of their names. In June it was disclosed in the Manila press that some Chinese had entered into fraudulent marriage relations with Filipino women, apparently for business reasons or else to ensure their residence permit in the country, but that no documents of the marriage ceremonies were ever filed in church parish or government archives (ibid.).

The CPP-ML, like the pro-Chinese Malayan Communist organization last year, issued a long statement on the impending diplomatic recognition of People's China, apparently designed to eliminate any expectation that the Philippine Maoists would cease their opposition to the Marcos regime. The CPP-ML statement, broadcast over the "Voice of the Malayan Revolution" on 17 April, portrayed Marcos as not really wanting to make the trip to China, and speculated that he was compelled by the "political and economic crises" in his country to do so, and that the United States was willing (in accordance with the logic of U.S. President Nixon's visit to China) for him to go. The CPP-ML statement also asserted that the Marcos regime remained a "puppet state of U.S. imperialism," that the establishment of Sino-Philippine relations was "the final and fatal blow to SEATO," and that, by developing its relations with the Philippines, People's China had countered the schemes of and acquired a balance to offset the influence of "U.S. imperialism" and "Soviet social imperialism" in Southeast Asia (*FBIS*, 30 April). It seems apparent that the CPP-ML, like the Malaysian Communist party, expects to keep at least the moral support of Peking in its guerrilla struggle.

Philippine relations with the USSR appear to be developing more slowly and hesitantly. On 29 December 1974 Marcos told a visiting three-man Soviet delegation that he strongly supported "wider cultural cooperation" with the USSR, and the following day a Soviet-Philippine cultural agreement was signed in Manila which provides for exchanges of scholars, tourists, and sports groups. Festivals, symposiums, lectures, and exhibitions are also scheduled to be held under the agreement (ibid., 30 December). Amid increasing speculation that formal Soviet-Philippine diplomatic ties would be forged in the course of 1975 it was first announced that Marcos would visit Moscow at the end of August for that purpose, but on 18 August it was announced in Manila, without explanation, that Marcos would not be making his Soviet trip at the end of the month. Despite this postponement, plans for the signing of a trade agreement were reportedly going forward. (Ibid., 19 August.)

A Soviet shipping executive, Valery V. Makorov, told a gathering of businessmen in Manila on 27 June that the USSR was particularly interested in importing copra and coconut oil, but was unable to do so as yet because of the "lack of formal relations" (*Guardian*, Rangoon, 29 June). Soviet comment on the regime has been qualifiedly approving, alternatingly commending Marcos for his agrarian reforms and painting a bleak picture of the Philippine economy generally (*World Affairs Report*, Stanford, 4, no. 3, 1974: 265; 5, no. 2, 1975: 201). There have also been repeated Soviet attacks on what is called the "splinter and adventurist" groups deriving their inspiration from Mao Tse-tung, which "stooped to terrorism" and allegedly discredited the "progressive forces" in the Philippines by their general "subversive" activities (*FBIS*, 10 March, and 18 June 1975).

Communist ascendancy in South Vietnam, Cambodia, and Laos during the first half of 1975 led to official Philippine announcements of the need to "re-assess" Philippine foreign policy, particularly (as Marcos put it on 16 April 1975) because the U.S. Congress refused to extend further aid to Indochina, thereby indicating, according to the Philippine president, that Southeast Asia was "no longer an area of vital interest" to the United States (ibid., 16, 18 April). On 25 June, Marcos offered support for membership of Communist South Vietnam and Communist Cambodia in ASEAN, adding: "In our response to the changing setting of Southeast Asia we look not merely toward our arms in maintaining our security, but to the benefits that neutrality and regional solidarity can offer" (*The Nation*, Bangkok, 26 June). On 20 April the Philippine government announced that it was "broadening" its contacts with North Vietnam, apparently as a step toward diplomatic relations. "Developments in Indochina" urgently required formation of a "direct communications line to Hanoi," Marcos said (*FBIS*, 21 April).

Meanwhile the Philippines has been refurbishing its image as an ally of the United States. On 6 July, Marcos said that his government wished full control of remaining U.S. bases in the Philippines, thus ending the "practice of extra-territoriality" in the country (*Philippines Evening Express*, 7 July). For more than a year negotiations have been going forward to redefine commercial and investment relationships (Astri Suhrke, "U.S.-Philippines: The End of a Special Relationship," *The World Today*, London, February 1975, pp. 80-88), although anti-Marcos Philippine sources, including some Philippine residents in the United States, stress that so long as martial law prevails special privileges are likely to remain in effect for American businesses in the Philippines (*The Philippines: Martial Law Protects U.S. Business Interests*. San Francisco, National Committee for the Restoration of Civil Liberties in the Philippines, n.d.). Anti-Marcos sentiment, though often disorganized, remains an influential factor among expatriate Filipinos, especially in the United States (*YICA, 1975*, p. 408). Pro-Marcos sympathizers in the U.S. organized the "Magdalo II June 22 Movement" in Pittsburg, California, on 22 June 1975, its founding resolution condemning the efforts of anti-Marcos organizations like the "Movement for a Free Philippines" (MFP) and the NPA's sympathizing Katipunan ng mga Demokratikong Pilipino (KDP) or "Movement for a Democratic Philippines" to halt U.S. aid to the Marcos government (*Ang Katipunan*, July, p. 5). On 19 November 1974, only a few hours after a distraught expatriate had seized the Philippine ambassador in Washington at gunpoint, Marcos announced an amnesty to Philippine political offenders living abroad and a liberalization of foreign travel by Filipinos (*FBIS*, 19 November).

Efforts to widen further the range of Philippine diplomatic relations with the Communist world have continued. On 23 August 1975 the government announced that during a forthcoming visit of Mrs. Imelda Marcos to Havana diplomatic relations between the Philippines and Cuba, broken for fourteen years, would be reestablished. The impending rapprochement was considered especially important because both Cuba and the Philippines are among the world's principal producers of sugar. (Ibid., 25 August.)

Publications. *Ang Bayan* ("The Nation"), appearing in both English and Tagalog, is the principal organ of the CPP-ML. Excerpts from its articles, or other statements by the Maoist wing of Philippine Communism, have appeared much less frequently in *Peking Review* and other People's Chinese media than was the case three years ago. *Indonesian Tribune*, the organ of the Indonesian Maoist Communist party (see *Indonesia*), and the "Voice of the Malayan Revolution" radio, principal sounding-board of the Communist Party of Malaya (see *Malaysia*), regularly have relayed CPP-ML statements. As in preceding years, the PKP's principal publication *Ang Kommunista* ("The Communist") appeared infrequently, the party relying principally on stenciled leaflets and instructional booklets. PKP statements occasionally appear in *World Marxist Review* and *Information Bulletin* (Prague). NPA victories occasionally are briefly reported by the New China News Agency.

University of Bridgeport   Justus M. van der Kroef

Singapore

There is no formal, distinctive Singapore Communist party, but the Barisan Sosialis Malaya (Malayan Socialist Front), usually called Barisan Sosialis or just Barisan, is the main legal front organization for Singapore Communists. Neither Malaysian nor Singapore Communists, nor a number of sympathizing non-Communist Leftists in both Malaysia and Singapore, regard the formation of Malaysia (composed of the states on the Malay Peninsula, Singapore, and the Borneo territories of Sarawak and Sabah) in 1963, and the subsequent secession of Singapore from Malaysia in 1965, as having occurred in a legal and democratic way. Technically, therefore, the underground Communist Party of Malaya (CPM), which since the late 1950s has favored a merger of Malaya proper and Singapore (permitting Sarawak and Sabah to seek their own independence), has functioned as the official party home for Singapore Communists.

The splits within the CPM (see *Malaysia*), as well as a movement among some (by no means all) Singapore Communists today to develop their own party attuned to the island state's particular political realities, has tended to make CPM affiliation a mere formality although the Barisan, like the CPM, regards the formation of Malaysia and secession of Singapore as having been unlawful and hence also persists in urging a Malaya-Singapore merger. There has been little or no evidence of direction of Singapore Communists by any CPM faction for many years. According to the Singapore government, a number of local Communists claim affiliation with the Malayan National Liberation Army (MNLA) (*YICA, 1975*, p. 417) for purposes of small-scale protest and embryo urban guerrilla activities within Singapore. It is not known, however, whether such claimed affiliation has in fact the sanction of the MNLA in the Malay Peninsula itself.

In 1975 the Barisan Sosialis, as during much of the past decade, beset by strict government supervision, internal leadership squabbles, and small membership, was capable of only very limited overt activity. In recent years Barisan spokesmen, in conversation with the author, have consistently blamed "repression" by Singapore's government—dominated by the People's Action Party (PAP)—for the Barisan's small numbers, for membership defection through intimidation, and for the party's inability to publish its papers. Government spokesmen put the Barisan's ineffectiveness in the context of the Singapore electorate's general aversion to "Communism," although Leftist, if non-Communist, opposition to the government remains not inconsiderable, especially among students and other young people (from 15 to 20 percent of the Singapore electorate may be considered as politically opposed to the PAP government).

The Barisan, in any case, has little attraction for non-Communist Singapore Leftist and other opposition circles, partly because of a lack of confidence in the leadership of the Barisan's fifty-seven-year-old chairman, Dr. Lee Siew Choh, in the party's Maoist-flavored, CPM-oriented general program (the view that the party is not really indigenous but merely Peking's cat's paw is widespread), or in the party's specific action demands. The latter, which frequently seek to stress the alleged plight of workers because of high taxes and because of government pressure to keep wages down (*YICA, 1974*, p. 416) have had some, but not overwhelming support in Singapore's occasionally troubled but generally flourishing economy. (Between 1967 and 1970, according to a Singapore

Finance Ministry spokesman, real Gross Domestic Product grew to 14 percent per year, as compared to 7 percent in previous years, while for 1976 the GDP increase is targeted at 10 percent and for the period 1977-80 at 13 percent a year, so that even significant shortages of labor must be anticipated. (*Straits Times*, Singapore, 6 July 1975.) There has been majority popular backing for the government's policy of creating a political environment conducive as much as possible to massive foreign investment. Between 1965 and 1971 foreign investment in Singapore increased ten times (from about $62 million to more than $620 million) (Seah Chee Meow, "Singapore in 1974: Consolidation amidst Uncertainties," in *Southeast Asian Affairs 1975*, Institute of Southeast Asian Studies, Singapore, 1975, p. 141).

In keeping with the racial composition of Singapore, and like the Communist movement in Malaysia, most Communists in Singapore are ethnic Chinese. (Of Singapore's 2.25 million inhabitants, 76 percent are Chinese, 15 percent Malays, and about 8 percent Indians and Pakistanis.) Since the first appearance of organized Communism in Singapore during the early 1920s, trade unions and the Chinese secondary schools have served as fronts, agitational channels, and recruiting grounds. During the 1950s and early 60s Communist-directed or -inspired labor unrest, street demonstrations, strikes, and general confrontations with the government reached a new high, and Nanyang University in Singapore, according to the Malaysian and Singapore governments, became a particularly significant source of Communist activity (see the Malaysian government's white paper, *Communism in the Nanyang University*, Kuala Lumpur, 1964). In the past decade, however, strict government control over both trade unions and the school system, as well as public life generally, have reduced the Communist potential to the vanishing point.

Organization and Tactics. Since its establishment on 26 July 1961 by dissident radicals and underground Communists in the dominant People's Action Party (PAP), the Barisan Sosialis Malaya has been the only above-ground and legal party through which Singapore Communists have been able to articulate their views. The Barisan has participated in all local and general elections. But, in part because of internal party dissension resulting from calls from a few leaders for a boycott of all parliamentary and constitutional activity, and in part because of the effects of a PAP-dominated political environment in which, in effect, any partisan political rhetoric or other action can become the basis for a charge of incitement to violence, of defamation of character, or other claimed statutory transgression, the Barisan (or for that matter any other Communist front group, or indeed any other opposition party) has little room for political maneuvering.

The expectation among some leading Barisan activists that the government's alleged "obsession" with preserving political stability so as to be able to draw a steady flow of foreign capital needed for sustained growth will sooner or later be repudiated by a more democratically oriented electorate is, at least in the near future, unlikely to be realized. Moreover, while the demand from the Barisan, as well as from student circles and other non-government parties, for a more liberal political atmosphere has some popular appeal, the Barisan, because of its Communist complexion, has not been able to unify and lead the fragmented opposition to the policies of Premier Lee Kuan Yew's regime. The call in the Barisan's general program for a "democratic" and "socialist" state composed of a merger of Malaya and Singapore, for controls over if not elimination of the foreign multinational corporations, and for a closer relationship with the "Socialist countries," presumably including People's China, all represent so many risky policy experiments to Singapore voters that they are likely to continue to be repudiated, even if they should be advocated by non-Communist quarters.

Lee Siew Choh's report to the Barisan's third party congress, in August 1969, continues to be distributed at party headquarters; it remains essentially the party's general line at present, as Barisan spokesmen have indicated to the author. In this report Lee Kuan Yew is excoriated as an American imperialist puppet, and the creation of Malaysia and Singapore as separate states is viewed as but reflecting the designs of British and U.S. imperialism which is engulfing the economies of both Malaysia and Singapore; Soviet "revisionism," moreover, is said to have aided these imperialistic designs. Both Malaysia and Singapore are complete "police states" the report asserts. On the other hand, the international situation is considered much more promising, particularly in Southeast Asia, where "the masses, fighting for their liberation," are scoring significant gains (as, e.g., in Vietnam). Lee's report notes the collaboration between the proletariat and the students in these popular liberation struggles, and predicts that these groups, along with peasants and petty bourgeoisie, will form united fronts in their anti-imperialist efforts. This united front also provides the basis for a single political party seeking to achieve national democracy in a unitary, multinational state. This party, according to Lee's report, will also assist in the "struggle for democracy" in neighboring countries like Burma, Thailand, Indonesia, and North Borneo, and would ally itself with People's China to halt the inroads of Soviet revisionism and "U.S. imperialism." (*Chairman Lee Siew Choh's Report to the Third Congress of Party Representatives*, Frontline Publishing Committee, 1970, esp. pp. 1-3, 7-10, 53, 59, 72-82.)

On 21 December 1974 five minor opposition parties—the Singapore Malays Organization, the Singapore Chinese Party, the United Malays National Organization of Singapore, the Singapore Justice Party, and the United National Front—decided to form a united front block in order to contest the PAP in future elections. The Barisan is not a member of the united front (reportedly it was neither asked to join, nor had it requested to do so), although the new front's program calls for Singapore's "close relationship" with and its eventual rejoining of Malaysia, as well as for a government based on "socialism, democracy and justice" (*FBIS*, 23 December 1974, p. 64).

Today, the Barisan's own structure of, at one time, extensive satellite organizations has virtually crumbled. Among these were now inactive or dissolved groups like the Partai (or Party) Rakyat (People's Party), founded in 1956 and appealing also to the radical Malay element in the trade unions, and the more moderate "People's Front," active primarily during 1971-72. As in previous decades, the Barisan's and the Singapore CPM's mainstay are a number of smaller trade unions of service and clerical workers, shop assistants and street hawkers, long at odds with the dominant National Trade Union Congress which the Barisan considers to have "sold out" to foreign business interests because of its policy of maintaining stability in labor relations and of only urging moderate wage demands. Additionally, the Barisan continues to find support among a few scores of militants in the Chinese schools and among journalists and a few other younger professionals. The Industrial Workers Union (IWU) has perhaps been the chief trade union supporter of the Barisan, but during 1974-75 the party lost ground here. Although in the last Singapore parliamentary elections, in September 1972, parties opposing the PAP government won nearly 20 percent of the total votes cast (the Barisan won 4.5 percent), no opposition candidate led in any constituency and hence all 65 seats at stake in the election went to the PAP. The significance of the anti-PAP vote, however, is attenuated by the division among the opposition splinter parties, and the Barisan, largely because of its Communist aura, has been unable to serve as a significant anti-government popular rallying point.

Malay radicals and younger Chinese professionals and Chinese students from the secondary schools and Nanyang University, who once provided either membership depth or much of the agitational dynamism to the Barisan, today appear more interested in finding a modus vivendi with the PAP or a non-Communist left-wing alternative, although opposition to the allegedly "repressive" policies of the Lee Kuan Yew government was particularly notable in Singapore student circles during the first months of 1975. In the past two years Barisan spokesmen have consistently claimed to the author that their party has about 6,000 members, but non-party observers in Singapore generally believe that less than a tenth that figure would be a more accurate estimate. The hard Barisan cadre core operating throughout the island republic today amounts to about thirty, and the very modest third-floor party headquarters in one of the older and less affluent sections of the city (although in keeping with its "proletarian" image) does not suggest a flourishing organization.

Though there is nominally a Central Executive Committee (CEC), the party's principal founder and present chairman, Dr. Lee Siew Choh, trained as a physician, wholly dominates the Barisan leadership. The actual role of other party officers (e.g., vice-chairman Chen Kiong and treasurer Tai Chen Kang), or of the CEC generally, is a matter of controversy and speculation in the light of reported periodic moves by younger Barisan and IWU activists to oust Lee and his chief lieutenants. A glimpse of the Barisan's internal difficulties was offered by the public appeal of Dr. Lee Siew Choh, early in July 1975, to all "old members" of the party who would be prepared to uphold its program and policies to "re-register" themselves at party headquarters. An appeal was also made to "newcomers." The Barisan Sosialis was being reorganized, Lee went on, so that it might again develop and carry on its work under "extremely difficult circumstances." (*Straits Times*, 4 July.) According to Lee, the re-registration drive was being held in part because "many old members" had changed their addresses and had "lost contact with the party for some time." Those old party members who wished to return, he said further, would be accepted "according to the circumstances of each application." Reportedly this campaign netted the Barisan no more than a score of old members and newcomers, even though Lee had warned those those who failed to re-register within a specified period would be "deemed to have relinquished their membership." (Ibid.)

The Barisan's declining membership and internal leadership squabbles (particularly the conflict between chairman Lee and young IWU activists who favor a less overtly radical, less CPM-oriented policy, designed to win support from among the non-Communist Left and liberal critics of the Lee Kuan Yew government) obscure the possibly improving long-term tactical prospects of the party, according to some observers. The government has been notably unenthusiastic about the trend among some of its Southeast Asian neighbors to rush into diplomatic relations with People's China, and the aftermath of the Communist ascendancy in Indochina is viewed with considerable apprehension in the PAP leadership. Yet is is realized that eventually some kind of diplomatic rapprochement with Peking is inevitable and that, despite Lee Kuan Yew's frequent call for a continuing and significant U.S. strategic presence in Southeast Asia, the influence of the Communist powers (the USSR, People's China, and the Hanoi-dominated Indochina states) is likely to increase in the region. Though known to be Peking-oriented and given in its official publications to following the Chinese megaphone of denunciations of Soviet "social imperialism" and "revisionism," the Barisan, being the *only* party sympathetic to and generally reflective of the policies and aspirations of Communists in the area, can hardly at present be ignored by any of the Communist states. The accelerating diplomatic accommodation of Peking in the region, coupled with significant, persistent, though by no means majority electorate opposition to the Lee Kuan Yew government's extensive application of its police and surveillance powers over the press, all public gatherings, and indeed over all political activity, forms a dynamic which probably cannot but redound to the advantage of the Barisan in the long run.

In conversations with the author over the years some Barisan spokesmen have insisted that the political polarization of opinion in the island republic caused by the PAP government's policies is (and will be even more so over time) the Barisan's principal asset, and that in serving as a catalyst of this polarization the Barisan's future is brighter than may now appear. It is precisely here, however, that differences appear to exist between Barisan chairman Lee and some younger cadres. The latter reportedly assert that in assisting in polarizing and mobilizing public opinion against the Lee Kuan Yew government the Barisan, because of its close hewing to the CPM line, has been unable to capture leadership of the Singapore opposition Left (the premier and his PAP associates still call themselves Socialists) and so is not reaping any benefits from its confrontations with the government. By stressing a more "indigenous," Singapore-oriented image and the adaptability of its radical ideology to local conditions, these younger critics of Lee Siew Choh assert, the Barisan might become more attractive to the other Left opposition groups and at the same time loosen the straitjacket on party operations imposed by the government.

The Lee leadership faction, on the other hand, regards the Barisan's orientation on the Communist Movement in Malaya, in the context of a "merger" of Singapore and Malaya, as a non-negotiable party policy priority and, rightly or wrongly, regards such an orientation as also reflecting People's China's policy preference for the region. The view that the Barisan under Lee Siew Choh remains essentially a vehicle for Peking's long-term interest is held widely among young Singapore Chinese Leftists who, otherwise, and also but for Lee Siew Choh's heavy leadership hand, would have remained within the Barisan's orbit. On the other hand, Lee Siew Choh has on occasion been criticized as too "compromise"-minded and, indeed, as not aggressive enough. The suspicion that there are Barisan militants who believe that, in keeping with the thought of more militant CPM elements, the time is ripe for "urban guerrilla warfare" both in Singapore and the Malayan towns has reportedly made Lee Siew Choh's position even more difficult in the past two years. Still, there is no prospect that any faction in the party will succeed in replacing him in the near future.

The severe restrictions on party operations imposed by the government—so that, except to a limited degree at election time, communication with the electorate through meetings, demonstrations, or the media is extremely difficult—have had their intended demoralizing effect on the Barisan rank and file. Barisan contact spokesmen in the island republic's separate constituencies are increasingly fewer, party congresses and CEC plenary meetings continue to be postponed, and there is less and less opportunity to articulate the party's general program line of the need for a "prosperous and socialist Singapore" as a part of a "genuinely independent and unified Malaya." During 1974-75 an occasional Barisan mimeographed release attacked (1) the policies of the National Wages Council in Singapore, which was accused of unjustly resisting workers' demands for wage increases, and (2) the Employment Act and Industrial Relations Amended Act, which was said to prevent workers from taking "industrial action" (i.e., strikes) to improve working conditions. "Big monopolies" which "squeeze huge profits from the people" remained a favorite target. Party spokesmen interpreting the future of the region after the U.S. debacle in Indochina were wont to stress that the multinational corporations are the vehicles of a covert "U.S. neo-colonialism and imperialism" throughout Southeast Asia, and that the Lee Kuan Yew government, in urging the United States to continue to play a role in the region was, in fact, turning Singapore into the area's main "neo-colonial" base.

While some allegedly Barisan-inspired student activists at the University of Singapore have occasionally taken up the cause of workers abruptly dismissed by some foreign corporations in the wake of the recent economic recession, the continuing relative prosperity does not, among other factors, provide much of a basis for an effective student-worker alliance. Singaporeans today are on the whole better educated and have more income than ever before. According to the Media Index surveys, conducted by Survey Research Singapore, 17 percent of all adult males in 1971 had jobs paying more than $3,600 per year, and by 1974 the proportion had risen to 28 percent. In 1974, 15 percent of all adults in Singapore lived in families with a total annual income of more than $12,000 per year. Women's literacy rose from 50 percent in 1971 to 66 percent in 1974 (the male rate in 1974 was 92 percent), with 95 percent literate among women in the age group between 15 and 20 years. Also in 1974, 32 percent of all women, and 51 percent of all men who were 15 or older had received at least a secondary education (*Asian Student*, San Francisco, 18 January 1975).

During 1975, unlike the previous year, there were no incidents of violence attributed to the Malayan National Liberation Army. The relationship of this terrorist underground group with Singapore Communism, or with the various factions in which the CPM now is divided (see *Malaysia*), remains obscure. However, the political repercussions of the arrests by the Singapore government in mid-1974 of 30 persons, some described as MNLA members, have continued. A number of those arrested (among them a lawyer, journalists, mechanics, construction workers, and students) were alleged to have ties with the Barisan. Protests by the University of Singapore Students' Union and the Singapore Polytechnic Students' Union that the arrests were "a blatant violation of basic democratic principles," and allegations of torture of the arrested made by the wife of one of them, who went on to denounce the "fascist PAP regime" (*Journal of Contemporary Asia*, 4, no. 3, 1974: 370-72, and no. 4: 564-66), aided in providing an impetus to the outburst of student protest in December 1974 (see below). No long-term significance for Barisan tactics can be attached, however, to the new upsurge of student protest. For it was not the alleged Barisan affiliation of some of the mid-1974 arrestees, but rather the government's constant readiness to apply its extensive police powers, including preventive arrests, and its alleged insensitivity to workers' rights, that sparked the student protest movement at the close of 1974.

Domestic Developments. After the June 1974 arrests, relations between the Lee Kuan Yew government and a minority of the Singapore University student body rapidly deteriorated. This was a relatively surprising development since for the better part of the past decade students at the Nanyang and Singapore universities and at other institutions of higher education in the island republic had been politically rather quiescent and had given the government little difficulty. During the latter half of 1974 the economic downturn in Singapore meant the unemployment of an additional 18,000 workers in industries ranging from textiles and electronics to construction and pleasure-boat building. The president of the University of Singapore Students' Union (USSU), Tan Wah Piow, was instrumental in establishing an unemployment relief center on the university campus, taking over a building in order to do so. Tan reportedly also told incoming university students "to do what the students of Thailand have already done" (in October 1973, Thai student demonstrations were the major cause of the overthrow of the Thanom Kittikachorn government in Bangkok). A USSU periodical, *Awakening*, began attacking the labor policies of the government and the pronouncements of the president of Singapore's largest labor federation, the National Trade Union Congress (NTUC), Devan Nair, who had urged unions to exercise self-restraint in wage demands during the economic recession period. Nair's appeal very much reflected Singapore government policy. *Awakening* charged, however, that workers' real wages were dropping sharply because of the 23 percent price jump. (Denzil Peiris, "Identifying Outside Subversion," *Far Eastern Economic Review*, Hong Kong, 3 January 1975, p. 10; *Intercontinental Press*, New York, 24 February, p. 247.)

The Singapore government retaliated swiftly. Tan, after a demonstration at a trade union office, was charged with criminal trespass and rioting; he and two Malaysian workers were brought to trial on 11 December 1974. On the same day six University of Singapore students (one from Hong Kong, the others from Malaysia) were ordered to leave the island republic, the government contending that these students, in violation of pledges given at the time they accepted scholarships, had engaged in political activity. As student publications and leaders meanwhile sought to whip up a radical temper on the university campus, a two-day boycott of classes occurred there (17-18 December) in protest against the dismissals of the six students. During the boycott, scores of university students, in an effort to further their solidarity with workers, went to workers' housing projects in order to engage in discussions of their protest. Meanwhile, students at Nanyang University—which, in contrast with previous years, had not become involved in the anti-government agitation this time—collected funds for families of workers who had perished in a recent ship explosion outside Singapore harbor. Government troops and police, though alerted, did not interfere in the boycott, which, it was soon apparent, only a few hundred students actively supported. (Peiris, op. cit.)

The government chose to use the boycott incident and the student restiveness generally for extended analysis of the nature of what its spokesmen called the "New Left" subversive threat. The foreign minister, S. Rajaratnam, in an address to a seminar on "Trends in Singapore," sponsored by the quasi-official Institute of Southeast Asian Studies, at the University of Singapore, dealt with the question of "non-Communist" or "New Left" subversion in the island state. This subversion, he said, though as yet amorphous and not even specifically indigenous to Singapore, nevertheless had already formulated a three-pronged attack on the Lee Kuan Yew government: (1) Singapore, because of its one-party, PAP-dominated government is rapidly turning into a dictatorship where arbitrary arrests prevail and fear stalks everywhere; (2) an independent Singapore is not economically, politically, or militarily viable, and, hence, a merger of Singapore with Malaya is necessary; and (3) the racial minorities in Singapore, particularly the Malays are suppressed, and the solution here lies in the creation of several communal (i.e., racial or ethnic) parties that can be brought together in an alliance, rather than in the formation of multiracial-membership parties like the PAP. According to Rajaratnam, much of the agitation against Singapore was inspired from abroad. For instance, the picture of Singapore as an incipient dictatorship had since 1970 been propagated by the press in the United Kingdom, Hong Kong, Australia, and the United States. On another occasion Rajaratnam had already named such publications as *The Guardian* and *The Times* in London, the *Far Eastern Economic Review*, and the U.S. periodical *Newsweek* and the *New York Times* as among those engaged in a "tortuous and consistent campaign" against the idea of an independent Singapore. (*Asia Research Bulletin*, Political Supplement, 31 December 1974, p. 38.)

Rajaratnam, in the same address, particularly criticized the Western press for its coverage of the PAP parliamentary election victories in 1968 and 1972, alleging that more attention was paid to the votes won by the opposition parties than to those won by the PAP. He also alleged the existence of a design framed by unnamed sources to establish a "mass-media network in Southeast Asia" which would support parliamentary opposition groups with a view to keeping the governments of the region, including Singapore's in check. According to the Singapore foreign minister, a prototypical "New Left" for Southeast Asia had begun to appear in Hong Kong, where an Asian Students Seminar, in March 1974, had developed a common "New Left" action program. Hong Kong "New Left" activists were making contact with revolutionary groups in Europe and South America as well as Asian countries, Rajaratnam said. (Ibid.)

In an interview at about the same time, Rajaratnam called attention also to the identification of Christian radical elements, including students and clergy, with this "New Left." He expressed concern that the Communists would exploit the instability and discontent created by student agitation; by themselves, he believed, the students were "manageable" and not a danger to the state. (Peiris, op. cit., pp. 10-11.)

While the government during 1975 forbore to take extensive or precipitate action against student dissidents, it made it plain that it would not tolerate further expressions of organized opposition. On 23 December 1974 the Singapore home affairs minister, Chua Sian Chin, replied to a letter from the University of Singapore Students' Union, which had protested the expulsion of six student leaders, noted above. Declaring that the six had deliberately challenged the authority of the government and knew the risk they were running, Chua charged that the USSU had been "converted into a political machine struggling for power," and that the expelled students shared responsibility for this. In support of his contention, Chua cited excerpts from an article in the December issue of the Singapore student periodical *Pelandok*. The excerpts noted the relative lack of success in the students' past struggle against "bureaucratic and bourgeois injustice and exploitation" and urged students to a "real commitment" and acceptance of "ultimate consequences" as a result of their actions. Poverty and persecution would be the logical consequences for those engaged in a "total struggle" against the existing "bourgeois capitalist system," the excerpts said. According to Chua, ever since the present USSU leadership had taken over there had been much internal conflict in the organization, as student officers of the USSU were attempting to "convert the campus into a sanctuary" where student power could be mobilized free from government or even the university administration's control. (*FBIS*, 24 December.)

The Singapore press, on critical public issues usually in accord with government policy, also reflected government views this time. On the subject of the recent student agitation the *Straits Times*, the leading English daily, editorialized on 24 December:

Campus activists might claim that their motives have been misunderstood or maligned. . . . That does not square with the line followed by USSU since a new council was elected early in 1974. USSU's first-ever girl president, a Malaysian, promised soon after her appointment to "revolutionize" the union. With her colleagues on the council, including foreign students, she brought USSU out into the streets to campaign on domestic issues, such as increases in bus fares—and also on non-Singaporean problems such as squatters in Johor Baru. Some of USSU's activities this past year could be explained in terms of legitimate student interest. But some of the methods used and some other issues taken up in recent months could not be classified by any stretch of the imagination as student affairs. Students who want to play politics should leave the sanctuary of the university and join a political party—and allow the vast majority of their contemporaries to study in peace.

In line with the government's view that a concerted attempt was being made to create "media pressure" on the government, the 11 November 1974 issue of *Newsweek* magazine became the basis of a contempt of court conviction and the imposition of fines ranging from $200 to $600 by the Singapore High Court on the distributor, the local circulation agent, and a local correspondent of the magazine. In this issue, *Newsweek*, under the title "Selective Justice," had criticized a not-guilty verdict rendered by the court on 1 November in the case of a PAP member of parliament who had been accused of libel by the small opposition Workers' Party during an election campaign. The article asserted that the High Court had chosen to "turn a blind eye to all precedents" in finding against the Workers' Party, and contrasted this verdict with an earlier judgment won by Premier Lee Kuan Yew and another PAP member of parliament in their libel action against opposition politicians in the recent parliamentary election. (*Asia Research Bulletin*, Political Supplement, 31 December, p. 38.)

On the other hand, the government has remained careful also to keep on making conciliatory gestures to its opponents. On 20 June 1975, for example, four of the group of 30 persons, described by the government as having MNLF or CPM connections or both, who had been arrested in June 1974 (*YICA, 1975*, p. 418) were released. According to the Home Affairs Ministry, the four had expressed their "deep regret" over their past involvement in Communist activities. (*The Nation*, Hong Kong, 21 June.) The release followed the pattern of similar arrests and releases of political prisoners set by the Lee Kuan Yew government in the past. Under the Internal Security Act the government is empowered to arrest and incarcerate persons without trial, but a declaration of regret, signed and voiced by a prisoner and usually promptly made public by the government, may bring release from detention. There are no exact data on the number of political prisoners being held; estimates range from 50 to 300, most of them with Barisan or suspected CPM connections. The Newspaper and Printing Act of 1974—designed, according to Singapore's minister of culture, to prevent "our newspapers from being used as instruments of subversion"—mandates that journalists in Singapore report the sources of foreign funds which they receive and that Singapore newspapers become public companies, facilitating complete supervision of their financial and other operations (Seah Chee Meow, op. cit. p. 147).

On 4 August Singapore radio reported that the Home Ministry had arrested five persons, one a woman, for alleged involvement in the CPM. How recent this involvement was did not become apparent. The government stated that one of the arrestees had allegedly directed acts of violence as long ago as 1965 and 1966, and claimed that the arrests, along with recovery of arms and ammunition from two of the arrestees, showed that the CPM was still active in Singapore. (*FBIS*, 4 August.) On 23 August the government announced that it had released ten political prisoners and expelled them to Malaysia and prohibited their re-entry into Singapore. The ten, six of them women, and all Chinese, also had been arrested last year for alleged involvement in MNLF activities. (Ibid., 2 September.)

Six members of an allegedly underground Communist organization were arrested on 3 October. Following their arrests, the Singapore government announced that it was stepping up its surveillance of CPM subversion attempts. The arrests involved members of the so-called "Mao Tse-tung Thought

League" or "Tung League," which the government claimed was now defunct but which since 1971, about a year after it had been founded, had sought contact with the Malayan National Liberation Front and had developed a network of "Communist cells." In the aftermath of the arrests, the government made a new appeal to the public to report to the police "individuals or groups behaving suspiciously" (FBIS, 3 October). On 4 November, the government announced three new arrests of men on grounds of "Communist activities." One of them was alleged to be a member of the Malayan National Liberation League and reportedly had also been "active in the Barisan Sosialis," while the other two were said to be "long standing members" of the CPM. The three were also charged with printing "Communist pamphlets" and disseminating a booklet containing texts of broadcasts from "The Voice of the Malayan Revolution." Urging the public to exercise "vigilance," a home affairs ministry statement declared further that it was the aim of the CPM "to stage a resurgence of armed revolution in Singapore" and that the Malayan National Liberation League was of the CPM's "underground satellite organizations" engaged in providing "a steady stream of new recruits for the CPM'" (FBIS, 5 November). It is difficult to assess the validity of these government charges since little or nothing of the details of the activities of those recently arrested is available.

Relations with Communist Countries. The ascendancy of Communism in Indochina during the first half of 1975 prompted a number of pessimistic forecasts by the Singapore premier, as at the same time his government cautiously seemed to move toward improving relations with the major Communist powers. Increased Sino-Soviet competition for power in Southeast Asia is, according to Lee Kuan Yew, one likely consequence of the present inability or unwillingness of the United States to intervene further in the Southeast Asian region. In an address to the National Press Club in Wellington, New Zealand, on 7 April, Lee said:

> The fear of the Southeast Asian countries is to be caught in the competitive clash between these two [i.e., the USSR and People's China]. China has the advantage of historic associations with the region. Memories of past tributes paid and an awareness of geographical proximity make Southeast Asia anxious not to take sides with the Soviet Union against the People's Republic of China, even though the Soviet Union is ahead on technology. Most hope to maintain equitable relations with both. . . . But this may not be possible unless these two communist countries cease to compete for ideological and nationalist supremacy—a remote prospect. (Asia Research Bulletin, Political Supplement, 30 April, p. 75.)

On this occasion Premier Lee urged the United States to maintain a naval presence and strong economic relationships with the Southeast Asian region, a theme he was to repeat in subsequent months.

In an interview heard over the BBC early in May, Lee expressed concern over the large supplies of weapons, including many of the most modern American manufacture, which as a result of the Communist victories in Indochina were believed to have fallen into the hands of Hanoi and its allies. These weapons, according to Lee, could become "a potential source of considerable mischief" if they came into possession of other insurgents in Asia and elsewhere. In this connection he foresaw a future course of political unrest as emanating not from a march of North Vietnamese or Khmer Rouge military forces into Thailand, or subsequently of Communist Thais marching into Peninsular Malaysia or Singapore. Rather, according to the Singapore premier, "the technique is a very subtle one of creating indigenous insurgencies with indigenous leaders and guerrillas and eventually indigenous counterarmies and countergovernment," culminating in a "grand victory parade." (FBIS, 5 May.)

On 30 April, Singapore defense minster Dr. Goh Keng Swee also said that the recent "military defect" in Indochina would result in increased pressures on Southeast Asian governments through "local insurgencies." Expansion of Communist influence would be gradual, in fact "sometimes almost imperceptible," he said, stressing that non-Communists did not understand the nature of the

Communist threat, since they viewed it primarily as military in nature. If Southeast Asian countries believed that military power and propaganda were all that was needed to defeat the Communists, Goh said, they they would likely meet the same fate as Vietnam. (Ibid., 30 April.)

Meanwhile Singapore's relations with the USSR and People's China appeared to be improving. On 4 July a new Soviet ambassador to Singapore, Y. I. Razdukhov, expressed the hope for "many additional areas" in the development of Soviet-Singapore relations. Razdukhov noted that on 7 November 1974 a cultural cooperation agreement had been signed between the two countries and that a program for specific cultural exchanges during 1975-76 would be signed in the near future. Sports exchanges were in the offing, and shortly a Leningrad theatrical group and a Soviet-Armenian orchestra would arrive in the island republic, he said. According to Razdukhov, Singapore's trade balance with Russia is quite favorable. Imports from the USSR during the first three months of 1975 were $1.3 million, and exports $45 million. (*Straits Times*, 5 July.) On 8 August an article in *Pravda* commemorating Singapore's tenth independence anniversary was basically very praiseworthy of Singapore's economic and cultural progress; ties with the USSR were described as good but with room for further improvement (*FBIS*, 15 August).

On 11 March Singapore foreign minister Rajaratnam said that his government continued to stand by an earlier statement that it would be the last of the five ASEAN nations (Association of Southeast Asian Nations, comprising Thailand, the Philippines, Malaysia, Singapore, and Indonesia) to complete formal diplomatic relations with People's China, adding however that "if world conditions change, then our policy will also change" (*FBIS*, 11 March). Yet, even as Rajaratnam was speaking, he was getting ready to depart at the head of a five-man Singapore delegation on an official visit to Peking, the first such visit ever made although there had been previous informal contacts between the two countries at the commercial and sports levels. Rajaratnam noted that his visit to Peking was the result of an invitation by Chinese foreign minister Chiao Kuan-hua the previous year, when Chiao headed the Peking government's delegation to the United Nations. Friendly but noncommittal was Rajaratnam's reaction to the press upon his return, although the trip almost certainly would result in improving trade and cultural relations. It has been speculated that China is particularly interested in Singapore's considerable experience in using offshore oil drilling and rigging equipment (*Far Eastern Economic Review*, 7 March, p. 32). There are two People's Chinese banks in Singapore, the Bank of China and the Kwantung Provincial Bank, and a number of retail outlets are permitted to import and sell Chinese manufactures. Singapore's total trade with China is currently valued at about $270 million per year (Kawin Wilairat, *Singapore's Foreign Policy*, Institute of Southeast Asian Studies Field Report, no. 10, Singapore, June 1975, p. 102).

Commercial and/or diplomatic relations with most East European nations remain correct and unspectacular. Singapore seems ready to proceed with recognition of the new Communist government of South Vietnam, although formal action will probably await the new South Vietnamese government's entry into the United Nations. On 19 April the Singapore government announced recognition of the Royal Government of National Union as the new sole and legal government of Cambodia, declaring that the Singapore Embassy staff which had departed at the height of the recent fighting would return to Phnom Penh as soon as circumstances permitted. In its recognition statement the Singapore government said that with the return of peace to Cambodia "under a new government headed by Prince Norodom Sihanouk" the Cambodian people would successfully rehabilitate their economy and "heal the wounds of war." (*FBIS*, 22 April.)

Publications. During 1975 the Barisan issued no regular publications, relying on occasional mimeographed leaflets. Neither the Barisan's biweekly *Plebeian* nor its Chinese-language *Chern Siau Pau* could, according to Barisan spokesmen, obtain publication permits from the government.

The CPM's clandestine radio transmitter, "Voice of the Malayan Revolution," which is thought to be located in China's southern Yunnan Province, has only rarely dealt with developments in Singapore in recent years. The CPM's major international mouthpiece, *Malayan Monitor and General News*, issued from London, has begun to appear less frequently. It carries but few reports on Singapore as such and has virtually no circulation there. According to Singapore police sources, the MNLF occasionally distributes handbills, but these are usually quickly confiscated and, like the "Voice" broadcasts, they have a minimal impact in the island republic. The Chinese government takes the position that the "Voice" is maintained and operated by "Malayan friends" and that it has no official connection with it.

University of Bridgeport   Justus M. van der Kroef

Sri Lanka

Sri Lanka's oldest Marxist party, the Lanka Sama Samaja Party (Ceylon Equal Society Party—LSSP), was formed in 1935. From the original LSSP, a number of parties and groups have emerged. The present LSSP, generally referred to as Trotskyist, although it was expelled from the Fourth International, is the country's major Marxist party.

The Ceylon Communist Party was formed in 1943 by an LSSP founder, S. A. Wickremasinghe. In 1963 it split into pro-Soviet and pro-Chinese factions led by Wickremasinghe and N. Sanmugathasan, respectively. Membership on the pro-Soviet Sri Lanka Communist Party (SLCP) is estimated at 2,000. That in the now divided pro-Chinese groups is probably less than 1,000.

In 1968 the LSSP and the SLCP subordinated their mutual antagonism and joined in the "United Front" (UF) with the social-democratic Sri Lanka Freedom Party (SLFP). Following the May 1970 general elections, the three parties formed a coalition government headed by the SLFP leader, Mrs. Sirimavo Bandaranaike. In September 1975, the LSSP was ousted from the coalition.

In the 1970 elections the LSSP had won 19 of the 151 seats contested and 8.7 percent of the popular vote. The SLCP won 6 seats and 3.4 percent of the vote. Sri Lanka's population is estimated at 13,700,000.

Leadership and Organization. *The LSSP.* The most prominent leaders of the LSSP are N. M. Perera, Colvin de Silva, and Leslie Goonewardena, who were cabinet ministers until September 1975. Bernard Soysa is general secretary.

The labor movement has long been identified politically with the Marxists, and the LSSP is a major influence in trade unionism. The party controls the Ceylon Federation of Labor and also receives support from the Government Workers' Trade Union Federation and the Government Clerical Service Union. (*YICA*, 1974, p. 543). The Ceylon Students Federation also supports the party.

The Pro-Soviet SLCP. In recent elections to the Politburo and Secretariat, Pieter Keuneman was chosen general secretary, S. A. Wickremasinghe as president, and K. P. Silva as secretary for organizational matters. (*Pravda*, Moscow, 16 September 1975.) Keuneman is also minister of housing.

Party affiliates include its Youth League, Women's Organization, and the Ceylon Federation of Trade Unions. Keuneman has claimed party leadership in unions with memberships totalling 250,000 and that youth leagues supporting the party have nearly 30,000 members. (*Ceylon Daily News*, 20 August.)

The Pro-Chinese Communist Parties. In 1972 Central Committee member Watson Fernando broke away from N. Sanmugathasan's pro-Chinese SLCP to establish the Communist Party of Sri Lanka (Marxist-Leninist). Sanmugathasan's faction is now called the Ceylon Communist Party (CCP) and has retained support of the Ceylon Trade Union Federation.

The Revolutionary JVP. In April 1971 the traditional Marxist parties found themselves challenged by a young radical movement—the Janatha Vimukthi Peramuna (JVP), or People's Liberation Front. Rohana Wijeweera and other JVP leaders had been members of the orthodox communist parties. Although their armed attempt in 1971 to overthrow the government failed, sporadic violence has continued. In December 1973, Wijeweera was sentenced to life imprisonment. Most of the 18,000 suspects originally detained had been released earlier.

Party Internal Affairs. The SLCP held its Ninth Congress on 20-24 August. A political report and program for the period preceding the 1977 general elections were adopted. The Congress also discussed the "devastating effects" of the "international capitalist crisis" on the third world and Sri Lanka, the need to complete the "national-democratic revolution," and the USSR's "numerous peace initiatives." (*Ceylon Daily News*, 20 August; *TASS* and *Pravda*, 22 August.)

Although less evident in the last year, internal divisions within the SLCP over the party's attitude toward participation in the coalition government apparently persist. The struggle between Keuneman's "soft-line" faction and Wickremasinghe's "hard-line" opposition to participation had led to a nine-month-long open split which was finally resolved in the 1974 reunification. (*YICA, 1975*, p. 423.)

Domestic Attitudes and Activities. *The LSSP.* Following the parliamentary path to power, the LSSP seeks extensive political and economic reforms, some of which have been achieved in government actions such as land reform, an income ceiling, greater press regulation, and the 1972 constitution. The younger, more militant party members consider the UF's progress toward socialism too slow, however, and their pressure probably contributed to the coalition's breakup this year.

The SLCP. The pro-Soviet SLCP has also followed the parliamentary strategy and officially supports the UF. The Wickremasinghe faction, however, has long criticized the government's failure to take over all foreign banks, industries and plantations and opposes Keuneman's participation in the cabinet. In September the party welcomed the government's proposed legislation on nationalizing plantations.

Other aims of the SLCP's current program, which focuses on the Ceylonese economic crisis, are a special price control agency, state monopoly of essential goods, people's committees to supervise distribution of goods, and wage increases. (*World Marxist Review*, May.) Party secretary K. P. Silva has noted, nevertheless, that the "absence within the left of a clear and consistent policy toward the economic crisis is a major obstacle to strengthening the left and democratic forces." (Ibid.)

Both the LSSP and SLCP were preoccupied during the year with the increasingly strained UF relationship and Prime Minister Bandaranaike's consequent expulsion of the LSSP. Mrs. Bandaranaike has maintained that the government would continue the social-democratic policies of her late husband, despite leftist pressures for more drastic policies. The LSSP's continuing public criticism of Mrs. Bandaranaike and her SLFP and the two parties' struggle for jurisdiction over the key plantation sector finally led to the break. In September she ousted the three LSSP ministers from the cabinet. The LSSP went into opposition and later proposed forming a "socialist UF" with the SLCP and the "centralized left" in Mrs. Bandaranaike's SLFP. (*New York Times*, 6 October.)

For its part, the SLCP attempted to mediate the dispute and, after the LSSP's departure, affirmed that it would remain in the UF.

The Pro-Chinese Communist Parties. Sanmugathasan has consistently advocated violent overthrow of the government, but Fernando's faction is apparently willing to support the UF's "progressive" measures.

International Views and Policies. *The LSSP.* Although the LSSP rejects Soviet domination (for example, it condemned the Soviet-led invasion of Czechoslovakia), it has supported the "socialist" USSR against "imperialism" and "capitalism." It has accused the U.S. of subversive activities in Sri Lanka and called the U.S. military presence in the Indian Ocean a threat to littoral states.

The SLCP. The party Congress in August approved the proposal for another international conference of communist and workers' parties and favored relaxation of tensions between states. Noting the need for a collective security system in Asia, it criticized China's "anti-Sovietism and cooperation with imperialism" (*TASS* and *Pravda*, 22 August.) Thirteen foreign communist delegations, including one from the CPSU, attended the Congress.

The Pro-Chinese CCP. Sanmugathasan sent a message of greeting to China's National Day celebration. (*NCNA*, Peking, 17 October.)

Party Publications. SLCP publications include *Aththa* and *Forward.* The current orientation of pro-Chinese Communist Party publications, such as *Kamkaruwa, Tolilali,* and *Red Flag*, is not clear. LSSP newspapers include *Samasamajaya* and *Janadina.*

Alexandria, Va.   Barbara Reid

Thailand

Communist activity in Thailand began in the 1920s when members of the Chinese Communist Party penetrated labor groups in Bangkok. During the 1920s and 1930s the purges of communists in China and Vietnam drove a large number of refugees with communist sympathies to seek refuge in Thailand and to establish the Indo-China Communist Party with its headquarters in Northeast Thailand. The first meeting of the Communist Party of Thailand (CPT) took place in 1942 and included Chinese and Vietnamese but no Thai. The CPT had only a negligible impact on the Thai citizenry. Except for a brief period following the Second World War when the Anti-Communist Act of 1933 was repealed (to gain Russia's support on entering the United Nations) the CPT has been declared illegal and vigorously suppressed. No more than several hundred members, almost entirely Chinese, has belonged to the Party until the last decade.

In the 1960s the Party formally resolved to resort to "revolutionary armed struggle" and protracted guerrilla warfare in Thailand. In 1960 the CPT announced the formation of a "Supreme Command" of the Thai Peoples' Liberation Armed Forces (TPLAF). Since that time the CPT has in some cases provided leadership for insurgency activity throughout the Kingdom, especially in those geographic areas where ethnic minorities predominate.

By 1975 the CPT comprised an estimated 8-10,000 members including the armed militia of the TPLAF. The estimate of CPT members is not reliable for several reasons. First, the CPT is an illegal and underground party and has never published membership statistics. Second, the criteria used to determine CPT members are inconsistent. If armed soldiers are excluded, for example, the number of civilian CPT members is estimated to be between 1 and 2,000. Third, the Thai Internal Security Operation Command (ISOC), the major counter-insurgency organization, tends to exaggerate the number of CPT members for its own purpose. The *Far Eastern Economic Review* (3 October 1975), quoting official Thai sources, estimated that almost 200,000 people (out of a total population of 40,000,000) are located in areas completely controlled by the CPT where the authority of the central government is not recognized. However, that figure has not been verified. The insurgency is operating intermittently in 37 of the country's 71 provinces involving more than one-third of the total population and territory.

Leadership and Organization. No information is available on the precise organizational structure and leading personalities of the CPT. The names of party leaders are not known nor is it known how much continuity exists in leadership positions over time. According to Thai intelligence sources, the Party is loosely organized with a Politburo and a Central Committee. The composition of these committees and the regularity and location of their meetings remain unknown factors. There appears to be no permanent Party headquarters. Instead, Party leaders move from place to place and meet only in small groups. Some efforts have been made to bring ethnic Thais into leadership positions, although Sino-Thai apparently still predominate.

The Party organization in each of the geographic regions of the country is autonomous with little coordination of activities. The military arm of the CPT is the TPLAF which consists of well-trained soldiers with modern weapons working out of jungle areas. The TPLAF is supported in turn by forces consisting of squad size units of youths who work around villages. These village soldiers have the task of supporting TPLAF operations. Over the past decade the TPLAF has steadily increased in numbers, strength, and sophistication of weaponry including the use of rocket-propelled grenades and possibly portable mortars. (*Far Eastern Economic Review* [FEER] 9 May; 3 October.)

Domestic Activities. In 1974-75 insurgency activity increased throughout the Kingdom but remained concentrated in three geographical areas: the Northeast, North, and South. These three regions share two important characteristics. They are the poorest regions and they are populated by ethnic minorities. Evidence is lacking on the precise role of the CPT in the planning and implementing of insurgency activity in these areas although some loose coordinating role seems clear.

In the North, insurgency is concentrated within the mountainous Hill tribe areas where some 500,000 hill tribesmen live. The aim of the insurgency is autonomy for the hill tribesmen from the Bangkok government and a lifting of restrictions on opium production and slash-and-burn agriculture. Since the ceasefire in Laos and with the rise of the Pathet Lao as the primary force in Laos, an estimated several hundred insurgents have crossed over the border into Thailand's northern and Northeastern region. There are an estimated 2,000-4,000 armed communists in the North. (*FEER*, 9

May.) Thai and American intelligence sources indicate that external support for the Communist insurgency in Northern Thailand comes from China.

The rural insurgency in the southern region is the most complex since it comprises several separate and diverse dissident organizations. (*Southeast Asia Spectrum*, April 1975). The non-communist Moslem separatist forces as well as bandit bands in the furthermost southern provinces which have engaged in terrorist activity, are often thought to be communist controlled. However, there is no documentation that proves either CPT or Malayan Communist Party (MCP) control or even coordination of Moslem separatist groups. The MCP retains a base area in the southernmost provinces of Thailand with 1,500 to 2,000 soldiers in Malaysia. CPT-led insurgency is concentrated further north of the Peninsula in the mid-southern provinces of Trang, Pattalung, Nakorn Sri Thammarat, and Surat Thani. There is no known organizational link between the MCP and the CTP.

Thai military sources reported that following the end of the Indochina war in the wake of communist victories, communist insurgents stepped up their activities in the South. Military officials stated that in the months of September and October, 1975, about 125 local government officials were killed by separatists, and/or communists. Almost daily, newspapers reported terrorist activities in the South including kidnappings, ambushes, and gun battles.

CPT insurgency began in the Northeast region where it has retained the largest and most active anti-government activity. Full-time communist forces (TPLAF) operate in Loei, Phitsanalok, and Petchabun provinces and in the Phu Phan mountain range in Nakhorn Phanom province.

In April, American intelligence analysts declassified a CIA-NSA document entitled "The 35th Pathet Lao/95th North Vietnamese Combined Command: External Support to the Thai Insurgency," which reported that North Vietnam has established a sophisticated system to support the Thai insurgency in the Northeast. According to the document, the joint Pathet Lao/North Vietnamese Command has its headquarters in Hanoi where it maintains communication with the CPT. The 35/95 Command is said to be training insurgents and to be coordinating the funneling of documents, currency, propaganda, weapons, and equipment to Thailand. (*Bangkok Post*, 6 April 1975.) The document states that over 700 Thai insurgents had been trained in Vietnam by the end of 1974, and over 300 in Peking and Nanking. A large number have also attended courses in Laos. Overall an estimated 2,500 Thai nationals have participated in these six month long training sessions. The intelligence document describes in detail the intricate communication and organization procedures established by the North Vietnamese and Laotians. It concludes that the Command is invulnerable and that communist border crossings into Thailand have scarcely been hindered even by the American-designed border security system. According to the CIA/NSA document, the Communist victory in Laos provides a "wholly permissive environment" for increased support of the Thai insurgency.

In September, the Cabinet proposed to repeal all anti-Communist legislation such as the Communist Activities Prevention Act of 1952, and numerous decrees laid down during the rule of Sarit Thannarat and Thanom Kittikachorn and to substitute a wide-ranging national security act. A special committee was to be set up to investigate and prosecute national security cases. The new act, if passed by the legislature, calls for stringent prison terms for those who (1) create panic or fear among the people and thereby prevent them from performing their duties; (2) create panic or fear among the state's officials with the aim of forcing the officials to ignore the laws of the land; (3) instigate or persuade people to destroy public or national property; and (4) persuade others to use weapons to force policy changes of the government or destroy the country's economy. (*The Nation*, Bangkok, 3 September.) The Voice of the People of Thailand (CPT radio broadcast) called the act a "move to deprive the people of their rights and liberties, a fascist law even more vicious than the former anticommunist act."

International Views and Policies. The CPT remained pro-Chinese in 1974 although there was some indication of factionalism with a minority supporting a Soviet-North Vietnamese orientation instead of a Chinese orientation. Speculation revolved around the theory that the Soviet Union was making a major effort to control the CPT's urban activities while leaving rural guerrilla efforts to the Chinese-oriented cadres.

A number of newspaper articles reported on the growing diplomatic and intelligence efforts of the Soviet Union *vis à vis* Thai students, politicians, labor leaders, and journalists. According to one report there are 223 Soviet citizens living in Bangkok, including women and children, most wives working in some capacity. Of these, 121 belong to the Embassy, 60 to the Soviet Trade office, 20 to the Economic and Social Commission for Asia and the Pacific, eight to Aeroflot, and the remainder to shipping companies and to Tass (*FEER*, 26 September). Newspaper stories report that an unsubstantiated number of these Soviet citizens are a part of the Soviet KGB.

The Thai government established diplomatic relations with the PRC on 1 July 1975. The two governments proclaimed that "all foreign aggression and subversion and all attempts by any country to control any other country or to interfere in internal affairs are impermissible and are to be condemned." The Thai government recognized the Government of the PRC as the sole legal government of China and acknowledged that Taiwan is an integral part of Chinese territory and that therefore all official representations from Taiwan would be removed by 1 August 1975.

Pravda charged that the establishment of diplomatic relations between Thailand and the PRC would be used by China for interference into the internal affairs of the country. The *Pravda* article stated that the ethnic Chinese in Thailand are a likely vehicle for Peking's efforts to extend its power in the country. (*New York Times*, 24 June 1975.)

Current official concerns focus more on Laos and the intentions of the Pathet Lao than on Vietnam, although until October 1975 the consistent public position of the Thai government officially has been to down-play incidents on the Lao riverine border. Major border incidents in October and November raised serious questions about Thailand's relations with Laos. Moreover, the initial diplomatic exchanges between Vietnam and Thailand reached an impasse. The establishment of diplomatic relations between the two nations was postponed indefinitely.

Insurgency appeared to have increased in 1974 although the rate of increase or the degree of CPT involvement could not be substantiated. Generally, the Thai press tends to exaggerate accounts of insurgent activity, often approaching outright fabrication, and such accounts are sometimes further distorted by foreign wire services and media.

Following the fall of Indochina, there was considerable apprehension among official Thai that an influx from Vietnam of captured weaponry would greatly increase insurgent activity. This influx has not occurred and many Thai officials have gradually realized that the communists have been hindered in their recruitment not by lack of arms but by the limited nature of their appeal on ideological grounds. Because of this apprehension, however, which was communicated to the press and public in various ways, several recent insurgent incidents have been inflated in the Thai press.

Northern Illinois University

Clark Neher

Vietnam: Democratic Republic of Vietnam

Communism came to Vietnam, which was then part of French Indochina, in the 1920s. Originally there were three streams of communist thought and organizational development: Stalinist, Trotskyite, and an indigenous youthful Marxist movement. In 1929 the Comintern ordered one of its agents in Asia, the man the world came to know as Ho Chi Minh, to effect a merger of these three movements. The effort was made in a meeting in Hong Kong, and although it failed to achieve the desired unity it did result in the birth, on 3 February 1930, of the Indochinese Communist Party (ICP), forerunner of today's Vietnam Dang Lao Dong or Vietnamese Workers Party.

Much of the challenge to French colonialism, as well as opposition to the ICP, during the 1930s came from what at the time were called the nationalists, primarily two clusters of organizations: the Dai Viet (Greater Vietnam) and the Viet Nam Quoc Dan Dang (Vietnamese Nationalist Party), the latter being patterned after Sun Yat Sen's Kuomintang.

The ICP moved into preeminence during World War II when Ho Chi Minh, who was an organizational genius, created the Viet Nam Doc Lap Dong Minh Hoi (or Viet Minh) as a united-front organization which opposed first the Japanese occupation of Indochina and then the returning French colonialists. With the Viet Minh as the mass-based organization and the Democratic Republic of Vietnam (DRV) as the administrative leader, the French were fought to victory in 1954.

In the following years the DRV was guided by the Lao Dong Party through initial economic development efforts and then through the Vietnam war. Throughout it was remarkably cohesive, rent by no serious factionalism nor by the purges common to communist parties. Most of the men who founded the party (the chief exception being the deceased Ho Chi Minh) were running it in 1975.

The Position in 1975. DRV hsitorians probably will record 1975 as the single most decisive year in the nation's history, even overshadowing 1945, the year of its birth, and 1954, the year of French colonialism's defeat.

January to May of 1975 were five months that changed the world for Vietnam. They witnessed the sudden and unexpected delivery of unification, that chimera-like goal which, since an initial gesture outside the Versailles conference hall in 1921 (by some of the men who today rule Vietnam) had been pursued with such single-minded devotion.

Again and again over the decades, the communists had found themselves at the gates of victory, only to see the gates hold and prevent them—by stubborn resistance of other Vietnamese, by their own allies, by fate itself—from taking that which they always considered was rightfully theirs.

Then suddenly, victory. South Vietnam fell, less to North Vietnamese moral or military superiority than to simple chaos and confusion. Unification was accomplished. The price may have been high—ten percent of the entire population war casualties, economic stagnation the worst in Asia, imposition of the most intrusive praetorian society on earth—but doubtless DRV wartime leaders, whatever others may conclude, will go to their graves convinced victory was worth it all.

It was a victory as unexpected as it was sudden. When 1975 began, the North Vietnamese were in a somber, even pessimistic mood. The future promised only interminable warfare, for neither armed struggle nor political struggle had been able to break the southern stalemate. The Paris agreements had neither delivered South Vietnam into the hands of Hanoi nor had they created sufficient political disarray to push the country toward the interim Third Force way-station. Socio-economic problems, which had been successfully held in check for so long, were generating overwhelming internal pressures, making it increasingly doubtful that rigid wartime policies could be maintained much longer.

A host of public statements—dealing with recent Lao Dong Party plenum resolutions (no. 22 in February 1974 and no. 23 in July 1974) plus reports and announcements by DRV premier Pham Van Dong and party secretary Le Duan at the end of 1974—assessed the DRV situation and the requisite tasks imposed on each:

—"Unite the people, preserve the peace, heal the wounds of war."

—"Rehabilitate and develop the economy and culture . . . build the material and technical foundations of socialism."

—"Closely combine economy with national defense" (i.e., balance allocation of resources between war in the South and economic development in the North). "Stabilize the economic situation and the people's standard of living" (i.e., improve both).

—"Step up the Three Revolutions"—revolution in means of production relationship (i.e., the economic organization of society), revolution in technology, (i.e., putting science and technology to work to solve various material problems), and revolution in culture (i.e., developing new socialist values and virtues).

—"Heighten vigilance and defeat all schemes of U.S. imperialism and its henchmen."

—"Fulfill our obligations to the revolutions in Laos and Cambodia."

—"Strive to fulfill our obligation in the revolutionary task aimed at completing independence and democracy in the South and proceed to the peaceful reunification of the country."

Such was the measure of things, the official parameters of DRV policy planning as the year began. The sense of these was delimiting and modest: concentrate on the most pressing economic problems and assume a static and unambitious military approach in the South. Ultimate objective was not changed, but priorities were reordered and the pace was slowed. Plainly the instructions were not marching orders to return to big-unit warfare in search of the knockout blow. Rather the theme running through the pronouncements was economic development at home, while working for eventual unification but, for the moment, with emphasis on the former.

Public statement was shored up by overt behavior. Air raid shelters were dismantled, their bricks and lumber going into new buildings. Anti-aircraft guns atop Hanoi roofs vanished as did the 130-mm artillery pieces in the suburbs. The state budget, long a military secret, was published for the first time in a decade and was found to be funding an ambitious program of constructing power stations, factories, dams, and hotels and fixing as the 1975 goal the increase of the GNP by 19.6 percent. In a hundred ways the regime communicated to the people that the country's "new stage" was primarily economic.

To make this shift palatable, or at least acceptable to party cadres, many of whom were unregenerate hawks, an intensive campaign was launched to tighten ideological discipline. A wide-ranging emulation campaign was ordered to institutionalize the changes. Middle-ranking cadres became particular targets in a purge-like attack on incompetency and sloth. It was led by party secretary Le Duan himself, who in a remarkably candid late 1974 speech had declared that only 30 to 40 percent of all party cadres were "active" (that is, energetic and diligent), while another 40 percent were only "middling," doing just enough to get by; he dismissed the remaining percent as "no good."

The organizational and communicational campaigns also were directed against the general population suffering from a deep sense of war weariness which manifested itself chiefly by massive indifference to whatever the regime was up to, whether war or economic development, and which in turn resulted in inadequate performance on farm and in factory, in and out of the party.

The military situation in the South was judged to have great long-range promise but at the moment was a stand-off, or was such that the massive force required to destroy the South Vietnamese army was unavailable, sources of supply too uncertain, and the outcome of such an undertaking too precarious to make it feasible in 1975.

Thus the twin factors of a bleak prospect for early progress in the South and a realization that war-generated pressures in the North had to be reduced temporarily, forced the leadership to pursue unification with less zeal without appearing to do so, and at the same time address the country's more pressing domestic economic problems.

This did not mean abandonment of the crusade of unification. But it sought to draw the war out, to return it to protracted conflict. Military pressure would continue in the South. PAVN (People's Army of Vietnam) generals would get adequate manpower and logistic supplies for this. They could have one or two limited-objective military campaigns during the year. But there would be no campaigns of the magnitude of Easter 1972, which saw every PAVN division except one outside DRV borders. Possibly, an all-out offensive would be authorized for 1976, cadres were told privately, but none in 1975.

Such was the thinking and planning of DRV leaders as the year began. Then came a limited offensive in Phuoc Long Province, probably as a sop to PAVN generals as much as anything else. The objective was to seize the northern portion of the province, an underpopulated area adjacent to Cambodia. It was a move of maneuver on a chessboard with many plays ahead. Surprisingly, ARVN (Army of the Republic of Vietnam) defenses collapsed. PAVN troops captured the province capital of Phuoc Binh on 7 January.

Phuoc Binh proved in retrospect to be the turning point in the entire Vietnam war. Officials in Saigon were puzzled and traumatized by the reversal. PAVN generals, unprepared for a general offensive, were unable to follow up the victory with a drive on Saigon not far to the south. Instead there came a lull, then a second limited-objective offensive in the Highland province of Ban Me Thuot. Here ARVN, having been alerted, was better prepared and was confident. But ARVN defenses again crumbled and the province capital fell on 17 March. Its capture, as it turned out, was the second and final blow to organized South Vietnamese resistance. The unravel began and never stopped until the war was over. The South Vietnamese army which had stood and fought so well—against greater odds and under worse conditions in the 1968 Tet offensive and again in 1972—hardly fought at all. Within days, chaos in decision making at the corps level and countermanded orders by Saigon made it impossible for ARVN to fight at all. PAVN divisions, in the next six weeks, did not defeat South Vietnamese troops in a series of battles. They simply moved forward into successive military vacuums: Da Nang, Hue, Nha Trang, Dalat, Saigon, and on into the Mekong Delta.

No one was more surprised by the collapse than the DRV leaders themselves. Pham Van Dong candidly admitted this to a foreign journalist: no, he had not expected Da Nang to fall as it did; yes, it came as a great surprise to him. The DRV leaders may have an unshakable faith in their cause but they scarcely could recognize success when it was thrust upon them.

The rest of the year 1975—May through December—were kaleidoscopic for the North Vietnamese. Unbelievably, the war was over. But also there came at once confrontation with a world vastly changed. In a country where for so long nothing changed, the next few months were marked by constant change and the syndrome of future shock appeared. The reports from Hanoi on life and anticipations and official plans became increasingly disjointed. The portrait of North Vietnam as totally coherent and one-dimensional gave way to a blurred, fragmented, out-of-focus picture.

Overnight North Vietnam's leaders found themselves plunged into a situation never anticipated, forced to make decisions on matters they had thought still years away and to which they had given no detailed attention. Beyond the problems were the ramifications of their responses. Hence, understandably, their behavior was marked by confusion. They were confused both as to assessment and to policy. It was at once apparent to them that much of what they had believed about the South obviously was incorrect, else they would have anticipated the collapse. If assumptions were wrong, policies based on them would be wrong. There was great uncertainty as how to proceed.

Clearly, what was desired was some systematic and comprhensive plan of action. But such a plan did not exist, nor was there time to produce one. The moment required all attention. What developed was a system of imperative priorities: quick day-by-day decisions addressed to the most demanding problems and letting all else go. Inevitably, as we shall see, this led to enormous chaos and confusion. There was great backing and filling. Orders by the party in Hanoi were contradicted by the party in Saigon. Recommendations from Saigon never reached Hanoi. Yesterday's decision was reversed today and reversed again tomorrow. What was policy in one province was forbidden in the neighboring province.

In sum, and this can easily be documented from the public record, in the last half of 1975 the DRV leadership reversed virtually every major policy at least once. Here is a quick index of such policy switches:

—Unification: from five-year (or three-year) timetable to immediate;

—Five-year plan (1976-80): from decision to proceed as originally determined, with a plan for the North only (as late as August) to integration of the South's economy into a new and broader plan;

—Economic development: from a plan "balanced" toward agriculture to one "balanced" toward industry;

—USSR relations: from fraternal but neutral to distinctly pro-USSR;

—Chinese relations: from fraternal but neutral to distinctly negative;

—Control mechanism for the South: from military occupation (Military Management Committee system) to separate mechanism (PRG/NFL/local security forces) to combined or DRV-integrated mechanism;

—United Nations: from militant hostility to application for membership, (from two Vietnams to one);

—Cambodian relations: from ignoring anti-Vietnamese excesses to a tough no-nonsense line;

—Japanese relations: from seeking full relations to seeking partial relations back to seeking full relations;

—U.S. relations: from let-the-dust-settle to quick embrace back to let-the-dust-settle.

All this is understandable. Indeed it could scarcely be otherwise. Being unprepared for enormously important decisions suddenly thrust upon them, the DRV leaders proceeded with caution and frequently reversed themselves. It was a pattern that quite likely would continue into 1976 and even beyond: the DRV has no well-worked-out blueprint for its future. Regardless of how assured its leaders may seem to be, lack of certitude dominates their thinking. Victory opened a whole new world of possibilities. There are great opportunities to be seized—also great dangers to avoid. Distinguishing between these two is no easy matter, for what appears to be promising venture can easily turn out to be a trap. Hence wisdom dictates clinging to a sense of the provisional.

As the year ended there loomed over the now one Vietnam a specter of still more enormous change. The leadership may soon be forced to leap the generational gap. Economic forces have been unleashed which could assume a life of their own and drive Vietnam in directions neither intended nor stoppable. Transition from war to peace is itself a major change. The young grow increasingly restive. The old verities lose their luster. PAVN generals, swelled by new and enormous status, could demand additional prerogatives, even a more central role in the country's affairs. Southern influence and example could prove seductive to Northerners in the South and a deadly virus to the status quo in the North. The winds of change which have buffeted the rest of the world for a decade but so curiously avoided North Vietnam are about to whip down with delayed fury. We cannot predict the course of this change, only the fact of it. And, as the world has so firmly learned in recent years, once the winds of change have passed nothing again is ever the same.

Party Leadership and Organization. The party celebrated its victory in formal Saigon ceremonies on 15-17 May. These were marked by the open acknowledgment of party control of the revolution since earliest days. Public references—many of them for the first time—brought to the surface an all-embracing party organization which long had blanketed and dominated operations in the South, quite at variance with the wartime public image of a struggle led by the Provisional Revolutionary Government of the Republic of South Vietnam (PRG) as administrative element, supported by the National Front for the Liberation of South Vietnam (NFL) as mass base, with the party merely acting as guide for the former and contributing to the latter.

Concomitantly with victory the party itself moved at once to organizational unification. In the 45 years of its existence it had successively transformed itself from a single monolith (the Indochinese Communist Party) to a national base (the Vietnam Communist Party, i.e., Dang Lao Dong or Workers Party), to a geographic division of the Lao Dong Party into Northern Branch and Southern Branch, to conversion (in 1963) of the Southern Branch into the People's Revolutionary Party (PRP) (which included the Central Committee Directorate for Southern Vietnam, or COSVN). Now, in May 1975, it was back to the Northern-Southern Branch arrangement. The PRP vanished from public reference, as did COSVN (the latter largely becoming the Military Management Committee, MMC, the occupation military government). However, the Southern party organization was foreshortened, incorporating only the southern part of South Vietnam, the Fifth Party Region, while the northern part of South Vietnam administratively now is under the party in Hanoi.

Quite probably this move presages an end to the two-branch system and return to a single all-Vietnam party, since formation of the separate branches and later the PRP, was required, it was explained at the time, by the vastly varied situations north and south and the consequent variance in tasks, as for example between a Haiphong stevedore and a Camau Peninsula guerrilla. It is conceivable the party will continue to run this old newsreel backward all the way to 1930 and eventually there will again emerge an Indochinese Communist Party incorporating the parties of Laos and Cambodia.

The Saigon ceremonies provided a rare glimpse into the leadership structure of the party, particularly in the South. Appearing for the first time in eight years was the shadowy Pham Hung, the Politburo member long believed, but until now never proven, to be the party's czar of the war in the South. At the Saigon celebration he was identified as the South Vietnam party organization secretary, also political commissar of the People's Liberation Armed Forces (PLAF).

The relevations now permit a reasonably clear reconstruction of party hierarchy in the South in recent years. The initial ranking official was Nguyen Van Linh (alias Nguyen Van Cuc, Muoi Ut, Muoi Cuc), who ran the Southern Branch prior to 1964. He is a Northerner born in 1913 who came to the South as a child and began his revolutionary career in the mid-1930s. Supposedly Le Duan has been his mentor since Viet Minh days.

In 1964, when the scope of the war enlarged and higher party authority was required, Linh was superseded by General Nguyen Chi Thanh, a Politburo member. Linh became Thanh's principal deputy. When Thanh was killed in mid-1967 he was replaced by Pham Hung and Linh stayed on. Hung then had three ranking deputies: Linh as the principal party deputy; Colonel General Tran Van Tra (alias Tu Chi) as his principal military deputy (and later representative to the Joint Military Commission established under the Paris agreements and still later, chief of the MMC); and Nguyen Van Dang (alias Pham Xuan Thai, Hai Van) as the principal "political" deputy, that is, liaison with various front organizations such as the NFL and the Alliance (VANDPF, Vietnam Alliance of Democratic Peace Forces).

Other party figures whose status was clarified were:

—Vo Chi Vong, the durable old Anastas Mikoyan of the party, identified as the ranking party official in the Fifth Party Organization or what is left of the PRP.

—Nguyen Van Ho, a Southerner identified as the ranking official of the all-important Saigon-Gia Dinh Municipal Party which divides with the Saigon MMC the task of running the Saigon metropolitan area (which at the fall included nearly 20 percent of the entire South Vietnamese population).

—Tran Nam Trung, former PRP secretary-general and PRG defense minister. He emerged as a high-ranking party figure. His appearance side-by-side with General Tran Van Tra settled the long-debated question of whether in fact Trung and Tra were not the same individual. It did not, however, prove the assertion made by some analysts in the mid-1960s that "Tran Nam Trung" was not an individual but a position (it means Loyal Southerner) held over the years by at least three different persons. In any event someone named Tran Nam Trung emerged and obviously commanded party deference.

—Generals Le Can Chan and Dong Van Cong were identified as PLAF deputy military commanders (apparently one serves as chief of staff and the other as deputy political commissar). Also present in the South is PAVN deputy chief of staff Lieutenant General Le Trong Tan, who apparently has supra-important security duties and reports directly to Hanoi.

For years it was known that the 1960 Third Party Congress elected at least ten "hidden" members to the party's Central Committee. But because these persons were working in the South, their names were never published, so as to protect them. This year's revelations in leadership make identity of some of these reasonably certain: Nguyen Van Linh (alias Nguyen Van Cuc, etc.); Nguyen Van Dang (alias Pham Xuan Thai, etc.); Vo Chi Cong; Tran Nam Trung, whatever his true name; Nguyen Van Ho, the party's financial and economic chief in the South; probably, Huynh Tan Phat, the PRG president; possibly, Le Van Kiet (alias Nguyen Van Kiet), who was (before being superseded by Nguyen Van Ho) the major (covert) party official in Saigon.

The amalgamation of the two branches probably will see most of the Southern cadres but few of the Southern members incorporated into the Lao Dong. At the year's beginning Lao Dong Party membership was estimated at 900,000 (or 3.9 percent of the DRV population of about 24,300,000). The PRP size, admittedly little more than an educated guess, was fixed at 180,000 members, of whom 30,000 could be termed cadres (this of course does not include Northern party members on duty in the South). A weeding-out process will greatly reduce the percentage of the 180,000 who actually join the ranks of the Lao Dong.

There were no changes in top party leadership during the year. The same Politburo which has been running the country virtually since its inception continued to do so (Le Duan, Truong Chinh, Pham Van Dong, Pham Hung, Vo Nguyen Giap, Le Duc Tho, Nguyen Duy Trinh, Le Thanh Nghi, Hoang Van Hoan, Tran Quoc Hoan, Van Tien Dung; minus of course the deceased Ho Chi Minh and Nguyen Chi Thanh). Their average age now is 65 (the Central Committee average is 64). Several leaders were reported ill during the year, none seriously. General Giap was said to have had a gallstone operation, and a year earlier was reported receiving radiation treatment for cancer in a Moscow hospital; he appeared in 1975 on at least two occasions looking frail but apparently healthy.

The party celebrated the 45th anniversary of its founding on 3 February. The theme of the observance was the complex and difficult nature of protracted conflict and the certain assurance of ultimate success. The speeches, as did much of the party output prior to May, had a grim undertone. Party members were harangued for their "many shortcomings and incorrect attitudes" and on the need to "strengthen the party ideologically, organizationally and politically." A serious effort was launched into systematic research of what was called "the science of party development," seeking to uncover reasons for party weaknesses and means to overcome these. A series of provincial-level party congresses was held to study Politburo resolutions and fix local tasks and guidelines.

Reliable reports from the Hanoi diplomatic community early in the year described a growing gap between younger and older party cadres, a not uncommon phenomenon, here termed the desire of the young to "liberate North Vietnam from old-guardism." One cutting edge in the youth-age issue was conservatism versus liberalism in doctrine; that is, questions of how orthodox must ideology be, or how far can ideology be bent without breaking it. Also involved was the matter of communist internationalism and its effects on domestic affairs, which in turn raised questions about the nature of proletarian solidarity and the reliability of the DRV's socialist allies. Surprisingly the young were reported as demonstrating isolationistic tendencies, maintaining that internationalism in fact meant outsider manipulation of DRV affairs.

Much of this, if it ever was serious, evaporated with victory. In fact all previous doctrinal disputes underwent radical alteration. Some, such as proper military strategy in the South, disappeared completely. Others—those over allocation of economic resources or over the best means of dealing with war-engendered social pathology—greatly diminished. Some doctrinal differences remained but even these were changed, chiefly the issues of generational transfer of party power, economic development strategy, and foreign relations. None could be termed serious factionalism. The year 1975 was an euphoric one for the party and doctrinal disputes lost, as least for the moment, their earlier grim quality.

Although predicted by many observers, no announcement came during the year that the long-delayed Fourth Party Congress would be convened. The Third Congress was held in 1960; party by-laws stipulate that a congress is to be held every four years; exigencies of war provided rationale for postponement in the past decade.

Year-end rumors in world communist capitals spoke of a Fourth Congress in April 1976. A 4 August 1975 party circular made indirect reference to a Central Committee resolution ordering a congress. Presumably there would be advance indication, since party by-laws require that, prior to a national congress, provincial congresses be held to elect delegates and discuss draft proposals. This had not been done as of December 1975.

It would appear mandatory that the Fourth Congress convene in 1976. Failure to do so would raise the most fundamental questions about the nature of the Lao Dong Party. What is involved is the basic concept of party democracy. Official dogma holds that the DRV has the highest form of democracy. It is the dictatorship of the proletariat (the vanguard, with the party as the vanguard of the vanguard) which stands on two immense legs, democratic centralism (diversity in debate, unity in action) and strict but voluntary discipline (party over self). In the war years it could be argued doctrinally that the principle of discipline was paramount and had supremacy over its twin, democratic centralism. Such an argument was persuasive among the faithful. But with the war's end there should be a return to standing on both legs, that is discipline and democratic centralism as represented by a party congress. Failure to stage a congress thus becomes failure in democracy communist-style. Such could possibly be justified but would have enormous adverse effect on party members, particularly the younger middle-ranking cadres. However, a party congress must be a thing prescribed, contained, under systematic control. The leadership must know what it wants from the congress and move carefully toward these results. To stage a congress with the leadership uncertain as how to proceed (which in fact is the case) or, worse, in disagreement over some major issue such as generational transfer of power, would be to risk even more adverse effects. An ill-prepared congress, for example, could unintentionally cause the now mildly disparate middle and upper-ranking cadres to coalesce into factions and blocs, thus unleashing new and largely uncontrollable political forces within the party. Further postponement might be the greater wisdom.

Party Internal Affairs. By far the major internal party development during 1975, the one on which virtually all others turned, involved unification of the two parts of the country.

Although unification for decades had been the goal, DRV leaders and planners were occupied with more short-range matters and thus had neither formed a contingency plan for communist management of all of South Vietnam, nor created the mechanism by which unification would be accomplished.

It had always been envisioned as a staged and probably slow-moving affair. Even at the time of Saigon's fall, DRV Foreign Ministry officials were telling diplomats in Hanoi that the DRV would not incorporate South Vietnam into the northern governmental structure. Rather they said they would create a government of national reconciliation in the framework of the 1973 Paris agreements which would administer the South until eventual unification. Thus, even at that late date the DRV continued to reinforce the contention which its apologists around the world had been making for a decade and a half, namely, that there were and would be two Vietnams, that the Southern element had a measure of independence and that separate identities could and would be preserved.

From initial statements in the immediate postwar days, including Le Duan's 15 May victory day speech, it appears the original Politburo scenario for the South was this:

(a) Establish a temporary military occupation government, called the Military Management Committee, administered by combat troops commanded by line officers and guided by a corps of party cadres flown in from Hanoi. The chief task of the MMC would be to preserve order, disarm the South Vietnamese; it would last perhaps five or six weeks.

(b) Replace the MMC with the PRG as the new civilian government, its chief task being:

(c) Stage a constituent assembly election to choose representatives who would come to Saigon and write a new constitution which would be promulgated and a people's republic installed.

(d) The new people's republic would operate for three to five years, chiefly devoting itself to developing sources of foreign economic aid.

(e) At the appropriate moment would come full formal unification.

Meantime and throughout the entire period, the party itself, now unified, would be the major (and sole) trans-national institution. Thus for a few years at least there would be an arrangement which could be described as two administrations, one party. Such appears to have been the Politburo intention in May 1975.

In June, Le Duan, Truong Chinh and Pham Van Dong flew to Saigon for meetings with Pham Hung and officials of the NFL and PRG. Probably their discussion dealt almost entirely with the question of South Vietnam's future. That same month the Fifth Session of the DRV Natinal Assembly issued a statement calling for unification, with Hanoi as capital of the entire nation. There were other indications: the Hanoi-based newspaper *Thong Nhat*, devoted to the cause of unification, ceased publication, its final editorial saying "our task has been completed."

But as late as early July the two administrations, one-party idea was still alive among DRV officials. Lack of firm control over the South, coupled with the vastly differing economic systems in the two sectors, it was argued, made it inevitable that unification would come slowly, perhaps in five years, three years at the earliest. This approach was widely and authoritatively asserted, and it was underscored by behavior, such as the dual application for U.N. membership.

Clearly the leadership changed its collective mind about the timetable for unification, speeding it up from three years to five years to immediately. The turning point appears to have been the party's 24th Plenum, which met in late July or early August (apparently in Dalat). At this session, it seems clear in retrospect, the issue of speed of unification was thrashed out. It was not an argument on unification versus non-unification, for southern separatists were not even in attendance. Nor was it simply an argument on slow versus fast. The theoretical base of the dispute turned on definition of stages of political and economic development, in the Marxist-Leninist framework. The three stages were:

—Stage One: People's national democratic revolutionary stage, the objective of which is to "create a national and democratic economy and culture," to quote Le Duan's 15 May address.

—Stage Two: Socialism-advancing-toward-communism stage, or the "stage of socialist revolution" as it is usually termed in North Vietnam.

—Stage Three: Achievement of communism, the utopian final stage in the historical process.

Originally, in these doctrinal terms, it had been decided that a national democratic regime would be created in the South, lasting three to five years, after which Stage Two would begin. The 24th Plenum reversed this decision and determined, by fiat, that Stage One would be skipped (or considered accomplished) and all of Vietnam was now by definition in Stage Two, the socialist revolution stage, although obviously the North was far more advanced in this stage than was the South. Premier Pham Van Dong at the 30th-anniversary celebration, 2 September, made it official and final: "The entire country is advancing toward Socialism." A Lao Dong Party circular issued earlier (4 August) had prepared the ground and alerted cadres that "unification must be urgently achieved."

It grew increasingly clear during late summer 1975 that what was involved in the unification issue was not the merging of two state administrations. After all, it was relatively easy to replace the discredited RVN and graft the revolutionary committee or rev-com system, long utilized in the liberated areas, onto the North's state system. What was involved was proper handling of the trends and forces in the Southern society—chiefly social and economic—so as to guide them in a direction consistent with previous and ongoing Northern plans and policies. South Vietnam remained a vital organism. It had a life of its own. It had a momentum which, if anything, was more dynamic than that in the North.

Thus, unification became a code word for control. In American parlance, the party wanted to get a handle on South Vietnam. To a degree control/unification had different meanings to different cadres. It meant control in the narrow physical sense, of security and order. But security as such did not loom inordinately large as a problem. Containment of such hostility and resistance as existed seemed well assured. Indeed, as contemporary history proves, maintenance of order offers a modern totalitarian state no great difficulty.

Control, more importantly perhaps, meant the imperative of following the DRV model—that is, the kind of organizational, managerial, communicational and manipulative control which makes the Northern system work. By nature it is total, unitary, all intrusive and completely alien to such notions as a two-administration arrangement. The more ideological cadres held that only such control would suffice and that the greater the delay, the harder would be its imposition.

Standing against this at the 24th Plenum were the arguments from the economic sector. All rationality dictated that the two parts of the country be gradually merged, and that meant temporary separate economic and political administrations, guided, of course, by party overseers. Anything else would be economically destructive and wasteful. Jamming together two non-meshing economic and political clusters would result in enormous dislocation and loss. But in the end the decision was immediate unification, whatever the price.

Probably what tipped the balance between the slow pace and the fast pace of unification—since the pragmatic economists and the ideological theoreticians were about equal in power—was the advent of the military, a new and major influence. The ideological arguments apparently were reinforced by the assertions of PAVN generals, now more influential and powerful than ever before, that military security required fast unification. PAVN generals always had seen the war in the South partly in old-fashioned terms, that is, a land enemy at the soft underbelly was to be eliminated so as to provide the protection of open water. Continued and extensive, if low-level, resistance by anti-government elements in the South contributed to their sense of urgency. Finally, as relations with China continued to worsen, the cautious and far viewing PAVN generals could argue with increased vigor that to go slow on unification was to risk losing control, an unnecessary risk and, should the China threat develop, a dangerous one.

PAVN's official needs were clearly indicated in the authoritative *Quan Doi Nhan Dan* (10 November):

> Our Army, which grew much stronger in 30 consecutive years of war and especially with the historic victory in completely defeating the U.S. war of aggression . . . will be an Army that fulfills all missions, overcomes all difficulties and defeats all enemies, a combatant who staunchly defends and contributes to building the independent, unified and socialist Vietnam. . . .
>
> An independent and socialist Vietnam with its important strategic location in Southeast Asia . . . will continue to make its glorious contributions to the common revolutionary struggle. . . .
>
> National unification should be realized as soon as possible because it will promote the building of a powerful country. . . .

The article in its entirety is an orthodox military response: assertion of the military's centrality; insistence that defense considerations override all others; the world and the future viewed largely in geopolitical terms of threat and opportunity. What has changed in the DRV is the increased importance of the military. It may be a temporary phenomenon. But for the moment PAVN is making a claim for a greater role in decision making, not simply as reward for winning a war, but because this is a new era for Vietnam requiring new attitudes toward national defense and the military. Vietnam must think big in strategic terms. Its armed forces, as never was the case in the past, must now become externally oriented.

On 15-21 November, the Political Consultative Conference on National Reunification met in Saigon and discussed the modalities of unification. A ten-person conference presidium was formed (Truong Chinh, Pham Hung, Hoang Van Hoan, Nguyen Huu Tho, Tran Huu Duc, Huynh Tan Phat, General Van Tien Dung, Trinh Dinh Thao, Xuan Thuy and Vo Chi Cong) to make the arrangements. Truong Chinh's 15 November speech set the tone and the parameters then echoed by others:

—Unification is to be treated as a process, not as a goal; there are many dimensions of unification—political, economic, social, ideological, psychic, etc.—and the conference is to be concerned with one, political or "state" unification.

—Unification represents a spiritual fulfillment for the Vietnamese people; it is an integral part of national independence. In fact independence is not possible without unification.

—Unification under a communized (versus capitalist) arrangement is the only acceptable and workable one. Unification is intermixed with economic development and will result in economic benefits for all.

—Security requirements make quick unification imperative (the implication being both internal and foreign security requirements are involved).

—The tasks of the party in the South, now that it is in the socialist revolution stage, are threefold. In Le Duan's words: "We deem it unnecessary [that] the South should carry out the people's national democratic revolution. . . . The great victory of the general offensive and uprising this spring concluded the stage of the people's national democratic revolution in the South and opened up for the southern people the new stage, the socialist revolution stage [which requires] building revolutionary administrations [,] repressing counter-revolutionaries and stamping out feudal land rights."

Truong Chinh outlined the various differences between North and South as the party officially views them (see accompanying Table).

Troung Chinh Compares North and South Vietnam

	NORTH	SOUTH
Economic components	State-run collective economic component	State-run economic component
	Individual economic component ("small number of people")	Collective economic component
		Joint state-private component
		Private capitalist component
		Individual economic component
Social classes	Working class	Working class
	Collectivized peasantry	Peasantry
	Socialist intelligentsia	Petty bourgeoisie
		National bourgeoisie
		Comprador bourgeoisie ("remnants of the feudal landlord class")
Economic planning	Planned economy	"Planning on a small-scale basis only"
State organization	Government National Assembly Constitution	Provisional government Advisory Council Promulgated regulations

Unification, it was made clear, means monolithism—not some federalized arrangement or even gesture to geographic regionalism. As Truong Chinh expressed it: "Unification means unifying the political and social systems, specifically in terms of economic structure, institutions, relationships in production, social strata, organization of the state, the constitution, law, culture and thinking [ideology]."`

The People's Liberation Armed Force will be absorbed into PAVN: "It is necessary . . . to unify the South Vietnam PLAF with the PAVN in the fields of name, functions, duties, rules, regulations, systems, and so forth."

The party also is unified: "To consolidate and improve the unified feature and similarities between the two zones it is necessary to strengthen the party's unified leadership over the revolutionary undertaking of the people throughout the country." Also out of the conference came indications that the NFL would be merged with its counterpart in the North, the Fatherland Front.

From conference reports it appeared that the unification scenario would be: (1) Hold general National Assembly elections in the first half of 1976, according to DRV voting practices; name a total of about 440 members (240 from the North, 200 from the South). Rather than a political party system, candidates would be sponsored by the two respective mass organizations, the Fatherland Front and the NFL. (2) The new expanded National Assembly will meet to receive and consider the draft of a new constitution (presumably prepared ahead of its meeting), elect a new all-Vietnam government and determine such matters as capital city, flag, national anthem, national emblem, and national colors. (3) Official and formal promulgation of unification.

Domestic Attitudes and Activities. The move to unification thus launched the people of Vietnam on a fateful journey whose actual destination was not at all clear. With the task of unification came two overriding considerations: control of the South and economic development of the nation.

The southern scene was marked by insecurity and opposition to the new rulers, by incidents of resistance, dissidence and lawlessness. This originated from hostility rooted in geographic regionalism, from fears by members of religious and cult organizations, and from ethno-linguistic differences. Other resistance was traceable to economic discontent and, of course, to anti-regime sentiment, for many South Vietnamese are militantly anti-communist.

Premier Pham Van Dong noted the condition in his National Day address and listed the four major cadre tasks in the South: "Stabilizing law and order, consolidating security, streamlining the revolutionary machine, and providing employment." A more precise outline of these duties came in a Radio Hanoi broadcast (22 October) to PAVN troops in the South: "Continue to attack and track down the enemy; repress counter-revolutionaries; firmly maintain law and order; strengthen our force in the South; build revolutionary administrations; and engage in other 'mass motivation' campaigns."

The authorities in the South did not seem particularly concerned with the resistance. The nine PAVN divisions stationed in the Saigon area ensured there would be no serious challenge to the new rule. (This also helped ease the Northern food shortage.) The South Vietnamese throughout 1975 were in a state of shock. If extensive and serious opposition to the new order were to develop, it would be only later, after the effects of the shock had passed.

Security in the North, in law and order terms, appeared better than in earlier years, although it never was a major problem. In Hanoi, certain civil defense activities were resumed in October after six months of inactivity. Possibly this was related to worsening relations with China. Mandatory morning physical exercises for cadres, bureaucrats and others were halted in May, then resumed in August.

As noted above, 1975 saw no demobilization by PAVN. In fact, the military draft in the North continued and military recruitment in the South was begun. PAVN not only was on garrison duty, but also was busy taking inventory of the vast stock of military hardware and supplies, estimated at US$6 billion, captured in the South. After inventory some of it was absorbed into the PAVN system. The fate of the rest apparently remained undetermined. There were persistent reports during the year that the DRV was in the process of selling war matériel abroad, to Libya, Pakistan, Mid-East terrorist organizations, Nigeria, even to the ASEAN nations. All reports were denied by the DRV and none could be substantiated during the year in the respective countries. In any event PAVN now is well provisioned and is in fact one of the largest, most experienced, best equipped and generally most formidable forces on the world's military scene.

During the year the regime continued to flog the average citizen's spirit with urgent calls to do one's duty militantly. It launched new and intensive emulation campaigns against what in 1972 was labeled in pejorative terms the "postwar mentality," by which was meant general ennui after years of maximum exertion, which was manifested not so much by lethargy as by increased complaints on the condition of life, demands for increased pay and benefits by cadres and workers alike, and a weakening of discipline among both civilians and military.

North Vietnam's national economic objective since early 1973 had been fastest possible economic development. So the leaders told the country. This had been pretense. To a very large degree national development was sacrificed to the war in the South. But with victory pretense could become reality and an all-out development effort be launched. Now for the first time there would be no need to siphon off most of the nation's resources and send them to war. No longer would the annual roundup of foreign economic aid put military needs over all else. The economic liability of war was past. In fact there had been an economic windfall, inheritance of a southern industrial plant valued at US$12 billion, an agricultural sector of four times the productivity of the North, plus some US$6 billion worth of military equipment and supplies.

The immediate situation, however, was worse than before victory. At the year's end, food was short by at least 300,000 tons of rice. Serious shortages of gasoline, raw materials and electric power developed (even though power during the year was restored to its prewar level). There were major transportation shortages. Rationing of rice (16-24 kilos per month); meat (500 grams to one kilogram per month) and cloth (4-5 meters per year) continued throughout the year, as did purchases on the so-called free market and black market, where virtually everything was available but at up to four times the state market price. DRV agriculture continued to decline from the 1960 high, chiefly due to neglect and lack of capital investment (machines, chemical fertilizer, water conservancy projects) on the communes and state farms. In short, despite the end of the war in May, in December frugality and austerity remained the dominant way of life in North Vietnam.

Some of the dislocation of course was traceable to events of the year, and was temporary, but by the year's end little of the economic snarl had been sorted out. What had developed or been accomplished of major importance at that time appeared to be as follows:

A short-run consumer-level economic improvement program had been launched to provide quick economic benefit to the North Vietnamese citizen. Cadres in the South dismantled consumer-goods factories and sent them north: a textile plant, a plant for monosodium glutamate (in chronic short supply in the DRV), a dairy processing plant, entire hospital and surgical units. They emptied Saigon warehouses of consumer goods: air conditioners, refrigerators, household electrical equipment, toys, clothing and chinaware. American automobiles and Japanese motorcycles appeared on the streets of Hanoi. There were systematic shipments of rice and other foodstuffs from Saigon to Haiphong. (Perhaps in answer to criticism, the DRV claimed in December that during the year it had shipped US$350 million in aid to South Vietnam.) The intent of this appeared to be to reduce consumer complaint in the DRV.

—The start was made on a full-scale economic development program. Premier Pham Van Dong, in his 2 September speech, declared: "The absolute priority objective is economic development . . . under the leading slogan: All for Production to Build Socialism."

The country's chronic labor shortage worsened with the end of the war. There was no demobilization, and recruitment continued. A large number of cadres and workers were ordered South to various tasks, perhaps as many as a half million, most of them going to Quang Tri and elsewhere in northern South Vietnam. At the same time more workers were assigned to housing construction and the transportation-communication sector, further draining labor from other sectors, chiefly agriculture, since 75 percent of the 10.5 million labor force was in agriculture.

The regime indicated that it plans rapid development of the country's petroleum reserves, even if this requires significant concessions to foreign capitalist enterprises. Quiet feelers were put out during the year to the multi-national oil corporations and to private and governmental oil interests in Japan, Italy and the United Kingdom. The DRV also showed interest in studying oil exploitation work in countries considered comparable to the DRV, such as Indonesia. Meantime, the DRV felt a serious shortage of gasoline and made several oil purchases from Japan.

The 1975 rice crop was only fair. The fifth-month crop was bountiful but the tenth-month crop was damaged by typhoons in late August which resulted in flash floods, waterlogging and loss of crops. There was no immediate progress in "solving the grain problem," as it is phrased—that is, making the country self-sufficient in food production. DRV rice production over the years has averaged about 2.9 million tons (milled rice), the high coming in 1959 (3.52 million tons) and the low in 1971 (2.45 million tons). The estimate for 1975 was 2.8 million tons, making the year slightly worse than average. Per capita availability of course continued to decrease, since the DRV population increases at a rate somewhere between 2.5 and 2.9 percent per annum. Given the windfall represented by victory in the South—its rice-producing capacity and its industry serving agriculture (and if the regime does not sabotage its own efforts with heavy-handed imposition of the commune system on the South) —agricultural production in Vietnam should show impressive increases in the next decade. But in 1975 the DRV remained dependent on outside sources (chiefly China) for some 15 percent of the food it consumed.

The country's new (and third) five-year plan (1976-80), which had been on the drafting boards for more than two years, was recast in August (after initial decision in May not to do so) to incorporate the South. The major aspects and characteristics of the plan as they stood at year's end were:

(1) The plan covered all phases of economic activity. Five-year plans are totally comprehensive, theoretically setting down the daily production task of each Vietnamese for five years. The planning approach remained essentially the same: plant concentration and centralization, use of simple economic institutions, and continued great faith in psychological motivation to increase productivity.

(2) Shift of emphasis from a plan "balanced toward agriculture" to one "balanced toward industry." While not entirely clear, this indicates somewhat greater allocation of resources to industry at the expense of agriculture. There will be more power-generating units, steel mills, truck assembly plants, and electronic factories. All this must be preceded by some rapid economic restoration work if the plan is to begin on schedule since Le Duan indicated at the August plenum that only 60 percent of the "All-Vietnam" industrial capability had been restored and that plants in operation were working at only two-thirds of capacity because of shortages of raw materials.

(3) The agricultural sector will be overhauled (an effort began in mid-1973). The commune managerial-administrative structure is to be reorganized. Increased authority will go to commune managers at the expense of the production brigade leaders. Commune consolidation will continue. Giant agro-factories are to be created, with 40,000 workers on a single 10,000-hectare commune. The work-point system is to be changed so as to increase individual farmer incentive. (The future of the private plot system, if it has been determined, had not been announced.) The decision is a momentous one. Of the total commune/state-farm land in production in North Vietnam (95 percent of all land is collectivized), some 95 percent of the acreage is centrally managed while 5 percent is "private" (plots farmed by individual families who are then free to dispose of their crop, usually garden vegetables, as they wish). Cadre studies in early 1973 revealed that 15 to 20 percent of North Vietnam's annual agricultural output comes from the private plots while only 80 to 85 percent comes

from the commune/state-farm managed land. Even so, private plots, which have tended to increase on many communes in recent years, are an ideological anathema since they represent, to quote Le Duan, "the daily rebirth of capitalism on the farm."

(4) Much of the agricultural burden will be shifted to the South. Under the plan, South Vietnam will become largely pastoral, a vast food-production and food-processing region with only scattered light industry. This involves a massive back-to-the-farm movement in the South, which already is under way.

(5) Efforts will be redoubled to increase agricultural yields. This will involve technology such as triple-cropping, more frequent vegetable plantings, new water conservancy projects, increased mechanization, greater availability of chemical fertilizer and other additives. It is apparent, however, that the planners remain parsimonious in allocating resources to agriculture, still unable to admit the high correlation between agricultural investment and agricultural productivity. Ideological blinders stay on. There remains the longstanding and persistent tendency to regard agricultural productivity not largely as a matter of capital and plant investment, but as a problem chiefly in management and psychology. DRV agricultural productivity is low and getting lower not because of unmotivated farmers or war damage (dike bombings is a myth), but because for years the agricultural sector has been starved and neglected. For decades the regime sought to increase yields largely by haranguing farmers and engaging them in endless emulation campaigns. The end of the war and greater availability of resources has not changed this thinking. Le Duan particularly continues to treat the "grain problem" not as a matter of land, labor, and capital investment but as a search for new ways to engender diligence, dynamism and perseverance among those who work the communes. Once it was believed he did this out of necessity. Now it appears it is a matter of principle.

(6) The plan calls for much tighter and more systematic control over the fruits of agriculture once they leave the fields. Despite strenuous efforts to control food distribution it is estimated that some 20 percent of the rice eaten in North Vietnam does not go through the state's hands.

(7) Work has begun on a master economic development plan, conceived as three consecutive five-year plans, which will take the country into the 1990s.

The five-year plan is certain to result in marked economic development of North Vietnam and significant improvement in the individual citizen's standard of living. This will hold true even if the plan falls short of its goals and fails to meet its various norms, which not only is possible but probable. Serious and intensive economic effort is under way, for the first time in a decade and a half, and this cannot help but mean improvement.

What is interesting but undeterminable is speculation on the precise motives of the leadership in this effort to lift Vietnam by its economic bootstraps. Quite possibly the leaders see themselves in a clear race with time. For years they have kept the lid tightly on North Vietnam, using the rationale of unification. Now the leaders may see that they must produce significant progress toward higher standards of living or face a socio-political explosion; that no agitprop campaign can shunt aside future expectations, only quick and demonstrable improvement in the quality of life in North Vietnam. Or, the leaders may take the exact opposite view, that the most dangerous course possible is to move away from the Spartan life and toward affluence. They may embrace what has been termed the Eric Hoffer thesis. Hoffer maintains that rulers in a modern totalitarian society of the Stalinist type can quite easily maintain control so long as they are totalitarian about it, but run great risks if they try to be less totalitarian even when they themselves are managing the liberalization. He uses the metaphor of a man holding down a tightly coiled spring. Keeping it fully compressed requires only some muscle power. If he tries to lessen the compression it becomes a matter of complex muscular coordination, not simple strength. The spring easily can fly out of control.

International Views and Activities. All of North Vietnam's external relationships changed at least to some degree during 1975 as the result of its military victory in the South. That victory may cause a basic shift in certain DRV national interests in foreign affairs, although this remained uncertain at year's end.

Five aspects of the DRV's foreign relations were of particular significance.

First, the DRV now sees itself, as indeed it is, as a major force in Asia. Overnight it achieved an irreversible quantum-jump in geopolitical power.

DRV theoreticians during the year outlined clearly the meaning of their victory for Vietnamese foreign affairs as well as their view of the current and future world scene. The major points they made were:

—The world's geopolitical strategic balance has been fundamentally and irrevocably altered by communist victory in Indochina.

—Three major forces now dominate the international scene and they largely will write the future of the world: (a) socialist world superiority: the power of socialist thinking coupled with its ever-growing military and economic strength; (b) the rise of new national attitudes of independence (xenophobic, anti-interdependent hostility toward outside influence) among smaller nations; (c) unification of the Third World, now bound together by common interest (hostility toward rich nations and determination to redress economic imbalance).

—The doctrine of protracted-conflict revolutionary war, as perfected in Vietnam, has been fully vindicated. Stimulated by Vietnam's victory, revolutionary forces world-wide can be expected to develop and flourish, enjoying new advantages, and destined to achieve ultimate victory over capitalism. In fact a new era of revolutionary warfare has been ushered in.

—The United States has declined as a superpower. The Vietnam war was a historic confrontation between the chief international imperialist reactionary and the forces of national independence/ socialism. In Asia, the changes will be the greatest because the U.S. defense line, maintained for decades, has collapsed.

The second major external change during the year was the immediate lessening of DRV entanglement in the Sino-Soviet dispute. Most of the wartime restraints, chiefly self-imposed, withered or died. DRV spokesmen during the closing months of the year repeatedly asserted that a major tenet of future foreign policy would be "independence" from both the USSR and the People's Republic of China. In general the Sino-Soviet dispute became less central to DRV thinking. Ironically, in the dispute itself, because of the Vietnamese victory, the stakes in the game were raised and the USSR-PRC rivalry was intensified both in Hanoi and throughout Asia.

DRV-PRC relations were deteriorating as 1975 began and continued to deteriorate throughout the year, reaching by December perhaps their lowest ebb ever. This was due partly to the rise of new contentious issues and partly to the exacerbation of old ones. As the year began the DRV considered that PRC war support was inadeuqate, that the PRC even might secretly be sabotaging clear-cut DRV victory. There were differences over the USSR, détente, and respective policies in Laos and Cambodia. There were conflicting claims to the Spratly, Paracel, and other islands in the South China Sea (an issue which remained a dark cloud on the horizon), and even unverified reports of hostile incidents along the 500-mile-long Vietnamese-Chinese border.

Clearly the DRV failed—as the USSR did not fail—to read correctly the course events would take in Indochina during 1975. By January the USSR had concluded that the DRV was going to win and quickly. It adjusted its behavior accordingly. Peking lost precious weeks clinging to its earlier estimate of indeterminate stalement for an indefinite period. In the wake of victory DRV-PRC relations were in a bruised condition. Nor was it lost on DRV leaders that the Chinese entertained distinctly mixed feelings about the stunning DRV victory. And they were aware of Peking's concern over increased DRV status and prestige in Southeast Asia. Finally there was the running undercurrent of difference over such issues as Portugal, India, and Sikkim.

At the year's end, then, the state of DRV-PRC relations could be described as generally poor, largely immobilized. The Vietnamese were heady with victory, the Chinese slightly embarrassed by it. Issues between the two countries for the moment were being held in abeyance as if by mutual consent. In peculiarly Asian fashion the two countries were in the process of delineating their new relationship and this act of redefinition was more important than any single issue.

USSR-DRV relations warmed steadily during the year although in basic terms nothing actually changed. The DRV remained dependent on the USSR for major economic assistance. The USSR responded to that need in a generous (but undetailed) manner, in part perhaps as an exchange for Le Duan's agreement in a September communiqué that "détente is irreversible." The USSR for its part continued to use the DRV as part of its broader anti-PRC campaign to increase USSR influence in countries bordering on China and lessening Chinese influence over individual Asian communist parties and governments. The USSR has a strategic and tactical disadvantage in Asia. Most of its moves there are moves from weakness. It believes, probably correctly, that the Chinese generally can undercut most USSR ventures in Asia just as the Chinese believe that the USSR can undercut most PRC ventures in the Middle East and elsewhere. Both probably are correct.

The USSR continued to press its advantage in Hanoi and appeared to act on the basis that Vietnam was the cornerstone of USSR policy in Southeast Asia. In Hanoi and elsewhere during the year it again offered its idea of a security-cooperation system for Asia which in essence is an anti-Chinese alliance with Moscow acting as senior guide. Where this failed it fell back on repeated warning on the folly of trying to move closer to Peking.

In Hanoi it suggested again the Soviet model for economic development. It built Ho Chi Minh's mausoleum (larger than Lenin's) for the North Vietnamese. It looked on reunification efforts with approval (and the Chinese did not). And, above all, it sought to maximize its chief advantage over China, which is economic, what it can offer by way of economic aid. In the long run this could prove advantageous but never so much so as to achieve what the USSR would truly like to see, a rupture of DRV-PRC relations.

It is possible, as some observers suggest, that the DRV leaders in 1975 decided that the postwar world required them to abandon their long-standing policy of neutralism in the Sino-Soviet dispute (or more correctly, carefully walking the line between the two contenders) and come down hard on the side of the USSR—on the grounds that only in this manner could the USSR largesse be encouraged and because the DRV may need a dependable ally since it is not entirely sure of a benign future China. More likely, however, what will prevail is something less drastic: the DRV leaders will conclude that China is too large and too close for any policy except accommodation; that, like it or not, the DRV must live with China, must bend when the Chinese become adamant over an issue, and must never permit a rupture to take place.

The third change was in the economic connection in foreign affairs. Economic need remained as great as ever, the change being in kind. DRV military hardware requirements all but vanished. They were replaced by new and even stronger requirements for economic development resources.

Possibly, although this was less clear at the year's end, the DRV external attitude shifted to a more pragmatic, less ideological coloration. In the final months of the year DRV pronouncements indicated that "economics is in command," as the Chinese phrase it, meaning that the measure of DRV policy toward other countries would turn on its estimates of how generous that country might be in economic aid.

The pronouncements also indicated that the DRV would seek aid from capitalist countries and in fact would be willing to borrow money if acceptable credit arrangements could be made. Chief needs, it was indicated, included construction equipment and materials such as steel, cement, and lumber; cranes and earth-moving equipment; transportation and communication systems and equipment; agricultural technology and means of mechanizing agriculture; oil-exploitation and mineral-extractive equipment and technical assistance; plus whatever gratis aid projects involving consumer goods or humanitarian aid could be garnered. The DRV claimed that it could offer, by way of trade (now or available shortly): coal, phosphates, gold, tungsten, manganese, and other metals and minerals; industrial crops (kenaf, ramie, rubber, seagrass matting); silk, rattan furniture, fish and seafood (chiefly shrimp and lobster), citrus fruits, and art objects. Its ability to deliver all these goods at the moment remained questionable.

Foreign aid, most of it gratis, increased in generosity during the year. Typical but not inclusive were the following: *USSR*: food, petroleum products, a chemical fertilizer plant, oil exploitation project, postal-telephone-telegraph equipment; truck assembly plant; public housing construction in Hanoi and the Ho mausoleum. *PRC*: food (large quantities of rice); consumer goods such as cooking equipment and ceramic ware: railway construction and maintenance; communications equipment. *France*: bicycle factory; hospital equipment; blankets; clothing; food such as condensed milk. *Sweden*: Bai Bang paper mill ($300 million project); two hospitals (Children's Hospital in Hanoi and Dung Be general hospital); earth-moving equipment; nursery school in Viet Tri. *Cuba*: Victory Hotel in Hanoi; Dong Hoi hospital; cattle-raising project. *Italy*: mobile hospital. *Belgium*: medicines and antibiotics. *Britain*: Ha Tinh hospital (private contributions). *Poland*: earth-moving equipment. *Australia*: cattle-raising project. *Japan*: a 13.5 billion yen loan (over a two-year span); marine and agricultural projects. *United States*: humanitarian aid (private donations).

Fourth, there was the obviously altered relationship with the United States. Wartime confrontation suddenly disappeared along with considerable bitterness and hatred on both sides. The Paris agreements, which had been the formal basis of the relationship, lay in shreds, their future legal relevance in doubt. There was a sort of psychological recoil by the United States, a momentary loss of certitude in attitude toward the United States by the North Vietnamese.

Then began a period of psychological adjustment to the new order of things. As if by tacit mutual consent both countries seemed to agree on the course and the timing of events in the relationship in the near future. There would be a period during which the dust would be allowed to settle, during which both sides would seek to prevent the relationship from becoming frozen, as was the case in U.S.-PRC relations after the Korean War. Eventually, in a year or two, there could begin a cautious effort toward normalizing relations in travel, trade, and diplomacy. All of this would be conditioned by the respective behavior of each, the United States carefully watching DRV actions in Thailand and elsewhere in Southeast Asia, the DRV watching for possible signs that the United States was organizing an anti-Vietnam alliance in Southeast Asia or was attempting to roll back communist control in Indochina.

DRV spokesmen late in the year asserted that normal relations with the United States were one of the DRV's three basic foreign policy goals ("independence" from the USSR and PRC and obtaining economic aid from all nations were the other two). This objective was not described in any detail. Nor was it restated in the form of overt behavior. The clearest indication from Hanoi on the subject involved oil exploitation, various signals sent to U.S. and multi-national oil corporations concerning resumption of work off South Vietnam (reportedly six wells were in operation there at the year's end). Oil exploitation could prove to be the thin entering wedge in U.S.-DRV relations.

Fifth, the idea of a Federation of Indochina once again surfaced and colored the DRV's relations with Laos and Cambodia and, in a different way, with Thailand. Not since the 1950s, when Ho Chi Minh spoke vaguely of a "French Indochina without the French," had the idea received any attention in Hanoi. Most of the attention in 1975 was negative, in the form of DRV denials that the idea was at all alive. Privately, cadres and others gave the subject considerable discussion.

Such a federation represents, or will come to represent, a major long-range DRV objective. Probably it will begin as a proposed loosely structured arrangement in confederation, established in such a way as to offer advantages to Laos and Cambodia, and based on equality, with Vietnam being first among the equals. Gradually, the Vietnamese would hope, the structure would become institutionalized, then formalized. Eventually would come full federation. To achieve this goal the Vietnamese must overcome two major forces: the historical fear and dislike by non-Vietnamese involved, and competition and resistance by the PRC and perhaps other countries in the region. There would be dangers to the Laotians and Cambodians inside such a federation, but other dangers outside; hence for Laos and Cambodia it would largely come down to a least-worse choice. During the year the DRV continued to take a strongly proprietary attitude toward Laos and Cambodia. It continued to assert in public statements the unique ties binding together the three countries as well as the need for ever more militant solidarity among the three peoples.

Cambodia, after the communist victory there, turned inward, shutting itself off from foreign (with the exception of Chinese) influence, a treatment barely tolerable to the DRV. Relations between the two countries had been strained for several years, marked by considerable ethnic-based hostility. Le Duan flew uninvited to Phnom Penh in August for meetings apparently dealing with the festering Cambodian-Vietnamese border, scene of a number of low-level incidents during the summer. Unofficial reports said Le Duan was stern. Late in the year relations improved somewhat. Cambodia came out of its self-imposed isolation to a degree. DRV and Khmer ambassadors were exchanged in November.

In Laos events during the year unfolded more to DRV liking. The country established a people's-republic style of government. DRV-Pathet Lao relations remained close and harmonious. There appeared to be some DRV concern over the prospect of Laos becoming the cockpit of competition among the USSR, PRC, and DRV. But with 30,000 troops still in the country, the DRV remained the dominant force. The DRV's chief interest in Laos—to force a diminution of U.S. influence and presence—was fully realized during the year.

The DRV mounted strong psychological pressure against Thailand, beginning in mid-1975, and relations were perhaps the most unpleasant of any DRV relationships. More than the other Southeast Asian countries, Thailand was traumatized by the communist victories in Indochina. For the DRV, Thailand became a case of dogma and opportunism battling caution and broader interests. Clearly, DRV behavior during the year was designed to push Thailand to the left, to isolate Thailand from its neighbors, to further internal differences, and to inhibit various Thai policies with respect to U.S. bases, Lao border challenges, Vietnam war matériel, Vietnamese refugees in Thailand, and the country's own insurgency. The Thais, beginning in January, sought diplomatic relations with the DRV, but made only modest progress.

The ASEAN nations, potential rivals of the DRV, sources of future challenge, or possible candidates for intimidation, presented the DRV with serious policy questions. But little commitment was made by the DRV. Hanoi said that it wanted normal relations with its Southeast Asian neighbors. It appeared to want to work through state mechanisms. But also it appeared quite willing to aid local insurgencies when this provided leverage. There was not, however, the dispatch into South Asia of war matériel captured in South Vietnam that had been feared by many in the region. DRV behavior toward the ASEAN nations was indecisive. It seemed to be straddling the contradiction arising from assurances of non-intervention in internal affairs and promises to contribute to the "revolution" in Southeast Asia.

Japan-DRV relations, after two years of on-again, off-again negotiations—marked by some strange and often callous behavior by Hanoi and some puzzling actions in the South—finally culminated in October with the establishment of full diplomatic relations. (The Japanese chargé d'affaires presented his credentials in Hanoi 11 October; the DRV ambassador to Japan had not arrived in Tokyo at the year's end.) The price was high: Japan agreed to give North Vietnam 13.5 billion yen in aid over a two-year period (negotiated upward by the DRV from an early 1975 figure of 5 billion yen).

Japan's interest in Vietnam concerns access to raw materials and markets, peace and stability in the region (to help keep the oil tanker routes from the Middle East open), closer political and cultural ties, general economic growth in the area, and, finally, a role for Japan in the future of the region.

The DRV leadership holds a complex view of Japan, regarding it both as a potential source of extensive economic assistance and an economic imperialist. It also apparently views Japan as something of a balance in the DRV relationship with the PRC and the USSR. The result, over the past several years, was that the DRV would woo and then rebuff Japan. It appeared that some X-factor, perhaps psychological, influenced DRV attitudes toward Japan.

The DRV's care in dealing with the ASEAN countries was indicative of its general attitude toward international organizations. It seemed quite apparent during 1975 that the DRV plans to build a systematic world-wide relationship with all appropriate regional and international groups (communist and non-communist alike). Although long militantly anti-United Nations, it applied for U.N. membership as well as membership in U.N. specialized organizations. Its reaction to the U.S. veto of its application in August was surprisingly mild, a reflection of its confusion over unification policy (one versus two Vietnams) and perhaps its conclusion that application for U.N. membership in 1975 was ill-timed and premature.

Publications. Most DRV and Lao Dong Party official statements and resolutions, plenum resolutions, Secretariat directives, and major speeches by leading party figures appear wholly or in part in *Nhan Dan* (The People), the party's daily newspaper (an edition of which now is printed in Saigon). *Hoc Tap* (Studies) is the party's theoretical monthly. *Quan Doi Nhan Dan* (People's Army) is the daily newspaper of the PAVN (which also publishes a monthly magazine called *Tap Chi Quan Doi Nhan Dan*). Other publications include *Tien Phong* (Vanguard), a party youth publication; *Lao Dong* (Worker), official publication of the Vietnam General Federation of Trade Unions, a major mass organization; *Cuu Quoc* (National Salvation) weekly organ of the Vietnam Fatherland Front; and *Nghien Cuu Kinh Te* (Economic Studies), which carries material on national planning and developments in the economic sector.

The "Voice of Vietnam" (Radio Hanoi) broadcasts in 10 languages on both medium- and short-wave frequencies. Books issue from several publishing houses, including (for English, French, Chinese, Russian and Spanish) the Foreign Language Publishing House, Hanoi.

Washington, D.C.   Douglas Pike

Vietnam: Republic of South Vietnam

The People's Revolutionary Party (Dang Nhan Dan Cach Mang; PRP) was founded on 1 January 1962 by remnants of the badly decimated southern organization of the Vietnam Workers' Party (Dang Lao Dong Vietnam; VWP), newly arrived cadres from North Vietnam (consisting mainly of Southern regroupees) and individuals who had formed an "Association of Former Resistance Fighters."

The PRP was formed because senior VWP leaders needed a political organization in South Vietnam which could function semi-autonomously during the period in which Vietnam was divided into two regions. Earlier, in September 1960 at the VWP's Third National Congress, the VWP had set itself two strategic tasks: socialist construction in the North and national liberation by means of a national democratic revolution in the South. The PRP was specifically formed to carry out this latter task.

In October 1961 the VWP reestablished a special directorate of its Central Committee with authority over party affairs in the South. Provision for this directorate, known popularly in the Western press as COSVN (Central Office for South Vietnam), was made in new party statutes adopted at the 1960 congress (article 24):

> The Central Executive Committee [of the VWP] may also assign a number of its members to set up a central directorate in charge of leading party activities in especially important party chapters. The central directorate is placed under the leadership of the Central Executive Committee. (*Nhan Dan*, Hanoi, 15 September 1960.)

According to an announcement made at the time of the PRP's formation, the PRP would "carry on the glorious and historic work of its revolutionary predecessor parties" (Liberation Press Agency [LAP], 13 January 1962.) It was clear from the context that the PRP was the present-day version of the Indochinese Communist Party, founded in 1930, which is the acknowledged predecessor of the VWP. After the Communist victory in South Vietnam on 30 April 1975, the party-controlled domestic press all but dropped reference to the PRP, referring instead to the South Vietnam organization of the VWP (Dang bo mien Nam Dang Lao Dong Viet Nam). Publications designed for circulation overseas have continued to refer to the PRP, albeit rarely (see *South Viet Nam in Struggle*, no. 305, 16 June, p. 2).

When the revolutionary armed forces under party control defeated the military units of the incumbent government of the Republic of Vietnam (RVN), forcing their unconditional surrender on 30 April, the party found itself in control of all Vietnam below the 17th parallel. At present the party has chosen to exercise its authority through the medium of military management committees (MMC's) and, in especially secure areas, through representation on people's revolutionary committees.

There are no reliable estimates of party strength in the South. In 1973 PRP membership was placed at around 60,000 (*YICA, 1974*, p. 560). This figure probably declined somewhat during the next year. In 1975 the party may have raised its membership to 180,000 as a result of a recruitment campaign (information provided privately to the author by American government officials). South Vietnam's population is estimated to be about 20,800,000.

Leadership and Organization. It would appear that party affairs in South Vietnam are run by three main committees: one for central Trung Bo (Zone 5 Committee), one for Nam Bo (COSVN) and the third for the Saigon (Ho Chi Minh City)—Gia Dinh special zone. It is as yet unclear whether separate committees exist for the Highlands (the "B-3" Front) and for the Tri-Thien-Hue area (embracing Quang Tri and Thua Thien provinces and Hue city).

The party's organization for Nam Bo (COSVN) appears to exercise control over what used to comprise the third and fourth military regions of the RVN, with the exception of the Saigon-Gia Dinh area. Mention of a party committee for eastern Nam Bo (Radio Hanoi, 30 June) suggests that an intermediate-level committee functions between COSVN and the provinces. It also implies the existence of party committees in western and central Nam Bo, a traditional division, although no mention was made of such. Provincial party committees have been reported operating in Bac Lieu (Liberation Radio, 25 June) and in Soc Trang (LPA, 18 August). It should be noted that party provincial boundaries are not congruent with those of the former RVN government.

The leadership of the party's committee for South Vietnam has been identified as follows: Pham Hung, secretary; Nguyen Van Linh and Phan Xuan Thai, deputy secretaries; and Tran Nam Trung, member. All are concurrent members of the VWP's Central Committee, and Pham Hung is ranked fourth in the VWP's Politburo. Nguyen Minh Duong has been identified as head of COSVN's Front Committee.

The Saigon-Gia Dinh area is organized separately under its own municipal party committee. Subordinate committees function at precinct and ward levels. The leadership of the Ho Chi Minh City (as Saigon is now called) party committee is as follows: Vo Van Kiet, secretary; Nguyen Ho (possibly Nguyen Van Ho) and Nguyen Van Tuong, standing committee members; and Sau Nhan, head of the propaganda and training department.

The Zone 5 Committee for central Trung Bo is headed by Vo Chi Cong, secretary of its executive committee. Cong, like his counterparts in Nam Bo, has also been identified as a concurrent member of the VWP Central Committee. Party committees were reported active in the following central provinces: Gia Lai (formerly Pleiku), Thua Thien-Hue (Le Tu Dong, secretary), Quang Nam-Da Nang (Ho Vinh, secretary), and Quang Tri.

Since 30 April two party youth groups have made their appearance: the Ho Chi Minh People's Revolutionary Youth Union (Doan Thanh Nien Nhan Dan Cach Mang Ho Chi Minh; HCM PRYU) in Nam Bo and the Ho Chi Minh Working Youth Union (HCM WYU) in Trung Bo. The latter is identical in name to the youth group operating in the Democratic Republic of Vietnam (DRV). The party's organization for pre-teens, the Ho Chi Minh Vanguard Youth League, claimed to have 120,000 members, of whom 33,000 resided in Saigon (LPA, 19 September). Although the activities of this group were reported, such as a recruitment drive in Ba Ria-Long Khanh Province, no leadership positions were mentioned.

Auxiliary and Mass Organizations. *Provisional Revolutionary Government of the Republic of South Vietnam (PRG).* Until 30 April the PRG was theoretically the insurgent government in areas of South Vietnam not controlled by the RVN. Its main purpose appears to have been to provide a facade administrative legitimacy to the outside world. The PRG was founded at a "congress of people's representatives" held during 4-6 June 1969. It consists of two main national bodies: the Council of Ministers and the Advisory Council. Membership for these bodies comprises mainly senior officials of the National Front for the Liberation of South Vietnam (NFL) and the Vietnam Alliance of National and Democratic Peace Forces (VANDPF).

Very little is known of the operations of the PRG below the national level. Last year it was announced that special PRG "representations" were being set up at the regional level; to date PRG representations have been reported in Central Trung Bo, southern Trung Bo (created at a congress of PRG representatives on 10-12 November 1974) and eastern Nam Bo only (whose first conference of the representation was held on 22-29 November 1974). The PRG administration extends downward at the provincial, district and village levels through the medium of people's revolutionary committees.

After 30 April, party leaders chose to exercise their authority through the military management committees. As security conditions have improved, these MMC's have been replaced by provisional people's revolutionary committees. During 1975, however, the PRG was not installed in office at the national level.

The present composition of the Council of Ministers is as follows:

President   Huynh Tan Phat

Vice-presidents: Phung Van Cung, Nguyen Doa, Nguyen Van Kiet

Minister of Economy and Finance   Duong Ky Hiep (acting)

Minister of Education and Youth   Nguyen Van Kiet

Deputy Ministers: Le Van Tri, Ho Huu Nhut

Minister of Foreign Affairs   Nguyen Thi Binh
Deputy Ministers: Le Quang Chanh, Hoang Bich Son

Minister of the Interior   Phung Van Cung
Deputy Minister: Nguyen Ngoc Thuong

Minister of Information and Culture   Luu Huu Phuoc
Deputy Ministers: Thanh Nghi, Lu Phuong

Minister of Justice   Truong Nhu Tang
Deputy Minister: Le Van Tha

Minister of National Defense   Tran Nam Trung
Deputy Ministers: Nguyen Chanh, Dong Van Cong

Minister of Public Health, Social   Duong Quynh Hoa
    Affairs and War Invalids
Deputy Minister: But Thi Me

Ministers in the President's Office: Ung Ngoc Ky, Tran Buu Kiem

Minister without Portfolio   Nguyen Van Hieu

The composition of the Advisory Council is:

President   Nguyen Huu Tho
Vice-President   Trinh Dinh Thao
Members: Huynh Cuong, Huynh Van Tri, Ibih Aleo, Nguyen Dinh Chi, Pham Ngoc Hung,
    Thich Don Hau, Vu Canh

There are several personnel changes of note. A permanent Economy and Finance minister has not been appointed; Duong Ky Hiep, the acting minister, replaced Nguyen Van Trieu. Lu Phuong, a deputy minister of Information and Culture, and Vu Canh, a member of the Advisory Council, are both new appointees. Ho Xuan Son, Le Van Giap and Nguyen Thi Dinh, although active in 1975 in other capacities, were not officially identified with their previous ministerial positions (*YICA, 1975*, pp. 444-45).

The PRG serves as the party's sounding board for both internal and external policies. In the months prior to the Communist victory the PRG's name was put behind all major statements concerned with the party's negotiating position vis-à-vis the RVN and the policies to be pursued in the post-victory period. On 21 March, after the successful assault on Ban Me Thuot had triggered the ill-fated ARVN (Army of the Republic of Vietnam) withdrawal from the Highlands, the PRG issued a statement outlining its current policies:

> The PRGRSV affirms its stand which was clearly outlined in its 8 October 1974 statement [see *YICA, 1975*, p. 448]. This stand is: resolutely demand that the United States completely and thoroughly end its military involvement and intervention in South Vietnam's internal affairs and withdraw all its military personnel disguised as civilians from South Vietnam, as specified in the Paris agreement, and [the] Nguyen Van Thieu clique—the main obstacle to the settlement of the present political problems in South Vietnam—be toppled so an administration which is really eager for peace, independence, democracy, and national concord and which will scrupulously implement the Paris agreement on Vietnam can be set up in Saigon. The PRGRSV is ready to negotiate with such an administration with a view to promptly solving South Vietnam's problems. (Liberation Radio, 21 March.)

On 25 March the PRG unveiled a new 7-point policy addressed to RVN officers, soldiers, policemen, public servants and their families. Each point dealt with a category of people, such as youths opposed to conscription, general officers and higher civil servants, and suggested actions which, if undertaken would be suitable rewarded. For example, point 6(C) stated:

> As to officers and general officers whose units revolt or mutiny under their command to join the revolutionary forces, they will be recognized as insurgent officers. They retain their rank, will receive important assignments and will be cited. Those who lead particularly meritorious actions will receive promotions. (Full text in *NYT*, 3 April.)

On 1 April the PRG issued a "10-point [statement of] policy toward the Newly Liberated Areas," and a 10-point "code of conduct for cadres and personnel in the newly liberated areas." The former, a guide to the PRG's current program, was as follows:

1. Completely eradicate the regime and its ruling apparatus, the armed forces, organizations, and rules and regulations and forms of repression and control of the puppet administration, and quickly establish the people's revolutionary administration at all levels in the newly liberated areas. All puppet agencies must come under revolutionary administration management. Public officials who worked for the puppet machinery are allowed to continue to work under the revolutionary administration and must correctly implement its policies and lines. Abolish all reactionary political parties and factions and all other political organizations which were lackeys of the U.S. imperialists and the puppet administration.

2. Implement the people's democratic liberties and achieve equality between men and women. Insure freedom of faith and unity and equality among the various religions. Respect the people's freedom of worship and protect pagodas, churches, and temples.

3. Implement a policy to achieve all-people unity and national reconciliation and concord and oppose aggressive imperialism. Strictly forbid all activities creating divisiveness, hatred, and suspicion among the people and among the various nationalities. Everyone, regardless of financial situation, nationality or political tendency, must unite, love and assist one another in developing the liberated areas and a peaceful, joyful and healthy life. Implement equality among the people of various nationalities, large and small. Positively assist the ethnic minority compatriots to develop their economic and cultural activities and improve their livelihood.

4. Everyone in the liberated areas will be allowed to continued their activities to earn a living and must maintain public order and security and support the revolution. The people's revolutionary administration will resolutely and promptly smash all enemy schemes and acts of sabotage and counterattacks; and it will severely punish those who oppose the revolutionary administration, sabotage public order and security, encroach on the people's livelihood, property and dignity and encroach or sabotage property managed by the revolutionary administration.

5. The property of the puppet administration will be managed by the PRGRSV.

6. Enterprises, industries and handicrafts, trading, and communications and transportation enterprises and other public utility projects must continue their activities to support the people's economy and normal activities. Restoration of production will be actively carried out and the urban people's livelihood will be stabilized. Unemployed workers and other working people will be given jobs. Industrialists' and traders' property will be guaranteed. They will be allowed to continue their business transactions if these are beneficial to national plans and the people's livelihood. Orphans, invalids, and the old and weak will be cared for.

7. Encourage and assist peasants in restoring and developing agricultural production, fishery, salt production and forestry; encourage the owners of plantations to grow industrial crops and fruit trees and continue their business.

8. All cultural, scientific and technical installations, schools and hospitals must continue their operations to serve the people. All reactionary, depraved and brain-poisoning organizations and activities of the U.S. imperialists and the puppet administration are banned. Encourage and develop healthy national cultural activities. Appreciate and employ persons of talent in the scientific and technical domains who are useful to national development.

9. Strictly implement the PRGRSV's policy promulgated on 25 March 1975 [see Liberation Radio, 26 March; *FBIS*, 27 March] toward officers and soldiers of the puppet administration. All servicemen,

officers, policemen, disabled troops, veterans and personnel of the puppet administration who have quit the enemy ranks to join the liberated areas, who have volunteered to stay in the liberated areas, who have reported to the organs of the revolutionary administration in accordance with regulations, or who have seriously complied with the laws of the revolutionary administration will be provided assistance in their business or allowed to return to their homes and participate in various activities according to their desires and ability. Those who have scored merits or who have atoned for their faults by achieving merits will be commended and rewarded. Those who resist the revolution will be seriously punished. Those guilty persons who have sincerely repented will be granted leniency.

10. Insure the lives and property of foreigners. All foreigners must respect the independence and sovereignty of Vietnam and must seriously implement all lines and policies of the revolutionary administration. Those foreigners who have contributed to the struggle for independence and freedom and in the nation building of the South Vietnamese people will be welcomed. (Liberation Radio, 3 April; *FBIS*, 3 April.)

The 10-point code of conduct was designed to assure the populace of the PRG's lenient policies and to provide a strict guide on behavior to party cadres and other personnel. From all accounts this code is being followed, much to the relief of the "newly liberated population," which had been led to expect much worse. As released by the Liberation Press Agency (3 April; *FBIS*, 4 April) the points were:

1. Firmly defend the revolutionary power, always remain vigilant, ready to smash all schemes of sabotage and opposition of the enemy.

2. Strictly implement all policies of the National Front for Liberation and all regulations defined by the revolutionary administration.

3. Strengthen solidarity among various strata of the population, among the cadres, combatants and the people, actively mobilize the people to carry out all policies and undertakings of the Front and the revolutionary administration in order to promote confidence and enthusiasm, step up production and fighting and consolidate the newly liberated areas in all fields.

4. Respect and protect the lives and property of the people, do not encroach upon even a needle and thread of the people, do not use the people's property without permission. Anyone who damages the people's property will be fined.

5. Ensure the democratic liberties of the people, respect the freedom of belief and the customs and habits of the people.

6. Protect public property, historical relics, cultural and art works and scientific research projects.

7. All documents, papers, weapons, property, money and other things captured from the enemy must be handed over to the revolutionary administration. It is forbidden to destroy or appropriate them or give them to others.

8. Be exemplary in observing public order, actively take part in checking and undoing all spying activities, and psychological warfare allegations of the enemy; fully observe the regulations concerning defense against enemy spies, keep the secrets of the revolution, mobilize the people to check and sweep away all kinds of depraved and reactionary culture.

9. It is forbidden to make arrests and to search persons or houses without warrants from the competent organs. In case a person is caught in the act of opposing the revolutionary administration and people by committing such acts as sabotage, robbery, murder, rape or causing disturbances to public security and order, he must be arrested and handed over immediately to the responsible organs for trial.

10. To preserve the revolutionary virtues: industry, thrift, integrity and public-mindedness. Strict forbiddance of all attitudes and actions harmful to the prestige of the revolution.

During the first three weeks of April most of South Vietnam north of Saigon came under the control of the revolutionary forces. Meanwhile the PRG convened a conference of "revolutionary administration at zonal and provincial levels in Nam Bo and southern Trung Bo to discuss the building of the liberated areas and the development of the role of the revolutionary administration in the new situation" (Liberation Radio, 6 April). Revolutionary administrations were soon reported in Hue, Da Nang and Quang Tri. Joint PRG-NFL delegations toured the Highlands and Lam Dong and Phuoc Long provinces.

During the final week of April attention focused on Saigon. Some 15 main force divisions had encircled the city while hurried negotiations were begun to save the capital from a destructive assault. At issue was whether or not RSV president Thieu would resign, and if so, whether a replacement acceptable to the PRG could be found. No doubt because of its increased strength the PRG changed the formulation of its acceptable conditions. On 19 April the United States was given an ultimatum, passed through diplomatic intermediaries, that Thieu must resign by midnight on 22 April in order to ensure that discussions would begin on a tripartite coalition government. After Thieu resigned on 21 April, his replacement by Tran Van Huong was dismissed by a PRG spokesman as "a ridiculous puppet dance" (AFP, Hong Kong, 22 April). On 26 April the PRG restated its negotiation position in two demands:

> 1. The U.S. government must seriously and fully observe Articles 1, 4 and 9 of the Paris agreement on Vietnam; really respect the fundamental national rights of the Vietnamese people and the right to self-determination of the South Vietnamese people [in other words, all U.S. personnel, including the U.S. ambassador, must first leave Vietnam].
> 2. The Saigon administration, an instrument of U.S. neo-colonialism, must be abolished. The present war machine and machinery of coercing and oppressing the people in South Vietnam must be abolished. As long as that administration, that war machine and that coercive and oppressive machinery remain, under whatever labels, the South Vietnamese people still have to endure suffering, misery and humiliation. (Vietnam News Agency [VNA], 26 April.)

Eventually, after a delay caused by President Huong's preference for constitutional niceties, the Huong government gave way to that of Duong Van Minh. The new president immediately entered into negotiations with PRG representatives. By this time, the PRG was no longer willing to delay victory through negotiations. On 30 April President Minh unconditionally surrendered the military and civil forces of the RVN to the PRG. On 1 May the Liberation Press Agency issued this announcement by the PRG's Foreign Ministry.

> As from April 30, 1975, the South Vietnamese people exercise full sovereignty throughout South Vietnam. The Provisional Revolutionary Government of the Republic of South Vietnam, the sole legal representative of the South Vietnamese people, is the manager of state affairs in the whole of South Vietnam.

The exact domestic role of the PRG has remained unclear. Major policy statements during the remainder of the year were mainly issued under the name of the Saigon-Gia Dinh Military Management Committee. Many of the MMC commissions and sections appear to duplicate ministries already set up within the PRG. Yet the PRG did not remain entirely inactive. On 4 June, the PRG's 6th anniversary, its cabinet held a much publicized meeting in Saigon. This did not result, however, in the expected formal displacement of the Saigon-Gia Dinh MMC by the PRG. In his opening address, President Phat listed "three big and pressing problems which we are striving to resolve urgently":

> 1. The problem of maintaining and safeguarding order and security and continuing to hunt down other remnants of the enemy troops and their die-hard lackeys who still remain in hiding to oppose the revolution and collude with hooligans and gangsters in sabotaging the people's order and security.
> 2. The problem of stabilizing the compatriots' life, building and developing the economy and culture and gradually improving the people's standard of living.
> 3. The problem of building and developing the revolutionary forces as well as building, strengthening and developing the revolutionary administration at various levels, particularly at the village, hamlet, ward and sub-ward basic levels. (Saigon domestic service, 5 June.)

The cabinet then heard several reports by the MMC ("on the state of the city management work, building the administration, safeguarding order and security, stabilizing the people's lives, helping the people return to their home towns, carrying out hunger relief work, promoting production and developing revolutionary culture") and the Economy and Finance and Foreign Affairs ministries. The final communiqué set out these "immediate tasks":

> 1. Enhance solidarity and initiate a forceful and widespread revolutionary movement among the masses to build and strengthen the revolutionary administration at various levels, smash counterrevolutionary acts and motivate the masses to strenuously engage in productive labor with a view to quickly overcoming the consequences of war, restoring the economy and advancing to build an independent, sovereign and prosperous economy.
> 2. Eliminate the decadent and reactionary culture and develop a democratic progressive and wholesome national culture.
> 3. Stabilize the material and cultural life of the people, complete the democratic national revolution and advance toward reunification of the Fatherland, reuniting the north and south under one roof. (Ibid; *FBIS*, 6 June.)

Throughtout the remainder of 1975 PRG ministers were reported to be mastering the intricacies of their portfolios, familiarizing themselves with the files and administration left by the RVN and, most importantly, conducting unpublicized meetings with their DRV counterparts on reunification. The latter took place in May in Saigon when high-level VWP-DRV officals came south to attend a series of victory celebrations and in August when a senior delegation of southern officials (including members of the PRG) went to Hanoi to attend the DRV's 30th anniversary celebrations. In November formal discussions commenced in Saigon between 25-member delegations from the North and South. According to one account:

> Especially important though will be discussions on how to extend the standardization and unification of government ministries and agencies. At the moment the system of education and social services in both North and South Vietnam have been considerably standardized and they will probably serve as models for other forms of administration. ("BBC World Roundup," Radio 3AR, Melbourne, 13 November.)

Although formal procedures had been agreed to (see "Domestic Attitudes and Activities"), it seems likely that before all-Vietnam elections are held the MMC's will be replaced, albeit temporarily, by the PRG and its subordinate people's revolutionary committees. Saigon Radio was reported to have stated:

> The people of Saigon have fulfilled their responsibilities in the building and reconstruction of the country toward socialism. The reestablishment of order has been rapidly effected. . . . Astonishingly, the Military Management of Saigon could be replaced this year by a popular [people's] revolutionary committee. (AFP, Hong Kong, 28 September.)

National Front for the Liberation of South Vietnam (NFL). The NFL's organizational structure consists of a national central committee, with a presidium and secretariat, and subordinate committees at regional, province, district and village level. During 1975 the following were officially identified as members of the presidium: Nguyen Huu Tho (president); Huynh Tan Phat (secretary-general); Ho Thu (deputy secretary-general); Ibih Aleo, Phung Van Cung, Tran Bach Dang, Tran Buu Kiem, Tran Nam Trung and Vo Chi Cong (vice presidents); Dang Tran Thi, Nguyen Huu The, Nguyen Thi Dinh, Nguyen Van Hieu, Nguyen Van Ngoi and Thich Thien Hao. Unofficial reports include Phan Xuan Thai. (*Est et Ouest* [Paris], 16-31 May.) Huynh Tan Phat and Ho Xuan Son were the only members of the secretariat to be so identified although it probably includes also Ho Thu, Le Van Huan and Ung Ngoc Ky.

During April, a combined NFL-PRG delegation made a quick tour through Thua Thien (20 April), Hue (22 April), Da Nang (24 April) and Quang Ngai (26 April). Nguyen Thi Binh represented the NFL on a tour of Da Nang on 27 April. Each visit provided an opportunity for the national NFL leaders to "show the flag" locally, introduce the members of the formerly clandestine NFL provincial committee and publicize the PRG's 10-point policy statement of 1 April.

Undoubtedly the most important event in the recent history of the NFL was the third congress of the Saigon-Gia Dinh NFL committee, held in Saigon on 27-29 July in the building that once housed the RVN National Assembly. A political report was delivered by Nguyen Van Chi (a heretofore obscure cadre). Other reports were given by representatives of the city party committee, the Liberation Armed Forces, the Liberation Federation of Trade Unions, the HCM PRYU, the Liberation Women's Association, various people's revolutionary committees, and cultural, political, religious, industrial and commercial organizations. A new Ho Chi Minh City NFL committee was appointed, comprising, in addition to veteran NFL cadres, a fair proportion of people from various walks of life (workers, peasants, etc.) including several prominent Third Force personalities. Nguyen Van Chi headed the 25-member presidium as chairman; Duong Van Bay (or Day) headed the secretariat; and a 30-odd-member central committee was also named (Saigon domestic service, 29 July; *FBIS*, 29, 31 July). The congress ended with an appeal addressed to all categories of persons (intellectuals, writers, teachers, bourgeoisie, religious personages, ethnic Chinese, former RVN personnel, etc.) assuring them that if they followed the NFL's policies they would all be able to "contribute their talents and energies to the task of healing the wounds of war, restoring the economy, stabilizing life, radically solving famine and unemployment; urging repatriation; and building an independent, sovereign economy."

In September the Saigon-Gia Dinh NFL committee convened for its first reported enlarged conference. It unanimously approved the PRG's new policies on "the restoration and development of industry and trade and the elimination of the comprador bourgeois monopolists" announced on 10 September (see "Domestic Attitudes and Activities").

There are four main headings under which organizations affiliated to the NFL and active in 1975 may be grouped: functional liberation associations; political parties; special interest groups; and foreign liaison associations.

(1) The South Vietnam Liberation Federation of Trade Unions (LFTU) assumed the duties of the former RVN General Confederation of Labor. Workers' committees were formed in all constituent labor unions. Those which had existed under the RVN were either dissolved or transformed into liberation unions affiliated to the LFTU. Organizing was focused on the Saigon-Bien Hoa industrial area, Da Nang, Hue and the rubber plantation in Tay Ninh Province. In May the "Third Force Committee to Defend Workers' Rights" was dissolved and its membership absorbed into the Saigon-Gia Dinh LFTU organization. A provisional LFTU committee in Da Nang was reported to have enrolled 22,000 or 90 percent of the members of former unions. The LFTU has undertaken to restore and return to production as many industries as possible, particularly public service ones, and to organize self-defense units within industries to provide security against sabotage.

The South Vietnam Liberation Women's Union (LWU) was charged with responsibility for organizing and managing the female population. It would appear that in the great shortage of technical and managerial personnel that the party has given top priority to mobilizing and training women. The dissolution of the "Third Force Women's Movement for the Right to Live" was announced. Members of this organization joined the LWU and some were given important posts.

It is unclear whether one or two organizations exist for high school and tertiary-level students. Press and radio accounts often described the activities of joint student and youth groups. After 30 April members of the South Vietnam Liberation Students' Association (SLA) were particularly active in the campaigns for eradicating all "depraved and reactionary literature" and more especially in cleaning up Saigon and removing the yellow-and-red RVN flags painted on offices and homes. No doubt the SLA, which formed the secret core of many of the urban student movements, will become more active as the new school year commences. The South Vietnam Liberation Youth Union (LYU) participated in the same campaigns as the SLA. During June and July, it was reported, some 40,000 youths in Bac Lieu Province attended political study courses and some 3,000 were accepted into LYU membership (LPA, 30 July).

The South Vietnam Liberation Peasants' Association (LPA) in November 1974 was reported to be issuing a paper called *Nong Thon* (Countryside). Except for occasional references to statements by this paper endorsing NFL and PRG policy announcements, very little was heard of the LPA in the first half of 1975. In August the LPA's executive committee reportedly had held its 4th plenary session. Possibly this meeting took the decision, announced later, to abolish the "land-to-the-tiller" program begun by the Thieu government (UPI, 18 October).

The South Vietnam Liberation Writers' and Artists' Association (LWAA) seems slated to serve as the organization that will enroll members of the intelligentsia. On 6 June a committee for the formation of a "Liberation Composers' Association" was announced. The LWAA will undoubtedly act as the umbrella organization for various associations in the arts.

In April it was reported that "art and cultural circles in Thua Thien-Hue" had met with representatives of the LWAA. In June an LWAA exhibition of paintings and writing in Saigon drew the attendance of prominent PRG personalities. The first "Liberation Writers' Conference" was held in Saigon on 17-18 June. The following month the first conference of the "South Vietnam Liberation Fine Arts Branch" was also convened in Saigon (July 4-5). It was attended by a delegation representing the DRV's Fine Arts Association. The importance of this meeting can be measured by the fact that Tran Bach Dang, head of the Saigon-Gia Dinh party committee's intellectual proselytizing section, addressed the delegates. The conference reached agreement on the "new trends and activities for creative purposes" to be pursued (the details of which are so far unreported). A 25-member "preparatory committee for the congress of various liberation artistic sectors" was announced (Saigon domestic service, 12 July).

(2) In April, Nguyen Thi Binh was asked about the role of political parties within the NFL in an interview by French radio. She stated: "We have three political parties, the Democratic Party, the Radical Socialist Party and the People's Revolutionary Party, and we have more than 20 mass organizations which represent all sections of the population." (Paris domestic service, 11 April; *FBIS*, 14 April.)

The only mention in 1975 of the existence of the "Democratic Party" and the "Radical Socialist Party" in the reports of the Foreign Broadcast Information Service came on 27 August when VNA released the names of Southern delegates to the DRV's 30th anniversary festivities. One of the delegates was identified as "deputy secretary-general of the Central Committee of the South Vietnam Democratic Party" and another as "deputy secretary-general of the South Vietnam Radical Socialist Party."

(3) Numerous special interest groups were active with the NFL in 1975. The "Association of God-Fearing and Patriotic Catholics" held a conference for social scientists in June which was attended by a delegation from the DRV. In September it was announced that the "Liaison and Information Committee for the Chinese" had begun a campaign to spread the use of Vietnamese language among the Chinese community of Saigon-Cholon. Other groups include the "Association of Patriotic Intellectuals," "Committee for the Protection of Teen-agers and Children," "Movement for the Autonomy of the Central Highlands," "Patriotic Buddhists" "Liaison Committee," "South Vietnam Buddhist Association," "South Vietnam Patriotic and Democratic Journalists' Association" and "South Vietnam Patriotic Teachers' Association" (PTA). In May the PTA held a conference for private school teachers in the Saigon-Gia Dinh area. Later in the year a PTA gathering unanimously supported a resolution calling for an end to private schools.

(4) Among the most active organizations affiliated with the NFL have been its foreign liaison associations. These would include the "Committee to Denounce War Crimes Committed by the U.S. Imperialists and Their Henchmen in South Vietnam," "South Vietnam Committee for the Defense of World Peace," "South Vietnam Committee for the Release of Patriotic and Peace-Loving People Still Detained by the Saigon Administration," "South Vietnam Committee for Solidarity with Cuba and Latin America," "South Vietnam Peace Committee" and "South Vietnam Red Cross Society."

People's Liberation Armed Forces (PLAF). The PLAF is supposedly the name for Southern-raised main force, regional and guerrilla troops operating under the command of the PRG. PAVN, the "People's Army of Vietnam," is the designation of the various armed forces under the command of DRV-VWP officials. In practice, PAVN and PLAF units have engaged in combined operations in South Vietnam. PRG officials, however, have repeatedly denied the presence of PAVN units in the South. An example is this exchange between a member of the PRG representation in Denmark and the correspondent for a Copenhagen newspaper (Aktuelt, 8 April): Question, "Are there North Vietnamese troops in South Vietnam?" Answer, "None at all."

In 1974 PLAF strength was estimated at 30,000 main force troops and 50,000 guerrillas (*YICA, 1975*, p. 441). As a result of increased recruitment the number of men in the main force category rose 60,000 to 80,000. The number of local guerrillas was estimated at 100,000 in early 1975. (*The Age*, Melbourne, 24 March; *The Economist*, 12 April; *The New Yorker*, 21 April, p. 132.) PAVN forces in the South remained relatively stable until the infiltration of a further seven divisions in January-March 1975 raised the total of their main force divisions to twenty.

On 9 February, at ceremonies commemorating the unification of the PLAF, its high command was identified as Tran Van Tra, Le Chan and Dong Van Cong. Later in the year Nguyen Thi Dinh was identified as a PLAF deputy commander and Nguyen Van Nghiem was listed as PLAF's deputy chief of staff.

In early March the PLAF Saigon-Gia Dinh Command held a congress to "welcome the outstanding achievements of the emulation combatants and the 'determined-to-win' valiant fighters" (Liberation Radio, 17 March). Reports were delivered over a three-day period on the achievements of local outstanding units, localities and individuals in 1974. At the last session "the delegates pledged their determination to score even greater achievements." Later that month RVN president Thieu undertook the strategic withdrawal from the Highlands which was quickly turned into a debacle by PLAF-PAVN commanders. A total rout soon followed as the revolutionary armed forces unleashed a highly mobile and effective offensive in central Vietnam causing in quick succession the loss of Quang Tri, Hue and Da Nang. By late March the PLAF high command was confidently calling for the surrender of all ARVN officers, NCO's and soldiers (*Vietnam Courier*, Hanoi, no. 36). The end came a month later when the RVN surrendered unconditionally.

After liberation the PLAF undertook to maintain order and security throughout the country, which in some cases meant scattered engagements with die-hard ARVN remnants. The PLAF also conducted a stepped-up recruitment campaign and undertook to modernize itself.

On 17-22 May, mid-level military cadres in central Nam Bo held a working session, according to Liberation Radio (29 May):

> the armed forces' current tasks are to continue to pursue and clean out the remaining obstinate elements; to maintain local order and security; to be ready to smash all enemy sabotage schemes in order to defend the people, the administration and the fruits of the revolution, to actively assist local areas, to carry out propaganda work, to motivate the masses; to quickly restore the people's activity to normal; to completely collect and fully utilize captured war booty; to energetically build and develop the armed forces in quality and quantity in order to build a modern regular army to defend the peace and the fatherland; to launch a movement for true culture and art; to reinforce healthy entertainment activities; and to eliminate the remaining vestiges of the enemy's degenerate culture.

In September an important military conference was held to review these tasks. Top priority was assigned to defeating the continuing resistance by ARVN remnants along the Cambodian border near Soc Trang and by Montagnard groups in the Highlands. Also this conference reviewed the program of implementing the PRG's policies toward former RVN personnel. It was stated that these policies had not been fully implemented and should be given close attention. Further, it was stated that due attention should be given to "problems of consolidating self-defense in the nearly liberated areas." (Liberation Radio, 21 September.)

Vietnam Alliance of National Democratic Peace Forces (VANDPF). Formed in 1969 as an organization of "patriotic bourgeoisie" (i.e., non-Communist nationalists who opposed the RVN government), the VANDPF played a crucial role throughout 1975 as a bridge between intellectual residents of the cities and the new revolutionary authorities. Its representatives toured South Vietnam with their NFL and PRG counterparts in the early days of liberation. VANDPF leaders were included in the Southern delegation to the DRV's 30th anniversary celebrations.

Current officials of the VANDPF include Trinh Dinh Thao, chairman; Ton That Duong Ky, secretary-general; Thanh Nghi, Duong Quynh Hoa and Le Hieu Dang, assistant secretary-generals; Thich Don Hau and Lam Van Tet; vice-chairmen; and Le Van Hao and Nguyen Van Kiet, permanent members.

Party Internal Affairs. Throughout the war, NFL and PRG leaders avoided discussion of the role of the PRP (the southern organization of the VWP). The PRP has maintained a discreet silence about itself and its leadership; consequently very little information has been made public about party plenums, discussions or decision-making. Nevertheless the party's key role has not gone unacknowledged, and since 30 April 1975 most speeches by senior NFL and PRG officials have made reference to its leading position.

In July, Nguyen Huu Tho, president of the PRG Advisory Council, was remarkably candid in an interview. Asked, "What is the relation between the NFL and the communists"? Tho replied:

> Communism has a party here—the southern section of the Vietnam Workers' Party. The people of South Vietnam know very well that since 1930—when this party was founded—the communists have been the vanguard of the fight for the fatherland's freedom and independence. The people therefore always showed deep admiration and great love for it. This truth must be known. (*Der Spiegel*, Hamburg, 30 June, pp. 62-65.)

It is now known that the military events of early 1975 followed upon decisions taken by the VWP Politburo in July-August 1974 (*The Age*, 24 March 1975; *Herald*, Melbourne, 31 March; *Time*, 10 March, p. 13). At that time the VWP carried out a major review of 18 months of implementation of the 1973 peace agreement. Party leaders reached the conclusion that no political settlement was possible as long as Thieu remained in office and therefore they would have to resort to "revolutionary violence" to overthrow his government. They reasoned that the balance of forces had begun to shift in their favor because of dwindling U.S. aid and internal RVN weaknesses. In addition, Thieu's refusal to deal with the PRG politically, coupled with his military offensives into its controlled areas and his pacification and economic blockade campaigns, meant that the party's position would be seriously challenged unless some change in strategy was made soon.

After this review a Politburo directive was dispatched to subordinate party organs in South Vietnam. Both COSVN (the party's organization for Nam Bo) and the Zone 5 Committee (for central Trung Bo) convened conferences to discuss the new guidelines.

According to the review undertaken by COSVN (translated and printed in *Viet-Nam Documents and Research Notes*, Saigon, No. 118), the Nam Bo party committee was in "full agreement" with the policies previously outlined in Resolution 21 of the Central Committee and COSVN's own Resolution 12 (see *YICA, 1975*, pp. 445-47). A review of policy implementation under these resolutions yielded four major conclusions:

1. During the first six months of the year we scored major full-scale and firm gains, blunted the enemy-initiated dry-season rice-looting plan, and set back and defeated by one major step his pacification and encroaching [schemes].

2. Our posture and force is being developed steadily, stronger than at the time we embarked on the '73-'74 dry season [offensive], stronger than at the time we made preparations for the offensives in 1968 and 1972.

3. *The Nguyen Van Thieu puppet army and government, although not yet being reduced to collapse, continue to face increasing difficulties in all respects and keep on declining both quantitatively and qualitatively in terms of posture and force.*

4. The current contest of strength between us and the enemy is occurring within the context of the world's situation, of the situation in Indochina, and even in the U.S., and is *highly favorable to our side and greatly disadvantageous to the enemy.* (Emphasis in original.)

COSVN forecast two future possibilities ("Capabilities" in the translation):

There exist two capabilities in the development of the revolution in the South. They are:

—If in the coming period the balance of forces between the enemy and us tilts to our side and the enemy meets with increased difficulties, they are compelled to cling to the Agreement and implement small parts of it to impede our advancement, save their deteriorating situation and sabotage the Accord.

—In case they do not want to carry out the Agreement and the present war gradually widens into a large-scale one we again have to win total victory.

These two capabilities exist side by side and are in the process of development. We must take advantage of Capability 1 and ready ourselves for Capability 2 and grasp revolutionary violence to secure victory regardless of what development will happen. The road to success for the revolution in the South is the road of violence based on political and military forces.

COSVN then set out five missions for "the period ahead" (i.e., for 1975):

The armed forces must in the coming period closely coordinate with the political, diplomatic and legal struggles with a view to fulfilling the following missions:

1. Vigorously pressing forward the gaining of the population and the population's control of their land in the lowlands and city-bordering areas; thwarting an important step in the enemy pacification, land-grabbing and boundary-delineating plan; recovering the areas occupied, pacified and expanded by the enemy; expanding and connecting penetration areas and disputed ones; turning the enemy-controlled areas into disputed and liberated ones; building up our reserve forces, manpower and material resources.

2. Our main forces must, on the one hand, engage in combat to wipe out the enemy; hold, expand and improve liberated areas and base areas; attract and hold the enemy in support of the gaining of the population in the lowlands; and, on the other, build up, strengthen and improve themselves in every respect in order to get prepared for a large-scale offensive when the need arises.

3. Vigorously pushing forward the urban movement, consolidating and developing mass organizations, rallying great numbers of the populace form all walks of life in various forms, pressing forward, step by step, the overt political struggle. Our operations in the lowlands as well as those of the main forces are geared to the backing of the urban movements so that they can move forward.

4. Strengthening and building up the liberated areas and base areas actively, urgently, and step by step; stabilizing the populace's living conditions; setting up on-the-spot rear service facilities; enlarging corridors; meeting immediate requirements and maintaining reserves; foiling the enemy plan of imposing a blockage against our economy; frustrating the economic development plan of the enemy; causing his economy to increasingly deteriorate.

5. Consolidating unity with Laos and Cambodia.

The Binh Dinh Province party committee held its third congress on 18-30 September 1974, apparently after the Zone 5 party committee had conducted a review similar to COSVN's. The resolution of this conference (ibid., pp. 26-55) parallels that of the COSVN directive in many respects and also makes it clear that the upsurge in fighting which occurred in November-December 1974 was not intended as the "final crushing military offensive" so long predicted by Western observers. However, after the capture of Phuoc Long Province in January 1975 and the successful 19-day offensive in the Highlands (5-23 March), the party revised these plans. According to Nguyen Huu Tho, "when the offensive against the city of Hue was about to be achieved . . . the determination to launch [the Ho Chi Min campaign] was officially laid down" (*Far Eastern Economic Review* [FEER], Hong Kong, 8 August, p. 22).

On 4 April the general order to prepare for an attack on Saigon was given, precipitating the events that brought the party to power.

On 19 May the anniversary of Ho Chi Minh's birth, the Hue VWP organization met and was addressed by its secretary, Le Tu Dong (Liberation Radio, 21 May). At the end of that month the Saigon-Gia Dinh municipal party committee's propaganda and training department held a conference attended by representatives from 21 districts in the Saigon area. They were addressed by "comrades of the leadership committee" (ban lanh dao); no further details were given (Saigon domestic service, 3 June).

In June it was reported that the party security organization in Saigon was operating under the cover of an "Intellectual Action Committee":

> Though it functions in the strictest secrecy, the committee is known to head several subcommittees, and these are said to control the numerous people's associations that have been springing up in all fields since the Communist take-over on April 30.
>
> There are, for example, associations of doctors, pharmacists, university professors, writers and artists. Communications between the subcommittees that oversee them reportedly must be made through the committee itself.
>
> This mysterious organization is believed to formulate the policies that are carried out by Saigon's Military Administrative Committee, under the leadership of Lieut. Gen. Tran Van Tra. (Dispatch from Saigon dated 3 June, originally published in *Le Monde*; reprinted, *NYT*, 4 June.)

Contact with this committee was arranged by another group called the People's Association of Professors (ibid.).

A conference on "propaganda and training" was convened by the Zone 8 committee on 7-9 June. The role of the party, party committees and chapters in organizing training for the ideological guidance of cadres was discussed (Liberation Radio, 11 June). On 15 June the propaganda and training department of the Saigon party committee opened a training course for 500 precinct- and ward-level cadres. Apparently one of the aims of this program was to produce basic-level cultural and information personnel (Saigon domestic service, 16 June).

According to Douglas Pike (see *Democratic Republic of Vietnam*), sometime during July a decision was taken to "unify" the VWP organization in North and South Vietnam. This accords with an account that "further confirmation of North Vietnamese dominance was provided by a high-ranking official in Hanoi, who told a Japanese newsman that the Communist parties and armed forces of North and South Vietnam have been merged" (*Intercontinental Press*, New York, no. 26, 7 July).

In August the VWP Central Committee (in Hanoi) issued a circular on the program for the DRV's 30th-anniversary celebrations which alluded to the need "to successfully implement the resolution [on] the 4th VWP Congress" (Hanoi Radio, 5 August; *FBIS*, 7 August). This congress has long been predicted by Western observers. The commencement of the DRV's second five-year-plan (1976-80) makes it seem likely that the congress will be held during the first half of 1976 (*Newsweek*, International edition, 24 November 1975, p. 13). No doubt, when held, it will be attended by party cadres from the south.

The Ho Chi Minh People's Revolutionary Youth Union has been active in two main areas: (1) organizational expansion and (2) conducting emulation campaigns. The 19 May anniversary of Ho Chi Minh's birth and the second founding anniversary of the HCM PRYU (30 June; see *YICA, 1974*, p. 563) were both used as public occasions to present PRYU committees and to outline the PRYU program. Its executive committee met at Thu Duc on 18 May to pay respects to "Uncle Ho." A festival of the "assault youth force" (luc luong thanh nien xung kich) in My Tho on 25 May celebrated the liberation of Vietnam. Three days later the PRYU issued a circular on plans for celebrating International Children's Day (1 June).

On May 31 the Saigon-Gia Dinh HCM PRYU held a ceremony to mark the start of the "sixth class of Ly Tu Trong cadres." Just prior to the start of festivities on June 1st the PRYU executive committee held a press conference to announce the commencement of four movements:

1. The movement to pursue evil elements who stubbornly hide from and sabotage the revolution; to smash in time all schemes to obstruct the revolution's progress; and to take a fundamental step in totally removing all counter-revolutionary and decadent social, literary, artistic, cultural, political and ideological vestiges and influence.

2. The movement to develop forces, motivate youths and youth union members to participate in military training and drills, build the armed forces and defend the revolution's fruits and administration.

3. The movement for mutual solidarity for production in which the rural youths must be in the vanguard in organizing labor exchanges, broadly expanding the area of and increasing productivity in agricultural production. Worker and laborer youths must develop technical innovations to raise output and improve quality, must be in the vanguard on all production fronts and must simultaneously organize and motivate male and female youths for readiness to participate in labor on all worksites and state farms which the party and government entrusts to youths.

4. The recreation movement in which youths must exert themselves in political and cultural studies, increasing their level of awareness to respond to the new demands of the revolution, and participating in healthy singing and recreation for a joyous and healthy building of the fatherland (Liberation Radio, 2 July; *FBIS*, 8 July.)

During the period 30 July-30 August, the Saigon-Gia Dinh HCM PRYU committee launched an emulation movement to mark the anniversaries of the August 1945 revolution and National Day, "to develop revolutionary forces, engage in productive labor, to eliminate decadent culture and social evils, tracking down tyrants, stepping up famine relief work, sanitation, disease protection and culture and art work to serve the people" (ibid., 4 August).

The Ho Chi Minh Working Youth Union, as the party's youth organization is called in Trung Bo, launched a program during May-July of sending cadres down to the villages, hamlets, wards and sub-wards to "guide youths and students in performing political study" and to launch the "three-assaults" movements: "to engage in productive labor to build the country, to defend the revolutionary administration and the Fatherland, to build a new life-style and a new breed of man" (Radio Hanoi, 5 July).

The Ho Chi Minh Vanguard Youth League organized rallies throughout May in western Nam Bo to "promulgate the five teachings of Uncle Ho." A massive recruitment drive raised membership to about 100,000 or 120,000 (LPA, 2 June, 19 September). In September the league's activities were reported as follows: to plant trees in memory of Ho Chi Minh, to clean the graves of fallen heroes, to clean the streets, to eradicate the vestiges of depraved culture and to confiscate reactionary and obscene books and literature (*FBIS*, 19 September).

Domestic Attitudes and Activities. The party's chosen instrument for administration in the immediate aftermath of victory was the so-called military management committee. The MMC's primary tasks were to maintain public order and security and to stabilize the life of the people. Generally, MMC's were composed of both civilian and military personnel, headed by a senior party official. For example, the Saigon-Gia Dinh MMC, announced on 3 May, consisted of four military officers. Tran Van Tra, the MMC chairman, was concurrently a member of COSVN and the VWP Central Committee. In Hue and Da Nang, joint MMC-people's revolutionary committee rule was established. The people's revolutionary committee (the PRG's basic governmental structure at all levels) theoretically is chosen by a congress of people's representatives at whatever level (province, district, village, etc.) it operates. After 30 April provisional people's revolutionary committees were established throughout South Vietnam. Eventually all MMC's were to be replaced by civilian-run people's revolutionary committees.

Problems confronting party leaders in 1975 were enormous as they undertook to design detailed programs for almost every facet of Vietnamese life. In short, the 10-point policy toward newly controlled areas had to be expanded to meet the needs of a formerly insurgent government become the administration of the day.

Public Order and Security. The collapse of the RVN left most of the ARVN forces still under arms at the very time the new Saigon MMC was installing itself. This situation enabled various factions and gangs to elude party control measures and engage in resistance. Not surprisingly, the first flood of communiqués broadcast over Saigon radio requested all civilian and military RVN personnel to turn in their arms, official documents and government property and report to various centers for registration. Special units provided security for various industries and public services. Workers and civil servants were urged to stay on and continue their operations. Many members of the former RVN administration were in fact covert party members (20,000 Viet Cong agents, according to an estimate based on U.S. intelligence calculations; *Washington Post*, 10 September).

The Saigon MMC was forced to extend the registration deadline twice. Former RVN personnel were divided into categories for this purpose—for example, police and intelligence operatives, general officers and senior civil servants, ordinary soldiers and low-ranking public servants. All members of reactionary political parties (i.e., anti-communist political groups) were likewise instructed to register. By late August it was estimated that only 300,000 men from Thieu's army of 1,000,000 had registered (*Le Monde*, 20 August).

On 12 May the "house and land management organ" of the MMC issued a communiqué "on the protection of houses and property of the state and the people" (Saigon domestic service, 13 May). Later in the month, population-control measures divided hamlets and neighborhoods into cells consisting of 10 to 12 families headed by a leader responsible for implementing MMC policy (AFP, Saigon, 28 May). The billeting of soldiers with the local population was also employed as a security measure (*NYT*, 23 May). The problem of law and order remained, as groups of "cowboys" (armed young toughs) began roaming the streets. Robbery was said to have registered an "alarming increase" (*FEER*, 13 June).

Armed remnants of the RVN regime—both police and military—continued isolated acts of resistance throughout the year despite the MMC's announced policy of reconciliation. During September, some 500 men operating in Soc Trang Province were captured (*NYT*, 19 October). The murder and assassination of NFL and PLAF cadres apparently continued. There was no bloodbath by way of response, however, although there were reports (often unconfirmed) of cases of reprisal or isolated incidents of revenge. There appears to be no credible evidence that any systematic elimination of former adversaries has occurred or is being planned (dispatch from Da Nang, AFP, 23 April; dispatch from Saigon, *NYT*, 31 May; *FEER*, 6 June, 28 November; *Christian Science Monitor*, 24 July; *Le Monde*, 16 July). This is not to say that no executions were meted out by "people's revolutionary courts" for offenses against the new order (see Radio Hanoi, 23 February, for a statement on revolutionary courts). The public execution of Nguyen Tu Sang on 29 May, which received international publicity, was but one example (*NYT*, 6 June).

Economic Affairs. The takeover of the Highlands and the major cities along the central coastline confronted the revolutionary authorities with staggering problems of feeding and maintaining the health of nearly 5 million people. PRG spokesmen made international appeals for aid against the danger of famine. The problem was compounded with the assumption of complete control of South Vietnam. PRG officials reckoned that there were 3.5 million unemployed to be cared for (1.5 million former soldiers, 1.5 million former government employees, and a half million "social cases") (*NYT*, 21 September). One of the first reactions to this problem was the setting up of anti-famine committees charged with overseeing a distribution program of free rice. Foodstuffs from overseas, carried mainly in Chinese and Russian ships, began to arrive after the ports resumed operations (Da Nang on 24 April and Saigon on 17 May).

Emergency measures were taken to get productive industries operating again. In this regard Vietnam faced critical shortages of petrol and other oil products which overseas shipments only partly alleviated. A policy was soon adopted to encourage the resettlement in their native villages of as many persons as possible. Those who chose to return were provided with transportation costs and food rations for the journey. Working committees were formed in the rural areas to handle this influx. Other problems arose from difficulties in locating land and farming tools. Land was temporarily allotted to groups who were expected to farm collectively, and collectives were assigned the task of reclaiming unused land, and labor exchange and mutual aid teams were formed to help solve problems related to the shortage of buffaloes and tools.

In July it was reported that 97 percent of the peasant households in Quang Tri province as of late May were organized collectively, 73 percent of which had joined "cooperative and production groups" (LPA, 15 July). By mid-July nearly one million persons were said to have voluntarily left the cities for their native villages (Liberation Radio, 16 July). The population of Da Nang presumably fell to just under one million as a result of a reported exodus of 600,000 (*NYT*, 16 August). By late September, 239,758 persons were said to have left Saigon for resettlement in their home villages (ibid., 19 October).

A policy of opening "new economic areas" was unveiled and by mid-August 150,000 Saigonese had registered to participate, of whom 35,820 were said to have been settled by early October (LPA, 3 October). Other areas were said to have been opened for "colonization" by PAVN troops slated for demobilization (the policy may have been in effect before victory; see *Newsweek*, international edition, 30 January). As noted earlier, the RVN's "land-to-the-tiller" program was abolished. An experimental land reform program got under way near Phu Bai in October when some 10,000 farmers received newly redistributed land, some of it confiscated from previous owners classified as "traitors" (UPI, Saigon, 18 October). Late in the year the Saigon MMC distributed ration cards to one million city households to enable them to buy set amounts of rice, condensed milk, sugar, soap and tobacco at fixed prices (ibid.).

In the urban areas there was a hiatus of several months during which all banks were kept closed. This caused a run on cash reserves, seriously disadvantaging the less well-off. In May it was announced that civil servants would be paid reduced wages consisting of food and cash. (Saigon domestic service, 25 May). That same month the entire banking system was effectively nationalized. On 10 June the National Bank of Vietnam resumed its operations, authorizing limited transactions in RVN currency. The following month, savings accounts were opened for restricted withdrawals and transfers. In August the PRG Council of Ministers discontinued the operations of private banks and credit firms.

The climax in currency developments came in September when quite unexpectedly the MMC authorities introduced a new currency system on a par with the DRV dong (one new piastre equivalent to US $0.65). Families were permitted to exchange their old piastres for any amount not exceeding 200 new piastres, thus disadvantaging those with large sums of old RVN currency. Shortly thereafter, on 22 September the MMC issued a decree fixing the price levels of certain goods. This was rescinded on 6 October because, according to a communiqué of the Saigon-Gia Dinh MMC, these price stabilization measures had caused "untoward difficulties" (AFP, Saigon, 7 October).

MMC policies in the industrial sector were aimed at restoring productivity in selected industries as quickly as possible by repairing war damage and reorganizing the managerial level by relying on worker-management committees. Toward this end the old regime's trade union structure was completely revamped, and newly appointed "liberation trade unions" appeared. Trade union activity was particularly active among workers employed by ESSO, Shell and Caltex in the Nha Be Area, the dockers in Saigon and workers at "idling middle-size enterprises" which were privately owned (Saigon domestic service, 25 May).

The most significant and potentially far-reaching decision announced in the economic sphere came on 10 September, when a statement entitled "On Some Policies on the Restoration and Development of Industry and Trade and the Elimination of "Comprador Bourgeoisie Monopolists' " was issued in the PRG's name. It outlined a 14-point economic policy:

1. The state will endeavor to build and strengthen state-run forces in various economic sectors . . .

2. The state will acclaim all Vietnamese bourgeoisie [who struggle to contribute their talents] to expanding business activities and developing the national economy in various sectors and occupations in the interests of national welfare and the people's livelihood in conformity with the lines and policies of the government. The property ownership and the right to legitimate profits will be protected by the state. The state will guide and help small enterprises and other business installations in solving problems concerning raw materials, materials and fuel and in the selling of their products. . . .

3. The state stands ready to [cooperate in conducting business activities] with the bourgeoisie who intend to use their money, capital, equipment, raw materials and knowledge—in cooperation with the state—to restore or build necessary enterprises according to the requirements of the production development plan. . . . In private enterprises it is necessary, on the one hand, to insure the state's right to leadership and management and the basic rights of the workers' and, on the other hand, to insure the bourgeoisie's right to participate in management and attain legitimate profits.

4. The state will do its utmost to encourage and help the bourgeoisie who contribute their capital, technical knowledge and talents to participating in building new economic areas.

5. There are special cases in which many bourgeoisie want to sell their production and business establishments to the state so they will be used for the benefit of the common economy. The state may examine and consider each particular case.

6. Intellectuals entrusted with scientific and technical tasks and having specialized skills in production techniques or management very helpful to the restoration and development of the state economy will be given important jobs and treated appropriately according to their abilities and the result of their actual contributions.

7. The state will pay great attention to encouraging, guiding and assisting small industrial and handicraft producers in implementing production guidelines and procedures on the supply of materials and raw materials and the consumption of products to restore and develop necessary occupations and branches, especially the traditional handicraft occupations of the people, and to contribute to producing as many goods as possible for the people's consumption and export.

8. Small merchants who will be guided and assisted by the state in their trade activities to earn a living in compliance with the government's policies and laws must not let the comprador bourgeoisie take advantage of them to monopolize, speculate in and hoard goods, upset prices or disrupt the market. . . .

9. The state is determined to eliminate all speculation, hoarding, and smuggling activities and to severely punish speculators and smugglers for monopolizing the economy, disrupting the market, upsetting prices, currency, and goods, launching false rumors, and stealing state economic secrets. . . .

10. Persons who are engaged in economic speculation and monopoly practices which disrupt the market and who collude with the present counterrevolutionaries will be arrested, detained and dealt with according to the gravity of their crime. Their property may be confiscated entirely or in part.

11. As for the comprador bourgeoisie who undertook speculation in wartime by relying on the U.S. imperialists and colluding with the ringleaders in the puppet armed forces and administration and who have fled abroad or still remain in the country, their entire property under state management will be confiscated completely or partly according to the gravity of their crimes.

12. Persons who formerly collaborated with the comprador bourgeoisie or acted as their agents, and who, since liberation, have continued to help these comprador bourgeoisie to carry out speculative and monopolizing activities, hoard goods, raise or lower prices, smuggle currencies, gold, silver, diamonds, and narcotics, and disperse their property will be considered as accomplices and treated and punished according to the gravity of their crimes.

13. Persons rendering meritorious service in exposing or helping state organs arrest speculators and monopolists who disrupt the market and disperse their property will be appropriately commended and rewarded materially and morally.

14. Cadres, state personnel, and combatants in the liberation armed forces must exemplarily and strictly implement government policies: if they reveal state economic secrets and harbor, collude with, or help in the carrying out of illegal activities, they will be severely punished. (Saigon domestic service, 10 September; *FBIS*, 10 September.)

Social Affairs. Immediately after the communists took over the reigns of power in Saigon they initiated a campaign to "eliminate enslaving and degrading culture" which sent thousands of youths and students through the city streets rounding up copies of Western "girlie" magazines and "reactionary material" of a political and anti-communist nature. On 28 May at a conference convened to make a preliminary assessment of this movement the chief of the information and cultural section of the MMC had to remind his enthusiastic audience that "decadent and reactionary" books and magazines were to be turned over to the authorities, not burned, and that the circulation of scientific and technical materials was permitted (Saigon domestic service, 30 May). On 27 October the newspaper *Giai Phong* (Liberation) carried an announcement that the MMC had decided to proscribe 489 books by 56 individual authors. In the meantime, a special publication service was churning out party-approved literature, histories and biographies of Ho Chi Minh. Several hundred tons of books were shipped from Hanoi to help fill the void.

After the deadline set by the Saigon-Gia Dinh MMC for the completion of registration by former officials and soldiers, it was announced that they would be required to attend "study reform" classes. Low ranking soldiers and officials were required to attend one three-day session; higher-ranking officials were slated for a one-month initial session. The announcements made it clear that this was only the first phase. The purpose of these particular classes was to convey the revolutionary viewpoint to men who had until recently opposed the revolution. Lectures on the history of the Vietnam war, U.S. neocolonialism, war crimes, and the like were given. Those in attendance were supposed to relate their own "crimes and misdeeds," thereby acknowledging their mistakes. On 11 June it was announced that due to "improper organization" the period of study reform would be extended until the end of the month (Saigon domestic service, 12 June).

The prolonged absence of higher-ranking personnel engaged in study reform led to a spate of rumors that they had been executed. Wives of several officers organized a demonstration to protest the lack of news (AFP, Saigon, 11 July). On 15 August it was announced that as certain of the courses had ended "officers and civil servants would be returning home" (*Le Monde*, 20 August). In September some 800 officers were released after the completion of their courses (*Washington Post*, 10 September). "Hundreds" of junior and field grade officers were permitted to return home in October.

An editorial in *Saigon Giai Phong*, (17 June) hinted that the "graduates would have to demonstrate their progress by their future acts. It suggested three things former RVN personnel could do: return to their native villages; perform productive labor; "help the people wipe out the counterrevolutionaries and wicked elements and detect and smash all enemy designs" (Saigon domestic service, 17 June).

The revolutionary authorities moved quickly to reopen primary and secondary schools. By mid-June it was claimed that all "primary and secondary and vocational schools" in central Trung Bo had "resumed their normal activities" (LPA, 13 June) and by 28 June both primary and secondary schools were said to have completed their final examinations (ibid., 6 July).

The Saigon-Gia Dinh Education Service set forth an ambitious program of eradication of illiteracy among all strata of the people and implementation of supplementary education to raise their cultural levels. The Mass Education Bureau set itself the goal of bringing literacy to 250,000 persons by the end of 1976 (Radio Hanoi, 5 July).

Teachers in both public and private schools were quickly organized and given summer vacation courses in a new curriculum which was introduced virtually wholesale from the DRV. During May and June various organizing conferences were held to discuss the "campaign for the eradication of illiteracy and improvement of the people's cultural standards" which was formally begun on 6 July (Liberation Radio, 10 July; *FBIS* editorial report, 21 July).

In August the PRG Ministry of Education and Youth provided the general education schools with "concrete guidance" for the commencement of the 1975-76 school year. In October, the Saigon MMC engineered a conference of the Patriotic Teacher's Association which "unanimously proposed to the PRG to turn private schools into public ones as soon as possible in time to open the new school year." The PTA members also unanimously expressed to wish "to become teachers of the people . . . to study politics and new teaching methods to overcome difficulties so as to accomplish well their duties as teachers." (LPA, 30 September.) Among the participants were representatives of the private Chinese, Vietnamese and religious schools.

The situation in the universities provided educational authorities with a few problems. According to enrollment figures for 1974, of 98,546 students, 260 were studying agriculture, 26,673 literature, 29,905 law and none either animal husbandry or forestry (*FEER*, 7 November). It therefore came as no surprise when it was announced that only the faculties of medicine, dentistry and pharmacy would be reopened (Saigon domestic service, 9 June). In October the Ministry of Education and Youth unveiled plans to select and train 1,000 of the best student members of the Liberation Youth Union as cadres in the eighteen public and private universities in South Vietnam. Their task would be to conduct political study courses for university students in the 1975-1976 school year (LPA, 2 October).

Neither the PRG nor the MMC has issued any statement on policies toward the ethnic minorities living in the Highlands. The administration which emerged there appeared to be Montagnard-dominated. Management of the rubber, coffee and tea plantations, however, appears to be supervised directly from Saigon. Otherwise, the Highlands seem to have a measure of budgetary autonomy (*FEER*, 27 June.)

On 19-22 August some 200 delegates of the Bahnar and Jarai ethnic minority groups attended a solidarity conference to "contribute their views to building their native places." Among those present were Ibih Aleo, representatives of the central Trung Bo region and the "comrade secretary" of the Gia Lai VWP province committee. In September Ibih Aleo was identified as a vice-chairman of the DRV Nationalities Commission (Liberation Radio, 6 September).

The Hoa Hao Buddhist Sect has been a focal point of resistance to the new revolutionary authorities. Liberation Radio has several times denounced the "evil, anti-religious, anti-people and counterrevolutionary Luong Trong Tuong-Huynh Van Nhiem clique" (Liberation Radio, 12 July; LPA, 26 August).

Problems with Catholics arose as "progressive" and "conservative" factions clashed. In June the Vatican representative was expelled, presumably for his close relations with the Thieu government (*NYT*, 6 June). In August the Archbishop of Saigon came under attack by progressives over the role played by his coadjutor. The affair seemingly ended when the latter undertook to "respect the political line put forward by the revolutionary authorities" and accepted a transfer to Nha Trang. There are estimated to be 2 million Catholics in South Vietnam, of whom 600,000 live in Saigon.

A special committee was formed for the purpose of spreading literacy in the Vietnamese language among the ethnic Chinese, who number some one million (*Tin Sang* [Saigon], 5 September). A "patriotic" Chinese businessman was appointed to the NFL committee for Saigon.

International Children's Day, 1 June, was chosen for launching a campaign to instruct children and teenagers in the teachings of Ho Chi Minh. "Liberation youth units" (doi thieu nien giai phong) were formed to step up "the teaching of Uncle Ho's five precepts to children" and to work in conjunction with other youth groups "in eliminating reactionary and decadent culture." These units were used to spearhead a drive to help children "abstain from reading decadent books, newspapers, and pictures and to resolutely wipe out the slavish, depraved and reactionary culture." (Liberation Radio, 1 June.)

Political Activities. When the communists seized control of Da Nang in March they did so with the cooperation of clandestine units which had been secretly organized within the city, composed mainly of students and teachers. At that time a Buddhist-influenced "National Reconciliation Force" made its debut and offered complete cooperation with the victorious revolutionaries. Elsewhere, Third Force personalities seem to have been co-opted into administrative positions, most noticeably on the Saigon city NFL committee. Seven members of the Third Force were appointed to the 25-member Southern delegation for the talks on unification between North and South which began in November. Their organizations, however, have one by one announced their own dissolution: "Anti-Hunger Front," "Committee to Defend the Workers' Rights," "Committee to Reform the Prison System," "Movement for the People's Right to Self-Determination," and the "Women's Movement for the Right to Life."

Political organizations deemed reactionary by the MMC were dissolved and their leaders required to register and to attend study reform classes. Among these were the Democratic Party (Dan Chu) Worker-Peasant Party, United Vietnam Nationalist Party, Can Lao Nhan Vi Party, Tan Dai Viet Party, Nhan Van Cach Mang Party, Vietnam Nationalist Party, Tu Du (Freedom) Party, Vietnam National Restoration Party, Dai Viet Party, Radical (Cap Tien) Party, and the Social Democratic Alliance.

Political expression has been placed under MMC control. On 1 May the MMC decided to suspend publication of various books, newspapers, magazines and related printed material and to require prior authorization for the distribution of all printed matter (Saigon domestic service, 1 May). In August, newspapers were no longer subject to prior censorship but under a provisional statute they had to "serve the national interest" (Australian Associated Press, Saigon, 15 August).

Unification. The question of a timetable for the unification of Vietnam was a never-ending source of speculation in the Western press during 1975. During May, high-level officials from the DRV were reportedly in Saigon discussing the issue (*FEER*, 30 May, 6 June, *The Age*, 2 June; *NYT*, 6 June; *The Economist*, 14 June). In August a Southern delegation went to Hanoi for the DRV's 30th anniversary. From the tenor of statements issued after their return it seemed almost certain that unification was once again on the agenda. In November it was announced that a 25-member delegation from the North would conduct talks with their Southern counterparts. At the end of five days of discussions, a joint communiqué was issued which settled the issue: elections were planned for the first half of 1976 at which voters would select a National Assembly charged with drawing up a new state constitution. The anomaly of "one party, one army and two governments" (quoted by the correspondent in Hanoi for the Australian Communist Party's *Tribune*, Sydney, in *FEER*, 1 August) was about to end.

International Views and Policies. No statements were issued by either the PRP or the VWP's southern organization which reflected official Party views on international affairs. Instead, statements on foreign affairs originated either from the PRG, the NFL or any one of a number of foreign liaison associations, such as those noted earlier. Two themes were dominant in the statements: militant support for the non-aligned bloc, and neutrality in the Sino-Soviet dispute.

In August, Nguyen Thi Binh attended the non-aligned foreign ministers' conference in Lima, Peru, as a representative of the PRG. En route, she gave the following statement to a press conference in Algiers:

> In addition to the links of friendship which we stressed, the PRGRSV adheres to the same principles as Algeria concerning international solidarity, the same concept and the same policy of solidarity with nations struggling against imperialism and colonialism, the same concept of building a new, free and dignified life for all. (*El Moudjahid*, Algiers, 7 June.)

In another interview the PRG foreign minister stressed that her government's "membership in the non-aligned movement will not be put into question by the reunification of Vietnam" (TANYUG, Belgrade, 13 June).

PRG officials made it clear that adherence to a posture of militant non-alignment meant neutrality in the Sino-Soviet dispute and opposition to foreign bases both in Vietnam and in the wider Southeast Asian region. PRG officials rarely commented on the former matter and it is, therefore, significant that Tran Van Tra, head of the Saigon-Gia Dinh MMC let himself be drawn on this issue at a press conference in Saigon on 8 May: "The general, who had Soviet military training, also made it clear that PRG would not get embroiled in the feud between Peking and Moscow when he thanked both China and the Soviet Union for aid." (*Canberra Times*, 13 May). This theme was reiterated by PRG president Huynh Tan Phat in a speech marking the PRG's 6th anniversary: "We pledge to constantly strengthen solidarity with the Soviet Union, China and the Socialist Countries; with the nonaligned countries; with the national liberation movements and the revolutionary movements." (Saigon domestic service, 7 June).

Persistent news reports that the Soviet Union had asked for the use of Cam Ranh port as a naval base (*The Age*, 12 May, 22 September, for example) were dismissed by PRG spokesmen as "dangerous speculation [designed] to sow discord among neighbors" (quoted, AFP, 12 June). The PRG stated that the Soviet Union has also denied making such a request. (A DRV official stated that the Soviet Union, if needed, would enjoy facilities at Cam Ranh similar to those given any other friendly country; *FEER*, 8 August.)

PRG officials, while opposing the presence of U.S. bases in Southeast Asia (especially in Thailand and the Philippines), expressed willingness to "normalize" relations with the United States. Advisory council president Nguyen Huu Tho has stated that the PRG was ready to establish diplomatic, economic, cultural and friendly relations with all countries "including the United States" on the basis of mutual respect for the independence, sovereignty and territorial integrity of each country and non-interference in each other's internal affairs (AFP, Hong Kong, 4 April).

During 1975 the United States twice vetoed applications for U.N. membership made by the PRG (U.S. Department of State, Bureau of Public Affairs, news release, 21 August; AAP-Reuter, 1 October). Nevertheless, with regard to foreign economic involvement in South Vietnam, a willingness to deal with U.S. firms was indicated. For example, a statement on the establishment of relations for "economic, scientific and technical cooperation" hinted that the PRG would welcome the participation of U.S. firms in oil exploration and exploitation: the PRG was "ready to discuss with foreign governments and oil companies desirous of taking part in the abovesaid undertaking, *including those companies having previously operated in this domain in South Vietnam*" (LPA, 9 August).

Party leaders have used both the South Vietnam Afro-Asian Solidarity Committee (SVN AASC) and the South Vietnam Peace Committee as platforms on which to comment on international affairs. In January the SVN AASC declared: "We fully and resolutely support the Arab people's just struggle against the U.S. and Israel for independence and sovereignty and demand that Israel completely withdraw its troops from the illegally occupied Arab territory and respect the authentic national rights of the Palestinian people." (LPA, 23 January.) In February the SVN AASC and the South Vietnam Peace Committee issued a joint statement condemning the Turkish invasion of Cyprus (VNA, 19 February). In July both organizations combined to stage a meeting which demanded the withdrawal of the United States from South Korea (ibid., 24 July).

International Activities and Contacts. In October a delegation of the VWP's South Vietnam committee, led by Tran Nam Trung, attended the 12th anniversary celebration of Laotian independence in Viengsay "at the invitation of the Lao People's Revolutionary Party." This was the only publicly reported party delegation to leave Vietnam in 1975. While party members are known to have traveled extensively overseas during the year, they were invariably identified in their non-party roles. Similarly, messages exchanged with overseas communist parties were signed by the Central Committee of the NFL and not by either the PRP or the VWP's COSVN. In 1975 messages of greeting were sent to communist parties in the USSR, China, the United States, Denmark, Sweden, Italy, Hungary, Romania, East Germany, North Korea and North Vietnam—45th anniversary of the VWP—all signed by the NFL. Vietnamese delegates who attended the Romanian Communist Party's congress in November 1974 and the Swedish Left Communist's Congress in March 1975 were identified as members of the NFL and not by any party affiliation. On this basis it seems certain that the independence of a communist party in South Vietnam is not recognized internationally. Nevertheless, party members have ample opportunity to make overseas contacts as members of delegations of various ostensibly non-party organizations.

In 1975, the following countries granted diplomatic recognition to the PRG (consult *YICA, 1974*, p. 569, and 1975, p. 453, for the earlier countries): Afghanistan, Australia, Austria, Belgium, Burma, Cambodia, Canada, Cyprus, Denmark, Finland, France, Guyana, Iceland, India, Indonesia, Italy, Ivory Coast, Jamaica, Japan, Kuwait, Laos, Libya, Luxembourg, Malagasy, Malasia, Maldives, Mexico, Mozambique, Netherlands, Nepal, New Zealand, Niger, Norway, Pakistan, Panama, Papua-New Guinea, Peru, Sierra Leone, Sweden, Switzerland, Thailand, United Kingdom, Upper Volta, Venezuela, and Zaire. Recognition was also granted by the Palestine Liberation Organization (PLO).

PRG authorities sought the removal from Saigon of all diplomats who had been accredited to the RVN. In June, diplomatic representatives from Algeria, Guinea, Mauritania, Uganda, Senegal, Tanzania, Mongolia, Yugoslavia, Poland, Burundi, and the PLO were invited to attend the PRG's 6th-anniversary celebration. In September the PRG permitted Cuba, Congo, Mauritania, Sweden, Denmark, Mexico, and the PLO to send ambassadors (a chargé d'affaires in the case of Burundi and a "representative" in the case of the PLO) to take up their posts in Saigon. Under unification it seems likely that Hanoi would be the national capital and diplomatic posts in Saigon would be downgraded. India was discouraged from sending a fully accredited ambassador to Saigon and in November reportedly was about to receive a Vietnamese ambassador representing the entire country (*FEER*, 28 November).

Various non-refundable aid agreements were signed with the PRG (for 1975-76) during late 1974 and during 1975 by the USSR, China, Bulgaria, and Mongolia, during late 1974 by Czechoslovakia, Albania, East Germany and Hungary, and during 1975 by Finland, Sweden, Algeria, Poland, Norway and Iraq.

The PRG kept up its round of international contacts through the indefatigable efforts of its foreign minister, Nguyen Thi Binh. Her itinerary included China (28 February-3 March); Afghanistan, Libya, Algeria, France, Congo and Tanzania (March-April); USSR, Algeria, Libya and Iraq (2 June-2 August); non-aligned conference in Peru (August); Venezuela, Cuba and Mexico (August-September); and East Germany (13-14 September). Nguyen Van Tien, the PRG's special representative in Hanoi, paid friendship visits to Mauritania, Guinea, Senegal, Libya, Sierra Leone and Zaire (25 December 1974-8 February 1975).

The Liberation Women's Union, the Liberation Students' and Youth Unions, the South Vietnam Peace Committee, and the Liberation Federation of Trade Unions sent numerous delegations overseas. Delegations to South Vietnam were few. Late in 1974 a Danish-Vietnam solidarity committee was welcomed in Quang Tri, as were two correspondents of TASS and NOSVOSTI who arrived in January 1975. A U.S. peace movement delegation, headed by Gabriel Kolko, was received by Mme Binh in Da Nang in April. Apparently, delegations were not received over the intervening months until September, when a combined delegation representing the World Peace Council, the Afro-Asian Peoples' Solidarity Organization, and the International Association of Democratic Lawyers, and a delegation of overseas Vietnamese were welcomed in Saigon.

Publications. No mention was made of the party's weekly *Nhan Dan* (The People) or its theoretical journal *Tien Phong* (Vanguard) by Liberation Radio during 1975. After 30 April, a paper entitled *Giai Phong* (Liberation) made its appearance. It was identified as a service of the VWP's Southern organization by another paper (*Saigon Giai Phong*, no. 26, 5 June). Its editorials were regularly broadcast by Saigon radio. On 23 July the LPA announced that the first issue of *Giai Phong* (same title), organ of the NFL, had made its appearance on 22 July. The official paper of the PLAF; *Quan Giai Phong* (Liberation Army) continued to be produced. *South Vietnam in Struggle*, distributed overseas in English and French as the "central organ" of the NFL, ceased publication on 1 September with a special issue, no. 314/315. Other news coverage was carried by *Saigon Giai Phong* (Liberated Saigon) which was printed on the city's modern offset presses soon after 30 April. Both Liberation Radio and the Liberation Press Agency continued to function.

Bendigo Institute of Technology   Carlyle A. Thayer
Victoria, Australia

THE AMERICAS

Argentina

The Communist Party of Argentina (Partido Comunista de Argentina; PCA) originated from the Partido Socialista Internacionalista, a split-off from the Partido Socialista. It was established in 1918 and its present name was taken in 1920. The PCA is strongly pro-Soviet.

The PCA in early 1975 claimed to have 147,527 members, reporting that 15,244 new affiliates had joined in the previous year. It announced that between 80 and 90 percent of the new members were former Peronistas. Non-communist sources put the party membership at a considerably lower figure, about 70,000. The population of Argentina is something over 25 million.

PCA membership, two thirds of which is said to be concentrated in the Federal Capital (city of Buenos Aires) and in Buenos Aires Province, is drawn mainly from the urban middle and lower classes. The class distribution of delegates to the last party congress on which such information was announced (1969) was 72 workers, 10 members of the liberal professions, 6 teachers, 6 writers and journalists, 4 peasants, 2 housewives, and one student. The party claims to have made substantial gains among peasants and students since then. The PCA is believed to be financially well off through its indirect participation in various commercial and banking enterprises. It claimed to have raised a billion pesos in its finance campaign in 1974; information is not available on its 1975 drive.

The PCA was legalized in May 1973 by then President Héctor Cámpora in one of his first acts in office. The party congress in August of that year was the first legal one in 27 years and only the second held under legal conditions since 1930. Although the party ran, and elected, some camouflaged candidates in the 1973 election, it was not until 1975 that it was able to run nominees under its own name, in the provincial election in Misiones, in April. None of its candidates was elected.

Other communist parties in Argentina include the Revolutionary Communist Party (Partido Comunista Revolucionario; PCR), and the Communist Vanguard (Vanguardia Comunista; VC), both of which are pro-Chinese, and the Trotskyist movement, split into various factions, at least one of which is dedicated to terrorism and guerrilla war.

In recent years, various small leftist groups composed of Castroite or Peronista extremists, or both, have emerged. While most do not espouse communist ideologies, they have a shared strategy of armed struggle to seize power. Their total membership—earlier estimated at between 6,000 and 7,000—probably increased considerably during 1975. Although the avowedly Peronista terrorist groups generally threw their support behind the Peronista governments of Héctor Cámpora (1973) and Juan Perón (1973-74), by the end of 1974 they had returned to terrorist activities against the government of President María Estela (Isabel) Martínez de Perón. During 1975 the largest Peronista guerrilla group, the Montoneros, appeared to have absorbed most of the others, and its terrorist activities surpassed those of the Trotskyite Ejército Revolucionario del Pueblo (People's Revolutionary Army; ERP) in volume and violence.

The PCA. Leadership and Organization. The PCA is led by Gerónimo Arnedo Alvarez, the secretary-general. Its national leadership tends to be rather old, including the Ghioldi brothers, Rodolfo (a founder of the party) and Orestes (who joined it in 1922), and Rubens Iscaro, Alcira de la Peña, and Héctor Agosti, who rose to national prominence in the late 1930s. Its leadership also includes its two national deputies, Jesús Mira and Juan Carlos Domínguez. The PCA is organized pyramidally from cells, neighborhood committees, and local committees on up to provincial committees, and the Central Committee, Executive Committee, and Secretariat.

The PCA youth movement, the Communist Youth Federation (Federación Juvenil Comunista; FJC), is organized along the same lines as the party. Early in 1975 it claimed 57,920 members, announcing that 17,206 had joined during the previous year. The FJC's strength is concentrated largely in the student movement, and it has benefited to some degree from the radicalization of the students in recent years.

The PCA is weak in the labor movement despite the presence of party units in many unions. The major trade union body, the General Confederation of Labor (Confederación General del Trabajo; CGT) was until 1975 absolutely dominated by Peronistas who completely rejected communist interference. Even the marked decline in control by the Peronista national CGT leadership over its regional and industrial affiliates during 1975 appears to have strengthened principally left-wing Peronistas and various pro-Maoist and pro-Trotskyist elements rather than the PCA.

The PCA controls the Movement for Trade Union Unity (Movimiento de Unidad y Coordinación Sindical; MUCS), which represents some small regional unions, mostly those centered in Córdoba and Mendoza provinces. PCA Central Committee member Rubens Iscaro is the MUCS secretary-general and is closely associated with the World Frederation of Trade Unions.

Although peasant organizations are mostly grouped under the non-communist Argentina Agrarian Federation (Federación Agraria Argentina; FAA), the PCA claims to be active in the Union of Agrarian Producers of Argentina (UPARA), formed in 1969. UPARA is composed of small and medium farmers, and claims to have 60,000 members.

Most PCA fronts, such as the Argentine League for the Rights of Men, the Union of Argentine Women, and the Argentine Peace Council, were illegal for many years until 1973.

PCA National Meetings. Three national meetings of the PCA were given particular publicity during 1975. These were a Central Committee Secretariat meeting in January and Central Committee plenums late in April and late in July.

In theory at least, the second-highest body within the PCA, after the party congress, is the plenum of its Central Committee, composed of members of the committee and representatives of various provincial organizations. In the interim, the Secretariat speaks for the party.

The Secretariat meeting in January received a report on the current situation in the country. It noted "unanimous" working-class support for "democratization and national liberation," and pointed to the "conspiratorial activity of the people's enemies." The report commented that the people should not submit to "fatalism," and that although the social and economic crisis was growing, it could be resolved. (*IB*, no. 2.)

The April plenum heard a speech by the party secretary-general which stressed the deterioration of the domestic political situation and called for government action against right-wing terrorists of the Argentine Anti-Communist Alliance (Alianza Anti-comunista Argentina; AAA) (ibid., no. 9). The July plenum came after the fall of José López Rega. It adopted a declaration to the effect that the CGT general strike which had resulted in the removal of López Rega and a reconstitution of the cabinet was an "important labor victory" (*Expreso PL*, 18 July).

Domestic Attitudes and Activities. The political and economic situation of the country deteriorated throughout 1975. The weakness and indecisiveness of the government of President Isabel Perón led to deep splits within the Peronista ranks, increased hostility toward her by the Opposition, and virtually complete lack of direction in economic and social affairs. Terrorism by both right- and left-wing extremists mounted, and rumors of impending coup attempts were frequent.

Increasingly critical of Isabel Peron, the PCA participated in the mid-year campaign against presidential adviser José López Rega, warned frequently of the danger of a coup, and continued to demand government action against terrorism, particularly that of the AAA.

In mid-December 1974, Communist deputies Jesús Mira and Juan Carlos Domínguez urged that Congress lift the state of siege, declared by Isabel Peron ostensibly to deal with terrorism. The deputies·argued that the state of siege "would serve as a pretext for persecuting the political forces supporting democracy, freedom, and national sovereignty and independence." (Radio La Nación, 18 December.)

On 22 March 1975 the PCA issued a statement denouncing a claim by the Ministry of Interior of the existence of a left-wing plot to paralyze the country's principal industrial centers. The statement said that the Ministry's claim was "issued at a time when pro-oligarchic and pro-imperialist circles are threatening a coup d'état, while the Argentine Anti-Communist Alliance is murdering people, and, when, on the other hand, political and social forces both within and outside the Justicialist Movement coming out in defense of democracy and against imperialism are demanding the continuation of the course begun in 1973." The PCA called for "joint action to beat back the offensive of the right-wing elements in the government," adding: "There is still time." (*IB*, no. 7.)

A couple of weeks later, the PCA Central Committee issued another statement, announcing its continued willingness to support the government in "carrying out its task and fulfilling the program promised to the people." But it warned that "one of the principal causes of the deterioration of the situation is the abandonment of the programmatic goals which were agreed upon by the coalition of political forces in 1973 as a plan for the progressive liberation of the country."

The Communist statement accused "North American imperialism" of trying to "frustrate definitively the democratic process begun in 1973." It also denounced the fact that the AAA was allowed to operate with "impunity."

The PCA then proposed that "Señora President María Estela Martínez must resume immediately a constructive dialogue, real, efficient, reaching common agreements which will be fulfilled." It went on to say that "this does not mean a simple change of personnel, but radical change of policy, altering direction and returning to the road initiated in 1973 and to the program of national and social liberation for which the people voted." (*Expreso PL*, 4 April.)

At the end of April, the Communist weekly *Nuestra Palabra* again urged the government to dismiss "officials who are not doing their job," and to change its policies. It particularly criticized the president for having met on 18 April with Chilean president General Augusto Pinochet. (*Granma*, Havana, English edition, 27 April.)

The PCA itself was a victim of right-wing terrorists on 14 June. A bomb exploded at its Córdoba provincial headquarters, and this attack was denounced the same day by the Radical Party, the major opposition group.

With the beginning in mid-June of the final struggle between José López Rega, Minister of Social Security as well as private secretary and principal confidant of President Isabel Perón, on the one hand, and his opponents inside and outside the Peronista movement, on the other, the PCA took its position firmly with the latter group. It sounded the tocsin in an article in *Nuestra Palabra* on 25 June. This article strongly attacked the economic plan put forward by Celestino Rodrigo, with support of López Rega. It said that this plan led to measures which, besides being "conducive to the further enrichment of foreign monopolies, the land-owning oligarchy, and big capital at the expense of worse conditions for the workers and other people," were "placing our country in even greater dependence on the general crisis of the world capitalist system."

The article went on to say: "The plan can be carried out only by reversing the gains of the working class and suppressing democratic freedoms. Economically, it is a turn to the right, masterminded by reactionary forces operating within the government.... Our Party will expose the situation with all the means at its disposal. It will struggle indefatigably for the unity of all patriotic, democratic and popular forces to bar the road to reaction and open the way to progress and a better life for our people." (*IB*, no. 13.)

The struggle culminated in mid-July, when the leadership of the CGT, of the military, and of the opposition parties demanded that the president dismiss López Rega. The CGT called a general strike to back up the demand. The president finally yielded, and López Rega went into exile in Spain, and most of the ministers associated with him were dismissed.

The PCA Central Committee proclaimed the defeat of López Rega "an important victory," noting that "the struggle which the working class began for economic reasons . . . was immediately transformed into a fully political strike." It added that "the democratic and popular victory is at the same time a defeat for the most reactionary sectors of the country and for the multinationals," in which "a positive role has been played by the democratic political parties, the Armed Forces, the progressive trade unions and cultural organizations." The PCA announced that it "insists on the need for constituting in Argentina a civil-military cabinet of wide democratic coalition, alert to the danger of reactionary countercoup." (*Expreso PL*, 18 July.)

On 22 July the PCA Executive Committee issued another commentary on the López Rega crisis. It urged that the CGT, the opposition parties, and others agree on a plan to deal with the country's problems: "Based on a common plan of national solutions, it will be possible to establish a solid civilian-military cabinet of a broad democratic coalition which can express the wish of the great majority of the nation." It added: "If the main forces hesitate to give the country an urgent political solution, the reactionary forces waiting for power, taking advantage of the general dissatisfaction, will have a chance to strike." (Radio Clarin, 24 July.)

Early in August the PCA weekly *Nuestra Palabra* renewed its attacks on the incumbent cabinet: "There is needed a cabinet with prestige and authority, capable of awakening the confidence and enthusiasm of the people." It again urged that the new cabinet be a civil-military one, which could "enjoy the firm support of the masses who are fighting against imperialism and the oligarchy." It ended saying that "in this way the economic crisis can be faced and a reactionary coup can be prevented." (*Expreso PL*, 8 August.)

On 9 August the PCA was invited by Minister of Economy Pedro Bonsani to present its ideas as to how to meet the economic and social crisis. The party leadership announced that it had proposed "freezing prices of staples and a minimum salary of 6,500 pesos, getting the National Institute of Remunerations . . . to function, enforcing the ruling of the labor-management commission and a flexible 82 and 75 percent pension for retired people and pension holders." It also desired that the "public sector be strengthened and strict control of bank, financial and especially foreign sectors be established." (Radio Telam, 9 August.) When a new cabinet was formed in mid-August, the PCA announced its support.

On 19 August the PCA placed a paid announcement in several Buenos Aires papers, commenting on recent changes in the government. A key part of this statement noted that "The Communist Party adopts an objective attitude regarding the new cabinet. It has repeatedly stated that it does not long for the failure of the government or the destruction of the Peronista party. Consequently, the new cabinet is to be judged according to its statements and, above all, by its concrete actions." (Radio Clarin, 19 August.)

On the same day, Fernando Nadra, editor of *Nuestra Palabra*, announced the dispatch of a letter to *La Opinión*, which had been attacking the PCA extensively. This letter emphasized several points concerning the then current position of the party: "As far as ultraleft terrorism is concerned, it is known that we have consistently fought against it. Our fight has been both ideological, political, and concrete, and through it we have shed much light and won the minds of many mistaken or hestitating youths. . . . With regard to the terrorism of the ultraright, and especially the AAA, which has ravaged the country during the last few years, [we] do not need to say anything, but only to emphasize the events. You know very well that we have been in the forefront of the fight to tear it out by its roots."

The letter emphasized the PCA's demand for release of all "political and labor prisoners. . . . Many of the 2,000 prisoners who have been arrested without cause or process and put at the disposal of the Executive Branch are members of our party. As you should know, we have various party buildings and houses of comrades which were destroyed by fire bombs, and many comrades were murdered after sadistic torture and the wanton mutilation of their bodies."

Fernando Nadra ended his letter with the comment: "We believe that a great deal of good is done for the armed forces, the country, the people and for democracy when problems are made clear and solutions are found and not merely by the simple expression of faith." (Radio La Opinión, 19 August.)

Early in October, the PCA issued an "open letter" in which it again denounced the terrorists and warned also against growing talk of a possible coup. It commented that "Neither the so-called guerrillas nor the unbridled and bloody actions of rightist bands resolve any problems; rather they aggravate them." It warned: "Democratic freedoms are clearly in danger. We must save them, saving the democratic institution to insure the realization of the electoral process in 1976 or in early 1977. This is the fundamental task in these danger-filled times for democrats and patriots, civilians and soldiers, who comprise the large majority in this country."

The PCA argued that a "serious dilemma presents itself: an authentic democracy to fulfill the dream of all Argentines to put an end to dependency—the deep cause of our evils—or a dictatorship of the monopolies, larger landowners and financiers." It went on to warn against "coupists of various types" and their slogan of "order or chaos" and their talk about "a profound moral crisis." It argued that coupists wished to give "free rein to the monopolies and the large landowners while placing the whole burden of the economic crisis on the back of the working people." (Ibid., 8 October.)

International Views and Contacts. During 1975 the PCA continued its traditionally pro-Soviet attitudes. Various PCA delegations visited Eastern Europe and the Soviet Union. In mid-year an Argentine delegation headed by Rodolfo Ghioldi participated in an "international symposium" held in Prague to celebrate the 40th anniversary of the Seventh Congress of the Communist International, sponsored by the *World Marxist Review*, the organ of the pro-Moscow section of international communism. Rubens Iscaro and Rodolfo Ghioldi were among the contributors to *World Marxist Review* during the year.

The PCA made clear its opposition to the Chinese line. Thus, the July plenum of the Central Committee accused the Maoists of being "bearers of petty bourgeois, chauvinist ideology." It accused the leaders of the Chinese party of "stubbornly sabotaging all measures aimed at strengthening peace," "impeding the settlement of international conflicts by peaceful negotiation," and "provoking the disruption of stability in various parts of the world." (Radio Pravda, 21 September.)

Publications. The PCA's *Nuestra Palabra* appears weekly. *Nueva Era* is the party's monthly theoretical journal. It also publishes the bimonthly *Cuadernos de Cultura*, catering mainly to intellectuals, and since August 1970 the *Bolletín de Informaciones Latinoamericanas*, a fortnightly report. The FJC has a fortnightly, *Juventud*. The party also publishes numerous pamphlets.

*   *   *

The PCR. The Revolutionary Communist Party (originally the Communist Party of Revolutionary Recovery) was created in January 1968 by dissidents from the PCA, especially the youth organization, who rejected the PCA's attempted "broad democratic front" as an effort at "class conciliation" and "conciliation with imperialism." César Otto Vargas is the PCR secretary-general; another leading figure is Guillermo Sánchez. Several PCR leaders held important positions in the FJC before expulsion from the PCA in 1967.

The PCR tends to be pro-Maoist, advocates armed struggle, and believes that leadership in the revolutionary moment must be held by the party, favoring only urban guerrilla struggle and contending that the "wide plains" of Argentina and the "highly developed agriculture of the coast" would not permit successful operations. There is no evidence of any recent participation in guerrilla activities.

On 29 May 1975 the Buenos Aires provincial police prohibited a meeting planned by the PCR in the packinghouse town of Berisso. The police said that they had acted because the PCR was not a legally registered party, and in conformity with the state of siege then in force (Radio Telam, 29 May). In October, the Chinese Communist Party announced that among the cables of congratulations on the 26th anniversary of the People's Republic was one from the Argentine PCR (Peking Radio, NCNA, 15 October).

The VC. The Communist Vanguard, probably founded in 1964, is pro-Chinese and enjoys recognition from the Chinese as the more or less official Maoist party of Argentina. In May a delegation of the VC Central Committee visited China, where it was received by Yao Wen-yuan, member of the Politburo of the Chinese party, and by Keng Piao, member of the Central Committee and head of its International Liaison Department. On the 26th anniversary of the founding of the People's Republic, Mao Tse-tung and Chou En-lai received telegrams of congratulation from the VC. (Peking radio, NCNA, 15 October).

*   *   *

Trotskyism is represented in Argentina by varied groups. The Socialist Workers' Party (Partido Socialista de Trabajadores; PST) and the Revolutionary Workers' Party (Partido Revolucionario de los Trabajadores; PRT) both have, or have had, affiliation with the United Secretariat of the Fourth International. The PRT has spawned the so-called People's Revolutionary Army (ERP), a guerrilla group. In 1973 the PRT and ERP split into factions. One declared that it no longer considered itself Trotskyist. The other reorganized as the Revolutionary Communist League (Liga Comunista Revolucionaria; LCR), which became a "sympathizing organization of the United Secretariat."

The Trotskyist Labor Party—Partido Obrero (Trotskista)—is aligned with the International Secretariat of the Fourth International, headed by J. Posadas, an Argentine. Politica Obrera is apparently an independent group. Another element of Trotskyite origins, the Partido Socialista de la Izquierda Nacional, has formally foresworn allegiance to Trotskyism, while still revering Trotsky.

The PRT-ERP. The PRT was founded in 1964 and divided in 1968, when two thirds of the members espoused the tactic of armed struggle. The views of the majority faction are expressed in *El Combatiente*, which still appears clandestinely, and those of the minority in *La Verdad*.

The "armed branch" of the majority faction is the ERP, in existence since August 1970. The ERP was at first particularly strong in Córdoba and Rosario, with some influence in Tucumán and Buenos Aires, and in recent years it has operated in virtually all parts of the country.

The principal ERP leaders, Mario Roberto Santucho Juárez and Enrique Harold Corrianán Merlo, are members of the 11-man Executive Committee of the PRT. The ERP follows a cellular type of organization; a political commisar in each cell is appointed by the PRT.

During 1975 the guerrilla activities of the ERP were confined largely to the northern province of Tucumán. It is not clear whether the ERP's retreat to the Tucumán mountains was due to serious casualties in its urban guerrilla activities, agreement with the Montoneros to leave urban operations to them, or belief by the ERP in the feasibility of organizing a Che Guevara "foco" type of guerrilla base in Tucumán. However, it is obvious that the ERP was able to maintain a relatively large-scale guerrilla operation in the northern province. At the end of August the military announced that they had either killed or captured 800 guerrillas. They did not mention their own casualties.

Early in August the ERP announced a major change in strategy, offering President Isabel Perón a truce "in exchange for the release of political prisoners and the lifting of its illegal status." It announced that it was offering an armistice because of the "disintegration of the Peronist government, the lack of potential of the military party in the face of the powerful mass mobilization and the continuous strengthening of the revolutionary forces." It urged formation of a "strong popular front" and called for a constituent assembly with "full popular participation" to adopt "just provisions to solve the crisis and preserve the interests of the majorities." (Radio EFE, Madrid, 4 August.)

The government paid little or no attention to the ERP "armistice" offer. Desultory fighting went on in Tucumán throughout the year.

The Liga Comunista Revolucionaria. In 1973, when the PRT-ERP split, the dissidents formed the Liga Comunista Revolucionaria (LCR). At the time of the killing of two LCR members during a police raid in January 1975, the LCR issued a statement which, according to *Intercontinental Press* (New York, 27 January) "described how the two revolutionists had become aware of a militarist and centrist deviation in the PRT and sided with the Fracción Roja (Red Faction), which began to raise criticisms of the organization's course."

The LCR statement noted, concerning its disagreements with the PRT-ERP, that, "as opposed to the guerrilla organizations that conceive of the armed struggle only as single combat isolated from the mass movement against the bourgeois repressive forces, we offer the example of these two compañeros. Following the orientation of our organization, they put their political and military capacities to the service of advancing the consciousness, organization, and arming of the workers' movement and other sectors of the poor masses. For them as for our organization, the socialist revolution, the seizure of power by the working class, involves unifying the struggles, building the independent organization, raising the level of consciousness, and arming the masses."

The LCR, avowedly Trotskyist, is associated with the United Secretariat of the Fourth International. It has a monthly periodical, *Combate.*

The PST. A veteran Trotskyist, Nahuel Moreno, headed the faction of the original PRT that opposed guerrilla activities. At the end of 1971 it joined with a faction of the Socialist Party headed by Juan Corral to form the Socialist Workers' Party. The party received legal recognition, and ran Corral as presidential candidate in the 1973 elections.

The PST was aligned with the opposition to the Perón regime during 1975. It supported the fight against López Rega, but thereafter urged the resignation of Isabel Perón, and urged Congress to "name a new provisional president, perhaps a representative of the CGT."

On 21 August, two months after the fall of López Rega, the PST warned of an impending coup attempt. In a statement in its periodical, *Avanzada Socialista*, it said that this was threatened because of "the fact that the workers' movement has not responded to the political, social and economic crisis with mass mobilizations. Although the masses have not been defeated and have emerged victoriously from the June general strike, they have been pulled offstage because of the break of the trade union leadership. Thus, the stage is dominated by actions of terrorist groups, by criminal provocations of fascist gangs, and finally by attempts at military "solutions." (*Intercontinental Press*, 5 September.)

Some PST members were victims of the right-wing terrorism which gripped the country throughout the year. On 5 September, five members of the party were killed, and on the following day three were kidnaped in La Plata.

Some members of the PST were jailed by the government during the year. Four were released early in September after an appeal by the PST to the Constitutional Affairs Committee of Congress.

It was reported at the time that at least eight others were still being held. (Ibid., 15 September.)

The PST continued to oppose guerrilla activities. In a statement issued early in the year, it proclaimed itself as committed "to continue opposing guerrilla activity because, ignoring and deprecating the consciousness of the masses, what they want and feel, the [guerrillas] launch terrorist actions against the government that the workers still support, particularly in the face of the menace of the ultra right" (ibid., 27 January).

During the early months of 1975 the PST was the center of a controversy within the United Secretariat of the Fourth International. The Secretariat issued an attack on the PST for having supported "institutionalization" of the Argentine political system, and having conferred with Peron at least once. The PST replied, defending its activities on the basis of its desire to form a mass party, and its belief that in the face of militarist and "fascist" menaces in Argentina, it had been correct in supporting return to a democratic system there in 1973. (Ibid.)

The Socialist Workers Party of the United States indicated its support of the PST by sponsoring Juan Antonio Corral in a tour of the United States in the autumn.

Other Trotskyist Groups. The Partido Obrero (Trotskista) of J. Posadas concentrated most of its activities during 1975 on its periodical *Voz Proletaria*. It tended to have a more friendly attitude, toward the government than did the PRT, LCR, or PST. The Partido Socialista de la Revolución Nacional supported the movement against López Rega and opposed the general aimlessness of the government of President Isabel Perón.

*   *   *

Peronista Extremist Groups. During 1975 the Montoneros were the principal extremist Peronista group. Throughout the year it engaged in guerrilla activities. For example, on 5 October a Montonero group attacked an army post, took over an airport, and hijacked a plane in the northern city of Formosa.

Montonero activity was carried on all over the country. An editorial in the *Christian Science Monitor* (9 October) underscored the significance of the group: "The Montonero challenge is serious. It may not be enough to bring down the government . . . but it adversely affects just about everything that happens in Argentina. Effective counteraction by government is needed."

Rutgers University   Robert J. Alexander

Bolivia

The Communist Party of Bolivia (Partido Comunista de Bolivia; PCB) was founded in 1950 and is pro-Soviet in orientation. A pro-Chinese splinter group became the Communist Party of Bolivia Marxist-Leninist (Partido Comunista de Bolivia, Marxista-Leninista; PCB-ML) in 1965. The Trotskyist Revolutionary Workers' Party (Partido Obrero Revolucionario; POR) is split into three factions. The National Liberation Army (Ejército de Liberación Nacional; ELN), founded in 1966, formed the

Bolivian Workers' Revolutionary Party (Partido Revolucionario de los Trabajadores de Bolivia; PRT-B) in March 1975. The Movement of the Revolutionary Left (Movimiento de Izquierda Revolucionaria; MIR) was formed in mid-1971 and reorganized after the 21 August 1971 coup in which rightist Colonel Hugo Banzer overthrew the government of leftist General Juan José Torres and seized the presidency for himself. Other revolutionary groups included the Union of Poor Peasants (Unión de Campesinos Pobres; UCP), the Tupac Katari, and other peasant-oriented organizations.

All of these parties were illegal during 1975. The PCB and PCB-ML are estimated to have 300 and 150 members, respectively. The population of Bolivia is 5,500,000 (estimated 1975).

Since the fall of General Torres, Bolivian leftist parties and organizations in the country and in exile have called for the formation of a united opposition to the Banzer government. The first and most important of several unsuccessful alliances was the Anti-Imperialist Revolutionary Front (Frente Revolucionario Anti-imperialista; FRA)—which included the PCB, the PCB-ML, the MIR, the ELN, and two factions of the POR—was formed in November 1971. In June 1973 a "Call to the Bolivian People" was issued by the PCB, PCB-ML, the Revolutionary Party of the Nationalist Left (PRIN), and the Leftist Revolutionary Nationalist Movement (MNRI) to overthrow the "fascist" Banzer government and its North American and Brazilian supporters. Despite several efforts to form an operational leftist front, unity was not achieved in 1974 or 1975 though calls came from everyone from former President Torres (*Granma*, Havana, English ed., 17 August 1975) to the PCB.

Disruptions in November 1974 led to the government establishment of a "new order" in Bolivia. Elections scheduled for 1975 were cancelled, the armed forces assuming "complete responsibility and total control of the government" until 1980. The "new order" further reduced the scope of political activities in the country. Some protests and demonstrations continued, just the same, by students, workers, and miners, in part through their respective outlawed organizations—the Bolivian University Confederation (CUB), the Bolivian Labor Central (COB), the Bolivian Mineworkers Federation (FSTMB)—and by Catholics—particularly early in the year through the Justice and Peace Commission (CJP). On a number of occasions the government announced the seizure of "subversive propaganda" of the PCB, MIR, ELN, and other groups, and charged that these organizations and others received aid from abroad.

The PCB. Leadership and Organization. The first secretary of the PCB is Jorge Kolle Cueto. Others prominent in the party include Mario Monje Molina, a former first secretary, and Central Committee members Simón Reyes, Arturo Lanza, and Carlos Alba. Luis Padilla, a member of the Central Committee as well, is the party's chief international spokesman.

The basic organization of the PCB is the cell, which consists of no fewer than three party members. District committees, elected at national congresses (the most recent of which was in June 1971), exist in each department and in most mining centers. The national congress of the party elects the Central Committee, the latter guiding the party between congresses. The Central Committee elects the Political and Control-Auditing Commissions and the first secretary, and convenes National conferences to discuss current organizational and political affairs not requiring the convocation of the national congress. District committees may hold district conferences with the approval of the Central Committee. (According to *WMR*, September 1973.)

According to Luis Padilla, the "brutal repression" of the PCB by the Banzer government since 1971 confirms the communist policy and Marxist-Leninist principles of the working class party. Among the most important is the combination of revolutionary strategy with flexible tactics suited to the actual situation, thus allowing PCB leaders to isolate and resolve problems arising from the often very abrupt and unexpected course of political events. Since 1971 the party has been "on the defensive, cutting back its mass actions" in order to "preserve the organization and create conditions for eventually taking the offensive." The recent past has confirmed communist participation in alliances and "broad democratic movements." (*WMR*, May 1975.) At present the party must, above all else, solve the problem of participation of the patriotic military in the working class and popular movement (ibid., August).

The PCB's youth organization, the Communist Youth of Bolivia (Juventud Comunista de Bolivia; JCB), is illegal. Among JCB leaders in recent years have been Jorge Escalera and Carlos Soría Galvarro. At an international conference in mid-1974, Lanza noted that left extremism in Bolivia was closely associated with the social behavior of students as part of the middle strata. He added that despite the ideological vagueness of the Bolivian student movement, there was a clear pattern: ingrained individualism, avant-guardism, voluntarism, anarchic terrorism, and other attributes of leftism. Though the students negate theory, they theorize about the absolute character of action. The youth struggle was acquiring a class dimension, according to Lanza, under the ideological influence of the proletariat. This new development was supported by the PCB while the party intensified its struggle against the "pseudo-left." (*WMR*, August 1974.)

Domestic and International Positions. The two urgent objectives of the PCB and the Bolivian revolutionary movement are: "to lay the foundations for united action of all social strata and political currents opposed to the dictatorship on the basis of a program reflecting the vital interests of the country and people, and second, to give impulse to anti-imperialist action and the people's struggle for vital demands by working up a revolutionary, patriotic and democratic spirit" (ibid., May 1975).

The experience of the final months of the Torres government, when "united anti-fascist actions" seemed to be possible, taught Bolivian revolutionaries several things about the Right and the ultra-left. With respect to the former, the Banzer takeover (as well as "counterrevolutionary coups" in Chile and Uruguay) shows that the "intermediate social strata" may take a neutral stand or even back counterrevolutionary or fascist positions, at least for a time. Thus, it is apparent that the revolutionary potential of these social strata is ultimately determined by the degree of organization, unity, and political maturity of the working class, spheres "in which the activity of Marxist-Leninist parties is of decisive importance." (Ibid., August.) The activities of the ultra-left groups during 1971 show that they wanted to make the popular front "an instrument for their own subjectivist, adventurist, anti-Communist and anti-Soviet designs." The most obvious evidence of this was their effort to impose a "military administration" in place of "collective political leadership," causing the front to break up. The practical lesson to be learned is that "it is not enough for a democratic movement seeking unity to reach a more or less broad mutual understanding concerning a *common program*. Views concerning the *ways* to the revolution should coincide in practice. There should be agreement on the *forms* and *means* of attaining the strategic objectives, the ultimate goal. The facts showed that these ways, forms and means of struggle are the result, first and foremost, of the *revolutionary experience of the Bolivian working class* (whose leading role was acknowledge and proclaimed by the members of the front). (Ibid., May; emphasis in original.)

Bolivia was represented at the Conference of Latin American and Caribbean Communist Parties which convened in Havana in June, and signed the strongly pro-Soviet declaration issued after that event. (See Cuba, Appendix.) After many years of conflict between the PCB and the Cuban government, the party now expresses its fullest support for the Communist Party of Cuba and its activities (see *WMR*, November).

Publication. The PCB paper is the irregular, clandestine *Unidad.*

* * *

The PCB-ML. The PCB-ML, which has suffered from internal disputes for several years, apparently remained under the leadership of its long-time secretary general, Oscar Zamora Medinacelli. It too claims to seek the unity of the Bolivian people in order to overthrow the Banzer government.

* * *

The ELN and the PRT-B. The ELN was founded in 1966 and under the leadership of Che Guevara issued its first communiqué in March-April 1967. Its chief leader in 1975 was either Osvaldo "Chato" Peredo or his brother, Antonio Peredo. Early in 1974 the ELN announced that it had joined an international Junta of Revolutionary Coordination (Junta de Coordinación Revolucionaria; JCR) with guerrilla-oriented groups from Argentina (the ERP), Chile (MIR), and Uruguay (MLN-Tupamaros) in order to advance revolutionary struggle in southern South America (see *YICA 1975*, pp. 484-86).

On 11 June 1975 the JCR press agency in Paris, APAL (Agencia de Prensa América Latina) announced that the ELN had formed the Bolivian Workers' Revolutionary Party (PRT-B) to grow into the vanguard for the Bolivian revolution. The ELN would not disappear, but be the "armed fist" or "military force of the working class and Bolivian people" under the "Marxist-Leninist leadership" of the new party. According to an article in the 1 September 1975 *El Proletario*, this vanguard will raise the struggle of the Bolivian proletariat "to the level of a revolutionary war against the bourgeoisie and imperialism." The statement admits that Che Guevara made "tactical errors" in 1966-67, but reiterates its conviction that as Guevara said, revolution must be by armed struggle and continental in scope. The statement repeated the charge of treasonous actions in 1966-67 by the PCB. (See *El Sol de México*, Mexico City, 6 October; *FBIS*, Latin America, 12 June; and *Review of the River Plate*, Buenos Aires, 21 August). An article in the JCR's journal, *Che Guevara* (November 1974), looked forward to a "prolonged war" in three stages; (1) a traditional guerrilla campaign, (2) an insurrection, and (3) a full scale war against intervening imperialist armies. An attack was leveled at Bolivian "reformists" who reject armed struggle in favor of "simple agitation" or a "pact with the bourgeoisie." In mid-December the government announced the arrest in the Siglo XX mining area of Antonio Peredo and a number of other Bolivians and foreigners—the latter variously reported as Argentines and Chileans— said to be the regional command of the PRT-B. According to the official reports, the arrests partially dismantled an "international conspiracy" against the Bolivian government which was to have been activated in Cochabamba in January or February 1975. (LATIN, Buenos Aires, 11 December; AFP, Paris, 11 December; *FBIS*, Latin America, 12 December; *Granma*, Havana, 12 and 15 December.)

Publications. The PRT-B publishes *El Proletario*, an irregular, clandestine paper.

Hoover Institution   William E. Ratliff
Stanford University

Brazil

The Brazilian Communist Party (Partido Comunista Brasileiro; PCB), which suffered from mass arrests during the year, is still the most important Marxist-Leninist organization in the nation. The pro-Soviet PCB was originally founded in 1922 as the Communist Party of Brazil (Partido Comunista do Brasil; PCdoB). During the 1930s several groups broke away or were expelled, and these formed a Trotskyist movement which still exists although split into several factions.

In a bid for legal recognition in 1960, the party dropped all international slogans from its statutes and changed its name to Brazilian Communist Party. A pro-Chinese element broke away the following year and in February 1962 adopted the original party name, Communist Party of Brazil (PCdoB). Still another source of present far-leftist groups was Popular Action (Acão Popular; AP), a left-Catholic group originating in the Catholic student movement in the late 1950s, which in the following decade proclaimed itself to be Marxist-Leninist.

Dissidence within the ranks of these parties after the military coup of 1964 led to the formation of numerous splinter groups, predominantly of Castroite tendency, that strongly advocated the use of armed violence to overthrow the government. Some of them, employing urban guerrilla tactics, gained considerable notoriety for a time, but between 1969 and 1972 the death of their most prominent leaders, the wholesale arrests of militants, and continued public indifference or hostility, drastically reduced the number and effectiveness of the terrorist groups.

In February 1973 four extremist organizations—the National Liberation Alliance (Alianca Libertadora Nacional; ALN), Marxist-Leninist Popular Action (Acão Popular Marxista-Leninista; APM-L), the Revolutionary Brazilian Communist Party (Partido Comunista Brasileiro Revolucionario; PCBR), and the Palmares Armed Revolutionary Vanguard (Vanguarda Armada Revolucionaria-Palmares; VAR-Palmares)—issued a joint statement recognizing the defeat of the guerrilla movement, at least in the short run. Although they called for a long "people's war," there is no evidence that any of the revolutionary leftist groups have had any role in leading the sporadic guerrilla outbursts in rural areas. In 1974 the PCdoB expressed its support of these armed efforts and some underground Marxist-Leninist publications carried news about them. The Guerrilla Forces of Araguaia (Forças Guerrilheiras do Araguaia; FGA), which operates in the state of Pará, has not acknowledged allegiance to any of the known groups.

The communist movement has been illegal in Brazil throughout most of its existence. Except for one year in the 1920s and for the years 1945-47 (when it reached its largest membership, about 150,000), the PCB has been outlawed. However, from 1947-64 the PCB was allowed to function with varying degrees of freedom, and its members ran for office on tickets of other parties. During the presidency of João Goulart (1961-64), the PCB succeeded in infiltrating and controlling important labor, student, political and bureaucratic bodies. At that time, its membership was estimated at 30,000. In this period other far-left groups, although not enjoying legal recognition, were also able to operate freely.

The military regime which came to power in March 1964 drove the PCB and other far-leftist groups underground and banned the existing communist influenced organizations. Since 1969 certain acts of subversion have been punishable by banishment or death. In practice the death penalty has not been applied by the courts though several dozen Brazilian terrorists have been exiled and others have been killed in shootouts with the police and military.

PCB membership is still estimated at the 1974 figure of about 6,000. The PCdoB was said to have had about 1,000 members in 1974, and no estimates were available for 1975. Little is known of the membership of the other Marxist-Leninist groups. The population of Brazil is estimated at 107,-000,000.

The PCB. Organization and Leadership. The PCB apparatus includes the 21-member Executive Commission (some of whose members reside abroad), the Central Committee (which functions chiefly in Brazil, although several of its members also reside abroad), state committees, municipal committees, and local cells in residential districts and places of employment. The Sixth Congress of the PCB, its latest, took place in December 1967. Party secretary general Luiz Carlos Prestes has resided in the Soviet Union since 1971; his stand-in, assistant secretary Giocondo Alves Dias, is presumably in Brazil.

The PCB claims it is playing the "prime role in the process of uniting the democratic forces, in orienting and coordinating the anti-fascist struggle" in Brazil and, in retaliation, "fascism is venting all its hate against the Communists, against our Central Committee." According to an official PCB statement circulated internationally at the end of the year, "the Brazilian dictatorship, unable to destroy our Party, is trying to behead it by imprisoning and physically eliminating its leaders." (*IB*, No. 17, 1975.) Leadership at all levels was indeed weakened by the wave of arrests which followed the discovery in January of clandestine printing operations in São Paulo and Rio de Janeiro. Among the PCB officials (Central Committee or higher) who were reportedly under arrest or "disappeared" during the year were: Osvaldo Pacheco da Silva, a labor union leader based in São Paulo, Aristeu Nogueira, in charge of party organization, Marco Antonio Tavares Coelho, Fernando Pereira Cristino, Elson Costa, Walter Ribeiro, and David Capistrano da Costa. (Others are listed in *IB*, No. 17.)

The investigations interrupted regional, state and municipal organizations in what seemed to be a large scale recruitment and training of new cadres. In Rio de Janeiro, 15 members of the Regional Committee were arrested, among others. The Fifth Military Region claims to have completely dismantled PCB structures in the state of Paraná, and has now begun operations in Santa Catarina where 38 detentions were reported in early December. Repression was also conspicuous in Bahia, Goiás, Rio Grande do Sul and—particularly—in São Paulo. Those arrested included salaried PCB organizers, students, teachers, journalists, professionals, merchants, union leaders, workers and lower echelons of the legal opposition party, Brazilian Democratic Movement (Movimento Brasileiro Democrático; MDB). In São Paulo, 23 officers, 25 non-coms and 15 enlisted men were indicted for subversive activity in the Military Police. Some of these had been members of the PCB "military sector" since 1949. Results of an investigation of a PCB "Jewish sector" have not been released.

Domestic Attitudes and Activities. An official PCB statement circulating toward the end of 1975 charges that living conditions in Brazil are very bad and deteriorating—unemployment and exploitation rise while the minimum wage and personal freedoms fall. Transnational monopolies are said to be moving a substantial part of their production to Brazil, "using the fascist dictatorship and cheap labour as a tool against the international working class." What is more, the deleterious effect of Brazilian "fascism" has reached beyond the country's borders. Brazil has become a "bastion of international imperialism" and a launching ground for actions against the "democratic regimes and peoples of Latin America." Confronted with serious economic problems, political isolation, and "growing protest and struggle of the people," the government is "openly raising the banner of anti-communism" and intensifying "political repression." The PCB statement charges that "ruthless violence" has "become an everyday occurrence."

> The official terror is aimed against public organisations, trade unions, the National Congress, judicial bodies, universities, religious organisations, youth, women's movement, intellectuals. Many Brazilians are persecuted, trade union leaders removed from their posts, teachers and students expelled from universities, clergymen are imprisoned and tortured, certain books and publications are banned, and newspapers, films and plays are censored. The adoption of Institutional Act No. 5 virtually annulled the Constitution and established absolute arbitrary rule on the part of the President of the Republic, introduced the death penalty for political offences, and infringes the principle of personal immunity." (*IB*, No. 17.)

In a February press conference in Moscow, Luiz Carlos Prestes said that protests from all sectors against the military dictatorship culminated in the victory of the MDB in last year's congressional elections: "The communist party, which called on the people to use the vote as a protest weapon, played a most important role in the campaign. It helped to provide conditions for the growth of a broad anti-fascist patriotic front that will isolate and defeat the military and police regime." (*IB*, no.

5.) Later in the year he stated that the PCB is being singled out for repression because "workers' strikes are increasing, the peasants are defending their land against capitalist penetration, and the dictatorship receives no support from intellectuals, employees or the church. The military has realized that in Brazil today the communist party is the only force directing and mobilizing these masses. The Justice Minister has said that the victory of the MDB is due to the communists. The PCB is the only party, existing as such, which has roots in the working class and the rural areas." (*L'Humanité*, Paris, 29 July.)

The deposition of Marco Antonio Coelho listed 23 MDB congressmen elected in 1974 as recipients of PCB support. Coelho said that the PCB platform was drafted at the meeting of the Central Committee in November 1973, and that, generally speaking, this platform was consistent with the pragmatic position adopted by the MDB in the elections. The PCB decided to reject the concept of blank and invalid ballots or abstention. In this situation they could only give their support to opposition candidates. According to Coelho, the PCB contributed to the holding of neighborhood and factory gate rallies, drafting and distributing propaganda, and fund raising campaigns for candidates. (*O Globo*, Rio de Janeiro, 26 April.)

An official communiqué of the Fifth Military Region states that the "basic program" of the PCB defends the following points: "Amnesty for political prisoners, direct elections at all levels, elimination of Institutional Act no. 5 and repeal of Decree Law 477 [which prohibits political activity in the universities], abolition of censorship, recognition of Habeas Corpus for crimes covered by the National Security Law, and convocation of a constituent assembly for the drafting of a new federal constitution" (*O Estado de São Paulo*, 8 October). The same issues form part of the MDB platform and are defended by all liberal sectors. Municipal elections are scheduled for November 1976, and direct elections for state governors and part of the national congress are slated to be held in 1978. Some observers feel that hard line opposition to President Ernesto Geisel's policies of relative liberalization may force the cancellation of these elections unless reforms which would assure a government victory are adopted.

In addition to the support which the PCB has given to opposition politicians, Coelho also revealed that the party maintained two business firms in São Paulo, received economic aid from Argentina, France, Italy, the U.S. and other countries, and organized a network to infiltrate union and political organizations. His testimony states that the state enterprises in which the PCB is most active are Petrobras, the Central Railroad of Brazil and the commercial aviation firms. (Serious accidents on the Central Railroad this year are attributed to communist sabotage.) Preventive prison was decreed for leaders of the transport, textile and metallurgical unions in São Paulo, and the coffee workers union in Paraná. Police reported the arrest of "agitators" in connection with a transport workers strike in Bahia in December, but did not give their affiliations.

No leftist organizations were mentioned in connection with a two-month walkout by students at the University of Bahia, but arrests indicate a high level of PCB activity in other universities, especially in Rio de Janeiro and São Paulo. The University of São Paulo went on strike for a week in October to protest the reported suicide in an army cell of journalist and USP professor Wladimir Herzog. Led by the journalists association, and joined by the church, the Order of Lawyers and numerous universities, the protest assumed national proportions. A major institutional crisis was narrowly averted by what seemed to be a last moment, undeclared truce. A seventh day ecumenical mass for Herzog was conducted in the metropolitan cathedral without demonstrations by students, and heavy security patrols were warned to offer no provocations. Investigation of Herzog's death is continuing. Repression of subversive activity by the II Army in São Paulo is generally conceded to be the most brutal in the country.

International Views and Positions. Luiz Carlos Prestes attended the Havana conference of Latin American and Caribbean communist parties which he termed an "historic event." "We composed a very good document ... which emphasizes the fact that capitalism has been affected by a structural crisis throughout Latin America. All parties have agreed that the solution to this crisis must take the form of anti-imperialistic struggle, and that imperialism is the main enemy. Therefore, we stressed the need to achieve agreements with all social forces willing to fight for Latin America's complete independence, it being understood that socialism is our final aim." (*L'Humanité*, 29 July.) In an earlier interview with the same paper, Prestes said that the Portuguese revolutionary process is a source of encouragement and has a positive influence in Brazil. The PCB leader was a guest of the PCF Central Committee, which promised to "intensify its already great and valuable solidarity with our party's and the Brazilian people's struggle." On several occasions during the year, the party echoed the appeal which appeared in the February *Voz Operária* for an international campaign to denounce the crimes of the Brazilian government (e.g., *IB*, No. 17).

Publications. Unable to seek new party members and inform the old in open meetings and publications, the PCB resorted to the clandestine publication of papers, magazines, and flyers. Though the government dismantled several printing operations early in the year, the party claims its publications still circulated thereafter often by the "pass it on" and "wind" methods. The official PCB organ is *Voz Operária*. The party reports that it publishes papers for a variety of interest groups: *Asa Vermelha* (Red Wing) circulated in the Air Force Academy, *Triangulo de Ferro* (Iron Triangle) for seamen, *Soldado Varmelho* (Red Soldier) for the army, *Rolo* (Roll) for textile workers, in addition to municipal papers *Trabalhador Ocupa Teo Posto!* in Pernambuco and *O Povo* in Rio Grande do Sul. (See *WMR*, November.)

*   *   *

The PCdoB. Organization and Leadership. The organizational structure of the PCdoB, which was founded by men who had long held leadership positions in the PCB, is believed to be patterned after that of the parent party. Little is known about the number or distribution of currently functioning units, but they are believed to exist in São Paulo, Rio de Janeiro, Espirito Santo, Bahia and the North East. Three founding members were killed in clashes with police in 1972. Locations of at least eight PCdoB members who have been arrested during 1975 have not been revealed. University students have traditionally played a major role in the activities and direction of the party.

Domestic Attitudes and Activities. Although the PCdoB Central Committee cheered the progress of guerrilla activity in the state of Pará in 1974, there was no information as to the degree of its participation in those struggles. Indeed, there is no indication of the party's involvement in any guerrilla fighting during the year. Simultaneously with that of the PCB, the government initiated an investigation of the PCdoB, but few results have been made available. In October, PCdoB members Urtiz Servulo da Silva and Arlindenor Pedro de Souza were charged with supporting MDB candidates in the 1974 elections, and publishing manifestos and propaganda in clandestine print shops. Other members arrested were simply noted as being accused of "crimes against national security." (*O Estado de São Paulo*, 10 and 14 October.) No terrorist activity has been mentioned in press reports of the trials.

International Views and Positions. The PCdoB was the first pro-Chinese communist party founded in Latin America and it has long joined the Chinese Communist Party in condemning "Soviet revisionism." Since the easing of Sino-U.S. relations, however, the PCdoB has been less outspoken in its praise of China and apparently has dropped Mao Tse-tung from its list of giants of international communism. For their part, the Chinese appear to have ceased giving publicity to the PCdoB.

Publications. The PCdoB publishes an irregular clandestine newspaper, *A Classe Operária*, and an occasional journal, *Resistencia Popular*. Its statements were until recently carried by Chinese and Albanian publications.   *   *   *

Castroite Organizations. Small subversive groups holding communist and left-nationalist views and advocating "armed struggle" tactics as the means to establish a socialist system proliferated in Brazil in the late 1960s. With the death of their outstanding leaders—Carlos Marighella, Joaquim Camara Ferreira and Carlos Lamarca—and under persistent persecution from security agencies, they have steadily declined in strength. The groups which have survived, at least in name, were in the news this year only as the result of the death, defection or final sentencing for old offenses of their members. Sergio Guarani Waldimirov Saulos, "O Grande," was killed by police in Rio. A former militant of the VPR, who was with Carlos Lamarca when the latter was killed in Bahia in 1971, Saulos had given up terrorism for the drug trade. Police claimed to have found a large arsenal of homemade bombs and machine guns in his home. (*O Estado de São Paulo*, 12 and 13 September.)

Father Gerson da Conceicao, arrested in 1972 in connection with subversive operations of the VAR-Palmares, was sentenced to one year by the Superior Military Court in September. The Superior Court also handed down decisions on appeals from members of the MR-8, the APM-L, and the ALN. Gilberto Marques, who is serving the last half of a five year term for his part in ALN terrorist activity, talked to the press in May to say he regretted his old connections. According to Marques, "terrorism has only been halted, not killed, and the ALN is one of the most active groups." (*Folha de São Paulo*, 17 May.) The ALN was the strongest of the terrorist groups. The ALN was founded by Carlos Marighella, a one-time PCB member of the Chamber of Deputies, who quit the party in 1967 and became the principal theoretician of urban guerrilla activity in Latin America.

Early this year, President Ernesto Geisel acknowledged the presence of guerrilla groups in Pará, Paraná and Goiás. Referring to them as "untiring termites," he said they must be controlled, but represent no threat to internal security. (*Latin American Report*, February 1975.) Strength and distribution of the guerrilla groups is not known, and their activity can easily be confused with legitimate self defense movements of squatters and "colons" in the pioneer territory opened up by the Trans-Amazon highway. Claims made by guerrilla leader João Lobo in Paris are considered inflated. Lobo said that the Guerrilla Forces of Araguaia (FGA) control 600,000 square kilometers in the state of Pará, in an area bounded by the Trans-Amazon highway and the Xingu and Araguaia Rivers. Directing peasant uprisings since 1972, the FGA has attracted recruits from neighboring states and young people from the cities. Its program calls for a general amnesty, elections, formation of a popular and democratic government, and implementation of a program of social justice. Operations consist of taking over towns to propagandize the masses, attacking police headquarters to seize arms and ammunition, and protecting peasants threatened with expulsion. No terrorism is employed. According to Lobo, 15,000 to 20,000 troops have participated in each of three unsuccessful military campaigns against the FGA. (AFP, Paris, 5 May.)

*   *   *

Trotskyist Groups. At least two Trotskyist groups exist in Brazil. One of these is the Partido Operário Revolucionário (Trotskista), affiliated with the International Secretariat of the Fourth International headed by J. Posadas. It occasionally issues an illegal periodical *Frente Operária*, largely filled with speeches by Posadas. The other is the Partido Operário Comunista, more or less aligned with the United Secretariat of the Fourth International. It has been officially committed to the strategy of guerrilla war although there is no evidence that it has undertaken any serious guerrilla activities. In an article in *Intercontinental Press* (21 July) it announced a program for mobilization of the working class which calls for a minimum monthly wage of $97.50, quarterly cost-of-living adjustments, free trade unions and reorganization of the CGT, and the reestablishment of democratic rights.

Latin American Report   Carole Merten

Canada

The Communist Party of Canada (CPC) was founded in 1921. It functions legally and has an estimated membership of 2,500. The population of Canada is 23,000,000 (estimated 1975).

There are several other communist parties or groups, of unascertainable membership, but all small. Among these, the following have some prominence. The Communist Party of Canada (Marxist-Leninist), or CPC(M-L), which is Maoist, is especially active in the province of Quebec and has its headquarters in Montreal. The League for Socialist Action/Ligue Socialist Ouvriere (LSA/LSO) is the most important Trotskyist organization in Canada. It has a youth wing, the Young Socialists. The Revolutionary Marxist Group (RMG) was founded in 1973 by LSA/LSO breakaways, the Red Circle group, composed of some left-wing members of the New Democratic Party, and the Old Mole, a student group at the University of Toronto. The Groupe Marxiste Revolutionnnaire (GMR) is the RMG's "sister organization in Quebec," its founders being French-Canadian Trotskyists who broke away from the LSA/LSO in the summer of 1972. The Workers League of Canada, which is the Canadian section of the International Committee of the Fourth International in Paris, confines its activities to Montreal. Its monthly, *Labor Press*, appears in English and French, and is printed in the United States. The Canadian Party of Labour (CPL) was founded by breakaways from the Progressive Workers Movement, the first pro-Maoist organization in Canada. Like the Progressive Labor Party in the United States, the CPL followed a pro-Maoist line until the improvement in Sino-U.S. relations. Its monthly, *Worker* (Toronto), publishes articles in English, French and Italian.

While most CPC are thought to be elderly, there has been active recruitment of younger members. In the provincial election in Ontario, 18 September 1975, there were 33 CPC candidates, more than half of whom were under 40 years old; none was elected, though altogether the candidates won 9,600 votes. The general membership continues to be composed of old-age pensioners, manual and white-collar workers, and a disproportionate number of persons of East European extraction. In the most recent federal election (8 July 1974), the CPC nominated 69 candidates of 264 constituencies, who won some 12,000 votes altogether, some 0.13 percent of the total cast. Thus the CPC has no representation in federal parliament in Ottawa nor in any of the ten provincial legislatures. There are some pro-communist members or sympathizers on municipal councils and local school boards.

The United Fishermen and the Allied Workers Union, on the West Coast, and the United Electrical, Radio, and Allied Workers Union are run by party members. Communists are influential on several district and town labor councils and in the British Columbia Federation of Labour. The CPC controls a half-dozen ethnic organizations of Canadians of East European origin.

CPC Leadership and Organization. William Kashtan continues as the CPC's national secretary. Alfred Dewhurst became editor of *Communist Viewpoint* in July 1975; he had been a member of the party's Central Executive Committee and director of its ideological work. Norman Freed, the former editor, undertook the assignment of writing a history of the CPC. Bruce Magnusson serves as labor secretary. William Stewart led the party in Ontario in the election campaign of September.

The Parti Communiste du Quebec (PCQ) continued to enjoy a certain autonomy within the CPC, and the Young Communist League (YCL) worked at increasing its membership.

Domestic Attitudes and Activities. In his main report to the CPC Central Committee in May, National Secretary Kashtan reviewed the "increasing difficulties" faced during the year by the Canadian economy and people, and charged that "state monopoly regulation of the economy, rather than bringing stability to capitalism, is deepening and sharpening all its contradictions." He concluded: "Indeed, what characterises the situation today, is the growing anti-monopoly and anti-imperialist sentiment which permeates ever wider sections of the Canadian population." (*IB*, No. 16.) The economic crisis gave the CPC numerous opportunities to be highly critical of the Canadian government's handling of inflation, unemployment, and strikes. In February the Central Executive Committee of the CPC issued a special attack on an agreement—known as the Syncrude Canada Ltd.—of the federal government and several provinces with various multi-national oil companies to develop the oil sands of Alberta. The CPC also attacked a government "green paper" on immigration policy as racist for its proposal to be more elective in accepting immigrants. Since 1975 was International Women's Year, special attention was given to the role of women in the labor movement, and much was made of the equality women have attained under Marxist-Leninist regimes.

In 1975, Progress Books published the official biography of Tim Buck, who headed the CPC for 32 years. The book, Oscar Ryan's *Tim Buck: A Conscience for Canada*, was praised by the CPC (*Communist Viewpoint*, May-June) with "the reader gets a true picture" and condemned by the LSA/LSO (*Labor Challenge*, 16 June) as "dishonest from beginning to end." Ivan Avakumovic's *The Communist Party in Canada*, published this year by McClelland and Stewart, Toronto, was regarded by the LSA/LSO as "written from a liberal academic point of view" incorporating a great deal of material drawn primarily from CP newspapers and magazines" (ibid.).

International Views and Policies. The CPC generally supports positions taken by the Communist Party of the Soviet Union (CPSU) on international issues. During 1975 it praised the efforts to continue détente and the signing of the Helsinki pact. It was critical of the junta in Chile and the Franco regime in Spain; it welcomed the withdrawal of the Portuguese from Angola, and supported the Communist leaders in the struggle in Portugal. It praised the measures taken by Indira Gandhi to suppress "the right" in India, and spoke well of the Palestine Liberation Organization in the Middle East, while condemning Israel. The space achievements of the USSR in the Soyuz flight were regarded as a great triumph; the fall of South Vietnam was a subject of special rejoicing. It continued to be especially critical of the United States and what it regarded as attempts to "Americanize" Canada. The CPC campaigned against Canada's participation in NATO and the renewal of the NORAD agreements with the United States for the defense of North America.

International Activities and Contacts. During 1975 members of the CPC Central Executive Committee made several trips to the East European communist countries. In February Samuel Walsh (Quebec) led a delegation of provincial secretaries to the USSR and Poland. In July, William Kashtan talked with party CP leaders in Poland and East Germany before going to Moscow to be received by B. N. Ponomarev, secretary of the CPSU Central Committee. The preparations for the 25th CPSU congress were discussed. In June, CPC representatives were observers at the conference of Latin American communist parties in Havana.

Publications. The CPC publishes a theoretical journal, *Communist Viewpoint*, six times per year, and two weeklies: *Canadian Tribune* (Toronto) and *Pacific Tribune* (Vancouver). The PCQ issues the fortnightly *Combat* (Montreal). The organ of the YCL, *Young Worker* (Toronto), appears irregularly and has a circulation of 5,000. Party members edit pro-communist weeklies in eight languages other than English and French.

The North American edition of the Prague-based *Problems of Peace and Socialism* is printed in

Toronto as the *World Marxist Review*. The fortnightly *Information Bulletin* is its companion publication.

The CPC(M-L) theoretical organ, *Mass Line*, continues to appear irregularly. The party's *People's Canada Daily News* (Toronto) appears regularly and republishes news items supplied by the New China News Agency, and covers the labor strife in Quebec quite closely.

The LSA/LSO publishes the fortnightly *Labor Challenge* (Toronto) and, in French, the monthly *Libération* (Montreal). It supported the New Democratic Party in the September election in Ontario. The *Young Socialist* (Toronto) is the organ of its youth wing, the Young Socialists.

University of San Francisco   Desmond J. FitzGerald

Chile

The Chilean Communist Party, which only a few years ago was the best organized and, for a time, the largest in the Western Hemisphere, has now practically ceased to function in Chile. Originally established as the Socialist Workers' Party by Luis Emilio Recabarrén in 1912, it adopted its name, Partido Comunista de Chile (PCCh), in 1922 after the leadership decided to join the Communist International in 1921. Its growth was slow but by 1938 it integrated the Popular Front which brought President Aguirre Cerda to power. In 1945, it was the second largest party in the Alianza Democrática which brought Gabriel Gonzales Videla to power. But in 1948 President Gonzales had the party declared illegal, and so it remained for a ten year period. The party did not lose its organizational cadres and it emerged in 1958 stronger than before. Between 1956 and 1969 the PCCh allied itself for electoral purposes with the Socialist Party of Chile (PSCh) in the Popular Action Front (Frente de Acción Popular; FRAP). These same parties with several smaller ones formed the Popular Unity (Unidad Popular; UP) in 1969 and their candidate, PSCh leader Salvador Allende, was elected president in 1970. The PCCh together with the PSCh dominated the executive branch of government in Chile until 11 September 1973 when the Chilean military ousted the UP in the midst of popular disillusionment after widespread national dislocations. Following the overthrow of Allende the PCCh, together with other parties in the UP, was declared illegal, many of its leaders imprisoned, its publications suspended, and its properties taken over by the State. The PCCh may still have 100,000 official members.

Other Marxist parties in Chile are the Movement of the Revolutionary Left (Movimiento de Izquierda Revolucionaria; MIR) and the Revolutionary Communist Party of Chile (Partido Comunista Revolucionario de Chile). The MIR was a party started by dissident students at the University of Concepción in 1965. It soon gathered other dissident groups which demanded a violent revolutionary alternative. The PCRCh was established in 1966 by Maoist dissidents who had been expelled from the PCCh in 1963. The PCRCh has practically ceased to exist. Its members have either joined the MIR, left the country or abandoned all political activity.

All three parties were illegal throughout 1975. The MIR was the only group engaging in revolutionary activities; it suffered severe losses and most of its leaders have been imprisoned, killed, or taken refuge abroad.

Unification Attempts. During 1975 several meetings were held among the leaders of the UP living in exile. An effort was made to unite all factions in an Anti-fascist Alliance which had been already loosely organized in 1974 (See *YICA, 1975*, pp. 477-79). No unity of command was achieved, however, and no agreements were made on concrete plans other than to publicly express their desire to see Chile free from the military junta.

In Chile itself, the MIR made a public declaration on 16 January in which it stated: "the lack of unity among the political leadership, the lack of a political front of resistance to the dictatorship, a front that should have been formed by the Communist Party, the Socialist Party, the MAPU-OC and the Christian Left, groups that represent the medium and small bourgeois and the anti-coup groups of the Christian Democrats and the MIR, has resulted in a grave cost to the Chilean people . . . We are calling upon all parties, at home and abroad, to leave aside their differences and join up against our principal enemy the gorilla dictatorship." (*El Mercurio*, Santiago, 16 January.)

The most important meeting of the UP forces took place in East Germany in July and resulted in the release of a long statement of problems to be overcome and objectives to be realized. The statement, dated 27 July, was signed by representatives of the Communist Party (Orlando Millas, Manuel Cantero, Julieta Campusano), the Christian Left, the MAPU, the MAPU Worker-Peasant Party, the Radical Party, and the Socialist Party (Carlos Altamirano, Adonis Sepulveda, Clodomiro Almeyda). The principal task of the day was "to put an end to the fascist junta," the military government the UP concluded was ever more isolated both from the Chilean people and from the international community. This would have to be done by the formation of a "popular-democratic alliance" which would be "politically, socially, and ideologically much broader than the Popular Unity," ranging from the MIR through the Christian Democrats and the members of the Christian church generally. (The UP recognized that it differed with the MIR on strategy and tactics and acknowledged that a common front with the Christian Democrats would only come from the cultivation of positive tendencies in the party.) It proposed a "real alternative" to the junta with the following program: (1) set into motion an "irrepressible mass movement" which would culminate in the overthrow of the junta; (2) establishment of a "popular, revolutionary, pluralist and democratic government with the aim of uprooting fascism"; (3) "implementation of economic measures to extricate the country from the bankruptcy and chaos into which fascism has plunged it and to ensure its planned development on the basis of state ownership and control over the basic wealth"; (4) an independent foreign policy; (5) the establishment of "new state institutions"; and (5) "undertaking to carry out profound changes in the armed forces and carabineros with a view to excluding for all time any possibility of their being used against a new government, converting them into an organisation serving the people." The UP urged the Chilean people and all representative organizations to develop specific platforms on the following three questions: (1) restoration of human rights and democratic freedoms; (2) concern for the people's living standard; and (3) defense of national sovereignty and the country's economy. Reliance always had to be on the masses and the struggle made it necessary to "establish close ties and coordination between the movement in the country and . . . the forces acting abroad." (*IB*, No. 16.)

On 1 November the Chilean government announced the seizure of documents alleging a Communist-Socialist plan from abroad to take over Chile. The existence of such a plan was denied by the PCCh (see *Daily World*, New York, 21 November).

The PCCh in Exile. Before the downfall of President Allende, the Communist Party's leadership was formed by a 75-member Central Committee, a 9-member Political Commission and a 7-member Secretariat. The Political Committee and the Central Committee have been broken up by deaths, exile and imprisonment, leaving only the Secretariat with some semblance of structure. Its Chairman, former senator Luis Corvalán, is being held prisoner in Chile. In 1975 the leading member of the PCCh, and most frequent spokesman for the party, was former senator Volodia Teitelboim. The release of political prisoners in Chile has not yet included any former PCCh leaders. Prominent Chilean Communists abroad are: Orlando Millas, Rodrigo Rojas, Luis Figueroa, Manuel Cantero, Gladys Marín, and Julieta Campusano.

The chief PCCh activity abroad during 1975 was involvement in a campaign of propaganda against the Chilean Junta which may even surpass in intensity a similar campaign launched by Marxists during the Spanish Civil War of 1936. Until it can return to Chile, the PCCh has taken to propaganda as its most effective weapon. A powerful voice in this campaign has been Moscow radio which broadcasts five daily programs in Spanish on several wave lengths. These programs are directed in part by the PCCh and frequently broadcast news from Chile not available through other sources. The former PCCh radio in Chile, Magallanes, has been resurrected in Moscow as a short wave station broadcasting to Chile. Several other communist countries broadcast programs aimed at Chile. The former president of the Single Center of Chilean Workers (CUTCh, or CUT), conducted an extensive propaganda campaign through communist dominated labor unions and front organizations around the world.

Although the PCCh has taken no credit for them, twenty-seven documented terrorist acts have been committed on Chilean embassies and legations abroad, all of which seemed to be aimed at propaganda rather than intimidation.

It is not known to what extent the PCCh has been involved in plans to support guerrilla activities in Chile, despite its public statements rejecting the tactic at the present time. A government communiqué issued on 11 November, for example, claimed that 1200 guerrillas trained in Cuba and elsewhere were ready to enter Chile from Argentina, but no mention was made of their possible party affiliations (*El Mercurio*, 11 November).

So far as is known, the PCCh has not established a headquarters anywhere outside of Chile. It has not organized a governing body in exile and continues to make reference to Luis Corvalán as the leader of the party in spite of his being detained in a Chilean jail.

Domestic Attitudes and Activities. During 1975 the PCCh called for the formation of an "anti-fascist" front, a task the party's clandestine organ described as "difficult but not impossible" (editorial from *Unidad antifascista*, June, quoted in *Nuestra Palabra*, Buenos Aires, 2 July). The objectives of the anti-fascist front, according to a party statement of December 1974, are the defeat of the dictatorship, the destruction of the totalitarian state it set up, and the construction of a new legal, democratic, anti-fascist, national, popular, pluralist state which would guarantee the rebirth of democracy and the total elimination of fascism, pushed forward by revolutionary change and national independence. The Front would take into consideration all involved sectors, not only the political, including the church. It rejects terrorism and insists on the need for mass action, legal and illegal. (Declaration excerpted in *Nuestra Palabra*, 22 January, and complete in *Boletín de Información*, Prague, supplement to No. 2, 1975.) A party statement in August attacked the military government and praised what it considered signs of increasing popular opposition, concluding that after the junta's fall a "new democracy" would be established with the following three "fundamental components": (1) "the building of a new, fully democratic state"; (2) "a minimum economic programme ensuring the country's independence"; and (3) an independent foreign policy. (*IB*, No. 17.)

Early in the year, a proclamation of the Chilean Communist Youth, supposedly issued in Chile, declared: "Chilean youth are aware of their responsibility. They will perform their tasks. Amidst crime, terror and repression, the organization and struggle of youth are growing. There are thousands who take part in the struggle all over the country: the youth organizations emerge in every community, trade unions, villages and schools working for the concrete interests of the youth and for their rights despite the terror unleashed by the regime. Illegal political organization has recovered its forces and directs the struggle. Every day anonymous young heroes write slogans on the walls, distribute leaflets and clandestine papers calling for struggle. They organize and step up the struggle for resistance of youth." (*WFDY*, February 1975.) Similarly, Teitelboim is reported as saying: "The PCCh and the UP work indefatigably: they are conducting a tireless struggle underground and they are ever expanding their ties with the masses. In this battle the ideological struggle is acquiring ever greater significance on all fronts. Our duty is to intensify it." (*Latiskaya America*, Moscow, Mar-Apr 1975.)

These two rather optimistic reports are not clearly corroborated by the facts in Chile. Hardly any PCCh activity has been noted. The very few leaflets and clandestine newspapers circulating are products of the MIR. Furthermore, the few communists captured by the military have been turned over by neighbors or suspicious citizens.

There seems to be a good network of PCCh communications across the country, however. News items sometimes reach Moscow radio faster than western wire services. This was in part explained on 22 June when a powerful radio was discovered in Copiapó. The station was used to relay information to other Latin American countries from which it was passed on to Moscow. The PCCh has also been able to coordinate some activities which reveal that some limited but highly effective organization is going on. For example, on the eve of the date set for the Human Rights Commission to visit Chile, a group of 22 persons, mostly former PCCh members, sought asylum in the Honduras Embassy in Santiago. The group changed its mind when it learned that the visit had been cancelled. It is suspected that similar groups were to ask for asylum in other embassies but only this group failed to get word of the cancellation on time.

Most of the properties of the PCCh have been taken over by the government. One notable exception is the house of the late poet and PCCh Central Committee member Pablo Neruda, which was registered as property of the PCCh though the government is negotiating with Neruda's widow to acquire it.

Numerous arms caches were discovered in Chile during 1975 and in the majority of cases it was charged they were "Communist Arsenals." At least seven of these discoveries resulted in the arrest of former PCCh party members. The weapons may have been left over from UP days but there is evidence that similar weapons, such as AKA automatic rifles, have been supplied to the MIR. General Gustavo Leigh, member of the ruling Junta, claims that "the Chilean Communists are hiding more than 10,000 rifles." He adds that the Chilean Armed Forces have seized 20 percent of the arms held by the Marxists, and that new weapons, manufactured in North Korea and the Soviet Union, are being introduced to Chile. (*FBIS*, Latin America, 5 November.)

A further erosion of PCCh influence in Chile took place in the labor unions. The CUT has been totally eliminated, leaving each union independent. No elections have been held and in the pro-UP unions the old leaders have been replaced with government appointees. According to a publication of the World Federation of Trade Unions (WFTU), "a very substantial number of Chilean trade-union leaders, almost 50 percent, have disappeared from their posts. These leaders have either been killed, executed, imprisoned, dismissed or forced to resign, or they have fled or simply disappeared." (*Flashes*, 18 June.) Furthermore, the military government has officially recognized 441 small trade-unions while 252 more are being considered for approval. The tendency is to create small unions in which all members know each other.

Volodia Teitelboim may be overly optimistic when he says: "Thousands of Communist Party primary organizations are now operating among the masses, waging struggle for the release of political prisoners, for human rights and for an end to the tortures. The Communist numbers are increasing. The Anti-fascist Unity Front is being forged and is embracing an increasingly broad strata of the people." But there is no doubt that his final remarks are true: " [The party] is alive, it is operating, it is leading." (*FBIS*, Latin America, 23 January.)

Publications. According to Mexican sources, Chilean resistance has a net of clandestine presses, of makeshift mimeos and ditto machines, and even homemade rubber stamps. Still, the official PCCh publication *Unidad Anti-Facista* has very limited clandestine circulation in Chile. It is impossible to verify the origin of certain documents and publications which the Communist world press claims originated in Chile.

*   *   *

The MIR. The Movement of the Revolutionary Left, founded in 1965, became an avowedly Castroite organization advocating the armed road to power enunciated at the Latin American Solidarity Organization (OLAS) conference held in Havana in 1967. The violent behavior of the MIR forced the government of President Eduardo Frei to declare it illegal in 1969. The Party went underground and did not reappear until after the election of Salvador Allende. Although the MIR never joined the UP, Allended pardoned all imprisoned "miristas" and the party responded by supporting him and even providing men for his own body guard. During the UP the MIR suffered the accidental loss of some of its leaders and was involved in many violent incidents against the police and opposition politicians. Heavy losses were reported by the MIR during the 11 September coup that deposed Allende in 1973 and the MIR was forced to go underground once more.

The secretary general of the MIR at the time of the coup was Miguel Enríquez, an original leader who held his position until his death in October 1974 during a shootout with the police. Most of the leaders in line to succeed him were in jail, so in December 1974 the leadership was officially assumed by Andrés Pascal Allende, nephew of the late president. Pascal has recently sought asylum in the Costa Rican Embassy where he remains.

Domestic Attitudes and Activities. At the end of 1974 the MIR seemed to be in serious disarray. However, it started the year with a new outlook and an increase in activity. The very first week of January it circulated a document through the mails and eventually released it to the press. In it, the MIR leaders claimed that since all efforts to unite the former parties of the UP had failed, they must fight on their own.

A month later, four imprisoned leaders of the MIR made an unusual appearance on Chile's National television network. They proceeded to declare that "the defeat of the MIR is political and military" and went on to say that there was no use in opposing "national reality." Besides reading a list of their dead and imprisoned comrades, they made a plea to end the fighting: "We don't want any more dead and no more arrests." (*El Mercurio*, 20 February.) The four claimed to speak for at least thirty other miristas who were in jail with them.

At that time the committees of the MIR had been decimated if not disappeared. The Political Committee was reduced to two members: Andrés Pascal and Nelsón Gutiérrez. These two and three newly appointed members used the mails to report that a trial had been held and their four former comrades had been condemned to death for their plea to stop the fighting. (*El Mercurio*, March 2, 1975.)

In spite of their heavy losses, which according to the magazine *Presencia* in La Paz amounted to 400 dead and 2,000 prisoners, the MIR went into a flurry of activity. (*Presencia* 18 August 1975.) Little was said in the Chilean press and the MIR itself reported only a state of continuous resistance in Chile. The discovery and closing of underground presses in Santiago in February and others in

Valparaíso in April, provided the government with numerous captured documents from which it was learned that the MIR was getting planning and support from the Argentinian ERP.

Prior to June there were few announcements of shootouts between the MIR and the armed forces, but in that month the MIR suffered serious setbacks. It was also learned that some miristas were fighting in Argentina with the ERP, though the publication in Argentina of a list of 60 dead miristas was not confirmed with proper identification of the dead. Prisoners in one Chilean camp went on a hunger strike, but no public demonstrations were observed. Further shootouts with the police brought about the death of Dagoberto Pérez, the number two man in the MIR, who had been earlier reported as fighting in Argentina. These confrontations were followed by a massive search that resulted in the seizure of arms deposits, explosives, and even a well equipped hospital. Documents captured by the government indicated that there were plans for a large scale uprising against the Junta with simultaneous action in nine Chilean cities. The MIR and all other Marxist parties were to form a Patriotic Front of National Liberation, (Frente Patriótico de Liberación Nacional; FPLN). The plan had three objectives: the killing of members of the Junta, primarily General Pinochet; armed actions against the armed forces; and the organization of a Marxist-Leninist government. The military government announced the arrest of several former members of the PCCH, PSCh and MIR. Although the authenticity of the plan was immediately questioned outside Chile, the government followed up on the information obtained. A house near Malloco in Santiago province was surrounded and a few miristas who managed to escape sought refuge in sympathetic Chilean and American religious communities. But the investigation continued and eventually resulted in the arrest of Humberto Hernández, the number three man in the MIR chain of command, found hiding in the house of a priest. Nelsón Gutiérrez and Andrés Pascal Allende managed to elude the search and eventually sought refuge in foreign embassies, where they remain at this writing.

In spite of these serious setbacks, the MIR gave no signs of being defeated. New confrontations occurred in November; at least five more miristas were killed and an undetermined number taken prisoner. The police also announced the capture of the top mirista in Copiapó, Héctor Echague. The government announced the discovery of two subversive plans: Boomerang I and Boomerang II. Aided by Argentinian security forces, the Chilean Army was able to prevent the entrance into Chile of 1,200 terrorists trained abroad to create chaos in the country. Among the documents found was a letter stating that the only way to revive the MIR was to bring Edgardo Enríquez back to Chile.

The MIR ended the year in a condition very similar to that of December 1974 with the known organization badly decimated. Only two members of the committees were still at large: Hernán Aguiló and Lautaro Videla. All secretaries of the nine Chilean regions and even their alternatives are either dead, in exile, or under arrest. As early as July 1975, Inter Press reported: "The loss of the militants and the political cadres, including some of the best, has been considerable. To a large extent the organization is mobilized to preserve its own continued existence, its own survival, which reduces its capacity to intervention accordingly. All these factors have created a situation that makes it particularly difficult to work out precise orientations, which is a necessary condition for an effective political intervention to reorganize the workers movement." (*Inter Press*, 28 July.)

In spite of its apparent defeat, the MIR caused serious problems for the Junta. The arrest and expulsion of foreign priests and nuns who protected the miristas adversely affected public opinion abroad, especially in the United States, and the arrest of Chilean priests created a conflict with the Cardinal.

Publications. Captured documents indicate that the MIR's most important goal during 1975 was the creation of a proper atmosphere in which future actions could take place. Instructions were given on how to build mimeographs. In Mexico, a MIR spokesman claimed to have printed 40,000 leaflets in Santiago and 15,000 in the provinces. The official publication *El Rebelde*, scheduled to appear once a week, was not available in Santiago. The only known issue was mailed out of Chile in January, a carefully prepared but badly printed 48-page pocket size edition with pictures of dead mirista leaders. In an article analyzing the situation of the MIR the author, an unknown mirista, lamented the disappearance of the leadership and adds, "the inevitable desertions which each blow brings with it have weakened the forces of the MIR."

Menlo College   Carlos López U.

Colombia

The communist movement in Colombia began within the ranks of the Socialist Revolutionary Party (Partido Socialista Revolucionario; PSR) shortly after the party's formation in December 1926. Contacts between the PSR and the Communist International during 1929 and 1930 inspired a group of PSR members to proclaim publicly the creation of the Communist Party of Colombia (Partido Comunista de Colombia; PCC) on 17 July 1930. The party has retained this designation ever since except for a short period (1944-47) during which it was called the Social Democratic Party (Partido Social Democrático). In July 1965 a schism within the PCC between pro-Soviet and pro-Chinese factions resulted in the latter's becoming the Communist Party of Colombia, Marxist-Leninist (Partido Comunista de Colombia, Marxista-Leninista; PCC-ML). Only the PCC has legal status. It has been allowed to participate in elections under its own banners since 1972. The PCC participated in the 1974 general elections as a member of the leftist coalition National Opposition Union (Unión de Oposición Nacional; UNO), founded in September 1972. The other parties comprising UNO are the pro-Chinese Independent Revolutionary Workers Movement (MOIR), and the Broad Colombian Movement (MAC). The coalition won two seats in the 112-member Senate (Antioquia, Cundinamarca), and 5 seats in the 199-member Lower Chamber (Antioquia, Cauca, Cundinamarca 2, and Santander). Of these, PCC members occupy one of the Lower Chamber seats from Cundinamarca and the seat from Cauca.

The PCC is estimated to have 10,000-12,000 members and exercises only marginal influence in national affairs. The population of Colombia is 24,000,000 (estimated 1975).

Guerrilla warfare, although not a serious threat to the government, has been a feature of Colombian life since the late 1940's, the current wave beginning in 1964. The three main guerrilla organizations are the Revolutionary Armed Forces of Colombia (FARC), long controlled by the PCC, the pro-Chinese People's Liberation Army (EPL), and the Castroite National Liberation Army (ELN). Estimates of membership rank the ELN first with 250-300 men, followed by the FARC and the EPL with fewer than 250 and 100 members respectively.

Speculation existed in April that the top leadership of the three guerrilla movements had met for the purpose of discussing a possible merger (*El Tiempo*, 2 April). Although ideological differences and leadership rivalries have militated against attempts at coordination in the past, a renewal of guerrilla activities showed signs of cooperation. The Ministry of National Defense reported on 5 April that a small town in Santander was attacked by guerrillas belonging to combined units of the FARC and the ELN (*El Siglo*, 6 April). Shortly thereafter, military intelligence sources announced the discovery of a "national guerrilla plan" which called for coordinated guerrilla attacks in several regions of the country, but without involving a formal alliance among the three groups. According to the report, predetermined regions for attacks carried out in Antioquia, Santander, Tolima, Boyacá, Cundinamarca, and Caquetá Intendancy were apparently agreed upon at the aforementioned meeting of guerrilla leaders (*El Tiempo*, 12 April). An FARC document released on 3 December reportedly indicates that this guerrilla organization is now at odds with its erstwhile patron, the PCC, and claims that the FARC is being "persecuted" by the EPL (EFE, Madrid, 3 December). Whether or not this "document" is authentic, the ideological commitments and rivalries of the various guerrilla organizations in recent years suggest that reports of unity should be regarded with caution. In any event, the resurgence of guerrilla activity during the year clearly belied military reports in late 1974 that the guerrilla threat had been virtually eliminated.

The reappearance of guerrilla activity in northern Colombia was specifically mentioned by President Alfonso López Michelsen in announcing the imposition of a general state of siege on 26 June (ibid., 27 June). However, most observers agreed that the declaration was made necessary in order to control more effectively a series of civil and political disturbances involving peasant movements, trade unions, student organizations, and the leftist press (*New York Times*, 28 June). The assassination of General José Rincón Quiñones in Bogotá on 8 September interrupted several months of relative calm in which guerrilla activities were limited primarily to ransom kidnapings of businessmen and landowners. Rincón had long been on the ELN's wanted list for his command of the successful operations carried out in 1974 against guerrillas operating in the Santander region. Military sources suggested that the guerrillas might well be using the state of siege for regrouping and were merely awaiting an auspicious time to renew their violence (*Christian Science Monitor*, 10 September). At a meeting of army commanders of the continent in November, General Luis Camacho Leyva asserted that "in Colombia guerrillas have been rendered powerless." He gave assurances that "at the present time subversive groups are no problem for the government," although he admitted that guerrillas were still operating in Antioquia, Magdalena, El César, Huila, and Santander Departments, supported by urban commandos in various cities (*El Tiempo*, 7 November). In view of the military's past optimism and the guerrillas' proven ability to survive, it would be prudent to conclude that in spite of extensive counterinsurgency operations, the government is not likely to eliminate completely the various revolutionary guerrilla groups in the near future.

The PCC. Leadership and Organization. The PCC is headed by its 12-member Executive Committee and 54-member Central Committee. The highest party authority is the Congress, convened by the Central Committee at four-year intervals. Gilberto Vieira is general secretary of the party. Members of the Executive Committee include, besides Vieira; Alvaro Vásquez, Joaquín Moreno, Jesús Villegas, Roso Osorio, Hernando Hurtado, Julio Posada, Gustavo Castro, Gustavo Osorio, Juan Viana, Manlio Lafont, and Manuel Cepeda Vargas.

The PCC held its 12th Congress from 5 to 9 December in Bogotá. The meeting, presided over by Vieira and the members of the National Executive Secretariat (Vásquez, Villegas, Moreno, and Osorio), was attended by more than 250 delegates and representatives of 19 communist parties, mainly from the socialist countries and Latin America (including Guyana, Costa Rica, Venezuela, Peru, Uruguay, and Ecuador). The political thesis, which served as the basis of discussions at the Congress, had reportedly been discussed and developed by party militants in more than 10,000 meetings throughout the country over the preceding four months. The delegates elected new party officials and discussed the development of mass struggles under present conditions in Colombia, organization of the labor and democratic movement, unity of leftist forces, and alliances between these and other democratic sectors. (See *Granma*, Havana, 3, 5, 6, and 9 December; the Congress will be covered in greater detail in the next edition of the *YICA*.)

A major source of the PCC's influence lies in its control over the Trade Union Confederation of Workers of Colombia (Confederación Sindical de Trabajadores de Colombia; CSTC), which claims a membership of over 200,000. The CSTC was granted legal status by the Colombian government in August 1974. At the time, CSTC president Pástor Pérez declared that "legal recognition would contribute significantly toward efforts to unite the Colombian working class" (WFTU, *Flashes*, 30 August 1974). However, at the 2nd Congress of the CSTC held in March 1975, reports indicated the existence of a serious split within the communist labor movement between the Moscow line represented by the CSTC and the Chinese-oriented MOIR. On 7 March the MOIR ordered the disaffiliation of more than 50 unions from the CSTC, including the National Union of Workers of the National Telecommunications Enterprise (SITTELECOM), the Colombian Association of Bank Employees (ACEB), the Colombian Teachers' Federation (FECODE), and employees of the Colombian Agrarian Reform Institute (INCORA) (*El Tiempo*, 8 March). CSTC delegates accused the MOIR leadership of "playing division and anarchy." The Congress' final document issued a call to all Colombian workers to create a single labor federation "as the only way to stand up to the pretensions of the bosses and the Colombian oligarchy." The declaration contained a strong proposal to work for "an integral agrarian reform" and reiterated CSTC demands for a 50 percent pay increase. The delegates who supported the CSTC's pleas for labor unity approved a declaration by the Executive Board in which they criticized the social-labor policy of the López government and the "giveaway" position of the major labor federations, namely the Union of Workers of Colombia (UTC) and the Confederation of Workers of Colombia (CTC). Pástor Pérez was reelected president of the CSTC at the final session, with Gustavo Osorio reelected as general secretary (ibid.). Other prominent leaders in the CSTC are Hernán Sabogal, Luis Carlos Pérez, Julio Poveda, and Alcibiades Aguirre. A strike against cement companies on the part of labor unions affiliated with the CSTC affected the construction industry throughout the country and contributed to the civil disturbances preceding the state of siege in late June. In August, *El Tiempo* reported that various labor leaders remained "discontented" with the CSTC's direction at the national and department levels. The possible separation of additional labor unions has presented the PCC with an organizational crisis in the labor sector that may "seriously and permanently" affect the CSTC (ibid., 22 August). The CSTC was represented at the 26th meeting of the General Council of the World Federation of Trade Unions (WFTU) held in Havana in October.

PCC efforts to expand its influence within the one-million member National Peasant Association of Land Users (Asociación Nacional de Usuarios Campesinos; ANUC) achieved no visible success in 1975. Although founded by the government in 1968 to encourage peasant participation in the development and implementation of agrarian reform, the ANUC soon established a militantly independent policy. It has retained its autonomous position under the presidency of Jesús Pérez, elected at ANUC's Third Congress held in September 1974. Under ANUC's leadership, the peasantry has become one of the most combative sectors of the Colombian population. PCC initiatives to capitalize on this fact have been hampered by ideological, sectarian, and personalist differences within the peasant leadership. The PCC's principal agrarian leaders affiliated with ANUC are Víctor Merchán and Gerardo González.

The PCC's youth organization, the Communist Youth of Colombia (Juventud Comunista de Colombia; JUCO) has an estimated membership of 2,000. JUCO has its own National Directorate, Executive Committee, and Central Committee. The general secretary is Carlos Romero, a member of the PCC's Central Committee. Other important JUCO leaders in recent years have been Jaime Caicedo, Leonardo Posada, Jaime Miller Chacón, Eduardo Martínez, Enrique Sierra, Lucio Lara, and Alvaro Oviedo. During the year, JUCO leadership issued repeated denials of the organization's involvement in the face of government accusations of "subversive disorders" in Colombia. A JUCO communiqué issued on 5 April accused the extreme right and the CIA of disrupting law and order and called upon all Colombians, especially students, to reject "anarchist provocations" (EFE, Madrid, 6 April). A similar denial took place in the wake of violent student disorders in Bogotá which included the burning of eight cars and an attack on the papal nuncio (*El Tiempo*, 19 April). Following the assassination of General Rincón, the JUCO published a declaration indicating its "emphatic rejection" of the Tupamaro tactics of urban guerrilla terrorism because "they run contrary to the recommended path for achieving revolutionary goals." The JUCO urged a "united front" against the ELN and called for support of the FARC (*Voz Proletaria*, 14-20 September). On 28 October JUCO reported the alleged murder of four peasant leaders belonging to its organization. In a message to President López, JUCO charged that military and civilian defense forces were responsible for the murders. Romero demanded a thorough investigation and called for guarantees for the activities of Communist youth and opposition parties in general (AFP, Paris, 28 October).

The PCC has controlled a peasant guerrilla group since 1966, the Revolutionary Armed Forces of Colombia (FARC), led by Manuel Marulanda Vélez. Although party spokesmen continue to hold that "armed revolutionary struggle is a necessary factor of the revolution in Colombia," the FARC has received only nominal support in recent years, especially before elections. This may account in party for the FARC's relative inactivity in 1974. Writing on the various forms of struggle of the Colombian Communists, Alvaro Mosquera acknowledged as a member of the Central Committee that "armed struggle cannot yet be the chief means of resistance. . . . The PCC is aware of this and does not make an absolute of the guerrilla form of the class struggle" (*WMR*, October). Nevertheless, FARC guerrilla units were unquestionably the most active of any guerrilla organization during the first half of 1975. On 10 April a FARC guerrilla force estimated at 200 temporarily occupied the town of Puerto Rico in Caquetá Intendancy, some 600 miles south of Bogotá. Food, drugs, and clothing were stolen, and prisoners released (*El Espectador*, 11 April). The guerrillas withdrew before army helicopters could arrive, although several were killed or captured in subsequent military operations. The assault was reportedly the fifth carried out by guerrillas since the first of the year, although not all were attributed to the FARC. On 2 June official sources reported that a group of about 50 FARC guerrillas occupied the town of San Vicente where they looted stores for supplies and distributed communist propaganda (*El Tiempo*, 3 June). In July the National Defense Ministry confirmed that FARC units had carried out similar attacks on small towns in Boyacá and Valle del Cauca (Radio Cadena Nacional, 28 July). Army patrols reported only moderate success in their pursuit of FARC units. The FARC appears to have expanded the traditional areas of its activities in the southern departments of Tolima, Huila, and Cauca to include operations in the northern departments of Antioquia, Boyacá, and Santander, nearer ELN territory. Whether or not the resurgence of FARC activities in 1975 will ultimately lead to a break with the PCC—and the alleged FARC statement of 3 December (see above) suggests that it may—is a matter of conjecture.

Domestic Attitudes and Activities. The PCC's domestic policy in 1975 was guided by its continued desire to strengthen and dominate coalition activity with other leftist parties through the National Opposition Union (UNO). However, Gilberto Vieira, writing about the political panorama of Colombia at mid-year, acknowledged that UNO's development since the 1974 elections has been "temporarily paralyzed by right-wing and ultra-leftist tendencies." A liberal faction emerged which advocated reconciliation with the administration of President López. Simultaneously, the MOIR shifted to a more sectarian position, prompting Vieira to criticize its supporters for "holding up and restricting the unity process" (*WMR*, July). Three Broad Colombian Movement deputies elected under UNO's banner in 1974 announced their intention to set up a socialist party "without foreign tutelage," an obvious objection to the PCC's efforts to dominate the coalition. Vieira expressed confidence that the crisis within UNO could be overcome by a "consistent policy of unity, expansion of membership, and defense and propaganda of its program," as outlined in June 1974 (see *Voz Proletaria*, 6-12 June 1974; also *YICA 1975*, pp. 490-91). With respect to the National Popular Alliance (Alianza Nacional Popular; ANAPO), Vieira stated that since the death of Rojas Pinilla in January, the PCC has been seeking joint action with left-wing ANAPO forces and is working in that party's mass local organizations. In addition to criticizing ANAPO's right-wing for pursuing "Peronism Colombian style," he attacked the Maoist and neo-Trotskyite groups for their "out-and-out anti-communism and rabid anti-Sovietism" (*WMR*, July).

According to Vieira, the two-party monopoly of Colombia's traditional Liberal and Conservative parties remains "a major obstacle to overcoming the structural crisis and expanding the popular struggle." In summarizing the PCC's views on domestic issues, he stressed the need (1) "to expand the struggle for genuine freedoms for the people, against the threats of declaring a state of emergency used by the authorities to blackmail the labor and popular movement; (2) for the rights of workers and their trade unions, against police surveillance of trade unions and the arbitration courts that function during strikes; (3) for the rights and freedoms of rural workers whose organizations are persecuted by the latifundists and the bureaucrats serving them and those lands have been occupied by army units under the pretext of fighting guerrillas; (4) for the repeal of all reactionary laws violating public freedoms, and against the reactionary military patronized by U.S. military missions, whose privileges are detrimental to national sovereignty and economic interests" (ibid.).

In late June the PCC's Executive Committee issued a communiqué condemning the state of siege and calling on all popular forces in the country to struggle against the decree. The communiqué attributed Colombia's difficult situation to "the high cost of living, unemployment, housing shortages, low salaries, a lack of land for peasants, and a decreased educational budget" (*Voz Proletaria*, 30 June-6 July). Alvaro Mosquera, in comments delivered at an international symposium in Prague on the topic of "Communists in the Struggle for the Unity of Democratic and Anti-Imperialist Forces," declared that the working class is the decisive political and economic factor in Colombia. However, he added that "it will be unable fully to lead a united front until it unites organizationally and politically in spite of the plots of pro-imperialist governments, reactionary dictatorships, the U.S. Embassy, and their abettors in the working-class movement" (*WMR*, August).

In September, the PCC condemned the acts of violence and disorder that were committed by students who claimed affiliation with the "extreme left." Editorial comment in the party organ stated that "the revolutionary process is not a friend of violence . . . and the battle must be waged with ideas" (*Voz Proletaria*, 17-24 September).

International Views and Positions. The PCC closely follows the Soviet Union in its international views. Vieira's summation of the 9-13 June Havana Conference of Latin American Communist parties praised "the Leninist policy of peaceful coexistence which is being resolutely pursued by the CPSU Central Committee." As a signatory to the conference's final declaration, the PCC reaffirmed its "resolute rejection of the slanderous fabrications against the CPSU and the Soviet Union resorted to by the imperialists, Maoists, and other revisionists united in a new 'holy alliance.'" (*Pravda*, July 19). In general, the PCC contends that recent events all over the world have made a positive impact on the situation in Colombia. Writing in the *World Marxist Review*, Vieira characterized the international situation by citing "favorable advances of the forces of peace, progress and socialism . . . highlighted by the policy of international detente and the struggle against imperialism" (*WMR*, July).

Hemispherically, the PCC expressed its approval of the reestablishment of diplomatic and commercial relations between Colombia and Cuba, an action to which it had long given verbal support (*Voz Proletaria*, 8-15 March). The PCC and the Venezuelan Communist Party signed a joint declaration in April blaming the CIA and the Pentagon for "encouraging the chauvinist manifestations that are taking place in both countries with the aim of creating a climate of tension, starting a new arms race, and sabotaging the Andean Pact." Both parties reaffirmed the validity of their 1970 declaration which pledged "resolute opposition to all those who try to bring about discord between Venezuelans and Colombians" (*Granma*, English edition, 11 May). At the Havana Conference, the PCC joined other Latin American Communist parties in condemning "the growing dependence on imperialist monopolies, particularly American ones, and the landowning system, as a result of which, with a rare exception [Cuba], the scandalous inequality which has existed for a century and a half is preserved." The PCC identifies itself with "the Latin American peoples' struggle against imperialist expropriation of their natural resources and against merciless capitalist exploitation of the working people." After denouncing "the bloody fascist coup in Chile," the document cites the anti-imperialist struggle of the armed forces of Peru and Panama and concludes that "wider opportunities have opened up for creating democratic governments which are ready to fight imperialism and pursue a progressive policy in the social sphere" (*Pravda*, 19 July; see Cuba, Appendix.)

Party Contacts. A study delegation of the PCC headed by Hernando Ortega visited Berlin in June to acquaint itself with the SED's agitation and propaganda work (GDR Domestic Service, 9 June). Also in June, a CPSU delegation headed by M. T. Iovchuck, rector of the CPSU Academy of Social Sciences, visited Colombia at the Invitation of the PCC (*Pravda*, 20 July). In September, Roso Osorio headed a delegaton of the PCC that met with members of the Romanian Communist Party in Bucharest. Members of a Czechoslovak parliamentary delegation visited Colombia in September. During their stay they met with Vieira and other members of the PCC's Executive Committee to discuss the development of relations between the two countries. The PCC sent a congratulatory message to the Central Committee of the CPSU on the occasion of the 58th anniversary of the October Revolution (*Pravda*, 11 November).

Publications. The PCC publishes a weekly newspaper, *Voz Proletaria*, founded in 1957, with a circulation of 25,000; a theoretical journal, *Documentos Politicos*, with a circulation of 5,000; and a Colombian edition of the *World Marxist Review*, with a circulation of 7,500. The FARC publishes a clandestine bulletin, *Resistencia*.

*   *   *

The PCC-ML. The Communist Party of Colombia Marxist-Leninist is firmly pro-Chinese. Although its leadership hierarchy is not clearly known, important positions have been held in recent years by first secretary Pedro León Arboleda, Francisco Garnica, and Pedro Vásquez. The party has an estimated membership of 1,000. In terms of national political life, the party's impact is insignificant.

Unlike the PCC, the PCC-ML has not attempted to obtain legal status. The party suffered a serious setback in July when military intelligence sources confirmed that León Arboleda had been killed by police while on a party assignment in Cali (*El Tiempo*, 29 July).

Within the labor movement, the PCC-ML has exercised some influence in the past over the Bloque Independiente, a small trade union organization with an estimated membership of 20,000. The Independent Revolutionary Worker's Movement (MOIR), established in 1971, also follows a pro-Chinese orientation. The MOIR's leadership was badly split by internal dissension arising over the policy to be followed at the CSTC's 2nd Congress in March. One faction, headed by José Antolínez, disagreed with the general approved list of conclusions, while a second group, led by Miguel Antonio Caro, rejected Antolínez's objectives and approved the Congress' final manifesto (*El Tiempo*, 8 March).

Among student activities, on 30 September pro-Peking students at the University of Antioquia approved a resolution backing General Rincón's killing and denouncng the "revisionist Communist

Party for siding with the imperialists and their lackeys" by rejecting Rincón's murder (*El Espectador*, 23 October).

The EPL guerrillas were reportedly led by Francisco Caraballo.

Publications. The organ of the PCC-ML is *Revolución*. PCC-ML statements are sometimes found in Chinese Communist publications and those of pro-Chinese parties in Europe and Latin America.

*   *   *

The ELN. The National Liberation Army was formed in Santander in 1964 under the inspiration of the Cuban Revolution. It undertook its first military action in January 1965.

Although much of the ELN's top leadership and its urban network have been eliminated since 1973, the movement still remains the largest and most active group in Colombia. It operates mainly in Antioquia, Santander, and Bolívar Departments. Despite heavy losses suffered in late 1974, the ELN regrouped under its principal founder and leader, Fabio Vásquez Castaño, and resumed its activities in February by ambushing an army patrol in southern Bolívar. Further operations were carried out on a small scale in April and May, including the continued purge of dissidents and suspected informers. In May, the ELN's clandestine publication, *Insurrección*, reported that one of its members had been executed in Antioquia for giving information to the military (Circuito Todelar, 3 May). On 8 June ELN units launched simultaneous attacks on three villages in Santander, executing several local community leaders accused of being army informers and holding others for ransom (*New York Times*, 12 June). On 24 June another ELN force ambushed an army patrol in an operation named in memory of Domingo Laín, the Spanish priest who was killed fighting the army in 1974. According to military sources, the force was commanded by another Spanish priest, Miguel García (ibid., 28 June). Approximately 50 ELN guerrillas occupied the town of Monterrey in Bolívar on 18 August where they publicly tried and shot a peasant accused of being an informer (*El Tiempo*, 19 August). According to military authorities in Bucaramanga, three additional peasants were killed by the ELN in the area of San Pablo in early September (ibid., 9 September). In its most spectacular activity of the year, the ELN assumed responsibility for the assassination of General Rincón on 8 September. In a communiqué issued on the day of the murder, the ELN announced that the assassination had been ordered because Rincón's services were "rendered in the service of the Colombian oligarchy and United States imperialism" and to show that the ELN is "vigilant, cannot be bribed, and struggling for our independence and for socialism" (*El Espectador*, 10 September). In response to the ELN's renewed activities, increased military operations in areas of Antioquia resulted in the death of Francisco Jaramillo and the capture of Oscar William Macías in late October. Macías had reportedly been the leader of an ELN band engaged in rustling, theft, and extortion in the northeastern sector of Antioquia for almost 10 years (*El Tiempo*, 29 October). It would appear that as long as Fabio Vásquez remains at large, any speculation as to the ELN's eventual demise would be unwarranted.

Washington College   Daniel L. Premo

Costa Rica

The Communist Party of Costa Rica (Partido Comunista de Costa Rica) was founded in 1931 and accepted as a full member of the Communist International in 1935. In 1943, following the wartime policy of many Latin American communist parties, the Costa Rican communists reorganized under a new name, the Popular Vanguard Party (Partido Vanguardia Popular; PVP). The PVP and its youth and labor affiliates basically follow Soviet-line policies.

The PVP was illegal between 1948 and 4 August 1974, when Article 98 of the Costa Rican constitution, which in effect proscribed the party, was rescinded. In recent years the PVP had operated with some freedom and in the February 1974 elections had run members as candidates of the legal Partido de Acción Socialista (PASO), a leftist coalition of splinter groups. Two PASO candidates were elected to the 57-seat National Assembly: Eduardo Mora Valverde, brother of PVP founder and secretary-general Manuel Mora Valverde, and Antonio Ferreto Segura, a full-time worker in PVP affairs for many years with under-secretary-general Humberto Vargas Carbonell. With the legitimization of the PVP, the PASO appears to be fading. In the Assembly its two deputies call themselves the PVP faction.

It is difficult to estimate the size of the PVP membership. Since the party has scheduled its Twelfth Congress for March 1976 and expects 600 delegates to attend, it probably has a membership of at least 600, but probably not more than 1,500. The population of Costa Rica is 2,000,000 (estimated 1975).

Although the PVP may be the best organized and most sophisticated communist party in Central America, it has not become a significant force in Costa Rican politics. Due to its small size and aging leadership, as well as general conditions in the country, it has faced an uphill struggle and little evidence of change is apparent. (See 1974 electon results in *YICA, 1975*, p. 493.)

Leadership and Organization. Manuel Mora Valverde has been secretary-general of the PVP since its founding. His brother Eduardo is assistant secretary-general and Ferreto Segura is organizational secretary.

The PVP-controlled General Confederation of Costa Rican Workers (Confederación General de Trabajadores Costarricenses; CGTC) is believed to enroll in its affiliates about 3,600 among the estimated 30,000 unionized workers in the country. The CGTC is strongest in the banana-growing coastal regions. A marked victory in 1975 was achieved with contracts covering some 200 workers in the African palm plantations in the Quepos area. Government intervention in the contract dispute did little to help either side. A new thrust of the CGTC is toward organization of employees in the semi-autonomous agencies of the government. Alvaro Montero Vega continues as secretary-general.

The PVP affiliate for work among young persons is the Vanguard Youth of Costa Rica (Juventud Vanguardia de Costa Rica; JVCR). For the second year in a row, the JVCR dominated the elections of the University Student Federation of Costa Rica (Federación Estudiantil Universidad de Costa Rica; FEUCR), Manual Delgado being elected president of the student government at the University of Costa Rica. Delgado ran on the Unidad Para Avanzar (UPA) ticket with a Young

Socialist (JS) member, Albino Devandas, who was elected vice president. The UPA platform focused on issues of scholarships, tuition, and administrative procedures, though framed in "anti-imperialist progressive" ideological terms.

Domestic and International Attitudes. The PVP has a threefold domestic aim of enlisting worker support through the CGTC, influencing and enrolling young persons at the universities, and improving its standing in the political arena with the hope of getting a larger role in decision-making processes after the national elections in 1978. It seems doubtful that the third objective can be reached with the current party leadership, particularly because of stigmas which go back to the 1948 revolution.

The party's Twelfth Congress is dedicated to deceased author Carlos Luis Fallas, whose most famous work is a novel entitled *Mamita Yunai*, the name popularly applied in the banana-growing regions to the United Fruit Company. The dedication to Fallas, whose works are still widely read, appears to reflect the PVP's effort to attain increased acceptance along with its new legality. According to Vargas (*Libertad*, 8 November 1975), the principal task of the congress will be to make party procedures and programs consistent with the PVP's legal status.

Considerable space in *Libertad* has been devoted to the importance of détente between the United States and the USSR. This led to at least one official visit by Manuel Mora Valverde to the United States Embassy in the latter part of 1975. It has also led to some muting of the traditional anti-imperialist position of the PVP. Mora, displaying some of the behavioral patterns of veteran communist leaders in Latin America, has during the past ten years been quite willing to accept diplomatic appointments from the government; in the late 1960s he visited Eastern Europe to push the purchase of Costa Rican coffee.

Publications. The weekly *Libertad* is the official PVP newspaper. The CGTC publishes *El Orientador*.

National University of Costa Rica   Charles F. Denton
Heredia, Costa Rica

Cuba

The Communist Party of Cuba (Partido Comunista de Cuba; PCC), is Cuba's ruling party and the only one allowed to function in the country. It was founded in August 1925 by Moscow-trained members of the Comintern. For over three decades, Cuban communist leaders followed faithfully the policies of Stalin. They collaborated closely with the regime of Fulgencio Batista, adapting to the prevailing political situations in Cuba. In 1940 the party supported Batista's candidacy for president and during his 1940-44 presidential term the Communists were rewarded with positions in the government and in the labor unions. In 1944 Carlos Rafael Rodríguez, one of the pro-Moscow communist leaders and today a member of the PCC's Political Bureau, became one of Batista's ministers without portfolio. In that year, the party changed its name to the People's Socialist Party (Partido Socialista Popular; PSP). It retained this name until July 1961, when it merged with Fidel Castro's victorious 26th of July Movement and the Revolutionary Directorate (a student anti-Batista group), to form the Integrated Revolutionary Organizations (Organizaciones Revolucionarias Integradas; ORI). In 1962 ORI, after a purge of its members, was transformed into the United Party of the Socialist Revolution (Partido Unido de la Revolución Socialista; PURS). On 5 October, 1965, PURS was dissolved and in its place the Communist Party of Cuba (PCC) was formed along orthodox Soviet-communist lines.

Leadership and Organization. Between 17 and 22 December 1975 the PCC held its First Congress, which had been in preparation practically since the party was formed ten years earlier. While there have been some indications that a number of PCC members were removed from the party—those who have displayed "apathy or indifference toward the vanguard tasks which the communists must perform among the masses" (*Granma*, Havana, 26 September 1975)—membership exceeded 200,000 by the end of 1975. (The population of Cuba is estimated at 9,300,000.) Since party members continued to be drawn from the so-called "vanguard workers," Castro and other party leaders acknowledge that the low educational level of the party leaders is a problem. Castro, in his report to the Congress, said that only 4 percent of party members and applicants went to college, and 20 percent have not reached the sixth grade. He said that the PCC would try to improve the educational level to a minimum of the eighth grade by the end of this decade. The party has its own school on Marxism-Leninism with 6,000 students, and a number of party leaders are studying in the Soviet Union, East Germany and Bulgaria (significantly the most orthodox Communist states), according to Castro. (*New York Times*, 21 December 1975.)

The organizational, pyramid-like structure of the party, in force since 1972, was confirmed with a few changes by the Congress. At the top of the pyramid is the PCC's Political Bureau, which was enlarged from eight to 13 members. They are: Fidel Castro, first secretary; Raúl Castro, second secretary; Osvaldo Dorticós Torrado, Juan Almeida Bosque, Ramiro Valdés Menéndez, Guillermo García Frías, Armando Hart Dávalos, Sergio del Valle Jiménez, Blas Roca Calderío, José Ramón Machado Ventura, Carlos Rafael Rodríguez, Pedro Miret Prieto and Arnaldo Milián Castro. (The five last men are the new members. Three of them—Blas Roca, Carlos Rafael Rodríguez and Arnaldo Milián—are members of the Old Guard leadership of the PSP, who allied themselves with the Castroite forces in late 1958.)

The party Secretariat was reduced from 12 to nine members. They are: Fidel Castro, Raúl Castro, Blas Roca, Carlos Rafael Rodríguez, Pedro Miret, Isidro Malmierca Peoli, Jorge Risquet Valdés, Antonio Pérez Herrera and Raúl García Pelaez. The dropping of Dorticós and Hart, both members of the Politburo, did not appear to be a demotion since Dorticós has acquired wide powers in the running of the economy and Hart is the top leader in Eastern Cuba, distant from Havana. Faure Chomón Mediavilla, in 1959 leader of the Student Directorate, one part of the then ruling troika, was obviously demoted, but he has remained a member of the Central Committee (CC).

One of the most important tasks of the Congress, attended by 3,136 delegates, was the election of the Central Committe, the PCC's ruling body between congresses, which in turn elected the Politburo and the Secretariat. The CC was enlarged from 100 to 112 members, with 12 alternates. The members are (in addition to those in the Politburo and the Secretariat): José Abrahantes, Rogelio Acevedo, Armando Acosta, Severo Aguirre, José Alvarez Bravo, José Arteaga, Emilio Aragonés, José Ramón Balaguer, Sixto Batista, Flavio Bravo, Julio Camacho Aguilera, Miguel José Cano, José Felipe Carneado, Senen Casas, Belarmino Castilla, Lino Carreras, Reinaldo Castro, Osmaní Cienfuegos, Leopoldo Cintras Frías, Abelardo Colomé, Jaime Crombet, Raúl Curbelo, Joel Chaveco, Faure Chomón, Manuel Díaz González, Joel Domenech, Luis Orlando Domínguez, Vilma Espín, José Ramón Fernández, Pilar Fernández, Marcelo Fernández, Oscar Fernández Mel, Haroldo Ferrer, Rafael

Francia, Calixto García, Julio García Olivera, Pedro M. García Pelaez, Rigoberto García Fernández, Elena Gil, Ladislao González Carvajal, Fabio Grobart, Pedro Guelmes, Nicolás Guillén, Raúl Guerra Bermejo, Secundino Guerra, Adolfo R. Hodge, Omar Iser Omjena, Reinerio Jiménez, Rolando Kindelán, César Lara, Jorge Lescano, Arturo Lince, Emilio Lo, Antonio Enrique Lusson, Juan Marinello, Zoilo Marinello, Facundo Martínez, José Joaquín Méndez Cominches, Jorge Enrique Mendoza, Alfredo Menéndez, Raúl Menéndez Tomassevich, Jesús Montané Oropesa, José A. Naranjo, Arnaldo Ochoa, Mario Oliva, Filiberto Olivera Moya, Ramón Pardo Guerra, Faustino Pérez, Carlos Pi Delgado, Humberto Pérez González, Manual Piñeiro, José Ramírez Cruz, Julián Rizo, Raúl Roa García, Hector Rodríguez Llompart, Pedro Rodríguez Peralta, Orlando Rodríguez, Ursinio Rojas, Ulises Rosales, Irving Ruiz Brito, Celia Sánchez, Haydeé Santamaria, Aldo Santamaria, René de los Santos, Asela de los Santos, José R. Silva, Leonel Soto, Diocles Torralbas, Felipe Torres, Raúl Valdés Vivó, Fernando Vecino Alegret, Roberto Veiga, Aníbal Velaz, Roberto Viera Estrada, and Luis Alfonso Zayas.

The alternate members are: Maria Julia Arredondo, Joaquín Bernal, Thelma Vornoz, Francisco Cabrera, Dora Carcano, Julio Casas, José Cuza, Electra Fernández, Rosario Fernández, Serafín Fernández, José A. Gutiérrez Muñiz and Francisco Pérez Olivera. (Havana Radio, 23 December.)

Virtually all of the members of the Central Committee are known to hold high administrative jobs, or are top commanders of the armed forces or the internal security force. At the Congress, the exact function of the CC and the frequency of its meetings were not made explicit. It appeared, therefore, that the CC would continue to play a subservient role to the Politburo and the Secretariat, even though it had selected those two bodies.

Below the three superior party levels are party secretariats in the provinces, municipalities and city districts. Further below are party cells that have been formed in practically all centers of work and in larger military units.

The Congress confirmed the leadership role of the Party in Socialist Cuba. "The Party must be the higher leading force of Cuban society and the Cuban State, it must organize and orient common efforts aimed at the construction of Socialism and the advance toward Communism. . . The Party must strengthen and perfect, to the maximum extent, the mechanisms of democratic centralism. . . All [Party] bodies must function on the basis of collective leadership . . . [but] all must observe Party discipline and the minority must subordinate itself to the majority; all decisions made by the [higher] bodies must be carried out obligatorily and unconditionally by lower-level Party and government organizations. . ." (Congress Platform Program of the PCC, *Verde Olivo*, Havana, 26 October.) The position of Fidel Castro was, if anything, strengthened. Not only did messages from foreign communist leaders praise his personal leadership, but Havana too, at the time of the Congress, constantly played up the theme: "The Party is the soul of the country, but Fidel is the soul of the Party."

The draft of Cuba's new Constitution (which is to replace that of 1940), the country's 1976-80 economic plan, and 25 other topics concerning all facets of national life were discussed and approved by the Congress. Under the Constitution, Cuba will have a new administrative division. By March 1976, Cuba's six provinces, established by the Spanish colonial administration in 1878, will become 14, and the island's 407 municipalities will be reduced to 179. The change was carried out, Castro explained, to eliminate several administrative levels—among them the region and the section—and thus to improve government efficiency. To the present provinces of Pinar del Río, Havana, Matanzas and Camagüey, will be added the new provinces City of Havana, Villaclara, Cienfuegos, Sancti Spiritus, Ciego de Avila, Las Tunas, Holguín, Granma, Santiago de Cuba and Guantánamo. The province of Granma, the name of the boat on which Castro and his supporters traveled from Mexico to Cuba in 1956 to begin revolutionary struggle against Batista, comprises the eastern regions of Bayamo and Manzanillo. The draft of the Constitution will be submitted to national referendum on 15 February

1976, and proclaimed as Cuba's basic charter on 24 February. Under the Charter, during the following eight months, elections are scheduled at municipal and provincial levels to create the organs of People's Government, local power, with the transfer of local administrative functions to those local assemblies completed by October. (The organs of the People's Government will be equivalent to the Soviets, the local councils or committees in the USSR.) On 2 December 1976 the National People's Assembly will be created, concluding the institutionalization of Socialist Cuba. The Assembly will elect the State Council which will meet every six months. Between sessions there will be a supreme organ that will have a chairman, a first deputy, five other deputy chairmen and 24 more members. This 31-member Executive Committee will be the supreme organ of the National Assembly. On 2 December 1976 the Assembly will also elect a Council of Ministers, which will have executive powers, and powers of passing executive resolutions. The State Council will have legislative powers.

Until 2 December 1976 the Cuban Government is expected to be made up of the Executive Committee of the Council of Ministers whose nine members are responsible for individual "sectors" of the country's life and who supervise 27 ministries and 17 independent agencies on sub-ministerial level. Premier Fidel Castro, chairman of the Executive Committee, is in charge of the Defense, Security and Non-Sugar Agriculture, responsibility which he shares with First Deputy Premier Raúl Castro.

President Dorticós is in charge of planning, banking and trade relations with non-Communist countries.

Deputy Premier Ramiro Valdés is in charge of the Construction Sector.

Deputy Premier Guillermo García is in charge of the Transportation and Communication Sector.

Deputy Premier Flavio Bravo Pardo is in charge of the Consumer Goods and Domestic Commerce and Industry Sector.

Deputy Premier Belarmino Castilla is in charge of the Education, Culture and Science Sector.

Deputy Premier Carlos Rafael Rodríguez is in charge of the Foreign Affairs Sector.

Deputy Premier Diocles Torralba Gonzáles is in charge of the Sugar Sector.

Mass Organizations. During 1975 Cuba's mass organizations were: the Confederation of Cuban Workers (Central de Trabajadores de Cuba; CTC), the National Association of Small Farmers (Asociación de Agricultores Pequeños; ANAP), the Committees for the Defense of the Revolution (Comités de Defensa de la Revolución; CDR), and the Federation of Cuban Women (Federación de Mujeres Cubanas; FMC). Four other groups, the Union of Young Communists (Unión de Jovenes Comunistas; UJC), the Union of Cuban Pioneers (Unión de Pioneros de Cuba; UPC), the University Student Federation (Federación Estudiantil Universitaria; FEU), and the Federation of High School Students (Federación de Estudiantes de la Enseñanza Media; FEEM), are not regarded as mass organizations. Rather, they are institutional stepping stones in the selection process of the ruling élite: the Communist Party and the governmental officialdom.

The CTC. The Confederation of Cuban Workers was headed by Roberto Veiga González, secretary-general of its National Committee, who was chosen for the post in March 1974. The CTC had in 1975 about 2.2 million members, a number that has remained unchanged for several years. Labor unions have as a principal task fulfilling production goals set by the government. This they do also by the so-called "volunteer labor" and by promoting and organizing "socialist competitions" in most places of work. Rewards—mostly scarce appliances such as refrigerators or motorcycles—are distributed through the unions to "exemplary workers." The average monthly wage in Cuba remained low—about $160—but with few items to purchase it provided a better standard of living for workers than enjoyed in many Latin American countries. At the Congress, CTC leaders pledged to "create and strengthen a conscious, Socialist labor discipline" and to broaden the scope of volunteer labor.

The ANAP. The National Association of Small Farmers was headed at the close of 1975 by CC-member José Ramírez Cruz. It is a party-controlled organization that exercises close control over the activities of independent farmers, whose farms make up more than 20 percent of the land under cultivation. In 1975, ANAP membership was about 170,000, a drop of some 10,000 as compared with 1974. Cuban private farmers have to sell virtually all they produce, mostly vegetables, tobacco and coffee, to the state. The disappearance of the private agricultural sector is only a question of time. At the Congress, Castro said that as a matter of PCC policy, private farmers would be "persuaded" to give up their land, which then would be incorporated into the state farms.

The CDR: The Committees for the Defense of the Revolution were headed by Jorge Lescano, their National Coordinator and member of the PCC Central Committee. In 1975, there were some 4.8 million members of the CDR (over 70 percent of the adult population), organized in about 74,000 committees formed in every city, city block, factory, farm and office in the country. Their principal task was to "defend the Revolution" by constant "revolutionary vigilance" toward every type of activity around them, many members apparently watching over the activities of other members. One task of the CDR during 1975 was to provide all Cubans of 16 years or older with an identity card to make them eligible for voting in the 15 February 1976 referendum.

The FMC. Since its inception in 1960, the Federation of Cuban Woman—an organization intended to bring Cuban women into revolutionary ranks and productive occupations—has been headed by Vilma Espín, the wife of Raúl Castro and member of the PCC Central Committee. Although the FMC had some 2 million members, and a quarter of Cuba's 2.4 million workers are women, Fidel Castro said at the Congress that efforts to minimize "machismo" have been less than successful in Cuba. Only 15 percent of the women were members of the PCC. No woman has been chosen to the Party's Politburo or the Secretariat and only six of the 112 CC members are women. Very few, if any, have occupied high positions within the government, and job opportunities for women have been limited. Because of the continuing scarcity of consumer products in Cuba, the traditional household chores performed by women have been burdensome and the government's goal of equality for women was far from fulfillment by the end of 1975.

The UJC. The Union of Young Communists is the Cuban counterpart of the Soviet Komsomol. An elitist group of young people chosen for their leadership qualities, the UJC had some 300,000 members by the end of 1975 (*The New York Times*, 21 December). It was headed by Luis O. Domínguez, a member of the PCC Central Committee. Cuban youth can join the UJC at the age of 14. At 27, if they pass an ideological test, some of them join the PCC. The UJC is organizationally independent of the PCC and its central function is to "draw the young people into the tasks of the Revolution . . . preparing them for joining the Party." (*Verde Olivo*, Havana, 26 October.) The UJC watches directly over the activities of the Union of Cuban Pioneers, the Federation of High School Students (headed in 1975 by Idalia Romero), and indirectly those of the University Student Federation (FEU), whose president was Carlos Lage.

The UPC. The Union of Cuban Pioneers, also equivalent to the Soviet Pioneers, was organized in 1961 to control activities of school children from the ages of 5 to 14. According to the Platform of the PCC Congress, the organization is a "great school in which our country's children prepare themselves for the future and in which begins the revolutionary life of the men and women of tomorrow. . . It inculcates in them profound patriotic and revolutionary sentiments . . . and directs their after-school activities." It is estimated that over 80 percent of Cuban children belong to the UPC.

The Revolutionary Armed Forces. The FAR (Fuerzas Armadas Revolucionarias), according to the Strategic Services Institute, had 116,000 men under arms by mid-1975, with 213,000 more organized in paramilitary groups. In the event of a serious conflict, the Institute estimated Cuba could mobilize up to 300,000 men in 48 hours and over one million during the first week of fighting, all with a high degree of military training. (*Ahora*, Santa Domingo, 18 August.) At the Congress, Fidel Castro said that during the 1976-80 period the FAR would be re-equipped with an "appreciable quantity of even more modern technology" (Havana Radio, 18 December). He also promised higher salaries for military commanders. Castro said that the role of the Soviet Union in the strengthening of Cuba's armed forces has been "decisive," and added that in 1975 the FAR was "highly trained, equipped with modern weapons and ready to fulfill any mission" (ibid.). While the FAR was essentially a defensive force, its intervention in the fighting in Angola in 1975 indicated that the Castro government had new offensive goals for the Cuban military. Castro, in a series of references to fighting in Africa, confirmed at the Congress that the Cuban army had "shed blood more than once in other countries threatened by imperialist aggression" and had helped to organize the armed forces and militia of "other progressive countries (*New York Times*, 19 December). In another Congress speech Castro, promising more aid to Angola, said: "We have supported the progressive governments and revolutionary movements in Africa since the triumph of the Revolution. And we shall continue to do so. The aid has been manifested in different forms. At times, we have sent weapons. Sometimes we have sent men. Other times, we have sent instructors, military instructors. At other times, we have sent doctors, construction people." (Ibid., 23 December.) While Castro did not comment on reports that about 5,000 Cuban troops were in Angola, he indicated that the number was considerable, and that even some of the delegates to the Congress were fighting in Africa. Cuba has a very highly politicized army; over 85 percent of the officers belonged either to the party or the UJC.

Domestic Affairs. 1975 was the "Year of the First Congress," and most of the domestic activities in Cuba were centered on preparations for that event. Thousands of meetings were held to discuss the draft of the Constitution and the party Platform in what was described as the continuing process of the country's institutionalization.

The performance of the economy is improving, though not dramatically. Rationing continued to be a permanent feature of the Cuban life in 1975, though more consumer goods produced domestically and imported from abroad were placed on sale. Cuban foreign trade increased because of high prices for sugar, the country's principal export. The 1975 sugar production was estimated at 5.7 million tons, practically the same as that of 1974. A severe drought, which also affected other lesser crops and cattle production, was blamed for the failure to harvest more sugar. About US$5 billion in Soviet development and balance-of-payment loans, given the Castro government since 1960, has permitted the Cuban economy to consume and invest beyond its means. Cuban imports are dominated by capital goods, raw materials for industries and petroleum—over 95 percent of the country's consumption.

While the high prices of sugar helped the Cuban trade balance, the country had to pay much more for its imports, too. The Cuban economy was affected by world inflationary pressures, which had a direct bearing on the country's future development. "The 1976-80 economic plan will concur with the present crisis in the world capitalist economy, which prevents us from making a definite forecast," said Osvaldo Dorticós. "The truth is that our economy is affected by the world capitalist economy . . . the inevitable limitations imposed by high costs of imports for our economy, which is notoriously dependent on foreign trade, compel us to keep the growth rate within foreign market possibilities." (*Granma*, Havana, 28 October.)

International Positions. The main premise of the Cuban foreign policy in 1975 was a complete agreement with the international position of the Soviet Union. The Soviet role in the formulation of

Cuban policies was emphasized during the party Congress by Castro, who repeatedly said that "our Soviet brothers have taught us our internationalist duties," and expressed his support for the policy of peaceful coexistence. "Eternal friendship, cooperation and political and ideological unity" exists between Cuba and the Soviet Union, said *Granma* earlier in 1975. "We [Cuba and the Soviet Union] have helped to speed up the pace of history in Latin America. We have given a new boost to the cohesion of the Socialist camp." (*Granma*, 2 February.)

In June 1975, a meeting of 24 communist parties of Latin America and the Caribbean was held in Havana. Indicating Cuba's allegiance to the Soviet Union, the final declaration of the meeting strongly chastized Communist China. "This Conference," the declaration said, "energetically condemns the foreign policy of the leadership of the Communist Party of China which flirts with Yankee imperialism, defends its presence in Asia and Europe, justifies NATO, attacks and slanders the USSR with the same viciousness of the worst spokesmen of international reaction. (*Granma International*, Havana, 23 June 1975. Represented at the 9-13 June 1975 meeting were the communist parties of: Argentina, Bolivia, Brazil, Chile, Colombia, Costa Rica, Cuba, the Dominican Republic, Ecuador, El Salvador, Guadeloupe, Guatemala, Guyana, Haiti, Honduras, Martinique, Mexico, Nicaragua, Panamá, Paraguay, Puerto Rico, Uruguay and Venezuela.) As for the Hemisphere, the declaration said that "true progress" will not be achieved "without political overthrow" of the ruling classes. Stating that "U.S. imperialism is the main common enemy," it called for political alliances with other non-communist governments and social groups which are not pro-American. (See Appendix below.)

Cuba, which already had diplomatic relations with Mexico, Perú and Argentina (relations with Chile were broken after the overthrow of President Allende), re-established in 1975 diplomatic ties with Colombia, Venezuela and Panamá, among other Latin and Caribbean countries. "We are a member of the Latin American family," declared Premier Castro to Mexico newsmen who traveled to Havana with President Luis Echeverría in August 1975.

Cuba's interest in non-aligned nations continued strong in 1976. In March, Premier Castro hosted a meeting of the Coordinating Bureau of Non-Aligned Countries. In essence, he pleaded with delegates to the conference that their governments align themselves with the Communist bloc and give support to national liberation movements. At the United Nations, Cuba has consistently voted with the Soviet Union and the Third World countries. In November, she joined all other members of the Communist bloc (except Romania) in supporting a resolution which equated Zionism with "Racism."

Cuba's position of supporting the Puerto Rican independence movement was as uncompromising as ever. In September Havana was the site of an International Conference of Solidarity for the Independence of Puerto Rico. "We assure the men and women of Puerto Rico of our firm solidarity," said Cuba's President Dorticós addressing the Conference. "Cuba reaffirms and ratifies in full her pledge of unlimited support to the Puerto Rican cause . . . Puerto Rico is not an internal affair of the United States." (*Granma*, 17 September.)

In July 1975, the Organization of American States (OAS), composed of 21 Western Hemisphere countries including the United States, overwhelmingly voted to end its sanctions against Cuba imposed a decade earlier. In August, the United States relaxed its commercial embargo by allowing foreign subsidiaries of U.S. firms to trade with Cuba. Both Washington and Havana indicated that the climate for re-establishment of diplomatic and commercial ties was improving. But the disclosure that Cuban troops were engaged in the Angolan conflict froze moves toward rapprochement. Replying to U.S. President Ford's statement in December that the Cuban action "destroys any opportunity for improvement in relations with the United States," Castro at the close of the party Congress said that he did not care if relations with the United States were not restored "for the next 100 years."

International Contacts. Some 86 foreign delegations were present for the party Congress.

Although Leonid Brezhnev was expected to head the Soviet delegation, Mikhail Suslov came instead. Among those present were: Todor Zhivkov, the Bulgarian Communist leader; Janos Kadar, head of the Hungarian Party, who made his first trip to Cuba; Henry Jablonski, president of the Polish State Council; General Vo Nguyen Giap of North Vietnam; and Alvaro Cunhal, secretary general of the Portuguese Communist Party.

In January, Edward Gierek, first secretary of the Polish Communist Party, visited Havana. So did Major Joao Bernardo Viera, Commissar of the Armed Forces of the Republic of Guinea-Bissau, and Juan Bosch, the Dominican opposition leader. In March, the visitors were: Carlos Altamirano, secretary-general of the Socialist Party of Chile; Rodney Arismendi, secretary-general of the Uruguayan Communist Party and Pierre Nze, member of the Politburo of the Congolese Party of Labor. The April visitors were: Peter Mladenov, Foreign Minister of Bulgaria; Alastair Gillespie, Canadian Minister of Bulgaria; Alastair Gillespie, Canadian Minister of Industry, Trade and Commerce; Forbes Burnham, Prime Minister of Guyana and Dr. Kenneth D. Kaunda, President of Zambia. In May Norbert Sengard, French Minister of Foreign Trade traveled to Cuba and in June, Eric Williams, Prime Minister of Trinidad-Tobago. In July visitors were Olaf Palme, Prime Minister of Sweden; Michael Manley, Prime Minister of Jamaica; and the then General Otelo Saraiva de Carvalho, a Portuguese military leader. President Luis Echeverría of Mexico paid a state visit to Cuba in August and President Marien Ngonabi of the People's Republic of the Congo in September. Few Cuban leaders traveled abroad because of the preparations for the Party Congress.

Publications. The official organ of the Central Committee is the Havana daily *Granma*, published six times a week. Its editor, Jorge Enrique Mendoza, is member of the Party's Central Committee. *Granma* also appears in weekly editions in Spanish, English and French. The average daily circulation is 600,000, and the paper has between 8 and 12 pages. There were six provincial newspapers, also controlled by the Party. The UJC publishes in Havana the daily *Juventud Rebelde*, the country's second national newspaper with a circulation of 200,000. *Verde Olivo*, a weekly, is the organ of the FAR, and *Bohemia* is a general news weekly national magazine, with a circulation of some 300,000.

University of Miami   George Volsky

APPENDIX

CONFERENCE OF COMMUNIST PARTIES OF LATIN AMERICA AND THE CARIBBEAN

The largest meeting of communist parties from Latin America and the Caribbean ever held in the hemisphere took place from 9 to 13 June 1975 in Havana. The 24 voting delegations represented the communist parties from all the Latin American countries as well as those from Puerto Rico, Martinique, and Guadeloupe. They were:

Communist Party of Argentina
Communist Party of Bolivia
Brazilian Communist Party
Communist Party of Chile
Communist Party of Colombia

People's Progressive Party of Guyana
Unified Party of Haitian Communists
Communist Party of Honduras
Martiniquian Communist Party
Mexican Communist Party

People's Vanguard Party of Costa Rica
Communist Party of Cuba
Dominican Communist Party
Communist Party of Ecuador
Communist Party of El Salvador
Guadeloupean Communist Party
Guatemalan Party of Labor

Socialist Party of Nicaragua
People's Party of Panama
Paraguayan Communist Party
Peruvian Communist Party
Communist Party of Puerto Rico
Communist Party of Uruguay
Communist Party of Venezuela

Delegations from the Communist Party of Canada and the Communist Party of the United States (three persons, headed by national chairman Henry Winston) also attended as observers. Conspicuously (and predictably) absent were representatives of competing Marxist-Leninist organizations, namely the pro-Chinese and Trotskyist parties and their armed branches (such as the Colombian EPL), Castroite movements (such as the Bolivian ELN, the Uruguayan Tupamaros, and the Chilean MIR), other chiefly guerrilla-oriented organizations (such as the Argentine Montoneros) and Venezuela's independent communist parties, the Movement Toward Socialism (MAS) and the Communist Vanguard (VC).

The first public call for this conference came in May 1974 from the Ninth Conference of Communist and Workers' Parties of Central America and Mexico. That conference's declaration, signed by parties from Mexico, Guatemala, El Salvador, Nicaragua, Costa Rica, and Panama, appealed for a preparatory meeting of all communist and workers' parties in Latin America to discuss organization, agenda, and related matters for a regional conference, concluding: "We believe that the revolutionary movement in Latin America would benefit from such a conference, held in the spirit of unity and aimed at clearing up common viewpoints on such questions as the present state of the revolutionary process, its successes and setbacks, the present alignment of forces, diverse forms and specific features of the revolutionary process, and at making a scientific analysis of possibilities for coordinated action of all our parties and all anti-imperialist forces."[1] According to a press release in the Cuban Communist Party organ *Granma* (14 June 1975), "the meeting was carefully prepared through a series of activities by the representatives of the Communist Parties of Latin America and the Caribbean, working as a committee to draft the document that served as the basis for discussion in the meeting." The press release continued that the meeting had demonstrated the "firm unity" of the parties and their "fundamental identity of opinion in appraising the international and Latin-American situations and the strategic bases and tactical concepts that serve the Communists and all the revolutionaries and patriots in Latin America and the Caribbean in their struggle against the main enemy, defined by the meeting as Yankee imperialism."[2]

The 20,000-word declaration signed on 13 June was solidly pro-Soviet in orientation though it relied in some instances on generalized formulas which are open to varying interpretations. The nine sections of the statement analyzed the socio-economic history of Latin America, the impact and importance of the Cuban Revolution, revolutionary developments in Latin America since the fall of Batista in 1959, the international aspects of this "epoch of revolutionary transition from capitalism to socialism," and communist strategies and tactics for the years ahead in Latin America. The document praised the governments in Ecuador, Panama, Venezuela, Mexico, and Peru (then under Juan Velasco), particularly the latter, and stressed the need for united anti-imperialist action with other leftists and certain "bourgeois sectors" in the "struggle for economic independence and national sovereignty." Nationalist tendencies can be transformed into anti-imperialist and revolutionary positions with sufficient decisive participation by the "people's forces." The Christian-Marxist dialogue strengthened cooperation between revolutionaries and the "reformist" and "advanced" sectors of the Church. The Chilean experience of the early 1970s showed that "revolutionary movements cannot discard any way of democratic access to power" but also that they must be "fully prepared and ready to defend, with the force of weapons the democratic achievements." The document called for a world conference of communist parties, as sought by the Soviet Union, and "energetically condemned" the "treasonous" foreign policy of the Communist Party of China. The extended passage on China was typical of those issued by most pro-Soviet parties for more than a decade, but was much more forceful than any endorsed by Cuba since 1966. The meeting marked the full return of the Communist Party of Cuba to the company of pro-Soviet communist parties in Latin America.[3]

[1] *Information Bulletin* (Prague), no. 14, 1974, pp. 32-33
[2] *Granma*, English edition, 22 June 1975
[3] Portions of this summary are based on my contribution to *Latin American Report* (San Francisco), June 1975.

Hoover Institution   William E. Ratliff
Stanford University

Dominican Republic

Intense disagreement over the leadership and policy issues, especially since the civil war of 1965, has led to fragmentation of the communist movement of the Dominican Republic. The three principal organizations are the Dominican Communist Party (Partido Comunista Dominicano; PCD), more or less officially recognized by the USSR; Dominican People's Movement (Movimiento Popular Dominicano, MPD), which has been pro-Chinese; and Revolutionary Movement of 14 June (Movimiento Revolucionario 14 de Junio; MR-1J4), pro-Chinese, but also the group most sympathetic toward Cuba. Splits within these groups have created several new factions and parties, including: the Popular Socialist Party (Partido Socialista Popular; PSP), the Communist Party of the Dominican Republic (Partido Comunista de la Republica Dominicana; PCRD or PACOREDO), and the Red Flag (Bandera Roja), Red Line (Línea Roja), Red Fatherland (Patria Roja),and Proletarian Voice (Voz Proletaria), factions of MR-1J4. Only the PCD appears clearly to enjoy recognition within the international communist movement.

Communism is officially proscribed in the Dominican Republic, under laws covering propaganda and subversive activities. President Joaquín Balaguer has allowed the various groups to operate with relative freedom, although a bill he sent to Congress in 1974 to give legal recognition to the PCD does not seem to have been acted upon. For their part, most of the Marxist-Leninist groups have tended to seek respectability in recent years; the more important of them have denounced terrorism.

Estimates of membership vary widely. On 2 October 1974 the *New York Times* reported that the MPD, which was rated the largest of the communist groups, had some 2,000 members. Reuters Agency in May 1974 credited the PCD with 300 members (*Christian Science Monitor*, 31 May). In contrast, the U.S. State Department estimated all of the leftist groups to have only about 1,400 members in 1974: PCD, 460; MPD, 385; MR-1J4, 300; PCRD, 145; VP, 65; and PSP 40 (*World*

Strength of the Communist Party Organizations, 1974, p. 162). The population of the Dominican Republic is about 4,700,000.

Politically motivated murders became an established feature of the Dominican scene after the 1965 civil war. Although victims were of all political colors, most were members of communist groups or of the major opposition party, the Dominican Revolutionary Party (Partido Revolucionario Dominicano; PRD). The killings were attributed both to feuds among communist groups and to actions by paramilitary gangs reportedly organized by the military and police, particularly the latter. Political assassinations continued during 1975, although on a somewhat reduced level; the most notable murder was that of a leading young journalist, PCD member Orlando Martínez.

Sources of communist support include the universities, secondary schools, and labor unions, and reflect the fragmentation of the movement. At the university level, the student movement is divided into the following organizations: "Fragua," led by the Red Line of the MR-1J4; Juventud Comunista, led by PCRD members, the Comité Universitario "Julio Antonio Mella," led by PCD members; and the Comité Flavio Sucre, led by MPD members. The powerful Federation of Dominican Students (Federación de Estudiantes Dominicanos; FED), which is said to enroll about 200,000 university and secondary school students, was after 1969 in the hands of non-communist but left-wing students of the PRD. The communist movement in the secondary schools is represented by the Union of Revolutionary Students (Unión de Estudiantes Revolucionarios; UER).

Within the labor movement, which generally has been weak since the 1965 civil war, communist support is more limited. The "Foupsa-Cesitrado" labor confederation, reportedly in MPD hands, is only one of several central labor bodies. There is also some communist influence in the General Confederation of Workers (Confederación General de Trabajadores; CGT). The largest is the Confederación Autónoma Sindical Cristiana, more or less associated with the Revolutionary Social Christian Party (Partido Revolucionario Social Cristiano; PRSC). The powerful "Unachosin" chauffeurs' union includes communist members, mostly of the MPD.

The PCD. The PCD was founded clandestinely in 1942. As the Popular Socialist Party (Partido Socialista Popular), it came into the open for a short while in 1946; in 1947 it was suppressed by the Trujillo dictatorship. During the military-civilian revolt in April 1965, the party took the PCD name, which it has used since. In 1967 the PCD adopted (verbally but not in practice) a Castroite line, advocating the concept of armed struggle for most Latin American countries, but soon abandoned that position. In recent years it has advocated the kind of popular front characteristic of the pro-Soviet parties in Latin America. In 1975, although part of the opposition, it professed to support President Balaguer against more reactionary elements of the Establishment.

Leadership and Organization. Narciso Isa Conde is the PCD secretary-general. Other leaders include Dr. Julian Pena and Mario González Córdova. The party claims to be organized on a national scale, with cells in most cities and in the countryside. It has a committee operating in New York City among persons of Dominican origin.

Domestic Attitudes and Activities. The PCD threw its support behind President Balaguer early in May 1975 when he faced a challenge from major figures in the military. When he sought to shift commands, the heads of all armed services protested and resigned; however, the great majority of armed forces leaders backed the president, who accepted the resignations which had been offered to him.

Narciso Isa Conde, explaining his party's support of Balaguer, identified him as "the principal exponent of the reformist tendency" in the government, in contrast to the "ultra-reactionaries" who had opposed him in the crisis. He accused the mutinous military men of being "a neo-fascist tendency aligned closely with the CIA," and attributed to them the responsibility for the wave of political murders. (*Expreso PL*, 23 May.)

Throughout the year, the PCD stressed the theme that the country's natural resources should remain in Dominican hands. In January, Narciso Isa Conde reported the PCD's endorsement of the decision of Venezuela's government to nationalize that country's iron and petroleum, and added: "I believe that the time has now come for our country to take up the cudgels resolutely in favor of the recovery of our bauxite, gold, ferronickel and sugar, which are today in the hands of giant foreign consortiums" (*El Caribe*, 27 January).

In October the PCD attacked the prospective profits of the Rosario Dominicana mining company as being "scandalous." It insisted that the government should annul the contract. (Radio Mil, Santo Domingo, 4 October.)

International Contacts. During 1975 the PCD moved to strengthen its position as the recognized Dominican member of the group of pro-Soviet communist parties. In July and August the party's secretary-general visited various countries of Eastern Europe, where he was received by leading figures in the ruling parties. In May the PCD sent a cable, published in *Pravda* (13 May), to the Central Committee of the Communist Party of the Soviet Union, congratulating the USSR on the 30th anniversary of the end of World War II in Europe.

Publication. The PCD publishes a clandestine weekly, *El Popular*. Its declarations are also published from time to time in the daily press of Santo Domingo.

*   *   *

The PSP. When the PCD adopted Castroite views and tactics—mostly limited to verbal declarations—in 1967, a split occurred within the party. The more moderate members, proclaiming support for the USSR and "peaceful coexistence," formed a new party, using the PCD's former name, Partido Socialista Popular. Despite its pro-Soviet stance, the PSP has not been recognized by the USSR, but it seems to maintain friendly relations with some pro-Soviet parties in Latin America.

The PSP was apparently relatively inactive during 1975.

*   *   *

The MPD. The MPD was formed by Dominican exiles in Havana in 1956. Originally its leaders included many persons who did not have communist sympathies. After the death of Trujillo in 1961 and the return of the founders to Santo Domingo, it quickly took on a Marxist-Leninist orientation, and those who were opposed to this left the party.

The MPD became a formal party only in August 1965. It was then pro-Chinese and was one of the most active and violent leftist groups, with considerable support among students and slum dwellers and some following in organized labor. More recently, like the PCD, it has sought a more respectable image, a development which has led to the desertion of its ranks by more violence-prone elements.

Among the leaders of the MPD is Julio de Peña Valdés, who has been secretary-general of the Foupsa-Cesitrado trade union group. Others include Rafael Tavares and Rafael Enrique Rivera Mejía. (For names of other leaders see *YICA, 1972*,, pp. 363-64). The party has some influence also in the General Confederation of Workers.

MPD activities received relatively little publicity during 1975. In June, MPD leader David Onelo Espaillat was arrested at the time of a guerrilla "invasion" (see below).

The MPD publishes an irregular clandestine paper, *Libertad*.

The 12 January Liberation Movement. As the MPD has sought a more respectable and recognized position in the national political spectrum, some more extremist elements have abandoned it. One such group formed the 12 January Liberation Movement in 1973 and since then has engaged in several terrorist actions.

The PCRD. The Communist Party of the Dominican Republic was formed by MPD dissidents after the 1965 civil war, and is considered very extreme. The secretary-general is Luis Adolfo Montas González. The membership is limited mostly to the city of Santo Domingo. The PCRD defines itself as a Marxist-Leninist party, "created in conformity with the thoughts of Mao Tse-tung." The party proclaims its major objective to be to install socialism and then communism, through a "democratic revolution" (statement by Montas González, Radio Continental, Santo Domingo, 17 January 1971). The PCRD seems to have been relatively inactive during 1975.

The PCRD's official organ is the clandestine *El Comunista.*

The MR-1J4. The Revolutionary Movement of 14 June derives its name from an unsuccessful attempt to overthrow the late dictator Trujillo on that day in 1959 by an invasion from Cuba. Although helped by Castro, many of the early leaders of the MR-1J4 felt that Cuban leaders had betrayed them and the party was not pro-communist until October 1963, when the government of President Juan Bosch was overthrown. Soon thereafter, the MR-1J4 attempted a guerrilla insurrection, which resulted in the death of its original leaders. Those who took over evolved quickly in the communist direction, particularly toward the Castro version of Marxism-Leninism. The MR-1J4 has subsequently split into several factions, most of which were Maoist by the middle 1970's. These include the so-called Red Flag, headed by Juan B. Mejía; Red Line, led by Juan Rodríquez; Red Fatherland; and Proletarian Voice. The Red Line faction was reported in June 1975 as being active in agitation concerning the size of the University of Santo Domingo budget. (*Intercontinental Press*, New York, 30 June). In October the Red Flag, Red Line, and Voz Proletaria groups were announced by the Chinese to have sent greetings to Mao Tse-tung and Chou En-lai on the occasion of the 26th anniversary of the proclaimation of the Peoples Republic of China (NCNA, 15 October).

Immediately after the death of Trujillo, the 14 June Movement was one of the three major political groups in the Dominican Republic, along with the PRD and the Union Civica Nacional. By 1975 all MR-1J4 factions were fringe groups in national politics. They had at most marginal influence in the student and labor movements, and little or no impact on the general political picture.

*   *   *

Guerrilla Activity. Although most of the extreme left groups are formally committed to the use of guerrilla war as the road to power, none of them has made any serious effort to mount such a war in recent years. In 1975, however, there was one attempt at guerrilla activity, launched from abroad.

Early in June it was announced that a guerrilla group had been landed. Within a few days, three Puerto Ricans, members of the Puerto Rican Socialist Party, were arrested. They were accused of having brought three Dominicans, Claudio Caamaño Grullen (nephew of Colonel Caamaño, leader of the Constitutionalist forces in the 1965 civil war), Toribio Peña Jáquez and Manfredo Casado Villar from Puerto Rico to launch a guerrilla effort. (Radio Latin, Buenos Aires, 24 June.) The three Puerto Ricans were sentenced to 30 years in jail (Radio Mil, 2 October) and then, in November, pardoned by President Balaguer (*Renovación*, Santo Domingo, 25 November).

This "invasion" was the occasion for the arrest of numerous members of the opposition. These included leaders of the General Confederation of Workers, as well as some leaders of the MPD, the Dominican Liberation Party of former president Juan Bosch, and the PRD. (Ibid., 7 June; *Intercontinental Press*, 29 July.) Most were soon released. In early October, Claudio Caamaño and Toribio Peña Jáquez were captured in the province of San Cristobal (ibid., 2 October). The "guerrillas" were not identified as being affiliated with any political group within the republic.

Rutgers University   Robert J. Alexander

Ecuador

In May 1926 the Socialist Party of Ecuador (Partido Socialista Ecuatoriano; PSE) was founded. Two years later Ricardo Paredes led the "Friends of Lenin" group of the PSE to join the Communist International, and in 1931 it adopted the name of Communist Party of Ecuador (Partido Comunista del Ecuador; PCE). A pro-Chinese splinter group, the Marxist-Leninist Communist Party of Ecuador (Partido Comunista Marxista-Leninista del Ecuador; PCMLE) dates from 1963. Factional divisions of the PSE have periodically produced other Marxist-Leninist groups, most notably the Revolutionary Socialist Party of Ecuador (Partido Socialista Revolucionario Ecuatoriano; PSRE). It broke away in 1962 as a frankly fidelista movement.

The PCE is estimated to have 500 members, although this figure may be conservative. PSE membership is roughly comparable. The PCMLE and PSRE number no more than 100 each. The population of Ecuador is 6,700,000.

The military junta that assumed power in July 1963 declared the PCE illegal, but the party remained intact through clandestine activities and its representation in various mass organizations. After 1966, when the government returned to civilian control, the party again began to function openly. In 1968 elections the PCE organized a coalition movement, the Popular Democratic Union (Unión Democrática Popular; UDP). Its candidates, Elías Gallegos Anda (president) and Gonzalo Villalba (vice-president), both finished last in a five-man race, with about 2 percent of the valid votes. In 1971 the PCE was joined by other small leftist organizations to form the Popular Unity in anticipation of elections scheduled for June 1972. Their efforts were halted by a military coup led by General Guillermo Rodríguez Lara on 15 February 1972 and elections were canceled. The PCE was legalized under that name in 1973.

Since that time the PCE has provided sturdy support for the Rodríguez regime, the only party to do so. A "confidential circular" issued 19 March 1975 and published in April spoke of the need to infiltrate the government and penetrate the ranks of the armed forces. This required continuing backing for the regime in its defense of natural resources (most notably petroleum) and in its pursuit of alignment with Third World nations.

The PCE was the only major party not represented in the "National Civic Junta" which in August 1975 issued a public call for national elections. Following an unsuccessful attempted coup against the government on 1 September 1975, the PCE reiterated its backing of General Rodríguez. The members of the National Civic Junta were in turn denounced for attempting to subvert the "revolutionary nationalist" regime.

Organization and Leadership. The PCE elected a new Central Committee of 27 full and 15 alternate members at its 9th Congress, in Guayaquil on 15-18 November 1973 (see *YICA, 1975*, p. 509). At subsequent meetings of the Central Committee plenum, the party has retained Pedro Antonio Saad as general secretary, a position he has held for three decades. Saad was a founder of the Communist-dominated Confederation of Ecuadorean Workers (Confederación de Trabajadores Ecuatorianos; CTE) in 1944 and has served several times as its general secretary.

The party's youth organization is the Communist Youth of Ecuador (Juventud Comunista Ecuatoriana; JCE). It has waged a constant struggle against the influence of "Maoist terrorist groups" in the universities, and especially the extreme right-wing paramilitary Association for the Armed Transformation of Lation America (Asociación para la Transformación Armada Latinoamericana; ATALA), sometimes known as the Student Struggle Front (Frente de Lucha Estudiantil; FLE). The most recent clash came on 16 May 1975 with the brief ATALA occupation of the National University in Quito (*El Tiempo*, Quito, 17 May). The JCE also exercises influence within the national Federation of Ecuadorean University Students (Federación Estudiantil Universitaria Ecuatoriana; FEUE), often clashing with rival groups of pro-Chinese and/or fidelista views.

The JCE held its Second Congress on 29 November-1 December in Guayaquil, electing Winston Alarcón as secretary general. The delegates examined the problems of the people of Ecuador in their struggle for "true national and social liberation," such as the strengthening of unity of the nation's "democratic forces." (*Granma*, Havana, 2 December.) Youth delegations were present from the communist parties of Cuba, Venezuela, Colombia, and Argentina, invited by the CTE Youth (Juventud de la CTE). The head of the Cuban delegation, Juan Pantaleón, commented that the Congress was an important step in the unification process of communist youth movements on the continent. (Ibid., 3 December.)

The PCE controls the Confederation of Ecuadorean Workers, until recently the largest labor organization in the country, with a claimed membership of 60,000. The CTE, a member of the World Federation of Trade Unions, is led by Juan Basquez Bastidas (president), Becquer Sánchez (vice-president), Leónidas Córdoba, and Bolívar Bolaños. At its 13th Congress, on 13-16 February 1975, the CTE called for "united action by the workers for revolutionary changes" and "food, land, a home, education, freedom, national sovereignty and democracy for the people" (*WFTU Flashes*, 26 March). Among the major points of its platform were: rejection of economic repression and threats of U.S. imperialism, firm defense of national sovereignty and natural resources, struggle for revolutionary social changes, and implementation of agrarian reform. A subsequent meeting of the PCE Central Committee reviewed the results of the CTE congress favorably, praising its importance for the working class and the Ecuadorean people (*IB*, no. 7). Peasant organizations under PCE influence are the Coastal Farm Workers Federation (Federación de Trabajadores Agrícolas del Litoral; FTAL) and the Ecuadorean Federation of Indians (Federación Ecuatoriana de Indias; FEI).

Party Internal Affairs. The most recent party congress was that of 15-18 November 1973 (*YICA, 1975*) Four plenums of the Central Committee were held in 1975 (*IB*, no. 4; *WMR*, no. 3; *IB*, no. 6-7; *IB*, no. 10).

Domestic Views. The "Political Resolution" of the 1973 PCE congress stated that "the sole way to freedom, well-being and progress is the national-liberation, anti-imperialist, anti-feudal and democratic revolution with its subsequent progress toward socialism." Some policies of the military government were regarded as at least partially constructive, while others were not.

The PCE views the existing agrarian reform law of 1973 as inadequate, since "genuine agrarian reform should mean a real change of structures," whereas "increased production based on maintaining outdated forms of land ownership, or on imposing capitalist-type enterprises on these structures, cannot be called agrarian reform" (*El Pueblo*, 1975). The 1975 CTE congress called for the end of feudal landownership; possession of the land by those who work it, whether collectively or individually; a limit to individual ownership of land; technical assistance for peasants, a guaranteed market for products at remunerative prices; and improvement of rural conditions of education, health, and housing (*WFTU Flashes*, 9 July).

Problems of inflation and monetization, resulting from the government's oil-related policies, are seen as having worsened the condition of the masses, and thus as constituting an "explosive weapon of popular intervention," enhancing revolutionary consciousness. Government policies intended to placate the "plutocratic sectors" contribute further to a radicalization of public opinion (*El Tiempo*, 17 April). In general, the PCE continues to follow the guidelines of the 1973 congress: the necessity of working with peasants and workers, appealing to the middle sectors, and maintaining that "a national-liberation front must be created as the main tool of our revolution" (*YICA, 1975*, pp. 509-10).

International Views. At its 1975 plenums the PCE Central Committee praised the Communist Party of the Soviet Union on the 30th anniversary of victory over Nazi Germany (*IB*, no. 6-7) and backed the government denunciation of the January 1975 U.S. Trade Act (*WMR*, no. 3). The Communist Party of Cuba continued to be viewed favorably, and a PCE delegation attended a conference of Latin American communist parties in Havana on 9-13 June (ibid., no. 8; see Cuba, Appendix.)

Publications. The PCE weekly *El Pueblo*, founded in 1946, is published in Guayaquil. Its 1,000th number appeared 24 April 1975.

*   *   *

The PCMLE. The Marxist-Leninist Communist Party of Ecuador was first established in 1963 and was split into three factions by 1968. One of these, led by Rafael Echeverría, has been regarded by the Chinese as the authentic PCMLE. *En Marcha*, organ of the PCMLE Central Committee, frequently denounces U.S. and Soviet "imperialism" in parallel terms (*Peking Review*, 5 September 1975).

University of North Carolina   John D. Martz

El Salvador

The Communist Party of El Salvador (Partido Comunista de El Salvador; PCES) was officially founded in March 1930, although communist groups had been active in the country since 1925. Since its attempted revolt in 1932, the party has been illegal. It currently operates through a front organization, the National Democratic Union (Unión Democrática Nacionalista; UDN). The guerrilla group known as the People's Revolutionary Army (Ejército Revolucionario del Pueblo; ERP) is the military arm of the party.

The PCES is estimated to have 100 to 200 members. El Salvador, the smallest and most densely populated country on the mainland of the Western Hemisphere, has a population of around 4.1 million.

The gap between wealthy and poor is great and continues to grow, with an unemployment rate of 20 percent and an annual inflation rate of 60 percent. Behind a semblance of democracy, the government is a military dictatorship, headed by President Colonel Arturo Armando Molina (see *YICA, 1975,* p. 511). The PCES is pro-Soviet.

Leadership and Organization. The PCES secretary-general is Jorge Shafick Handal. A prominent figure, and well-known poet and intellectual, was Roque Dalton García (see below).

In addition to its legal embodiment in the UDN, the PCES controls a major labor organization, the United Federation of Salvadorian Unions (Federación Unida de Sindicatos Salvadoreños; FUSS), which enrolls some 12,000 workers.

The communist front organization, the UDN, has joined with the Christian Democratic Party and the left-wing but non-communist National Revolutionary Movement to form the National Opposition Union (Unión Nacional Opositara; UNO).

In addition to the PCES-backed and Moscow-oriented ERP, there are a number of small Marxist guerrilla movements, the most prominent of which are the Maoist-Castroite Popular Liberation Forces (Fuerzas Populares de Liberación; FPL), the National Liberation Front (Frente Nacional de Liberación; FNL), and the Workers Revolutionary Organization (Organización Revolucionario de Trabajadores; ORT).

Domestic Activities. The year 1975 witnessed a continuation of the violence so marked in 1974, along with growing internal disputes within the Marxist movements. In November 1974 the government itself gave fresh impetus to the violence by massacring a peaceful demonstration at Cayetana where peasants, under the leadership of a radical priest, were demanding genuine land reform. In retaliation, the FPL kidnaped an important coffee grower on 6 December. Several political leaders were assassinated around the same time.

In May 1975, Roque Dalton García, the leader of the ERP, was murdered by a dissident element of that group. The ERP accused the dissidents of "manifestations of a petty bourgeois deviation that attempts to impose itself on the proletarian consciousness of the great majority of the ERP cadres." (*Latin America*, 22 August.) To call attention to this pronouncement, the ERP set off two small bombs on the campus of the National University in early June. A bomb was also exploded by the ORT at the Salvadorian Tourist Institute on 19 July. No one was hurt, although the bomb was of considerable magnitude. The ORT communiqué announced: "If the bourgeoisie and imperialists give us violence, we will give them violence also" (*FBIS*, 23 July).

In July the "Miss Universe Contest" at San Salvador gave rise to violent demonstrations against the 1.5 million dollars the government spent on it. When these demonstrations were quashed, a massive rally of university students and unionists followed on 30 July. The National Guard fired on this gathering, killing 12 and wounding numerous others, and President Molina put the blame on "a communist plot." (*Latin America*, 22 August.)

The UNO parties led a demonstration against the massacre on 13 August and the ERP took over 2 radio stations to broadcast propaganda. On 16 August, police raided an ERP hideout and after a battle captured three terrorists and the tapes which had been played over the air, along with a quantity of arms and ammunition.

On 22 September the ERP attempted to kidnap Rodolfo Dutriz, assistant director of *La Prensa Gráfica* and member of one of the ruling families. Though he was seriously wounded, the attempt failed. Evidently in retaliation, Rafael Aquiñada Carranza, the secretary-general of FUSS, was murdered by the right-wing terrorist group known as the Falange.

Evidence of continuing dissent within the communist party was shown when the ERP seized control of eight radio stations on 2 November. According to the official government information bulletin, the ERP broadcast a message attacking UDN participation in the UNO coalition for the national and municipal elections scheduled for March 1976. (*FBIS*, 3 November.) At the end of the month, members of the ERP wounded a policeman who had discovered them painting slogans on the walls of the national stadium. The ERP—which the Argentine news agency LATIN (1 December; *FBIS*, 3 December) identified as "the armed wing of the outlawed Marxist-Leninist Salvadorian Revolutionary Party (PRS)"—warned the police not to interfere in their activities.

International Activities and Contacts. PCES secretary-general Jorge Shafick Handal visited Romania in July 1975 at the request of the Central Committee of that country's communist party and met with its secretary-general, Nicolae Ceauşescu. Their communiqué pledged solidarity and an intention to expand ties and interests. (*FBIS*, 18 July.)

Eastern Connecticut State College   Thomas P. Anderson

Guadeloupe

The Guadeloupean Communist Party (Parti Communiste Guadeloupéen; PCG) originated in 1944 as the Guadeloupe Federation of the French Communist Party, which in March 1958 transformed itself into the present autonomous party. In recent years the PCG has been plagued by conflict and expulsions, and the communist left in Guadeloupe is now represented by several diffuse groups in addition to the PCG.

The PCG is legal. It claimed 1,500 members in 1972 (*WMR*, April 1972). The United States State Department has estimated its membership as 3,000 (*World Strength of the Communist Party Organizations*, Washington, D.C., 1974). The population of Guadeloupe is 352,000 (estimated 1975).

The PCG is an active and effective participant in Guadeloupe's political life, on both local and departmental levels. (As one of France's overseas departments, Guadeloupe is an integral part of the French Republic.) With one seat in the French National Assembly (Hégésippe Ibéné) and 10 of the 31 seats in the Guadeloupe General Council, the PCG is the strongest single party on the council and the most powerful communist party in any of the French overseas departments (see *L'Humanité*, Paris, 2 October 1973). In elections held in January and February 1975 to the newly created Departmental Commission and Regional Council (see below), two PCG leaders, Paul Lacave and Hermann Songeons, were appointed. According to the official organ of the PCG, both organizations were dominated by leftist parties (*L'Etincelle*, 22 February).

Leadership and Organization. The PCG is headed by Guy Daninthe as first secretary. Other prominent leaders include Réné Georges, Bernard Alexis, Gerty Archimede, Henri Bangou, Jérôme Cléry, H. Ibéné, P. Lacave, Raymond Baron, Serge Pierre-Justin, H. Songeons, Dunières Talis, and Pierre Tarer. Bangou is mayor of Point-à-Pitre, the largest city of Guadeloupe. Cléry is mayor of Basse Terre, its capital. Ibéné and Lacave are also mayors.

The PCG, according to G. Daninthe, is organized in 11 "sections" and 50 "nuclei." A large number of its members are said to be workers, many of whom are engaged in the growing of sugar cane, the island's main economic activity. (*WMR*, April 1972.)

The PCG has strong influence in Guadeloupe's largest trade Union, the General Confederation of Labor of Guadeloupe (Confédération Générale du Travail de la Guadeloupe; CGTC), which has some 5,000 members. H. Songeons is the current CGTC secretary-general. The party's youth front, the Union of Communist Youth of Guadeloupe (Union de la Jeunesse Communiste de la Guadeloupe; UJCG), has limited influence among young people. The party is influential also within the Union of Guadeloupean Women (Union des Femmes Guadeloupéenes; UFG), which is affiliated with the Soviet-controlled Women's International Democratic Federation. The president of the UFG is Marcelle Bangou.

Departmental and National Views and Positions. The PCG-initiated movement to attain the right of self-determination for Guadeloupe picked up strength during 1975. The alliance of leftist parties, developed in 1974 with the French presidential elections, culminated on 15 January 1975 in the formation of a Permanent Committee of the Left in Guadeloupe (Comité Permanent de la Gauche en Guadeloupe; CPGG). This common front, composed of the PCG, the Socialist Movement of Guadeloupe, the Progressive Movement of Guadeloupe, and the Socialist Federation of Guadeloupe, declared itself to be "ready to draft a statute to give Guadeloupe decision-making power within the framework of the French Republic" (*L'Etincelle*, 18-25 January).

The member parties of the CPGG published a statement deploring the present economic situation of the island, which they described as characterized by a high rate of unemployment, inflation, a threatened sugar cane growing and sugar industry, and a constant exodus of its young people to France (ibid., 18-25 January). In February, the CPGG organized a protest in Abymes to demand 100 francs per ton of sugar cane for the small and medium-sized sugar cane growers.

Following French President Giscard d'Estaing's decision to establish a policy of "economic departmentalization" in the French overseas territories, elections were held with Guadeloupe's General Council to form a Departmental Commission and a Regional Council. PCG members Lacave and Songeons were elected to the seven-member Departmental Council while various sympathetic non-Communist leftists were elected to the Regional Council. In reporting this news, the PCG party organ noted that while the main objective of the left is to secure Guadeluope's self-determination, it had decided to participate in these new bodies to "thwart the prefect's power, oppose the creation of new taxes, demonstrate the vanity of the [French] institutions, and use these bodies as a springboard toward the triumph of the right to self-determination" (ibid., 22 February).

In various statements throughout the year, the PCG continued to express its concern regarding what was perceived as a serious and deteriorating economic crisis in Guadeloupe. In Central Committee communiqués (ibid., 1 February, 30 March, and 11 October), the party noted the increase in the number of strikes, the extensive migration of the Guadeloupean youth to France, and the accentuated cultural alienation. In addition, the PCG called for a rate of 100 francs per ton of sugar cane cut in 1974 and a minimum rate of 110 francs for that cut in 1975.

The party organ reported successful actions undertaken by the CGTG in various strikes by dock and banana workers. Reportedly, such strikes resulted in higher wages and improved working conditions (ibid., 5 April). A CGTG-organized work stoppage held on 10 July in Pointe-à-Pitre and Basse Terre to protest the island's economic situation was said to have resulted in a high participation of banana, construction, dock, and petrochemical plant workers (ibid., 19 July).

The two CPG front organizations, the UFG and the UJCG, engaged in minor activities during the year. The UFG celebrated the International Women's Day on 8 March, with an attendance claimed to be close to 1,000 women.

In relations between the PCG and its parent French Communist Party (PCF), the most important event of 1975 was the holding of a meeting in Paris on 28-30 January between the leaders of the communist parties of Guadeloupe, Réunion, and Martinique and the French Communist Party. A similar meeting had taken place in 1966, at which time apparently the communist parties of the French territories had expressed their position in favor of self-determination. At the end of the 1975 meeting, the four parties issued a joint communiqué in which the PCF restated that "France must allow the people of the Antilles and Réunion to have the right to self-determination." The same communiqué stated that a popular and democratic autonomy in these islands would include: a) a legislative assembly elected by universal suffrage, b) an executive responsible to the Assembly, and c) a permanent body for cooperation with France. (Ibid., 8 February.) The same communiqué described as "dangerous concessions" the recent military, political, and economic plans agreed upon by France and the USA. A second meeting between the PCG and PCF occurred on 7-12 April when a delegation of the PCF, led by Etienne Fajon, Secretary of the Central Committee, visited Guadeloupe, where similar matters were discussed. The French delegation visited several factories in the island and reportedly met with labor leaders. In addition, it held a "friendly talk" with representatives of the CPGG.

International Views and Positions. The PCG continued to be a strong supporter of the Soviet Union and its party organ frequently ran articles about life under socialism in the USSR. Its Şecretary-General Daninthe was in the Soviet Union early in November where he met with B. Ponomarev, member of the Central Committee of the Communist Party of the Soviet Union (*Pravda*, 4 November).

PCG representatives attended meetings in Cuba on 17 January-7 February (to serve in a jury of Latin American writers and literary critics) and on 5-7 September (to attend the International Conference of Solidarity with Puerto Rico). Early in the year, Juan Solís Castro, member of the Central Committee of the Communist Party of Ecuador, visited Guy Daninthe in Guadeloupe. Solís Castro was reported to have said that his party was offering critical support to the military government of Ecuador in its program of nationalization, struggle against imperialism, and cooperation with socialist nations (ibid., 18-28 January).

Publications. The PCG publishes a weekly newspaper, *L'Etincelle*, with a claimed circulation of 9,000 (occasionally reaching 15,000 during special events).

*   *   *

In addition to the PCG there are at least two other Marxist-Leninist parties in Guadeloupe: The Combat Ouvrier (Worker Combat) and the G.O.N.G. (Guadeloupe National Organization Group). Combat Ouvrier joined the PCG, the CGTG, the UFG, and the UJCG in the creation of the Guadeloupe Committee of Solidarity with and Support to the Independence of Puerto Rico in July (*L'Etincelle*, 2 August). No news was reported during the year of the activities carried out by the G.O.N.G.

Guadeloupe has also a Trotskyist group, the Socialist Revolution Group (GRS), formed in 1973 and which represents the Fourth International in the Antilles. No developments were reported for this group, which appeared to concentrate its activities in Martinique during 1975.

The PCG organ carried an article on 22 February announcing that former members of the Guadeloupe Federation of the Socialist Party had formed a new party, the Guadeloupe Socialist Party.

Mountain View, Calif.   Eric Stromquist

Guatemala

The communist party in Guatemala, which since 1952 has been called the Guatemalan Party of Labor (Partido Guatemalteco del Trabajo; PGT), originated in the predominantly communist-controlled "Socialist Labor Unification," founded in 1921. This group became the Communist Party of Guatemala (Partido Comunista de Guatemala; PCG) in 1923 and joined the Communist International in 1924. Increasing communist activities among workers during the mid-1920s were cut off by the end of the decade and were kept at a minimum throughout the dictatorship of Jorge Ubico (1921-1944). In 1946-47 new Marxist groups appeared in the trade union and student movements, organized in the clandestine "Democratic Vanguard." At an underground Congress held in 1949 this group took the name PCG. A prominent communist labor leader founded a second and parallel communist party in 1950, called the "Revolutionary Workers' Party of Guatemala." The two groups merged into a single PCG in 1951. In 1952 the PCG adopted the name PGT, which it has continued to use. The PGT operated legally between 1951 and 1954 and played an active role in the administration of Jacobo Arbenz. The party was outlawed in 1954 following the overthrow of Arbenz. It has operated underground since then. Although the party has some influence among students, intellectuals, and workers, it does not play any significant role in national affairs. The last national election was held in March 1974 with the Conservative coalition candidate General Kjell Laugerud García winning a disputed victory over his non-Communist Left opponent.

The PGT is estimated to have 750 members. The population of Guatemala is 5,850,000 (1974 estimate).

Three guerrilla groups have operated in Guatemala in recent years; the Revolutionary Armed Forces, which is the military arm of the PGT; the Rebel Armed Forces, at least some of whose members claim affiliation with the PGT (Fuerzas Armadas Rebeldes; FAR); and the 13 November Revolutionary Movement (Movimiento Revolucionario 13 de Noviembre; MR-13). The Revolutionary Armed Forces and the FAR are believed to have fewer than 100 members each, plus several hundred sympathizers. If the MR-13 continues to exist, its activities are no longer specifically identified with the movement in the Guatemalan press. Both the size of membership and the scope of operations of all three groups were severely reduced by the effective counterinsurgency tactics of the Guatemalan military during the "law-and-order" administration of General Carlos Arana Osorio (1970-1974). Official statements concerning the existence and activities of the FAR and "other" guerrilla bands during 1975 were highly contradictory (see "Domestic Views and Activities"). The guerrilla situation is further complicated by the continued presence of non-ideological groups of bandits who engage in kidnapings and other acts of violence.

Political violence documented in 1974 does not appear to have diminished appreciably, if at all, in 1975. Amnesty International compiled a dossier of 134 cases of political murder reported in the Guatemalan press between 1 July 1974 and 31 January 1975. AI's report concluded that the torture and murder of political dissidents "is tacitly condoned, if not expressly supported," by the Guatemalan government (*Intercontinental Press*, 8 September). In December 1974 the Director General of the National Police complained about the insufficient number of policemen to control what he characterized as "communist subversion" and the "latent guerrilla threat that may possibly be in a reorganizational phase" (*El Imparcial*, 12 December). During a series of press conferences in February, the Guatemalan Minister of Government referred to "the dramatic climate of violence in the country" and stated that "political violence and common delinquency would be uncontrollable even if we had an additional 20,000 police agents." General Vassaux attributed the resurgence of violence in general to "armed bands representing diverse ideologies, the absence of moral and ethical values, the increase in drug consumption, personal vengeance and land disputes, and the more general social problems related to unemployment, alcoholism, and population growth." The Minister predicted no decrease in the levels of violence until the root causes were attacked. In a revealing statement, it was disclosed that Guatemala, with a population of almost six million, employs only 4,000 police agents, 2,000 of whom are located in the capital. Of these 4,000, over 300 agents had been discharged recently for "unethical behavior," and 90 percent of those were under indictment for "serious breeches of conduct." (Ibid., 6 and 14 February.) Government officials have speculated that large numbers of ex-policemen are responsible for the organization of delinquent bands whose activities are frequently indistinguishable from those of guerrilla units. One such agent was discovered to be the leader of an extortionist band that had been operating in the region of Esquintla for nine months (ibid., 7 August).

Acts of violence by leftist organizations and clandestine movements of the right occurred with alarming frequency during 1975 and continued to spread fear among residents in both urban and rural areas. The self-named "Death Squadron" created in 1974 claimed its first victim in January (*El Imparcial*, 18 January), and the extreme right-wing Organized Anti-Communist Movement (MANO) was reportedly active at mid-year (ibid., 22 July). One Guatemalan daily reported that "paid killers" were being imported to "create chaos and confusion" and "to punish those who cooperated with subversive leftist organizations" (*La Tarde*, 3 April). The murder of a news correspondent for *La Nación* in El Progreso on 19 July prompted the influential Association of Guatemalan Journalists (APG) to appeal to the government for stronger guarantees for freedom of the press (*El Imparcial*, 21 July). A former member of Arbenz' General Staff, Roberto Cruz Wer, was murdered several days later in the same province, apparently the victim of one of the extreme rightist organizations. Leftist organizations of unidentified origins were equally active in perpetrating political crimes. In January the Duarte Villeda brothers who had collaborated with the government in its effective anti-guerrilla campaign in the early 1970s were murdered within two days of each other (ibid., 24 January). At least 20 peasants suspected of being government informers were brutally murdered in separate incidents in the San Marcos and Zacapa areas between April and June (ibid., 19 April, 30 May, 14 and 26 June). In mid-December a new group calling itself the People's Guerrilla Army (Ejército Guerillero del Pueblo; EGP) killed a congressional deputy and promised that similar executions of anti-communists would follow (*FBIS*, Latin America, 15 December). Despite the obvious continuation of political violence emanating from both extremes of the political spectrum, the Guatemalan Minister of Defense announced on 5 August that "Communist guerrillas do not exist in Guatemala" and the country is experiencing "complete tranquility (ibid., 6 August).

Leadership and Organization. Little information is available on the present leadership and organization of the PGT. As reported last year, the bullet-riddled body of Humberto Alvarado Arellano, general secretary of the PGT, was found on 21 December. According to PGT and other Communist sources, Alvarado was arrested, tortured, and assassinated by "repressive agencies of Guatemala" (*IB*, No. 1, 1975). According to official government sources, Alvarado was wounded while police were attempting to rescue a kidnap victim, but no responsibility was assumed for the appearance of his body the following day. Alvarado was eulogized by the Communist press as "a leading member of the international communist and labor movement and a staunch fighter against imperialism and local oligarchy" (*WMR*, February). As a member of the PGT since its founding, he was accused by the government of having organized previous kidnapings and of having served as an intermediary for the PGT in Mexico for supplying money from the Soviet Union to support the FAR (*El Imparcial*, 23 December 1974). (The incident is reminiscent of September 1972 when six members of the PGT's Central Committee were killed, including general secretary Bernardo Alvarado Monzón, apparently by the police or the army). Alvarado Arrellano, who frequently wrote under the alias Miguel Rodríguez, has been succeeded as general secretary by Isías de León. Other prominent members of the Central Committee are Pedro Gonzales Torres and Otto Sánchez. The PGT publishes an illegal newspaper, *Verdad.*

The PGT has a youth auxiliary, the Patriotic Youth of Labor (Juventud Patriótica del Trabajo). Student agitators are active at both the secondary and university levels, although any affiliation with the PGT is disclaimed. PGT youth members were undoubtedly responsible in part for the "subversive plan" operating through the secondary schools that was denounced by President Laugerud in February (ibid., 28 February). However, the student group believed to have been supported by the PGT was unsuccessful in its effort to win the student elections held at San Carlos University in May. Members of the PGT's youth movement attended a two-week seminar on the Cuban Revolution held in Havana in June (*Granma*, English edition, 13 July).

The PGT also controls the clandestine Guatemalan Autonomous Federation of Trade Unions (Federación Autónoma Guatemalteca), a small and relatively unimportant labor organization. The Federation became an affiliated member of the World Federation of Trade Unions (WFTU) in October 1974. The WFTU expressed its "indignation" over the assassination of Alvarado and called for an end to "fascist violence" in Guatemala (*WFTU Bulletin*, 30 January).

Domestic Attitudes and Activities. During talks with Soviet leaders in March, the PGT's new general secretary stressed the difficulties of conducting party activities under "conditions of terror and persecution." De León spoke of the Guatemalan communists' resolve to continue their "courageous struggle in defense of the Guatemalan working people's vital interests, against the domination of imperialist monopolies and the local oligarchy, and for democracy and social progress" (*Pravda*, 13 March).

Writing in the *World Marxist Review* (August), Central Committee member Otto Sánchez defined the party's tactics as "designed to stimulate the growth of the democratic movement that has been in evidence since 1973. . . . Following a policy of unity is a difficult but feasible task for our Party. Experience shows that diverse democratic and progressive parties and organizations can join a united front given a broad and specific program expressing their common interests. It is on the basis of using all potentialities and relying on the masses . . . that we try to assure the hegemony of the working class as we build up the worker-peasant alliance." Although not an official statement of party policy, Sánchez' remarks represent a change in emphasis from the position formulated at the PGT's last Congress in 1969 when the main struggle of the party was "to carry out an agrarian anti-imperialist people's revolution" (*WMR*, January 1974).

In its analysis of the domestic political situation, the PGT hopes to "narrow the social and political base of counter-revolution, isolate it and aggravate its internal antagonisms" (ibid., August). In this respect, the internal divisions and "antagonisms" that have occurred both within and between the coalition of parties that elected President Laugerud in 1974 have required no visible agitation from the PGT. By mid-year, the extreme right-wing National Liberation Party (MLN) had lost much of its influence within the ruling coalition, receiving only two of the top seven posts in Congress. The Institutional Democratic Party (PID) and the Organized Aranista Coalition (CAO) divided the rest. Guatemala's major opposition parties, the Revolutionary Party (PR) and the Christian Democratic Party (PDC) allied themselves with the PID and the CAO in return for the chairmanship of some of the key 15 congressional committees (*Latin America*, 27 June).

In September, reports by the Government Ministry and the National Police accused the PGT of intensifying its clandestine propaganda activities throughout the country on the occasion of its 26th anniversary. In addition to "exploding bombs" and "painting placards," a brochure called *Voz Proletaria* was distributed in the capital (*El Imparcial*, 1 October).

The resurgence of guerrilla activity in various parts of the country cannot be attributed solely to the influence of the PGT. However, it does appear that the FAR's activities in 1975 were more closely associated with the PGT than at any since the late 1960s. Three persons captured in connection with the FAR kidnaping of industrialist Robert Abularach in December 1974 reportedly confessed their affiliation with the PGT (ibid., 23 December 1974). In late April the Defense Minister affirmed that "all guerrillas have been eradicated from Guatemala" and that "the assaults and robberies now being committed in the countryside are the work of common criminals" (*Prensa Libre*, 1 May). However, within weeks police announced the existence of guerrilla outbursts in the zone around San Marcos and Quetzaltenango. It was reported that a high leader within the FAR's ranks, Leopoldo Lucas Jollave, was killed in one skirmish. Lucas had been sought for six months as the coordinator of various guerrilla cells operating in the region (*El Imparcial*, 22 May). In July, military patrols skirmished with an alleged guerrilla band operating in Alta Verapaz and continued a sweeping search covering a wide sector of the Las Minas Mountain region of Chiquimula and Zacapa. The latter patrol was reported to be in pursuit of a guerrilla unit headed by Valentín Ramos (ibid., 7 July). Public spokesmen for the military initially denied the existence of any guerrillas operating in the region and announced that the military was cooperating with civil authorities in their struggle against the recent increase in "banditry" headed by Ramos. The reported skirmish of 5 July was attributed to "routine training maneuvers" (ibid., 8 July). However, on 9 July the National Defense Minister, General Romeo Lucas García, announced that "in view of the resurgence of guerrilla activity in northwestern Guatemala, the army has assumed absolute control of the nation's security to prevent attacks." The discovery of a number of arms caches in Quiché and Huehuetenango confirmed the existence of several guerrilla bands of undetermined size, although military sources described them as "so few in number that they do not pose a threat to the nation" (ibid., 9 July). On 5 August General Lucas admitted to the fact that "the communist subversion" had attempted recently to indoctrinate peasants in the region of El Quiché, but that the group "had been quickly discovered and dispersed" (ibid., 6 August). Toward year's end, government officials were directing their attention—and that of the public—toward themes of economic nationalism and the renewel of threats to reclaim Belize (British Honduras).

International Positions and Contacts. The PGT's positions on international issues follow those of the Soviet Union. Delegates attended a meeting of the communist parties of Latin America and the Caribbean in Havana on 9-13 June. The final document emerging from the conference reaffirmed socialism as "the only system capable of truly guaranteeing the development of Latin America." The conference energetically condemned the foreign policy of China for "flirting with Yankee imperialism, attacking the Communist parties, and frequently acting as enemy agents within the revolutionary movement." Encomiums for the military were reserved for such countries as Peru and Panama where the armed forces have become "elements of progress and even of revolutionary potentiality." The Chilean experience was cited as confirmation of "the urgency of closing ranks for the defense of democracy and against fascist threats in Latin America and its inseparable unity with anti-imperialist struggle." The document called for "unity of action" as a necessary condition to consolidate trade union unity. It defined the struggle for "democratic agrarian reform" as one of the essential elements of the worker-peasant alliance. The parties expressed their firm willingness to struggle for the future economic integration and the political unity of Latin Ameica, which they consider "an indispensable condition for survival and development." After lauding the examples of Cuba and particularly the Soviet Union, the document concluded with an appeal to struggle "for complete national liberation and full independence of our countries, for democracy, people's welfare, world peace and socialism." (*Granma*, English edition, 16 June.)

During de León's visit to Moscow in March, he reaffirmed the PGT's full support for the CPSU's measures to implement the peace program adopted by the 24th Congress and he wished the Soviet people "further great successes in resolving the tasks of building communism." Representatives of the two countries expressed themselves in favor of "the further cohesion of the ranks of the international communist movement on the basis of the principles of Marxism-Leninism and proletarian interna-tionalism." De León expressed the PGT's "profound gratitude" to the CPSU and the Soviet people for "their broad proletarian solidarity with the communists and all Guatemalan democrats" (*Pravda*, 13 March).

Washington College   Daniel L. Premo

Guyana

The People's Progressive Party (PPP) of Guyana was founded in 1950. At its First Congress, in 1951, it declared itself a nationalist party, committed to socialism, national independence, and Caribbean unity. During the nearly two decades following, the leadership of the PPP claimed to be Marxist-Leninist, but the party was not officially affiliated with the international communist movement. In 1969 the leader of the party, Cheddi Jagan, moved unequivocally to align the PPP with the Soviet Union and, in turn, the PPP was recognized by Soviet leaders as a bona fide communist party.

The PPP is a legal organization and represents the major opposition to the ruling People's National Congress (PNC), a party led by one-time PPP member, the present prime minister, Forbes Burnham. Particularly after Burnham's break with the PPP in the mid-1950s, Guyanese politics followed closely the ethnic differences in the country—roughly half of the population is East Indian (and supported the PPP) while the other half is black (and supported the PNC). In July 1973 elections, however, Burnham was reelected for his third term and the PNC obtained a two-thirds majority in the parliament. When the PPP, claiming to be the majority party in the country, obtained only 26 percent of the votes (and 14 out of 53 seats in parliament), Jagan protested that fraud and illegal maneuvers had prevailed. The PPP boycotted the parliament during 1975 since, as Jagan charged at the party's 1974 Congress, it was "not representative of the people" (*Thunder*, October-December 1974). PPP influence has also been reduced by the rapidly expanding socialist policies of the PNC, ranging from nationalizations to continuous contacts between the government and socialist and Third World countries.

The membership of the PPP is unknown, though the number of active and influential Marxist-Leninists is probably less than 100. The population of Guyana is 825,000 (estimated 1975).

Leadership and Organization. Cheddi Jagan was relected secretary general of the PPP at the

August 1974 congress. Other prominent party leaders include: Ranji Chandisingh (vice-chairman), Ram Karran (member of the General Council), and Janet Jagan (secretary for international affairs). Balchand Persaud, former organizing secretary, was expelled from the PPP at mid-year for "antiparty activities."

The Progressive Youth Organization (PYO), the official youth group of the PPP, has traditionally been a source of strong personal support for Cheddi Jagan. At its Eighth Congress in April 1974, the PYO expressed its determination to help transform the PPP into a "more disciplined Marxist-Leninist party, to heal the racial wounds exacerbated by the PNC, to forge links between the working people and the youth of the country," and to increase its own effectiveness and discipline (*Thunder*, April-June 1974). The Guyana Agricultural Workers' Union (GAWU), headed by Cheddi Jagan, is made up primarily of workers in the sugar industry. The GAWU was active in several long and costly strikes among sugar workers during the year. The PPP also sponsors the Women's Progressive Organization.

Party Internal Affairs. The PPP held its 18th Congress in Georgetown on 3-5 August 1974; in attendance were 479 delegates and 170 observers from Guyana, as well as representatives from several other Latin American communist parties (see *Thunder*, October-December 1974). The party held its 25th anniversary conference in early August 1975.

According to Ranji Chandisingh, Guyana must have a mass-based Marxist-Leninist party to lead the working class in organizing and guiding the masses in the building of socialism. This party must be "equipped with the ideology of scientific socialism (Marxism-Leninism) and an understanding of the objective laws of social development" and made up of the "most advanced, conscious, and dedicated members of the working class and other working people." (*Thunder*, April-August 1975.) Party leaders insist that they must play a vanguard role firstly in educating the masses by explaining "why things are bad, why they will get worse, and what must be done to make them better," and secondly, in "organizing the people to take power—anti-imperialist, pro-democratic and pro-socialist power" (ibid., April-June 1974). At the 1974 congress, Jagan said the PPP must improve its links with the masses in order to prepare the people at all levels—workers, farmers, students, revolutionary intellectuals, small businessmen, and professionals—in every possible way "to confront the corrupt minority regime" of the PNC (ibid., October-December 1974). Special attention had to be devoted to exposing the ideological trends designed to sow confusion in and weaken the anti-imperialist struggle, namely Maoism, neo-Trotskyism, neo-pan Africanism, black capitalism, and national communism (see ibid., and *IB*, No. 17, 1974).

PPP Program from 18th Congress. At the 1974 Congress, Cheddi Jagan proclaimed the "anti-imperialist, democratic and pro-socialist" program of the PPP for the coming period. Among its points were: (1) nationalization of foreign and comprador capitalist-owned and controlled mines, plantations, factories, banks, insurance, and foreign trade; (2) planned proportional development of the economy under centralized planning and control with emphasis simultaneously on industry and agriculture instead of infrastructure; (3) transformation of the economy from primary to integrated production by making the sugar, lumber, and bauxite industries into complexes; (4) development of an all-embracing agricultural policy with land reform, diversification, and expanded production of rice, corn, bananas, livestock, and dairy products, for domestic consumption and export; (5) withdrawal from the Caribbean Common Market, which the PPP regards as an "imperialist-dominated" organization, and strengthening of Caribbean anti-imperialist unity; (6) establishment and protection of industries to replace imports wherever practicable and feasible, based on a policy of import substitution; (7) measures to curb conspicuous consumption; (8) a strict system of foreign exchange control; (9) full democracy and popular participation in all levels of government operations;

(10) a genuine policy of non-alignment with meaningful diplomatic, economic, and cultural relations with the socialist world; (11) training of administrative, diplomatic, technical, and professional personnel in socialist states; (12) imbuing the people with the "revolutionary scientific socialist (Marxist-Leninist) ideology"; (13) revising the National Insurance Scheme to provide for unemployment relief, earlier pensions, and a national health service; (14) a national house-building program; (15) effective rent and price controls; (16) settlement of border issues so that they cannot be used for launching attacks against Guyana; (17) ending corruption, nepotism, favoritism, discrimination, extravagance, "squandermania," and exclusion of depressed groups. (*Thunder*, October-December 1974.)

Domestic Attitudes and Activities. The PPP attitude toward the PNC underwent a major change during the year. Prior to the August 1975 conference, criticism was unrelenting. The PNC was described as "a minority regime manoeuvring and utilising certain aspects of socialist phraseology and concepts to serve ends that are diametrically opposite to the development of real people's democracy and socialism." Political power was in the hands of "a petty-bourgeois nationalist intelligentsia and bureaucratic capitalist elite." According to Jagan, in Guyana nationalization was "leading to state and bureaucratic capitalism coupled with corruption, extravagance, racial and political discrimination and without basic democracy at the trade union, industrial, and central and local government levels." The minority regime was "rapidly expanding the military bureaucratic apparatus, not so much to defend national sovereignty and territorial integrity as to hold down the vast majority of the people and to deny them their fundamental rights." The regime's response to growing criticism and dissatisfaction was "repression, denial of civil liberties, and extensive electoral fraud." (*Thunder*, April-August 1975.) Early in the year Jagan charged that Guyana was moving towards a "fascist, one-party state" (*Mirror*, 14 February). The 1975 budget—which the government had cleverly labeled a "people's budget"—was just another routine through which the ruling bureaucracy could "increase the sums it intends to squander on itself, and on its half-baked anti-popular schemes" (*Thunder*, January-March 1975).

Then, at the August conference, Jagan said that in order to play a vanguard role in society, the PPP had to properly assess the present situation. He noted that whereas for years the PNC government had been "obviously pro-imperialist," the situation had become less clear cut. The PNC, pushed along by changing international conditions, PPP pressure, and the lack of mass support, had in recent years undertaken some policies which called for a "more flexible approach" on the part of the PPP. Some of these were policies the PPP had long advocated, such as recognition of socialist states, support for the nonaligned and African liberation movements, attacks on capitalism, nationalizations, support for Latin American and Caribbean cooperation, and advocacy of socialism and Marxism-Leninism. In view of these changes the PPP was prepared to give its "critical support" to the PNC: "This means supporting the government in all progressive measures, criticising it for its shortcomings, and pressing it to advance boldly." Jagan declared that the PPP had never claimed to have a monopoly on socialism; if the PNC was really prepared to take the noncapitalist road and build socialism, the PPP would give its support. (*Mirror*, 5 August.) The government responded to this PPP opening by allowing Jagan wider access to the media, including his first nationally broadcast press conference in some years. Although within a month the PPP was charging the government with harassments which might jeopardize the policy of "critical support," informal meetings between Jagan and Burnham—the first in several years—began in November.

International Positions and Relations. Cheddi Jagan attended the Conference of Communist Parties of Latin America and the Caribbean held in Havana in June. In his speech to that assembly, he expressed his party's agreement with the main line of the conference declaration, namely that "the main enemy of the peoples of the Americas is U.S. imperialism; that it is the duty of all the Latin American communist parties to take the lead in uniting all the possible forces against imperialism; to isolate, weaken and destroy it." The PPP also agreed that while the immediate goal of the communist parties is anti-imperialism, it should never be forgotten that their ultimate objective is socialism. Jagan noted that anti-imperialist parties and individuals sometimes delayed or betrayed the revolutions in their countries in the end, as had Víctor Paz Estenssoro in Bolivia. He added that the petty-bourgeois regimes of Latin America were currently following two tendencies; some were moving towards authoritarian or even fascist dictatorship, whereas others were taking steps against imperialism. Jagan noted that in Guyana and other countries where positive steps were taken, the communist parties should give their support, a hint of his subsequent declaration of "critical support" for the PNC made at the August conference in Guyana. (*Thunder*, April-August 1975.)

Publications. The PPP daily newspaper is *Mirror*, edited by Janet Jagen, and the party's theoretical and discussion journal is *Thunder*, a slightly irregular quarterly, edited by Ranji Chandisingh.

Hoover Institution   William E. Ratliff
Stanford University

Haiti

The United Party of Haitian Communists (Parti Unifié des Communistes Haitiens; PUCH) was formed in 1969 by the merging of the Party of the Union of Haitian Democrats and the People's Entente Party. (For background on these parties, see *YICA, 1973*, p. 356.) The membership of the PUCH is unknown, but presumed to be less than several hundred persons. The population of Haiti is 5,100,000 (estimated 1975).

All political parties in Haiti have been outlawed since 1949. In April 1969 a law was passed declaring all forms of communist activity crimes against the state, the penalty for which would be both confiscation of property and death. The government's anti-communist campaign which followed, under François Duvalier (until his death in April 1971) and his son Jean-Claude, has decimated the ranks of the PUCH. (*Nuestra Palabra*, Buenos Aires, 28 May 1975.) Much PUCH activity has been carried on outside Haiti among exiles in Europe (especially the Soviet Union) and Cuba. The PUCH says it is disseminating revolutionary ideas, starting more cells in industry and agriculture, and forging links between the party and the workers, peasants, and other sectors of the population. The Party's national newspaper is *Bouean*, printed illegally in Haiti. Several PUCH press organs are published in Canada, Mexico and France.

Domestic and International Views. The PUCH has attempted to call national attention to what it alleges are the central dilemmas of the government of Jean-Claude Duvalier: the influence of foreign capital, inflation, political corruption, repression against all forms of opposition (especially against PUCH members), exploitation of the country's resources and the very nature of the regime itself. In its most recent "Letter to the Membership," the PUCH Central Committee wrote:

> The major tendencies of the national situation can be presented in the following manner: on the one hand, the Duvalier dictatorship, which, entangled in its own contradictions, reveals itself more and more incapable of meeting the serious problems of the country, is rotting, decomposing, and uses desperate efforts to hang on to power. On the other hand, discontent reaches more and more layers of the population, becomes deeper, wider and responds better to the efforts of our Party to channel and organize it.
>
> Despite the serious difficulties, despite appearances, the revolutionary movement sees opening before it very promising perspectives which are within the ability of our organization to bring to fruition. (*Political Affairs*, New York, October 1975.)

The party claims to be working to unite all anti-government forces against a regime that it contends is supported by outside assistance, particularly from the United States (*Nuestra Palabra*, 28 May). The Central Committee letter of 1975 went on to state: "Everywhere, even among the people in the government, there is a feeling that the situation cannot continue, that something must happen. The mafia in power is supported only by a handful of profiteers and by their foreign masters." The PUCH claims that the continued penetration of Haiti by the Pentagon and CIA only invigorates the revolutionary movement and hastens the day when the regime must fall.

The PUCH is firmly pro-Soviet in its international position. In November 1975, for example, the party sent the following telegram to the CPSU Central Committee:

> The Central Committee of the United Party of Haitian Communists sends you, dear comrades, its fraternal congratulations on the occasion of the 58th anniversary of the Great October Socialist Revolution. The Haitian communists reaffirm their unbreakable solidarity with your great party and the Soviet people, who are successfully building communism. (*Pravda*, 9 November.)

Hoover Institution   John J. Tierney, Jr.
Stanford University

Honduras

The Communist Party of Honduras (Partido Comunista de Honduras; PCH) was organized in 1927, disbanded in 1932, and reorganized in 1954. In 1967 a dispute over strategy and tactics led to a division of the PCH into rival factions. Since 1971 there has been a self-proclaimed pro-Chinese Communist Party of Honduras/Marxist-Leninist; (PCH-ML). A later division within the PCH led to the formation of the Honduran Workers' Party (Partido de los Trabajadores Hondureños; PTH).

The PCH has been illegal since 1957. In December 1972 the armed forces of Honduras overthrew the government of President Ramón Cruz in a non-violent coup. Under the leadership of General Oswaldo López Arellano (previously president 1963-1971), the situation in Honduras relaxed and the PCH, although still formally illegal, was able to operate more openly than before with occasional public meetings, radio broadcasts, and the opportunity to distribute party and other Marxist-Leninist literature in bookstores in the largest cities. On 22 April 1975, General López was replaced by Colonel Juan Alberto Melgar Castro after charges that the former accepted a $1.25 million bribe from United Brands to reduce export taxes imposed on bananas in 1974. There have been no significant changes in the status or activities of the PCH under the Melgar regime. The membership of the PCH is estimated at 500. The PCH-ML and the PTH have estimated memberships of 100 and 150 respectively. The populaton of Honduras is 2,750,000 (estimated 1975).

Leadership and Organization. The secretary general of the PCH is Dionisio Ramos Bejarano. Other important leaders are Rigoberto Padilla Rush, Secretary of the Central Committee, Milton Rene Paredes, a Central Committee member, and Mario Sosa Navarro, a member of the Political Commission. Padilla and Paredes were the PCH's principal spokesmen in international affairs and Sosa the principal spokesman in domestic affairs in 1975. Mario Morales, PCH first secretary for many years, Longino Becerra, and José Pérez, two other well-known PCH leaders in the late 1960's and early 1970's, have not engaged in public activities since 1972 for unknown reasons.

The party has been active in recruiting work among students, urban workers, banana workers on the plantations operated by United Brands and Standard Fruit Company on the North Coast and the peasant movement but is still "often forced to work underground" in certain local areas according to Paredes. (*WMR*, April 1975.)

The PCH claims that students make up 20 percent of its members. The PCH sponsors the Socialist Student Front (Frente Estudiantil Socialista; FES) and the Federation of Secondary Students (FESS). The FES is probably the second most important university student organization in the country and operates freely on the campuses of the National Autonomous University of Honduras in Tegucigalpa, the capital, and San Pedro Sula, the most important city on the North Coast. The FESS, now in its fifth year, claims a membership of more than 40,000 and Paredes writes that PCH influence "predominates" (ibid.).

The PCH has tried to influence both the National Innovation and Unity Party (Partido Inovación Unidad; PINU) and the Christian Democratic Party (PDC), neither of which has been able to obtain legal recognition. It is not known whether the PCH is attempting to influence the National Reconstruction Committee (Comité de la Reconstrución Nacional; COREN) which asked 28 May 1975, "that all ideologies be recognized and that the right to belong to any political party (*militáncia*) be established." (*FBIS*, Latin America, 21 May 1975.)

The PCH generally has been publicly silent about the currents dividing the armed forces, especially the 22-man supreme council where political power is concentrated, although the PCH recognized that factionalism exists. Currently, the supreme council is divided into three factions: conservatives, reformists, and radicals or *peruanistas* who look to Peru for models that might be implemented, especially in the area of agrarian reform.

The PCH claims to have party nuclei in the leadership of the North Coast Workers' Federation (Federación Sindical de Trabajadores Norteños de Honduras; FESITRANH) and the Central Federation of Unions of Free Workers (Federación Central de Sindicatos de Trabajadores Libres; FECESITLH), both of which are affiliated with the Inter-American Regional Organization of Workers (ORIT). Paredes also claims that PCH members have been elected to the Executive Committee of the National Association of Honduran Peasants (Asociación Nacional de Campesinos Hondureños; ANACH) "despite fierce opposition from the reactionaries," a probable reference to ORIT-influence in

FESITRANH and the Honduran Workers Confederation (CTH). (*WMR*, April 1975) Paredes admits that the PCH "would like to draw on the achievements of fraternal parties" in correcting shortcomings in the party's communications network between its leaders and individuals "in the basic units" or "nuclei." The PCH could not say that it had "made optimal use of the new situation." a reference to the return to rule under General López in a country where peasant occupation of untilled public and private land has been the principal focus of national politics since mid-1972. "In some areas, Party growth has been very slow, due primarily to sectarianism and amateurism, underestimation of mass work and reluctance to adopt new methods." (Ibid.)

Domestic Views. Shortly after General López was ousted from the presidency, the Central Committee of the PCH held its 16th Enlarged Plenum and issued a resolution on 25 May 1975 which recognized that the new government under Colonel Melgar was "made up of two warring factions. One of them comprises advocates of preserving the existing economic and political structures and the other, those who regard social change as the only way to remedy the grave state of the nation." (*IB*, No. 13.) The Party's current policy is to "promote the popular struggle for the national development plan, first of all the agrarian reform law [enacted on 20 December 1974, and promulgated 14 January 1975]." Secondly, the party must be on "guard against an eventual conspiracy of the ultra-rightist forces of imperialism and its domestic allies aimed at giving power back to the landowner and bourgeois oligarchy through various pre-election stratagems or brutal repression of the people." In addition, "Communists have a great stake in ending the division of democratic and left forces ... resolutely seeking unity of action of progressive political quarters and democratic organizations. This will be the phase preceding the formation of a democratic and anti-imperialist front." (Ibid.)

Earlier, on 5 February, the Political Commission of the PCH Central Committee issued a statement in which it analyzed the new agrarian reform law which, while it had some "positive provisions," was "essentially capitalist" in character (*IB*, No. 7). The "essentially capitalist character of the Law" was reflected in its goal of increasing the output and productivity of farming (Article 1) and of setting a "four-year time limit for uncultivated estates to be efficiently exploited." (Article 41). Among the "positive provisions," according to the PCH, was Article 35 which legalized the group occupation of untilled land (*assentamientos*) under Decree No. 8 of 26 December 1972, because the Article legalized action "carried forward through direct action by the peasants." Among the "negative provisions of the law" was Article 89 which provided that peasants would pay for the land in installments over a 20-year period, thus diverting funds "which could be used for developing agricultural production." In addition, the PCH Political Commission was unhappy with Article 170 which suspended benefits of the law "for up to two years," while also not prohibiting penal sanctions, for those who instigated or promoted the occupation of lands. Given the "contradiction of the law" and the "factionalism of the armed forces," a fundamental task of the worker-peasant alliance is (1) to see to it that the Law is applied, "not according to its negative provisions but according to the positive ones"; (2) to prevent a "rightist reform of the Law" by the National Federation of Farmers and Cattlemen of Honduras (FENAGH); (3) to seek a revision of "the most negative provisions," and (4) to demand "changes in the composition of the National Agrarian Council" (CNA) so that the number of peasants on that 8-member body would be increased over the present two as well as to see to it that "the organized working class [with no representatives at present on the CNA] is likewise represented." (Ibid.)

International Activities and Contacts. The PCH attended the meeting of the Communist Parties of Latin America and the Caribbean held 9-13 June in Havana, Cuba. Surprisingly, although the lengthy Declaration issued by the Conference on 13 June hailed the "creation of the Union of Banana Producing Countries"—without mentioning General López who was instrumental in its creation—

nothing else was said about developments in Honduras. (*Granma*, English, 22 June 1975.)

On 6 August AGERPRESS in Bucharest announced that Nicolas Ceauşescu, General Secretary of the Romanian Communist Party, met Dionisio Ramos at the seaside resort of Neptun, Romania. Besides discussing the international political situation, and communist responsibilities such as essential support for the Helsinki Treaty, the two leaders emphasized the need for their parties' "independent development on the path of economic and social progress, for a new international political and economic order. In this context, underlined was the importance of the Latin American peoples' struggle for taking the national riches into their own hands." (*FBIS*, East Europe, 7 August 1975.)

On 9 October the Honduran Government announced that it would "shortly reestablish commercial relations with Cuba and other socialist countries" in order to increase the country's export base, damaged by Hurricane Fifi in 1974 and the currently deteriorated international economic situation (*FBIS*, Latin America, 10 October).

Publications. The PCH publishes *El Trabajo*, a theoretical, political and informational journal, and a weekly newspaper *Vanguardia Revolucionaria*. Party statements are often found in the *World Marxist Review* and that journal's *Information Bulletin*.

Texas Tech University   Neale J. Pearson

Martinique

The Martinique Communist Party (Parti Communiste Martiniquais; PCM) traces its founding to July 1921. In September 1957 it became the autonomous PCM. The party is legal.

The PCM is estimated to have 1,000 members. The population of Martinique is 347,000 (estimated 1975).

The PCM is an active participant in Martinique's political life, on both local and departmental levels. (As one of France's overseas departments Martinique is an integral part of the French Republic.) In 1956 the party suffered a serious setback when one of its leaders, Aimé Césaire, withdrew to create the left-wing non-communist Martinique Progressive Party (Parti Progressiste Martiniquais; PPM). The PCM controls several municipal governments in Martinique and holds 4 seats on the 36-member General Council. The PCM has no representatives in the French National Assembly.

Leadership and Organization. The PCM's Fifth Congress was held in late December 1972. A Central Committee of 35 members and Control Commission of 3 members were elected, and Armand Nicolas was reelected secretary-general. In January 1973 the Central Committee elected a new 13-member Political Bureau: Armand Nicolas, Luc Bourgeois (propaganda secretary), René Bramban, Philipbert Duféal (organization secretary), Mathurin Gottin, Georges Gratiant, Walter Guitteaud, Victor Lamon, Gabriel Lordinot, Georges Mauvois, René Ménil, Edgar Nestoret, and Albert Platon.

The PCM controls the General Confederation of Labor of Martinique (Confédération Générale du Travail de la Martinique; CGTM) which, under the leadership of PCM Political Bureau member Lamon, is the largest trade union organization in Martinique, with some 4,000 members. The party's youth organization is the Union of Communist Youth of Martinique (Union de la Jeunesse Communiste de la Martinique; UJCM). The UJCM, disbanded in 1969 (see *YICA, 1970*), held its first congress as a reconstituted organization on 27 July. The Union of Women of Martinique (Union des Femmes de la Martinique; UFM), led by Solange Fitte-Duval, also is controlled by the PCM. In 1975, the International Women's Year, the UFM was particularly active organizing meetings and being represented at a number of domestic and international gatherings. The Second Congress of the UFM was held on 14 July 1975.

Departmental and National Views and Positions. The year 1975 was relatively uneventful for the PCM. The party concerned itself mainly with the state of the economy, its proposal for autonomy, an alliance of leftist forces, and the threat from the extreme left.

Articles in the PCM organ *Justice* identified the outstanding economic problems of the island as being low wages and massive unemployment, created largely by inappropriate measures instituted by French President Valery Giscard d'Estaing and leaders of his party (the Gaullist Union of Democrats for the Republic; UDR) in Martinique. The decline of sugar production and other industries on the island was said to be creating a consumer economy more heavily dependent on France. The Europeans within the Common Market reportedly do not want the rum, bananas, or pineapples produced in Martinique (*Justice*, 20 February). Furthermore, sugar, it was argued, could be sold to the Common Market countries at a much higher price from outside than from within. Additionally, large scale migration to an uncertain future in France by young persons from Martinique was allegedly depleting the island of an important resource (though this presumably is helping Martinique's own unemployment problem).

These problems have suggested to the PCM that the fundamental solution is political rather than the program of economic resurgence (*relance*) proposed by the French government, and that many of Martinique's economic woes would disappear or diminish significantly if the island were allowed to make its own economic decisions. The PCM, at its Fourth Congress in 1968, elaborated a program for autonomy within the French system, rather than complete independence. It has undertaken a continuous campaign to defend and promote this view since that time. The proposal would allow Martinique to direct its own affairs so that it might pursue "economic development, social progress, and a flowering of the Martinique personality," "while conserving the advantages acquired [from France] as defined at the Convention of Morne Rouge [Martinique] in 1971." (Resolution of the Central Committee of the PCM, 23 December 1974; in *Justice*, 2 January.)

The PCM apparently had mixed feelings when France granted independence to the Comoro Islands in mid-1975. Noting that the Comoro archipelago is roughly the size of Martinique, but with fewer people, a *Justice* editorial reiterated the party's position on autonomy. It condemned the splitting the Comoro Islands by retaining one of the islands under the "colonial regime" with the "pretext that there is a majority there that rejects independence" (ibid., 10 July). It was understood, the editorial concluded, that the government of the Comoro Islands had decided to accept independence in this manner and to fight for its territorial integrity in the United Nations.

The autonomy movement was supported by a coalition of leftist forces that grew out of the presidential campaign of 1974. The "Permanent Committee of the Martinique Left" (Comité Permanent de la Gauche Martiniquaise; CPGM), including the PCM, the PPM, the Socialist Federation of Martinique, the CGTM, and five other organizations, is a somewhat larger group than the island's representation at Morne Rouge in 1971. The PCM has expressed concern over statements by the Socialist Federation and the PPM which have proposed versions of autonomy slightly different from that favored by the PCM (ibid., 30 January and 27 February).

The PCM continued in 1975 to suffer attacks from the extreme left. The Trotskyist Socialist Revolution Group (GRS) concentrated on the PCM's association with the CPGM. The CPGM was, according to a GRS brochure "The Bloc of May" by Philippe Pierre-Charles, "electoralist, assimilationist, reformist, [and] dedicated to inaction, if not failure" (ibid., 27 February). The CPGM, Pierre-Charles contended, possessed an "evident desire to isolate the extreme left, and particularly the GRS." The GRS held further that it was the "nature of unity itself that it is always formed on the basis of the program of the weakest partner." The PCM denied both charges, explained its position— that revolution requires alliances of "diverse social strata and different political forces among which the degree of combativeness is also different"—and launched its counterattack. Trotskyism, according to the *Justice* account, was the "great grave-digger of revolutionary movements"; while the Leninist practice of unity has proven successful, the Trotskyist method has "never led a single working class nor any people to take power." The *Justice* article affirmed that the PCM has worked with the CPGM "without having renounced a single of the policies of its Fifth Congress." After listing a series of somewhat minor actions by the CPGM, the article indicated that one of the most important achievements has been an increasing mutual understanding of its representative organizations. *Justice* also took advantage of the opportunity to call for growth and greater mobilizing actions for the CPGM, qualifying this call by adding that this depended ultimately on the working masses of Martinique, who were well represented in the CPGM.

The PCM was threatened also by Maoists during the year. The group, "G.A.P.," whose members "camouflage themselves without saying their names," according to *Justice* (16 January), has reportedly "begun war" against the CGTM. These Maoists have allegedly sought to attract CGTM members to their own Union of Agricultural Workers of Martinique.

Two major meetings between the PCM and its parent French Communist Party (PCF) occurred during 1975. On 27-30 January Secretary-General Nicolas and Secretary Roland Leroy met in Paris with PCF leaders and leaders of communist parties from other overseas departments. The talks centered on subjects of mutual interest—self-determination of the overseas departments, immigration policies, and application of French credits in these departments. The PCF lent its "full support" to the objectives of the Convention of Morne Rouge. On 1-7 April, a PCF delegation, led by Etienne Fajon, member of the Secretariat and deputy of the National Assembly, reiterated many of the PCF statements made in Paris and was shown through the municipal strongholds of the PCM.

International Views and Positions. The PCM position on international affairs coincides in all important respects with that of the French Communist Party, which it praises as its chief ally in the struggle against "anti-colonialism." The party condemns the leaders of the People's Republic of China (PRC) and carries articles on pro-Soviet or non-aligned communist parties on major occasions. On 4 December, *Justice* carried an article characterizing leaders of the PRC as "irresponsible" for their negative attitude toward efforts for a Soviet-American détente. *Justice* declared that "to isolate Maoism is the duty of all communists."

The nation receiving perhaps the greatest coverage in the PCM press during 1975 was Cuba. The founding assembly of the Martinique-Cuba Association, held on 25 June at Fort-de-France, was sponsored or at least fully supported by the PCM. Secretary-General Nicolas represented the PCM, which was one of the five communist parties from the Antilles attending the Conference of Latin American and Caribbean Communist parties in Havana on 9-13 June.

The PCM applauded the "liberation" of South Vietnam and Cambodia during the year. The party expressed "total solidarity with the revolutionary and progressive forces in Portugal, particularly the Portuguese Communist Party," which were fighting to "block fascism" and "open the path to socialism in favor of the working masses" (ibid., 28 August). Representatives of the CPGM attended an International Conference of Solidarity with Puerto Rico, which took place in Havana on 5-7 September.

Publications. The PCM publishes a weekly newspaper, *Justice*, which claims a circulation of 8,000. It has also an irregular theoretical journal, *Action*.

Mountain View, Calif.   Eric Stromquist

Mexico

The Mexican Communist Party (Partido Comunista Mexicano; PCM) was founded in 1919. Originally the party was called the Communist Party of the Mexican Proletariat to distinguish it from another communist organization then in existence. In the spring of 1920, after the assassination of Venustiano Carranza and the demise of the other communist group, the party changed its name to the Mexican Communist Party and was recognized as such by the Comintern (the Communist International).

The PCM is composed primarily of intellectuals, students and elements of the middle class; it is not, and never has been, a party of the workers and peasants. Over the last few years, the estimated size of the party has been approximately 5,000 members. Although the PCM has legal status, it has not been able to meet the legal membership requirement of 65,000 to enter candidates in national elections. There are no communist party members in Congress. However, the PCM claims that it does fulfill the qualifications for registration as a party, and participation in the 1976 presidential elections, but that it does not wish to submit the names and addresses of its members to the government.

Several other Marxist-Leninist political parties and groups continue to operate, and we can divide these into socialists, Trotskyites and guerrillas. There are three political parties which refer to themselves as socialist. In 1947 the Partido Popular was founded by the late Vicente Lombardo Toledano, and the following year it became the Popular Socialist Party (Partido Popular Socialista; PPS). In 1963 the party merged with the communist-oriented Partido Obrero y Campesino de México. Like the PCM, the PPS appeals primarily to some intellectuals and certain elements of the middle class. However, unlike the PCM, the PPS in recent years has been able to meet the minimum legal number for registration to have candidates on the printed ballot. The party continues to claim 75,000 members. In recent elections the PPS received just under 500,000 votes, approximately 3.5 percent, allowing it to have 10 seats in congress (4.4 percent).

In 1972 several student leaders of the 1968 movement met with others to discuss the possibility of forming a new workers' party. The group eventually split and two political parties emerged: the Mexican Workers Party (Partido Mexicano de los Trabajadores; PMT) in 1974 and the Socialist Workers Party (Partido Socialista de los Trabajadores; PST) in 1975. Neither party registered the minimum number of voters to be placed on the ballot for the 1976 elections. The PMT claims 45,000 members. The PST claims 45,000 members. The PST claims that it registered over 100,000 voters, almost double the minimum requirement to be placed on the ballot, but the deadline had passed.

Other groups which refer to themselves as socialist are the Unified Socialist Action Movement

(Movimiento de Acción Unificada Socialista; MAUS), the Socialist Organization Movement (Movimiento de Organización Socialista; MOS), the Socialist Popular Youth (Juventud Popular Socialista; JPS), and the National Confederation of Democratic Youth (Confederación Nacional de Jóvenes Democráticos; CNJD), formed in 1975.

There are two Trotskyite groups which are "sympathizing organizations" of the Fourth International in Mexico. The Internationalist Communist Group (Grupo Comunista Internacionalista; GCI) was founded in 1968. The Socialist League (Liga Socialista; LS) was formed a few years later as a result of a split in the GCI.

Another group is the Mexican section of the "Latin American Labor Committee," described by its members as a "Marxist-Luxemburgist" movement.

Various guerrilla groups have been operating for several years. However, in contrast to 1974, when at least eight identifiable guerrilla groups were active, only the 23 September Communist League (Liga Comunista 23 Septiembre; the League) carried on sustained activities in 1975. Established in 1967 and taking its name from an abortive guerrilla attack on a Chihuahua army post that same year, the League operated in 1975 through various affiliates—the Red Brigade (Brigada Roja), the 15 June Brigade (Brigada 15 Junio) and the 23 September Bolshevik Brigade (Brigada 23 Septiembre Bolchevique). Although there were rumors of a new guerrilla leader in the state of Guerrero, the Party of the Poor (Partido de Los Pobres), also established in 1967, did not recover from the death of its leader Lucio Cabañas Barrientos.

The Setting. There are four political parties represented in Congress—the Institutional Revolutionary Party (Partido Revolucionario Institucional; PRI), the National Action Party (Partido de Acción Nacional, PAN), the Authentic Party of the Mexican Revolution (Partido Auténtico de la Revolución Mexicana; PARM), and the PPS. The PRI is the outgrowth of the political apparatus which has dominated Mexican politics and government since 1929. To the right is the conservative PAN and somewhat to the left of the PRI is the PARM, which usually supports the PRI positions and presidential candidates. Of the four, only the PPS is a Marxist-Leninist party. As far as legal representation is concerned, the PCM and the other Marxist-Leninist parties and groups are outside the political spectrum.

Although Mexico's oil findings have recently made the country a petroleum exporter, dire poverty continues to be a problem in various parts of the country. In the state of Guerrero, for example, a peon earns 10 pesos per day from sunrise to sundown. The landowners have gunmen guarding the livestock and the peons. Wages are paid in corn, salt, sugar and mezcal; thus, the equivalent of the company store still exists (*Revista de Revistas*, 9 April 1975). Such conditions are fodder for violence.

In addition to guerrilla attacks, various incidents of violence occurred in 1975 resulting in strong government reaction. At the beginning of the year, several members of the Socialist League (LS) were killed by an anti-communist group called "Los Gavilanes" (The Hawks). In March, several hundred students shouted abuse at President Echeverría when he tried to address a meeting which opened the academic year of the National University. Later, as he left the campus after cutting short his visit, he and his bodyguards were showered with bottles and pieces of brick. An official spokesman said the President was slightly grazed but not seriously hurt. According to *The New York Times* (14 March), extreme left-wing groups interpreted the President's visit as a challenge. The PCM and the PPS denounced the violence.

Early in the year, the mysterious death in jail of a PCM leader caused opposition groups to accuse the government of preparing a wave of repression against the left.

The year 1975 also witnessed serious rural unrest. Reports of clashes between squatters and state or federal police or former owners of expropriated lands came from Chihuahua and Colima. In

Hidalgo and Veracruz, peasants were shot and killed fighting for possession of farmland. In an interview with the daily *El Día* (25 August), anthropologist Salomon Nahman Sitton, associate director of the National Institute for Indian Affairs (INI), charged that the National Cattlemen's Confederation covered up such matters as the razing of the town of Canada de Colotlan in Puebla, the slaughtering of peasants in Huejutla de Reyes, and other acts of violence committed against peasants. The Mexican Agrarian Council secretary general, Humberto Seranno, petitioned the government for arms to protect the peasants from "cattlemen who are organizing a White Guards Army throughout the nation" (EFE), Madrid, 25 August). In Guerrero, where Lucio Cabañas was killed, the Professors' Union of the Autonomous University reported the disappearance of more than 800 peasants and "an undeclared state of war" against the civilian population of the state. They accused the army and the police of carrying out the persecution (EFE, Madrid, 9 August).

The event which most aroused the Mexican and foreign press occurred in the state of Sonora. On 23 October, several hundred peasants who occupied land, allegedly promised them years before, were ejected by the army and police using tear gas, machine-guns and small arms; seven people were killed, 20 seriously wounded and 60 arrested (*Latin America*, 28 November). President Echeverría dismissed the state governor, Carlos Armando Biebrich, and the state police chief fled to avoid arrest. Celestino Salcedo Monteón, leader of the powerful National Peasants Confederation (CNC), described the incident as "conceivable only in dictatorial regimes such as those of (Francisco) Franco and (Augusto) Pinochet" (LATIN, Buenos Aires, 25 October).

But while the government confronted leftist militancy within the country, it closely identified with the leftist militancy of the developing world in its foreign policy. Mexico was a founding member of the Latin American Economic System (SELA), comprised of most hemispheric countries excluding the United States, whose primary goal is to increase Latin America's power of negotiation with the more industrialized countries. The government applauded the communist victory in South Vietnam, and Secretary of the Presidency Hugo Cervantes del Rio and Foreign Secretary Emilio O. Rabasa stated, "The principles of people's self-determination and of nonintervention have won in Vietnam" (INFORMEX, Mexico City, 2 May). President Echeverría received President Nicolai Ceauşescu of Romania in the first visit by a communist head of state. Mexico also hosted the First International Congress of Third World Teachers. In the summer, President Echeverría made an extended trip to nine countries, primarily of the Middle East and Africa; he also visited Cuba and received the National Order of José Martí. Identifying with the position of many of the Third World (and communist) countries, particularly the Arab states, Mexico joined Brazil as the two Latin American countries which voted for the United Nations General Assembly resolution equating Zionism with racism and racial discrimination. (Several other Latin American countries abstained.)

The PRI nominated the Minister of Finance, José López Portillo, to be the party's presidential candidate in the 1976 electons. The party's nomination is tantamount to election. The population continued to grow at a high rate, and Mexico is estimated to have a population of 58,000,000.

The PCM. Leadership and Organization. The leading organizational bodies of the PCM are the Politburo, the Central Committee and the Executive Commission of the Central Committee. The secretary-general is Arnoldo Martínez Verdugo, a leader in the party since the 1940s. Members of the Central Committee include Reynaldo Rosas, Pablo Gómez, Liberato Terán Olguin, Gerardo Unzueta and Jesús Sosa Castro. The Executive Commission members include J. E. Pérez and Arturo Martínez Nateras.

Auxiliary and Mass Organizations. The auxiliary organizations of the party include the Mexican Communist Youth (Juventud Comunista Mexicana; JCM). The party also has several regional organizations, such as the Nadiezha Krupaskaya in Morelos.

Party Internal Affairs. At the end of December 1974, the PCM held a national conference in Mexico City. The conference summed up the party's activities since the 16th Congress (October 1973) and discussed the domestic political situation. A conference resolution noted that since the 16th Congress, party membership had grown by 35 percent.

The Central Committee met 5-6 April. Those invited to attend the plenary session included the secretaries general of regional committees and members of national commissions. The main item on the agenda was a discussion of the report "Tactical Problems of the Party at Present," presented by Arnoldo Martínez Verdugo. The Central Committee also adopted a resolution on convening the 17th Party Congress and drafted a political resolution to be submitted to the forthcoming congress for discussion. The Central Committee agreed on the following agenda for the congress: report on PCM activities since the 16th Congress, party tactics in the 1976 presidential elections, steps to improve the work of the PCM leadership and the election of a new Central Committee. Details on the congress, held in mid-December, were not available at this writing, and will be presented in next year's article.

Domestic Attitudes and Activities. At the PCM conference in December 1974, it was pointed out that "class struggle in Mexico is sharpening, there is a polarization of political forces, and pressure on the present government by imperialism and domestic big proprietors is increasing. In these conditions ... the country's democratic and anti-imperialistic forces must unite to intensify the revolutionary struggle." (*IB*, No. 2, 1975.)

The April Central Committe meeting applied Lenin's analysis of the stages of capitalism to Mexico, pointing out that the country was experiencing "tendencies toward a closer alliance of the oligarchy, government and transnational imperialist monopolies of mixed enterprises, indicating the trend toward state-monopoly capitalism." But the Central Committee also observed the appearance of new progressive organizations and parties and what it considered to be highly favorable conditions for united action by the "democratic and revolutionary forces." Because of the contradictions in the ruling class and state apparatus, mainly in connection with the change of president, the Central Committee believed it was appropriate to consider such action seriously. (*IB*, No. 11.)

For at least a year, the PCM had been calling for the creation of a leftist bloc of parties and groups which would formulate a common program and oppose the PRI in the forthcoming election. In an interview with the newspaper *El Día*, Martínez Verdugo specified who should comprise the proposed bloc of "democratic and leftist forces"—the PCM, the PPS, the PMT, the PST, the MAUS and the MOS. He also included advanced currents in the church, elements of the university, "patriotic groups" from the army, popular sectors within the PRI, and the workers' and peasants' movement. In the spring, the PCM, PMT, MAUS, and MOS formed a bloc which sought unsuccessfully to change the electoral law and to coordinate activities in the pre-electoral period. The formation of the bloc reflected a change in tactics by the PCM. Whereas in 1974 the party had been very critical of President Echeverría and called for a new revolution in Mexico, in 1975 it was careful not to criticize the president and, rather than urging a new revolution, it supported the leftist bloc to realize "authentic democratization." In a speech to party members on 22 June, Martínez Verdugo discussed in detail the "chief obstacle to the working people's upholding their rights and interests," namely the "lack of political freedoms." The present electoral system, excluding participation by the PCM and "revolutionaries and democrats" from other classes, was designed to uphold the interests of the present rulers; though there were shades of differences between the potential PRI candidates, their real or imagined differences "do not go beyond the framework of the interests of the ruling group." In the upcoming electoral campaign, "the Left in our country can play a historic role only if it acts as an independent force, with its own alternative on all issues and as a vehicle of complete renewal of economic, political and social life, and not an amorphous, scattered stream, or one that mingles with the ruling bourgeois group." (*IB*, No. 16.)

In its draft resolution to be presented to the 17th National Party Congress, the PCM strongly criticized the government's economic policy and demanded that profound changes be made. The party proposed, among other things, "the nationalization of all land, introduction of the sliding salary scale into labor laws, freezing of rents on the people's housing, active defense of world peace and solidarity with people who struggle for independence and against imperialist aggression." The party criticized reactionary forces within the country who were opposing President Echeverría. (*El Día*, 26 July.)

Throughout the latter part of 1975, the PCM continued the effort to present itself as an alternative in the forthcoming election. It criticized both the PAN and the more conservative elements within the PRI. The Central Committee condemned the method of selecting the PRI presidential candidate, and in the fall, the party issued a manifesto officially opposing the presidential candidacy of José López Portillo, accusing him of being the candidate of the Mexican and foreign financial oligarchy. The manifesto pointed out that the electoral campaign began under ominous signs, such as the negation of the political rights of the leftist parties and groups. (The government refused to amend the electoral statute.) The PCM contended that the task of giving the Mexican people an independent, leftist political alternative was becoming more important in the elections against the PRI, and its candidate, and against the PAN reactionaries. The manifesto added that it was increasingly important to struggle for a platform of change in economic policy to lighten the burdens on the exploited and oppressed people and that the leftist, democratic and progressive forces could demonstrate that there was a historic force in the country which was capable of opening a new road for the people. The PCM reiterated its condemnation of the electoral system at the congress in December and, as a symbolic gesture, nominated its own candidate, the veteran peasant leader, Valentín Campa (*El Día*, Mexico City, 15 December).

Although the PCM continued to support President Echeverría, as exemplified by the party's acceptance of the president's invitation to send a delegation to accompany him on his visit to Cuba, PCM-government relations were strained at times. The police arrested more than 20 members of the PCM, accusing them of plotting against the governments of Guatemala, El Salvador, and Honduras. A PCM leader charged with forging and printing blank birth certificates, identification documents, and passports—so that nationals of El Salvador and Guatemala could return to their countries to carry out criminal acts against their respective governments—was found dead in his cell at the beginning of the year. The police said he had committed suicide. The party's Central Committee issued a statement denying any guilt and blamed the "rightist forces" said to have infiltrated the police rather than the government of President Echeverría. In an 18 January *Pravda* article, K. Kurin viewed the incident as a "campaign of provocation" by reactionaries and imperialists seeking to "goad the official authorities to anti-communist actions."

International Views and Policies. The resolution convening the 17th Congress also analyzed international developments. The party was encouraged by the gains (as of April) of "progressive forces" in Spain and Portugal. Party leaders believed the communist victories in Cambodia and South Vietnam reflected a changed relation of world forces and were an important stimulus for the Mexican people's struggle. They supported U.S.-Soviet détente and criticized those who tried to undermine it. At the same time, "the sharpening of the general crisis of capitalism and the defeats that drive the imperialists into despair, warn us of the danger of local wars and of even bigger acts of vandalism on the international scene" (*Oposición*, 30 April). The PCM was careful not to condemn the People's Republic of China (PRC) in the Sino-Soviet dispute. It was reported (AFP, Paris, 19 June) that the PCM opposed the condemnation of the PRC, and the joint call for a world conference of communist parties, in the declaration of the June conference of Latin American communist parties in Havana.

Throughout the year the party supported the foreign policy of the Echeverría administration and joined Soviet leaders in approving such actions of the Mexican government as breaking relations with the Chilean government and improving relations with Cuba. Martínez Verdugo openly attacked the Chinese Communist Party at the 17th Congress for its policies toward the Pinochet government in Chile and the "pro-imperialist forces" in Angola, as well as for its efforts to split communist and workers parties (*FBIS*, Soviet Union, 29 December.)

International Activities and Contacts. In addition to attending the Havana conference of communist parties, representatives of the PCM participated in the Second Congress for Sovereignty and Peace in Costa Rica (August 1975), urging the Congress to include a discussion of the U.S. "colonialist enclave in Panama." In August, Martínez Verdugo and Sosa Castro visited East Germany and held talks with East German communist officials. The East German and Mexican communists reaffirmed their support for the "democratic struggle of the Portuguese people" and called upon the government of Chile to release Chilean communist leader Luis Corvalán and all other political prisoners without further delay.

Publications. The history of the communist press in Mexico goes back over 50 years. The newspaper *El Machete*, founded in 1924, was succeeded by *La Voz de México* (1938-1970). The journal *Oposición* dates back to the same period, and it was recently converted into a weekly. The party also has a theoretical journal, *Nueva Epoca.*

*   *   *

Other Marxist-Leninist Parties and Groups. The PPS. The largest Marxist-Leninist political party continues to be the Popular Socialist Party. Jorge Cruickshank has been the secretary-general since 1968, and other members of the Central Committee include Francisco Ortiz Mendoza, Deputy Miguel Hernández González and Lázaro Rubio Félix.

The PPS held several meetings during the year to determine its position in the forthcoming elections. Early in the year, the party said it would support a joint presidential candidate of the "democratic and revolutionary alliance" who would be prepared to "follow the positive path which Echeverría has maintained at the head of the country in domestic and international affairs" (*El Día*, 11 January). The PCM had hoped that the PPS would join the bloc of "leftist forces," but the latter declined the invitation. In September, even before the PRI nominated José López Portillo, the PPS announced, as it had done since 1958, that it would support the presidential candidate of the PRI.

The PPS ran its own candidates in the spring state and local elections. The party nominated Antonio Miselen Asufra to be governor of Quintana Roo; seven candidates ran for local deputy seats and seven ran for municipal presidents. The party also nominated Gustavo G. Velázquez as candidate for the governorship of the state of México; candidates for deputy in 15 electoral districts of the state were also nominated. The mayor of Tepic, Alejandro Gascon Mercade, was nominated to be the party's candidate for governor of Nayarit.

The PPS emphasized that it was opposed to force and violence and expressed its support for constitutional legitimacy and the peaceful path. Cruickshank condemned the attack on President Echeverría at the National University as a "vulgar provocation" by rightist groups. Although the party supported the president, it felt free to attack key figures within the government. The Agriculture Secretary, Oscar Brauer, was accused of being controlled by Rockefeller money, under the influence of U.S. agricultural monopolies, and therefore opposed to the improvement of the rural masses. The PPS also asked for the removal of Commerce and Industry Secretary, José Campillo Sáinz, whom they accused of being an agent of private enterprise and powerful economic forces.

In addition to opposing what it considered to be powerful economic interests in the country, the PPS strongly criticized the traditional right and U.S. imperialism. The party maintains that transnational corporations control too much of the Mexican economy. In the international sphere, the PPS has always been a strong supporter of the Soviet Union while criticizing the PRC for maintaining diplomatic ties with the Chilean military government.

The principal informational organ of the PPS is *Viva México*.

The PMT. The secretary-general of the Mexican Workers Party is Heberto Castillo, reportedly a former close aide of the late President Lázaro Cárdenas. The party leaders complained that "obstacles" have been placed in their political path, its organizers have been arrested, and the party's attempts to hold public meetings disrupted.

The PST. The secretary-general of the Socialist Workers Party is Rafael Aguiler Talamantes. Other leaders include Rafael Fernández and César del Angel, peasant leader and former congressman. At the beginning of the year, the army arrested del Angel on charges of possessing illegal firearms. His arrest came when the army blocked a peasant protest march to Mexico City. The PST leader, who had been involved in organizing tobacco and sugar farmers, was released on bail. (*NYT*, 18 January.)

PST leaders stated that the popular alliance (with the PCM and others) will permit them to join "the small and middle bourgeoisie and the progressive sectors of the bureaucracy in order to struggle against imperialism, the great monopolistic bourgeoisie, and their politicians." According to the PST, "the monopolistic bourgeoisie" and imperialism had hopes for a "Brazilian style" political hegemony as a means to prevent "revolutionary development, such as Cuba's or Chile's, which would lead to socialism" (LATIN, Buenos Aires, 2 May 1975).

In the summer, Aguilar Talamantes announced that the PST had embarked upon a national mobilization against rural and urban latifundism in order to eliminate all vestiges of abuse with respect to land ownership. He said that in Veracruz, Coahuila, Jalisco, San Luis Potosí and other areas, activities had been organized similar to the one held by the PST in Mexico City to oppose the large latifundia which still persisted in the country.

The MAUS. The Unified Socialist Action Movement is led by Aroche Parra.

The GCI. The GCI held its first national congress in mid-December 1974. Delegates came from Baja California, Oaxaca, Guerrero, Chihuahua, Monterrey, Colima, Morelos, Puebla, Sonora, the state of México and the Federal District. One of the principal items under discussion was the possible fusion of the GCI and the LS. The two organizations formed a joint commission to prepare for eventual unification. The congress issued a call "for the unity of revolutionary forces to oppose the frontist alternative (referring to the bloc of the PCM and other groups) that the bourgeoisie is now preparing." The congress also called for the class struggle, particularly in the labor movement, and moving the Mexican revolutionary movement beyond narrow nationalist limits to unite in the building of an international revolutionary Marxist organization. (*Inprecor*, Mexico City, 13 February 1975.) The GCI continues to publish its newspaper, *Bandera Roja*.

The LS. In the summer, the Socialist League (LS) published an article (translated and published by *Intercontinental Press*, June 1975) which was highly critical of the bloc of leftist forces proposed by the PCM. The LS rejected the formation of a "popular front" of organizations which allegedly represented the far right of the groupings in Mexico that claimed to be socialist. The article pointed out that a coalition that invited joint participation with bourgeois forces in an electoral contest could not represent the interests of the working class. "In Mexico, the PCM is creating illusions that the bloc it is proposing can lead to the conquest of democratic goals without a workers' revolution having occurred first." The article concluded that the bloc's purpose was to support the foreign policy of Echeverría, an attitude consistent with Brezhnev's hollow policy of détente. The LS continues to publish its fortnightly newspaper *El Socialista*.

The "Latin American Labor Committee." In the spring, police arrested three leaders of the Mexican section of the Committee, Carlos Arturo de Hoyos, José Carlos Trujillo and Héctor Apolinar Iribe, who claimed they were part of a movement which sought to control the world through armed struggle (INFORMEX, Mexico City, to ANSA, Buenos Aires, 7 April). During the raid, police uncovered files with up-to-date classified data on Mexican politics, economy, basic industries, electricity, oil, army installations with specification of military zones, location and names of military commanders, and outlines of army activities. All this information was being sent to a central office in New York which, in turn, distributed it to branch offices in the United States, Canada, Italy, Germany, Belgium, Switzerland, Denmark, France, the Netherlands, Japan, and Australia. The information was also being used for publication of the newspaper *Nueva Solidaridad*, which is published in English, Spanish, French, German, Italian, Swedish, Greek, and Turkish. The Mexican section covers Latin America with 80 active members, some of whom were identified. The three arrested persons reported that Patricio Estevez and his wife Cecilia Soto González, who were in charge of training group members, went to Bogotá, Colombia to organize a committee in that country.

Guerrillas. For all practical purposes, the guerrilla movement of 1975 was synonymous with the activities of the 23 September Communist League, which usually concentrates on urban rather than rural areas. The tactics shifted because the League abandoned spectacular kidnappings in favor of assassination, primarily of policemen. Authorities suspected that this was part of the League's campaign to create panic among the police force. During the year, more than a dozen policemen died, as well as a number of civilians, in League attacks which involved bombings and bank robberies in various cities. The guerrillas also succeeded in stealing a fairly large quantity of weapons.

Police killed several League members and apprehended others, while some eluded capture. The police continued to search for "La Nera," 23-year-old María de Refugio Jauregui Aguirre, who took part in an assault in which seven people were killed. Demetrio Torralva Alvarez, one of the League's leaders, was reported captured.

In the summer, the police killed two accused League members on the campus of the National University, one identified as "Mariano" and the other as Teresa Hernández Antonio. Apparently to seek revenge for his wife's death, League member David Jiménez Sarmiento led an attack on a Mexico City restaurant killing two policemen and three inspectors from the Ministry of Industry and Commerce. Leaflets left behind said the attackers were members of the League. A few weeks later Jiménez Sarmiento led the 15 June Brigade (the date when the police killed Teresa Hernández Antonio) in an attack against a naval medical center during which two marines were killed and a supply of weapons stolen.

Several days later the police claimed to have arrested 27 militants of the League. Authorities hinted that the League had been virtually immobilized with these arrests, since it did not have a large membership, and several of its leaders were among those arrested. An article in *The New York Times* (30 August) stated that the League had been decimated by the arrests, and in provincial cities such as Monterrey and Guadalajara, where the League was once powerful, it appeared to have been crushed. The article quoted a top government official who said, "This is a problem that is difficult to eliminate entirely. Fringe groups of this sort will always be with us. But they are under control in the sense that they cannot threaten the security of the state."

The Party of the Poor in the state of Guerrero was inactive during most of 1975. Carmelo Cortes took command of the Party after the death of Lucio Cabañas Barrientos in December 1974. Cortes was accused of shooting a police commissioner in August, of being wounded himself in the process, and of abandoning a suitcase containing some 450,000 pesos (U.S. $36,000).

Grand Valley State Colleges   Donald L. Herman

Nicaragua

The Socialist Party of Nicaragua (Partido Socialista de Nicaragua; PSN) was founded in 1937 and held its first official congress in 1944. One year later it was declared illegal and has been a clandestine organization ever since.

The Sandinist Liberation Front (Frente Sandinista de Liberación; FSN) is a guerrilla organization founded in 1961 by Carlos Fonseca Amador.

The PSN is a pro-Soviet party. In 1967 an internal struggle resulted in the expulsion of some party leaders who then organized an anti-Soviet Communist Party of Nicaragua (Partido Comunista de Nicaragua; PCN). The population of Nicaragua is 2,150,000 (estimated 1975).

The PSN has a negligible effect on the national political situation. This is due to its small, scattered membership, internal splintering and the thorough suppression of such groups by the government of Anastasio Somoza. A slight rise in communist activities followed the disastrous earthquake of December 1972. The leadership of the PSN has undergone numerous changes in recent years. Luis Domingo Sánchez Sancho is presently believed to be the head of the party.

Domestic and International Views. At its 10th Congress, the party stated that the present "independence of Nicaragua is entirely nominal, being merely the facade of a semi-colonial and feudal regime fully devoted to imperialism." The Party program said that the immediate goal was to free Nicaragua from U.S. domination. Tactically, the PSN calls for a united front of workers, students, peasants, middle class and other "progressives" against the Somoza government. While the PSN believes in armed struggle, it considers that the conditions in Nicaragua are still lacking. At this stage, it prefers building up its influence among the above sectors of the population until conditions are more propitious for violent action. The General Confederation of Labor, for example, operates under communist leadership.

Internationally, the PSN has consistently reaffirmed its pro-Soviet stance. In the recent past, it has condemned the military coup which toppled the Allende government in Chile and has attacked those in Central America that have sought to initiate violent action. The PSN attended the Conference of Latin American Communist Parties in Havana in June.

*   *   *

The FSLN. Founded in 1961 by Carlos Fonseca Amador as a Castroite guerrilla organization, the FSLN has consistently maintained the necessity for direct action against the Somoza regime. Throughout most of its history, however, it has been largely inactive. After the exile of Fonseca to Cuba in 1970, the FSLN went completely underground, confining its operations to propaganda statements issued by its leader. In a 1971 interview published in Chile, Fonseca said armed struggle "involves the most difficult course," but is "the only sure one." When the FSLN "takes up the guerrilla rifle, it inculcates a class consciousness. For the peasants in the mountains, for the poor in the suburbs, for the students in remote towns, the revolutionaries, the rebels, the communists, are the members of the Sandinist Front."

In attempting to establish a guerrilla-foothold in the peasant society of northern Nicaragua, the

505

FSLN is emulating the individual after which it was named: Augusto C. Sandino, a Nicaraguan revolutionary killed by government forces in 1934. Sandino is a true hero to the Nicaraguan left and, indeed, has become a legendary figure among the present generation of Latin American revolutionaries. For six years (1927-1933) Sandino and his band of rebels occupied northern and eastern Nicaragua and waged a classic guerrilla war against both the U.S. Marines and the National Guard of Nicaragua. With a propaganda arm that was truly worldwide, Sandino succeeded in eluding his enemies until January 1933, when the last American soldier departed from Nicaragua. Almost immediately thereafter, Sandino made a truce with the Nicaraguan government and lived the last year of his life in semi-retirement. Although the contemporary movement (with approximately 150 members) does not evidence the power of the original Sandino, it parallels the earlier one in the nature of its operations and is reportedly winning sympathy among peasants in the north, students in Managua and León, and among certain middle-class professionals.

Although the movement in the north seems to be gaining some momentum, the Somoza government is in full-strength against it. In addition to the energetic pursuit of rebel bands and their sympathizers, it has retained the state of emergency first declared in December 1974. That means that all constitutional guarantees have been suspended, including a strict censorship of all newspapers and radio stations. All references to guerrilla activities are also eliminated from dispatches sent out by foreign correspondents. No indication of the real extent of the campaign, therefore, is possible at the moment.

Domestic Activities. In a 1971 statement, Fonseca declared that "United States imperialism is renewing its century-old covetousness of Nicaragua" and has continued its "traditional utilization" of Nicaragua as a base for "acts of aggression against other countries in the area." Since the December 1974 raid on a Christmas party in Managua (see *YICA, 1975*, p. 539), the United States has sent military advisors to assist Nicaraguan counter-insurgency forces against the guerrillas and has supplied some $4 million in military aid. Against what it calls this "new U.S. imperialist intervention," the FSLN issued a communiqué in April 1975 stating that American military aid "demonstrates the imperialists' desperate determination to maintain their power bases against the resolute actions of the revolutionary movements which repeatedly defeat them."

In getting ready for the armed struggle in Nicaragua, FSLN members have been active in the northern regions of the country, where they claim to have reached a comparatively high degree of organization. However, even though the FSLN says it exerts tremendous influence on the labor movement it expects its attempted overthrow of the government to require a protracted guerrilla war. In the process, the FSLN seeks to isolate the Somoza government by uniting all "progressive" sectors of society—from the proletariat to members of the church.

International Attitudes. Avowedly castroite since its beginning in 1961, the FSLN has always had moral blessings from Cuba; those members that participated in the 1974 kidnapping flew directly to Havana afterward. In a 1971 statement sent to the CPSU Congress, Fonseca declared that the FSLN was "the successor of the Bolshevist October Revolution." The FSLN, he continued, will follow the revolutionary path of Lenin: "The ideals of the immortal Lenin, founder of the CPSU, are a guiding star in the struggle which the revolutionaries of our country are waging with the aim of overthrowing the reactionary regime."

The FSLN supports any force which can curtail the spread of U.S. influence. The 1970 election of Salvador Allende as president of Chile, for example, was hailed as an "important victory for the revolutionary movement in Latin America." Those regimes that are supported by the United States are condemned by the FSLN as reactionary. U.S. support for the Nicaraguan government's anti-guerrilla war against the FSLN has intensified the anti-American tone of FSLN propaganda. The members now feel that their war is as much against Washington directly as it is against President Somoza.

Hoover Institution   John J. Tierney, Jr.
Stanford University

Panama

The Communist Party of Panama (Partido Comunista de Panama) was founded in 1930 but was dissolved in 1943 in favor of the People's Party of Panama (Partido del Pueblo de Panamá; PDP). This party has been illegal since 1953, though a general relaxation of political repression by the government of General Omar Torrijos Herrera has, since the regime's inception in 1968, permitted the PDP a measure of freedom for its activities. The PDP has a membership of approximately 500. The population of Panama is 1,650,000 (estimated 1975).

Other leftist groups in Panama include the Revolutionary Unity Movement (Movimiento de Unidad Revolucionario; MUR), The National Action Vanguard (Vanguardia de Acción Nacional; VAN), the Panamanian Revolutionary Union (Unión Revolucionaria Panameña; URP) and the National Liberation Movement of 29 November (MLN-29-11). During the past few years these groups have been virtually inactive, with most of their leaders either exiled or imprisoned. During 1975 a new organization was formed, the Revolutionary Socialist Faction (Fracción Socialista Revolucionaria; FSR).

PDP. Leadership and Organization. Since 1951 the secretary general of the PDP has been Ruben Darío Sousa. Other leaders are Hugh Víctor, Miguel Parcell and Luther Thomas.

The PDP exerts little influence on mass organizations in Panama. Its labor affiliate is the Trade Union Federation of the Workers of the Republic of Panama (Federación Sindical de Trabajadores de la República de Panamá; FST), which was disbanded by the government in 1968. The PDP works with students largely through the University Reform Front (Frente Reformista Universitaria; FRU), but has also exerted a degree of influence over the 18,000 member Federation of Students of Panama (Federación de Estudiantes de Panama; FEP). Direct PDP influence over the FEP is not substantial, although the views of both groups often coincide.

Party Internal Affairs. In April the PDP celebrated its 45th anniversary. Communists and other socialist "progressives" held an anniversary meeting in the capital. Speaking to the assemblage, Darío Sousa pointed out the prominent role which the party, according to Marxist-Leninist principles, has played in the struggle against imperialism and for national liberation. The theme of his speech was the necessity to build a socialist society in Panama. The secretary general also praised the "patriotic, democratic and anti-imperialist" program being carried out under the leadership of General Torrijos, head of government, and Demetrio Lakas, President of the Republic. He ended by praising the government's foreign policy, especially in its pursuit of further contacts with the developing and socialist countries.

Domestic Views and Activities. The PDP has been for a long time an admittedly pro-Soviet party and, in line with that stand, has consistently advocated the adoption of united-front tactics for the revolutionary struggle in Panama. The great praise which Darío Sousa gave to the Torrijos government in his April speech is indicative of the long way in which the party has come in its espousal of mass action coordinated with non-communist elements. The PDP now views the 1968 coup which brought the regime into power as a revolutionary action. It has supported the government in its efforts to rid Panama of foreign influence, although the party has, in the past, criticized the government for its alleged toleration of the American presence. During the U.S.-Panamanian negotiations over the future of the canal, the Panamanian government indicated that it would consider a continuation of the American presence for at least another 25 years.

It its efforts to arouse coordinated action against the U.S., the PDP has long urged all "patriotic and progressive" forces to rely on the masses in order to build a united front of workers, peasants, intellectuals, students, small proprietors and "progressive" military and bourgeoisie. The PDP has achieved a degree of success in this type of program, particularly among the FEP student group and with workers from unions such as the National Workers Union (CNT) and peasant organizations like the Confederation of Panamanian Settlements (CONAC).

A split among Panama's leftist groups, however, has led to internal strife which became even more manifest during 1975. Pro-Chinese organizations such as the Federation of Revolutionary Students (FER) and the newly-formed Revolutionary Socialist Faction, for example, rioted in front of the American Embassy in September, knocking out at least 100 windows, as they shouted anti-U.S. slogans and demanded an immediate American withdrawal from the Canal Zone. These were the worst anti-American disturbances in Panama since 1964. Rival leftist student groups also fought with each other in October at the Panama National University. The proliferation of left-wing and socialist groups in Panama, with the infighting that always attends such rivalry, has diluted the efforts of the PDP to form a united front with anything resembling a national coalition. The strong identification of the party with the government's program, furthermore, has undermined its appeal with the more radical, action-oriented elements of the Panamanian left.

International Views and Contacts. The PDP reaffirmed its position on the issue of U.S. control of the Canal Zone. During the negotiations of 1975 between representatives of Panama and the United States over the future of the canal, the PDP criticized Washington's alleged failure to respect the sovereignty of the Panamanian people. The party supported the attempts of the Torrijos government to extract a favorable transferral of authority within a reasonable length of time and consistent with the economic needs of the people of Panama. The PDP also publicly supported the government in the international support which it has lined up for its position regarding the Canal. At this stage the PDP feels that it can best bring about a truly socialist, anti-oligarchic country by a continuing endorsement of the anti-imperialist features of the domestic and foreign policies of General Torrijos.

Hoover Institution   John J. Tierney, Jr.
Stanford University

Paraguay

The Paraguayan Communist Party (Partido Comunista Paraguayo; PCP) was founded in 1928. It has been illegal since that time except for a six-month period in late 1946-early 1947. The party has traditionally been aligned with the Soviet Union. One-time secretary general Oscar Creydt formed a rival PCP in 1965 which has maintained an essentially pro-Chinese stance.

The membership of the PCP, including all factions and sympathizers, is estimated at approximately 3500 persons, many of whom are exiled in various Latin American and European countries, particularly Argentina. The party claims to have been growing rapidly in the past three years. The population of Paraguay is 2,550,000 (estimated 1975).

Organization and Internal Affairs. The pro-Soviet PCP is headed by Miguel Angel Soler (sometimes identified as "Comrade Marin"). Other party leaders include Pedro Vásquez (member of the Political Commission), Mario Bruno, and Carlos Masiel. The present Central Committee members were elected at the Third Party Congress in 1971. According to the paper of the Paraguayan Radical Liberal Party, Antonio Maidana, the PCP chairman who was imprisoned in the late 1950s, died in prison in late 1974 (*El Radical*, cited in *WMR*, November 1974).

In accordance with the directives of the Third Congress, the party has sought to develop its influence on Paraguayan youth through the Young Communist League, a revitalized organization said to be preparing to hold a national conference.

The PCP has devoted much of its time in recent years to trying to resolve the disputes which have separated Paraguayan communists in recent years. According to Vásquez, a major step forward occurred in December 1974 when a general agreement was reached among party members regarding the essential dedication of communists to Marxism-Leninism and proletarian internationalism. The agreement emphasized that the program, rules, and policies approved at the Third Congress were binding on party members. Responding to critics of the right and left, he argued that "international assistance" received by the PCP during its period of reorganization did not undermine the party's independence; such "bourgeois" interpretations were based on nationalist rather than internationalist criteria. (*WMR*, June.)

The unity theme was advanced at a Central Committee plenum early in 1975. By mid-year the party thought it was becoming a "powerful and potentially explosive force." Its priority task for the present was to prepare for the Fourth Party Congress, which would consolidate the monolithic unity of the PCP and help solve a variety of remaining problems, including those involved in the organization and development of the national anti-dictatorial front. (*WMR*, June.) According to an earlier PCP report, the next congress would be held under the guidelines—cohesion, common outlook, unity of organization and action, and no concessions to factionalism (ibid., April 1974).

Domestic Views and Activities. The PCP argues that Paraguayan president Alfredo Stroessner (in office since 1954; reelected in 1973) is a spiritual descendant a Hitler, a hatchetman subservient to the CIA, the Pentagon, and the Brazilian militarists. He is selling out much of the country to the U.S.

monopolies and threatening to turn Paraguay into an "associated state" (indeed, a province) of Brazil. According to the PCP, the degree of prosperity in Paraguay has not touched the bulk of the population whose standard of living continues to fall. (Ibid.)

Paraguay's problems are due to the "triple evil" of latifundism, imperialism, and dictatorship. The PCP argues that the country's obsolescent social, economic, and political system, combined with the radicalization of all sections, is bound to produce an unprecedented national political crisis fraught with revolution. The Stroessner government will not collapse on its own, however, but must be pushed by the Paraguayan people in a national, anti-dictatorial front.

The formation of the front was the key problem of the day. The scale and social base of the front, according to Vásquez, would depend chiefly on its ability to voice the interests and direct the struggle of all classes and strata of society suffering from the dictatorship. The PCP should center its efforts on mobilizing, organizing, and uniting the masses; the workers and peasants should form the core of the front and the masses in general its overall strength. It was essential to develop a network of unity committees and coordinating councils to carry out these activities. Several problems had to be faced and overcome. First, the working class in Paraguay was not yet able to play the revolutionary role it is destined to play, due in large part to its high percentage of people of non-proletarian ideology. Uniting the proletariat and giving it a more distinct class character should be done in the beginning by making the trade unions the militant weapon of the working class. But beyond this, the party had to decide who it should bring into the united front and for what purpose. From the standpoint of class alliances, the anti-dictatorial front could not be limitless. The line of demarcation should not be between communists and non-communists, but between the "real opposition working for political freedoms" and the "sham opposition using the poison of anti-communism to disrupt and paralyze the revolutionary democratic movement." Communists should also realize that those who want to steer a "middle course" can be dangerous since they do not want to create revolutionary upheavals and class struggle, but are willing instead to settle for a limited degree of opposition permitted by the dictatorship.

Finally, the PCP sees itself as the "motive force" behind the anti-dictatorial front, and recognizes that in order to be successful it must demonstrate a high standard of political leadership capable of shrewdly assessing the alignment of class forces and the best ways of changing the alignment in favor of the people. Vásquez admitted that many of the PCP setbacks in the past were attributable to its "inability to assess the correlation of forces and the changing political situation." (*WMR*, June; *Granma*, Havana, English ed., 2 March.) According to the London-based *Latin America* (7 March), PCP efforts to form a front seem to have led to a degree of cooperation with the Partido Febrerista Revolucionario and the Movimiento Popular Colorado. The PCP is thought to be the driving force behind the Movement in Defense of the Fatherland (Movimiento de Defensa del Patria; MODEPA), an early stage of the popular front which already includes several communist and other Marxist groups, which met in Argentina at mid-year to work out ways to obstruct the hydro-electric project on the Paraná River called Itaipú (*Review of the River Plate*, Buenos Aires, 21 August).

Publications. The PCP claims that, despite the wave of arrests in Paraguay in late 1974-early 1975, its paper, *Adelante*, continued to reach working class readers. The party also claims to publish a bi-monthly edition of *World Marxist Review*.

San Francisco, Calif.   Lynn Ratliff

Peru

The Peruvian Communist Party (Partido Comunista Peruano; PCP) had its origins in the Peruvian Socialist Party, founded in 1928. As a result of orders from the Communist International, it took its present name in 1930. Since 1964 the movement has been divided into a pro-Soviet party and several pro-Chinese splinter groups, some of them using the PCP name.

There also exist in Peru various Marxist-Leninist organizations to the left of the PCP. These include the Castroite Movement of the Revolutionary Left (Movimiento de Izquierda Revolucionaria; MIR), and Army of National Liberation (Ejercito de Liberación Nacional; ELN) and the Trotskyite Revolutionary Left Front (Frente de Izquierda Revolucionaria; FIR), Partido Obrero Revolucionario (Trotskista), and Revolutionary Vanguard (Vanguardia Revolucionaria; VR).

Membership of the pro-Soviet PCP has been estimated at 2,000 and that of the pro-Chinese PCP groups at 1,200. This perhaps overestimates the latter. Other Marxist-Leninist groups are small, the FIR and VIR having perhaps the largest memberships. The population of Peru is about 14,800,000.

Communist membership is predominantly urban, mainly drawn from workers, students, and professional groups. Pro-Chinese elements seem to have the strongest hold in the universities. Communist influence in the trade movement is exercised mainly by the pro-Soviet PCP, which controls the General Confederation of Workers of Peru (Confederación General de Trabajadores del Peru; CGTP). Some of the more extremist groups have influence in independent unions, particularly in the mining areas. The FIR and MIR at one time had some influence among the peasants, although in recent years that has largely dissipated. The pro-Soviet PCP, through the CGTP, has increased its influence among the peasants in recent years.

A constitutional provision prohibits communist parties from participating in Peruvian elections, which are not being held in any case under the present military government; but the Communists have been allowed to operate under varying degrees of police surveillance and harassment. The government led by General Juan Velasco Alvarado, who was ousted from the presidency in August 1975, permitted the pro-Soviet PCP to function freely, but kept considerable control over other leftist groups and deported several pro-Chinese and Trotskyite leaders. On 1 December 1971 a law was passed providing for the death penalty or 25-year prison terms in cases of terrorist attacks causing death, serious injury, or property destruction. The Velasco government also sought to co-opt leaders of various Marxist-Leninist groups. Policies toward the Communists and groups to their left only changed marginally with the substitution of General Morales Bermudez for General Velasco in the presidency.

The Pro-Soviet PCP. Leadership and Organization. The highest organ of the pro-Soviet PCP is officially the national congress, which is supposed to meet every three years. Its Sixth Congress, the most recent, met in November 1973. The principal party leaders are Jorge del Prado, secretary-general, and Raúl Acosta Salas, undersecretary-general. Central Committee member Gustavo Espinoza is secretary-general of the CGTP.

The pro-Soviet party is organized from cells upward through local and regional committees, to its

Central Committee. Regional committees exist in at least 22 cities. Lima has the largest number of local committees, concentrated in low-income neighborhoods and in the slum areas which the government now refers to as "new towns."

A report delivered at the PCP's 1973 congress stated that 56 percent of the party members were urban workers. The rest included 8 percent peasants, 21 percent intellectuals, 4 percent students, and 9 percent undifferentiated. It also reported that the average party member had belonged for nine and a half years, and that the average age was 34 years. (*WMR*, January 1974.)

The pro-Soviet PCP has a youth group, the Peruvian Communist Youth (Juventud Comunista Peruano; JCP), which is small and operates mainly in the universities. The party also controls several front organizations, including the Popular Union of Peruvian Women (Unión Popular de Mujeres Peruanas).

The CGTP. The most influential organization under control of the pro-Soviet PCP is the CGTP. It was organized three months before the military coup of October 1968 and was given legal recognition a few months after the military took power. By the beginning of 1975 it had become the largest of the country's central labor organizations, largely as a result of sympathetic treatment it received from the Velasco government.

For several years, however, the CGTP has had to face competition from the Central Organization of Workers of the Peruvian Revolution (Central de Trabajadores de la Revolución Peruana; CTRP), organized under the direct sponsorship of the military regime. For many purposes, however, the CGTP and CTRP have been able to cooperate, as in March 1975 when they joined with a small Catholic-oriented group, the CNT, and a new National Confederation of Agricultural Workers (Confederación Nacional de Agricultores; CNA) to organize what they called the Coordinating Committee for the Defense of the Peruvian Revolution (*Flashes*, World Federation of Trade Unions bulletin, 12 March).

During 1975 the CGTP faced much more serious difficulties. For one thing, its Miners Federation disaffiliated because its leaders broke with the Communist party. For another, elements within the military government who were opposed to growing Communist influence in the labor movement organized what they called the Revolutionary Labor Movement (Movimiento Laboral Revolucionario; MLR). It proclaimed itself an arm of the CTRP, and concentrated on taking affiliates from the CGTP and having them join the CTRP. It enjoyed the editorial support of the daily newspaper *Ultima Hora*, headed by a former Trotskyite supporter of the military government. It also was supported by elements of SINAMOS, the government's organ for mobilizing popular support for its regime. (*Unidad*, 8 May.)

The MLR succeeded in getting control of some fishermen's unions and of some in the metal industry, but had not been able by the end of the year substantially to weaken the CGTP. It was consistently attacked by the Communist press throughout the year.

In an effort to consolidate its forces, the CGTP held a National Organization Conference for three days in mid-July. It paid particular attention to the problem of training lower and middle ranks of CGTP leadership. Because of the rapid growth of the CGTP in previous years, a large proportion of its leadership was relatively inexperienced.

Party Internal Affairs. The pro-Soviet PCP held several national meetings during 1975. There were Central Committee plenums in February, March, and May, a National Organization Conference in April, a National Trade Union Conference in July, and a National Conference of the JCP at the end of May.

The plenum of 15-16 February issued a defense of the party from attacks made on it for alleged participation in disturbances which occurred on 5 February. It "called on the working people to close their ranks in the struggle to defend the revolutionary process" (*IB*, No. 7). The next plenum, 15-16

March was also primarily concerned with reactions to the events of 5 February. A document stating the conclusions of the meeting noted that the government had issued an official statement of "Ideological Bases of the Peruvian Revolution" and was taking steps to establish its own political organization. In the face of these measures, the Communist Party reemphasized its support of the revolutionary government and called for unification of the people behind it. (*Unidad*, 20 March.)

The National Organization Conference of 12-13 April brought together 100 leaders representing 20 regional, zonal, and local party committees. Its agenda consisted of a political report by secretary-general Jorge del Prado, and a report by the organizational secretary. The major thrust of the second report was insistence on the need for more thorough training of local party and youth leaders. (Ibid., 18 April.)

The official report on the plenum of 31 May-1 June carried some implied criticisms of the military regime. It complained of the lack of popular participation in the work of the government, indicated that its "next step" should be to move in a "socialist" direction, and warned against "infiltration" into the regime by elements of the opposition Aprista party. On the other hand, it defended the party's support of the military regime against criticism by elements to the left of the PCP.

The Trade Union Conference, 6-7 July, was largely devoted to presenting arguments in defense of the government's economic measures, which imposed a considerable degree of austerity and, it is to be presumed, generated some discontent among the party's labor supporters (ibid., 11 July).

The party youth conference, at the end of May, was principally concerned with the problem of groups to the left of the PCP, the principal rivals of the JCP in the student field. Party secretary-general Jorge del Prado warned that such leftists were in fact "imperialist agents." He also stressed that the government enjoyed wide support from the "socialist camp." (TASS, 1 June.)

Domestic Attitudes and Activities. During much of 1975 the party was on the defensive. There was growing concern among elements in the military about the alignment of the regime with the PCP, and the party had to meet increasing criticism from these people. In August it was faced with a change in the top echelons of the government which was motivated in part by the fears of those opposed to Communist influence.

One factor which aroused the anti-Communists among the military was the rioting of 5 February. The day's events started as a march of students who were critical of the government. It soon deteriorated into rioting and vandalism in some of the central parts of Lima. The police were on strike, so they were not available to suppress the rioting. Only after many hours were elements of the Army called out, and they put down the rioting only with many casualties.

The Communists claimed that the opposition Aprista Party had been behind the 5 February events, and frequently criticized the government for not punishing the Apristas. However, elements of the military were convinced that it was the Communists who attempted to take advantage of the chaos of that day for their own ends.

For the rest of the year, the Communists were particularly concerned to demonstrate their continuing loyalty to the military regime. Probably their most important efforts in this regard were their defense of economic measures taken by the regime on June 30. Among these was a decision not to devaluate the sol, and one to end subsidies of a number of basic products, thus allowing their prices to rise.

A statement by the PCP, published in the 4 July issue of the party paper, *Unidad*, defended the government against charges that it was responsible for the price increases of recent years, and stated: "The PCP considers it valuable and noteworthy that the Government did not recur to devaluation as have the governments which are victims of the world crisis of capitalism."

With regard to the end of subsidies, the PCP statement said, "The PCP considers that the sacrifices for the workers and popular masses imposed by the elimination of subsidies of feed and combustible products constitute the precious and inestimable contribution of the Peruvian people to carrying out economic and social development, because they substantially increase the capacity of investment of the State, which is playing a fundamental role in the promotion of the economic development of the country."

The party's most serious crisis was presented by the overthrow of President Juan Velasco on 29 August and the ascension to the presidency of General Francisco Morales Bermudez. Morales was generally considered a member of the anti-Communist element among the military, and he proceeded to remove a number of pro-PCP military men from key positions.

Early in September the PCP issued a statement of its position, affirming "that the changes in the presidency of the republic and in the cabinet are important as they are to strengthen and deepen the Peruvian revolution and eliminate the deviations and errors in guiding it which in the past 10 months made popular support difficult." It congratulated the armed forces on having maintained their unity, and commented that in this "the government has given evidence of maintaining unchanged the revolutionary spirit."

The statement went on: "The PCP once again reaffirms its revolutionary sentiments and is sure that in this stage which is beginning in the process of change, the anti-imperialist and anti-oligarchic trend will be consolidated and deepened." It then issued a call to "its members and the people" to stay on the alert for "provocations" by "reactionaries and imperialism," and ended by sending "revolutionary greetings" to the new president. (*Expreso*, 4 September.)

International Views and Positions. The PCP continued in 1975 to maintain a very close pro-Soviet alignment. In April a delegation of the Central Committee visited Eastern Europe, and two months later a group representing the JCP did the same.

Publication. The official organ of the pro-Soviet PCP is the weekly newspaper *Unidad*, which claims a circulation of more than 10,000. When the government took over all of the Lima daily newspapers in mid-1974, most of them were placed under the editorial direction of Communists or fellow-travelers. With the overthrow of President Velasco, his successor began to remove these pro-Communist editors.

*   *   *

The Pro-Chinese Communists. Leadership and Organization. The PCP organ *Unidad* asserted on 31 January 1974 that there were as many as 30 far-left groups in Peru. Most of these, certainly, were tiny organizations with little more than a name, a handful of members, and a rubber stamp for their stationery. However, some of the more important ones fell into more or less easily identifiable categories. One of these consists of pro-Chinese parties.

Virtually from their inception, the pro-Chinese communists have experienced internal dissension and splits. There are at least three factions of the pro-Chinese PCP. The one which enjoys more or less official recognition from the Chinese Communist Party is headed by Saturnino Paredes Macedo and, from its somewhat sporadic periodical, *Bandera Roja*, is generally known as the Bandera Roja PCP. The so-called Sotomayor faction has its principal center of influence in the southern city of Arequipa. The Red Fatherland faction, so-called because of its periodical, *Patria Roja*, is said to have the largest following of all pro-Chinese groups among the students. It was reported to have sent greetings to Mao Tse-tung and Chou En-lai on the anniversary of the founding of the People's Republic of China in October (Peking radio, 15 October 1975). All Maoist factions have opposed the military regime. The TASS news agency in a Moscow broadcast (28 June) attacked another Maoist group, the Movimiento Revolucionario de Trabajadores, not otherwise identified.

The pro-Chinese parties had limited activity during 1975. They had some influence in the miners' federation formerly affiliated with CGTP, and in the teachers' unions. They won renewed control of the Teachers' Federation in elections in July.

The several Marxist-Leninist parties and groups of Castroite and Trotskyite orientation in Peru that reached their apogee in the early 1960s are now small in membership, although they have some ideological influence among young people, particularly students. The Castroite groups include the MIR, ELN, and a faction of the VR. Trotskyites comprise the FIR, POR(T), and POMR.

*   *   *

The MIR. The Movement of the Revolutionary Left was first organized as the Partido Aprista Rebelde in the late 1950s by a group of young people who felt that the country's traditional democratic leftist group, the Partido Aprista, had abandoned its early militancy. After the Castro Revolution, it came under Castroite influence and adopted the present name. In 1965 it launched a major guerrilla war effort, in which its then leader was killed and the membership suffered many casualties. The extent of current membership is not known, but the MIR has some influence in the universities. Ricardo Gadea, brother of Che Guevara's first wife, is the principal leader. He was deported from Peru by President Velasco shortly before Velasco's overthrow, but was allowed to return by the new president, General Morales Bermudez. The MIR has consistently opposed the military regime since 1968.

The ELN. The ELN, founded in 1962 by former PCP members, participated in the peasant guerrilla movement in 1965. Its main leader, Héctor Béjar, was released from prison in December 1970 in a general political amnesty. Subsequently he was named head of the Youth Section of SINAMOS. Angel Castro Lavarelle is now president of the ELN.

*   *   *

The VR. The VR is a Marxist-Leninist party founded by former Aprista Party members in 1965. It advocates armed confrontation as a means of achieving socialism, but holds that its members should have theoretical and practical training before engaging in actual struggle. There is no evidence that it has so far engaged in any guerrilla movement. Although composed primarily of intellectuals, it includes some workers. It is reported to have considerable influence among the mining workers of the central part of Peru, in the former holdings of the Cerro de Pasco corporation.

The VR split in 1971. One faction formed the Marxist Revolutionary Workers Party (Partido Obrero Marxista Revolucionario). The leaders describe the party as "Leninist-Trotskyist," but it has no affiliation with any of the international factions of Trotskyism.

The FIR. The FIR is a Trotskyist party associated with the United Secretariat faction of the Fourth International. Its principal figure is Hugo Blanco, who in 1962 led a movement of peasants near Cuzco to seize land, culminating in an armed uprising. He was captured and kept in prison until December 1970, when he was released in a general amnesty. Because of his criticisms of the military government, he was deported in September 1973.

The FIR has a youth group, the Vanguard Socialist Youth (Juventud Avanzada Socialista). It also publishes a periodical, *Palabra Socialista.*

During 1975 Hugo Blanco carried on continuous criticism of the military regime from abroad. There was no indication of important activity by the group within Peru.

The POR(T). The POR(T) is a Trotskyite faction associated with the International Secretariat of the Fourth International, the Posadas faction. It has supported the government since 1968. As in previous years, the POR(T) concentrated most of its efforts in 1975 on distributing its periodicals and pamphlets, most of which are written by Posadas.

Rutgers University

Robert J. Alexander

Puerto Rico

The Puerto Rican Communist Party (Partido Comunista Puertorriqueño; PCP) is closely associated with the Communist Party of the United States (CPUSA) and shares its pro-Soviet orientation. The Puerto Rican Socialist League (Liga Socialista Puertorriqueña; LSP) is on good terms with the Progressive Labor Party (PLP) of the United States and, like the PLP, dropped its original pro-Chinese orientation in 1971. The Popular Socialist Movement (Movimiento Socialista Popular; MSP), which held its first congress in late 1974, maintains a generally Maoist stance. The Young Communist League (Liga de Juventud Comunista; LJC), founded in the fall of 1974, is Trotskyist in orientation. The Armed Forces of Puerto Rican National Liberation (Fuerzas Armadas de Liberación Nacional Puertorriqueña; FALN), which gained international recognition in October 1974, may have had its origins in earlier terrorist groups (see below). The Puerto Rican Socialist Party (Partido Socialista Puertorriqueño; PSP), an outgrowth of the Pro-Independence Movement (MPI), with close ties to Cuba, is independent in the Sino-Soviet dispute.

The LSP, MSP, and LJC probably have fewer than 50 members each, while the PCP may have slightly more than 100. FALN membership is estimated at about one dozen (*NYT*, 28 October 1975). PSP membership seems to have grown steadily since the party's formation in 1971 and, by the end of 1975, probably totaled several thousand (*NYT*, 9 November), with perhaps ten times that many supporters. The population of Puerto Rico is 900,000 (estimated 1975).

The PCP. The Puerto Rican Communist Party was founded in 1934, dissolved in 1944, and founded again in 1946. Little is known of its organizational structure, except that it appears to operate both in Puerto Rico and the United States (particularly New York City). Among its leaders are Félix Ojeda Ruiz (secretary general), Franklyn Irrizarri (organizing secretary), Sergio Kentish (labor secretary), Manuel Méndez del Toro (Politburo member), Gertrudis Ménéndez (in charge of the women's front), Alfredo Matos, and Alberto Rodríguez. The party claims to be organized in residential and working areas, with branches united in territorial organizations led by municipal committees. The party congress, held once every five years, elects a Central Committee, which in turn elects a Political Commission. The party says its social composition is: wage-earners (70 percent), peasants (5), salary-earners (20), and other categories (5). Women constitute 15 percent and persons under 30 years of age constitute 60 percent. (*WMR*, July 1974.)

Domestic and International Views. The domestic and international views of the PCP mirror those of the CPUSA. At a press conference in Havana, Ojeda stated that the serious economic crisis in Puerto Rico during 1975 was chiefly a result of "enormous Yankee investments" in the island, adding that "the economic crisis being experienced by the United States hits Puerto Rico much harder" than it does the governing colonial power (the U.S.) itself. The island's problems are reflected in the high rates of inflation and unemployment, which the "colonial government" seeks to resolve only by "demagoguery." The class struggle intensified under deteriorating economic conditions in 1975, according to Kentish, despite the fact that the labor movement in Puerto Rico has long been heavily influenced by ideas imported from the U.S. labor unions. Ojeda reports that the PCP is working on a new party program and expects to hold a congress. (*Granma*, Havana, English, 16 March.) The PCP actively supported the International Conference of Solidarity with the Independence of Puerto Rico which was held in Havana in early September.

Occasional PCP publications are *El Pueblo* and *El Proletario*.

*   *   *

The LSP. The Puerto Rican Socialist League, apparently operating in both Puerto Rico and New York City, is led by its secretary general, Juan Antonio Corretjer. The LSP still calls for "people's war" in Puerto Rico. Its organs, which appear irregularly, are *Pabellón* and *El Socialista*. Occasional information on the LSP is found in the PLP paper *Challenge/Desafio*.

*   *   *

The FALN. The Armed Forces of National Liberation is known chiefly for large-scale bombing attacks between October 1974 and October 1975 against U.S. government buildings, corporate offices, and banks, mostly in New York City. The origins of the group are unclear. A *New York Times* study (7 February 1975) utilizing information from unnamed detectives and FBI agents involved in FALN investigations, reported that the terrorist organization may be the outgrowth of the Armed Revolutionary Independence Movement (MIRA), apparently organized in Cuba in 1966. MIRA began incendiary raids in the U.S. and Puerto Rico in 1969 but was rendered inoperative by arrests in 1971. Investigators suggest that remaining MIRA members may have then formed the United Armed Revolutionary Force for Independence (FURIA), which subsequently became the Armed Commandos for Liberation (CAL). The FALN was formed from former militants of the FURIA and CAL. The Communist Party of the U.S. claims that the FALN is a CIA-inspired and financed group made up of Cuban counterrevolutionaries which is intended to discredit the Puerto Rican independence movement (*Daily World*, New York, 6 December 1975). The FALN's main activities have been disclaimed and criticized by the PCP, the PSP, and other independence-oriented groups in Puerto Rico.

The FALN, in messages delivered after its periodic attacks, demands independence for Puerto Rico and the release of alleged political prisoners (imprisoned Puerto Rican nationalists, one convicted of trying to assassinate U.S. President Harry Truman in 1950 and four of shooting congressmen in the U.S. House of Representatives in 1954). The organization claims to be carrying out a "coordinated attack against Yankee government and monopoly capitalist institutions."

The most spectacular of the 25 bombings now attributed to the FALN since August 1974 are: 1) the almost simultaneous explosions outside five Manhattan banks in October 1974, the first attack for which the FALN claimed responsibility; 2) the mid-day bombing in New York's crowded Fraunces Tavern in January 1975; and 3) the almost simultaneous bombing of government, corporation, and banking offices in New York, Chicago, and Washington, in October 1975.

*   *   *

The LJC. The Young Communist League was formed by members of a small Trotskyist study circle in the fall of 1974. Among its leaders is Tony Merle, a former PSP member who came within six votes of being elected president of the student council of the Natural Sciences Faculty at the Rio Piedras campus of the University of Puerto Rico in September 1974. (*Militant*, New York, 12 September 1975.) During 1975 the LJC participated in organizing student activities.

*   *   *

The MSP. The Popular Socialist Movement, a self-proclaimed Marxist-Leninist organization, held its first congress in November 1974. Its secretary genral is Luis Angel Torres, a member of the Puerto Rican legislature (elected while a member of the Puerto Rican Independence Party–PIP). The MSP claims to be working toward the formation of a "genuine Marxist-Leninist party in Puerto Rico," arguing that none exists at present. The MSP disagrees with the classification of Puerto Rico as a "classical colony," insisting that it is an "industrial colony." Unlike the "classical" colonies, there is no significant peasantry, no patriotic bourgeoisie, and few members of the petty-bourgeoisie who are not on the side of "U.S. imperialism." Thus, the struggle for Puerto Rican independence must be fundamentally a struggle for socialism. The basic strategy for achieving national liberation in Puerto Rico is armed struggle and "protracted revolutionary war." Torres charges that the PIP relies too much on the election process and that its strategy is best characterized as "militant pacifism." PSP strategy is described as one of "insurrection," but without a coherent plan for the protracted struggle.

The MSP has played an active role in the United Workers' Movement (Movimiento Obrero Unido; MOU), a militant federation of some 40 unions and 100 locals which the leaders of the PSP say has laid the groundwork for a central labor organization. The MSP urged participation in the international conference on Puerto Rican independence, viewing it as an opportunity to confront such "revisionists" as those on the sponsoring World Peace Council. (*Guardian*, New York, 9 July 1975.)

*   *   *

The PSP. The Puerto Rican Socialist Party was formed in November 1971 at the Eighth National Assembly of the Pro-Independence Movement. Its leaders include Juan Mari Bras (secretary general), Julio Vives Vásquez (chairman), and Political Commission members Pedro Baiges (also first secretary of the Central Committee), Ramón Arbona (also editor of the party paper, *Claridad*), and Digna Sánchez. Carlos Gallisa is the only PSP member in the Puerto Rican legislature, having been elected while a member of the PIP. Other party leaders and spokespersons include: Pedro Grant (coordinator of the United Workers' Movement), José Alberto Alvarez, Angel Gandía, Gervasio Morales, Néstor Nazario, Carlos Rivera, Florencio Merced (delegate to the United States), and Andrés Torres (secretary of labor affairs in New York). Mari Bras told the editor of a radical U.S. weekly in December that the PSP was prepared to go underground if necessary, adding that the party would be able to continue its diverse activities under backup leadership even if all present national leaders were suddenly arrested (*Guardian*, New York, 24 December).

The PSP is now said to have an organizational presence in every important population center in Puerto Rico, with the largest and most active organizations in the key industrial areas. Arbona states that since 1971 the number of party organizations, nuclei and zones has increased seven-fold. (Ibid.) The PSP is carrying on "intensive activity" in the United States, according to Mari Bras, and a system of organizations has been built up paralleling the one in Puerto Rico (*Bohemia*, Havana, 27 September 1974). The most important activity of 1976 will be the "growth and consolidation of the first Marxist-Leninist party of the Puerto Rican working class" (according to Mari Bras, *Guardian*, 17 December).

The PSP held its Second Congress in San Juan on 28 November-7 December, reportedly drawing some 10,000 supporters to the closing event in the Roberto Clemente Coliseum. Official delegates numbered 296, including approximately 100 trade union members. Some 350 observers were present from the United States. (*Guardian*, 17 December.) Summarizing the main accomplishments of the Congress, Mari Bras stated on 6 December:

> [It] consolidated the organization of the party . . . demonstrated the great support that the leadership of the party, as a collective, has won . . . and achieved what was one of our major goals, the program of the party as the result of all the several theses that we have published in the last eighteen years. It is the first time that a program has been approved by a Marxist-Leninist party with such a background of experience in Puerto Rico. (Ibid., 24 December.)

The PSP is active in the United Workers Movement and assorted efforts to create a broadly-based general confederation of workers, in the Puerto Rican Peace Council, in activities among students, faculty and staff in educational establishments, and in endeavors to create a broad national liberation or united front. The party, and in particular its secretary-general, played a leading role in setting up the International Conference of Solidarity with the Independence of Puerto Rico (see below).

Domestic Attitudes and Activities. The PSP held that Puerto Rico is an exploited colony and that the present institutional structure serves only the intersts of U.S. imperialism and Puerto Rican reactionaries. At an extraordinary congress of the party in early 1974, the PSP approved its "Socialist Alternative," calling for an independence movement which will develop all existing forms of struggle to overthrow the colonial regime and proclaim a Workers Democratic Republic (*Granma*, English, 17 March 1974). This program was developed at the December 1975 congress with plans to move from a national liberation front to the Workers Republic and the foundations of socialism.

Delivering the major address of the Second Congress, Mari Bras said that Puerto Rico was "rapidly coming to the end of the pre-revolutionary period." All of the objective factors for revolution already existed and, with the accelerating growth of the key subjective force—the party of the proletariat—the Puerto Rican people will soon be entering a full "revolutionary period." (*Guardian*, 17 December 1975.) The national liberation movement in Puerto Rico, according to Mari Bras, will include "all the classes and social groups and segments of the population who have an objective interest in defeating colonialism and winning full sovereignty for the people of Puerto Rico." This national unity of the "vast majority" will incorporate the small bourgeoisie, intellectuals, professionals, and "all of the working masses, besides the working class as such." The only sectors excluded will be the "very powerful intermediate and bureaucratic bourgeoisie." Politically, the unity efforts aim at incorporating all political parties (including the PIP) and other organizations that support the independence movement. (Ibid., 24 December.)

A major policy shift occurred at the Second Congress when the PSP decided—not without considerable opposition from within (see *Daily World*, New York, 6 December)—to run candidates in the 1976 elections. Party leaders say this does not mean that the PSP expects to achieve national independence by the "parliamentary" road, but merely, as the party resolution states, that elections will be used to denounce the "bourgeois" and "colonial" character of the electoral system. The elections will put the PSP program—the "Socialist Alternative"—up in contrast to the programs of the "bourgeois parties," thus "forcing a discussion of our ideological positions vis-à-vis the position adopted by the parties of colonialism." Mari Bras stated that the PSP hopes to summon up a significant protest vote from those who want socialism and independence, hopefully broadening the basis of the party, organizing a wide periphery of sympathizers, and giving the PSP a voice in the House of Representatives and municipal assemblies. (*Granma*, Spanish edition, 9 December; *Guardian*, 24 December.)

The PSP secretary general insisted in his address that this electoral participation did not mean the party had rejected armed struggle. He reportedly brought the crowd to its feet with a powerful ovation when he quoted Fidel Castro: "There can be no victorious revolution if you have the arms and you do not have the masses. But there cannot be a victorious revolution without arms." Armed struggle, he concluded, is the "inalienable right of all oppressed people." (*Guardian*, 17 and 24 December; *Granma*, 9 December.)

The party attitude toward terrorism—as carried out by the FALN—became clearer during 1975. Though some PSP commentaries in late 1974 gave the impression that the PSP approved some FALN actions (see *Militant*, New York, 25 July 1975), Mari Bras stated after the January 1975 tavern bombing that "indiscriminate and irresponsible terrorism obviously directed at the death of innocent persons is contrary to the practice of revolutionary warfare" (*Intercontinental Press*, New York, 3 February), a position repeated at length by José A. Alvarez in the 29 June weekly edition of *Claridad* circulated in the United States (see *Militant*, 25 July). In an interview on 6 December, Mari Bras said the PSP rejected "isolated terrorism, particularly acts that demobilize the masses and those that victimize people from the working class who are our allies," giving the tavern bombing as an example. Then he added: "But we do not give up the right of utilizing all means and forms of struggle, including all the various forms of armed struggle, in the development of the mass actions against colonialism and capitalism in Puerto Rico." (*Guardian*, 24 December.)

International Views and Attitudes. The PSP maintains an independent stance in international affairs, supporting or criticizing the socialist countries on an issue-by-issue basis. Though it seeks and generally receives support from the Soviet bloc in its independence campaign, the PSP expresses reservations about some aspects of "detente" and wants close ties with the People's Republic of China (PRC). The PSP praised the Chinese for their refusal to allow the mayor of San Juan to visit China as a member of a U.S. mayors' delegation, but objected to Chinese policies toward Chile and Angola. (*Guardian*, 17 December; also, *Granma*, Spanish edition, 10 December.) Though the PSP does not always agree with the Cuban government, Cuba has always been its strongest ally. Cuba has long led the international movement in support of Puerto Rican independence through its activities at the United Nations, among the nonaligned countries, and in governmental forums. This process reached its peak with the 5-7 September 1975 International Conference of Solidarity with the Independence of Puerto Rico in Havana (see Mari Bras comments in *Granma*, English edition, 14 September). [The conference drew 291 delegates and 34 observers from 79 nations, 18 international organizations; see General Statement in ibid., 21 September.]

The PSP has long sought to "make an international matter of the case of Puerto Rico" (Mari Bras, ibid., 14 September). With this objective in mind, the party in 1975 continued to wage its campaign against the United States in the United Nations, receiving full encouragement and support from Cuba. Mari Bras appeared before the U.N. Special Committee on the Situation with Regard to the Implementation of the Declaration of the Granting of Independence to Colonial Countries and Peoples (the Decolonization Committee) on 14 August, urging passage of a resolution which would have recognized "the national liberation movement of Puerto Rico as representing the legitimate aspirations of the Puerto Rican people struggling for independence." The PSP leader was particularly critical of admitted and alleged FBI efforts to harass the Puerto Rican independence movement between 1960 and 1971, charging that "persecution" has increased in the past few years. [One PSP Political Commission member told a sympathetic foreign editor that he did not expect the party to be able to operate legally for much longer (*Guardian*, 17 December).]

Publication. The PSP publishes *Claridad.* This paper has reportedly grown from a 24-page weekly with 15,000 distribution in 1971 to a "full service" daily in 1975 with a daily circulation of 20,000 and a weekend edition of 30,000. *Claridad* has a full-time staff of 86 under editor Arbona. (*Guardian*, 17 December.)

Hoover Institution   William E. Ratliff
Stanford University

United States of America

The Communist Party, USA (CPUSA) is the largest and most influential Marxist-Leninist organization in the United States. It is descended from the Communist Labor Party and the Communist Party, both formed in 1919. At various times the CPUSA has also been called the Workers Party and, for a brief period during World War II, the Communist Political Association.

The Socialist Workers Party (SWP) is the leading Trotskyite party. Organized in 1938, it traces its origin to 1928, when several CPUSA members were expelled for supporting Leon Trotsky. The SWP has spawned numerous other Trotskyite groups, including the Workers' World Party.

The Progressive Labor Party (PLP) came into existence in 1965 following the expulsion of several CPUSA members for ultra-leftism. The PLP strongly supported Maoism until 1971. Its present ideological posture is rigidly Stalinist.

The two most important Maoist sects are the Revolutionary Union (RU) and the October League (OL). A commitment to Marxism-Leninism is also proclaimed by such groups as the Weather Underground Organization (WUO), Prairie Fire Distributing Committee (PFDC), the Marxist-Leninist Organizing Committee, the Communist Labor Party, the Revolutionary Student Brigade, the Revolutionary Workers' Congress, and the August 29th Movement. All of these emerged, at least in their Marxist-Leninist guise, in the early 1970s, usually under the direction of veterans of the now defunct Students for a Democratic Society (SDS).

The CPUSA is a legal party. Restrictive laws which hindered access to the ballot in some states have been removed or are under legal attack and the party hopes to run candidates in all 50 states in 1976. At present it has no representation either in Congress or any state legislature. During 1975 a CPUSA candidate for mayor in New Haven, Connecticut, received a little over 1 percent of the vote despite an intensive campaign. A party member in Berkeley, California, running in a non-partisan election, received 35 percent. Two party figures won election: one to a New York City community board, the other to a school board in Brooklyn (*Daily World*, 24 July).

The CPUSA claims to have about 15,000 members; the FBI estimate is only 4,200 (*Christian Science Monitor*, 25 July). Membership is mainly concentrated in a few industrial states and recruitment efforts are particularly aimed at minorities (blacks, Puerto Ricans, Chicanos) and young industrial workers. The party claims that membership among minorities (including also Asians and American Indians) "is approximately in proportion to their percentage of the population" but deems that the percentages are not good enough, since these groups are heavily working class (*Daily World*, 2 July). The population of the United States is about 215 million.

The SWP, like the CPUSA, runs candidates for state, local, and national office. None have been elected. There are perhaps 2,500 party members. The SWP, although concentrated in the industrial states, has established strong local chapters in some places (e.g., Atlanta, Georgia) where the CPUSA has made no headway.

The PLP does not run candidates for office. Neither does it provide information about membership. It is unlikely that there are more than 1,000 members. Neither the RU nor the OL provides such information, but neither has more than a few hundred members. The other groups are smaller.

The CPUSA and SWP are active in broad-scale left movements, such as support of school busing and black causes, and attacks on the Chilean junta. The smaller sects, whose origins go back to the campus turmoil of the 1960s, no longer appear to wield much influence in the colleges and universities. In general, the continuing economic problems in the United States have not stimulated any noticeable growth in Marxist-Leninist influence, but an increasing attraction toward Marxism-Leninism is apparent among the remnants of the New Left.

The CPUSA. Leadership and Organization. There were few changes within the party leadership in 1975. The 21st Convention of the CPUSA elected a 68-member Central Committee and 136-member National Council, the latter including most Central Committee members. The new Central Committee unanimously reelected Gus Hall as general secretary and Henry Winston as national chairman. Arnold Bechetti is organizational secretary, Betty Smith is national administrative secretary, and Sid Taylor was selected for a new post, national treasurer. Other important party leaders include: Helen Winter (international affairs secretary), James Jackson (national education director), Grace Mora (chairwoman, Puerto Rican Commission), Alva Buxenbaum (chairwoman, Commission for Women's Equality), George Meyers (chairman, National Labor Commission), Lorenzo Torres (chairman, National Chicano Commission), Arnold Johnson (public relations director), William Petterson and Roscoe Proctor (co-chairmen, Black Liberation Commission), Victor Perlo (chairman, Economics Commission), Hyman Lumer (editor, *Political Affairs* and *Jewish Affairs*), Carl Bloice (editor, *People's World*), Carl Winter (editor, *Daily World*), Danny Rubin (chairman, Commission on Unemployment), and Si Gerson, Claude Lightfoot, Angela Davis, Charlene Mitchell, and Herbert Aptheker (Central Committee members).

Among the party leaders in important states are Jarvis Tyner (New York), Jim West (Ohio), Ishmael Flory and Jack Kling (Illinois), William Taylor and Al Lima (California), Tom Dennis (Michigan), Thomas Crenshaw (Missouri), Lee Dlugin (New Jersey), Ed Teixeira (New England).

The CPUSA does not officially have any auxiliary organizations. The Young Workers Liberation League (YWLL), related to but not affiliated with the party, serves as the CPUSA's youth organization. It has about 4,000 members. YWLL leaders are active within the party, and the group's policies and programs, "following the lead of our great Communist Party," are identical with those of the CPUSA (*Daily World*, 25 June). The YWLL Third National Convention in Philadelphia on 13-16 December 1974 was attended by 700 delegates and guests. Leaders claimed that 50 percent of the delegates were workers, 40 percent black and another 7 percent of other minorities, and 25 percent were college students. A 55-member Central Committee was elected. Officers included Jim Steele (national chairman), Roque Ristorucci (executive secretary), Jay Schaffner (education director), Matthew Berkellhammer (organizational secretary), Victoria Missick (national student secretary) and Jill Harris (editor, *Young Worker*). The YWLL called for a Youth Rights Campaign to demand, among other things, that the federal government create a million youth jobs at union wages out of the military budget. The convention attacked Chile, South Africa, and U.S. "domination" of Puerto Rico. Speakers urged a united front with other U.S. youth groups, such as the YMCA, to fight racism and suggested that a black-white youth movement for jobs would have prevented the outbreak of racism in Boston (ibid., 18 January, 15 February 1975). Active in efforts to support school busing, the YWLL attacked the Trotskyite Young Socialist Alliance (YSA) for its role in the National Student Conference Against Racism, charging the YSA with ignoring and denigrating the need for whites to organize in the white community in support of busing (ibid., 13 March). In May 1975 the YWLL sent a delegation led by Jim Steele to Cuba (ibid., 27 May). CPUSA chief Gus Hall declared that the YWLL was "moving sizable numbers of youth" toward Marxism-Leninism and that the CPUSA would be unable to overcome weaknesses in the youth area without a strong YWLL (ibid., 2 July).

Several other organizations, while not party-affiliated, maintain close ties with the CPUSA and either follow its lead or cooperate closely with it. The most prominent of the CPUSA's united-front organizations continues to be the National Alliance Against Racist and Political Repression (NARPR). Charlene Mitchell, CPUSA presidential candidate in 1968, is executive secretary of the NARPR and Angela Davis is prominent in the organization. The *Daily World* (15 October 1975) has called the NARPR "an essential organization." The Third National Conference of the NARPR, held in November 1975, focused on efforts to defeat S.B.1, a U.S. Senate bill to reform the federal criminal code which the CPUSA had labeled repressive (ibid., 8 October). In addition the organization sponsored a Washington march which attracted several thousand people to protest the conviction of the "Wilmington 10" in North Carolina and called for the release of the Puerto Ricans whose random gunfire wounded 5 members of Congress in 1954 (ibid., 3 June, 26 September).

The continued economic difficulties in the United States have encouraged the CPUSA to try to expand its influence within the labor movement. There are two major front groups active in this area. The National Coalition to Fight Inflation and Unemployment (NCFIU) has worked closely with the party. Gus Hall noted its importance and indicated that the CPUSA was active within its ranks (*Political Affairs*, April 1975). Sidney Von Luther is NCFIU chairman and Elizabeth Merkelson is executive secretary. The coalition was active in promoting the "April 26th Rally for Jobs in Washington" organized by a number of industrial unions, and sponsored demonstrations in various cities for federal programs to create jobs. It has planned a united front rally in Washington for January 1976 to "demand full employment now" (*Daily World*, 11 November).

The other front, the National Co-ordinating Committee for Trade Union Action and Democracy (TUAD), was founded in 1970 to increase party influence in the trade union movement. Among TUAD leaders are Rayfield Mooty, Fred Gaboury, and Bill Scott. It is believed that, as a center of class-struggle trade unionism, the TUAD provides the opportunity for a united front with non-party workers (ibid., 28 June), and that it has "played a role in bringing together already established rank-and-file groups" (ibid., 9 August). Gus Hall has termed TUAD and its publication, *Labor Today*, as essential in the continuance of the rank-and-file upsurge in the unions, and has insisted that it "call for broad united action" and "become a greater force" by seeking to go beyond rank-and-file appeals and aiming at a coalition with sections of the unions' leadership (*Political Affairs*, April). TUAD has stressed the need for alliances with other insurgent groups in various unions.

Other party-dominated organizations include the National Anti-Imperialist Movement in Solidarity with African Liberation, led by Anthony Monteiro, a CPUSA Central Committee member, which has collected signatures urging the expulsion of South Africa from the United Nations; the Chile Solidarity Committee; the Committee for a Just Peace in the Middle East; Women for Racial and Economic Equality; and the National Council of American-Soviet Friendship.

Party Internal Affairs. The 21st National Convention of the CPUSA was held in Chicago on 26-29 June 1975. The convention concluded with a "People's Bicentennial Rally" attended by 6,000 persons. The party hailed the convention as symbolizing CPUSA's role as the "most viable, most influential" and "best organized, most youthful" force on the U.S. left (*Daily World*, 2 July). The 357 delegates reportedly represented an increase of 40 percent over the number attending the 1972 convention and thus reflected the party's growth. In line with the convention theme that there is not and cannot be "any contradiction between Party work and mass work," the building of the party was called the chief priority for all levels (*Political Affairs*, September). Also a decision was made to begin work on redrafting the party program, adopted in 1969.

Gus Hall, in his report to the convention, stressed the opportunities for party gains, but also pinpointed specific areas of weakness. The party remained invisible in a number of severely depressed areas, and still had to "begin serious work with farmers" and in the field of public education. Further work in the cultural field, where a new journal, *Cultural Reporter* was established, was also mentioned. (*Daily World*, 2 July.) Earlier, Hall revealed certain disagreements within the party over the formation of coalitions within some unions to elect insurgent candidates, and criticized "some comrades" who were too sectarian to appreciate the benefits of united struggle (*Political Affairs*, January).

The CPUSA's opposition to the ratification of the Equal Rights Amendment (ERA) for women has also generated disagreement. Afraid that the working women whom they wish to attract would be harmed by the elimination of existing protective legislation, the party has officially opposed ERA and supported instead a legislative program for extending women's rights. The SWP and other leftist groups have consistently criticized this stand, and some members have joined the debate. Hall indicated in his convention report that the Central Committee would appoint a study committee to examine the issue in greater depth (*Daily World*, 28 June).

Although Jews no longer form as large a component of the membership as they once did, the CPUSA's sensitivity on the Middle East issue indicates that it remains a source of tension within the party. The resolution passed by the convention did not make explicit mention of Israel's continued right to exist, as previous statements had done. Instead, the resolution upheld the Palestinian right to "establish national authority over lands relinquished by the Israeli aggressors" and the "right of the Palestinian people to return to their homelands with full democratic rights" (ibid., 27 August). Although other references indicated the party supports a Middle East agreement based on U.N. resolutions to be reached at Geneva, and a report called for safe borders for Israel (ibid., 3 July), the language of the convention resolution and what it omits seem to suggest a retreat from previous statements criticizing the Palestine Liberation Organization's call for a democratic, secular state in Palestine (see *YICA, 1975*, p. 560). Hyman Lumer insisted that the party's main struggle must be against the "racist, aggressive character of Zionism" and that, while critical of those calling for the dissolution of Israel, the CPUSA supports the Palestinians (*Daily World*, 8 November).

Domestic Attitudes and Activities. At the CPUSA convention Gus Hall inisted that a socialist revolution in the United State is "blowing in the wind." The strategy he projected was designed to enable the CPUSA to become a factor in the 1976 elections. Citing the record number of non-voters and the increasing number of political independents, Hall argued that there was a vacuum in U.S. political leadership: "independents are now the largest single grouping . . . but [they have] no organized centers, programs or leadership." Predicting that both major parties would run "rightist" candidates, Hall described the possibilities for a new alternative on the left as "much greater now than they were four years ago, or two years ago." Seeing both parties as captives of "monopoly capital," the CPUSA rejected efforts to work within the Democratic Party. Instead, it called on "all progressives, independents and anti-monpoly forces to join in a dialogue now, a common electoral front against the monarchs of monopoly capitalism." Although such a united front might not reach fruition in the 1976 elections, the party would continue to push for it. The focus of the united front was to be the struggle against monopoly capital which was seen as increasingly in conflict with the outlook of the bulk of the population. This anti-monopoly theme, according to Hall, would unify and direct separate struggles against the military, imperialism, the ultra-right, and fascism. While seeking a united front against monopoly, the party would not insist on agreement on other issues but would continue to press its own views: "We are for the broadest unity possible," Hall declared, not even insisting on an acceptance of socialism. The only precondition for allies was a rejection of both racism and anti-communism. (*Daily World*, 1 July 1975.) Hall called for an electoral alliance which could support such figures as Ramsey Clark, Shirley Chisholm, and Bella Abzug, along with Communists, in an effort to achieve a balance of power. (*Political Affairs*, January.) Henry Winston insisted that such a united front concept is a permanent, not temporary part of the CPUSA line (*Daily World*, 1 July).

According to Hall, a united front is essential because monopoly capitalism has launched an offensive against the working class and democracy. Hall criticized President Gerald Ford's administration for seeking to improve profits at the expense of the population and for failing to take action against the recession. The energy crisis, he charged, had been "manufactured to keep prices up." Among the other tactics imputed to monopoly were a speedup, the financial strangulation of the cities, and efforts to increase repression and racism (ibid., 23 January, 27 June). New York City's financial crisis was laid at the feet of the banks and monopolies, which were trying to "smash the trade union movement" and reduce social services. Such efforts, it was argued, could only be combated with a mass struggle to gain federal aid and force the banks and big business to absorb the financial burden (ibid., 25, 28 October).

George Meyers saw the economic crisis and consequent efforts to force the working class to reduce its standard of living as causing a record number of strikes. The growing radicalization of the rank and file meant increasing pressure on the top union leadership to modify or abandon its class-collaborationist policies. While attacking George Meany, head of the American Federation of Labor and Congress of Industrial Organizations (AFL-CIO), Meyers did suggest that a statement of Meany expressing dissatisfaction with the two-party system "requires closer examination." (Ibid., 18 March.) The new militant trend in labor, sparked by such organization as TUAD, the Coalition of Black Trade Unionists, and the Coalition of Labor Union Women suggested to Hall that such party demands as a 30-hour work week with no cut in pay and an end to discrimination were within reach (ibid., 3 July). Other party proposals to deal with the economic crisis included a 20 percent cut in prices of non-farm products, government jobs for the unemployed, and an end to all taxes for families with incomes under $25,000 (ibid., 23 January).

The CPUSA repeatedly called for elimination of the Central Intelligence Agency and the Federal Bureau of Investigation, charging both with violations of the law and repression. The CIA was accused of being subversive of democracy, anti-labor, and racist (ibid., 11 July). Some ultra-leftist organizations, such as the National Caucus of Labor Committees (see *YICA, 1975*, p. 556), were alleged to be CIA fronts (*Daily World*, 18 September). The FBI was denounced for its "Operation Hoodwink," which was said to be designed to encourage underworld attacks on the CPUSA. A woman who was charged with an attempt to assassinate President Ford was described by the CPUSA as an FBI informer and the actions of such persons were said to "objectively serve only the ruling class" (ibid., 24 September). Similarly when a Puerto Rican terrorist group carried out a bombing in New York, the action was denounced as the work of provocateurs (ibid., 28 June).

When the final report on the Watergate affair was issued, the CPUSA charged that it only perpetuated the cover-up of former President Nixon (ibid., 17 October). The Watergate affair was seen as part of a conspiracy by monopoly capitalism aimed at "preparing the political and ideological soil and the climate in which fascism can come to power" (ibid., 27 June).

International Views and Policies. The CPUSA remained wedded to a defense of both the domestic and foreign policies of the Soviet Union. During 1975 there are no discernible differences on any policy issues. The CPUSA convention endorsed a call for the early convening of a conference of all communist parties, which would presumably read Communist China out of the world movement (*Daily World*, 3 July). Maoism was a frequent target for editorial writers and party leaders. Henry Winston denounced Maoism for supporting U.S. imperialism, destroying the cadres of the Chinese Communist Party, and abandoning internal democracy (*Political Affairs*, September). Gus Hall argued that the Chinese were appealing for a "front of aggression based on a U.S. imperialist-Maoist axis." (*Daily World*, 21 October).

The CPUSA continued to campaign for U.S.-Soviet détente, criticizing those elements in the United States which have questioned the value of the relationship. The Apollo-Soyuz space flight was prominently featured as a symbol of international cooperation (ibid., 13 July) and the Helsinki meeting hailed for marking "the closing of the period of the cold war" (ibid., 23 July). AFL-CIO chief Meany was denounced for opposing grain shipments to the USSR; his concern over high food prices was alleged to be a cover-up for his anti-détente effort, which also included AFL-CIO dinners honoring Alexander Solzhenitsyn (ibid., 20 August). The adoption of Senator Henry M. Jackson's amendment to the U.S.-Soviet trade agreement was blasted as having sacrificed jobs for U.S. workers; détente and expanded trade were seen as generating jobs for the U.S. unemployed (ibid., 16 January, 13 March). The U.S. military budget was attacked as being far too large, deflecting money from social services, and being unnecessary in an age of détente (ibid., 18 October); the arms budget, it was claimed, could be cut entirely without jeopardizing national security: "no military enemy is waiting to pounce on the United States" (ibid., 22 October). While endorsing détente, the draft resolution of the CPUSA convention made it clear that détente was "a special form of the class struggle, not its negation, not its abandoment" (ibid., 27 June).

Developments in Portugal were closely observed during the year, and strong support was given to the Portuguese Communist Party. The Portuguese Socialists, led by Mario Soares, were attacked for inciting violence (ibid., 13 July), and Soares himself was said to be helping the "CIA and world imperialism" by his attacks on the Communists (ibid., 29 July). The *República* case was called a provocation (ibid., 21 June). There were warnings that Portugal was becoming another Chile and that U.S. interference must end: "Let everyone who cherishes democracy act now, for the cause of Portugal is the cause of democracy" (ibid., 23 August). Barely a month before, the same paper had defended Alvaro Cunhal's attack on bourgeois democracy (24 July).

During the early part of the year, the CPUSA frequently argued that the United States should not provide any aid to the Thieu government in South Vietnam. Secretary of Defense Schlesinger was attacked for not ruling out future aid to Southeast Asia (ibid., 21 January). The crumbling of the Saigon regime was viewed as "a defeat for U.S. imperialism and a victory for the American people," and the Ford administration was called upon to abide by the Paris agreements and send aid to the Provisional Revolutionary Government (ibid., 4, 9 April). Gus Hall condemned the airlift of Vietnamese orphans as "kidnaping" and suggested that consideration be given to impeaching Ford and Kissinger for asking for authority to use troops to evacuate U.S. citizens (ibid., 11, 12 April). When the new Cambodian government seized the *Mayaguez*, the party reaction was that it was "another Tonkin provocation" and the U.S. rescue effort was a "criminal brutal act of aggression" to disguise the defeat of U.S. imperialism in Southeast Asia (ibid., 14, 16 May).

The appointment of Patrick Moynihan as U.S. ambassador to the United Nations was, Henry Winston charged, an effort to implement a "racist ruling-class philosophy" internationally (ibid., 16 August). When Moynihan called Ugandan director Amin a racist murderer, the CPUSA urged that the "swaggering bully-boy and arrogant mouthpiece of U.S. imperialist ruling circles" be dismissed (ibid., 8 October). An editorial applauded the U.N. resolution on Zionism and charged that the real anti-Semites were Ford and Moynihan since the United States tolerated Nazi Party activities (ibid., 28 October). The CPUSA also supported "unconditional independence for Puerto Rico" (ibid., 1 July).

International Activities and Contacts. Roscoe Proctor and Charlene Mitchell were CPUSA representatives at the Second Congress of the Congolese Party of Workers, held in December 1974 in Brazzaville. In January 1975, Henry Winston led a CPUSA delegation to France for discussions with French Communist Party leaders; a communiqué was issued calling for increased solidarity in the face of the present crisis of capitalism (*Daily World*, 21 January). Another delegation led by Winston stopped in Moscow in August en route to Hanoi for the celebration of North Vietnam's 30th anniversary of independence. In October Gus Hall was awarded the Order of People's Friendship by the Presidium of the USSR Supreme Soviet (ibid., 17 October).

Party Publications. The *Daily World*, published five times a week in New York, is the CPUSA's major publication. *Political Affairs* is a theoretical journal. Other party-linked papers are *People's World*, a San Francisco weekly; *Freedomways*, a black quarterly; *New World Review*, a bimonthly journal on international affairs; *Jewish Affairs*, a bimonthly newsletter; *Cultural Reporter*; *African Agenda*; *Labor Today*; and *Korea Forum*. International Publishers in New York has long been identified as the party's publishing outlet. There are plans to begin publishing a new party journal for blacks in January 1976 (*Daily World*, 10 July).

*　　*　　*

The SWP. Jack Barnes is national secretary and Barry Sheppard is organizational secretary of the Socialist Workers Party. Linda Jenness and Ed Heisler head the party's 1976 National Campaign Committee. Peter Camejo and Willie Mae Reid will be the SWP candidates for President and Vice-President. Other party leaders include Fred Halstead, Tony Thomas, Andrew Pulley, Elizabeth Stone, Pedro Vásquez, Ray Markey, Omari Musa, Catarino Garza, and Frank Lovell. Mary-Alice Waters is editor of the SWP newspaper, *The Militant*.

The Young Socialist Alliance, the party's youth group and its largest and most important auxiliary, is headed by Mailk Miah. The YSA's 15th Convention, to be held in late December 1975 in Milwaukee, planned to vote on a resolution urging resistance to an expected government "offensive against education," whose "first victims" would be women and minorities (*Militant*, 21 November), and calling for government guarantees of jobs for youth and free education (*Young Socialist*, November). The YSA has taken an active role in the National Student Coalition Against Racism, one of whose leaders, Maceo Dixon, is an SWP leader. The coalition has organized demonstrations in support of school busing in Boston, a city whose troubles over busing were described by the SWP as "harbinger of future struggles" (*Militant*, 3 October). The YSA and SWP urged the federal government to "use all necessary force" to protect black children being bused, including federal troops (ibid., 19 September). The YSA role in the coalition provoked attacks from other leftist groups, including the YWLL and various Maoist groups.

The Political Rights Defense Fund was formed to press the SWP's suit against alleged harassment by the FBI and CIA. Syd Stapleton is national secretary for the fund.

The 26th National Convention of the SWP, held in Ohio on 17-21 August, attracted 1,600 delegates and alternates. A convention report noted that 43 percent of this number were women. The convention saw signs that the radicalization of the working class was beginning and that the period ahead would be one of class polarization and struggle requiring a shift in SWP activities. Recognizing that the party was a "relatively small nucleus," the convention noted that it must "champion the progressive demands and support the struggles of all sectors of the oppressed, [and] press for revolutionary unity based on support for the demands of the most oppressed." (*Militant*, 9 September; *International Socialist Review*, November). Because of the impending capitalist offensive against workers, the convention believed that rapid party growth is possible (*Militant*, 26 September). The party supports such groups as La Raza Unida (Chicano political parties) and the demands of other "oppressed minorities" (*International Socialist Review*, November). The coming socialist revolution, it argues, will be a combined one—to end capitalist exploitation of the working class and to allow self-determination of Blacks (*Militant*, 3 October). The SWP strongly supports the Equal Rights Amendment and has sharply attacked the CPUSA for opposing it (ibid., 26 September, 14 November).

In its positions on foreign policy, the SWP is critical of all the major powers. The United States is regarded as the stronghold of world imperialism. The USSR is attacked for its betrayal of democracy, as is China. The major foreign policy preoccupation in 1975, however, was Portugal, on which the SWP convention spent a third of its time. There are two tendencies of roughly equal strength within the Fourth International (both of which originated in the late 1960s out of debates over the role of guerrilla warfare in Latin America), the International Majority Tendency and the Leninist Trotskyist Faction, which have some fundamental disagreements in regard to Portugal. The latter, supported by the SWP leadership, refuses to minimize the struggle for democracy in Portugal and, while critical of Soares' Socialist Party, urges a united front and insists that a socialist revolution must be a majority revolution involving a defense of democratic rights (ibid., 10 October).

The SWP has supported the view that Zionism is racism and argued that as a settler state, Israel has no right to exist (ibid., 31 October). The party hailed the Communist victory in Vietnam (ibid., 18 October), but has attacked the Soviet Union for its denial of civil liberties and for posing as the representative of socialism (ibid., 21 March).

The SWP publishes *The Militant* every week. Its *Young Socialist* and *International Socialist Review* are monthlies.

*   *   *

The PLP. The Progressive Labor Party does not provide information about its membership or its leading cadres. The party's founders were Milt Rosen and Mort Scheer. Other key figures appear to be Levi Laub, formerly associated with the SDS, and John Harris.

The PLP's most important front group is the Committee Against Racism (CAR) whose chairman is Finley Campbell. Among its other activities, the CAR has encouraged disruption of speeches on genetics and intelligence by William Shockley and has defended PLP members who disrupted classes on this theme taught by Edward Banfield. The PLP has urged that "racists" such as Banfield be put on trial for genocide (*Challenge*, 30 January 1975). Active in the Boston school busing controversy, the PLP sponsored a May Day march there which drew 2,500 people and was denounced as a provocation by the CPUSA and SWP (ibid., 22 May). The PLP contended that "a mass fascist movement is growing in our country," centered in Boston and led by Louise Day Hicks and a parents' group, ROAR (Restore Our Alienated Rights) (ibid., 6 February, 15 May). The party argued that this fascist offensive is supported by liberal politicians such as Senator Edward Kennedy and "liberal racist theorists at places like Harvard" (ibid., 6 February). The anti-busing movement was seen as a diversion to destroy working-class unity. The PLP thus stressed the need to forge worker-student alliances and urged anti-racist teach-ins, priority for workers' demands, dismissal of racist professors, and support for ghetto rebellions (ibid., 13 February).

In domestic activities focusing on workers' needs, the PLP stressed support for "30 for 40" (30 hours' work for 40 hours' pay), which it contends will end unemployment. Declaring that the "fight for workers' powers in the unions begins with the development of caucuses organized by the rank-and-file with the participation and leadership of communists" (ibid., 16 January), the PLP has been active in such rank-and-file caucuses and has managed to attain influence in several local unions. It argues that such developments will eventually give workers the power to shut down production, but that only after the workers employ their ultimate weapon—the general strike—will they be able to seize power (ibid., 16 January). The economic difficulties of New York City were blamed on "bankers, big bosses and their politician flunkies" who were committing crimes against workers (ibid., 14 August), and labor leaders in the city were accused of selling out their workers (ibid., 31 July).

PLP's foreign policy positions include criticism of both the USSR and China. U.S.-Soviet imperialist clashes were regarded as threatening to bring World War III (ibid., 27 February). In China, right-wingers were said to have been in control since Chou En-lai engineered the defeat of the Cultural Revolution (ibid., 6 February). The U.S. withdrawal in Southeast Asia was seen as "strengthening the position of the Soviet and Chinese bosses vis-à-vis the U.S. bosses" (ibid., 29 May), and as merely one instance of a faltering of U.S. imperialism around the world. In response to such crises, said the PLP, ruling-class circles in the United States had initiated an exposé of the CIA in order to "return the CIA securely to the grip of the big bosses who are controlled by [Vice President Nelson] Rockefeller" (ibid., 23 January).

According to the PLP, "the current situation of world capitalism is ripe for socialist revolutions," but in order to take advantage of the crisis "a new Communist movement has to be built world-wide" (ibid, 3 April). The character visualized for that movement was clearly indicated in PLP's defense of Stalin and its comment that his only fault was that he was too liberal (ibid., 19 June). The PLP also insisted that it is "not a pacifist organization" (ibid., 15 May).

The PLP publishes *Challenge/Desafio*, an English-Spanish weekly, and *Progressive Labor*, a theoretical journal.

*   *   *

Maoist Groups. There are a number of Maoist groups in the United States which proclaim their devotion to "Marxism-Leninism Mao Tse-tung Thought." The two largest are the Revolutionary Union—recently renamed the Revolutionary Communist Party (RCP)—and the October League. The OL chairman is Michael Klonsky, a former SDS leader.

Both RU and OL are committed to an armed seizure of power by the working class. Both vigorously condemn the CPUSA as revisionist—the OL has insisted that "a critical part of making revolution in the U.S. is educating the masses of people to the danger of the CP's revisionism" (*Guardian*, 9 April)—and attack the Soviet Union as imperialist. Both have also supported the concept of self-determination in the Black Belt (the lower South) for American Negroes. A series of disagreements has thwarted efforts to form a "new" communist party: these include the RU's opposition to busing, which it regards as a manifestation of narrow nationalism, and its hostility to the Equal Rights Amendment for women (ibid., 8 January, 9 April). The OL has set up "fight-back committees" in various cities to coordinate and initiate economic struggles. It has also achieved considerable influence in the Southern Conference Educational Fund, formerly dominated by the CPUSA, but has recently become embroiled in controversy with other revolutionary groups because of its hostility to homosexual liberation movements. The OL's youth arm, the Communist Youth Organization, was established in 1975.

The RU publishes *Revolution*. The OL's major journal is *The Call*. *The Guardian*, which takes an independent Maoist line, is published weekly in New York and is the most influential paper among U.S. Maoists.

*   *   *

Weather Underground Organization. The small but active Weather Underground Organization was originally a part of the Students for a Democratic Society. It went underground after a number of its leaders were indicted for their activities in a series of Chicago riots. It is headed by Bernadine Dohrn, Bill Ayers, and Jeff Jones. The WUO, which considers Marxism-Leninism "a necessary guide" for understanding capitalist society and deciding on a revolutionary strategy, has taken credit for "25 armed actions" including bombings at the Pentagon and State Department (*Ossawatomie*, Spring 1975).

During 1975 an open support group, The Prairie Fire Distributing Committee (PFDC), issued several publications giving the WUO perspective. The PFDC also held a national conference in July where the leadership included Jennifer Dohrn (sister of Bernadine), Alan Berkman, and Sylvia Baraldini. The WUO has also apparently gained the support of former Yippie leader Abbie Hoffman, at present a fugitive from a drug charge, who has recommended the formation of a new communist party (*NYT*, 19 May 1975).

The WUO finds inspiration in such countries as North Vietnam, Cuba, and China, and insists that "the quality of life of a Chinese peasant is better than ours" (*Prairie Fire*, 1974). The group's goal is to "build a mass anti-imperialist organization," "a Marxist-Leninist party to lead the people" (*Groundswell*, February 1975). The estimated membership of the WUO is 40 and that of the PFDC a few hundred.

Emory University   Harvey Klehr

Uruguay

The Communist Party of Uruguay (Partido Comunista del Uruguay; PCU) dates from September 1920, when a congress of the Socialist Party voted to join the Comintern. The present name was adopted in April 1921. On 1 December 1973 the PCU was declared illegal for the first time in its history. It is firmly pro-Soviet.

Numerous leftist organizations operate in Uruguay and display Soviet, Chinese, Cuban, or nationalist leanings or combinations thereof. Among the more important are the Socialist Party of Uruguay (Partido Socialista del Uruguay; PSU), the Movement of the Revolutionary Left (Movimiento de Izquierda Revolucionaria; MIR), and the National Liberation Movement (Movimiento de Liberación Nacional; MLN), the latter better known as the Tupamaros.

The Revolutionary Workers' Party (Partido Obrero Revolucionario; POR), originally formed in 1944 as the Revolutionary Workers' League, and the Socialist Workers' Party of Uruguay (Partido Socialista de los Trabajadores del Uruguay; PSTU), are Trotskyist in orientation.

Except for the PCU, these groups are apparently small (no precise membership figures are known). The PCU is estimated to have 30,000 members, with workers accounting for about 73 percent, with its youth group and sympathizers added, the total may be 35,000 to 40,000. The population of Uruguay is 3,075,000 (estimated 1975).

The Broad Front. PCU electoral strength long resided in the Leftist Liberation Front (Frente Izquierda de Liberación; FIDEL), founded by the PCU in 1962 and composed of some 10 small political and cultural groups. In an extremely complex electoral system which discourages voting for minority party candidates, FIDEL had never done very well (less than 6 percent of the vote in 1966). In 1971 FIDEL took part in the national election as part of a much larger coalition, the Broad Front (Frente Amplio; FA), made up of 17 leftist and anti-government parties and groups, including also the PSU, POR, the Christian Democratic Party (Partido Demócrata Cristiano; PDC), a faction of the liberal Colorado Party led by Senator Zelmar Michelini, a faction of the conservative National (Blanco) Party led by Senator Francisco Ridríguez Camusso, and independent leftists. The FA won 18 percent of the vote. It had 18 members in the Chamber of Deputies and 5 in the Senate until 27 June 1973 when President Juan Bordaberry with military backing dissolved the Congress, charging the FA congressmen with "criminal actions of conspiracy against the constitution."

The PCU. Organization and Leadership. On 1 January 1975, President Bordaberry by decree made permanent the outlawing of the PCU, the December 1973 decree making the party illegal having left the time period indefinite (*El Día*, Montevideo, 2 January). Long-time PCU head and first secretary Rodney Arismendi, in prison since 8 May 1974 on charges of subversion, was released on 4 January 1975 and exiled to Moscow. He said that Soviet party chief Brezhnev helped in his release by communication with Uruguayan military leaders interested in trade with the Soviet Union (TASS, 10 January).

The PCU Central Committee has 48 members and 27 alternates. The five-member Secretariat consists of Arismendi, Enrique Pastorino, Jaime Pérez, Enrique Rodríguez, and Alberto Suárez. At an underground headquarters, the Secretariat has a coordinator. Pérez was arrested in November 1974 after calling for a "provisional regime to end the dictatorship." Charged with attacking the morale of the armed forces and attempting to overthrow the government, he was sentenced in February 1975 to 18 months in jail (AP, 27 February). Suárez was organization secretary until deposed for "not preparing party members for coping with the circumstances of the PCU being outlawed" (according to the Cuban news agency, Prensa Latina, 2 January 1975). He was also blamed for not warning party members about the changed attitude of FA leader and retired general Liber Seregni, who was released from jail in November 1974. Seregni broke with the PCU and urged PDC and other non-Marxist FA members not to cooperate with the PCU.

The PCU Executive Committee has 15 members: the five Secretariat members, Félix Díaz, Eduardo Viera, Alberto Altesor, Leopoldo Bruera, José L. Massera, Rosario Pietrarroia, César Reyes Daglio, Gerardo Cuesta, Jorge Mazzarovich, and Wladímir Turiansky. Díaz has been in prison since 1973; Viera was imprisoned for three months in 1973, released, and then indicted and convicted of subversion in May 1975 (*Granma*, Havana, 11 May). Among those in prison for all or part of the year, according to Arismendi, were Mazzarovich, Pérez, Massera, Altesor, and Eduardo Bleir (*Unidad*, Lima, 20 February; *Granma*, 1 December). Late in the year PCU leaders charged that a new wave of "fascist terror" had been unleashed in Uruguay (*L'Unità*, Rome, 29 November; *Granma*, 1 and 17 December). Early in December the Armed Forces charged the PCU with selecting and financing Uruguayan students studying subversive techniques in the Soviet Union (EFE, Madrid, 10 December).

The National Convention of Workers (Convención Nacional de Trabajadores; CNT), established in 1966 as the largest federation of labor unions, has been led by PCU officials, including Pastorino, Díaz, and Turiansky. After the CNT called a general strike, the government on 30 June 1973 suspended all CNT activities. The CNT nonetheless makes periodic statements regarding the state of the nation, calling for pay increases and deficit government spending, and charging that new currency policies have simply made business calculations easier but not reduced inflation (*Crisis*, Buenos Aires, September).

Pastorino remains president of the pro-Soviet World Federation of Trade Unions (WFTU), and through the International Labor Office has been given United Nations diplomatic immunity. He arranged the 1974 Havana meeting of the WFTU Council and the 1975 CNT report on diminished purchasing power of Uruguayan workers (*Granma 9*, February).

The WFTU in telegrams to the Uruguayan government and letters to workers' groups declared its solidarity with the CNT (*WFTU Flashes*, 29 January, 16 April). On 11 March, police arrested leaders of the Uruguayan Railways Workers Union and released them after questioning about CNT plans for work stoppages (*Granma*, 30 March). Also in March, police raided the headquarters of the Association of Secondary Education Unions (Associación Integremial de Enseñanza Secundaria; AIES), the teachers' unions federation, and arrested outlawed CNT officials. The government announced that the raid yielded documents of CNT plans for disturbances and shutdowns in public schools. On 13 April, the Interior Ministry suspended AIES operations and impounded its funds (AP, Montevideo 14 April). As a follow-up, on 26 June, the director of secondary education announced that the government would eliminate social science textbooks sympathetic to the PCU (*Latin America*, 4 July).

On 24 April, at the construction site of the Salto Grande hydroelectric project on the Argentine border, police arrested for questioning 1,800 protesting labor union members. The government charged that the CNT had called rallies to plan work stoppages for 1 May to bankrupt the economy (*Le Monde*, Paris, 30 April). About 100 youths were arrested in Montevideo after distributing CNT leaflets calling for May Day demonstrations (*Latin*, 30 April). The WFTU called on the CNT to aid socialist solidarity by supporting the U.N. "International Women's Year" and by protesting on 27

June—the second anniversary of Bordaberry's dissolving of Congress (*WFTU Flashes*, 9 July). In July, police arrested two CNT leaders, one the head of the Telecommunications Workers Union and the other the head of the Transport Workers Union (ibid., 6 August).

The PCU-influenced Federation of University Students of Uruguay (Federación de Estudiantes Universitarios del Uruguay; FEUU), an affiliate of the Soviet-front International Union of Students, was outlawed along with the party in 1973. The FEUU secretary-general, Horacio Bazzano, was arrested in March 1975 for denouncing the government. Evelio Oribe, PCU liaison adviser for FEUU, has been in prison since April 1974.

The PCU's youth organization, the Union of Communist Youth (Unión de la Juventud Comunista; UJC), was founded in 1955. It had a claimed membership of 22,000 when it was outlawed in 1973.

The army announced 30 April, that in Trienta y Tres city, 60 PCU and UJC men and women, of whom 25 were teen-agers, were arrested for recruiting students throughout Treinta y tres department into the UJC (Radio El Espectador, Montevideo, 30 April). On 17 July 1975 a military court ordered the trial of 20 UJC members in San José city for conducting "Marxist-Leninist indoctrination meetings for youth" in San José department and for publishing a clandestine newspaper (ibid., 17 July).

Domestic Attitudes and Activities. With its publications outlawed, and the Marxist weekly *Marcha* closed since 26 November 1974, the PCU during 1975 issued statements in the mimeographed *Carta Semanal* and leaflets that were circulated clandestinely, and through the Cuban news agency, Prensa Latina. In May a Montevideo court tried three PCU members on charges of circulating party periodicals (Radio El Espectador, 6 May). A presidential decree in June banned the circulation of any Marxist printed or recorded material and authorized the Postal Service to confiscate Marxist periodicals, books, tapes, and films (*Latin*, Montevideo, 6 June).

Differences over economic policies prompted the PCU to speculate over divisions between President Bordaberry and the military leaders, but in August Bordaberry said that the military will continue to support the government, and that Uruguay will not return to the multiparty political system which paralyzed the economy. He also forecast major constitutional reforms in 1976 whereby the PCU, PSU, and other socialist parties would be excluded from future elections. (*Latin*, 29 August.)

International Views and Positions. On 17 July 1975 the Interior Ministry carried out a presidential decree dissolving the Uruguay-Soviet Union Cultural Institute for violating the law against participating in PCU activities (Radio Carve, Montevideo, 17 July). On 20 September, the Central Committee of the Communist Party of the Soviet Union (CPSU) sent greetings to Uruguayan communists on the 55th anniversary of the PCU (TASS, 20 September).

Exiled PCU first secretary Arismendi on television in Moscow on 26 January launched a series of interviews which he continued in various countries during 1975. In Havana on 14 March he was awarded the Playa Girón medal by Fidel Castro on behalf of the Cuban Communist Party for furthering the cause of Marxism (*Granma*, 23 March). After touring the Cuban provinces, Arismendi flew to Rome to attend the congress of the Italian Communist Party, where he expressed confidence that Third World as well as socialist nations would continue to help the PCU in its struggle against the Uruguayan government (*L'Unità*, 30 March). On 7 April Arismendi spoke in Prague at the Czechoslovak symposium on "Problems of Peace and Socialism" (*FBIS*, 9 April).

Arismendi stated in Moscow on 1 May that the former dean of the engineering faculty in Montevideo and also the former director of the Pedagogical Institute were in prison in Uruguay for PCU activities (ibid., 7 May). On 20 May, Arismendi spoke before the Central Committee of the

Uzbekistan republic CPSU organization in Tashkent. On 27 June he spoke in Havana to Cuban party groups. During 9-14 July he conferred in Sofia with Todor Zhivkov, first secretary, and the Central Committee of the Bulgarian Communist Party (ibid., 14 July). On 25 July, in Belgrade, Arismendi conferred with the executive secretary of the League of Communists of Yugoslavia on promoting solidarity of workers' parties in various nations, and opposition to the Organization of American States (ibid., 25 July).

Publications. The principal PCU publications, the daily newspaper *El Popular* and the theoretical journal *Estudios*, outlawed by the government, did not come out during 1975. An underground weekly, *Carta Semanal del Partido Comunista,* begun in March 1974, appeared irregularly in clandestine distribution during 1975 reportedly reaching "tens of thousands of readers" (*WMR*, November 1975). To replace the *Estudios*, the PCU mimeographed and irregularly issued *Ensayos.* On 19 October, the government closed the United Peoples Publishing House (Editorial Pueblos Unidos; EPU) in Montevideo, charging that EPU was a propaganda front for the PCU (ANSA, 19 October).

*   *   *

The MLN (Tupamaros). The idea of the MLN arose among Uruguayan leftists in the early 1960s. The organization made its first raid in July 1963. In 1970-71 it attracted international attention by kidnaping several foreign nationals in Uruguay. By 1973 the army had captured most of the MLN guerrillas, and their leaders, following conviction on charges of subversion, have been imprisoned since April of that year. On 28 November 1974 an MLN document reported that the organization had split into two competing sections (*El Combatiente*, Buenos Aires, 15 January).

A book, *The Tupamaros: The Unmentionables*, by Carlos Wilson of Berkeley, California, was published in Boston in 1974 by Branden Press and was intended to be sympathetic to the MLN, but MLN exiles in Argentina called it "unreadable, not helping in our quest for people's justice" (Prensa Latina, 9 May).

MLN leader Pedro Larena, arrested in Montevideo in May 1975, died in a prison hospital in October (*Latin America*, 17 October).

In a letter to Professor Kenneth Golby of York University in Canada, President Bordaberry denied the charges of harsh treatment of MLN prisoners made in the propaganda campaign by the Golby Committee, pointing out that neither the International Red Cross nor Amnesty International found cases of claimed mistreatment (*El País*, Montevideo, 2 March).

On 11 April in Buenos Aires, police arrested 21 Argentines and 4 Uruguayan Tupamaros in an arsenal headquarters of the Revolutionary Coordinating Junta (*UPI*, 12 April). On 4 June at a ranch in Buenos Aires province, police arrested 13 Argentine guerrillas and confiscated dozens of weapons and documents indicating MLN Uruguayans had been involved (*Clarín*, Buenos Aires, 6 June).

Between 25 May and 10 July in Montevideo, police and the army arrested 22 Tupamaros, most of whom had secretly returned from exile in Argentina and Bolivia (*Washington Post*, 18 July). Police arrested two Tupamaros on 29 May in Palmira, a city on the Uruguay River (AFP, 30 May).

On 26 June in Montevideo, the armed forces announced that by arresting 20 Tupamaros and killing three others in raids the government had nullified a plan to reactivate the MLN (Radio El Espectador, Montevideo, 26 June). On 10 July the armed forces announced that among Tupamaros arrested in Solís with weapons at a target-practice range were four linked to the MLN Sector for the Support of Teachers and the First of May Group (ibid., 10 July).

On 10 July, the French government expelled three diplomats of the Cuban Embassy in Paris for activity in the international terrorist group led by Carlos Ramírez Sánchez, whose membership includes several MLN Uruguayans. The indictment of Ramírez charged that the MLN helped in a raid on the French Embassy in The Hague in September 1974 and the killing of three French intelligence agents in Paris on 27 June 1975 (AP, 11 July).

Tupamaros were among the Argentine guerrillas who killed U.S. consul John Egan on 28 February in Córdoba, kidnaped a Buenos Aires provincial supreme court justice on the same date, and fought the army in Tucumán on 30 August, according to the Argentine general directing the Tucumán anti-guerrilla campaign (AP, 31 August).

Arizona State University   Marvin Alisky

Venezuela

The Communist Party of Venezuela (Partido Comunista de Venezuela; PCV), the oldest of the extreme leftist groups in the country, was founded in 1931. In recent years two serious splits have greatly undermined the party's strength and influence. One took place in December 1970, when most of its youth organization and substantial elements of the adult party broke away to form the Movimiento al Socialismo (MAS); the other in mid-1974, when a group of party leaders split away to form the Vanguardia Comunista (VC).

Another Marxist-Leninist group, the Movement of the Revolutionary Left (Movimiento de Izquierda Revolucionaria; MIR), originated in 1960 from a split in the Democratic Action Party (Acción Democrática; AD), which controlled the government from 1959 to 1969 and returned to power early in 1974. Two other new elements on the far left have appeared in recent years—a Maoist movement and a Trotskyist group, the latter established early in 1973. Finally, there remain some active remnants of the urban and rural guerrilla movement which had its high point in the early 1960s, when both the PCV and the MIR participated; these have had little more than nuisance value since the major elements of both parties withdrew from guerrilla activities in 1965-66.

Much of the activity of the Venezuelan Marxist-Leninists in 1975 centered on the question of the country's oil industry. The nationalization of petroleum, Venezuela's participation in the Organization of Petroleum Exporting Countries, and the reaction of the United States and other industrial countries to OPEC policies were the principal subjects of discussion.

The PCV. Organization and Leadership. The top leadership of the PCV is its 13-member Politburo. The body includes, among others: Gustavo Machado, party chairman; Jesús Faría, secretary general; and Radames Larrazabal, who in recent years has been the principal public spokesman for the party.

Until the December 1970 split of the PCV, the party's Venezuelan Communist Youth (Juventud Comunista Venezolana; JCV) was the largest political group in the student movement. The split deprived the JCV of most of its leaders and members, and threw it into such confusion that it was not until February 1972 that the JCV held its Third National Congress. The split reduced PCV influence in the student movement to minor proportions, its former leading position being taken by the youth group of the MAS.

The principal center of PCV influence in the labor movement has long been the United Workers' Confederation of Venezuela (Confederación Unitaria de Trabajadores de Venezuela CUTV), established in the early 1960s, when the PCV lost virtually all influence in the majority Confederation of Workers of Venezuela (Confederación de Trabajadores de Venezuela; CTV). The Communists apparently had no representation in the Seventh Congress of the CTV in May 1975, although Radames Larrazabal indicated a desire for rapprochement with the AD by voicing support for several measures announced by Venezuelan president Carlos Andres Pérez at the opening session of the CTV Congress.

During 1975 there was some limited cooperation between the CTV and the Communists' CUTV. Thus, in May these two groups and the Catholic Confederación de Sindicatos Autonomes (CODESA) issued a joint declaration against U.S. hostility towards the OPEC. It is also notable that a delegation of the CTV visited Cuba in January, as guests of the Castro regime's Confederación de Trabajadores de Cuba. (*Granma*, Havana, 18 January.)

Domestic Attitudes and Activities. During much of 1975 the PCV was involved in the discussion around President Carlos Andrés Pérez's initiative to nationalize the country's oil industry. In mid-January the PCV Politburo adopted a resolution indicating general support for Pérez, saying that in face of aggressive behavior by the United States against OPEC, "Venezuela, through its president and the National Congress, has been expressing increasing resistance to these threats, which has merited the support of the national majorities." (*Tribuna Popular*, 18 January.)

A plenum of the PCV Central Committee, 23-25 January, adopted a long resolution which proclaimed that "the fundamental task of the Party and the Communist Youth League, as well as of the masses, must be to set up the Patriotic Front." It added that "to unite the majority of the nation ... it is necessary to have explicit aims and a firm orientation." The plenum resolution set forth, as part of a suggested "program for patriotic unity," its position on the issue of oil nationalization: "Support the draft law prepared by a presidential commission on transferring the fuel industry and the sale of its output to the state. The law should provide for paying compensation to the enterprises and for the possibility of concluding working contracts." (*IB*, No. 5.) This position was in contrast to that taken by Radamés Larrazabal, the PCV representative in the president's oil commission, who had opposed compensation for the foreign oil companies.

Two months later, the PCV apparently reversed its position with regard to the conditions for oil nationalization. In March it joined with the other opposition parties against Article 5 of President Pérez's bill which provided that the government "shall be enabled to enter into such agreements as may be necessary for fulfillment of its functions, without allowing such arrangements in any case to interfere with the essence of its control of the appointed activities," and that the State may "enter into agreements of limited duration with private interests, but must retain such participation as guarantee state control." (*Latin America*, 21 March.)

The oil nationalization law was finally passed, largely as it had been proposed by Pérez. However, the oil issue continued to preoccupy the PCV. The party supported the government's backing of increased oil prices at the OPEC meeting which began on 24 September. Shortly before, the Politburo of the PCV declared itself to be in "permanent session," giving as its reason the need to "follow the course of relations between the United States and Venezuela, in view of the threats made by President Ford and Secretary of State Kissinger" (*Ultimas Noticias*, Caracas, 21 September).

International Views and Positions. The PCV's loyalty to Moscow remained strong during 1975. Several delegations from the Venezuelan party visited East Europe, including Czechoslovakia, Hungary, Yugoslavia, and Bulgaria. The PCV also participated in the conference of 24 Latin American Communist parties held in Cuba in June.

The PCV further underscored its loyalty by a statement entitled "Struggle against the Chinese leaders' policy which has betrayed the principles of proletarian internationalism," issued by the Politburo in September. The statement claimed "that the present Chinese leaders are separating China from the socialist community," and added that "the Chinese leaders could constitute a threat to world peace with their militarist plans and their national policy of total preparation for war." It charged that "the Maoist leaders cooperate with the reactionary forces throughout the world." (Radio Moscow, 17 September.)

Publications. The principal organ of the PCV is the daily newspaper *Tribuna Popular.* It also issues a theoretical periodical, *Documentos Políticos*, which has had some difficulty in coming out since the MAS split.

*   *   *

VC. The launching of the Vanguardia Comunista in June 1974, was significant because it represented a split in the "old guard" of the Venezuelan Communist movement. Particularly interesting was the presence in its leadership of Eduardo Machado. In all previous divisions of the communist party, the Machado brothers, Gustavo and Eduardo, had always been aligned together. Another member of the PCV old guard who helped form Vanguardia Comunista was Guillermo García Ponce.

The VC held its First Congress in early November 1974. This meeting proclaimed the new group to be a "Marxist-Leninist party . . . faithful to the traditions of international solidarity." It urged nationalization of all basic industries of Venezuela. Eduardo Machado was elected president of the party, and Guillermo García Ponce secretary general. (*El Nacional*, Caracas, 4 November.)

Seven weeks after the congress it was announced that the VC was contemplating merger with the Movimiento de Izquierda Revolucionaria. A MIR spokesman said that such a merger arose from "an ideological, political, and organizational convergence which has come about in the course of everyday actions" (Radio EFE, Madrid, 22 December 1974).

Late in January 1975, committees representing the VC and MIR began negotiating the unification of the two groups. At the beginning of these meetings, Guillermo Garcia Ponce stated: "within the two organizations there is a sentiment in favor of inviting all of the socialist groups of Venezuela to participate in this work with a view to the constitution of one great revolutionary party" (*El Nacional*, 24 January).

Negotiations between VC and MIR had not brought about unification by the middle of the year. This was indicated by the publication in late July of a statement by the VC Politburo denouncing a suggestion by President Alfonso López Michelson of Colombia that there be co-dominion by Colombia and Venezuela over the Gulf of Venezuela. Eduardo Machado, speaking for the VC, declared: "The Colombian oligarchy's claim to Venezuelan territory does not correspond to the interests of the Colombian people. It is not a stand in defense of the sister republic's sovereignty or territory, [but] a maneuver to negotiate, at a later date, the exploitation of the rich oil deposits in the Gulf of Venezuela with the large international companies."

Although a small group, Vanguardia Communista further undermined the already reduced ranks of the PCV. The new party's following seems to be largely confined to Caracas.

*   *   *

The MAS. The "Movement toward Socialism" was formed late in 1970 as the result of a split in the PCV. Its principal leaders include former PCV Politburo member Pompeyo Márquez, the MAS secretary general, and Alexis Adam, Eleazar Díaz Rangel, Germán Lairet, Augusto León, Freddy Muñoz, Alfredo Padilla, Teodoro Petkoff, Tirso Pinto, Héctor Rodríguez Bauza, and Eloy Torres, the last one of the principal trade union leaders of the PCV after 1958. The MAS took with it a large part of the intermediary leadership cadres of the PCV; it seems certain that a majority of the former PCV rank-and-file and virtually all of the JCV joined the MAS.

The MAS Youth organization is the Juventud Comunista-MAS (JC-MAS). Upon its formation, the JC-MAS dominated most of the student bodies of Venezuelan universities. Although subsequently its influence has somewhat declined, it still remains the largest political group operating in the student movement.

The MAS had some influence at its inception in the CUTV trade union movement. Those who went with MAS first formed the CUT Clasista, as a rival organization. However, in July 1974 the MAS Central Committee decided to have its supporters enter the Confederación de Trabajadores de Venezuela, the majority union group. The MAS was reported as having 2.1 percent of the delegates to the Seventh Congress of the CTV, held late in April 1975 (*Expreso PL*, 18 April).

In January 1975 the MAS announced that it was establishing a secretariat. The leadership had until then been in the hands of a National Directorate and an Executive Committee. (*Punto*, 15 January.)

Domestic Attitudes and Activities. Although in the months following the ascension to power of President Carlos Andres Pérez of the Democratic Action Party, the MAS had maintained a position of "critical support" of Pérez, its attitude changed during 1975. It was reported in February that "from the recent policy discussions within the MAS, the line espoused by Teodoro Petkoff and Pompeyo Márquez, appears to have emerged triumphant. The MAS will now be seen to take a rather more critical attitude towards the government, emphasizing its incapacity to solve the country's social problems within the framework of capitalist development" (*Latin America*, 21 February).

In April the MAS in a two-day meeting defined its attitude toward the government: "The first year of the present administration began with competition between popular reforms announced through a series of measures and decrees and the development of private capital in the government's benefits and programs. [But] private capital development has been gaining ground while the popular reforms have been losing out since the measures decreed for the popular sectors are not being implemented." (EFE, Madrid, 21 April.)

The MAS's new attitude was emphasized in its position with regard to the oil nationalization bill submitted by President Pérez to Congress. The party joined other opposition groups in strongly fighting Article 5, which would permit the government under certain circumstances to sign service contracts with private oil companies (*Latin America*, 12 March).

The new position of MAS evoked a hostile reply from within Acción Democrática. Former president Romulo Betancourt, addressing the AD national convention in July, strongly attacked the MAS, calling it "extremely dangerous" and accusing it of trying to infiltrate the armed forces. He was answered by José Vicente Rangel, the MAS presidential candidate in 1973, who said that the MAS was sponsoring a "dialogue" with the military, but had no intentions of carrying out a coup. (Ibid., 25 July.) However, Pompeyo Márquez completely denied any attempt by MAS to infiltrate the armed forces (Radio Rumbos, 5 August).

The MAS was also attacked by the ring-wing Caracas newspaper *Ultimas Noticias*, which on 27 September accused it of trying to ape Salvador Allende's "Chilean Road to Socialism" in Venezuela. It reminded its readers that many MAS leaders had been in the guerrilla forces in the early 1960s, and expressed doubts that the MAS would be able to repeat the performance of the Chilean Unidad Popular.

In September MAS held a large rally in Valencia for the purpose of denouncing the attitude of the United States government toward the OPEC and toward Venezuela in particular (Radio Rumbos, 23 September).

International Views. During 1975, the MAS continued to maintain an independent attitude in its relations with foreign parties and governments.

Publication. The principal organ of publicity of the MAS is the afternoon newspaper *Punto* edited by Pompeyo Márquez.

*   *   *

The LSDP. Late in 1974 a new group made its appearance in the Venezuelan far left, the Socialist League for the Rights of the People (Liga Socialista de Derechos del Pueblo; LSDP). It was formed by 76 groups which had urged a blank vote in the 1973 election, and was headed by Jorge Rodríguez and Augstín Calzadilla. In announcing its formation, Rodríguez said: "There has been an effort to falsify socialism, without understanding that this is a theory and practice that is possible only with control of the state by the working class, which in our opinion continues to be the irreplaceable vanguard of the socialist revolution. On this point, we believe that certain leaders of the MAS are attempting to weaken the struggle for socialism, speaking in the name of it, but practicing reformism." He proclaimed that the LSDP was in complete opposition to the Pérez government "since we believe that the policy used is directed toward favoring the economically powerful sectors, both external and domestic." (*Ultimas Noticias*, 1 November 1974.)

There was little evidence of activity on the part of the LSDP during 1975.

The MIR. The MIR was established in 1960 by dissidents from the AD, including most of that party's youth movement. In 1962 it joined in launching a guerrilla effort which lasted for several years. A large element of the party leadership and rank and file, headed by Domingo Alberto Rangel, withdrew from guerrilla activities in 1965-66 and later quit the party. The MIR officially foreswore participation in guerrilla activities in 1969.

The most publicized activity of the MIR during 1975 was its celebration of the 15th anniversary of the party, in April. It held a series of meetings around the country and issued a long statement of its position. It was reported that this statement "ratifies its opposition to the current administration; demands the nationalization of all oil without any joint public and private companies; . . . announces that it will wage a continuing fight against corruption; and supports the unity of all socialist forces."

With regard to this last point, the MIR statement said: "For us, it is obvious that today, no socialist force can win a decisive battle acting alone. For that reason, we proclaim our willingness to make the necessary efforts aimed at unifying the greatest possible number of forces so as to develop successfully and on a national level the struggles of the people, accelerate the process of social change and achieve the great victory of socialism." (*El Nacional*, 9 April.)

Its one step in the direction of "socialist unity," negotiations with the Vanguardia Comunista, did not seem to have reached fruition during the year.

In June the MIR received some publicity for its demand that $90 million be deducted from whatever compensation was planned to be given to the Texaco Corporation under the oil nationalization law. The MIR charged that Texaco had evaded taxes worth that amount.

*   *   *

The Maoists. Maoist elements in Venezuela appear to be divided into two groups: the Patria Nueva movement and the Party of the Venezuelan Revolution (Partido de la Revolución Venezolana; PRV). The PRV is reportedly led by Douglas Bravo, one-time Politburo member of the PCV.

The Trotskyists. A Trotskyist party was officially founded in Venezuela for the first time in 1973. This group, which first took the name Socialist Workers Party (Partido Socialista de los Trabajadores), but later changed it to Socialist League (Liga Socialista; LS), is the Venezuelan section of the United Secretariat of the Fourth International. It publishes a fortnightly periodical, *Voz Socialista*. In early 1975 it strongly opposed the bill sponsored by the Pérez government to nationalize the iron industry, on the grounds that the bill sought continuation of foreign influence in the iron mining industry, and particularly attacked the MAS for not taking a strong position against the measure (*Intercontinental Press*, New York, 24 February). It later protested against alleged "harassment" by police (ibid., 30 June).

The Guerrillas. Isolated guerrilla groups continued sporadic activities during 1975, although they had no noticeable impact on the country's general political situation. At the beginning of the year considerable publicity was provoked by the escape of 23 guerrilla leaders from the San Carlos military prison. They were associated with the Bandera Roja, Punto Cero, and Fuerzas Armadas de Liberación Nacional guerrilla groups. (*Latin America*, 31 January.) In October two former guerrilla leaders, Gregorio Lunar Márquez and Luben Petkov, met with President Pérez for forty minutes (Radio Latin, Buenos Aires, 21 October).

Rutgers University   Robert J. Alexander

MIDDLE EAST AND AFRICA

Egypt

The first communist group in Egypt was formed in 1921, and had a purely alien membership, mostly Russian Jews, Greeks, and Italians. More than a decade later the first native Egyptian communist party took shape as the Communist Party of Egypt (al-Hizb al-Shuyu'i al-Misri; CPE). Neither that party nor any subsequent communist party in Egypt was granted official recognition by any of the Egyptian governments, though President Nasir, who throughout 1958-59 had suppressed the CPE, gave it tacit recognition in 1965. In that year, under pressure from the Soviet Union, the CPE dissolved its membership as a gesture of solidarity and joined the Arab Socialist Union (ASU), the only legal party in the country. The CPE leaders, who took on the appellation of Marxists, were absorbed into Egyptian cabinets.

The ouster of some prominent figures of the left, 'Ali Sabri and his faction, in 1971, showed a rift in the alliance between the left and the Egyptian government. The rift widened in 1973 when President Sadat accused "leftist Marxist ideology" of fomenting student unrest, and in consequence 90 ASU members were expelled from the party. The Beirut *Arab World Weekly* of 10 February 1973 then wrote that the Marxists might go underground in preparation for regrouping.

Subsequent to the October 1973 war, the leaders of the Egyptian left revived the Nasir cult in opposition to President Sadat's liberalization policies. They feared that Egypt's rapprochement with the United States and Saudi Arabia would result in their virtual elimination from political life. In answer President Sadat denounced publicly what he termed the "Rejectionist Left" (*Arab World Weekly*, 26 July 1975), but he did not then identify the elements in that faction. The July disengagement agreement with Israel brought the newly formed CPE out into the open. Throughout 1974 there had been rumors that the CPE was re-constituting itself. Many leftists believed that the dissolution of the CPE had been a mistake and that a re-evaluation of the past decade was necessary. While some other Arab communist parties, such as the Lebanese, favored the revival of the CPE, others, such as the Syrian, opposed it. The CPE, however, published a manifesto in the Beirut newspaper *al-Safir* on 4 August 1975, signing it "The Secretariat of the Communist Party of Egypt."

The manifesto (*Arab World Weekly*, Documents Sections, 9 August) accused the Egyptian authorities of "deviations . . . from the nationalist and progressive policies of the Nasirite regime"; of abandoning the "strategic alliance" with the Soviet Union; and of accepting an "American" solution to the Arab-Israeli dispute, which would lead to a unilateral settlement with Israel, a trend described as "capitulationist" and a betrayal of pan-Arab commitments and the Arab national liberation movement. The manifesto denounced the Sadat government's economic liberalization policies which were bent on liquidating the public sector and encouraging the private sector, seeking thereby to tie the Egyptian economy to the "international imperialist economic bloc." The manifesto did not, however, call for an overthrow of the government; to do so would be "an adolescent stand that ignores the presence of nationalist elements and factions within the government." Instead, it called for working within the government in order to "paralyze the hesitant forces which increasingly tend to make a truce with imperialism" and to encourage as well the "nationalist elements which oppose the capitulationist trends." There was no official Egyptian reaction to the manifesto, but in an interview with the Lebanese weekly *al-Hawadith*, broadcast on Cairo Radio on 21 August, President Sadat drew a distinction between the Egyptian left and the communists. He said that while the Egyptian left supported Egypt's aspirations, the communists remained prisoners of their old theories and had no weight or power in Egypt.

The CPE has never in the past been particularly numerous; during its heyday its membership never exceeded 5,000. Who the leaders of the new CPE are remains unknown as yet, but the prominent older members seem to have been discarded. Presumably they had become less radical and perhaps even discredited because of their previous collaboration with the authorities. For the moment the activities of the CPE concentrate on two areas. The first is industrial labor, notably among the workers of Helwan and Shubra al-Khaimah outside Cairo, where a struggle for power between the leftists and the labor union affiliated with the ASU is going on. Secondly, CPE activity seems to be branching out among the rural workers. A recent modification of the land law defining the relationship between tenants and landowners has created dissatisfaction among the peasantry, thus providing fertile ground for recruitment. This is a new departure, as previous CPE efforts were concentrated in the urban environment. What role, if any, the CPE will play in the future depends to a large extent on the outcome of the Arab-Israeli conflict.

University of California   Afaf Lutfi al-Sayyid Marsot
Los Angeles

Iran

The precursors of organized communist activity in Iran were two political groups organized in Tiflis and Baku during the first two decades of the 20th century. The Persian Social Democratic Party was formed in 1904, while in 1917 a group of Iranian Azerbaijani intellectuals founded the Hezb-e 'Adalat (Justice Party). At the first major party congress convened in Pahlavi (Enzeli) in 1920, the Justice Party changed its name to the Communist Party of Iran. In 1931, the government of Iran enacted a law banning communist activity in the country. This, combined with the Stalinist purges taking place in the neighboring Soviet Union, caused the Communist Party of Iran to disband.

In 1941, a group of German-educated Marxist intellectuals formed the present communist party of Iran known as the Tudeh Party ("Party of the Masses"). During the 1941-1953 period of relative political freedom in Iran, the Tudeh burgeoned in size and influence until it became the largest party in the country. By 1946, it had opened branches in every town with a population over 10,000. Its affiliated labor organizations, presided over by the Central Council of United Trade Unions, enrolled approximately 400,000 members and counted 75 percent of the industrial labor force within their memberships. In August 1946, the Iranian government was directed by a coalition cabinet that included three Tudeh ministers.

A major split in the organized communist movement in Iran developed in 1945-46. The Tudeh organization in the province of Azerbaijan broke away from the main party and formed the Democratic Party of Azerbaijan. This division stemmed both from the reluctance of the Tudeh Party to emphasize the ethnic problems peculiar to Azerbaijan and from the Soviet drive to support a friendly provincial government to counter the pro-Western central government in Tehran. In 1946, the Democratic Party of Azerbaijan was outlawed after the Iranian army reoccupied the province. In 1949, the Tudeh Party itself was banned when a member of the Central Council of United Trade Unions attempted to assassinate the Shah. Despite the ban, the Tudeh Party grew during the Mosaddeq period between 1951 and 1953. After the coup d'état and the return of the Shah to power in late 1953, the Tudeh Party was effectively suppressed. Some 500 army officers who belonged to the party were arrested; of these, 27 were executed. A number of the party leaders managed to escape to Europe and reorganized the Tudeh Party in East Germany.

Today Tudeh Party activity is confined almost entirely to organizations operating outside Iran. Within a country whose 1975 population was an estimated 34,000,000, Tudeh Party membership probably does not exceed a thousand. There are, however, perhaps 15,000 to 20,000 Iranians associated with other Marxist-Leninist groupings and engaged in opposition activities of various kinds. Among them are the following four organizations, all of which have been formed since 1960 and all of which have a presence both within and outside the country:

(1) The Revolutionary Tudeh Party (*Hezb-e Tudeh-e Iran*) was formed in 1965 by a Maoist group that had been expelled from the Tudeh Party. This group publishes *Setareh-i Sorkh* ("Red Star").

(2) The Organization of Marxist-Leninists (*Sazman-e Marxist-Leninist*) was organized in 1967 by two Maoist members of the Central Committee of the Tudeh Party. This group publishes the periodical *Tufan* ("Storm").

(3) The Guerrilla Organization of the Devotees for the People (*Cheraki Feda-ye Khalq*) was formed in Iran in 1971. A number of its founders were former members of the Tudeh Party's youth organization. These individuals had left the party because of the latter's opposition to guerrilla warfare. This group is well organized and has been responsible for a number of violent incidents directed against the government. Since 1971, approximately 100 members of this organization have been either killed in action or executed. This group tends to identify more with Latin American revolutionaries than with either Russia or China.

(4) A section of the National Front (*Jebheh-e Melli*) which supported Dr. Mosaddeq has become Marxist since 1972. This group publishes *Bakhtar-e Emruz* ("Today's West").

Although Marxist-Leninist-oriented groups such as the above have decidedly gained in strength and appeal, the Tudeh Party remains the major communist organization directly concerned with Iran in the international context.

Tudeh Party Leadership and Organization. Iradj Eskandari has been first secretary of the Tudeh Party since 1971. The party seldom publishes names of members, partly because of the government's repressive policy towards this particular group. Most pronouncements are issued in the name of the Central Committee of the Iranian Tudeh Party.

The leadership of the Tudeh Party places great stress on the need to turn the Iranian masses against the regime in power. In the May 1975 issue of the *World Marxist Review*, Tudeh theoretician Hamid Safari wrote that "our main purpose is to build a mass basis for the revolutionary movement." The Tudeh Party works to implement this goal primarily through its operation of the clandestine radio station, "Radio Iran Courier." This station, which is believed to be broadcasting from the German Democratic Republic, continues to harass the Iranian government through its programs of sharp social and political criticism. Major policy pronouncements concerning opposition tactics are also communicated through this channel. An important case in point was a statement issued by the Secretariat of the Central Committee of the Tudeh Party on April 17, 1975. In this message, the Tudeh leadership urged opposition elements in Iran to join the regime and the various police organizations. From here they were urged to subvert and destroy the system from within.

The Tudeh Position on Domestic Issues. The Tudeh Party has consistently attacked the leadership of the Shah in Iran while stressing his regime's alleged oppression, injustice, backwardness, and corruption. In 1975, the Tudeh Party held its Fifteenth Plenum of the Central Committee somewhere in Europe. Among the policies ratified was a political report entitled "Our party's task is to make the overthrow of the Shah's despotic regime the primary aim of all the national progressive forces in Iran." Among the printed resolutions that touch on domestic issues are the following five:

(1) The party condemned the Iranian government's use of terror, violence, and torture against its opponents and critics;

(2) The party demanded freedom for all political prisoners in Iran;

(3) The party called upon all patriotic and democratic organizations to assist the Iranian workers in their strikes and conflicts;

(4) The party called upon all patriotic and democratic organizations to unite in a common effort against the present regime in Iran; and

(5) The party demanded that the people of Iran be accorded their democratic rights.

The Tudeh Position on International Issues. The Tudeh Party of Iran has been a strong supporter of the Soviet Union in the competition among the super powers. The United States and the People's Republic of China are considered implacable enemies of both the people and the Tudeh Party itself. Maoist China has gradually become a major target of Tudeh attack in the international arena. The Fifteenth Plenum of the Central Committee condemned the subversive role of Maoism, which in its hostility to the Soviet Union had chosen to consort with reactionary regimes such as the one in power in Iran. Among the specific resolutions adopted were the following five:

(1) The party supported the Soviet Union's policy of peaceful coexistence with the capitalist countries;

(2) The party applauded the social and economic advances made in the socialist countries;

(3) The party condemned the Maoist policy of collaborating intimately with the enemies of the socialist countries;

(4) The party condemned the Iranian government's policy of serving as an American policeman in the Persian Gulf and Indian Ocean; and

(5) The party condemned the government of Iran's interference designed to thwart the people's struggle in Oman.

Publications. The two major publications of the Tudeh Party are *Mardom* ("People") and *Donya* ("World"). These papers are published in Eastern Europe and contain a mixture of articles that deal with Marxist-Leninist theory, international politics and economics, and the Iranian social and political scene. Some space is devoted to the history, social structure, and party development in Iran.

Austin, Texas   James A. Bill

Iraq

The Iraqi Communist Party (al-Hizb al-Shuyuʻi al-ʻIraqi, ICP) was founded in 1934 through a merger of various communist groups. It is pro-Soviet. ICP leaders are primarily intellectuals and professionals (doctors, lawyers, and teachers, and many are of Kurdish origin, including the secretary general, ʻAziz Muhammad (known as Nazim ʻAli).

In 1946 the ICP held its First Congress, which elected a Central Committee and adopted a national charter. Until 1973 the party was illegal and until 1958 was severely repressed. In 1948 the government executed three prominent ICP leaders. Between July 1958 and February 1963, while remaining illegal, the party carried on activities with comparative ease and one member succeeded in obtaining a cabinet post. This relative success was followed by a setback in the period from February 1963 to 1972 during which some 3,000 members reportedly were killed and many others were imprisoned.

In 1972 the ICP's relationship with the ruling Baʻth party improved significantly, and legalization came in the following year with the signing of the National Action Charter (see below). Unprecedented freedom in conducting the party's affairs came in 1974 but was followed in 1975 by signs of strain between the ICP and the ruling party. Reports in 1975 indicated the existence of ICP branch offices in major cities and towns of Iraq. The current party membership is estimated at 2,000. The population of Iraq is about 11,500,000.

The ICP and the Baʻth Party. Between 1958 and 1972 the ICP and the ruling Baʻth Party regarded each other with mutual suspicion, evidenced by violence and bloodshed. In 1972 a shift in the relationship occurred, culminating in their signing of the National Action Charter on 1 July 1973. The charter was the basis for the National Front, granting legality to the ICP for the first time. Appointment to the Supreme Committee of the National Front of three ICP Central Committee members was made on 30 March 1974 (INA, Baghdad, 30 March 1974).

Difficulties between the ICP and the Baʻth Party returned in 1975. On 16 March 1975 an accord was signed wherein Iraq agreed to share equally with Iran the waterway of the Shatt al-ʻArab (the lower course of the Tigris and Euphrates) and Iran agreed to end its support of the Kurdish revolt in northern Iraq. The accord took the ICP and the Soviet Union by surprise, and by creating new conditions in Iraq lessened the Baʻth Party's need for ICP and Soviet support. The ICP's complaints were numerous. An important policy move had been taken by the Baʻth leadership and the Revolutionary Command Council which governs Iraq without consulting the ICP (*Arab World Weekly*, Beirut, 19 July). Baʻth members had been moving into the North and had gained complete control of the Kurdish areas, pushing communists completely into the background, ICP offices were being closed, and the opening of new offices in the North has been forbidden (ibid., 19 July). Baʻthists had removed a number of leading communists from high-level positions (*An-Nahar Arab Report*, Beirut, 24 February), and the two ICP members in the cabinet were functioning as no more than civil servants.

ICP complaints continued on the international level. Disapproval was expressed over Iraq's new policy of turning to the West for "know-how" and giving an increasing number of contracts to Western companies—the U.S. share of total imports had risen from 3 percent in 1972 to 10 percent in 1974 (*Christian Science Monitor*, 28 January). Iraqi officials privately complained about the poor quality of machinery received from communist countries intended for use on Iraqi projects.

Domestic Attitudes. The ICP's views on domestic policy emphasize the importance of the National Front and support the creation of constitutional institutions, the strengthening and furthering of self-government in Kurdistan, and the improving of the standard of living of the entire population.

The ICP's newspaper *Tariq al-Sha'b* complained of government censorship. It stated that the government had warned against the publishing of articles that attacked states having normal relations with Iraq. The ICP stated that the commitment of the parties of the National Front to each other did not wipe out the differences among them (MENA, 16 October 1975).

Arab Policy. Within the Arab world, the ICP condemns all attempts at a partial solution to the Arab-Israeli conflict. It calls for a "stepping-up" of the struggle against concluding any truce with U.S. imperialism and urges the convening of the Geneva conference to discuss a solution. Total liberation of all Arab land occupied in June 1967 is viewed as basic for any lasting peace in the area. Another ICP tenet is support of the Palestinian Arabs, under the leadership of the Palestine Liberation Organization. The ICP affirms their right to return to their homeland and to determine their own destiny.

The ICP calls for strengthening Arab solidarity against the forces of imperialism and Zionism by working through national fronts, but attacks the "defeatist" action of the Egyptian government in concluding a separate interim agreement with Israel on Sinai.

In the Gulf area, ICP publications support the revolt against the government of Oman in Dhofar, and attack Iran's policy of trying to dominate the area. The party claims that Iran is implementing an imperialist scheme to preserve and extend U.S. interests there.

Relations with other Communist Parties. During 1975, ICP delegations led by Central Committee members visited the USSR, Romania, and Bulgaria. The ICP also received many delegations of other communist parties, including the party in Syria.

The ICP took part in the meeting of Arab communist parties in April 1975 at an undisclosed place (see the Introduction, p. xxviii).

The ICP also participated in several conferences held in Iraq and abroad, including the 10th session of the World Federation of Trade Unions, held at Baghdad in April, and the meeting of the Asian Peace Force for Peace and Security in Asia, in February.

International Views and Activities. *Tariq al-Sha'b* in numerous articles in 1975 hailed the gains and achievements of the forces of peace, liberation, and socialism which found expression in détente; the increasing strength of the world socialist system; and the victory of the democrats in Portugal and Greece; and of the liberation movements in Angola and Mozambique. In the party's view, the situation was ripe for the convening of an international meeting of communist and worker parties (*IB*, June). The ICP called also for intensifying Iraq's economic, political, and scientific relations with the entire socialist bloc.

Publications. The ICP publishes a daily newspaper, *Tariq al-Sha'b* ("People's Road"). In addition, it distributes with relative freedom a number of illegal publications: the daily *Ittihad al-Sha'b* ("People's Union"), which is circulated within the party ranks; *al-Fikr al-Jadid* ("New Thought"), a cultural weekly which also carries articles on political topics and a literary-political monthly, *al-Thaqafah al-Jadidah* ("New Culture"). ICP information is also regularly disseminated through the publications of the Lebanese Communist Party, *al-Nida'* and *al-Akhbar*.

California State University   Ayad Al-Qazzaz
Sacramento

Israel

The first communist party in Palestine, the Socialist Workers' Party, was established in 1919-20. In 1922 some of its members broke away and established a new party, the Palestine Communist Party (PCP), which affiliated with the Comintern in 1924. Further rifts occurred, the most serious of which was in 1943, when the PCP split into chiefly Jewish and Arab factions. Although these factions reunited in October 1948 within the Israel Communist Party (Miflaga Komunistit Isre'elit; MAKI), tensions continued between nationalist Arabs and Jews with pro-Israel (although not necessarily Zionist) sympathies. In August 1965 a deeper rift occurred; a small faction, composed almost exclusively of Jews, was still called MAKI, while the larger group came to be called the New Communist List (Reshima Komunistit Hadasha; RAKAH). Most of the latter's members—an estimated 70 percent—are Arabs, although Jews hold some of the leading positions. Although RAKAH is now Israel's main communist party, it still has a relatively small membership, estimated at about 1,000 to 1,500. In 1975 the population of Israel (exclusive of the Israeli-held territories) was about 3,500,000.

At the second session of MAKI's Seventeenth Convention, held on 20-21 June 1975, it was decided by a vote of 121 to 14, with 2 abstentions, to merge with MOKED ("Focus"), a Zionist-Socialist but not avowedly Marxist group formed before the December 1973 national elections. In those elections, MAKI had not run on its own for the Knesset (Israel's parliament), but had cooperated with the "Blue-Red" group, the core of MOKED. On 20 July MAKI officially merged with MOKED, thus disappearing from the map of Israel's political parties.

Other Marxist-Leninist groups are tiny, extra-parliamentary, and devoid of any palpable influence on Israeli politics. The Israel Socialist Organization (Irgun Sotziyalisti Isre'eli; ISO), a small group of intellectuals whose core left MAKI in 1962, is chiefly known for its journal *Matzpen* ("Compass"). In 1970-71 it split into four fragments (*'Al ha-Mishmar*, Tel-Aviv, 15 December 1972, p. 5; *Pi ha-Aton*, Jerusalem, 8 May 1974, p. 7): the original group; the Revolutionary Communist League (Brit Komunistit Mahapkhanit; RCL); the Workers' League (Brit ha-Po'alim; WL); and the Revolutionary Communist Alliance-Struggle (Brit Komunistit Mahapkhanit-Ma'avak; RCAS). Another group, the Israel New Left (Smo'l Isre'eli Hadash; INL), was set up in 1968-69 by leftist intellectuals, angry with MAPAM, the Israeli left-wing labor party, for having formed a political alignment with the Israel Labor Party, thus ostensibly joining the Establishment. A few MAKI members, disappointed with leader Moshe Sneh's "nationalist" line, joined INL later. A forum for Marxist ideological debate,

INL's small number dwindled further in mid-1975, when its Tel-Aviv group joined MOKED at the same time MAKI did.

All the above groups are legal, but, because of their negation of the Zionist ideology embraced by the vast majority of Israel's Jews, their role is marginal in national politics, except for RAKAH's sustained activity among Israel's Arab minority. RAKAH has four seats in the 120-seat Knesset elected in 1973, and MOKED has one, for its leader, Me'ir Pa'il. RAKAH has four and MAKI three seats in the Histadrut (Trade Union) Executive Committee.

RAKAH. Leadership and Organization. RAKAH's organization follows the usual pattern of communist parties in non-communist states—its Central Committee and Supervisory Board are elected by the party convention; the Political Bureau and the Secretariat are in turn elected by the Central Committee. The party convention has met in 1965, 1969, aand 1972—in each case not long before a national electoral contest, to give the party a boost for its campaign. Among RAKAH's leaders are its four knesset members: Me'ir Vilner, secretary-general; Taufiq Tubi, coordinator of the Secretariat; Avraham Levenbraun, member of the Political Bureau; and Taufiq Ziyad, poet and journalist in the Arabic press. Others are Wolff Ehrlich, chairman of the party's Supervisory Board and editor of 'Arakhim; David Khenin, member of the Political Bureau and secretary of the Central Committee; Tamar Gozansky and Hans Lebrecht, members of the Central Committee; Emile Tuma, member of the Political Bureau and one of the party's main theoreticians; and Yehoshu'a Irga, RAKAH's chief delegate in the Executive Committee of the Histadrut.

Auxiliary Organizations. RAKAH supports the Young Communist League, the League of Democratic Women, the Israel-Soviet Union Friendship Movement, the Israeli Association of Anti-Fascist Fighters and Victims of Nazism, and several Youth Circles.

Domestic Attitudes and Activities. On the internal scene in 1975, RAKAH's main activities were in four areas: (a) intensificiation of printed propaganda, supporting every strike and attacking the inflationary process, which it feared would result in "a further deterioration of the standard of living" and in unemployment (Khenin, in *WMR*, no. 2, p. 115); (b) speeches in the Knesset, such as that of Vilner, in which he attacked Israeli rule in the Israeli-held territories, or of Tubi, in which he attributed a hate campaign against RAKAH to the Israeli security services; (c) defending the social and economic rights of workers through its representatives in the Histadrut's Executive Committee; and (d) electoral campaigning.

RAKAH achieved an impressive advance in the Histadrut elections to the Builders' Union on 23 November, when it increased its share of the vote from 4.5 percent to about 9 percent. This was probably due to the relatively large number of Arab members in this union, over a fifth. However, the municipal elections in all-Arab Nazareth, the largest Arab town in Israel (population about 40,000), were the central event for RAKAH in 1975. A joint slate of RAKAH and local Arab intellectuals (i.e., members of the liberal professions) called itself the Pro-Nazareth Democratic Front (PNDF); it ran against two groups sponsored by the Israel Labor Party and two sponsored by the National Religious Party. RAKAH's campaign was managed by ex-Knesset member Emile Habibi. It emphasized mainly the government's neglect of municipal affairs, but also adopted a strongly nationalist Arab line. The campaign's effectiveness was proven on 9 December. Out of 19,662 having the right to vote, 14,777 turned out and cast 14,125 valid votes. Participation was 75.2 percent, compared to 85 percent in the previous municipal elections in 1970. The PNDF obtained 9,510 votes, an unprecedented 67.3 percent of the total; in 1970 RAKAH had received only 39.4 percent. Although in 1975 the PNDF's support was strongest in Nazareth's Muslim and Greek Orthodox quarters, it received more than half the vote in Greek Catholic polls as well. It gained 11 of the 17 seats on the municipal council (as against 7 in 1970). For the first time Nazareth got a Communist mayor, 46-year-old Taufiq Ziyad, a

RAKAH Knesset member and a former secretary of the party's local branch. The other ten PNDF municipal councilors were equally divided between RAKAH members and affiliated young intellectuals (not previously identified with RAKAH), who were partly responsible for the support given the PNDF by many of the approximately 4,000 young voters who had received the right to vote for the first time.

International Views and Policies. RAKAH repeatedly maintained that safeguarding the public's standard of living was closely linked to the struggle for peace, as a reduction in military expenses would benefit the civilian economy (Levenbraun, in the Knesset, 20 January 1975). The party's understanding of peace was closely modeled on Moscow's; it strove to present the image of a peace party and demonstrated concern about the imminence of another war in the Middle East (*L'Unità*, Rome, 8 February). In 1975, however, RAKAH's dilemma was how to account for the apparent contradiction between its cardinal policy of advocating peace based on withdrawal from Israeli-held territories and its condemnation of U.S. secretary of state Kissinger's mediation moves between Israel and Egypt, which excluded the Soviet Union completely. The failure of Kissinger's efforts in March enabled the party to solve the dilemma by proclaiming on 25 March that Kissinger's failure was the failure of U.S. policy itself: the United States allegedly aimed at avoiding the Geneva peace conference by implementing a step-by-step policy intended to enhance divisiveness among the Arab states and perpetuate a situation of no-peace-no-war, thus prolonging the Israeli-Arab conflict (*IB*, no. 9, pp. 47-48). RAKAH advocated Israel's withdrawal from all territories held since 1967, recognition of the sovereignty and territorial integrity of both Israel and the Arab states, the right of the Palestinian Arabs to self-determination and the establishment of a state of their own side by side with Israel, and the solving of Arab refugee problems.

On 22-23 May the 18th plenary session of RAKAH's Central Committee reiterated the above and accused the Israeli government of sabotaging peace efforts by refusing to attend the Geneva conference and by pursuing an "annexationist and militarist policy" (*al-Ittihad*, 30 May; *Zo ha-Derekh*, 4 June). It warned that, because of oil interests, U.S. policy was now less committed to Israel (Tuma, in *WMR*, no. 6, pp. 91-97). On the other hand, according to Vilner, back from a Moscow visit, the Soviet Union was ready to share in all peace arrangements and even resume relations with Israel (*Summary of World Broadcasts*, 19 June). In September, the 21st plenary meeting of RAKAH's Central Committee condemned the second stage of disengagement between Israel and Egypt, on the grounds that a U.S. presence introduced a new element of tension into the area (*TASS*, in English, 3 September). An article in RAKAH's organ *'Arakhim* (no. 5, October, pp. 3-12) claimed that the disengagement had achieved at most a brief respite, with the danger of war still present and arms pouring in.

International Activities and Contacts. RAKAH was increasingly recognized by communist parties abroad as Israel's only communist party; they repeatedly referred to it as the Communist Party of Israel. MAKI's fusion into MOKED reinforced RAKAH's claims. In practical terms, this meant the visit of a RAKAH delegation to Italy in February, where Tuma participated in the 14th Congress of the Italian Communist Party; the visit in June of a RAKAH delegation to Poland and to Moscow (where it met Soviet party secretary Boris Ponomarev), and of another to Romania. Further, RAKAH was host to a Soviet delegation that visited Israel on the 30th anniversary of the Russian victory in World War II.

Publications. The main RAKAH newspapers are the Hebrew weekly *Zo ha-Derekh* ("This Is the Way"), edited by Me'ir Vilner in Tel-Aviv; and the Arabic *al-Ittihad* ("Unity"), edited by Taufiq Tubi and published twice a week in Haifa. Two theoretical journals in Hebrew, *'Arakhim* ("Values") and *Be'ayot ha-shalom ve-ha-sotziyalizm* ("Problems of Peace and Socialism") fused into one in August 1975, combining both names—*'Arakhim–Be'ayot ha-shalom ve-ha-sotziyalizm*. It is edited by Wolff

Ehrlich in Tel-Aviv and appears irregularly (about every two months). Other RAKAH Journals are in Arabic: *al-Jadid* ("The New"), a literary monthly, is edited by Hanna Naqara in Haifa; *al-Ghad* ("Tomorrow"), a political-literary monthly, allegedly edited by Salim Jubran, appears in Haifa; *al-Darb* ("The Road") is a theoretical journal, published about twice a year and edited by Emile Habibi in Haifa. *Der Weg* ("The Road") is a Yiddish weekly, edited by Vilner in Tel-Aviv. *Tovaye Putyam* ("This Is the Way") is a Bulgarian fortnightly, published in Jaffa. The *Information Bulletin* appears at irregular intervals.

MAKI. Until its merger into MOKED in mid-1975, MAKI was organized in a manner similar to RAKAH and other communist parties. The rapprochement with Blue-Red and pending fusion with MOKED caused tension among party leaders and the departure of several veterans. Shmu'el Mikunis, MAKI's previous secretary-general, a long-time communist and a former member of the Knesset, resigned his position on 14 November 1974 (see *YICA, 1975*, p. 588). In April 1975 he left MAKI altogether, protesting the party's retreat from internationalism (*Ha-Aretz*, Tel-Aviv, 29 April); he reportedly joined Esther Vilenska in the tiny Israel Communist Opposition (Opozitziya Komunistit Isre'elit), whose organ is the Hebrew monthly *Hedim* ("Echoes"), edited in Tel-Aviv by Vilenska from 1974 until her death on 8 November 1975. MAKI's leading figures in 1975 were Ya'ir Tzaban, chairman of the Political Bureau and MAKI's chief delegate in the Histadrut's Executive Committee; Raoul Teitelbaum, chairman of the Central Committee; Berl Balti, member of the Political Bureau and editor of *Kol ha-'Am* ("Voice of the People"); and Eliyahu Druckman, member of the Political Bureau.

In February, MAKI affiliated with the World Jewish Congress and participated, for the first time, in its plenary session. However, its domestic activities during the first half of 1975 were almost exclusively devoted to preparations for its merger with MOKED. These preoccupations limited even further MAKI's international activities and contacts, which had already suffered since RAKAH had been recognized abroad as Israel's only communist party. Nevertheless, MAKI's spokesmen have repeatedly claimed relations, on a personal basis, with communist leaders in Europe.

The main publication of MAKI was the Hebrew fortnightly *Kol ha-'Am*, published in Tel-Aviv. Upon the merger with MOKED, *Kol ha-'Am* ceased to appear after the issue of 30 July. *Fray Isro'el* ("Free Israel"), MAKI's Yiddish monthly, appearing in Tel-Aviv, has been publsihed by MOKED since August 1975. *Naroden Glas* ("The Popular Voice") was a Bulgarian irregular newspaper, edited in Bat Yam by Albert Beni; it seems to have ceased publication in March 1975. MAKI members were enjoined to contribute to the leftist Hebrew monthly *'Emda* ("Position"), which has been published in Tel-Aviv since September 1974.

ISO. The Israel Socialist Organization has been considerably weakened by its 1970-1971 split and probably comprises at most a few dozen regular members, mostly intellectuals (20 members only, according to *The New Middle East*, London, nos. 42-43, March-April 1972, p. 20). Its most articulate leaders are Moshe Mahower, 'Oded Pilawsky (Me'ir Pa'il's brother), and Hayim Hanegbi. The ISO maintains that Zionism is a colonialist ideology and that there was no need to establish the state of Israel as a solution to the Jewish problem. Consequently, it strives for "the de-Zionization of Israel," the liquidation of the State, and the substitution of a supra-national socialist state as a step towards a socialist union of the Middle East. In Israel itself, the ISO organizes demonstrations and distributes leaflets at universities and schools. Abroad, its intensive anti-Israeli propaganda—linked with the international New Left—has brought it more fame than its small size warrants. Its main organ is the quarterly *Matzpen*, appearing in Tel-Aviv in Hebrew and Arabic, whose publisher and editor are Moshe Mahower and 'Oded Pilawsky.

RCL. The Revolutionary Communist League, until February 1975 called "Matzpen-Marxist," is a relatively moderate Trotskyite splinter, numbering but a few members. One of its main theoreticians, Jabra Niqula, died in London on 28 December 1974. A veteran Arab member of the PCP until the 1940s, Niqula had been one of the ISO's leading theoreticians since 1963, writing under the pseudonym of Abu Sa'id, but he later moved closer to the RCL (*Red Weekly*, London, 9 Jan., quoted in *Intercontinental Press Correspondence*, 31 Jan.). Michael Warshavski is prominent among the current leaders. The RCL is linked to the Fourth (Trotskyite) International. It advocates, with a zeal equal to ISO's, the liquidation of Zionism and the destruction of Israel by undermining the effectiveness of the Israel Defence Forces, sharpening the economic crisis in Israel, and setting up an internationalist alternative with the Palestinian organizations and the Arab revolutionary movement. The RCL publishes a Hebrew and Arabic monthly in Jerusalem, edited by I. Feifman. Formerly named *Matzpen Marksisti*, it is now called (since March 1975) *Kol ha-Ma'amad* in Hebrew and *Saut al-Tabaqah* in Arabic ("Voice of the Class"); it claims a circulation of close to 1,500 (*Kol ha-Ma'amad*, no. 11 (76), March, p. 1). *Hafarperet* ("Male") is the group's youth journal.

WL. The tiny Workers' League is more orthodoxly Trotskyite than the RCL. Among the WL's leading figures is Menahem Karmi. Ideologically, its attitudes are not very different from the RCL's, although its propaganda is more intense and apparently more worker-oriented. Also, the WL proclaims even more frankly that it is "a partner in the Palestinian struggle for National Liberation" (*Kol ha-Po'el*, Jerusalem, no. 22, July-August 1975, p. 2). The WL's monthly appears in both Hebrew and Arabic and is named, respectively, *Kol ha-Po'el* and *Saut al-'Amil* ("Voice of the Worker"). Published in Jerusalem, it is edited by Menahem Karmi and distributed chiefly among urban workers. *Avangard* ("Vanguard") is the WL's theoretical organ in Hebrew, published in Jerusalem irregularly and edited by Menahem Karmi.

RCAS. The Revolutionary Communist Alliance-Struggle is a tiny Maoist group with Marius Shneider one of its most articulate exponents. The group's organ is *Ma'avak* ("Struggle"), published sporadically in Jerusalem.

INL. The Israel New Left has consistently abstained from any formal organizational structures and has preferred a "participating democracy," maintaining the character of a debating forum, although it has taken part in some demonstrations. Until mid-1975 it was made up of two discussion groups, chiefly composed of students at Tel-Aviv University and the Hebrew University of Jerusalem respectively. Although avowedly Marxist, the two groups differed in their interpretation of the Socialist-Zionist synthesis. Most INL adherents see Zionism as a national liberation movement but argue for the recognition of the Palestinian liberation movement as well; they call this approach the "doctrine of national symmetry." However, the Tel-Aviv group, with more empathy toward Zionism and Israel, led by Ran Cohen, joined MOKED in July 1975. The Jerusalem group shows greater affinity to the concerns of the Left on the international scene; it was the only INL group active in late 1975. Its main theoretician is Aryeh Arnon. *Siah* (a Hebrew acronym meaning INL) is published irregularly in Jerusalem in Hebrew as a forum for INL discussions. *Israleft* is an English-language fortnightly, recently published on a monthly basis. It appears in Jerusalem, avowing that "Israleft News Service is a non-profit project of members of Siah (Israel New Left) in Jerusalem." It provides mimeographed translations of excerpts from articles and news items in the Hebrew press.

The Hebrew University   Jacob M. Landau
Jerusalem, Israel

Jordan

The Communist Party of Jordan (al-Hizb al-Shuyu'i al-Urdunni; CPJ) was officially established in June 1951. However, communist activity on the West Bank of the Jordan River, annexed by the Hashemite Kingdom of Jordan after the 1948 Arab-Israeli War, can be traced back to the founding in September 1943 of the Palestinian National Liberation League (PNLL) in Haifa. The partition of Palestine, supported by the Soviet Union, caused splits among local communists, the PNLL initially opposing Jordan's takeover of the West Bank and denouncing the "Hashemite army of occupation." Nonetheless, members of the PNLL ultimately joined with like-minded Jordanians to form the CPJ.

Under constant government pressure since the early 1950s, the party has operated under the guise of various popular front organizations. Its center of activity has been on the West Bank, where it drew support from students, teachers, professional workers, and the "lower middle classes." Although it had probably no more than 1,000 members at the time, mostly Palestinians, the CPJ was reportedly the strongest party in Jordan during the country's first decade of independence beginning in 1946. An anti-communist law adopted in 1953 failed to suppress the organization, and repressive tactics appeared to be counter-productive. The CPJ retained its image as an enemy of "feudalism" and "imperialism," and in October 1956 a communist-led front elected three CPJ members to the Jordanian parliament. The party exercised considerable political influence through alliance with the Ba'th Party and Sulaiman al-Nabulsi's National Socialists. A CPJ member was appointed minister of agriculture, the first communist in the Arab world to receive a ministerial portfolio.

In reaction to the party's growing power, King Husain warned the country in February 1957 of the dangers of communist infiltration and urged Prime Minister al-Nabulsi to eliminate "destructive propaganda." As a result, all local communist publications were banned, along with films and newspapers. On 25 April 1957, following an abortive attempt by "left-wing nationalists" to overturn the monarchy, the king declared the CPJ illegal and disbanded all other parties. Hundreds of communists were arrested, including the CPJ parliamentary deputies, who were sentenced to long prison terms.

The CPJ has been illegal since 1957, although the government's normally repressive measures occasionally have been relaxed. For example, two communist deputies were elected to parliament as "independents" in 1961. More significantly, under a political amnesty granted at the outbreak of the 1967 Arab-Israeli War, all communists were released from Jordanian jails, and the party's secretary-general, Fu'ad Nassar, was allowed to return from exile. For a time the CPJ operated semi-legally. Repressive measures were resumed in 1972, and at present communist party membership is punishable by jail sentences of from 3 to 15 years. Few radical organizations other than the communists are active in Jordan. Various Palestinian groups, such as the Marxist-oriented Popular Front for the Liberation of Palestine, embittered by "repression" of the Palestinians during 1970-1971, urge the overthrow of King Husain, but they appear to have little overt influence in Jordan itself. Communist party membership has been estimated by Israeli authorities at no more than 400 persons, mostly Palestinians, out of a total Jordanian population of about 2,750,000 (January 1976 estimate), including more than 700,000 in Israel-occupied East Jerusalem and the West Bank.

Leadership and Organization. The CPJ is said to be a "tightly organized, well disciplined network of small cells" (*NYT*, 23 August 1974). Secrecy is highly valued, and little information on party leadership is available. The current secretary-general, and only one to hold that position, is Fu'ad Nassar, born in 1915, a Palestinian of Christian origin without formal education. Other prominent party members reportedly include 'Abd al-Muhsin Abu Maizar, also of the Palestine National Front (PNF), and Ishaq al-Khatib. 'Arabi 'Awad is a member of the CPJ's Central Committee and a PNF leader; he reportedly leads the West Bank branch of the party and has spent over 10 years in Jordanian and Israeli prisons. Other members of the Central Committee include 'Isa Madanat and Na'im Ashhab. Jiryas Qawwas, an association of 'Awad, is also a prominent West Bank communist, PNF official, and former teacher, who claims to have spent more than 13 years in Jordanian and Israeli jails.

The CPJ since its decline in the late 1950s has been known as a "passive political underground movement" confined to the West Bank (*NYT*, 23 August 1974). In recent years, however, party activities have increased, and the CPJ claims to be the only party really active in Jordan. Nonetheless, Fu'ad Nassar declared in an interview late in 1973 (Budapest Radio, 29 December) that the party operates "under very difficult circumstances" on both sides of the river, pointing to the frequent arrests of CPJ members by the authorities in Amman and the difficulties imposed by the Israelis, who have regularly rounded up communists, among others, and deported them to the East Bank. In December 1973, for instance, the Israelis deported eight West Bank Palestinians, including 'Arabi 'Awad and Jiryas Qawwas, who were accused of being "top figures" in the CPJ in addition to being members of the PNF. Another Israeli security campaign began in late 1974 to counter the upsurge in activity by the Palestine Liberation Organization (PLO), whose supporters include CPJ and PNF members. In January 1975, Bashir Barghuti, a West Bank resident, was tried by the Israelis on charges of spying for the "Communist-led" PNF. The Soviet news agency TASS denounced the "trumped-up charges," stating that Barghuti had simply written a letter to Amman referring to Israeli news accounts of the arrest and torture of PNF members (*Arab Report and Record*, London, 16-31 January 1975). Another West Banker, Mahu Yasin, was reportedly sentenced by an Israeli military court to 8 years' imprisonment for membership in the PNF (ibid.).

Auxiliary and Mass Organizations. On 15 August 1973, the Palestinian National Front, composed of professional and labor union representatives as well as "patriotic personalities," was established on the West Bank, evidently at CPJ instigation. The PNF generally follows the PLO line: it advocates creating an independent Palestinian state on the West Bank together with the Gaza Strip and urges Palestinian participation in the Geneva peace talks. Its program also includes mass political struggle and armed resistance in the occupied territories.

Not until after the October 1973 Arab-Israeli War did the PNF emerge as an "active pro-Palestinian organizatin." In an "Interview with the Palestine National Front" (*MERIP Reports*, Beirut, November 1974), Jiryas Qawwas and 'Arabi 'Awad noted that the PNF had organized the Arab boycott of the Israeli trade union elections in Jerusalem in September 1973 as well as of the Israeli parliamentary elections the following December. During the October War, the PNF issued leaflets opposing the Israeli war effort and organized strikes of Arab workers in Israeli factories. Other activities have included campaigns against high Israeli taxes and prices, opposition to Jewish settlement in Nablus, and attacks against Israeli police posts, labor offices, and banks in the West Bank. The PNF has also begun "systematic political training." It reportedly organized the "popular uprising" of 13-23 November 1974 on the West Bank, on the occasion of Yasir 'Arafat's speech to the General Assembly of the United Nations.

Although the PNF's precise relationship to the CPJ is unknown, Israeli officials have stated that the CPJ is the core of the group's strength. The PNF is a member of the PLO, and its Central Committee includes representatives of most Palestinian factions and commando organizations. At least some of its leadership comes from the CPJ, but Muhammad Yasin, a West Bank engineer and communist arrested by the Israelis, denied Israeli charges that the PNF was an appendage of the CPJ; he declared that the PNF "represents every political and democratic force in the occupied territories" (*Le Monde; Atlas World Press Review*, August 1975). It is clear, nonetheless, that West Bank communists have become closely associated with Palestinian nationalist forces, and Qawwas and 'Awad have stated that the PNF mission "is to lead the struggle from inside the occupied territories" (*MERIP Reports*, November 1974).

A statement issued over Aden Radio's "Voice of Oman" (4 April 1975; *FBIS*, 10 April 1975) referred to a number of Jordanian "progressive parties," "forces," and "popular organizations," including the Jordanian Revolutionary National Movement; the General Federation of Jordanian Trade Unions (disbanded by the Jordanian government in the early 1970s); the Federation of Jordanian Students; the Jordanian Revolutionary Popular Party; the Socialist Arab Ba'th Party, Jordan Region; the Unified Palestinian Organization; and the CPJ. Except for the Ba'th, it is probable that these groups are little more than paper organizations, and their links with the CPJ, if any, are unknown.

Party Internal Affairs. In a June 1975 statement (*WMR*), Na'im Ashhab described the CPJ as "the working-class party of two fraternal peoples—Jordanian and Palestinian." It is apparent, however, that the CPJ, despite its support of Palestinian statehood, remains somewhat suspicious of the PLO. In 1975, West Bank communists began signing official statements with the name "Communist Party of the West Bank," as did affiliated student, labor, and women's associations. Moreover, the newspaper *al-Watan* also appeared under the name "Palestine Communist Party." This change of name was evidently taken by West Bank cells without prior approval by the CPJ's central committee, which operates outside the West Bank (*Le Matin—An-Nahar Arab Report*, Beirut, 3 February 1975)

Domestic Attitudes and Activities. As a party oriented more toward Palestine than toward Jordan, the CPJ seemingly has devoted little attention to purely domestic issues. Like other anti-Husain Palestinians of whatever ideological persuasion, Fu'ad Nassar has denounced the "reactionary regime" in Amman and its links to "imperialism" and has advocated the establishment in Jordan of "a democratic, independent state" whose goal is social development. The party's 1974 program called for a "national and liberated regime in Jordan which alone would be capable of ending the policy of subservience to imperialism that led to Jordan's isolation from its Arab brothers" (*The Arab World*, 14 May 1974). The April 1975 "Voice of Oman" statement (*FBIS*, 10 April 1975) denounced the "agent regime" in Jordan, which was said to deny general liberties and suppress the "masses' struggle," and criticized Jordanian military aid to Sultan Qabus of Oman. In addition, the statement referred to "the national liberation movement" in Jordan, proposed the establishment of "a national progressive regime" in Amman, as well as "a national front" to be closely allied with the Palestinian and Arab national liberation movements.

The Palestine issue has vexed the party since its inception. As a generally pro-Soviet organization, the CPJ evidently has not been entirely free to take an independent stand on Palestine and consequently has lost support to more committed and radical Palestinian liberation movements. The CPJ's basic position on Palestine is similar to that of the main Palestinian liberation groups. The party recognized the PLO as the sole representative of the Palestinian people, and its 1974 program emphasized the Palestinians' right to "determine their destiny freely, including the right to establish their independent national state on lands evacuated by Israel" (*The Arab World*, 3 June 1974).

International Activities and Contacts. In early April 1975 the CPJ took part in a summit conference of Arab communist parties at an undisclosed location (see the Introduction, p. xxviii). However, the CPJ's role at the conference was not detailed. CPJ relations with the Lebanese communists were said to have deteriorated in 1975 because of the LCP's alleged encouragement of the West Bank communists in their break with the CPJ (*Le Matin–An-Nahar Arab Report*, 24 March 1975).

Fu'ad Nassar traveled to Moscow in May, where he celebrated his birthday and was feted by high Soviet officials. Nassar stressed his party's loyalty to the Soviet Union and was presented with the Friendship of the People's Order, for his "great services" to the national liberation movement, his participation in the anti-imperialist struggle, and his role in strengthening Soviet-Arab friendship. The two sides also emphasized the need for the Israelis to withdraw from all occupied Arab territories and supported the establishment of an independent Palestinian state (TASS, 13, 19 May 1975; *FBIS*, 14, 21 May 1975). In an article in *WMR* (June 1975), Na'im Ashhab analyzed the growing strength of the liberation movement in the Middle East and noted the importance of Arab unity in foiling U.S.-Israeli plots in the region.

Publications. The CPJ publishes a journal, *al-Jamahir* ("The Masses"), and an underground newspaper, *al-Watan* ("The Homeland"), both of which appear irregularly. *Al-Watan* was closed on the West Bank for 8 months in 1974, following arrests of party members in April and May 1974, but resumed publication on 1 January 1975. The party also issues a political and theoretical journal, *al-Haqiqah* ("The Truth"), and special pamphlets. These publications are distributed clandestinely on both sides of the Jordan River, except for *al-Watan*, which seems to be restricted mainly to the West Bank. PNF began publication, evidently in 1974, of its own newspaper, *Filastin* ("Palestine"). News of CPJ activities also appears in the organs of the Lebanese Communist Party, *al-Akhbar* and *al-Nida'*.

U.S. Department of Commerce   Norman F. Howard*
Washington, D.C.

* The views expressed in this article are the author's own and do not represent those of the Department of Commerce.

Lebanon

The Lebanese Communist Party (al-Hizb al-Shuyu'i al-Lubnani; LCP) was established in 1924. During the period of the French mandates it accepted members from both Lebanon and Syria. What is generally considered its First Congress was held in January 1944, a little more than two years after Syria and Lebanon were first proclaimed independent states. This congress decided to establish separate Lebanese and Syrian communist parties.

In 1965 the LCP decided to break away from its policy of working independently of other Lebanese political groups. Since then it has become a member of the Front of Progressive Parties and National Forces (FPPNF) under the leadership of the Progressive Socialists, a party headed by Kamal Jumblat. The LCP is also a member of the Arab Front for Participation in the Palestine Revolution (AFPPR). The LCP was banned by the government until 13 August 1970, when it gained recognition along with other controversial parties.

Recent estimates of LCP strength count 2,000-3,000 Lebanese among its members and sympathizers, with a Lebanese population in 1975 of about 2,500,000.

Leadership and Organization. The congress, which is to be convened every four years, is the supreme organ of the party. The most recent congress, the Third, was held in Beirut in January 1972 with delegates from more than 30 foreign communist parties attending (*YICA 1972*, pp. 252-259). This was the first formal congress ever held openly by an Arab communist party. Between congresses authority is vested in the 24-member Central Committee, which in turn selects and invests authority in the 11-member Politburo and the 5-member Secretariat. The secretary-general, Niqula al-Shawi, and his second in command, George Hawi, who is head of the Secretariat, are both Greek Orthodox. Other members of the Secretariat include Karim Muruwwah, Nadim 'Abd al-Samad, and Khalil al-Dibs.

Domestic Views and Activities. 1975 was a year of severe crisis in Lebanon. Thousands of Lebanese and Palestinians were killed, many more were wounded, and certain areas of Lebanon's major cities were devastated as a result of domestic warfare. The major periods of fighting were in the spring, fall, and winter. Just before the first serious clashes broke out in April, George Hawi wrote that "the country is today on the verge of admitting that the present administration in every sphere—economic, social, and political—can no longer be maintained." He proposed that fundamental political and constitutional reforms were necessary in order to establish a modern, secular, and democratic government "to which the state, administration, military, and civil apparatus are fully subordinated." He stressed that "a broad alliance or broad national front is the basic condition for solving all the sensitive and dangerous questions posed by the present crisis" (*IB*, no. 11, 1975).

Late in April the LCP joined with other leftist parties in condemning the right-wing Christian Phalangist Party. An LCP editorial charged that the Phalangists had revealed themselves as a fascist group working against the Palestinian resistance, the general national struggle, and efforts toward bringing about democratic and social changes. In early June the Military Prosecutor in the northern district of 'Akkar issued summonses to fifty leaders of the leftist movement, including LCP leaders, ostensibly to question them in connection with charges of disturbing the peace and breaking the law. The leftist leaders rejected the summonses. They questioned why no similar action was taken against Phalangists. At a meeting in Beirut on 7 June they characterized the action as "arbitrary, aimed at terrorizing the progressive movement and restricting democratic freedoms" (*Arab World*, Beirut, 9 June). Throughout the spring and summer LCP representatives participated in various rallies of leftist parties opposing military- or rightist-dominated cabinets.

The weekly *al-Hawadith* quoted assurances by George Hawi in August declaring that the LCP would not use force to deal with other parties. Noting that the situation in Lebanon is special, Hawi explained that "if we communists were to reach a position of power, we would rule in the special Lebanese way . . ." (*Arab World*, 6 August). The LCP joined with other leftist parties on 18 August in holding a press conference in which they called for the end of the confessional system and the reorganization of the army, as well as reform of the administration, the electoral system, and the system of popular representation. Just before the domestic situation exploded again in September, Nadim 'Abd al-Samad reiterated the LCP line by charging that the Phalangists had formed a fascist-type militia and had kindled religious strife through outright and also subtle lies in order to stymie the fundamental progressive reforms that would lead the way out of the domestic crisis. In an article in *The New York Times* of 5 October reporting on external sources of aid to the various factions, it was noted that "Moscow reportedly has provided significant amounts of aid to the leftist forces through the LCP."

The LCP and the Middle East. The general policy of the LCP in regard to the Middle East essentially followed Soviet policy. It reaffirmed support of the Palestine Liberation Organization (PLO) as the sole legitimate representative of the Palestinian people. In June, Shawi called for the reconvening of the Geneva conference and stressed that a solution to the Middle East conflict could only be achieved if all occupied Arab territories were evacuated and Palestinian rights guaranteed. The LCP strongly opposed the Egyptian-Israeli disengagement agreement. At a meeting in mid-October the LCP and the newly re-surfaced Communist Party of Egypt joined in rejecting the agreement as a hostile scheme meant to end the state of war without securing either Palestinian rights or total withdrawal. The agreement was condemned as dividing the Arab cause, strengthening the Zionist enemy, and providing U.S. imperialism with a military foothold in Arab Sinai (*al-Nida'*, 14 October).

Members of the LCP were involved in fighting against Israel. In the first week of 1975 Mahmud Muhammad Ka'k, a teacher and secretary of the LCP organization in the village of al-Taibah in southern Lebanon, was killed during an Israeli raid on the village. On 23 July members of the Popular Guard strongly resisted an Israeli attack on the village of Kfar Kila. This group was formed as the result of a call by the LCP in January 1970 for all progressive and national forces to enlist popular guards to defend southern villages, lands, and citizens. Despite disapproval by other Arab communist parties, the LCP encouraged the West Bank branch of the Jordanian Communist Party (JCP) led by 'Arabi 'Awad to secede from the JCP and organize itself as the Palestinian Communist Party.

The LCP met with seven other Arab communist parties at the beginning of April to discuss various issues of vital concern to the people of the Arab world (see the Introduction, p. xxviii).

International Contacts. The LCP maintained active contact throughout the year with communist parties of Eastern Europe and the Soviet Union. In May Muruwwah and 'Abd al-Samad were guests of communist parties in East Germany and Bulgaria; in June, Shawi and 'Abd al-Samad, alone or in concert, visited Hungary, the Soviet Union, East Germany, Czechoslovakia, and Romania; and in August Shawi met communist leaders of East Germany and Romania. In September the chairman of the LCP Central Control and Auditing Commission met his Bulgarian counterpart. In early October Artin Madoyan met the First Secretary of the Armenian Communist Party Central Committee in Yerevan.

Publications. The LCP publishes a daily newspaper, *al-Nida'* ("The Call"), a weekly magazine *al-Akhbar* ("The News"), and a literary and ideological monthly *al-Tariq* ("The Road"). In an article in the Lebanese weekly *al-Diyar*, the editor of *al-Akhbar*, Milhim Abu Rizq, complained that advertising agencies were boycotting party publications, using advertisements as political leverage rather than for purposes of trade. He noted that in 1974 the LCP magazine ran up a deficit, but he claimed that it is one of the most widely distributed magazines in Lebanon (*Arab World*, 15 February).

*   *   *

Other Communist Organizations. The Organization of Communist Action in Lebanon (OCAL) is led by its secretary-general, Muhsin Ibrahim. Like the LCP, it is a member of both the Front of Progressive Parties and National Froces and the Arab Front for Participation in the Palestine Revolution. On the domestic situation Muhsin Ibrahim was quoted as saying that "we [leftists] believe that the present system cannot continue, and that the system will change within one year" (*Arab World*, 6 August). The OCAL joined other leftist parties in Lebanon in calling for sweeping reforms to solve the domestic crisis and took part in leftist rallies opposing military and rightist cabinets. The left exercised its greatest influence under the Rashid al-Sulh government, but an OCAL editorial in April stressed that the left did not support its becoming a strong government. Rather, the aim of the left was to oppose any "strong government" and to protect and strengthen the gains realized by the popular movement (*al-Hurriyah*, 9 April). Northern leaders of OCAL were among the leftists issued summonses in June, which they rejected as being arbitrary and directed against the progressive movement (see LCP above).

An OCAL delegation led by Muhsin Ibrahim visited Aden in mid-April at the invitation of the National Front of the People's Democratic Republic of Yemen. In a joint communiqué the OCAL explained the Lebanese situation in terms of intensified reactionary provocations meant to disrupt Lebanese unity, liquidate "the valiant Palestine resistance," and strike at the nationalist and progressive movement. The OCAL pointed out the rise in the level of struggle of the popular movement and in Lebanese-Palestinian cohesion. The two organizations sharply criticized Kissinger's mission to the Middle East, objecting to partial solutions and efforts to strike at Arab solidarity. They renewed support for "the valiant Palestine resistance . . . within the framework of the PLO, the sole legal representative of the Palestinian people." They expressed support for the people of Oman in their struggle against colonialism, Iran, and "the reactionary regime [of Oman]. They condemned "the fascist military clique in Chile . . . [and] the white minority regimes in Rhodesia and South Africa" (*Aden Home Service* in *Summary of World Broadcasts*, 17 April).

Muhsin Ibrahim escaped an assassination attempt by unidentified persons on 10 September. His bodyguard was killed and an OCAL Politburo member was wounded. The OCAL publishes the weekly *al-Hurriyah* ("Freedom") in partnership with the Popular Democratic Front for the Liberation of Palestine (PFLP), led by Nayif Hawatmah.

*   *   *

The Arab Communist Organization (ACO) was founded in Lebanon some years ago with the expressed aim of replacing Arab communist parties it considered to be deviationist and revisionist. The ACO is composed of small cells·linked together under larger commands with an overall command for the Arab world, decentrally organized in such a way that members can operate freely without exposing others in the party. It is not known how big it is or how closely it is related to other organizations such as the PFLP. ACO membership includes Arabs of various nationalities, with cells in a number of Arab countries. Both the LCP and the OCAL denounce the ACO. The ACO was refused membership in the Arab Front for Participation in the Palestine Revolution. The ACO began to undertake urban guerrilla operations in 1974 after being joined by former members of the now defunct Lebanese Revolutionary Socialist Organization. Since the summer of 1974 the ACO has been primarily engaged in bank robberies and sabotage activities against commercial establishments in Lebanon as well as in Syria and Kuwait. In mid-July 25 members were arrested in Lebanon for establishing cells in the military and were charged with responsibility for explosions in military and police quarters. Lebanese leftists denounced the campaign of arrests, charging that the ACO was being used as a pretext to liquidate national and progressive views in the military. Earlier in July ten other ACO members were arrested in Lebanon with the close cooperation of the intelligence services of Lebanon, Syria, Kuwait, Jordan, and Egypt, while at the same time other members were apprehended in Syria and Kuwait for terrorist activities.

Hoover Institution   Michel Nabti
Stanford University

The Maghreb

ALGERIA

The Algerian Communist Party (Parti Communiste Algérien; PCA), like the other communist parties of the Maghreb, was originally related to the French occupation of these areas. It evolved in 1920 as a part of the French Communist Party but did not flourish in the atmosphere of Islam. During World War II most communist groups in the French orbit were active in the French resistance. Though their cadres suffered persecution and death during the war, many new adherents joined the party during these years. In the course of the Algerian revolution, 1954-1962, the PCA attempted to gain an important foothold in the Algerian National Liberation Front (FLN), but the PCA's longstanding French and Russian orientation made it a doubtful ally in the revolutionary struggle. A number of Algerian communists were liquidated during the revolution.

In 1962 when the newly independent government of Algeria under Ahmad Ben Bella came to power, Algeria tried to reach an accommodation with various leftist and moderate political tendencies. For a short time the PCA was a legal organization.

Leadership and Party Affairs. Following the coup d'état of Houari Boumedienne in June 1965, his one-party Islamic socialist and military government banned the PCA. It became a clandestine operation under the title of Socialist Vanguard Party (Parti de l'Avant-Garde-Socialiste; PAGS). In 1974 the PAGS obtained minimal legality in Algeria and was active in strengthening relations with various communist parties abroad. It is thus considered the direct descendant of the old PCA. The PAGS is controlled by Secretary Sadiq Hadjeres, and its membership is estimated at 400. The population of Algeria is nearly 17,000,000.

International Activities. Boumedienne in 1974 allowed the PAGS more leeway in international affairs and released some communists from jail. The PAGS does not press a Marxist-Leninist or Trotskyite program for Algeria; instead it has moderated orthodox communist views for closer accord with the FLN's Islamic socialist program, which contains a mixture of state capitalism, socialism, and private industry and land-holding.

Since the FLN has maintained cordial relations with the USSR and its allies in the communist world and claims to be a neutralist nationalist party, the position of the PAGS remains of no great importance. However, it is useful in meetings with communist workers' parties in various places. A PAGS delegation attended the meeting of a group of Arab communist parties held in April 1975 (see the Introduction, p. xxviii). The delegates confirmed their desire to cooperate closely with the FLN in Algeria.

In 1975 many delegations were sent from Algeria to communist countries. These visits were usually made by FLN leaders or FLN revolutionary cadres and were not directly connected with activities of the PAGS. The FLN also entertained many visiting communist envoys. *L'Unità* of Rome reported on the visit of a delegation of the Italian Communist Party led by Gian Carlo Pajetta to the Algerian FLN (16-21 January 1975). Algeria's delegates were led by Sharif Messadia. Discussions were held on the improvements of commercial ties.

A delegation headed by the Algerian secretary of state for planning, 'Abd Allah Kodjha, went to Hungary on 3 February 1975 to acquaint that nation with the Algerian Second Four-year Plan and to visit automated projects there.

In May 1975 Boumedienne and the FLN received a delegation of the Korean Workers' Party of the Democratic People's Republic of Korea. President Kim Il-song, the party leader, was met by the Revolutionary Council of Algeria and accorded much honor by the Algerian government, which supports the reunification of Korea (Algiers Domestic Service, 2 June).

In June foreign minister Nguyen Thi Binh of the Revolutionary Government of South Vietnam visited Algiers. She was received by 'Abd al-Malik Ben Habyles, secretary general of the foreign ministry. Boumedienne promised support to the new country in its energy development program (Algiers Domestic Service, 14 June).

Similar visits by representatives of other communist or progressive governments were reported in the summer months. They included one by Pham Van Dong, premier of the Democratic Republic of Vietnam; Todor Zhivkov, first secretary of the Bulgarian Communist Party Central Committee and chairman of the State Council of the Bulgarian People's Republic; and Mexican President Luis Echeverria, a friend and colleague of Houari Boumedienne (Algiers Domestic Service, July).

Publications. The PAGS issues *Saut al-Sha'b* ("The Voice of the People"), a clandestine journal.

MOROCCO

The Moroccan Communist Party (Parti Communiste Marocaine; PCM), founded in 1943 as a branch of the French Communist Party, originally contained no Moroccan members. By 1945, when Comintern-trained Moroccan students returned home and 'Ali Yata became secretary-general, this condition changed. Declared illegal, along with Istiqlal (Independence Party), by the French Protectorate (1952), banned again by King Muhammad V in 1959, it resurfaced in 1968 as the Party of Liberation and Socialism (Parti de la Libération et du Socialisme; PLS) to be outlawed once again in 1969 by King Hasan II. By August 1974 the pro-Soviet Communist group, granted legal status in return for favors rendered to Hasan II, called itself the Party of Progress and Socialism (Parti du Progrès et du Socialisme; PPS) (*The Guardian*, 22 March 1975).

Another group composed largely of intellectuals espousing Marxist-Leninist principles, which denied any validity to the existing government or the other political parties, works both underground and in exile. Bearing no name, it publishes *Souffles* ('Whispers") irregularly, which identifies the movement. Its leader is Abraham Serfaty, a brilliant forty-nine-year-old mining engineer of Jewish birth, formerly chief of the technical department of the Moroccan Phosphates Office. Judging from the vitriol it receives from the PPS, it is a serious rival, attracting especially the youth, 150 of whom were arrested. The usually efficient Moroccan police have not been able to lay hands on Muhammad al-Basri, formerly of the Socialist Union of National Forces (Union Socialiste des Forces Nationales; USFP), an exiled Berber, classified like Serfaty as "New Left, or [one of] those who do not play the game" (*Jeune Afrique*, 14 December 1974). Other lesser elements of the left are the Progressive Liberal Party (Parti Progressive Libéral; PPL) and the Action Party (Parti de l'Action; PA), both newly formed in late 1974 after Hasan II announced future parliamentary elections, which were later postponed. An estimated 500 persons might be labeled communist. Morocco's population numbers about 17,300,000.

Domestic Attitudes, Activities and Leadership. Royal sanction of the PPS resulted from 'Ali Yata's active support of Hasan II's claims to the Spanish Sahara and from the king's desire to broaden his political base after two unsuccessful assassination attempts on his life. The PPS held its party congress on 21-23 February 1975. It confirmed 'Ali Yata as general party secretary and created a Secretariat of Yata, 'Abd Allah Layashi, and 'Abd al-Salam Burquia. The congress named a seven-man Politburo which included the three Secretariat members plus 'Abd al-'Aziz Belay, an attorney; Simon Levy; Muhammad Shu'aib Rifi; and Muhammad Musharik (*WMR*, No. 5, 1975). According to *WMR* (No. 7, July 1975), 338 delegates attended the congress. The same source analyzed their social composition as "workers and employees 43 percent, poor peasants 16, intelligentsia 41. Among them were more than twenty women. Ages: 43 percent up to 30 years, 40 percent 30-40 years, 17 percent over 40." At the congress the PPS viewed itself as "the vanguard of the Moroccan working class" and sought with Moscow's support to build a "popular front." "Representatives of 16 communist and a number of revolutionary-democratic parties and the Palestine Liberation Organization attended the congress" (*WMR*, No. 7, 1975). Bu 'Abid, the leader of the USFP, also attended, as did representatives of the trade unions and student organizations.

The PPS advocated gradual scientific socialism. Its specific targets included nationalization of banks, insurance companies, electricity, gas and oil distribution, sugar, cement, and pharmaceuticals. Mines in which foreign banks were large holders were also signaled out for nationalization. The elimination of "feudal land tenure," support of Moroccan workers in France, and elimination of wage discrimination against women rounded out the domestic economic program.

International Attitudes and Activities. Abroad, total support for Morocco's claims to the Spanish Sahara became the life blood of all above-ground political parties, including the PPS. Rapprochement between Morocco and the Soviet Union served both the PPS and gathering Soviet strength in the Mediterranean. The PPS denounced imperialism and Zionism, at the same time calling for the return of all Arab lands by Israel and asserting the national rights of Arabs to Palestine. The PPS was represented at the gathering of Arab communist parties in April (see the Introduction, p. xxviii).

Publications. 'Ali Yata edits *al-Bayan* ("*The Bulletin*"), a weekly appearing in Rabat.

TUNISIA

The Communist Party of Tunisia (Parti Communiste Tunisien; PCT) was founded in 1919, predating by one year the Algerian Communist Party. The PCT, like its sister Maghrebian parties, was originally a part of the French Communist Party and in general suffered the same fate as its sisters. The PCT became independent in 1934 and had at its peak some 2,000 members.

When Tunisia, under the leadership of Habib Bourguiba and the Neo-Destour (later the Destourian Socialist Party), gained its independence from France in 1956, the PCT lost the basis of its power, as it had been an urban workers' party aligned with the French trade unionists and other leftist elements. The moderate elements of Neo-Destour also destroyed the right wing conservative Destour. However, the PCT was not formally banned until 1962, when all parties except the Destourian Socialist were prohibited from engaging in political activity.

After the Arab-Israeli war of 1967, anti-Jewish outbursts were blamed on the Tunisian political left. A number of Tunisian communists were jailed. Accordingly, the politics of Tunisia seemed to be avoiding a drift towards the strongly socialist bent of its Algerian neighbor. In 1974 the number of communists in Tunisia was estimated to be 100. The population of Tunisia in 1975 was estimated to be 5,000,000.

Domestic Attitudes and Activities. In 1974 President Bourguiba became president for life. This development was accepted with apparent good will by the greater part of the nation, although Ahmad Ben Salah, the former minister of economy and planning who had been interested in agrarian socialization, was arrested for treason at this time. In the event of Bourguiba's death it is expected that Hadi Nouira, the present prime minister and a man of moderate views, would take over the presidency. Therefore, there seems little likelihood of an important PCT movement.

Clandestine elements of the PCT published an article in *IB* (May 1974) outlining the party's objectives. They were low-keyed, stressing the need for alteration of the capitalist system in the direction of socialism and advocating the removal of the ban on communist party institutions, along with the granting of the right to strike and trade union freedoms.

International Attitudes and Activities. The same article in *IB* called for an alliance with other socialist nations to sustain anti-imperialist and territorial struggles such as that of the Palestinians and in general a pro-Arab stance vis-à-vis the Israeli question and world energy problems.

In March 1975, Soviet experts carried out a survey for the construction of a dam on a Tunisian river and sent specialists and hydroelectric equipment to aid in the supply of water to thousands of hectares of Tunisian land.

In April members of the PCT attended the congress of Arab communist parties (see the Introduction, p. xxviii).

In May 1975, President Bourguiba entertained USSR Chairman Aleksei Kosygin and complimented him on his continuing battle to help the nations still under the yoke of imperialism and capitalism. Bourguiba especially thanked the Russian people for their support in the Arab-Israeli dispute and for backing other national liberation groups in their attempts to achieve political freedom and social democracy (Tunis Domestic Service, 15 May).

Publications. With the banning of the PCT came the banning of its publications *al-Tali 'ah* ("The Vanguard") and *Tribune du Progrès*. The PCT now has no official journal. News of the activities of other Tunisian leftists, Marxists, and Trotskyites had been included in *Tunisian Perspectives* and *The Tunisian Worker* published by leftist, mostly student groups, members of which suffered arrest and persecution in 1974. Prison sentences ranging from six months to ten years were given to 175 persons.

Oakland University

Joan Brace
Richard Brace

Réunion

The Réunion Communist Party (Parti Communiste Réunnionais; PCR) was founded in 1959 by the transformation of the Réunion Federation of the French Communist Party into an autonomous organization.

The PCR is legal. In 1967 the party claimed 3,500 members. No new figures were released at the party's Third Congress, in July 1972. The U.S. State Department has estimated PCR membership at 800 (*World Strength of the Communist Party Organizations*, Washington, D.C., 1973, p. 127). Réunion has a population of 470,000 (estimated 1972).

The PCR is an active participant in Réunion political life, on both local and departmental levels. (As one of France's overseas departments, Réunion is an integral part of the French Republic.) The PCR is the only party with a local organization; elected candidates of other parties are normally French, without permanent organizaion in Réunion. In 1974 the PCR held 6 seats on the 36-member General Council. The PCR won none of the three contested seats for the French National Assembly in March 1973. It repeatedly charged fraud and unsuccessfully called for the annulment of the September 1973 election.

PCR secretary-general Paul Vergès is the mayor of the island's main city. Vergès was reelected secretary-general of the PCR at the Third Congress, but no other leadership positions were announced in the party organ. A special party conference, scheduled to occur on 21 April 1974, was indefinitely postponed because of a time conflict with presidential elections in France.

The PCR controls the largest trade union, the General Confederation of Labor of Réunion (Confédération Générale du Travail de la Réunion; CGTR), led by Bruny Payet, who is also a member of the General Council. The party is also influential in the Réunion Front of Autonomous Youth (Front de la Jeunesse Autonomiste de la Réunion; FJAR), headed by Elie Hoarau, and the Union of Réunion Women (Union des Femmes de la Réunion; UFR).

Departmental and National Views and Positions. The PCR continued its quest for self-determination for Réunion, by supporting the Réunion Coordination Committee for Self-Determination (CRCA). It worked closely with other organizations it controls or influences, such as the UFR, the CGTR, and the FJAR. On 8 November Vergès, in a major speech in Mont Vert, reaffirmed the commitment of the party to "a profound change" and to prepare the masses for autonomy.

The party also continued opposing an expanded emigration policy to remove "surplus" population from Réunion, complaining that the government's action would "seriously reduce the genetic potential" of the country. Gervais Barret, in the name of the group of communist deputies of the Conseil Régional, condemned birth control measures for Réunion as proposed by the government, charging that together with emigration it would lead to the rapid aging of the population (*Témoignages*, 17 November). The PCR took particular aim at Michel Debré, who defended these policies in a national debate on demographic problems in the National Assembly in Paris.

Paul Vergés led a group of more than 500 dissatisfied tenants to victory in a court case against A. Minatchy, a large landlord who had cut off services to tenants. The court decision forced the restoration of the services and was hailed as a sign of party influence on the Union of Tenants of Réunion (Syndicat des Locataires de la Réunion; SDLR). Vergès congratulated the tenants on the victory, emphasizing the "role of solidarity" of the PCR and the decisive contribution of the party organ, *Témoignages.*

Significant space and publicity were given to the trip of three women from Réunion to the World Congress for International Women's Year in Berlin in October. Odette Mofy, the leader of the delegation, spoke to the Third Commission on Women and Development, charging that the condition of women was so difficult in Réunion, where 30 percent are still illiterate, that women will have to take their affairs in their own hands from now on. Mme. Vergès told the Seventh Commission that "the solidarity of women and peoples of the world is necessary for the workers' battle for self-determination." She also attacked the military bases at Diego-Garcia and Simonstown in South Africa as "menaces to the liberty" of people in the Indian Ocean area.

A women's conference with over 1,000 delegates to the URF was held in Port in October; autonomy was also a major concern of this fourth meeting which took as its theme: "The liberation of woman is not complete until the country is liberated from colonialism." Prominent signs proclaimed "Democratic and popular autonomy," and "Liberty for the people of Réunion to direct their own affairs." Delegates were invited from women's organizations in Madagascar, Mauritius, and the Seychelles. Both Paul Vergès and Bruny Payet of the CGTR welcomed the delegates, aided by Jean-Philippe Rivière of the FJAR.

Elie Hoarau, secretary of the FJAR, was briefly implicated in the aftermath of the bombing of the Paris residence of Michel Debrè; for several days, French police sought M. Hoarau, but he was on an official visit to Romania and disclaimed any connection with the incident. *Témoignages* used the incident to launch further attacks against Michel Debré and the French police.

International Views and Contacts. The PCR continued its opposition to militarization efforts in the Indian Ocean, especially those attributed to the United States and France, as well as its attacks on the racial policies of the Republic of South Africa.

The PCR also vigorously opposed the attempt of the French government to bring about a new vote on Mayotte, one of the islands of the newly independent country of the Comoros. Charging Paris with colonialist intervention, the party denounced Debré and large landowner Marcel Henri with conspiring to regain independent territory for French colonialist interests. *Témoignages* gave considerable coverage to political development in the Comoros, especially to the acceptance by the United Nations of the new country's bid for membership.

In September Vergès and Elie Hoarau visited Moscow, to attend the conference of the Organization of Solidarity of Peoples of Africa and Asia; Paris, where Hoarau met with leaders of the Ligue Populaire Africaine pour l'Indépendance de Djibouti; and Bucharest.

Publication. The daily organ of the PCR is *Témoignages.*

University of California
Santa Barbara

G. Wesley Johnson

Senegal

The African Independence Party (Parti Africain de l'Indépendance; PAI) of Senegal was founded in 1957, declaring itself a Marxist-Leninist party supporting the political line and objectives of the international communist movement. Originally operating as a federated organization, the PAI carried out activities in several French possessions in Africa. Since 1962 the party has restricted its activities to Senegal on the grounds that France had by then been forced to grant autonomy or independence to the territories of its former colonial federations. (*WMR*, June.)

The PAI, illegal since 1960, has been torn by internal dissension during the past decade; it is now apparently split into two main factions, pro-Soviet and pro-Chinese in orientation, although no information is available on the latter. No membership figures have been released on the pro-Soviet party, which seems to draw most of its support from intellectuals, particularly students, many of whom reside in Paris.

Senegalese politics is dominated by President Léopold Sédar Senghor and the official Union Progressiste Sénégalaise. Senghor claims to be a socialist and to think that only socialism can solve Senegal's problems (interview, *Vjesnik*, Zagreb, 7-8 September). All opposition parties were outlawed and many political opponents incarcerated during the 1960s and early 1970s. Following an amnesty for some political prisoners in 1974, the government authorized the formation of one opposition party while continuing to suppress the PAI. Possible legalization of the PAI was discussed at the end of 1975 (see below). The population of Senegal is 4,100,000 (estimated 1975).

Party Affairs. The PAI held its First Congress in 1962 and its Second Congress ten years later. The party is run by its Central Committee, Political Bureau, and Secretariat.

Domestic Policies and Activities. At its First Congress the PAI called for the unity of democratic and patriotic forces in Senegal in order to fight effectively for the elimination of foreign influence in the country and for the formation of an anti-imperialist government with a powerful state sector and democratic freedoms. This platform was reaffirmed at the Second Congress. In mid-1975 the PAI emphasized the need for a broad united front to eliminate the Senghor government (which it considered pro-imperialist), to achieve "full national independence," to undertake what it calls a genuine democratic policy in the interests of the entire nation, and to pursue a non-capitalist development leading to socialism. (*WMR*, June.)

According to an article published in Prague at mid-year, the PAI claimed its policies had won considerable public support and were forcing the government to seek an accommodation. Specifically, it maintained that "ruling circles" in Senegal were now willing to legalize the PAI if the party would get rid of its "foreign agents." (The party denies the presence of such agents and attacks the government for banning democratic organizations, trade unions, youth and student organizations, on the pretext that they are influenced or used by the PAI.) At the end of the year President Senghor proposed making Senegal a three-party nation, with one of the three having a Marxist-Leninist orientation. In mid-November the PAI Central Committee issued a declaration in Dakar rejecting the proposal, calling instead for the simultaneous recognition of the PAI and the elimination of all restrictions on the formation of other legal political parties. The November declaration went on to demand the annulment of existing laws and decrees affecting elections and political organizations generally, the dissolution of the state's security court and a government guarantee of freedom of expression, concluding that the PAI was prepared to cooperate with all the nation's political forces and leaders within a program of national interest. At the same time, the PAI reaffirmed its commitment to the class struggle and socialism. (AFP, 18 November, in *FBIS*, Sub-Saharan Africa, 19 November.)

Publications. The PAI publishes the monthly *La Lutte* (Struggle) and the weekly *Momsarev* (Independence). Reports of party activities and positions appear periodically in the publications of other pro-Soviet parties and organizations. The PAI is represented on the Editorial Council of the *World Marxist Review*.

San Francisco, Calif.   Lynn Ratliff

South Africa

Africa's oldest Marxist-Leninist party celebrates its fifty-fifth anniversary on July 30, 1976. Founded in 1921 as the legal Communist Party of South Africa, outlawed and dissolved in 1950, and reconstituted as the South African Communist Party (SACP) in 1953, the SACP has operated underground since its rebirth twenty-three years ago. The top leadership of the party resides outside South Africa, but cadres of the SACP operate within the country, occasionally publishing clandestine broadsheets. The party's membership is drawn from all races but its precise composition and numerical strength are unknown; probably membership does not exceed several hundred. The population of South Africa is 25,000,000 (estimated 1975).

The SACP regards itself as an essential component of "our national liberation front headed by the mass organization of the most exploited and oppressed section of our people—the ANC" (*African Communist*, no. 60, p. 27). The ANC, the African National Congress, historically the country's most prominent national African political organization, has also operated underground and in exile since its banning in 1960. It is linked within the liberation front to the South African Indian Congress (SAIC), the South African Coloured People's Congress, and the South African Congress of Trade Unions (SACTU). Elements of the SAIC, particularly those within the revived Natal Indian Congress, and small groups affiliated to SACTU, operate legally within the country, although they are often harassed by government authorities.

Leadership and Organization. The publicly identified leadership of the SACP remains in the hands of longtime party members who were active in South Africa both before and after the banning of the original CPSA in 1950. Dr. Yusuf M. Dadoo, a 66-year-old Indian leader who left South Africa in 1960, continues as chairman, a post to which he was elected by a plenary session of the party held in exile in December, 1972, Moses Kotane, a 70-year-old African, retains the post of general secretary to which he was elected in 1939. Since shortly after suffering a heart attack in Dar es Salaam in 1968, Kotane has been under medical care in the Soviet Union; he has been able to participate only intermittently in party affairs during his convalescence. Bram Fischer, a prominent Afrikaans-speaking white lawyer who headed the underground party in the early 1960's and was imprisoned for life in 1966, died in South Africa in May at the age of 67 after a long bout with cancer. Other leading party officials, almost all of whom are certainly in exile, are not identified except by pseudonyms in the party press.

In the view of Dr. Dadoo the SACP is "the party of the most advanced class, and the propagandist of Marxism," with an "indispensable role, both as an independent organization and as an integral part of the national liberation movement" (*World Marxist Review*, February, 1975). Dedicated to maintaining itself as "an organization of professional revolutionaries" (*African Communist*, no. 43), the SACP regards the ANC as the key mass organization for the successful mobilization of the African population in a national struggle to overthrow white domination as a step towards socialism.

Domestic Activities and Attitudes. The SACP has reaffirmed its commitment to guidelines for action laid down at its plenary session in December, 1972 (*World Marxist Review*, Febuary). The prime task is seen as the creation of "conditions in which organized physical resistance will begin to play a bigger and bigger part." To this end a high premium is placed upon the strengthening of underground organization and links with "all organized centers of opposition in town and country," but in addition calls are made for the "simultaneous intensification of mass struggles in the course of which the people will feel their strength and gain more and more confidence in their capacity to meet and challenge the enemy on his own ground." The black working class, in particular, is to be mobilized both in the cities and on white-owned farms, and a special role is assigned to black youth "in helping to elaborate and to spread the policies and program of the liberation front." (Ibid.)

Articles in the SACP party journal view recent shifts of government policy within South Africa and moves by the Nationalist government towards "détente" with black Africa as both an opportunity and danger for the SACP and its allies within the liberation front. On the one hand the final disintegration of Portuguese colonialism and the accession of FRELIMO to power in neighboring Mozambique was regarded as a dramatic exposure of the myth of white supremacy and a direct spur to heightened resistance within South Africa (*African Communist*, no. 62). The white ruling class was estimated to be showing "signs that its confidence and cohesiveness are becoming less assured" (*African Communist*, no. 60). On the other hand it was conceded that the government reacted in a sophisticated fashion to changes beyond South Africa's borders and "the new strategy of the establishment should not be underestimated." Specific warnings against the pitfalls of black collaborationism within the framework of the Bantustans were made in tandem with calls for new theoretical clarity drawing upon both the experience of revolutionaries in Vietnam, Cuba, and Mozambique and that of the struggle within the peculiar conditions of South Africa itself (*African Communist*, no. 63).

International Views and Activities. The focus of recent international activities of the SACP has been Mozambique, Portugal, and Western Europe while at the same time the strong pro-Soviet stance which has characterized the party in the past has been maintained. Upon the occasion of Mozambican independence, the Central Committee of the SACP sent a warm letter to Samora Machel, President of

FRELIMO; earlier in the year the party journal published an exclusive interview with Alvaro Cunhal, General Secretary of the Portuguese Communist Party (PCP), and a delegation from the SACP met with a delegation from the PCP in Lisbon. Analogous meetings were held during the year with delegations of the British and French Communist Parties. Although no explicit attacks were made upon China, the SACP and the PCP "pledged to continue contributing actively to the strengthening of the unity and cohesion of the world communist movement on the basis of the principles of Marxism-Leninism and of the resolutions of the Moscow Conference of 1969" (*African Communist*, no. 61).

Publications. The SACP publishes from London the *African Communist*, a quarterly printed in the German Democratic Republic. Within South Africa it distributes an illegal mimeographed party journal, *Inkululeko-Freedom*. It has also welcomed the appearance of a sister underground publication, *Vukani-Awake*, committed to support of the liberation front headed by the ANC.

Duke University   Sheridan Johns

Sudan

The Sudanese Communist Party (SCP) traces its origins to 1944, although it was not until 1947 that communists formed a political party, the Sudanese Movement for National Liberation, with 'Abd al-Khaliq Mahjub as its secretary-general. The SCP, as it was later named, operated clandestinely at times, and at other times in relative freedom and with considerable power and influence. Some of its members were elected representatives to the national legislature. Even Ja'far Numairi, President of the Sudan since May 1969, at one time had two communist members in his cabinet. The SCP gradually became a focal point of opposition, however, successfully infiltrating a number of professional, student, and labor groups. Implication in the abortive coup d'état of 19 July 1971 led to severe repression of the party (see *YICA, 1972*, pp. 290-292). Numerous SCP leaders were executed, including Mahjub. Thousands of party members were arrested and held without trial.

No reliable figures exist concerning present SCP membership, which before the 1971 attempted coup was estimated at from 5,000 to 10,000 active members. An undisclosed number are continuing party activities in exile or clandestinely within the Sudan.

Leadership and Organization. Names of party leaders have consistently been absent from international press reports on the SCP. Due to the suppression of the party in the Sudan, statements issued by the party itself have also withheld any names. However, leading figures identified in 1974

were Ibrahim Nuqud, then in exile; Mahjub ·'Uthman and al-Faijani al-Tayyib, arrested in October 1974 after returning from exile; and Dr. 'Izz al-Din 'Ali Amir and Ibrahim Zakariya, whose whereabouts were unknown.

Domestic Views and Activities. Until 1971 the SCP was considered the most highly organized political force in the Sudan. Its effectiveness derived from its tradition of militancy and its ability to mobilize popular support and the support of the trade unions and student organizations. The party remains in direct opposition to the government of Ja'far Numairi, whose power base lies in the military.

The SCP has been primarily concerned with domestic issues. Early in 1975 it was reported that the party had forged an alliance with the more radical section of the Ummah Party, forming a united National Front along with the Unionist Party and the conservative Moslem Brotherhood. On 3 March at least 50 students were injured in clashes at Khartoum University. The cause of the incident was an attempt by student members of the SCP and the Moslem Brotherhood to prevent student members of the pro-government Sudanese Socialist Union from setting up an exhibition to mark the anniversary of the Addis Ababa agreement which officially resolved the civil war in Sudan.

In early April, anti-government leaflets were distributed in the town of Sennar by the SCP during the President's visit there. In reaction to such activities President Numairi, who in 1974 would not publicly acknowledge the revival of the SCP, charged on April 14 that "the SCP has launched a sabotage campaign against the regime" (*al-Usbu' al-'Arabi*, Beirut, 28 April). He accused the communists of trying to undermine the people's confidence in their economic system, "exploiting what they [the SCP] termed the traditional cowardice of capitalism inside and outside the Sudan." Numairi in a broadcast to the nation assured the people that the government would not interfere with private property and that nationalization and confiscation were policies of the past which would not be re-adopted. Numairi also accused the SCP of encouraging divisiveness between the northern and southern regions of the Sudan through rumors that hundreds of northern Sudanese had been killed in the south and that he and Libya's Colonel Mu'ammar al-Qadhdhafi had been attacked during celebrations marking the anniversary of the Addis Ababa agreement (*Arab Report and Record*, London, 1-15 April).

On 4-5 May *Le Monde* of Paris reported an appeal by the SCP to "the union of popular opposition forces." urging it to struggle to liberate political prisoners and have "the reactionary fascist law on internment" repealed. The SCP accused the Sudanese government of imprisoning people without charge and for longer than the legal time limit. The party urged those involved to demand release or trial without delay of the political prisoners. The appeal noted that those imprisoned included 91 people from various occupations, primarily workers, civil servants, and students.

President Numairi charged in June that "a communist plot to take over power had been foiled a few months ago." He called the SCP an "alien organization in the country" constituting a "diabolical presence" (*al-Sahafah*, Khartoum, 16 June).

International Views and Activities. The SCP follows a pro-Soviet line. It maintains contact with other Arab communist parties. A number of reports during the year suggested that the SCP had made common cause with Egyptian Communists. The SCP participated in a congress of Arab communist parties in early April (see the Introduction, p. xxviii). No specific mention was made of the Sudan in the official communiqué.

Publications. As the SCP is under severe repression in the Sudan, the party does not have a regular party organ, but it publishes and distributes leaflets clandestinely. News of the party is printed in publications of the Lebanese Communist Party, *al-Nida'* and *al-Akhbar*.

Stanford University   Patricia Mihaly

Syria

The Syrian Communist Party (al-Hizb al-Shuyu'i al-Suri; SCP) is an offshoot of the Lebanese Communist Party established in 1924 (see *Lebanon*). Under the French mandates all communist activity was proscribed in 1939. This ban was continued after Syria and Lebanon were proclaimed independent states in 1941 and the separate SCP was formed in 1944. Despite illegality, the SCP has enjoyed several periods of considerable political freedom. The last begin in 1966 when a communist was named to a cabinet post for the first time. The communist position improved even further after the bloodless coup of Lieutenant General Hafiz al-Asad in November 1970. As a result of changes brought about by al-Asad, two cabinet posts have been held by communists since 1971. In March 1972 the SCP gained de facto legality through its participation in the National Progressive Front formed by al-Asad. Plagued with internal disputes since early 1971, the SCP finally split into two parties in December 1973 (see *YICA, 1974* and 1975).

Combined membership in the SCP is believed to range between 3,000 and 4,000 with perhaps another 10,000 sympathizers. The population of Syria is about 7,500,000 (estimated 1975).

Leadership and Organization. The SCP is led by Khalid Bakdash, a Syrian Kurd who has been secretary-general of the SCP—except for a brief period in 1968—since the inception of the party. At the party's Fourth Congress in 1974 Bakdash was reelected secretary-general and Yusuf Faisal deputy secretary-general, a new post created by the Congress. The following were elected to the new ten-member Politburo: Bakdash; three former dissidents—Daniel Ni'mah, Dhahir 'Abd al-Samad, and Ibrahim Bakri; and five new members—Murad Yusuf, Ramu Shaikhu, 'Umar Siba'i, Maurice Salibi, and Khalid Hammami. Siba'i is minister of communications and 'Abd al-Samad minister of state in the Syrian cabinet. Bakdash and Ni'mah are the SCP representatives in the National Progressive Front.

Very little was written during 1975 regarding the faction that split from the SCP in 1973. Under the leadership of Riyad al-Turk this dissident group, also identifying itself as the SCP, held what it called its Fourth Congress at the end of December 1973. The Central Committee formed at that time met in January 1974 and elected a Politburo comprised of Riyad al-Turk, first secretary of the party; Badr al-Tawil, 'Umar Qashshash, Wasil Faisal, and Yusuf Nimr, Secretariat members; and Ahmad Fayiz al-Fawwaz, Michel Jirji 'Isa, and Nuri Rifa'i. This faction was officially expelled from the SCP of Bakdash at its Fourth Congress in September 1974. Unlike the SCP of Bakdash, the SCP of al-Turk does not have representation in the Syrian cabinet or the National Progressive Front. From the lack of current information on this group one may speculate that it has felt compelled to operate clandestinely. Further references to the SCP in this profile apply to the SCP led by Khalid Bakdash.

Party Internal Affairs. The SCP held its most recent congress, its Fourth, on 26-28 September 1974, after two postponements occasioned by its lack of unity. It was reported that 170 members attended. The Congress received greetings from 42 foreign communist parties. On 13-14 March 1975 the Central Committee of the SCP held plenary meetings in Damascus. Discussions concentrated primarily on the political situation in the Middle East and on the activities of the party's representatives in the National Progressive Front.

In an interview in January, "Yusuf Faisal stressed that the recent party congress has helped to strengthen the ideological and organizational unity of the party and brought to a successful conclusion the several-year-old struggle against the secessionist actions pursued by a group of opportunists" (*Summary of World Broadcasts; SWB*, 3 February). It was suggested by a Beirut journal in March, however, that Yusuf Faisal himself was challenging the unity of leadership of the party on a number of domestic issues.

In June, Boris Ponomarev of the CPSU visited SCP leaders in Damacsus. It is believed that one reason for his visit was to attempt to resolve differences within the SCP which had led to its split into two factions in 1973.

Domestic Views and Activities. According to Khalid Bakdash, cooperation between the SCP and the ruling Ba'th Party goes back to 1966. In the nine years since then this cooperation has extended to the People's Council, the trade unions, and the student movement, leading ultimately to the organization of the National Progressive Front in 1972. Noting that there have been difficulties obstructing cooperation, Bakdash outlined the principles guiding SCP policy toward the "progressive forces" which include the Ba'th: "First, cooperation with all patriotic forces within and outside the government; secondly, upholding the independence of our party on all fundamental questions and pressing political issues; thirdly, all-out support for the demands and interests of the masses (*WMR*, July 1975). The Plenum in March reaffirmed the SCP policy "of consolidation of the front, the intensification of its role in the country's life, and the deepening of cooperation between its participants, and particularly between the communist party and the Ba'th Party" (*FBIS*, 25 March).

In January, Yusuf Faisal explained that the SCP and the Ba'th Party "are linked by a convergence or identity of viewpoints on such problems as the struggle against imperialism, cooperation with the socialist states, and struggle for the solution of the Middle East problem." He noted that "any differences that may exist" relate to certain domestic problems (*SWB*, 3 February). Several of these domestic problems threatened unity within the SCP. One such problem concerned the Association of Syrian Students Abroad, an organization of Syrian students in Europe which had always been under the control of the SCP. The Ba'th Party wanted the association to be integrated into the Ba'th-controlled Union of Syrian Students Abroad. Faisal approved the plan but Bakdash opposed it. In the end, despite considerable reservations by association members, the change was made. Another such issue concerned the conflict between the Popular Front for the Liberation of Palestine (PFLP) and the Ba'th Party. Bakdash felt the SCP should maintain a neutral stance, but Faisal expressed violent opposition to the PFLP, charging it with complicity with the Arab Communist Organization (see below).

In the March Plenum the SCP resolved to support the Syrian government's policy of strengthening the public sector and giving more control of it to the masses. The SCP urged more vigorous action against "the parasitic bourgeoisie" such as the big middlemen and called for studying such mass problems as high prices and the housing shortage. It noted the importance of lightening the burden of the masses and increasing their support of the regime.

The SCP and the Middle East. Khalid Bakdash outlined SCP policy regarding the Arab-Israeli conflict in an article in January. He stressed that a just and stable peace could only be achieved through a withdrawal of Israeli troops from occupied Arab territories and an end to the Israeli policy of expansion and aggression. He noted that "we [Arabs] will strive to liberate our land by peaceful means. However, if that proves ineffective, we will resort to other means." He urged resumption of the Geneva Conference, with the equal participation of the Palestine Liberation Organization (PLO), which the SCP recognizes as the sole legitimate representative of the Arab people of Palestine. He reaffirmed SCP support for United Nations Security Council Resolutions 242 and 338. In addition, he reaffirmed SCP belief in the right of the Palestinian people to create a national homeland, noting further that a solution to the conflict could not be achieved without participation by the Soviet Union (*FBIS*, 30 January). The Plenum in March reiterated these principles once again, though in regard to the Palestinians it spoke of their "right to an independent state" rather than a "homeland." As U.S. negotiations with Egypt and Israel were in progress, the Plenum strongly rejected "the partial and separate solution U.S. imperialism is trying to impose." The Plenum urged consolidation of Arab solidarity and proposed that the fighting capability of the Syrian army should be raised in order to repel any future Israeli aggression (*IB*, no. 6-7, 1975). A joint communiqué issued by the SCP and the Bulgarian Communist Party stated that one important basis for peace in the Middle East was "insuring the legitimate national rights of the Arab people of Palestine, including the right to create their own state and including the right of self-determination." The communiqué urged the resumption of the Geneva conference "after efficient preliminary preparations" (*FBIS*, 23 June).

The Politburo of the SCP expressed sharp criticism of the Egyptian-Israeli Sinai disengagement agreement. It charged that the agreement insured continued Israeli occupation of Arab territories, giving the Israelis a new chance to strengthen their occupation by implanting militarized settlements in occupied lands. The SCP stated that the agreement isolated Egypt from the Arab struggle and imposed new difficulties for the struggle to achieve a comprehensive settlement which would grant the Arab people of Palestine their legitimate national rights. In addition, the agreement pictured the United States as a mediator, whereas it is actually a participant in the conflict, hostile to the Arab cause. The SCP supported the Syrian government and the PLO leadership in denouncing such partial and separate settlements and urged greater cooperation among "Arab patriotic forces," both among themselves and with their "true ally," the Soviet Union (TASS, 3 September).

The SCP maintained contact with other Arab communist parties. Early in March an SCP delegation led by Khalid Bakdash met leaders of the Iraqi Communist Party in Baghdad. In a joint communiqué the two parties "expressed identical views" on various problems, including the Middle East conflict. They stressed their cooperation and alliance with the Ba'th parties in their respective countries and with "national progressive forces" (*Pravda*, 14 March). It is believed that Bakdash visited Iraq with the official approval of the Syrian government and that one purpose of his visit was to smooth Iraqi-Syrian relations, which had deteriorated due to conflicting Ba'thist ideologies and a dispute over sharing the water of the Euphrates River.

In March Bakdash made serious efforts to have Arab communist parties approve the convening of a joint conference. One of his motivations was to secure his position in the SCP. He also wanted to resolve conflicts among the Arab communist parties in regard to the PLO and other leftist groups, the creation of the Palestinian Communist Party of 'Arabi 'Awad and the reintegration of certain dissident factions into a number of Arab Communist parties (*An-Nahar Arab Report*, Beirut, 24 March). The summit conference which Bakdash had proposed was held in an undisclosed Arab capital early in April (see the Introduction, p. xxviii). According to some Arab observers, several delegates accused the Syrian and Iraqi national fronts of rightist tendencies and of denying the local communist parties any political power. Despite opposition by others, these delegates urged the undermining of the two regimes. *Al-Nida'*, organ of the Lebanese Communist Party, chose not to acknowledge any discord, reporting that the meeting "was characterized by the spirit of camaraderie and a consensus of opinion on all subjects" (*al-Nida'*, 5 April). The summit called for strengthening

the nationalist and progressive regimes in Syria, Iraq, Algeria and South Yemen, promoting cooperation with the Syrian and Iraqi Baʻth parties and the national front parties in Algeria and South
Yemen. The summit expressed support for the struggle of the Moroccan people to liberate all parts of
their homeland and expressed respect for the nationalist rights of the Kurdish people, supporting the
application of the autonomy law within the framework of the Iraqi Republic. It also acknowledged
the right of other nationalist minorities in the Arab countries (*al-Akhbar*, Beirut, 5 April).

International Views and Activities. The SCP maintained active contact with various communist
parties of Eastern Europe and the Soviet Union. In February Andrei Gromyko met SCP leaders in
Damascus and Yusuf Faisal met communist party leaders in Bulgaria. In March the SCP Plenum
stressed the need for Syria to have "closer political, economic and military cooperation with [its]
friend, the Soviet Union" (*IB*, no. 6-7). In April Khalid Bakdash visited leaders of the Communist
Party of Czechoslovakia. On 10 May Bakdash addressed a meeting in Damascus commemorating the
30th anniversary of the Soviet victory over fascism. He called it "the biggest and most important
event of the 20th century after the Great October Socialist Revolution" (TASS, 10 May). On 10-16
June a delegation of the SCP toured Sofia and held meetings with leaders of the Bulgarian Communist
Party, the National Council of the Fatherland Front, and the Central Council of the Bulgarian Trade
Unions. A communiqué issued by the two communist parties in effect outlined SCP international
policies. It stressed the need for a speedy conclusion of the European Security and Cooperation
Conference and the reduction of armed forces and armaments in central Europe. It welcomed the
victories of the peoples of Vietnam, Cambodia, and Laos. The communiqué expressed solidarity with
the struggle of the Cypriot people and urged the withdrawal of all foreign troops and the elimination
of foreign military bases in Cyprus. It also expressed solidarity with the "progressive forces in
Portugal and Greece." The communiqué condemned the military junta in Chile and demanded the
immediate liberation of Comrade Luis Corvelan and "all other Chilean patriots." The two parties
strongly condemned "the anti-Leninist and chauvinist policy of the present Chinese leadership and its
adventurous line." To intensify relations the two parties adopted a protocol on cooperation for the
1975-77 period (*FBIS*, 23 June). A Soviet delegation led by Boris Ponomarev visited Damascus in
mid-June. Along with discussing the internal issues mentioned earlier, the two parties discussed the
Middle East conflict and the strengthening of cooperation between Syria and the Soviet Union.

Publications. The party organ of the SCP is the fortnightly newspaper *Nidal al-Shaʻb* ("People's
Struggle"). The paper is officially banned, but it has been circulated freely since the party joined the
National Progressive Front. The party disseminates most of its news through the two legal publica-
tions of the Lebanese Communist party in Beirut, *al-Nida'* and *al-Akhbar*.

*   *   *

The Arab Communist Organization (ACO). The ACO began in Lebanon some years ago (see
Lebanon). The organization, whose members are all between the ages of 16 and 24, denounces both
the Soviet and Chinese leaderships and seeks changes in Arab social and political systems through
force and sabotage. The ACO claimed responsibility in Syria in 1975 for explosions at the United
States Pavilion at the Damascus International Fair, the offices of the American firm National Cash
Register, the Egyptian Affairs Bureau, and the Jordanian Embassy. In July, Syrian authorities
captured what they believed to be all members of the ACO operating in Syria, including its founder
and leader, a Palestinian named ʻAli Ghadban. The Supreme State Security Court tried the ACO
members, and death sentences were passed against five of the accused, including Ghadban. Other
sentences ranged from 15 years to life imprisonment. The Syrian media pointed out that the stiff
sentences were meant to deter other subversive activities in the country. The death sentences were
carried out August 2 despite pleas by the Soviet Ambassador to stay the executions. The Syrian

regime at one point suspected the ACO of being affiliated with the Popular Front for the Liberation of Palestine (PFLP) and in fact, the Syrian-sponsored Palestinian guerrilla group al-Sa'iqah accused the PFLP of being paid by Iraq to undertake the ACO's subversive campaign. When Israel charged that the SCP was behind the explosions at the Egyptian and Jordanian buildings, Yusuf Faisal denied any connection between the SCP and the ACO and condemned the PFLP for these acts of sabotage. The SCP circulated a statement explaining that the ACO had "nothing in common with communism ideologically, politically, or organizationally." The statement stressed that the ACO used the word "communist" for "purely provocative purposes" (*FBIS*, 30 July).

Stanford University   Patricia Mihaly

INTERNATIONAL COMMUNIST FRONT ORGANIZATIONS

Afro-Asian Peoples' Solidarity Organization. The Afro-Asian Peoples' Solidarity Organization (AAPSO) was set up in Cairo in 1958 as an "anti-colonial" offshoot of the World Peace Council (WPC). During the first few years of its existence it was jointly controlled by the Soviet Union, China, and the United Arab Republic. The Sino-Soviet dispute led to disruption of AAPSO conferences in Moshi, Tanzania, in February 1963, and Winneba, Ghana, in May 1965, and finally to a split in the organization following the WPC meeting in Nicosia, Cyprus, in February 1967. The Chinese boycotted the Nicosia meeting, which decided to hold the fifth AAPSO conference in Algiers in 1967 rather than in Peking as originally planned. Since then, Soviet domination of the AAPSO has continued.

Structure and Leadership. From the AAPSO's inception, its organizational structure has been relatively loose. Although Congress and Council meetings have been held during this period, in a practical sense the Secretariat has been the key organizational unit. The 11th Council meeting, March 1974, established the Presidium, which apparently will bear primary responsibility along with the Secretariat for the development and execution of policy.

Yusuf el-Sebai, the AAPSO's secretary-general since its foundation, was reelected to that position at the 11th Council. He was also elected chairman of the Presidum. Since Yusuf el-Sebai is secretary-general not only of AAPSO but also of AAWPB-Cairo (see below), these two organizations have in effect an "overlapping directorate." Additional linkages are noticeable if the AAPSO and AAWPB-Cairo are juxtaposed: both are headquartered in Cairo and both focus on problems of the same geographical area; thus to an extent they have analogous functions. The AAPSO at present appears to be the more active and important of the two organizations.

Views and Activities. On 18 January 1975 the AAPSO sponsored a "Conference of Support for Reunification of Korea" in Baghdad. The 800 delegates represented 100 "progressive and democratic organizations" in 80 countries. Aziz Sharif, secretary-general of the Iraq National Council for Peace and Solidarity, opened the meeting. The Conference demanded the immediate withdrawal of all foreign troops from South Korea. An action-program was drawn up which vigorously supported the "Korean people's struggle for unification," including a political campaign to begin on 9 September aimed at the recognition of North Korea as the sole legitimate government of a united Korea (*Baghdad Observer*, 14-18 January; TASS, 17 January; Iraqi News Agency, 18-20 January).

Aziz Sharif (Iraq) and Akil Salimov (USSR) were the main speakers at an AAPSO conference in Cairo on 13 April, marking the anniversary of the Bandung Conference. Yusuf el-Sebai reported that socialism had become a decisive factor in world development. Much of the credit, he said, was due to the contribution of the Soviet Union. Other issues discussed were Zionism and the liberation struggles of the Palestinians and the peoples of Africa (*Baghdad Observer*, 11, 14, 17 April; TASS, 12-13 April).

The 2nd Presidium meeting took place in Nicosia on 15 May. Heading the delegates were el-Sebai, Aziz Sharif, and Vassos Lyssarides (Cyprus), and representatives of the World Federation of Trade Unions (WFTU) and the Women's International Democratic Federation (WIDF). Speakers were from Iraq, the USSR, East Germany, India, and South-West Africa. A message from Archbishop Makarios, president of Cyprus, welcomed the delegates and praised the leading role of the AAPSO in the struggles of the peoples of Africa and Asia for liberty and independence. Throughout his remarks, he denounced Turkey for invading the island republic and called on all nations to respect the resolutions on Cyprus adopted by the U.N. General Assembly and Security Council (Nicosia domestic service, 15 May). Lyssarides, president of the Cyprus Committee of the AAPSO, stressed in his address that the Cyprus problem "is not a local issue [but] an integral part of the general anti-imperialist problem," and that Cyprus had "the same enemies as the people who are engaged in this struggle: world imperialism headed by the United States," and "the same allies," the latter being "the Soviet Union, socialist countries, nonaligned countries and the Arab progressive countries" (ibid., 15 May). The meeting issued a general declaration declaring the support of the African and Asian peoples in the struggle for Cyprus. The declaration also called for a settlement in the Middle East based on the complete withdrawal of Israeli forces from Arab lands and the implementation of the national rights of the Palestinian people. In order to achieve these ends, a speedy convocation of the Geneva conference was demanded (ibid., 16 May). To pursue on a continuing basis the struggle in Cyprus, the Presidium established "a permanent body for coordinating international solidarity with Cyprus in conjunction with all democratic organizations." Practical support would include the formation of special national committees and other bodies. Member committees were called upon to participate in a week of solidarity with the people of Cyprus on 15-22 July (Nicosia radio, 15-16 May).

Shortly after the Nicosia session, many of the participants along with representatives of the WPC, WFTU, WIDF, World Federation of Democratic Youth (WFDY), and International Union of Students (IUS) attended a meeting in Beirut (17 May) of Arab "Committees for Peace and Solidarity," sponsored by the Palestine Liberation Organization (PLO). The head of the Palestine National Council, Khalid al-Fahoum, called for stronger PLO relations with the Afro-Asian solidarity organizations and the WPC (al Moharrer, Lebanon, 18 May).

The 12th session of the AAPSO Council met in Moscow on 17 September, at which the key topic, reported in advance by TASS (15-16 September), was the development of the Afro-Asian national liberation movements. The Council opened with delegates from 70 countries and international and regional organizations in attendance. The chairman of the Soviet Committee of Solidarity of Asian and African Countries expressed hope that the meeting would serve to strengthen the unity of the movement. Aziz Sharif, deputy chairman of the AAPSO, took note of the location: "Moscow has always been and is our dear city which attracts the eyes of all fighters against imperialism and colonialism." (Ibid., 17 September.) Khalid al-Fahoum, head of the Palestine National Council, stressed that so-called partial agreements could not solve the Middle East question; the same view was expressed by the assistant secretary of the Syrian Ba'th party (ibid., 18 September). Representatives of Laos, Morocco, Kuwait, and other countries said that the success of the national liberation movements in Asia and Africa were primarily connected with the unity of world socialism and national liberation movements. In its final declaration, the Council stated that the task of the AAPSO is to lend all-round assistance and support to the former Portuguese territories, mobilize international public support of the national liberation forces in Angola, and to mobilize further world public support of the struggle of the Arab peoples against imperialism and Zionism. The session called on all national groups of the solidarity movement to render effective moral, political, and material assistance to the Palestine movement. (Ibid., 19 September.) Writing in New Times, Alexander Dzasokhov, executive-secretary of the Soviet Afro-Asian Solidarity Committee, stated that the session gave proof of the growing activity of the movement and the wide international recognition of the peace program adopted by the 24th Congress of the Communist Party of the Soviet Union (CPSU). Dzasokhov continued: "The opponents of anti-imperialist solidarity sought to hamper the striving of the peoples of two continents for unity with socialist countries. Now we may say that this time has passed. The majority of the participants in the movement are well aware who their real friends are and were able to bar the attempts of imperialist circles to isolate this movement from socialist countries, from the Soviet Union." Maoist policy "isolating the Chinese people from the democratic movement," was said to be harmful to the unity of the movement. Although the Peking leaders abstained unilaterally from the initiatives of the AAPSO, according to Dzasokhov there were "irrefutable facts" revealing that Maoist emissaries were "involved in the splitting activities." (Ibid., 24 September.)

At the time of the political crisis in India, the AAPSO urged full support for the measures taken by the government to protect national sovereignty. It further asked all its national committees and all peace forces of the world to give assistance and support to the Indian government. (Ibid., 8 July.)

Afro-Asian Writers' Permanent Bureau. The Afro-Asian Writers' Permanent Bureau (AAWPB) was originally set up by the Soviets at an "Afro-Asian Writers' Conference" in Tashkent in October 1958. Following a second conference, in Cairo in February 1962, a "Permanent Bureau" was established with headquarters in Colombo, Ceylon. The Chinese communists gained control of the organization at a meeting of its Executive Committee in Bali, Indonesia, in July 1963, and established a new Executive Secretariat in Peking on 15 August 1966. Thus, while the AAWPB is still officially based in Colombo, it operates exclusively from Peking. A pro-Soviet faction—the AAWPB-Cairo—broke away after the Chinese began to dominate the organization. The AAWPB-Peking, which has not yet held a third conference, appears to have no activities outside its irregular publication, *The Call*, and occasional statements carried by the New China News Agency.

The AAWPB-Cairo. The pro-Soviet faction of the AAWPB was founded on 19-21 June 1966 at an "extraordinary meeting" attended by delegations from Cameroun, Ceylon, India, Sudan, the Soviet Union, and the United Arab Republic. Its relatively successful "Third Afro-Asian Writers' Conference," held at Beirut in 1967 and attended by some 150 delegates from 42 countries, was the first serious blow to the pro-Chinese AAWPB. Since then, the pro-Soviet organization appears to have consolidated and augmented its base of support.

The secretary-general of the AAWPB-Cairo is Yusuf el-Sebai (Egypt), secretary-general also of the AAPSO and a member of the Presidential Committee of the WPC. The assistant secretary-general is Edward el-Kharat (Egypt). The AAWPB-Cairo has a 10-member Permanent Bureau, with members from India, Japan, Lebanon, Mongolia, the former Portuguese colonies, Senegal, South Africa, the Soviet Union, Sudan, and Egypt. There is also a 30-member Executive Committee.

The 15th session of the Permanent Bureau met in Moscow on 28-30 June 1975. Representatives attended from 18 countries, including Algeria, India, Sudan, and the German Democratic Republic. Yusuf el-Sebai spoke of the growing importance of contacts among "men of letters" of the two continents and seemed particularly satisfied with contacts in Algeria and Iraq. A resolution supported the "initiative by the USSR and other countries of the Socialist community on détente, and stressed that the AAWPB would continue its struggle against aggression, colonialism, apartheid, and zionism." The international literary *Lotus* prizes for 1975 were awarded to writers from Pakistan, Iran, and Nigeria. The meeting also decided to establish an AAWPB regional center in Dacca, Bangladesh. (TASS, 28-30 June; *Bangladesh Observer*, 27 June.)

AAWPB-Peking. The pro-Chinese AAWPB, the continuation of the original body, is led by Frederik L. Risakotta (Indonesia), of the Peking-based Delegation of the Communist Party of Indoesia's Central Committee, as "acting head ad interim" of the AAWPB Secretariat. The AAWPB-Peking was relatively inactive in 1975.

Publications. The main AAWPB-Cairo organ is a "literature, arts and sociopolitical quarterly,"

Lotus, which appears in English, French, and Arabic editions. Books by various Afro-Asian "men of letters" have been published in the USSR by the AAWPB-Cairo.

The AAWPB-Peking bulletin, *The Call*, is issued from Peking at irregular intervals.

International Association of Democratic Lawyers. The International Association of Democratic Lawyers (IADL) was founded at an "International Congress of Jurists" held in Paris in October 1946 under the auspices of a para-communist organization, the "Mouvement National Judiciaire," and attended by lawyers from 25 countries. Although it originally included elements of various political orientations, the leading role was played by leftist French lawyers, and by 1949 most non-communists had resigned. The IADL was originally based in Paris but was expelled by the French government in 1950. It then moved to Brussels, where it remains; some organizational work has also been carried out from Warsaw.

Membership is open to lawyers' organizations or groups and to individual lawyers, and may be on a "corresponding," "donation," or "permanent" basis. Lawyers holding membership through organizations or individually are estimated to number about 25,000. The IADL claims to be supported by membership fees and donations; no details of its finances are published.

The IADL holds consultative status Category C with the U.N. Economic and Social Council.

Structure and Leadership. The highest organ of the IADL is the congress, in which each member organization is represented. There have been ten congresses to date, the latest in Algiers in April 1975. The congress elects the IADL Council, which is supposed to meet yearly and consists of the Bureau, the Secretariat, and a representative of each member organization. Several changes were made in the leadership at the General Council meeting which took place in Algeria directly after the 10th Congress. Robert Dachet (Belgium) replaced Joe Nordmann as secretary-general. Dachet, previously executive secretary of the IADL, was formerly a member of the Central Committee of the Communist Party of Belgium and an editor of the party organ, *Le Drapeau Rouge.* Nordmann was named deputy president. Reelected were Pierre Cot (France), president, and Heinrich Toeplitz (GDR), IADL treasurer. Others elected to the Secretariat were from Algeria (two), Hungary, and South Vietnam. (TASS, 2 April; *El Moudjahid*, Algiers; 4-9 April; *Izvestiia*, 21 April.)

Views and Activities. Meeting in Warsaw on 26 January 1975, the Secretariat decided to hold the IADL's 10th Congress in April in Algiers (Warsaw radio, 26 January). In February it was announced that in accordance with "new demands for a new economic and juridical order brought about by the advent of the non-aligned movement as a power on the international scene" the congress would be open to non-members from Asia, Africa, the Middle East, Latin America, Western Europe, and the Communist countries (*El Moudjahid*, 18 February).

The congress opened in Algiers on 2 April 1975. In attendance were more than 500 lawyers from 64 countries and 13 international organizations, including members of the Stockholm Conference on Vietnam War Crimes (TASS, 2 April). The agenda, developed early in 1975, was concerned with (1) law and its function in the struggle against imperialism, colonialism and neo-colonialism, racism, and apartheid; (2) problems of peace and international security in a climate of co-existence of countries with different social systems; (3) legal aspects of problems of economic development, including the sovereignty of states and their natural resources, nationalization, multi-national firms, and principles of economic and technical aid; (4) protection of the environment; and (5) the role of lawyers and the law in the development of democracy, the rights of man, and social progress. Resolutions were passed urging all lawyers to give disinterested and effective aid to developing countries, to intercede with the United Nations and other international organizations as well as with governments, to act against multi-national firms, and to help the trend toward economic, cultural, scientific, and technical cooperation on the basis of equality, non-discrimination and non-interference in internal affairs.

Support was proclaimed for the rights of Palestinians and others "struggling against colonialism." The IADL stated its firm backing for a just settlement in the Middle East. (Ibid., *El Moudjahid*, 4-9 April; Algiers radio, 6 April.)

The IADL protested the fact that a lawyer of the Antwerp bar was prevented from attending as an observer at the trial of two Basques in Spain (*L'Humanité*, Paris, 30 August).

U.N. commissioner Sean MacBride visited Dakar in the spring, accompanied by the secretaries-general of the Institute of Human Rights (Strasbourg), the International Commission of Jurists (ICJ) and by an IADL secretary. Following their visit, a national commission on human rights in Namibia was set up. (*Le Soleil*, Dakar, 8 April.) The IADL, the Institute of Human Rights, and the ICJ are to organize a seminar on human rights in Namibia, set for 5-8 January 1976, which 300 delegates are expected to attend.

Publications. The IADL's two principal publications, *Review of Contemporary Laws* and *Information Bulletin*, appear irregularly in English and French. The IADL also issues pamphlets on questions of topical interest.

International Federation of Resistance Fighters. The International Federation of Resistance Fighters (*Federation Internationale des Resistants*; FIR) was founded in 1951 in Vienna as the successor to the International Federation of Former Political Prisoners (Federation Internationale des Anciens Prisonniers Politiques). With the name change, membership eligibility was widened to include former partisans and resistance fighters, and all victims of Nazism and fascism and their descendants.

In 1959 the FIR had a membership of four million; no recent figures have been announced. On its 20th anniversary, in 1971, the FIR claimed affiliated groups and representation in every country of Europe (*Resistance Unie*, no. 14). The headquarters of the FIR is in Vienna; a small Secretariat is maintained in Paris. In 1972 the FIR was granted Category B status with the U.N. Economic and Social Council (ECOSOC).

Structure and Leadership. The organs of the FIR are the Congress, General Council, Bureau, and Secretariat. Until the Sixth Congress (Venice, 1969), the Congress was convened every three years; it was then decided that this body should meet every four years. The Congress elects the FIR president, vice-presidents, and members of the Bureau, and determines and ratifies members of the General Council after they have been nominated by national associations. The General Council is supposed to meet at least once a year. The Bureau supervises the implementation of decisions reached by the Congress and General Council; it is also responsible for the budget, and from among its members it elects the Secretariat. Arialdo Banfi (Italy) is president, and Alex Lhote (France) is secretary-general. (For other officers see *YICA, 1975*, p. 618.)

Views and Activities. There was relatively little FIR activity during 1975. The most important gathering was that of the Bureau in Vienna on 18-19 March. The meeting discussed FIR activities for the 30th anniversary of the end of World War II; a European symposium of ex-servicemen for disarmament; World Disarmament Week (14-20 April), proclaimed by ECOSOC; and the FIR delegation's appearance before the U.N. Human Rights Commission. The meeting issued an appeal asking that détente be fully supported. (*Informationsdienst*, no. 3.) In line with the Bureau's efforts to further disarmament, the FIR, along with the European Confederation of Ex-Servicemen, the International Confederation of Former Prisoners of War, and the World Veterans Federation, began in April preparations for a "European Symposium of Ex-Servicemen for Disarmament." Paris was chosen as the site and 27 November as the tentative date. (Ibid.)

The FIR condemned the Franco government in Spain and called on it to end torture and free political prisoners (Statement, 6 June). When tensions mounted in Portugal, the FIR expressed its solidarity with the "democratic forces" and urged all resistance fighters to support them (Statement, 21 August).

Publications. The FIR publishes a journal in French and German, *Resistance Unie* and *Widerstandskämpfer.* News reports are disseminated occasionally through the French-language *Service d'Information de la FIR* and its German counterpart, *Informationsdienst der FIR.*

International Organization of Journalists. The International Organization of Journalists (IOJ) was founded in June 1946 in Copenhagen. Merging with it at that time were the International Federation of Journalists (IFJ) and the International Federation of Journalists of Allied and Free Countries. By 1952 the participating non-communist unions had withdrawn in order to re-found the IFJ. Since 1955 the IOJ has made unsuccessful overtures to the IFJ for forming a new world organization of journalists. It was for the purpose of bridging differences with the IFJ that the IOJ founded in 1955 the International Committee for Cooperation of Journalists (ICCJ). No IFJ member is known to have become affiliated with the ICCJ—perhaps because most ICCJ officers are also leading members of the parent IOJ. The IOJ headquarters, originally in London, was moved to Prague in 1947.

In 1963 a rival organization was established by pro-Chinese journalists, the Afro-Asian Journalists' Association (AAJA; see below).

The IOJ was awarded consultative and information Category B status with UNESCO in 1969. It also holds consultative status, Category II, with the U.N. Economic and Social Council.

Structure and Leadership. National Unions and groups are eligible for membership in the IOJ, as are also individual journalists. Some 150,000 members are claimed in 67 organizations in 58 countries (TASS, 14 June 1971).

The highest IOJ body is the Congress, which is supposed to meet every four years. The Congress elects the Executive Committee, made up of the Presidium (president, vice-president, and secretary-general), other officers (secretaries and treasurer), and ordinary members. The leadership remained the same in 1975: Jean-Maurice Hermann (France), president, and Jiří Kubka (Czechoslovakia), secretary-general (for other names and details on structure see *YICA, 1972*, pp. 615-16).

Views and Activities. Throughout 1975 the IOJ appeared to put its main effort on establishing and expanding contacts in the developing world. Communications with the Arab world were extended with the introduction of Arabic as a working language in IOJ publications. Thus the IOJ will now be publishing in Arabic, English, French, Russian, and Spanish. (*Baghdad Observer*, 17 February.) Late in 1974, a delegation from the "Palestinian Writers' and Journalists Union" arrived in Prague for talks with IOJ officials. Subsequently it was announced that a "Palestinian Center" would be set up in the IOJ Prague office. (CTK, 9-11 December.) Early in 1975, journalists from both Portugal and Ethiopia visited Prague. The latter visit resulted in an offer by the IOJ to train young Ethiopian journalists in Budapest (ibid., 31 January). The Guinea-Bissau Ministry of Information invited the IOJ to discuss cooperation with the Union of Journalists of Guinea-Bissau. Burundi also expressed interest in developing a working relationship with the IOJ. (*Ghanian Times*, Accra, 4 April.) In the spring, the IOJ was invited to attend the First Latin American Journalists' Congress in Lima in October. The initial preparations for this Congress were made in Cuernavaca, Mexico, in April; in August a second preparatory meeting, in Lima, decided to postpone the congress until February 1976 because of the organizers' feeling that the Peruvian government was becoming increasingly hostile to it (*La Prensa*, Lima, 13 August; *El Nacional*, Caracas, 19 August).

The establishment of contacts has, of course, the aim of influencing key individuals in the developing areas. The process of influence goes beyond mere contacts; indeed, the contacts are cultivated in various ways. Among these are the use of special training programs run by the IOJ.

During 1975, for example, the deputy chairman of the East German Association of Journalists opened a six-month course at the International Solidarity School, in East Berlin. Attending the course were young journalists from Egypt, Syria, Iraq, South Yemen, the Palestine Liberation Organization, Somalia, Ghana, Bangladesh, and "Zimbabwe" (*ADN*, 22 January). Complementing this school is the International Center for Journalist Training, in Budapest, which admitted more than 40 students in 1975 (*Journalists' Affairs*, no. 4). In addition to the schools in Eastern Europe, the IOJ runs regional centers. The IOJ center in Cairo was active in 1975 in bringing together journalists from Africa and the Middle East (ibid., no. 8).

The IOJ Secretariat welcomed resolutions of the 18th UNESCO Conference (November 1974) on strengthening peace and international security, the struggle against colonialism and racial discrimination, and the strengthening of cooperation and understanding. It complained that UNESCO leaders had been under attack from sections of the mass media representing monopoly interests and colonialists, with some member states threatening to stop their contributions; this was "contrary to the interests of international relations" (CTK, 25 March). An IOJ secretary and the head of the UNESCO department for the development of information had talks at the IOJ headquarters on professional cooperation between the two organizations. They also discussed the organizing of an international seminar on the problems of training journalists from developing countries. (*Journalists' Affairs*, no. 9/10.)

A third meeting of representatives of the IOJ and the IFJ drew up an agreement on mutual cooperation on matters relating to the Conference on Security and Cooperation in Europe and expressed agreement on problems facing Chile. Both sides wanted to see development of bilateral and regional contacts between national organizations of journalists which could lead to the conclusion of specific agreements. (CTK, 3 July.) The meeting of IOJ-IFJ representatives was preceded by a four-day meeting of European journalists, attended by representatives of journalist organizations in 21 countries. A closing document outlined the tasks of journalists in the interest of peace and understanding among nations. IOJ delegates met with the leadership of the National Federation of the Italian Press, and the two organizations were said to have formed plans for cooperation. (Ibid.) Both gatherings took place on Capri in late June.

Publications. The IOJ issues a monthly journal, the *Democratic Journalist*, in English, French, Russian, and Spanish. The IOJ's *Information Bulletin* apparently is no longer published. A new fortnightly publication, *Journalists' Affairs*, is being distributed in English, French, Spanish, and Russian.

The AAJA. The Afro-Asian Journalists' Association was set up in Djakarta in April 1963 with an Afro-Asian Press Bureau and a permanent Secretariat. Until the attempted coup in Indonesia (1965), the AAJA appeared to represent a possibly serious rival to the pro-Soviet IOJ, particularly in developing countries. At that juncture, AAJA headquarters were "temporarily" moved to Peking. Djawoto, the AAJA's Indonesian secretary-general, who was dismissed from his post as Indonesia's ambassador to China, has since headed the Secretariat in Peking, which has become the permanent seat of AAJA operations.

The Secretariat met in Peking on 24 April to celebrate Afro-Asian Journalists' Day and the 12th anniversary of the founding of the AAJA. Attending were Secretariat members from Indonesia, China, Sri Lanka, and Tanzania, and others from China, New Zealand, and "Palestine" (NCNA, 24 April).

There is little indication that the AAJA has succeeded in winning over the allegiance of IOJ members or member organizations. Few jouranlists' organizations and governments have expressed open support for the AAJA or indicated that they would send delegates to an eventual AAJA conference. The AAJA devotes its energies mainly to propagating the Chinese view on international political affairs.

The AAJA's main publication, *Afro-Asian Journalist*, appears irregularly. Pamphlets on topical issues are published from time to time.

International Union of Students. The International Union of Students (IUS) was founded in August 1946 at a congress in Prague attended by students of varying political persuasions. This diversity of views lasted until 1951, when most of the non-communist student unions withdrew because of domination of the IUS by pro-Soviet groups. The 1960s were marked by bitter debates between pro-Soviet and pro-Chinese students. In the middle 1960s the Chinese withdrew from active participation.

The IUS has consultative Category C status with UNESCO; applications for Category B status have been repeatedly deferred.

Structure and Leadership. The highest governing body of the IUS is its Congress. Constitutional amendments approved by the Tenth Congress (Bratislava, January 1971) changed the requirements regarding the frequency that the Congress assembles from once every two years to once every three years. The terms of representation remain the same: each affiliate or associate organization is permitted to send delegates to the Congress. The Executive Committee meets once a year. The Congress elects the national unions to be represented on the Executive Committee; the national unions then determine which individual(s) will represent them. (For additional details on organizational structure see *YICA, 1975*, p. 620.)

Dusan Ulcak (Czechoslovakia) is the IUS president; Fathi Muhammad al-Fadi (Sudan) is the secretary-general.

Views and Activities. Early in 1975 Dusan Ulcak announced IUS plans for the year. The highest priority was given to strengthening the involvement of the international progressive student movement in the solving of the world's problems. For the IUS this would include cultivating solidarity with the peoples of Chile, Vietnam, and the Arab countries; supporting activities connected with European security and cooperation; participating in the observance of International Women's Year; and preparing for the 11th World Youth Festival. Looking back over 1974, Ulcak declared that the most successful activities of the IUS had been the international campaign of solidarity with Chile and the support given the students of the Arab world. (CTK, 6 January.)

On 10 June, in Leipzig, representatives from approximately 50 national student organizations attended the Executive Committee meeting. The session was devoted to a discussion of the reports presented by the IUS Secretariat on its activities since the 11th Congress, preparations for the 11th World Youth Festival, affiliations to the IUS, and the adoption of documents and resolutions. Among the activities mentioned were the fund-raising campaign for the construction of the Nguyen Van Troi School in the Republic of South Vietnam, support for international youth and student solidarity conference on Chile (in Mexico), the organizing of a solidarity tour through Western Europe for a delegation of Arab student organizations, and the holding of an international student work camp in Portugal. During the session, a member of the coordinating committee to establish a progressive students' union in Portugal said that his committee was seeking to merge the progressive students from Portugal's three universities into a single progressive organization. As far as the World Youth Festival, the Executive Committee appealed to all students to make efforts on the national, regional, and international levels to mobilize the broadest possible masses of students. (The festival is scheduled for Havana, Cuba, in the summer of 1978.) Admitted into the IUS as full members were the national unions of students in Oman and in Bahrain. At the close, resolutions were adopted dealing with European security and cooperation, Angola, students' contribution to the peoples' struggle for full rights over the disposal of their raw materials, and support for students in Chile. (*ADN*, 12, 16, 17 June; TASS, 13 June.) (For a detailed discussion of the Executive Committee session see *World Student News*, no. 9/10.)

Throughout the spring and early summer, the IUS stressed the importance of the Conference on Security and Cooperation in Europe (CSCE). The *World Student News* (no. 4) printed numerous statements of the various IUS national unions on this matter. In all of them, the term "détente" appeared to be used interchangeably with "European security and cooperation." The statement of the Soviet student union, taking the stand that: "The Process of Détente Must Be Made Irreversible," goes on to discuss in some detail the relationship between security and cooperation in Europe and détente. Both "political détente" and "military détente" were cited as key elements in the new relationship between East and West. To support the continued development of this relationship, the statement called for the further expansion of mass movements of progressive students. In its article the Free German Youth (FDJ) stressed the benefits derived from détente, and pointed to the "link" between cooperation and détente. Looking to the future, the FDJ held that the achievement of cooperation will depend on the elaboration of the "principles which will directly prevent new military conflicts, guarantee the inviolability of borders, recognize territorial integrity and proclaim the renunciation of violence." The Finnish Students Union (SYL) called for closer cooperation within the European student movement and suggested that although progress had been made toward détente, primarily as a result of "the initiatives of the Soviet Union and other socialist countries," there remained forces opposed to cooperation. Cited as obstructionist was "the often highly unrepresentative but influential Western European conservative press." To counter negative factors, the SYL urged cooperation by students on both the national and the all-European levels. In the latter, the leadership role of the IUS was considered particularly important, for it could take the lead in organizing all-European student seminars, regional meetings, and such specific gatherings as the proposed "Conference on Youth and Student Tourism." While the statements gave full support to détente, particularly with reference to the appropriate political and military relations among states, there was no mention of "basket three" of the CSCE—that is, the question of greater freedom for individuals within countries.

The IUS also moved in a more concrete way to rally support for the CSCE. The "International Committee for European Security and Cooperation" had met in November 1974 in Brussels. This body, which includes the IUS, is an umbrella organization within which various groups worked to mobilize public opinion on behalf of the security conference. At the Brussels meeting it was decided to sponsor an "Assembly of European Public Opinion" which would "provide an opportunity for a broad dialogue among all public forces working to safeguard peace and to promote détente and cooperation." The assembly took place on 26 April 1975 in Brussels, attended by representatives from 30 countries and 47 international organizations. Its final declaration urged complete support for the CSCE and the broadening of détente. After the assembly, special meetings of trade unionists, women's and youth organizations, clergymen, and so on were held. The youth and student section was attended by 10 international and 54 national youth and student groups. In addition to specific questions related to the CSCE, the students discussed the "Meeting of European Youth and Students" scheduled for Warsaw in 1976. (*IUS News Service*, no. 10.)

In June, more than 100 representatives of youth and student organizations in 70 countries came to Espoo, Finland, for a youth meeting on security and cooperation sponsored by the IUS and the SYL. Five commissions reviewed peace, security, and cooperation, solidarity, natural resources and independence, democratic education, and cooperation with the United Nations. A spokesman of the IUS looked to the Helsinki high-level meeting to open up a significant new stage in the establishment of a durable peace. Within this new framework "political détente must be supplemented by military détente." This meant that attention would have to be focused on the problems of military alliances and such negotiations as SALT and MBFR. It also meant an expansion of détente from Europe to other areas where it could take tangible form, as in an Asian collective defense arrangement and an Indian Ocean zone of peace. The final communiqué stressed the leading role of the USSR and other socialist states on the questions of peace, détente and security, and called for the adoption of measures to ensure additional relaxation of tension after the CSCE. (TASS, 16-19 June; *World Student News*, No. 9-10.)

In September the IUS and the FAOJ ("an organization linked to the National Union of Portuguese Students") with the collaboration of the Armed Forces Movement held an international youth camp in Portugal on the theme "for unity and anti-imperialist solidarity." One specific objective of the camp was to prepare young Portuguese workers and students for the 11th World Youth Festival (*Diario de Noticias*, Lisbon, 4 August). The importance given détente, particularly as a regional issue, and the swift movement of the IUS to link itself more firmly with the students of Portugal, reveals one dominating feature of current IUS policy, which is to expand and solidify its influence in Western Europe. Several articles in *World Student News* were preceded by a map of all of Europe, clearly indicating that the IUS sees itself as operating extensively in the West; the increased emphasis on European meetings of the national student unions is another indicator.

At the invitation of the IUS Secretariat, a delegation from the World Student Christian Federation (WSCF) visited Prague on 20 January. Within an atmosphere of cordiality, a broad exchange of views took place. Both organizations confirmed the convergence of opinion with regard to significant problems of concern to the international student movement. They also agreed to cooperate in the struggle against racism, colonialism, neo-colonialism, and fascism, and to intensify their efforts in the battle for liberation. Plans for the 11th World Youth Festival were reviewed, and both the IUS and the WSCF expressed "their particular satisfaction" over the choice of Havana as the site. Finally, the two organizations agreed to intensify mutual, regular collaboration in action programs. (*IUS News Service*, No. 6.)

An article in *World Student News* (No. 2, February) reported that the IUS scholarship program was helping to overcome the shortage of specialists in the developing countries. By 1975 the program had enabled nearly 3,000 students to pursue higher studies in the Soviet Union, Czechoslovakia, Hungary, Poland, the GDR, and Bulgaria. Henceforth grants are to be made available for study in Finland and Syria as well.

Throughout the year the IUS sought to promote support for students suffering under military rule in Chile. On several occasions the IUS headquarters in Prague received exiled Chilean students. Plans were developed for an international seminar on Chile in London to be jointly sponsored by the Chilean Students' Union, the British National Union of Students (NUS), and the IUS (*Main Mail*, NUS publication, 4 July).

The IUS continued its backing of the Irish Republican Army. Early in 1975 the Russian vice-president of the IUS arrived in London and announced the launching of a campaign for an "end of internment, withdrawal of troops, and new civil liberties." An "international week of solidarity for a free Northern Ireland" was designated for February. (*Daily Mail*, London, 17 January.)

Publications. The principal IUS publications are a monthly magazine, *World Student News*, published in English, French, German, and Spanish, and a fortnightly bulletin, *IUS News Service*, in English, French, and Spanish. Published once a year is the *Magazine on the Democratization and Reform of Education*.

Women's International Democratic Federation. The Women's International Democratic Federation (WIDF) was founded in Paris in December 1945 at a "Congress of Women" organized by the communist-dominated Union dès Femmes Françaises. The WIDF headquarters was in Paris until 1951, when it was expelled by the French government. It was then moved to East Berlin. The WIDF holds Category A status with the U.N. Economic and Social Council, and Category B with UNESCO. It is also on the Special List of the International Labor Organization, and chairs the Non-governmental Organization's (NGO) Sub-Committee on the Status of Women in the framework of the NGO's Human Rights Commission. At present the WIDF has 120 national affiliated organizations in 103 countries. (*International Associations*, Brussels, no. 8/9, 1975.)

Structure and Leadership. The WIDF's highest governing body is the Congress, which meets every four years. Next in authority is the Council, which meets annually and is in control between Congresses; it elects the Bureau and the Secretariat. The Bureau meets at least twice a year and implements decisions taken by the Congress and the Council; it is assisted by the Secretariat. Fanny Edelman (Argentina) continued in 1975 as secretary-general. Freda Brown (Australia) was elected president at the 7th Congress, East Berlin, in October.

Membership in the WIDF is open to all women's organizations and groups and in exceptional cases to individuals. Total membership in 1971 exceeded 200 million. The WIDF seeks to maintain contact with non-affiliated women's groups through its International Liaison Bureau, which has its general headquarters in Copenhagen and a secretariat in Brussels.

Views and Activities. WIDF activities in 1975 centered on the World Congress of Women, sponsored by the WIDF to mark International Women's Year. (It was the WIDF that originally called for 1975 to be designated as International Women's Year.)

In November 1974 some 150 delegates from 100 women's organizations, along with representatives of youth and trade union organizations, the World Peace Council, the World Council of Churches, and various U.N. organizations and committees attended a conference organized by the National Council of Hungarian Women in Tihany, Hungary. This conference was called to prepare for the World Congress of Women to be held in East Berlin on 20-24 October, 1975. The Conference was sponsored by the Women's International League for Peace and Freedom, Pan-African Women's Organization, International Federation of Women in Legal Careers, the Liaison Bureau formed at the 1960 International Assembly of Women, the Women's Bureau of the Afro-Asian People's Solidarity Organization, and the WIDF. Fanny Edelman addressed the meeting, which set up an international preparatory committee and an international executive committee for the congress. Freda Brown was made chairman of both committees. The conference decided to call the congress formally the "World Congress for International Women's Year" and to form five commissions, on equal rights for women, women and development, women in society, women and peace, and women in a changing world. (MTI, 4-6 November; *Neues Deutschland*, East Berlin, 5-7 November.) The WIDF called on "all people of good will" to use 1975 to eliminate discrimination against women, ensure their full participation in national development, and make possible their intensified work for peace. The first meeting of the International Preparatory Committee (IPC) was announced for East Berlin in late January. (*Neues Deutschland*, 3-15 December.) An East German preparatory committee was established, and Edelman announced that "regional" meetings in support of the Congress were being planned: a meeting in Alexandria of Afro-Asian women, a seminar in cooperation with the Women's International League for Peace and Freedom in New York, and a session of the executive committee of the IPC (ibid., 1-2 February).

The IPC executive committee meeting, in East Berlin on 4-5 February, drew representatives of the WIDF, Women's International League for Peace and Freedom, International Federation of Women in Legal Careers, Pan-African Women's Organization, AAPSO, WFTU, World Federation of U.N. Associations, WPC International Peace Bureau, WFDY, International Student Movement for the U.N., International Federation for the Rights of Man, German Democratic Women's Union, All-Arab Women's Federation, and the Council for European National Youth Committee. The communiqué issued by the IPC committee indicated that an international fund was being established to help guarantee participation at the congress. (Ibid., 7 February.) At a press conference Brown stated that 2,000 delegates were expected and more than 70 national committees had been set up to support preparations (ibid., 18 February; TASS, 17 February).

Edelman and delegates from more than 50 countries attended the Afro-Asian Women's Conference in Alexandria on 8 March, held under WIDF and AAPSO auspices. A resolution stressed that full equality for the women of Asia and Africa was linked with the fight for national independence, peace, democracy and social progress. Obstacles in the way of improving their situation were said to include the consequences of colonialism, racial discrimination, exploitation, poverty and illiteracy. (*Neues Deutschland*, 12 March.)

Brown, visiting Moscow in April, met with delegates to a preparatory meeting for the World Meeting of Girls, held in Moscow in October (see *World Federation of Democratic Youth*). Later, in Helsinki, Brown and members of the WPC Secretariat issued a joint communiqué stressing WPC support for both the Congress and International Women's Year. The communiqué also indicated that the WPC was organizing seminars to study the problems facing women and peace. (TASS, 9 April; *Peace Courier*, No. 3.)

On 22 April a WIDF Bureau meeting in Bucharest adopted measures in connection with the World Congress of Women and the 7th WIDF Congress, both scheduled for East Berlin in October.

The IPC Executive Committee, in Berlin on 27 May, recommended that small groups representing different national and international organizations should begin drafting working papers for nine commissions to discuss at the 7th WIDF Congress (*Neues Deutschland*, 29-30 May; TASS, 29 May).

The committee met in Prague on 29 July with representatives of 35 international and regional organizations, and 65 preparatory committees and national organizations from 61 countries. Freda Brown stated that the congress was a historic event and that the preparations in Prague were the "more encouraging in view of the fact that these were being held on the eve of the opening of the Conference on Security and Cooperation in Europe (CSCE)." She added that women from 117 countries and representatives from 773 organizations were interested in attending the congress, to which invitations were being issued to "the highest representatives" of various countries. (CTK, 25, 27, 29, 31 July; ADN, 31 July.)

On 20 October the "World Congress for International Women's Year" convened in East Berlin. Erich Honecker, first secretary of the Central Committe of the ruling party in the GDR, delivered the opening address to some 2,000 delegates. He applauded the work of women in the development of social progress, spoke of the need for peace and security, stressed the necessity for disarmament, and praised the role of the Soviet Union in achieving these things (East Berlin TV service, 20 October). Messages to the congress came from communist party chiefs in Bulgaria, Cuba, Czechoslovakia, and Hungary, and from Yasir Arafat of the Palestine Liberation Organization and Ahmad Hasan al-Bakr of the Ba'th Party in Iraq. A final declaration gave total support to the "complete emancipation of women" and warned that in Africa, Asia, and Latin America imperialism still discriminated against people. The Congress called for each country to condemn fascist and racist regimes, to respect the right of nations to their natural resources, and to support the motto of International Women's Year, "Equal Rights, Development, Peace."(Ibid., 24 October.)

Immediately afterward, the 7th WIDF Congress convened, with some 500 delegates from 120 national organizations in 103 countries. Edelman reviewed for the delegates the importance of the World Congress. A Romanian delegate and member of the Executive Committee of the Romanian ruling party called on the WIDF to establish more active links in a broader spirit of collaboration with other democratic, progressive, anti-imperialist women's organizations and movements." The WIDF's general plan over the next five years was discussed. (East Berlin domestic service, 26 October; ADN, 26 October; AGERPRES, 28 October.)

During the year the WIDF issued numerous statements and protests. A message to the Organization of African Unity (OAU) reaffirmed solidarity with the struggle of the African peoples against colonialism and for their liberation (ADN, 26 May). Several strong protests were issued against "the continued Israeli aggression" (e.g., ibid., 8 May). The WIDF submitted a report to the United Nations on the treatment of a Chilean women patriot in a "concentration camp" (*Voice of the GDR*, 8 July). A message to the National Federation of Indian Women expressed solidarity with their struggle against reactionary forces (ADN, 5 July). Several statements expressed support for the struggle of the people of Angola; in each the WIDF charged the Front for the National Liberation of Angola with "criminal attacks against the genuine liberation movement" (e.g., ibid., 6 August).

Publications. The WIDF publishes an illustrated quarterly magazine, *Women of the Whole World*, in English, German, Spanish, French, and Russian, and issues pamphlets and bulletins on specific issues.

World Federation of Democratic Youth. The World Federation of Democratic Youth (WFDY) was founded in November 1945 at a "World Youth Conference" convened in London by the World Youth Council. Although the WFDY appeared to represent varying shades of political opinion, key offices were quickly taken by communists. By 1950 most non-communists had withdrawn and established their own organization, the World Assembly of Youth. Originally based in Paris, the WFDY was expelled by the French government in 1951. Its headquarters has since been in Budapest.

All youth organizations that contribute to the safeguarding of the activities of young persons are eligible for membership in the WFDY, which claims more than 100 million persons, in 200 organizations in 90 countries.

Structure and Leadership. The highest governing body of the WFDY is the Assembly, which convenes every three years and to which all affiliated organizations send representatives. The Assembly elects the Executive Committee, which meets at least twice a year. Day-to-day work is conducted by the Bureau and its Secretariat. Piero Lapiccirella (Italy) is president; Jean-Charles Negre (France) is secretary-general. (For other officers and subsidiary organizations see *YICA, 1975*, p. 626.)

Views and Activities. The WFDY held no major meetings in 1975, but participated in numerous gatherings and action programs. The year was also its 30th anniversary. At the outset, leaders denied charges in "Western media" that the WFDY is a communist youth international. Rather, the WFDY argued, "socialist, social democratic, liberal and radical youth organizations are also represented in its membership," and described it as "a political organization that rallies the progressive youth movements of the globe in the struggle against imperialism and encourages united action for the solution of international political problems" (MTI, Budapest, 5 February).

A WFDY-organized seminar on "the problems of peace in Europe and the solution of the Cyprus question" was held in Athens on 8 April, attended by representatives of 26 youth organizations in 16 European countries and 10 international organizations. Messages were received from Archbishop Makarios and the General Confederation of Greek Workers. The final communiqué called for an immediate withdrawal of all foreign military forces from Cyprus, the safe return of all refugees, and talks within the framework of the United Nations on a just settlement of the problem. It ended with an appeal for active solidarity with Cyprus. (*Kathimerini*, Athens, 8 April; *WFTU Flashes*, No. 15.)

At the request of the Finnish National Committee of Youth and Student Organization for Security and Cooperation, representatives of the WFDY, the International Union of Socialist Youth, the Council of European National Youth Committees, and youth organizations from the USSR, Poland, and Hungary met in Helsinki in late February to discuss a possible all-European youth meeting in 1976. The participants accepted a proposal by the Federation of Socialist Unions of Polish Youth that this meeting be held in Warsaw in June 1976 (TASS, 11 March). An earlier report (ibid., 28 February) stated that Finnish youth organization supported the suggestion of the Soviet Young

Communist League for such a meeting. On 31 May-2 June, representatives of the WFDY, IUS, and a number of European youth organizations "of various political trends" attended the 3d consultative meeting of European youth and student organizations in Balatonalmadi, Hungary, where they discussed methods of cooperation toward convening the meeting (MTI, 31 May). By June, developments were far enough along for the Polish News Agency (PAP, 10 June) to report that 1,500 delegates were expected to participate and to work toward a new program of youth activity within the conditions prevailing after the end of the Conference on Security and Cooperation in Europe.

An international consultative conference to prepare for the WFDY-sponsored World Meeting of Girls was held in Moscow on 3 April. Representatives from 32 countries attended. The chairman of the USSR Committee of Youth Organizations said that the meeting would provide a forum for discussion on the role of young women in the struggle against exploitation, oppression, and discrimination, and would also deal with international security, national independence, and social progress (Moscow radio, 3 April; TASS, 4 April).

The WFDY and the Hungarian Communist Youth League organized an international round table conference on fascism in Budapest on 15 April. Delegates attended from 22 countries and 5 international organizations. The meeting paid tribute to the role of the Soviet Union in crushing Hitlerite Fascism. (MTI, 15 April, and WFDY pamphlet.)

The WFDY sent a delegation to Angola for "May Day celebrations," comprising members from the USSR, East Germany, West Germany, Czechoslovakia, Romania, Finland, and Congo. The whole group was arrested in Luanda on the orders of Angola's minister of the interior, the representative of the National Front for the Liberation of Angola (FNLA) in the country's transitional government. The FNLA called the group "professional agitators" who had entered Angola unlawfully with the assistance of the Popular Movement for the Liberation of Angola (MPLA). One report described the arrest as a crude political maneuver (TASS, 5 May); another version was that the group had entered Angola masquerading as journalists and schoolteachers and using passes issued by the MPLA (*Sunday Telegraph*, London, 5 May).

In April it was announced that there would be an "International Meeting for National Independence and the Return of the Natural Resources of Latin American Countries" in Maracaibo (*Tribuna Popular*, Caracas, 12 April). The sponsors of the meeting were the WFDY, the IUS, the United Political Youth of Venezuela, International Union of Socialist Youth, International Student Movement for the United Nations, International Young Christian Workers, and World Student Christian Federation. In preparation for the meeting a WFDY delegation visited a number of Latin American countries. In Caracas the delegation announced that the meeting would be attended by 150 people (ibid., 25-31 July). No specific date for this meeting was announced.

In April the WFDY stated that it was following with deep attention the process taking place in Portugal (TASS, 19 April). By August, alarmed and highly critical of the developments, the WFDY charged that Portuguese reactionary forces were carrying out their anti-communist campaign with the intention of destroying Portuguese democracy (MTI, 26 August).

The dispute between the WFDY and the Yugoslav youth organizations, which has continued on and off since the late 1940s, flared up again over differences in the editorial policies of the WFDY magazine. As related by *Belgrade NIN* (20 July), a member of the Secretariat of the Socialist Youth of Yugoslavia, visiting in Bucharest, came upon a "particular kind of deceit committed against our young people by the editors of *Youth of the World*," having obtained a copy of the magazine's April issue devoted to the 30th anniversary of the victory over fascism and discovered that, "contrary to an agreement between the Federation of Socialist Youth of Yugoslavia and the journal's editors, this issue did not include any articles on the participation of Yugoslav youth in the national liberation struggle." Although an article submitted by the Yugoslavs was printed in the subsequent issue, this did not mollify the Yugoslav Federation, because "our dissatisfaction over certain occurrences in the work of the World Federation of Democratic Youth is based on somewhat wider foundations and has older origins—foundations and origins which this latest event have made current." Others in Yugoslavia made similar comments.

At the time of the "political trials" in Spain, the WFDY issued a series of statements charging that ruthless oppression was growing in Spain and was aimed at democratic and anti-fascist elements (MTI, 25 September). After the executions, the WFDY protested vigorously.

World Youth Festival. The WFDY began preparations for the 11th World Youth Festival early in 1975. The International Preparatory Committee (IPC) held its constituent meeting in East Berlin on 13 February, with representatives of 95 organizations in 62 countries and 14 regional and international youth and student organizations attending. It was decided that the 11th Festival should be held in Havana in 1978 (the original date was expected to be 1976). Speakers said there were new prospects for the Festival movement in the light of international détente and increasing cooperation between countries with different socio-economic systems. These improvements had been made possible, so the speakers said, by the consistent and constructive foreign policies of the USSR and other countries of the socialist community. The session adopted a solidarity statement with the people and youth of Chile and sent a message of greeting to Vietnamese youth. Havana was chosen for the next session of the IPC, which would determine the content and slogans of the event. (*Neues Deutschland*, 12, 14, 16 February; TASS, 12, 13, 15 February.)

Publications. The WFDY publishes a bi-monthly magazine, *World Youth*, in English, French, German, and Arabic. The monthly WFDY *News* appears in English, French, and Spanish. Other publications, directed to specific areas of interest, include special magazines and pamphlets to commemorate congresses, festivals, and other events.

World Federation of Scientific Workers. The World Federation of Scientific Workers (WFSW) was founded in London in 1946 at the initiative of the British Association of Scientific Workers, with 18 organizations of scientists from 14 countries taking part. Although it purported to be a scientific rather than a political organization, communists obtained most official posts at the start and have kept control since. The headquarters is in London, but the secretary-general's office is in Paris.

WFSW membership is open to organizations of scientific workers everywhere and to individual scientists in countries where no affiliated groups are active. The WFSW claims to represent 300,000 scientists in 30 countries; most of the membership derives from 14 groups in communist-ruled countries. The only large non-communist affiliate, the British Association of Scientific Workers, has 21,000 members. Scientists of distinction who do not belong to an affiliated organization may be nominated for "corresponding membership." The WFSW has a constitution and a "Charter for Scientific Workers" to which affiliates must subscribe (see *YICA, 1968*, p. 736).

Structure and Leadership. The governing body of the WFSW is the General Assembly, in which all affiliated organizations are represented. Ten Assembly meetings have been held, the latest in September 1973 in Varna, Bulgaria. Between these, the Executive Council and its Bureau are responsible for the operation of the WFSW. There are also three standing committees: the Science Policy Committee, the Socio-Economic Committee, and the Committee on Peace and Disarmament. No change occurred in the leadership in 1975. Eric Burhop (United Kingdom) remained as president and chairman of the Executive Council and Pierre Biguard as secretary-general.

The WFSW has consultative status Category A with UNESCO.

Views and Activities. The WFSW Bureau meeting in Berlin in December 1974 decided, at the suggestion of its Disarmament Committee, to hold a Disarmament Symposium in the USSR in the summer of 1975. It was indicated that this symposium would seek closer cooperation with trade unions in the struggle for disarmament. (*Voice of the GDR*, 7 December.) The preparatory committee for the symposium met in Moscow in February and subsequently reported that 450 representatives of scientific organizations from 60 to 70 countries were expected to attend. (*Neues Deutschland*, 19 February.)

The agenda for the symposium, distributed in March, provided for five commissions which would discuss (1) social and economic aspects of disarmament, the economic burden of the arms race, and the problems of scientific workers; (2) the interdependence of détente and disarmament, and how scientific workers' organizations can promote détente; (3) ending the arms race and eliminating the danger of nuclear war; (4) the banning of chemical, biological and geophysical weapons; and (5) forms of cooperation of scientific workers and their organizations with the broad movement for peace and disarmament. It was further noted that several Soviet organizations had joined with the WFSW in sponsoring the symposium: All-Union Central Council of Trade Unions, the Education and Scientific Workers' Union of the USSR, the Soviet Committee of the World Congress of Peace Forces, and the Academy of Science of the USSR. (Circular, 1 March 1975.)

The Disarmament Symposium opened in Moscow on 15 July with 442 scientists from 62 countries and 20 international organizations attending. Among the international organizations were the United Nations, UNESCO, the World Peace Council (WPC), World Federation of Trade Unions, Stockholm International Peace Research Institute, and European Center on Nuclear Research. In his initial remarks, Burhop criticized arms expenditures, particularly those of the United States. He then called for an "atmosphere which led 50 million people to sign the Stockholm Appeal against nuclear weapons in 1950." Romesh Chandra, speaking on behalf of the WPC, linked the activities of the WFSW and the WPC, and noted that the decision to set up the WPC came from people who were directly involved with the WFSW. The reference to the Stockholm Appeal and the linkage of the WPC and the WFSW undoubtedly suggests a common effort by these two organizations to undertake a campaign on behalf of "disarmament" and détente.

The commission discussing the social and economic aspects of disarmament stressed the "negative" impact of the arms race. In particular it noted that the war orientation of many countries restricted the development of science and technology. As a response to this socio-economic problem, the commission recommended regional seminars to educate the people against "arms expenditures." The second commission concluded that détente and peaceful co-existence would expand international cooperation, and urged scientists to participate in appropriate social movements supporting peaceful co-existence. The third and fourth commissions condemned the spread of nuclear and biological weapons. The fifth commission called on all scientists to carry out the recommendations of the symposium. Specifically, scientists were asked to support the WPC's New Stockholm Appeal (see *World Peace Council*) and the World Forum for Disarmament in York, England, in 1976. In their final appeal, the delegates demanded a halt to the further stockpiling and development of nuclear weapons, and to the spread of these weapons. All scientists were urged to prevent a return to the era of the cold war and to assist in the development of détente (*Pravda*, 16 July; Conference Documents.)

A British delegate, Joseph Hanlon wrote shortly afterward in *New Scientist* (31 July) that although the symposium had been billed as a discussion on disarmament, it was in fact intended to be a "mass blessing for U.S./USSR détente." After pointing out that the Soviets paid the expenses of delegates, he went on to say: "The meeting was sponsored by the WFSW, a Soviet-dominated trade union group set up to build bridges between Eastern and Western scientists. But at this meeting, adherence to the line of Soviet-U.S. detente was more important than bridge-building. Most attendees were chosen for their long service to the WFSW rather than for any disarmament or weapons expertise." Burhop in reply criticized Hanlon's article as being full of innuendos, inaccuracies, and half-truths, but in an interview with TASS he affirmed that the symposium fully supported U.S./USSR détente. (*New Scientist*, 7 August; TASS, 13 August.)

Publications. The official publication of the WFSW is *Scientific World*, issued quarterly in English, French, Russian, German, Spanish, and Czech. The WFSW *Bulletin*, issued irregularly and only to members, is published in English, French, German, and Russian. "Science and Mankind" is the general title of a series of WFSW booklets in several languages. The WFSW publishes pamphlets of specific subjects from time to time.

World Federation of Trade Unions. The World Federation of Trade Unions (WFTU), set up at the initiative of the British Trade Union Congress, held its founding congress in October 1945 in Paris, where its first headquarters was established. Expelled from Paris and next from Vienna for subversive activities, the headquarters has been in Prague since 1956. At Soviet insistence, Louis Saillant (France), the WFTU's first secretary-general, is generally considered responsible for bringing the WFTU Secretariat and other ruling bodies under communist control. Some non-communist affiliates in 1949 gave up their membership to found an alternative organization, the International Conference of Free Trade Unions (ICFTU). Since 1949, however, the WFTU has grown. Today, by its calculations, there are 160 to 170 million members, in 68 countries, as against 64 million in 56 countries at the time of its founding (TASS, 9 October 1975).

Structure and Leadership. The highest WFTU authority is the Congress. It meets every four years and is composed of delegates from affiliates in proportion to the number of their members. The latest Congress was held in Varna, Bulgaria, in the fall of 1973. The Congress, which has no policy-making function and is too large to transact much specific business, elects the General Council, Executive Bureau, and Secretariat. The General Council is composed of approximately 66 regular and 68 deputy members representing the national affiliates and 11 Trade Union Internationals (TUIs). The 1973 Congress reelected Enrique Pastorino (Uruguay) as president and Pierre Gensous (France) as secretary-general. Two seats on the General Council have been left vacant for China and Indonesia. The Executive Bureau is the most powerful body of the WFTU, having assumed much of the authority which before 1969 was enjoyed by the Secretariat. The Secretariat was revamped by the 1969 Congress and reduced to six members, including the secretary-general.

The TUIs represent workers of particular trades and crafts. One of their main purposes is to recruit local unions which do not, through their national centers, belong to the WFTU. Though the TUIs are in theory independent (each TUI has its own offices and officials, holds its own meetings, and publishes its own bulletin), their policies and finances are controlled by the WFTU department having supervision over their particular areas. The WFTU General Council in December 1966 decided that each TUI should have its own constitution; this move, taken to bolster the appearance of independence, had the purpose of allowing the TUIs to join international bodies as individual organizations.

In recent years the WFTU has moved vigorously to establish working relationships with non-communist trade unions and intergovernmental organizations. In this area of operation one of the most important structural linkages is the WFTU's "Special Commission on U.N. Agencies," created in 1967 to facilitate WFTU activities in the United Nations. The WFTU enjoys Category A Status with a number of U.N. agencies, and has permanent representatives at the United Nations in New York and at the International Labor Organization (ILO), the Food and Agriculture Agency (FAO), and UNESCO.

One of the founders of the WFTU and its former vice-President, Benoit Frachon, died in August 1975. He was also a member of the Political Bureau of the French Communist Party and general-secretary and president of the CGT (*L'Humanité*, Paris, 8 August).

For a brief review of the history of the WFTU see *Flashes*, 1 October 1975.

Views and Activities. At the end of January 1975 an "extraordinary session of the WFTU

Bureau" was held in East Berlin. (For detailed reports see *Flashes*, 12 February, and *The Worsening of the Crisis of the Capitalist World*, a special WFTU document.) The session was called to discuss "the deepening economic crisis in the Capitalist countries," put forward solutions for overcoming the crisis, decide on the WFTU's specific tacks, and take action toward international trade union unity (*Flashes*, 12 February). Attending the session were Pastorino, Gensous, and Bureau members from Czechoslovakia, France, Hungary, East Germany, Poland, and the USSR. Two fundamental aspects of the situation underlied the discussions: "The international coordination of the struggle against the multinational companies which bear overwhelming responsibility for the worsening of the crisis, and the organization of international working class solidarity in the struggle for the complete political and economic independence of all peoples." Pastorino spoke of the development of the contradictions of the capitalist regimes and the concomitant requirement of a joint platform of the workers and their trade union organizations to deal with the crisis. Gensous continued the theme and talked of the need to continue to be extremely vigilant even though the balance of power in the world had shifted in favor of peace and socialism. In specific terms he denounced the U.S. Foreign Trade Bill as "flagrant American interference in the domestic affairs of the USSR." A. Shelepin (USSR) argued:

> [The] working class, all the working people and the trade unions in capitalist countries have entered a new, difficult and, most likely, prolonged period of trials, tough class confrontations in the complex crisis conditions. The crisis of capitalism has been accelerated by the energy crisis. The monopolies themselves brought on oil hunger because higher oil prices spelled great benefits for them. They are trying to blackmail the oil-producing countries and conceal from the world public and the workers of their countries the fact that the crisis flows direclty from their policy of aggression against developing countries.

He proposed that the WFTU Secretariat draw up a policy document on united action of the working people and the trade unions in defense of their economic, social, and political rights in the context of a sharpened general crisis of capitalism. At the end of the session, Sandor Gaspar (Hungary) stated:

> During the session our opinion grew stronger that what is happening in Western Europe today as a consequence of the crisis is not a matter for the workers of the capitalist countries alone but is the common cause of the European working class.... We, who come out in defense of the working people, have a duty to put the capitalist system and the capitalists, the real culprits of the crisis, on trial. The attraction of the socialist countries is increasing in the countries hit by the crisis and this is also a reason for the attempts to conceal the causes of the crisis.... It is in the joint interest of West European workers and the trade union movements of the socialist countries to set the united strength of the millions of organized workers against these plans. For this very reason it is important for us to understand each other and for our fellow workers to belong to other international trade union organizations. There is hope that in Geneva, where the second meeting of European trade union leaders will take place at the end of February, besides the originally fixed agenda, these pressing problems will be discussed.

The Bureau adopted a communiqué which emphasized the need to strengthen trade union unity in the face of the growing crisis in the capitalist world. A message to the executives of the International Confederation of Free Trade Unions (ICFTU) and the World Confederation of Labor (WCL), asking them for concrete action against the policies of the multi-national companies, was approved. At a press conference, Gensous stated that there was no crisis in the Socialist countries—only in the capitalist world because of the economic system. He went on to say that a struggle had to be waged against the monopolies and against the governments which supported them. He urged the workers in Western Europe not to give up their struggle for higher wages. Pointing to specific tasks, he first stressed that it was especially important to bring to a head the struggle with the multi-national companies; second, he suggested that the commission of the three world trade union organizations cooperating within the United Nations should publish as soon as possible its report on multi-national companies; and third, that on the basis of the consultative status enjoyed by the trade union within the United Nations that at the next session of UNESCO a draft memorandum be drawn up dealing with the demands of the workers and the problem of unemployment. (*Flashes*, 12 February; *Voice of the GDR*, 30 January; MTI, 30 January; TASS, 28 January; *Trud*, 29 January.)

It seems that the WFTU sees the "economic crisis" in the West as an opportunity to gain two specific ends: greater unity of the "working class" under the influence of the WFTU and a weakening of the multinationals by characterizing them as the culprits in the crisis.

Shortly after the close of the extraordinary Bureau session, the Trade Union Conference mentioned by Gaspar opened in Geneva on 28 February. Attending were representatives from 44 trade unions and 10 international and regional organizations. As stated by the WFTU, the main significance of the conference lay in the fact that the European trade union leaders managed to sit down together around a conference table. Furthermore, concrete action was taken toward improving the safety, health, and welfare of workers. As for the future, the conference agreed to work together within certain bodies of the ILO, and to seek closer relations among all labor groups. Indeed, the main thrust of the conference was the previously mentioned goal of greater trade union unity. In the United States, the meeting was severely criticized by the AFL-CIO labor federation, which stated that "the East-West trade union conference, to be held under the roof of the ILO this month in Geneva, is another example of a long-sought Soviet political goal, finally won through patient cultivation of Western European labor centers through exchange visits and mutual endeavor" (*Flashes*, 12 March).

The 12th Session of the Bureau, in Baghdad on 23 April, was a follow-up to the extraordinary session in East Berlin. It dealt with (1) the coordination of the struggle against the effects of the economic crisis in the capitalist world, especially with reference to the multi-national companies, and (2) joint support by "the labor world" for the legitimate struggle of the workers and people of the Third World to recover their national wealth, achieve political and economic independence, and establish a new international economic order. The latter point was reconfirmed when a Sudan representative spoke of the WFTU's solidarity with the struggle of the Arab people. A TASS (25 April) report on the session noted that the present world situation "creates fresh opportunities for the development of the class struggle in capitalist countries, for the upsurge of the national-liberation movement and the progress of socialism."

The 26th Session of the WFTU General Council opened in Paris on 7 October with delegates in attendance from 90 countries. Gensous declared that the changes taking place in the world, particularly the crisis of capitalism, required that the WFTU follow its long standing policy of trade union unity (*Trud*, 8 October; TASS, 9 October). This theme of "trade union unity" was reiterated repeatedly throughout the Session. Indeed, the message sent by Soviet party chief Brezhnev was devoted almost exclusively to this subject. In a long speech to the Council, Karel Hoffmann, chairman of the Czechoslovak Central Council of Trade Unions, detailed the strategy and tactics that the WFTU should employ in achieving this unity. It is quoted here at length because an understanding of these tactics is critical to understanding the behavior of the WFTU, particularly as it relates to non-communist labor groups.

> The report [given by Gensous] correctly emphasized that the WFTU, Trade Union Internationals (TUIs), and its member centers must continue to put the main emphasis—particularly in the existing situation—on the question of unity and cooperation. We believe that the member centers should help more in this matter and regularly inform the WFTU about their bilateral and multilateral relations with non-member organizations, because the WFTU then can use this information in its initiatives toward the ICFTU and the WCL. The same applies also to relations between trade unions and TUI's non-member unions. With the assistance of these bilateral relations of its centers, the WFTU could strive to establish

contacts with representatives of non-member organizations in concrete spheres of the trade unions extensive activity.

To Intensify Propaganda Activity

To achieve success in establishing contacts with our partners in non-member organizations and particularly in international centers presumes that we know them, and above all know them well. That means to know their programs, their activities, their tactics, actions, changes in orientation, various currents and tendencies of views and so forth. It would be of help in this respect if the WFTU provided still better substantiated and, above all, more rapid information as far as the situation in the ICFTU and WCL is concerned.

All this information and a whole number of various other pertinent statements and speeches by representatives of the ICFTU and WCL are particularly useful in connection with the need to oppose the activity of enemies of unity and cooperation. If we do not know these standpoints and attitudes of our opponents in time, we cannot react to them promptly, and disprove with appropriate arguments the numerous false and unsubstantiated assertions, thus leaving a free scope for activity to our opponents.

Also closely connected with this is the general concept of WFTU propaganda activity. . . . WFTU propaganda instruments are still inadequately offensive and militant, and particularly too little differentiated according to the individual spheres in which we want to be active. . . . In the sphere of information the existing system will not suffice either.

To Coordinate Actions Purposefully

We regard the part of the report devoted to the WFTU regional activity on individual continents as particularly obligatory. This question is extraordinarily important at the present time, when the specific development of the situation and particularly of the trade union movement, is subject to rapid changes, on which one has to flexibly and promptly react if we do not wish the WFTU to lag behind this development of events. We are of the opinion that the main weak spot in the WFTU and TUI's regional activity was that this activity was of too general a nature, and that too little attention was paid to the implementation side of the WFTU activity. Yet we all know well that it is precisely the TUI's that can play a substantially greater role in this direction than has been the case until now. We, therefore, welcome the elaboration of the main orientation according to individual continents. We fully identify ourselves with the view that until now there is no effective coordination not only of WFTU actions, but also of TUI's actions, and particularly on national centers.

In view of the different conditions on individual continents and the binding problems which stem from this, we suggest for consideration whether the time has not arrived for each continent (and maybe also for the Arab countries) to have initiative commissions or groups of representatives of members' centers of the pertinent continent attached to the WFTU Secretariat, which would submit concrete recommendations for the activity of the WFTU and TUI's and eventually also for the activity of individual organizations.

We believe that another main shortcoming of coordination is being manifested in the sphere of schooling of trade union cadres of the developing countries, where we are often unnecessarily splintering our power to achieve proper effect. The following should remain especially valid here: concentration of more means, more educational actions to be organized directly in the given country or continent. . . .

At the end of the Council Session, all the delegates accepted the mandate for greater trade union unity. Without question the drive for unity was the main preoccupation of the WFTU in 1975.

The importance of national trade centers in helping to establish trade union unity was clearly seen at the annual British TUC (*Flashes*, 24 September). At this meeting the chairman of the TUC International Committee spoke to the point that the British TUC had always been a leader in the movement toward greater trade union unity, that Europe includes both East and West, and that further steps should be taken to bring the sides together. At the same meeting the Amalgamated Union of Engineering Workers proposed successfully a resolution urging the WFTU and the ICFTU to work more closely together. The attitudes and actions of certain British labor groups were similar to those of groups affiliated with the WFTU in other West European countries.

Within the United Nations, ILO, and FAO, the WFTU continued to press for a larger role. The 60th Session of the ILO conference in Geneva (4 June) saw a number of WFTU members elected to key positions. At the session the WFTU put forward suggestions for making the structure of the ILO more democratic and up-to-date in the interests of the workers. Shortly after the ILO gathering, the first official meeting between the international trade union organizations and the United Nations took place in Geneva on 17 July. At the meeting the WFTU submitted a proposal for action to "tackle the crisis of the capitalist world." For the most part the proposal contained demands for the extension of trade union rights and participation in the decision-making apparatus of public and private organizations. This included, for example, the "right of workers and peoples to exercise control over the activities of the multinational companies." The WFTU considered the meeting highly successful (ibid., special, July.)

In *Flashes*, 28 May, the WFTU announced that one of its aims had been met; there would be on-going contact between trade union officials within the FAO. The FAO had informed the WFTU that ad hoc meetings would be replaced by yearly contact. The 4th Consultation between the FAO and the trade unions took place in Rome on 19 September. Two important decisions were reached. First, the FAO agreed to cooperate with trade unions on a regional and continental basis. In line with this agreement, a Latin American regional Consultation was scheduled for 1976 and a Middle East Consultation for 1977. Second, it was decided that rural workers and their trade unions would take an active part in drawing up and implementing all FAO-sponsored national plans for the economic and social development of rural areas. (Ibid., 1 October.)

The WFTU was preoccupied off and on in 1975 with what it called "the fight for disarmament." At conferences dealing with all sorts of matters, the WFTU repeatedly brought up its demand that arms be curtailed. Interestingly, the bulk of the WFTU's discussion on disarmament dealt with the relationship between excessive military spending and the problems in the capitalist societies. Thus, the call for disarmament became a call for reduced military spending in the West.

Members of the WFTU Secretariat visited Latin America on several occasions. Pastorino toured Colombia, Cuba, Mexico, Panama, Peru, and Venezuela. During this tour he addressed the First International Congress of Third World Teachers in Acapulco on 5 August. In June and July the WFTU issued two special *Flashes* on the situation in Chile. These issues expressed severe criticism of the junta and support for the "anti-fascist struggle" against the Chilean government.

The WFTU voiced "increasing concern over the events in Portugal" and called for massive support to save Portuguese democracy (ibid., special, August). On 8 September in Prague, European member organizations of the WFTU met to discuss the situation and determined that counter-revolutionary forces openly supported by foreign fascists and multi-national companies were seeking to destroy the democratic elements in Portugal (MTI, 13 September).

As the WFTU described the situation in Angola, the Popular Movement for the Liberation of Angola (MPLA), which had led the struggle for independence, was under attack by "international imperialism" and was in danger of falling to the "reactionaries." The WFTU expressed its complete solidarity with and support of the struggle of the MPLA. (Ibid., special, August.)

The general secretary of the Singapore National Trade Union Congress, an affiliate of the ICFTU, said that West European international trade union groupings, "would, if they ever chose to institutionalize relations with the Moscow-based WFTU, provoke Peking and perhaps Hanoi to initiate their own competing versions of Asian Labor solidarity." He went on: "I must state that if any international trade secretariat indulges in political adventurism we in Singapore will find ourselves obliged to opt out of the International Trade Secretariat [of the ICFTU]." (*Straits Times*, 29 May.)

Publications. The most important publication of the WFTU is an illustrated magazine, *World Trade Union Movement*, circulated in some 70 countries, in English, French, Spanish, German, Russian, and other languages. *Flashes*, published several times a month in four languages, is an information bulletin of 4-5 pages containing brief reports and documents.

World Peace Council. The "world peace" movement headed by the World Peace Council (WPC) dates from August 1948, when a "World Congress of Intellectuals for Peace" in Wroclaw, Poland, set up an organization called the "International Liaison Committee of Intellectuals." This committee in April 1949 convened a "First World Peace Congress" in Paris. The Congress launched a "World Committee of Partisans of Peace," which in November 1950 was renamed the World Peace Council. Originally based in Paris, the WPC was expelled in 1951 by the French government. It moved first to Prague and then, in 1954, to Vienna, where it adopted the name "World Council of Peace." Although outlawed in Austria in 1957, the World Council of Peace continued its operations in Vienna under the cover of a new organization, the International Institute of Peace (IIP). The IIP has subsequently been referred to by WPC members as the "scientific-theoretical workshop of the WPC" (CTK, 16 December 1971). In September 1968 the World Council of Peace transferred its headquarters to Helsinki, while the IIP remained in Vienna. Although no formal announcement was made, the World Council of Peace has reverted to its earlier name, the World Peace Council.

Structure and Leadership. The WPC is organized on a national basis, with Peace Committees and other affiliated groups in more than 80 countries. No exact figure is available on the total individual membership. The highest authority is the Council, with 600 members. The Council elects the 101-member Presidential Committee, which in turn elects the 24-member Bureau and 18-member Secretariat, with memberships divided among representatives from various countries. International communist front organizations such as the IUS, WFDY, WFSW, WFTU, and WIDF are represented on the Presidential Committee.

Amendments adopted at the February 1974 meeting of the Council require it to meet every three years instead of every two and urge the national peace movements (Peace Committees) to meet annually, while the Presidential Committee will meet only once a year instead of twice. The Bureau will normally meet three or four times a year to review international events and the Council's work, and to execute decisions of the Presidential Committee. It appears that the Bureau has authority to act independently on a wide range of matters. The executive bodies of the IIP—ostensibly independent of those of the WPC, but in fact elected by the Council—are the 7-member Presidium and 30-member Executive Committee. Romesh Chandra (India) is the WPC secretary-general.

The WPC has "Consultation and Association—Category A" status with UNESCO.

Views and Activities. As noted above, the 1974 Council urged the national Peace Committees to meet annually. On 6 December 1974, the first annual conference of these movements took place in Prague. (For a detailed report see the WPC pamphlet *Conference of Representatives of National Peace Movements, Prague, December 6-9, 1974.*) Some 250 delegates from 100 countries attended, and also representatives of the Palestine Liberation Organization (PLO). Tasks of the world peace movement and a report on International Women's Year were debated, and reports of commissions on the mass media and on peace research were heard. Three commissions were established, on Security and Cooperation in Europe, Disarmament, and Economic Development and the Right of all Nations to Own Their Natural Resources. In his main address, Chandra said that mankind "owes a great debt of gratitude to the Soviet people, the Soviet Government and the Communist Party of the Soviet Union for their actions to implement the Soviet peace program in all fields," and that the cold-war advocates who oppose détente had received a major setback. Détente, he stressed, must be made irreversible. He noted that with the help of the Socialist countries, the Third World countries had made gigantic strides to wrest control of their wealth from imperialists and multi-national companies. To further this effort, he called for a "world development conference" to be held in 1976. On the Middle East, he demanded complete withdrawal of all Israeli forces from occupied Arab lands and full recognition of the rights of the Palestinian people. In support of the reconvening of the Geneva conference on the Middle East with the PLO present, Chandra indicated that the WPC was planning wide-scale activities.

Finally, he called for full backing of the work going on toward European security. At the end of the conference, resolutions were passed on the following subjects: *On Unity in the Struggle for Development*, dealing with independent control over resources; *On Asian Security and Cooperation*, calling for an Asian collective security arrangement; *On the Indian Ocean*, supporting the decisions reached at the International Conference on the Indian Ocean, Against Foreign Military Bases and for a Zone of Peace (New Delhi, 14 November 1974); and *On Actions to End the Arms Race and for Disarmament*, calling for a number of actions, such as support of World Disarmament Week, for a reduction in the arms race. (CTK, 4-9 December 1974; TASS, 6-19 December; Prague radio, 7-9 December.) Shortly after the conference, Chandra announced some future activities of the WPC: the convening in Aden of an international conference of solidarity in support of revolutionary movements in Yemen; an international tribunal to consider the crimes of the Chilean military junta, in Mexico; and a conference of Asian countries, in Baghdad (Prague radio, 10 December; TASS, 19 December).

On 18 February 1975 the 3d session of the "Commission on Crimes of the Chilean Junta" began in Mexico City. It was opened by Mexican president Echeverría, who stated that Latin America could not remain passive toward situations like the one which provoked the fall of the Allende regime and toward "foreign interference." Some 130 persons attended, including representatives from various international organizations. The final document called for an end to "fascist terror" in Chile. To achieve this, the session proposed a world-wide solidarity campaign to isolate the junta. Messages were sent to the U.S. government demanding that it cease support of the junta, and to the U.S. Senate Foreign Relations Committee demanding that its inquiry into Chile be made public. (TASS, 19-20 February; *Le Monde*, Paris, 23-24 February.)

The 2d Conference for Peace and Security in Asia was held in Baghdad on 24 February. (For details see *For Peace and Security in Asia: Conference of Asian Peace Forces*, published by Continuing Liaison Council, World Congress of Peace Forces.) Present were 250 delegates from 35 countries and 14 international organizations. The theme of Asian security ran through the conference and was linked to a call for an Asian collective security arrangement which would stand against imperialism. Members of the conference fully supported the resolutions of the International Conference on the Indian Ocean; in particular the delegates condemned proposed U.S. bases on Diego Garcia and inside the Arab Gulf. Full support was also given to the liberation movements operating in the Gulf area. At the end of the conference, resolutions were adopted on these topics, along with resolutions condemning U.S. efforts to break the Arab-Soviet alliance, Zionist aggression, and the threat of the United States to intervene in the oil-producing states. The "peace forces" in the Gulf area and in the countries bordering the Indian Ocean were urged to fight against the plots of U.S. imperialism and the CIA. A special resolution praised the fraternal help of the Socialist community, particularly the USSR. A telegram from Iraq's president Ahmad Hasan al-Bakr expressed full solidarity with the Arab liberation movement against Iran and demanded that Iran stop interfering in Iraqi internal affairs and change its expansionist policy in the Gulf area. (*Baghdad Observer*, 12, 22, 25, 27 February; Iraqi News Agency, 24-26 February). The apparent preoccupation of the conference with U.S. imperialism and the countermove to create an Asian collective security arrangement failed to touch on a significant variable in the Asian equation: the role of China. In June, at the Stockholm session of the Presidential Committee, strong support was again given to the Soviet idea of an Asian collective security system, and the purpose of this security system was clarified when, in an interview, the chairman of the Great People's Assembly of Mongolia condemned Chinese aggressive intentions (TASS, 6 June).

An enlarged meeting of the Presidential Committee and Bureau was held in East Berlin on 18 April. GDR foreign minister Oskar Fischer welcomed the delegates. Chandra, in his address, paid tribute to the Soviet Union as the most powerful guarantor of world peace. Prominent on the agenda was détente, and the struggle to promote it in the face of "rightwing extremists and conservatives" actively opposing it, particularly in "West Germany and the United States." The resolution on détente proclaimed that "The peace forces sincerely hope that everything will be done to ensure the complete success of the Conference for Security and Cooperation in Europe," appealed to all peace-loving forces to "achieve the total isolation of the enemies of detente ... and expose their activites," and demanded that political détente be complemented by military détente. On the issue of Cyprus, the Bureau declared that the situation on the island resulted from NATO "maneuvers" which were designed to eliminate the independence of Cyprus. Full support was given to the U.N. resolution on Cyprus, and the WPC determined to campaign for this end. The Bureau continued the WPC's commitment to "national rights of the Arab people in Palestine," and called for the convening of the Geneva conference. Also receiving the Bureau's attention were the problems of Portugal's struggle for democracy, the liberation movements in Africa, and women in their struggle for freedom. (*Peace Courier*, May; ADN, 18-20 April; GDR domestic service, 18 April.)

The second Assembly of European Public Opinion met in Brussels on 26 April. (The first was held in Brussels in June 1971.) The WPC was represented by nine persons; nearly 500 delegates, from 29 countries and 49 international organizations, were present. The main discussion was on security and cooperation in Europe. Thus, the Assembly urged full support for the upcoming Conference on Security and Cooperation in Europe (CSCE) in Helsinki, and called for the continuing development of "political détente," which should be "complemented by military détente." This latter point referred to such negotiations as the Non-proliferation Treaty talks and the Mutual Balanced Force Reduction. Discussion also took place on the exchange of technology between East and West. Although the Assembly dealt with the rights of individuals "to engage and advance without restraint in the process of democracy," it apparently avoided the subject of free movement of people between and within countries, a topic which would come under review at Helsinki. (*Peace Courier*, June; TASS, 26, 28 April.)

One of the main preoccupations of the WPC throughout 1975 was what it described as the "need to end the arms race." At the "Conference of Representatives of National Peace Movements" in Prague (6 December 1974) the "problem" of the arms race was fully explored. Although the delegates concluded that much progress had been made (i.e., SALT I), they also determined that "public opinion should continue its work" (*Peace Courier*, February, March 1975). Early in the year, national efforts were begun to organize public opinion behind this drive against "the arms race." A total of 180 delegates, among whom were representatives from the British Trade Unions, the WPC, the WFTU, the Communist Party of Great Britain, and the Committee for European Security and Cooperation, met in London on 28 February at the request of the All-Britain Peace Liaison Group to discuss the problem of disarmament. (The British group had been set up after discussions at the World Congress of Peace Forces in Moscow, October 1973.) Arthur Booth, vice-chairman of the International Continuing Liaison Council of the World Congress of Peace Forces and chairman of the International Peace Bureau, announced plans for an "International Disarmament Conference" at York University in March. The All-Britain Liaison Peace Group called on delegates to take up the proposal that the government be asked what preparations it was making toward an intergovernmental world disarmament conference and that at the same time the government prepare plans on the transfer of manpower from war to peace projects. (*Morning Star*, London, 17, 24 February.) In the United States, WPC representatives attended a "National Conference for a Drastic Cut in Military Spending," in Chicago on 5 April. The major theme of the conference was the proposed nationwide campaign for a 50 percent reduction in the U.S. defense budget (*Peace Courier*, May). On an international level, the WPC Presidential Committee, meeting in Stockholm on 2 June, launched a "New Stockholm Movement" for "general and complete disarmament." This meeting, which occurred on the 25th anniversary of the Stockholm Appeal for banning the atomic bomb, sought to work out an action program for disarmament (see *World Federation of Scientific Workers*), and appealed to all governments to "join hands" in this effort. After debates in four commissions and seven regional meetings, participants proposed the following activities in connection with détente and disarmament: an international week against weapons of mass destruction on 6-13 August (to mark the 30th anniversary of the bombing of Hiroshima); an international week for the convocation of a world disarmament conference, in September; and campaigns for the creation of nuclear-free zones in Africa, the Middle East, and northern Europe. Support was voiced for the Soviet idea of setting up a collective security system in Asia. Adopted at the end was an appeal to all peace-loving forces to launch a new world-wide offensive in favor of détente and disarmament and to convene quickly a world disarmament conference. Other documents were related to European security and cooperation, and to the need to reduce military spending in order to achieve greater economic development. (*Peace Courier*, June, July; TASS, 6 June; *L'Humanité*, Paris, 10 June). (For detailed information on the meeting see the WPC pamphlet *World Peace Council Presidential Committee, Stockholm, May 31-June 2.*) The documents relating to the appeal "to end the arms race and for disarmament" have been issued in a special WPC pamphlet entitled *New Stockholm Movement.* These documents will apparently serve as the basis for the campaign now being launched by the WPC. In Moscow during the week of 6-12 October there was support for the WPC's "week for a world conference on disarmament." A Soviet writer stressed that the "task of strengthening political détente with military détente has now become very important," and declared that in this connection the "latest initiative of the Soviet Union, which has put forward proposals to the current session of the U.N. General Assembly for banning the development and production of new forms of weapons of mass destruction . . . is of great significance." To ensure that this initiative received the needed support, backing for the WPC's world disarmament conference was urged to confront governments with the need to reduce arms expenditures. (TASS, 6 October.) The linkage of arms expenditures with disarmament continued to be a constant theme in WPC discussions. Repeatedly, WPC officials described the amount of money spent in NATO countries on arms, and the adverse consequences of this on the people of these countries. Indeed, it might be concluded that the WPC's real concern is twofold: containment of the development of weapons of mass destruction, and the reduction of arms expenditures in the West.

After the heads of state, in Helsinki, concluded the Conference on Security and Cooperation in Europe, the WPC gave vigorous approval to what it called the significance of the event. In a letter to national Peace Committees, the WPC drew attention to the necessity of "taking maximum advantage of the new possibilities which are opening up after the Conference." The letter set a number of tasks for the Peace Committees: to publicize widely the final CSCE documents and demand that the governments which signed the documents also give wide-scale publicity to them; to struggle against those who sought to prevent the conference; and to organize study committees, meetings, lectures, seminars and mass meetings to link the CSCE with the WPC-proposed world disarmament conference, the MBFR talks, and the world development conference planned by the WPC in 1976. (*Peace Courier*, October.) An article in *Izvestiia* indicated that the final act of the CSCE had aroused fresh enthusiasm among champions of peace, and connected the CSCE with the world disarmament conference which "will be convened by non-governmental organizations in Great Britain in March 1976." The article went on: "This conference is to play a significant role in mobilizing masses in all countries for the support of the Helsinki decisions." (TASS, 12 September.)

The WPC organized two major meetings relating to the Middle East in 1975. The first was an "International Conference for a Just and Peaceful Solution to the Middle East Problem" in Paris on 3 May. TASS (26 March) reported that the WPC had decided to convene this conference quickly to support the convocation of a Geneva conference on the Middle East. Present were 115 delegates from 30 countries. In opening remarks, Chandra spoke of the "failure" of the step-by-step approach of U.S. secretary of state Henry Kissinger which, according to Chandra, "was directed—and is still directed—at weakening the unity of the Arab peoples." The WPC leader went on to say that the proper path to a true solution to the problem was through the convening of a Geneva conference which would include the Palestine Liberation Organization. In the final declaration, the gathering called for a wide-ranging effort to mobilize public opinion on behalf of a Geneva conference. (*Peace Courier*, May; *Geneva Conference: Way to Peace and Justice in the Middle East*, Paris, 3-4 May.) Another conference, the "2nd Conference of Peace and Justice in the Middle East," was held in Rome on 10 July. This gathering had its origin in a similar conference in Bologna in 1972, and the subsequent preparatory efforts by the Italian Peace Committee (see *YICA, 1975*, p. 638). The exact groups behind the Rome meeting were the Italian Committee for Peace and Justice in the Middle East, the Italian Forum for Security and Cooperation in Europe and the Mediterranean, and the National Commission for Peace and Friendship among Peoples. Representatives from almost all countries bordering the Mediterranean attended along with delegates from a number of communist parties in Europe and from all Arab states. At the end, an appeal was issued for withdrawal of Israeli troops from Arab lands and recognition of the rights of the Palestinian people, a speedy convening of the Geneva conference, which would include the PLO, and recognition of the PLO by the Italian government (*L'Unità*, Rome, 10-13 July; *Baghdad Observer*, 8 July).

The WPC's Bureau met in Guinea-Bissau on 8 September. Present were representatives of most of the international front organizations (IUS, WFDY, WFTU, etc.). In his opening remarks, Romesh Chandra stressed the contributions to world peace of the national liberation movements, which could always count on the support and solidarity of the Soviet Union and other socialist countries. Resolutions were adopted dealing with the struggles going on in the Middle East and Africa. (*Peace Courier*, October.) In October, WPC delegation in Lisbon spoke on the situation in Angola: "The World Peace Council opposes foreign interference in the affairs of the Angolan people. We think that power in Angola should be handed to the sole legitimate proponent of the people's interests, the Popular Movement for the Liberation of Angola." (TASS, 29 October.)

Among WPC pamphlets on particular issues in 1975 were *Our Task: Isolate Chile's Fascist Junta* and *Israeli Violation of Human Rights in the Occupied Arab Territories*.

Christian Peace Conference. The Christian Peace Conference (CPC), which has been under Soviet domination since 1968, is noted here because it operates in tandem with the WPC. The CPC's relatively high level of activity in 1974 (see *YICA, 1975*, p. 640) included a meeting of its International Secretariat in Prague on 9 December. The secretary-general, Dr. Karoly Toth (Hungary), reported on the conference of WPC national Peace Committees, held there on 6 December. Also discussed were activities planned for 1975, particularly the upcoming "Asian Christian Peace Conference" in Kottayam, India. (*CPC Information*, 16 December.)

The Asian Christian Peace Conference opened on 8 January 1975 with 100 representatives from 22 countries attending. Four commissions discussed theology, politics, economics, and culture. Lectures were given on collective security in Asia, and China after the Cultural Revolution. The conference adopted a resolution and a statement on Korea demanding the full reunification of that country in accordance with the principles of the five-point proposal of the North Korean government. At the end, it established a commission to investigate the question of political prisoners in Asian countries and a continuing committee responsible for carrying out the conference's decisions. (Ibid., nos., 169, 171.)

On 24 January in West Berlin, 80 participants from eastern and western Europe, North America, Africa, and Asia attended a seminar on "What Is the Meaning of the World Christian in the Work for Peace." This seminar was held at the suggestion of the CPC president, Metropolitan Nikodim (USSR). In a message to the seminar, Nikodim noted that the gathering was the first opportunity in years for leading members of the CPC to enter into discussion with former members of the movement and with representatives of other Christian peace groups. Hope was expressed that ways could be found to continue this "fellowship." (Ibid., no. 172.)

On 24 February the International Secretariat met in Moscow, where it discussed plans for a "Working Committee," scheduled to meet in Sofia in April (ibid., no. 174). The Working Committee, which included 50 leading church representatives, met on 10 April, with Nikodim presiding. The theme of the session was "The Co-existence of Christians, Jews and Muslims and the Problems of Peace in the Middle East." Touched on in the discussions were the contributions Christians could make in resolving the Middle East conflict, the general problems facing the international system, and the possibilities for further cooperation with anti-imperialist forces. Nikodim pointed out the necessity of putting an end to Zionism's misuse of religious ideas for justifying Israel's aggressive policy. The meeting pledged support for the Ethiopian Orthodox church and progressive forces in Ethiopia, and for the "International Conference of Solidarity for the Independence of Puerto Rico," called by the WPC and scheduled for Havana in September. (BTA, 10 April; *CPC Information*, no. 177.)

A Theological Commission meeting was held in Romania on 27 May. Representatives from Africa, Asia, Europe, and North and South America attended. On 5 June the International Secretariat met in Zwefall, West Germany, to discuss security and disarmament in connection with the CSCE. (*CPC Information*, no. 180.)

Publications. The WPC issues a semi-monthly bulletin, *Peace Courier*, in English, French, Spanish, and German, and a quarterly journal, *New Perspectives*, in English and French. The WPC also distributes occasionally a *Letter to National Committees*, and a *Letter* to members. Issued on a more limited basis are *Middle East News Letter* and *Spotlight on Africa*. Documents, statements, and press releases are issued in connection with conferences and campaigns.

California State College   Paul F. Magnelia
Stanislaus

BIOGRAPHIES OF PROMINENT INTERNATIONAL COMMUNIST FIGURES

ENRICO BERLINGUER
(Italy)

Enrico Berlinguer, currently undisputed leader of the Italian Communist Party (PCI), was born on 25 May 1922 into a patrician family at Sassari on the island of Sardinia. His father, Mario, a prominent left-wing socialist, served as associate high commissioner during the anti-fascist purge. Already clandestinely active in the illegal socialist-communist youth movement as a teen-ager, Enrico served as secretary to the local Communist youth organization in Sassari. After the liberation of Rome, he moved to the youth movement's central office. In 1945, because of his father's position, he was placed on the PCI Central Committee. He held the posts of general secretary for the youth movement from 1949 to 1956 and chairman of the World Federation of Democratic Youth from 1950 to 1953. These appointments resulted in his elevation to candidate membership on the PCI Directorate.

After 1956, Berlinguer's career in the party apparatus included directorship of the Higher Party School, two years as regional PCI secretary for Sardinia, and, in 1959, full membership on the PCI Directorate with responsibility for organizational affairs. After work on the Secretariat, he was elected in January 1966 to the Politburo. By May 1968, when he first ran for parliament at the head of the Rome Province list in Palmiro Togliatti's former constituency, he had become one of Italy's top four or five communists. Not as well known as the eloquent and prolific Giorgio Amendola, Pietro Ingrao, or Giancarlo Pajetta, he had a better grasp of the party apparatus. On 15 February 1969 Berlinguer was made deputy secretary, in effect acting on behalf of the ailing leader Luigi Longo. Two years later he officially became secretary-general.

Enrico Berlinguer has led many party delegations on visits abroad. During the first of these, to the French Communist Party congress in 1964, he attacked the Chinese for ideological impurity. Since a trip to Hanoi in 1966 he has maintained silence on China and has kept the PCI from any contact with pro-Chinese communists. In contrast, Berlinguer's second major visit abroad was to meet the new Soviet team which had succeeded Khrushchev. Under his leadership, PCI delegations have visited the USSR very often. In 1975 Berlinguer presided over a regular session of the PCI Secretariat in Moscow. His speech that same year to the PCI congress included praise for the "superior moral climate," which he believed to exist in the Soviet Union and contained a succinct answer to those who might wish to detach the PCI from the USSR: "No, never! "

Berlinguer's domestic policy is based on his belief that, in its march toward power, the party cannot afford to arouse more opposition than it can successfully deal with at any given time. Communist participation in a government, which would leave the Christian Democrats intact as a powerful opposition, is far more dangerous for the PCI than an alliance with the Christian Democrats in the exercise of government power. Through such an alliance the latter would become transformed gradually into PCI partners or, in any case, become incapable of opposing the PCI.

Enrico Berlinguer is a short, wiry man of courtly manners and impassive visage, apparently endowed with a well-disciplined temper. Interviewers have found it impossible to elicit anything beyond what he wishes to convey. In his personal life, the aristocratic Berlinguer differs from previous Italian communist leaders—who were of petty-bourgeois origin—in that he does not show a taste for *la dolce vita*. The party, eager for respectability, emphasizes that Berlinguer is married to a practicing Catholic and has three children.

SANTIAGO CARRILLO
(Spain)

Carrillo was born on 18 January 1915 in Gijon (Asturias), the son of a workman who was both a militant syndicalist and a socialist deputy. In 1928 he worked as a typographical apprentice. He joined the Socialist Youth Federation, was elected a member of its Executive Committee in 1932, edited its official organ *Renovación*, and was promoted to secretary-general in 1934. In early 1936 he made his first trip to the USSR and upon his return merged the socialist and communist youth groups into one single organization of which he was secretary-general. During that same year he joined the Spanish Communist Party (PCE) and in 1937 became both a member of its Central Committee and alternate member of its Politburo.

At the outbreak of the Spanish civil war Carrillo was at first political commissar of a battalion in Madrid and then a member of the Junta in charge of defending the capital. Later, until the beginning of 1938, he was active in Valencia and in 1939, when Republican Spain was defeated, he escaped to France.

At the end of 1939 Carrillo crossed Nazi Germany to establish himself in Moscow where for six months he was secretary of the Communist Youth International. He then became its emissary, spending six months in the United States and later residing in Cuba and Mexico. In 1944 he went to Algeria, anticipating anti-Francoist action. From there he traveled to France and was promoted to membership in the PCE Politburo in 1945. In March 1946 he was named minister without portfolio in the Republican Government in exile presided over by José Giral. He retained that title until January 1947.

After World War II, Carrillo lived mainly in France, frequently visiting countries of Eastern Europe. In 1954 he became a member of the Secretariat of the Central Committee of the PCE and in January 1960, at the Sixth Party Congress, was elected secretary-general. He had worked partially in that capacity since 1956, alongside Dolores Ibarruri. On 21 August 1968, the day of the Soviet invasion of Czechoslovakia, he was in the Crimea. He left immediately to convene the Political Bureau of the PCE, which condemned the Soviet intevention. In June 1969 he headed the Spanish delegation to the world conference of communist parties in Moscow and presented a speech in behalf of his party. Since then Carrillo has cultivated political relations with the communist regimes of Romania and Yugoslavia, and in October-November 1971 he led a PCE delegation to China. In 1974 he was one of the organizers of the Democratic Junta, an anti-Francoist coalition formed around the PCE.

CHANG CH'UN-CH'IAO
(China)

Chang Ch'un-ch'iao, who together with Teng Hsiao-p'ing stands among those who might succeed to the post of premier following the departure of Chou En-lai, was born in about 1919. In the thirties he was a member of the League of Left-Wing Writers and during World War II he was active in fighting against the Japanese as a member of communist guerrilla groups. In 1949, he joined the staff of *Liberation Daily* and by 1950 had become director of the East China branch of the New China News

Agency and deputy director of the News and Publications Bureau of the East China Military and Administrative Committee. By 1954, he had become director of the *Liberation Daily* and in 1955 he became vice-chairman of the All-China Federation of Journalists. In the latter half of the fifties he was active in campaigns against deviant intellectuals and rightists and was associated with the Shanghai municipal committee of the Chinese Communist Party (CCP) in 1958, joining its Standing Committee in 1959. He became director of the Propaganda Department in 1963, alternate secretary in 1964, and secretary in 1965. He became associated with Chiang Ch'ing in 1963-64 during her attempt to reform the classical Chinese opera, and took a part in writing the article attacking the play *Hai Jui Dismissed from Office*, often considered the beginning point of the Cultural Revolution. During the Cultural Revolution he played a prominent part, and was most probably in charge of the Culture and Art Section of the Cultural Revolution Group. Chang remained in Mao's favor and was seventh on the Presidium of the Ninth CCP Congress in April 1969. He was elected to the CCP Politburo and in 1971 became first secretary of the CCP Committee of Shanghai. At the Tenth CCP Congress in August 1973, he was elected secretary general of the Presidium and became a Standing Committee member of the new Politburo. He was appointed a deputy premier in 1975 and is also director of the General Political Department of the People's Liberation Army. It was Chang who reported on the revised draft constitution of the People's Republic of China that was produced at the Fourth National People's Congress in January 1975.

ALVARO CUNHAL
(Portugal)

Born on 10 November 1913 in Coimbra into a middle-class family, Cunhal was the son of an attorney. Between 1931 and 1935, while studying law at the University of Lisbon, he became a militant communist. In 1931 he joined a communist youth organization; he headed communist activities at the university, and in 1935 he was promoted to secretary-general of the Association of Communist Youth of Portugal. In the autumn of that year he visited the Soviet Union for the first time, to attend the Sixth Congress of the Communist Youth International in Moscow.

In 1936 Cunhal joined the Central Committee of the Portuguese Communist Party (PCP). After the outbreak of civil war in Spain he went there and stayed until the beginning of 1937. He then returned to Portugal and in 1938 was elected member of the Secretariat of the PCP Central Committee. In 1937-38 and 1940 he was briefly under arrest. Then, for almost a decade, he pursued his political activities without apprehension. In 1949 he was seized; tried in 1950, he was condemned to a four-and-a-half-year prison term. In 1953, while he was still in jail, the sentence was extended to ten years. In January 1960 he managed to escape with a group of communist leaders and from then on lived in Moscow and various East European capitals, most importantly Prague. In 1961 he became secretary-general of the PCP, a position he still holds.

During his exile Cunhal was the leader and spokesman of the PCP at all important meetings held in the Soviet capital. In October 1961 he attended the Twenty-second Congress of the CPSU; in March-April 1966, its Twenty-third; in November 1967 he was present at the celebration of the 50th anniversary of the October Revolution; in June 1969 he participated in the world conference of communist parties; and in March-April 1971 he attended the Twenty-fourth CPSU congress. On 22 August 1968, on the morrow of the Soviet invasion of Czechoslovakia, Cunhal approved Moscow's course of action in the name of his party.

Upon his return to Portugal, one week after the coup d'état of 25 April 1974, Cunhal was named state secretary without portfolio in the government of Palma Carlos. He maintained that post in the first government formed by Colonel Vasco Gonçalves on 17 July as well as through all its successive alterations. However, in July 1975, following the resignation of ministers from the Socialist and Popular Democratic parties, Gonçalves was entrusted to establish a new government without the participation of the principal leaders of political parties and Cunhal was out of office.

In October 1974, at the Seventh Congress of the PCP, held in Lisbon, Cunhal was reelected secretary-general of the party. At the end of that month he made an official visit to Moscow in the name of the Portuguese government.

KHIEU SAMPHAN
(Cambodia)

Khieu Samphan was born on 27 July 1931 in the province of Svay Rieng in eastern Cambodia. He worked his way through school and earned scholarships allowing him to study in France from 1954 to 1959, where he obtained his doctorate in economics from the Sorbonne. During his period of study in France, he served as general secretary of the Federation of Cambodian Students, a group with a communist orientation. Upon his return to Cambodia, he declared himself to be a liberal Marxist, and became active in politics. As a consequence, he came into frequent conflict with the then anti-communist policy of Norodom Sihanouk, and was arrested for a brief time in 1960 on a charge of engaging in subversive activities. In 1962 he was elected to the National Assembly and also appointed by Sihanouk to the post of state secretary in the Ministry of Trade. As a result of his reformist approach, he became very popular among young Cambodian intellectuals, a popularity that prompted his resignation from the Ministry of Trade under pressure from Sihanouk. He was reelected to the National Assembly in 1966.

In early 1967 the Battambang peasant uprising occurred in the Samlaut district of northeastern Cambodia for which Sihanouk held Khieu Samphan responsible. At this point the latter disappeared from sight, going underground and later joining the Khmer Rouge. Following the coup of 18 March 1970 in which Sihanouk was deposed and the Khmer Republic established under Lon Nol, the Khmer Rouge joined the followers of Sihanouk in a united front, known as the United National Front of Cambodia, which established the Royal Government of National Union in May 1970 with Khieu Samphan as deputy premier and minister of defense. Actual leadership of the government as a whole was most probably also in his hands. He has continued in his dominant position since the Khmer Rouge took control of Cambodia in the spring of 1975. It is virtually certain that he is a member of Central Committee of the Khmer Communist Party and hence, with the other two deputy premiers, one of the dominant political personalities in Phnom Penh. He is regarded as a Khmer nationalist, a man of rare integrity, and an opponent of the Vietnamese.

GEORGE MARCHAIS
(France)

Marchais was born on 7 June 1920 in Hoguette (Calvados). At the age of 20 he was a lathe worker in the Paris region. He was mobilized for the war in December 1942, during the German occupation, and worked in Germany at the Messerschmitt factories. He claims to have returned to France in 1943, though the date is controversial.

After the liberation of France, Marchais continued as a specialized worker in an Issy-les-Moulineaux (suburb of Paris) factory and in 1947 joined the French Communist Party (PCF). At the end of 1949 he attended a trade union school for cadres and in 1950 was named secretary-general of the metal workers' trade union of Issy-les-Moulineaux. The following year he left the factory and became a permanent member of the apparatus—first of the General Confederation of Labor (CGT) and then of the PCF. In 1951 he was one of the leaders of the party's Seine federation and after its reorganization in Paris was named secretary of the Seine-Sud federation in 1954. At the Fourteenth Congress of the PCF, in July 1956, he was elected alternate member of the Central Committee and at the next congress, in 1959, was promoted to full membership besides being named alternate member of the Politburo. In 1961 he joined the Politburo as a full member and became secretary of the Central Committee in charge of organization. In February 1970, at the Nineteenth Congress of the PCF, he was named adjunct secretary-general. At the following congress, in December 1972, he replaced Valdeck Rochet as secretary-general.

During 1968-69 Marchais took part in numerous international meetings convened to organize the world conference of communist parties which finally took place in June 1969 in Moscow. He was a member of the French delegation at the gathering and chaired one of its sessions.

On 27 June 1972 he headed a delegation of the PCF to sign a joint Communist-Socialist program. In March 1973 he was elected deputy to the National Assembly for the first time. That same year he published a book entitled *Le Défi démocratique* (Democratic Challenge). In January 1975 he suffered a coronary complication but promptly recuperated and in April attended a meeting of the Central Committee.

NGUYEN HUU THO
(South Vietnam)

Nguyen Huu Tho was born in Cholon, South Vietnam, on 10 July 1910. In his early twenties (1929-32) he went to France, where he studied law. After receiving his degree, he returned to Vietnam and went into practice as a lawyer. He became actively engaged in politics after World War II, when he aligned himself with those seeking Vietnam's independence from the French. He was arrested by the government in 1950 for his part in initiating mass demonstrations on 19 March of that year protesting the arrival of U.S. ships and airplanes. He was not released from prison until 1952. In 1954 he resumed his law practice and became deputy chairman of the "Fight for Peace Committee" of the Saigon-Cholon district, a group engaged in agitation against the Ngo Dinh Diem government and the United States. Subsequently imprisoned, he escaped in 1961, at which time he disappeared from view, apparently devoting himself to activities in opposition to the Ngo Dinh Diem regime.

He was chosen as presiding chairman of the Central Committee of the National Liberation Front both at the First Congress, which was held from February to March 1962, and at the Second Congress in January 1964. When a "provisional government" was formed at the "Congress of People's Representatives of South Vietnam," which was held from 6 to 8 June 1969, he was selected as chairman of the Advisory Council of the "Provisional Revolutionary government of the Republic of South Vietnam" (PRG), a position he has retained since. He has also served as president of the Council of Wise Men. Although he may now be in poor health, he has continued to be a spokesman for the PRG since the communist assumption of power in the south.

CARLOS RAFAEL RODRÍGUEZ
(Cuba)

Carlos Rafael Rodríguez, who has long been the most important "old communist" in Fidel Castro's government, was born of middle-class stock on 23 May 1913. After receiving a solid Jesuit education, he gained highest distinctions while taking doctorates in law and social sciences. Rodríguez's early leftist activities occurred during his student days. In the early 1930s he agitated against the Machado government as a leader of the Student Directorate in his home town, Cienfuegos. He spent most of the 1935-39 period at the university and at the end of the decade promoted anti-Batista activities as a leader of the communist-dominated Ala Izquierda Estudiantil, which controlled university politics in Havana.

Rodríguez joined the Cuban Communist Party in 1937, and in only two years was elected to its Central Committee. By 1940 the communists had decided to collaborate with the Batista regime, and in 1944 Batista appointed Rodríguez minister without portfolio, with special responsibilities for education. In 1944 the communists adopted the People's Socialist Party (PSP) name and Rodríguez was elected to the party's Executive Bureau. Long interested in journalism, he edited leftist publications from the 1930s; between the late 1930s and the mid-1960s he served in editorial positions for several communist publications, most importantly the PSP theoretical journal, *Cuba Socialista*, and the party newspaper, *Hoy*.

Rodríguez was one of the first Cuban communists to become an ardent admirer of Fidel Castro. He went to the Sierra Cristal to see Raúl Castro in July 1958 and then on to the Sierra Maestra to see Fidel, remaining in the mountains most of the time between then and the fall of Batista in January 1959. As editor of *Hoy*, he was one of Castro's strongest supporters among Cuban communists from the beginning of 1959. In the early 1960s he was a professor of political science at Havana University and a member of the Higher Committee on University Reform; in March 1962 he became director of the National Institute of Agrarian Reform. In the mid-1960s he was once again appointed minister without portfolio, but this time by Fidel Castro, with special responsibilities for economic development in general and trade with the Soviet Bloc in particular. In this capacity he traveled frequently to Eastern Europe and the Soviet Union. During the early 1970s he attended conferences sponsored by the United Nations and other meetings in Europe and Latin America.

Carlos Rafael Rodríguez has had greater influence on Fidel Castro than any other "old communist," and more than most of Castro's 26th of July Movement followers, both as a member of the Secretariat of Castro's Communist Party, founded in 1965, and as a personal adviser to the premier. When the Executive Committee of the Council of Ministers was set up in November 1972, Rodríguez was put in charge of the Foreign Affairs Sector, a position he retained at the end of 1975. At the First Congress of the Cuban Communist Party in December 1975 he was reelected to the party Secretariat and appointed as well to the Political Bureau.

TENG HSIAO-P'ING
(China)

Teng Hsiao-p'ing, undoubtedly the effective leader of the Chinese government at this writing, was born in 1904 in western Szechuan province. He studied in France (where he joined the Chinese Communist Party in 1924), Belgium, and the Soviet Union, returning to China in 1926 to serve as political advisor to Feng Yu-hsiang. In 1927, Teng became advisor to Li Li-san, who headed the CCP at that time. In 1929, he served as commissar of the newly formed Red Seventh Army, which shifted its headquarters to Kiangsi Province. As a member of the Kiangsi army, Teng was known as a propagandist. During the decade of the thirties Teng had an active military career, participating in the Long March of 1934-35, contributing to Civil War victories by the Second Field Army, and becoming commissar of the 129th Division of the Eighth Route Army. In the forties his career moved into a political phase and by 1943 he had become director of the General Political Department of the CCP Revolutionary Military Committee. At the Seventh Congress of the party, in 1945, he was elected to the Central Committee.

In 1952 he was chosen to be on the National Committee of the Central Committee. He became as well deputy premier under Chou En-lai, and in 1953 was selected as vice-chairman of the Finance and Economic Committee, a post he held until 1954 when he became secretary-general of the Central Committee. He was active in national politics for the remainder of the decade and by 1960 was seventh in the list of party leaders. His career ran into trouble during the Cultural Revolution, at which time he was attacked on various posters. He disappeared completely from sight for a six-year period beginning in December 1966. It was alleged that he was an ally of Liu Shao-ch'i and he was blamed for sabotaging agricultural policy and the Socialist Education movement of the early sixties. He was finally rehabilitated in 1973, appearing at a banquet in April of that year, and not long after was reinstated as deputy premier. His membership on the Central Committee was reinstated at the Tenth Party Congress in August. At the National Party Conference in 1975 he was elected first among 10 deputy premiers and was made chief of staff of the People's Liberation Army.

With both Mao and Chou En-lai in apparent ill health, Teng now with little doubt has strong control of the government and may emerge as the new leader of China at some point in the near future. On the other hand, the fact that he appears to have made a good number of enemies in the party over the years should not be discounted as a potential source of opposition to him.

SELECT BIBLIOGRAPHY 1974-75

GENERAL ON COMMUNISM

Asprey, Robert B. *War in the Shadows: The Guerrilla in History*. Garden City, N.Y., Doubleday, 1975. 730 pp.

Clutterbuck, Richard. *Protest and the Urban Guerrilla*. New York, Abelard-Schuman, 1974. 309 pp.

Crozier, Brian (ed.). *Annual of Power and Conflict, 1974-75: Survey of Political Violence and International Influence*. London, Institute for the Study of Conflict, 1975. 167 pp.

——. *A Theory of Conflict*. New York, Scribner, 1975. 245 pp.

Dalton, George. *Economic Systems and Society: Capitalism, Communism and the Third World*. Baltimore, Penguin, 1974. 250 pp.

Deakin, F. W., H. Shukman, and H. T. Willetts. *A History of World Communism*. London, Weidenfeld & Nicolson, 1975. 177 pp.

Debray, Régis. *La critique des armes*. Paris, Seuil, 1974. 323 pp.

Fairbairn, Geoffrey. *Revolutionary Guerrilla Warfare: The Countryside Version*. Baltimore, Penguin, 1974. 400 pp.

Florence, Ronald. *Marx's Daughters: Eleanor Marx, Rosa Luxemburg, Angelica Balabanoff*. New York, Dial, 1975. 258 pp.

Hammond, Thomas T., and Robert Farrell (eds.). *The Anatomy of Communist Takeovers*. New Haven, Yale University Press, 1975. 664 pp.

Hook, Sidney. *Revolution, Reform, & Social Justice: Studies in the Theory and Practice of Marxism*. New York, New York University Press, 1975. 325 pp.

Hyams, Edward. *Terrorists and Terrorism*. New York, St. Martin's Press, 1974. 200 pp.

Jordan, Z. A. (ed.). *Karl Marx: Economy, Class and Social Revolution*. New York, Scribner, 1974. 332 pp.

Kiernan, E. Victor Gordon. *Marxism and Imperialism: Studies*. London, E. Arnold, 1974. 260 pp.

Leonhard, Wolfgang. *Three Faces of Marxism: The Political Concepts of Soviet Ideology, Maoism, and Humanist Marxism*. New York, Holt, Rinehart, 1974. 497 pp.

Martić, Miloš. *Insurrection: Five Schools of Revolutionary Thought*. New York, Dunellen, 1975. 342 pp.

McKnight, Gerald. *The Terrorist Mind: Why They Hijack, Kidnap, Bomb and Kill*. Indianapolis, Bobbs-Merrill, 1974. 182 pp.

Mesa-Lago, Carmelo, and Carl Beck (eds.). *Comparative Socialist Systems*. Pittsburgh, Center for International Studies, University of Pittsburgh, 1975. 441 pp.

Migdal, Joel S. *Peasants, Politics and Revolution*. Princeton, Princeton University Press, 1974. 310 pp.

Nagorski, Zygmunt, Jr. *The Psychology of East-West Trade: Illusions and Opportunities*. Mason & Lipscomb, 1974. 228 pp.

Niezing, Johan (ed.). *Urban Guerrilla*. Rotterdam, University Press, 1974. 149 pp.

Ozinga, James R. *Communism: A Tarnished Promise–The Story of an Idea.* Rochester, Mich., Oakland University, 1975. 264 pp.

Paepe, César de. *Entre Marx et Bakounine.* Paris, Maspero, 1974. 316 pp.

Prpić, George J. *A Century of World Communism.* Woodbury, N.Y., Barron's, 1974. 322 pp.

Radel, J.-Lucien. *Roots of Totalitarianism.* New York, Crane Russak, 1975. 218 pp.

Rubinstein, Alvin Z. (ed.). *Soviet and Chinese Influence in the Third World.* New York, Praeger, 1975. 231 pp.

Rush, Myron. *How Communist States Change Their Rulers.* Ithaca, N.Y., Cornell University Press, 1974. 346 pp.

Staar, Richard F. (ed.). *Yearbook on International Communist Affairs, 1975.* Stanford, Calif., Hoover Institution Press, 1975. 678 pp.

Weinstein, Warren (ed.). *Chinese and Soviet Aid to Africa.* New York, Praeger, 1975. 291 pp.

Wilkinson, Paul. *Political Terrorism.* New York, Wiley, 1975. 159 pp.

EASTERN EUROPE AND THE SOVIET UNION

Beyme, Klaus von. *Ökonomie und Politik im Sozialismus.* Munich, Piper, 1975. 411 pp.

Bociurkiw, Bohdan R., and John W. Strong (eds.). *Religion and Atheism in the U.S.S.R. and Eastern Europe.* Toronto, University of Toronto Press, 1975. 412 pp.

Burghardt, Andrew F. (ed.). *Development Regions in the Soviet Union, Eastern Europe, and Canada.* New York, Praeger, 1975. 192 pp.

Csikós-Nagy, Béla. *Socialist Price Theory and Price Policy.* Budapest, Kiadó Kossuth, 1975. 628 pp.

Ezergailis, Andrew. *The 1917 Revolution in Latvia.* New York, Columbia University Press, 1974. 281 pp.

Faber, Bernard Lewis (ed.). *The Social Structure of Eastern Europe.* New York, Praeger, 1975. 450 pp.

Fallenbuchl, Zbigniew M. (ed.). *Economic Development in the Soviet Union and Eastern Europe.* New York, Praeger, 1975. 2 vols.

Gawenda, Jerzy. *The Soviet Domination of Eastern Europe in the Light of International Law.* Richmond, Surrey, Foreign Affairs Publ., 1974. 200 pp.

Jahn, Wolfgang. *Sozialistische Integration zum Wohle unserer Völker.* East Berlin, Staatsverlag der DDR, 1974. 157 pp.

Kovaly, Pavel. *Rehumanization or Dehumanization? Philosophical Essays on Current Issues of Marxist Humanism.* Boston, Branden Press, 1974. 153 pp.

Kovrig, Bennett. *The Myth of Liberation: East-Central Europe in U.S. Diplomacy and Politics since 1941.* Baltimore, Johns Hopkins University Press, 1974. 360 pp.

Lavigne, Marie. *The Socialist Economies of the Soviet Union and Europe.* White Plains, N.Y., International Arts & Sciences, 1974. 396 pp.

Mellor, Roy E. H. *Eastern Europe: A Geography of the Comecon Countries.* New York, Columbia University Press, 1975. 358 pp.

Mieczkowski, Bogdan. *Personal and Social Consumption in Eastern Europe.* New York, Praeger, 1975. 344 pp.

Révész, László. *Militärische Ausbildung in Osteuropa.* Bern, Schweizerisches Ost-Institut, 1975. 302 pp.

Shanor, Donald R. *Soviet Europe.* New York, Harper & Row, 1975. 252 pp.

Simon, Jeffrey. *Ruling Communist Parties and Détente.* Washington, D.C., American Enterprise Institute, 1975. 314 pp.

Starr, Robert. *East-West Business Transactions.* New York, Praeger, 1974. 596 pp.

Steele, Alexander. *How to Spy on the U.S.* New Rochelle, N.Y., Arlington House, 1974. 185 pp.

Steele, Jonathan (ed.). *Eastern Europe since Stalin.* New York, Crane Russak, 1974. 215 pp.

Sydov, Werner (ed.). *Forschung und Entwicklung im RGW.* Berlin, Die Wirtschaft, 1974. 218 pp.

Szporluk, Roman (ed.). *The Influence of East Europe on the USSR.* New York, Praeger, 1975. 280 pp.

Volgyes, Ivan (ed.). *Political Socialization in Eastern Europe.* New York, Praeger, 1975. 199 pp.

Wädekin, Karl-Eugen. *Sozialistische Agrarpolitik in Osteuropa.* Berlin, Duncker & Humblot, 1974. 238 pp.

Wilczyński, Józef. *Technology in Comecon.* New York, Praeger, 1975. 379 pp.

EASTERN EUROPE

Adam, Jan. *Wage, Price and Taxation Policy in Czechoslovakia, 1948-1970.* Berlin, Duncker & Humblot, 1974. 231 pp.

Akademie der Wissenschaften. *DDR, Werden und Wachsen.* East Berlin, Dietz, 1974. 576 pp.

Bardhosi, Besim, and Theodhor Kareco. *The Economic and Social Development of the People's Republic of Albania During Thirty Years of the People's Power.* Tirana, "8 Nëntori," 1974. 247 pp.

Clissold, Stephen. *Yugoslavia and the Soviet Union, 1939-1973: A Documentary Survey.* London, Oxford University Press, 1975. 368 pp.

Dedijer, Vladimir, et al. *History of Yugoslavia.* New York, McGraw-Hill, 1974. 752 pp.

Devedjiev, Hristo H. *Stalinization of the Bulgarian Society, 1949-1953.* Philadelphia, Dorrance, 1975. 216 pp.

Djilas, Milovan. *Parts of a Lifetime.* New York, Harcourt, Brace, Jovanovich, 1975. 442 pp.

Dubey, Vinod. *Yugoslavia: Development with Decentralization.* Baltimore, Johns Hopkins University Press, 1975. 490 pp.

Farkas, Richard P. *Yugoslav Economic Development and Political Change.* New York, Praeger, 1975. 133 pp.

Fiedler, Helene. *SED und Staatsmacht.* East Berlin, Dietz, 1974. 387 pp.

Gabanyi, Anneli Ute. *Partei und Literatur in Rumaenien seit 1945.* Munich, Oldenbourg, 1975. 209 pp.

Gilberg, Trond. *Modernization in Romania since World War II.* New York, Praeger, 1975. 261 pp.

Gorupić, Vlado. *The Enterprise and the Development of the Yugoslav Economic System.* Zagreb, Ekonomski Institut, 1974. 159 pp.

Hacker, Jens. *Der Rechtsstatus Deutschlands aus der Sicht der DDR.* Cologne, Wissenschaft & Politik, 1974. 508 pp.

Hagemann, Michael, and Alenka Klemenčič. *Die Sozialistische Marktwirtschaft Jugoslawiens.* Stuttgart, Fischer, 1974. 303 pp.

History of the Revolutionary Workers' Movement in Hungary, 1944-1962. Budapest, Corvina, 1974. 387 pp.

Hoxha, Enver. *Selected Works.* Tirana, "8" Nëntori," 1974. 850 pp.

Institut für Marxismus-Leninismus. *Studien zur Geschichte der Kommunistischen Internationale.* East Berlin, Dietz, 1974. 800 pp.

——. *Dokumente und Materialien der Zusammenarbeit der SED und der KPSU, 1971-1974.* East Berlin, Dietz, 1975. 256 pp.

Janković, Dragoslav, et al. (eds.). *Historiography of Yugoslavia.* Belgrade, Association of Yugoslav Historical Societies, 1975. 522 pp.

Komorowski, Eugeniusz. *Night Never Ending.* Chicago, Regnery, 1974. 285 pp.

Leptin, Gert (ed.). *Die Rolle der DDR in Osteuropa.* Berlin, Duncker & Humblot, 1974. 122 pp.

Lindemann, Hans, and Kurt Mueller. *Auswärtige Kulturpolitik der DDR.* Bad Godesberg, Neue Gesellschaft, 1974. 212 pp.

Lorenz, Lothar. *Volksrepublik Albanien.* Giessen, Achenbach, 1974. 204 pp.

Lukacs, Georg. *Tactics and Ethics: Political Essays, 1919-1929.* New York, Harper & Row, 1974. 257 pp.

Marmullaku, Ramadan. *Albania and the Albanians.* Hamden, Conn., Archon, 1975. 178 pp.

Miller, Marshall Lee. *Bulgaria during the Second World War.* Stanford, Calif., Stanford University Press, 1975. 290 pp.

Mitzscherling, Peter, et al. *D.D.R.-Wirtschaft.* Frankfurt/Main, Fischer, 1974. 462 pp.

Murgescu, Costin. *Romania's Socialist Economy.* Bucharest, Meridiane, 1974. 78 pp.

Orlik, I. I., et al. *Sotsialisticheskaia Respublika Rumyniia.* Moscow, Nauka, 1974. 190 pp.

Otetea, Andrea. *History of the Romanian People.* Bucharest, Scientific Publ., 1975. 637 pp.

Party of Labour of Albania on the Building and the Life of the Party. Tirana, "8 Nëntori," 1975. 336 pp.

Piekalkiewicz, Jaroslaw. *Communist Local Government: A Study of Poland.* Athens, Ohio, Ohio University Press, 1975. 282 pp.

Pinkus, Theo (ed.). *Conversations with Lukács.* Cambridge, Mass., MIT Press, 1975. 155 pp.

Programme of the Romanian Communist Party for the Building of the Multilaterally Developed Socialist Society and Romania's Advance toward Communism. Bucharest, Agerpres, 1975. 219 pp.

Ratiu, Ion. *Contemporary Romania.* Richmond, Surrey, Foreign Affairs Publ., 1975. 138 pp.

Rodionov, N. N., and I. Mariai (eds.). *Sovetsko-Vengerskie otnosheniia, 1948-1970 gg.: dokumenty i materialy.* Moscow, Politizdat, 1974. 726 pp.

Ronneberger, Franz, and Borislav Radovanović (eds.). *Sozialer Wandel in Jugoslawien.* Cologne, Wissenschaft & Politik, 1974. 380 pp.

Sindermann, Horst. *Erfolgreich voran auf dem Kurs des VIII. Parteitages.* East Berlin, Dietz, 1975. 513 pp.

Smaus, Gerlinda. *Der Kulturarbeiter der CSSR.* Bern, Lang, 1974. 207 pp.

Staar, Richard F. *Poland, 1944-1962.* Westport, Conn., Greenwood Press, 1975. 300 pp.

Starrels, John M., and Anita M. Mallinckrodt. *Politics in the German Democratic Republic.* New York, Praeger, 1975. 350 pp.

Ulč, Otto. *Politics in Czechoslovakia.* San Francisco, Freeman, 1974. 181 pp.

Valori, Giancarlo Elia. *Ceaușescu.* Paris, Grasset & Fasquelle, 1975. 185 pp.

Weber, Hermann. *Die SED nach Ulbricht.* Hanover, Fackelträger, 1974. 135 pp.

Zhivkov, Todor. *Modern Bulgaria: Problems and Tasks of Building an Advanced Socialist Society.* New York, International Publ., 1974. 238 pp.

Zukin, Sharon. *Beyond Marx and Tito.* New York, Cambridge University Press, 1975. 272 pp.

SOVIET UNION

Aminova, R. Kh., et al. (eds.). *Ocherki istorii kommunisticheskoi partii Uzbekistana.* Tashkent, "Uzbekistan," 1974. 768 pp.

Anweiler, Oskar. *The Soviets.* New York, Pantheon, 1974. 337 pp.

Bernier, Wolfgang, et al. (eds.). *Sowjetunion 1974/75.* Munich, Hanser, 1975. 298 pp.

Bethell, Nicholas. *The Last Secret.* New York, Basic Books, 1974. 224 pp.

Borisov, O. B., and V. T. Koloskov. *Sino-Soviet Relations, 1945-1973.* Moscow, Progress, 1975. 336 pp.

Bortoli, Georges. *The Death of Stalin.* New York, Praeger, 1975. 214 pp.

Brezhnev, Leonid I. *The CPSU in the Struggle for Unity of all Revolutionary and Peace Forces.* Moscow, Progress, 1975. 300 pp.

Brokhim, Yuri. *Sex and Crime in Russia Today.* New York, Dial, 1975. 203 pp.

Carmichael, Joel. *Trotsky.* New York, St. Martin's Press, 1975. 512 pp.

Chalidze,. Valery. *To Defend These Rights.* New York, Random House, 1974. 340 pp.

Chambre, Henri. *L'evolution du marxisme sovietique.* Paris, Seuil, 1974. 475 pp.

Clem, Ralph S. (ed.). *The Soviet West.* New York, Praeger, 1975. 161 pp.

Denikin, Anton I. *The Career of a Tsarist Officer.* Minneapolis, University of Minnesota Press, 1975. 333 pp.

Desanti, Dominique. *Les staliniens 1944-1956: une expérience politique.* Paris, Fayard, 1975. 383 pp.

Dolgun, Alexander, with Patrick Watson. *Alexander Dolgun's Story: An American in the Gulag.* New York, Knopf, 1975. 370 pp.

Dziuba, Ivan. *Internationalism or Russification?* New York, Monad, 1974. 262 pp.

Edmonds, Robin. *Soviet Foreign Policy, 1962-1973.* New York, Oxford University Press, 1975. 197 pp.

Eichenbaum, V. M. (pseud., Voline). *The Unknown Revolution, 1917-1921.* New York, Free Life, 1974. 717 pp.

Eissenstat, Bernard W. (ed.). *The Soviet Union.* Lexington, Mass., Heath, 1975. 356 pp.

Elleinstein, Jean. *Histoire du Phénomène Stalinien.* Paris, Grasset, 1975. 248 pp.

Evans, Michael. *Karl Marx.* Bloomington, Indiana University Press, 1975. 215 pp.

Feldbrugge, F. J. M. *Samizdat and Political Dissent in the Soviet Union.* Leyden, Sijthoff, 1975. 255 pp.

Freedman, Robert O. *Soviet Policy toward the Middle East since 1970.* New York, Praeger, 1975. 198 pp.

Geyer, Georgie Anne. *The Young Russians.* Homewood, Ill., ETC, 1975. 295 pp.

Gilison, Jerome M. *The Soviet Image of Utopia.* Baltimore, Johns Hopkins University Press, 1975. 192 pp.

Girke, Wolfgang, and Helmut Jachnow (eds.). *Sprache und Gesellschaft in der Sowjetunion.* Munich, Fink, 1975. 381 pp.

Goldhamer, Herbert. *The Soviet Soldier: Soviet Military Management at the Troop Level.* New York, Crane Russak, 1975. 348 pp.

Goldman, Marshall I. *Détente and Dollars.* New York, Basic Books, 1975. 337 pp.

Gouré, Leon, and Morris Rothenberg. *Soviet Penetration of Latin America.* Coral Gables, Fla., Center for Advanced International Studies, 1975. 204 pp.

Gruber, Helmut. *Soviet Russia Masters the Comintern.* Garden City, N.Y., Doubleday, 1974. 544 pp.

Haimson, Leopold H. (ed.). *The Mensheviks.* Chicago, University of Chicago Press, 1974. 476 pp. Published with the Hoover Institution.

Kanet, Robert E., and Donna Bahry (eds.). *Soviet Economic and Political Relations with the Developing World.* New York, Praeger, 1975. 300 pp.

Katz, Zev, Rosemarie Rogers, and Frederic Harned (eds.). *Handbook of Major Soviet Nationalities.* New York, Free Press, 1975. 481 pp.

Kirk, Irina. *Profiles in Russian Resistance.* New York, Quadrangle, 1975. 297 pp.

Kohler, Foy D., and Mose L. Harvey (eds.). *The Soviet Union: Yesterday, Today, Tomorrow.* Coral Gables, Fla., Center for Advanced International Studies, 1975. 220 pp.

Lane, David Stuart. *Roots of Russian Communism.* University Park, Pennsylvania State University Press, 1975. 256 pp.

Lenin, V. I., and Leon Trotsky. *Lenin's Fight against Stalinism.* New York, Pathfinder, 1975. 160 pp.

Lewin, Moshe. *Political Undercurrents in Soviet Economic Debates.* Princeton, Princeton University, 1974. 374 pp.

Liebman, Marcel. *Leninism under Lenin.* London, Cape, 1975. 477 pp.

Liegle, Ludwig. *The Family's Role in Soviet Education.* New York, Springer, 1975. 186 pp.

Lobusov, V., et al. (comps.). *Organizatsionno-ustavnye voprosy komsomol'skoi raboty.* Moscow, Molodaya Gvardiya, 1974. 175 pp.

Lourie, Richard. *Letters to the Future: An Approach to Siniavskii-Tertz.* Ithaca, N.Y., Cornell University Press, 1975. 221 pp.

Mandel, William M. *Soviet Women.* New York, Doubleday, 1975. 350 pp.

McCauley, Martin (ed.). *The Russian Revolution and the Soviet State, 1917-1921: Documents.* New York, Barnes & Noble, 1975. 315 pp.

McLane, Charles B. *Soviet-African Relations.* London, Central Asian Research Centre, 1974. 190 pp.

McLaurin, Ronald De. *The Middle East in Soviet Policy.* Lexington, Mass., Heath, 1975. 206 pp.

McNeal, Robert H. *The Bolshevik Tradition: Lenin, Stalin, Khrushchev, Brezhnev.* Englewood Cliffs, N.J., Prentice-Hall, 1975. 210 pp.

Medvedev, Roy A. *On Socialist Democracy.* New York, Knopf, 1975. 405 pp.

Mehnert, Klaus. *Moscow and the New Left.* Berkeley and Los Angeles, University of California Press, 1975. 275 pp.

Moroz, Valentyn. *Report from the Beria Reserve.* Chicago, Cataract, 1974. 162 pp.

Morozov, Michael. *L'establishment soviétique.* Paris, Fayard, 1974. 257 pp.

Morton, Henry W., and Rudolf L. Tökés (eds.). *Soviet Politics and Society in the 1970's.* New York, Free Press, 1974. 401 pp.

Navrozov, Lev. *The Education of Lev Navrozov.* New York, Harper's Magazine, 1975. 628 pp.

Nicolaevsky, Boris I. *Power and the Soviet Elite.* Ann Arbor, University of Michigan Press, 1975. 275 pp.

Nove, Alec. *Stalinism and After.* London, Allen & Unwin, 1975. 205 pp.

Pearson, Michael. *The Sealed Train.* New York, Putnam, 1975. 320 pp.

Pethybridge, Roger. *The Social Prelude to Stalinism.* New York, St. Martin's Press, 1974. 343 pp.

Powell, David E. *Antireligious Propaganda in the Soviet Union.* Cambridge, Mass., MIT Press, 1975. 206 pp.

Remnek, Richard B. *Soviet Scholars and Soviet Foreign Policy.* Durham, N.C., Carolina Academic Press, 1975. 343 pp.

Rosenstone, Robert A. *Romantic Revolutionary: A Biography of John Reed.* New York, Knopf, 1975. 430 pp.

Rosenthal, Gérard. *Avocat de Trotsky.* Paris, Laffont, 1975. 330 pp.

Ryavec, Karl W. *Implementation of Soviet Economic Reforms.* New York, Praeger, 1975. 360 pp.

Sakharov, Andrei D. *My Country and The World.* New York, Knopf, 1975. 109 pp.

Schwartz, Morton. *The Foreign Policy of the USSR.* Encino, Calif., Dickenson, 1975. 214 pp.

Serge, Victor, and Natalia Sedova Trotsky. *The Life and Death of Leon Trotsky.* New York, Basic Books, 1975. 296 pp.

Smith, Canfield F. *Vladivostok under Red and White Rule: Revolution and Counterrevolution in the Russian Far East, 1920-1922.* Seattle, University of Washington Press, 1975. 286 pp.

Solzhenitsyn, Aleksandr I. *The Gulag Archipelago, 1918-1956.* Vol. 2. New York, Harper & Row, 1975. 712 pp.

——. *Lenin v. Zurikhe*. Paris, YMCA Press, 1975. 240 pp.

——. *Mir i nasilie*. Frankfurt/Main, Possev, 1974. 103 pp.

——. *Pis'mo vozhdiam Sovetskogo Soiiuza*. Paris, YMCA Press, 1974. 50 pp.

——, et al. *Iz pod glyb*. Paris, YMCA Press, 1974. 276 pp.

Suslov, Mikhail. *Marxism-Leninism–The International Teaching of the Working Class*. Moscow, Progress, 1975. 245 pp.

Szamuely, Tibor. *The Russian Tradition*. New York, McGraw-Hill, 1974. 443 pp.

Tarsis, Valerii. *Palata no. 7*. Frankfurt/Main, Possev, 1974. 148 pp.

Tökés, Rudolf L. (ed.). *Dissent in the USSR*. Baltimore, Johns Hopkins University Press, 1975. 453 pp.

Trepper, Leopold. *Die Wahrheit: Ich War der Chef der Roten Kapelle*. Munich, Kindler, 1975. 440 pp.

Tucker, Robert C. (ed.). *The Lenin Anthology*. New York, Norton, 1975. 764 pp.

Ulam, Adam. *The Russian Political System*. New York, Random House, 1974. 180 pp.

Unger, Aryeh L. *The Totalitarian Party*. New York, Cambridge University Press, 1974. 286 pp.

Vloyantes, John P. *Silk Glove Hegemony: Finnish-Soviet Relations, 1944-1974*. Kent, Ohio, Kent State University Press, 1975. 208 pp.

Wassmund, Hans. *Kontinuität im Wandel*. Cologne, Böhlau, 1974. 125 pp.

Wilson, Edward Thomas. *Russia and Black Africa before World War II*. New York, Holmes & Meier, 1974. 397 pp.

WESTERN EUROPE

Abril, abril: Textos escritores comunistas. Lisbon, Avante, 1975. 196 pp.

Alfonsi, Philippe, and Patrick Pesnot. *Vivre à gauche*. Paris, Albin Michel, 1975. 475 pp.

Andreu, Anne, and Jean-Louis Mignalon. *L'adhésion: les nouveaux communistes de 1975*. Paris, Calman Lévy, 1975. 240 pp.

Auciello, Nicola. *Socialismo e egemonia en Gramsci e Togliatti*. Bari, De Donato, 1974. 201 pp.

Berlinguer, Enrico. *Unita del popolo per salvare l'Italia*. Rome, Riuniti, 1975. 112 pp.

Birchall, Ian H. *Workers against the Monolith: The Communist Parties since 1943*. London, Pluto, 1974. 256 pp.

Black, Robert. *Stalinism in Britain*. London, Park, 1975. 440 pp.

Blackmer, Donald L. M., and Sidney Tarrow (eds.). *Communism in Italy and France*. Princeton, Princeton University Press, 1975. 492 pp.

Brown, Bernard E. *Protest in Paris: Anatomy of a Revolt*. Morristown, N.J., General Learning Press, 1974. 240 pp.

Carillo, Santiago. *Amanhã a Espanha*. Lisbon, Europa-América, 1975. 223 pp.

——. *A Espanha após o franquismo*. Lisbon, Futura, 1975. 107 pp.

Cunhal, Alvaro. *The Democratic and National Revolution*. New York, International Publ., 1975. 216 pp.

——. *Discursos políticos*. Lisbon, Avante, 1975. 2 vols.

——. *Relatório da actividade do Comité Central ao VI congresso do PCP*. Lisbon, Avante, 1975. 215 pp.

——. *Rumo a vitória*. Lisbon, Avante, 1975. 221 pp.

A defesa acusa: os comunistas Portuguêses perante a polícia e os tribunais fascistas. Lisbon, Avante, 1975. 246 pp.

Deutschland dem deutschen Volk: Erklärung des ZK der KPD/ML zur nationalen Frage. Hamburg, Roter Morgen, 1974. 44 pp.

Dreyfus, François-Georges. *Histoire des gauches en France (1940-1974).* Paris, Grasset, 1974. 376 pp.

Dupuy, Fernand. *Etre maire communiste.* Paris, Calman Levy, 1975. 254 pp.

Filipec, Jindrich, et al. *Sozialismus-Imperialismus-wissenschaftlich-technische Revolution.* Frankfurt/Main, Marxistische Blätter, 1974. 128 pp.

Franz, Hans Werner, and Santiago Tovar. *Klassenkämpfe in Spanien heute.* Frankfurt/Main, Marxistische Blätter, 1974. 160 pp.

Harris, André, and Alain de Sédouy. *Voyage à l'intérieur du Parti Communiste.* Paris, Seuil, 1974. 440 pp.

Hermet, Guy. *The Communists in Spain.* Lexington, Mass., Heath, 1974. 238 pp.

La Huelga general de Pamplona: un balance por ETA-VI. Lausanne, Liga Marxista Revolucionaria, 1974. 64 pp.

Kukko, Lüsa, and H. Keim. *Klassenkämpfe in Finnland heute.* Frankfurt/Main, Marxistische Blätter, 1974. 160 pp.

Landau, Jacob M. *Radical Politics in Modern Turkey.* Leiden, Brill, 1974. 315 pp.

Latouche, Serge. *Le projet marxiste.* Paris, Presses Universitaires, 1975. 208 pp.

Lindemann, Albert S. *The Red Years: European Socialism versus Bolshevism, 1919-1921.* Berkeley and Los Angeles, University of California Press, 1974. 349 pp.

López Trujillo, Alfonso. *Liberación marxista y liberación cristiana.* Madrid, Católica, 1974. 276 pp.

Macciocchi, Maria Antonietta. *Letters from Inside the Italian Communist Party to Louis Althusser.* Atlantic Highlands, N.J., Humanities Press, 1975. 341 pp.

MacStiofáin, Séan. *Revolutionary in Ireland.* New York, Atheneum, 1975. 372 pp.

Marchais, Georges. *La politique du Parti Communiste Français.* Paris, Editions Sociales, 1974. 96 pp.

Matkovskiy, N. V., et al. (eds.). *Polozhenie i bor'ba britanskogo rabochego klassa.* Moscow, Nauka, 1974. 352 pp.

McInnes, Neil. *The Communist Parties of Western Europe.* London, Oxford University Press, 1975. 209 pp.

Nenni, Pietro. *I nodi della politica estera Italiana.* Milan, Sugar, 1975. 315 pp.

Norris, Russell Bradner. *God, Marx, and the Future: Dialogue with Roger Garaudy.* Philadelphia, Fortress Press, 1974. 210 pp.

Oliveira, Cesar. *O primeiro Congresso do PCP.* Lisbon, Seara Nova, 1975. 98 pp.

Oliveira, Franklin. *A resposta comunista ás nossas perguntas.* Braga, Oliveira, 1975. 131 pp.

A palavra do PCP: discursos de camaradas do CC do PCP em comícios. Lisbon, Avante, 1975. 236 pp.

Parti Communiste Français. *Congrès national.* Paris, 1974. 130 pp.

Partido Comunista Português. *Documentos do Comitê central, 1965-1974.* Lisbon, Avante, 1975. 446 pp.

———. *Programa e estatutos do PCP: aprovados no VI congresso (extraordinario).* Lisbon, Avante, 1974. 111 pp.

Partito Communista Italiano. *VI. conferenza operaia del PCI.* Rome, Riuniti, 1974. 336 pp.

Pereira de Abreu, Miguel. *Portugal: Rumo ao comunismo?* Porto, Autor, 1974. 79 pp.

A revolução das Flores. Lisbon, Aster, 1974-1975. 3 vols.

La ricera storica marxista in Italia. Rome, Riuniti, 1974. 160 pp.

Sociologie du communisme en Italie. Paris, Armand Colin, 1974. 245 pp.

Soulie, Michel. *Le cartel des gauches et la crise présidentielle.* Paris, Dullis, 1974. 334 pp.

Terceiro congresso de oposiçao democrática, aveiro 4 a 8 de abril de 1973: teses. Lisbon, Seara Nova, 1974. 259 pp.

Thälmann, Paul. *Wo die Freiheit stirbt: Stationen eines politischen Kampfes.* Munich, Walter, 1974. 270 pp.

Togliatti, Palmiro. *Opere scelte.* Rome, Riuniti, 1974. 1,190 pp.

Vieuguet, André. *Français et immigrés: le combat du Parti Communiste Français.* Paris, Editions Sociales, 1975. 221 pp.

ASIA AND THE PACIFIC

Baum, Richard. *Prelude to Revolution: Mao, the Party and the Peasant Question, 1962-66.* New York, Columbia University Press, 1975. 222 pp.

Cayrac-Blanchard, Francoise. *Le Parti Communiste Indonésien.* Paris, Armand Colin, 1973. 217 pp.

Chai, Winberg. *In Search for a New China.* New York, Putnam, 1975. 316 pp.

Communist Party of India. *Guidelines of the History of the Communist Party of India.* New Delhi, Sengupta, 1974. 134 pp.

Dai, Shen-Yu. *China, the Superpowers and the Third World: A Handbook on Comparative World Politics.* Hong Kong, The Chinese University, 1974. 420 pp.

Deacon, Richard. *The Chinese Secret Service.* New York, Taplinger, 1974. 523 pp.

Delleyne, Jan. *The Chinese Economy.* New York, Harper & Row, 1974. 207 pp.

Dittmer, Lowell. *Liu Shao-Ch'i and the Chinese Cultural Revolution.* Berkeley and Los Angeles, University of California Press, 1974. 386 pp.

Elvin, Mark, and G. William Skinner (eds.). *The Chinese City between Two Worlds.* Stanford, Calif., Stanford University Press, 1974. 471 pp.

Étienne, Gilbert. *La Voie chinoise: la Longue Marche de l'économie, 1949-1974.* Paris, Presses Universitaires, 1974. 357 pp.

Fan, K. H., and K. T. Fan (eds.). *From the Other Side of the River: A Self Portrait of China Today.* New York, Doubleday, 1975. 429 pp.

Fletcher, Merton Don. *Workers and Commissars: Trade Union Policy in the People's Republic of China.* Bellingham, Western Washington State College, 1974. 148 pp.

Garth, Bryant G., et al. (eds.). *China's Changing Role in the World Economy.* New York, Praeger, 1975. 250 pp.

Giap, Vo Nguyen. *People's War against U.S. Aeronaval War.* Hanoi, Foreign Languages Publ., 1975. 223 pp.

———. *To Arm the Revolutionary Masses, to Build the People's Army.* Hanoi, Foreign Languages Publ., 1975. 233 pp.

Graff, Violette. *Les partis communistes Indiens.* Paris, Fondation Nationale des Sciences Politiques, 1974. 333 pp.

Horvath, Janos. *The Net Cost of Chinese Foreign Aid.* New York, Praeger, 1975. 250 pp.

Hsiung, James Chieh (ed.). *The Logic of "Maoism."* New York, Praeger, 1974. 231 pp.

Karol, K. S. (pseud., Karol Kewes). *The Second Chinese Revolution.* New York, Hill & Wang, 1975. 472 pp.

Kim, Ilpyong J. *Communist Politics in North Korea.* New York, Praeger, 1975. 140 pp.

Kim, Joung-won Alexander. *Divided Korea: The Politics of Development, 1945-1972.* Cambridge, Mass., Harvard University Press, 1975. 471 pp.

Kotovskiy, G. G., and P. V. Kutsobin (eds.). *Respublika Shri Lanka.* Moscow, Nauka, 1974. 230 pp.

Leigh, Michael B. *The Rising Moon: Political Change in Sarawak.* Sydney, University Press, 1974. 232 pp.

Lien, Chan (ed.). *Proceedings of the Third Sino-American Conference on Mainland China.* Taipei, Tong-Hsing, 1974. 986 pp.

Schram, Stuart (ed.). *Chairman Mao Talks to the People.* New York, Pantheon, 1974. 352 pp.

Short, Anthony. *The Communist Insurrection in Malaya: 1948-1960.* New York, Crane Russak, 1975. 546 pp.

Simmons, Robert R. *The Strained Alliance: Peking, Pyongyang, Moscow and the Politics of the Korean Civil War.* New York, Free Press, 1975. 270 pp.

Snow, Lois Wheeler. *A Death with Dignity: When the Chinese Came.* New York, Random House, 1975. 148 pp.

Thurston, Donald R. *Teachers and Politics in Japan.* Princeton, Princeton University Press, 1974. 352 pp.

Turner, Robert F. *Vietnamese Communism: Its Origins and Development.* Stanford, Calif., Hoover Institution Press, 1975. 517 pp.

Varkey, Ouseph. *At the Crossroads: The Sino-Indian Border Dispute and the Communist Party in India, 1959-1963.* Calcutta, Minerva, 1974. 304 pp.

Yeh Ch'ing (Jen Tso-hsuan). *Inside Mao Tse-tung Thought.* Hicksville, N.Y., Exposition Press, 1975. 336 pp.

Yu, George T. *China's African Policy: A Study of Tanzania.* New York, Praeger, 1975. 224 pp.

Zasloff, Joseph J., and MacAlister Brown (eds.). *Communism in Indochina.* Lexington, Mass., Heath, 1975. 295 pp.

THE AMERICAS

Alisky, Marvin. *Peruvian Political Perspective.* Tempe, Ariz., Center for Latin American Studies, Arizona State University, 1975. 44 pp.

Avakumovic, Ivan. *The Communist Party in Canada.* Toronto, McClelland & Stewart, 1975. 309 pp.

Baini, Alberto. *Pro y contra Castro.* Madrid, Edifrans & Mandadori, 1975. 159 pp.

Bender, Lynn Darrell. *The Politics of Hostility: Castro's Revolution and U.S. Policy.* Hato Rey, P.R., Inter-American University Press, 1975. 156 pp.

Breve historia de la Unidad Popular. Santiago, El Mercurio, 1974. 510 pp.

Broderick, Walter J. *Camilo Torres: A Biography of the Priest-Guerrillero.* Garden City, N.Y., Doubleday, 1975. 370 pp.

Caute, David. *Cuba, Yes?* New York, McGraw-Hill, 1974. 206 pp.

Cerda, Carlos. *Génocide au Chili.* Paris, Maspero, 1974. 134 pp.

Córdova-Claure, Luis Eduardo. *Los años 60, Cuba vs. USA.* Buenos Aires, Cuarto Mundo, 1974. 133 pp.

Cotler, Julio, and Richard R. Fagen (eds.). *Latin America and the United States: The Changing Political Realities.* Stanford, Calif., Stanford University Press, 1974. 428 pp.

Debray, Régis. *La guérilla du Che.* Paris, Seuil, 1974. 187 pp.

Deslois, Christian. *Chili, 1970-1974.* Paris, Tautin, 1974. 151 pp.

Goodsell, James Nelson (comp.). *Fidel Castro's Personal Revolution in Cuba, 1959-1973.* New York, Knopf, 1975. 349 pp.

Hodges, Donald C. *The Latin-American Revolution: Politics and Strategy from Apro-Marxism to Guevarism.* New York, Morrow, 1974. 287 pp.

Jackson, Sir Geoffrey. *Surviving the Long Night: An Autobiographical Account of a Political Kidnapping.* New York, Vanguard, 1974. 226 pp.

Jackson, James E. *Revolutionary Tracings.* New York, International Publ., 1974. 263 pp.

Jaffe, Philip J. *The Rise and Fall of American Communism.* New York, Horizon, 1975. 236 pp.

Joxe, Alain. *Le Chili sous Allende.* Paris, Gallimard/Julliard, 1974. 263 pp.

Lipschütz, Alexander. *Marx y Lenin en la América Latina y los problemas idigenistas.* Havana, Casa de las Américas, 1974. 224 pp.

Macaulay, Neill. *The Prestes Column: Revolution in Brazil.* New York, New Viewpoints, 1974. 281 pp.

Mankiewicz, Frank, and Kirby Jones. *With Fidel: A Portrait of Castro and Cuba.* New York, Simon & Schuster, 1975. 269 pp.

Matthews, Herbert L. *Revolution in Cuba: An Essay in Understanding.* New York, Scribner, 1975. 468 pp.

Mesa-Lago, Carmelo. *Cuba in the 1970s: Pragmatism and Institutionalization.* Albuquerque, University of New Mexico Press, 1974. 179 pp.

Nicholson, Joe, Jr. *Inside Cuba.* New York, Sheed & Ward, 1974. 235 pp.

O'Brien, Philip (ed.). *Allende's Chile.* New York, Praeger, 1975. 225 pp.

Orrego Vicuña, Francisco (ed.). *Chile: The Balanced Views.* Santiago, Institute of International Studies, University of Chile, 1975. 297 pp.

Rama, Carlos M. *Chile: mil días entre la revolución y el fascismo.* Barcelona, Planeta, 1974. 233 pp.

Raptis, Michel. *Revolution and Counter-Revolution in Chile.* New York, St. Martin's Press, 1975. 174 pp.

Ravines, Eudocio. *El rescate de Chile.* Mexico, G. de Anda, 1974. 303 pp.

Ritter, Archibald R. M. *The Economic Development of Revolutionary Cuba.* New York, Praeger, 1974. 394 pp.

Spilimbergo, Jorge Enea. *La cuestión nacional en Marx.* Buenos Aires, Ediciones Octubre, 1974. 226 pp.

Szajkowski, Zosa. *The Impact of the 1919-20 Red Scare on American Jewish Life.* New York, Ktav Publ., 1974. 398 pp.

Thomas, Tony (comp.). *Black Liberation and Socialism.* New York, Pathfinder, 1974. 207 pp.

Vergara, Jose Manuel, and Florence Varas. *Coup! Allende's Last Day.* New York, Stein & Day, 1975. 182 pp.

Vickers, George R. *Formation of the New Left: The Early Years.* Lexington, Mass., Heath, 1975. 166 pp.

Weather Underground. *Prairie Fire: Politics of Revolutionary Anti-Imperialism.* San Francisco, Communications Co., 1974. 186 pp.

White, Judy (ed.). *Chile's Days of Terror.* New York, Pathfinder, 1974. 124 pp.

Wilson, Major Carlos. *The Tupamaros; the Unmentionables.* Boston, Branden Press, 1974. 171 pp.

MIDDLE EAST AND AFRICA

Africa Information Service. *Return to the Source: Selected Speeches of Amilcar Cabral.* New York, Monthly Review, 1974. 110 pp.

Alla, Malumud Ata. *Arab Struggle for Economic Independence.* Moscow, Progress, 1974. 272 pp.

Beliaev, I. L., and E. M. Primakov. *Egipet vremia Prezidenta Nasera.* Moscow, Mysl, 1974. 399 pp.

Bertogli, Paola. *Il Marocco tra nazionalismo e rivoluzione.* Milan, Marsorati, 1974. 371 pp.

Beshir, Mohamed Omer. *Revolution and Nationalism in the Sudan.* New York, Barnes & Noble, 1974. 314 pp.

Bill, James, and Carl Leiden. *The Middle East: Politics and Power.* Boston, Allyn & Bacon, 1974. 287 pp.

Bunting, Brian. *Moses Kotane, South African Revolutionary: A Political Biography of the General Secretary of the South African Communist Party.* London, Inkululeko, 1975. 309 pp.

Dekmejian, R. Hrair. *Patterns of Political Leadership: Egypt, Israel, Lebanon.* Albany, State University of New York Press, 1975. 310 pp.

Faddah, Mohammad. *The Middle East in Transition.* New York, Asia Publishing House, 1974. 339 pp.

Humbaraci, Arslan, and Nicole Muchnik. *Portugal's African Wars.* New York, Third Press, 1975. 250 pp.

Kapungu, Leonard T. *Rhodesia: The Struggle for Freedom.* Mary Knoll, N.Y., Orbis Books, 1974. 117 pp.

Kazziha, Walid W. *Revolutionary Transformation in the Arab World: Habash and His Comrades from Nationalism to Marxism.* New York, St. Martin's Press, 1975. 118 pp.

Lenczowski, George (ed.). *Political Elites in the Middle East.* Washington, D.C., American Enterprise Institute, 1975. 227 pp.

Morris, Michael. *Armed Conflict in Southern Africa.* Cape Town, Jeremy Spence, 1974. 357 pp.

Naamani, Israel, David Rudavsky, and Abraham Katsh (eds.). *Israel: Its Politics and Philosophy.* New York, Behrmann, 1974. 434 pp.

Rudebeck, Lars. *Guinea-Bissau: A Study of Political Mobilization.* New York, Africana Publ., 1975. 277 pp.

Thompson, Virginia, and Richard Adloff. *Historical Dictionary of the People's Republic of the Congo (Congo-Brazzaville).* Metuchen, N.J., Scarecrow Press, 1974. 139 pp.

Vatin, Jean-Claude. *L'Algérie, politique, histoire et société.* Paris, Fondation Nationale des Sciences Politiques, 1974. 312 pp.

Venter, Al J. *The Zambesi Salient: Conflict in Southern Africa.* Old Greenwich, Conn., Devin-Adair, 1974. 395 pp.

INDEX OF NAMES

Llakaj, Veli, 7-8
Lleshi, Haxhi, 4
Lo, Emilio, 465
Lo Jui-ching, 262
Lobo, João, 446
Locke, Keith, 353
Lon Nol, 250-51, 604
Longo, Luigi, 15, 178, 191
López Arellano, Oswaldo, 492-93
López Michelsen, Alfonso, 456, 458
López Portillo, José, 501-2
López Rega, José, 432-34, 437
Lordinot, Gabriel, 494
Lorenz, Peter, 156, 158
Losonczi, Pál, 39, 43
Lovell, Frank, 527
Lu Phuong, 410
Lubonja, Todi, 3
Lucas García, Romeo, 486
Lucas Jollave, Leopoldo, 486
Ludviger, Emil, 99
Lugovskiy, Y., 296
Lukaszewicz, Jerzy, 52, 57
Lukman, Abdul Hamid, 368
Lumer, Hyman, 522, 524
Luneta, Jess, 366
Luong Trong Tuong, 426
Lussón, Antonio E., 465
von Luther, Sidney, 523
Luu Huu Phuoc, 410
Luvsanvandan, 347
Luxemburg, Rosa, 143, 147
Lyssarides, Vassos, 114, 117, 121, 574-75

Macapagal, Felicisimo, 363-65
MacArthur, Douglas A., 300, 302
MacBride, Sean, 578
Machado, Eduardo, 536
Machado, Gustavo, 534
Machado, José Ramón, 464
Machel, Samora, 566
Macovescu, Gheorghe, 66-67, 100
Madanat, 'Isa, 552
Madoyan, Artin, 556
Magnin, Armand, 224
Magnusson, Bruce, 447
Magsaysay, Ramon, 360
Mahendra (King), 350-51
Mahjub, 'Abd al-Khaliq, 567
Mahower, Moshe, 549
Maidana, Antonio, 509
Maidar, 347
Maidin, Abdul Rashid bin, 338
Maihofer, Werner, 144
Maiskii, Ivan, 349
Maisouk Saisompheng, 329
Makarios (Archbishop), 113-14, 116-22, 575, 586
Makorov, Valery V., 370
Malaka, Tan, 288
Malhotra, Avtar Singh, 280
Malik, Adam, 292, 295
Malmierca, Isidro, 464
Malo, Javer, 8
Maloney, Joan, 264

Mamaqi, Dashnor, 5-6
Manca, Alessandro, 186
Mandel, Ernest, 234-35
Mănescu, Manea, 59, 64-65, 67, 101
Manson, John Andrew, 353-54
Mao Tse-tung, 99,247-48, 252, 257-59, 261-67, 269, 273, 275-76, 310, 334-36, 338, 361, 369, 370, 379, 445, 607
Marchais, Georges, 15, 112, 130-38, 140-43, 153, 604-5
Marchenko, Anatoly, 76
Marcos, Ferdinand, 361-64, 366-71, 369
Marcos, Imelda, 369
Mari Bras, Juan, 518-20
Marighella, Carlos, 446
Marín, Gladys, 451
Marinello, Juan, 465
Marinello, Zoilo, 465
Markey, Ray, 527
Marklund, Eivor, 219
Marko, Rita, 1, 3
Marković, Mihajlo, 95
Maron, Karl, 26
Maróthy, László, 39-40, 42-43
Marquez, Gilberto, 446
Márquez, Gregorio Lunar, 539
Márquez, Pompeyo, 536-37
Martínez Eduardo, 457
Martínez, Facundo, 465
Martínez Nateras, Arturo, 499
Martínez Verdugo, Arnoldo, 499-500, 502
de Martino, Francesco, 177, 191
Marulanda Vélez, Manuel, 458
Masherov, Piotr M., 69
Masiel, Carlos, 509
Masjkur, Kjai H., 297
Massera, José L., 531
Matos, Alfredo, 516
Matsuhara Harushige, 301
Matthews, Betty, 161
Matthews, George, 161
Mauroy, Pierre, 135
Mauvois, Georges, 494
Mazari, Sherbaz Khan, 357
Mazumdar, Charu, 286
Mazurov, Kiril T., 69, 71, 86
Mazzarovich, Jorge, 531
McAra, Peter Wilfred George ("Bill"), 353-54
McBride, John, 303
McLennan, Gordon, 161-62
Meany, George, 525-26
Mecollari, Sami, 7
Medvedev, Roy, 75-76
Meinhof, Ulrike, 225
Melgar Castro, Juan Alberto, 492-93
Men San, 255
Méndez, José Joaquín, 465
Méndez del Toro, Manuel, 516
Mendoza, Jorge Enrique, 465, 470
Menéndez, Alfredo, 465
Menéndez, Gertrudis, 516
Menéndez, Raúl, 465
Ménil, René, 494
Merced, Florencio, 518